D0456325

Collins
Pocket
German
Dictionary

German ≫ English   English ≫ German

HarperCollins*Publishers*

fifth edition/fünfte Auflage 2001

© **HarperCollins Publishers 1996, 1998, 1999, 2001**
© William Collins Sons & Co. Ltd. 1990

HarperCollins Publishers
Westerhill Road, Bishopbriggs, Glasgow G64 2QT,
Great Britain

The HarperCollins website address is
www.**fire**and**water**.com

ISBN 0-00-472437-2

HarperCollins Publishers, Inc.
10 East 53rd Street, New York, NY 10022

ISBN 0-00-472437-2

CIP information is available on request

The HarperCollins USA website address is
www.harpercollins.com

Typeset by Morton Word Processing Ltd, Scarborough

*Printed and bound in Great Britain by
Omnia Books Ltd, Glasgow, G64*

editors/Redaktion
Veronika Schnorr • Ute Nicol • Peter Terrell
Bob Grossmith • Helga Holtkamp • Horst Kopleck
Beate Wengel • John Whitlam

editorial staff/Manuskriptbearbeitung
Joyce Littlejohn • Elspeth Anderson
Christine Bahr • John Podbielski

series editor/Gesamtleitung
Lorna Sinclair Knight

INTRODUCTION

We are delighted you have decided to buy the Collins Pocket German Dictionary and hope you will enjoy and benefit from using it at home, at school, on holiday or at work.

The innovative use of colour guides you quickly and efficiently to the word you want, and the comprehensive wordlist provides a wealth of modern and idiomatic phrases not normally found in a dictionary this size.

In addition, the supplement provides you with guidance on using the dictionary, along with entertaining ways of improving your dictionary skills.

We hope that you will enjoy using it and that it will significantly enhance your language studies.

ZUM GEBRAUCH IHRES COLLINS TASCHENWÖRTERBUCHS

Das Wörterbuch enthält eine Fülle von Informationen, die mithilfe von unterschiedlichen Schriften und Schriftgrößen, Symbolen, Abkürzungen und Klammern vermittelt werden. Die dabei verwendeten Regeln und Symbole werden in den folgenden Abschnitten erklärt.

Stichwörter
Die Wörter, die Sie im Wörterbuch nachschlagen — „Stichwörter" — sind alphabetisch geordnet. Sie sind **in Farbe** gedruckt, damit man sie schnell erkennt. Die beiden Stichwörter oben links und rechts auf jeder Doppelseite geben das erste bzw. letzte Wort an, das auf den betreffenden Seiten behandelt wird.

Informationen zur Verwendung oder zur Form bestimmter Stichwörter stehen in Klammern hinter der Lautschrift. Sie erscheinen meist in abgekürzter Form und sind kursiv gedruckt (z. B. (*fam*), (*COMM*)).

Wo es angebracht ist, werden mit dem Stichwort verwandte Wörter im selben Artikel behandelt (z. B. **accept, acceptance**). Sie sind wie das Stichwort fett, aber etwas kleiner gedruckt.

Häufig verwendete Ausdrücke, in denen das Stichwort vorkommt (z. B. **to be cold**), sind in einer anderen Schrift halbfett gedruckt.

Lautschrift
Die Lautschrift für jedes Stichwort (zur Angabe seiner Aussprache) steht in eckigen Klammern direkt hinter dem Stichwort (z. B. **Quark** [kvark]; **knead** [niːd]). Die Symbole der Lautschrift sind auf Seite xii erklärt.

Übersetzungen
Die Übersetzungen des Stichworts sind normal gedruckt. Wenn es mehr als eine Bedeutung oder Verwendung des Stichworts gibt, sind diese durch ein Semikolon voneinander getrennt. Vor den Übersetzungen stehen oft andere, kursiv gedruckte Wörter in Klammern. Sie geben an, in welchem Zusammenhang das Stichwort erscheinen könnte (z. B. **rough** (*voice*) oder (*weather*)), oder sie sind Synonyme (z. B. **rough** (*violent*)).

Schlüsselwörter
Besonders behandelt werden bestimmte deutsche und englische Wörter, die man als „Schlüsselwörter" der jeweiligen Sprache betrachten kann. Diese Wörter kommen beispielsweise sehr häufig vor oder werden unterschiedlich verwendet (z. B. **sein, auch; get, that**). Mithilfe von Rauten und Ziffern können Sie die verschiedenen Wortarten und Verwendungen unterscheiden. Weitere nützliche Hinweise finden Sie kursiv und in Klammern in der jeweiligen Sprache des Benutzers.

Grammatische Informationen
Wortarten stehen in abgekürzter Form kursiv gedruckt hinter der Aussprache des

Stichworts (z. B. *vt, adv, conj*).

Die unregelmäßigen Formen englischer Substantive und Verben stehen in Klammern vor der Wortart (z. B. **man** (*pl* **men**) *n*, **give** (*pt* **gave**, *pp* **given**) *vt*).

Die deutsche Rechtschreibreform

Dieses Wörterbuch folgt durchweg der reformierten deutschen Rechtschreibung. Alle Stichwörter auf der deutsch-englischen Seite, die von der Rechtschreibreform betroffen sind, sind mit ▲ gekennzeichnet. Alte Schreibungen, die sich wesentlich von der neuen Schreibung unterscheiden und an einem anderen alphabetischen Ort erscheinen, sind jedoch weiterhin aufgeführt und werden zur neuen Schreibung verwiesen. Diese alten Schreibungen sind mit △ gekennzeichnet.

USING YOUR COLLINS POCKET DICTIONARY

A wealth of information is presented in the dictionary, using various typefaces, sizes of type, symbols, abbreviations and brackets. The conventions and symbols used are explained in the following sections.

Headwords

The words you look up in a dictionary — "headwords" — are listed alphabetically. They are printed in **colour** for rapid identification. The two headwords appearing at the top left and top right of each double page indicate the first and last word dealt with on the pages in question.

Information about the usage or form of certain headwords is given in brackets after the phonetic spelling. This usually appears in abbreviated form and in italics (e.g. (*umg*), (*COMM*)).

Where appropriate, words related to headwords are grouped in the same entry (**Glück, glücken**) in a slightly smaller bold type than the headword.

Common expressions in which the headword appears are shown in a different bold roman type (e.g. **Glück haben**).

Phonetic spellings

The phonetic spelling of each headword (indicating its pronunciation) is given in square brackets immediately after the headword (e.g. **Quark** [kvark]). A list of these symbols is given on page xii.

Meanings

Headword translations are given in ordinary type and, where more than one meaning or usage exists, these are separated by a semi-colon. You will often find other words in italics in brackets before the translations. These offer suggested contexts in which the headword might appear (e.g. **eng** (*Kleidung*) or (*Freundschaft*)) or provide synonyms (e.g. **eng** (*fig: Horizont*)).

"Key" words

Special status is given to certain German and English words which are considered as "key" words in each language. They may, for example, occur very frequently or have several types of usage (e.g. **sein, auch; get, that**). A combination of lozenges and numbers helps you to distinguish different parts of speech and different meanings. Further helpful information is provided in brackets and in italics in the relevant language for the user.

Grammatical information

Parts of speech are given in abbreviated form in italics after the phonetic spellings of headwords (e.g. *vt, adv, konj*).

Genders of German nouns are indicated as follows: *m* for a masculine and *f* for a feminine and *nt* for a neuter noun. The genitive and plural forms of regular nouns are shown on the table on page xi. Nouns which do not follow these rules have the genitive and plural in brackets immediately preceding the gender (e.g. **Spaß**, (-es, -̈e), *m*).

Adjectives are normally shown in their basic form (e.g. **groß** *adj*), but where they are only used attributively (i.e. before a noun) feminine and neuter endings follow in brackets (**hohe (r, s)** *adj attrib*).

German spelling reform
The German spelling reform has been fully implemented in this dictionary. All headwords on the German-English side which are affected by the spelling changes are marked with ▲, but old spellings which are markedly different from the new ones and have a different alphabetical position are still listed and are cross-referenced to the new spellings. The old spellings are marked with △.

ABKÜRZUNGEN

ABBREVIATIONS

Abkürzung	abk, abbr	abbreviation
Akkusativ	acc	accusative
Adjektiv	adj	adjective
Adverb	adv	adverb
Landwirtschaft	AGR	agriculture
Akkusativ	akk	accusative
Anatomie	ANAT	anatomy
Architektur	ARCHIT	architecture
Astrologie	ASTROL	astrology
Astronomie	ASTRON	astronomy
attributiv	attrib	attributive
Kraftfahrzeuge	AUT	automobiles
Hilfsverb	aux	auxiliary
Luftfahrt	AVIAT	aviation
besonders	bes	especially
Biologie	BIOL	biology
Botanik	BOT	botany
britisch	BRIT	British
Chemie	CHEM	chemistry
Film	CINE	cinema
Handel	COMM	commerce
Komparativ	compar	comparative
Computer	COMPUT	computing
Konjunktion	conj	conjunction
Kochen und Backen	COOK	cooking
zusammengesetztes Wort	cpd	compound
Dativ	dat	dative
bestimmter Artikel	def art	definite article
Diminutiv	dimin	diminutive
kirchlich	ECCL	ecclesiastical
Eisenbahn	EISENB	railways
Elektrizität	ELEK, ELEC	electricity
besonders	esp	especially
und so weiter	etc	et cetera
etwas	etw	something
Euphemismus, Hüllwort	euph	euphemism
Interjektion, Ausruf	excl	exclamation
Femininum	f	feminine
übertragen	fig	figurative
Finanzwesen	FIN	finance
nicht getrennt gebraucht	fus	(phrasal verb) inseparable
Genitiv	gen	genitive
Geografie	GEOG	geography
Geologie	GEOL	geology
Grammatik	GRAM	grammar

Geschichte	HIST	history
unpersönlich	impers	impersonal
unbestimmter Artikel	indef art	indefinite article
umgangssprachlich (! vulgär)	inf(!)	informal (! particularly offensive)
Infinitiv, Grundform	infin	infinitive
nicht getrennt gebraucht	insep	inseparable
unveränderlich	inv	invariable
unregelmäßig	irreg	irregular
jemand	jd	somebody
jemandem	jdm	(to) somebody
jemanden	jdn	somebody
jemandes	jds	somebody's
Rechtswesen	JUR	law
Kochen und Backen	KOCH	cooking
Komparativ	kompar	comparative
Konjunktion	konj	conjunction
Sprachwissenschaft	LING	linguistics
Literatur	LITER	of literature
Maskulinum	m	masculine
Mathematik	MATH	mathematics
Medizin	MED	medicine
Meteorologie	MET	meteorology
Militär	MIL	military
Bergbau	MIN	mining
Musik	MUS	music
Substantiv, Hauptwort	n	noun
nautisch, Seefahrt	NAUT	nautical, naval
Nominativ	nom	nominative
Neutrum	nt	neuter
Zahlwort	num	numeral
Objekt	obj	object
oder	od	or
sich	o.s.	oneself
Parlament	PARL	parliament
abschätzig	pej	pejorative
Fotografie	PHOT	photography
Physik	PHYS	physics
Plural	pl	plural
Politik	POL	politics
Präfix, Vorsilbe	pp	prefix
Präposition	präp, prep	preposition
Typografie	PRINT	printing
Pronomen, Fürwort	pron	pronoun
Psychologie	PSYCH	psychology
1. Vergangenheit, Imperfekt	pt	past tense
Radio	RAD	radio
Eisenbahn	RAIL	railways
Religion	REL	religion

jemand(-en, -em)	sb	someone, somebody
Schulwesen	SCH	school
Naturwissenschaft	SCI	science
Singular, Einzahl	sg	singular
etwas	sth	something
Konjunktiv	sub	subjunctive
Subjekt	subj	(grammatical) subject
Superlativ	superl	superlative
Technik	TECH	technology
Nachrichtentechnik	TEL	telecommunications
Theater	THEAT	theatre
Fernsehen	TV	television
Typografie	TYP	printing
umgangssprachlich (! vulgär)	umg(!)	informal (! particularly offensive)
Hochschulwesen	UNIV	university
unpersönlich	unpers	impersonal
unregelmäßig	unreg	irregular
(nord)amerikanisch	US	(North) America
gewöhnlich	usu	usually
Verb	vb	verb
intransitives Verb	vi	intransitive verb
reflexives Verb	vr	reflexive verb
transitives Verb	vt	transitive verb
Zoologie	ZOOL	zoology
zusammengesetztes Wort	zW	compound
zwischen zwei Sprechern	—	change of speaker
ungefähre Entsprechung	≅	cultural equivalent
eingetragenes Warenzeichen	®	registered trademark

Warenzeichen

Wörter, die unseres Wissens eingetragene Warenzeichen darstellen, sind als solche gekennzeichnet. Es ist jedoch zu beachten, dass weder das Vorhandensein noch das Fehlen derartiger Kennzeichnungen die Rechtslage hinsichtlich eingetragener Warenzeichen berührt.

Note on trademarks

Words which we have reason to believe constitute trademarks have been designated as such. However, neither the presence nor the absence of such designation should be regarded as affecting the legal status of any trademark.

REGULAR GERMAN NOUN ENDINGS

nom		gen	pl
-ant	*m*	-anten	-anten
-anz	*f*	-anz	-anzen
-ar	*m*	-ar(e)s	-are
-chen	*nt*	-chens	-chen
-e	*f*	-	-n
-ei	*f*	-ei	-eien
-elle	*f*	-elle	-ellen
-ent	*m*	-enten	-enten
-enz	*f*	-enz	-enzen
-ette	*f*	-ette	-etten
-eur	*m*	-eurs	-eure
-euse	*f*	-euse	-eusen
-heit	*f*	-heit	-heiten
-ie	*f*	-ie	-ien
-ik	*f*	-ik	-iken
-in	*f*	-in	-innen
-ine	*f*	-ine	-inen
-ion	*f*	-ion	-ionen
-ist	*m*	-isten	-isten
-ium	*nt*	-iums	-ien
-ius	*m*	-ius	-iusse
-ive	*f*	-ive	-iven
-keit	*f*	-keit	-keiten
-lein	*nt*	-leins	-lein
-ling	*m*	-lings	-linge
-ment	*nt*	-ments	-mente
-mus	*m*	-mus	-men
-schaft	*f*	-schaft	-schaften
-tät	*f*	-tät	-täten
-tor	*m*	-tors	-toren
-ung	*f*	-ung	-ungen
-ur	*f*	-ur	-uren

PHONETIC SYMBOLS / LAUTSCHRIFT

[:] *length mark/Längezeichen* ['] *stress mark/Betonung*
[|] *glottal stop/Knacklaut*

all vowel sounds are approximate only
alle Vokallaute sind nur ungefähre Entsprechungen

bet	[b]	**Ball**		[e]	Metall
dim	[d]	**dann**		[e:]	geben
face	[f]	**Fass**	set	[ɛ]	hässlich
go	[g]	**Gast**		[ɛ̃:]	Cousin
hit	[h]	**Herr**	pity	[ɪ]	Bischof
you	[j]	**ja**		[i]	vital
cat	[k]	**kalt**	green	[i:]	viel
lick	[l]	**Last**	rot	[ɔ]	Post
must	[m]	**Mast**	board	[ɔ:]	
nut	[n]	**Nuss**		[o]	Moral
bang	[ŋ]	**lang**		[o:]	oben
pepper	[p]	**Pakt**		[õ]	Champignon
red	[r]	**Regen**		[ø]	ökonomisch
sit	[s]	**Rasse**		[œ]	gönnen
shame	[ʃ]	**Schal**	full	[u]	kulant
tell	[t]	**Tal**	root	[u:]	Hut
chat	[tʃ]	**tschüs**	come	[ʌ]	
vine	[v]	**was**		[ʊ]	Pult
wine	[w]			[y]	physisch
loch	[x]	**Bach**		[y:]	für
	[ç]	**ich**		[ʏ]	Müll
zero	[z]	**Hase**	above	[ə]	bitte
leisure	[ʒ]	**Genie**	girl	[ə:]	
join	[dʒ]				
thin	[θ]		lie	[aɪ]	weit
this	[ð]		now	[au]	
	[a]	**Hast**		[aʊ]	Haut
hat	[æ]		day	[eɪ]	
	[ɑ:]	**Bahn**	fair	[ɛə]	
farm	[ɑ:]		beer	[ɪə]	
	[ã]	**Ensemble**	toy	[ɔɪ]	
fiancé	[ɑ̃:]			[ɔʏ]	Heu
			pure	[uə]	

[ʳ] r can be pronounced before a vowel; Bindungs-R

ZAHLEN

NUMBERS

ein(s)	1	one
zwei	2	two
drei	3	three
vier	4	four
fünf	5	five
sechs	6	six
sieben	7	seven
acht	8	eight
neun	9	nine
zehn	10	ten
elf	11	eleven
zwölf	12	twelve
dreizehn	13	thirteen
vierzehn	14	fourteen
fünfzehn	15	fifteen
sechzehn	16	sixteen
siebzehn	17	seventeen
achtzehn	18	eighteen
neunzehn	19	nineteen
zwanzig	20	twenty
einundzwanzig	21	twenty-one
zweiundzwanzig	22	twenty-two
dreißig	30	thirty
vierzig	40	forty
fünfzig	50	fifty
sechzig	60	sixty
siebzig	70	seventy
achtzig	80	eighty
neunzig	90	ninety
hundert	100	a hundred
hunderteins	101	a hundred and one
zweihundert	200	two hundred
zweihunderteins	201	two hundred and one
dreihundert	300	three hundred
dreihunderteins	301	three hundred and one
tausend	1000	a thousand
tausend(und)eins	1001	a thousand and one
fünftausend	5000	five thousand
eine Million	1000000	a million

erste(r, s)	1.	first	1st
zweite(r, s)	2.	second	2nd
dritte(r, s)	3.	third	3rd
vierte(r, s)	4.	fourth	4th
fünfte(r, s)	5.	fifth	5th
sechste(r, s)	6.	sixth	6th

siebte(r, s)	7.	seventh	7th
achte(r, s)	8.	eighth	8th
neunte(r, s)	9.	ninth	9th
zehnte(r, s)	10.	tenth	10th
elfte(r, s)	11.	eleventh	11th
zwölfte(r, s)	12.	twelfth	12th
dreizehnte(r, s)	13.	thirteenth	13th
vierzehnte(r, s)	14.	fourteenth	14th
fünfzehnte(r, s)	15.	fifteenth	15th
sechzehnte(r, s)	16.	sixteenth	16th
siebzehnte(r, s)	17.	seventeenth	17th
achtzehnte(r, s)	18.	eighteenth	18th
neunzehnte(r, s)	19.	nineteenth	19th
zwanzigste(r, s)	20.	twentieth	20th
einundzwanzigste(r, s)	21.	twenty-first	21st
dreißigste(r, s)	30.	thirtieth	30th
hundertste(r, s)	100.	hundredth	100th
hunderterste(r, s)	101.	hundred-and-first	101st
tausendste(r, s)	1000.	thousandth	1000th

Brüche usw.

Fractions etc.

ein Halb	$\frac{1}{2}$	a half	
ein Drittel	$\frac{1}{3}$	a third	
ein Viertel	$\frac{1}{4}$	a quarter	
ein Fünftel	$\frac{1}{5}$	a fifth	
null Komma fünf	0,5	(nought) point five	0.5
drei Komma vier	3,4	three point four	3.4
sechs Komma acht neun	6,89	six point eight nine	6.89
zehn Prozent	10%	ten per cent	
hundert Prozent	100%	a hundred per cent	

Beispiele

Examples

er wohnt in Nummer 10	he lives at number 10
es steht in Kapitel 7	it's in chapter 7
auf Seite 7	on page 7
er wohnt im 7. Stock	he lives on the 7th floor
er wurde 7.	he came in 7th
Maßstab eins zu zwanzigtausend	scale one to twenty thousand

UHRZEIT

THE TIME

wie viel Uhr ist es?, wie spät ist es?

what time is it?

es ist ...

it's ...

Mitternacht, zwölf Uhr nachts
ein Uhr (morgens *or* früh)
fünf nach eins, ein Uhr fünf
zehn nach eins, ein Uhr zehn
Viertel nach eins, ein Uhr fünfzehn
fünf vor halb zwei, ein Uhr
  fünfundzwanzig
halb zwei, ein Uhr dreißig
fünf nach halb zwei, ein Uhr
  fünfunddreißig
zwanzig vor zwei, ein Uhr vierzig
Viertel vor zwei, ein Uhr
  fünfundvierzig
zehn vor zwei, ein Uhr fünfzig
zwölf Uhr (mittags), Mittag
halb eins (mittags *or* nachmittags),
  zwölf Uhr dreißig
zwei Uhr (nachmittags)

halb acht (abends)

midnight
one o'clock (in the morning), one (a.m.)
five past one
ten past one
a quarter past one, one fifteen
twenty-five past one, one twenty-five

half past one, one thirty
twenty-five to two, one thirty-five

twenty to two, one forty
a quarter to two, one forty-five

ten to two, one fifty
twelve o'clock, midday, noon
half past twelve, twelve thirty (p.m.)

two o'clock (in the afternoon), two
  (p.m.)
half past seven (in the evening), seven
  thirty (p.m.)

um wie viel Uhr?

at what time?

um Mitternacht
um sieben Uhr

at midnight
at seven o'clock

in zwanzig Minuten
vor fünfzehn Minuten

in twenty minutes
fifteen minutes ago

DEUTSCH – ENGLISCH
GERMAN – ENGLISH

A, a

Aal [aːl] *(-(e)s, -e)* *m* eel
Aas [aːs] *(-es, -e od Äser)* *nt* carrion

SCHLÜSSELWORT
---

ab [ap] *präp +dat* from; **Kinder ab 12 Jahren** children from the age of 12; **ab morgen** from tomorrow; **ab sofort** as of now
♦ *adv* **1** off; **links ab** to the left; **der Knopf ist ab** the button has come off; **ab nach Hause!** off you go home
2 *(zeitlich)*: **von da ab** from then on; **von heute ab** from today, as of today
3 *(auf Fahrplänen)*: **München ab 12.20** leaving Munich 12.20
4: **ab und zu** *od* **an** now and then *od* again

Abänderung [ˈapˌɛndərʊŋ] *f* alteration
Abbau [ˈapbaʊ] *(-(e)s)* *m* *(+gen)* dismantling; *(Verminderung)* reduction (in); *(Verfall)* decline (in); *(MIN)* mining; quarrying; *(CHEM)* decomposition; **a~en** *vt* to dismantle; *(MIN)* to mine; to quarry; *(verringern)* to reduce; *(CHEM)* to break down
abbeißen [ˈapbaɪsən] *(unreg)* *vt* to bite off
abbekommen [ˈapbəkɔmən] *(unreg)* *vt* *(Deckel, Schraube, Band)* to loosen; **etwas ~** *(beschädigt werden)*: **a~en** *vt* to get damaged; *(: Person)* to get injured
abbestellen [ˈapbəʃtɛlən] *vt* to cancel
abbezahlen [ˈapbətsaːlən] *vt* to pay off
abbiegen [ˈapbiːgən] *(unreg)* *vi* to turn off; *(Straße)* to bend ♦ *vt* to bend; *(verhindern)* to ward off
abbilden [ˈapbɪldən] *vt* to portray; **Abbildung** *f* illustration
abblenden [ˈapblɛndən] *vt, vi* *(AUT)* to dip *(BRIT)*, to dim *(US)*
Abblendlicht [ˈapblɛntlɪçt] *nt* dipped *(BRIT)* *od* dimmed *(US)* headlights *pl*

abbrechen [ˈapbrɛçən] *(unreg)* *vt, vi* to break off; *(Gebäude)* to pull down; *(Zelt)* to take down; *(aufhören)* to stop; *(COMPUT)* to abort
abbrennen [ˈapbrɛnən] *(unreg)* *vt* to burn off; *(Feuerwerk)* to let off ♦ *vi* *(aux sein)* to burn down
abbringen [ˈapbrɪŋən] *(unreg)* *vt*: **jdn von etw ~** to dissuade sb from sth; **jdn vom Weg ~** to divert sb
abbröckeln [ˈapbrœkəln] *vt, vi* to crumble off *od* away
Abbruch [ˈapbrʊx] *m* *(von Verhandlungen etc)* breaking off; *(von Haus)* demolition; **jdm/ etw ~ tun** to harm sb/sth; **a~reif** *adj* only fit for demolition
abbrühen [ˈapbryːən] *vt* to scald; **abgebrüht** *(umg)* hard-boiled
abbuchen [ˈapbuːxən] *vt* to debit
abdanken [ˈapdaŋkən] *vi* to resign; *(König)* to abdicate; **Abdankung** *f* resignation; abdication
abdecken [ˈapdɛkən] *vt* *(Loch)* to cover; *(Tisch)* to clear; *(Plane)* to uncover
abdichten [ˈapdɪçtən] *vt* to seal; *(NAUT)* to caulk
abdrehen [ˈapdreːən] *vt* *(Gas)* to turn off; *(Licht)* to switch off; *(Film)* to shoot ♦ *vi* *(Schiff)* to change course
Abdruck [ˈapdrʊk] *m* *(Nachdrucken)* reprinting; *(Gedrucktes)* reprint; *(Gipsabdruck, Wachsabdruck)* impression; *(Fingerabdruck)* print; **a~en** *vt* to print, to publish
abdrücken [ˈapdrʏkən] *vt* *(Waffe)* to fire; *(Person)* to hug, to squeeze
Abend [ˈaːbənt] *m* *(-s, -e)* *m* evening; **guten ~** good evening; **zu ~ essen** to have dinner *od* supper; **heute ~** this evening; **~brot** *nt* supper; **~essen** *nt* supper; **~garderobe** *f*

evening dress; **~kasse** *f* box office; **~kleid**
nt evening dress; **~kurs** *m* evening classes
pl; **~land** *nt* (*Europa*) West; **a~lich** *adj*
evening; **~mahl** *nt* Holy Communion; **~rot**
nt sunset; **a~s** *adv* in the evening

Abenteuer ['a:bəntɔyər] (**-s, -**) *nt* adventure;
a~lich *adj* adventurous; **~urlaub** *m*
adventure holiday

Abenteurer (**-s, -**) *m* adventurer; **~in** *f*
adventuress

aber ['a:bər] *konj* but; (*jedoch*) however
♦ *adv*: **das ist ~ schön** that's really nice;
nun ist ~ Schluss! now that's enough!;
vielen Dank – ~ bitte! thanks a lot – you're
welcome; **A~glaube** *m* superstition;
~gläubisch *adj* superstitious

aberkennen ['ap|ɛrkɛnən] (*unreg*) *vt* (*JUR*):
jdm etw ~ to deprive sb of sth, to take sth
(away) from sb

abermals ['a:bəma:ls] *adv* once again

Abertausend, abertausend
['a:bətauzənt] *indef pron* **tausend** *od*
Tausend und ~ thousands upon thousands

Abf. *abk* (= *Abfahrt*) dep.

abfahren ['apfa:rən] (*unreg*) *vi* to leave, to
depart ♦ *vt* to take *od* cart away; (*Strecke*)
to drive; (*Reifen*) to wear; (*Fahrkarte*) to use

Abfahrt ['apfa:rt] *f* departure; (*SKI*) descent;
(*Piste*) run; **~szeit** *f* departure time

Abfall ['apfal] *m* waste; (*von Speisen etc*)
rubbish (*BRIT*), garbage (*US*); (*Neigung*)
slope; (*Verschlechterung*) decline; **~eimer** *m*
rubbish bin (*BRIT*), garbage can (*US*); **a~en**
(*unreg*) *vi* (*auch fig*) to fall *od* drop off; (*sich
neigen*) to fall *od* drop away

abfällig ['apfɛlɪç] *adj* disparaging,
deprecatory

abfangen ['apfaŋən] (*unreg*) *vt* to intercept;
(*Person*) to catch; (*unter Kontrolle bringen*) to
check

abfärben ['apfɛrbən] *vi* to lose its colour;
(*Wäsche*) to run; (*fig*) to rub off

abfassen ['apfasən] *vt* to write, to draft

abfertigen ['apfɛrtɪgən] *vt* to prepare for
dispatch, to process; (*an der Grenze*) to
clear; (*Kundschaft*) to attend to

Abfertigungsschalter *m* (*Flughafen*)
check-in desk

abfeuern ['apfɔyərn] *vt* to fire

abfinden ['apfɪndən] (*unreg*) *vt* to pay off
♦ *vr* to come to terms; **sich mit jdm ~/
nicht ~** to put up with/not get on with sb

Abfindung *f* (*von Gläubigern*) payment;
(*Geld*) sum in settlement

abflauen ['apflauən] *vi* (*Wind, Erregung*) to
die away, to subside; (*Nachfrage, Geschäft*)
to fall *od* drop off

abfliegen ['apfli:gən] (*unreg*) *vi* (*Flugzeug*) to
take off; (*Passagier auch*) to fly ♦ *vt* (*Gebiet*)
to fly over

abfließen ['apfli:sən] (*unreg*) *vi* to drain
away

Abflug ['apflu:k] *m* departure; (*Start*) take-
off; **~halle** *f* departure lounge; **~zeit** *f*
departure time

Abfluss ▲ ['apflʊs] *m* draining away;
(*Öffnung*) outlet; **~rohr** *nt* drain pipe; (*von
sanitären Anlagen auch*) waste pipe

abfragen ['apfra:gən] *vt* (*bes SCH*) to test
orally (on)

Abfuhr ['apfu:r] (**-, -en**) *f* removal; (*fig*)
snub, rebuff

abführen ['apfy:rən] *vt* to lead away;
(*Gelder, Steuern*) to pay ♦ *vi* (*MED*) to have a
laxative effect

Abführmittel ['apfy:rmɪtəl] *nt* laxative,
purgative

abfüllen ['apfylən] *vt* to draw off; (*in
Flaschen*) to bottle

Abgabe ['apga:bə] *f* handing in; (*von Ball*)
pass; (*Steuer*) tax; (*eines Amtes*) giving up;
(*einer Erklärung*) giving

Abgang ['apgaŋ] *m* (*von Schule*) leaving;
(*THEAT*) exit; (*Abfahrt*) departure; (*der Post,
von Waren*) dispatch

Abgas ['apga:s] *nt* waste gas; (*AUT*) exhaust

abgeben ['apge:bən] (*unreg*) *vt* (*Gegenstand*)
to hand *od* give in; (*Ball*) to pass; (*Wärme*)
to give off; (*Amt*) to hand over; (*Schuss*) to
fire; (*Erklärung, Urteil*) to give; (*darstellen,
sein*) to make ♦ *vr*: **sich mit jdm/etw ~** to
associate with sb/bother with sth; **jdm etw
~** (*überlassen*) to let sb have sth

abgebrüht ['apgəbry:t] (*umg*) *adj* (*skrupellos*)

hard-boiled

abgehen ['apgeːən] (*unreg*) *vi* to go away, to leave; (*THEAT*) to exit; (*Knopf etc*) to come off; (*Straße*) to branch off ♦ *vt* (*Strecke*) to go *od* walk along; **etw geht jdm ab** (*fehlt*) sb lacks sth

abgelegen ['apgəleːgən] *adj* remote

abgemacht ['apgəmaxt] *adj* fixed; **~!** done!

abgeneigt ['apgənaɪkt] *adj* disinclined

abgenutzt ['apgənʊtst] *adj* worn

Abgeordnete(r) ['apgəʔɔrdnətə(r)] *f(m)* member of parliament; elected representative

abgeschlossen ['apgəʃlɔsən] *adj attrib* (*Wohnung*) self-contained

abgeschmackt ['apgəʃmakt] *adj* tasteless

abgesehen ['apgəzeːən] *adj*: **es auf jdn/ etw ~ haben** to be after sb/sth; **~ von ...** apart from ...

abgespannt ['apgəʃpant] *adj* tired out

abgestanden ['apgəʃtandən] *adj* stale; (*Bier auch*) flat

abgestorben ['apgəʃtɔrbən] *adj* numb; (*BIOL, MED*) dead

abgetragen ['apgətraːgən] *adj* shabby, worn out

abgewinnen ['apgəvɪnən] (*unreg*) *vt*: **einer Sache etw/Geschmack ~** to get sth/ pleasure from sth

abgewöhnen ['apgəvøːnən] *vt*: **jdm/sich etw ~** to cure sb of sth/give sth up

abgrenzen ['apgrɛntsən] *vt* (*auch fig*) to mark off; to fence off

Abgrund ['apgrʊnt] *m* (*auch fig*) abyss

abhacken ['aphakən] *vt* to chop off

abhaken ['aphaːkən] *vt* (*auf Papier*) to tick off

abhalten ['aphaltən] (*unreg*) *vt* (*Versammlung*) to hold; **jdn von etw ~** (*fern halten*) to keep sb away from sth; (*hindern*) to keep sb from sth

abhanden [ap'handən] *adj*: **~ kommen** to get lost

Abhandlung ['aphandlʊŋ] *f* treatise, discourse

Abhang ['aphaŋ] *m* slope

abhängen ['aphɛŋən] *vt* (*Bild*) to take down; (*Anhänger*) to uncouple; (*Verfolger*) to shake off ♦ *vi* (*unreg*: *Fleisch*) to hang; **von jdm/ etw ~** to depend on sb/sth

abhängig ['aphɛŋɪç] *adj*: **~ (von)** dependent (on); **A~keit** *f*: **A~keit (von)** dependence (on)

abhärten ['aphɛrtən] *vt, vr* to toughen (o.s.) up; **sich gegen etw ~** to inure o.s. to sth

abhauen ['aphauən] (*unreg*) *vt* to cut off; (*Baum*) to cut down ♦ *vi* (*umg*) to clear off *od* out

abheben ['apheːbən] (*unreg*) *vt* to lift (up); (*Karten*) to take; (*Geld*) to withdraw, to take out ♦ *vi* (*Flugzeug*) to take off; (*Rakete*) to lift off ♦ *vr* to stand out

abheften ['apheftən] *vt* (*Rechnungen etc*) to file away

abhetzen ['aphetsən] *vr* to wear *od* tire o.s. out

Abhilfe ['aphɪlfə] *f* remedy; **~ schaffen** to put things right

abholen ['aphoːlən] *vt* (*Gegenstand*) to fetch, to collect; (*Person*) to call for; (*am Bahnhof etc*) to pick up, to meet

abholzen ['aphɔltsən] *vt* (*Wald*) to clear

abhorchen ['aphɔrçən] *vt* (*MED*) to listen to a patient's chest

abhören ['aphøːrən] *vt* (*Vokabeln*) to test; (*Telefongespräch*) to tap; (*Tonband etc*) to listen to

Abhörgerät *nt* bug

Abitur [abi'tuːr] (*-s, -e*) *nt* German school-leaving examination; **~i'ent(in)** *m(f)* candidate for school-leaving certificate

---

Abitur

> ⓘ The **Abitur** is the German school-leaving examination taken in four subjects by pupils at a **Gymnasium** at the age of 18 or 19. It is necessary for entry to university.

Abk. *abk* (= *Abkürzung*) abbr.

abkapseln ['apkapsəln] *vr* to shut *od* cut o.s. off

abkaufen ['apkaufən] *vt*: **jdm etw ~** (*auch fig*) to buy sth from sb

abkehren ['apkeːrən] *vt* (*Blick*) to avert, to turn away ♦ *vr* to turn away

abklingen ['apklıŋən] (*unreg*) *vi* to die away; (*Radio*) to fade out

abknöpfen ['apknœpfən] *vt* to unbutton; **jdm etw ~** (*umg*) to get sth off sb

abkochen ['apkɔxən] *vt* to boil

abkommen ['apkɔmən] (*unreg*) *vi* to get away; **von der Straße/von einem Plan ~** to leave the road/give up a plan; **A~** (**-s, -**) *nt* agreement

abkömmlich ['apkœmlıç] *adj* available, free

abkratzen ['apkratsən] *vt* to scrape off ♦ *vi* (*umg*) to kick the bucket

abkühlen ['apkyːlən] *vt* to cool down ♦ *vr* (*Mensch*) to cool down *od* off; (*Wetter*) to get cool; (*Zuneigung*) to cool

abkürzen ['apkʏrtsən] *vt* to shorten; (*Wort auch*) to abbreviate; **den Weg ~** to take a short cut

Abkürzung *f* (*Wort*) abbreviation; (*Weg*) short cut

abladen ['aplaːdən] (*unreg*) *vt* to unload

Ablage ['aplaːgə] *f* (*für Akten*) tray; (*für Kleider*) cloakroom

ablassen ['aplasən] (*unreg*) *vt* (*Wasser, Dampf*) to let off; (*vom Preis*) to knock off ♦ *vi*: **von etw ~** to give sth up, to abandon sth

Ablauf ['aplaʊf] *m* (*Abfluss*) drain; (*von Ereignissen*) course; (*einer Frist, Zeit*) expiry (*BRIT*), expiration (*US*); **a~en** (*unreg*) *vi* (*abfließen*) to drain away; (*Ereignisse*) to happen; (*Frist, Zeit, Pass*) to expire ♦ *vt* (*Sohlen*) to wear (down *od* out)

ablegen ['apleːgən] *vt* to put *od* lay down; (*Kleider*) to take off; (*Gewohnheit*) to get rid of; (*Prüfung*) to take, to sit; (*Zeugnis*) to give

Ableger (**-s, -**) *m* layer; (*fig*) branch, offshoot

ablehnen ['apleːnən] *vt* to reject; (*Einladung*) to decline, to refuse ♦ *vi* to decline, to refuse

ablehnend *adj* (*Haltung, Antwort*) negative; (*Geste*) disapproving; **ein ~er Bescheid** a rejection

Ablehnung *f* rejection; refusal

ableiten ['aplaɪtən] *vt* (*Wasser*) to divert; (*deduzieren*) to deduce; (*Wort*) to derive; **Ableitung** *f* diversion; deduction; derivation; (*Wort*) derivative

ablenken ['aplɛŋkən] *vt* to turn away, to deflect; (*zerstreuen*) to distract ♦ *vi* to change the subject; **Ablenkung** *f* distraction

ablesen ['apleːzən] (*unreg*) *vt* to read out; (*Messgeräte*) to read

ablichten ['aplıçtən] *vt* to photocopy

abliefern ['apliːfərn] *vt* to deliver; **etw bei jdm ~** to hand sth over to sb

Ablieferung *f* delivery

ablösen ['apløːzən] *vt* (*abtrennen*) to take off, to remove; (*in Amt*) to take over from; (*Wache*) to relieve

Ablösung *f* removal; relieving

abmachen ['apmaxən] *vt* to take off; (*vereinbaren*) to agree; **Abmachung** *f* agreement

abmagern ['apmaːgərn] *vi* to get thinner

Abmagerungskur *f* diet; **eine ~ machen** to go on a diet

abmarschieren ['apmarʃiːrən] *vi* to march off

abmelden ['apmɛldən] *vt* (*Zeitungen*) to cancel; (*Auto*) to take off the road ♦ *vr* to give notice of one's departure; (*im Hotel*) to check out; **jdn bei der Polizei ~** to register sb's departure with the police

abmessen ['apmɛsən] (*unreg*) *vt* to measure; **Abmessung** *f* measurement

abmontieren ['apmɔntiːrən] *vt* to take off

abmühen ['apmyːən] *vr* to wear o.s. out

Abnahme ['apnaːmə] *f* (*+gen*) removal; (*COMM*) buying; (*Verringerung*) decrease (in)

abnehmen ['apneːmən] (*unreg*) *vt* to take off, to remove; (*Führerschein*) to take away; (*Prüfung*) to hold; (*Maschen*) to decrease ♦ *vi* to decrease; (*schlanker werden*) to lose weight; (**jdm**) **etw ~** (*Geld*) to get sth (out of sb); (*kaufen, umg: glauben*) to buy sth (from sb); **jdm Arbeit ~** to take work off sb's shoulders

Abnehmer (**-s, -**) *m* purchaser, customer

Abneigung ['apnaɪgʊŋ] *f* aversion, dislike

abnorm [ap'nɔrm] *adj* abnormal

abnutzen ['apnʊtsən] *vt* to wear out; **Abnutzung** *f* wear (and tear)

Abo ['abo] (*umg*) *nt abk* = **Abonnement**

Abonnement [abɔn(ə)'mãː] (**-s, -s**) *nt* subscription; **Abonnent(in)** [abɔ'nɛnt(ɪn)] *m(f)* subscriber; **abonnieren** *vt* to subscribe to

Abordnung ['apɔrdnʊŋ] *f* delegation

abpacken ['appakən] *vt* to pack

abpassen ['appasən] *vt* (*Person, Gelegenheit*) to wait for

Abpfiff ['appfɪf] *m* final whistle

abplagen ['appla:gən] *vr* to wear o.s. out

abprallen ['appralən] *vi* to bounce off; to ricochet

abraten ['apra:tən] (*unreg*) *vi*: **jdm von etw ~ to advise or warn sb against sth**

abräumen ['aprɔʏmən] *vt* to clear up *od* away

abreagieren ['apreagi:rən] *vt*: **seinen Zorn (an jdm/etw) ~ to work one's anger off (on sb/sth)** ♦ *vr* to calm down

abrechnen ['aprɛçnən] *vt* to deduct, to take off ♦ *vi* to settle up; (*fig*) to get even

Abrechnung *f* settlement; (*Rechnung*) bill

Abrede ['apre:də] *f*: **etw in ~ stellen** to deny *od* dispute sth

Abreise ['apraɪzə] *f* departure; **a~n** *vi* to leave, to set off

abreißen ['apraɪsən] (*unreg*) *vt* (*Haus*) to tear down; (*Blatt*) to tear off

abrichten ['aprɪçtən] *vt* to train

abriegeln ['apri:gəln] *vt* (*Straße, Gebiet*) to seal off

Abruf ['apru:f] *m*: **auf ~** on call; **a~en** (*unreg*) *vt* (*Mensch*) to call away; (*COMM*: *Ware*) to request delivery of

abrunden ['aprʊndən] *vt* to round off

abrupt [a'brʊpt] *adj* abrupt

abrüsten ['aprʏstən] *vi* to disarm; **Abrüstung** *f* disarmament

abrutschen ['aprʊtʃən] *vi* to slip; (*AVIAT*) to sideslip

Abs. *abk* (= *Absender*) sender, from

Absage ['apza:gə] *f* refusal; **a~n** *vt* to cancel, to call off; (*Einladung*) to turn down

♦ *vi* to cry off; (*ablehnen*) to decline

absahnen ['apza:nən] *vt* to skim ♦ *vi* (*fig*) to rake in

Absatz ['apzats] *m* (*COMM*) sales *pl*; (*Bodensatz*) deposit; (*neuer Abschnitt*) paragraph; (*Treppenabsatz*) landing; (*Schuhabsatz*) heel; **~gebiet** *nt* (*COMM*) market

abschaffen ['apʃafən] *vt* to abolish, to do away with; **Abschaffung** *f* abolition

abschalten ['apʃaltən] *vt, vi* (*auch umg*) to switch off

abschätzen ['apʃɛtsən] *vt* to estimate; (*Lage*) to assess; (*Person*) to size up

abschätzig ['apʃɛtsɪç] *adj* disparaging, derogatory

Abschaum ['apʃaʊm] (**-(e)s**) *m* scum

Abscheu ['apʃɔʏ] (**-(e)s**) *m* loathing, repugnance; **~ erregend** repulsive, loathsome; **a~lich** [ap'ʃɔʏlɪç] *adj* abominable

abschicken ['apʃɪkən] *vt* to send off

abschieben ['apʃi:bən] (*unreg*) *vt* to push away; (*Person*) to pack off; (: *POL*) to deport

Abschied ['apʃi:t] (**-(e)s, -e**) *m* parting; (*von Armee*) discharge; (**von jdm**) **~ nehmen** to say goodbye (to sb), to take one's leave (of sb); **seinen ~ nehmen** (*MIL*) to apply for discharge; **~sbrief** *m* farewell letter; **~sfeier** *f* farewell party

abschießen ['apʃi:sən] (*unreg*) *vt* (*Flugzeug*) to shoot down; (*Geschoss*) to fire

abschirmen ['apʃɪrmən] *vt* to screen

abschlagen ['apʃla:gən] (*unreg*) *vt* (*abhacken, COMM*) to knock off; (*ablehnen*) to refuse; (*MIL*) to repel

abschlägig ['apʃlɛ:gɪç] *adj* negative

Abschlagszahlung *f* interim payment

Abschlepp- ['apʃlɛp] *zW*: **~dienst** *m* (*AUT*) breakdown service (*BRIT*), towing company (*US*); **a~en** *vt* to (take in) tow; **~seil** *nt* towrope

abschließen ['apʃli:sən] (*unreg*) *vt* (*Tür*) to lock; (*beenden*) to conclude, to finish; (*Vertrag, Handel*) to conclude ♦ *vr* (*sich isolieren*) to cut o.s. off; **~d** *adj* concluding

Abschluss ▲ ['apʃlʊs] *m* (*Beendigung*) close,

conclusion; (*COMM: Bilanz*) balancing; (*von Vertrag, Handel*) conclusion; **zum ~** in conclusion; **~feier** *f* (*SCH*) end of term party; **~prüfung** *f* final exam

abschneiden ['apʃnaɪdən] (*unreg*) *vt* to cut off ♦ *vi* to do, to come off

Abschnitt ['apʃnɪt] *m* section; (*MIL*) sector; (*Kontrollabschnitt*) counterfoil; (*MATH*) segment; (*Zeitabschnitt*) period

abschrauben ['apʃraʊbən] *vt* to unscrew

abschrecken ['apʃrɛkən] *vt* to deter, to put off; (*mit kaltem Wasser*) to plunge in cold water; **~d** *adj* deterrent; **~des Beispiel** warning

abschreiben ['apʃraɪbən] (*unreg*) *vt* to copy; (*verloren geben*) to write off; (*COMM*) to deduct

Abschrift ['apʃrɪft] *f* copy

Abschuss ▲ ['apʃʊs] *m* (*eines Geschützes*) firing; (*Herunterschießen*) shooting down; (*Tötung*) shooting

abschüssig ['apʃʏsɪç] *adj* steep

abschwächen ['apʃvɛçən] *vt* to lessen; (*Behauptung, Kritik*) to tone down ♦ *vr* to lessen

abschweifen ['apʃvaɪfən] *vi* to digress

abschwellen ['apʃvɛlən] (*unreg*) *vi* (*Geschwulst*) to go down; (*Lärm*) to die down

abschwören ['apʃvøːrən] *vi* (+*dat*) to renounce

absehbar ['apzeːbaːr] *adj* foreseeable; **in ~er Zeit** in the foreseeable future; **das Ende ist ~** the end is in sight

absehen ['apzeːən] (*unreg*) *vt* (*Ende, Folgen*) to foresee ♦ *vi*: **von etw ~** to refrain from sth; (*nicht berücksichtigen*) to leave sth out of consideration

abseilen ['apzaɪlən] *vr* (*Bergsteiger*) to abseil (down)

abseits ['apzaɪts] *adv* out of the way ♦ *präp* +*gen* away from; **A~** *nt* (*SPORT*) offside

absenden ['apzɛndən] (*unreg*) *vt* to send off, to dispatch

Absender (-s, -) *m* sender

absetzen ['apzɛtsən] *vt* (*niederstellen, aussteigen lassen*) to put down; (*abnehmen*) to take off; (*COMM: verkaufen*) to sell; (*FIN: abziehen*) to deduct; (*entlassen*) to dismiss; (*König*) to depose; (*streichen*) to drop; (*hervorheben*) to pick out ♦ *vr* (*sich entfernen*) to clear off; (*sich ablagern*) to be deposited

Absetzung *f* (*FIN: Abzug*) deduction; (*Entlassung*) dismissal; (*von König*) deposing

absichern ['apzɪçərn] *vt* to make safe; (*schützen*) to safeguard ♦ *vr* to protect o.s.

Absicht ['apzɪçt] *f* intention; **mit ~** on purpose; **a~lich** *adj* intentional, deliberate

absinken ['apzɪŋkən] (*unreg*) *vi* to sink; (*Temperatur, Geschwindigkeit*) to decrease

absitzen ['apzɪtsən] (*unreg*) *vi* to dismount ♦ *vt* (*Strafe*) to serve

absolut [apzoˈluːt] *adj* absolute; **A~ismus** *m* absolutism

absolvieren [apzɔlˈviːrən] *vt* (*SCH*) to complete

absonder- ['apzɔndər] *zW*: **~lich** *adj* odd, strange; **~n** *vt* to separate; (*ausscheiden*) to give off, to secrete ♦ *vr* to cut o.s. off; **A~ung** *f* separation; (*MED*) secretion

abspalten ['apʃpaltən] *vt* to split off

abspannen ['apʃpanən] *vt* (*Pferde*) to unhitch; (*Wagen*) to uncouple

abspeisen ['apʃpaɪzən] *vt* (*fig*) to fob off

abspenstig ['apʃpɛnstɪç] *adj*: **(jdm) ~ machen** to lure away (from sb)

absperren ['apʃpɛrən] *vt* to block *od* close off; (*Tür*) to lock; **Absperrung** *f* (*Vorgang*) blocking *od* closing off; (*Sperre*) barricade

abspielen ['apʃpiːlən] *vt* (*Platte, Tonband*) to play; (*SPORT: Ball*) to pass ♦ *vr* to happen

Absprache ['apʃpraːxə] *f* arrangement

absprechen ['apʃprɛçən] (*unreg*) *vt* (*vereinbaren*) to arrange; **jdm etw ~** to deny sb sth

abspringen ['apʃprɪŋən] (*unreg*) *vi* to jump down/off; (*Farbe, Lack*) to flake off; (*AVIAT*) to bale out; (*sich distanzieren*) to back out

Absprung ['apʃprʊŋ] *m* jump

abspülen ['apʃpyːlən] *vt* to rinse; (*Geschirr*) to wash up

abstammen ['apʃtamən] *vi* to be descended; (*Wort*) to be derived; **Abstammung** *f* descent; derivation

Abstand ['apʃtant] *m* distance; (*zeitlich*) interval; **davon ~ nehmen, etw zu tun** to refrain from doing sth; **mit ~ der Beste** by far the best

abstatten ['apʃtatən] *vt* (*Dank*) to give; (*Besuch*) to pay

abstauben ['apʃtaʊbən] *vt, vi* to dust; (*umg: stehlen*) to pinch; (: *schnorren*) to scrounge

Abstecher ['apʃtɛçər] **(-s, -)** *m* detour

abstehen ['apʃteːən] (*unreg*) *vi* (*Ohren, Haare*) to stick out; (*entfernt sein*) to stand away

absteigen ['apʃtaɪgən] (*unreg*) *vi* (*vom Rad etc*) to get off, to dismount; **(in die zweite Liga) ~** to be relegated (to the second division)

abstellen ['apʃtɛlən] *vt* (*niederstellen*) to put down; (*entfernt stellen*) to pull out; (*hinstellen: Auto*) to park; (*ausschalten*) to turn *od* switch off; (*Missstand, Unsitte*) to stop

Abstellraum *m* storage room

abstempeln ['apʃtɛmpəln] *vt* to stamp

absterben ['apʃtɛrbən] (*unreg*) *vi* to die; (*Körperteil*) to go numb

Abstieg ['apʃtiːk] **(-(e)s, -e)** *m* descent; (*SPORT*) relegation; (*fig*) decline

abstimmen ['apʃtɪmən] *vi* to vote ♦ *vt:* **~ (auf +akk)** (*Instrument*) to tune to); (*Interessen*) to match (with), (*Termine, Ziele*) to fit in (with) ♦ *vr* to agree

Abstimmung *f* vote

Abstinenz [apstiˈnɛnts] *f* abstinence; teetotalism; **~ler(in) (-s, -)** *m(f)* teetaller

abstoßen ['apʃtoːsən] (*unreg*) *vt* to push off *od* away; (*verkaufen*) to unload; (*anekeln*) to repel, to repulse; **~d** *adj* repulsive

abstrakt [apˈstrakt] *adj* abstract ♦ *adv* abstractly, in the abstract

abstreiten ['apʃtraɪtən] (*unreg*) *vt* to deny

Abstrich ['apʃtrɪç] *m* (*Abzug*) cut; (*MED*) smear; **~e machen** to lower one's sights

abstufen ['apʃtuːfən] *vt* (*Hang*) to terrace; (*Farben*) to shade; (*Gehälter*) to grade

Absturz ['apʃtʊrts] *m* fall; (*AVIAT*) crash

abstürzen ['apʃtʏrtsən] *vi* to fall; (*AVIAT*) to crash

absuchen ['apzuːxən] *vt* to scour, to search

absurd [apˈzʊrt] *adj* absurd

Abszess ▲ [apsˈtsɛs] **(-es, -e)** *m* abscess

Abt [apt] **(-(e)s, ⁺e)** *m* abbot

Abt. *abk* (– *Abteilung*) dept.

abtasten ['aptastən] *vt* to feel, to probe

abtauen ['aptaʊən] *vt, vi* to thaw

Abtei [apˈtaɪ] **(-, -en)** *f* abbey

Abteil [apˈtaɪl] **(-(e)s, -e)** *nt* compartment; **'a~n** *vt* to divide up; (*abtrennen*) to divide off; **~ung** *f* (*in Firma, Kaufhaus*) department; (*in Krankenhaus*) section; (*MIL*) unit

abtippen ['aptɪpən] *vt* (*Text*) to type up

abtransportieren ['aptranspɔrtiːrən] *vt* to take away, to remove

abtreiben ['aptraɪbən] (*unreg*) *vt* (*Boot, Flugzeug*) to drive off course; (*Kind*) to abort ♦ *vi* to be driven off course; to abort

Abtreibung *f* abortion

abtrennen ['aptrɛnən] *vt* (*lostrennen*) to detach; (*entfernen*) to take off; (*abteilen*) to separate off

abtreten ['aptreːtən] (*unreg*) *vt* to wear out; (*überlassen*) to hand over, to cede ♦ *vi* to go off; (*zurücktreten*) to step down

Abtritt ['aptrɪt] *m* resignation

abtrocknen ['aptrɔknən] *vt, vi* to dry

abtun ['aptuːn] (*unreg*) *vt* (*fig*) to dismiss

abwägen ['apvɛːgən] (*unreg*) *vt* to weigh up

abwälzen ['apvɛltsən] *vt* (*Schuld, Verantwortung*): **~ (auf +akk)** to shift (onto)

abwandeln ['apvandəln] *vt* to adapt

abwandern ['apvandərn] *vi* to move away; (*FIN*) to be transferred

abwarten ['apvartən] *vt* to wait for ♦ *vi* to wait

abwärts ['apvɛrts] *adv* down

Abwasch ['apvaʃ] **(-(e)s)** *m* washing-up; **a~en** (*unreg*) *vt* (*Schmutz*) to wash off; (*Geschirr*) to wash (up)

Abwasser ['apvasər] **(-s, -wässer)** *nt* sewage

abwechseln ['apvɛksəln] *vi, vr* to alternate; (*Personen*) to take turns; **~d** *adj* alternate; **Abwechslung** *f* change; **abwechslungsreich** *adj* varied

abwegig ['apveːgɪç] *adj* wrong

Spelling Reform: ▲ new spelling △ old spelling (to be phased out)

Abwehr ['apveːr] (-) *f* defence; (*Schutz*) protection; (*~dienst*) counterintelligence (service); **a~en** *vt* to ward off; (*Ball*) to stop

abweichen ['apvaiçən] (*unreg*) *vi* to deviate; (*Meinung*) to differ

abweisen ['apvaizən] (*unreg*) *vt* to turn away; (*Antrag*) to turn down; **~d** *adj* (*Haltung*) cold

abwenden ['apvɛndən] (*unreg*) *vt* to avert ♦ *vr* to turn away

abwerfen ['apvɛrfən] (*unreg*) *vt* to throw off; (*Profit*) to yield; (*aus Flugzeug*) to drop; (*Spielkarte*) to discard

abwerten ['apvɛrtən] *vt* (*FIN*) to devalue

abwertend *adj* (*Worte, Sinn*) pejorative

Abwertung *f* (*von Währung*) devaluation

abwesend ['apveːzənt] *adj* absent

Abwesenheit ['apveːzənhait] *f* absence

abwickeln ['apvikəln] *vt* to unwind; (*Geschäft*) to wind up

abwimmeln ['apviməln] (*umg*) *vt* (*Menschen*) to get shot of

abwischen ['apviʃən] *vt* to wipe off *od* away; (*putzen*) to wipe

Abwurf ['apvʊrf] *m* throwing off; (*von Bomben etc*) dropping; (*von Reiter, SPORT*) throw

abwürgen ['apvʏrgən] (*umg*) *vt* to scotch; (*Motor*) to stall

abzahlen ['aptsaːlən] *vt* to pay off

abzählen ['aptsɛːlən] *vt, vi* to count (up)

Abzahlung *f* repayment; **auf ~ kaufen** to buy on hire purchase

abzapfen ['aptsapfən] *vt* to draw off; **jdm Blut ~** to take blood from sb

abzäunen ['aptsɔʏnən] *vt* to fence off

Abzeichen ['aptsaiçən] *nt* badge; (*Orden*) decoration

abzeichnen ['aptsaiçnən] *vt* to draw, to copy; (*Dokument*) to initial ♦ *vr* to stand out; (*fig: bevorstehen*) to loom

abziehen ['aptsiːən] (*unreg*) *vt* to take off; (*Tier*) to skin; (*Bett*) to strip; (*Truppen*) to withdraw; (*subtrahieren*) to take away, to subtract; (*kopieren*) to run off ♦ *vi* to go away; (*Truppen*) to withdraw

abzielen ['aptsiːlən] *vi*: **~ auf** +*akk* to be aimed at

Abzug ['aptsuːk] *m* departure; (*von Truppen*) withdrawal; (*Kopie*) copy; (*Subtraktion*) subtraction; (*Betrag*) deduction; (*Rauchabzug*) flue; (*von Waffen*) trigger

abzüglich ['aptsyːkliç] *präp* +*gen* less

abzweigen ['aptsvaigən] *vi* to branch off ♦ *vt* to set aside

Abzweigung *f* junction

ach [ax] *excl* oh; **~ ja!** (oh) yes; **~ so!** I see; **mit A~ und Krach** by the skin of one's teeth

Achse ['aksə] *f* axis; (*AUT*) axle

Achsel ['aksəl] (-, -n) *f* shoulder; **~höhle** *f* armpit

acht [axt] *num* eight; **~ Tage** a week; **A~¹** (-, -en) *f* eight; (*beim Eislaufen etc*) figure eight

Acht² (-, -en) *f*: **~ geben (auf** +*akk*) to pay attention (to); **sich in ~ nehmen (vor** +*dat*) to be careful (of), to watch out (for); **etw außer ~ lassen** to disregard sth; **a~bar** *adj* worthy

acht- *zW*: **~e(r, s)** *adj* eighth; **A~el** *num* eighth; **~en** *vt* to respect ♦ *vi*: **~en (auf** +*akk*) to pay attention (to); **~en, dass ...** to be careful that ...

ächten ['ɛçtən] *vt* to outlaw, to ban

Achterbahn ['axtər-] *f* roller coaster

acht- *zW*: **~fach** *adj* eightfold; **~geben** △ (*unreg*) *vi siehe* **Acht²**; **~hundert** *num* eight hundred; **~los** *adj* careless; **~mal** *adv* eight times; **~sam** *adj* attentive

Achtung ['axtʊŋ] *f* attention; (*Ehrfurcht*) respect ♦ *excl* look out!; (*MIL*) attention!; **alle ~!** good for you/him *etc*

achtzehn *num* eighteen

achtzig *num* eighty

ächzen ['ɛçtsən] *vi* to groan

Acker ['akər] (-s, ˝) *m* field; **a~n** *vt, vi* to plough; (*umg*) to slog away

ADAC [aːdeːˈaˌtseː] *abk* (= *Allgemeiner Deutscher Automobil-Club*) ≃ AA, RAC

Adapter [aˈdaptər] (-s, -) *m* adapter

addieren [aˈdiːrən] *vt* to add (up); **Addition** [aditsiˈoːn] *f* addition

Adel ['aːdəl] (-s) *m* nobility; **a~ig** *adj* noble;

a~n vt to raise to the peerage

Ader ['aːdər] (-, -n) f vein

Adjektiv ['atjektiːf] (-s, -e) nt adjective

Adler ['aːdlər] (-s, -) m eagle

adlig adj noble

Adopt- zW: **a~ieren** [adɔp'tiːrən] vt to adopt; **~ion** [adɔptsi'oːn] f adoption; **~iveltern** pl adoptive parents; **~ivkind** nt adopted child

Adressbuch ▲ nt directory; (privat) address book

Adress- zW: **~e** [a'drɛsə] f address; **a~ieren** [adrɛ'siːrən] vt: **a~ieren (an** +akk) to address (to)

Adria ['aːdria] (-) f Adriatic

Advent [at'vɛnt] (-(e)s, -e) m Advent; **~skalender** m Advent calendar; **~skranz** m Advent wreath

Adverb [at'vɛrp] nt adverb

Aerobic [ae'roːbik] nt aerobics sg

Affäre [a'fɛːrə] f affair

Affe ['afə] (-n, -n) m monkey

Affekt [a'fɛkt] (-(e)s, -e) m: **im ~ handeln** to act in the heat of the moment; **a~iert** [afɛk'tiːrt] adj affected

Affen- zW: **a~artig** adj like a monkey; **mit a~artiger Geschwindigkeit** like a flash; **~hitze** (umg) f incredible heat

affig ['afɪç] adj affected

Afrika ['aːfrika] (-s) nt Africa; **~ner(in)** [-'kaːnər(ɪn)] (-s, -) m(f) African; **a~nisch** adj African

AG [aː'geː] abk (= Aktiengesellschaft) ≈ plc (BRIT); ≈ Inc. (US)

Agent [a'gɛnt] m agent; **~ur** f agency

Aggregat [agre'gaːt] (-(e)s, -e) nt aggregate; (TECH) unit

Aggress- zW: **~ion** [agrɛsi'oːn] f aggression; **a~iv** [agrɛ'siːf] adj aggressive; **~ivität** [agrɛsivi'tɛːt] f aggressiveness

Agrarpolitik [a'graːr-] f agricultural policy

Ägypten [ɛ'gʏptən] (-s) nt Egypt; **ägyptisch** adj Egyptian

aha [a'haː] excl aha

ähneln ['ɛːnəln] vi +dat to be like, to resemble ♦ vr to be alike od similar

ahnen ['aːnən] vt to suspect; (Tod, Gefahr) to have a presentiment of

ähnlich ['ɛːnlɪç] adj (+dat) similar (to); **Ä~keit** f similarity

Ahnung ['aːnʊŋ] f idea, suspicion; presentiment; **a~slos** adj unsuspecting

Ahorn ['aːhɔrn] (-s, -e) m maple

Ähre ['ɛːrə] f ear

Aids [eːdz] nt AIDS sg

Airbag ['ɛːəbɛk] (-s, -s) m airbag

Akademie [akade'miː] f academy; **Aka'demiker(in)** (-s, -) m(f) university graduate; **akademisch** adj academic

akklimatisieren [aklimati'ziːrən] vr to become acclimatized

Akkord [a'kɔrt] (-(e)s, -e) m (MUS) chord; **im ~ arbeiten** to do piecework

Akkordeon [a'kɔrdeɔn] (-s, -s) nt accordion

Akku ['aku] (-s, -s) m rechargeable battery

Akkusativ ['akuzatiːf] (-s, -e) m accusative

Akne ['aknə] f acne

Akrobat(in) [akro'baːt(ɪn)] (-en, -en) m(f) acrobat

Akt [akt] (-(e)s, -e) m act; (KUNST) nude

Akte ['aktə] f file

Akten- zW: **~koffer** m attaché case; **a~kundig** adj on the files; **~schrank** m filing cabinet; **~tasche** f briefcase

Aktie ['aktsiə] f share

Aktien- zW: **~gesellschaft** f public limited company; **~index** (-(es), -e od -indices) m share index; **~kurs** m share price

Aktion [aktsi'oːn] f campaign; (Polizeiaktion, Suchaktion) action

Aktionär [aktsio'nɛːr] (-s, -e) m shareholder

aktiv [ak'tiːf] adj active; (MIL) regular; **~ieren** [-'viːrən] vt to activate; **A~i'tät** f activity

Aktualität [aktuali'tɛːt] f topicality; (einer Mode) up-to-dateness

aktuell [aktu'ɛl] adj topical; up-to-date

Akupunktur [akupʊŋk'tuːər] f acupuncture

Akustik [a'kʊstɪk] f acoustics pl

akut [a'kuːt] adj acute

Akzent [ak'tsɛnt] m accent; (Betonung) stress

akzeptabel [aktsɛp'taːbl] adj acceptable

akzeptieren [aktsɛp'tiːrən] vt to accept

Alarm [a'larm] (-(e)s, -e) m alarm; **a~bereit** adj standing by; **~bereitschaft** f stand-by;

Spelling Reform: ▲ *new spelling* △ *old spelling (to be phased out)*

a~ieren [-'miːrən] *vt* to alarm
Albanien [al'baːniən] (**-s**) *nt* Albania
albanisch *adj* Albanian
albern ['albərn] *adj* silly
Albtraum ▲ ['alptraʊm] *m* nightmare
Album ['albʊm] (**-s, Alben**) *nt* album
Alge ['algə] *f* algae
Algebra ['algebra] (**-**) *f* algebra
Algerier(in) [al'geːriːr(ɪn)] (**-s, -**) *m(f)* Algerian
algerisch *adj* Algerian
alias ['aːlias] *adv* alias
Alibi ['aːlibi] (**-s, -s**) *nt* alibi
Alimente [ali'mɛntə] *pl* alimony *sg*
Alkohol ['alkohol] (**-s, -e**) *m* alcohol; **a~frei**
  adj non-alcoholic; **~iker(in)**
  [alko'hoːlikər(ɪn)] (**-s, -**) *m(f)* alcoholic;
  a~isch *adj* alcoholic; **~verbot** *nt* ban on
  alcohol
All [al] (**-s**) *nt* universe
all'abendlich *adv* every evening
'allbekannt *adj* universally known

alle(r, s) ['alə(r,s)] *adj* 1 (*sämtliche*) all; **wir
  alle** all of us; **alle Kinder waren da** all the
  children were there; **alle Kinder mögen ...**
  all children like ...; **alle beide** both of us/
  them; **sie kamen alle** they all came; **alles
  Gute** all the best; **alles in allem** all in all
  2 (*mit Zeit- oder Maßangaben*) every; **alle
  vier Jahre** every four years; **alle fünf
  Meter** every five metres
  ♦ *pron* everything; **alles was er sagt**
  everything he says, all that he says
  ♦ *adv* (*zu Ende, aufgebraucht*) finished; **die
  Milch ist alle** the milk's all gone, there's
  no milk left; **etw alle machen** to finish sth
  up

Allee [a'leː] *f* avenue
allein [a'laɪn] *adv* alone; (*ohne Hilfe*) on one's
  own, by oneself ♦ *konj* but, only; **nicht ~**
  (*nicht nur*) not only; **~ stehend** single;
  A~erziehende(r) *f(m)* single parent;
  A~gang *m*: **im A~gang** on one's own
allemal ['aləˈmaːl] *adv* (*jedes Mal*) always;
  (*ohne weiteres*) with no bother; *siehe* **Mal**

allenfalls ['alənˈfals] *adv* at all events;
  (*höchstens*) at most
aller- ['alər] *zW*: **~beste(r, s)** *adj* very best;
  ~dings *adv* (*zwar*) admittedly; (*gewiss*)
  certainly
Allergie [aler'giː] *f* allergy; **al'lergisch** *adj*
  allergic
aller- *zW*: **~hand** (*umg*) *adj inv* all sorts of;
  das ist doch ~hand! that's a bit much;
  ~hand! (*lobend*) good show!; **A~'heiligen**
  nt All Saints' Day; **~höchstens** *adv* at the
  very most; **~lei** *adj inv* all sorts of;
  ~letzte(r, s) *adj* very last; **A~seelen** (**-s**)
  nt All Souls' Day; **~seits** *adv* on all sides;
  prost ~seits! cheers everyone!

i **Allerheiligen** (*All Saints' Day*) is
  celebrated on November 1st and is a
  public holiday in some parts of Germany
  and in Austria. **Allerseelen** (*All Souls'
  Day*) is celebrated on November 2nd in the
  Roman Catholic Church. It is customary to
  visit cemeteries and place lighted candles on
  the graves of relatives and friends.

Allerwelts- *in zW* (*Durchschnitts-*) common;
  (*nichts sagend*) commonplace
alles *pron* everything; **~ in allem** all in all; **~
  Gute!** all the best!
Alleskleber (**-s, -**) *m* multi-purpose glue
allgemein ['algəmaɪn] *adj* general; **im A~en**
  in general; **~ gültig** generally accepted;
  A~wissen *nt* general knowledge
Alliierte(r) [ali'iːrtə(r)] *m* ally
all- *zW*: **~jährlich** *adj* annual; **~mächtig**
  adj almighty; **~mählich** *adj* gradual;
  A~tag *m* everyday life; **~täglich** *adj, adv*
  daily; (*gewöhnlich*) commonplace; **~tags**
  adv on weekdays; **~'wissend** *adj*
  omniscient; **~zu** *adv* all too; **~ oft** all too
  often; **~ viel** too much
Allzweck- ['altsvɛk-] *in zW* multi-purpose
Alm [alm] (**-, -en**) *f* alpine pasture
Almosen ['almoːzən] (**-s, -**) *nt* alms *pl*
Alpen ['alpən] *pl* Alps; **~vorland** *nt* foothills
  pl of the Alps

Alphabet [alfa'be:t] (**-(e)s, -e**) *nt* alphabet; **a~isch** *adj* alphabetical

Alptraum ['alptraum] = **Albtraum**

┌─────────────────────────────┐
│ *SCHLÜSSELWORT* │
└─────────────────────────────┘

als [als] *konj* **1** (*zeitlich*) when; (*gleichzeitig*) as; **damals, als ...** (in the days) when ...; **gerade, als ...** just as ...
2 (*in der Eigenschaft*) than; **als Antwort** as an answer; **als Kind** as a child
3 (*bei Vergleichen*) than; **ich kam später als er** I came later than he (did) *od* later than him; **lieber ... als ...** rather ... than ...; **nichts als Ärger** nothing but trouble
4: **als ob/wenn** as if

also ['alzo:] *konj* so; (*folglich*) therefore; **~ gut** *od* **schön!** okay then; **~, so was!** well really!; **na ~!** there you are then!

Alsterwasser ['alstər-] *nt* shandy (*BRIT*), beer and lemonade

Alt [alt] (**-s, -e**) *m* (*MUS*) alto

alt *adj* old; **alles beim A~en lassen** to leave everything as it was

Altar [al'ta:r] (**-(e)s, -äre**) *m* altar

Alt- *zW*: **~bau** *m* old building; **a~bekannt** *adj* long-known; **~bier** *nt* top-fermented German dark beer; **~'eisen** *nt* scrap iron

Alten(wohn)heim *nt* old people's home

Alter ['altər] (**-s, -**) *nt* age; (*hohes*) old age; **im ~ von** at the age of; **a~n** *vi* to grow old, to age

Alternativ- [alterna'ti:f] *in zW* alternative; **~e** *f* alternative

Alters- *zW*: **~grenze** *f* age limit; **~heim** *nt* old people's home; **~rente** *f* old age pension; **a~schwach** *adj* (*Mensch*) frail; **~versorgung** *f* old age pension

Altertum ['altərtu:m] *nt* antiquity

alt- *zW*: **A~glas** *nt* glass for recycling; **A~glascontainer** *m* bottle bank; **~klug** *adj* precocious; **~modisch** *adj* old-fashioned; **A~papier** *nt* waste paper; **A~stadt** *f* old town

Alufolie ['a:lufo:liə] *f* aluminium foil

Aluminium [alu'mi:niom] (**-s**) *nt* aluminium, aluminum (*US*)

Alzheimerkrankheit ['altshaimər'kraŋkhait] *f* Alzheimer's (disease)

am [am] = **an dem**; **~ Schlafen**; (*umg*) sleeping; **~ 15. März** on March 15th; **~ besten/schönsten** best/most beautiful

Amateur [ama'tø:r] *m* amateur

Amboss ▲ ['ambɔs] (**-es, -e**) *m* anvil

ambulant [ambu'lant] *adj* outpatient; **Ambulanz** *f* outpatients *sg*

Ameise ['a:maizə] *f* ant

Ameisenhaufen *m* ant hill

Amerika [a'me:rika] (**-s**) *nt* America; **~ner(in)** [-'ka:nər(in)] (**-s, -**) *m(f)* American; **a~nisch** [-'ka:nɪʃ] *adj* American

Amnestie [amnɛs'ti:] *f* amnesty

Ampel ['ampəl] (**-, -n**) *f* traffic lights *pl*

amputieren [ampu'ti:rən] *vt* to amputate

Amsel ['amzəl] (**-, -n**) *f* blackbird

Amt [amt] (**-(e)s, -er**) *nt* office; (*Pflicht*) duty; (*TEL*) exchange; **a~ieren** [am'ti:rən] *vi* to hold office; **a~lich** *adj* official

Amts- *zW*: **~richter** *m* district judge; **~stunden** *pl* office hours; **~zeichen** *nt* dialling tone; **~zeit** *f* period of office

amüsant [amy'zant] *adj* amusing

amüsieren [amy'zi:rən] *vt* to amuse ♦ *vr* to enjoy o.s.

Amüsierviertel *nt* nightclub district

┌─────────────────────────────┐
│ *SCHLÜSSELWORT* │
└─────────────────────────────┘

an [an] *präp +dat* **1** (*räumlich: wo?*) at; (*auf, bei*) on; (*nahe bei*) near; **an diesem Ort** at this place; **an der Wand** on the wall; **zu nahe an etw** too near to sth; **unten am Fluss** down by the river; **Köln liegt am Rhein** Cologne is on the Rhine
2 (*zeitlich: wann?*) on; **an diesem Tag** on this day; **an Ostern** at Easter
3: **arm an Fett** low in fat; **an etw sterben** to die of sth; **an (und für) sich** actually
♦ *präp +akk* **1** (*räumlich: wohin?*) to; **er ging ans Fenster** he went (over) to the window; **etw an die Wand hängen/schreiben** to hang/write sth on the wall
2 (*zeitlich: woran?*): **an etw denken** to think of sth
3 (*gerichtet an*) to; **ein Gruß/eine Frage**

Spelling Reform: ▲ *new spelling* △ *old spelling (to be phased out)*

an dich greetings/a question to you
♦ *adv* 1 (*ungefähr*) about; **an die hundert** about a hundred
2 (*auf Fahrplänen*): **Frankfurt an 18.30** arriving Frankfurt 18.30
3 (*ab*): **von dort/heute an** from there/today onwards
4 (*angeschaltet, angezogen*) on; **das Licht ist an** the light is on; **ohne etwas an** with nothing on; *siehe auch* **am**

---

analog [ana'lo:k] *adj* analogous; **A~ie** [-'gi:] *f* analogy
Analphabet(in) [an|alfa'be:t(ɪn)] (**-en, -en**) *m(f)* illiterate (person)
Analyse [ana'ly:zə] *f* analysis
analysieren [analy'zi:rən] *vt* to analyse
Ananas ['ananas] (**-, -** *od* **-se**) *f* pineapple
Anarchie [anar'çi:] *f* anarchy
Anatomie [anato'mi:] *f* anatomy
anbahnen ['anba:nən] *vt, vr* to open up
Anbau ['anbaʊ] *m* (*AGR*) cultivation; (*Gebäude*) extension; **a~en** *vt* (*AGR*) to cultivate; (*Gebäudeteil*) to build on
anbehalten ['anbəhaltən] (*unreg*) *vt* to keep on
anbei [an'baɪ] *adv* enclosed
anbeißen ['anbaɪsən] (*unreg*) *vt* to bite into ♦ *vi* to bite; (*fig*) to swallow the bait; **zum A~** (*umg*) good enough to eat
anbelangen ['anbəlaŋən] *vt* to concern; **was mich anbelangt** as far as I am concerned
anbeten ['anbe:tən] *vt* to worship
Anbetracht ['anbətraxt] *m*: **in ~** +*gen* in view of
anbieten ['anbi:tən] (*unreg*) *vt* to offer ♦ *vr* to volunteer
anbinden ['anbɪndən] (*unreg*) *vt* to tie up; **kurz angebunden** (*fig*) curt
Anblick ['anblɪk] *m* sight; **a~en** *vt* to look at
anbraten ['anbra:tən] *vt* to brown
anbrechen ['anbreçən] (*unreg*) *vt* to start; (*Vorräte*) to break into ♦ *vi* to start; (*Tag*) to break; (*Nacht*) to fall
anbrennen ['anbrenən] (*unreg*) *vi* to catch fire; (*KOCH*) to burn

anbringen ['anbrɪŋən] (*unreg*) *vt* to bring; (*Ware*) to sell; (*festmachen*) to fasten
Anbruch ['anbrʊx] *m* beginning; **~ des Tages/der Nacht** dawn/nightfall
anbrüllen ['anbrʏlən] *vt* to roar at
Andacht ['andaxt] (**-, -en**) *f* devotion; (*Gottesdienst*) prayers *pl*; **andächtig** *adj* ['andɛçtɪç] devout
andauern ['andaʊərn] *vi* to last, to go on; **~d** *adj* continual
Anden ['andən] *pl* Andes
Andenken ['andɛŋkən] (**-s, -**) *nt* memory; souvenir
andere(r, s) ['andərə(r, z)] *adj* other; (*verschieden*) different; **ein ~s Mal** another time; **kein ~r** nobody else; **von etw ~m sprechen** to talk about something else; **~rseits** *adv* on the other hand
andermal *adv*: **ein ~** some other time
ändern ['ɛndərn] *vt* to alter, to change ♦ *vr* to change
andernfalls ['andərnfals] *adv* otherwise
anders ['andərs] *adv*: **~ (als)** differently (from); **wer ~?** who else?; **jd/irgendwo ~** sb/somewhere else; **~ aussehen/klingen** to look/sound different; **~artig** *adj* different; **~herum** *adv* the other way round; **~wo** *adv* somewhere else; **~woher** *adv* from somewhere else
anderthalb ['andərt'halp] *adj* one and a half
Änderung ['ɛndərʊŋ] *f* alteration, change
Änderungsschneiderei *f* tailor (*who does alterations*)
anderweitig ['andər'vaɪtɪç] *adj* other ♦ *adv* otherwise; (*anderswo*) elsewhere
andeuten ['andɔʏtən] *vt* to indicate; (*Wink geben*) to hint at; **Andeutung** *f* indication; hint
Andrang ['andraŋ] *m* crush
andrehen ['andre:ən] *vt* to turn *od* switch on; **jdm etw ~** (*umg*) to unload sth onto sb
androhen ['andro:ən] *vt*: **jdm etw ~** to threaten sb with sth
aneignen ['an|aɪgnən] *vt*: **sich** *dat* **etw ~** to acquire sth; (*widerrechtlich*) to appropriate sth

---

Rechtschreibreform: ▲ *neue Schreibung* △ *alte Schreibung (auslaufend)*

aneinander [an|aɪˈnandər] *adv* at/on/to *etc* one another *od* each other; ~ **geraten** to clash

Anekdote [anɛkˈdoːtə] *f* anecdote

anekeln [ˈan|eːkəln] *vt* to disgust

anerkannt [ˈan|ɛrkant] *adj* recognized, acknowledged

anerkennen [ˈan|ɛrkɛnən] (*unreg*) *vt* to recognize, to acknowledge; (*würdigen*) to appreciate; **~d** *adj* appreciative

Anerkennung *f* recognition, acknowledgement; appreciation

anfachen [ˈanfaxən] *vt* to fan into flame; (*fig*) to kindle

anfahren [ˈanfaːrən] (*unreg*) *vt* to deliver; (*fahren gegen*) to hit; (*Hafen*) to put into; (*fig*) to bawl out ♦ *vi* to drive up; (*losfahren*) to drive off

Anfahrt [ˈanfaːrt] *f* (~*sweg*, ~*szeit*) journey

Anfall [ˈanfal] *m* (*MED*) attack; **a~en** (*unreg*) *vt* to attack; (*fig*) to overcome ♦ *vi* (*Arbeit*) to come up; (*Produkt*) to be obtained

anfällig [ˈanfɛlɪç] *adj* delicate; ~ **für etw** prone to sth

Anfang [ˈanfaŋ] (*-(e)s*, *-fänge*) *m* beginning, start; **von ~ an** right from the beginning; **zu ~** at the beginning; ~ **Mai** at the beginning of May; **a~en** (*unreg*) *vt*, *vi* to begin, to start; (*machen*) to do

Anfänger(in) [ˈanfɛŋar(ɪn)] (*-s*, *-*) *m(f)* beginner

anfänglich [ˈanfɛŋlɪç] *adj* initial

anfangs *adv* at first; **A~buchstabe** *m* initial *od* first letter; **A~gehalt** *nt* starting salary

anfassen [ˈanfasən] *vt* to handle; (*berühren*) to touch ♦ *vi* to lend a hand ♦ *vr* to feel

anfechten [ˈanfɛçtən] (*unreg*) *vt* to dispute

anfertigen [ˈanfɛrtɪgən] *vt* to make

anfeuern [ˈanfɔyərn] *vt* (*fig*) to spur on

anflehen [ˈanfleːən] *vt* to implore

anfliegen [ˈanfliːgən] (*unreg*) *vt* to fly to

Anflug [ˈanfluːk] *m* (*AVIAT*) approach; (*Spur*) trace

anfordern [ˈanfɔrdərn] *vt* to demand; (*COMM*) to requisition

Anforderung *f* (+*gen*) demand (for)

Anfrage [ˈanfraːgə] *f* inquiry; **a~n** *vi* to inquire

anfreunden [ˈanfrɔyndən] *vr* to make friends

anfügen [ˈanfyːgən] *vt* to add; (*beifügen*) to enclose

anfühlen [ˈanfyːlən] *vt*, *vr* to feel

anführen [ˈanfyːrən] *vt* to lead; (*zitieren*) to quote; (*umg: betrügen*) to lead up the garden path

Anführer *m* leader

Anführungszeichen *pl* quotation marks, inverted commas

Angabe [ˈangaːbə] *f* statement; (*TECH*) specification; (*umg: Prahlerei*) boasting; (*SPORT*) service

angeben [ˈangeːbən] (*unreg*) *vt* to give; (*anzeigen*) to inform on; (*bestimmen*) to set ♦ *vi* (*umg*) to boast; (*SPORT*) to serve

Angeber (-s, -) (*umg*) *m* show-off; **Angebe'rei** (*umg*) *f* showing off

angeblich [ˈangeːplɪç] *adj* alleged

angeboren [ˈangəboːrən] *adj* inborn, innate

Angebot [ˈangəboːt] *nt* offer; ~ (*an* +*dat*) (*COMM*) supply (of)

angebracht [ˈangəbraxt] *adj* appropriate, in order

angegriffen [ˈangəgrɪfən] *adj* exhausted

angeheitert [ˈangəhaɪtərt] *adj* tipsy

angehen [ˈangeːən] (*unreg*) *vt* to concern; (*angreifen*) to attack; (*bitten*): **jdn ~ (um)** to approach sb (for) ♦ *vi* (*Feuer*) to light; (*umg: beginnen*) to begin; ~**d** *adj* prospective

angehören [ˈangəhøːrən] *vi* (+ *dat*) to belong to; (*Partei*) to be a member of

Angehörige(r) *f(m)* relative

Angeklagte(r) [ˈangəklaːktə(r)] *f(m)* accused

Angel [ˈaŋəl] (*-*, *-n*) *f* fishing rod; (*Türangel*) hinge

Angelegenheit [ˈangəleːgənhaɪt] *f* affair, matter

Angel- *zW*: ~**haken** *m* fish hook; **a~n** *vt* to catch ♦ *vi* to fish; ~**n** (*-s*) *nt* angling, fishing; ~**rute** *f* fishing rod; ~**schein** *m* fishing permit

angemessen [ˈangəmɛsən] *adj* appropriate, suitable

Spelling Reform: ▲ *new spelling* △ *old spelling (to be phased out)*

angenehm ['angəneːm] *adj* pleasant; ~! (*bei Vorstellung*) pleased to meet you

angeregt [angəreːkt] *adj* animated, lively

angesehen ['angəzeːən] *adj* respected

angesichts ['angəzɪçts] *präp* +*gen* in view of, considering

angespannt ['angəʃpant] *adj* (*Aufmerksamkeit*) close; (*Arbeit*) hard

Angestellte(r) ['angəʃtɛltə(r)] *f(m)* employee

angestrengt ['angəʃtrɛŋt] *adv* as hard as one can

angetan ['angətaːn] *adj*: **von jdm/etw ~ sein** to be impressed by sb/sth; **es jdm ~ haben** to appeal to sb

angetrunken ['angətrʊŋkən] *adj* tipsy

angewiesen ['angəviːzən] *adj*: **auf jdn/etw ~ sein** to be dependent on sb/sth

angewöhnen ['angəvøːnən] *vt*: **jdm/sich etw ~** to get sb/become accustomed to sth

Angewohnheit ['angəvoːnhaɪt] *f* habit

angleichen ['anglaɪçən] (*unreg*) *vt, vr* to adjust

Angler ['aŋlər] (**-s, -**) *m* angler

angreifen ['angraɪfən] (*unreg*) *vt* to attack; (*beschädigen*) to damage

Angreifer (**-s, -**) *m* attacker

Angriff ['angrɪf] *m* attack; **etw in ~ nehmen** to make a start on sth

Angst (**-, ⁛e**) *f* fear; **jdm ist a~** sb is afraid *od* scared; **~ haben** (**vor** +*dat*) to be afraid *od* scared (of); **~ haben um jdn/etw** to be worried about sb/sth; **jdm ~ machen** to scare sb; **~hase** (*umg*) *m* chicken, scaredy-cat

ängst- ['ɛŋst] *zW*: **~igen** *vt* to frighten ♦ *vr*: **sich ~igen** (**vor** +*dat od* **um**) to worry (o.s.) (about); **~lich** *adj* nervous; (*besorgt*) worried; **Ä~lichkeit** *f* nervousness

anhaben ['anhaːbən] (*unreg*) *vt* to have on; **er kann mir nichts ~** he can't hurt me

anhalt- ['anhalt] *zW*: **~en** (*unreg*) *vt* to stop ♦ *vi* to stop; (*andauern*) to persist; (**jdm**) **etw ~en** to hold sth up (against sb); **jdn zur Arbeit/Höflichkeit ~en** to make sb work/be polite; **~end** *adj* persistent;

A~er(in) (**-s, -**) *m(f)* hitch-hiker; **per A~er fahren** to hitch-hike; **A~spunkt** *m* clue

anhand [an'hant] *präp* +*gen* with

Anhang ['anhaŋ] *m* appendix; (*Leute*) family; supporters *pl*

anhäng- ['anhɛŋ] *zW*: **~en** (*unreg*) *vt* to hang up; (*Wagen*) to couple up; (*Zusatz*) to add (on); **A~er** (**-s, -**) *m* supporter; (*AUT*) trailer; (*am Koffer*) tag; (*Schmuck*) pendant; **A~erschaft** *f* supporters *pl*; **~lich** *adj* devoted; **A~lichkeit** *f* devotion; **A~sel** (**-s, -**) *nt* appendage

Anhäufung ['anhɔʏfʊŋ] *f* accumulation

anheben ['anheːbən] (*unreg*) *vt* to lift up; (*Preise*) to raise

anheizen ['anhaɪtsən] *vt* (*Stimmung*) to lift; (*Moral*) to boost

Anhieb ['anhiːb] *m*: **auf ~** at the very first go; (*kurz entschlossen*) on the spur of the moment

Anhöhe ['anhøːə] *f* hill

anhören ['anhøːrən] *vt* to listen to; (*anmerken*) to hear ♦ *vr* to sound

animieren [ani'miːrən] *vt* to encourage, to urge on

Anis [a'niːs] (**-es, -e**) *m* aniseed

Ank. *abk* (= *Ankunft*) arr.

Ankauf ['ankauf] *m* (*von Wertpapieren, Devisen, Waren*) purchase; **a~en** *vt* to purchase, to buy

Anker ['aŋkər] (**-s, -**) *m* anchor; **vor ~ gehen** to drop anchor

Anklage ['anklaːgə] *f* accusation; (*JUR*) charge; **~bank** *f* dock; **a~n** *vt* to accuse; **jdn (eines Verbrechens) a~n** (*JUR*) to charge sb (with a crime)

Ankläger ['anklɛːgər] *m* accuser

Anklang ['anklaŋ] *m*: **bei jdm ~ finden** to meet with sb's approval

Ankleidekabine *f* changing cubicle

ankleiden ['anklaɪdən] *vt, vr* to dress

anklicken ['anklɪkən] *vt* (*COMPUT*) to click on

anklopfen ['anklɔpfən] *vi* to knock

anknüpfen ['anknʏpfən] *vt* to fasten *od* tie on; (*fig*) to start ♦ *vi* (*anschließen*): **~ an** +*akk* to refer to

ankommen ['ankɔmən] (*unreg*) *vi* to arrive;

(*näher kommen*) to approach; (*Anklang finden*): **bei jdm (gut) ~** to go down well with sb; **es kommt darauf an** it depends; (*wichtig sein*) that (is what) matters; **es darauf ~ lassen** to let things take their course; **gegen jdn/etw ~** to cope with sb/sth; **bei jdm schlecht ~** to go down badly with sb

ankreuzen ['ankrɔytsən] *vt* to mark with a cross; (*hervorheben*) to highlight

ankündigen ['ankʏndıgən] *vt* to announce; **Ankündigung** *f* announcement

Ankunft ['ankunft] (**-, -künfte**) *f* arrival; **~szeit** *f* time of arrival

ankurbeln ['ankurbəln] *vt* (*fig*) to boost

Anlage ['anlaːgə] *f* disposition; (*Begabung*) talent; (*Park*) gardens *pl*; (*Beilage*) enclosure; (*TECH*) plant; (*FIN*) investment; (*Entwurf*) layout

Anlass ▲ ['anlas] (**-es, -lässe**) *m*: **~ (zu)** cause (for); (*Ereignis*) occasion; **aus ~** +*gen* on the occasion of; **~ zu etw geben** to give rise to sth; **etw zum ~ nehmen** to take the opportunity of sth

anlassen (*unreg*) *vt* to leave on; (*Motor*) to start ♦ *vr* (*umg*) to start off

Anlasser (**-s, -**) *m* (*AUT*) starter

anlässlich ▲ ['anlesliç] *prap* +*gen* on the occasion of

Anlauf ['anlauf] *m* run-up; **a~en** (*unreg*) *vi* to begin; (*neuer Film*) to show; (*SPORT*) to run up; (*Fenster*) to mist up; (*Metall*) to tarnish ♦ *vt* to call at; **rot a~en** to blush; **angelaufen kommen** to come running up

anlegen ['anleːgən] *vt* to put; (*anziehen*) to put on; (*gestalten*) to lay out; (*Geld*) to invest ♦ *vi* to dock; **etw an etw** *akk* **~** to put sth against *od* on sth; **ein Gewehr ~ (auf** +*akk*) to aim a weapon (at); **es auf etw** *akk* **~** to be out for sth/to do sth; **sich mit jdm ~** (*umg*) to quarrel with sb

Anlegestelle *f* landing place

anlehnen ['anleːnən] *vt* to lean; (*Tür*) to leave ajar; **(sich) an etw** *akk* **~** to lean on/against sth

Anleihe ['anlaɪə] *f* (*FIN*) loan

anleiten ['anlaɪtən] *vt* to instruct;

Anleitung *f* instructions *pl*

anliegen ['anliːgən] (*unreg*) *vi* (*Kleidung*) to cling; **A~ (-s, -)** *nt* matter; (*Wunsch*) wish; **~d** *adj* adjacent; (*beigefügt*) enclosed

Anlieger (**-s, -**) *m* resident; **„~ frei"** "residents only"

anmachen ['anmaxən] *vt* to attach; (*ELEK*) to put on; (*Zigarette*) to light; (*Salat*) to dress

anmaßen ['anmaːsən] *vt*: **sich** *dat* **etw ~** (*Recht*) to lay claim to sth; **~d** *adj* arrogant

Anmaßung *f* presumption

anmelden ['anmɛldən] *vt* to announce ♦ *vr* (*sich ankündigen*) to make an appointment; (*polizeilich, für Kurs etc*) to register

Anmeldung *f* announcement; appointment; registration

anmerken ['anmɛrkən] *vt* to observe; (*anstreichen*) to mark; **sich** *dat* **nichts ~ lassen** to not give anything away

Anmerkung *f* note

anmieten ['anmiːtən] *vt* to rent; (*auch Auto*) to hire

Anmut ['anmuːt] (**-**) *f* grace; **a~en** *vt* to give a feeling; **a~ig** *adj* charming

annähen ['anneːən] *vt* to sew on

annähern ['anneːərn] *vr* to get closer; **~d** *adj* approximate

Annäherung *f* approach

Annäherungsversuch *m* advances *pl*

Annahme ['annaːmə] *f* acceptance; (*Vermutung*) assumption

annehm- ['anneːm] *zW*: **~bar** *adj* acceptable; **~en** (*unreg*) *vt* to accept; (*Namen*) to take; (*Kind*) to adopt; (*vermuten*) to suppose, to assume ♦ *vr* (+*gen*) to take care (of); **A~lichkeit** *f* comfort

Annonce [a'nõːsə] *f* advertisement

annoncieren [anõ'siːrən] *vt*, *vi* to advertise

annullieren [anʊ'liːrən] *vt* to annul

anonym [ano'nyːm] *adj* anonymous

Anorak ['anorak] (**-s, -s**) *m* anorak

anordnen ['anɔrdnən] *vt* to arrange; (*befehlen*) to order

Anordnung *f* arrangement; order

anorganisch ['anɔrganıʃ] *adj* inorganic

anpacken ['anpakən] *vt* to grasp; (*fig*) to tackle; **mit ~** to lend a hand

anpassen ['anpasən] *vt:* **(jdm)** ~ to fit (on sb); *(fig)* to adapt ♦ *vr* to adapt
anpassungsfähig *adj* adaptable
Anpfiff ['anpfɪf] *m (SPORT)* (starting) whistle; kick-off; *(umg)* rocket
anprallen ['anpralən] *vi:* ~ **(gegen** *od* **an** +*akk)* to collide (with)
anprangern ['anpraŋərn] *vt* to denounce
anpreisen ['anpraɪzən] *(unreg) vt* to extol
Anprobe ['anproːbə] *f* trying on
anprobieren ['anprobiːrən] *vt* to try on
anrechnen ['anrɛçnən] *vt* to charge; *(fig)* to count; **jdm etw hoch** ~ to think highly of sb for sth
Anrecht ['anrɛçt] *nt:* ~ **(auf** +*akk)* right (to)
Anrede ['anreːdə] *f* form of address; a~n *vt* to address; *(belästigen)* to accost
anregen ['anreːgən] *vt* to stimulate; **angeregte Unterhaltung** lively discussion; ~**d** *adj* stimulating
Anregung *f* stimulation; *(Vorschlag)* suggestion
anreichern ['anraɪçərn] *vt* to enrich
Anreise ['anraɪzə] *f* journey; a~n *vi* to arrive
Anreiz ['anraɪts] *m* incentive
Anrichte ['anrɪçtə] *f* sideboard; a~n *vt* to serve up; **Unheil a~n** to make mischief
anrüchig ['anrʏçɪç] *adj* dubious
anrücken ['anrʏkən] *vi* to approach; *(MIL)* to advance
Anruf ['anruːf] *m* call; ~**beantworter** [-bə-'|antvɔrtər] **(-s, -)** *m* answering machine; a~en *(unreg) vt* to call out to; *(bitten)* to call on; *(TEL)* to ring up, to phone, to call
ans [ans] = **an das**
Ansage ['anzaːgə] *f* announcement; a~n *vt* to announce ♦ *vr* to say one will come; ~**r(in)** **(-s, -)** *m(f)* announcer
ansammeln ['anzaməln] *vt (Reichtümer)* to amass ♦ *vr (Menschen)* to gather, to assemble; *(Wasser)* to collect; **Ansammlung** *f* collection; *(Leute)* crowd
ansässig ['anzɛsɪç] *adj* resident
Ansatz ['anzats] *m* start; *(Haaransatz)* hairline; *(Halsansatz)* base; *(Verlängerungsstück)* extension; *(Veranschlagung)* estimate; ~**punkt** *m* starting point

anschaffen ['anʃafən] *vt* to buy, to purchase; **Anschaffung** *f* purchase
anschalten ['anʃaltən] *vt* to switch on
anschau- ['anʃaʊ] *zW:* ~**en** *vt* to look at; ~**lich** *adj* illustrative; **A~ung** *f (Meinung)* view; **aus eigener A~ung** from one's own experience
Anschein ['anʃaɪn] *m* appearance; **allem ~ nach** to all appearances; **den ~ haben** to seem, to appear; a~end *adj* apparent
anschieben ['anʃiːbən] *vt* to push
Anschlag ['anʃlaːk] *m* notice; *(Attentat)* attack; *(COMM)* estimate; *(auf Klavier)* touch; *(Schreibmaschine)* character; a~en ['anʃlaːgən] *(unreg) vt* to put up; *(beschädigen)* to chip; *(Akkord)* to strike; *(Kosten)* to estimate ♦ *vi* to hit; *(wirken)* to have an effect; *(Glocke)* to ring; **an etw** *akk* **a~en** to hit against sth
anschließen ['anʃliːsən] *(unreg) vt* to connect up; *(Sender)* to link up ♦ *vi:* **an etw** *akk* ~ to adjoin sth; *(zeitlich)* to follow sth ♦ *vr:* **sich jdm/etw** ~ to join sb/sth; *(beipflichten)* to agree with sb/sth; **sich an etw** *akk* ~ to adjoin sth; ~**d** *adj* adjacent; *(zeitlich)* subsequent ♦ *adv* afterwards
Anschluss ▲ ['anʃlʊs] *m (ELEK, EISENB)* connection; *(von Wasser etc)* supply; **im ~ an** +*akk* following; ~ **finden** to make friends; ~**flug** *m* connecting flight
anschmiegsam ['anʃmiːkzaːm] *adj* affectionate
anschnallen ['anʃnalən] *vt* to buckle on ♦ *vr* to fasten one's seat belt
anschneiden ['anʃnaɪdən] *(unreg) vt* to cut into; *(Thema)* to introduce
anschreiben ['anʃraɪbən] *(unreg) vt* to write (up); *(COMM)* to charge up; *(benachrichtigen)* to write to
anschreien ['anʃraɪən] *(unreg) vt* to shout at
Anschrift ['anʃrɪft] *f* address
Anschuldigung ['anʃʊldɪgʊŋ] *f* accusation
anschwellen ['anʃvelən] *(unreg) vi* to swell (up)
anschwindeln ['anʃvɪndəln] *vt* to lie to
ansehen ['anzeːən] *(unreg) vt* to look at;

jdm etw ~ to see sth (from sb's face);
jdn/etw als etw ~ to look on sb/sth as sth;
~ für to consider; **A~ (-s)** *nt* respect; *(Ruf)*
reputation

ansehnlich ['anzeːnlɪç] *adj* fine-looking;
(beträchtlich) considerable

ansetzen ['anzɛtsən] *vt (festlegen)* to fix;
(entwickeln) to develop; *(Fett)* to put on;
(Blätter) to grow; *(zubereiten)* to prepare
♦ *vi (anfangen)* to start, to begin;
(Entwicklung) to set in; *(dick werden)* to put
on weight ♦ *vr (Rost etc)* to start to
develop; **~ an** *+akk (anfügen)* to fix on to;
(anlegen, an Mund etc) to put to

Ansicht ['anzɪçt] *f (Anblick)* sight; *(Meinung)*
view, opinion; **zur ~** on approval; **meiner ~**
nach in my opinion; **~skarte** *f* picture
postcard; **~ssache** *f* matter of opinion

ansonsten [an'zɔnstən] *adv* otherwise

anspannen ['anʃpanən] *vt* to harness;
(Muskel) to strain; **Anspannung** *f* strain

anspielen ['anʃpiːlən] *vi (SPORT)* to start
play; **auf etw** *akk* **~** to refer *od* allude to
sth

Anspielung *f*: **~ (auf** *+akk)* reference (to),
allusion (to)

Anspitzer ['anʃpɪtsər] *m* **(-s, -)** *m* pencil
sharpener

Ansporn ['anʃpɔrn] **(-(e)s)** *m* incentive

Ansprache ['anʃpraːxə] *f* address

ansprechen ['anʃprɛçən] *(unreg)* *vt* to speak
to; *(bitten, gefallen)* to appeal to ♦ *vi* **(auf**
etw *akk)* **~** to react (to sth); **jdn auf etw**
akk **(hin)** **~** to ask sb about sth; **~d** *adj*
attractive

anspringen ['anʃprɪŋən] *(unreg)* *vi (AUT)* to
start ♦ *vt* to jump at

Anspruch ['anʃprʊx] *m (Recht)*: **~ (auf** *+akk)*
claim (to); **hohe Ansprüche stellen/**
haben to demand/expect a lot; **jdn/etw in**
~ nehmen to occupy sb/take up sth;
a~slos *adj* undemanding; **a~svoll** *adj*
demanding

anstacheln ['anʃtaxəln] *vt* to spur on

Anstalt ['anʃtalt] **(-, -en)** *f* institution; **~en**
machen, etw zu tun to prepare to do sth

Anstand ['anʃtant] *m* decency

anständig ['anʃtɛndɪç] *adj* decent; *(umg)*
proper; *(groß)* considerable

anstandslos *adv* without any ado

anstarren ['anʃtarən] *vt* to stare at

anstatt [an'ʃtat] *präp* +gen instead of ♦ *konj*:
~ etw zu tun instead of doing sth

Ansteck- ['anʃtɛk] *zW*: **a~en** *vt* to pin on;
(MED) to infect; *(Pfeife)* to light; *(Haus)* to
set fire to ♦ *vr*: **ich habe mich bei ihm**
angesteckt I caught it from him ♦ *vi (fig)*
to be infectious; **a~end** *adj* infectious;
~ung *f* infection

anstehen ['anʃteːən] *(unreg)* *vi* to queue
(up) *(BRIT)*, to line up *(US)*

ansteigen ['anʃtaɪɡən] *vt (Straße)* to climb;
(Gelände, Temperatur, Preise) to rise

anstelle, an Stelle [an'ʃtɛlə] *präp* +gen in
place of; **~n** ['an-] *vt (einschalten)* to turn
on; *(Arbeit geben)* to employ; *(machen)* to
do ♦ *vr* to queue (up) *(BRIT)*, to line up *(US)*;
(umg) to act

Anstellung *f* employment; *(Posten)* post,
position

Anstieg ['anʃtiːk] **(-(e)s, -e)** *m (+gen)* climb;
(fig: von Preisen etc) increase (in)

anstiften ['anʃtɪftən] *vt (Unglück)* to cause;
jdn zu etw ~ to put sb up to sth

anstimmen ['anʃtɪmən] *vt (Lied)* to strike up
with; *(Geschrei)* to set up

Anstoß ['anʃtoːs] *m* impetus; *(Ärgernis)*
offence; *(SPORT)* kick-off; **der erste ~** the
initiative; **~ nehmen an** *+dat* to take
offence at; **a~en** *(unreg)* *vt* to push; *(mit*
Fuß) to kick ♦ *vi* to knock, to bump; *(mit der*
Zunge) to lisp; *(mit Gläsern)*: **a~en (auf**
+akk) to drink (to), to drink a toast (to)

anstößig ['anʃtøːsɪç] *adj* offensive, indecent

anstreichen ['anʃtraɪçən] *(unreg)* *vt* to paint

anstrengen ['anʃtrɛŋən] *vt* to strain; *(JUR)* to
bring ♦ *vr* to make an effort; **~d** *adj* tiring

Anstrengung *f* effort

Anstrich ['anʃtrɪç] *m* coat of paint

Ansturm ['anʃtʊrm] *m* rush; *(MIL)* attack

Antarktis [ant'ʔarktɪs] **(-)** *f* Antarctic

antasten ['antastən] *vt* to touch; *(Recht)* to
infringe upon; *(Ehre)* to question

Anteil ['antaɪl] **(-s, -e)** *m* share; *(Mitgefühl)*

Spelling Reform: ▲ *new spelling* △ *old spelling (to be phased out)*

sympathy; **~ nehmen (an** +*dat*) to share (in); (*sich interessieren*) to take an interest (in); **~nahme** (-) *f* sympathy

Antenne [an'tɛnə] *f* aerial

Anti- ['anti] *in zW* anti; **~alko'holiker** *m* teetotaller; **a~autori'tär** *adj* anti-authoritarian; **~babypille** *f* contraceptive pill; **~biotikum** [antibi'oːtikʊm] **(-s, -ka)** *nt* antibiotic

antik [an'tiːk] *adj* antique; **A~e** *f* (*Zeitalter*) ancient world

Antiquariat [antikvari'aːt] **(-(e)s, -e)** *nt* secondhand bookshop

Antiquitäten [antikvi'tɛːtən] *pl* antiques; **~händler** *m* antique dealer

Antrag ['antraːk] **(-(e)s, -träge)** *m* proposal; (*PARL*) motion; (*Gesuch*) application; **~steller(in)** **(-s, -)** *m(f)* claimant; (*für Kredit*) applicant

antreffen ['antrɛfən] (*unreg*) *vt* to meet

antreiben ['antraɪbən] (*unreg*) *vt* to drive on; (*Motor*) to drive

antreten ['antreːtən] (*unreg*) *vt* (*Amt*) to take up; (*Erbschaft*) to come into; (*Beweis*) to offer; (*Reise*) to start, to begin ♦ *vi* (*MIL*) to fall in; (*SPORT*) to line up; **gegen jdn ~** to play/fight (against) sb

Antrieb ['antriːp] *m* (*auch fig*) drive; **aus eigenem ~** of one's own accord

antrinken ['antrɪŋkən] (*unreg*) *vt* (*Flasche, Glas*) to start to drink from; **sich** *dat* **Mut/ einen Rausch ~** to give o.s. Dutch courage/get drunk; **angetrunken sein** to be tipsy

Antritt ['antrɪt] *m* beginning, commencement; (*eines Amts*) taking up

antun ['antuːn] (*unreg*) *vt*: **jdm etw ~** to do sth to sb; **sich** *dat* **Zwang ~** to force o.s.; **sich** *dat* **etwas ~** to (try to) take one's own life

Antwort ['antvɔrt] **(-, -en)** *f* answer, reply; **a~en** *vi* to answer, to reply

anvertrauen ['anfɛrtraʊən] *vt*: **jdm etw ~** to entrust sb with sth; **sich jdm ~** to confide in sb

anwachsen ['anvaksən] (*unreg*) *vi* to grow; (*Pflanze*) to take root

Anwalt ['anvalt] **(-(e)s, -wälte)** *m* solicitor; lawyer; (*fig*) champion

Anwältin ['anvɛltɪn] *f siehe* **Anwalt**

Anwärter ['anvɛrtər] *m* candidate

anweisen ['anvaɪzən] (*unreg*) *vt* to instruct; (*zuteilen*) to assign

Anweisung *f* instruction; (*COMM*) remittance; (*Postanweisung, Zahlungsanweisung*) money order

anwend- ['anvɛnd] *zW*: **~bar** *adj* practicable, applicable; **~en** (*unreg*) *vt* to use, to employ; (*Gesetz, Regel*) to apply; **A~ung** *f* use; application

anwesend ['anveːzənt] *adj* present; **die A~en** those present

Anwesenheit *f* presence

anwidern ['anviːdərn] *vt* to disgust

Anwohner(in) ['anvoːnər(ɪn)] **(-s, -)** *m(f)* neighbour

Anzahl ['antsaːl] *f*: **~ (an** +*dat*) number (of); **a~en** *vt* to pay on account; **~ung** *f* deposit, payment on account

Anzeichen ['antsaɪçən] *nt* sign, indication

Anzeige ['antsaɪɡə] *f* (*Zeitungsanzeige*) announcement; (*Werbung*) advertisement; (*bei Polizei*) report; **~ erstatten gegen jdn** to report sb (to the police); **a~n** *vt* (*zu erkennen geben*) to show; (*bekannt geben*) to announce; (*bei Polizei*) to report

anziehen ['antsiːən] (*unreg*) *vt* to attract; (*Kleidung*) to put on; (*Mensch*) to dress; (*Seil*) to pull tight; (*Schraube*) to tighten; (*Knie*) to draw up ♦ *vr* to get dressed; **~d** *adj* attractive

Anziehung *f* (*Reiz*) attraction; **~skraft** *f* power of attraction; (*PHYS*) force of gravitation

Anzug ['antsuːk] *m* suit; (*Herankommen*): **im ~ sein** to be approaching

anzüglich ['antsyːklɪç] *adj* personal; (*anstößig*) offensive; **A~keit** *f* offensiveness; (*Bemerkung*) personal remark

anzünden ['antsʏndən] *vt* to light

anzweifeln ['antsvaɪfəln] *vt* to doubt

apathisch [a'paːtɪʃ] *adj* apathetic

Apfel ['apfəl] **(-s, ᵘ)** *m* apple; **~saft** *m* apple juice; **~sine** [-'ziːnə] *f* orange; **~wein** *m* cider

Apostel [a'pɔstəl] **(-s, -)** *m* apostle

Apotheke [apo'te:kə] *f* chemist's (shop), drugstore (*US*); **a~npflichtig** [-pflıçtıç] *adj* available only at a chemist's shop (*BRIT*) or pharmacy; **~r(in) (-s, -)** *m(f)* chemist, druggist (*US*)

Apotheke

ⓘ *The* **Apotheke** *is a pharmacy selling medicines available only on prescription and toiletries. The pharmacist is qualified to give advice on medicines and treatments.*

Apparat [apa'ra:t] **(-(e)s, -e)** *m* piece of apparatus; camera; telephone; (*RADIO, TV*) set; **am ~!** speaking!; **~ur** [-'tu:r] *f* apparatus

Appartement [apart(ə)'mã:] **(-s, -s)** *nt* flat

appellieren [ape'li:rən] *vi:* **~ (an** +*akk*) to appeal (to)

Appetit [ape'ti:t] **(-(e)s, -e)** *m* appetite; **guten ~!** enjoy your meal; **a~lich** *adj* appetizing; **~losigkeit** *f* lack of appetite

Applaus [ap'laʊs] **(-es, -e)** *m* applause

Aprikose [apri'ko:zə] *f* apricot

April [a'prıl] **(-(s), -e)** *m* April

Aquarell [akva'rɛl] **(-s, -e)** *nt* watercolour

Äquator [ɛ'kva:tɔr] **(-s)** *m* equator

Arab- ['arab] *zW:* **~er(in) (-s, -)** *m(f)* Arab; **~ien** [a'ra:biən] **(-s)** *nt* Arabia; **a~isch** [a'ra:bıʃ] *adj* Arabian

Arbeit ['arbaıt] **(-, -en)** *f* work *no art*; (*Stelle*) job; (*Erzeugnis*) piece of work; (*wissenschaftliche*) dissertation; (*Klassenarbeit*) test; **das war eine ~** that was a hard job; **a~en** *vi* to work ♦ *vt* to work, to make; **~er(in) (-s, -)** *m(f)* worker; (*ungelernt*) labourer; **~erschaft** *f* workers *pl*, labour force; **~geber (-s, -)** *m* employer; **~nehmer (-s, -)** *m* employee

Arbeits- *in zW* labour; **a~am** *adj* industrious; **~amt** *nt* employment exchange; **~erlaubnis** *f* work permit; **a~fähig** *adj* fit for work, able-bodied; **~gang** *m* operation; **~kräfte** *pl* (*Mitarbeiter*) workforce; **a~los** *adj* unemployed, out-of-work; **~lose(r)** *f(m)* unemployed person; **~losigkeit** *f* unemployment; **~markt** *m* job market; **~platz** *m* job; place of work; **a~scheu** *adj* workshy; **~tag** *m* work(ing) day; **a~unfähig** *adj* unfit for work; **~zeit** *f* working hours *pl*; **~zimmer** *nt* study

Archäologe [arçɛo'lo:gə] **(-n, -n)** *m* archaeologist

Architekt(in) [arçi'tɛkt(ın)] **(-en, -en)** *m(f)* architect; **~ur** [-'tu:r] *f* architecture

Archiv [ar'çi:f] **(-s, -e)** *nt* archive

arg [ark] *adj* bad, awful ♦ *adv* awfully, very

Argentinien [argen'ti:niən] **(-s)** *nt* Argentina, the Argentine

argentinisch *adj* Argentinian

Ärger ['ɛrgər] **(-s)** *m* (*Wut*) anger; (*Unannehmlichkeit*) trouble; **ä~lich** (*zornig*) angry; (*lästig*) annoying, aggravating; **ä~n** *vt* to annoy ♦ *vr* to get annoyed

arg- *zW:* **~listig** *adj* cunning, insidious; **~los** *adj* guileless, innocent

Argument [argu'mɛnt] *nt* argument

argwöhnisch *adj* suspicious

Arie ['a:riə] *f* aria

Aristokrat [aristo'kra:t] **(-en, -en)** *m* aristocrat; **~ie** [-'ti:] *f* aristocracy

Arktis ['arktıs] **(-)** *f* Arctic

Arm [arm] **(-(e)s, -e)** *m* arm, (*Flussarm*) branch

arm *adj* poor

Armatur [arma'tu:r] *f* (*ELEK*) armature; **~enbrett** *nt* instrument panel; (*AUT*) dashboard

Armband *nt* bracelet; **~uhr** *f* (wrist) watch

Arme(r) *f(m)* poor man (woman); **die ~n** the poor

Armee [ar'me:] *f* army

Ärmel ['ɛrməl] **(-s, -)** *m* sleeve; **etw aus dem ~ schütteln** (*fig*) to produce sth just like that; **~kanal** *m* English Channel

ärmlich ['ɛrmlıç] *adj* poor

armselig *adj* wretched, miserable

Armut ['armu:t] **(-)** *f* poverty

Aroma [a'ro:ma] **(-s, Aromen)** *nt* aroma; **~therapie** *f* aromatherapy; **a~tisch**

[aro'ma:tɪʃ] *adj* aromatic

arrangieren [arã:'ʒi:rən] *vt* to arrange ♦ *vr* to come to an arrangement

Arrest [a'rɛst] (-(e)s, -e) *m* detention

arrogant [aro'gant] *adj* arrogant

Arsch [arʃ] (-es, ᵘe) (*umg!*) *m* arse (*BRIT!*), ass (*US!*)

Art [a:rt] (-, -en) *f* (*Weise*) way; (*Sorte*) kind, sort; (*BIOL*) species; **eine ~ (von) Frucht** a kind of fruit; **Häuser aller ~** houses of all kinds; **es ist nicht seine ~, das zu tun** it's not like him to do that; **ich mache das auf meine ~** I do that my (own) way

Arterie [ar'te:riə] *f* artery; **~nverkalkung** *f* arteriosclerosis

artig ['a:rtɪç] *adj* good, well-behaved

Artikel [ar'ti:kəl] (-s, -) *m* article

Artillerie [artɪlə'ri:] *f* artillery

Artischocke [artɪ'ʃɔkə] *f* artichoke

Artist(in) [ar'tɪst(ɪn)] (-en, -en) *m(f)* (circus/ variety) artiste *od* performer

Arznei [a:rts'naɪ] *f* medicine; **~mittel** *nt* medicine, medicament

Arzt [a:rtst] (-es, ᵘe) *m* doctor; **~helferin** *f* (doctor's) receptionist

Ärztin ['ɛ:rtstɪn] *f* doctor

ärztlich ['ɛ:rtstlɪç] *adj* medical

As △ [as] (-ses, -se) *nt* = **Ass**

Asche ['aʃə] *f* (-, -n) ash, cinder

Aschen- *zW:* **~bahn** *f* cinder track; **~becher** *m* ashtray

Aschermittwoch *m* Ash Wednesday

Äser ['ɛ:zər] *pl von* **Aas**

Asiat(in) [azi'a:t(ɪn)] (-en, -en) *m(f)* Asian; **asiatisch** [-'a:tɪʃ] *adj* Asian

Asien ['a:ziən] (-s) *nt* Asia

asozial ['azotsia:l] *adj* antisocial; (*Familien*) asocial

Aspekt [as'pɛkt] (-(e)s, -e) *m* aspect

Asphalt [as'falt] (-(e)s, -e) *m* asphalt

Ass ▲ [as] (-es, -e) *nt* ace

aß *etc* [a:s] *vb siehe* **essen**

Assistent(in) [asɪs'tɛnt(ɪn)] *m(f)* assistant

Assoziation [asotsiatsi'o:n] *f* association

Ast [ast] (-(e)s, ᵘe) *m* bough, branch

ästhetisch [ɛs'te:tɪʃ] *adj* aesthetic

Asthma ['astma] (-s) *nt* asthma; **~tiker(in)**

(-s, -) *m(f)* asthmatic

Astro- [astro] *zW:* **~loge (-n, -n)** *m* astrologer; **~lo'gie** *f* astrology; **~'naut** (-en, -en) *m* astronaut; **~'nom (-en, -en)** *m* astronomer; **~no'mie** *f* astronomy

Asyl [a'zy:l] (-s, -e) *nt* asylum; (*Heim*) home; (*Obdachlosenasyl*) shelter; **~ant(in)** [azy'lant(ɪn)] (-en, -en) *m(f)* asylum-seeker; **~bewerber(in)** *m(f)* asylum-seeker

Atelier [atəli'e:] (-s, -s) *nt* studio

Atem ['a:təm] (-s) *m* breath; **den ~ anhalten** to hold one's breath; **außer ~** out of breath; **a~beraubend** *adj* breathtaking; **a~los** *adj* breathless; **~not** *f* difficulty in breathing; **~pause** *f* breather; **~zug** *m* breath

Atheismus [ate'ɪsmʊs] *m* atheism

Atheist *m* atheist; **a~isch** *adj* atheistic

Athen [a'te:n] (-s) *nt* Athens

Äthiopien [ɛti'o:piən] (-s) *nt* Ethiopia

Athlet [at'le:t] (-en, -en) *m* athlete

Atlantik [at'lantɪk] (-s) *nt* Atlantic (Ocean)

Atlas ['atlas] (- *od* -ses, -se *od* **Atlanten**) *m* atlas

atmen ['a:tmən] *vt, vi* to breathe

Atmosphäre [atmo'sfɛ:rə] *f* atmosphere; **atmosphärisch** *adj* atmospheric

Atmung ['a:tmʊŋ] *f* respiration

Atom [a'to:m] (-s, -e) *nt* atom; **a~ar** *adj* atomic; **~bombe** *f* atom bomb; **~energie** *f* atomic *od* nuclear energy; **~kern** *m* atomic nucleus; **~kraftwerk** *nt* nuclear power station; **~krieg** *m* nuclear *od* atomic war; **~müll** *m* atomic waste; **~strom** *m* (electricity generated by) nuclear power; **~versuch** *m* atomic test; **~waffen** *pl* atomic weapons; **a~waffenfrei** *adj* nuclear-free; **~zeitalter** *nt* atomic age

Attentat [atɛn'ta:t] (-(e)s, -e) *nt:* **~ (auf +akk)** (attempted) assassination (of)

Attentäter [atɛn'tɛ:tər] *m* (would-be) assassin

Attest [a'tɛst] (-(e)s, -e) *nt* certificate

Attraktion [atraktsi'o:n] *f* (*Tourismus, Zirkus*) attraction

attraktiv [atrak'ti:f] *adj* attractive

Attrappe [a'trapə] *f* dummy

Attribut [atri'buːt] **(-(e)s, -e)** *nt* (GRAM) attribute

ätzen ['ɛtsən] *vi* to be caustic; ~**d** *adj* (Säure) corrosive; (fig: Spott) cutting

au [aʊ] *excl* ouch!; ~ **ja!** oh yes!

Aubergine [obɛr'ʒiːnə] *f* aubergine, eggplant

| SCHLÜSSELWORT |
---

auch [aʊx] *adv* **1** (ebenfalls) also, too, as well; **das ist auch schön** that's nice too *od* as well; **er kommt - ich auch** he's coming - so am I, me too; **auch nicht** not ... either; **ich auch nicht** nor I, me neither; **oder auch** or; **auch das noch!** not that as well! **2** (selbst, sogar) even; **auch wenn das Wetter schlecht ist** even if the weather is bad; **ohne auch nur zu fragen** without even asking **3** (wirklich) really; **du siehst müde aus - bin ich auch** you look tired - (so) I am; **so sieht es auch aus** it looks like it too **4** (auch immer): **wer auch** whoever; **was auch** whatever; **wie dem auch sei** be that as it may; **wie sehr er sich auch bemühte** however much he tried

---
| SCHLÜSSELWORT |
---

auf [aʊf] *präp +dat* (wo?) on; **auf dem Tisch** on the table; **auf der Reise** on the way; **auf der Post/dem Fest** at the post office/ party; **auf der Straße** on the road; **auf dem Land/der ganzen Welt** in the country/the whole world
♦ *präp +akk* **1** (wohin?) on(to); **auf den Tisch** on(to) the table; **auf die Post gehen** go to the post office; **auf das Land** into the country; **etw auf einen Zettel schreiben** to write sth on a piece of paper **2**: **auf Deutsch** in German; **auf Lebenszeit** for my/his lifetime; **bis auf ihn** except for him; **auf einmal** at once; **auf seinen Vorschlag (hin)** at his suggestion
♦ *adv* **1** (offen) open; **auf sein** (umg) (Tür, Geschäft) to be open; **das Fenster ist auf** the window is open

2 (hinauf) up; **auf und ab** up and down; **auf und davon** up and away; **auf!** (los!) come on! **3** (aufgestanden) up; **auf sein** to be up; **ist er schon auf?** is he up yet?
♦ *konj*: **auf dass** (so) that

---

aufatmen ['aʊfʔaːtmən] *vi* to heave a sigh of relief

aufbahren ['aʊfbaːrən] *vt* to lay out

Aufbau ['aʊfbaʊ] *m* (Bauen) building, construction; (Struktur) structure; (aufgebautes Teil) superstructure; **a~en** *vt* to erect, to build (up); (Existenz) to make; (gestalten) to construct; **a~en (auf** *dat)* (gründen) to found *od* base (on)

aufbauschen ['aʊfbaʊʃən] *vt* to puff out; (fig) to exaggerate

aufbekommen ['aʊfbəkɔmən] (unreg) *vt* (öffnen) to get open; (Hausaufgaben) to be given

aufbessern ['aʊfbɛsərn] *vt* (Gehalt) to increase

aufbewahren ['aʊfbəvaːrən] *vt* to keep; (Gepäck) to put in the left-luggage office (BRIT) *od* baggage check (US)

Aufbewahrung *f* (safe)keeping; (Gepäckaufbewahrung) left-luggage office (BRIT), baggage check (US)

aufbieten ['aʊfbiːtən] (unreg) *vt* (Kraft) to summon (up); (Armee, Polizei) to mobilize

aufblasen ['aʊfblaːzən] (unreg) *vt* to blow up, to inflate ♦ *vr* (umg) to become bigheaded

aufbleiben ['aʊfblaɪbən] (unreg) *vi* (Laden) to remain open; (Person) to stay up

aufblenden ['aʊfblɛndən] *vt* (Scheinwerfer) to switch on full beam ♦ *vi* (Fahrer) to have the lights on full beam; (AUT: Scheinwerfer) to be on full beam

aufblicken ['aʊfblɪkən] *vi* to look up; ~ **zu** to look up at; (fig) to look up to

aufblühen ['aʊfblyːən] *vi* to blossom, to flourish

aufbrauchen ['aʊfbraʊxən] *vt* to use up

aufbrausen ['aʊfbraʊzən] *vi* (fig) to flare up; ~**d** *adj* hot-tempered

Spelling Reform: ▲ *new spelling* △ *old spelling (to be phased out)*

aufbrechen ['aʊfbrɛçən] (*unreg*) *vt* to break *od* prise (*BRIT*) open ♦ *vi* to burst open; (*gehen*) to start, to set off

aufbringen ['aʊfbrɪŋən] (*unreg*) *vt* (*öffnen*) open; (*in Mode*) to bring into fashion; (*beschaffen*) to procure; (*FIN*) to raise; (*ärgern*) to irritate; **Verständnis für etw ~** to be able to understand sth

Aufbruch ['aʊfbrʊx] *m* departure

aufbrühen ['aʊfbryːən] *vt* (*Tee*) to make

aufbürden ['aʊfbʏrdən] *vt*: **jdm etw ~** to burden sb with sth

aufdecken ['aʊfdɛkən] *vt* to uncover

aufdrängen ['aʊfdrɛŋən] *vt*: **jdm etw ~** to force sth on sb ♦ *vr* (*Mensch*): **sich jdm ~** to intrude on sb

aufdrehen ['aʊfdreːən] *vt* (*Wasserhahn etc*) to turn on; (*Ventil*) to open up

aufdringlich ['aʊfdrɪŋlɪç] *adj* pushy

aufeinander [aʊflaɪˈnandər] *adv* on top of each other; (*schießen*) at each other; (*vertrauen*) each other; **~ folgen** to follow one another; **~ folgend** consecutive; **~ prallen** to hit one another

Aufenthalt ['aʊflɛnthalt] *m* stay; (*Verzögerung*) delay; (*EISENB: Halten*) stop; (*Ort*) haunt

Aufenthaltserlaubnis *f* residence permit

auferlegen ['aʊflɛrleːgən] *vt*: (**jdm**) **~** to impose (upon sb)

Auferstehung ['aʊflɛrʃteːʊŋ] *f* resurrection

aufessen ['aʊflɛsən] (*unreg*) *vt* to eat up

auffahr- ['aʊffaːr] *zW*: **~en** (*unreg*) *vi* (*herankommen*) to draw up; (*hochfahren*) to jump up; (*wütend werden*) to flare up; (*in den Himmel*) to ascend ♦ *vt* (*Kanonen, Geschütz*) to bring up; **~en auf** +*akk* (*Auto*) to run *od* crash into; **~end** *adj* hot-tempered; **A~t** *f* (*Hausauffahrt*) drive; (*Autobahnauffahrt*) slip road (*BRIT*), (*freeway*) entrance (*US*); **A~unfall** *m* pile-up

auffallen ['aʊffalən] (*unreg*) *vi* to be noticeable; **jdm ~** to strike sb

auffällig ['aʊffɛlɪç] *adj* conspicuous, striking

auffangen ['aʊffaŋən] (*unreg*) *vt* to catch; (*Funkspruch*) to intercept; (*Preise*) to peg

auffassen ['aʊffasən] *vt* to understand, to comprehend; (*auslegen*) to see, to view

Auffassung *f* (*Meinung*) opinion; (*Auslegung*) view, concept; (*auch:* **~sgabe**) grasp

auffindbar ['aʊffɪntbaːr] *adj* to be found

auffordern ['aʊffɔrdərn] *vt* (*befehlen*) to call upon, to order; (*bitten*) to ask

Aufforderung *f* (*Befehl*) order; (*Einladung*) invitation

auffrischen ['aʊffrɪʃən] *vt* to freshen up; (*Kenntnisse*) to brush up; (*Erinnerungen*) to reawaken ♦ *vi* (*Wind*) to freshen

aufführen ['aʊffyːrən] *vt* (*THEAT*) to perform; (*in einem Verzeichnis*) to list, to specify ♦ *vr* (*sich benehmen*) to behave

Aufführung *f* (*THEAT*) performance; (*Liste*) specification

Aufgabe ['aʊfgaːbə] *f* task; (*SCH*) exercise; (*Hausaufgabe*) homework; (*Verzicht*) giving up; (*von Gepäck*) registration; (*von Post*) posting; (*von Inserat*) insertion

Aufgang ['aʊfgaŋ] *m* ascent; (*Sonnenaufgang*) rise; (*Treppe*) staircase

aufgeben ['aʊfgeːbən] (*unreg*) *vt* (*verzichten*) to give up; (*Paket*) to send, to post; (*Gepäck*) to register; (*Bestellung*) to give; (*Inserat*) to insert; (*Rätsel, Problem*) to set ♦ *vi* to give up

Aufgebot ['aʊfgəboːt] *nt* supply; (*Eheaufgebot*) banns *pl*

aufgedunsen ['aʊfgədʊnzən] *adj* swollen, puffed up

aufgehen ['aʊfgeːən] (*unreg*) *vi* (*Sonne, Teig*) to rise; (*sich öffnen*) to open; (*klar werden*) to become clear; (*MATH*) to come out exactly; **~ (in** +*dat*) (*sich widmen*) to be absorbed (in); **in Rauch/Flammen ~** to go up in smoke/flames

aufgelegt ['aʊfgəleːkt] *adj*: **gut/schlecht ~ sein** to be in a good/bad mood; **zu etw ~ sein** to be in the mood for sth

aufgeregt ['aʊfgəreːkt] *adj* excited

aufgeschlossen ['aʊfgəʃlɔsən] *adj* open, open-minded

aufgeweckt ['aʊfgəvɛkt] *adj* bright, intelligent

aufgießen ['aʊfgiːsən] (*unreg*) *vt* (*Wasser*) to

pour over; (*Tee*) to infuse

aufgreifen ['aʊfɡraɪfən] (*unreg*) *vt* (*Thema*) to take up; (*Verdächtige*) to pick up, to seize

aufgrund, auf Grund [aʊf'ɡrʊnt] *präp +gen* on the basis of, (*wegen*) because of

aufhaben ['aʊfhaːbən] (*unreg*) *vt* to have on; (*Arbeit*) to have to do

aufhalsen ['aʊfhalzən] (*umg*) *vt*: **jdm etw ~** to saddle *od* lumber sb with sth

aufhalten ['aʊfhaltən] (*unreg*) *vt* (*Person*) to detain; (*Entwicklung*) to check; (*Tür, Hand*) to hold open; (*Augen*) to keep open ♦ *vr* (*wohnen*) to live; (*bleiben*) to stay; **sich mit etw ~** to waste time over sth

aufhängen ['aʊfhɛŋən] (*unreg*) *vt* (*Wäsche*) to hang up; (*Menschen*) to hang ♦ *vr* to hang o.s.

Aufhänger (**-s, -**) *m* (*am Mantel*) loop; (*fig*) peg

aufheben ['aʊfheːbən] (*unreg*) *vt* (*hochheben*) to raise, to lift; (*Sitzung*) to wind up; (*Urteil*) to annul; (*Gesetz*) to repeal, to abolish; (*aufbewahren*) to keep ♦ *vr* to cancel itself out; **bei jdm gut aufgehoben sein** to be well looked after at sb's; **viel A~(s) machen (von)** to make a fuss (about)

aufheitern ['aʊfhaɪtərn] *vt*, *vr* (*Himmel, Miene*) to brighten; (*Mensch*) to cheer up

aufhellen ['aʊfhɛlən] *vt*, *vr* to clear up; (*Farbe, Haare*) to lighten

aufhetzen ['aʊfhɛtsən] *vt* to stir up

aufholen ['aʊfhoːlən] *vt* to make up ♦ *vi* to catch up

aufhorchen ['aʊfhɔrçən] *vi* to prick up one's ears

aufhören ['aʊfhøːrən] *vi* to stop; **~, etw zu tun** to stop doing sth

aufklappen ['aʊfklapən] *vt* to open

aufklären ['aʊfklɛːrən] *vt* (*Geheimnis etc*) to clear up; (*Person*) to enlighten; (*sexuell*) to tell the facts of life to; (*MIL*) to reconnoitre ♦ *vr* to clear up

Aufklärung *f* (*von Geheimnis*) clearing up; (*Unterrichtung, Zeitalter*) enlightenment; (*sexuell*) sex education; (*MIL, AVIAT*) reconnaissance

aufkleben ['aʊfkleːbən] *vt* to stick on;

Aufkleber (**-s, -**) *m* sticker

aufknöpfen ['aʊfknœpfən] *vt* to unbutton

aufkommen ['aʊfkɔmən] (*unreg*) *vi* (*Wind*) to come up; (*Zweifel, Gefühl*) to arise; (*Mode*) to start; **für jdn/etw ~** to be liable *od* responsible for sb/sth

aufladen ['aʊflaːdən] (*unreg*) *vt* to load

Auflage ['aʊflaːɡə] *f* edition; (*Zeitung*) circulation; (*Bedingung*) condition

auflassen ['aʊflasən] (*unreg*) *vt* (*offen*) to leave open; (*aufgesetzt*) to leave on

auflauern ['aʊflaʊərn] *vi*: **jdm ~** to lie in wait for sb

Auflauf ['aʊflaʊf] *m* (*KOCH*) pudding; (*Menschenauflauf*) crowd

aufleben ['aʊfleːbən] *vi* (*Mensch, Gespräch*) to liven up; (*Interesse*) to revive

auflegen ['aʊfleːɡən] *vt* to put on; (*Telefon*) to hang up; (*TYP*) to print

auflehnen ['aʊfleːnən] *vt* to lean on ♦ *vr* to rebel

Auflehnung *f* rebellion

auflesen ['aʊfleːzən] (*unreg*) *vt* to pick up

aufleuchten ['aʊflɔʏçtən] *vi* to light up

auflisten ['aʊflɪstən] *vt* to list

auflockern ['aʊflɔkərn] *vt* to loosen; (*fig: Eintönigkeit etc*) to liven up

auflösen ['aʊfløːzən] *vt* to dissolve; (*Haare etc*) to loosen; (*Missverständnis*) to sort out ♦ *vr* to dissolve; to come undone; to be resolved; (**in Tränen) aufgelöst sein** to be in tears

Auflösung *f* dissolving; (*fig*) solution

aufmachen ['aʊfmaxən] *vt* to open; (*Kleidung*) to undo; (*zurechtmachen*) to do up ♦ *vr* to set out

Aufmachung *f* (*Kleidung*) outfit, get-up; (*Gestaltung*) format

aufmerksam ['aʊfmɛrkzaːm] *adj* attentive; **jdn auf etw** *akk* **~ machen** to point sth out to sb; **A~keit** *f* attention, attentiveness

aufmuntern ['aʊfmʊntərn] *vt* (*ermutigen*) to encourage; (*erheitern*) to cheer up

Aufnahme ['aʊfnaːmə] *f* reception; (*Beginn*) beginning; (*in Verein etc*) admission; (*in Liste etc*) inclusion; (*Notieren*) taking down; (*PHOT*) shot; (*auf Tonband etc*) recording;

Spelling Reform: ▲ *new spelling* △ *old spelling (to be phased out)*

a~**fähig** adj receptive; ~**prüfung** f entrance test

aufnehmen ['aʊfneːmən] (unreg) vt to receive; (hochheben) to pick up; (beginnen) to take up; (in Verein etc) to admit; (in Liste etc) to include; (fassen) to hold; (notieren) to take down; (fotografieren) to photograph; (auf Tonband, Platte) to record; (FIN: leihen) to take out; **es mit jdm ~ können** to be able to compete with sb

aufopfern ['aʊfɔpfərn] vt, vr to sacrifice; ~**d** adj selfless

aufpassen ['aʊfpasən] vi (aufmerksam sein) to pay attention; **auf jdn/etw ~** to look after od watch sb/sth; **aufgepasst!** look out!

Aufprall ['aʊfpral] (-s, -e) m impact; a~**en** vi to hit, to strike

Aufpreis ['aʊfpraɪs] m extra charge

aufpumpen ['aʊfpʊmpən] vt to pump up

aufräumen ['aʊfrɔymən] vt, vi (Dinge) to clear away; (Zimmer) to tidy up

aufrecht ['aʊfrɛçt] adj (auch fig) upright; ~**erhalten** (unreg) vt to maintain

aufreg- ['aʊfreːg] zW: ~**en** vt to excite ♦ vr to get excited; ~**end** adj exciting; **A~ung** f excitement

aufreibend ['aʊfraɪbənt] adj strenuous

aufreißen ['aʊfraɪsən] (unreg) vt (Umschlag) to tear open; (Augen) to open wide; (Tür) to throw open; (Straße) to take up

aufreizen ['aʊfraɪtsən] vt to incite, to stir up; ~**d** adj exciting, stimulating

aufrichten ['aʊfrɪçtən] vt to put up, to erect; (moralisch) to console ♦ vr to rise; (moralisch): **sich ~ (an** +dat) to take heart (from)

aufrichtig ['aʊfrɪçtɪç] adj sincere, honest; **A~keit** f sincerity

aufrücken ['aʊfrʏkən] vi to move up; (beruflich) to be promoted

Aufruf ['aʊfruːf] m summons; (zur Hilfe) call; (des Namens) calling out; a~**en** (unreg) vt (Namen) to call out; (auffordern): **jdn a~en (zu)** to call upon sb (for)

Aufruhr ['aʊfruːr] (-(e)s, -e) m uprising, revolt

aufrührerisch ['aʊfryːrərɪʃ] adj rebellious

aufrunden ['aʊfrʊndən] vt (Summe) to round up

Aufrüstung ['aʊfrʏstʊŋ] f rearmament

aufrütteln ['aʊfrʏtəln] vt (auch fig) to shake up

aufs [aʊfs] = **auf das**

aufsagen ['aʊfzaːgən] vt (Gedicht) to recite

aufsässig ['aʊfzɛsɪç] adj rebellious

Aufsatz ['aʊfzats] m (Geschriebenes) essay; (auf Schrank etc) top

aufsaugen ['aʊfzaʊgən] (unreg) vt to soak up

aufschauen ['aʊfʃaʊən] vi to look up

aufscheuchen ['aʊfʃɔyçən] vt to scare od frighten away

aufschieben ['aʊfʃiːbən] (unreg) vt to push open; (verzögern) to put off, to postpone

Aufschlag ['aʊfʃlaːk] m (Ärmelaufschlag) cuff; (Jackenaufschlag) lapel; (Hosenaufschlag) turn-up; (Aufprall) impact; (Preisaufschlag) surcharge; (Tennis) service; a~**en** [-gən] (unreg) vt (öffnen) to open; (verwunden) to cut; (hochschlagen) to turn up; (aufbauen: Zelt, Lager) to pitch, to erect; (Wohnsitz) to take up ♦ vi (aufprallen) to hit; (teurer werden) to go up; (Tennis) to serve

aufschließen ['aʊfʃliːsən] (unreg) vt to open up, to unlock ♦ vi (aufrücken) to close up

aufschlussreich ▲ adj informative, illuminating

aufschnappen ['aʊfʃnapən] vt (umg) to pick up ♦ vi to fly open

aufschneiden ['aʊfʃnaɪdən] (unreg) vt (Brot) to cut up; (MED) to lance ♦ vi to brag

Aufschneider (-s, -) m boaster, braggart

Aufschnitt ['aʊfʃnɪt] m (slices of) cold meat

aufschrauben ['aʊfʃraʊbən] vt (festschrauben) to screw on; (lösen) to unscrew

aufschrecken ['aʊfʃrɛkən] vt to startle ♦ vi (unreg) to start up

aufschreiben ['aʊfʃraɪbən] (unreg) vt to write down

aufschreien ['aʊfʃraɪən] (unreg) vi to cry out

Aufschrift ['aʊfʃrɪft] f (Inschrift) inscription; (auf Etikett) label

Aufschub ['aʊfʃuːp] **(-(e)s, -schübe)** *m* delay, postponement

Aufschwung ['aʊfʃvʊŋ] *m* (*Elan*) boost; (*wirtschaftlich*) upturn, boom; (*SPORT*) circle

aufsehen ['aʊfzeːən] (*unreg*) *vi* to look up; **~ zu** to look up at; (*fig*) to look up to; **A~ (-s)** *nt* sensation, stir; **~ erregend** sensational

Aufseher(in) **(-s, -)** *m(f)* guard; (*im Betrieb*) supervisor; (*Museumsaufseher*) attendant; (*Parkaufseher*) keeper

auf sein ▲ *siehe* **auf**

aufsetzen ['aʊfzɛtsən] *vt* to put on; (*Dokument*) to draw up ♦ *vr* to sit up(right) ♦ *vi* (*Flugzeug*) to touch down

Aufsicht ['aʊfzɪçt] *f* supervision; **die ~ haben** to be in charge

Aufsichtsrat *m* (supervisory) board

aufsitzen ['aʊfzɪtsən] (*unreg*) *vi* (*aufrecht hinsitzen*) to sit up; (*aufs Pferd, Motorrad*) to mount, to get on; (*Schiff*) to run aground; **jdm ~** (*umg*) to be taken in by sb

aufsparen ['aʊfʃpaːrən] *vt* to save (up)

aufsperren ['aʊfʃpɛrən] *vt* to unlock; (*Mund*) to open wide

aufspielen ['aʊfʃpiːlən] *vr* to show off

aufspießen ['aʊfʃpiːsən] *vt* to spear

aufspringen ['aʊfʃprɪŋən] (*unreg*) *vi* (*hochspringen*) to jump up; (*sich öffnen*) to spring open; (*Hände, Lippen*) to become chapped; **auf etw** *akk* **~** to jump onto sth

aufspüren ['aʊfʃpyːrən] *vt* to track down, to trace

aufstacheln ['aʊfʃtaxəln] *vt* to incite

Aufstand ['aʊfʃtant] *m* insurrection, rebellion; **aufständisch** ['aʊfʃtɛndɪʃ] *adj* rebellious, mutinous

aufstehen ['aʊfʃteːən] (*unreg*) *vi* to get up; (*Tür*) to be open

aufsteigen ['aʊfʃtaɪgən] (*unreg*) *vi* (*hochsteigen*) to climb; (*Rauch*) to rise; **auf etw** *akk* **~** to get onto sth

aufstellen ['aʊfʃtɛlən] *vt* (*aufrecht stellen*) to put up; (*aufreihen*) to line up; (*nominieren*) to nominate; (*formulieren: Programm etc*) to draw up; (*leisten: Rekord*) to set up

Aufstellung *f* (*SPORT*) line-up; (*Liste*) list

Aufstieg ['aʊfʃtiːk] **(-(e)s, -e)** *m* (*auf Berg*) ascent; (*Fortschritt*) rise; (*beruflich, SPORT*) promotion

aufstocken ['aʊfʃtɔkən] *vt* (*Kapital*) to increase

aufstoßen ['aʊfʃtoːsən] (*unreg*) *vt* to push open ♦ *vi* to belch

aufstützen ['aʊfʃtʏtsən] *vt* (*Körperteil*) to prop, to lean; (*Person*) to prop up ♦ *vr*: **sich auf etw** *akk* **~** to lean on sth

aufsuchen ['aʊfzuːxən] *vt* (*besuchen*) to visit; (*konsultieren*) to consult

Auftakt ['aʊftakt] *m* (*MUS*) upbeat; (*fig*) prelude

auftanken ['aʊftaŋkən] *vi* to get petrol (*BRIT*) *od* gas (*US*) ♦ *vt* to refuel

auftauchen ['aʊftaʊxən] *vi* to appear; (*aus Wasser etc*) to emerge; (*U-Boot*) to surface; (*Zweifel*) to arise

auftauen ['aʊftaʊən] *vt* to thaw ♦ *vi* to thaw; (*fig*) to relax

aufteilen ['aʊftaɪlən] *vt* to divide up; (*Raum*) to partition; **Aufteilung** *f* division; partition

Auftrag ['aʊftraːk] **(-(e)s, -träge)** *m* order; (*Anweisung*) commission; (*Aufgabe*) mission; **im ~ von** on behalf of; **a~en** [-gən] (*unreg*) *vt* (*Essen*) to serve; (*Farbe*) to put on; (*Kleidung*) to wear out; **jdm etw a~en** to tell sb sth; **dick a~en** (*fig*) to exaggerate; **~geber (-s, -)** *m* (*COMM*) purchaser, customer

auftreiben ['aʊftraɪbən] (*unreg*) *vt* (*umg: beschaffen*) to raise

auftreten ['aʊftreːtən] (*unreg*) *vt* to kick open ♦ *vi* to appear; (*mit Füßen*) to tread; (*sich verhalten*) to behave; **A~ (-s)** *nt* (*Vorkommen*) appearance; (*Benehmen*) behaviour

Auftrieb ['aʊftriːp] *m* (*PHYS*) buoyancy, lift; (*fig*) impetus

Auftritt ['aʊftrɪt] *m* (*des Schauspielers*) entrance; (*Szene: auch fig*) scene

aufwachen ['aʊfvaxən] *vi* to wake up

aufwachsen ['aʊfvaksən] (*unreg*) *vi* to grow up

Aufwand ['aʊfvant] **(-(e)s)** *m* expenditure; (*Kosten auch*) expense; (*Luxus*) show

Spelling Reform: ▲ *new spelling* △ *old spelling (to be phased out)*

aufwändig ▲ ['aufvɛndɪç] *adj* costly

aufwärmen ['aufvɛrmən] *vt* to warm up; *(alte Geschichten)* to rake up

aufwärts ['aufvɛrts] *adv* upwards; **A~entwicklung** *f* upward trend

Aufwasch ['aufvaʃ] *m* washing-up

aufwecken ['aufvɛkən] *vt* to wake up, to waken up

aufweisen ['aufvaɪzən] *(unreg) vt* to show

aufwenden ['aufvɛndən] *(unreg) vt* to expend; *(Geld)* to spend; *(Sorgfalt)* to devote

aufwendig *adj siehe* **aufwändig**

aufwerfen ['aufvɛrfən] *(unreg) vt (Fenster etc)* to throw open; *(Probleme)* to throw up, to raise

aufwerten ['aufvɛrtən] *vt (FIN)* to revalue; *(fig)* to raise in value

aufwickeln ['aufvɪkəln] *vt (aufrollen)* to roll up; *(umg: Haar)* to put in curlers

aufwiegen ['aufviːgən] *(unreg) vt* to make up for

Aufwind ['aufvɪnt] *m* up-current

aufwirbeln ['aufvɪrbəln] *vt* to whirl up; **Staub ~** *(fig)* to create a stir

aufwischen ['aufvɪʃən] *vt* to wipe up

aufzählen ['auftsɛːlən] *vt* to list

aufzeichnen ['auftsaɪçnən] *vt* to sketch; *(schriftlich)* to jot down; *(auf Band)* to record

Aufzeichnung *f (schriftlich)* note; *(Tonbandaufzeichnung)* recording; *(Filmaufzeichnung)* record

aufzeigen ['auftsaɪgən] *vt* to show, to demonstrate

aufziehen ['auftsiːən] *(unreg) vt (hochziehen)* to raise, to draw up; *(öffnen)* to pull open; *(Uhr)* to wind; *(umg: necken)* to tease; *(großziehen: Kinder)* to raise, to bring up; *(Tiere)* to rear

Aufzug ['auftsuːk] *m (Fahrstuhl)* lift, elevator; *(Aufmarsch)* procession, parade; *(Kleidung)* get-up; *(THEAT)* act

aufzwingen ['auftsvɪŋən] *(unreg) vt:* **jdm etw ~** to force sth upon sb

Augapfel ['aukˌapfəl] *m* eyeball; *(fig)* apple of one's eye

Auge ['augə] *(-s, -n) nt* eye; *(Fettauge)*

globule of fat; **unter vier ~n** in private

Augen- *zW:* **~blick** *m* moment; **im ~blick** at the moment; **a~blicklich** *adj (sofort)* instantaneous; *(gegenwärtig)* present; **~braue** *f* eyebrow; **~optiker(in)** *m(f)* optician; **~weide** *f* sight for sore eyes; **~zeuge** *m* eye witness

August [au'gust] *(-(e)s od -, -e) m* August

Auktion [auktsi'oːn] *f* auction

Aula ['aula] *(-, Aulen od -s) f* assembly hall

SCHLÜSSELWORT

---

aus [aus] *präp +dat* **1** *(räumlich)* out of; *(von ... her)* from; **er ist aus Berlin** he's from Berlin; **aus dem Fenster** out of the window

2 *(gemacht/hergestellt aus)* made of; **ein Herz aus Stein** a heart of stone

3 *(auf Ursache deutend)* out of; **aus Mitleid** out of sympathy; **aus Erfahrung** from experience; **aus Spaß** for fun

4: aus ihr wird nie etwas she'll never get anywhere

♦ *adv* **1** *(zu Ende)* finished, over; **aus sein** to be over; **aus und vorbei** over and done with

2 *(ausgeschaltet, ausgezogen)* out; *(Aufschrift an Geräten)* off; **aus sein** *(nicht brennen)* to be out; *(abgeschaltet sein: Radio, Herd)* to be off; **Licht aus!** lights out!

3 *(nicht zu Hause)*: **aus sein** to be out

4 *(in Verbindung mit von)*: **von Rom aus** from Rome; **vom Fenster aus** out of the window; **von sich aus** *(selbstständig)* of one's own accord; **von ihm aus** as far as he's concerned

---

ausarbeiten ['ausˌarbaɪtən] *vt* to work out

ausarten ['ausˌartən] *vi* to degenerate

ausatmen ['ausˌaːtmən] *vi* to breathe out

ausbaden ['ausˌbaːdən] *(umg) vt:* **etw ~ müssen** to carry the can for sth

Ausbau ['ausbau] *m* extension, expansion; removal; **a~en** *vt* to extend, to expand; *(herausnehmen)* to take out, to remove; **a~fähig** *adj (fig)* worth developing

ausbessern ['ausbɛsərn] *vt* to mend, to

Rechtschreibreform: ▲ neue Schreibung △ alte Schreibung (auslaufend) repair

ausbeulen ['ausbɔʏlən] *vt* to beat out

Ausbeute ['ausbɔʏtə] *f* yield; (*Fische*) catch; **a~n** *vt* to exploit; (*MIN*) to work

ausbild- ['ausbɪld] *zW:* **~en** *vt* to educate; (*Lehrling, Soldat*) to instruct, to train; (*Fähigkeiten*) to develop; (*Geschmack*) to cultivate; **A~er (-s, -)** *m* instructor; **A~ung** *f* education; training, instruction; development; cultivation

ausbleiben ['ausblaɪbən] (*unreg*) *vi* (*Personen*) to stay away, not to come; (*Ereignisse*) to fail to happen, not to happen

Ausblick ['ausblɪk] *m* (*auch fig*) prospect, outlook, view

ausbrechen ['ausbrɛçən] (*unreg*) *vi* to break out ♦ *vt* to break off; **in Tränen/Gelächter ~** to burst into tears/out laughing

ausbreiten ['ausbraɪtən] *vt* to spread (out); (*Arme*) to stretch out ♦ *vr* to spread; **sich über ein Thema ~** to expand *od* enlarge on a topic

ausbrennen ['ausbrɛnən] (*unreg*) *vt* to scorch; (*Wunde*) to cauterize ♦ *vi* to burn out

Ausbruch ['ausbrʊx] *m* outbreak; (*von Vulkan*) eruption; (*Gefühlsausbruch*) outburst; (*von Gefangenen*) escape

ausbrüten ['ausbry:tən] *vt* (*auch fig*) to hatch

Ausdauer ['ausdauər] *f* perseverance, stamina; **a~nd** *adj* persevering

ausdehnen ['ausde:nən] *vt, vr* (*räumlich*) to expand; (*zeitlich, auch Gummi*) to stretch; (*Nebel, fig: Macht*) to extend

ausdenken ['ausdɛŋkən] (*unreg*) *vt:* **sich** *dat* **etw ~** to think sth up

Ausdruck ['ausdrʊk] *m* expression, phrase; (*Kundgabe, Gesichtsausdruck*) expression; (*COMPUT*) print-out, hard copy; **a~en** *vt* (*COMPUT*) to print out

ausdrücken ['ausdrʏkən] *vt* (*auch vr: formulieren, zeigen*) to express; (*Zigarette*) to put out; (*Zitrone*) to squeeze

ausdrücklich *adj* express, explicit

ausdrucks- *zW:* **~los** *adj* expressionless, blank; **~voll** *adj* expressive; **A~weise** *f*

mode of expression

auseinander [ausaɪ'nandər] *adv* (*getrennt*) apart; **~ schreiben** to write as separate words; **~ bringen** to separate; **~ fallen** to fall apart; **~ gehen** (*Menschen*) to separate; (*Meinungen*) to differ; (*Gegenstand*) to fall apart; **~ halten** to tell apart; **~ nehmen** to take to pieces, to dismantle; **~ setzen** (*erklären*) to set forth, to explain; **sich ~ setzen** (*sich verständigen*) to come to terms, to settle; (*sich befassen*) to concern o.s.; **A~setzung** *f* argument

ausfahren ['ausfa:rən] (*unreg*) *vt* (*spazieren fahren: im Auto*) to take for a drive; (: *im Kinderwagen*) to take for a walk; (*liefern*) to deliver

Ausfahrt *f* (*des Zuges etc*) leaving, departure; (*Autobahnausfahrt*) exit; (*Garagenausfahrt etc*) exit, way out; (*Spazierfahrt*) drive, excursion

Ausfall ['ausfal] *m* loss; (*Nichtstattfinden*) cancellation; (*MIL*) sortie; (*radioaktiv*) fallout; **a~en** (*unreg*) *vi* (*Zähne, Haare*) to fall *od* come out; (*nicht stattfinden*) to be cancelled; (*wegbleiben*) to be omitted; (*Person*) to drop out; (*Lohn*) to be stopped; (*nicht funktionieren*) to break down; (*Resultat haben*) to turn out; **~straße** *f* arterial road

ausfertigen ['ausfɛrtɪgən] *vt* (*förmlich: Urkunde, Pass*) to draw up; (*Rechnung*) to make out

Ausfertigung ['ausfɛrtɪgʊŋ] *f* drawing up; making out; (*Exemplar*) copy

ausfindig ['ausfɪndɪç] *adj:* **~ machen** to discover

ausfließen ['ausfli:sən] (*unreg*) *vt* (*her~*): **~ (aus)** to flow out (of); (*auslaufen: Öl etc*): **~ (aus)** to leak (out of)

Ausflucht ['ausflʊxt] (-, **-flüchte**) *f* excuse

Ausflug ['ausflu:k] *m* excursion, outing; **Ausflügler** ['ausfly:klər] (**-s, -**) *m* tripper

Ausflugslokal *nt* tourist café

Ausfluss ▲ ['ausflʊs] *m* outlet; (*MED*) discharge

ausfragen ['ausfra:gən] *vt* to interrogate, to question

ausfressen ['ausfrɛsən] (*unreg*) *vt* to eat up;

Spelling Reform: ▲ *new spelling* △ *old spelling (to be phased out)*

(*aushöhlen*) to corrode; (*umg: anstellen*) to be up to

Ausfuhr ['aʊsfuːr] (-, -en) *f* export, exportation ♦ *in zW* export

ausführ- ['aʊsfyːr] *zW*: **~en** *vt* (*verwirklichen*) to carry out; (*Person*) to take out; (*Hund*) to take for a walk; (*COMM*) to export; (*erklären*) to give details of; **~lich** *adj* detailed ♦ *adv* in detail; **A~lichkeit** *f* detail; **A~ung** *f* execution, performance; (*Durchführung*) completion; (*Herstellungsart*) version; (*Erklärung*) explanation

ausfüllen ['aʊsfʏlən] *vt* to fill up; (*Fragebogen etc*) to fill in; (*Beruf*) to be fulfilling for

Ausgabe ['aʊsgaːbə] *f* (*Geld*) expenditure, outlay; (*Aushändigung*) giving out; (*Gepäckausgabe*) left-luggage office; (*Buch*) edition; (*Nummer*) issue; (*COMPUT*) output

Ausgang ['aʊsgaŋ] *m* way out, exit; (*Ende*) end; (*~spunkt*) starting point; (*Ergebnis*) result; (*Ausgehtag*) free time, time off; **kein ~** no exit

Ausgangs- *zW*: **~punkt** *m* starting point; **~sperre** *f* curfew

ausgeben ['aʊsgeːbən] (*unreg*) *vt* (*Geld*) to spend; (*austeilen*) to issue, to distribute ♦ *vr*: **sich für etw/jdn ~** to pass o.s. off as sth/sb

ausgebucht ['aʊsgəbuːxt] *adj* (*Vorstellung, Flug, Maschine*) fully booked

ausgedient ['aʊsgədiːnt] *adj* (*Soldat*) discharged; (*verbraucht*) no longer in use; **~ haben** to have done good service

ausgefallen ['aʊsgəfalən] *adj* (*ungewöhnlich*) exceptional

ausgeglichen ['aʊsgəglɪçən] *adj* (well-) balanced; **A~heit** *f* balance; (*von Mensch*) even-temperedness

ausgehen ['aʊsgeːən] *vi* to go out; (*zu Ende gehen*) to come to an end; (*Benzin*) to run out; (*Haare, Zähne*) to fall *od* come out; (*Feuer, Ofen, Licht*) to go out; (*Strom*) to go off; (*Resultat haben*) to turn out; **mir ging das Benzin aus** I ran out of petrol (*BRIT*) *od* gas (*US*); **von etw ~** (*wegführen*) to lead away from sth; (*herrühren*) to come

from sth; (*zugrunde legen*) to proceed from sth; **wir können davon ~, dass ...** we can take as our starting point that ...; **leer ~** to get nothing

ausgelassen ['aʊsgəlasən] *adj* boisterous, high-spirited

ausgelastet ['aʊsgəlastət] *adj* fully occupied

ausgelernt ['aʊsgəlɛrnt] *adj* trained, qualified

ausgemacht ['aʊsgəmaxt] *adj* settled; (*umg: Dummkopf etc*) out-and-out, downright; **es war eine ~e Sache, dass ...** it was a foregone conclusion that ...

ausgenommen ['aʊsgənɔmən] *präp* +*gen* except ♦ *konj* except; **Anwesende sind ~** present company excepted

ausgeprägt ['aʊsgəprɛːkt] *adj* distinct

ausgerechnet ['aʊsgəreçnət] *adv* just, precisely; **~ du/heute** you of all people/ today of all days

ausgeschlossen ['aʊsgəʃlɔsən] *adj* (*unmöglich*) impossible, out of the question

ausgeschnitten ['aʊsgəʃnɪtən] *adj* (*Kleid*) low-necked

ausgesprochen ['aʊsgəʃprɔxən] *adj* (*Faulheit, Lüge etc*) out-and-out; (*unverkennbar*) marked ♦ *adv* decidedly

ausgezeichnet ['aʊsgətsaɪçnət] *adj* excellent

ausgiebig ['aʊsgiːbɪç] *adj* (*Gebrauch*) thorough, good; (*Essen*) generous, lavish; **~ schlafen** to have a good sleep

ausgießen ['aʊsgiːsən] *vt* to pour out; (*Behälter*) to empty

Ausgleich ['aʊsglaɪç] (-(e)s, -e) *m* balance; (*Vermittlung*) reconciliation; (*SPORT*) equalization; **zum ~ einer Sache** *gen* in order to offset sth; **a~en** (*unreg*) *vt* to balance (out); to reconcile; (*Höhe*) to even up ♦ *vi* (*SPORT*) to equalize

ausgraben ['aʊsgraːbən] (*unreg*) *vt* to dig up; (*Leichen*) to exhume; (*fig*) to unearth

Ausgrabung *f* excavation; (*Ausgraben auch*) digging up

Ausguss ▲ ['aʊsgʊs] *m* (*Spüle*) sink; (*Abfluss*) outlet; (*Tülle*) spout

aushalten ['aʊshaltən] (*unreg*) *vt* to bear, to

stand; (*Geliebte*) to keep ♦ *vi* to hold out;
das ist nicht zum A~ that is unbearable
aushandeln ['aʊshandəln] *vt* to negotiate
aushändigen ['aʊshɛndɪgən] *vt*: **jdm etw ~**
to hand sth over to sb
Aushang ['aʊshaŋ] *m* notice
aushängen ['aʊshɛŋən] (*unreg*) *vt* (*Meldung*)
to put up; (*Fenster*) to take off its hinges
♦ *vi* to be displayed
ausharren ['aʊsharən] *vi* to hold out
ausheben ['aʊshe:bən] (*unreg*) *vt* (*Erde*) to
lift out; (*Grube*) to hollow out; (*Tür*) to take
off its hinges; (*Diebesnest*) to clear out; (*MIL*)
to enlist
aushecken ['aʊshɛkən] (*umg*) *vt* to cook up
aushelfen ['aʊshɛlfən] (*unreg*) *vi*: **jdm ~** to
help sb out
Aushilfe ['aʊshɪlfə] *f* help, assistance;
(*Person*) (temporary) worker
Aushilfs- *zW*: **~kraft** *f* temporary worker;
a~weise *adv* temporarily, as a stopgap
ausholen ['aʊsho:lən] *vi* to swing one's arm
back; (*zur Ohrfeige*) to raise one's hand;
(*beim Gehen*) to take long strides
aushorchen ['aʊshɔrçən] *vt* to sound out,
to pump
auskennen ['aʊskɛnən] (*unreg*) *vr* to know a
lot; (*an einem Ort*) to know one's way
about; (*in Fragen etc*) to be knowledgeable
Ausklang ['aʊsklaŋ] *m* end
auskleiden ['aʊsklaɪdən] *vr* to undress ♦ *vt*
(*Wand*) to line
ausklingen ['aʊsklɪŋən] (*unreg*) *vi* (*Ton, Lied*)
to die away; (*Fest*) to peter out
ausklopfen ['aʊsklɔpfən] *vt* (*Teppich*) to
beat; (*Pfeife*) to knock out
auskochen ['aʊskɔxən] *vt* to boil; (*MED*) to
sterilize; **ausgekocht** (*fig*) out-and-out
Auskommen (**-s**) *nt*: **sein A~ haben** to
have a regular income; **a~** (*unreg*) *vi*: **mit**
jdm a~ to get on with sb; **mit etw a~** to
get by with sth
auskosten ['aʊskɔstən] *vt* to enjoy to the
full
auskundschaften ['aʊskʊntʃaftən] *vt* to
spy out; (*Gebiet*) to reconnoitre
Auskunft ['aʊskʊnft] (**-, -künfte**) *f*

information; (*nähere*) details *pl*, particulars
pl; (*Stelle*) information office; (*TEL*) directory
inquiries *sg*
auslachen ['aʊslaxən] *vt* to laugh at, to
mock
ausladen ['aʊsla:dən] (*unreg*) *vt* to unload;
(*umg: Gäste*) to cancel an invitation to
Auslage ['aʊsla:gə] *f* shop window (display);
~n *pl* (*Ausgabe*) outlay *sg*
Ausland ['aʊslant] *nt* foreign countries *pl*;
im ~ abroad; **ins ~** abroad
Ausländer(in) ['aʊslɛndər(ɪn)] (**-s, -**) *m(f)*
foreigner
ausländisch *adj* foreign
Auslands- *zW*: **~gespräoh** *nt*
international call; **~reise** *f* trip abroad;
~schutzbrief *m* international travel cover
auslassen ['aʊslasən] (*unreg*) *vt* to leave
out; (*Wort etc auch*) to omit; (*Fett*) to melt;
(*Kleidungsstück*) to let out ♦ *vr*: **sich über**
etw *akk* **~** to speak one's mind about sth;
seine Wut *etc* **an jdm ~** to vent one's rage
etc on sb
Auslassung *f* omission
Auslauf ['aʊslaʊf] *m* (*für Tiere*) run; (*Ausfluss*)
outflow, outlet; **a~en** (*unreg*) *vi* to run out;
(*Behälter*) to leak; (*NAUT*) to put out (to
sea); (*langsam aufhören*) to run down
Ausläufer ['aʊslɔʏfər] *m* (*von Gebirge*) spur;
(*Pflanze*) runner; (*MET: von Hoch*) ridge;
(: *von Tief*) trough
ausleeren ['aʊsle:rən] *vt* to empty
auslegen ['aʊsle:gən] *vt* (*Waren*) to lay out;
(*Köder*) to put down; (*Geld*) to lend;
(*bedecken*) to cover; (*Text etc*) to interpret
Auslegung *f* interpretation
ausleiern ['aʊslaɪərn] *vi* (*Gummi*) to wear
out
Ausleihe ['aʊslaɪə] *f* issuing; (*Stelle*) issue
desk; **a~n** (*unreg*) *vt* (*verleihen*) to lend; **sich**
dat **etw a~n** to borrow sth
Auslese ['aʊsle:zə] *f* selection; (*Elite*) elite;
(*Wein*) choice wine; **a~n** (*unreg*) *vt* to
select; (*umg: zu Ende lesen*) to finish
ausliefern ['aʊsli:fərn] *vt* to deliver (up), to
hand over; (*COMM*) to deliver; **jdm/etw**
ausgeliefert sein to be at the mercy of

sb/sth

ausloggen ['aʊslɔgən] *vi* (*COMPUT*) to log off

auslöschen ['aʊslœʃən] *vt* to extinguish; (*fig*) to wipe out, to obliterate

auslosen ['aʊsloːzən] *vt* to draw lots for

auslösen ['aʊsløːzən] *vt* (*Explosion, Schuss*) to set off; (*hervorrufen*) to cause, to produce; (*Gefangene*) to ransom; (*Pfand*) to redeem

ausmachen ['aʊsmaxən] *vt* (*Licht, Radio*) to turn off; (*Feuer*) to put out; (*entdecken*) to make out; (*vereinbaren*) to agree; (*beilegen*) to settle; (*Anteil darstellen, betragen*) to represent; (*bedeuten*) to matter; **macht es Ihnen etwas aus, wenn ...?** would you mind if ...?

ausmalen ['aʊsmaːlən] *vt* to paint; (*fig*) to describe; **sich** *dat* **etw ~** to imagine sth

Ausmaß ['aʊsmaːs] *nt* dimension; (*fig auch*) scale

ausmessen ['aʊsmɛsən] (*unreg*) *vt* to measure

Ausnahme ['aʊsnaːmə] *f* exception; **~fall** *m* exceptional case; **~zustand** *m* state of emergency

ausnahms- *zW:* **~los** *adv* without exception; **~weise** *adv* by way of exception, for once

ausnehmen ['aʊsneːmən] (*unreg*) *vt* to take out, to remove; (*Tier*) to gut; (*Nest*) to rob; (*umg: Geld abnehmen*) to clean out; (*ausschließen*) to make an exception of ♦ *vr* to look, to appear; **~d** *adj* exceptional

ausnützen ['aʊsnʏtsən] *vt* (*Zeit, Gelegenheit*) to use, to turn to good account; (*Einfluss*) to use; (*Mensch, Gutmütigkeit*) to exploit

auspacken ['aʊspakən] *vt* to unpack

auspfeifen ['aʊspfaɪfən] (*unreg*) *vt* to hiss/boo at

ausplaudern ['aʊsplaʊdərn] *vt* to blab

ausprobieren ['aʊsprobiːrən] *vt* to try (out)

Auspuff ['aʊspʊf] (**-(e)s, -e**) *m* (*TECH*) exhaust; **~rohr** *nt* exhaust (pipe)

ausradieren ['aʊsradiːrən] *vt* to erase, to rub out; (*fig*) to annihilate

ausrangieren ['aʊsrãʒiːrən] (*umg*) *vt* to chuck out

ausrauben ['aʊsraʊbən] *vt* to rob

ausräumen ['aʊsrɔʏmən] *vt* (*Dinge*) to clear away; (*Schrank, Zimmer*) to empty; (*Bedenken*) to dispel

ausrechnen ['aʊsrɛçnən] *vt* to calculate, to reckon

Ausrede ['aʊsreːdə] *f* excuse; **a~n** *vi* to have one's say ♦ *vt:* **jdm etw a~n** to talk sb out of sth

ausreichen ['aʊsraɪçən] *vi* to suffice, to be enough; **~d** *adj* sufficient, adequate; (*SCH*) adequate

Ausreise ['aʊsraɪzə] *f* departure; **bei der ~** when leaving the country; **~erlaubnis** *f* exit visa; **a~n** *vi* to leave the country

ausreißen ['aʊsraɪsən] (*unreg*) *vt* to tear *od* pull out ♦ *vi* (*Riss bekommen*) to tear; (*umg*) to make off, to scram

ausrenken ['aʊsrɛŋkən] *vt* to dislocate

ausrichten ['aʊsrɪçtən] *vt* (*Botschaft*) to deliver; (*Gruß*) to pass on; (*Hochzeit etc*) to arrange; (*in gerade Linie bringen*) to get in a straight line; (*angleichen*) to bring into line; (*TYP*) to justify; **ich werde es ihm ~** I'll tell him; **etwas/nichts bei jdm ~** to get somewhere/nowhere with sb

ausrotten ['aʊsrɔtən] *vt* to stamp out, to exterminate

Ausruf ['aʊsruːf] *m* (*Schrei*) cry, exclamation; (*Bekanntmachung*) proclamation; **a~en** (*unreg*) *vt* to cry out, to exclaim; to call out; **~ezeichen** *nt* exclamation mark

ausruhen ['aʊsruːən] *vt, vr* to rest

ausrüsten ['aʊsrʏstən] *vt* to equip, to fit out

Ausrüstung *f* equipment

ausrutschen ['aʊsrʊtʃən] *vi* to slip

Aussage ['aʊszaːgə] *f* (*JUR*) statement; **a~n** *vt* to say, to state ♦ *vi* (*JUR*) to give evidence

ausschalten ['aʊsʃaltən] *vt* to switch off; (*fig*) to eliminate

Ausschank ['aʊsʃaŋk] (**-(e)s, -schänke**) *m* dispensing, giving out; (*COMM*) selling; (*Theke*) bar

Ausschau ['aʊsʃaʊ] *f:* **~ halten (nach)** to look out (for), to watch (for); **a~en** *vi:* **a~en (nach)** to look out (for), to be on the look-out (for)

ausscheiden ['aʊsʃaɪdən] (*unreg*) *vt* to take

out; (MED) to secrete ♦ vi: ~ **(aus)** to leave; (SPORT) to be eliminated (from) od knocked out (of)

Ausscheidung f separation; secretion; elimination; (aus Amt) retirement

ausschenken ['aʊsʃɛŋkən] vt (Alkohol, Kaffee) to pour out; (COMM) to sell

ausschildern ['aʊsʃɪldɐn] vt to signpost

ausschimpfen ['aʊsʃɪmpfən] vt to scold, to tell off

ausschlafen ['aʊsʃlaːfən] (unreg) vi, vr to have a good sleep ♦ vt to sleep off; **ich bin nicht ausgeschlafen** I didn't have od get enough sleep

Ausschlag ['aʊsʃlaːk] m (MED) rash; (Pendelausschlag) swing; (Nadelausschlag) deflection; **den ~ geben** (fig) to tip the balance; **a~en** [-gən] (unreg) vt to knock out; (auskleiden) to deck out; (verweigern) to decline ♦ vi (Pferd) to kick out; (BOT) to sprout; **a~gebend** adj decisive

ausschließen ['aʊsʃliːsən] (unreg) vt to shut od lock out; (fig) to exclude

ausschließlich adj exclusive ♦ adv exclusively ♦ präp +gen exclusive of, excluding

Ausschluss ▲ ['aʊsʃlʊs] m exclusion

ausschmücken ['aʊsʃmʏkən] vt to decorate; (fig) to embellish

ausschneiden ['aʊsʃnaɪdən] (unreg) vt to cut out; (Büsche) to trim

Ausschnitt ['aʊsʃnɪt] m (Teil) section; (von Kleid) neckline; (Zeitungsausschnitt) cutting; (aus Film etc) excerpt

ausschreiben ['aʊsʃraɪbən] (unreg) vt (ganz schreiben) to write out (in full); (ausstellen) to write (out); (Stelle, Wettbewerb etc) to announce, to advertise

Ausschreitung ['aʊsʃraɪtʊŋ] f (usu pl) riot

Ausschuss ▲ ['aʊsʃʊs] m committee, board; (Abfall) waste, scraps pl; (COMM: auch: ~**ware**) reject

ausschütten ['aʊsʃʏtən] vt to pour out; (Eimer) to empty; (Geld) to pay ♦ vr to shake (with laughter)

ausschweifend ['aʊsʃvaɪfənt] adj (Leben) dissipated, debauched; (Fantasie) extravagant

aussehen ['aʊszeːən] (unreg) vi to look; **es sieht nach Regen aus** it looks like rain; **es sieht schlecht aus** things look bad; **A~ (-s)** nt appearance

aus sein ▲ siehe aus

außen ['aʊsən] adv outside; (nach ~) outwards; ~ **ist es rot** it's red (on the) outside

Außen- zW: ~**dienst** m: **im ~dienst sein** to work outside the office; ~**handel** m foreign trade; ~**minister** m foreign minister; ~**ministerium** nt foreign office; ~**politik** f foreign policy; **a~politisch** adj (Entwicklung, Lage) foreign; ~**seite** f outside; ~**seiter (-s, -)** m outsider; ~**stände** pl outstanding debts; ~**stehende(r)** f(m) outsider; ~**welt** f outside world

außer ['aʊsɐ] präp +dat (räumlich) out of; (abgesehen von) except ♦ konj (ausgenommen) except; ~ **Gefahr** out of danger; ~ **Zweifel** beyond any doubt; ~ **Betrieb** out of order; ~ **Dienst** retired; ~ **Landes** abroad; ~ **sich** dat **sein** to be beside o.s.; ~ **sich** akk **geraten** to go wild; ~ **wenn** unless; ~ **dass** except; ~**dem** konj besides, in addition

äußere(r, s) ['ɔʏsərə(r,s)] adj outer, external

außergewöhnlich adj unusual

außerhalb präp +gen outside ♦ adv outside

äußerlich adj external

äußern vt to utter, to express; (zeigen) to show ♦ vr to give one's opinion; (Krankheit etc) to show itself

außerordentlich adj extraordinary

außerplanmäßig adj unscheduled

äußerst ['ɔʏsɐst] adv extremely, most; ~**e(r, s)** adj utmost; (räumlich) farthest; (Termin) last possible; (Preis) highest

Äußerung f remark, comment

aussetzen ['aʊszɛtsən] vt (Kind, Tier) to abandon; (Boote) to lower; (Belohnung) to offer; (Urteil, Verfahren) to postpone ♦ vi (aufhören) to stop; (Pause machen) to have a break; **jdm/etw ausgesetzt sein** to be exposed to sb/sth; **an jdm/etw etwas ~** to find fault with sb/sth

Aussicht ['aʊszɪçt] *f* view; (*in Zukunft*) prospect; **etw in ~ haben** to have sth in view

Aussichts- *zW:* **a~los** *adj* hopeless; **~punkt** *m* viewpoint; **a~reich** *adj* promising; **~turm** *m* observation tower

aussöhnen ['aʊszø:nən] *vt* to reconcile ♦ *vr* to reconcile o.s., to become reconciled

aussondern ['aʊszɔndərn] *vt* to separate, to select

aussortieren ['aʊszɔrti:rən] *vt* to sort out

ausspannen ['aʊsʃpanən] *vt* to spread *od* stretch out; (*Pferd*) to unharness; (*umg: Mädchen*): (**jdm**) **jdn ~** to steal sb (from sb) ♦ *vi* to relax

aussperren ['aʊsʃpɛrən] *vt* to lock out

ausspielen ['aʊsʃpi:lən] *vt* (*Karte*) to lead; (*Geldprämie*) to offer as a prize ♦ *vi* (*KARTEN*) to lead; **jdn gegen jdn ~** to play sb off against sb; **ausgespielt haben** to be finished

Aussprache ['aʊsʃpra:xə] *f* pronunciation; (*Unterredung*) (frank) discussion

aussprechen ['aʊsʃprɛçən] (*unreg*) *vt* to pronounce; (*äußern*) to say, to express ♦ *vr* (*sich äußern*): **sich ~ (über** +*akk*) to speak (about); (*sich anvertrauen*) to unburden o.s. (about *od* on); (*diskutieren*) to discuss ♦ *vi* (*zu Ende sprechen*) to finish speaking

Ausspruch ['aʊsʃprʊx] *m* saying, remark

ausspülen ['aʊsʃpy:lən] *vt* to wash out; (*Mund*) to rinse

Ausstand ['aʊsʃtant] *m* strike; **in den ~ treten** to go on strike

ausstatten ['aʊsʃtatən] *vt* (*Zimmer etc*) to furnish; (*Person*) to equip, to kit out

Ausstattung *f* (*Ausstatten*) provision; (*Kleidung*) outfit; (*Aufmachung*) make-up; (*Einrichtung*) furnishing

ausstechen ['aʊsʃtɛçən] (*unreg*) *vt* (*Augen, Rasen, Graben*) to dig out; (*Kekse*) to cut out; (*übertreffen*) to outshine

ausstehen ['aʊsʃte:ən] (*unreg*) *vt* to stand, to endure ♦ *vi* (*noch nicht da sein*) to be outstanding

aussteigen ['aʊsʃtaɪgən] (*unreg*) *vi* to get

out, to alight

ausstellen ['aʊsʃtɛlən] *vt* to exhibit, to display; (*umg: ausschalten*) to switch off; (*Rechnung etc*) to make out; (*Pass, Zeugnis*) to issue

Ausstellung *f* exhibition; (*FIN*) drawing up; (*einer Rechnung*) making out; (*eines Passes etc*) issuing

aussterben ['aʊsʃtɛrbən] (*unreg*) *vi* to die out

Aussteuer ['aʊsʃtɔyər] *f* dowry

Ausstieg ['aʊsʃti:k] (**-(e)s, -e**) *m* exit

ausstopfen ['aʊsʃtɔpfən] *vt* to stuff

ausstoßen ['aʊsʃto:sən] (*unreg*) *vt* (*Luft, Rauch*) to give off, to emit; (*aus Verein etc*) to expel, to exclude; (*Auge*) to poke out

ausstrahlen ['aʊsʃtra:lən] *vt, vi* to radiate; (*RADIO*) to broadcast

Ausstrahlung *f* radiation; (*fig*) charisma

ausstrecken ['aʊsʃtrɛkən] *vt, vr* to stretch out

ausstreichen ['aʊsʃtraɪçən] (*unreg*) *vt* to cross out; (*glätten*) to smooth (out)

ausströmen ['aʊsʃtrø:mən] *vi* (*Gas*) to pour out, to escape ♦ *vt* to give off; (*fig*) to radiate

aussuchen ['aʊszu:xən] *vt* to select, to pick out

Austausch ['aʊstaʊʃ] *m* exchange; **a~bar** *adj* exchangeable; **a~en** *vt* to exchange, to swap

austeilen ['aʊstaɪlən] *vt* to distribute, to give out

Auster ['aʊstər] (**-, -n**) *f* oyster

austoben ['aʊsto:bən] *vr* (*Kind*) to run wild; (*Erwachsene*) to sow one's wild oats

austragen ['aʊstra:gən] (*unreg*) *vt* (*Post*) to deliver; (*Streit etc*) to decide; (*Wettkämpfe*) to hold

Australien [aʊs'tra:liən] (**-s**) *nt* Australia; **Australier(in)** (**-s, -**) *m(f)* Australian; **australisch** *adj* Australian

austreiben ['aʊstraɪbən] (*unreg*) *vt* to drive out, to expel; (*Geister*) to exorcize

austreten ['aʊstre:tən] (*unreg*) *vi* (*zur Toilette*) to be excused ♦ *vt* (*Feuer*) to tread out, to trample; (*Schuhe*) to wear out; (*Treppe*) to

wear down; **aus etw ~** to leave sth
austrinken ['aʊstrɪŋkən] vt (unreg) vt (Glas) to
drain; (Getränk) to drink up ♦ vi to finish
one's drink, to drink up
Austritt ['aʊstrɪt] m emission; (aus Verein,
Partei etc) withdrawal
austrocknen ['aʊstrɔknən] vt, vi to dry up
ausüben ['aʊsʔyːbən] vt (Beruf) to practise,
to carry out; (Funktion) to perform; (Einfluss)
to exert; **einen Reiz auf jdn ~** to hold an
attraction for sb; **eine Wirkung auf jdn ~**
to have an effect on sb
Ausverkauf ['aʊsferkaʊf] m sale; **a~en** vt to
sell out; (Geschäft) to sell up; **a~t** adj
(Karten, Artikel) sold out; (THEAT: Haus) full
Auswahl ['aʊsvaːl] f: **eine ~ (an** +dat) a
selection (of), a choice (of)
auswählen ['aʊsvɛːlən] vt to select, to
choose
Auswander- ['aʊsvandər] zW: **~er** m
emigrant; **a~n** vi to emigrate; **~ung** f
emigration
auswärtig ['aʊsvɛrtɪç] adj (nicht am/vom Ort)
out-of-town; (ausländisch) foreign
auswärts ['aʊsvɛrts] adv outside; **~ essen** to eat out;
A~spiel ['aʊsvɛrtsʃpiːl] nt away game
auswechseln ['aʊsvɛksəln] vt to change, to
substitute
Ausweg ['aʊsveːk] m way out, **a~los** adj
hopeless
ausweichen ['aʊsvaɪçən] (unreg) vi: **jdm/
etw ~** to move aside od make way for sb/
sth; (fig) to side-step sb/sth; **~d** adj evasive
ausweinen ['aʊsvaɪnən] vr to have a (good)
cry
Ausweis ['aʊsvaɪs] (**-es, -e**) m identity card;
passport; (Mitgliedsausweis, Bibliotheksausweis
etc) card; **a~en** [-zən] (unreg) vt to expel, to
banish ♦ vr to prove one's identity;
~kontrolle f identity check; **~papiere** pl
identity papers; **~ung** f expulsion
ausweiten ['aʊsvaɪtən] vt to stretch
auswendig ['aʊsvɛndɪç] adv by heart
auswerten ['aʊsveːrtən] vt to evaluate;
Auswertung f evaluation, analysis;
(Nutzung) utilization

auswirken ['aʊsvɪrkən] vr to have an effect;
Auswirkung f effect
auswischen ['aʊsvɪʃən] vt to wipe out; **jdm
eins ~** (umg) to put one over on sb
Auswuchs ['aʊsvuːks] m (out)growth; (fig)
product
auszahlen ['aʊstsaːlən] vt (Lohn, Summe) to
pay out; (Arbeiter) to pay off; (Miterbe) to
buy out ♦ vr (sich lohnen) to pay
auszählen ['aʊstsɛːlən] vt (Stimmen) to
count
auszeichnen ['aʊstsaɪçnən] vt to honour;
(MIL) to decorate; (COMM) to price ♦ vr to
distinguish o.s.
Auszeichnung f distinction; (COMM)
pricing; (Ehrung) awarding of decoration;
(Ehre) honour; (Orden) decoration; **mit ~**
with distinction
ausziehen ['aʊstsiːən] (unreg) vt (Kleidung)
to take off; (Haare, Zähne, Tisch etc) to pull
out; (nachmalen) to trace ♦ vr to undress
♦ vi (aufbrechen) to leave; (aus Wohnung) to
move out
Auszubildende(r) ['aʊstsubɪldəndə(r)] f(m)
trainee
Auszug ['aʊstsuːk] m (aus Wohnung)
removal; (aus Buch etc) extract; (Konto~)
statement; (Ausmarsch) departure
Auto ['aʊto] (**-s, -s**) nt (motor)car; **~ fahren**
to drive; **~atlas** m road atlas; **~bahn** f
motorway; **~bahndreieck** nt motorway
junction; **~bahngebühr** f toll;
~bahnkreuz nt motorway intersection;
~bus m bus; **~fähre** f car ferry;
~fahrer(in) m(f) motorist, driver; **~fahrt** f
drive; **a~gen** [-'geːn] adj autogenous;
~'gramm nt autograph

Autobahn

i An **Autobahn** is a motorway. In former
West Germany there is a widespread
motorway network but in the former **DDR**
the motorways are somewhat less extensive.
There is no overall speed limit but a limit of
130 km/hour is recommended and there are
lower mandatory limits on certain stretches
of road. As yet there are no tolls payable on

German Autobahnen. However, a yearly toll is payable in Switzerland and tolls have been introduced in Austria.

Auto- *zW:* **~'mat (-en, -en)** *m* machine; **~matik** [aʊto'maːtɪk] *f (AUT)* automatic; **a~'matisch** *adj* automatic; **a~nom** [-'noːm] *adj* autonomous

Autor(in) ['aʊtɔr(ɪn)] **(-s, -en)** *m(f)* author

Auto- *zW:* **~radio** *nt* car radio; **~reifen** *m* car tyre; **~reisezug** *m* motorail train; **~rennen** *nt* motor racing

autoritär [aʊtori'tɛːr] *adj* authoritarian

Autorität *f* authority

Auto- *zW:* **~telefon** *nt* car phone; **~unfall** *m* car *od* motor accident; **~vermietung** *m* car hire *(BRIT) od* rental *(US)*; **~waschanlage** *f* car wash

Axt [akst] **(-, ⁺e)** *f* axe

B, b

Baby ['beːbi] **(-s, -s)** *nt* baby; **~nahrung** *f* baby food; **~sitter (-s, -)** *m* baby-sitter

Bach [bax] **(-(e)s, ⁺e)** *m* stream, brook

Backbord (-(e)s, -e) *nt (NAUT)* port

Backe ['bakə] *f* cheek

backen ['bakən] *(unreg) vt, vi* to bake

Backenzahn *m* molar

Bäcker ['bɛkɑr(ɪn)] **(-s, -)** *m* baker; **~ei** *f* bakery; *(~eiladen)* baker's (shop)

Back- *zW:* **~form** *f* baking tin; **~obst** *nt* dried fruit; **~ofen** *m* oven; **~pflaume** *f* prune; **~pulver** *nt* baking powder; **~stein** *m* brick

Bad [baːt] **(-(e)s, ⁺er)** *nt* bath; *(Schwimmen)* bathe; *(Ort)* spa

Bade- ['baːdə] *zW:* **~anstalt** *f* (swimming) baths *pl;* **~anzug** *m* bathing suit; **~hose** *f* bathing *od* swimming trunks *pl;* **~kappe** *f* bathing cap; **~mantel** *m* bath(ing) robe; **~meister** *m* baths attendant; **b~n** *vi* to bathe, to have a bath ♦ *vt* to bath; **~ort** *m* spa; **~tuch** *nt* bath towel; **~wanne** *f* bath (tub); **~zimmer** *nt* bathroom

Bagatelle [baga'tɛlə] *f* trifle

Bagger ['bagər] **(-s, -)** *m* excavator; *(NAUT)* dredger; **b~n** *vt, vi* to excavate; to dredge

Bahn [baːn] **(-, -en)** *f* railway, railroad *(US); (Weg)* road, way; *(Spur)* lane; *(Rennbahn)* track; *(ASTRON)* orbit; *(Stoffbahn)* length; **b~brechend** *adj* pioneering; **~Card** ['baːnkaːrd] **(-, -s)** Ⓡ *f* ≈ railcard; **~damm** *m* railway embankment; **b~en** *vt:* **sich/ jdm einen Weg b~en** to clear a way/a way for sb; **~fahrt** *f* railway journey; **~fracht** *f* rail freight; **~hof (-, -s)** *m* station; **auf dem ~hof** at the station; **~hofshalle** *f* station concourse; **~linie** *f* (railway) line; **~steig** *m* platform; **~übergang** *m* level crossing, grade crossing *(US)*

Bahre ['baːrə] *f* stretcher

Bakterien [bak'teːriən] *pl* bacteria *pl*

Balance [ba'lãːsə] *f* balance, equilibrium

balan'cieren *vt, vi* to balance

bald [balt] *adv (zeitlich)* soon; *(beinahe)* almost; **~ig** ['baldɪç] *adj* early, speedy

Baldrian ['baldriaːn] **(-s, -e)** *m* valerian

Balkan ['balkaːn] **(-s)** *m:* **der ~** the Balkans *pl*

Balken ['balkən] **(-s, -)** *m* beam; *(Tragbalken)* girder; *(Stützbalken)* prop

Balkon [bal'kõː] **(-s, -s** *od* **-e)** *m* balcony; *(THEAT)* (dress) circle

Ball [bal] **(-(e)s, ⁺e)** *m* ball; *(Tanz)* dance, ball

Ballast ['balast] **(-(e)s, -e)** *m* ballast; *(fig)* weight, burden

Ballen ['balən] **(-s, -)** *m* bale; *(ANAT)* ball; **b~** *vt (formen)* to make into a ball; *(Faust)* to clench ♦ *vr (Wolken etc)* to build up; *(Menschen)* to gather

Ballett [ba'lɛt] **(-(e)s, -e)** *nt* ballet

Ballkleid *nt* evening dress

Ballon [ba'lõː] **(-s, -s** *od* **-e)** *m* balloon

Ballspiel *nt* ball game

Ballungsgebiet ['balʊŋsgəbiːt] *nt* conurbation

Baltikum ['baltikʊm] **(-s)** *nt:* **das ~** the Baltic States

Banane [ba'naːnə] *f* banana

Band¹ [bant] **(-(e)s, ⁺e)** *m (Buchband)* volume

Band² (-(e)s, ⁻er) *nt* (*Stoffband*) ribbon, tape; (*Fließband*) production line; (*Tonband*) tape; (*ANAT*) ligament; **etw auf ~ aufnehmen** to tape sth; **am laufenden ~** (*umg*) non-stop

Band³ (-(e)s, -e) *nt* (*Freundschaftsband etc*) bond

Band⁴ [bɛnt] (-, -s) *f* band, group

band *etc vb siehe* **binden**

Bandage [ban'daːʒə] *f* bandage

banda'gieren *vt* to bandage

Bande ['bandə] *f* band; (*Straßenbande*) gang

bändigen ['bɛndɪɡən] *vt* (*Tier*) to tame; (*Trieb, Leidenschaft*) to control, to restrain

Bandit [ban'diːt] (-en, -en) *m* bandit

Band- *zW:* **~nudel** *f* (*KOCH: gew pl*) ribbon noodles *pl*; **~scheibe** *f* (*ANAT*) disc; **~wurm** *m* tapeworm

bange ['baŋə] *adj* scared; (*besorgt*) anxious; **jdm wird es ~** sb is becoming scared; **jdm B~ machen** to scare sb; **~n** *vi*: **um jdn / etw ~** to be anxious *od* worried about sb/sth

Bank¹ [baŋk] (-, ⁻e) *f* (*Sitz~*) bench; (*Sand~ etc*) (sand)bank, (sand)bar

Bank² [baŋk] (-, -en) *f* (*Geldbank*) bank; **~anweisung** *f* banker's order; **~einzug** *m* direct debit

Bankett [baŋ'kɛt] (-(e)s, -e) *nt* (*Essen*) banquet; (*Straßenrand*) verge (*BRIT*), shoulder (*US*)

Bankier [baŋki'eː] (-s, -s) *m* banker

Bank- *zW:* **~konto** *nt* bank account; **~leitzahl** *f* bank sort code number; **~note** *f* banknote; **~raub** *m* bank robbery

Bankrott [baŋ'krɔt] (-(e)s, -e) *m* bankruptcy; **~ machen** to go bankrupt; **b~ adj** bankrupt

Bankverbindung *f* banking arrangements *pl*; **geben Sie bitte Ihre ~ an** please give your account details

Bann [ban] (-(e)s, -e) *m* (*HIST*) ban; (*Kirchenbann*) excommunication; (*fig: Zauber*) spell; **b~en** *vt* (*Geister*) to exorcize; (*Gefahr*) to avert; (*bezaubern*) to enchant; (*HIST*) to banish

Banner (-s, -) *nt* banner, flag

Bar (-, -s) *f* bar

bar [baːr] *adj* (+*gen*) (*unbedeckt*) bare; (*frei von*) lacking (in); (*offenkundig*) utter, sheer; **~e(s) Geld** cash; **etw (in) ~ bezahlen** to pay sth (in) cash; **etw für ~e Münze nehmen** (*fig*) to take sth at its face value

Bär [bɛːr] (-en, -en) *m* bear

Baracke [ba'rakə] *f* hut

barbarisch [bar'baːrɪʃ] *adj* barbaric, barbarous

Bar- *zW:* **b~fuß** *adj* barefoot; **~geld** *nt* cash, ready money; **b~geldlos** *adj* non-cash

Barkauf *m* cash purchase

Barkeeper ['baːrkiːpər] (-s, -) *m* barman, bartender

barmherzig [barm'hɛrtsɪç] *adj* merciful, compassionate

Baron [ba'roːn] (-s, -e) *m* baron; **~in** *f* baroness

Barren ['barən] (-s, -) *m* parallel bars *pl*; (*Goldbarren*) ingot

Barriere [bari'ɛːrə] *f* barrier

Barrikade [bari'kaːdə] *f* barricade

Barsch [barʃ] (-(e)s, -e) *m* perch

barsch [barʃ] *adj* brusque, gruff

Bar- *zW:* **~schaft** *f* ready money; **~scheck** *m* open *od* uncrossed cheque (*BRIT*), open check (*US*)

Bart [baːrt] (-(e)s, ⁻e) *m* beard; (*Schlüsselbart*) bit; **bärtig** ['bɛːrtɪç] *adj* bearded

Barzahlung *f* cash payment

Base ['baːzə] *f* (*CHEM*) base; (*Kusine*) cousin

Basel ['baːzəl] *nt* Basle

Basen *pl von* **Base; Basis**

basieren [ba'ziːrən] *vt* to base ♦ *vi* to be based

Basis ['baːzɪs] (-, **Basen**) *f* basis

Bass ▲ [bas] (-es, ⁻e) *m* bass

Bassin [ba'sɛ̃ː] (-s, -s) *nt* pool

basteln ['bastəln] *vt* to make ♦ *vi* to do handicrafts

bat *etc* [baːt] *vb siehe* **bitten**

Bataillon [batal'joːn] (-s, -e) *nt* battalion

Batik ['baːtɪk] *f* (*Verfahren*) batik

Batterie [batə'riː] *f* battery

Bau [bau] (-(e)s) *m* (~en) building,

construction; (*Aufbau*) structure; (*Körperbau*) frame; (*~stelle*) building site; (*pl ~e*: *Tierbau*) hole, burrow; (: *MIN*) working(s); (*pl ~ten*: *Gebäude*) building; **sich im ~ befinden** to be under construction; **~arbeiten** *pl* building *od* construction work *sg*; **~arbeiter** *m* building worker

Bauch [baʊx] **(-(e)s, Bäuche)** *m* belly; (*ANAT auch*) stomach, abdomen; **~fell** *nt* peritoneum; **b~ig** *adj* bulbous; **~nabel** *m* navel; **~redner** *m* ventriloquist; **~schmerzen** *pl* stomachache; **~weh** *nt* stomachache

Baudenkmal *nt* historical monument

bauen ['baʊən] *vt, vi* to build; (*TECH*) to construct; **auf jdn/etw ~** to depend *od* count upon sb/sth

Bauer¹ ['baʊər] **(-n** *od* **-s, -n)** *m* farmer; (*Schach*) pawn

Bauer² ['baʊər] **(-s, -)** *m od nt* (bird)cage

Bäuerin ['bɔʏərɪn] *f* farmer; (*Frau des Bauers*) farmer's wife

bäuerlich *adj* rustic

Bauern- *zW*: **~haus** *nt* farmhouse; **~hof** *m* farm(yard)

Bau- *zW*: **b~fällig** *adj* dilapidated; **~gelände** *f* building site; **~genehmigung** *f* building permit; **~gerüst** *nt* scaffolding; **~herr** *m* purchaser; **~kasten** *m* box of bricks; **~land** *nt* building land; **b~lich** *adj* structural

Baum [baʊm] **(-(e)s, Bäume)** *m* tree

baumeln ['baʊməln] *vi* to dangle

bäumen ['bɔʏmən] *vr* to rear (up)

Baum- *zW*: **~schule** *f* nursery; **~stamm** *m* tree trunk; **~stumpf** *m* tree stump; **~wolle** *f* cotton

Bau- *zW*: **~plan** *m* architect's plan; **~platz** *m* building site

bauspar- *zW*: **~en** *vi* to save with a building society; **B~kasse** *f* building society; **B~vertrag** *m* building society savings agreement

Bau- *zW*: **~stein** *m* building stone, freestone; **~stelle** *f* building site; **~teil** *nt* prefabricated part (of building); **~ten** *pl von* **Bau**; **~unternehmer** *m* building

contractor; **~weise** *f* (method of) construction; **~werk** *nt* building; **~zaun** *m* hoarding

Bayern ['baɪərn] *nt* Bavaria

bayrisch ['baɪrɪʃ] *adj* Bavarian

Bazillus [ba'tsɪlʊs] **(-, Bazillen)** *m* bacillus

beabsichtigen [bə'apzɪçtɪgən] *vt* to intend

beacht- [bə'axt] *zW*: **~en** *vt* to take note of; (*Vorschrift*) to obey; (*Vorfahrt*) to observe; **~lich** *adj* considerable; **B~ung** *f* notice, attention, observation

Beamte(r) [bə'amtə(r)] **(-n, -n)** *m* official; (*Staatsbeamte*) civil servant; (*Bankbeamte etc*) employee

Beamtin *f siehe* **Beamte(r)**

beängstigend [bə'ɛŋstɪgənt] *adj* alarming

beanspruchen [bə'anʃprʊxən] *vt* to claim; (*Zeit, Platz*) to take up, to occupy; **jdn ~** to take up sb's time

beanstanden [bə'anʃtandən] *vt* to complain about, to object to

beantragen [bə'antra:gən] *vt* to apply for, to ask for

beantworten [bə'antvɔrtən] *vt* to answer; **Beantwortung** *f* (+*gen*) reply (to)

bearbeiten [bə'arbaɪtən] *vt* to work; (*Material*) to process; (*Thema*) to deal with; (*Land*) to cultivate; (*CHEM*) to treat; (*Buch*) to revise; (*umg: beeinflussen wollen*) to work on

Bearbeitung *f* processing; cultivation; treatment; revision

Bearbeitungsgebühr *f* handling charge

Beatmung [bə'a:tmʊŋ] *f* respiration

beaufsichtigen [bə'aʊfzɪçtɪgən] *vt* to supervise; **Beaufsichtigung** *f* supervision

beauftragen [bə'aʊftra:gən] *vt* to instruct; **jdn mit etw ~** to entrust sb with sth

Beauftragte(r) *f(m)* representative

bebauen [bə'baʊən] *vt* to build on; (*AGR*) to cultivate

beben ['be:bən] *vi* to tremble, to shake; **B~ (-s, -)** *nt* earthquake

Becher ['bɛçər] **(-s, -)** *m* mug; (*ohne Henkel*) tumbler

Becken ['bɛkən] **(-s, -)** *nt* basin; (*MUS*) cymbal; (*ANAT*) pelvis

---

Rechtschreibreform: ▲ *neue Schreibung* △ *alte Schreibung (auslaufend)*

bedacht [bə'daxt] *adj* thoughtful, careful; **auf etw** *akk* ~ **sein** to be concerned about sth

bedächtig [bə'dɛçtɪç] *adj* (*umsichtig*) thoughtful, reflective; (*langsam*) slow, deliberate

bedanken [bə'daŋkən] *vr*: **sich (bei jdm)** ~ to say thank you (to sb)

Bedarf [bə'darf] **(-(e)s)** *m* need, requirement; (*COMM*) demand; **je nach** ~ according to demand; ~ **an etw** *dat* **haben** to be in need of sth

Bedarfs- *zW*: ~**fall** *m* case of need; ~**haltestelle** *f* request stop

bedauerlich [bə'dauərlɪç] *adj* regrettable

bedauern [bə'dauərn] *vt* to be sorry for; (*bemitleiden*) to pity; **B~ (-s)** *nt* regret; ~**swert** *adj* (*Zustände*) regrettable; (*Mensch*) pitiable, unfortunate

bedecken [bə'dɛkən] *vt* to cover

bedeckt *adj* covered; (*Himmel*) overcast

bedenken [bə'dɛŋkən] (*unreg*) *vt* to think over, to consider

Bedenken (-s, -) *nt* (*Überlegen*) consideration; (*Zweifel*) doubt; (*Skrupel*) scruple

bedenklich *adj* doubtful; (*bedrohlich*) dangerous, risky

Bedenkzeit *f* time to think

bedeuten [bə'dɔytən] *vt* to mean; to signify; (*wichtig sein*) to be of importance; ~**d** *adj* important; (*beträchtlich*) considerable

bedeutsam *adj* (*wichtig*) significant

Bedeutung *f* meaning; significance; (*Wichtigkeit*) importance; **b~slos** *adj* insignificant, unimportant; **b~svoll** *adj* momentous, significant

bedienen [bə'di:nən] *vt* to serve; (*Maschine*) to work, to operate ♦ *vr* (*beim Essen*) to help o.s.; **sich jds/einer Sache** ~ to make use of sb/sth

Bedienung *f* service; (*Kellnerin*) waitress; (*Verkäuferin*) shop assistant; (*Zuschlag*) service (charge)

Bedienungsanleitung *f* operating instructions *pl*

bedingen [bə'dɪŋən] *vt* (*verursachen*) to cause

bedingt *adj* (*Richtigkeit, Tauglichkeit*) limited; (*Zusage, Annahme*) conditional

Bedingung *f* condition; (*Voraussetzung*) stipulation; **b~slos** *adj* unconditional

bedrängen [bə'drɛŋən] *vt* to pester, to harass

bedrohen [bə'dro:ən] *vt* to threaten; **Bedrohung** *f* threat, menace

bedrücken [bə'drʏkən] *vt* to oppress, to trouble

bedürf- [bə'dʏrf] *zW*: ~**en** (*unreg*) *vi* +*gen* to need, to require; **B~nis (-ses, -se)** *nt* need; ~**tig** *adj* in need, poor, needy

beeilen [bə'|ailən] *vr* to hurry

beeindrucken [bə'|aindrukən] *vt* to impress, to make an impression on

beeinflussen [bə'|ainflusən] *vt* to influence

beeinträchtigen [bə'|aintrɛçtɪgən] *vt* to affect adversely; (*Freiheit*) to infringe upon

beend(ig)en [bə'|ɛnd(ɪg)ən] *vt* to end, to finish, to terminate

beengen [bə'|ɛŋən] *vt* to cramp; (*fig*) to hamper, to oppress

beerben [bə'|ɛrbən] *vt*: **jdn** ~ to inherit from sb

beerdigen [bə'|e:rdɪgən] *vt* to bury; **Beerdigung** *f* funeral, burial

Beere ['be:rə] *f* berry; (*Traubenbeere*) grape

Beet [be:t] **(-(e)s, -e)** *nt* bed

befähigen [bə'fɛːɪgən] *vt* to enable

befähigt *adj* (*begabt*) talented; ~ **(für)** (*fähig*) capable (of)

Befähigung *f* capability; (*Begabung*) talent, aptitude

befahrbar [bə'fa:rba:r] *adj* passable; (*NAUT*) navigable

befahren [bə'fa:rən] (*unreg*) *vt* to use, to drive over; (*NAUT*) to navigate ♦ *adj* used

befallen [bə'falən] (*unreg*) *vt* to come over

befangen [bə'faŋən] *adj* (*schüchtern*) shy, self-conscious; (*voreingenommen*) biased

befassen [bə'fasən] *vr* to concern o.s.

Befehl [bə'fe:l] **(-(e)s, -e)** *m* command, order; **b~en** (*unreg*) *vt* to order ♦ *vi* to give orders; **jdm etw b~en** to order sb to do sth; ~**sverweigerung** *f* insubordination

befestigen [bə'fɛstɪgən] *vt* to fasten;
(*stärken*) to strengthen; (*MIL*) to fortify; **~ an**
+*dat* to fasten to
Befestigung *f* fastening; strengthening;
(*MIL*) fortification
befeuchten [bə'fɔʏçtən] *vt* to damp(en), to
moisten
befinden [bə'fɪndən] (*unreg*) *vr* to be; (*sich
fühlen*) to feel ♦ *vt*: **jdn/etw für** *od* **als etw
~** to deem sb/sth to be sth ♦ *vi*: **~ (über**
+*akk*) to decide (on), to adjudicate (on);
B~ (-s) *nt* health, condition; (*Meinung*)
view, opinion
befolgen [bə'fɔlgən] *vt* to comply with, to
follow
befördern [bə'fœrdərn] *vt* (*senden*) to
transport, to send; (*beruflich*) to promote;
Beförderung *f* transport; promotion
befragen [bə'fraːgən] *vt* to question
befreien [bə'fraɪən] *vt* to set free; (*erlassen*)
to exempt; **Befreiung** *f* liberation, release;
(*Erlassen*) exemption
befreunden [bə'frɔʏndən] *vr* to make
friends; (*mit Idee etc*) to acquaint o.s.
befreundet *adj* friendly
befriedigen [bə'friːdɪgən] *vt* to satisfy; **~d**
adj satisfactory
Befriedigung *f* satisfaction, gratification
befristet [bə'frɪstət] *adj* limited
befruchten [bə'frʊxtən] *vt* to fertilize; (*fig*)
to stimulate
Befruchtung *f*: **künstliche ~** artificial
insemination
Befugnis [bə'fuːknɪs] **(-, -se)** *f* authorization,
powers *pl*
befugt *adj* authorized, entitled
Befund [bə'fʊnt] **(-(e)s, -e)** *m* findings *pl*;
(*MED*) diagnosis
befürchten [bə'fʏrçtən] *vt* to fear;
Befürchtung *f* fear, apprehension
befürworten [bə'fyːrvɔrtən] *vt* to support,
to speak in favour of; **Befürworter (-s, -)**
m supporter, advocate
begabt [bə'gaːpt] *adj* gifted
Begabung [bə'gaːbʊŋ] *f* talent, gift
begann *etc* [bə'gan] *vb siehe* **beginnen**
begeben [bə'geːbən] (*unreg*) *vr* (*gehen*) to

betake o.s.; (*geschehen*) to occur; **sich ~
nach** *od* **zu** to proceed to(wards); **B~heit** *f*
occurrence
begegnen [bə'geːgnən] *vi*: **jdm ~** to meet
sb; (*behandeln*) to treat sb; **einer Sache** *dat*
~ to meet with sth
Begegnung *f* meeting
begehen [bə'geːən] (*unreg*) *vt* (*Straftat*) to
commit; (*abschreiten*) to cover; (*Straße etc*)
to use, to negotiate; (*Feier*) to celebrate
begehren [bə'geːrən] *vt* to desire
begehrt *adj* in demand; (*Junggeselle*) eligible
begeistern [bə'gaɪstərn] *vt* to fill with
enthusiasm, to inspire ♦ *vr*: **sich für etw ~**
to get enthusiastic about sth
begeistert *adj* enthusiastic
Begierde [bə'giːrdə] *f* desire, passion
begierig [bə'giːrɪç] *adj* eager, keen
begießen [bə'giːsən] (*unreg*) *vt* to water;
(*mit Alkohol*) to drink to
Beginn [bə'gɪn] **(-(e)s)** *m* beginning; **zu ~** at
the beginning; **b~en** (*unreg*) *vt, vi* to start,
to begin
beglaubigen [bə'glaʊbɪgən] *vt* to
countersign; **Beglaubigung** *f*
countersignature
begleichen [bə'glaɪçən] (*unreg*) *vt* to settle,
to pay
Begleit- [bə'glaɪt] *zW*: **b~en** *vt* to
accompany; (*MIL*) to escort; **~er (-s, -)** *m*
companion; (*Freund*) escort; (*MUS*)
accompanist; **~schreiben** *nt* covering
letter; **~umstände** *pl* concomitant
circumstances; **~ung** *f* company; (*MIL*)
escort; (*MUS*) accompaniment
beglücken [bə'glʏkən] *vt* to make happy, to
delight
beglückwünschen [bə'glʏkvʏnʃən] *vt*: **~
(zu)** to congratulate (on)
begnadigen [bə'gnaːdɪgən] *vt* to pardon;
Begnadigung *f* pardon, amnesty
begnügen [bə'gnyːgən] *vr* to be satisfied, to
content o.s.
begonnen *etc* [bə'gɔnən] *vb siehe* **beginnen**
begraben [bə'graːbən] (*unreg*) *vt* to bury;
Begräbnis (-ses, -se) *nt*
burial, funeral

begreifen [bəˈgraɪfən] (*unreg*) *vt* to understand, to comprehend

begreiflich [bəˈgraɪflɪç] *adj* understandable

begrenzen [bəˈgrɛntsən] *vt* (*beschränken*) to limit

Begrenztheit [bəˈgrɛntsthaɪt] *f* limitation, restriction; (*fig*) narrowness

Begriff [bəˈgrɪf] **(-(e)s, -e)** *m* concept, idea; **im ~ sein, etw zu tun** to be about to do sth; **schwer von ~** (*umg*) slow, dense

begriffsstutzig *adj* slow, dense

begründ- [bəˈgrʏnd] *zW*: **~en** *vt* (*Gründe geben*) to justify; **~et** *adj* well-founded, justified; **B~ung** *f* justification, reason

begrüßen [bəˈgryːsən] *vt* to greet, to welcome; **Begrüßung** *f* greeting, welcome

begünstigen [bəˈgʏnstɪɡən] *vt* (*Person*) to favour; (*Sache*) to further, to promote

begutachten [bəˈguːtˌaxtən] *vt* to assess

begütert [bəˈgyːtərt] *adj* wealthy, well-to-do

behaart [bəˈhaːrt] *adj* hairy

behagen [bəˈhaːgən] *vi*: **das behagt ihm nicht** he does not like it

behaglich [bəˈhaːklɪç] *adj* comfortable, cosy; **B~keit** *f* comfort, cosiness

behalten [bəˈhaltən] (*unreg*) *vt* to keep, to retain; (*im Gedächtnis*) to remember

Behälter [bəˈhɛltɐ] **(-s, -)** *m* container, receptacle

behandeln [bəˈhandəln] *vt* to treat; (*Thema*) to deal with; (*Maschine*) to handle

Behandlung *f* treatment; (*von Maschine*) handling

beharren [bəˈharən] *vi*: **auf etw** *dat* **~** to stick *od* keep to sth

beharrlich [bəˈharlɪç] *adj* (*ausdauernd*) steadfast, unwavering; (*hartnäckig*) tenacious, dogged; **B~keit** *f* steadfastness; tenacity

behaupten [bəˈhaʊptən] *vt* to claim, to assert, to maintain; (*sein Recht*) to defend ♦ *vr* to assert o.s.

Behauptung *f* claim, assertion

beheben [bəˈheːbən] (*unreg*) *vt* to remove

behelfen [bəˈhɛlfən] (*unreg*) *vr*: **sich mit etw ~** to make do with sth

behelfsmäßig *adj* improvised, makeshift; (*vorübergehend*) temporary

behelligen [bəˈhɛlɪɡən] *vt* to trouble, to bother

beherbergen [bəˈhɛrbɛrɡən] *vt* to put up, to house

beherrsch- [bəˈhɛrʃ] *zW*: **~en** *vt* (*Volk*) to rule, to govern; (*Situation*) to control; (*Sprache, Gefühle*) to master ♦ *vr* to control o.s.; **~t** *adj* controlled; **B~ung** *f* rule; control; mastery

beherzigen [bəˈhɛrtsɪɡən] *vt* to take to heart

beherzt *adj* courageous, brave

behilflich [bəˈhɪlflɪç] *adj* helpful; **jdm ~ sein (bei)** to help sb (with)

behindern [bəˈhɪndərn] *vt* to hinder, to impede

Behinderte(r) *f(m)* disabled person

Behinderung *f* hindrance; (*Körperbehinderung*) handicap

Behörde [bəˈhøːrdə] *f* (*auch pl*) authorities *pl*

behördlich [bəˈhøːrtlɪç] *adj* official

behüten [bəˈhyːtən] *vt* to guard; **jdn vor etw** *dat* **~** to preserve sb from sth

behutsam [bəˈhuːtzaːm] *adj* cautious, careful; **B~keit** *f* caution, carefulness

---

SCHLÜSSELWORT

bei [baɪ] *präp* +*dat* **1** (*nahe bei*) near; (*zum Aufenthalt*) at, with; (*unter, zwischen*) among; **bei München** near Munich; **bei uns** at our place; **beim Friseur** at the hairdresser's; **bei seinen Eltern wohnen** to live with one's parents; **bei einer Firma arbeiten** to work for a firm; **etw bei sich haben** to have sth on one; **jdn bei sich haben** to have sb with one; **bei Goethe** in Goethe; **beim Militär** in the army

2 (*zeitlich*) at, on; (*während*) during; (*Zustand, Umstand*) in; **bei Nacht** at night; **bei Nebel** in fog; **bei Regen** if it rains; **bei solcher Hitze** in such heat; **bei meiner Ankuft** on my arrival; **bei der Arbeit** when I'm *etc* working; **beim Fahren** while driving

---

beibehalten [ˈbaɪbəhaltən] (*unreg*) *vt* to keep, to retain

beibringen ['baɪbrɪŋən] (*unreg*) *vt* (*Beweis, Zeugen*) to bring forward; (*Gründe*) to adduce; **jdm etw ~** (*lehren*) to teach sb sth; (*zu verstehen geben*) to make sb understand sth; (*zufügen*) to inflict sth on sb

Beichte ['baɪçtə] *f* confession; **b~n** *vt* to confess ♦ *vi* to go to confession

beide(s) ['baɪdə(s)] *pron, adj* both; **meine ~n Brüder** my two brothers, both my brothers; **die ersten ~n** the first two; **wir ~** we two; **einer von ~n** one of the two; **alles ~s** both (of them)

beider- ['baɪdər] *zW*: **~lei** *adj inv* of both; **~seitig** *adj* mutual, reciprocal; **~seits** *adv* mutually ♦ *präp +gen* on both sides of

beieinander [baɪaɪˈnandər] *adv* together

Beifahrer ['baɪfaːrər] *m* passenger

Beifall ['baɪfal] (**-(e)s**) *m* applause; (*Zustimmung*) approval

beifügen ['baɪfyːgən] *vt* to enclose

beige ['beːʒ] *adj* beige, fawn

beigeben ['baɪgeːbən] (*unreg*) *vt* (*zufügen*) to add; (*mitgeben*) to give ♦ *vi* (*nachgeben*) to give in

Beihilfe ['baɪhɪlfə] *f* aid, assistance; (*Studienbeihilfe*) grant; (*JUR*) aiding and abetting

beikommen ['baɪkɔmən] (*unreg*) *vi +dat* to get at; (*einem Problem*) to deal with

Beil [baɪl] (**-(e)s, -e**) *nt* axe, hatchet

Beilage ['baɪlaːgə] *f* (*Buchbeilage etc*) supplement; (*KOCH*) vegetables and potatoes *pl*

beiläufig ['baɪlɔyfɪç] *adj* casual, incidental ♦ *adv* casually, by the way

beilegen ['baɪleːgən] *vt* (*hinzufügen*) to enclose, to add; (*beimessen*) to attribute, to ascribe; (*Streit*) to settle

Beileid ['baɪlaɪt] *nt* condolence, sympathy; **herzliches ~** deepest sympathy

beiliegend ['baɪliːgənt] *adj* (*COMM*) enclosed

beim [baɪm] = **bei dem**

beimessen ['baɪmesən] (*unreg*) *vt* (**+dat**) to attribute (to), to ascribe (to)

Bein [baɪn] (**-(e)s, -e**) *nt* leg

beinah(e) ['baɪnaː(ə)] *adv* almost, nearly

Beinbruch *m* fracture of the leg

beinhalten [bəˈɪnhaltən] *vt* to contain

Beipackzettel ['baɪpaktsetəl] *m* instruction leaflet

beipflichten ['baɪpflɪçtən] *vi*: **jdm/etw ~** to agree with sb/sth

beisammen [baɪˈzamən] *adv* together; **B~sein** (**-s**) *nt* get-together

Beischlaf ['baɪʃlaːf] *m* sexual intercourse

Beisein ['baɪzaɪn] (**-s**) *nt* presence

beiseite [baɪˈzaɪtə] *adv* to one side, aside; (*stehen*) on one side, aside; **etw ~ legen** (*sparen*) to put sth by

beisetzen ['baɪzetsən] *vt* to bury; **Beisetzung** *f* funeral

Beisitzer ['baɪzɪtsər] (**-s, -**) *m* (*bei Prüfung*) assessor

Beispiel ['baɪʃpiːl] (**-(e)s, -e**) *nt* example; **sich +dat an jdm ein ~ nehmen** to take sb as an example; **zum ~** for example; **b~haft** *adj* exemplary; **b~los** *adj* unprecedented; **b~sweise** *adv* for instance *od* example

beißen ['baɪsən] (*unreg*) *vt, vi* to bite; (*stechen: Rauch, Säure*) to burn ♦ *vr* (*Farben*) to clash; **~d** *adj* biting, caustic; (*fig auch*) sarcastic

Beistand ['baɪʃtant] (**-(e)s, ⁺e**) *m* support, help; (*JUR*) adviser

beistehen ['baɪʃteːən] (*unreg*) *vi*: **jdm ~** to stand by sb

beisteuern ['baɪʃtɔyərn] *vt* to contribute

Beitrag ['baɪtraːk] (**-(e)s, ⁺e**) *m* contribution; (*Zahlung*) fee, subscription; (*Versicherungsbeitrag*) premium; **b~en** ['baɪtraːgən] (*unreg*) *vt, vi*: **b~en (zu)** to contribute (to); (*mithelfen*) to help (with)

beitreten ['baɪtreːtən] (*unreg*) *vi +dat* to join

Beitritt ['baɪtrɪt] *m* joining, membership

Beiwagen ['baɪvaːgən] *m* (*Motorradbeiwagen*) sidecar

beizeiten [baɪˈtsaɪtən] *adv* in time

bejahen [bəˈjaːən] *vt* (*Frage*) to say yes to, to answer in the affirmative; (*gutheißen*) to agree with

bekämpfen [bəˈkɛmpfən] *vt* (*Gegner*) to fight; (*Seuche*) to combat ♦ *vr* to fight;

Bekämpfung f fight, struggle

bekannt [bə'kant] adj (well-)known; (nicht fremd) familiar; **~ geben** to announce publicly; **mit jdm ~ sein** to know sb; **~ machen** to announce; **jdn mit jdm ~ machen** to introduce sb to sb; **das ist mir ~** I know that; **es/sie kommt mir ~ vor** it/she seems familiar; **B~e(r)** f(m) acquaintance; friend; **B~enkreis** m circle of friends; **~lich** adv as is well known, as you know; **B~machung** f publication; announcement; **B~schaft** f acquaintance

bekehren [bə'ke:rən] vt to convert ♦ vr to be od become converted

bekennen [bə'kɛnən] (unreg) vt to confess; (Glauben) to profess; **Farbe ~** (umg) to show where one stands

Bekenntnis [bə'kɛntnɪs] (-ses, -se) nt admission, confession; (Religion) confession, denomination

beklagen [bə'kla:gən] vt to deplore, to lament ♦ vr to complain

bekleiden [bə'klaɪdən] vt to clothe; (Amt) to occupy, to fill

Bekleidung f clothing

beklemmen [bə'klɛmən] vt to oppress

beklommen [bə'kləmən] adj anxious, uneasy

bekommen [bə'kəmən] (unreg) vt to get, to receive; (Kind) to have, (Zug) to catch, to get ♦ vi: **jdm ~** to agree with sb

bekömmlich [bə'kœmlɪç] adj easily digestible

bekräftigen [bə'krɛftɪgən] vt to confirm, to corroborate

bekreuzigen [bə'krɔʏtsɪgən] vr to cross o.s.

bekunden [bə'kundən] vt (sagen) to state; (zeigen) to show

belächeln [bə'lɛçəln] vt to laugh at

beladen [bə'la:dən] (unreg) vt to load

Belag [bə'la:k] (-(e)s, ¬e) m covering, coating; (Brotbelag) spread; (Zahnbelag) tartar; (auf Zunge) fur; (Bremsbelag) lining

belagern [bə'la:gərn] vt to besiege; **Belagerung** f siege

Belang [bə'laŋ] (-(e)s) m importance; **~e** pl (Interessen) interests, concerns; **b~los** adj trivial, unimportant

belassen [bə'lasən] (unreg) vt (in Zustand, Glauben) to leave; (in Stellung) to retain

belasten [bə'lastən] vt to burden; (fig: bedrücken) to trouble, to worry; (COMM: Konto) to debit; (JUR) to incriminate ♦ vr to weigh o.s. down; (JUR) to incriminate o.s.; **~d** adj (JUR) incriminating

belästigen [bə'lɛstɪgən] vt to annoy, to pester; **Belästigung** f annoyance, pestering

Belastung [bə'lastʊŋ] f load; (fig: Sorge etc) weight; (COMM) charge, debit(ing); (JUR) incriminatory evidence

belaufen [bə'laʊfən] (unreg) vr: **sich ~ auf** +akk to amount to

beleben [bə'le:bən] vt (anregen) to liven up; (Konjunktur, jds Hoffnungen) to stimulate ♦ vr (Augen) to light up; (Stadt) to come to life

belebt [bə'le:pt] adj (Straße) busy

Beleg [bə'le:k] (-(e)s, -e) m (COMM) receipt; (Beweis) documentary evidence, proof; (Beispiel) example; **b~en** vt to cover; (Kuchen, Brot) to spread; (Platz) to reserve, to book; (Kurs, Vorlesung) to register for; (beweisen) to verify, to prove; (MIL: mit Bomben) to bomb; **~schaft** f personnel, staff; **b~t** adj: **b~tes Brot** open sandwich

belehren [bə'le:rən] vt to instruct, to teach; **Belehrung** f instruction

beleibt [bə'laɪpt] adj stout, corpulent

beleidigen [bə'laɪdɪgən] vt to insult, to offend; **Beleidigung** f insult; (JUR) slander, libel

beleuchten [bə'lɔʏçtən] vt to light, to illuminate; (fig) to throw light on

Beleuchtung f lighting, illumination

Belgien ['bɛlgiən] nt Belgium; **Belgier(in)** m(f) Belgian; **belgisch** adj Belgian

belichten [bə'lɪçtən] vt to expose

Belichtung f exposure; **~smesser** m exposure meter

Belleben [bə'li:bən] nt: **(ganz) nach ~** (just) as you wish

beliebig [bə'li:bɪç] adj any you like ♦ adv as you like; **ein ~es Thema** any subject you like od want; **~ viel/viele** as much/many as you like

beliebt [bə'li:pt] *adj* popular; **sich bei jdm ~ machen** to make o.s. popular with sb; **B~heit** *f* popularity

beliefern [bə'li:fərn] *vt* to supply

bellen ['bɛlən] *vi* to bark

belohnen [bə'lo:nən] *vt* to reward; **Belohnung** *f* reward

Belüftung [bə'lʏftʊŋ] *f* ventilation

belügen [bə'ly:gən] (*unreg*) *vt* to lie to, to deceive

belustigen [bə'lʊstɪgən] *vt* to amuse; **Belustigung** *f* amusement

bemalen [bə'ma:lən] *vt* to paint

bemängeln [bə'mɛŋəln] *vt* to criticize

bemerk- [bə'mɛrk] *zW:* **~bar** *adj* perceptible, noticeable; **sich ~bar machen** (*Person*) to make od get o.s. noticed; (*Unruhe*) to become noticeable; **~en** *vt* (*wahrnehmen*) to notice, to observe; (*sagen*) to say, to mention; **~enswert** *adj* remarkable, noteworthy; **B~ung** *f* remark; (*schriftlich auch*) note

bemitleiden [bə'mɪtlaɪdən] *vt* to pity

bemühen [bə'my:ən] *vr* to take trouble *od* pains; **Bemühung** *f* trouble, pains *pl*, effort

benachbart [bə'naxba:rt] *adj* neighbouring

benachrichtigen [bə'na:xrɪçtɪgən] *vt* to inform; **Benachrichtigung** *f* notification, information

benachteiligen [bə'na:xtaɪlɪgən] *vt* to put at a disadvantage; to victimize

benehmen [bə'ne:mən] (*unreg*) *vr* to behave; **B~ (-s)** *nt* behaviour

beneiden [bə'naɪdən] *vt* to envy; **~swert** *adj* enviable

benennen [bə'nɛnən] (*unreg*) *vt* to name

Bengel ['bɛŋəl] **(-s, -)** *m* (little) rascal *od* rogue

benommen [bə'nɔmən] *adj* dazed

benoten [bə'no:tən] *vt* to mark

benötigen [bə'nø:tɪgən] *vt* to need

benutzen [bə'nʊtsən] *vt* to use

Benutzer (-s, -) *m* user

Benutzung *f* utilization, use

Benzin [bɛnt'si:n] **(-s, -e)** *nt* (*AUT*) petrol

(*BRIT*), gas(oline) (*US*); **~kanister** *m* petrol (*BRIT*), gas tank (*US*) can; **~tank** *m* petrol tank (*BRIT*), gas tank (*US*); **~uhr** *f* petrol (*BRIT*) *od* gas (*US*) gauge

beobachten [bə'o:baxtən] *vt* to observe; **Beobachter (-s, -)** *m* observer; (*eines Unfalls*) witness; (*PRESSE, TV*) correspondent; **Beobachtung** *f* observation

bepacken [bə'pakən] *vt* to load, to pack

bequem [bə'kve:m] *adj* comfortable; (*Ausrede*) convenient; (*Person*) lazy, indolent; **~en** *vr:* **sich ~en(, etw zu tun)** to condescend (to do sth); **B~lichkeit** [-'lɪçkaɪt] *f* convenience, comfort; (*Faulheit*) laziness, indolence

beraten [bə'ra:tən] (*unreg*) *vt* to advise; (*besprechen*) to discuss, to debate ♦ *vr* to consult; **gut/schlecht ~ sein** to be well/ill advised; **sich ~ lassen** to get advice

Berater (-s, -) *m* adviser

Beratung *f* advice; (*Besprechung*) consultation; **~sstelle** *f* advice centre

berauben [bə'raʊbən] *vt* to rob

berechenbar [bə'rɛçənba:r] *adj* calculable

berechnen [bə'rɛçnən] *vt* to calculate; (*COMM: anrechnen*) to charge; **~d** *adj* (*Mensch*) calculating, scheming

Berechnung *f* calculation; (*COMM*) charge

berechtigen [bə'rɛçtɪgən] *vt* to entitle; to authorize; (*fig*) to justify

berechtigt [bə'rɛçtɪçt] *adj* justifiable, justified

Berechtigung *f* authorization; (*fig*) justification

bereden [bə're:dən] *vt* (*besprechen*) to discuss; (*überreden*) to persuade ♦ *vr* to discuss

Bereich [bə'raɪç] **(-(e)s, -e)** *m* (*Bezirk*) area; (*PHYS*) range; (*Ressort, Gebiet*) sphere

bereichern [bə'raɪçərn] *vt* to enrich ♦ *vr* to get rich

bereinigen [bə'raɪnɪgən] *vt* to settle

bereisen [bə'raɪzən] *vt* (*Land*) to travel through

bereit [bə'raɪt] *adj* ready, prepared; **zu etw ~ sein** to be ready for sth; **sich ~ erklären** to declare o.s. willing; **~en** *vt* to prepare, to make ready; (*Kummer, Freude*) to cause;

~halten (*unreg*) *vt* to keep in readiness; **~legen** *vt* to lay out; **~machen** *vt*, *vr* to prepare, to get ready; **~s** *adv* already; **B~schaft** *f* readiness; (*Polizei*) alert; **B~schaftsdienst** *m* emergency service; **~stehen** (*unreg*) *vi* (*Person*) to be prepared; (*Ding*) to be ready; **~stellen** *vt* (*Kisten, Pakete etc*) to put ready; (*Geld etc*) to make available; (*Truppen, Maschinen*) to put at the ready; **~willig** *adj* willing, ready; **B~willigkeit** *f* willingness, readiness

bereuen [bəˈrɔyən] *vt* to regret

Berg [bɛrk] **(-(e)s, -e)** *m* mountain; hill; **b~ab** *adv* downhill; **~arbeiter** *m* miner; **b~auf** *adv* uphill; **~bahn** *f* mountain railway; **~bau** *m* mining

bergen [ˈbɛrgən] (*unreg*) *vt* (*retten*) to rescue; (*Ladung*) to salvage; (*enthalten*) to contain

Berg- *zW*: **~führer** *m* mountain guide; **~gipfel** *m* peak, summit; **b~ig** [ˈbɛrgɪç] *adj* mountainous; hilly; **~kette** *f* mountain range; **~mann** (*pl* **~leute**) *m* miner; **~rettungsdienst** *m* mountain rescue team; **~rutsch** *m* landslide; **~steigen** *nt* mountaineering; **~steiger(in)** **(-s, -)** *m(f)* mountaineer, climber; **~tour** *f* mountain climb

Bergung [ˈbɛrgʊŋ] *f* (*von Menschen*) rescue; (*von Material*) recovery; (*NAUT*) salvage

Berg- *zW*: **~wacht** *f* mountain rescue service; **~wanderung** *f* hike in the mountains; **~werk** *nt* mine

Bericht [bəˈrɪçt] **(-(e)s, -e)** *m* report, account; **b~en** *vt*, *vi* to report; **~erstatter** **(-s, -)** *m* reporter; (*newspaper*) correspondent

berichtigen [bəˈrɪçtɪgən] *vt* to correct; **Berichtigung** *f* correction

Bernstein [ˈbɛrnʃtaɪn] *m* amber

bersten [ˈbɛrstən] (*unreg*) *vi* to burst, to split

berüchtigt [bəˈrʏçtɪçt] *adj* notorious, infamous

berücksichtigen [bəˈrʏkzɪçtɪgən] *vt* to consider, to bear in mind; **Berücksichtigung** *f* consideration

Beruf [bəˈruːf] **(-(e)s, -e)** *m* occupation, profession; (*Gewerbe*) trade; **b~en** (*unreg*)

vt: **b~en zu** to appoint to ♦ *vr*: **sich auf jdn/etw b~en** to refer *od* appeal to sb/sth ♦ *adj* competent, qualified; **b~lich** *adj* professional

Berufs- *zW*: **~ausbildung** *f* job training; **~berater** *m* careers adviser; **~beratung** *f* vocational guidance; **~geheimnis** *nt* professional secret; **~leben** *nt* professional life; **~schule** *f* vocational *od* trade school; **~sportler** [-ʃpɔrtlər] *m* professional (sportsman); **b~tätig** *adj* employed; **b~unfähig** *adj* unfit for work; **~verkehr** *m* rush-hour traffic

Berufung *f* vocation, calling; (*Ernennung*) appointment; (*JUR*) appeal; **~ einlegen** to appeal

beruhen [bəˈruːən] *vi*: **auf etw** *dat* **~** to be based on sth; **etw auf sich ~ lassen** to leave sth at that

beruhigen [bəˈruːɪgən] *vt* to calm, to pacify, to soothe ♦ *vr* (*Mensch*) to calm (o.s.) down; (*Situation*) to calm down

Beruhigung *f* soothing; (*der Nerven*) calming; **zu jds ~** (in order) to reassure sb; **~smittel** *nt* sedative

berühmt [bəˈryːmt] *adj* famous; **B~heit** *f* (*Ruf*) fame; (*Mensch*) celebrity

berühren [bəˈryːrən] *vt* to touch; (*gefühlsmäßig bewegen*) to affect; (*flüchtig erwähnen*) to mention, to touch on ♦ *vr* to meet, to touch

Berührung *f* contact

besagen [bəˈzaːgən] *vt* to mean

besänftigen [bəˈzɛnftɪgən] *vt* to soothe, to calm

Besatz [bəˈzats] **(-es, ⁺e)** *m* trimming, edging

Besatzung *f* garrison; (*NAUT, AVIAT*) crew

Besatzungsmacht *f* occupying power

beschädigen [bəˈʃɛːdɪgən] *vt* to damage; **Beschädigung** *f* damage; (*Stelle*) damaged spot

beschaffen [bəˈʃafən] *vt* to get, to acquire ♦ *adj*: **das ist so ~, dass** that is such that; **B~heit** *f* (*von Mensch*) constitution, nature

Beschaffung *f* acquisition

beschäftigen [bəˈʃɛftɪgən] *vt* to occupy;

(*beruflich*) to employ ♦ *vr* to occupy *od* concern o.s.

beschäftigt *adj* busy, occupied

Beschäftigung *f* (*Beruf*) employment; (*Tätigkeit*) occupation; (*Befassen*) concern

beschämen [bə'ʃɛːmən] *vt* to put to shame; ~**d** *adj* shameful; (*Hilfsbereitschaft*) shaming

beschämt *adj* ashamed

Bescheid [bə'ʃaɪt] **(-(e)s, -e)** *m* information; (*Weisung*) directions *pl*; ~ **wissen (über** +*akk*) to be well-informed (about); **ich weiß ~** I know; **jdm ~ geben** *od* **sagen** to let sb know

bescheiden [bə'ʃaɪdən] (*unreg*) *vr* to content o.s. ♦ *adj* modest; **B~heit** *f* modesty

bescheinen [bə'ʃaɪnən] (*unreg*) *vt* to shine on

bescheinigen [bə'ʃaɪnɪɡən] *vt* to certify; (*bestätigen*) to acknowledge

Bescheinigung *f* certificate; (*Quittung*) receipt

beschenken [bə'ʃɛŋkən] *vt*: **jdn mit etw ~** to give sb sth as a present

bescheren [bə'ʃeːrən] *vt*: **jdm etw ~** to give sb sth as a Christmas present; **jdn ~** to give Christmas presents to sb

Bescherung *f* giving of Christmas presents; (*umg*) mess

beschildern [bə'ʃɪldərn] *vt* to put signs/a sign on

beschimpfen [bə'ʃɪmpfən] *vt* to abuse; **Beschimpfung** *f* abuse; insult

Beschlag [bə'ʃlaːk] **(-(e)s, ⁻e)** *m* (*Metallband*) fitting; (*auf Fenster*) condensation; (*auf Metall*) tarnish; finish; (*Hufeisen*) horseshoe; **jdn/etw in ~ nehmen** *od* **mit ~ belegen** to monopolize sb/sth; **b~en** [bə'ʃlaːɡən] (*unreg*) *vt* to cover; (*Pferd*) to shoe ♦ *vi, vr* (*Fenster etc*) to mist over; **b~en sein (in** *od* **auf** +*dat*) to be well versed (in); **b~nahmen** *vt* to seize, to confiscate; to requisition; ~**nahmung** *f* confiscation, sequestration

beschleunigen [bə'ʃlɔynɪɡən] *vt* to accelerate, to speed up ♦ *vi* (*AUT*) to accelerate; **Beschleunigung** *f* acceleration

beschließen [bə'ʃliːsən] (*unreg*) *vt* to decide on; (*beenden*) to end, to close

Beschluss ▲ [bə'ʃlʊs] **(-es, ⁻e)** *m* decision, conclusion; (*Ende*) conclusion, end

beschmutzen [bə'ʃmʊtsən] *vt* to dirty, to soil

beschönigen [bə'ʃøːnɪɡən] *vt* to gloss over

beschränken [bə'ʃrɛŋkən] *vt, vr*: **(sich) ~ (auf** +*akk*) to limit *od* restrict (o.s.) (to)

beschränk- *zW*: ~**t** *adj* confined, restricted; (*Mensch*) limited, narrow-minded; **B~ung** *f* limitation

beschreiben [bə'ʃraɪbən] (*unreg*) *vt* to describe; (*Papier*) to write on

Beschreibung *f* description

beschriften [bə'ʃrɪftən] *vt* to mark, to label; **Beschriftung** *f* lettering

beschuldigen [bə'ʃʊldɪɡən] *vt* to accuse; **Beschuldigung** *f* accusation

Beschuss ▲ [bə'ʃʊs] *m*: **jdn/etw unter ~ nehmen** (*MIL*) to open fire on sb/sth

beschützen [bə'ʃʏtsən] *vt*: **~ (vor** +*dat*) to protect (from); **Beschützer (-s, -)** *m* protector

Beschwerde [bə'ʃveːrdə] *f* complaint; (*Mühe*) hardship; ~**n** *pl* (*Leiden*) trouble

beschweren [bə'ʃveːrən] *vt* to weight down; (*fig*) to burden ♦ *vr* to complain

beschwerlich *adj* tiring, exhausting

beschwichtigen [bə'ʃvɪçtɪɡən] *vt* to soothe, to pacify

beschwindeln [bə'ʃvɪndəln] *vt* (*betrügen*) to cheat; (*belügen*) to fib to

beschwingt [bə'ʃvɪŋt] *adj* in high spirits

beschwipst [bə'ʃvɪpst] (*umg*) *adj* tipsy

beschwören [bə'ʃvøːrən] (*unreg*) *vt* (*Aussage*) to swear to; (*anflehen*) to implore; (*Geister*) to conjure up

beseitigen [bə'zaɪtɪɡən] *vt* to remove; **Beseitigung** *f* removal

Besen ['beːzən] **(-s, -)** *m* broom; ~**stiel** *m* broomstick

besessen [bə'zɛsən] *adj* possessed

besetz- [bə'zɛts] *zW*: ~**en** *vt* (*Haus, Land*) to occupy; (*Platz*) to take, to fill; (*Posten*) to fill; (*Rolle*) to cast; (*mit Edelsteinen*) to set; ~**t** *adj* full; (*TEL*) engaged, busy; (*Platz*) taken;

Rechtschreibreform: ▲ *neue Schreibung* △ *alte Schreibung (auslaufend)*

(*WC*) engaged; **B~tzeichen** *nt* engaged tone; **B~ung** *f* occupation; filling; (*von Rolle*) casting; (*die Schauspieler*) cast

besichtigen [bəˈzɪçtɪɡən] *vt* to visit, to have a look at; **Besichtigung** *f* visit

besiegen [bəˈziːɡən] *vt* to defeat, to overcome

besinn- [bəˈzɪn] *zW:* **~en** (*unreg*) *vr* (*nachdenken*) to think, to reflect; (*erinnern*) to remember; **sich anders ~en** to change one's mind; **B~ung** *f* consciousness; **zur B~ung kommen** to recover consciousness; (*fig*) to come to one's senses; **~ungslos** *adj* unconscious

Besitz [bəˈzɪts] (**-es**) *m* possession, (*Eigentum*) property; **b~en** (*unreg*) *vt* to possess, to own; (*Eigenschaft*) to have; **~er(in)** (**-s, -**) *m(f)* owner, proprietor; **~ergreifung** *f* occupation, seizure

besoffen [bəˈzɔfən] (*umg*) *adj* drunk, stoned

besohlen [bəˈzoːlən] *vt* to sole

Besoldung [bəˈzɔldʊŋ] *f* salary, pay

besondere(r, s) [bəˈzɔndərə(r, s)] *adj* special; (*eigen*) particular; (*gesondert*) separate; (*eigentümlich*) peculiar

Besonderheit [bəˈzɔndɐhaɪt] *f* peculiarity

besonders [bəˈzɔndɐs] *adv* especially, particularly; (*getrennt*) separately

besonnen [bəˈzɔnən] *adj* sensible, level-headed

besorg- [bəˈzɔrg] *zW:* **~en** *vt* (*beschaffen*) to acquire; (*kaufen auch*) to purchase; (*erledigen: Geschäfte*) to deal with; (*sich kümmern um*) to take care of; **B~nis** (**-, -se**) *f* anxiety, concern; **~t** [bəˈzɔrçt] *adj* anxious, worried; **B~ung** *f* acquisition; (*Kauf*) purchase

bespielen [bəˈʃpiːlən] *vt* to record

bespitzeln [bəˈʃpɪtsəln] *vt* to spy on

besprechen [bəˈʃprɛçən] (*unreg*) *vt* to discuss; (*Tonband etc*) to record, to speak onto; (*Buch*) to review ♦ *vr* to discuss, to consult; **Besprechung** *f* meeting, discussion; (*von Buch*) review

besser [ˈbɛsɐ] *adj* better; **es geht ihm ~** he is feeling better; **~n** *vt* to make better, to improve ♦ *vr* (*Menschen*) to

reform; **B~ung** *f* improvement; **gute B~ung!** get well soon!; **B~wisser** (**-s, -**) *m* know-all

Bestand [bəˈʃtant] (**-(e)s, ⁓e**) *m* (*Fortbestehen*) duration, stability; (*Kassenbestand*) amount, balance; (*Vorrat*) stock; **~ haben, von ~ sein** to last long, to endure

beständig [bəˈʃtɛndɪç] *adj* (*ausdauernd: auch fig*) constant; (*Wetter*) settled; (*Stoffe*) resistant; (*Klagen etc*) continual

Bestandsaufnahme [bəˈʃtantsaʊfnaːmə] *f* stocktaking

Bestandteil *m* part, component; (*Zutat*) ingredient

bestärken [bəˈʃtɛrkən] *vt*: **jdn in etw** *dat* **~** to strengthen *od* confirm sb in sth

bestätigen [bəˈʃtɛːtɪɡən] *vt* to confirm; (*anerkennen, COMM*) to acknowledge; **Bestätigung** *f* confirmation; acknowledgement

bestatten [bəˈʃtatən] *vt* to bury

Bestattung *f* funeral

Bestattungsinstitut *nt* funeral director's

bestaunen [bəˈʃtaʊnən] *vt* to marvel at, gaze at in wonder

beste(r, s) [ˈbɛstə(r, s)] *adj* best; **so ist es am ~n** it's best that way; **am ~n gehst du gleich** you'd better go at once; **jdn zum B~n haben** to pull sb's leg; **einen Witz** *etc* **zum B~n geben** to tell a joke *etc*; **aufs B~** *od* **~** in the best possible way; **zu jds B~n** for the benefit of sb

bestechen [bəˈʃtɛçən] (*unreg*) *vt* to bribe; **bestechlich** *adj* corruptible; **Bestechung** *f* bribery, corruption

Besteck [bəˈʃtɛk] (**-(e)s, -e**) *nt* knife, fork and spoon, cutlery; (*MED*) set of instruments

bestehen [bəˈʃteːən] (*unreg*) *vi* to be; to exist; (*andauern*) to last ♦ *vt* (*Kampf, Probe, Prüfung*) to pass; **~ auf** +*dat* to insist on; **~ aus** to consist of

bestehlen [bəˈʃteːlən] (*unreg*) *vt*: **jdn (um etw) ~** to rob sb (of sth)

besteigen [bəˈʃtaɪɡən] (*unreg*) *vt* to climb, to ascend; (*Pferd*) to mount; (*Thron*) to ascend

Bestell- [bə'ʃtɛl] zW: **~buch** nt order book; **b~en** vt to order; (*kommen lassen*) to arrange to see; (*nominieren*) to name; (*Acker*) to cultivate; (*Grüße, Auftrag*) to pass on; **~formular** nt order form; **~nummer** f order code; **~ung** f (*COMM*) order; (*~en*) ordering

bestenfalls ['bɛstən'fals] adv at best

bestens ['bɛstəns] adv very well

besteuern [bə'ʃtɔyərn] vt (*jdn, Waren*) to tax

Bestie ['bɛstiə] f (*auch fig*) beast

bestimm- [bə'ʃtɪm] zW: **~en** vt (*Regeln*) to lay down; (*Tag, Ort*) to fix; (*beherrschen*) to characterize; (*vorsehen*) to mean; (*ernennen*) to appoint; (*definieren*) to define; (*veranlassen*) to induce; **~t** adj (*entschlossen*) firm; (*gewiss*) certain, definite; (*Artikel*) definite ♦ adv (*gewiss*) definitely, for sure; **suchen Sie etwas B~tes?** are you looking for something in particular?; **B~theit** f firmness; certainty; **B~ung** f (*Verordnung*) regulation; (*Festsetzen*) determining; (*Verwendungszweck*) purpose; (*Schicksal*) fate; (*Definition*) definition; **B~ungsland** nt (country of) destination; **B~ungsort** m (place of) destination

Bestleistung f best performance

bestmöglich adj best possible

bestrafen [bə'ʃtraːfən] vt to punish; **Bestrafung** f punishment

bestrahlen [bə'ʃtraːlən] vt to shine on; (*MED*) to treat with X-rays

Bestrahlung f (*MED*) X-ray treatment, radiotherapy

Bestreben [bə'ʃtreːbən] (*-s*) nt endeavour, effort

bestreiten [bə'ʃtraɪtən] (*unreg*) vt (*abstreiten*) to dispute; (*finanzieren*) to pay for, to finance

bestreuen [bə'ʃtrɔyən] vt to sprinkle, to dust; (*Straße*) to grit

bestürmen [bə'ʃtʏrmən] vt (*mit Fragen, Bitten etc*) to overwhelm, to swamp

bestürzend [bə'ʃtʏrtsənd] adj (*Nachrichten*) disturbing

bestürzt [bə'ʃtʏrtst] adj dismayed

Bestürzung f consternation

Besuch [bə'zuːx] (*-(e)s, -e*) m visit; (*Person*) visitor; **einen ~ machen bei jdm** to pay sb a visit od call; **~ haben** to have visitors; **bei jdm auf** od **zu ~ sein** to be visiting sb; **b~en** vt to visit; (*SCH etc*) to attend; **gut b~t** well-attended; **~er(in)** (*-s, -*) m(f) visitor, guest; **~szeit** f visiting hours pl

betätigen [bə'tɛːtɪgən] vt (*bedienen*) to work, to operate ♦ vr to involve o.s.; **sich als etw ~** to work as sth

Betätigung f activity; (*beruflich*) occupation; (*TECH*) operation

betäuben [bə'tɔybən] vt to stun; (*fig: Gewissen*) to still; (*MED*) to anaesthetize

Betäubung f (*Narkose*): **örtliche ~** local anaesthetic

Betäubungsmittel nt anaesthetic

Bete ['beːtə] f: **Rote ~** beetroot (*BRIT*), beet (*US*)

beteilig- [bə'taɪlɪg] zW: **~en** vr: **sich ~en (an +dat)** to take part (in), to participate (in), to share (in); (*an Geschäft: finanziell*) to have a share (in) ♦ vt: **jdn ~en (an +dat)** to give sb a share od interest (in); **B~te(r)** f(m) (*Mitwirkender*) partner; (*finanziell*) shareholder; **B~ung** f participation; (*Anteil*) share, interest; (*Besucherzahl*) attendance

beten ['beːtən] vt, vi to pray

beteuern [bə'tɔyərn] vt to assert; (*Unschuld*) to protest

Beton [be'tõː] (*-s, -s*) m concrete

betonen [be'toːnən] vt to stress

betonieren [beto'niːrən] vt to concrete

Betonung f stress, emphasis

betr. abk (*= betrifft*) re

Betracht [bə'traxt] m: **in ~ kommen** to be considered od relevant; **etw in ~ ziehen** to take sth into consideration; **außer ~ bleiben** not to be considered; **b~en** vt to look at; (*fig*) to look at, to consider; **~er(in)** (*-s, -*) m(f) observer

beträchtlich [bə'trɛçtlɪç] adj considerable

Betrachtung f (*Ansehen*) examination; (*Erwägung*) consideration

Betrag [bə'traːk] (*-(e)s, ⁻e*) m amount; **b~en** (*unreg*) vt to amount to ♦ vr to behave; **~en** (*-s, -*) nt behaviour

Betreff *m:* ~ **Ihr Schreiben vom ...** re your letter of ...

betreffen [bə'trɛfən] (*unreg*) *vt* to concern, to affect; **was mich betrifft** as for me; **~d** *adj* relevant, in question

betreffs [bə'trɛfs] *präp +gen* concerning, regarding; (*COMM*) re

betreiben [bə'traɪbən] (*unreg*) *vt* (*ausüben*) to practise; (*Politik*) to follow; (*Studien*) to pursue; (*vorantreiben*) to push ahead; (*TECH: antreiben*) to drive

betreten [bə'tre:tən] (*unreg*) *vt* to enter; (*Bühne etc*) to step onto ♦ *adj* embarrassed; **B~ verboten** keep off/out

Betreuer(in) [bə'trɔyər(ɪn)] (**-s, -**) *m(f)* (*einer Person*) minder; (*eines Gebäudes, Arbeitsgebiets*) caretaker; (*SPORT*) coach

Betreuung *f* care

Betrieb [bə'tri:p] (**-(e)s, -e**) *m* (*Firma*) firm, concern; (*Anlage*) plant; (*Tätigkeit*) operation; (*Treiben*) traffic; **außer ~ sein** to be out of order; **in ~ sein** to be in operation

Betriebs- *zW:* **~ausflug** *m* works outing; **b~bereit** *adj* operational; **b~fähig** *adj* in working order; **~ferien** *pl* company holidays (*BRIT*), company vacation *sg* (*US*); **~klima** *nt* (working) atmosphere; **~kosten** *pl* running costs; **~rat** *m* workers' council; **b~sicher** *adj* safe (to operate); **~störung** *f* breakdown; **~system** *nt* (*COMPUT*) operating system; **~unfall** *m* industrial accident; **~wirtschaft** *f* economics

betrinken [bə'trɪŋkən] (*unreg*) *vr* to get drunk

betroffen [bə'trɔfən] *adj* (*bestürzt*) full of consternation; **von etw ~ werden** *od* **sein** to be affected by sth

betrüben [bə'try:bən] *vt* to grieve

betrübt [bə'try:pt] *adj* sorrowful, grieved

Betrug [bə'tru:k] (**-(e)s**) *m* deception, fraud; (*JUR*) fraud

betrügen [bə'try:gən] (*unreg*) *vt* to cheat; (*JUR*) to defraud; (*Ehepartner*) to be unfaithful to ♦ *vr* to deceive o.s.

Betrüger (**-s, -**) *m* cheat, deceiver; **b~isch** *adj* deceitful; (*JUR*) fraudulent

betrunken [bə'trʊŋkən] *adj* drunk

Bett [bɛt] (**-(e)s, -en**) *nt* bed; **ins** *od* **zu ~ gehen** to go to bed; **~bezug** *m* duvet cover; **~decke** *f* blanket; (*Daunenbett*) quilt; (*Überwurf*) bedspread

Bettel- ['bɛtəl] *zW:* **b~arm** *adj* very poor, destitute; **~ei** [bɛtə'laɪ] *f* begging; **b~n** *vi* to beg

bettlägerig ['bɛtlɛ:gərɪç] *adj* bedridden

Bettlaken *nt* sheet

Bettler(in) ['bɛtlər(ɪn)] (**-s, -**) *m(f)* beggar

Bett- *zW:* **~tuch** ▲ *nt* sheet; **~vorleger** *m* bedside rug; **~wäsche** *f* bed linen; **~zeug** *nt* bed linen *pl*

beugen ['bɔygən] *vt* to bend; (*GRAM*) to inflect ♦ *vr* (*sich fügen*) to bow

Beule ['bɔylə] *f* bump, swelling

beunruhigen [bə'ʊnru:ɪgən] *vt* to disturb, to alarm ♦ *vr* to become worried

Beunruhigung *f* worry, alarm

beurlauben [bə'u:rlaubən] *vt* to give leave *od* a holiday to (*BRIT*), to grant vacation time to (*US*)

beurteilen [bə'ʊrtaɪlən] *vt* to judge; (*Buch etc*) to review

Beurteilung *f* judgement; review; (*Note*) mark

Beute ['bɔytə] (**-**) *f* booty, loot

Beutel (**-s, -**) *m* bag; (*Geldbeutel*) purse; (*Tabakbeutel*) pouch

Bevölkerung [bə'fœlkərʊŋ] *f* population

bevollmächtigen [bə'fɔlmɛçtɪgən] *vt* to authorize

Bevollmächtigte(r) *f(m)* authorized agent

bevor [bə'fo:r] *konj* before; **~munden** *vt* *insep* to treat like a child; **~stehen** (*unreg*) *vi:* (**jdm**) **~stehen** to be in store (for sb); **~stehend** *adj* imminent, approaching; **~zugen** *vt* *insep* to prefer

bewachen [bə'vaxən] *vt* to watch, to guard

Bewachung *f* (*Bewachen*) guarding; (*Leute*) guard, watch

bewaffnen [bə'vafnən] *vt* to arm

Bewaffnung *f* (*Vorgang*) arming; (*Ausrüstung*) armament, arms *pl*

bewahren [bə'va:rən] *vt* to keep; **jdn vor jdm/etw ~** to save sb from sb/sth

bewähren [bə'vɛːrən] *vr* to prove o.s.; (*Maschine*) to prove its worth

bewahrheiten [bə'vaːrhaɪtən] *vr* to come true

bewährt *adj* reliable

Bewährung *f (JUR)* probation

bewältigen [bə'vɛltɪgən] *vt* to overcome; (*Arbeit*) to finish; (*Portion*) to manage

bewandert [bə'vandərt] *adj* expert, knowledgeable

bewässern [bə'vɛsərn] *vt* to irrigate

Bewässerung *f* irrigation

bewegen [bə'veːgən] *vt, vr* to move; **jdn zu etw ~** to induce sb to do sth; **~d** *adj* touching, moving

Beweg- [bə'veːk] *zW*: **~grund** *m* motive; **b~lich** *adj* movable, mobile; (*flink*) quick; **b~t** *adj* (*Leben*) eventful; (*Meer*) rough; (*ergriffen*) touched

Bewegung *f* movement, motion; (*innere*) emotion; (*körperlich*) exercise; **~sfreiheit** *f* freedom of movement; (*fig*) freedom of action; **b~ungslos** *adj* motionless

Beweis [bə'vaɪs] **(-es, -e)** *m* proof; (*Zeichen*) sign; **b~en** [-zən] (*unreg*) *vt* to prove; (*zeigen*) to show; **~mittel** *nt* evidence

Bewerb- [bə'vɛrb] *zW*: **b~en** (*unreg*) *vr* to apply (for); **~er(in)** **(-s, -)** *m(f)* applicant; **~ung** *f* application

bewerkstelligen [bə'vɛrkʃtɛlɪgən] *vt* to manage, to accomplish

bewerten [bə'veːrtən] *vt* to assess

bewilligen [bə'vɪlɪgən] *vt* to grant, to allow

Bewilligung *f* granting

bewirken [bə'vɪrkən] *vt* to cause, to bring about

bewirten [bə'vɪrtən] *vt* to feed, to entertain (to a meal)

bewirtschaften [bə'vɪrtʃaftən] *vt* to manage

Bewirtung *f* hospitality

bewog *etc* [bə'voːk] *vb siehe* **bewegen**

bewohn- [bə'voːn] *zW*: **~bar** *adj* habitable; **~en** *vt* to inhabit, to live in; **B~er(in) (-s, -)** *m(f)* inhabitant; (*von Haus*) resident

bewölkt [bə'vœlkt] *adj* cloudy, overcast

Bewölkung *f* clouds *pl*

Bewunder- [bə'vʊndər] *zW*: **~er (-s, -)** *m* admirer; **b~n** *vt* to admire; **b~nswert** *adj* admirable, wonderful; **~ung** *f* admiration

bewusst ▲ [bə'vʊst] *adj* conscious; (*absichtlich*) deliberate; **sich** *dat* **einer Sache** *gen* **~ sein** to be aware of sth; **~los** *adj* unconscious; **B~losigkeit** *f* unconsciousness; **B~sein** *nt* consciousness; **bei B~sein** conscious

bezahlen [bə'tsaːlən] *vt* to pay for

Bezahlung *f* payment

bezaubern [bə'tsaʊbərn] *vt* to enchant, to charm

bezeichnen [bə'tsaɪçnən] *vt* (*kennzeichnen*) to mark; (*nennen*) to call; (*beschreiben*) to describe; (*zeigen*) to show, to indicate; **~d** *adj*: **~d (für)** characteristic (of), typical (of)

Bezeichnung *f* (*Zeichen*) mark, sign; (*Beschreibung*) description

bezeugen [bə'tsɔʏgən] *vt* to testify to

Bezichtigung *f* accusation

beziehen [bə'tsiːən] (*unreg*) *vt* (*mit Überzug*) to cover; (*Bett*) to make; (*Haus, Position*) to move into; (*Standpunkt*) to take up; (*erhalten*) to receive; (*Zeitung*) to subscribe to, to take ♦ *vr* (*Himmel*) to cloud over; **etw auf jdn/etw ~** to relate sth to sb/sth; **sich ~ auf** +*akk* to refer to

Beziehung *f* (*Verbindung*) connection; (*Zusammenhang*) relation; (*Verhältnis*) relationship; (*Hinsicht*) respect; **~en haben** (*vorteilhaft*) to have connections *od* contacts; **b~sweise** *adv* or; (*genauer gesagt auch*) that is, or rather

Bezirk [bə'tsɪrk] **(-(e)s, -e)** *m* district

Bezug [bə'tsuːk] **(-(e)s, -̈e)** *m* (*Hülle*) covering; (*COMM*) ordering; (*Gehalt*) income, salary; (*Beziehung*): **~ (zu)** relation(ship) (to); **in ~ auf** +*akk* with reference to; **~ nehmen auf** +*akk* to refer to

bezüglich [bə'tsyːklɪç] *präp* +*gen* concerning, referring to ♦ *adj* (*GRAM*) relative; **auf etw** *akk* **~** relating to sth

bezwecken [bə'tsvɛkən] *vt* to aim at

bezweifeln [bə'tsvaɪfəln] *vt* to doubt, to query

Rechtschreibreform: ▲ *neue Schreibung* △ *alte Schreibung (auslaufend)*

BH *m abk von* **Büstenhalter**

Bhf. *abk* (= *Bahnhof*) station

Bibel ['bi:bəl] (-, -n) *f* Bible

Biber ['bi:bər] (-s, -) *m* beaver

Biblio- [bi:blio] *zW*: **~grafie** ▲ [-gra'fi:] *f* bibliography; **~thek** [-'te:k] (-, -en) *f* library; **~thekar(in)** [-te'ka:r(in)] (-s, -e) *m(f)* librarian

biblisch ['bi:blɪʃ] *adj* biblical

bieder ['bi:dər] *adj* upright, worthy; (*Kleid etc*) plain

bieg- ['bi:g] *zW*: **~en** (*unreg*) *vt, vr* to bend ♦ *vi* to turn; **~sam** ['bi:k-] *adj* flexible; **B~ung** *f* bend, curve

Biene ['bi:nə] *f* bee

Bienenhonig *m* honey

Bienenwachs *nt* beeswax

Bier [bi:r] (-(e)s, -e) *nt* beer; **~deckel** *m* beer mat; **~garten** *m* beer garden; **~krug** *m* beer mug; **~zelt** *nt* beer tent

Biest [bi:st] (-s, -er) (*umg: pej*) *nt* (*Tier*) beast, creature; (*Mensch*) beast

bieten ['bi:tən] (*unreg*) *vt* to offer; (*bei Versteigerung*) to bid ♦ *vr* (*Gelegenheit*): **sich jdm ~** to present itself to sb; **sich** *dat* **etw ~ lassen** to put up with sth

Bikini [bi'ki:ni] (-s, -s) *m* bikini

Bilanz [bi'lants] *f* balance; (*fig*) outcome; **~ziehen (aus)** to take stock (of)

Bild [bɪlt] (-(e)s, -er) *nt* (*auch fig*) picture; photo; (*Spiegelbild*) reflection; **~bericht** *m* photographic report

bilden ['bɪldən] *vt* to form; (*erziehen*) to educate; (*ausmachen*) to constitute ♦ *vr* to arise; (*erziehen*) to educate o.s.

Bilderbuch *nt* picture book

Bilderrahmen *m* picture frame

Bild- *zW*: **~fläche** *f* screen; (*fig*) scene; **~hauer** (-s, -) *m* sculptor; **b~hübsch** *adj* lovely, pretty as a picture; **b~lich** *adj* figurative; pictorial; **~schirm** *m* television screen; (*COMPUT*) monitor; **~schirmschoner** *m* (*COMPUT*) screen saver; **b~schön** *adj* lovely

Bildung [bɪldʊŋ] *f* formation; (*Wissen, Benehmen*) education

Billard ['bɪljart] (-s, -e) *nt* billiards *sg*; **~kugel** *f* billiard ball

billig ['bɪlɪç] *adj* cheap; (*gerecht*) fair, reasonable; **~en** ['bɪlɪgən] *vt* to approve of

Binde ['bɪndə] *f* bandage; (*Armbinde*) band; (*MED*) sanitary towel; **~gewebe** *nt* connective tissue; **~glied** *nt* connecting link; **~hautentzündung** *f* conjunctivitis; **b~n** (*unreg*) *vt* to bind, to tie; **~strich** *m* hyphen

Bindfaden ['bɪnt-] *m* string

Bindung *f* bond, tie; (*Skibindung*) binding

binnen ['bɪnən] *präp* (+*dat od gen*) within; **B~hafen** *m* river port; **B~handel** *m* internal trade

Bio- [bio-] *in zW* bio-: **~chemie** *f* biochemistry; **~grafie** ▲ [-gra'fi:] *f* biography; **~laden** *m* wholefood shop; **~loge** [-'lo:gə] (-n, -n) *m* biologist; **~logie** [-lo'gi:] *f* biology; **b~logisch** [-'lo:gɪʃ] *adj* biological; **~top** *m od nt* biotope

---
Bioladen
---

i A *Bioladen* is a shop specializing in environmentally-friendly products such as phosphate-free washing powders, recycled paper and organically-grown vegetables.

Birke ['bɪrkə] *f* birch

Dirne [bɪrnə] *f* pear; (*ELEK*) (light) bulb

SCHLÜSSELWORT
---

bis [bɪs] *präp* +*akk*, *adv* **1** (*zeitlich*) till, until; (*bis spätestens*) by; **Sie haben bis Dienstag Zeit** you have until *od* till Tuesday; **bis Dienstag muss es fertig sein** it must be ready by Tuesday; **bis auf weiteres** until further notice; **bis in die Nacht** into the night; **bis bald/gleich** see you later/soon **2** (*räumlich*) (up) to; **ich fahre bis Köln** I'm going to *od* I'm going as far as Cologne; **bis an unser Grundstück** (right *od* up) to our plot; **bis hierher** this far **3** (*bei Zahlen*) up to; **bis zu** up to **4**: **bis auf etw** *akk* (*außer*) except sth; (*einschließlich*) including sth ♦ *konj* **1** (*mit Zahlen*) to; **10 bis 20** 10 to 20 **2** (*zeitlich*) till, until; **bis es dunkel wird** till

---

od until it gets dark; **von ... bis ...** from ... to ...

Bischof ['bɪʃɔf] **(-s, ⁻e)** *m* bishop; **bischöflich** ['bɪʃøːflɪç] *adj* episcopal

bisher [bɪs'heːr] *adv* till now, hitherto; **~ig** *adj* till now

Biskuit [bɪs'kviːt] **(-(e)s, -s** *od* **-e)** *m od nt* (fatless) sponge

Biss ▲ [bɪs] **(-es, -e)** *m* bite

biss ▲ *etc vb siehe* **beißen**

bisschen ▲ ['bɪsçən] *adj, adv* bit

Bissen ['bɪsən] **(-s, -)** *m* bite, morsel

bissig ['bɪsɪç] *adj* (*Hund*) snappy; (*Bemerkung*) cutting, biting

bist [bɪst] *vb siehe* **sein**

bisweilen [bɪs'vaɪlən] *adv* at times, occasionally

Bitte ['bɪtə] *f* request; **b~** *excl* please; (*wie b~?*) (I beg your) pardon? ♦ *interj* (*als Antwort auf Dank*) you're welcome; **darf ich? – aber b~!** may I? – please do; **b~ schön!** it was a pleasure; **b~n** (*unreg*) *vt, vi*: **b~n (um)** to ask (for); **b~nd** *adj* pleading, imploring

bitter ['bɪtər] *adj* bitter; **~böse** *adj* very angry; **B~keit** *f* bitterness; **~lich** *adj* bitter

Blähungen ['blɛːʊŋən] *pl* (*MED*) wind *sg*

blamabel [bla'maːbəl] *adj* disgraceful

Blamage [bla'maːʒə] *f* disgrace

blamieren [bla'miːrən] *vr* to make a fool of o.s., to disgrace o.s. ♦ *vt* to let down, to disgrace

blank [blaŋk] *adj* bright; (*unbedeckt*) bare; (*sauber*) clean, polished; (*umg: ohne Geld*) broke; (*offensichtlich*) blatant

blanko ['blaŋko] *adv* blank; **B~scheck** *m* blank cheque

Blase ['blaːzə] *f* bubble; (*MED*) blister; (*ANAT*) bladder; **~balg (-(e)s, -bälge)** *m* bellows *pl*; **b~n** (*unreg*) *vt, vi* to blow; **~nentzündung** *f* cystitis

Blas- ['blaːs] *zW*: **~instrument** *nt* wind instrument; **~kapelle** *f* brass band

blass ▲ [blas] *adj* pale

Blässe ['blɛsə] **(-)** *f* paleness, pallor

Blatt [blat] **(-(e)s, ⁻er)** *nt* leaf; (*von Papier*)

sheet; (*Zeitung*) newspaper; (*KARTEN*) hand

blättern ['blɛtərn] *vi*: **in etw** *dat* **~** to leaf through sth

Blätterteig *m* flaky *od* puff pastry

blau [blaʊ] *adj* blue; (*umg*) drunk, stoned; (*KOCH*) boiled; (*Auge*) black; **~er Fleck** bruise; **Fahrt ins B~e** mystery tour; **~äugig** *adj* blue-eyed

Blech [blɛç] **(-(e)s, -e)** *nt* tin, sheet metal; (*Backblech*) baking tray; **~büchse** *f* tin, can; **~dose** *f* tin, can; **b~en** (*umg*) *vt, vi* to fork out; **~schaden** *m* (*AUT*) damage to bodywork

Blei [blaɪ] **(-(e)s, -e)** *nt* lead

Bleibe ['blaɪbə] *f* roof over one's head; **b~n** (*unreg*) *vi* to stay, to remain; **~ lassen** to leave alone; **b~nd** *adj* (*Erinnerung*) lasting; (*Schaden*) permanent

bleich [blaɪç] *adj* faded, pale; **~en** *vt* to bleach

Blei- *zW*: **b~ern** *adj* leaden; **b~frei** *adj* (*Benzin*) lead-free; **~stift** *m* pencil

Blende ['blɛndə] *f* (*PHOT*) aperture; **b~n** *vt* to blind, to dazzle; (*fig*) to hoodwink; **b~nd** (*umg*) *adj* grand; **b~nd aussehen** to look smashing

Blick [blɪk] **(-(e)s, -e)** *m* (*kurz*) glance, glimpse; (*Anschauen*) look; (*Aussicht*) view; **b~en** *vi* to look; **sich b~en lassen** to put in an appearance; **~fang** *m* eye-catcher

blieb *etc* [bliːp] *vb siehe* **bleiben**

blind [blɪnt] *adj* blind; (*Glas etc*) dull; **~er Passagier** stowaway; **B~darm** *m* appendix; **B~darmentzündung** *f* appendicitis; **B~enschrift** ['blɪndən-] *f* Braille; **B~heit** *f* blindness; **~lings** *adv* blindly

blink- ['blɪŋk] *zW*: **~en** *vi* to twinkle, to sparkle; (*Licht*) to flash, to signal; (*AUT*) to indicate ♦ *vt* to flash, to signal; **B~er (-s, -)** *m* (*AUT*) indicator; **B~licht** *nt* (*AUT*) indicator; (*an Bahnübergängen usw*) flashing light

blinzeln ['blɪntsəln] *vi* to blink, to wink

Blitz [blɪts] **(-es, -e)** *m* (flash of) lightning; **~ableiter** *m* lightning conductor; **b~en** *vi* (*aufleuchten*) to flash, to sparkle; **es b~t**

(MET) there's a flash of lightning; **~licht** nt flashlight; **b~schnell** adj lightning ♦ adv (as) quick as a flash

Block [blɔk] **(-(e)s, "e)** m block; *(von Papier)* pad; **~ade** [blɔ'ka:də] f blockade; **~flöte** f recorder; **b~frei** adj *(POL)* unaligned; **~haus** nt log cabin; **b~ieren** [blɔ'ki:rən] vt to block ♦ vi *(Räder)* to jam; **~schrift** f block letters pl

blöd [blø:t] adj silly, stupid; **~eln** ['blø:dəln] *(umg)* vi to act the goat *(fam)*, to fool around; **B~sinn** m nonsense; **~sinnig** adj silly, idiotic

blond [blɔnt] adj blond, fair-haired

bloß [blo:s] adj **1** *(unbedeckt)* bare; *(nackt)* naked; **mit der bloßen Hand** with one's bare hand; **mit bloßem Auge** with the naked eye

2 *(alleinig, nur)* mere; **der bloße Gedanke** the very thought; **bloßer Neid** sheer envy ♦ adv only, merely; **lass das bloß!** just don't do that!; **wie ist das bloß passiert?** how on earth did that happen?

Blöße ['blø:sə] f bareness; nakedness; *(fig)* weakness

bloßstellen vt to show up

blühen ['bly:ən] vi to bloom *(lit)*, to be in bloom; *(fig)* to flourish; **~d** adj *(Pflanze)* blooming; *(Aussehen)* blooming, radiant; *(Handel)* thriving, booming

Blume ['blu:mə] f flower; *(von Wein)* bouquet

Blumen- zW: **~kohl** m cauliflower; **~topf** m flowerpot; **~zwiebel** f bulb

Bluse ['blu:zə] f blouse

Blut [blu:t] **(-(e)s)** nt blood; **b~arm** adj anaemic; *(fig)* penniless; **b~befleckt** adj bloodstained; **~bild** nt blood count; **~druck** m blood pressure

Blüte ['bly:tə] f blossom; *(fig)* prime

Blut- zW: **b~en** vi to bleed; **~er** m *(MED)* haemophiliac; **~erguss** ▲ m haemorrhage; *(auf Haut)* bruise

Blütezeit f flowering period; *(fig)* prime

Blut- zW: **~gruppe** f blood group; **b~ig** adj bloody; **b~jung** adj very young; **~probe** f blood test; **~spender** m blood donor; **~transfusion** f *(MED)* blood transfusion; **~ung** f bleeding, haemorrhage; **~vergiftung** f blood poisoning; **~wurst** f black pudding

Bö [bø:] **(-, -en)** f squall

Bock [bɔk] **(-(e)s, "e)** m buck, ram; *(Gestell)* trestle, support; *(SPORT)* buck; **~wurst** f type of pork sausage

Boden ['bo:dən] **(-s, ")** m ground; *(Fußboden)* floor; *(Meeresboden, Fassboden)* bottom; *(Speicher)* attic; **b~los** adj bottomless; *(umg)* incredible; **~nebel** m ground mist; **~personal** nt *(AVIAT)* ground staff; **~schätze** pl mineral resources; **~see** m: **der ~see** Lake Constance; **~turnen** nt floor exercises pl

Böe ['bø:ə] f squall

Bogen ['bo:gən] **(-s, -)** m *(Biegung)* curve; *(ARCHIT)* arch; *(Waffe, MUS)* bow; *(Papier)* sheet

Bohne ['bo:nə] f bean

bohnern vt to wax, to polish

Bohnerwachs nt floor polish

Bohr- [bo:r] zW: **b~en** vt to bore; **~er** **(-s, -)** m drill; **~insel** f oil rig; **~maschine** f drill; **~turm** m derrick

Boiler ['bɔylər] **(-s, -)** m (hot-water) tank

Boje ['bo:jə] f buoy

Bolzen ['bɔltsən] **(-s, -)** m bolt

bombardieren [bɔmbar'di:rən] vt to bombard; *(aus der Luft)* to bomb

Bombe ['bɔmbə] f bomb

Bombenangriff m bombing raid

Bombenerfolg *(umg)* m smash hit

Bon [bɔŋ] **(-s, -s)** m voucher, chit

Bonbon [bõ'bõ:] **(-s, -s)** m od nt sweet

Boot [bo:t] **(-(e)s, -e)** nt boat

Bord [bɔrt] **(-(e)s, -e)** m *(AVIAT, NAUT)* board ♦ nt *(Brett)* shelf; **an ~** on board

Bordell [bɔr'dɛl] **(-s, -e)** nt brothel

Bordstein m kerb(stone)

borgen ['bɔrgən] vt to borrow; **jdm etw ~** to lend sb sth

borniert [bɔr'ni:rt] adj narrow-minded

Börse ['bœːrzə] f stock exchange; (*Geldbörse*) purse; **~nmakler** m stockbroker

Borte ['bɔrtə] f edging; (*Band*) trimming

bös [bøːs] adj = **böse**

bösartig ['bøːz-] adj malicious

Böschung ['bœʃʊŋ] f slope; (*Uferböschung etc*) embankment

böse ['bøːzə] adj bad, evil; (*zornig*) angry

boshaft ['boːshaft] adj malicious, spiteful

Bosheit f malice, spite

Bosnien ['bɔsniən] (**-s**) nt Bosnia; ~ **und Herzegowina** [-hɛrtsə'goːvina] nt Bosnia (and) Herzegovina

böswillig ['bøːsvɪlɪç] adj malicious

bot etc [boːt] vb siehe **bieten**

Botanik [bo'taːnɪk] f botany; **botanisch** adj botanical

Bot- ['boːt] zW: **~e** (**-n, -n**) m messenger; **~schaft** f message, news; (*POL*) embassy; **~schafter** (**-s, -**) m ambassador

Bottich ['bɔtɪç] (**-(e)s, -e**) m vat, tub

Bouillon [bu'ljɔ:] (**-, -s**) f consommé

Bowle ['boːlə] f punch

Box- ['bɔks] zW: **b~en** vi to box; **~er** (**-s, -**) m boxer; **~kampf** m boxing match

boykottieren [bɔykɔ'tiːrən] vt to boycott

brach etc [braːx] vb siehe **brechen**

brachte etc ['braxtə] vb siehe **bringen**

Branche ['brãːʃə] f line of business

Branchenverzeichnis nt Yellow Pages® pl

Brand [brant] (**-(e)s, ⁺e**) m fire; (*MED*) gangrene; **b~en** ['brandən] vi to surge; (*Meer*) to break; **b~marken** vt to brand; (*fig*) to stigmatize; **~salbe** f ointment for burns; **~stifter** [-ʃtɪftər] m arsonist, fire raiser; **~stiftung** f arson; **~ung** f surf

Branntwein ['brantvaɪn] m brandy

Brasilien [bra'ziːliən] nt Brazil

Brat- ['braːt] zW: **~apfel** m baked apple; **b~en** (*unreg*) vt to roast; to fry; **~en** (**-s, -**) m roast, joint; **~hähnchen** nt roast chicken; **~huhn** nt roast chicken; **~kartoffeln** pl fried od roast potatoes; **~pfanne** f frying pan

Bratsche ['braːtʃə] f viola

Bratspieß m spit

Bratwurst f grilled/fried sausage

Brauch [braux] (**-(e)s, Bräuche**) m custom; **b~bar** adj usable, serviceable; (*Person*) capable; **b~en** vt (*bedürfen*) to need; (*müssen*) to have to; (*umg: verwenden*) to use

Braue ['brauə] f brow

brauen ['brauən] vt to brew

Braue'rei f brewery

braun [braun] adj brown; (*von Sonne auch*) tanned; ~ **gebrannt** tanned

Bräune ['brɔynə] (**-**) f brownness; (*Sonnenbräune*) tan; **b~n** vt to make brown; (*Sonne*) to tan

Brause ['brauzə] f shower bath; (*von Gießkanne*) rose; (*Getränk*) lemonade; **b~n** vi to roar; (*auch vr: duschen*) to take a shower

Braut [braut] (**-, Bräute**) f bride; (*Verlobte*) fiancée

Bräutigam ['brɔytɪgam] (**-s, -e**) m bridegroom; fiancé

Brautpaar nt bride and (bride)groom, bridal pair

brav [braːf] adj (*artig*) good; (*ehrenhaft*) worthy, honest

bravo ['braːvo] excl well done

BRD ['beː'ɛr'deː] (**-**) f abk = **Bundesrepublik Deutschland**

> **BRD**

The BRD (Bundesrepublik Deutschland) is the official name for the Federal Republic of Germany. It comprises 16 Länder (see Land). It was formerly the name given to West Germany as opposed to East Germany (the DDR). The two Germanies were reunited on 3rd October 1990.

Brech- ['brɛç] zW: **~eisen** nt crowbar; **b~en** (*unreg*) vt, vi to break; (*Licht*) to refract; (*fig: Mensch*) to crush; (*speien*) to vomit; **~reiz** m nausea, retching

Brei [braɪ] (**-(e)s, -e**) m (*Masse*) pulp; (*KOCH*) gruel; (*Haferbrei*) porridge

breit [braɪt] adj wide, broad; **sich ~ machen** to spread o.s. out; **B~e** f width; (*bes bei*

Maßangaben) breadth; (*GEOG*) latitude; **~en** *vt*: **etw über etw** *akk* **~en** to spread sth over sth; **B~engrad** *m* degree of latitude; **~treten** (*unreg*) (*umg*) *vt* to go on about

Brems- ['brɛms] *zW*: **~belag** *m* brake lining; **~e** [-zə] *f* brake; (*ZOOL*) horsefly; **b~en** [zən] *vi* to brake ♦ *vt* to brake; (*fig*) to slow down; **~flüssigkeit** *f* brake fluid; **~licht** *nt* brake light; **~pedal** *nt* brake pedal; **~spur** *f* skid mark(*s pl*); **~weg** *m* braking distance

Brenn- ['brɛn] *zW*: **b~bar** *adj* inflammable; **b~en** (*unreg*) *vi* to burn, to be on fire; (*Licht, Kerze etc*) to burn ♦ *vt* (*Holz etc*) to burn; (*Ziegel, Ton*) to fire; (*Kaffee*) to roast; **darauf b~en, etw zu tun** to be dying to do sth; **~nessel** ▲ *f* stinging nettle; **~punkt** *m* (*PHYS*) focal point; (*Mittelpunkt*) focus; **~stoff** *m* fuel

brenzlig ['brɛntslıç] *adj* (*fig*) precarious

Bretagne [bra'tanjə] *f*: **die ~** Brittany

Brett [brɛt] (*-(e)s, -er*) *nt* board, plank; (*Bord*) shelf; (*Spielbrett*) board; **~er** *pl* (*SKI*) skis; (*THEAT*) boards; **schwarzes ~** notice board; **~erzaun** *m* wooden fence; **~spiel** *nt* board game

Brezel ['bre:tsəl] (*-, -n*) *f* pretzel

brichst *etc* [brıçst] *vb siehe* **brechen**

Brief [bri:f] (*-(e)s, -e*) *m* letter; **~freund** *m* penfriend; **~kasten** *m* letterbox; **b~lich** *adj, adv* by letter; **~marke** *f* (*postage*) stamp; **~papier** *nt* notepaper; **~tasche** *f* wallet; **~träger** *m* postman; **~umschlag** *m* envelope; **~waage** *f* letter scales; **~wechsel** *m* correspondence

brief *etc* [bri:t] *vb siehe* **braten**

Brikett [bri'kɛt] (*-s, -s*) *nt* briquette

brillant [brɪl'jant] *adj* (*fig*) brilliant; **B~** (*-en, -en*) *m* brilliant, diamond

Brille ['brɪlə] *f* spectacles *pl*; (*Schutzbrille*) goggles *pl*; (*Toilettenbrille*) (toilet) seat; **~ngestell** *nt* (spectacle) frames

bringen ['brɪŋən] (*unreg*) *vt* to bring; (*mitnehmen, begleiten*) to take; (*einbringen: Profit*) to bring in; (*veröffentlichen*) to publish; (*THEAT, CINE*) to show; (*RADIO, TV*) to broadcast; (*in einen Zustand versetzen*) to

get; (*umg: tun können*) to manage; **jdn dazu ~, etw zu tun** to make sb do sth; **jdn nach Hause ~** to take sb home; **jdn um etw ~** to make sb lose sth; **jdn auf eine Idee ~** to give sb an idea

Brise ['bri:zə] *f* breeze

Brit- ['bri:t] *zW*: **~e** *m* Briton; **~in** *f* Briton; **b~isch** *adj* British

bröckelig ['brœkəlıç] *adj* crumbly

Brocken ['brɔkən] (*-s, -*) *m* piece, bit; (*Felsbrocken*) lump of rock

brodeln ['bro:dəln] *vi* to bubble

Brokkoli ['brɔkoli] *pl* (*BOT*) broccoli

Brombeere ['brɔmbe:rə] *f* blackberry, bramble (*BRIT*)

Bronchien ['brɔnçiən] *pl* bronchia(l tubes) *pl*

Bronchitis [brɔn'çi:tıs] (*-*) *f* bronchitis

Bronze ['brõ:sə] *f* bronze

Brosche ['brɔʃə] *f* brooch

Broschüre [brɔ'ʃy:rə] *f* pamphlet

Brot [bro:t] (*-(e)s, -e*) *nt* bread; (*Laib*) loaf

Brötchen ['brø:tçən] *nt* roll

Bruch [brʊx] (*-(e)s, ⁻e*) *m* breakage; (*zerbrochene Stelle*) break; (*fig*) split, breach; (*MED: Eingeweidebruch*) rupture, hernia; (*Beinbruch etc*) fracture; (*MATH*) fraction

brüchig ['brʊçıç] *adj* brittle, fragile; (*Haus*) dilapidated

Bruch- *zW*: **~landung** *f* crash landing; **~strich** *m* (*MATH*) line; **~stück** *nt* fragment; **~teil** *m* fraction; **~zahl** [brʊxtsa:l] *f* (*MATH*) fraction

Brücke ['brʊkə] *f* bridge; (*Teppich*) rug

Bruder ['bru:dər] (*-s, ⁻*) *m* brother; **brüderlich** *adj* brotherly

Brühe ['bry:ə] *f* broth, stock; (*pej*) muck

brüllen ['brʊlən] *vi* to bellow, to roar

brummen ['brʊmən] *vi* (*Bär, Mensch etc*) to growl; (*Insekt*) to buzz; (*Motoren*) to roar; (*murren*) to grumble

brünett [bry'nɛt] *adj* brunette, dark-haired

Brunnen ['brʊnən] (*-s, -*) *m* fountain; (*tief*) well; (*natürlich*) spring

Brust [brʊst] (*-, ⁻e*) *f* breast; (*Männerbrust*) chest

brüsten ['brʊstən] *vr* to boast

Spelling Reform: ▲ *new spelling* △ *old spelling (to be phased out)*

Brust- *zW:* **~kasten** *m* chest; **~schwimmen** *nt* breast-stroke

Brüstung ['brʏstʊŋ] *f* parapet

Brut [bruːt] (-, -en) *f* brood; (*Brüten*) hatching

brutal [bru'taːl] *adj* brutal

Brutali'tät *f* brutality

brüten ['bryːtən] *vi* (*auch fig*) to brood

Brutkasten *m* incubator

brutto ['brʊto] *adv* gross; **B~einkommen** *nt* gross salary; **B~gehalt** *nt* gross salary; **B~gewicht** *nt* gross weight; **B~lohn** *m* gross wages *pl*; **B~sozialprodukt** *nt* gross national product

BSE *f abk* (= *Bovine Spongiforme Enzephalopathie*) BSE

Bube ['buːbə] (-n, -n) *m* (*Schurke*) rogue; (*KARTEN*) jack

Buch [buːx] (-(e)s, ᵘer) *nt* book; (*COMM*) account book; **~binder** *m* bookbinder; **~drucker** *m* printer

Buche *f* beech tree

buchen *vt* to book; (*Betrag*) to enter

Bücher- ['byːçər] *zW:* **~brett** *nt* bookshelf; **~ei** [-'raɪ] *f* library; **~regal** *nt* bookshelves *pl*, bookcase; **~schrank** *m* bookcase

Buch- *zW:* **~führung** *f* book-keeping, accounting; **~halter(in)** (-s, -) *m(f)* bookkeeper; **~handel** *m* book trade; **~händler(in)** *m(f)* bookseller; **~handlung** *f* bookshop

Büchse ['bʏksə] *f* tin, can; (*Holzbüchse*) box; (*Gewehr*) rifle; **~nfleisch** *nt* tinned meat; **~nmilch** *f* (*KOCH*) evaporated milk, tinned milk; **~nöffner** *m* tin *od* can opener

Buchstabe (-ns, -n) *m* letter (of the alphabet)

buchstabieren [buːxʃta'biːrən] *vt* to spell

buchstäblich ['buːxʃtɛːplɪç] *adj* literal

Bucht ['bʊxt] (-, -en) *f* bay

Buchung ['buːxʊŋ] *f* booking; (*COMM*) entry

Buckel ['bʊkəl] (-s, -) *m* hump

bücken ['bʏkən] *vr* to bend

Bude ['buːdə] *f* booth, stall; (*umg*) digs *pl* (*BRIT*)

Büfett [bʏ'fet] (-s, -s) *nt* (*Anrichte*) sideboard; (*Geschirrschrank*) dresser; **kaltes ~** cold buffet

Büffel ['bʏfəl] (-s, -) *m* buffalo

Bug [buːk] (-(e)s, -e) *m* (*NAUT*) bow; (*AVIAT*) nose

Bügel ['byːgəl] (-s, -) *m* (*Kleider~*) hanger; (*Steig~*) stirrup; (*Brillen~*) arm; **~brett** *nt* ironing board; **~eisen** *nt* iron; **~falte** *f* crease; **b~frei** *adj* crease-resistant, noniron; **b~n** *vt, vi* to iron

Bühne ['byːnə] *f* stage; **~nbild** *nt* set, scenery

Buhruf ['buːruːf] *m* boo

buk *etc* [buːk] *vb siehe* **backen**

Bulgarien [bʊl'gaːriən] *nt* Bulgaria

Bull- ['bʊl] *zW:* **~auge** *nt* (*NAUT*) porthole; **~dogge** *f* bulldog; **~dozer** ['bʊldoːzər] (-s, -) *m* bulldozer; **~e** (-n, -n) *m* bull

Bumerang ['buːməraŋ] (-s, -e) *m* boomerang

Bummel ['bʊməl] (-s, -) *m* stroll; (*Schaufensterbummel*) window-shopping; **~ant** [-'lant] *m* slowcoach; **~ei** [-'laɪ] *f* wandering; dawdling; skiving; **b~n** *vi* to wander, to stroll; (*trödeln*) to dawdle; (*faulenzen*) to skive, to loaf around; **~streik** ['bʊməlʃtraɪk] *m* go-slow

Bund¹ [bʊnt] (-(e)s, ᵘe) *m* (*Freundschaftsbund etc*) bond; (*Organisation*) union; (*POL*) confederacy; (*Hosenbund, Rockbund*) waistband

Bund² (-(e)s, -e) *nt* bunch; (*Strohbund*) bundle

Bündel ['bʏndəl] (-s, -) *nt* bundle, bale; **b~n** *vt* to bundle

Bundes- ['bʊndəs] *in zW* Federal; **~bürger** *m* German citizen; **~hauptstadt** *f* Federal capital; **~kanzler** *m* Federal Chancellor; **~land** *nt* Land; **~liga** *f* football league; **~präsident** *m* Federal President; **~rat** *m* upper house of German Parliament; **~regierung** *f* Federal government; **~republik** *f* Federal Republic (of Germany); **~staat** *m* Federal state; **~straße** *f* Federal road; **~tag** *m* German Parliament; **~wehr** *f* German Armed Forces *pl*; **b~weit** *adj* nationwide

Rechtschreibreform: ▲ *neue Schreibung* △ *alte Schreibung (auslaufend)*

Bundespräsident

i The **Bundespräsident** *is the head of state of the Federal Republic of Germany. He is elected every 5 years - no-one can be elected more than twice - by the members of the* **Bundesversammlung**, *a body formed especially for this purpose. His role is to represent Germany at home and abroad. In Switzerland the* **Bundespräsident** *is the head of the government, known as the* **Bundesrat**. *The* **Bundesrat** *is the Upper House of the German Parliament whose 68 members are nominated by the parliaments of the* **Länder**. *Its most important function is to approve federal laws concerned with the jurisdiction of the* **Länder**; *it can raise objections to other laws, but can be outvoted by the* **Bundestag**. *In Austria the* **Länder** *are also represented in the* **Bundesrat**.

Bundestag

i The **Bundestag** *is the Lower House of the German Parliament and is elected by the people by proportional representation. There are 672 MPs, half of them elected directly from the first vote (***Erststimme***), and half from the regional list of parliamentary candidates resulting from the second vote (***Zweitstimme***). The* **Bundestag** *exercises parliamentary control over the government.*

Bündnis ['bʏntnɪs] **(-ses, -se)** *nt* alliance
bunt [bʊnt] *adj* coloured; *(gemischt)* mixed; **jdm wird es zu ~** it's getting too much for sb; **B~stift** *m* coloured pencil, crayon
Burg [bʊrk] **(-, -en)** *f* castle, fort
Bürge ['bʏrɡə] **(-n, -n)** *m* guarantor; **b~n** *vi:* **b~n für** to vouch for
Bürger(in) ['bʏrɡər(ɪn)] **(-s, -)** *m(f)* citizen; member of the middle class; **~krieg** *m* civil war; **b~lich** *adj (Rechte)* civil; *(Klasse)* middle-class; *(pej)* bourgeois; **~meister** *m*

mayor; **~recht** *nt* civil rights *pl;* **~schaft** *f (Vertretung)* City Parliament; **~steig** *m* pavement
Bürgschaft *f* surety; **~ leisten** to give security
Büro [by'roː] **(-s, -s)** *nt* office; **~angestellte(r)** *f(m)* office worker; **~klammer** *f* paper clip; **~kra'tie** *f* bureaucracy; **b~'kratisch** *adj* bureaucratic; **~schluss** ▲ *m* office closing time
Bursche ['bʊrʃə] **(-n, -n)** *m* lad, fellow; *(Diener)* servant
Bürste ['bʏrstə] *f* brush; **b~n** *vt* to brush
Bus [bʊs] **(-ses, -se)** *m* bus; **~bahnhof** *m* bus/coach *(BRIT)* station
Busch [bʊʃ] **(-(e)s, ⁀e)** *m* bush, shrub
Büschel ['bʏʃəl] **(-s, -)** *nt* tuft
buschig *adj* bushy
Busen ['buːzən] **(-s, -)** *m* bosom; *(Meerbusen)* inlet, bay
Bushaltestelle *f* bus stop
Buße ['buːsə] *f* atonement, penance; *(Geld)* fine
büßen ['byːsən] *vi* to do penance, to atone ♦ *vt* to do penance for, to atone for
Bußgeld ['buːsɡɛlt] *nt* fine; **~bescheid** *m* notice of payment due *(for traffic offence etc)*
Büste ['bʏstə] *f* bust; **~nhalter** *m* bra
Butter ['bʊtər] **(-)** *f* butter; **~blume** *f* buttercup; **~brot** *nt* (piece of) bread and butter; *(umg)* sandwich; **~brotpapier** *nt* greaseproof paper; **~dose** *f* butter dish; **~milch** *f* buttermilk; **b~weich** ['bʊtərvaɪç] *adj* soft as butter; *(fig, umg)* soft
b. w. *abk (= bitte wenden)* p.t.o.
bzgl. *abk (= bezüglich)* re
bzw. *abk* = **beziehungsweise**

C, c

ca. [ka] *abk (= circa)* approx.
Café [ka'feː] **(-s, -s)** *nt* café
Cafeteria [kafete'riːa] **(-, -s)** *f* cafeteria
Camcorder **(-s, -)** *m* camcorder
Camp- ['kɛmp] *zW:* **c~en** *vi* to camp; **~er**

(**-s, -**) *m* camper; **~ing** (**-s**) *nt* camping;
~ingführer *m* camping guide (book);
~ingkocher *m* camping stove; **~ingplatz**
m camp(ing) site
CD-Spieler *m* CD (player)
Cello ['tʃɛlo] (**-s, -s** *od* **Celli**) *nt* cello
Celsius ['tsɛlziʊs] (**-**) *nt* centigrade
Cent [sɛnt] (**-s, -s**) *m* cent
Champagner [ʃam'panjər] (**-s, -**) *m*
champagne
Champignon ['ʃampɪnjõ] (**-s, -s**) *m* button
mushroom
Chance ['ʃã:s(ə)] *f* chance, opportunity
Chaos ['ka:ɔs] (**-, -**) *nt* chaos; **chaotisch**
[ka'o:tɪʃ] *adj* chaotic
Charakter [ka'raktər, *pl* karak'te:rə] (**-s, -e**) *m*
character; **c~fest** *adj* of firm character,
strong; **c~i'sieren** *vt* to characterize;
c~istisch [karakte'rɪstɪʃ] *adj*: **c~istisch (für)**
characteristic (of), typical (of); **c~los** *adj*
unprincipled; **~losigkeit** *f* lack of principle;
~schwäche *f* weakness of character;
~stärke *f* strength of character; **~zug** *m*
characteristic, trait
charmant [ʃar'mant] *adj* charming
Charme [ʃarm] (**-s**) *m* charm
Charterflug ['tʃartərflu:k] *m* charter flight
Chauffeur [ʃɔ'fø:r] *m* chauffeur
Chauvinist [ʃovi'nɪst] *m* chauvinist, jingoist
Chef [ʃɛf] (**-s, -s**) *m* head; (*umg*) boss; **~arzt**
m senior consultant; **~in** (*umg*) *f* boss
Chemie [çe'mi:] (**-**) *f* chemistry; **~faser** *f*
man-made fibre
Chemikalie [çemi'ka:liə] *f* chemical
Chemiker ['çe:mikər] (**-s, -**) *m* (industrial)
chemist
chemisch ['çe:mɪʃ] *adj* chemical; **~e**
Reinigung dry cleaning
Chicorée ['ʃikore:] (**-s**) *m od f* chicory
Chiffre ['ʃɪfrə] *f* (*Geheimzeichen*) cipher; (*in*
Zeitung) box number
Chile ['tʃi:le] *nt* Chile
Chin- ['çi:n] *zW*: **~a** *nt* China; **~akohl** *m*
Chinese leaves; **~ese** [-'ne:zə] *m* Chinese;
~esin *f* Chinese; **c~esisch** *adj* Chinese
Chip [tʃɪp] (**-s, -s**) *m* (*Kartoffelchips*) crisp
(*BRIT*), chip (*US*); (*COMPUT*) chip; **~karte** *f*

smart card
Chirurg [çi'rʊrg] (**-en, -en**) *m* surgeon; **~ie**
[-'gi:] *f* surgery; **c~isch** *adj* surgical
Chlor [klo:r] (**-s**) *nt* chlorine; **~o'form** (**-s**)
nt chloroform
cholerisch [ko'le:rɪʃ] *adj* choleric
Chor [ko:r] (**-(e)s, ⁀e**) *m* choir; (*Musikstück,*
THEAT) chorus; **~al** [ko'ra:l] (**-s, -äle**) *m*
chorale
Choreograf ▲ [koreo'gra:f] (**-en, -en**) *m*
choreographer
Christ [krɪst] (**-en, -en**) *m* Christian; **~baum**
m Christmas tree; **~entum** *nt* Christianity;
~in *f* Christian; **~kind** *nt* ≈ Father
Christmas; (*Jesus*) baby Jesus; **c~lich** *adj*
Christian; **~us** (**-**) *m* Christ
Chrom [kro:m] (**-s**) *nt* chromium; chrome
Chron- ['kro:n] *zW*: **~ik** *f* chronicle; **c~isch**
adj chronic; **c~ologisch** [-o'lo:gɪʃ] *adj*
chronological
circa ['tsɪrka] *adv* about, approximately
Clown [klaʊn] (**-s, -s**) *m* clown
Cocktail ['kɔkte:l] (**-s, -s**) *m* cocktail
Cola ['ko:la] (**-, -s**) *f* Coke ®
Computer [kɔm'pju:tər] (**-s, -**) *m* computer;
~spiel *nt* computer game
Cord [kɔrt] (**-s**) *m* cord, corduroy
Couch [kaʊtʃ] (**-, -es** *od* **-en**) *f* couch
Coupon [ku'põ] (**-s, -s**) *m* = **Kupon**
Cousin [ku'zɛ̃:] (**-s, -s**) *m* cousin; **~e**
[ku'zi:nə] *f* cousin
Creme [krɛːm] (**-, -s**) *f* cream; (*Schuhcreme*)
polish; (*Zahncreme*) paste; (*KOCH*) mousse;
c~farben *adj* cream(-coloured)
cremig ['kre:mɪç] *adj* creamy
Curry ['kari] (**-s**) *m od nt* curry powder;
~pulver *nt* curry powder; **~wurst** *f* curried
sausage

D, d

SCHLÜSSELWORT

da [da:] *adv* **1** (*örtlich*) there; (*hier*) here; **da**
draußen out there; **da sein** to be there; **da**

Rechtschreibreform: ▲ *neue Schreibung* △ *alte Schreibung (auslaufend)*

bin ich here I am; **da, wo** where; **ist noch Milch da?** is there any milk left?
2 (zeitlich) then; (folglich) so
3: da haben wir Glück gehabt we were lucky there; **da kann man nichts machen** nothing can be done about it
♦ konj (weil) as, since

dabehalten (unreg) vt to keep
dabei [da'baɪ] adv (räumlich) close to it; (noch dazu) besides; (zusammen mit) with them; (zeitlich) during this; (obwohl doch) but, however; **was ist schon ~?** what of it?; **es ist doch nichts ~, wenn ...** it doesn't matter if ...; **bleiben wir ~** let's leave it at that; **es bleibt ~** that's settled; **das Dumme/Schwierige ~** the stupid/difficult part of it; **er war gerade ~ zu gehen** he was just leaving; **~ sein** (anwesend) to be present; (beteiligt) to be involved; **~stehen** (unreg) vi to stand around

Dach [dax] (-(e)s, ¨er) nt roof; **~boden** m attic, loft; **~decker** (-s, -) m slater, tiler; **~fenster** nt skylight; **~gepäckträger** m roof rack; **~luke** f skylight; **~pappe** f roofing felt; **~rinne** f gutter

Dachs [daks] (-es, -e) m badger
dachte etc ['daxtə] vb siehe **denken**
Dackel ['dakəl] (-s, -) m dachshund
dadurch [da'dʊrç] adv (räumlich) through it; (durch diesen Umstand) thereby, in that way; (deshalb) because of that, for that reason
♦ konj: **~, dass** because

dafür [da'fyːr] adv for it; (anstatt) instead; **er kann nichts ~** he can't help it; **er ist bekannt ~** he is well-known for that; **was bekomme ich ~?** what will I get for it?

dagegen [da'geːgən] adv against it; (im Vergleich damit) in comparison with it; (bei Tausch) for it/them ♦ konj however; **ich habe nichts ~** I don't mind; **ich war ~** I was against it; **~ kann man nichts tun** one can't do anything about it; **~halten** (unreg) vt (vergleichen) to compare with it; (entgegnen) to object to it; **~sprechen** (unreg) vi: **es spricht nichts ~** there's no reason why not

daheim [da'haɪm] adv at home; **D~** (-s) nt home

daher [da'heːr] adv (räumlich) from there; (Ursache) from that ♦ konj (deshalb) that's why

dahin [da'hɪn] adv (räumlich) there; (zeitlich) then; (vergangen) gone; **~ gehend** on this matter; **~'gegen** konj on the other hand; **~gestellt** adv: **~gestellt bleiben** to remain to be seen; **~gestellt sein lassen** to leave open od undecided

dahinten [da'hɪntən] adv over there
dahinter [da'hɪntər] adv behind it; **~ kommen** to get to the bottom of it

dalli ['dali] (umg) adv chop chop
damalig ['daːmaːlɪç] adj of that time, then
damals ['daːmaːls] adv at that time, then

Dame ['daːmə] f lady; (SCHACH, KARTEN) queen; (Spiel) draughts sg; **~nbinde** f sanitary towel od napkin (US); **d~nhaft** adj ladylike; **~ntoilette** f ladies' toilet od restroom (US); **~nwahl** f ladies' excuse-me

damit [da'mɪt] adv with it; (begründend) by that ♦ konj in order that, in order to; **was meint er ~?** what does he mean by that?; **genug ~!** that's enough!

dämlich ['dɛːmlɪç] (umg) adj silly, stupid
Damm [dam] (-(e)s, ¨e) m dyke; (Staudamm) dam; (Hafendamm) mole; (Bahndamm, Straßendamm) embankment

dämmen ['dɛmən] vt (Wasser) to dam up; (Schmerzen) to keep back

dämmer- zW: **~ig** adj dim, faint; **~n** vi (Tag) to dawn; (Abend) to fall; **D~ung** f twilight; (Morgendämmerung) dawn; (Abenddämmerung) dusk

Dampf [dampf] (-(e)s, ¨e) m steam; (Dunst) vapour; **d~en** vi to steam

dämpfen ['dɛmpfən] vt (KOCH) to steam; (bügeln) to iron with a damp cloth; (fig) to dampen, to subdue

Dampf- zW: **~schiff** nt steamship; **~walze** f steamroller

danach [da'naːx] adv after that; (zeitlich) after that, afterwards; (gemäß) accordingly; according to which; according to that; **er sieht ~ aus** he looks it

Däne ['dɛːnə] (-n, -n) *m* Dane
daneben [da'neːbən] *adv* beside it; (*im Vergleich*) in comparison; **~benehmen** (*unreg*) *vr* to misbehave; **~gehen** (*unreg*) *vi* to miss; (*Plan*) to fail
Dänemark ['dɛːnəmark] *nt* Denmark; **Dänin** *f* Dane; **dänisch** *adj* Danish
Dank [daŋk] (-(e)s) *m* thanks *pl*; **vielen** *od* **schönen ~** many thanks; **jdm ~ sagen** to thank sb; **d~** *präp* (+*dat od gen*) thanks to; **d~bar** *adj* grateful; (*Aufgabe*) rewarding; **~barkeit** *f* gratitude; **d~e** *excl* thank you, thanks; **d~en** *vi* +*dat* to thank; **d~enswert** *adj* (*Arbeit*) worthwhile; rewarding; (*Bemühung*) kind; **d~sagen** *vi* to express one's thanks
dann [dan] *adv* then; **~ und wann** now and then
daran [da'ran] *adv* on it; (*stoßen*) against it; **es liegt ~, dass ...** the cause of it is that ...; **gut/schlecht ~ sein** to be well-/badly off; **das Beste/Dümmste ~** the best/ stupidest thing about it; **ich war nahe ~ zu ...** I was on the point of ...; **er ist ~ gestorben** he died from it *od* of it; **~gehen** (*unreg*) *vi* to start; **~setzen** *vt* to stake
darauf [da'rauf] *adv* (*räumlich*) on it; (*zielgerichtet*) towards it; (*danach*) afterwards; **es kommt ganz ~ an, ob ...** it depends whether ...; **die Tage ~** the days following *od* thereafter; **am Tag ~** the next day; **~ folgend** (*Tag, Jahr*) next, following; **~ legen** to lay *od* put on top
daraus [da'raus] *adv* from it; **was ist ~ geworden?** what became of it?; **~ geht hervor, dass ...** this means that ...
Darbietung ['daːrbiːtʊŋ] *f* performance
darf *etc* [darf] *vb siehe* **dürfen**
darin [da'rɪn] *adv* in (there), in it
darlegen ['daːrleːgən] *vt* to explain, to expound, to set forth; **Darlegung** *f* explanation
Darleh(e)n (-s, -) *nt* loan
Darm [darm] (-(e)s, ⁻e) *m* intestine; (*Wurstdarm*) skin; **~grippe** *f* (*MED*) gastric influenza *od* flu

darstell- ['daːrʃtɛl] *zW:* **~en** *vt* (*abbilden, bedeuten*) to represent; (*THEAT*) to act; (*beschreiben*) to describe ♦ *vr* to appear to be; **D~er(in)** (-s, -) *m(f)* actor (actress); **D~ung** *f* portrayal, depiction
darüber [da'ryːbər] *adv* (*räumlich*) over it, above it; (*fahren*) over it; (*mehr*) more; (*währenddessen*) meanwhile; (*sprechen, streiten*) about it; **~ geht nichts** there's nothing like it
darum [da'rʊm] *adv* (*räumlich*) round it ♦ *konj* that's why; **er bittet ~** he is pleading for it; **es geht ~, dass ...** the thing is that ...; **er würde viel ~ geben, wenn ...** he would give a lot to ...; **ich tue es ~, weil ...** I am doing it because ...
darunter [da'rʊntər] *adv* (*räumlich*) under it; (*dazwischen*) among them; (*weniger*) less; **ein Stockwerk ~** one floor below (it); **was verstehen Sie ~?** what do you understand by that?
das [das] *def art* the ♦ *pron* that
Dasein ['daːzain] (-s) *nt* (*Leben*) life; (*Anwesenheit*) presence; (*Bestehen*) existence
da sein ▲ *siehe* **da**
dass ▲ [das] *konj* that
dasselbe [das'zɛlbə] *art, pron* the same
dastehen ['daːʃteːən] (*unreg*) *vi* to stand there
Datei [da'tai] *f* file
Daten- ['daːtən] *zW:* **~bank** *f* data base; **~schutz** *m* data protection; **~verarbeitung** *f* data processing
datieren [da'tiːrən] *vt* to date
Dativ ['daːtiːf] (-s, -e) *m* dative (case)
Dattel ['datəl] (-, -n) *f* date
Datum ['daːtʊm] (-s, **Daten**) *nt* date; **Daten** *pl* (*Angaben*) data *pl*
Dauer ['dauər] (-, -n) *f* duration; (*gewisse Zeitspanne*) length; (*Bestand, Fortbestehen*) permanence; **es war nur von kurzer ~** it didn't last long; **auf die ~** in the long run; (*auf längere Zeit*) indefinitely; **~auftrag** *m* standing order; **d~haft** *adj* lasting, durable; **~karte** *f* season ticket; **~lauf** *m* jog(ging); **d~n** *vi* to last; **es hat sehr lang gedauert, bis er ...** it took him a long time to ...;

d~nd adj constant; **~parkplatz** m long-stay car park; **~welle** f perm, permanent wave; **~wurst** f German salami; **~zustand** m permanent condition

Daumen ['daʊmən] (-s, -) m thumb

Daune ['daʊnə] f down; **~ndecke** f down duvet, down quilt

davon [da'fɔn] adv of it; (räumlich) away; (weg von) from it; (Grund) because of it; **das kommt ~!** that's what you get; **~ abgesehen** apart from that; **~ sprechen/wissen** to talk/know of od about it; **was habe ich ~?** what's the point?; **~kommen** (unreg) vi to escape; **~laufen** (unreg) vi to run away

davor [da'fo:r] adv (räumlich) in front of it; (zeitlich) before (that); **~ warnen** to warn about it

dazu [da'tsu:] adv (legen, stellen) by it; (essen, singen) with it; **und ~ noch** and in addition; **ein Beispiel/seine Gedanken ~** one example for/his thoughts on this; **wie komme ich denn ~?** why should I?; **~ fähig sein** to be capable of it; **sich ~ äußern** to say something on it; **~gehören** vi to belong to it; **~kommen** (unreg) vi (Ereignisse) to happen too; (an einen Ort) to come along

dazwischen [da'tsvɪʃən] adv in between; (räumlich auch) between (them); (zusammen mit) among them; **~kommen** (unreg) vi (hineingeraten) to get caught in it; **es ist etwas ~gekommen** something cropped up; **~reden** vi (unterbrechen) to interrupt; (sich einmischen) to interfere; **~treten** (unreg) vi to intervene

DDR ⌐

i The **DDR** (*Deutsche Demokratische Republik*) was the name by which the former Communist German Democratic Republic was known. It was founded in 1949 from the Soviet-occupied zone. After the Berlin Wall was built in 1961 it was virtually sealed off from the West. Mass demonstrations and demands for reform forced the opening of the borders in 1989 and the **DDR** merged in 1990 with the **BRD**.

Debatte [de'batə] f debate

Deck [dɛk] (-(e)s, -s od -e) nt deck; **an ~ gehen** to go on deck

Decke f cover; (Bettdecke) blanket; (Tischdecke) tablecloth; (Zimmerdecke) ceiling; **unter einer ~ stecken** to be hand in glove; **~l** (-s, -) m lid; **d~n** vt to cover ♦ vr to coincide

Deckung f (Schützen) covering; (Schutz) cover; (SPORT) defence; (Übereinstimmen) agreement

Defekt [de'fɛkt] (-(e)s, -e) m fault, defect; **d~** adj faulty

defensiv [defɛn'si:f] adj defensive

definieren [defi'ni:rən] vt to define;

Definition [definitsi'o:n] f definition

Defizit ['de:fitsɪt] (-s, -e) nt deficit

deftig ['dɛftɪç] adj (Essen) large; (Witz) coarse

Degen ['de:gən] (-s, -) m sword

degenerieren [degene'ri:rən] vi to degenerate

dehnbar ['de:nba:r] adj elastic; (fig: Begriff) loose

dehnen vt, vr to stretch

Deich [daɪç] (-(e)s, -e) m dyke, dike

deichseln (umg) vt (fig) to wangle

dein(e) [daɪn(ə)] adj your; **~e(r, s)** pron yours; **~er** (gen von du) pron of you; **~erseits** adv on your part; **~esgleichen** pron people like you; **~etwegen** adv (für dich) for your sake; (wegen dir) on your account; **~etwillen** adv: **um ~etwillen = deinetwegen**; **~ige** pron: **der/die/das ~ige** od **D~ige** yours

Deklination [deklinatsi'o:n] f declension

deklinieren [dekli'ni:rən] vt to decline

Dekolleté, Dekolletee ▲ [dekɔl'te:] (-s, -s) nt low neckline

Deko- [deko] zW: **~rateur** [-ra'tø:r] m window dresser; **~ration** [-ratsi'o:n] f decoration; (in Laden) window dressing; **d~rativ** [-ra'ti:f] adj decorative; **d~rieren** [-'ri:rən] vt to decorate; (Schaufenster) to dress

Spelling Reform: ▲ *new spelling* △ *old spelling (to be phased out)*

Delegation [delegatsi'o:n] *f* delegation
delegieren [dele'gi:rən] *vt*: ~ **an** +*akk*
(*Aufgaben*) to delegate to
Delfin ▲ [dɛl'fi:n] (**-s, -e**) *m* dolphin
delikat [deli'ka:t] *adj* (*zart, heikel*) delicate;
(*köstlich*) delicious
Delikatesse [delika'tɛsə] *f* delicacy; **~n** *pl*
(*Feinkost*) delicatessen food; **~ngeschäft** *nt*
delicatessen
Delikt [de'lɪkt] (**-(e)s, -e**) *nt* (*JUR*) offence
Delle [dɛlə] (*umg*) *f* dent
Delphin △ [dɛl'fi:n] (**-s, -e**) *m* = **Delfin**
dem [de(:)m] *art dat von* **der**
Demagoge [dema'go:gə] (**-n, -n**) *m*
demagogue
dementieren [demɛn'ti:rən] *vt* to deny
dem- *zW*: **~gemäß** *adv* accordingly;
~nach *adv* accordingly; **~nächst** *adv*
shortly
Demokrat [demo'kra:t] (**-en, -en**) *m*
democrat; **~ie** [-'ti:] *f* democracy; **d~isch**
adj democratic; **d~isieren** [-i'zi:rən] *vt* to
democratize
demolieren [demo'li:rən] *vt* to demolish
Demon- [demɔn] *zW*: **~strant(in)** [-'stra-
nt(ɪn)] *m(f)* demonstrator; **~stration** [-stra-
tsi'o:n] *f* demonstration; **d~strativ** [-stra'ti:f]
adj demonstrative; (*Protest*) pointed; **d~st-
rieren** [-'stri:rən] *vt, vi* to demonstrate
Demoskopie [demosko'pi:] *f* public opinion
research
Demut ['de:mu:t] (**-**) *f* humility
demütig ['de:my:tɪç] *adj* humble; **~en**
['de:my:tɪgən] *vt* to humiliate; **D~ung** *f*
humiliation
demzufolge ['de:mtsu'fɔlgə] *adv* accordingly
den [de(:)n] *art akk von* **der**
denen ['de:nən] *pron dat pl von* **der**; **die**;
das
Denk- ['dɛŋk] *zW*: **d~bar** *adj* conceivable;
~en (**-s**) *nt* thinking; **d~en** (*unreg*) *vt, vi*
to think; **d~faul** *adj* lazy; **~fehler** *m* logical
error; **~mal** (**-s, ⁻er**) *nt* monument;
~malschutz *m* protection of historical
monuments; **unter ~malschutz stehen** to
be classified as a historical monument;
d~würdig *adj* memorable; **~zettel** *m*: **jdm**

einen ~zettel verpassen to teach sb a
lesson
denn [dɛn] *konj* for ♦ *adv* then; (*nach
Komparativ*) than; **warum ~?** why?
dennoch ['dɛnnɔx] *konj* nevertheless
Denunziant [denʊntsi'ant(m)] *m* informer
Deodorant [de|odo'rant] (**-s, -s** *od* **-e**) *nt*
deodorant
Deponie [depo'ni:] *f* dump
deponieren [depo'ni:rən] *vt* (*COMM*) to
deposit
Depot [de'po:] (**-s, -s**) *nt* warehouse;
(*Busdepot, EISENB*) depot; (*Bankdepot*)
strongroom, safe (*US*)
Depression [deprɛsi'o:n] *f* depression;
depres'siv *adj* depressive
deprimieren [depri'mi:rən] *vt* to depress

SCHLÜSSELWORT

---

der [de(:)r] (*f* **die**, *nt* **das**, *gen* **des, der, des**,
dat **dem, der, dem**, *akk* **den, die, das**, *pl*
die) *def art* the; **der Klaus** (*umg*) Klaus; **der
Frau** (*im
Allgemeinen*) women; **der Tod/das Leben**
death/life; **der Fuß des Berges** the foot of
the hill; **gib es der Frau** give it to the
woman; **er hat sich die Hand verletzt** he
has hurt his hand

♦ *relativ pron* (*bei Menschen*) who, that; (*bei
Tieren, Sachen*) which, that; **der Mann, den
ich gesehen habe** the man who *od* whom
od that I saw

♦ *demonstrativ pron* he/she/it; (*jener, dieser*)
that; (*pl*) those; **der/die war es** it was
him/her; **der mit der Brille** the one with
glasses; **ich will den (da)** I want that one

---

derart ['de:r|a:rt] *adv* so; (*solcher Art*) such;
~ig *adj* such, this sort of
derb [dɛrp] *adj* sturdy; (*Kost*) solid; (*grob*)
coarse
der- *zW*: **'~'gleichen** *pron* such; **'~jenige**
pron he; she; it; the one (who); that
(which); **'~'maßen** *adv* to such an extent,
so; **'~'selbe** *art, pron* the same; **'~'weil(en)**
adv in the meantime; **'~'zeitig** *adj* present,
current; (*damalig*) then

Rechtschreibreform: ▲ *neue Schreibung* △ *alte Schreibung (auslaufend)*

des [dɛs] *art gen von* **der**

desertieren [dezɛr'tiːrən] *vi* to desert

desgleichen ['dɛs'glaiçən] *adv* likewise, also

deshalb ['dɛs'halp] *adv* therefore, that's why

Desinfektion [dezɪnfɛktsi'oːn] *f* disinfection; **~smittel** *nt* disinfectant

desinfizieren [dezɪnfi'tsiːrən] *vt* to disinfect

dessen ['dɛsən] *pron gen von* **der**; **das**; **~ ungeachtet** nevertheless, regardless

Dessert [dɛ'seːr] **(-s, -s)** *nt* dessert

destillieren [dɛstɪ'liːrən] *vt* to distil

desto ['dɛsto] *adv* all the, so much the; **~ besser** all the better

deswegen ['dɛs'veːgən] *konj* therefore, hence

Detail [de'tai] **(-s, -s)** *nt* detail

Detektiv [detɛk'tiːf] **(-s, -e)** *m* detective

deut- ['dɔyt] *zW:* **~en** *vt* to interpret, to explain ♦ *vi:* **~en (auf** +*akk*) to point (to *od* at); **~lich** *adj* clear; (*Unterschied*) distinct; **D~lichkeit** *f* clarity; distinctness

Deutsch [dɔytʃ] *nt* German

deutsch *adj* German; **auf D~** in German; **D~e Demokratische Republik** (*HIST*) German Democratic Republic, East Germany; **~es Beefsteak** ≃ hamburger; **D~e(r)** *mf* German; **ich bin D~er** I am German, **D~land** *nt* Germany

Devise [de'viːzə] *f* motto, device; **~n** *pl* (*FIN*) foreign currency, foreign exchange

Dezember [de'tsɛmbər] **(-s, -)** *m* December

dezent [de'tsɛnt] *adj* discreet

dezimal [detsi'maːl] *adj* decimal; **D~system** *nt* decimal system

d. h. *abk* (= *das heißt*) i.e.

Dia ['diːa] **(-s, -s)** *nt* (*PHOT*) slide, transparency

Diabetes [dia'beːtɛs] **(-, -)** *m* (*MED*) diabetes

Diagnose [dia'gnoːzə] *f* diagnosis

diagonal [diago'naːl] *adj* diagonal

Dialekt [dia'lɛkt] **(-(e)s, -e)** *m* dialect; **d~isch** *adj* dialectal; (*Logik*) dialectical

Dialog [dia'loːk] **(-(e)s, -e)** *m* dialogue

Diamant [dia'mant] *m* diamond

Diaprojektor ['diːaprojɛktɔr] *m* slide projector

Diät [di'ɛːt] **(-, -en)** *f* diet

dich [dɪç] (*akk von du*) *pron* you; yourself

dicht [dɪçt] *adj* dense; (*Nebel*) thick; (*Gewebe*) close; (*undurchlässig*) (water)tight; (*fig*) concise ♦ *adv:* **~ an/bei** close to; **~ bevölkert** densely *od* heavily populated; **D~e** *f* density; thickness; closeness; (water)tightness; (*fig*) conciseness

dichten *vt* (*dicht machen*) to make watertight, to seal; (*NAUT*) to caulk; (*LITER*) to compose, to write ♦ *vi* to compose, to write

Dichter(in) **(-s, -)** *m(f)* poet; (*Autor*) writer; **d~isch** *adj* poetical

dichthalten (*unreg*) (*umg*) *vi* to keep one's mouth shut

Dichtung *f* (*TECH*) washer; (*AUT*) gasket; (*Gedichte*) poetry; (*Prosa*) (piece of) writing

dick [dɪk] *adj* thick; (*fett*) fat; **durch ~ und dünn** through thick and thin; **D~darm** *m* (*ANAT*) colon; **D~e** *f* thickness; fatness; **~flüssig** *adj* viscous; **D~icht** **(-s, -e)** *nt* thicket; **D~kopf** *m* mule; **D~milch** *f* soured milk

die [diː] *def art siehe* **der**

Dieb(in) [diːp, 'diːbɪn] **(-(e)s, -e)** *m(f)* thief; **d~isch** *adj* thieving; (*umg*) immense; **~stahl** **(-(e)s, ⁓e)** *m* theft; **~stahlversicherung** *f* insurance against theft

Diele [diːlə] *f* (*Brett*) board; (*Flur*) hall, lobby

dienen ['diːnən] *vi:* (*jdm*) **~** to serve (sb)

Diener **(-s, -)** *m* servant; **~in** *f* (maid)servant; **~schaft** *f* servants *pl*

Dienst [diːnst] **(-(e)s, -e)** *m* service; **außer ~** retired; **~ haben** to be on duty; **~ habend** (*Arzt*) on duty

Dienstag ['diːnstaːk] *m* Tuesday; **d~s** *adv* on Tuesdays

Dienst- *zW:* **~bote** *m* servant; **~geheimnis** *nt* official secret; **~gespräch** *nt* business call; **~leistung** *f* service; **d~lich** *adj* official; **~mädchen** *nt* (house)maid; **~reise** *f* business trip; **~stelle** *f* office; **~vorschrift** *f* official regulations *pl*; **~weg** *m* official channels *pl*; **~zeit** *f* working hours *pl*; (*MIL*) period of service

Spelling Reform: ▲ *new spelling* △ *old spelling (to be phased out)*

dies [di:s] *pron (demonstrativ: sg)* this; (: *pl*) these; ~**bezüglich** *adj (Frage)* on this matter; ~**e(r, s)** ['di:zə(r, s)] *pron* this (one)

Diesel ['di:zəl] *m (Kraftstoff)* diesel

dieselbe [di:'zɛlbə] *pron, art* the same

Dieselmotor *m* diesel engine

diesig ['di:zɪç] *adj* drizzly

dies- *zW:* ~**jährig** *adj* this year's; ~**mal** *adv* this time; ~**seits** *präp +gen* on this side; **D~seits** (-) *nt* this life

Dietrich ['di:trɪç] (-**s, -e**) *m* picklock

diffamieren [dɪfa'mi:rən] *(pej) vt* to defame

Differenz [dɪfə'rɛnts] (-, -en) *f (Unterschied)* difference; ~**en** *pl (Meinungsverschiedenheit)* difference (of opinion); **d~ieren** *vt* to make distinctions in; **d~iert** *adj (Mensch etc)* complex

differenzial ▲ [dɪferɛntsia:l] *adj* differential; **D~rechnung** *f* differential calculus

digital [digi'ta:l] *adj* digital; **D~fernsehen** *f* digital TV

Dikt- [dɪkt] *zW:* ~**afon, ~aphon** [-a'fo:n] *nt* dictaphone; ~**at** [-'ta:t] (-(e)s, -e) *nt* dictation; ~**ator** [-'ta:tɔr] *m* dictator; **d~atorisch** [-a'to:rɪʃ] *adj* dictatorial; ~**atur** [-a'tu:r] *f* dictatorship; **d~ieren** [-'ti:rən] *vt* to dictate

Dilemma [di'lɛma] (-**s, -s** *od* -**ta**) *nt* dilemma

Dilettant [dile'tant] *m* dilettante, amateur; **d~isch** *adj* amateurish, dilettante

Dimension [dimɛnzi'o:n] *f* dimension

DIN *f abk (= Deutsche Industrie-Norm)* German Industrial Standard

Ding [dɪŋ] (-(e)s, -e) *nt* thing, object; **d~lich** *adj* real, concrete; ~**s(bums)** ['dɪŋks(bʊms)] (-) *(umg) m* thingummybob

Diplom [di'plo:m] (-(e)s, -e) *nt* diploma, certificate; ~**at** [-'ma:t] (-en, -en) *m* diplomat; ~**atie** [-a'ti:] *f* diplomacy; **d~atisch** [-'ma:tɪʃ] *adj* diplomatic; ~**ingenieur** *m* qualified engineer

dir [di:r] *(dat von du) pron* (to) you

direkt [di'rɛkt] *adj* direct; **D~flug** *m* direct flight; **D~or** *m* director; *(SCH)* principal, headmaster; **D~übertragung** *f* live broadcast

Dirigent [diri'gɛnt(ɪn)] *m* conductor

dirigieren [diri'gi:rən] *vt* to direct; *(MUS)* to conduct

Diskette [dɪs'kɛtə] *f* diskette, floppy disk

Diskont [dɪs'kɔnt] (-**s, -e**) *m* discount; ~**satz** *m* rate of discount

Diskothek [dɪsko'te:k] (-, -en) *f* disco(theque)

diskret [dɪs'kre:t] *adj* discreet; **D~ion** *f* discretion

diskriminieren [dɪskrimi'ni:rən] *vt* to discriminate against

Diskussion [dɪskʊsi'o:n] *f* discussion; debate; **zur ~ stehen** to be under discussion

diskutieren [dɪsku'ti:rən] *vt, vi* to discuss; to debate

Distanz [dɪs'tants] *f* distance; **distan'zieren** *vr:* **sich von jdm/etw d~ieren** to distance o.s. from sb/sth

Distel ['dɪstəl] (-, -n) *f* thistle

Disziplin [dɪstsi'pli:n] *f* discipline

Dividende [divi'dɛndə] *f* dividend

dividieren [divi'di:rən] *vt:* **(durch etw) ~** to divide (by sth)

DM [de:'|ɛm] *abk (= Deutsche Mark)* German Mark

D-Mark ['de:mark] *f* D Mark, German Mark

SCHLÜSSELWORT

doch [dɔx] *adv* 1 *(dennoch)* after all; *(sowieso)* anyway; **er kam doch noch** he came after all; **du weißt es ja doch besser** you know better than I do anyway; **und doch ...** and yet ...

2 *(als bejahende Antwort)* yes I do/it does *etc*; **das ist nicht wahr - doch!** that's not true - yes it is!

3 *(auffordernd)*: **komm doch** do come; **lass ihn doch** just leave him; **nicht doch!** oh no!

4: **sie ist doch noch so jung** but she's still so young; **Sie wissen doch, wie das ist** you know how it is (, don't you?); **wenn doch** if only

♦ *konj (aber)* but; *(trotzdem)* all the same;

und doch hat er es getan but still he did
it

Docht [dɔxt] **(-(e)s, -e)** m wick

Dock [dɔk] **(-s, -s** od **-e)** nt dock

Dogge ['dɔgə] f bulldog

Dogma ['dɔgma] **(-s, -men)** nt dogma;
d~tisch adj dogmatic

Doktor ['dɔktɔr, pl -'toːrən] **(-s, -en)** m
doctor

Dokument [doku'mɛnt] nt document

Dokumentar- [dokumɛn'taːr] zW: **~bericht**
m documentary; **~film** m documentary
(film); **d~isch** adj documentary

Dolch [dɔlç] **(-(e)s, -e)** m dagger

dolmetschen ['dɔlmɛtʃən] vt, vi to
interpret; **Dolmetscher(in) (-s, -)** m(f)
interpreter

Dom [doːm] **(-(e)s, -e)** m cathedral

dominieren [domi'niːrən] vt to dominate
♦ vi to predominate

Donau ['doːnaʊ] f Danube

Donner ['dɔnər] **(-s, -)** m thunder; **d~n** vi
unpers to thunder

Donnerstag ['dɔnərstaːk] m Thursday

doof [doːf] (umg) adj daft, stupid

Doppel ['dɔpəl] **(-s, -)** nt duplicate; (SPORT)
doubles; **~bett** nt double bed; **d~deutig**
adj ambiguous; **~fenster** nt double
glazing; **~gänger (-s, -)** m double;
~punkt m colon; **~stecker** m two-way
adaptor; **d~t** adj double; **in d~ter
Ausführung** in duplicate; **~verdiener** m
person with two incomes; (pl: Paar) two-
income family; **~zentner** m 100 kilograms;
~zimmer nt double room

Dorf [dɔrf] **(-(e)s, "er)** nt village;
~bewohner m villager

Dorn [dɔrn] **(-(e)s, -en)** m (BOT) thorn; **d~ig**
adj thorny

Dörrobst ['dœroːpst] nt dried fruit

Dorsch [dɔrʃ] **(-(e)s, -e)** m cod

dort [dɔrt] adv there; **~ drüben** over there;
~her adv from there; **~hin** adv (to) there;
~ig adj of that place; in that town

Dose ['doːzə] f box; (Blechdose) tin, can

Dosen pl von **Dose**; **Dosis**

Dosenöffner m tin od can opener

Dosis ['doːzɪs] **(-, Dosen)** f dose

Dotter ['dɔtər] **(-s, -)** m (egg) yolk

Drache ['draxə] **(-n, -n)** m (Tier) dragon

Drachen (-s, -) m kite; **~fliegen (-s)** nt
hang-gliding

Draht [draːt] **(-(e)s, "e)** m wire; **auf ~ sein**
to be on the ball; **d~ig** adj (Mann) wiry;
~seil nt cable; **~seilbahn** f cable railway,
funicular

Drama ['draːma] **(-s, Dramen)** nt drama,
play; **~tiker** [-'maːtikər] **(-s, -)** m dramatist;
d~tisch [-'maːtɪʃ] adj dramatic

dran [dran] (umg) adv: **jetzt bin ich ~!** it's
my turn now; siehe **daran**

Drang [draŋ] **(-(e)s, "e)** m (Trieb): **~ (nach)**
impulse (for), urge (for), desire (for);
(Druck) pressure

drängeln ['drɛŋəln] vt, vi to push, to jostle

drängen ['drɛŋən] vt (schieben) to push, to
press; (antreiben) to urge ♦ vi (eilig sein) to
be urgent; (Zeit) to press; **auf etw** akk **~** to
press for sth

drastisch ['drastɪʃ] adj drastic

drauf [draʊf] (umg) adv = **darauf;
D~gänger (-s, -)** m daredevil

draußen ['draʊsən] adv outside

Dreck [drɛk] **(-(e)s)** m mud, dirt; **d~ig** adj
dirty, filthy

Dreh- ['dreː] zW: **~arbeiten** pl (CINE)
shooting sg; **~bank** f lathe; **~buch** nt
(CINE) script; **d~en** vt to turn, to rotate;
(Zigaretten) to roll; (Film) to shoot ♦ vi to
turn, to rotate ♦ vr to turn; (handeln von):
es d~t sich um ... it's about ...; **~orgel** f
barrel organ; **~tür** f revolving door; **~ung** f
(Rotation) rotation; (Umdrehung, Wendung)
turn; **~zahl** f rate of revolutions;
~zahlmesser m rev(olution) counter

drei [draɪ] num three; **~ viertel** three
quarters; **D~eck** nt triangle; **~eckig** adj
triangular; **~einhalb** num three and a half;
~erlei adj inv of three kinds; **~fach** adj
triple, treble ♦ adv three times; **~hundert**
num three hundred; **D~königsfest** nt
Epiphany; **~mal** adv three times; **~malig**
adj three times

dreinreden ['draɪnreːdən] *vi*: **jdm ~**
(*dazwischenreden*) to interrupt sb; (*sich
einmischen*) to interfere with sb
Dreirad *nt* tricycle
dreißig ['draɪsɪç] *num* thirty
dreist [draɪst] *adj* bold, audacious
drei- *zW*: **~viertel** △ *num siehe* **drei**;
D~viertelstunde *f* three-quarters of an
hour; **~zehn** *num* thirteen
dreschen ['drɛʃən] (*unreg*) *vt* (*Getreide*) to
thresh; (*umg*: *verprügeln*) to beat up
dressieren [drɛˈsiːrən] *vt* to train
drillen ['drɪlən] *vt* (*bohren*) to drill, to bore;
(*MIL*) to drill; (*fig*) to train
Drilling *m* triplet
drin [drɪn] (*umg*) *adv* = **darin**
dringen ['drɪŋən] (*unreg*) *vi* (*Wasser, Licht,
Kälte*): **~ (durch/in** +*akk*) to penetrate
(through/into); **auf etw** *akk* **~** to insist on
sth
dringend ['drɪŋənt] *adj* urgent
Dringlichkeit *f* urgency
drinnen ['drɪnən] *adv* inside, indoors
dritte(r, s) [drɪtə(r, s)] *adj* third; **D~ Welt**
Third World; **D~s Reich** Third Reich; **D~l**
(-s, -) *nt* third; **~ns** *adv* thirdly
DRK [deːˈɛrˈkaː] *nt abk* (= *Deutsches Rotes
Kreuz*) German Red Cross
droben ['droːbən] *adv* above, up there
Droge ['droːgə] *f* drug
drogen *zW*: **~abhängig** *adj* addicted to
drugs; **D~händler** *m* drug pedlar, pusher
Drogerie [droːgəˈriː] *f* chemist's shop

Drogerie

i The **Drogerie** as opposed to the
Apotheke sells medicines not requiring
*a prescription. It tends to be cheaper
and also sells cosmetics, perfume and
toiletries.*

Drogist [droˈgɪst] *m* pharmacist, chemist
drohen ['droːən] *vi*: **(jdm) ~** to threaten
(sb)
dröhnen ['drøːnən] *vi* (*Motor*) to roar;
(*Stimme, Musik*) to ring, to resound
Drohung ['droːʊŋ] *f* threat

drollig ['drɔlɪç] *adj* droll
Drossel ['drɔsəl] **(-, -n)** *f* thrush
drüben ['dryːbən] *adv* over there, on the
other side
drüber ['dryːbər] (*umg*) *adv* = **darüber**
Druck [drʊk] **(-(e)s, -e)** *m* (*PHYS*: *Zwang*)
pressure; (*TYP*: *Vorgang*) printing; (: *Produkt*)
print; (*fig*: *Belastung*) burden, weight;
~buchstabe *m* block letter
drücken ['drʏkən] *vt* (*Knopf, Hand*) to press;
(*zu eng sein*) to pinch; (*fig*: *Preise*) to keep
down; (: *belasten*) to oppress, to weigh
down ♦ *vi* to press; to pinch ♦ *vr*: **sich vor
etw** *dat* **~** to get out of (doing) sth; **~d** *adj*
oppressive
Drucker **(-s, -)** *m* printer
Drücker **(-s, -)** *m* button; (*Türdrücker*)
handle; (*Gewehrdrücker*) trigger
Druck- *zW*: **~erei** *f* printing works, press;
~erschwärze *f* printer's ink; **~fehler** *m*
misprint; **~knopf** *m* press stud, snap
fastener; **~sache** *f* printed matter;
~schrift *f* block *od* printed letters *pl*
drum [drʊm] (*umg*) *adv* = **darum**
drunten ['drʊntən] *adv* below, down there
Drüse ['dryːzə] *f* gland
Dschungel ['dʒʊŋəl] **(-s, -)** *m* jungle
du [duː] (*nom*) *pron* you; **~ sagen** = **duzen**
Dübel ['dyːbəl] **(-s, -)** *m* Rawlplug ®
ducken ['dʊkən] *vt* (*Kopf, Person*) to duck;
(*fig*) to take down a peg or two ♦ *vr* to
duck
Duckmäuser ['dʊkmɔʏzər] **(-s, -)** *m* yes
man
Dudelsack ['duːdəlzak] *m* bagpipes *pl*
Duell [duˈɛl] **(-s, -e)** *nt* duel
Duft [dʊft] **(-(e)s, -̈e)** *m* scent, odour; **d~en**
vi to smell, to be fragrant; **d~ig** *adj* (*Stoff,
Kleid*) delicate, diaphanous
dulden ['dʊldən] *vt* to suffer; (*zulassen*) to
tolerate ♦ *vi* to suffer
dumm [dʊm] *adj* stupid; (*ärgerlich*)
annoying; **der D~e sein** to be the loser;
~erweise *adv* stupidly; **D~heit** *f* stupidity;
(*Tat*) blunder, stupid mistake; **D~kopf** *m*
blockhead
dumpf [dʊmpf] *adj* (*Ton*) hollow, dull; (*Luft*)

Rechtschreibreform: ▲ *neue Schreibung* △ *alte Schreibung (auslaufend)*

musty; (*Erinnerung, Schmerz*) vague
Düne ['dy:nə] f dune
düngen ['dyŋən] vt to manure
Dünger (-s, -) m dung, manure; (*künstlich*)
fertilizer
dunkel ['dʊŋkəl] adj dark; (*Stimme*) deep;
(*Ahnung*) vague; (*rätselhaft*) obscure;
(*verdächtig*) dubious, shady; **im D~n
tappen** (*fig*) to grope in the dark
Dunkel- zW: **~heit** f darkness; (*fig*)
obscurity; **~kammer** f (PHOT) darkroom;
d~n vi unpers to grow dark; **~ziffer** f
estimated number of unreported cases
dünn [dʏn] adj thin; **~flüssig** adj watery,
thin
Dunst [dʊnst] (-es, ᵘe) m vapour; (*Wetter*)
haze
dünsten ['dʏnstən] vt to steam
dunstig ['dʊnstɪç] adj vaporous; (*Wetter*)
hazy, misty
Duplikat [dupliˈkaːt] (-(e)s, -e) nt duplicate
Dur [duːr] (-, -) nt (MUS) major

| SCHLÜSSELWORT |
---

durch [dʊrç] präp +akk 1 (*hindurch*) through;
durch den Urwald through the jungle;
durch die ganze Welt reisen to travel all
over the world
2 (*mittels*) through, by (means of);
(*aufgrund*) due to, owing to; **Tod durch
Herzschlag/den Strang** death from a
heart attack/by hanging; **durch die Post**
by post; **durch seine Bemühungen**
through his efforts
♦ adv 1 (*hindurch*) through; **die ganze
Nacht durch** all through the night; **den
Sommer durch** during the summer; **8 Uhr
durch** past 8 o'clock; **durch und durch**
completely
2 (*durchgebraten etc*): **(gut) durch** well-done

---

durch- zW: **~arbeiten** vt, vi to work
through ♦ vr to work one's way through;
~'aus adv completely; (*unbedingt*)
definitely; **~aus nicht** absolutely not
Durchblick ['dʊrçblɪk] m view; (*fig*)
comprehension; **d~en** vi to look through;

(*umg: verstehen*): **(bei etw) d~en** to
understand (sth); **etw d~en lassen** (*fig*) to
hint at sth
durchbrechen ['dʊrçbrɛçən] (*unreg*) vt, vi to
break
durch'brechen [dʊrçˈbrɛçən] (*unreg*) vt
insep (*Schranken*) to break through;
(*Schallmauer*) to break; (*Gewohnheit*) to
break free from
durchbrennen ['dʊrçbrɛnən] (*unreg*) vi
(*Draht, Sicherung*) to burn through; (*umg*) to
run away
durchbringen (*unreg*) vt (*Kranken*) to pull
through; (*umg: Familie*) to support;
(*durchsetzen: Antrag, Kandidat*) to get
through; (*vergeuden: Geld*) to get through,
to squander
Durchbruch ['dʊrçbrʊx] m (*Öffnung*)
opening; (MIL) breach; (*von Gefühlen etc*)
eruption; (*der Zähne*) cutting; (*fig*)
breakthrough; **zum ~ kommen** to break
through
durch- zW: **~dacht** [-'daxt] adj well
thought-out; **~'denken** (*unreg*) vt to think
out; **~drehen** vt (*Fleisch*) to mince ♦ vi
(*umg*) to crack up
durcheinander [dʊrçʔaɪˈnandər] adv in a
mess, in confusion; (*umg: verwirrt*)
confused; **~ bringen** to mess up; (*verwirren*)
to confuse; **~ reden** to talk at the same
time; **D~ (-s)** nt (*Verwirrung*) confusion;
(*Unordnung*) mess
durch- zW: **~fahren** (*unreg*) vi (~ *Tunnel
usw*) to drive through; (*ohne Unterbrechung*)
to drive straight through; (*ohne anzuhalten*):
der Zug fährt bis Hamburg ~ the train
runs direct to Hamburg; (*ohne Umsteigen*):
können wir ~fahren? can we go direct?,
can we go non-stop?; **D~fahrt** f transit;
(*Verkehr*) thoroughfare; **D~fall** m (MED)
diarrhoea; **~fallen** (*unreg*) vi to fall
through; (*in Prüfung*) to fail; **~finden**
(*unreg*) vr to find one's way through;
~fragen vr to find one's way by asking
durchführ- ['dʊrçfy:r] zW: **~bar** adj
feasible, practicable; **~en** vt to carry out;
D~ung f execution, performance

Durchgang ['dʊrçgaŋ] *m* passage(way); (*bei Produktion, Versuch*) run; (*SPORT*) round; (*bei Wahl*) ballot; **„~ verboten"** "no thoroughfare"

Durchgangsverkehr *m* through traffic

durchgefroren ['dʊrçgəfroːrən] *adj* (*Mensch*) frozen stiff

durchgehen ['dʊrçgeːən] (*unreg*) *vt* (*behandeln*) to go over ♦ *vi* to go through; (*ausreißen: Pferd*) to break loose; (*Mensch*) to run away; **mein Temperament ging mit mir durch** my temper got the better of me; **jdm etw ~ lassen** to let sb get away with sth; **~d** *adj* (*Zug*) through; (*Öffnungszeiten*) continuous

durch- *zW:* **~greifen** (*unreg*) *vi* to take strong action; **~halten** (*unreg*) *vi* to last out ♦ *vt* to keep up; **~kommen** (*unreg*) *vi* to get through; (*überleben*) to pull through; **~'kreuzen** *vt insep* to thwart, to frustrate; **~lassen** (*unreg*) *vt* (*Person*) to let through; (*Wasser*) to let in; **~lesen** (*unreg*) *vt* to read through; **~'leuchten** *vt insep* to X-ray; **~machen** *vt* to go through; **die Nacht ~machen** to make a night of it

Durchmesser (**-s, -**) *m* diameter

durch- *zW:* **~'nässen** *vt insep* to soak (through); **~nehmen** (*unreg*) *vt* to go over; **~nummerieren** ▲ *vt* to number consecutively; **~'queren** [dʊrç'kveːrən] *vt insep* to cross; **D~reise** *f* transit; **auf der D~reise** passing through; (*Güter*) in transit; **~ringen** (*unreg*) *vr* to reach a decision after a long struggle

durchs [dʊrçs] = **durch das**

Durchsage ['dʊrçzaːgə] *f* intercom *od* radio announcement

durchschauen ['dʊrçʃaʊən] *vi* to look *od* see through; (*Person, Lüge*) to see through

durchscheinen ['dʊrçʃaɪnən] (*unreg*) *vi* to shine through; **~d** *adj* translucent

Durchschlag ['dʊrçʃlaːk] *m* (*Doppel*) carbon copy; (*Sieb*) strainer; **d~en** [-gən] (*unreg*) *vt* (*entzweischlagen*) to split (in two); (*sieben*) to sieve ♦ *vi* (*zum Vorschein kommen*) to emerge, to come out ♦ *vr* to

get by

durchschlagend *adj* resounding

durchschneiden ['dʊrçʃnaɪdən] (*unreg*) *vt* to cut through

Durchschnitt ['dʊrçʃnɪt] *m* (*Mittelwert*) average; **über/unter dem ~** above/below average; **im ~** on average; **d~lich** *adj* average ♦ *adv* on average

Durchschnittswert *m* average

durch- *zW:* **D~schrift** *f* copy; **~sehen** (*unreg*) *vt* to look through; **~setzen** *vt* to enforce ♦ *vr* (*Erfolg haben*) to succeed; (*sich behaupten*) to get one's way; **seinen Kopf ~setzen** to get one's way; **~'setzen** *vt insep* to mix

Durchsicht ['dʊrçzɪçt] *f* looking through, checking; **d~ig** *adj* transparent

durch- *zW:* **'~sprechen** (*unreg*) *vt* to talk over; **'~stehen** (*unreg*) *vt* to live through; **~stellen** *vt* (*an Telefon*) to put through; **~stöbern** (*auch untr*) *vt* (*Kisten*) to rummage through, to rifle through; (*Haus, Wohnung*) to ransack; **'~streichen** (*unreg*) *vt* to cross out; **~'suchen** *vt insep* to search; **D~'suchung** *f* search; **~'wachsen** *adj* (*Speck*) streaky; (*fig: mittelmäßig*) so-so; **D~wahl** *f* (*TEL*) direct dialling; **~weg** *adv* throughout, completely; **~ziehen** (*unreg*) *vt* (*Faden*) to draw through ♦ *vi* to pass through; **D~zug** *m* (*Luft*) draught; (*von Truppen, Vögeln*) passage

---

SCHLÜSSELWORT

---

dürfen ['dʏrfən] (*unreg*) *vi* **1** (*Erlaubnis haben*) to be allowed to; **ich darf das** I'm allowed to (to do that); **darf ich?** may I?; **darf ich ins Kino?** can *od* may I go to the cinema?; **es darf geraucht werden** you may smoke

2 (*in Verneinungen*): **er darf das nicht** he's not allowed to (to do that); **das darf nicht geschehen** that must not happen; **da darf sie sich nicht wundern** that shouldn't surprise her

3 (*in Höflichkeitsformeln*): **darf ich Sie bitten, das zu tun?** may *od* could I ask you to do that?; **was darf es sein?** what can I do for you?

4 (*können*): **das dürfen Sie mir glauben** you can believe me
5 (*Möglichkeit*): **das dürfte genug sein** that should be enough; **es dürfte Ihnen bekannt sein, dass ...** as you will probably know ...

---

dürftig ['dʏrftɪç] *adj* (*ärmlich*) needy, poor; (*unzulänglich*) inadequate
dürr [dʏr] *adj* dried-up; (*Land*) arid; (*mager*) skinny, gaunt; **D~e** *f* aridity; (*Zeit*) drought; (*Magerkeit*) skinniness
Durst [dʊrst] (-(e)s) *m* thirst; **~ haben** to be thirsty; **d~ig** *adj* thirsty
Dusche ['duʃə] *f* shower; **d~en** *vi, vr* to have a shower
Düse ['dy:zə] *f* nozzle; (*Flugzeugdüse*) jet
Düsen- *zW*: **~antrieb** *m* jet propulsion; **~flugzeug** *nt* jet (plane); **~jäger** *m* jet fighter
Dussel ['dʊsəl] (-s, -) (*umg*) *m* twit
düster ['dy:star] *adj* dark; (*Gedanken, Zukunft*) gloomy
Dutzend ['dʊtsənt] (-s, -e) *nt* dozen; **~(e) od d~(e) Mal(e)** a dozen times
duzen ['du:tsən] *vt*: (**jdn**) **~** to use the familiar form of address "du" (to *od* with sb)

---
duzen
---

i There are two different forms of address in Germany: du and Sie. **Duzen** means addressing someone as 'du' - used with children, family and close friends - and **siezen** means addressing someone as 'Sie' - used for all grown-ups and older teenagers. Students almost always use 'du' to each other.

Dynamik [dy'na:mɪk] *f* (*PHYS*) dynamics *sg*; (*fig: Schwung*) momentum; (*von Mensch*) dynamism; **dynamisch** *adj* (*auch fig*) dynamic
Dynamit [dyna'mi:t] (-s) *nt* dynamite
Dynamo [dy'na:mo] (-s, -s) *m* dynamo
DZ *nt abk* = **Doppelzimmer**
D-Zug ['de:tsu:k] *m* through train

E, e

Ebbe ['ɛbə] *f* low tide
eben ['e:bən] *adj* level, flat; (*glatt*) smooth
♦ *adv* just; (*bestätigend*) exactly; **~ deswegen** just because of that; **~bürtig** *adj*: **jdm ~bürtig sein** to be sb's equal; **E~e** *f* plain; (*fig*) level; **~falls** *adv* likewise; **~so** *adv* just as
Eber ['e:bər] (-s, -) *m* boar
ebnen ['e:bnən] *vt* to level
Echo ['ɛço] (-s, -s) *nt* echo
echt [ɛçt] *adj* genuine; (*typisch*) typical; **E~heit** *f* genuineness
Eck- ['ɛk] *zW*: **~ball** *m* corner (kick); **~e** *f* corner; (*MATH*) angle; **e~ig** *adj* angular; **~zahn** *m* eye tooth
ECU [e'ky:] (-, -s) *m* (*FIN*) ECU
edel ['e:dəl] *adj* noble; **E~metall** *nt* rare metal; **E~stahl** *m* high-grade steel; **E~stein** *m* precious stone
EDV [e:de:'fau] (-) *f abk* (= *elektronische Datenverarbeitung*) electronic data processing
Efeu ['e:fɔy] (-s) *m* ivy
Effekt [ɛ'fɛkt] (-s, -e) *m* effect
Effekten [ɛ'fɛktən] *pl* stocks
effektiv [ɛfɛk'ti:f] *adj* effective, actual
EG ['e:'ge:] *f abk* (= *Europäische Gemeinschaft*) EC
egal [e'ga:l] *adj* all the same
Ego- [e:go] *zW*: **~ismus** [-'ɪsmʊs] *m* selfishness, egoism; **~ist** [-'ɪst] *m* egoist; **e~istisch** *adj* selfish, egoistic
Ehe ['e:ə] *f* marriage
ehe *konj* before
Ehe- *zW*: **~beratung** *f* marriage guidance (counselling); **~bruch** *m* adultery; **~frau** *f* married woman; wife; **~leute** *pl* married people; **e~lich** *adj* matrimonial; (*Kind*) legitimate
ehemalig *adj* former
ehemals *adv* formerly
Ehe- *zW*: **~mann** *m* married man; husband; **~paar** *nt* married couple

---

Spelling Reform: ▲ *new spelling* △ *old spelling (to be phased out)*

eher ['e:ər] *adv* (*früher*) sooner; (*lieber*) rather, sooner; (*mehr*) more

Ehe- *zW:* **~ring** *m* wedding ring; **~schließung** *f* marriage ceremony

eheste(r, s) ['e:əstə(r, s)] *adj* (*früheste*) first, earliest; **am ~n** (*liebsten*) soonest; (*meist*) most; (*wahrscheinlichst*) most probably

Ehr- ['e:r] *zW:* **e~bar** *adj* honourable, respectable; **~e** *f* honour; **e~en** *vt* to honour

Ehren- ['e:rən] *zW:* **e~amtlich** *adj* honorary; **~gast** *m* guest of honour; **e~haft** *adj* honourable; **~platz** *m* place of honour *od* (*US*) honor; **~runde** *f* lap of honour; **~sache** *f* point of honour; **e~voll** *adj* honourable; **~wort** *nt* word of honour

Ehr- *zW:* **~furcht** *f* awe, deep respect; **e~fürchtig** *adj* reverent; **~gefühl** *nt* sense of honour; **~geiz** *m* ambition; **e~geizig** *adj* ambitious; **e~lich** *adj* honest; **~lichkeit** *f* honesty; **e~los** *adj* dishonourable; **~ung** *f* honour(ing); **e~würdig** *adj* venerable

Ei [aɪ] (**-(e)s, -er**) *nt* egg

Eich- *zW:* **~e** ['aɪçə] *f* oak (tree); **~l** (**-, -n**) *f* acorn; **~hörnchen** *nt* squirrel

Eichmaß *nt* standard

Eid ['aɪt] (**-(e)s, -e**) *m* oath

Eidechse ['aɪdɛksə] *f* lizard

eidesstattlich *adj:* **~e Erklärung** affidavit

Eidgenosse *m* Swiss

Eier- *zW:* **~becher** *m* eggcup; **~kuchen** *m* omelette; pancake; **~likör** *m* advocaat; **~schale** *f* eggshell; **~stock** *m* ovary; **~uhr** *f* egg timer

Eifer ['aɪfər] (**-s**) *m* zeal, enthusiasm; **~sucht** *f* jealousy; **e~süchtig** *adj:* **e~süchtig (auf** +*akk*) jealous (of)

eifrig ['aɪfrɪç] *adj* zealous, enthusiastic

Eigelb ['aɪgɛlp] (**-(e)s, -**) *nt* egg yolk

eigen ['aɪgən] *adj* own; (~*artig*) peculiar; **mit der/dem Ihm ~en ...** with that ... peculiar to him; **sich** *dat* **etw zu E~ machen** to make sth one's own; **E~art** *f* peculiarity; characteristic; **~artig** *adj* peculiar; **E~bedarf** *m:* **zum E~bedarf** for (one's own) personal use/domestic requirements; **der Vermieter machte E~bedarf geltend**

the landlord showed he needed the house/flat for himself; **~händig** *adj* with one's own hand; **E~heim** *nt* owner-occupied house; **E~heit** *f* peculiarity; **~mächtig** *adj* high-handed; **E~name** *m* proper name; **~s** *adv* expressly, on purpose; **E~schaft** *f* quality, property, attribute; **E~sinn** *m* obstinacy; **~sinnig** *adj* obstinate; **~tlich** *adj* actual, real ♦ *adv* actually, really; **E~tor** *nt* own goal; **E~tum** *nt* property; **E~tümer(in)** (**-s, -**) *m(f)* owner, proprietor; **~tümlich** *adj* peculiar; **E~tümlichkeit** *f* peculiarity; **E~tumswohnung** *f* freehold flat

eignen ['aɪgnən] *vr* to be suited; **Eignung** *f* suitability

Eil- ['aɪl] *zW:* **~bote** *m* courier; **~brief** *m* express letter; **~e** *f* haste; **es hat keine ~e** there's no hurry; **e~en** *vi* (*Mensch*) to hurry; (*dringend sein*) to be urgent; **e~ends** *adv* hastily; **~gut** *nt* express goods *pl*, fast freight (*US*); **e~ig** *adj* hasty, hurried; (*dringlich*) urgent; **es e~ig haben** to be in a hurry; **~zug** *m* semi-fast train, limited stop train

Eimer ['aɪmər] (**-s, -**) *m* bucket, pail

ein ['aɪn] *adv:* **nicht ~ noch aus wissen** not to know what to do

ein(e) ['aɪn(ə)] *num* one ♦ *indef art* a, an

einander [aɪ'nandər] *pron* one another, each other

einarbeiten ['aɪn|arbaɪtən] *vt* to train ♦ *vr:* **sich in etw** *akk* **~** to familiarize o.s. with sth

einatmen ['aɪn|a:tmən] *vt, vi* to inhale, to breathe in

Einbahnstraße ['aɪnba:nʃtra:sə] *f* one-way street

Einband ['aɪnbant] *m* binding, cover

einbauen ['aɪnbauən] *vt* to build in; (*Motor*) to install, to fit

Einbaumöbel *pl* built-in furniture *sg*

einbegriffen ['aɪnbəgrɪfən] *adj* included

einberufen ['aɪnbəru:fən] (*unreg*) *vt* to convene, to call up; (*MIL*) to call up

Einbettzimmer *nt* single room

einbeziehen ['aɪnbətsi:ən] (*unreg*) *vt* to

include

einbiegen ['aɪnbiːgən] (*unreg*) *vi* to turn

einbilden ['aɪnbɪldən] *vt*: **sich** *dat* **etw ~** to imagine sth

Einbildung *f* imagination; (*Dünkel*) conceit; **~skraft** *f* imagination

Einblick ['aɪnblɪk] *m* insight

einbrechen ['aɪnbreçən] (*unreg*) *vi* (*in Haus*) to break in; (*Nacht*) to fall; (*Winter*) to set in; (*durchbrechen*) to break; **~ in** +*akk* (*MIL*) to invade

Einbrecher (-s, -) *m* burglar

einbringen ['aɪnbrɪŋən] (*unreg*) *vt* to bring in; (*Geld, Vorteil*) to yield; (*mitbringen*) to contribute

Einbruch ['aɪnbrʊx] *m* (*Hauseinbruch*) break-in, burglary; (*Eindringen*) invasion; (*des Winters*) onset; (*Durchbrechen*) break; (*MET*) approach; (*MIL*) penetration; (**bei/vor**) **der Nacht** at/before nightfall; **e~sicher** *adj* burglar-proof

einbürgern ['aɪnbʏrgərn] *vt* to naturalize ♦ *vr* to become adopted

einbüßen ['aɪnbyːsən] *vt* to lose, to forfeit

einchecken ['aɪntʃɛkən] *vt, vi* to check in

eincremen ['aɪnkreːmən] *vt* to put cream on

eindecken ['aɪndɛkən] *vr*: **sich (mit etw) ~** to lay in stocks (of sth); to stock up (with sth)

eindeutig ['aɪndɔʏtɪç] *adj* unequivocal

eindringen ['aɪndrɪŋən] (*unreg*) *vi*: **~ (in** +*akk*) to force one's way in(to); (*in Haus*) to break in(to); (*in Land*) to invade; (*Gas, Wasser*) to penetrate; (**auf jdn**) **~** (*mit Bitten*) to pester (sb)

eindringlich *adj* forcible, urgent

Eindringling *m* intruder

Eindruck ['aɪndrʊk] *m* impression

eindrücken ['aɪndrʏkən] *vt* to press in

eindrucksvoll *adj* impressive

eine(r, s) *pron* one; (*jemand*) someone

eineiig ['aɪnʔaɪɪç] *adj* (*Zwillinge*) identical

eineinhalb ['aɪnʔaɪn'halp] *num* one and a half

einengen ['aɪnʔɛŋən] *vt* to confine, to restrict

einer- ['aɪnər] *zW*: **'E~'lei (-s)** *nt* sameness; **'~'lei** *adj* (*gleichartig*) the same kind of; **es ist mir ~lei** it is all the same to me; **~seits** *adv* on the one hand

einfach ['aɪnfax] *adj* simple; (*nicht mehrfach*) single ♦ *adv* simply; **E~heit** *f* simplicity

einfädeln ['aɪnfɛːdəln] *vt* (*Nadel, Faden*) to thread; (*fig*) to contrive

einfahren ['aɪnfaːrən] (*unreg*) *vt* to bring in; (*Barriere*) to knock down; (*Auto*) to run in ♦ *vi* to drive in; (*Zug*) to pull in; (*MIN*) to go down

Einfahrt *f* (*Vorgang*) driving in; pulling in; (*MIN*) descent; (*Ort*) entrance

Einfall ['aɪnfal] *m* (*Idee*) idea, notion; (*Lichteinfall*) incidence; (*MIL*) raid; **e~en** (*unreg*) *vi* (*Licht*) to fall; (*MIL*) to raid; (*einstürzen*) to fall in, to collapse; (*einstimmen*): (**in etw** *akk*) **e~en** to join in (with sth); **etw fällt jdm ein** sth occurs to sb; **das fällt mir gar nicht ein** I wouldn't dream of it; **sich** *dat* **etw e~en lassen** to have a good idea

einfältig ['aɪnfɛltɪç] *adj* simple(-minded)

Einfamilienhaus [aɪnfa'miːliənhaʊs] *nt* detached house

einfarbig ['aɪnfarbɪç] *adj* all one colour; (*Stoff etc*) self-coloured

einfetten ['aɪnfɛtən] *vt* to grease

einfließen ['aɪnfliːsən] (*unreg*) *vi* to flow in

einflößen ['aɪnfløːsən] *vt*: **jdm etw ~** to give sb sth; (*fig*) to instil sth in sb

Einfluss ▲ ['aɪnflʊs] *m* influence; **~bereich** *m* sphere of influence

einförmig ['aɪnfœrmɪç] *adj* uniform; **E~keit** *f* uniformity

einfrieren ['aɪnfriːrən] (*unreg*) *vi* to freeze (up) ♦ *vt* to freeze

einfügen ['aɪnfyːgən] *vt* to fit in; (*zusätzlich*) to add

Einfuhr ['aɪnfuːr] (-) *f* import; **~beschränkung** *f* import restrictions *pl*; **~bestimmungen** *pl* import regulations

einführen ['aɪnfyːrən] *vt* to bring in; (*Mensch, Sitten*) to introduce; (*Ware*) to import

Einführung *f* introduction

Eingabe ['aɪngaːbə] f petition; (COMPUT) input

Eingang ['aɪngaŋ] m entrance; (COMM: Ankunft) arrival; (Erhalt) receipt

eingeben ['aɪngeːbən] (unreg) vt (Arznei) to give; (Daten etc) to enter

eingebildet ['aɪngəbɪldət] adj imaginary; (eitel) conceited

Eingeborene(r) ['aɪngəboːrənə(r)] f(m) native

Eingebung f inspiration

eingefleischt ['aɪngəflaɪʃt] adj (Gewohnheit, Vorurteile) deep-rooted

eingehen ['aɪngeːən] (unreg) vi (Aufnahme finden) to come in; (Sendung, Geld) to be received; (Tier, Pflanze) to die; (Firma) to fold; (schrumpfen) to shrink ♦ vt to enter into; (Wette) to make; **auf etw** akk ~ to go into sth; **auf jdn** ~ to respond to sb; **jdm** ~ (verständlich sein) to be comprehensible to sb; **~d** adj exhaustive, thorough

Eingemachte(s) ['aɪngəmaːxtə(s)] nt preserves pl

eingenommen ['aɪngənɔmən] adj: ~ **(von)** fond (of), partial (to); ~ **(gegen)** prejudiced (against)

eingeschrieben ['aɪngəʃriːbən] adj registered

eingespielt ['aɪngəʃpiːlt] adj: **aufeinander ~ sein** to be in tune with each other

Eingeständnis ['aɪngəʃtɛntnɪs] (-ses, -se) nt admission, confession

eingestehen ['aɪngəʃteːən] (unreg) vt to confess

eingestellt ['aɪngəʃtɛlt] adj: **auf etw ~ sein** to be prepared for sth

eingetragen ['aɪngətraːgən] adj (COMM) registered

Eingeweide ['aɪngəvaɪdə] (-s, -) nt innards pl, intestines pl

Eingeweihte(r) ['aɪngəvaɪtə(r)] f(m) initiate

eingewöhnen ['aɪngəvøːnən] vr: **sich ~ in** +akk to settle (down) in

eingleisig ['aɪnglaɪzɪç] adj single-track

eingreifen ['aɪngraɪfən] (unreg) vi to intervene, to interfere; (Zahnrad) to mesh

Eingriff ['aɪngrɪf] m intervention,

interference; (Operation) operation

einhaken ['aɪnhaːkən] vt to hook in ♦ vr: **sich bei jdm** ~ to link arms with sb ♦ vi (sich einmischen) to intervene

Einhalt ['aɪnhalt] m: ~ **gebieten** +dat to put a stop to; **e~en** (unreg) vt (Regel) to keep ♦ vi to stop

einhändigen ['aɪnhɛndɪgən] vt to hand in

einhängen ['aɪnhɛŋən] vt to hang; (Telefon) to hang up ♦ vi (at TEL) to hang up; **sich bei jdm** ~ to link arms with sb

einheimisch ['aɪnhaɪmɪʃ] adj native; **E~e(r)** f(m) local

Einheit ['aɪnhaɪt] f unity; (Maß, MIL) unit; **e~lich** adj uniform; **~spreis** m standard price

einholen ['aɪnhoːlən] vt (Tau) to haul in; (Fahne, Segel) to lower; (Vorsprung aufholen) to catch up with; (Verspätung) to make up; (Rat, Erlaubnis) to ask ♦ vi (einkaufen) to shop

einhüllen ['aɪnhylən] vt to wrap up

einhundert ['aɪn'hʊndərt] num one hundred, a hundred

einig ['aɪnɪç] adj (vereint) united; ~ **gehen** to agree; **sich** dat ~ **sein** to be in agreement; ~ **werden** to agree

einige(r, s) ['aɪnɪgə(r, s)] adj, pron some ♦ pl some; (mehrere) several; ~ **Mal** a few times

einigen vt to unite ♦ vr: **sich ~ (auf** +akk) to agree (on)

einigermaßen adv somewhat; (leidlich) reasonably

einig- zW: **E~keit** f unity; (Übereinstimmung) agreement; **E~ung** f agreement; (Vereinigung) unification

einkalkulieren ['aɪnkalkuliːrən] vt to take into account, to allow for

Einkauf ['aɪnkaʊf] m purchase; **e~en** vt to buy ♦ vi to shop; **e~en gehen** to go shopping

Einkaufs- zW: **~bummel** m shopping spree; **~korb** m shopping basket; **~wagen** m shopping trolley; **~zentrum** nt shopping centre

einklammern ['aɪnklamərn] vt to put in brackets, to bracket

Einklang ['aɪnklaŋ] m harmony

einklemmen ['aɪnklɛmən] vt to jam

einkochen ['aɪnkɔxən] vt to boil down; (Obst) to preserve, to bottle

Einkommen ['aɪnkɔmən] (-s, -) nt income; ~(s)steuer f income tax

Einkünfte ['aɪnkʏnftə] pl income sg, revenue sg

einladen ['aɪnla:dən] (unreg) vt (Person) to invite; (Gegenstände) to load; **jdn ins Kino ~** to take sb to the cinema

Einladung f invitation

Einlage ['aɪnla:gə] f (Programm~) interlude; (Spar~) deposit; (Schuh~) insole; (Fußstütze) support; (Zahn~) temporary filling; (KOCH) noodles pl, vegetables pl etc in soup

einlagern ['aɪnla:gərn] vt to store

Einlass ▲ ['aɪnlas] (-es, ⁻e) m (Zutritt) admission

einlassen ['aɪnlasən] (unreg) vt to let in; (einsetzen) to set in ♦ vr: **sich mit jdm/auf etw** akk ~ to get involved with sb/sth

Einlauf ['aɪnlaʊf] m arrival; (von Pferden) finish; (MED) enema; **e~en** (unreg) vi to arrive, to come in; (in Hafen) to enter; (SPORT) to finish; (Wasser) to run in; (Stoff) to shrink ♦ vt (Schuhe) to break in ♦ vr (SPORT) to warm up; (Motor, Maschine) to run in; **jdm das Haus e~en** to invade sb's house

einleben ['aɪnle:bən] vr to settle down

einlegen ['aɪnle:gən] vt (einfügen: Blatt, Sohle) to insert; (KOCH) to pickle; (Pause) to have; (Protest) to make; (Veto) to use; (Berufung) to lodge; (AUT: Gang) to engage

einleiten ['aɪnlaɪtən] vt to introduce, to start; (Geburt) to induce; **Einleitung** f introduction; induction

einleuchten ['aɪnlɔʏçtən] vi: **(jdm) ~** to be clear od evident (to sb); ~**d** adj clear

einliefern ['aɪnli:fərn] vt: ~ **(in** +akk) to take (into)

Einlieferungsschein m certificate of posting

Einliegerwohnung ['aɪnli:gərvo:nʊŋ] f self-contained flat; (für Eltern, Großeltern) granny flat

einloggen ['aɪnlɔgən] vi (COMPUT) to log on

einlösen ['aɪnlø:zən] vt (Scheck) to cash; (Schuldschein, Pfand) to redeem; (Versprechen) to keep

einmachen ['aɪnmaxən] vt to preserve

einmal ['aɪnma:l] adv once; (erstens) first; (zukünftig) sometime; **nehmen wir ~ an** just let's suppose; **noch ~** once more; **nicht ~** not even; **auf ~** all at once; **es war ~** once upon a time there was/were; **E~eins** nt multiplication tables pl; ~**ig** adj unique; (einmal erforderlich) single; (prima) fantastic

Einmarsch ['aɪnmarʃ] m entry; (MIL) invasion; **e~ieren** vi to march in

einmischen ['aɪnmɪʃən] vr: **sich ~ (in** +akk) to interfere (with)

einmütig ['aɪnmy:tɪç] adj unanimous

Einnahme ['aɪnna:mə] f (von Medizin) taking; (MIL) capture, taking; ~**n** pl (Geld) takings, revenue sg; ~**quelle** f source of income

einnehmen ['aɪnne:mən] (unreg) vt to take; (Stellung, Raum) to take up; ~ **für/gegen** to persuade in favour of/against; ~**d** adj charming

einordnen ['aɪnɔrdnən] vt to arrange, to fit in ♦ vr to adapt; (AUT) to get into lane

einpacken ['aɪnpakən] vt to pack (up)

einparken ['aɪnparkən] vt to park

einpendeln ['aɪnpɛndəln] vr to even out

einpflanzen ['aɪnpflantsən] vt to plant; (MED) to implant

einplanen ['aɪnpla:nən] vt to plan for

einprägen ['aɪnprɛ:gən] vt to impress, to imprint; (beibringen): **(jdm) ~** to impress (on sb); **sich** dat **etw ~** to memorize sth

einrahmen ['aɪnra:mən] vt to frame

einräumen ['aɪnrɔʏmən] vt (ordnend) to put away; (überlassen: Platz) to give up; (zugestehen) to admit, to concede

einreden ['aɪnre:dən] vt: **jdm/sich etw ~** to talk sb/o.s. into believing sth

einreiben ['aɪnraɪbən] (unreg) vt to rub in

einreichen ['aɪnraɪçən] vt to hand in; (Antrag) to submit

Einreise ['aɪnraɪzə] f entry;

~**bestimmungen** *pl* entry regulations;
~**erlaubnis** *f* entry permit;
~**genehmigung** *f* entry permit; **e~n** *vi*:
(in ein Land) e~n to enter (a country)
einrichten [ˈaɪnrɪçtən] *vt* (*Haus*) to furnish;
(*schaffen*) to establish, to set up;
(*arrangieren*) to arrange; (*möglich machen*) to
manage ♦ *vr* (*in Haus*) to furnish one's
house; **sich ~ (auf** +*akk*) (*sich vorbereiten*) to
prepare o.s. (for); (*sich anpassen*) to adapt
(to)
Einrichtung *f* (*Wohnungseinrichtung*)
furnishings *pl*; (*öffentliche Anstalt*)
organization; (*Dienste*) service
einrosten [ˈaɪnrɔstən] *vi* to get rusty
einrücken [ˈaɪnrʏkən] *vi* (*MIL: in Land*) to
move in
Eins [aɪns] **(-, -en)** *f* one; **e~** *num* one; **es ist
mir alles e~** it's all one to me
einsam [ˈaɪnzaːm] *adj* lonely, solitary;
E~keit *f* loneliness, solitude
einsammeln [ˈaɪnzaməln] *vt* to collect
Einsatz [ˈaɪnzats] *m* (*Teil*) inset; (*an Kleid*)
insertion; (*Verwendung*) use, employment;
(*Spieleinsatz*) stake; (*Risiko*) risk; (*MIL*)
operation; (*MUS*) entry; **im ~** in action;
e~bereit *adj* ready for action
einschalten [ˈaɪnʃaltən] *vt* (*einfügen*) to
insert; (*Pause*) to make; (*ELEK*) to switch on;
(*Anwalt*) to bring in ♦ *vr* (*dazwischentreten*)
to intervene
einschärfen [ˈaɪnʃɛrfən] *vt*: **jdm etw ~** to
impress sth (up)on sb
einschätzen [ˈaɪnʃɛtsən] *vt* to estimate, to
assess ♦ *vr* to rate o.s.
einschenken [ˈaɪnʃɛŋkən] *vt* to pour out
einschicken [ˈaɪnʃɪkən] *vt* to send in
einschl. *abk* (= *einschließlich*) incl.
einschlafen [ˈaɪnʃlaːfən] (*unreg*) *vi* to fall
asleep, to go to sleep
einschläfernd [ˈaɪnʃlɛːfərnt] *adj* (*MED*)
soporific; (*langweilig*) boring; (*Stimme*)
lulling
Einschlag [ˈaɪnʃlaːk] *m* impact; (*fig:
Beimischung*) touch, hint; **e~en** [-gən]
(*unreg*) *vt* to knock in; (*Fenster*) to smash, to
break; (*Zähne, Schädel*) to smash in; (*AUT:*

Räder) to turn; (*kürzer machen*) to take up;
(*Ware*) to pack, to wrap up; (*Weg, Richtung*)
to take ♦ *vi* to hit; (*sich einigen*) to agree;
(*Anklang finden*) to work, to succeed; **in etw**
akk / **auf jdn e~en** to hit sth/sb
einschlägig [ˈaɪnʃlɛːgɪç] *adj* relevant
einschließen [ˈaɪnʃliːsən] (*unreg*) *vt* (*Kind*) to
lock in; (*Häftling*) to lock up; (*Gegenstand*)
to lock away; (*Bergleute*) to cut off;
(*umgeben*) to surround; (*MIL*) to encircle;
(*fig*) to include, to comprise ♦ *vr* to lock
o.s. in
einschließlich *adv* inclusive ♦ *präp* +*gen*
inclusive of, including
einschmeicheln [ˈaɪnʃmaɪçəln] *vr*: **sich ~
(bei)** to ingratiate o.s. (with)
einschnappen [ˈaɪnʃnapən] *vi* (*Tür*) to click
to; (*fig*) to be touchy; **eingeschnappt sein**
to be in a huff
einschneidend [ˈaɪnʃnaɪdənt] *adj* drastic
Einschnitt [ˈaɪnʃnɪt] *m* cutting; (*MED*)
incision; (*Ereignis*) decisive point
einschränken [ˈaɪnʃrɛŋkən] *vt* to limit, to
restrict; (*Kosten*) to cut down, to reduce
♦ *vr* to cut down (on expenditure);
Einschränkung *f* restriction, limitation;
reduction; (*von Behauptung*) qualification
Einschreib- [ˈaɪnʃraɪb] *zW*: **~(e)brief** *m*
recorded delivery letter; **e~en** (*unreg*) *vt* to
write in; (*Post*) to send recorded delivery
♦ *vr* to register; (*UNIV*) to enrol; **~en** *nt*
recorded delivery letter
einschreiten [ˈaɪnʃraɪtən] (*unreg*) *vi* to step
in, to intervene; **~ gegen** to take action
against
einschüchtern [ˈaɪnʃʏçtərn] *vt* to intimidate
einschulen [ˈaɪnʃuːlən] *vt*: **eingeschult
werden** (*Kind*) to start school
einsehen [ˈaɪnzeːən] (*unreg*) *vt* (*hineinsehen
in*) to realize; (*Akten*) to have a look at;
(*verstehen*) to see; **E~ (-s)** *nt*
understanding; **ein E~ haben** to show
understanding
einseitig [ˈaɪnzaɪtɪç] *adj* one-sided
Einsend- [ˈaɪnzɛnd] *zW*: **e~en** (*unreg*) *vt* to
send in; **~er (-s, -)** *m* sender, contributor;
~ung *f* sending in

einsetzen ['aɪnzɛtsən] vt to put (in); (in Amt) to appoint, to install; (Geld) to stake; (verwenden) to use; (MIL) to employ ♦ vi (beginnen) to set in; (MUS) to enter, to come in ♦ vr to work hard; **sich für jdn/ etw ~** to support sb/sth

Einsicht ['aɪnzɪçt] f insight; (in Akten) look, inspection; **zu der ~ kommen, dass ...** to come to the conclusion that ...; **e~ig** adj (Mensch) judicious; **e~slos** adj unreasonable; **e~svoll** adj understanding

einsilbig ['aɪnzɪlbɪç] adj (auch fig) monosyllabic; (Mensch) uncommunicative

einspannen ['aɪnʃpanən] vt (Papier) to insert; (Pferde) to harness; (umg: Person) to rope in

Einsparung ['aɪnʃpaːrʊŋ] f economy, saving

einsperren ['aɪnʃpɛrən] vt to lock up

einspielen ['aɪnʃpiːlən] vr (SPORT) to warm up ♦ vt (Film: Geld) to bring in; (Instrument) to play in; **sich aufeinander ~** to become attuned to each other; **gut eingespielt** running smoothly

einsprachig ['aɪnʃpraːxɪç] adj monolingual

einspringen ['aɪnʃprɪŋən] (unreg) vi (aushelfen) to help out, to step into the breach

Einspruch ['aɪnʃprʊx] m protest, objection; **~srecht** nt veto

einspurig ['aɪnʃpuːrɪç] adj (EISENB) single-track; (AUT) single-lane

einst [aɪnst] adv once; (zukünftig) one day, some day

einstecken ['aɪnʃtɛkən] vt to stick in, to insert; (Brief) to post; (ELEK: Stecker) to plug in; (Geld) to pocket; (mitnehmen) to take; (überlegen sein) to put in the shade; (hinnehmen) to swallow

einstehen ['aɪnʃteːən] (unreg) vi: **für jdn/ etw ~** to guarantee sb/sth; (verantworten): **für etw ~** to answer for sth

einsteigen ['aɪnʃtaɪɡən] (unreg) vi to get in od on; (in Schiff) to go on board; (sich beteiligen) to come in; (hineinklettern) to climb in

einstellen ['aɪnʃtɛlən] vt (aufhören) to stop; (Geräte) to adjust; (Kamera etc) to focus;

(Sender, Radio) to tune in; (unterstellen) to put; (in Firma) to employ, to take on ♦ vi (Firma) to take on staff/workers ♦ vr (anfangen) to set in; (kommen) to arrive; **sich auf jdn ~** to adapt to sb; **sich auf etw** akk **~** to prepare o.s. for sth

Einstellung f (Aufhören) suspension; adjustment; focusing; (von Arbeiter etc) appointment; (Haltung) attitude

Einstieg ['aɪnʃtiːk] (-(e)s, -e) m entry; (fig) approach

einstig ['aɪnstɪç] adj former

einstimmig ['aɪnʃtɪmɪç] adj unanimous; (MUS) for one voice

einstmals adv once, formerly

einstöckig ['aɪnʃtœkɪç] adj two-storeyed

Einsturz ['aɪnʃtʊrts] m collapse

einstürzen ['aɪnʃtʏrtsən] vi to fall in, to collapse

einst- zW: **~weilen** adv meanwhile; (vorläufig) temporarily, for the time being; **~weilig** adj temporary

eintägig ['aɪntɛːɡɪç] adj one-day

eintauschen ['aɪntaʊʃən] vt: **~ (gegen** od **für)** to exchange (for)

eintausend ['aɪntaʊzənt] num one thousand

einteilen ['aɪntaɪlən] vt (in Teile) to divide (up); (Menschen) to assign

einteilig adj one-piece

eintönig ['aɪntøːnɪç] adj monotonous

Eintopf ['aɪntɔpf] m stew

Eintracht ['aɪntraxt] (-) f concord, harmony; **einträchtig** ['aɪntrɛçtɪç] adj harmonious

Eintrag ['aɪntraːk] (-(e)s, ⁻e) m entry; **amtlicher ~** entry in the register; **e~en** [-ɡən] (unreg) vt (in Buch) to enter; (Profit) to yield ♦ vr to put one's name down

einträglich ['aɪntrɛːklɪç] adj profitable

eintreffen ['aɪntrɛfən] (unreg) vi to happen; (ankommen) to arrive

eintreten ['aɪntreːtən] (unreg) vi to occur; (sich einsetzen) to intercede ♦ vt (Tür) to kick open; **~ in** +akk to enter; (in Klub, Partei) to join

Eintritt ['aɪntrɪt] m (Betreten) entrance; (Anfang) commencement; (in Klub etc)

Spelling Reform: ▲ *new spelling* △ *old spelling (to be phased out)*

joining

Eintritts- *zW*: **~geld** *nt* admission charge; **~karte** *f* (admission) ticket; **~preis** *m* admission charge

einüben ['ain|y:bən] *vt* to practise

Einvernehmen ['ainferne:mən] (**-s, -**) *nt* agreement, harmony

einverstanden ['ainferʃtandən] *excl* agreed, okay ♦ *adj*: **~ sein** to agree, to be agreed

Einverständnis ['ainferʃtɛntnis] *nt* understanding; (*gleiche Meinung*) agreement

Einwand ['ainvant] (**-(e)s, ˙e**) *m* objection

Einwand- *zW*: **~erer** ['ainvandərər] *m* immigrant; **e~ern** *vi* to immigrate; **~erung** *f* immigration

einwandfrei *adj* perfect ♦ *adv* absolutely

Einweg- ['ainve:g-] *zW*: **~flasche** *f* no-deposit bottle; **~spritze** *f* disposable syringe

einweichen ['ainvaiçən] *vt* to soak

einweihen ['ainvaiən] *vt* (*Kirche*) to consecrate; (*Brücke*) to open; (*Gebäude*) to inaugurate; **~ (in** +*akk*) (*Person*) to initiate (in); **Einweihung** *f* consecration; opening; inauguration; initiation

einweisen ['ainvaizən] (*unreg*) *vt* (*in Amt*) to install; (*in Arbeit*) to introduce; (*in Anstalt*) to send

einwenden ['ainvɛndən] (*unreg*) *vt*: **etwas ~ gegen** to object to, to oppose

einwerfen ['ainvɛrfən] (*unreg*) *vt* to throw in; (*Brief*) to post; (*Geld*) to put in, to insert; (*Fenster*) to smash; (*äußern*) to interpose

einwickeln ['ainvikəln] *vt* to wrap up; (*fig: umg*) to outsmart

einwilligen ['ainviligən] *vi*: **~ (in** +*akk*) to consent (to), to agree (to); **Einwilligung** *f* consent

einwirken ['ainvirkən] *vi*: **auf jdn/etw ~** to influence sb/sth

Einwohner ['ainvo:nər] (**-s, -**) *m* inhabitant; **~'meldeamt** *nt* registration office; **~schaft** *f* population, inhabitants *pl*

Einwurf ['ainvurf] *m* (*Öffnung*) slot; (*von Münze*) insertion; (*von Brief*) posting; (*Einwand*) objection; (*SPORT*) throw-in

Einzahl ['aintsa:l] *f* singular; **e~en** *vt* to pay

in; **~ung** *f* paying in; **~ungsschein** *m* paying-in slip, deposit slip

einzäunen ['aintsɔynən] *vt* to fence in

Einzel ['aintsəl] (**-s, -**) *nt* (*TENNIS*) singles; **~fahrschein** *m* one-way ticket; **~fall** *m* single instance, individual case; **~handel** *m* retail trade; **~handelspreis** *m* retail price; **~heit** *f* particular, detail; **~kind** *nt* only child; **e~n** *adj* single; (*vereinzelt*) the odd ♦ *adv* singly; **e~n angeben** to specify; **der/die E~ne** the individual; **das E~ne** the particular; **ins E~ne gehen** to go into detail(s); **~teil** *nt* component (part); **~zimmer** *nt* single room; **~zimmerzuschlag** *m* single room supplement

einziehen ['aintsi:ən] (*unreg*) *vt* to draw in, to take in; (*Kopf*) to duck; (*Fühler, Antenne, Fahrgestell*) to retract; (*Steuern, Erkundigungen*) to collect; (*MIL*) to draft, to call up; (*aus dem Verkehr ziehen*) to withdraw; (*konfiszieren*) to confiscate ♦ *vi* to move in; (*Friede, Ruhe*) to come; (*Flüssigkeit*) to penetrate

einzig ['aintsiç] *adj* only; (*ohnegleichen*) unique; **das E~e** the only thing; **der/die E~e** the only one; **~artig** *adj* unique

Einzug ['aintsu:k] *m* entry, moving in

Eis [ais] (**-es, -**) *nt* ice; (*Speiseeis*) ice cream; **~bahn** *f* ice *od* skating rink; **~bär** *m* polar bear; **~becher** *m* sundae; **~bein** *nt* pig's trotters *pl*; **~berg** *m* iceberg; **~café** *nt* ice-cream parlour (*BRIT*) *od* parlor (*US*); **~decke** *f* sheet of ice; **~diele** *f* ice-cream parlour

Eisen ['aizən] (**-s, -**) *nt* iron

Eisenbahn *f* railway, railroad (*US*); **~er** (**-s, -**) *m* railwayman, railway employee, railroader (*US*); **~schaffner** *m* railway guard; **~wagen** *m* railway carriage

Eisenerz *nt* iron ore

eisern ['aizərn] *adj* iron; (*Gesundheit*) robust; (*Energie*) unrelenting; (*Reserve*) emergency

Eis- *zW*: **e~frei** *adj* clear of ice; **~hockey** *nt* ice hockey; **e~ig** ['aiziç] *adj* icy; **e~kalt** *adj* icy cold; **~kunstlauf** *m* figure skating; **~laufen** *nt* ice skating; **~pickel** *m* ice axe; **~schrank** *m* fridge, icebox (*US*); **~würfel**

m ice cube; **~zapfen** *m* icicle; **~zeit** *f* ice age

eitel ['aɪtəl] *adj* vain; **E~keit** *f* vanity

Eiter ['aɪtər] **(-s)** *m* pus; **e~ig** *adj* suppurating; **e~n** *vi* to suppurate

Eiweiß (-es, -e) *nt* white of an egg; *(CHEM)* protein

Ekel[1] ['eːkəl] **(-s, -)** *nt (umg: Mensch)* nauseating person

Ekel[2] ['eːkəl] **(-s)** *m* nausea, disgust; **~erregend** nauseating, disgusting; **e~haft** *adj* nauseating, disgusting; **e~ig** *adj* nauseating, disgusting; **e~n** *vt* to disgust ♦ *vr:* **sich e~n (vor** *+dat)* to loathe, to be disgusted (at); **es e~t jdn** *od* **jdm** sb is disgusted; **eklig** *adj* nauseating, disgusting

Ekstase [ɛk'staːzə] *f* ecstasy

Ekzem [ɛk'tseːm] **(-s, -e)** *nt (MED)* eczema

Elan [e'lã] **(-s)** *m* elan

elastisch [e'lastɪʃ] *adj* elastic

Elastizität [elastitsi'tɛːt] *f* elasticity

Elch [ɛlç] **(-(e)s, -e)** *m* elk

Elefant [ele'fant] *m* elephant

elegant [ele'gant] *adj* elegant

Eleganz [ele'gants] *f* elegance

Elek- [e'lek] *zW:* **~triker** [-trɪkər] **(-s, -)** *m* electrician; **e~trisch** [-trɪʃ] *adj* electric; **e~trisieren** [-tri'ziːrən] *vt (auch fig)* to electrify; *(Mensch)* to give an electric shock to ♦ *vr* to get an electric shock; **~trizität** [tritsi'tɛːt] *f* electricity; **~trizitätswerk** *nt* power station; *(Gesellschaft)* electric power company

Elektro- [e'lɛktro] *zW:* **~de** [-'troːdə] *f* electrode; **~gerät** *nt* electrical appliance; **~herd** *m* electric cooker; **~n (-s, -en)** *nt* electron; **~nik** *f* electronics *sg;* **e~nisch** *adj* electronic; **~rasierer** *m* electric razor; **~technik** *f* electrical engineering

Element [ele'mɛnt] **(-s, -e)** *nt* element; *(ELEK)* cell, battery; **e~ar** [-'taːr] *adj* elementary; *(naturhaft)* elemental

Elend ['eːlɛnt] **(-(e)s)** *nt* misery; **e~** *adj* miserable; **~sviertel** *nt* slum

elf [ɛlf] *num* eleven; **E~ (-, -en)** *f (SPORT)* eleven

Elfe *f* elf

Elfenbein *nt* ivory

Elfmeter *m (SPORT)* penalty (kick)

Elite [e'liːtə] *f* elite

Ell- *zW:* **~bogen** *m* elbow; **~e** ['ɛlə] *f* ell; *(Maß)* yard; **~enbogen** *m* elbow; **~(en)bogenfreiheit** *f (fig)* elbow room

Elsass ▲ ['ɛlzas] **(- od -es)** *nt:* **das ~** Alsace

Elster ['ɛlstər] **(-, -n)** *f* magpie

Eltern ['ɛltərn] *pl* parents; **~beirat** *m (SCH)* ≈ PTA *(BRIT),* parents' council; **~haus** *nt* home; **e~los** *adj* parentless

E-Mail ['iːmeːl] **(-, -s)** *f* E-mail; **~-Adresse** *f* e-mail address

Emaille [e'maljə] **(-s, -s)** *nt* enamel

emaillieren [ema'jiːrən] *vt* to enamel

Emanzipation [emantsipatsi'oːn] *f* emancipation

emanzipieren [eman'tsi'piːrən] *vt* to emancipate

Embryo ['ɛmbryo] **(-s, -s** *od* **Embryonen)** *m* embryo

Emi- *zW:* **~'grant(in)** *m(f)* emigrant; **~gration** *f* emigration; **e~grieren** *vi* to emigrate

Emissionen [emisi'oːnən] *fpl* emissions

Empfang [ɛm'pfaŋ] **(-(e)s, ⁺e)** *m* reception; *(Erhalten)* receipt; **in ~ nehmen** to receive; **e~en** *(unreg) vt* to receive ♦ *vi (schwanger werden)* to conceive

Empfäng- [ɛm'pfɛŋ] *zW:* **~er (-s, -)** *m* receiver; *(COMM)* addressee, consignee; **~erabschnitt** *m* receipt slip; **e~lich** *adj* receptive, susceptible; **~nis (-, -se)** *f* conception; **~nisverhütung** *f* contraception

Empfangs- *zW:* **~bestätigung** *f* acknowledgement; **~dame** *f* receptionist; **~schein** *m* receipt; **~zimmer** *nt* reception room

empfehlen [ɛm'pfeːlən] *(unreg) vt* to recommend ♦ *vr* to take one's leave; **~swert** *adj* recommendable

Empfehlung *f* recommendation

empfiehlst *etc* [ɛm'pfiːlst] *vb siehe* **empfehlen**

empfind- [ɛm'pfɪnt] *zW:* **~en** [-dən] *(unreg) vt* to feel; **~lich** *adj* sensitive; *(Stelle)* sore; *(reizbar)* touchy; **~sam** *adj* sentimental;

E~ung [-dʊŋ] f feeling, sentiment
empfohlen etc [ɛmˈpfoːlən] vb siehe
empfehlen
empor [ɛmˈpoːr] adv up, upwards
empören [ɛmˈpøːrən] vt to make indignant;
to shock ♦ vr to become indignant; **~d** adj
outrageous
Emporkömmling [ɛmˈpoːrkœmlɪŋ] m
upstart, parvenu
Empörung f indignation
emsig [ˈɛmzɪç] adj diligent, busy
End- [ˈɛnd] in zW final; **~e** (-s, -n) nt end;
am ~e at the end; (schließlich) in the end;
am ~e sein to be at the end of one's
tether; **~e Dezember** at the end of
December; **zu ~e sein** to be finished;
e~en vi to end; **e~gültig** [ˈɛnt-] adj final,
definite
Endivie [ɛnˈdiːviə] f endive
End- zW: **e~lich** adj final; (MATH) finite
♦ adv finally; **e~lich!** at last!; **komm e~lich!**
come on!; **e~los** adj endless, infinite;
~spiel nt final(s); **~spurt** m (SPORT) final
spurt; **~station** f terminus; **~ung** f ending
Energie [enɛrˈgiː] f energy; **~bedarf** m
energy requirement; **~los** adj lacking in
energy, weak; **~verbrauch** m energy
consumption; **~versorgung** f supply of
energy; **~wirtschaft** f energy industry
energisch [eˈnɛrgɪʃ] adj energetic
eng [ɛŋ] adj narrow; (Kleidung) tight; (fig:
Horizont) narrow, limited; (Freundschaft,
Verhältnis) close; **~ an etw** dat close to sth
Engagement [ãgaʒəˈmãː] (-s, -s) nt
engagement; (Verpflichtung) commitment
engagieren [ãgaˈʒiːrən] vt to engage ♦ vr to
commit o.s.
Enge [ˈɛŋə] f (auch fig) narrowness;
(Landenge) defile; (Meerenge) straits pl; **jdn
in die ~ treiben** to drive sb into a corner
Engel [ˈɛŋəl] (-s, -) m angel; **e~haft** adj
angelic
England [ˈɛŋlant] nt England;
Engländer(in) m(f) Englishman(-woman);
englisch adj English
Engpass ▲ m defile, pass; (fig, Verkehr)
bottleneck

en gros [ãˈgro] adv wholesale
engstirnig [ˈɛŋʃtɪrnɪç] adj narrow-minded
Enkel [ˈɛŋkəl] (-s, -) m grandson; **~in** f
granddaughter; **~kind** nt grandchild
enorm [eˈnɔrm] adj enormous
Ensemble [ãˈsãbəl] (-s, -s) nt company,
ensemble
entbehr- [ɛntˈbeːr-] zW: **~en** vt to do
without, to dispense with; **~lich** adj
superfluous; **E~ung** f deprivation
entbinden [ɛntˈbɪndən] (unreg) vt (+gen) to
release (from); (MED) to deliver ♦ vi (MED)
to give birth; **Entbindung** f release; (MED)
confinement; **Entbindungsheim** nt
maternity hospital
entdeck- [ɛntˈdɛk] zW: **~en** vt to discover;
E~er (-s, -) m discoverer; **E~ung** f
discovery
Ente [ˈɛntə] f duck; (fig) canard, false report
enteignen [ɛntˈʔaɪɡnən] vt to expropriate;
(Besitzer) to dispossess
enterben [ɛntˈʔɛrbən] vt to disinherit
entfallen [ɛntˈfalən] (unreg) vi to drop, to
fall; (wegfallen) to be dropped; **jdm ~**
(vergessen) to slip sb's memory; **auf jdn ~**
to be allotted to sb
entfalten [ɛntˈfaltən] vt to unfold; (Talente)
to develop ♦ vr to open; (Mensch) to
develop one's potential; **Entfaltung** f
unfolding; (von Talenten) development
entfern- [ɛntˈfɛrn] zW: **~en** vt to remove;
(hinauswerfen) to expel ♦ vr to go away, to
withdraw; **~t** adj distant; **weit davon ~t
sein, etw zu tun** to be far from doing sth;
E~ung f distance; (Wegschaffen) removal
entfremden [ɛntˈfrɛmdən] vt to estrange, to
alienate; **Entfremdung** f alienation,
estrangement
entfrosten [ɛntˈfrɔstən] vt to defrost
Entfroster (-s, -) m (AUT) defroster
entführ- [ɛntˈfyːr] zW: **~en** vt to carry off,
to abduct; to kidnap; **E~er** m kidnapper;
E~ung f abduction; kidnapping
entgegen [ɛntˈgeːgən] präp +dat contrary to,
against ♦ adv towards; **~bringen** (unreg) vt
to bring; **jdm etw ~bringen** (fig) to show
sb sth; **~gehen** (unreg) vi +dat to go to

meet, to go towards; **~gesetzt** *adj* opposite; *(widersprechend)* opposed; **~halten** *(unreg) vt (fig)* to object; **E~kommen** *nt* obligingness; **~kommen** *(unreg) vi +dat* to approach; to meet; *(fig)* to accommodate; **~kommend** *adj* obliging; **~nehmen** *(unreg) vt* to receive, to accept; **~sehen** *(unreg) vi +dat* to await; **~setzen** *vt* to oppose; **~treten** *(unreg) vi +dat* to step up to; *(fig)* to oppose, to counter; **~wirken** *vi +dat* to counteract

entgegnen [ɛnt'geːgnən] *vt* to reply, to retort

entgehen [ɛnt'geːən] *(unreg) vi (fig)*: **jdm ~** to escape sb's notice; **sich** *dat* **etw ~ lassen** to miss sth

Entgelt [ɛnt'gɛlt] **(-(e)s, -e)** *nt* compensation, remuneration

entgleisen [ɛnt'glaɪzən] *vi (EISENB)* to be derailed; *(fig: Person)* to misbehave; **~ lassen** to derail

entgräten [ɛnt'grɛːtən] *vt* to fillet, to bone

Enthaarungscreme [ɛnt'haːrʊŋs-] *f* hair-removing cream

enthalten [ɛnt'haltən] *(unreg) vt* to contain ♦ *vr:* **sich (von etw) ~** to abstain (from sth), to refrain (from sth)

enthaltsam [ɛnt'haltzaːm] *adj* abstinent, abstemious

enthemmen [ɛnt'hɛmən] *vt:* **jdn ~** to free sb from his inhibitions

enthüllen [ɛnt'hʏlən] *vt* to reveal, to unveil

Enthusiasmus [ɛntʊzi'asmʊs] *m* enthusiasm

entkommen [ɛnt'kɔmən] *(unreg) vi:* **~ (aus** *od +dat)* to get away (from), to escape (from)

entkräften [ɛnt'krɛftən] *vt* to weaken, to exhaust; *(Argument)* to refute

entladen [ɛnt'laːdən] *(unreg) vt* to unload; *(ELEK)* to discharge ♦ *vr (ELEK: Gewehr)* to discharge; *(Ärger etc)* to vent itself

entlang [ɛnt'laŋ] *adv* along; **~ dem Fluss, den Fluss ~** along the river; **~gehen** *(unreg) vi* to walk along

entlarven [ɛnt'larfən] *vt* to unmask, to expose

entlassen [ɛnt'lasən] *(unreg) vt* to discharge; *(Arbeiter)* to dismiss; **Entlassung** *f* discharge; dismissal

entlasten [ɛnt'lastən] *vt* to relieve; *(Achse)* to relieve the load on; *(Angeklagten)* to exonerate; *(Konto)* to clear

Entlastung *f* relief; *(COMM)* crediting

Entlastungszug *m* relief train

entlegen [ɛnt'leːgən] *adj* remote

entlocken [ɛnt'lɔkən] *vt:* **(jdm etw) ~** to elicit (sth from sb)

entmutigen [ɛnt'muːtɪgən] *vt* to discourage

entnehmen [ɛnt'neːmən] *(unreg) vt (+dat)* to take out (of), to take (from); *(folgern)* to infer (from)

entreißen [ɛnt'raɪsən] *(unreg) vt:* **jdm etw ~** to snatch sth (away) from sb

entrichten [ɛnt'rɪçtən] *vt* to pay

entrosten [ɛnt'rɔstən] *vt* to remove rust from

entrümpeln [ɛnt'rʏmpəln] *vt* to clear out

entrüst- [ɛnt'rʏst] *zW:* **~en** *vt* to incense, to outrage ♦ *vr* to be filled with indignation; **~et** *adj* indignant, outraged; **E~ung** *f* indignation

entschädigen [ɛnt'ʃɛːdɪgən] *vt* to compensate; **Entschädigung** *f* compensation

entschärfen [ɛnt'ʃɛrfən] *vt* to defuse; *(Kritik)* to tone down

Entscheid [ɛnt'ʃaɪt] **(-(e)s, -e)** *m* decision, **e~en** [-dən] *(unreg) vt, vi, vr* to decide; **e~end** *adj* decisive; *(Stimme)* casting; **~ung** *f* decision

entschieden [ɛnt'ʃiːdən] *adj* decided; *(entschlossen)* resolute; **E~heit** *f* firmness, determination

entschließen [ɛnt'ʃliːsən] *(unreg) vr* to decide

entschlossen [ɛnt'ʃlɔsən] *adj* determined, resolute; **E~heit** *f* determination

Entschluss ▲ [ɛnt'ʃlʊs] *m* decision; **e~freudig** *adj* decisive; **~kraft** *f* determination, decisiveness

entschuldigen [ɛnt'ʃʊldɪgən] *vt* to excuse ♦ *vr* to apologize

Entschuldigung *f* apology; *(Grund)*

excuse; **jdn um ~ bitten** to apologize to sb;
~! excuse me; (*Verzeihung*) sorry
entsetz- [ɛntˈzɛts] *zW:* **~en** *vt* to horrify;
(*MIL*) to relieve ♦ *vr* to be horrified *od*
appalled; **E~en (-s)** *nt* horror, dismay;
~lich *adj* dreadful, appalling; **~t** *adj*
horrified
Entsorgung [ɛntˈzɔrgʊŋ] *f* (*von Kraftwerken,
Chemikalien*) (waste) disposal
entspannen [ɛntˈʃpanən] *vt, vr* (*Körper*) to
relax; (*POL: Lage*) to ease
Entspannung *f* relaxation, rest; (*POL*)
détente; **~spolitik** *f* policy of détente
entsprechen [ɛntˈʃprɛçən] (*unreg*) *vi +dat* to
correspond to; (*Anforderungen, Wünschen*) to
meet, to comply with; **~d** *adj* appropriate
♦ *adv* accordingly
entspringen [ɛntˈʃprɪŋən] (*unreg*) *vi* (+*dat*)
to spring (from)
entstehen [ɛntˈʃteːən] (*unreg*) *vi*: **~ (aus** *od*
durch) to arise (from), to result (from)
Entstehung *f* genesis, origin
entstellen [ɛntˈʃtɛlən] *vt* to disfigure;
(*Wahrheit*) to distort
entstören [ɛntˈʃtøːrən] *vt* (*RADIO*) to
eliminate interference from
enttäuschen [ɛntˈtɔʏʃən] *vt* to disappoint;
Enttäuschung *f* disappointment
entwaffnen [ɛntˈvafnən] *vt* (*lit, fig*) to
disarm
entwässern [ɛntˈvɛsərn] *vt* to drain;
Entwässerung *f* drainage
entweder [ɛntˈveːdɐ] *konj* either
entwenden [ɛntˈvɛndən] (*unreg*) *vt* to
purloin, to steal
entwerfen [ɛntˈvɛrfən] (*unreg*) *vt* (*Zeichnung*)
to sketch; (*Modell*) to design; (*Vortrag,
Gesetz etc*) to draft
entwerten [ɛntˈveːrtən] *vt* to devalue;
(*stempeln*) to cancel
Entwerter (-s, -) *m* ticket punching
machine
entwickeln [ɛntˈvɪkəln] *vt, vr* (*auch PHOT*) to
develop; (*Mut, Energie*) to show (o.s.), to
display (o.s.)
Entwicklung [ɛntˈvɪklʊŋ] *f* development;
(*PHOT*) developing

Entwicklungs- *zW:* **~hilfe** *f* aid for
developing countries; **~land** *nt* developing
country
entwöhnen [ɛntˈvøːnən] *vt* to wean;
(*Süchtige*): **(einer Sache** *dat od* **von etw) ~**
to cure (of sth)
Entwöhnung *f* weaning; cure, curing
entwürdigend [ɛntˈvʏrdɪgənt] *adj*
degrading
Entwurf [ɛntˈvʊrf] *m* outline, design;
(*Vertragsentwurf, Konzept*) draft
entziehen [ɛntˈtsiːən] (*unreg*) *vt* (+*dat*) to
withdraw (from), to take away (from);
(*Flüssigkeit*) to draw (from), to extract
(from) ♦ *vr* (+*dat*) to escape (from); (*jds
Kenntnis*) to be outside *od* beyond; (*der
Pflicht*) to shirk (from)
Entziehung *f* withdrawal; **~sanstalt** *f*
drug addiction/alcoholism treatment
centre; **~skur** *f* treatment for drug
addiction/alcoholism
entziffern [ɛntˈtsɪfərn] *vt* to decipher; to
decode
entzücken [ɛntˈtsʏkən] *vt* to delight; **E~
(-s)** *nt* delight; **~d** *adj* delightful, charming
entzünden [ɛntˈtsʏndən] *vt* to light, to set
light to; (*fig, MED*) to inflame; (*Streit*) to
spark off ♦ *vr* (*auch fig*) to catch fire; (*Streit*)
to start; (*MED*) to become inflamed
Entzündung *f* (*MED*) inflammation
entzwei [ɛntˈtsvai] *adv* broken; in two;
~brechen (*unreg*) *vt, vi* to break in two;
~en *vt* to set at odds ♦ *vr* to fall out;
~gehen (*unreg*) *vi* to break (in two)
Enzian [ˈɛntsiaːn] (**-s, -e**) *m* gentian
Epidemie [epideˈmiː] *f* epidemic
Epilepsie [epileˈpsiː] *f* epilepsy
Episode [epiˈzoːdə] *f* episode
Epoche [eˈpɔxə] *f* epoch; **~ machend**
epoch-making
Epos [ˈeːpɔs] (**-s, Epen**) *nt* epic (poem)
er [eːr] (*nom*) *pron* he; it
erarbeiten [ɛrˈʔarbaitən] *vt* to work for, to
acquire; (*Theorie*) to work out
erbarmen [ɛrˈbarmən] *vr* (+*gen*) to have pity
od mercy (on); **E~ (-s)** *nt* pity
erbärmlich [ɛrˈbɛrmlɪç] *adj* wretched,

pitiful; **E~keit** f wretchedness

erbarmungslos [ɛr'barmʊŋsloːs] adj pitiless, merciless

erbau- [ɛr'baʊl zW: **~en** vt to build, to erect; (fig) to edify; **E~er** (-s, -) m builder; **~lich** adj edifying

Erbe[1] ['ɛrbə] (-n, -n) m heir

Erbe[2] ['ɛrbə] nt inheritance; (fig) heritage

erben vt to inherit

erbeuten [ɛr'bɔʏtən] vt to carry off; (MIL) to capture

Erb- [ɛrb] zW: **~faktor** m gene; **~folge** f (line of) succession; **~in** f heiress

erbittern [ɛr'bɪtərn] vt to embitter; (erzürnen) to incense

erbittert [ɛr'bɪtərt] adj (Kampf) fierce, bitter

erblassen [ɛr'blasən] vi to (turn) pale

erblich ['ɛrplɪç] adj hereditary

erblinden [ɛr'blɪndən] vi to go blind

erbrechen [ɛr'brɛçən] (unreg) vt, vr to vomit

Erbschaft f inheritance, legacy

Erbse ['ɛrpsə] f pea

Erbstück nt heirloom

Erd- ['eːrd] zW: **~achse** f earth's axis; **~atmosphäre** f earth's atmosphere; **~beben** nt earthquake; **~beere** f strawberry; **~boden** m ground; **~e** f earth; **zu ebener ~e** at ground level; **e~en** vt (ELEK) to earth

erdenklich [ɛr'dɛŋklɪç] adj conceivable

Erd- zW: **~gas** nt natural gas; **~geschoss** ▲ nt ground floor; **~kunde** f geography; **~nuss** ▲ f peanut; **~öl** nt (mineral) oil

erdrosseln [ɛr'drɔsəln] vt to strangle, to throttle

erdrücken [ɛr'drʏkən] vt to crush

Erd- zW: **~rutsch** m landslide; **~teil** m continent

erdulden [ɛr'dʊldən] vt to endure, to suffer

ereignen [ɛr'|aɪɡnən] vr to happen

Ereignis [ɛr'|aɪɡnɪs] (-ses, -se) nt event; **e~los** adj uneventful; **e~reich** adj eventful

ererbt [ɛr'|ɛrpt] adj (Haus) inherited; (Krankheit) hereditary

erfahren [ɛr'faːrən] (unreg) vt to learn, to find out; (erleben) to experience ♦ adj experienced

Erfahrung f experience; **e~sgemäß** adv according to experience

erfassen [ɛr'fasən] vt to seize; (fig: einbeziehen) to include, to register; (verstehen) to grasp

erfind- [ɛr'fɪnd] zW: **~en** (unreg) vt to invent; **E~er** (-s, -) m inventor; **~erisch** adj inventive; **E~ung** f invention

Erfolg [ɛr'fɔlk] (-(e)s, -e) m success; (Folge) result; **~ versprechend** promising; **e~en** [-ɡən] vi to follow; (sich ergeben) to result; (stattfinden) to take place; (Zahlung) to be effected; **e~los** adj unsuccessful; **~losigkeit** f lack of success; **e~reich** adj successful

erforderlich adj requisite, necessary

erfordern [ɛr'fɔrdərn] vt to require, to demand

erforschen [ɛr'fɔrʃən] vt (Land) to explore; (Problem) to investigate; (Gewissen) to search; **Erforschung** f exploration; investigation; searching

erfreuen [ɛr'frɔʏən] vr: **sich ~ an** +dat to enjoy ♦ vt to delight; **sich einer Sache** gen **~** to enjoy sth

erfreulich [ɛr'frɔʏlɪç] adj pleasing, gratifying; **~erweise** adv happily, luckily

erfrieren [ɛr'friːrən] (unreg) vi to freeze (to death); (Glieder) to get frostbitten; (Pflanzen) to be killed by frost

erfrischen [ɛr'frɪʃən] vt to refresh; **Erfrischung** f refreshment

Erfrischungs- zW: **~getränk** nt (liquid) refreshment; **~raum** m snack bar, cafeteria

erfüllen [ɛr'fʏlən] vt (Raum etc) to fill; (fig: Bitte etc) to fulfil ♦ vr to come true

ergänzen [ɛr'ɡɛntsən] vt to supplement, to complete ♦ vr to complement one another; **Ergänzung** f completion; (Zusatz) supplement

ergeben [ɛr'ɡeːbən] (unreg) vt to yield, to produce ♦ vr to surrender; (folgen) to result ♦ adj devoted, humble

Ergebnis [ɛr'ɡeːpnɪs] (-ses, -se) nt result; **e~los** adj without result, fruitless

ergehen [ɛr'ɡeːən] (unreg) vi to be issued, to go out ♦ vi unpers: **es ergeht ihm gut /**

Spelling Reform: ▲ *new spelling* △ *old spelling (to be phased out)*

schlecht he's faring *od* getting on well/badly ♦ *vr*: **sich in etw** *dat* ~ to indulge in sth; **etw über sich ~ lassen** to put up with sth

ergiebig [ɛrˈgiːbɪç] *adj* productive

Ergonomie [ɛrgonoˈmiː] *f* ergonomics *sg*

Ergonomik [ɛrgoˈnoːmɪk] *f* = **Ergonomie**

ergreifen [ɛrˈgraɪfən] (*unreg*) *vt* (*auch fig*) to seize; (*Beruf*) to take up; (*Maßnahmen*) to resort to; (*rühren*) to move; **~d** *adj* moving, touching

ergriffen [ɛrˈgrɪfən] *adj* deeply moved

Erguss ▲ [ɛrˈgʊs] *m* discharge; (*fig*) outpouring, effusion

erhaben [ɛrˈhaːbən] *adj* raised, embossed; (*fig*) exalted, lofty; **über etw** *akk* ~ **sein** to be above sth

erhalten [ɛrˈhaltən] (*unreg*) *vt* to receive; (*bewahren*) to preserve, to maintain; **gut ~** in good condition

erhältlich [ɛrˈhɛltlɪç] *adj* obtainable, available

Erhaltung *f* maintenance, preservation

erhärten [ɛrˈhɛrtən] *vt* to harden; (*These*) to substantiate, to corroborate

erheben [ɛrˈheːbən] (*unreg*) *vt* to raise; (*Protest, Forderungen*) to make; (*Fakten*) to ascertain, to establish ♦ *vr* to rise (up)

erheblich [ɛrˈheːplɪç] *adj* considerable

erheitern [ɛrˈhaɪtərn] *vt* to amuse, to cheer (up)

Erheiterung *f* exhilaration; **zur allgemeinen ~** to everybody's amusement

erhitzen [ɛrˈhɪtsən] *vt* to heat ♦ *vr* to heat up; (*fig*) to become heated

erhoffen [ɛrˈhɔfən] *vt* to hope for

erhöhen [ɛrˈhøːən] *vt* to raise; (*verstärken*) to increase

erhol- [ɛrˈhoːl] *zW*: **~en** *vr* to recover; (*entspannen*) to have a rest; **~sam** *adj* restful; **E~ung** *f* recovery; relaxation, rest; **~ungsbedürftig** *adj* in need of a rest, run-down; **E~ungsgebiet** *nt* ≈ holiday area; **E~ungsheim** *nt* convalescent home

erhören [ɛrˈhøːrən] *vt* (*Gebet etc*) to hear; (*Bitte etc*) to yield to

erinnern [ɛrˈ|ɪnərn] *vt*: **~ (an** +*akk*) to

remind (of) ♦ *vr*: **sich (an** *akk* **etw)** ~ to remember (sth)

Erinnerung *f* memory; (*Andenken*) reminder

erkältet [ɛrˈkɛltət] *adj* with a cold; ~ **sein** to have a cold

Erkältung *f* cold

erkennbar *adj* recognizable

erkennen [ɛrˈkɛnən] (*unreg*) *vt* to recognize; (*sehen, verstehen*) to see

erkennt- *zW*: **~lich** *adj*: **sich ~lich zeigen** to show one's appreciation; **E~lichkeit** *f* gratitude; (*Geschenk*) token of one's gratitude; **E~nis** (-, -se) *f* knowledge; (*das Erkennen*) recognition; (*Einsicht*) insight; **zur E~nis kommen** to realize

Erkennung *f* recognition

Erkennungszeichen *nt* identification

Erker [ˈɛrkər] (-s, -) *m* bay

erklär- [ɛrˈklɛːr] *zW*: **~bar** *adj* explicable; **~en** *vt* to explain; **~lich** *adj* explicable; (*verständlich*) understandable; **E~ung** *f* explanation; (*Aussage*) declaration

erkranken [ɛrˈkraŋkən] *vi* to fall ill; **Erkrankung** *f* illness

erkund- [ɛrˈkʊnd] *zW*: **~en** *vt* to find out, to ascertain; (*bes MIL*) to reconnoitre, to scout; **~igen** *vr*: **sich ~igen (nach)** to inquire (about); **E~igung** *f* inquiry; **E~ung** *f* reconnaissance, scouting

erlahmen [ɛrˈlaːmən] *vi* to tire; (*nachlassen*) to flag, to wane

erlangen [ɛrˈlaŋən] *vt* to attain, to achieve

Erlass ▲ [ɛrˈlas] (-es, ⁻e) *m* decree; (*Aufhebung*) remission

erlassen (*unreg*) *vt* (*Verfügung*) to issue; (*Gesetz*) to enact; (*Strafe*) to remit; **jdm etw** ~ to release sb from sth

erlauben [ɛrˈlaʊbən] *vt*: **(jdm etw)** ~ to allow *od* permit (sb (to do) sth) ♦ *vr* to permit o.s., to venture

Erlaubnis [ɛrˈlaʊpnɪs] (-, -se) *f* permission; (*Schriftstück*) permit

erläutern [ɛrˈlɔytərn] *vt* to explain; **Erläuterung** *f* explanation

erleben [ɛrˈleːbən] *vt* to experience; (*Zeit*) to live through; (*miterleben*) to witness; (*noch* *miterleben*) to live to see

Erlebnis [ɛr'leːpnɪs] **(-ses, -se)** *nt* experience

erledigen [ɛr'leːdɪɡən] *vt* to take care of, to deal with; (*Antrag etc*) to process; (*umg: erschöpfen*) to wear out; (: *ruinieren*) to finish; (: *umbringen*) to do in

erleichtern [ɛr'laɪçtərn] *vt* to make easier; (*fig: Last*) to lighten; (*lindern, beruhigen*) to relieve; **Erleichterung** *f* facilitation; lightening; relief

erleiden [ɛr'laɪdən] (*unreg*) *vt* to suffer, to endure

erlernen [ɛr'lɛrnən] *vt* to learn, to acquire

erlesen [ɛr'leːzən] *adj* select, choice

erleuchten [ɛr'lɔʏçtən] *vt* to illuminate; (*fig*) to inspire

Erleuchtung *f* (*Einfall*) inspiration

Erlös [ɛr'løːs] **(-es, -e)** *m* proceeds *pl*

erlösen [ɛr'løːzən] *vt* to redeem, to save; **Erlösung** *f* release; (*REL*) redemption

ermächtigen [ɛr'mɛçtɪɡən] *vt* to authorize, to empower; **Ermächtigung** *f* authorization; authority

ermahnen [ɛr'maːnən] *vt* to exhort, to admonish; **Ermahnung** *f* admonition, exhortation

ermäßigen [ɛr'mɛsɪɡən] *vt* to reduce; **Ermäßigung** *f* reduction

ermessen [ɛr'mɛsən] (*unreg*) *vt* to estimate, to gauge; **E~ (-s)** *nt* estimation; discretion; **in jds E~ liegen** to lie within sb's discretion

ermitteln [ɛr'mɪtəln] *vt* to determine; (*Täter*) to trace ♦ *vi*: **gegen jdn ~** to investigate sb

Ermittlung [ɛr'mɪtlʊŋ] *f* determination; (*Polizeiermittlung*) investigation

ermöglichen [ɛr'møːklɪçən] *vt* (*+dat*) to make possible (for)

ermorden [ɛr'mɔrdən] *vt* to murder

ermüden [ɛr'myːdən] *vt, vi* to tire; (*TECH*) to fatigue; **~d** *adj* tiring; (*fig*) wearisome

Ermüdung *f* fatigue

ermutigen [ɛr'muːtɪɡən] *vt* to encourage

ernähr- [ɛr'nɛːr] *zW:* **~en** *vt* to feed, to nourish; (*Familie*) to support ♦ *vr* to support o.s., to earn a living; **sich ~en von** to live

on; **E~er (-s, -)** *m* breadwinner; **E~ung** *f* nourishment; nutrition; (*Unterhalt*) maintenance

ernennen [ɛr'nɛnən] (*unreg*) *vt* to appoint; **Ernennung** *f* appointment

erneu- [ɛr'nɔʏ] *zW:* **~ern** *vt* to renew; to restore; to renovate; **E~erung** *f* renewal; restoration; renovation; **~t** *adj* renewed, fresh ♦ *adv* once more

ernst [ɛrnst] *adj* serious; **~ gemeint** meant in earnest, serious; **E~ (-es)** *m* seriousness; **das ist mein E~** I'm quite serious; **im E~** in earnest; **E~ machen mit etw** to put sth into practice; **E~fall** *m* emergency; **~haft** *adj* serious; **E~haftigkeit** *f* seriousness; **~lich** *adj* serious

Ernte ['ɛrntə] *f* harvest; **e~n** *vt* to harvest; (*Lob etc*) to earn

ernüchtern [ɛr'nʏçtərn] *vt* to sober up; (*fig*) to bring down to earth

Erober- [ɛr'|oːbər] *zW:* **~er (-s, -)** *m* conqueror; **e~n** *vt* to conquer; **~ung** *f* conquest

eröffnen [ɛr'|œfnən] *vt* to open ♦ *vr* to present itself; **jdm etw ~** to disclose sth to sb

Eröffnung *f* opening

erörtern [ɛr'|œrtərn] *vt* to discuss

Erotik [e'roːtɪk] *f* eroticism; **erotisch** *adj* erotic

erpress- [ɛr'prɛs] *zW:* **~en** *vt* (*Geld etc*) to extort; (*Mensch*) to blackmail; **E~er (-s, -)** *m* blackmailer; **E~ung** *f* extortion; blackmail

erprobt [ɛr'proːpt] *adj* (*Gerät, Medikamente*) proven, tested

erraten [ɛr'raːtən] (*unreg*) *vt* to guess

erreg- [ɛr'reːg] *zW:* **~en** *vt* to excite; (*ärgern*) to infuriate; (*hervorrufen*) to arouse, to provoke ♦ *vr* to get excited *od* worked up; **E~er (-s, -)** *m* causative agent; **E~ung** *f* excitement

erreichbar *adj* accessible, within reach

erreichen [ɛr'raɪçən] *vt* to reach; (*Zweck*) to achieve; (*Zug*) to catch

errichten [ɛr'rɪçtən] *vt* to erect, to put up; (*gründen*) to establish, to set up

Spelling Reform: ▲ *new spelling* △ *old spelling (to be phased out)*

erringen [ɛrˈrɪŋən] (*unreg*) *vt* to gain, to win

erröten [ɛrˈrøːtən] *vi* to blush, to flush

Errungenschaft [ɛrˈrʊŋənʃaft] *f* achievement; (*umg*: *Anschaffung*) acquisition

Ersatz [ɛrˈzats] (**-es**) *m* substitute; replacement; (*Schadenersatz*) compensation; (*MIL*) reinforcements *pl*; **~dienst** *m* (*MIL*) alternative service; **~reifen** *m* (*AUT*) spare tyre; **~teil** *nt* spare (part)

erschaffen [ɛrˈʃafən] (*unreg*) *vt* to create

erscheinen [ɛrˈʃaɪnən] (*unreg*) *vi* to appear; **Erscheinung** *f* appearance; (*Geist*) apparition; (*Gegebenheit*) phenomenon; (*Gestalt*) figure

erschießen [ɛrˈʃiːsən] (*unreg*) *vt* to shoot (dead)

erschlagen [ɛrˈʃlaːgən] (*unreg*) *vt* to strike dead

erschöpf- [ɛrˈʃœpf] *zW*: **~en** *vt* to exhaust; **~end** *adj* exhaustive, thorough; **E~ung** *f* exhaustion

erschrecken [ɛrˈʃrɛkən] *vt* to startle, to frighten ♦ *vi* to be frightened *od* startled; **~d** *adj* alarming, frightening

erschrocken [ɛrˈʃrɔkən] *adj* frightened, startled

erschüttern [ɛrˈʃʏtərn] *vt* to shake; (*fig*) to move deeply; **Erschütterung** *f* shaking; shock

erschweren [ɛrˈʃveːrən] *vt* to complicate

erschwinglich *adj* within one's means

ersetzen [ɛrˈzɛtsən] *vt* to replace; **jdm Unkosten** *etc* **~** to pay sb's expenses *etc*

ersichtlich [ɛrˈzɪçtlɪç] *adj* evident, obvious

ersparen [ɛrˈʃpaːrən] *vt* (*Ärger etc*) to spare; (*Geld*) to save

Ersparnis (**-, -se**) *f* saving

SCHLÜSSELWORT

erst [eːrst] *adv* **1** first; **mach erst mal die Arbeit fertig** finish your work first; **wenn du das erst mal hinter dir hast** once you've got that behind you

2 (*nicht früher als, nur*) only; (*nicht bis*) not till; **erst gestern** only yesterday; **erst morgen** not until tomorrow; **erst als** only when, not until; **wir fahren erst später**

we're not going until later; **er ist (gerade) erst angekommen** he's only just arrived

3: **wäre er doch erst zurück!** if only he were back!

---

erstatten [ɛrˈʃtatən] *vt* (*Kosten*) to (re)pay; **Anzeige** *etc* **gegen jdn ~** to report sb; **Bericht ~** to make a report

Erstattung *f* (*von Kosten*) refund

Erstaufführung [ˈeːrstˌʔaʊffyːrʊŋ] *f* first performance

erstaunen [ɛrˈʃtaʊnən] *vt* to astonish ♦ *vi* to be astonished; **E~** (**-s**) *nt* astonishment

erstaunlich *adj* astonishing

erst- [ˈeːrst] *zW*: **E~ausgabe** *f* first edition; **~beste(r, s)** *adj* first that comes along; **~e(r, s)** *adj* first

erstechen [ɛrˈʃtɛçən] (*unreg*) *vt* to stab (to death)

erstehen [ɛrˈʃteːən] (*unreg*) *vt* to buy ♦ *vi* to (a)rise

erstens [ˈeːrstəns] *adv* firstly, in the first place

ersticken [ɛrˈʃtɪkən] *vt* (*auch fig*) to stifle; (*Mensch*) to suffocate; (*Flammen*) to smother ♦ *vi* (*Mensch*) to suffocate; (*Feuer*) to be smothered; **in Arbeit ~** to be snowed under with work

erst- *zW*: **~klassig** *adj* first-class; **~malig** *adj* first; **~mals** *adv* for the first time

erstrebenswert [ɛrˈʃtreːbənsveːrt] *adj* desirable, worthwhile

erstrecken [ɛrˈʃtrɛkən] *vr* to extend, to stretch

ersuchen [ɛrˈzuːxən] *vt* to request

ertappen [ɛrˈtapən] *vt* to catch, to detect

erteilen [ɛrˈtaɪlən] *vt* to give

Ertrag [ɛrˈtraːk] (**-(e)s, ⁻e**) *m* yield; (*Gewinn*) proceeds *pl*

ertragen [ɛrˈtraːgən] (*unreg*) *vt* to bear, to stand

erträglich [ɛrˈtrɛːklɪç] *adj* tolerable, bearable

ertrinken [ɛrˈtrɪŋkən] (*unreg*) *vi* to drown; **E~** (**-s**) *nt* drowning

erübrigen [ɛrˈʔyːbrɪgən] *vt* to spare ♦ *vr* to be unnecessary

erwachen [ɛrˈvaxən] *vi* to awake

Rechtschreibreform: ▲ *neue Schreibung* △ *alte Schreibung (auslaufend)*

erwachsen [ɛr'vaksən] *adj* grown-up; **E~e(r)** *f(m)* adult; **E~enbildung** *f* adult education

erwägen [ɛr'vɛːgən] (*unreg*) *vt* to consider; **Erwägung** *f* consideration

erwähn- [ɛr'vɛːn] *zW*: **~en** *vt* to mention; **~enswert** *adj* worth mentioning; **E~ung** *f* mention

erwärmen [ɛr'vɛrmən] *vt* to warm, to heat ♦ *vr* to get warm, to warm up; **sich ~ für** to warm to

Erwarten *nt*: **über meinen/unseren** *usw* ~ beyond my/our *etc* expectations; **wider ~** contrary to expectations

erwarten [ɛr'vartən] *vt* to expect; (*warten auf*) to wait for; **etw kaum ~ können** to be hardly able to wait for sth

Erwartung *f* expectation

erwartungsgemäß *adv* as expected

erwartungsvoll *adj* expectant

erwecken [ɛr'vɛkən] *vt* to rouse, to awake; **den Anschein ~** to give the impression

Erweis [ɛr'vais] (**-es, -e**) *m* proof; **e~en** (*unreg*) *vt* to prove ♦ *vr*: **sich e~en (als)** to prove (to be); **jdm einen Gefallen/Dienst e~en** to do sb a favour/service

Erwerb [ɛr'vɛrp] (**-(e)s, -e**) *m* acquisition; (*Beruf*) trade; **e~en** [-bən] (*unreg*) *vt* to acquire

erwerbs- *zW*: **~los** *adj* unemployed; **E~quelle** *f* source of income; **~tätig** *adj* (gainfully) employed

erwidern [ɛr'viːdərn] *vt* to reply; (*vergelten*) to return

erwischen [ɛr'vɪʃən] (*umg*) *vt* to catch, to get

erwünscht [ɛr'vʏnʃt] *adj* desired

erwürgen [ɛr'vʏrgən] *vt* to strangle

Erz [ɛːrts] (**-es, -e**) *nt* ore

erzähl- [ɛr'tsɛːl] *zW*: **~en** *vt* to tell ♦ *vi*: **sie kann gut ~en** she's a good story-teller; **E~er (-s, -)** *m* narrator; **E~ung** *f* story, tale

Erzbischof *m* archbishop

erzeug- [ɛr'tsɔyg] *zW*: **~en** *vt* to produce; (*Strom*) to generate; **E~nis (-ses, -se)** *nt* product, produce; **E~ung** *f* production; generation

erziehen [ɛr'tsiːən] (*unreg*) *vt* to bring up; (*bilden*) to educate, to train; **Erzieher(in) (-s, -)** *m(f)* (*Berufsbezeichnung*) teacher; **Erziehung** *f* bringing up; (*Bildung*) education; **Erziehungsbeihilfe** *f* educational grant; **Erziehungsberechtigte(r)** *f(m)* parent; guardian

erzielen [ɛr'tsiːlən] *vt* to achieve, to obtain; (*Tor*) to score

erzwingen [ɛr'tsvɪŋən] (*unreg*) *vt* to force, to obtain by force

es [ɛs] (*nom, akk*) *pron* it

Esel ['eːzəl] (**-s, -**) *m* donkey, ass

Eskalation [ɛskalatsi'oːn] *f* escalation

ess- ▲ ['ɛs] *zW*: **~bar** ['ɛsbaːr] *adj* eatable, edible; **E~besteck** *nt* knife, fork and spoon; **E~ecke** *f* dining area

essen ['ɛsən] (*unreg*) *vt, vi* to eat; **E~ (-s, -)** *nt* meal; food

Essig ['ɛsɪç] (**-s, -e**) *m* vinegar

Ess- ▲ *zW*: **~kastanie** *f* sweet chestnut; **~löffel** *m* tablespoon; **~tisch** *m* dining table; **~waren** *pl* foodstuffs, provisions; **~zimmer** *nt* dining room

etablieren [eta'bliːrən] *vr* to become established; to set up in business

Etage [e'taːʒə] *f* floor, storey; **~nbetten** *pl* bunk beds; **~nwohnung** *f* flat

Etappe [e'tapə] *f* stage

Etat [e'taː] (**-s, -s**) *m* budget

etc *abk* (= *et cetera*) etc

Ethik ['eːtɪk] *f* ethics *sg*; **ethisch** *adj* ethical

Etikett [eti'kɛt] (**-(e)s, -e**) *nt* label; tag; **~e** *f* etiquette, manners *pl*

etliche ['ɛtlɪçə] *pron pl* some, quite a few; **~s** *pron* a thing or two

Etui [ɛt'viː] (**-s, -s**) *nt* case

etwa ['ɛtva] *adv* (*ungefähr*) about; (*vielleicht*) perhaps; (*beispielsweise*) for instance; **nicht ~** by no means; **~ig** ['ɛtvaɪç] *adj* possible

etwas *pron* something; anything; (*ein wenig*) a little ♦ *adv* a little

euch [ɔyç] *pron* (*akk von* **ihr**) you; yourselves; (*dat von* **ihr**) (to) you

euer ['ɔyər] *pron* (*gen von* **ihr**) of you ♦ *adj* your

Spelling Reform: ▲ *new spelling* △ *old spelling (to be phased out)*

Eule ['ɔylə] f owl

eure ['ɔyrə] adj f siehe **euer**

eure(r, s) ['ɔyrə(r, s)] pron yours; **~rseits**
adv on your part; **~s** adj nt siehe **euer**;
~sgleichen pron people like you;
~twegen adv (für euch) for your sakes;
(wegen euch) on your account; **~twillen**
adv: um **~twillen = euretwegen**

eurige ['ɔyrɪgə] pron: **der/die/das ~** od **E~**
yours

Euro ['ɔyro:] m (-, -s) m (FIN) euro

Euro- zW: **~pa** [ɔy'ro:pa] nt Europe;
~päer(in) [ɔyro'pɛːər(ɪn)] m(f) European;
e~päisch adj European; **~pameister**
[ɔy'ro:pə-] m European champion;
~paparlament nt European Parliament;
~scheck m (FIN) eurocheque

Euter ['ɔytər] (-s, -) nt udder

ev. abk = **evangelisch**

evakuieren [evaku'iːrən] vt to evacuate

evangelisch [evaŋ'geːlɪʃ] adj Protestant

Evangelium [evaŋ'geːliʊm] nt gospel

eventuell [eventu'ɛl] adj possible ♦ adv
possibly, perhaps

evtl. abk = **eventuell**

EWG [eːveː'geː] (-) f abk (= Europäische
Wirtschaftsgemeinschaft) EEC, Common
Market

ewig ['eːvɪç] adj eternal; **E~keit** f eternity

EWU [eːveː'uː] f abk (= Europäische
Währungsunion) EMU

exakt [ɛ'ksakt] adj exact

Examen [ɛ'ksaːmən] (-s, - od **Examina**) nt
examination

Exemplar [ɛksɛm'plaːr] (-s, -e) nt specimen;
(Buchexemplar) copy; **e~isch** adj exemplary

Exil [ɛ'ksiːl] (-s, -e) nt exile

Existenz [ɛksɪs'tɛnts] f existence; (Unterhalt)
livelihood, living; (pej: Mensch) character;
~minimum (-s) nt subsistence level

existieren [ɛksɪs'tiːrən] vi to exist

exklusiv [ɛksklu'ziːf] adj exclusive; **~e** adv
exclusive of, not including ♦ präp +gen
exclusive of, not including

exotisch [ɛ'ksoːtɪʃ] adj exotic

Expedition [ɛkspeditsi'oːn] f expedition

Experiment [ɛksperi'mɛnt] nt experiment;

e~ell [-'tɛl] adj experimental; **e~ieren**
[-'tiːrən] vi to experiment

Experte [ɛks'pɛrtə] (-n, -n) m expert,
specialist; **Expertin** f expert, specialist

explo- [ɛksplo] zW: **~dieren** [-'diːrən] vi to
explode; **E~sion** [-zi'oːn] f explosion; **~siv**
[-'ziːf] adj explosive

Export [ɛks'pɔrt] (-(e)s, -e) m export; **~eur**
[-'tøːr] m exporter; **~handel** m export
trade; **e~ieren** [-'tiːrən] vt to export; **~land**
nt exporting country

Express- ▲ [ɛks'prɛs] zW: **~gut** nt express
goods pl, express freight; **~zug** m express
(train)

extra ['ɛkstra] adj inv (umg: gesondert)
separate; (besondere) extra ♦ adv (gesondert)
separately; (speziell) specially; (absichtlich)
on purpose; (vor Adjektiven, zusätzlich)
specially; **E~** (-s, -s) nt extra; **E~ausgabe** f special
edition; **E~blatt** nt special edition

Extrakt [ɛks'trakt] (-(e)s, -e) m extract

extravagant [ɛkstrava'gant] adj extravagant

extrem [ɛks'treːm] adj extreme; **~istisch**
[-'mɪstɪʃ] adj (POL) extremist; **E~itäten**
[-mi'tɛːtən] pl extremities

exzentrisch [ɛks'tsɛntrɪʃ] adj eccentric

EZ nt abk = **Einzelzimmer**

EZB f abk (= Europäische Zentralbank) ECB

F, f

Fa. abk (= Firma) firm; (in Briefen) Messrs

Fabel ['faːbəl] (-, -n) f fable; **f~haft** adj
fabulous, marvellous

Fabrik [fa'briːk] f factory; **~ant** [-'kant] m
(Hersteller) manufacturer; (Besitzer)
industrialist; **~arbeiter** m factory worker;
~at [-'kaːt] (-(e)s, -e) nt manufacture,
product; **~gelände** nt factory site

Fach [fax] (-(e)s, "er) nt compartment;
(Sachgebiet) subject; **ein Mann vom ~** an
expert; **~arbeiter** m skilled worker; **~arzt**
m (medical) specialist; **~ausdruck** m
technical term

Fächer ['fɛçər] (-s, -) m fan

Fach- zW: **~geschäft** nt specialist shop;

~**hochschule** f technical college; ~**kraft** f skilled worker, trained employee; **f~kundig** adj expert, specialist; **f~lich** adj professional; expert; ~**mann** (pl -**leute**) m specialist; **f~männisch** adj professional; ~**schule** f technical college; **f~simpeln** vi to talk shop; ~**werk** nt timber frame

Fackel ['fakəl] (-, -n) f torch

fad(e) [faːt, 'faːdə] adj insipid; (langweilig) dull

Faden ['faːdən] (-s, ˮ) m thread; **f~scheinig** adj (auch fig) threadbare

fähig ['fɛːɪç] adj: ~ (**zu** od +gen) capable (of); able (to); **F~keit** f ability

fahnden ['faːndən] vi: ~ **nach** to search for; **Fahndung** f search

Fahndungsliste f list of wanted criminals, wanted list

Fahne ['faːnə] f flag, standard; **eine ~ haben** (umg) to smell of drink; ~**nflucht** f desertion

Fahr- zW: ~**ausweis** m ticket; ~**bahn** f carriageway (BRIT), roadway

Fähre ['fɛːrə] f ferry

fahren ['faːrən] (unreg) vt to drive; (Rad) to ride; (befördern) to drive, to take; (Rennen) to drive in ♦ vi (sich bewegen) to go; (Schiff) to sail; (abfahren) to leave; **mit dem Auto/Zug ~** to go od travel by car/train; **mit der Hand ~ über** +akk to pass one's hand over

Fahr- zW: ~**er(in)** (-s, -) m(f) driver; ~**erflucht** f hit-and-run; ~**gast** m passenger; ~**geld** nt fare; ~**karte** f ticket; ~**kartenausgabe** f ticket office; ~**kartenautomat** m ticket machine; ~**kartenschalter** m ticket office; **f~lässig** adj negligent; **f~lässige Tötung** manslaughter; ~**lehrer** m driving instructor; ~**plan** m timetable; **f~planmäßig** adj scheduled; ~**preis** m fare; ~**prüfung** f driving test; ~**rad** nt bicycle; ~**radweg** m cycle lane; ~**schein** m ticket; ~**scheinentwerter** m (automatic) ticket stamping machine

Fährschiff ['fɛːrʃɪf] nt ferry(boat)

Fahr- zW: ~**schule** f driving school; ~**spur** f lane; ~**stuhl** m lift (BRIT), elevator (US)

Fahrt [faːrt] (-, -en) f journey; (kurz) trip; (AUT) drive; (Geschwindigkeit) speed; **gute ~!** have a good journey

Fährte ['fɛːrtə] f track, trail

Fahrt- zW: ~**kosten** pl travelling expenses; ~**richtung** f course, direction

Fahrzeit f time for the journey

Fahrzeug nt vehicle; ~**brief** m log book; ~**papiere** pl vehicle documents

fair [fɛːr] adj fair

Fakt [fakt] (-(e)s, -en) m fact

Faktor ['faktɔr] m factor

Fakultät [fakʊl'tɛːt] f faculty

Falke ['falkə] (-n, -n) m falcon

Fall [fal] (-(e)s, ˮe) m (Sturz) fall; (Sachverhalt, JUR, GRAM) case; **auf jeden ~**, **auf alle Fälle** in any case; (bestimmt) definitely; **auf keinen ~!** no way!

Falle f trap

fallen (unreg) vi to fall; **etw ~ lassen** to drop sth; (Bemerkung) to make sth; (Plan) to abandon sth, to drop sth

fällen ['fɛlən] vt (Baum) to fell; (Urteil) to pass

fällig ['fɛlɪç] adj due

falls [fals] adv in case, if

Fallschirm m parachute; ~**springer** m parachutist

falsch [falʃ] adj false; (unrichtig) wrong

fälschen ['fɛlʃən] vt to forge

fälsch- zW: ~**lich** adj false; ~**licherweise** adv mistakenly; **F~ung** f forgery

Falte ['faltə] f (Knick) fold, crease; (Hautfalte) wrinkle; (Rockfalte) pleat; **f~n** vt to fold; (Stirn) to wrinkle

faltig ['faltɪç] adj (Hände, Haut) wrinkled; (zerknittert: Rock) creased

familiär [famili'ɛːr] adj familiar

Familie [fa'miːliə] f family

Familien- zW: ~**betrieb** m family business; ~**kreis** m family circle; ~**mitglied** nt member of the family; ~**name** m surname; ~**stand** m marital status

Fanatiker [fa'naːtikər] (-s, -) m fanatic; **fanatisch** adj fanatical

fand etc [fant] vb siehe **finden**

Fang [faŋ] (-(e)s, ˮe) m catch; (Jagen) hunting; (Kralle) talon, claw; **f~en** (unreg) vt to catch ♦ vr to get caught; (Flugzeug) to level out; (*Mensch: nicht fallen*) to steady o.s.; (*fig*) to compose o.s.; (*in Leistung*) to get back on form

Fantasie ▲ [fanta'ziː] *f* imagination; **f~los** *adj* unimaginative; **f~ren** *vi* to fantasize; **f~voll** *adj* imaginative

fantastisch ▲ [fan'tastɪʃ] *adj* fantastic

Farb- ['farb] *zW:* **~abzug** *m* colour print; **~aufnahme** *f* colour photograph; **~band** *m* typewriter ribbon; **~e** *f* colour; (*zum Malen etc*) paint; (*Stoffarbe*) dye; **f~echt** *adj* colourfast

färben ['fɛrbən] *vt* to colour; (*Stoff, Haar*) to dye

farben- ['farbən] *zW:* **~blind** *adj* colour-blind; **~freudig** *adj* colourful; **~froh** *adj* colourful, gay

Farb- *zW:* **~fernsehen** *nt* colour television; **~film** *m* colour film; **~foto** *nt* colour photograph; **f~ig** *adj* coloured; **~ige(r)** *f(m)* coloured (person); **~kasten** *m* paintbox; **f~lich** *adj* colour; **f~los** *adj* colourless; **~stift** *m* coloured pencil; **~stoff** *m* dye; **~ton** *m* hue, tone

Färbung ['fɛrbʊŋ] *f* colouring; (*Tendenz*) bias

Farn [farn] *(-(e)s, -e)* *m* fern; bracken

Fasan [fa'zaːn] *(-(e)s, -e(n))* *m* pheasant

Fasching ['faʃɪŋ] *(-s, -e od -s)* *m* carnival

Faschismus [fa'ʃɪsmʊs] *m* fascism

Faschist *m* fascist

Faser ['faːzər] *(-, -n)* *f* fibre; **f~n** *vi* to fray

Fass ▲ [fas] *(-es, ᵘer)* *nt* vat, barrel; (*für Öl*) drum; **Bier vom ~** draught beer

Fassade [fa'saːdə] *f* façade

fassen ['fasən] *vt* (*ergreifen*) to grasp, to take; (*inhaltlich*) to hold; (*Entschluss etc*) to take; (*verstehen*) to understand; (*Ring etc*) to set; (*formulieren*) to formulate, to phrase ♦ *vr* to calm down; **nicht zu ~** unbelievable

Fassung ['fasʊŋ] *f* (*Umrahmung*) mounting; (*Lampenfassung*) socket; (*Wortlaut*) version; (*Beherrschung*) composure; **jdn aus der ~ bringen** to upset sb; **f~slos** *adj* speechless

fast [fast] *adv* almost, nearly

fasten ['fastən] *vi* to fast; **F~zeit** *f* Lent

Fastnacht *f* Shrove Tuesday; carnival

faszinieren [fastsi'niːrən] *vt* to fascinate

fatal [fa'taːl] *adj* fatal; (*peinlich*) embarrassing

faul [faul] *adj* rotten; (*Person*) lazy; (*Ausreden*) lame; **daran ist etwas ~** there's something fishy about it; **~en** *vi* to rot; **~enzen** *vi* to idle; **F~enzer** *(-s, -)* *m* idler, loafer; **F~heit** *f* laziness; **~ig** *adj* putrid

Faust [faust] *(-, Fäuste)* *f* fist; **auf eigene ~** off one's own bat; **~handschuh** *m* mitten

Favorit [favo'riːt] *(-en, -en)* *m* favourite

Fax [faks] *(-, -(e))* *nt* fax

faxen ['faksən] *vt* to fax; **jdm etw ~** to fax sth to sb

FCKW *m abk* (= *Fluorchlorkohlenwasserstoff*) CFC

Februar ['feːbruaːr] *(-(s), -e)* *m* February

fechten ['fɛçtən] *(unreg)* *vi* to fence

Feder ['feːdər] *(-, -n)* *f* feather; (*Schreibfeder*) pen nib; (*TECH*) spring; **~ball** *m* shuttlecock; **~bett** *nt* continental quilt; **~halter** *m* penholder, pen; **f~leicht** *adj* light as a feather; **f~n** *vi* (*nachgeben*) to be springy; (*sich bewegen*) to bounce ♦ *vt* to spring; **~ung** *f* (*AUT*) suspension

Fee [feː] *f* fairy

fegen ['feːgən] *vt* to sweep

fehl [feːl] *adj:* **~ am Platz** *od* **Ort** out of place; **F~betrag** *m* deficit; **~en** *vi* to be wanting *od* missing; (*abwesend sein*) to be absent; **etw ~t jdm** sb lacks sth; **du ~st mir** I miss you; **was ~t ihm?** what's wrong with him?; **F~er** *(-s, -)* *m* mistake, error; (*Mangel, Schwäche*) fault; **~erfrei** *adj* faultless; without any mistakes; **~erhaft** *adj* incorrect; faulty; **~erlos** *adj* flawless, perfect; **F~geburt** *f* miscarriage; **~gehen** *(unreg)* *vi* to go astray; **F~griff** *m* blunder; **F~konstruktion** *f* badly designed thing; **~schlagen** *(unreg)* *vi* to fail; **F~start** *m* (*SPORT*) false start; **F~zündung** *f* (*AUT*) misfire, backfire

Feier ['faɪər] *(-, -n)* *f* celebration; **~abend** *m* time to stop work; **~abend machen** to stop, to knock off; **jetzt ist ~abend!** that's enough!; **f~lich** *adj* solemn; **~lichkeit** *f* solemnity; **~lichkeiten** *pl* (*Veranstaltungen*) festivities; **f~n** *vt, vi* to celebrate; **~tag** *m*

Rechtschreibreform: ▲ *neue Schreibung* △ *alte Schreibung (auslaufend)*

holiday

felg(e) [faɪk, 'faɪgə] *adj* cowardly

Feige ['faɪgə] *f* fig

Feigheit *f* cowardice

Feigling *m* coward

Feile ['faɪlə] *f* file

feilschen ['faɪlʃən] *vi* to haggle

fein [faɪn] *adj* fine; (*vornehm*) refined; (*Gehör etc*) keen; **~!** great!

Feind [faɪnt] **(-(e)s, -e)** *m* enemy; **f~lich** *adj* hostile; **~schaft** *f* enmity; **f~selig** *adj* hostile

Fein- *zW:* **f~fühlig** *adj* sensitive; **~gefühl** *nt* delicacy, tact; **~heit** *f* fineness; refinement; keenness; **~kostgeschäft** *nt* delicatessen (shop); **~schmecker** **(-s, -)** *m* gourmet; **~wäsche** *f* delicate clothing (*when washing*); **~waschmittel** *nt* mild detergent

Feld [fɛlt] **(-(e)s, -er)** *nt* field; (*SCHACH*) square; (*SPORT*) pitch; **~herr** *m* commander; **~stecher** **(-s, -)** *m* binoculars *pl*; **~weg** *m* path; **~zug** *m* (*fig*) campaign

Felge ['fɛlgə] *f* (wheel) rim

Fell [fɛl] **(-(e)s, -e)** *nt* fur; coat; (*von Schaf*) fleece; (*von toten Tieren*) skin

Fels [fɛls] **(-en, -en)** *m* rock; (*Klippe*) cliff

Felsen ['fɛlzən] **(-s, -)** *m* = Fels; **f~fest** *adj* firm

feminin [femi'niːn] *adj* feminine

Fenster ['fɛnstər] **(-s, -)** *nt* window; **~bank** *f* windowsill; **~laden** *m* shutter; **~leder** *nt* chamois (leather); **~scheibe** *f* windowpane

Ferien ['feːriən] *pl* holidays, vacation *sg* (*US*); **~ haben** to be on holiday; **~bungalow** [-bʊngalo] **(-s, -s)** *m* holiday bungalow; **~haus** *nt* holiday home; **~kurs** *m* holiday course; **~lager** *nt* holiday camp; **~reise** *f* holiday; **~wohnung** *f* holiday apartment

Ferkel ['fɛrkəl] **(-s, -)** *nt* piglet

fern [fɛrn] *adj, adv* far-off, distant; **~ von hier** a long way (away) from here; **der F~e Osten** the Far East; **~ halten** to keep away; **F~bedienung** *f* remote control; **F~e** *f* distance; **~er** *adj* further ♦ *adv* further; (*weiterhin*) in future; **F~gespräch** *nt* trunk call; **F~glas** *nt* binoculars *pl*; **F~licht** *nt*

(*AUT*) full beam; **F~rohr** *nt* telescope; **F~ruf** *m* (*förmlich*) telephone number; **F~schreiben** *nt* telex; **F~sehapparat** *m* television set; **F~sehen** **(-s)** *nt* television; **im F~sehen** on television; **~sehen** (*unreg*) *vi* to watch television; **F~seher** *m* television; **F~sehturm** *m* television tower; **F~sprecher** *m* telephone; **F~steuerung** *f* remote control; **F~straße** *f* ≃ 'A' road (*BRIT*), highway (*US*); **F~verkehr** *m* long-distance traffic

Ferse ['fɛrzə] *f* heel

fertig ['fɛrtɪç] *adj* (*bereit*) ready; (*beendet*) finished; (*gebrauchsfertig*) ready-made; **~ bringen** (*fähig sein*) to be capable of; **~ machen** (*beenden*) to finish; (*umg: Person*) to finish; (: *körperlich*) to exhaust; (: *moralisch*) to get down; **sich ~ machen** to get ready; **~ stellen** to complete; **F~gericht** *nt* precooked meal; **F~haus** *nt* kit house, prefab; **F~keit** *f* skill

Fessel ['fɛsəl] **(-, -n)** *f* fetter; **f~n** *vt* to bind; (*mit ~n*) to fetter; (*fig*) to spellbind; **f~nd** *adj* fascinating, captivating

Fest **(-(e)s, -e)** *nt* party; festival; **frohes ~!** Happy Christmas!

fest [fɛst] *adj* firm; (*Nahrung*) solid; (*Gehalt*) regular; **~e Kosten** fixed cost ♦ *adv* (*schlafen*) soundly; **~ angestellt** permanently employed; **~binden** (*unreg*) *vt* to tie, to fasten; **~bleiben** (*unreg*) *vi* to stand firm; **F~essen** *nt* banquet; **~halten** (*unreg*) *vt* to seize, to hold fast; (*Ereignis*) to record ♦ *vr:* **sich ~halten (an** +*dat*) to hold on (to); **~igen** *vt* to strengthen; **F~igkeit** *f* strength; **F~ival** ['fɛstɪval] **(-s, -s)** *nt* festival; **F~land** *nt* mainland; **~legen** *vt* to fix ♦ *vr* to commit o.s.; **~lich** *adj* festive; **~liegen** (*unreg*) *vi* (*~stehen: Termin*) to be confirmed, be fixed; **~machen** *vt* to fasten; (*Termin etc*) to fix; **F~nahme** *f* arrest; **~nehmen** (*unreg*) *vt* to arrest; **F~preis** *m* (*COMM*) fixed price; **F~rede** *f* address; **~setzen** *vt* to fix, to settle; **F~spiele** *pl* (*Veranstaltung*) festival *sg*; **~stehen** (*unreg*) *vi* to be certain; **~stellen** *vt* to establish; (*sagen*) to remark; **F~tag** *m*

feast day, holiday; **F~ung** f fortress;
F~wochen pl festival sg

Fett [fɛt] **(-(e)s, -e)** nt fat, grease

fett adj fat; (*Essen etc*) greasy; (*TYP*) bold;
~arm adj low fat; **~en** vt to grease;
F~fleck m grease stain; **~ig** adj greasy,
fatty

Fetzen ['fɛtsən] **(-s, -)** m scrap

feucht [fɔʏçt] adj damp; (*Luft*) humid;
F~igkeit f dampness; humidity;
F~igkeitscreme f moisturizing cream

Feuer ['fɔʏər] **(-s, -)** nt fire; (*zum Rauchen*) a
light; (*fig: Schwung*) spirit; **~alarm** nt fire
alarm; **f~fest** adj fireproof; **~gefahr** f
danger of fire; **f~gefährlich** adj
inflammable; **~leiter** f fire escape ladder;
~löscher (-s, -) m fire extinguisher;
~melder (-s, -) m fire alarm; **f~n** vt, vi
(*auch fig*) to fire; **~stein** m flint; **~treppe** f
fire escape; **~wehr (-, -en)** f fire brigade;
~wehrauto nt fire engine; **~wehrmann**
m fireman; **~werk** nt fireworks pl; **~zeug**
nt (cigarette) lighter

Fichte ['fɪçtə] f spruce, pine

Fieber ['fiːbər] **(-s, -)** nt fever, temperature;
f~haft adj feverish; **~thermometer** nt
thermometer; **fiebrig** adj (*Erkältung*)
feverish

fiel etc [fiːl] vb siehe **fallen**

fies [fiːs] (*umg*) adj nasty

Figur [fiˈguːr] **(-, -en)** f figure; (*Schachfigur*)
chessman, chess piece

Filet [fiˈleː] **(-s, -s)** nt (*KOCH*) fillet

Filiale [filiˈaːlə] **(-, -n)** f (*COMM*) branch

Film [fɪlm] **(-(e)s, -e)** m film; **~aufnahme** f
shooting; **f~en** vt, vi to film; **~kamera** f
cine camera

Filter ['fɪltər] **(-s, -)** m filter; **f~n** vt to filter;
~papier nt filter paper; **~zigarette** f
tipped cigarette

Filz [fɪlts] **(-es, -e)** m felt; **f~en** vt (*umg*) to
frisk ◆ vi (*Wolle*) to mat; **~stift** m felt-tip
pen

Finale [fiˈnaːlə] **(-s, -(s))** nt finale; (*SPORT*)
final(s)

Finanz [fiˈnants] f finance; **~amt** nt Inland
Revenue office; **~beamte(r)** m revenue

officer; **f~iell** [-tsiˈɛl] adj financial; **f~ieren**
[-ˈtsiːrən] vt to finance; **f~kräftig** adj
financially strong; **~minister** m Chancellor
of the Exchequer (*BRIT*), Minister of Finance

Find- ['fɪnd] zW: **f~en** (*unreg*) vt to find;
(*meinen*) to think ◆ vr to be (found); (*sich
fassen*) to compose o.s.; **ich f~e nichts
dabei, wenn** ... I don't see what's wrong if
...; **das wird sich f~en** things will work
out; **~er (-s, -)** m finder; **~erlohn** m
reward (*for sb who finds sth*); **f~ig** adj
resourceful

fing etc [fɪŋ] vb siehe **fangen**

Finger ['fɪŋər] **(-s, -)** m finger; **~abdruck** m
fingerprint; **~nagel** m fingernail; **~spitze** f
fingertip

fingiert adj made-up, fictitious

Fink [fɪŋk] **(-en, -en)** m finch

Finn- [fɪn] zW: **~e (-n, -n)** m Finn; **~in** f
Finn; **f~isch** adj Finnish; **~land** nt Finland

finster ['fɪnstər] adj dark, gloomy;
(*verdächtig*) dubious; (*verdrossen*) grim;
(*Gedanke*) dark; **F~nis** f darkness, gloom

Firma ['fɪrma] **(-, -men)** f firm

Firmen- ['fɪrmən] zW: **~inhaber** m owner
of firm; **~schild** nt (shop) sign; **~wagen**
m company car; **~zeichen** nt trademark

Fisch [fɪʃ] **(-(e)s, -e)** m fish; **~e** pl (*ASTROL*)
Pisces sg; **f~en** vt, vi to fish; **~er (-s, -)** m
fisherman; **~e'rei** f fishing, fishery; **~fang**
m fishing; **~geschäft** nt fishmonger's
(shop); **~gräte** f fishbone; **~stäbchen**
[-ʃtɛːpçən] nt fish finger (*BRIT*), fish stick (*US*)

fit [fɪt] adj fit; **'F~ness** ▲ **(-, -)** f (physical)
fitness

fix [fɪks] adj fixed; (*Person*) alert, smart; **~ und
fertig** finished; (*erschöpft*) done in;
F~er(in) m(f) (*umg*) junkie; **F~erstube** f
(*umg*) junkies centre; **~ieren** [fiˈksiːrən] vt
to fix; (*anstarren*) to stare at

flach [flax] adj flat; (*Gefäß*) shallow

Fläche ['flɛçə] f area; (*Oberfläche*) surface

Flachland nt lowland

flackern ['flakərn] vi to flare, to flicker

Flagge ['flagə] f flag; **f~n** vi to fly a flag

flämisch ['flɛːmɪʃ] adj (*LING*) Flemish

Flamme ['flamə] f flame

Rechtschreibreform: ▲ *neue Schreibung* △ *alte Schreibung (auslaufend)*

Flandern ['flandərn] *nt* Flanders

Flanke ['flaŋkə] *f* flank; (*SPORT: Seite*) wing

Flasche ['flaʃə] *f* bottle; (*umg: Versager*) wash-out

Flaschen- *zW:* **~bier** *nt* bottled beer; **~öffner** *m* bottle opener; **~zug** *m* pulley

flatterhaft *adj* flighty, fickle

flattern ['flatərn] *vi* to flutter

flau [flau] *adj* weak, listless; (*Nachfrage*) slack; **jdm ist ~** sb feels queasy

Flaum [flaum] (**-(e)s**) *m* (*Feder*) down; (*Haare*) fluff

flauschig ['flauʃɪç] *adj* fluffy

Flaute ['flautə] *f* calm; (*COMM*) recession

Flechte ['flɛçtə] *f* plait; (*MED*) dry scab; (*BOT*) lichen; **f~n** (*unreg*) *vt* (*Kranz*) to twine

Fleck [flɛk] (**-(e)s, -e**) *m* spot; (*Schmutzfleck*) stain; (*Stofffleck*) patch; (*Makel*) blemish; **nicht vom ~ kommen** (*auch fig*) not to get any further; **vom ~ weg** straight away

Flecken (**-s, -**) *m* = Fleck; **f~los** *adj* spotless; **~mittel** *nt* stain remover; **~wasser** *nt* stain remover

fleckig *adj* spotted; stained

Fledermaus ['fleːdərmaus] *f* bat

Flegel ['fleːgəl] (**-s, -**) *m* (*Mensch*) lout; **f~haft** *adj* loutish, unmannerly; **~jahre** *pl* adolescence *sg*

flehen ['fleːən] *vi* to implore; **~tlich** *adj* imploring

Fleisch ['flaɪʃ] (**-(e)s**) *nt* flesh; (*Essen*) meat; **~brühe** *f* beef tea, meat stock; **~er** (**-s, -**) *m* butcher; **~e'rei** *f* butcher's (shop); **f~ig** *adj* fleshy; **f~los** *adj* meatless, vegetarian

Fleiß ['flaɪs] (**-es**) *m* diligence, industry; **f~ig** *adj* diligent, industrious

fletschen ['flɛtʃən] *vt* (*Zähne*) to show

flexibel [flɛ'ksiːbəl] *adj* flexible

Flicken ['flɪkən] (**-s, -**) *m* patch; **f~** *vt* to mend

Flieder ['fliːdər] (**-s, -**) *m* lilac

Fliege ['fliːgə] *f* fly; (*Kleidung*) bow tie; **f~n** (*unreg*) *vt, vi* to fly; **auf jdn/etw f~n** (*umg*) to be mad about sb/sth; **~npilz** *m* toadstool; **~r** (**-s, -**) *m* flier, airman

fliehen ['fliːən] (*unreg*) *vi* to flee

Fliese ['fliːzə] *f* tile

Fließ- ['fliːs] *zW:* **~band** *nt* production *od* assembly line; **f~en** (*unreg*) *vi* to flow; **f~end** *adj* flowing; (*Rede, Deutsch*) fluent; (*Übergänge*) smooth

flimmern ['flɪmərn] *vi* to glimmer

flink [flɪŋk] *adj* nimble, lively

Flinte ['flɪntə] *f* rifle; shotgun

Flitterwochen *pl* honeymoon *sg*

flitzen ['flɪtsən] *vi* to flit

Flocke ['flɔkə] *f* flake

flog *etc* [floːk] *vb siehe* **fliegen**

Floh [floː] (**-(e)s, Ꞌe**) *m* flea; **~markt** *m* flea market

florieren [floˈriːrən] *vi* to flourish

Floskel ['flɔskəl] (**-, -n**) *f* set phrase

Floß [floːs] (**-es, Ꞌe**) *nt* raft, float

floss ▲ *etc vb siehe* **fließen**

Flosse ['flɔsə] *f* fin

Flöte ['fløːtə] *f* flute; (*Blockflöte*) recorder

flott [flɔt] *adj* lively; (*elegant*) smart; (*NAUT*) afloat; **F~e** *f* fleet, navy

Fluch [fluːx] (**-(e)s, Ꞌe**) *m* curse; **f~en** *vi* to curse, to swear

Flucht [fluxt] (**-, -en**) *f* flight; (*Fensterflucht*) row; (*Zimmerflucht*) suite; **f~artig** *adj* hasty

flücht- ['flʏçt] *zW:* **~en** *vi, vr* to flee, to escape; **~ig** *adj* fugitive; (*vergänglich*) transitory; (*oberflächlich*) superficial; (*eilig*) fleeting; **F~igkeitsfehler** *m* careless slip; **F~ling** *m* fugitive, refugee

Flug [fluːk] (**-(e)s, Ꞌe**) *m* flight; **~blatt** *nt* pamphlet

Flügel ['flyːgəl] (**-s, -**) *m* wing; (*MUS*) grand piano

Fluggast *m* airline passenger

Flug- *zW:* **~gesellschaft** *f* airline (company); **~hafen** *m* airport; **~lärm** *m* aircraft noise; **~linie** *f* airline; **~plan** *m* flight schedule; **~platz** *m* airport; (*klein*) airfield; **~reise** *f* flight; **~schein** *m* (*Ticket*) plane ticket; (*Pilotenschein*) pilot's licence; **~steig** [-ʃtaɪk] (**-(e)s, -e**) *m* gate; **~verbindung** *f* air connection; **~verkehr** *m* air traffic; **~zeug** *nt* (aero)plane, airplane (*US*); **~zeugentführung** *f* hijacking of a plane; **~zeughalle** *f* hangar; **~zeugträger**

m aircraft carrier

Flunder ['flʊndər] (-, -n) *f* flounder

flunkern ['flʊŋkərn] *vi* to fib, to tell stories

Fluor ['fluːɔr] (-s) *nt* fluorine

Flur [fluːr] (-(e)s, -e) *m* hall; (*Treppenflur*) staircase

Fluss ▲ [flʊs] (-es, ⁻e) *m* river; (*Fließen*) flow

flüssig ['flʏsɪç] *adj* liquid; ~ **machen** (*Geld*) to make available; **F~keit** *f* liquid; (*Zustand*) liquidity

flüstern ['flʏstərn] *vt, vi* to whisper

Flut [fluːt] (-, -en) *f* (*auch fig*) flood; (*Gezeiten*) high tide; **f~en** *vi* to flood; **~licht** *nt* floodlight

Fohlen ['foːlən] (-s, -) *nt* foal

Föhn¹ [føːn] (-(e)s, -e) *m* (*warmer Fallwind*) föhn

Föhn² ▲ (-(e)s, -e) *m* (*Haartrockner*) hairdryer; **f~en** ▲ *vt* to (blow) dry; **~frisur** ▲ *f* blow-dry hairstyle

Folge ['fɔlɡə] *f* series, sequence; (*Fortsetzung*) instalment; (*Auswirkung*) result; **in rascher ~** in quick succession; **etw zur ~ haben** to result in sth; **~n haben** to have consequences; **einer Sache** *dat* ~ **leisten** to comply with sth; **f~n** *vi* +*dat* to follow; (*gehorchen*) to obey; **jdm f~n können** (*fig*) to follow *od* understand sb; **f~nd** *adj* following; **f~ndermaßen** *adv* as follows, in the following way; **f~rn** *vt*: **f~rn (aus)** to conclude (from); **~rung** *f* conclusion

folglich ['fɔlklɪç] *adv* consequently

folgsam ['fɔlkzaːm] *adj* obedient

Folie ['foːliə] *f* foil

Folklore ['fɔlkloːər] *f* folklore

Folter ['fɔltər] (-, -n) *f* torture; (*Gerät*) rack; **f~n** *vt* to torture

Fön [føːn] (-(e)s, -e) ℗ *m* hair dryer

Fondue [fõdy:] (-s, -s *od* -, -s) *nt od f* (*KOCH*) fondue

fönen △ *vt siehe* **föhnen**

Fönfrisur △ *f siehe* **Föhnfrisur**

Fontäne [fɔn'tɛːnə] *f* fountain

Förder- ['fœrdər] *zW*: **~band** *nt* conveyor belt; **~korb** *m* pit cage; **f~lich** *adj* beneficial

fordern ['fɔrdərn] *vt* to demand

fördern ['fœrdərn] *vt* to promote; (*unterstützen*) to help; (*Kohle*) to extract

Forderung ['fɔrdərʊŋ] *f* demand

Förderung ['fœrdərʊŋ] *f* promotion; help; extraction

Forelle [fo'rɛlə] *f* trout

Form [fɔrm] (-, -en) *f* shape; (*Gestaltung*) form; (*Gussform*) mould; (*Backform*) baking tin; **in ~ sein** to be in good form *od* shape; **in ~ von** in the shape of

Formali'tät *f* formality

Format [fɔr'maːt] (-(e)s, -e) *nt* format; (*fig*) distinction

formbar *adj* malleable

Formblatt *nt* form

Formel (-, -n) *f* formula

formell [fɔr'mɛl] *adj* formal

formen *vt* to form, to shape

Formfehler *m* faux pas, gaffe; (*JUR*) irregularity

formieren [fɔr'miːrən] *vt* to form ♦ *vr* to form up

förmlich ['fœrmlɪç] *adj* formal; (*umg*) real; **F~keit** *f* formality

formlos *adj* shapeless; (*Benehmen etc*) informal

Formular [fɔrmu'laːr] (-s, -e) *nt* form

formulieren [fɔrmu'liːrən] *vt* to formulate

forsch [fɔrʃ] *adj* energetic, vigorous

forsch- *zW*: **~en** *vi*: **~en (nach)** to search (for); (*wissenschaftlich*) to (do) research; **~end** *adj* searching; **F~er** (-s, -) *m* research scientist; (*Naturforscher*) explorer; **F~ung** *f* research

Forst [fɔrst] (-(e)s, -e) *m* forest

Förster ['fœrstər] (-s, -) *m* forester; (*für Wild*) gamekeeper

fort [fɔrt] *adv* away; (*verschwunden*) gone; (*vorwärts*) on; **und so ~** and so on; **in einem ~** on and on; **~bestehen** (*unreg*) *vi* to survive; **~bewegen** *vt, vr* to move away; **~bilden** *vr* to continue one's education; **~bleiben** (*unreg*) *vi* to stay away; **F~dauer** *f* continuance; **~fahren** (*unreg*) *vi* to depart; (*~setzen*) to go on, to continue; **~führen** *vt* to continue, to carry on; **~gehen** (*unreg*) *vi* to go away;

~**geschritten** adj advanced; ~**pflanzen** vr to reproduce; **F~pflanzung** f reproduction

fort- zW: ~**schaffen** vt to remove; ~**schreiten** (unreg) vi to advance

Fortschritt ['fɔrtʃrɪt] m advance; ~**e machen** to make progress; **f~lich** adj progressive

fort- zW: ~**setzen** vt to continue; **F~setzung** f continuation; (folgender Teil) instalment; **F~setzung folgt** to be continued; ~**während** adj incessant, continual

Foto ['foːto] (-s, -s) nt photo(graph); ~**apparat** m camera; ~'**graf** m photographer; ~**gra'fie** f photography; (Bild) photograph; **f~gra'fieren** vt to photograph ♦ vi to take photographs; ~**kopie** f photocopy

Fr. abk (= Frau) Mrs, Ms

Fracht [fraxt] (-, -en) f freight; (NAUT) cargo; (Preis) carriage; ~ **zahlt Empfänger** (COMM) carriage forward; ~**er** (-s, -) m freighter, cargo boat; ~**gut** nt freight

Frack [frak] (-(e)s, ⁼e) m tails pl

Frage ['fraːɡə] (-, -n) f question; **jdm eine ~ stellen** to ask sb a question, to put a question to sb; siehe **infrage**; ~**bogen** m questionnaire; **f~n** vt, vi to ask; ~**zeichen** nt question mark

fraglich adj questionable, doubtful

fraglos adv unquestionably

Fragment [fraˈɡmɛnt] nt fragment

fragwürdig ['fraːkvʏrdɪç] adj questionable, dubious

Fraktion [fraktsiˈoːn] f parliamentary party

frankieren [fraŋˈkiːrən] vt to stamp, to frank

franko ['fraŋko] adv post-paid; carriage paid

Frankreich ['fraŋkraɪç] (-s) nt France

Franzose [franˈtsoːzə] m Frenchman; **Französin** [franˈtsøːzɪn] f Frenchwoman; **französisch** adj French

fraß etc [fras] vb siehe **fressen**

Fratze ['fratsə] f grimace

Frau [frau] (-, -en) f woman; (Ehefrau) wife; (Anrede) Mrs, Ms; ~ **Doktor** Doctor

Frauen- zW: ~**arzt** m gynaecologist; ~**bewegung** f feminist movement; ~**haus**

nt women's refuge; ~**zimmer** nt female, broad (US)

Fräulein ['frɔʏlaɪn] nt young lady; (Anrede) Miss, Ms

fraulich ['fraʊlɪç] adj womanly

frech [frɛç] adj cheeky, impudent; **F~heit** f cheek, impudence

frei [fraɪ] adj free; (Stelle, Sitzplatz) free, vacant; (Mitarbeiter) freelance; (unbekleidet) bare; **von etw ~ sein** to be free of sth; **im F~en** in the open air; ~ **sprechen** to talk without notes; ~ **Haus** (COMM) carriage paid; ~**er Wettbewerb** (COMM) fair/open competition; **F~bad** nt open-air swimming pool; ~**bekommen** (unreg) vt: **einen Tag ~bekommen** to get a day off; ~**beruflich** adj self-employed; ~**gebig** adj generous; ~**halten** (unreg) vt to keep free; ~**händig** adv (fahren) with no hands; **F~heit** f freedom; ~**heitlich** adj liberal; **F~heitsstrafe** f prison sentence; **F~karte** f free ticket; ~**lassen** (unreg) vt to (set) free; ~**legen** vt to expose; ~**lich** adv certainly, admittedly; **ja ~lich** yes of course; **F~lichtbühne** f open-air theatre; **F~lichtmuseum** nt open-air museum; ~**machen** vt (Post) to frank ♦ vr to arrange to be free; (entkleiden) to undress; **Tage ~machen** to take days off; ~**nehmen** ▲ (unreg) vt: **sich** dat **einen Tag ~nehmen** to take a day off; ~**sprechen** (unreg) vt: ~**sprechen (von)** to acquit (of); **F~spruch** m acquittal; ~**stehen** (unreg) vi: **es steht dir ~, das zu tun** you're free to do that; (leer stehen: Wohnung, Haus) to lie/stand empty; ~**stellen** vt: **jdm etw ~stellen** to leave sth (up) to sb; **F~stoß** m free kick

Freitag m Friday; ~**s** adv on Fridays

frei- zW: ~**willig** adj voluntary; **F~zeit** f spare od free time; **F~zeitpark** m amusement park; **F~zeitzentrum** nt leisure centre; ~**zügig** adj liberal, broad-minded; (mit Geld) generous

fremd [frɛmt] adj (unvertraut) strange; (ausländisch) foreign; (nicht eigen) someone else's; **etw ist jdm ~** sth is foreign to sb; ~**artig** adj strange; **F~enführer** ['frɛmdən-]

m (tourist) guide; **F~enverkehr** *m*
tourism; **F~enverkehrsamt** *nt* tourist
board; **F~enzimmer** *nt* guest room;
F~körper *m* foreign body; **~ländisch** *adj*
foreign; **F~sprache** *f* foreign language;
F~wort *nt* foreign word

Frequenz [fre'kvɛnts] *f (RADIO)* frequency
fressen ['frɛsən] *(unreg) vt, vi* to eat
Freude ['frɔʏdə] *f* joy, delight
freudig *adj* joyful, happy
freuen ['frɔʏən] *vt unpers* to make happy *od*
pleased ♦ *vr* to be glad *od* happy; **freut
mich!** pleased to meet you; **sich auf etw**
akk ~ to look forward to sth; **sich über etw**
akk ~ to be pleased about sth
Freund ['frɔʏnt] **(-(e)s, -e)** *m* friend;
boyfriend; **~in** [-dɪn] *f* friend; girlfriend;
f~lich *adj* kind, friendly; **f~licherweise**
adv kindly; **~lichkeit** *f* friendliness,
kindness; **~schaft** *f* friendship;
f~schaftlich *adj* friendly
Frieden ['fri:dən] **(-s, -)** *m* peace; **im ~** in
peacetime
Friedens- *zW:* **~schluss** ▲ *m* peace
agreement; **~vertrag** *m* peace treaty;
~zeit *f* peacetime
fried- ['fri:t] *zW:* **~fertig** *adj* peaceable;
F~hof *m* cemetery; **~lich** *adj* peaceful
frieren ['fri:rən] *(unreg) vt, vi* to freeze; **ich
friere, es friert mich** I'm freezing, I'm cold
Frikadelle [frika'dɛlə] *f* rissole
Frikassee [frika'se:] **(-s, -s)** *nt (KOCH)*
fricassee
frisch [frɪʃ] *adj* fresh; *(lebhaft)* lively; **~
gestrichen!** wet paint!; **sich ~ machen** to
freshen (o.s.) up; **F~e** *f* freshness; liveliness;
F~haltefolie *f* cling film
Friseur [fri'zøːr] *m* hairdresser
Friseuse [fri'zøːzə] *f* hairdresser
frisieren [fri'zi:rən] *vt* to do (one's hair);
(fig: Abrechnung) to fiddle, to doctor ♦ *vr* to
do one's hair
Frisiersalon *m* hairdressing salon
frisst ▲ [frɪst] *vb siehe* **fressen**
Frist [frɪst] **(-, -en)** *f* period; *(Termin)*
deadline; **f~gerecht** *adj* within the
stipulated time *od* period; **f~los** *adj*

(Entlassung) instant
Frisur [fri'zu:r] *f* hairdo, hairstyle
frivol [fri'vo:l] *adj* frivolous
froh [fro:] *adj* happy, cheerful; **ich bin ~,
dass ...** I'm glad that ...
fröhlich ['frøːlɪç] *adj* merry, happy; **F~keit** *f*
merriness, gaiety
fromm [frɔm] *adj* pious, good; *(Wunsch)*
idle; **Frömmigkeit** ['frœmɪçkaɪt] *f* piety
Fronleichnam [froːn'laɪçnaːm] **(-(e)s)** *m*
Corpus Christi
Front [frɔnt] **(-, -en)** *f* front; **f~al** [frɔn'taːl]
adj frontal
fror *etc* [froːr] *vb siehe* **frieren**
Frosch [frɔʃ] **(-(e)s, ˮe)** *m* frog; *(Feuerwerk)*
squib; **~mann** *m* frogman; **~schenkel** *m*
frog's leg
Frost [frɔst] **(-(e)s, ˮe)** *m* frost; **~beule** *f*
chilblain
frösteln ['frœstəln] *vi* to shiver
frostig *adj* frosty
Frostschutzmittel *nt* antifreeze
Frottier(hand)tuch [frɔ'tiːr(hant)tuːx] *nt*
towel
Frucht [frʊxt] **(-, ˮe)** *f (auch fig)* fruit;
(Getreide) corn; **f~bar** *adj* fruitful, fertile;
~barkeit *f* fertility; **f~ig** *adj (Geschmack)*
fruity; **f~los** *adj* fruitless; **~saft** *m* fruit juice
früh [fryː] *adj, adv* early; **heute ~** this
morning; **F~aufsteher (-s, -)** *m* early riser;
F~e *f* early morning; **~er** *adj* earlier;
(ehemalig) former ♦ *adv* formerly; **~er war
das anders** that used to be different;
~estens *adv* at the earliest; **F~jahr** *nt*,
F~ling *m* spring; **~reif** *adj* precocious;
F~stück *nt* breakfast; **~stücken** *vi* to
(have) breakfast; **F~stücksbüfett** *nt*
breakfast buffet; **~zeitig** *adj* early; *(pej)*
untimely
frustrieren [frʊs'triːrən] *vt* to frustrate
Fuchs [fʊks] **(-es, ˮe)** *m* fox; **f~en** *(umg) vt*
to rile, to annoy; **f~teufelswild** *adj*
hopping mad
Fuge ['fuːgə] *f* joint; *(MUS)* fugue
fügen ['fyːgən] *vt* to place, to join ♦ *vr:* **sich
~ (in** +*dat)* to be obedient (to); *(anpassen)*
to adapt oneself (to) ♦ *vr unpers* to happen

fühl- *zW:* **~bar** *adj* perceptible, noticeable; **~en** *vt, vi, vr* to feel; **F~er** (-s, -) *m* feeler

fuhr *etc* [fu:r] *vb siehe* **fahren**

führen ['fy:rən] *vt* to lead; (*Geschäft*) to run; (*Name*) to bear; (*Buch*) to keep ♦ *vi* to lead ♦ *vr* to behave

Führer ['fy:rər] (-s, -) *m* leader; (*Fremdenführer*) guide; **~schein** *m* driving licence

Führung ['fy:rʊŋ] *f* leadership; (*eines Unternehmens*) management; (*MIL*) command; (*Benehmen*) conduct; (*Museumsführung*) conducted tour; **~szeugnis** *nt* certificate of good conduct

Fülle ['fʏlə] *f* wealth, abundance; **f~n** *vt* to fill; (*KOCH*) to stuff ♦ *vr* to fill (up)

Füll- *zW:* **~er** (-s, -) *m* fountain pen; **~federhalter** *m* fountain pen; **~ung** *f* filling; (*Holzfüllung*) panel

fummeln ['fʊməln] (*umg*) *vi* to fumble

Fund [fʊnt] (-(e)s, -e) *m* find

Fundament [fʊnda'mɛnt] *nt* foundation; **fundamen'tal** *adj* fundamental

Fund- *zW:* **~büro** *nt* lost property office, lost and found (*US*); **~grube** *f* (*fig*) treasure trove

fundiert [fʊn'di:rt] *adj* sound

fünf [fʏnf] *num* five; **~hundert** *num* five hundred; **~te(r, s)** *adj* fifth; **F~tel** (-s, -) *nt* fifth; **~zehn** *num* fifteen; **~zig** *num* fifty

Funk [fʊŋk] (-s) *m* radio, wireless; **~e** (-ns, -n) *m* (*auch fig*) spark; **f~eln** *vi* to sparkle; **~en** (-s, -) *m* (*auch fig*) spark; **f~en** *vi* (*durch Funk*) to signal, to radio; (*umg: richtig funktionieren*) to work ♦ *vt* (*Funken sprühen*) to shower with sparks; **~er** (-s, -) *m* radio operator; **~gerät** *nt* radio set; **~rufempfänger** *m* pager, paging device; **~streife** *f* police radio patrol; **~telefon** *nt* cellphone

Funktion [fʊŋktsi'oːn] *f* function; **f~ieren** [-'niːrən] *vi* to work, to function

für [fyːr] *präp +akk* for; **was ~** what kind *od* sort of; **das F~ und Wider** the pros and cons *pl*; **Schritt ~ Schritt** step by step

Furche ['fʊrçə] *f* furrow

Furcht [fʊrçt] (-) *f* fear; **f~bar** *adj* terrible, frightful

fürchten ['fʏrçtən] *vt* to be afraid of, to fear ♦ *vr:* **sich ~ (vor** +*dat*) to be afraid (of)

fürchterlich *adj* awful

furchtlos *adj* fearless

füreinander [fyːrʔaɪˈnandər] *adv* for each other

Furnier [fʊr'niːr] (-s, -e) *nt* veneer

fürs [fyːrs] = **für das**

Fürsorge ['fyːrzɔrgə] *f* care; (*Sozialfürsorge*) welfare; **~r(in)** (-s, -) *m(f)* welfare worker; **~unterstützung** *f* social security, welfare benefit (*US*); **fürsorglich** *adj* attentive, caring

Fürsprache *f* recommendation; (*um Gnade*) intercession

Fürsprecher *m* advocate

Fürst [fʏrst] (-en, -en) *m* prince; **~entum** *nt* principality; **~in** *f* princess; **f~lich** *adj* princely

Fuß [fuːs] (-es, ᵘe) *m* foot; (*von Glas, Säule etc*) base; (*von Möbel*) leg; **zu ~** on foot; **~ball** *m* football; **~ballplatz** *m* football pitch; **~ballspiel** *nt* football match; **~ballspieler** *m* footballer; **~boden** *m* floor; **~bremse** *f* (*AUT*) footbrake; **~ende** *nt* foot; **~gänger(in)** (-s, -) *m(f)* pedestrian; **~gängerzone** *f* pedestrian precinct; **~nagel** *m* toenail; **~note** *f* footnote; **~spur** *f* footprint; **~tritt** *m* kick; (*Spur*) footstep; **~weg** *m* footpath

Futter ['fʊtər] (-s, -) *nt* fodder, feed; (*Stoff*) lining; **~al** [-'raːl] (-s, -e) *nt* case

füttern ['fʏtərn] *vt* to feed; (*Kleidung*) to line

Futur [fu'tuːr] (-s, -e) *nt* future

G, g

g *abk* = **Gramm**

gab *etc* [gaːp] *vb siehe* **geben**

Gabe ['gaːbə] *f* gift

Gabel ['gaːbəl] (-, -n) *f* fork; **~ung** *f* fork

gackern ['gakərn] *vi* to cackle

gaffen ['gafən] *vi* to gape

Gage ['gaːʒə] *f* fee; salary

gähnen ['gɛːnən] *vi* to yawn

Galerie [galə'riː] f gallery

Galgen ['galgən] (-s, -) m gallows sg; ~**frist** f respite; ~**humor** m macabre humour

Galle ['galə] f gall; (Organ) gall bladder; ~**nstein** m gallstone

gammeln ['gaməln] (umg) vi to bum around; **Gammler(in)** (-s, -) (pej) m(f) layabout, loafer (inf)

Gämse ▲ ['gɛmzə] f chamois

Gang [gaŋ] (-(e)s, ⁺e) m walk; (Botengang) errand; (~art) gait; (Abschnitt eines Vorgangs) operation; (Essensgang, Ablauf) course; (Flur etc) corridor; (Durchgang) passage; (TECH) gear; **in ~ bringen** to start up; (fig) to get off the ground; **in ~ sein** to be in operation; (fig) to be under way

gang adj: ~ **und gäbe** usual, normal

gängig ['gɛŋɪç] adj common, current; (Ware) in demand, selling well

Gangschaltung f gears pl

Ganove [ga'noːvə] (-n, -n) (umg) m crook

Gans [gans] (-, ⁺e) f goose

Gänse- ['gɛnzə] zW: ~**blümchen** nt daisy; ~**füßchen** (umg) pl (Anführungszeichen) inverted commas; ~**haut** f goose pimples pl; ~**marsch** m: **im ~marsch** in single file; ~**rich** (-s, -e) m gander

ganz [gants] adj whole; (vollständig) complete ♦ adv quite; (völlig) completely; ~ **Europa** all Europe; **sein ~es Geld** all his money; ~ **und gar nicht** not at all; **es sieht ~ so aus** it really looks like it; **aufs G~e gehen** to go for the lot

gänzlich ['gɛntslɪç] adj complete, entire ♦ adv completely, entirely

Ganztagsschule f all-day school

gar [gaːr] adj cooked, done ♦ adv quite; ~ **nicht/nichts/keiner** not/nothing/nobody at all; ~ **nicht schlecht** not bad at all

Garage [ga'raːʒə] f garage

Garantie [garan'tiː] f guarantee; **g~ren** vt to guarantee; **er kommt g~rt** he's guaranteed to come

Garbe ['garbə] f sheaf

Garde ['gardə] f guard

Garderobe [gardə'roːbə] f wardrobe; (Abgabe) cloakroom; ~**nfrau** f cloakroom attendant

Gardine [gar'diːnə] f curtain

garen ['gaːrən] vt, vi to cook

gären ['gɛːrən] (unreg) vi to ferment

Garn [garn] (-(e)s, -e) nt thread; yarn (auch fig)

Garnele [gar'neːlə] f shrimp, prawn

garnieren [gar'niːrən] vt to decorate; (Speisen, fig) to garnish

Garnison [garni'zoːn] (-, -en) f garrison

Garnitur [garni'tuːr] f (Satz) set; (Unterwäsche) set of (matching) underwear; **erste ~** (fig) top rank; **zweite ~** (fig) second rate

garstig ['garstɪç] adj nasty, horrid

Garten ['gartən] (-s, ⁺) m garden; ~**arbeit** f gardening; ~**gerät** nt gardening tool; ~**lokal** nt beer garden; ~**tür** f garden gate

Gärtner(in) ['gɛrtnər(ɪn)] (-s, -) m(f) gardener; ~**ei** [-'raɪ] f nursery; (Gemüsegärtnerei) market garden (BRIT), truck farm (US)

Gärung ['gɛːrʊŋ] f fermentation

Gas [gaːs] (-es, -e) nt gas; ~ **geben** (AUT) to accelerate, to step on the gas; ~**hahn** m gas tap; ~**herd** m gas cooker; ~**kocher** m gas cooker; ~**leitung** f gas pipe; ~**pedal** nt accelerator, gas pedal

Gasse ['gasə] f lane, alley

Gast [gast] (-es, ⁺e) m guest; (in Lokal) patron; **bei jdm zu ~ sein** to be sb's guest; ~**arbeiter(in)** m(f) foreign worker

Gäste- ['gɛstə] zW: ~**buch** nt visitors' book, guest book; ~**zimmer** nt guest od spare room

Gast- zW: **g~freundlich** adj hospitable; ~**geber** (-s, -) m host; ~**geberin** f hostess; ~**haus** nt hotel, inn; ~**hof** m hotel, inn; **g~ieren** [-'tiːrən] vi (THEAT) to (appear as a) guest; **g~lich** adj hospitable; ~**rolle** f guest role; ~**spiel** nt (THEAT) guest performance; ~**stätte** f restaurant; pub; ~**wirt** m innkeeper; ~**wirtschaft** f hotel, inn

Gaswerk nt gasworks sg

Gaszähler m gas meter

Gatte ['gatə] (-n, -n) m husband, spouse

Gattin f wife, spouse

Rechtschreibreform: ▲ *neue Schreibung* △ *alte Schreibung (auslaufend)*

Gattung ['gatʊŋ] *f* genus; kind
Gaudi ['gaʊdi] (*umg: SÜDD, ÖSTERR*) *nt od f* fun
Gaul [gaʊl] (**-(e)s, Gäule**) *m* horse; nag
Gaumen ['gaʊmən] (**-s, -**) *m* palate
Gauner ['gaʊnər] (**-s, -**) *m* rogue; **~ei** [-'raɪ] *f* swindle
geb. *abk* = **geboren**
Gebäck [gə'bɛk] (**-(e)s, -e**) *nt* pastry
gebacken [gə'bakən] *adj* baked; (*gebraten*) fried
Gebälk [gə'bɛlk] (**-(e)s**) *nt* timberwork
Gebärde [gə'bɛːrdə] *f* gesture; **g~n** *vr* to behave
gebären [gə'bɛːrən] (*unreg*) *vt* to give birth to, to bear
Gebärmutter *f* uterus, womb
Gebäude [gə'bɔʏdə] (**-s, -**) *nt* building; **~komplex** *m* (building) complex
geben ['geːbən] (*unreg*) *vt, vi* to give; (*Karten*) to deal ♦ *vb unpers*: **es gibt** there is/are; there will be ♦ *vr* (*sich verhalten*) to behave, to act; (*aufhören*) to abate; **jdm etw ~** to give sb sth *od* sth to sb; **was gibts?** what's up?; **was gibt es im Kino?** what's on at the cinema?; **sich geschlagen ~** to admit defeat; **das wird sich schon ~** that'll soon sort itself out
Gebet [gə'beːt] (**-(e)s, -e**) *nt* prayer
gebeten [gə'beːtən] *vb siehe* **bitten**
Gebiet [gə'biːt] (**-(e)s, -e**) *nt* area; (*Hoheitsgebiet*) territory; (*fig*) field; **g~en** (*unreg*) *vt* to command, to demand; **g~erisch** *adj* imperious
Gebilde [gə'bɪldə] (**-s, -**) *nt* object
gebildet *adj* cultured, educated
Gebirge [gə'bɪrgə] (**-s, -**) *nt* mountain chain
Gebiss [gə'bɪs] (**-es, -e**) *nt* teeth *pl*; (*künstlich*) dentures *pl*
gebissen *vb siehe* **beißen**
geblieben [gə'bliːbən] *vb siehe* **bleiben**
geblümt [gə'blyːmt] *adj* (*Kleid, Stoff, Tapete*) floral
geboren [gə'boːrən] *adj* born; (*Frau*) née
geborgen [gə'bɔrgən] *adj* secure, safe
Gebot [gə'boːt] (**-(e)s, -e**) *nt* command; (*REL*) commandment; (*bei Auktion*) bid

geboten [gə'boːtən] *vb siehe* **bieten**
Gebr. *abk* (= *Gebrüder*) Bros.
gebracht [gə'braxt] *vb siehe* **bringen**
gebraten [gə'braːtən] *adj* fried
Gebrauch [gə'braʊx] (**-(e)s, Gebräuche**) *m* use; (*Sitte*) custom; **g~en** *vt* to use
gebräuchlich [gə'brɔʏçlɪç] *adj* usual, customary
Gebrauchs- *zW:* **~anweisung** *f* directions *pl* for use; **g~fertig** *adj* ready for use; **~gegenstand** *m* commodity
gebraucht [gə'braʊxt] *adj* used; **G~wagen** *m* secondhand *od* used car
gebrechlich [gə'brɛçlɪç] *adj* frail
Gebrüder [gə'bryːdər] *pl* brothers
Gebrüll [gə'brʏl] (**-(e)s**) *nt* roaring
Gebühr [gə'byːr] (**-, -en**) *f* charge, fee; **nach ~** fittingly; **über ~** unduly; **g~en** *vi*: **jdm g~en** to be sb's due *od* due to sb ♦ *vr* to be fitting; **g~end** *adj* fitting, appropriate ♦ *adv* fittingly, appropriately
Gebühren- *zW:* **~einheit** *f* (*TEL*) unit; **~erlass ▲** *m* remission of fees; **~ermäßigung** *f* reduction of fees; **g~frei** *adj* free of charge; **~ordnung** *f* scale of charges, tariff; **g~pflichtig** *adj* subject to a charge
gebunden [gə'bʊndən] *vb siehe* **binden**
Geburt [gə'buːrt] (**-, -en**) *f* birth
Geburtenkontrolle *f* birth control
Geburtenregelung *f* birth control
gebürtig [gə'bʏrtɪç] *adj* born in, native of; **~e Schweizerin** native of Switzerland
Geburts- *zW:* **~anzeige** *f* birth notice; **~datum** *nt* date of birth; **~jahr** *nt* year of birth; **~ort** *m* birthplace; **~tag** *m* birthday; **~urkunde** *f* birth certificate
Gebüsch [gə'bʏʃ] (**-(e)s, -e**) *nt* bushes *pl*
gedacht [gə'daxt] *vb siehe* **denken**
Gedächtnis [gə'dɛçtnɪs] (**-ses, -se**) *nt* memory; **~feier** *f* commemoration
Gedanke [gə'daŋkə] (**-ns, -n**) *m* thought; **sich über etw** *akk* **~n machen** to think about sth
Gedanken- *zW:* **~austausch** *m* exchange of ideas; **g~los** *adj* thoughtless; **~strich** *m* dash; **~übertragung** *f* thought

transference, telepathy

Gedeck [gə'dɛk] **(-(e)s, -e)** *nt* cover(ing); (*Speisenfolge*) menu; **ein ~ auflegen** to lay a place

gedeihen [gə'daɪən] (*unreg*) *vi* to thrive, to prosper

Gedenken *nt*: **zum ~ an jdn** in memory of sb

gedenken [gə'dɛŋkən] (*unreg*) *vi +gen* (*beabsichtigen*) to intend; (*sich erinnern*) to remember

Gedenk- *zW*: **~feier** *f* commemoration; **~minute** *f* minute's silence; **~stätte** *f* memorial; **~tag** *m* remembrance day

Gedicht [gə'dɪçt] **(-(e)s, -e)** *nt* poem

gediegen [gə'diːgən] *adj* (good) quality; (*Mensch*) reliable, honest

Gedränge [gə'drɛŋə] **(-s)** *nt* crush, crowd

gedrängt *adj* compressed; **~ voll** packed

gedrückt [gə'drʏkt] *adj* (*deprimiert*) low, depressed

gedrungen [gə'drʊŋən] *adj* thickset, stocky

Geduld [gə'dʊlt] *f* patience; **g~en** [gə'dʊldən] *vr* to be patient; **g~ig** *adj* patient, forbearing; **~sprobe** *f* trial of (one's) patience

gedurft [gə'dʊrft] *vb siehe* **dürfen**

geehrt [gə'|eːrt] *adj*: **Sehr ~e Frau X!** Dear Mrs X

geeignet [gə'|aɪgnət] *adj* suitable

Gefahr [gə'faːr] **(-, -en)** *f* danger; **~ laufen, etw zu tun** to run the risk of doing sth; **auf eigene ~** at one's own risk

gefährden [gə'fɛːrdən] *vt* to endanger

Gefahren- *zW*: **~quelle** *f* source of danger; **~zulage** *f* danger money

gefährlich [gə'fɛːrlɪç] *adj* dangerous

Gefährte [gə'fɛːrtə] **(-n, -n)** *m* companion; (*Lebenspartner*) partner

Gefährtin [gə'fɛːrtɪn] *f* (female) companion; (*Lebenspartner*) (female) partner

Gefälle [gə'fɛlə] **(-s, -)** *nt* gradient, incline

Gefallen¹ [gə'falən] **(-s, -)** *m* favour

Gefallen² [gə'falən] **(-s)** *nt* pleasure; **an etw** *dat* **~finden** to derive pleasure from sth

gefallen *pp von* **fallen ♦** *vi*: **jdm ~** to please

sb; **er/es gefällt mir** I like him/it; **das gefällt mir an ihm** that's one thing I like about him; **sich** *dat* **etw ~ lassen** to put up with sth

gefällig [gə'fɛlɪç] *adj* (*hilfsbereit*) obliging; (*erfreulich*) pleasant; **G~keit** *f* favour; helpfulness; **etw aus G~keit tun** to do sth out of the goodness of one's heart

gefangen [gə'faŋən] *adj* captured; (*fig*) captivated; **~ halten** to keep prisoner; **~ nehmen** to take prisoner; **G~e(r)** *f(m)* prisoner, captive; **G~nahme** *f* capture; **G~schaft** *f* captivity

Gefängnis [gə'fɛŋnɪs] **(-ses, -se)** *nt* prison; **~strafe** *f* prison sentence; **~wärter** *m* prison warder; **~zelle** *f* prison cell

Gefäß [gə'fɛːs] **(-es, -e)** *nt* vessel; (*auch* ANAT) container

gefasst ▲ [gə'fast] *adj* composed, calm; **auf etw** *akk* **~ sein** to be prepared *od* ready for sth

Gefecht [gə'fɛçt] **(-(e)s, -e)** *nt* fight; (MIL) engagement

Gefieder [gə'fiːdər] **(-s, -)** *nt* plumage, feathers *pl*

gefleckt [gə'flɛkt] *adj* spotted, mottled

geflogen [gə'floːgən] *vb siehe* **fliegen**

geflossen [gə'flɔsən] *vb siehe* **fließen**

Geflügel [gə'flyːgəl] **(-s)** *nt* poultry

Gefolgschaft [gə'fɔlkʃaft] *f* following

gefragt [ge'fraːkt] *adj* in demand

gefräßig [gə'frɛːsɪç] *adj* voracious

Gefreite(r) [gə'fraɪtə(r)] *m* lance corporal; (NAUT) able seaman; (AVIAT) aircraftman

Gefrierbeutel *m* freezer bag

gefrieren [gə'friːrən] (*unreg*) *vi* to freeze

Gefrier- *zW*: **~fach** *nt* icebox; **~fleisch** *nt* frozen meat; **g~getrocknet** [-gətrɔknət] *adj* freeze-dried; **~punkt** *m* freezing point; **~schutzmittel** *nt* antifreeze; **~truhe** *f* deep-freeze

gefroren [gə'froːrən] *vb siehe* **frieren**

Gefühl [gə'fyːl] **(-(e)s, -e)** *nt* feeling; **etw im ~ haben** to have a feel for sth; **g~los** *adj* unfeeling

gefühls- *zW*: **~betont** *adj* emotional; **G~duselei** [-duːzə'laɪ] *f* over-sentimentality;

~mäßig adj instinctive
gefüllt [gə'fʏlt] adj (KOCH) stuffed
gefunden [gə'fundən] vb siehe **finden**
gegangen [gə'gaŋən] vb siehe **gehen**
gegeben [gə'ge:bən] vb siehe **geben** ♦ adj
given; **zu ~er Zeit** in good time
gegebenenfalls [gə'ge:bənənfals] adv if
need be

SCHLÜSSELWORT

gegen ['ge:gən] präp +akk **1** against; **nichts
gegen jdn haben** to have nothing against
sb; **X gegen Y** (SPORT, JUR) X versus Y; **ein
Mittel gegen Schnupfen** something for
colds
2 (in Richtung auf) towards; **gegen Osten**
to(wards) the east; **gegen Abend** towards
evening; **gegen einen Baum fahren** to
drive into a tree
3 (ungefähr) round about; **gegen 3 Uhr**
around 3 o'clock
4 (gegenüber) towards; (ungefähr) around;
gerecht gegen alle fair to all
5 (im Austausch für) for; **gegen bar** for cash;
gegen Quittung against a receipt
6 (verglichen mit) compared with

Gegenangriff m counter-attack
Gegenbeweis m counter-evidence
Gegend ['ge:gənt] (-, -en) f area, district
Gegen- zW: **g~ei'nander** adv against one
another; **~fahrbahn** f oncoming
carriageway; **~frage** f counter-question;
~gewicht nt counterbalance; **~gift** nt
antidote; **~leistung** f service in return;
~maßnahme f countermeasure; **~mittel**
nt antidote, cure; **~satz** m contrast; **~sätze
überbrücken** to overcome differences;
g~sätzlich adj contrary, opposite;
(widersprüchlich) contradictory; **g~seitig** adj
mutual, reciprocal; **sich g~seitig helfen** to
help each other; **~spieler** m opponent;
~sprechanlage f (two-way) intercom;
~stand m object; **~stimme** f vote against;
~stoß m counterblow; **~stück** nt
counterpart; **~teil** nt opposite; **im ~teil** on
the contrary; **g~teilig** adj opposite,

contrary
gegenüber [ge:gən'|y:bər] präp +dat
opposite; (zu) to(wards); (angesichts) in the
face of ♦ adv opposite; **G~** (-s, -) nt person
opposite; **~liegen** (unreg) vr to face each
other; **~stehen** (unreg) vr to be opposed
(to each other); **~stellen** vt to confront;
(fig) to contrast; **G~stellung** f
confrontation; (fig) contrast; **~treten**
(unreg) vi +dat to face
Gegen- zW: **~verkehr** m oncoming traffic;
~vorschlag m counterproposal; **~wart** f
present; **g~wärtig** adj present ♦ adv at
present; **das ist mir nicht mehr g~wärtig**
that has slipped my mind; **~wert** m
equivalent; **~wind** m headwind;
g~zeichnen vt, vi to countersign
gegessen [gə'gesən] vb siehe **essen**
Gegner ['ge:gnər] (-s, -) m opponent;
g~isch adj opposing
gegr. abk (= gegründet) est.
gegrillt [gə'grɪlt] adj grilled
Gehackte(s) [gə'haktə(s)] nt mince(d meat)
Gehalt¹ [gə'halt] (-(e)s, -e) m content
Gehalt² [gə'halt] (-(e)s, ⁻er) nt salary
Gehalts- zW: **~empfänger** m salary
earner; **~erhöhung** f salary increase;
~zulage f salary increment
gehaltvoll [gə'haltfɔl] adj (nahrhaft)
nutritious
gehässig [gə'hesɪç] adj spiteful, nasty
Gehäuse [gə'hɔyzə] (-s, -) nt case; casing;
(von Apfel etc) core
Gehege [gə'he:gə] (-s, -) nt reserve; (im Zoo)
enclosure
geheim [gə'haɪm] adj secret; **~ halten** to
keep secret; **G~dienst** m secret service,
intelligence service; **G~nis** (-ses, -se) nt
secret; mystery; **~nisvoll** adj mysterious;
G~polizei f secret police
gehemmt [gə'hemt] adj inhibited, self-
conscious
gehen ['ge:ən] (unreg) vt, vi to go; (zu Fuß ~)
to walk ♦ vb unpers: **wie geht es (dir)?**
how are you od things?; **~ nach** (Fenster) to
face; **mir/ihm geht es gut** I'm/he's (doing)
fine; **geht das?** is that possible?; **gehts**

noch? can you manage?; **es geht** not too bad, O.K.; **das geht nicht** that's not on; **es geht um etw** it has to do with sth, it's about sth; **sich ~ lassen** (*unbeherrscht sein*) to lose control (of o.s.); **jdn ~ lassen** to let/leave sb alone; **lass mich ~!** leave me alone!

geheuer [gə'hɔyər] *adj:* **nicht ~** eerie; (*fragwürdig*) dubious

Gehilfe [gə'hɪlfə] **(-n, -n)** *m* assistant; **Gehilfin** *f* assistant

Gehirn [gə'hɪrn] **(-(e)s, -e)** *nt* brain; **~erschütterung** *f* concussion; **~hautentzündung** *f* meningitis

gehoben [gə'ho:bən] *pp von* **heben** ♦ *adj* (*Position*) elevated; high

geholfen [gə'hɔlfən] *vb siehe* **helfen**

Gehör [gə'hø:r] **(-(e)s)** *nt* hearing; **musikalisches ~** ear; **~ finden** to gain a hearing; **jdm ~ schenken** to give sb a hearing

gehorchen [gə'hɔrçən] *vi +dat* to obey

gehören [gə'hø:rən] *vi* to belong ♦ *vr unpers* to be right *od* proper

gehörig *adj* proper; **~ zu** *od +dat* belonging to; part of

gehörlos *adj* deaf

gehorsam [gə'ho:rza:m] *adj* obedient; **G~ (-s)** *m* obedience

Geh- [ge:-] *zW:* **~steig** *m* pavement, sidewalk (*US*); **~weg** *m* pavement, sidewalk (*US*)

Geier ['gaɪər] **(-s, -)** *m* vulture

Geige ['gaɪgə] *f* violin; **~r (-s, -)** *m* violinist

geil [gaɪl] *adj* randy (*BRIT*), horny (*US*)

Geisel ['gaɪzəl] **(-, -n)** *f* hostage

Geist [gaɪst] **(-(e)s, -er)** *m* spirit; (*Gespenst*) ghost; (*Verstand*) mind

geisterhaft *adj* ghostly

Geistes- *zW:* **g~abwesend** *adj* absent-minded; **~blitz** *m* brainwave; **~gegenwart** *f* presence of mind; **g~krank** *adj* mentally ill; **~kranke(r)** *f(m)* mentally ill person; **~krankheit** *f* mental illness; **~wissenschaften** *pl* the arts; **~zustand** *m* state of mind

geist- *zW:* **~ig** *adj* intellectual; mental;

(*Getränke*) alcoholic; **~ig behindert** mentally handicapped; **~lich** *adj* spiritual, religious; clerical; **G~liche(r)** *m* clergyman; **G~lichkeit** *f* clergy; **~los** *adj* uninspired, dull; **~reich** *adj* clever; witty; **~voll** *adj* intellectual; (*weise*) wise

Geiz [gaɪts] **(-es)** *m* miserliness, meanness; **g~en** *vi* to be miserly; **~hals** *m* miser; **g~ig** *adj* miserly, mean; **~kragen** *m* miser

gekannt [gə'kant] *vb siehe* **kennen**

gekonnt [gə'kɔnt] *adj* skilful ♦ *vb siehe* **können**

gekünstelt [ge'kynstəlt] *adj* artificial, affected

Gel [ge:l] **(-s, -e)** *nt* gel

Gelächter [gə'lɛçtər] **(-s, -)** *nt* laughter

geladen [ge'la:dən] *adj* loaded; (*ELEK*) live; (*fig*) furious

gelähmt [gə'lɛ:mt] *adj* paralysed

Gelände [gə'lɛndə] **(-s, -)** *nt* land, terrain; (*von Fabrik, Sportgelände*) grounds *pl*; (*Bau~*) site; **~lauf** *m* cross-country race

Geländer [gə'lɛndər] **(-s, -)** *nt* railing; (*Treppengeländer*) banister(s)

gelangen [gə'laŋən] *vi:* **~ (an +akk od zu)** to reach; (*erwerben*) to attain; **in jds Besitz** *akk* **~** to come into sb's possession

gelangweilt [gə'laŋvaɪlt] *adj* bored

gelassen [gə'lasən] *adj* calm, composed; **G~heit** *f* calmness, composure

Gelatine [ʒela'ti:nə] *f* gelatine

geläufig [gə'lɔyfɪç] *adj* (*üblich*) common; **das ist mir nicht ~** I'm not familiar with that

gelaunt [gə'laʊnt] *adj:* **schlecht / gut ~** in a bad/good mood; **wie ist er ~?** what sort of mood is he in?

gelb [gɛlp] *adj* yellow; (*Ampellicht*) amber; **~lich** *adj* yellowish; **G~sucht** *f* jaundice

Geld [gɛlt] **(-(e)s, -er)** *nt* money; **etw zu ~ machen** to sell sth off; **~anlage** *f* investment; **~automat** *m* cash dispenser; **~beutel** *m* purse; **~börse** *f* purse; **~geber (-s, -)** *m* financial backer; **~gierig** *adj* avaricious; **~schein** *m* banknote; **~schrank** *m* safe, strongbox; **~strafe** *f* fine; **~stück** *nt* coin; **~wechsel**

m exchange (of money)

Gelee [ʒeˈleː] **(-s, -s)** *nt od m* jelly

gelegen [ɡəˈleːɡən] *adj* situated; *(passend)* convenient, opportune ♦ *vb siehe* **liegen**; **etw kommt jdm ~** sth is convenient for sb

Gelegenheit [ɡəˈleːɡənhaɪt] *f* opportunity; *(Anlaß)* occasion; **bei jeder ~** at every opportunity; **~sarbeit** *f* casual work; **~skauf** *m* bargain

gelegentlich [ɡəˈleːɡəntlɪç] *adj* occasional ♦ *adv* occasionally; *(bei Gelegenheit)* some time (or other) ♦ *präp +gen* on the occasion of

gelehrt [ɡəˈleːrt] *adj* learned; **G~e(r)** *f(m)* scholar; **G~heit** *f* scholarliness

Geleise [ɡəˈlaɪzə] **(-s, -)** *nt* = **Gleis**

Geleit [ɡəˈlaɪt] **(-(e)s, -e)** *nt* escort; **g~en** *vt* to escort

Gelenk [ɡəˈlɛŋk] **(-(e)s, -e)** *nt* joint; **g~ig** *adj* supple

gelernt [ɡəˈlɛrnt] *adj* skilled

Geliebte(r) [ɡəˈliːptə(r)] *f(m)* sweetheart, beloved

geliehen [ɡəˈliːən] *vb siehe* **leihen**

gelind(e) [ɡəˈlɪnd(ə)] *adj* mild, light; *(fig: Wut)* fierce; **~ gesagt** to put it mildly

gelingen [ɡəˈlɪŋən] *(unreg) vi* to succeed; **es ist mir gelungen, etw zu tun** I succeeded in doing sth

geloben [ɡəˈloːbən] *vt, vi* to vow, to swear

gelten [ˈɡɛltən] *(unreg) vt (wert sein)* to be worth ♦ *vi (gültig sein)* to be valid; *(erlaubt sein)* to be allowed ♦ *vb unpers:* **es gilt, etw zu tun** it is necessary to do sth; **jdm viel/wenig ~** to mean a lot to/not to mean much to sb; **was gilt die Wette?** what do you bet?; **etw ~ lassen** to accept sth; **als od für etw ~** to be considered to be sth; **jdm od für jdn ~** *(betreffen)* to apply to od for sb; **~d** *adj* prevailing; **etw ~d machen** to assert sth; **sich ~d machen** to make itself/o.s. felt

Geltung [ˈɡɛltʊŋ] *f:* **~ haben** to have validity; **sich/etw** *dat* **~ verschaffen** to establish one's position/the position of sth; **etw zur ~ bringen** to show sth to its best advantage; **zur ~ kommen** to be seen/

heard *etc* to its best advantage

Geltungsbedürfnis *nt* desire for admiration

Gelübde [ɡəˈlʏpdə] **(-s, -)** *nt* vow

gelungen [ɡəˈlʊŋən] *adj* successful

gemächlich [ɡəˈmɛːçlɪç] *adj* leisurely

Gemahl [ɡəˈmaːl] **(-(e)s, -e)** *m* husband; **~in** *f* wife

Gemälde [ɡəˈmɛːldə] **(-s, -)** *nt* picture, painting

gemäß [ɡəˈmɛːs] *präp +dat* in accordance with ♦ *adj (+dat)* appropriate (to)

gemäßigt *adj* moderate; *(Klima)* temperate

gemein [ɡəˈmaɪn] *adj* common; *(niederträchtig)* mean; **etw ~ haben (mit)** to have sth in common (with)

Gemeinde [ɡəˈmaɪndə] *f* district, community; *(Pfarrgemeinde)* parish; *(Kirchengemeinde)* congregation; **~steuer** *f* local rates *pl*; **~verwaltung** *f* local administration; **~wahl** *f* local election

Gemein- *zW:* **g~gefährlich** *adj* dangerous to the public; **~heit** *f* commonness; mean thing to do/to say; **g~nützig** *adj* charitable; **g~nütziger Verein** non-profit-making organization; **g~sam** *adj* joint, common *(AUCH MATH)* ♦ *adv* together, jointly; **g~same Sache mit jdm machen** to be in cahoots with sb; **etw g~sam haben** to have sth in common; **~samkeit** *f* community, having in common; **~schaft** *f* community; **in ~schaft mit** jointly *od* together with; **g~schaftlich** *adj* = **gemeinsam**; **~schaftsarbeit** *f* teamwork; team effort; **~sinn** *m* public spirit

Gemenge [ɡəˈmɛŋə] **(-s, -)** *nt* mixture; *(Handgemenge)* scuffle

gemessen [ɡəˈmɛsən] *adj* measured

Gemetzel [ɡəˈmɛtsəl] **(-s, -)** *nt* slaughter, carnage, butchery

Gemisch [ɡəˈmɪʃ] **(-es, -e)** *nt* mixture; **g~t** *adj* mixed

gemocht [ɡəˈmɔxt] *vb siehe* **mögen**

Gemse △ [ˈɡɛmzə] *f siehe* **Gämse**

Gemurmel [ɡəˈmʊrməl] **(-s)** *nt* murmur(ing)

Gemüse [ɡəˈmyːzə] **(-s, -)** *nt* vegetables *pl*; **~garten** *m* vegetable garden; **~händler** *m* greengrocer

gemusst ▲ [gəˈmʊst] *vb siehe* **müssen**

gemustert [gəˈmʊstərt] *adj* patterned

Gemüt [gəˈmyːt] (-(e)s, -er) *nt* disposition, nature; person; **sich** *dat* **etw zu ~e führen** (*umg*) to indulge in sth; **die ~er erregen** to arouse strong feelings; **g~lich** *adj* comfortable, cosy; (*Person*) good-natured; **~lichkeit** *f* comfortableness, cosiness; amiability

Gemüts- *zW:* **~mensch** *m* sentimental person; **~ruhe** *f* composure; **~zustand** *m* state of mind

Gen [geːn] (-s, -e) *nt* gene

genannt [gəˈnant] *vb siehe* **nennen**

genau [gəˈnaʊ] *adj* exact, precise ♦ *adv* exactly, precisely; **etw ~ nehmen** to take sth seriously; **~ genommen** strictly speaking; **G~igkeit** *f* exactness, accuracy; **~so** *adv* just the same; **~so gut** just as good

genehm [gəˈneːm] *adj* agreeable, acceptable; **~igen** *vt* to approve, to authorize; **sich** *dat* **etw ~igen** to indulge in sth; **G~igung** *f* approval, authorization; (*Schriftstück*) permit

General [geneˈraːl] (-s, -e *od* ̈e) *m* general; **~direktor** *m* director general; **~konsulat** *nt* consulate general; **~probe** *f* dress rehearsal; **~streik** *m* general strike; **g~überholen** *vt* to overhaul thoroughly; **~versammlung** *f* general meeting

Generation [generatsiˈoːn] *f* generation

Generator [geneˈraːtɔr] *m* generator, dynamo

generell [genəˈrɛl] *adj* general

genesen [geˈneːzən] (*unreg*) *vi* to convalesce, to recover; **Genesung** *f* recovery, convalescence

genetisch [geˈneːtɪʃ] *adj* genetic

Genf [ˈgɛnf] *nt* Geneva; **der ~er See** Lake Geneva

genial [geniˈaːl] *adj* brilliant

Genick [gəˈnɪk] (-(e)s, -e) *nt* (back of the) neck

Genie [ʒeˈniː] (-s, -s) *nt* genius

genieren [ʒeˈniːrən] *vt* to bother ♦ *vr* to feel awkward *od* self-conscious

genieß- *zW:* **~bar** *adj* edible; drinkable; **~en** [gəˈniːsən] (*unreg*) *vt* to enjoy; to eat; to drink; **G~er** (-s, -) *m* epicure; pleasure lover; **~erisch** *adj* appreciative ♦ *adv* with relish

genmanipuliert [ˈgeːnmanipuliːrt] *adj* genetically modified

genommen [gəˈnɔmən] *vb siehe* **nehmen**

Genosse [gəˈnɔsə] (-n, -n) *m* (*bes POL*) comrade, companion; **~nschaft** *f* cooperative (association)

Genossin *f* (*bes POL*) comrade, companion

Gentechnik [ˈgeːntɛçnɪk] *f* genetic engineering

genug [gəˈnuːk] *adv* enough

Genüge [gəˈnyːgə] *f:* **jdm / etw ~ tun** *od* **leisten** to satisfy sb/sth; **g~n** *vi* (+*dat*) to be enough (for); **g~nd** *adj* sufficient

genügsam [gəˈnyːkzaːm] *adj* modest, easily satisfied; **G~keit** *f* moderation

Genugtuung [gəˈnuːktuːʊŋ] *f* satisfaction

Genuss ▲ [gəˈnʊs] (-es, ̈e) *m* pleasure; (*Zusichnehmen*) consumption; **in den ~ von etw kommen** to receive the benefit of sth

genüsslich ▲ [gəˈnʏslɪç] *adv* with relish

Genussmittel ▲ *pl* (semi-)luxury items

geöffnet [gəˈœfnət] *adj* open

Geograf ▲ [geoˈgraːf] (-en, -en) *m* geographer; **Geografie** ▲ *f* geography; **g~isch** *adj* geographical

Geologe [geoˈloːgə] (-n, -n) *m* geologist; **Geologie** *f* geology

Geometrie [geomeˈtriː] *f* geometry

Gepäck [gəˈpɛk] (-(e)s) *nt* luggage, baggage; **~abfertigung** *f* luggage office; **~annahme** *f* luggage office; **~aufbewahrung** *f* left-luggage office (*BRIT*), baggage check (*US*); **~aufgabe** *f* luggage office; **~ausgabe** *f* luggage office; (*AVIAT*) luggage reclaim; **~netz** *nt* luggage rack; **~träger** *m* porter; (*Fahrrad*) carrier; **~versicherung** *f* luggage insurance; **~wagen** *m* luggage van (*BRIT*), baggage car (*US*)

gepflegt [gəˈpfleːkt] *adj* well-groomed; (*Park etc*) well looked after

Gerade [gə'ra:də] f straight line; **g~'aus** adv straight ahead; **g~he'raus** adv straight out, bluntly; **g~stehen** (unreg) vi: **für jdn/etw g~stehen** to be answerable for sb('s actions)/sth; **g~wegs** adv direct, straight; **g~zu** adv (beinahe) virtually, almost

---
SCHLÜSSELWORT
---

gerade [gə'ra:də] adj straight; (aufrecht) upright; **eine gerade Zahl** an even number

♦ adv 1 (genau) just, exactly; (speziell) especially; **gerade deshalb** that's just od exactly why; **das ist es ja gerade!** that's just it!; **gerade du** you especially; **warum gerade ich?** why me (of all people)?; **jetzt gerade nicht!** not now!; **gerade neben** right next to

2 (eben, soeben) just; **er wollte gerade aufstehen** he was just about to get up; **gerade erst** only just; **gerade noch** (only) just

---

gerannt [gə'rant] vb siehe **rennen**
Gerät [gə'rɛːt] (-(e)s, -e) nt device; (Werkzeug) tool; (SPORT) apparatus; (Zubehör) equipment no pl
geraten [gə'ra:tən] (unreg) vi (gedeihen) to thrive; (gelingen): **(jdm) ~** to turn out well (for sb); **gut/schlecht ~** to turn out well/ badly; **an jdn ~** to come across sb; **in etw** akk **~** to get into sth; **nach jdm ~** to take after sb
Geratewohl [gəra:tə'vo:l] nt: **aufs ~** on the off chance; (bei Wahl) at random
geräuchert [gə'rɔʏçərt] adj smoked
geräumig [gə'rɔʏmɪç] adj roomy
Geräusch [gə'rɔʏʃ] (-(e)s, -e) nt sound, noise; **g~los** adj silent
gerben ['gɛrbən] vt to tan
gerecht [gə'rɛçt] adj just, fair; **jdm/etw ~ werden** to do justice to sb/sth; **G~igkeit** f justice, fairness
Gerede [gə're:də] (-s) nt talk, gossip
geregelt [gə're:gəlt] adj (Arbeit) steady, regular; (Mahlzeiten) regular, set

gereizt [gə'raɪtst] adj irritable; **G~heit** f irritation
Gericht [gə'rɪçt] (-(e)s, -e) nt court; (Essen) dish; **mit jdm ins ~ gehen** (fig) to judge sb harshly; **das Jüngste ~** the Last Judgement; **g~lich** adj judicial, legal ♦ adv judicially, legally
Gerichts- zW: **~barkeit** f jurisdiction; **~hof** m court (of law); **~kosten** pl (legal) costs; **~medizin** f forensic medicine; **~saal** m courtroom; **~verfahren** nt legal proceedings pl; **~verhandlung** f trial; **~vollzieher** m bailiff
gerieben [gə'ri:bən] adj grated; (umg: schlau) smart, wily ♦ vb siehe **reiben**
gering [gə'rɪŋ] adj slight, small; (niedrig) low; (Zeit) short; **~fügig** adj slight, trivial; **~schätzig** adj disparaging
geringste(r, s) adj slightest, least; **~nfalls** adv at the very least
gerinnen [gə'rɪnən] (unreg) vi to congeal; (Blut) to clot; (Milch) to curdle
Gerippe [gə'rɪpə] (-s, -) nt skeleton
gerissen [gə'rɪsən] adj wily, smart
geritten [gə'rɪtən] vb siehe **reiten**
gern(e) ['gɛrn(ə)] adv willingly, gladly; **~ haben, ~ mögen** to like; **etwas ~ tun** to like doing something; **ich möchte ~ ...** I'd like ...; **ja, ~** yes, please; yes, I'd like to; **~ geschehen** it's a pleasure
gerochen [gə'rɔxən] vb siehe **riechen**
Geröll [gə'rœl] (-(e)s, -e) nt scree
Gerste ['gɛrstə] f barley; **~nkorn** nt (im Auge) stye
Geruch [gə'rʊx] (-(e)s, "e) m smell, odour; **g~los** adj odourless
Gerücht [gə'rʏçt] (-(e)s, -e) nt rumour
geruhsam [gə'ru:za:m] adj (Leben) peaceful; (Nacht, Zeit) peaceful, restful; (langsam: Arbeitsweise, Spaziergang) leisurely
Gerümpel [gə'rʏmpəl] (-s) nt junk
Gerüst [gə'rʏst] (-(e)s, -e) nt (Baugerüst) scaffold(ing); frame
gesalzen [gə'zaltsən] pp von **salzen** ♦ adj (umg: Preis, Rechnung) steep
gesamt [gə'zamt] adj whole, entire; (Kosten) total; (Werke) complete; **im G~en** all in all;

~deutsch *adj* all-German; **G~eindruck** *m* general impression; **G~heit** *f* totality, whole; **G~schule** *f* ≈ comprehensive school

Gesamtschule

i *The Gesamtschule is a comprehensive school for pupils of different abilities. Traditionally pupils go to either a* **Gymnasium***,* **Realschule** *or* **Hauptschule***, depending on ability. The Gesamtschule seeks to avoid the elitism of many Gymnasien. However, these schools are still very controversial, with many parents still preferring the traditional education system.*

gesandt [gə'zant] *vb siehe* **senden**
Gesandte(r) [gə'zantə(r)] *m* envoy
Gesandtschaft [gə'zantʃaft] *f* legation
Gesang [gə'zaŋ] **(-(e)s, ⁻e)** *m* song; (*Singen*) singing; **~buch** *nt* (*REL*) hymn book
Gesäß [gə'zɛːs] **(-es, -e)** *nt* seat, bottom
Geschäft [gə'ʃɛft] **(-(e)s, -e)** *nt* business; (*Laden*) shop; (*~sabschluß*) deal; **g~ig** *adj* active, busy; (*pej*) officious; **g~lich** *adj* commercial ♦ *adv* on business
Geschäfts- *zW:* **~bedingungen** *pl* terms *pl* of business; **~bericht** *m* financial report; **~frau** *f* businesswoman; **~führer** *m* manager; (*Klub*) secretary; **~geheimnis** *nt* trade secret; **~jahr** *nt* financial year; **~lage** *f* business conditions *pl*; **~mann** *m* businessman; **g~mäßig** *adj* businesslike; **~partner** *m* business partner; **~reise** *f* business trip; **~schluss** ▲ *m* closing time; **~stelle** *f* office, place of business; **g~tüchtig** *adj* business-minded; **~viertel** *nt* business quarter; shopping centre; **~wagen** *m* company car; **~zeit** *f* business hours *pl*
geschehen [gə'ʃeːən] (*unreg*) *vi* to happen; **es war um ihn ~** that was the end of him
gescheit [gə'ʃait] *adj* clever
Geschenk [gə'ʃɛŋk] **(-(e)s, -e)** *nt* present, gift
Geschichte [gə'ʃɪçtə] *f* story; (*Sache*) affair;

(*Historie*) history
geschichtlich *adj* historical
Geschick [gə'ʃɪk] **(-(e)s, -e)** *nt* aptitude; (*Schicksal*) fate; **~lichkeit** *f* skill, dexterity; **g~** *adj* skilful
geschieden [gə'ʃiːdən] *adj* divorced
geschienen [gə'ʃiːnən] *vb siehe* **scheinen**
Geschirr [gə'ʃɪr] **(-(e)s, -e)** *nt* crockery; pots and pans *pl*; (*Pferdegeschirr*) harness; **~spülmaschine** *f* dishwasher; **~spülmittel** *nt* washing-up liquid; **~tuch** *nt* dish cloth
Geschlecht [gə'ʃlɛçt] **(-(e)s, -er)** *nt* sex; (*GRAM*) gender; (*Gattung*) race; family; **g~lich** *adj* sexual
Geschlechts- *zW:* **~krankheit** *f* venereal disease; **~teil** *nt* genitals *pl*; **~verkehr** *m* sexual intercourse
geschlossen [gə'ʃlɔsən] *adj* shut ♦ *vb siehe* **schließen**
Geschmack [gə'ʃmak] **(-(e)s, ⁻e)** *m* taste; **nach jds ~** to sb's taste; **~ finden an etw** *dat* to (come to) like sth; **g~los** *adj* tasteless; (*fig*) in bad taste; **~ssinn** *m* sense of taste; **g~voll** *adj* tasteful
geschmeidig [gə'ʃmaidɪç] *adj* supple; (*formbar*) malleable
Geschnetzelte(s) [gə'ʃnɛtsəltə(s)] *nt* (*KOCH*) *strips of meat stewed to produce a thick sauce*
geschnitten [gə'ʃnɪtən] *vb siehe* **schneiden**
Geschöpf [gə'ʃœpf] **(-(e)s, -e)** *nt* creature
Geschoss ▲ [gə'ʃɔs] **(-es, -e)** *nt* (*MIL*) projectile, missile; (*Stockwerk*) floor
geschossen [gə'ʃɔsən] *vb siehe* **schießen**
geschraubt [gə'ʃraupt] *adj* stilted, artificial
Geschrei [gə'ʃrai] **(-s)** *nt* cries *pl*, shouting; (*fig: Aufheben*) noise, fuss
geschrieben [gə'ʃriːbən] *vb siehe* **schreiben**
Geschütz [gə'ʃyts] **(-es, -e)** *nt* gun, cannon; **ein schweres ~ auffahren** (*fig*) to bring out the big guns
geschützt *adj* protected
Geschw. *abk siehe* **Geschwister**
Geschwätz [gə'ʃvɛts] **(-es)** *nt* chatter, gossip; **g~ig** *adj* talkative
geschweige [gə'ʃvaigə] *adv*: **~ (denn)** let

alone, not to mention

geschwind [gə'ʃvɪnt] *adj* quick, swift;
G~igkeit [-dɪçkaɪt] *f* speed, velocity;
G~igkeitsbeschränkung *f* speed limit;
G~igkeitsüberschreitung *f* exceeding
the speed limit

Geschwister [gə'ʃvɪstər] *pl* brothers and
sisters

geschwommen [gə'ʃvɔmən] *vb siehe*
schwimmen

Geschworene(r) [gə'ʃvoːrənə(r)] *f(m)* juror;
~n *pl* jury

Geschwulst [gə'ʃvʊlst] (-, ⁺e) *f* swelling;
growth, tumour

geschwungen [gə'ʃvʊŋən] *pp von*
schwingen ♦ *adj* curved, arched

Geschwür [gə'ʃvyːr] (-(e)s, -e) *nt* ulcer

Gesell- [gə'zɛl] *zW:* **~e** (-n, -n) *m* fellow;
(*Handwerksgeselle*) journeyman; **g~ig** *adj*
sociable; **~igkeit** *f* sociability; **~schaft** *f*
society, (*Begleitung, COMM*) company;
(*Abendgesellschaft etc*) party; **g~schaftlich**
adj social; **~schaftsordnung** *f* social
structure; **~schaftsschicht** *f* social
stratum

gesessen [gə'zɛsən] *vb siehe* **sitzen**

Gesetz [gə'zɛts] (-es, -e) *nt* law; **~buch** *nt*
statute book; **~entwurf** *m* (draft) bill;
~gebung *f* legislation; **g~lich** *adj* legal,
lawful; **g~licher Feiertag** statutory holiday;
g~los *adj* lawless; **g~mäßig** *adj* lawful;
g~t *adj* (*Mensch*) sedate; **g~widrig** *adj*
illegal, unlawful

Gesicht [gə'zɪçt] (-(e)s, -er) *nt* face; **das
zweite ~** second sight; **das ist mir nie zu
~ gekommen** I've never laid eyes on that

Gesichts- *zW:* **~ausdruck** *m* (facial)
expression; **~creme** *f* face cream; **~farbe**
f complexion; **~punkt** *m* point of view;
~wasser *nt* face lotion; **~züge** *pl* features

Gesindel [gə'zɪndəl] (-s) *nt* rabble

gesinnt [gə'zɪnt] *adj* disposed, minded

Gesinnung [gə'zɪnʊŋ] *f* disposition; (*Ansicht*)
views *pl*

gesittet [gə'zɪtət] *adj* well-mannered

Gespann [gə'ʃpan] (-(e)s, -e) *nt* team;
(*umg*) couple

gespannt *adj* tense, strained; (*begierig*)
eager; **ich bin ~, ob** I wonder if *od*
whether; **auf etw/jdn ~ sein** to look
forward to sth/meeting sb

Gespenst [gə'ʃpɛnst] (-(e)s, -er) *nt* ghost,
spectre

gesperrt [gə'ʃpɛrt] *adj* closed off

Gespött [gə'ʃpœt] (-(e)s) *nt* mockery; **zum ~
werden** to become a laughing stock

Gespräch [gə'ʃprɛːç] (-(e)s, -e) *nt*
conversation; discussion(s); (*Anruf*) call;
g~ig *adj* talkative

gesprochen [gə'ʃprɔxən] *vb siehe* **sprechen**

gesprungen [gə'ʃprʊŋən] *vb siehe* **springen**

Gespür [gə'ʃpyːr] (-s) *nt* feeling

Gestalt [gə'ʃtalt] (-, -en) *f* form, shape;
(*Person*) figure; **in ~ von** in the form of, **~
annehmen** to take shape; **g~en** *vt* (*formen*)
to shape, to form; (*organisieren*) to arrange,
to organize ♦ *vr:* **sich g~en (zu)** to turn out
(to be); **~ung** *f* formation; organization

gestanden [gə'ʃtandən] *vb siehe* **stehen**

Geständnis [gə'ʃtɛntnɪs] (-ses, -se) *nt*
confession

Gestank [gə'ʃtaŋk] (-(e)s) *m* stench

gestatten [gə'ʃtatən] *vt* to permit, to allow;
~ Sie? may I?; **sich dat ~, etw zu tun** to
take the liberty of doing sth

Geste l'gɛstəl *f* gesture

gestehen [gə'ʃteːən] (*unreg*) *vt* to confess

Gestein [gə'ʃtaɪn] (-(e)s, -e) *nt* rock

Gestell [gə'ʃtɛl] (-(e)s, -e) *nt* frame; (*Regal*)
rack, stand

gestern ['gɛstərn] *adv* yesterday; **~ Abend/
Morgen** yesterday evening/morning

Gestirn [gə'ʃtɪrn] (-(e)s, -e) *nt* star;
(*Sternbild*) constellation

gestohlen [gə'ʃtoːlən] *vb siehe* **stehlen**

gestorben [gə'ʃtɔrbən] *vb siehe* **sterben**

gestört [gə'ʃtøːrt] *adj* disturbed

gestreift [gə'ʃtraɪft] *adj* striped

gestrichen [gə'ʃtrɪçən] *adj* cancelled

gestrig ['gɛstrɪç] *adj* yesterday's

Gestrüpp [gə'ʃtrʏp] (-(e)s, -e) *nt*
undergrowth

Gestüt [gə'ʃtyːt] (-(e)s, -e) *nt* stud farm

Gesuch [gə'zuːx] (-(e)s, -e) *nt* petition;

(Antrag) application; **g~t** *adj (COMM)* in demand; wanted; *(fig)* contrived

gesund [gəˈzʊnt] *adj* healthy; **wieder ~ werden** to get better; **G~heit** *f* health(iness); **G~heit!** bless you!; **~heitlich** *adj* health *attrib*, physical ♦ *adv*: **wie geht es Ihnen ~heitlich?** how's your health?; **~heitsschädlich** *adj* unhealthy; **G~heitswesen** *nt* health service; **G~heitszustand** *m* state of health

gesungen [gəˈzʊŋən] *vb siehe* **singen**

getan [gəˈtaːn] *vb siehe* **tun**

Getöse [gəˈtøːzə] *(-s) nt* din, racket

Getränk [gəˈtrɛŋk] *(-(e)s, -e) nt* drink; **~ekarte** *f* wine list

getrauen [gəˈtraʊən] *vr* to dare, to venture

Getreide [gəˈtraɪdə] *(-s, -) nt* cereals *pl*, grain; **~speicher** *m* granary

getrennt [gəˈtrɛnt] *adj* separate

Getriebe [gəˈtriːbə] *(-s, -) nt (Leute)* bustle; *(AUT)* gearbox

getrieben *vb siehe* **treiben**

getroffen [gəˈtrɔfən] *vb siehe* **treffen**

getrost [gəˈtroːst] *adv* without any bother

getrunken [gəˈtrʊŋkən] *vb siehe* **trinken**

Getue [gəˈtuːə] *(-s) nt* fuss

geübt [gəˈyːpt] *adj* experienced

Gewächs [gəˈvɛks] *(-es, -e) nt* growth; *(Pflanze)* plant

gewachsen [gəˈvaksən] *adj*: **jdm/etw ~ sein** to be sb's equal/equal to sth

Gewächshaus *nt* greenhouse

gewagt [gəˈvaːkt] *adj* daring, risky

gewählt [gəˈvɛːlt] *adj (Sprache)* refined, elegant

Gewähr [gəˈvɛːr] *(-) f* guarantee; **keine ~ übernehmen für** to accept no responsibility for; **g~en** *vt* to grant; *(geben)* to provide; **g~leisten** *vt* to guarantee

Gewahrsam [gəˈvaːrzaːm] *(-s, -e) m* safekeeping; *(Polizeigewahrsam)* custody

Gewalt [gəˈvalt] *(-, -en) f* power; *(große Kraft)* force; *(~taten)* violence; **mit aller ~** with all one's might; **~anwendung** *f* use of force; **g~ig** *adj* tremendous; *(Irrtum)* huge; **~marsch** *m* forced march; **g~sam** *adj* forcible; **g~tätig** *adj* violent

Gewand [gəˈvant] *(-(e)s, ⁻er) nt* gown, robe

gewandt [gəˈvant] *adj* deft, skilful; *(erfahren)* experienced; **G~heit** *f* dexterity, skill

gewann *etc* [gəˈvaːn] *vb siehe* **gewinnen**

Gewässer [gəˈvɛsər] *(-s, -) nt* waters *pl*

Gewebe [gəˈveːbə] *(-s, -) nt (Stoff)* fabric; *(BIOL)* tissue

Gewehr [gəˈveːr] *(-(e)s, -e) nt* gun; rifle; **~lauf** *m* rifle barrel

Geweih [gəˈvaɪ] *(-(e)s, -e) nt* antlers *pl*

Gewerbe- [gəˈvɛrbə] *zW*: **~e** *(-s, -) nt* trade, occupation; **Handel und ~e** trade and industry; **~eschule** *f* technical school; **~ezweig** *m* line of trade

Gewerkschaft [gəˈvɛrkʃaft] *f* trade union; **~ler** *(-s, -) m* trade unionist; **~sbund** *m* trade unions federation

gewesen [gəˈveːzən] *pp von* **sein**

Gewicht [gəˈvɪçt] *(-(e)s, -e) nt* weight; *(fig)* importance

gewieft [gəˈviːft] *adj* shrewd, cunning

gewillt [gəˈvɪlt] *adj* willing, prepared

Gewimmel [gəˈvɪməl] *(-s) nt* swarm

Gewinde [gəˈvɪndə] *(-s, -) nt (Kranz)* wreath; *(von Schraube)* thread

Gewinn [gəˈvɪn] *(-(e)s, -e) m* profit; *(bei Spiel)* winnings *pl*; **~ bringend** profitable; **etw mit ~ verkaufen** to sell sth at a profit; **~~ und Verlustrechnung** *(COMM)* profit and loss account; **~beteiligung** *f* profit-sharing; **g~en** *(unreg) vt* to win; *(erwerben)* to gain; *(Kohle, Öl)* to extract ♦ *vi* to win; *(profitieren)* to gain; **an etw** *dat* **g~en** to gain (in) sth; **g~end** *adj (Lächeln, Aussehen)* winning, charming; **~er(in)** *(-s, -) m(f)* winner; **~spanne** *f* profit margin; **~ung** *f* winning; gaining; *(von Kohle etc)* extraction

Gewirr [gəˈvɪr] *(-(e)s, -e) nt* tangle; *(von Straßen)* maze

gewiss ▲ [gəˈvɪs] *adj* certain ♦ *adv* certainly

Gewissen [gəˈvɪsən] *(-s, -) nt* conscience; **g~haft** *adj* conscientious; **g~los** *adj* unscrupulous

Gewissens- *zW*: **~bisse** *pl* pangs of conscience, qualms; **~frage** *f* matter of conscience; **~konflikt** *m* moral conflict

gewissermaßen [gəvɪsərˈmaːsən] *adv* more

or less, in a way

Gewissheit ▲ [gəˈvɪshaɪt] f certainty

Gewitter [gəˈvɪtər] **(-s, -)** nt thunderstorm; **g~n** vi unpers: **es g~t** there's a thunderstorm

gewitzt [gəˈvɪtst] adj shrewd, cunning

gewogen [gəˈvoːɡən] adj (+dat) well-disposed (towards)

gewöhnen [gəˈvøːnən] vt: **jdn an etw** akk **~** to accustom sb to sth; (erziehen zu) to teach sb sth ♦ vr: **sich an etw** akk **~** to get used od accustomed to sth

Gewohnheit [gəˈvoːnhaɪt] f habit; (Brauch) custom; **aus ~** from habit; **zur ~ werden** to become a habit

Gewohnheits- zW: **~mensch** m creature of habit; **~recht** nt common law

gewöhnlich [gəˈvøːnlɪç] adj usual; ordinary; (pej) common; **wie ~** as usual

gewohnt [gəˈvoːnt] adj usual; **etw ~ sein** to be used to sth

Gewöhnung f: **~ (an** +akk) getting accustomed (to)

Gewölbe [gəˈvœlbə] **(-s, -)** nt vault

gewollt [gəˈvɔlt] adj affected, artificial

gewonnen [gəˈvɔnən] vb siehe **gewinnen**

geworden [gəˈvɔrdən] vb siehe **werden**

geworfen [gəˈvɔrfən] vb siehe **werfen**

Gewühl [gəˈvyːl] **(-(e)s)** nt throng

Gewürz [gəˈvʏrts] **(-es, -e)** nt spice, seasoning; **g~t** adj spiced

gewusst ▲ [gəˈvʊst] vb siehe **wissen**

Gezeiten [gəˈtsaɪtən] pl tides

gezielt [gəˈtsiːlt] adj with a particular aim in mind, purposeful; (Kritik) pointed

gezogen [gəˈtsoːɡən] vb siehe **ziehen**

Gezwitscher [gəˈtsvɪtʃər] **(-s)** nt twitter(ing), chirping

gezwungen [gəˈtsvʊŋən] adj forced; **~ermaßen** adv of necessity

ggf. abk von **gegebenenfalls**

gibst etc [ɡiːpst] vb siehe **geben**

Gicht [ɡɪçt] **(-)** f gout

Giebel [ˈɡiːbəl] **(-s, -)** m gable; **~dach** nt gable(d) roof; **~fenster** nt gable window

Gier [ɡiːr] **(-)** f greed; **g~ig** adj greedy

gießen [ˈɡiːsən] (unreg) vt to pour; (Blumen)

to water; (Metall) to cast; (Wachs) to mould

Gießkanne f watering can

Gift [ɡɪft] **(-(e)s, -e)** nt poison; **g~ig** adj poisonous; (fig: boshaft) venomous; **~müll** m toxic waste; **~stoff** m toxic substance; **~zahn** m fang

ging etc [ɡɪŋ] vb siehe **gehen**

Gipfel [ˈɡɪpfəl] **(-s, -)** m summit, peak; (fig: Höhepunkt) height; **g~n** vi to culminate; **~treffen** nt summit (meeting)

Gips [ɡɪps] **(-es, -e)** nt plaster; (MED) plaster (of Paris); **~abdruck** m plaster cast; **g~en** vt to plaster; **~verband** m plaster (cast)

Giraffe [ɡiˈrafə] f giraffe

Girlande [ɡɪrˈlandə] f garland

Giro [ˈʒiːro] **(-s, -s)** nt giro; **~konto** nt current account

Gitarre [ɡiˈtarə] f guitar

Gitter [ˈɡɪtər] **(-s, -)** nt grating, bars pl; (für Pflanzen) trellis; (Zaun) railing(s); **~bett** nt cot; **~fenster** nt barred window; **~zaun** m railing(s)

Glanz [ɡlants] **(-es)** m shine, lustre; (fig) splendour

glänzen [ˈɡlɛntsən] vi to shine (also fig), to gleam ♦ vt to polish; **~d** adj shining; (fig) brilliant

Glanz- zW: **~leistung** f brilliant achievement; **g~los** adj dull; **~zeit** f heyday

Glas [ɡlaːs] **(-es, ¨er)** nt glass; **~er (-s, -)** m glazier; **~faser** f fibreglass; **g~ieren** [ɡlaˈziːrən] vt to glaze; **g~ig** adj glassy; **~scheibe** f pane; **~ur** [ɡlaˈzuːr] f glaze; (KOCH) icing

glatt [ɡlat] adj smooth; (rutschig) slippery; (Absage) flat; (Lüge) downright; **Glätte** f smoothness; slipperiness

Glatteis nt (black) ice; **jdn aufs ~ führen** (fig) to take sb for a ride

glätten vt to smooth out

Glatze [ˈɡlatsə] f bald head; **eine ~ bekommen** to go bald

Glaube [ˈɡlaʊbə] **(-ns, -n)** m: **~ (an** +akk) faith (in); belief (in); **g~n** vt, vi to believe; to think; **jdm g~n** to believe sb; **an etw** akk **g~n** to believe in sth; **daran g~n müssen**

(*umg*) to be for it
glaubhaft ['glaʊbhaft] *adj* credible
gläubig ['glɔʏbɪç] *adj* (*REL*) devout; (*vertrauensvoll*) trustful; **G~e(r)** *f(m)* believer; **die G~en** the faithful; **G~er (-s, -)** *m* creditor
glaubwürdig ['glaʊbvʏrdɪç] *adj* credible; (*Mensch*) trustworthy; **G~keit** *f* credibility; trustworthiness
gleich [glaɪç] *adj* equal; (*identisch*) (the) same, identical ♦ *adv* equally; (*sofort*) straight away; (*bald*) in a minute; **es ist mir ~** it's all the same to me; **~ bleibend** constant; **~ gesinnt** like-minded; **2 mal 2 ~ 4** 2 times 2 is *od* equals 4; **~ groß** the same size; **~ nach/an** right after/at; **~altrig** *adj* of the same age; **~artig** *adj* similar; **~bedeutend** *adj* synonymous; **G~berechtigung** *f* equal rights *pl*; **~en** (*unreg*) *vi*: **jdm/etw ~en** to be like sb/sth ♦ *vr* to be alike; **~falls** *adv* likewise; **danke ~falls!** the same to you; **G~förmigkeit** *f* uniformity; **G~gewicht** *nt* equilibrium, balance; **~gültig** *adj* indifferent; (*unbedeutend*) unimportant; **G~gültigkeit** *f* indifference; **G~heit** *f* equality; **~kommen** (*unreg*) *vi +dat* to be equal to; **~mäßig** *adj* even, equal; **~sam** *adv* as it were; **G~schritt** *m*: **im G~schritt gehen** to walk in step; **~stellen** *vt* (*rechtlich etc*) to treat as (an) equal; **G~strom** *m* (*ELEK*) direct current; **~tun** (*unreg*) *vi*: **es jdm ~tun** to match sb; **G~ung** *f* equation; **~viel** *adv* no matter; **~wertig** *adj* (*Geld*) of the same value; (*Gegner*) evenly matched; **~zeitig** *adj* simultaneous
Gleis [glaɪs] (**-es, -e**) *nt* track, rails *pl*; (*Bahnsteig*) platform
gleiten ['glaɪtən] (*unreg*) *vi* to glide; (*rutschen*) to slide
Gleitzeit *f* flex(i)time
Gletscher ['glɛtʃər] (**-s, -**) *m* glacier; **~spalte** *f* crevasse
Glied [gliːt] (**-(e)s, -er**) *nt* member; (*Arm, Bein*) limb; (*von Kette*) link; (*MIL*) rank(s); **g~ern** [-dərn] *vt* to organize, to structure; **~erung** *f* structure, organization

glimmen ['glɪmən] (*unreg*) *vi* to glow, to gleam
glimpflich ['glɪmpflɪç] *adj* mild, lenient; **~ davonkommen** to get off lightly
glitschig ['glɪtʃɪç] *adj* (*Fisch, Weg*) slippery
glitzern ['glɪtsərn] *vi* to glitter; to twinkle
global [glo'baːl] *adj* global
Globus ['gloːbʊs] (**- *od* -ses, Globen** *od* **-se**) *m* globe
Glocke ['glɔkə] *f* bell; **etw an die große ~ hängen** (*fig*) to shout sth from the rooftops
Glocken- *zW*: **~blume** *f* bellflower; **~geläut** *nt* peal of bells; **~spiel** *nt* chime(s); (*MUS*) glockenspiel; **~turm** *m* bell tower
Glosse ['glɔsə] *f* comment
glotzen ['glɔtsən] (*umg*) *vi* to stare
Glück [glʏk] (**-(e)s**) *nt* luck, fortune; (*Freude*) happiness; **~ haben** to be lucky; **viel ~!** good luck!; **zum ~** fortunately; **g~en** *vi* to succeed; **es g~te ihm, es zu bekommen** he succeeded in getting it
gluckern ['glʊkərn] *vi* to glug
glück- *zW*: **~lich** *adj* fortunate; (*froh*) happy; **~licherweise** *adv* fortunately; **~'selig** *adj* blissful
Glücks- *zW*: **~fall** *m* stroke of luck; **~kind** *nt* lucky person; **~sache** *f* matter of luck; **~spiel** *nt* game of chance
Glückwunsch *m* congratulations *pl*, best wishes *pl*
Glüh- ['glyː] *zW*: **~birne** *f* light bulb; **g~en** *vi* to glow; **~wein** *m* mulled wine; **~würmchen** *nt* glow-worm
Glut [gluːt] (**-, -en**) *f* (*Röte*) glow; (*Feuersglut*) fire; (*Hitze*) heat; (*fig*) ardour
GmbH [geːʔɛmbeː'haː] *f abk* (= *Gesellschaft mit beschränkter Haftung*) limited company, Ltd
Gnade ['gnaːdə] *f* (*Gunst*) favour; (*Erbarmen*) mercy; (*Milde*) clemency
Gnaden- *zW*: **~frist** *f* reprieve, respite; **g~los** *adj* merciless; **~stoß** *m* coup de grâce
gnädig ['gnɛːdɪç] *adj* gracious; (*voll Erbarmen*) merciful
Gold [gɔlt] (**-(e)s**) *nt* gold; **g~en** *adj* golden; **~fisch** *m* goldfish; **~grube** *f* goldmine;

g~ig ['gɔldɪç] (*umg*) *adj* (*fig: allerliebst*) sweet, adorable; **~regen** *m* laburnum; **~schmied** *m* goldsmith

Golf¹ [gɔlf] (**-(e)s, -e**) *m* gulf

Golf² [gɔlf] (**-s**) *nt* golf; **~platz** *m* golf course; **~schläger** *m* golf club

Golfstrom *m* Gulf Stream

Gondel ['gɔndəl] (**-, -n**) *f* gondola; (*Seilbahn*) cable car

gönnen ['gœnən] *vt*: **jdm etw ~** not to begrudge sb sth; **sich** *dat* **etw ~** to allow o.s. sth

Gönner (**-s, -**) *m* patron; **g~haft** *adj* patronizing

Gosse ['gɔsə] *f* gutter

Gott [gɔt] (**-es, ¨er**) *m* god; **mein ~!** for heaven's sake!; **um ~es Willen!** for heaven's sake!; **grüß ~!** hello; **~ sei Dank!** thank God!; **~heit** *f* deity

Göttin ['gœtɪn] *f* goddess

göttlich *adj* divine

gottlos *adj* godless

Götze ['gœtsə] (**-n, -n**) *m* idol

Grab [gra:p] (**-(e)s, ¨er**) *nt* grave; **g~en** ['gra:bən] (*unreg*) *vt* to dig; **~en** (**-s, ¨**) *m* ditch; (*MIL*) trench; **~stein** *m* gravestone

Grad [gra:t] (**-(e)s, -e**) *m* degree

Graf [gra:f] (**-en, -en**) *m* count, earl

Grafiker(in) ▲ ['gra:fikər(ɪn)] (**-s, -**) *m(f)* graphic designer

grafisch ▲ ['gra:fɪʃ] *adj* graphic

Gram [gra:m] (**-(e)s**) *m* grief, sorrow

grämen ['grɛ:mən] *vr* to grieve

Gramm [gram] (**-s, -e**) *nt* gram(me)

Grammatik [gra'matɪk] *f* grammar

Granat [gra'na:t] (**-(e)s, -e**) *m* (*Stein*) garnet

Granate *f* (*MIL*) shell; (*Handgranate*) grenade

Granit [gra'ni:t] (**-s, -e**) *m* granite

Gras [gra:s] (**-es, ¨er**) *nt* grass; **g~en** ['gra:zən] *vi* to graze; **~halm** *m* blade of grass

grassieren [gra'si:rən] *vi* to be rampant, to rage

grässlich ▲ ['grɛslɪç] *adj* horrible

Grat [gra:t] (**-(e)s, -e**) *m* ridge

Gräte ['grɛ:tə] *f* fishbone

gratis ['gra:tɪs] *adj, adv* free (of charge);

G~probe *f* free sample

Gratulation [gratulatsi'o:n] *f* congratulation(s)

gratulieren [gratu'li:rən] *vi*: **jdm ~ (zu otw)** to congratulate sb (on sth); **(ich) gratuliere!** congratulations!

grau [grau] *adj* grey

Gräuel ▲ ['grɔyəl] (**-s, -**) *m* horror, revulsion; **etw ist jdm ein ~** sb loathes sth

Grauen (**-s**) *nt* horror; **g~** *vi unpers*: **es graut jdm vor etw** sb dreads sth, sb is afraid of sth ♦ *vr*: **sich g~ vor** to dread, to have a horror of; **g~haft** *adj* horrible

grauhaarig *adj* grey-haired

gräulich ▲ ['grɔylɪç] *adj* horrible

grausam ['grauza:m] *adj* cruel; **G~keit** *f* cruelty

Grausen ['grauzən] (**-s**) *nt* horror; **g~** *vb* = **grauen**

gravieren [gra'vi:rən] *vt* to engrave; **~d** *adj* grave

graziös [gratsi'ø:s] *adj* graceful

greifbar *adj* tangible, concrete; **in ~er Nähe** within reach

greifen ['graifən] (*unreg*) *vt* to seize; to grip; **nach etw ~** to reach for sth; **um sich ~** (*fig*) to spread; **zu etw ~** (*fig*) to turn to sth

Greis [grais] (**-es, -e**) *m* old man; **g~enhaft** *adj* senile; **~in** *f* old woman

grell [grɛl] *adj* harsh

Grenz- ['grɛnts] *zW*: **~beamte(r)** *m* frontier official; **~e** *f* boundary; (*Staatsgrenze*) frontier; (*Schranke*) limit; **g~en** *vi*: **g~en (an +akk)** to border (on); **g~enlos** *adj* boundless; **~fall** *m* borderline case; **~kontrolle** *f* border control; **~übergang** *m* frontier crossing

Greuel △ ['grɔyəl] (**-s, -**) *m siehe* **Gräuel**

greulich △ *adj siehe* **gräulich**

Griech- ['gri:ç] *zW*: **~e** (**-n, -n**) *m* Greek; **~enland** *nt* Greece; **~in** *f* Greek; **g~isch** *adj* Greek

griesgrämig ['gri:sgrɛ:mɪç] *adj* grumpy

Grieß [gri:s] (**-es, -e**) *m* (*KOCH*) semolina

Griff [grɪf] (**-(e)s, -e**) *m* grip; (*Vorrichtung*) handle; **g~bereit** *adj* handy

Grill [grɪl] *m* grill; **~e** *f* cricket; **g~en** *vt* to grill; **~fest** *nt* barbecue party

Grimasse [grɪ'masə] *f* grimace

grimmig ['grɪmɪç] *adj* furious; *(heftig)* fierce, severe

grinsen ['grɪnzən] *vi* to grin

Grippe ['grɪpə] *f* influenza, flu

grob [groːp] *adj* coarse, gross; *(Fehler, Verstoß)* gross; **G~heit** *f* coarseness; coarse expression

grölen ['grøːlən] *(pej) vt* to bawl, to bellow

Groll [grɔl] **(-(e)s)** *m* resentment; **g~en** *vi (Donner)* to rumble; **g~en (mit** *od* **+dat)** to bear ill will (towards)

groß [groːs] *adj* big, large; *(hoch)* tall; *(fig)* great ♦ *adv* greatly; **im G~en und Ganzen** on the whole; **bei jdm ~ geschrieben werden** to be high on sb's list of priorities; **~artig** *adj* great, splendid; **G~aufnahme** *f (CINE)* close-up; **G~britannien** *nt* Great Britain

Größe ['grøːsə] *f* size; *(Höhe)* height; *(fig)* greatness

Groß- *zW:* **~einkauf** *m* bulk purchase; **~eltern** *pl* grandparents; **g~enteils** *adv* mostly; **~format** *nt* large size; **~handel** *m* wholesale trade; **~händler** *m* wholesaler; **~macht** *f* great power; **~mutter** *f* grandmother; **~rechner** *m* mainframe (computer); **g~schreiben** *(unreg) vt (Wort)* to write in block capitals; *siehe* **groß**; **g~spurig** *adj* pompous; **~stadt** *f* city, large town

größte(r, s) ['grøːstə(r, s)] *adj superl von* **groß**; **größtenteils** *adv* for the most part

Groß- *zW:* **g~tun** *(unreg) vi* to boast; **~vater** *m* grandfather; **g~ziehen** *(unreg) vt* to raise; **g~zügig** *adj* generous; *(Planung)* on a large scale

grotesk [gro'tesk] *adj* grotesque

Grotte ['grɔtə] *f* grotto

Grübchen ['gryːpçən] *nt* dimple

Grube ['gruːbə] *f* pit; mine

grübeln ['gryːbəln] *vi* to brood

Gruft [gruft] **(-, ¨e)** *f* tomb, vault

grün [gryːn] *adj* green; **der ~e Punkt** green spot symbol on recyclable packaging

---

grüner Punkt

i *The* **grüner Punkt** *is a green spot which appears on packaging that should be kept separate from normal household refuse to be recycled through the recycling company,* **DSD** *(Duales System Deutschland). The recycling is financed by licences bought by the packaging manufacturer from* **DSD***. These costs are often passed on to the consumer.*

Grünanlage *f* park

Grund [grʊnt] **(-(e)s, ¨e)** *m* ground; *(von See, Gefäß)* bottom; *(fig)* reason; **im ~e genommen** basically; *siehe* **aufgrund**; **~ausbildung** *f* basic training; **~besitz** *m* land(ed property), real estate; **~buch** *nt* land register

gründen ['gryndən] *vt* to found ♦ *vr:* **sich ~ (auf** *+dat)* to be based (on); **~ auf** *+akk* to base on; **Gründer (-s, -)** *m* founder

Grund- *zW:* **~gebühr** *f* basic charge; **~gesetz** *nt* constitution; **~lage** *f* foundation; **g~legend** *adj* fundamental

gründlich *adj* thorough

Grund- *zW:* **g~los** *adj* groundless; **~regel** *f* basic rule; **~riss ▲** *m* plan; *(fig)* outline; **~satz** *m* principle; **g~sätzlich** *adj* fundamental; *(Frage)* of principle ♦ *adv* fundamentally; *(prinzipiell)* on principle; **~schule** *f* elementary school; **~stein** *m* foundation stone; **~stück** *nt* estate; plot

Grundwasser *nt* ground water

Grundschule

i *The* **Grundschule** *is a primary school which children attend for 4 years from the age of 6 to 10. There are no formal examinations in the* **Grundschule** *but parents receive a report on their child's progress twice a year. Many children attend a* **Kindergarten** *from 3-6 years before going to the* **Grundschule***, though no formal instruction takes place in the* **Kindergarten***.*

Grünstreifen *m* central reservation
grunzen ['grʊntsən] *vi* to grunt
Gruppe ['grʊpə] *f* group; **~nermäßigung** *f* group reduction; **g~nweise** *adv* in groups
gruppieren [grʊ'piːrən] *vt, vr* to group
gruselig *adj* creepy
gruseln ['gruːzəln] *vi unpers*: **es gruselt jdm vor etw** sth gives sb the creeps ♦ *vr* to have the creeps
Gruß [gruːs] **(-es, ¨e)** *m* greeting; (*MIL*) salute; **viele Grüße** best wishes; **mit freundlichen Grüßen** yours sincerely; **Grüße an** +*akk* regards to
grüßen ['gryːsən] *vt* to greet; (*MIL*) to salute; **jdn von jdm ~** to give sb sb's regards; **jdn ~ lassen** to send sb one's regards
gucken ['gʊkən] *vi* to look
gültig ['gʏltɪç] *adj* valid; **G~keit** *f* validity
Gummi ['gʊmi] **(-s, -s)** *nt od m* rubber; (*~harze*) gum; **~band** *nt* rubber *od* elastic band; (*Hosenband*) elastic; **~bärchen** *nt* ≈ jelly baby (*BRIT*); **~baum** *m* rubber plant; **g~eren** [gu'miːrən] *vt* to gum; **~stiefel** *m* rubber boot
günstig ['gʏnstɪç] *adj* convenient; (*Gelegenheit*) favourable; **das habe ich ~ bekommen** it was a bargain
Gurgel ['gʊrgəl] **(-, -n)** *f* throat; **g~n** *vi* to gurgle; (*im Mund*) to gargle
Gurke ['gʊrkə] *f* cucumber; **saure ~** pickled cucumber, gherkin
Gurt [gʊrt] **(-(e)s, -e)** *m* belt
Gürtel ['gʏrtəl] **(-s, -)** *m* belt; (*GEOG*) zone; **~reifen** *m* radial tyre
GUS *f abk* (= *Gemeinschaft unabhängiger Staaten*) CIS
Guss ▲ [gʊs] **(-es, ¨e)** *m* casting; (*Regenguss*) downpour; (*KOCH*) glazing; **~eisen** *nt* cast iron

gut *adj* good; **alles Gute** all the best; **also gut** all right then
♦ *adv* well; **gut gehen** to work, to come off; **es geht jdm gut** sb's doing fine; **gut gemeint** well meant; **gut schmecken** to

taste good; **jdm gut tun** to do sb good; **gut, aber ...** OK, but ...; **(na) gut, ich komme** all right, I'll come; **gut drei Stunden** a good three hours; **das kann gut sein** that may well be; **lass es gut sein** that'll do

Gut [guːt] **(-(e)s, ¨er)** *nt* (*Besitz*) possession; **Güter** *pl* (*Waren*) goods; **~achten** **(-s, -)** *nt* (expert) opinion; **~achter** **(-s, -)** *m* expert; **g~artig** *adj* good-natured; **g~bürgerlich** *adj* (*Küche*) (good) plain; **~dünken** *nt*: **nach ~dünken** at one's discretion
Güte ['gyːtə] *f* goodness, kindness; (*Qualität*) quality
Güter- *zW*: **~abfertigung** *f* (*EISENB*) goods office; **~bahnhof** *m* goods station; **~wagen** *m* goods waggon (*BRIT*), freight car (*US*); **~zug** *m* goods train (*BRIT*), freight train (*US*)
Gütezeichen *nt* quality mark; ≈ kite mark
gut- *zW*: **~gehen** △ (*unreg*) *vi unpers siehe* **gut**; **~gemeint** △ *adj siehe* **gut**; **~gläubig** *adj* trusting; **G~haben** **(-s)** *nt* credit; **~heißen** (*unreg*) *vt* to approve (of)
gütig ['gyːtɪç] *adj* kind
Gut- *zW*: **g~mütig** *adj* good-natured; **~schein** *m* voucher; **g~schreiben** (*unreg*) *vt* to credit; **~schrift** *f* (*Betrag*) credit; **g~tun** △ (*unreg*) *vi siehe* **gut**; **g~willig** *adj* willing
Gymnasium [gym'naːziʊm] *nt* grammar school (*BRIT*), high school (*US*)

Gymnasium

ⓘ *The* **Gymnasium** *is a selective secondary school. After nine years of study pupils sit the* **Abitur** *so they can go on to higher education. Pupils who successfully complete six years at a* **Gymnasium** *automatically gain the* **mittlere Reife***.*

Gymnastik [gym'nastɪk] *f* exercises *pl*, keep fit

H, h

Haag [haːk] *m*: **Den ~** the Hague

Haar [haːr] (-(e)s, -e) *nt* hair; **um ein ~** nearly; **an den ~en herbeigezogen** (*umg: Vergleich*) very far-fetched; **~bürste** *f* hairbrush; **h~en** *vi, vr* to lose hair; **~esbreite** *f*: **um ~esbreite** by a hair's-breadth; **~festiger** (-s, -) *m* (hair) setting lotion; **h~genau** *adv* precisely; **h~ig** *adj* hairy; (*fig*) nasty; **~klammer** *f* hairgrip; **~nadel** *f* hairpin; **h~scharf** (*beobachten*) very sharply; (*daneben*) by a hair's breadth; **~schnitt** *m* haircut; **~spange** *f* hair slide; **h~sträubend** *adj* hair-raising; **~teil** *nt* hairpiece; **~waschmittel** *nt* shampoo

Habe [ˈhaːbə] (-) *f* property

haben [ˈhaːbən] (*unreg*) *vt, vb aux* to have; **Hunger/Angst ~** to be hungry/afraid; **woher hast du das?** where did you get that from?; **was hast du denn?** what's the matter (with you)?; **du hast zu schweigen** you're to be quiet; **ich hätte gern** I would like; **H~** (-s, -) *nt* credit

Habgier *f* avarice; **h~ig** *adj* avaricious

Habicht [ˈhaːbɪçt] (-s, -e) *m* hawk

Habseligkeiten [ˈhaːpzeːlɪçkaɪtən] *pl* belongings

Hachse [ˈhaksə] *f* (*KOCH*) knuckle

Hacke [ˈhakə] *f* hoe; (*Ferse*) heel; **h~n** *vt* to hack, to chop; (*Erde*) to hoe

Hackfleisch *nt* mince, minced meat

Hafen [ˈhaːfən] (-s, ⁻) *m* harbour, port; **~arbeiter** *m* docker; **~rundfahrt** *f* boat trip round the harbour; **~stadt** *f* port

Hafer [ˈhaːfər] (-s, -) *m* oats *pl*; **~flocken** *pl* rolled oats; **~schleim** *m* gruel

Haft [haft] (-) *f* custody; **h~bar** *adj* liable, responsible; **~befehl** *m* warrant (for arrest); **h~en** *vi* to stick, to cling; **h~en für** to be liable *od* responsible for; **h~en bleiben** (**an** +*dat*) to stick (to); **Häftling** *m* prisoner; **~pflicht** *f* liability; **~pflichtversicherung** *f* (*AUT*) third party

insurance; **~schalen** *pl* contact lenses; **~ung** *f* liability; **~ungsbeschränkung** *f* limitation of liability

Hagebutte [ˈhaːgəbʊtə] *f* rose hip

Hagel [ˈhaːgəl] (-s) *m* hail; **h~n** *vi unpers* to hail

hager [ˈhaːgər] *adj* gaunt

Hahn [haːn] (-(e)s, ⁻e) *m* cock; (*Wasserhahn*) tap, faucet (*US*)

Hähnchen [ˈhɛːnçən] *nt* cockerel; (*KOCH*) chicken

Hai(fisch) [ˈhaɪ(fɪʃ)] (-(e)s, -e) *m* shark

häkeln [ˈhɛːkəln] *vt* to crochet

Haken [ˈhaːkən] (-s, -) *m* hook; (*fig*) catch; **~kreuz** *nt* swastika; **~nase** *f* hooked nose

halb [halp] *adj* half; **~ eins** half past twelve; **~ offen** half-open; **ein ~es Dutzend** half a dozen; **H~dunkel** *nt* semi-darkness

halber [ˈhalbər] *präp* +*gen* (*wegen*) on account of; (*für*) for the sake of

Halb- *zW*: **~heit** *f* half-measure; **h~ieren** *vt* to halve; **~insel** *f* peninsula; **~jahr** *nt* six months; (*auch*: *COMM*) half-year; **h~jährlich** *adj* half-yearly; **~kreis** *m* semicircle; **~leiter** *m* semiconductor; **~mond** *m* half-moon; (*fig*) crescent; **~pension** *f* half-board; **~schuh** *m* shoe; **h~tags** *adv*: **h~tags arbeiten** to work part-time, to work mornings/afternoons; **h~wegs** *adv* halfway; **h~wegs besser** more or less better; **~zeit** *f* (*SPORT*) half; (*Pause*) half-time

Halde [ˈhaldə] *f* (*Kohlen*) heap

half [half] *vb siehe* **helfen**

Hälfte [ˈhɛlftə] *f* half

Halfter [ˈhalftər] (-s, -) *m od nt* (*für Tiere*) halter

Halle [ˈhalə] *f* hall; (*AVIAT*) hangar; **h~n** *vi* to echo, to resound; **~nbad** *nt* indoor swimming pool

hallo [haˈloː] *excl* hello

Halluzination [halʊtsinatsiˈoːn] *f* hallucination

Halm [halm] (-(e)s, -e) *m* blade; stalk

Halogenlampe [haloˈgeːnlampə] *f* halogen lamp

Hals [hals] (**-es, ˵e**) *m* neck; (*Kehle*) throat; ~ **über Kopf** in a rush; **~band** *nt* (*von Hund*) collar; **~kette** *f* necklace; **~Nasen-Ohren-Arzt** *m* ear, nose and throat specialist; **~schmerzen** *pl* sore throat *sg*; **~tuch** *nt* scarf

Halt [halt] (**-(e)s, -e**) *m* stop; (*fester ~*) hold; (*innerer ~*) stability; ~ *od* **h~!** stop!, halt!; ~ **machen** to stop; **h~bar** *adj* durable; (*Lebensmittel*) non-perishable; (*MIL, fig*) tenable; **~barkeit** *f* durability; (non-) perishability

halten ['haltən] (*unreg*) *vt* to keep; (*festhalten*) to hold ♦ *vi* to hold; (*frisch bleiben*) to keep; (*stoppen*) to stop ♦ *vr* (*frisch bleiben*) to keep; (*sich behaupten*) to hold out; ~ **für** to regard as; ~ **von** to think of; **an sich** ~ to restrain o.s.; **sich rechts/links** ~ to keep to the right/left

Halte- *zW*: **~stelle** *f* stop; **~verbot** *nt*: **hier ist ~verbot** there's no waiting here

Halt- *zW*: **h~los** *adj* unstable; **h~machen** △ *vi siehe* **Halt**; **~ung** *f* posture; (*fig*) attitude; (*Selbstbeherrschung*) composure

Halunke [ha'luŋkə] (**-n, -n**) *m* rascal

hämisch ['hɛːmɪʃ] *adj* malicious

Hammel ['haməl] (**-s, ˵ od -**) *m* wether; **~fleisch** *nt* mutton

Hammer ['hamər] (**-s, ˵**) *m* hammer

hämmern ['hɛmərn] *vt, vi* to hammer

Hämorr(ho)iden [hɛmɔro'iːdən, hɛmɔ'riːdn] *pl* haemorrhoids

Hamster ['hamstər] (**-s, -**) *m* hamster; **~ei** [-'rai] *f* hoarding; **h~n** *vi* to hoard

Hand [hant] (**-, ˵e**) *f* hand; **~arbeit** *f* manual work; (*Nadelarbeit*) needlework; **~ball** *m* (*SPORT*) handball; **~bremse** *f* handbrake; **~buch** *nt* handbook, manual

Händedruck ['hɛndədrʊk] *m* handshake

Handel ['handəl] (**-s**) *m* trade; (*Geschäft*) transaction

Handeln ['handəln] (**-s**) *nt* action

handeln *vi* to trade; (*agieren*) to act ♦ *vr unpers*: **sich ~ um** to be a question of, to be about; ~ **von** to be about

Handels- *zW*: **~bilanz** *f* balance of trade;

~kammer *f* chamber of commerce; **~reisende(r)** *m* commercial traveller; **~schule** *f* business school; **h~üblich** *adj* customary; (*Preis*) going *attrib*; **~vertreter** *m* sales representative

Hand- *zW*: **~feger** (**-s, -**) *m* hand brush; **h~fest** *adj* hefty; **h~gearbeitet** *adj* handmade; **~gelenk** *nt* wrist; **~gemenge** *nt* scuffle; **~gepäck** *nt* hand luggage; **h~geschrieben** *adj* handwritten; **h~greiflich** *adj* palpable; **h~greiflich werden** to become violent; **~griff** *m* flick of the wrist; **h~haben** *vt insep* to handle

Händler ['hɛndlər] (**-s, -**) *m* trader, dealer

handlich ['hantlɪç] *adj* handy

Handlung ['handluŋ] *f* act(ion); (*in Buch*) plot; (*Geschäft*) shop

Hand- *zW*: **~schelle** *f* handcuff; **~schrift** *f* handwriting; (*Text*) manuscript; **~schuh** *m* glove; **~stand** *m* (*SPORT*) handstand; **~tasche** *f* handbag; **~tuch** *nt* towel; **~umdrehen** *nt*: **im ~umdrehen** in the twinkling of an eye; **~werk** *nt* trade, craft; **~werker** (**-s, -**) *m* craftsman, artisan; **~werkzeug** *nt* tools *pl*

Handy ['hɛndɪ] (**-s, -s**) *nt* mobile (telephone)

Hanf [hanf] (**-(e)s**) *m* hemp

Hang [haŋ] (**-(e)s, ˵e**) *m* inclination; (*Abhang*) slope

Hänge- ['hɛŋə] *in zW* hanging; **~brücke** *f* suspension bridge; **~matte** *f* hammock

hängen ['hɛŋən] (*unreg*) *vi* to hang ♦ *vt*: **etw (an etw** *akk*) ~ to hang sth (on sth); ~ **an** +*dat* (*fig*) to be attached to; **sich ~ an** +*akk* to hang on to, to cling to; ~ **bleiben** to be caught; (*fig*) to remain, to stick; ~ **bleiben an** +*dat* to catch *od* get caught on; ~ **lassen** (*vergessen*) to leave; **den Kopf ~ lassen** to get downhearted

Hannover [ha'noːfər] (**-s**) *nt* Hanover

hänseln ['hɛnzəln] *vt* to tease

Hansestadt ['hanzəʃtat] *f* Hanse town

hantieren [han'tiːrən] *vi* to work, to be busy; **mit etw ~** to handle sth

hapern ['haːpərn] *vi unpers*: **es hapert an etw** *dat* there is a lack of sth

Happen ['hapən] **(-s, -)** *m* mouthful

Harfe ['harfə] *f* harp

Harke ['harkə] *f* rake; **h~n** *vt, vi* to rake

harmlos ['harmloːs] *adj* harmless; **H~igkeit** *f* harmlessness

Harmonie [harmo'niː] *f* harmony; **h~ren** *vi* to harmonize

harmonisch [har'moːnɪʃ] *adj* harmonious

Harn ['harn] **(-(e)s, -e)** *m* urine; **~blase** *f* bladder

Harpune [har'puːnə] *f* harpoon

harren ['harən] *vi*: **~ (auf** +*akk*) to wait (for)

hart [hart] *adj* hard; (*fig*) harsh; **~ gekocht** hard-boiled

Härte ['hɛrtə] *f* hardness; (*fig*) harshness

hart- *zW*: **~herzig** *adj* hard-hearted; **~näckig** *adj* stubborn

Harz [haːrts] **(-es, -e)** *nt* resin

Haschee [ha'ʃeː] **(-s, -s)** *nt* hash

Haschisch ['haʃɪʃ] **(-)** *nt* hashish

Hase ['haːzə] **(-n, -n)** *m* hare

Haselnuss ▲ ['haːzəlnʊs] *f* hazelnut

Hasenscharte *f* harelip

Hass ▲ [has] **(-es)** *m* hate, hatred

hassen ['hasən] *vt* to hate

hässlich ▲ ['hɛslɪç] *adj* ugly; (*gemein*) nasty; **H~keit** *f* ugliness; nastiness

Hast [hast] *f* haste

hast *vb siehe* **haben**

hasten *vi* to rush

hastig *adj* hasty

hat [hat] *vb siehe* **haben**

hatte *etc* ['hatə] *vb siehe* **haben**

Haube ['haʊbə] *f* hood; (*Mütze*) cap; (*AUT*) bonnet, hood (*US*)

Hauch [haʊx] **(-(e)s, -e)** *m* breath; (*Lufthauch*) breeze; (*fig*) trace; **h~dünn** *adj* extremely thin

Haue ['haʊə] *f* hoe, pick; (*umg*) hiding; **h~n** (*unreg*) *vt* to hew, to cut; (*umg*) to thrash

Haufen ['haʊfən] **(-s, -)** *m* heap; (*Leute*) crowd; **ein ~ (x)** (*umg*) loads *od* a lot (of x); **auf einem ~** in one heap

häufen ['hɔyfən] *vt* to pile up ♦ *vr* to accumulate

haufenweise *adv* in heaps; in droves; **etw ~ haben** to have piles of sth

häufig ['hɔyfɪç] *adj* frequent ♦ *adv* frequently; **H~keit** *f* frequency

Haupt [haʊpt] **(-(e)s, Häupter)** *nt* head; (*Oberhaupt*) chief ♦ *in zW* main; **~bahnhof** *m* central station; **h~beruflich** *adv* as one's main occupation; **~darsteller(in)** *m(f)* leading actor (actress); **~fach** *nt* (*SCH, UNIV*) main subject, major (*US*); **~gericht** *nt* (*KOCH*) main course

Häuptling ['hɔyptlɪŋ] *m* chief(tain)

Haupt- *zW*: **~mann** (*pl* **-leute**) *m* (*MIL*) captain; **~person** *f* central figure; **~quartier** *nt* headquarters *pl*; **~rolle** *f* leading part; **~sache** *f* main thing; **h~sächlich** *adj* chief ♦ *adv* chiefly; **~saison** *f* high season, peak season; **~schule** *f* ≈ secondary school; **~stadt** *f* capital; **~straße** *f* main street; **~verkehrszeit** *f* rush-hour, peak traffic hours *pl*

Hauptschule

ⓘ The **Hauptschule** *is a non-selective school which pupils may attend after the* **Grundschule***. They complete five years of study and most go on to do some vocational training.*

Haus [haʊs] **(-es, Häuser)** *nt* house; **~ halten** (*sparen*) to economize; **nach ~e** home; **zu ~e** at home; **~apotheke** *f* medicine cabinet; **~arbeit** *f* housework; (*SCH*) homework; **~arzt** *m* family doctor; **~aufgabe** *f* (*SCH*) homework; **~besitzer(in)** *m(f)* house owner; **~besuch** *m* (*von Arzt*) house call; **~durchsuchung** *f* police raid; **h~eigen** *adj* belonging to a/ the hotel/firm

Häuser- ['hɔyzər] *zW*: **~block** *m* block (of houses); **~makler** *m* estate agent (*BRIT*), real estate agent (*US*)

Haus- *zW*: **~flur** *m* hallway; **~frau** *f* housewife; **h~gemacht** *adj* home-made; **~halt** *m* household; (*POL*) budget; **h~halten** (*unreg*) *vi* △ *siehe* **Haus**; **~hälterin** *f* housekeeper; **~haltsgeld** *nt* housekeeping (money); **~haltsgerät** *nt*

---

domestic appliance; **~herr** *m* host;
(*Vermieter*) landlord; **h~hoch** *adv*: **h~hoch
verlieren** to lose by a mile
hausieren [hau'zi:rən] *vi* to peddle
Hausierer (**-s, -**) *m* pedlar (*BRIT*), peddler
(*US*)
häuslich ['hɔyslıç] *adj* domestic
Haus- *zW*: **~meister** *m* caretaker, janitor;
~nummer *f* street number; **~ordnung** *f*
house rules *pl*; **~putz** *m* house cleaning;
~schlüssel *m* front door key; **~schuh** *m*
slipper; **~tier** *nt* pet; **~tür** *f* front door;
~wirt *m* landlord; **~wirtschaft** *f* domestic
science; **~zelt** *nt* frame tent
Haut [haut] (**-, Häute**) *f* skin; (*Tierhaut*) hide;
~creme *f* skin cream; **h~eng** *adj* skin-
tight; **~farbe** *f* complexion, **~krebs** *m* skin
cancer
Haxe ['haksə] *f* = **Hachse**
Hbf. *abk* = **Hauptbahnhof**
Hebamme ['he:p|amə] *f* midwife
Hebel ['he:bəl] (**-s, -**) *m* lever
heben ['he:bən] (*unreg*) *vt* to raise, to lift
Hecht [hɛçt] (**-(e)s, -e**) *m* pike
Heck [hɛk] (**-(e)s, -e**) *nt* stern; (*von Auto*)
rear
Hecke ['hɛkə] *f* hedge
Heckenschütze *m* sniper
Heckscheibe *f* rear window
Heer [he:r] (**-(e)s, -e**) *nt* army
Hefe ['he:fə] *f* yeast
Heft ['hɛft] (**-(e)s, -e**) *nt* exercise book;
(*Zeitschrift*) number; (*von Messer*) haft;
h~en *vt*: **h~en (an** +*akk*) to fasten (to);
(*nähen*) to tack ((on) to); **etw an etw** *akk*
h~en to fasten sth to sth; **~er** (**-s, -**) *m*
folder
heftig *adj* fierce, violent; **H~keit** *f*
fierceness, violence
Heft- *zW*: **~klammer** *f* paper clip;
~pflaster *nt* sticking plaster; **~zwecke** *f*
drawing pin
hegen ['he:gən] *vt* (*Wild, Bäume*) to care for,
to tend; (*fig, geh: empfinden: Wunsch*) to
cherish; (: *Misstrauen*) to feel
Hehl [he:l] *m od nt*: **kein(en) ~ aus etw
machen** to make no secret of sth; **~er** (**-s,
-**) *m* receiver (of stolen goods), fence
Helde[1] ['haidə] (**-n, -n**) *m* heathen, pagan
Heide[2] ['haidə] *f* heath, moor; **~kraut** *nt*
heather
Heidelbeere *f* bilberry
Heidentum *nt* paganism
Heidin *f* heathen, pagan
heikel ['haikəl] *adj* awkward, thorny
Heil [hail] (**-(e)s**) *nt* well-being; (*Seelenheil*)
salvation; **h~** *adj* in one piece, intact; **~and**
(**-(e)s, -e**) *m* saviour; **h~bar** *adj* curable;
h~en *vt* to cure ♦ *vi* to heal; **h~froh** *adj*
very relieved
heilig ['hailıç] *adj* holy; **~ sprechen** to
canonize; **H~abend** *m* Christmas Eve;
H~e(r) *f(m)* saint; **~en** *vt* to sanctify, to
hallow; **H~enschein** *m* halo; **H~keit** *f*
holiness; **H~tum** *nt* shrine; (*Gegenstand*)
relic
Heil- *zW*: **h~los** *adj* unholy; (*fig*) hopeless;
~mittel *nt* remedy; **~praktiker(in)** *m(f)*
non-medical practitioner; **h~sam** *adj* (*fig*)
salutary; **~sarmee** *f* Salvation Army; **~ung**
f cure
Helm [haim] (**-(e)s, -e**) *nt* home; **h~** *adv*
home
Heimat ['haima:t] (**-, -en**) *f* home (town/
country *etc*); **~land** *nt* homeland; **h~lich**
adj native, home *attrib*; (*Gefühle*) nostalgic;
h~los *adj* homeless; **~ort** *m* home town/
area
Heim- *zW*: **~computer** *m* home computer;
h~fahren (*unreg*) *vi* to drive home; **~fahrt**
f journey home; **h~gehen** (*unreg*) *vi* to go
home; (*sterben*) to pass away; **h~isch** *adj*
(*gebürtig*) native; **sich h~isch fühlen** to feel
at home; **~kehr** (**-, -en**) *f* homecoming;
h~kehren *vi* to return home; **h~lich** *adj*
secret; **~lichkeit** *f* secrecy; **~reise** *f*
journey home; **~spiel** *nt* (*SPORT*) home
game; **h~suchen** *vt* to afflict; (*Geist*) to
haunt; **~trainer** *m* exercise bike;
h~tückisch *adj* malicious; **~weg** *m* way
home; **~weh** *nt* homesickness; **~werker**
(**-s, -**) *m* handyman; **h~zahlen** *vt*: **jdm etw
h~zahlen** to pay sb back for sth
Heirat ['haira:t] (**-, -en**) *f* marriage; **h~en** *vt*

Spelling Reform: ▲ *new spelling* △ *old spelling (to be phased out)*

to marry ♦ *vi* to marry, to get married ♦ *vr* to get married; **~santrag** *m* proposal

heiser ['haɪzər] *adj* hoarse; **H~keit** *f* hoarseness

heiß [haɪs] *adj* hot; **~e(s) Eisen** (*umg*) hot potato; **~blütig** *adj* hot-blooded

heißen ['haɪsən] (*unreg*) *vi* to be called; (*bedeuten*) to mean ♦ *vt* to command; (*nennen*) to name ♦ *vi unpers*: **es heißt** it says; it is said; **das heißt** that is (to say)

Heiß- *zW*: **~hunger** *m* ravenous hunger; **h~laufen** (*unreg*) *vi*, *vr* to overheat

heiter ['haɪtər] *adj* cheerful; (*Wetter*) bright; **H~keit** *f* cheerfulness; (*Belustigung*) amusement

Heiz- ['haɪts] *zW*: **h~bar** *adj* heated; (*Raum*) with heating; **h~en** *vt* to heat; **~körper** *m* radiator; **~öl** *nt* fuel oil; **~sonne** *f* electric fire; **~ung** *f* heating

hektisch ['hɛktɪʃ] *adj* hectic

Held [hɛlt] (**-en, -en**) *m* hero; **h~enhaft** *adj* heroic; **~in** *f* heroine

helfen ['hɛlfən] (*unreg*) *vi* to help; (*nützen*) to be of use ♦ *vb unpers*: **es hilft nichts, du musst ...** it's no use, you'll have to ...; **jdm (bei etw) ~** to help sb (with sth); **sich dat zu ~ wissen** to be resourceful

Helfer (**-s, -**) *m* helper, assistant; **~shelfer** *m* accomplice

hell [hɛl] *adj* clear, bright; (*Farbe, Bier*) light; **~blau** *adj* light blue; **~blond** *adj* ash blond; **H~e** (**-**) *f* clearness, brightness; **~hörig** *adj* (*Wand*) paper-thin; **~hörig werden** (*fig*) to prick up one's ears; **H~seher** *m* clairvoyant; **~wach** *adj* wide-awake

Helm [hɛlm] (**-(e)s, -e**) *m* (*auf Kopf*) helmet

Hemd [hɛmt] (**-(e)s, -en**) *nt* shirt; (*Unterhemd*) vest; **~bluse** *f* blouse

hemmen ['hɛmən] *vt* to check, to hold up; **gehemmt sein** to be inhibited; **Hemmung** *f* check; (*PSYCH*) inhibition; **hemmungslos** *adj* unrestrained, without restraint

Hengst [hɛŋst] (**-es, -e**) *m* stallion

Henkel ['hɛŋkəl] (**-s, -**) *m* handle

Henker (**-s, -**) *m* hangman

Henne ['hɛnə] *f* hen

SCHLÜSSELWORT

her [heːr] *adv* **1** (*Richtung*): **komm her zu mir** come here (to me); **von England her** from England; **von weit her** from a long way away; **her damit!** hand it over!; **wo hat er das her?** where did he get that from? **2** (*Blickpunkt*): **von der Form her** as far as the form is concerned **3** (*zeitlich*): **das ist 5 Jahre her** that was 5 years ago; **wo bist du her?** where do you come from?; **ich kenne ihn von früher her** I know him from before

herab [hɛ'rap] *adv* down(ward(s)); **~hängen** (*unreg*) *vi* to hang down; **~lassen** (*unreg*) *vt* to let down ♦ *vr* to condescend; **~lassend** *adj* condescending; **~setzen** *vt* to lower, to reduce; (*fig*) to belittle, to disparage

heran [hɛ'ran] *adv*: **näher ~!** come up closer!; **~ zu mir!** come up to me!; **~bringen** (*unreg*) *vt*: **~bringen (an +akk)** to bring up (to); **~fahren** (*unreg*) *vi*: **~fahren (an +akk)** to drive up (to); **~kommen** (*unreg*) *vi*: (**an jdn/etw) ~kommen** to approach (sb/sth), to come near (to sb/sth); **~machen** *vr*: **sich an jdn ~machen** to make up to sb; **~treten** (*unreg*) *vi*: **mit etw an jdn ~treten** to approach sb with sth; **~wachsen** (*unreg*) *vi* to grow up; **~ziehen** (*unreg*) *vt* to pull nearer; (*aufziehen*) to raise; (*ausbilden*) to train; **jdn zu etw ~ziehen** to call upon sb to help in sth

herauf [hɛ'raʊf] *adv* up(ward(s)), up here; **~beschwören** (*unreg*) *vt* to conjure up, to evoke; **~bringen** (*unreg*) *vt* to bring up; **~setzen** *vt* (*Preise, Miete*) to raise, put up

heraus [hɛ'raʊs] *adv* out; **~bekommen** (*unreg*) *vt* to get out; (*fig*) to find *od* figure out; **~bringen** (*unreg*) *vt* to bring out; (*Geheimnis*) to elicit; **~finden** (*unreg*) *vt* to find out; **~fordern** *vt* to challenge; **H~forderung** *f* challenge; provocation; **~geben** (*unreg*) *vt* to hand over, to surrender; (*zurückgeben*) to give back; (*Buch*) to edit; (*veröffentlichen*) to publish; H~geber (-s, -) *m* editor; (*Verleger*) publisher; ~gehen (*unreg*) *vi*: aus sich ~gehen to come out of one's shell; ~halten (*unreg*) *vr*: sich aus etw ~halten to keep out of sth; ~hängen¹ *vt* to hang out; ~hängen² (*unreg*) *vi* to hang out; ~holen *vt*: ~holen (aus) to get out (of); ~kommen (*unreg*) *vi* to come out; dabei kommt nichts ~ nothing will come of it; ~nehmen (*unreg*) *vt* to remove (from), take out (of); sich *dat* etw ~nehmen to take liberties; ~reißen (*unreg*) *vt* to tear out; to pull out; ~rücken *vt* (*Geld*) to fork out, to hand over; mit etw ~rücken (*fig*) to come out with sth; ~stellen *vr*: sich ~stellen (als) to turn out (to be); ~suchen *vt*: sich *dat* jdn/etw ~suchen to pick sb/sth out; ~ziehen (*unreg*) *vt* to pull out, to extract

herb [hɛrp] *adj* (slightly) bitter, acid; (*Wein*) dry; (*fig: schmerzlich*) bitter

herbei [hɛr'baɪ] *adv* (over) here; ~führen *vt* to bring about; ~schaffen *vt* to procure

herbemühen ['hɛːrbəmyːən] *vr* to take the trouble to come

Herberge ['hɛrbɛrgə] *f* shelter; hostel, inn

Herbergsmutter *f* warden

Herbergsvater *m* warden

herbitten (*unreg*) *vt* to ask to come (here)

Herbst [hɛrpst] (-(e)s, -e) *m* autumn, fall (*US*); h~lich *adj* autumnal

Herd [hɛrt] (-(e)s, -e) *m* cooker; (*fig, MED*) focus, centre

Herde ['hɛːrdə] *f* herd; (*Schafherde*) flock

herein [hɛ'raɪn] *adv* in (here), here; ~! come in!; ~bitten (*unreg*) *vt* to ask in; ~brechen (*unreg*) *vi* to set in; ~bringen (*unreg*) *vt* to bring in; ~fallen (*unreg*) *vi* to be caught, to be taken in; ~fallen auf +*akk* to fall for; ~kommen (*unreg*) *vi* to come in; ~lassen (*unreg*) *vt* to admit; ~legen *vt*: jdn ~legen to take sb in; ~platzen (*umg*) *vi* to burst in

Her- *zW*: ~fahrt *f* journey here; h~fallen (*unreg*) *vi*: h~fallen über +*akk* to fall upon; ~gang *m* course of events; h~geben

(*unreg*) *vt* to give, to hand (over); sich zu etw h~geben to lend one's name to sth; h~gehen (*unreg*) *vi*: hinter jdm h~gehen to follow sb; es geht hoch h~ there are a lot of goings-on; h~halten (*unreg*) *vt* to hold out; h~halten müssen (*umg*) to have to suffer; h~hören *vi* to listen

Hering ['heːrɪŋ] (-s, -e) *m* herring

her- [hɛr] *zW*: ~kommen (*unreg*) *vi* to come; komm mal ~! come here!; ~kömmlich *adj* traditional; H~kunft (-, -künfte) *f* origin; H~kunftsland *nt* country of origin; H~kunftsort *m* place of origin; ~laufen (*unreg*) *vi*: ~laufen hinter +*dat* to run after

hermetisch [hɛr'meːtɪʃ] *adj* hermetic ♦ *adv* hermetically

her'nach *adv* afterwards

Heroin [hero'iːn] (-s) *nt* heroin

Herr [hɛr] (-(e)n, -en) *m* master; (*Mann*) gentleman; (*REL*) Lord; (*vor Namen*) Mr.; mein ~! sir!; meine ~en! gentlemen!

Herren- *zW*: ~haus *nt* mansion; ~konfektion *f* menswear; h~los *adj* ownerless; ~toilette *f* men's toilet *od* restroom (*US*)

herrichten ['hɛːrɪçtən] *vt* to prepare

Herr- *zW*: ~in *f* mistress; h~isch *adj* domineering; h~lich *adj* marvellous, splendid; ~lichkeit *f* splendour, magnificence; ~schaft *f* power, rule; (*und ~in*) master and mistress; meine ~schaften! ladies and gentlemen!

herrschen ['hɛrʃən] *vi* to rule; (*bestehen*) to prevail, to be

Herrscher(in) (-s, -) *m(f)* ruler

her- *zW*: ~rühren *vi* to arise, to originate; ~sagen *vt* to recite; ~stellen *vt* to make, to manufacture; H~steller (-s, -) *m* manufacturer; H~stellung *f* manufacture

herüber [hɛ'ryːbər] *adv* over (here), across

herum [hɛ'rʊm] *adv* about, (a)round; um etw ~ around sth; ~führen *vt* to show around; ~gehen (*unreg*) *vi* to walk about; um etw ~gehen to walk *od* go round sth; ~kommen (*unreg*) *vi* (um Kurve etc) to come round, to turn (round); ~kriegen

(*umg*) *vt* to bring *od* talk around; **~lungern**
(*umg*) *vi* to hang about *od* around;
~sprechen (*unreg*) *vr* to get around, to be
spread; **~treiben** *vi, vr* to drift about;
~ziehen *vi, vr* to wander about

herunter [hɛ'rʊntər] *adv* downward(s),
down (there); **~gekommen** *adj* run-down;
~kommen (*unreg*) *vi* to come down; (*fig*)
to come down in the world; **~laden** *unreg*
vt (*COMPUT*) to download; **~machen** *vt* to
take down; (*schimpfen*) to have a go at

hervor [hɛr'foːr] *adv* out, forth; **~bringen**
(*unreg*) *vt* to produce; (*Wort*) to utter;
~gehen (*unreg*) *vi* to emerge, to result;
~heben (*unreg*) *vt* to stress; (*als Kontrast*) to
set off; **~ragend** *adj* (*fig*) excellent; **~rufen**
(*unreg*) *vt* to cause, to give rise to; **~treten**
(*unreg*) *vi* to come out (from behind/
between/below); (*Adern*) to be prominent

Herz [hɛrts] (**-ens, -en**) *nt* heart; (*KARTEN*)
hearts *pl*; **~anfall** *m* heart attack; **~fehler**
m heart defect; **h~haft** *adj* hearty

herziehen ['hɛːrtsiːən] (*unreg*) *vi*: **über jdn/
etw ~** (*umg*) to pull sb/sth to pieces (*inf*)

Herz- *zW*: **~infarkt** *m* heart attack;
~klopfen *nt* palpitation; **h~lich** *adj*
cordial; **h~lichen Glückwunsch**
congratulations *pl*; **h~liche Grüße** best
wishes; **h~los** *adj* heartless

Herzog ['hɛrtsoːk] (**-(e)s, ⁺e**) *m* duke; **~tum**
nt duchy

Herz- *zW*: **~schlag** *m* heartbeat; (*MED*)
heart attack; **~stillstand** *m* cardiac arrest;
h~zerreißend *adj* heartrending

Hessen ['hɛsən] (**-s**) *nt* Hesse

hessisch *adj* Hessian

Hetze ['hɛtsə] *f* (*Eile*) rush; **h~n** *vt* to hunt;
(*verfolgen*) to chase ♦ *vi* (*eilen*) to rush;
jdn/etw auf jdn/etw h~n to set sb/sth on
sb/sth; **h~n gegen** to stir up feeling
against; **h~n zu** to agitate for

Heu [hɔy] (**-(e)s**) *nt* hay; **Geld wie ~** stacks
of money

Heuch- ['hɔyç] *zW*: **~elei** [-ə'laı] *f* hypocrisy;
h~eln *vt* to pretend, to feign ♦ *vi* to be
hypocritical; **~ler(in)** (**-s, -**) *m(f)* hypocrite;
h~lerisch *adj* hypocritical

heulen ['hɔylən] *vi* to howl; to cry

Heurige(r) ['hɔyrıgə(r)] *m* new wine

Heu- *zW*: **~schnupfen** *m* hay fever;
'**~schrecke** *f* grasshopper; locust

heute ['hɔytə] *adv* today; **~ Abend/früh** this
evening/morning

heutig ['hɔytıç] *adj* today's

heutzutage ['hɔytsutaːgə] *adv* nowadays

Hexe ['hɛksə] *f* witch; **h~n** *vi* to practise
witchcraft; **ich kann doch nicht h~n** I can't
work miracles; **~nschuss** ▲ *m* lumbago;
~'rei *f* witchcraft

Hieb [hiːp] (**-(e)s, -e**) *m* blow; (*Wunde*) cut,
gash; (*Stichelei*) cutting remark; **~e**
bekommen to get a thrashing

hielt *etc* [hiːlt] *vb siehe* **halten**

hier [hiːr] *adv* here; **~ behalten** to keep
here; **~ bleiben** to stay here; **~ lassen** to
leave here; **~auf** *adv* thereupon; (*danach*)
after that; **~bei** *adv* herewith, enclosed;
~durch *adv* by this means; (*örtlich*)
through here; **~her** *adv* this way, here;
~hin *adv* here; **~mit** *adv* hereby; **~nach**
adv hereafter; **~von** *adv* about this, hereof;
~zulande, ~ zu Lande *adv* in this
country

hiesig ['hiːzıç] *adj* of this place, local

hieß *etc* [hiːs] *vb siehe* **heißen**

Hilfe ['hılfə] *f* help; aid; **erste ~** first aid; **~!**
help!

Hilf- *zW*: **h~los** *adj* helpless; **~losigkeit** *f*
helplessness; **h~reich** *adj* helpful

Hilfs- *zW*: **~arbeiter** *m* labourer;
h~bedürftig *adj* needy; **h~bereit** *adj*
ready to help; **~kraft** *f* assistant, helper

hilfst [hılfst] *vb siehe* **helfen**

Himbeere ['hımbeːrə] *f* raspberry

Himmel ['hıml] (**-s, -**) *m* sky; (*REL, auch fig*)
heaven; **~bett** *nt* four-poster bed; **h~blau**
adj sky-blue; **~fahrt** *f* Ascension;
~srichtung *f* direction

himmlisch ['hımlıʃ] *adj* heavenly

SCHLÜSSELWORT
---

hin [hın] *adv* **1** (*Richtung*): **hin und zurück**
there and back; **hin und her** to and fro;
bis zur Mauer hin up to the wall; **wo ist**

er hin? where has he gone?; **Geld hin,
Geld her** money or no money
2 (*auf ... hin*): **auf meine Bitte hin** at my
request; **auf seinen Rat hin** on the basis of
his advice
3: mein Glück ist hin my happiness has
gone

hinab [hɪ'nap] *adv* down; **~gehen** (*unreg*) *vi*
to go down; **~sehen** (*unreg*) *vi* to look
down

hinauf [hɪ'nauf] *adv* up; **~arbeiten** *vr* to
work one's way up; **~steigen** (*unreg*) *vi* to
climb

hinaus [hɪ'naus] *adv* out; **~gehen** (*unreg*) *vi*
to go out; **~gehen über** +*akk* to exceed;
~laufen (*unreg*) *vi* to run out; **~laufen auf**
+*akk* to come to, to amount to;
~schieben (*unreg*) *vt* to put off, to
postpone; **~werfen** (*unreg*) *vt* (*Gegenstand,
Person*) to throw out; **~wollen** *vi* to want
to go out; **~wollen auf** +*akk* to drive at, to
get at

Hinblick ['hɪnblɪk] *m*: **in** *od* **im ~ auf** +*akk* in
view of

hinder- ['hɪndər] *zW*: **~lich** *adj*: **~lich sein**
to be a hindrance *od* nuisance; **~n** *vt* to
hinder, to hamper; **jdn an etw** *dat* **~n** to
prevent sb from doing sth; **H~nis** (**-ses,
-se**) *nt* obstacle; **H~nisrennen** *nt*
steeplechase

hindeuten ['hɪndɔʏtən] *vi*: **~ auf** +*akk* to
point to

hindurch [hɪn'dʊrç] *adv* through; across;
(*zeitlich*) through(out)

hinein [hɪ'naɪn] *adv* in; **~fallen** (*unreg*) *vi* to
fall in; **~fallen in** +*akk* to fall into; **~gehen**
(*unreg*) *vi* to go in; **~gehen in** +*akk* to go
into, to enter; **~geraten** (*unreg*) *vi*:
~geraten in +*akk* to get into; **~passen** *vi*
to fit in; **~passen in** +*akk* to fit into; (*fig*) to
fit in with; **~steigern** *vr*: **sich ~steigern in** +*akk* to get worked up;
~versetzen *vr*: **sich ~versetzen in** +*akk* to
put o.s. in the position of; **~ziehen** (*unreg*)
vt to pull in ♦ *vi* to go in

hin- ['hɪn] *zW*: **~fahren** (*unreg*) *vi* to go; to
drive ♦ *vt* to take; to drive; **H~fahrt** *f*

journey there; **~fallen** (*unreg*) *vi* to fall
(down); **~fällig** *adj* frail; (*fig: ungültig*)
invalid; **H~flug** *m* outward flight; **H~gabe**
f devotion; **~geben** (*unreg*) *vr* +*dat* to give
o.s. up to, to devote o.s. to; **~gehen**
(*unreg*) *vi* to go; (*Zeit*) to pass; **~halten**
(*unreg*) *vt* to hold out; (*warten lassen*) to put
off, to stall

hinken ['hɪŋkən] *vi* to limp; (*Vergleich*) to be
unconvincing

hinkommen (*unreg*) *vi* (*an Ort*) to arrive

hin- ['hɪn] *zW*: **~legen** *vt* to put down ♦ *vr*
to lie down; **~nehmen** (*unreg*) *vt* (*fig*) to
put up with, to take; **H~reise** *f* journey
out; **~reißen** (*unreg*) *vt* to carry away, to
enrapture; **sich ~reißen lassen, etw zu
tun** to get carried away and do sth;
~richten *vt* to execute; **H~richtung** *f*
execution; **~setzen** *vt* to put down ♦ *vr* to
sit down; **~sichtlich** *präp* +*gen* with regard
to; **~stellen** *vt* to put (down) ♦ *vr* to place
o.s.

hinten ['hɪntən] *adv* at the back; behind;
~herum *adv* round the back, (*fig*) secretly

hinter ['hɪntər] *präp* (+*dat od akk*) behind;
(*: nach*) after; **~ jdm her sein** to be after
sb; **H~achse** *f* rear axle; **H~bliebene(r)**
f(m) surviving relative; **~e(r, s)** *adj* rear,
back; **~einander** *adv* one after the other;
H~gedanke *m* ulterior motive; **~gehen**
(*unreg*) *vt* to deceive; **H~grund** *m*
background; **H~halt** *m* ambush; **~hältig**
adj underhand, sneaky; **~her** *adv*
afterwards, after; **H~hof** *m* backyard;
H~kopf *m* back of one's head; **~lassen**
(*unreg*) *vt* to leave; **~'legen** *vt* to deposit;
H~list *f* cunning, trickery; (*Handlung*) trick,
dodge; **~listig** *adj* cunning, crafty;
H~mann *m* person behind; **H~rad** *nt*
back wheel; **H~radantrieb** *m* (*AUT*) rear
wheel drive; **~rücks** *adv* from behind;
H~tür *f* back door; (*fig: Ausweg*) loophole;
~'ziehen (*unreg*) *vt* (*Steuern*) to evade

hinüber [hɪ'ny:bər] *adv* across, over;
~gehen (*unreg*) *vi* to go over *od* across

hinunter [hɪ'nʊntər] *adv* down; **~bringen**
(*unreg*) *vt* to take down; **~schlucken** *vt*

(*auch fig*) to swallow; **~steigen** (*unreg*) *vi*
to descend

Hinweg ['hɪnveːk] *m* journey out

hinweghelfen [hɪn'veːk-] (*unreg*) *vi*: **jdm**
über etw *akk* **~** to help sb to get over sth

hinwegsetzen [hɪn'veːk-] *vr*: **sich ~ über**
+*akk* to disregard

hin- ['hɪn] *zW*: **H~weis (-es, -e)** *m*
(*Andeutung*) hint; (*Anweisung*) instruction;
(*Verweis*) reference; **~weisen** (*unreg*) *vi*:
~weisen auf +*akk* (*anzeigen*) to point to;
(*sagen*) to point out, to refer to; **~werfen**
(*unreg*) *vt* to throw down; **~ziehen** (*unreg*)
vr (*fig*) to drag on

hinzu [hɪn'tsuː] *adv* in addition; **~fügen** *vt*
to add; **~kommen** (*unreg*) *vi* (*Mensch*) to
arrive, to turn up; (*Umstand*) to ensue

Hirn [hɪrn] **(-(e)s, -e)** *nt* brain(s); **~gespinst**
(-(e)s, -e) *nt* fantasy

Hirsch [hɪrʃ] **(-(e)s, -e)** *m* stag

Hirt ['hɪrt] **(-en, -en)** *m* herdsman; (*Schafhirt*,
fig) shepherd

hissen ['hɪsən] *vt* to hoist

Historiker [hɪs'toːrikər] **(-s, -)** *m* historian

historisch [hɪs'toːrɪʃ] *adj* historical

Hitze ['hɪtsə] **(-)** *f* heat; **h~beständig** *adj*
heat-resistant; **h~frei** *adj*: **h~frei haben** *to*
have time off school because of excessively
hot weather; **~welle** *f* heat wave

hitzig ['hɪtsɪç] *adj* hot-tempered; (*Debatte*)
heated

Hitzkopf *m* hothead

Hitzschlag *m* heatstroke

hl. *abk von* **heilig**

H-Milch ['haːmɪlç] *f* long-life milk

Hobby ['hɔbi] **(-s, -s)** *nt* hobby

Hobel ['hoːbəl] **(-s, -)** *m* plane; **~bank** *f*
carpenter's bench; **h~n** *vt*, *vi* to plane;
~späne *pl* wood shavings

Hoch (-s, -s) *nt* (*Ruf*) cheer; (*MET*)
anticyclone

hoch [hoːx] (*attrib* **hohe(r, s)**) *adj* high;
♦ *adv*: **~ achten** to respect; **~ begabt**
extremely gifted; **~ dotiert** highly paid;
H~achtung *f* respect, esteem;
~achtungsvoll *adv* yours faithfully;
H~amt *nt* high mass; **~arbeiten** *vr* to

work one's way up; **H~betrieb** *m* intense
activity; (*COMM*) peak time; **H~burg** *f*
stronghold; **H~deutsch** *nt* High German;
H~druck *m* high pressure; **H~ebene** *f*
plateau; **H~form** *f* top form; **H~gebirge**
nt high mountains *pl*; **H~glanz** *m* (*PHOT*)
high gloss print; **etw auf H~glanz bringen**
to make sth sparkle like new; **H~halten**
(*unreg*) *vt* to hold up; (*fig*) to uphold, to
cherish; **H~haus** *nt* multi-storey building;
~heben (*unreg*) *vt* to lift (up);
H~konjunktur *f* boom; **H~land** *nt*
highlands *pl*; **~leben** *vi*: **jdn ~leben**
lassen to give sb three cheers; **H~mut** *m*
pride; **~mütig** *adj* proud, haughty; **~näsig**
adj stuck-up, snooty; **H~ofen** *m* blast
furnace; **~prozentig** *adj* (*Alkohol*) strong;
H~rechnung *f* projection; **H~saison** *f*
high season; **H~schule** *f* college;
university; **H~sommer** *m* middle of
summer; **H~spannung** *f* high tension;
H~sprung *m* high jump

höchst [høːçst] *adv* highly, extremely

Hochstapler ['hoːxstaːplər] **(-s, -)** *m*
swindler

höchste(r, s) *adj* highest; (*äußerste*)
extreme

Höchst- *zW*: **h~ens** *adv* at the most;
~geschwindigkeit *f* maximum speed;
h~persönlich *adv* in person; **~preis** *m*
maximum price; **h~wahrscheinlich** *adv*
most probably

Hoch- *zW*: **~verrat** *m* high treason;
~wasser *nt* high water; (*Überschwemmung*)
floods *pl*

Hochzeit ['hɔxtsaɪt] **(-, -en)** *f* wedding;
~sreise *f* honeymoon

hocken ['hɔkən] *vi*, *vr* to squat, to crouch

Hocker (-s, -) *m* stool

Höcker ['hœkər] **(-s, -)** *m* hump

Hoden ['hoːdən] **(-s, -)** *m* testicle

Hof [hoːf] **(-(e)s, ⁺e)** *m* (*Hinterhof*) yard;
(*Bauernhof*) farm; (*Königshof*) court

hoff- ['hɔf] *zW*: **~en** *vi*: **~en (auf** +*akk*) to
hope (for); **~entlich** *adv* I hope, hopefully;
H~nung *f* hope

Hoffnungs- *zW*: **h~los** *adj* hopeless;

~losigkeit f hopelessness; **h~voll** adj hopeful

höflich ['høːflɪç] adj polite, courteous; **H~keit** f courtesy, politeness

hohe(r, s) ['hoːə(r, s)] adj attrib siehe **hoch**

Höhe ['høːə] f height; (Anhöhe) hill

Hoheit ['hoːhaɪt] f (POL) sovereignty; (Titel) Highness

Hoheits- zW: **~gebiet** nt sovereign territory; **~gewässer** nt territorial waters pl

Höhen- ['høːən] zW: **~luft** f mountain air; **~messer** (-s, -) m altimeter; **~sonne** f sun lamp; **~unterschied** m difference in altitude

Höhepunkt m climax

hoher adj, adv higher

hohl [hoːl] adj hollow

Höhle ['høːlə] f cave, hole; (Mundhöhle) cavity; (fig, ZOOL) den

Hohlmaß nt measure of volume

Hohn [hoːn] (-(e)s) m scorn

höhnisch adj scornful, taunting

holen ['hoːlən] vt to get, to fetch; (Atem) to take; **jdn/etw ~ lassen** to send for sb/sth

Holland ['hɔlant] nt Holland; **Holländer** ['hɔlɛndər] m Dutchman; **holländisch** adj Dutch

Hölle ['hœlə] f hell

höllisch ['hœlɪʃ] adj hellish, infernal

holperig ['hɔlpərɪç] adj rough, bumpy

Holunder [ho'lʊndər] (-s, -) m elder

Holz [hɔlts] (-es, ̈er) nt wood

hölzern ['hœltsərn] adj (auch fig) wooden

Holz- zW: **~fäller** (-s, -) m lumberjack, woodcutter; **h~ig** adj woody; **~kohle** f charcoal; **~schuh** m clog; **~weg** m (fig) wrong track; **~wolle** f fine wood shavings pl

Homöopathie [homøopa'tiː] f homeopathy

homosexuell [homozɛksu'ɛl] adj homosexual

Honig ['hoːnɪç] (-s, -e) m honey; **~melone** f (BOT, KOCH) honeydew melon; **~wabe** f honeycomb

Honorar [hono'raːr] (-s, -e) nt fee

Hopfen ['hɔpfən] (-s, -) m hops pl

hopsen ['hɔpsən] vi to hop

Hörapparat m hearing aid

hörbar adj audible

horchen ['hɔrçən] vi to listen; (pej) to eavesdrop

Horde ['hɔrdə] f horde

hör- ['høːr] zW: **~en** vt, vi to hear; **Musik/ Radio ~en** to listen to music/the radio; **H~er** (-s, -) m hearer; (RADIO) listener; (UNIV) student; (Telefonhörer) receiver; **H~funk** (-s) m radio; **~geschädigt** [-gəʃeːdɪçt] adj hearing-impaired

Horizont [hori'tsɔnt] (-(e)s, -e) m horizon; **h~al** [-'taːl] adj horizontal

Hormon [hɔr'moːn] (-s, -e) nt hormone

Hörmuschel f (TEL) earpiece

Horn [hɔrn] (-(e)s, ̈er) nt horn; **~haut** f horny skin

Hornisse [hɔr'nɪsə] f hornet

Horoskop [horo'skoːp] (-s, -e) nt horoscope

Hörspiel nt radio play

Hort [hɔrt] (-(e)s, -e) m (SCH) day centre for schoolchildren whose parents are at work

horten ['hɔrtən] vt to hoard

Hose ['hoːzə] f trousers pl, pants pl (US)

Hosen- zW: **~anzug** m trouser suit; **~rock** m culottes pl; **~tasche** f (trouser) pocket; **~träger** m braces pl (BRIT), suspenders pl (US)

Hostie ['hɔstiə] f (REL) host

Hotel [ho'tɛl] (-s, -s) nt hotel; **~ier** (-s, -s) [hoteli'eː] m hotelkeeper, hotelier; **~verzeichnis** nt hotel register

Hubraum ['huːp-] m (AUT) cubic capacity

hübsch [hʏpʃ] adj pretty, nice

Hubschrauber ['huːpʃraʊbər] (-s, -) m helicopter

Huf ['huːf] m hoof; **~eisen** nt horseshoe

Hüft- ['hʏft] zW: **~e** f hip; **~gürtel** m girdle; **~halter** (-s, -) m girdle

Hügel ['hyːgəl] (-s, -) m hill; **h~ig** adj hilly

Huhn [huːn] (-(e)s, ̈er) nt hen; (KOCH) chicken

Hühner- ['hyːnər] zW: **~auge** nt corn; **~brühe** f chicken broth

Hülle ['hʏlə] f cover(ing); wrapping; **in ~**

und Fülle galore; **h~n** vt: **h~n (in** +akk**)** to cover (with); to wrap (in)

Hülse ['hʏlzə] f husk, shell; **~nfrucht** f pulse

human [hu'maːn] adj humane; **~i'tär** adj humanitarian; **H~i'tät** f humanity

Hummel ['hʊməl] (-, -n) f bumblebee

Hummer ['hʊmər] (-s, -) m lobster

Humor [hu'moːr] (-s, -e) m humour; **~ haben** to have a sense of humour; **~ist** [-'rɪst] m humorist; **h~voll** adj humorous

humpeln ['hʊmpəln] vi to hobble

Humpen ['hʊmpən] (-s, -) m tankard

Hund [hʊnt] (-(e)s, -e) m dog

Hunde- [hʊndə] zW: **~hütte** f (dog) kennel; **h~müde** (umg) adj dog-tired

hundert ['hʊndərt] num hundred; **H~'jahrfeier** f centenary; **~prozentig** adj, adv one hundred per cent

Hundesteuer f dog licence fee

Hündin ['hʏndɪn] f bitch

Hunger ['hʊŋər] (-s) m hunger; **~ haben** to be hungry; **h~n** vi to starve; **~snot** f famine

hungrig ['hʊŋrɪç] adj hungry

Hupe ['huːpə] f horn; **h~n** vi to hoot, to sound one's horn

hüpfen ['hʏpfən] vi to hop; to jump

Hürde ['hʏrdə] f hurdle; (für Schafe) pen; **~nlauf** m hurdling

Hure ['huːrə] f whore

hurtig ['hʊrtɪç] adj brisk, quick ♦ adv briskly, quickly

huschen ['hʊʃən] vi to flit; to scurry

Husten ['huːstən] (-s) m cough; **h~** vi to cough; **~anfall** m coughing fit; **~bonbon** m od nt cough drop; **~saft** m cough mixture

Hut¹ [huːt] (-(e)s, ᵘe) m hat

Hut² [huːt] (-) f care; **auf der ~ sein** to be on one's guard

hüten ['hyːtən] vt to guard ♦ vr to watch out; **sich ~, zu** to take care not to; **sich ~ (vor)** to beware (of), to be on one's guard (against)

Hütte ['hʏtə] f hut; cottage; (Eisen~) forge

Hütten- zW: **~käse** m (KOCH) cottage cheese; **~schuh** m slipper sock

Hydrant [hy'drant] m hydrant

hydraulisch [hy'draʊlɪʃ] adj hydraulic

Hygiene [hygi'eːnə] (-) f hygiene

hygienisch [hygi'eːnɪʃ] adj hygienic

Hymne ['hʏmnə] f hymn; anthem

Hypno- [hʏp'noː] zW: **~se** f hypnosis; **h~tisch** adj hypnotic; **~tiseur** [-ti'zøːr] m hypnotist; **h~ti'sieren** vt to hypnotize

Hypothek [hypo'teːk] (-, -en) f mortgage

Hypothese [hypo'teːzə] f hypothesis

Hysterie [hʏste'riː] f hysteria

hysterisch [hʏs'teːrɪʃ] adj hysterical

I, i

ICE [iːtseː'eː] m abk = **Intercity-Expresszug**

Ich (-(s), -(s)) nt self; (PSYCH) ego

ich [ɪç] pron I; **~ bins!** it's me!

Icon ['aɪkɔn] (-s, -s) nt (COMPUT) icon

Ideal [ide'aːl] (-s, -e) nt ideal; **ideal** adj ideal; **idealistisch** [-'lɪstɪʃ] adj idealistic

Idee [i'deː, pl i'deːən] f idea

identifizieren [identifi'tsiːrən] vt to identify

identisch [i'dɛntɪʃ] adj identical

Identität [identi'tɛːt] f identity

Ideo- [ideo] zW: **~loge** [-'loːgə] (-n, -n) m ideologist; **~logie** [-lo'giː] f ideology; **ideologisch** [-'loːgɪʃ] adj ideological

Idiot [idi'oːt] (-en, -en) m idiot; **idiotisch** adj idiotic

idyllisch [i'dʏlɪʃ] adj idyllic

Igel ['iːgəl] (-s, -) m hedgehog

ignorieren [ɪgno'riːrən] vt to ignore

ihm [iːm] (dat von **er, es**) pron (to) him; (to) it

ihn [iːn] (akk von **er, es**) pron him; it; **~en** (dat von **sie** pl) pron (to) them; **Ihnen** (dat von **Sie** pl) pron (to) you

---
SCHLÜSSELWORT
---

ihr [iːr] pron 1 (nom pl) you; **ihr seid es** it's you

2 (dat von sie) to her; **gib es ihr** give it to her; **er steht neben ihr** he is standing beside her

♦ possessiv pron 1 (sg) her; (: bei Tieren,

Dingen) its; **ihr Mann** her husband
2 *(pl)* their; **die Bäume und ihre Blätter**
the trees and their leaves

ihr(e) [iːr] *adj (sg)* her, its; *(pl)* their; **Ihr(e)**
adj your
ihre(r, s) *pron (sg)* hers, its; *(pl)* theirs;
Ihre(r, s) *pron* yours; **~r** *(gen von* **sie** *sg/pl)*
pron of her/them; **Ihrer** *(gen von* **Sie**) *pron*
of you; **~rseits** *adv* for her/their part;
~sgleichen *pron* people like her/them;
(von Dingen) others like it; **~twegen** *adv*
(für sie) for her/its/their sake; *(wegen ihr)* on
her/its/their account; **~twillen** *adv:* **um**
~twillen = **ihretwegen**
ihrige [ˈiːrɪgə] *pron:* **der / die / das ~** *od* **I~**
hers; its; theirs
illegal [ˈɪlegaːl] *adj* illegal
Illusion [ɪluziˈoːn] *f* illusion
illusorisch [ɪluˈzoːrɪʃ] *adj* illusory
illustrieren [ɪlʊsˈtriːrən] *vt* to illustrate
Illustrierte *f* magazine
im [ɪm] = **in dem**
Imbiss ▲ [ˈɪmbɪs] **(-es, -e)** *m* snack;
~stube *f* snack bar
imitieren [imiˈtiːrən] *vt* to imitate
Imker [ˈɪmkər] **(-s, -)** *m* beekeeper
immatrikulieren [ɪmatrikuˈliːrən] *vi, vr* to
register
immer [ˈɪmar] *adv* always; **~ wieder** again
and again; **~ noch** still; **~ noch nicht** still
not; **für ~** forever; **~ wenn ich ...** every
time I ...; **~ schöner / trauriger** more and
more beautiful/sadder and sadder; **was /**
wer (auch) ~ whatever/whoever; **~hin** *adv*
all the same; **~zu** *adv* all the time
Immobilien [ɪmoˈbiːliən] *pl* real estate *sg*;
~makler *m* estate agent *(BRIT)*, realtor *(US)*
immun [ɪˈmuːn] *adj* immune; **Immunität**
[-iˈtɛːt] *f* immunity; **Immunsystem** *nt*
immune system
Imperfekt [ˈɪmperfɛkt] **(-s, -e)** *nt* imperfect
(tense)
Impf- [ˈɪmpf] *zW:* **impfen** *vt* to vaccinate;
~stoff *m* vaccine, serum; **~ung** *f*
vaccination
imponieren [ɪmpoˈniːrən] *vi* +*dat* to impress

Import [ɪmˈpɔrt] **(-(e)s, -e)** *m* import; **~eur**
m importer; **importieren** *vt* to import
imposant [ɪmpoˈzant] *adj* imposing
impotent [ˈɪmpotɛnt] *adj* impotent
imprägnieren [ɪmprɛˈɡniːrən] *vt* to
(water)proof
improvisieren [ɪmproviˈziːrən] *vt, vi* to
improvise
Impuls [ɪmˈpʊls] **(-es, -e)** *m* impulse;
impulsiv [-ˈziːf] *adj* impulsive
imstande, im Stande [ɪmˈʃtandə] *adj:* **~**
sein to be in a position; *(fähig)* to be able

SCHLÜSSELWORT

in [ɪn] *präp* +*akk* **1** *(räumlich: wohin?)* in, into;
in die Stadt into town; **in die Schule**
gehen to go to school

2 *(zeitlich):* **bis ins 20. Jahrhundert** into *od*
up to the 20th century

♦ *präp* +*dat* **1** *(räumlich: wo)* in; **in der Stadt**
in town; **in der Schule sein** to be at
school

2 *(zeitlich: wann):* **in diesem Jahr** this year;
(in jenem Jahr) in that year; **heute in zwei**
Wochen two weeks today

Inanspruchnahme [ɪnˈʔanʃprʊxnaːmə] *f*
(+gen) demands *pl* (on)
Inbegriff [ˈɪnbəɡrɪf] *m* embodiment,
personification; **inbegriffen** *adv* included
indem [ɪnˈdeːm] *konj* while; **~ man etw**
macht *(dadurch)* by doing sth
Inder(in) [ˈɪndər(ɪn)] *m(f)* Indian
indes(sen) [ɪnˈdes(ən)] *adv* however;
(inzwischen) meanwhile ♦ *konj* while
Indianer(in) [ɪndiˈaːnər(ɪn)] **(-s, -)** *m(f)*
American Indian, native American;
indianisch *adj* Red Indian
Indien [ˈɪndiən] *nt* India
indirekt [ˈɪndirɛkt] *adj* indirect
indisch [ˈɪndɪʃ] *adj* Indian
indiskret [ˈɪndɪskreːt] *adj* indiscreet
indiskutabel [ˈɪndɪskutaːbəl] *adj* out of the
question
individuell [ɪndividuˈɛl] *adj* individual
Individuum [ɪndiˈviːduʊm] **(-s, -en)** *nt*
individual

Spelling Reform: ▲ *new spelling* △ *old spelling (to be phased out)*

Indiz [ɪn'diːts] **(-es, -ien)** *nt (JUR)* clue; ~ **(für)** sign (of)

industrialisieren [ɪndʊstriaˌliˈziːrən] *vt* to industrialize

Industrie [ɪndʊsˈtriː] *f* industry ♦ *in zW* industrial; ~**gebiet** *nt* industrial area; ~- **und Handelskammer** *f* chamber of commerce; ~**zweig** *m* branch of industry

ineinander [ɪnˌaɪˈnandər] *adv* in(to) one another *od* each other

Infarkt [ɪnˈfarkt] **(-(e)s, -e)** *m* coronary (thrombosis)

Infektion [ɪnfɛktsiˈoːn] *f* infection; ~**skrankheit** *f* infectious disease

Infinitiv [ˈɪnfinitiːf] **(-s, -e)** *m* infinitive

infizieren [ɪnfiˈtsiːrən] *vt* to infect ♦ *vr:* **sich (bei jdm)** ~ to be infected (by sb)

Inflation [ɪnflatsiˈoːn] *f* inflation

inflationär [ɪnflatsioˈnɛːr] *adj* inflationary

infolge [ɪnˈfɔlgə] *präp +gen* as a result of, owing to; ~**dessen** [-ˈdɛsən] *adv* consequently

Informatik [ɪnfɔrˈmatɪk] *f* information studies *pl*

Information [ɪnfɔrmatsiˈoːn] *f* information *no pl*

informieren [ɪnfɔrˈmiːrən] *vt* to inform ♦ *vr:* **sich** ~ **(über** +*akk***)** to find out (about)

infrage, in Frage *adv:* ~ **stellen** to question sth; **nicht** ~ **kommen** to be out of the question

Ingenieur [ɪnʒeniˈøːr] *m* engineer; ~**schule** *f* school of engineering

Ingwer [ˈɪŋvər] **(-s)** *m* ginger

Inh. *abk* (= *Inhaber*) prop.; (= *Inhalt*) contents

Inhaber(in) [ˈɪnhaːbər(ɪn)] **(-s, -)** *m(f)* owner; (*Hausinhaber*) occupier; (*Lizenzinhaber*) licensee, holder; (*FIN*) bearer

inhaftieren [ɪnhafˈtiːrən] *vt* to take into custody

inhalieren [ɪnhaˈliːrən] *vt, vi* to inhale

Inhalt [ˈɪnhalt] **(-(e)s, -e)** *m* contents *pl*; (*eines Buchs etc*) content; (*MATH*) area; volume; **inhaltlich** *adj* as regards content

Inhalts- *zW:* ~**angabe** *f* summary; ~**verzeichnis** *nt* table of contents

inhuman [ˈɪnhumaːn] *adj* inhuman

Initiative [initsiaˈtiːvə] *f* initiative

inklusive [ɪnkluˈziːvə] *präp +gen* inclusive of ♦ *adv* inclusive

In-Kraft-Treten [ɪnˈkraftˌtreːtən] **(-s)** *nt* coming into force

Inland [ˈɪnlant] **(-(e)s)** *nt* (*GEOG*) inland; (*POL, COMM*) home (country); ~**flug** *m* domestic flight

inmitten [ɪnˈmɪtən] *präp +gen* in the middle of; ~ **von** amongst

innehaben [ˈɪnəhaːbən] (*unreg*) *vt* to hold

innen [ˈɪnən] *adv* inside; **Innenarchitekt** *m* interior designer; **Inneneinrichtung** *f* (interior) furnishings *pl*; **Innenhof** *m* inner courtyard; **Innenminister** *m* minister of the interior, Home Secretary (*BRIT*); **Innenpolitik** *f* domestic policy; ~**politisch** *adj* (*Entwicklung, Lage*) internal, domestic; **Innenstadt** *f* town/city centre

inner- [ˈɪnər] *zW:* ~**e(r, s)** *adj* inner; (*im Körper, inländisch*) internal; **Innere(s)** *nt* inside; (*Mitte*) centre; (*fig*) heart; **Innereien** [-ˈraɪən] *pl* innards; ~**halb** *adv* within; (*räumlich*) inside ♦ *präp +gen* within; inside; ~**lich** *adj* internal; (*geistig*) inward; ~**ste(r, s)** *adj* innermost; **Innerste(s)** *nt* heart

innig [ˈɪnɪç] *adj* (*Freundschaft*) close

inoffiziell [ˈɪnˌɔfitsiɛl] *adj* unofficial

ins [ɪns] = **in das**

Insasse [ˈɪnzasə] **(-n, -n)** *m* (*Anstalt*) inmate; (*AUT*) passenger

Insassenversicherung *f* passenger insurance

insbesondere [ɪnsbəˈzɔndərə] *adv* (e)specially

Inschrift [ˈɪnʃrɪft] *f* inscription

Insekt [ɪnˈzɛkt] **(-(e)s, -en)** *nt* insect

Insektenschutzmittel *nt* insect repellent

Insel [ˈɪnzəl] **(-, -n)** *f* island

Inser- *zW:* ~**at** [ɪnzeˈraːt] **(-(e)s, -e)** *nt* advertisement; ~**ent** [ɪnzeˈrɛnt] *m* advertiser; **inserieren** [ɪnzeˈriːrən] *vt, vi* to advertise

insgeheim [ɪnsgəˈhaɪm] *adv* secretly

insgesamt [ɪnsgəˈzamt] *adv* altogether, all in all

Rechtschreibreform: ▲ *neue Schreibung* △ *alte Schreibung (auslaufend)*

insofern[ɪnzo'fɛrn] *adv* in this respect ♦ *konj* if; *(deshalb)* (and) so; ~ **als** in so far as

insoweit[ɪnzo'vaɪt] = **insofern**

Installateur[ɪnstala'tøːr] *m* electrician; plumber

Instandhaltung[ɪn'ʃtanthaltʊŋ] *f* maintenance

inständig[ɪn'ʃtɛndɪç] *adj* urgent

Instandsetzung[ɪn'ʃtant-] *f* overhaul; *(eines Gebäudes)* restoration

Instanz[ɪn'stants] *f* authority; *(JUR)* court

Instinkt[ɪn'stɪŋkt] **(-(e)s, -e)** *m* instinct; **instinktiv**[-'tiːf] *adj* instinctive

Institut[ɪnsti'tuːt] **(-(e)s, -e)** *nt* institute

Instrument[ɪnstru'mɛnt] *nt* instrument

Intell-[ɪntɛl] *zW:* **intellektuell**[-ɛktu'ɛl] *adj* intellectual; **intelligent**[-i'gɛnt] *adj* intelligent; **~igenz**[-i'gɛnts] *f* intelligence; *(Leute)* intelligentsia *pl*

Intendant[ɪntɛn'dant] *m* director

intensiv[ɪntɛn'ziːf] *adj* intensive; **Intensivstation** *f* intensive care unit

Intercity-[ɪntɐr'sɪti] *zW:* **~-Expresszug**▲ *m* high-speed train; **~-Zug** *m* intercity (train); **~-Zuschlag** *m* intercity supplement

Interess- *zW:* **i~ant**[ɪntere'sant] *adj* interesting; **i~anterweise** *adv* interestingly enough; **~e**[ɪnte'resə] **(-s, -n)** *nt* interest; **~e haben an** +*dat* to be interested in; **~ent**[ɪntere'sɛnt] *m* interested party; **i~ieren**[ɪntere'siːrən] *vt* to interest ♦ *vr:* **sich i~ieren für** to be interested in

intern[ɪn'tɛrn] *adj (Angelegenheiten, Regelung)* internal; *(Besprechung)* private

Internat[ɪntɐr'naːt] **(-(e)s, -e)** *nt* boarding school

inter-[ɪntɐr] *zW:* **~national**[-natsio'naːl] *adj* international; **I~net**['ɪntɐrnɛt] **(-s)** *nt:* **das I~net** the Internet; **I~net-Anbieter** *m* Internet Service Provider, ISP, **I~net-Café** *nt* Internet café; **~pretieren**[-pre'tiːrən] *vt* to interpret; **I~vall**[-'val] **(-s, -e)** *nt* interval; **I~view**[-'vjuː] **(-s, -s)** *nt* interview; **~viewen**[-'vjuːən] *vt* to interview

intim[ɪn'tiːm] *adj* intimate; **Intimität** *f* intimacy

intolerant['ɪntolerant] *adj* intolerant

Intrige[ɪn'triːgə] *f* intrigue, plot

Invasion[ɪnvazi'oːn] *f* invasion

Inventar[ɪnvɛn'taːr] **(-s, -e)** *nt* inventory

Inventur[ɪnvɛn'tuːr] *f* stocktaking; ~ **machen** to stocktake

investieren[ɪnvɛs'tiːrən] *vt* to invest

inwie-[ɪnvi] *zW:* **~fern** *adv* how far, to what extent; **~weit** *adv* how far, to what extent

inzwischen[ɪn'tsvɪʃən] *adv* meanwhile

Irak[i'raːk] **(-s)** *m:* **der ~** Iraq; **irakisch** *adj* Iraqi

Iran[i'raːn] **(-s)** *m:* **der ~** Iran; **iranisch** *adj* Iranian

irdisch['ɪrdɪʃ] *adj* earthly

Ire['iːrə] **(-n, -n)** *m* Irishman

irgend['ɪrgɛnt] *adv* at all; **wann/was/wer ~** whenever/whatever/whoever; **~etwas** *pron* something/anything; **~jemand** *pron* somebody/anybody; **~ein(e, s)** *adj* some, any; **~einmal** *adv* sometime or other; *(fragend)* ever; **~wann** *adv* sometime; **~wie** *adv* somehow; **~wo** *adv* somewhere; anywhere; **~wohin** *adv* somewhere; anywhere

Irin['iːrɪn] *f* Irishwoman

Irland['ɪrlant] **(o)** *nt* Ireland

Ironie[iro'niː] *f* irony; **ironisch**[i'roːnɪʃ] *adj* ironic(al)

irre['ɪrə] *adj* crazy, mad; **Irre(r)** *f(m)* lunatic; **~führen** *vt* to mislead; **~machen** *vt* to confuse; **~n** *vi* to be mistaken; *(umherirren)* to wander, to stray ♦ *vr* to be mistaken; **Irrenanstalt** *f* lunatic asylum

Irr- *zW:* **~garten** *m* maze; **i~ig**['ɪrɪç] *adj* incorrect, wrong; **i~itieren**[ɪri'tiːrən] *vt (verwirren)* to confuse; *(ärgern)* to irritate; *(stören)* to annoy; **irrsinnig** *adj* mad, crazy; *(umg)* terrific; **~tum**(-s, **-tümer)** *m* mistake, error; **irrtümlich** *adj* mistaken

Island['iːslant] **(-s)** *nt* Iceland

Isolation[izolatsi'oːn] *f* isolation; *(ELEK)* insulation

Isolier-[izo'liːr] *zW:* **~band** *nt* insulating tape; **isolieren** *vt* to isolate; *(ELEK)* to insulate; **~station** *f (MED)* isolation ward;

~ung *f* isolation; (*ELEK*) insulation
Israel ['israeːl] (**-s**) *nt* Israel; **~i** (**-s, -s**) [-'eːli] *m* Israeli; **israelisch** *adj* Israeli
isst ▲ [ist] *vb siehe* **essen**
ist [ist] *vb siehe* **sein**
Italien [i'taːliən] (**-s**) *nt* Italy; **~er(in)** (**-s**) *m(f)* Italian; **italienisch** *adj* Italian
i. V. *abk* = **in Vertretung**

J, j

ja [jaː] *adv* **1** yes; **haben Sie das gesehen? - ja** did you see it? - yes(, I did); **ich glaube ja** (yes) I think so
2 (*fragend*) really?; **ich habe gekündigt - ja?** I've quit - have you?; **du kommst, ja?** you're coming, aren't you?
3: sei ja vorsichtig do be careful; **Sie wissen ja, dass ...** as you know, ...; **tu das ja nicht!** don't do that!; **ich habe es ja gewusst** I just knew it; **ja, also ...** well you see ...

Jacht [jaxt] (**-, -en**) *f* yacht
Jacke ['jakə] *f* jacket; (*Wolljacke*) cardigan
Jackett [ʒa'kɛt] (**-s, -s** *od* **-e**) *nt* jacket
Jagd [jaːkt] (**-, -en**) *f* hunt; (*Jagen*) hunting; **~beute** *f* kill; **~flugzeug** *nt* fighter; **~hund** *m* hunting dog
jagen ['jaːɡən] *vi* to hunt; (*eilen*) to race ♦ *vt* to hunt; (*wegjagen*) to drive (off); (*verfolgen*) to chase
Jäger ['jɛːɡər] (**-s, -**) *m* hunter; **~schnitzel** *nt* (*KOCH*) pork in a spicy sauce with mushrooms
jäh [jɛː] *adj* sudden, abrupt; (*steil*) steep, precipitous
Jahr [jaːr] (**-(e)s, -e**) *nt* year; **j~elang** *adv* for years
Jahres- *zW*: **~abonnement** *nt* annual subscription; **~abschluss** ▲ *m* end of the year; (*COMM*) annual statement of account; **~beitrag** *m* annual subscription; **~karte** *f*

yearly season ticket; **~tag** *m* anniversary; **~wechsel** *m* turn of the year; **~zahl** *f* date; year; **~zeit** *f* season
Jahr- *zW*: **~gang** *m* age group; (*von Wein*) vintage; **~'hundert** (**-s, -e**) *nt* century; **jährlich** ['jɛːrliç] *adj, adv* yearly; **~markt** *m* fair; **~tausend** *nt* millennium; **~'zehnt** *nt* decade
Jähzorn ['jɛːtsɔrn] *m* sudden anger; hot temper; **j~ig** *adj* hot-tempered
Jalousie [ʒalu'ziː] *f* venetian blind
Jammer ['jamər] (**-s**) *m* misery; **es ist ein ~, dass ...** it is a crying shame that ...
jämmerlich ['jɛmərlɪç] *adj* wretched, pathetic
jammern *vi* to wail ♦ *vt unpers*: **es jammert jdn** it makes sb feel sorry
Januar ['januaːr] (**-(s), -e**) *m* January
Japan ['jaːpan] (**-s**) *nt* Japan; **~er(in)** [-'paːnər(ɪn)] (**-s**) *m(f)* Japanese; **j~isch** *adj* Japanese
jäten ['jɛːtən] *vt*: **Unkraut ~** to weed
jauchzen ['jauxtsən] *vi* to rejoice
jaulen ['jaulən] *vi* to howl
jawohl [ja'voːl] *adv* yes (of course)
Jawort ['jaːvɔrt] *nt* consent
Jazz [dʒæz] (**-**) *m* Jazz

je [jeː] *adv* **1** (*jemals*) ever; **hast du so was je gesehen?** did you ever see anything like it?
2 (*jeweils*) every, each; **sie zahlten je 3 Mark** they paid 3 marks each
♦ *konj* **1: je nach** depending on; **je nachdem** it depends; **je nachdem, ob ...** depending on whether ...
2: je eher, desto *od* **umso besser** the sooner the better

Jeans [dʒiːnz] *pl* jeans
jede(r, s) ['jeːdə(r, s)] *adj* every, each ♦ *pron* everybody; (*~ Einzelne*) each; **~s Mal** every time, each time; **ohne ~ x** without any x
jedenfalls *adv* in any case
jedermann *pron* everyone
jederzeit *adv* at any time

jedoch [jeˈdɔx] *adv* however
jeher [ˈjeːheːr] *adv*: **von/seit ~** always
jemals [ˈjeːmaːls] *adv* ever
jemand [ˈjeːmant] *pron* somebody; anybody
jene(r, s) [ˈjeːnə(r, s)] *adj* that ♦ *pron* that one
jenseits [ˈjeːnzaɪts] *adv* on the other side ♦ *präp* +gen on the other side of, beyond
Jenseits *nt*: **das ~** the hereafter, the beyond
jetzig [ˈjɛtsɪç] *adj* present
jetzt [jɛtst] *adv* now
jeweilig *adj* respective
jewells *adv*: **~ zwei zusammen** two at a time; **zu ~ 5 DM** at 5 marks each; **~ das Erste** the first each time
Jh. *abk* = **Jahrhundert**
Job [dʒɔp] (**-s, -s**) *m* (*umg*) job; **j~ben** [ˈdʒɔbən] *vi* (*umg*) to work
Jockei [ˈdʒɔke] (**-s, -s**) *m* jockey
Jod [joːt] (**-(e)s**) *nt* iodine
jodeln [ˈjoːdəln] *vi* to yodel
joggen [ˈdʒɔgən] *vi* to jog
Jog(h)urt [ˈjoːgʊrt] (**-s, -s**) *m od nt* yogurt
Johannisbeere [joˈhanɪsbeːrə] *f* redcurrant; **schwarze ~** blackcurrant
johlen [ˈjoːlən] *vi* to yell
jonglieren [ʒõˈgliːrən] *vi* to juggle
Journal- [ʒʊrnal] *zW*: **~ismus** [-ˈlɪsmʊs] *m* journalism; **~ist(in)** [-ˈlɪst(ɪn)] *m(f)* journalist; **journaˈlistisch** *adj* journalistic
Jubel [ˈjuːbəl] (**-s**) *m* rejoicing; **j~n** *vi* to rejoice
Jubiläum [jubiˈlɛːʊm] (**-s, Jubiläen**) *nt* anniversary; jubilee
jucken [ˈjʊkən] *vi* to itch ♦ *vt*: **es juckt mich am Arm** my arm is itching
Juckreiz [ˈjʊkraɪts] *m* itch
Jude [ˈjuːdə] (**-n, -n**) *m* Jew
Juden- *zW*: **~tum** (**-**) *nt* Judaism; Jewry; **~verfolgung** *f* persecution of the Jews
Jüdin [ˈjyːdɪn] *f* Jewess
jüdisch [ˈjyːdɪʃ] *adj* Jewish
Jugend [ˈjuːgənt] (**-**) *f* youth; **j~frei** *adj* (*CINE*) U (*BRIT*), G (*US*), suitable for children; **~herberge** *f* youth hostel; **~herbergsausweis** *m* youth hostelling

card; **j~lich** *adj* youthful; **~liche(r)** *f(m)* teenager, young person
Jugoslaw- [jugoˈslaːv] *zW*: **~ien** (**-s**) *nt* Yugoslavia; **j~isch** *adj* Yugoslavian
Juli [ˈjuːli] (**-(s), -s**) *m* July
jun. *abk* (= *junior*) jr.
jung [jʊŋ] *adj* young; **J~e** (**-n, -n**) *m* boy, lad ♦ *nt* young animal; **J~en** *pl* (*von Tier*) young *pl*
Jünger [ˈjʏŋər] (**-s, -**) *m* disciple
jünger *adj* younger
Jung- *zW*: **~frau** *f* virgin; (*ASTROL*) Virgo; **~geselle** *m* bachelor; **~gesellin** *f* unmarried woman
jüngst [jʏŋst] *adv* lately, recently; **~e(r, s)** *adj* youngest; (*neueste*) latest
Juni [ˈjuːni] (**-(s), -s**) *m* June
Junior [ˈjuːnɪɔr] (**-s, -en**) *m* junior
Jurist [juˈrɪst] *m* jurist, lawyer; **j~isch** *adj* legal
Justiz [jʊsˈtiːts] (**-**) *f* justice; **~beamte(r)** *m* judicial officer; **~irrtum** *m* miscarriage of justice; **~minister** *m* ≈ Lord (High) Chancellor (*BRIT*), ≈ Attorney General (*US*)
Juwel [juˈveːl] (**-s, -en**) *nt od m* jewel
Juwelier [juveˈliːr] (**-s, -e**) *m* jeweller; **~geschäft** *nt* jeweller's (shop)
Jux [jʊks] (**-es, -e**) *m* joke, lark

K, k

Kabarett [kabaˈrɛt] (**-s, -e** *od* **-s**) *nt* cabaret; **~ist** [-ˈtɪst] *m* cabaret artiste
Kabel [ˈkaːbəl] (**-s, -**) *nt* (*ELEK*) wire; (*stark*) cable; **~fernsehen** *nt* cable television
Kabeljau [ˈkaːbəljau] (**-s, -e** *od* **-s**) *m* cod
Kabine [kaˈbiːnə] *f* cabin; (*Zelle*) cubicle
Kabinenbahn *f* cable railway
Kabinett [kabiˈnɛt] (**-s, -e**) *nt* (*POL*) cabinet
Kachel [ˈkaxəl] (**-, -n**) *f* tile; **k~n** *vt* to tile; **~ofen** *m* tiled stove
Käfer [ˈkɛːfər] (**-s, -**) *m* beetle
Kaffee [ˈkafe] (**-s, -s**) *m* coffee; **~haus** *nt* café; **~kanne** *f* coffeepot; **~löffel** *m* coffee spoon
Käfig [ˈkɛːfɪç] (**-s, -e**) *m* cage

Spelling Reform: ▲ *new spelling* △ *old spelling (to be phased out)*

kahl [kaːl] *adj* bald; ~ **geschoren** shaven, shorn; ~**köpfig** *adj* bald-headed

Kahn [kaːn] (-(e)s, ⁼e) *m* boat, barge

Kai [kaɪ] (-s, -e *od* -s) *m* quay

Kaiser ['kaɪzər] (-s, -) *m* emperor; ~**in** *f* empress; **k~lich** *adj* imperial; ~**reich** *nt* empire; ~**schnitt** *m* (*MED*) Caesarian (section)

Kakao [ka'kaːo] (-s, -s) *m* cocoa

Kaktee [kak'teː(ə)] (-, -n) *f* cactus

Kaktus ['kaktʊs] (-, -teen) *m* cactus

Kalb [kalp] (-(e)s, ⁼er) *nt* calf; **k~en** ['kalbən] *vi* to calve; ~**fleisch** *nt* veal; ~**sleder** *nt* calf(skin)

Kalender [ka'lɛndər] (-s, -) *m* calendar; (*Taschenkalender*) diary

Kaliber [ka'liːbər] (-s, -) *nt* (*auch fig*) calibre

Kalk [kalk] (-(e)s, -e) *m* lime; (*BIOL*) calcium; ~**stein** *m* limestone

kalkulieren [kalku'liːrən] *vt* to calculate

Kalorie [kalo'riː] *f* calorie

kalt [kalt] *adj* cold; **mir ist (es)** ~ I am cold; ~ **bleiben** (*fig*) to remain unmoved; ~ **stellen** to chill; ~**blütig** *adj* cold-blooded; (*ruhig*) cool

Kälte ['kɛltə] (-) *f* cold; coldness; ~**grad** *m* degree of frost *od* below zero; ~**welle** *f* cold spell

kalt- *zW*: ~**herzig** *adj* cold-hearted; ~**schnäuzig** *adj* cold, unfeeling; ~**stellen** *vt* (*fig*) to leave out in the cold

kam *etc* [kaːm] *vb siehe* **kommen**

Kamel [ka'meːl] (-(e)s, -e) *nt* camel

Kamera ['kamera] (-, -s) *f* camera

Kamerad [kamə'raːt] (-en, -en) *m* comrade, friend; ~**schaft** *f* comradeship; **k~schaftlich** *adj* comradely

Kameramann (-(e)s, -männer) *m* cameraman

Kamille [ka'mɪlə] *f* camomile; ~**ntee** *m* camomile tea

Kamin [ka'miːn] (-s, -e) *m* (*außen*) chimney; (*innen*) fireside, fireplace; ~**kehrer** (-s, -) *m* chimney sweep

Kamm [kam] (-(e)s, ⁼e) *m* comb; (*Bergkamm*) ridge; (*Hahnenkamm*) crest

kämmen ['kɛmən] *vt* to comb ♦ *vr* to comb one's hair

Kammer ['kamər] (-, -n) *f* chamber; small bedroom

Kammerdiener *m* valet

Kampagne [kam'panjə] *f* campaign

Kampf [kampf] (-(e)s, ⁼e) *m* fight, battle; (*Wettbewerb*) contest; (*fig: Anstrengung*) struggle; **k~bereit** *adj* ready for action

kämpfen ['kɛmpfən] *vi* to fight

Kämpfer (-s, -) *m* fighter, combatant

Kampf- *zW*: ~**handlung** *f* action; **k~los** *adj* without a fight; ~**richter** *m* (*SPORT*) referee; (*TENNIS*) umpire; ~**stoff** *m*: **chemischer/biologischer ~stoff** chemical/biological weapon

Kanada ['kanada] (-s) *nt* Canada; **Kanadier(in)** (-s, -) [kə'naːdiər(ɪn)] *m(f)* Canadian; **ka'nadisch** *adj* Canadian

Kanal [ka'naːl] (-s, Kanäle) *m* (*Fluss*) canal; (*Rinne, Ärmelkanal*) channel; (*für Abfluss*) drain; ~**inseln** *pl* Channel Islands; ~**isation** [-izatsi'oːn] *f* sewage system; ~**tunnel** *m*: **der ~tunnel** the Channel Tunnel

Kanarienvogel [ka'naːriənfoːgəl] *m* (*ZOOL*) canary

kanarisch [ka'naːrɪʃ] *adj*: **K~e Inseln** Canary Islands, Canaries

Kandi- [kandi] *zW*: ~**dat** [-'daːt] (-en, -en) *m* candidate; ~**datur** [-da'tuːr] *f* candidature, candidacy; **k~dieren** [-'diːrən] *vi* to stand, to run

Kandis(zucker) ['kandɪs(tsʊkər)] (-) *m* candy

Känguru ▲ ['kɛŋguru] (-s, -s) *nt* kangaroo

Kaninchen [ka'niːnçən] *nt* rabbit

Kanister [ka'nɪstər] (-s, -) *m* can, canister

Kännchen ['kɛnçən] *nt* pot

Kanne ['kanə] *f* (*Krug*) jug; (*Kaffeekanne*) pot; (*Milchkanne*) churn; (*Gießkanne*) can

kannst *etc* [kanst] *vb siehe* **können**

Kanone [ka'noːnə] *f* gun; (*HIST*) cannon; (*fig: Mensch*) ace

Kantate [kan'tatə] *f* cantata

Kante ['kantə] *f* edge

Kantine [kan'tiːnə] *f* canteen

Kanton [kan'toːn] (-s, -e) *m* canton

Kanton

> *i* **Kanton** *is the term for a state or region of Switzerland. Under the Swiss constitution the* **Kantone** *enjoy considerable autonomy. The Swiss* **Kantone** *are Aargau, Appenzell, Basel, Bern, Fribourg, Geneva, Glarus, Graubünden, Luzern, Neuchâtel, St. Gallen, Schaffhausen, Schwyz, Solothurn, Ticino, Thurgau, Unterwalden, Uri, Valais, Vaud, Zug and Zürich.*

Kanu ['ka:nu] (-s, -s) *nt* canoe
Kanzel ['kantsəl] (-, -n) *f* pulpit
Kanzler ['kantslər] (-s, -) *m* chancellor
Kap [kap] (-s, -s) *nt* cape (GEOG)
Kapazität [kapatsi'tɛ:t] *f* capacity; (*Fachmann*) authority
Kapelle [ka'pɛlə] *f* (*Gebäude*) chapel; (*MUS*) band
kapieren [ka'pi:rən] (*umg*) *vt, vi* to get, to understand
Kapital [kapi'ta:l] (-s, -e *od* -ien) *nt* capital; **~anlage** *f* investment; **~ismus** [-'lɪsmʊs] *m* capitalism; **~ist** [-'lɪst] *m* capitalist; **k~istisch** *adj* capitalist
Kapitän [kapi'tɛ:n] (-s, -e) *m* captain
Kapitel [ka'pɪtəl] (-s, -) *nt* chapter
Kapitulation [kapitulatsi'o:n] *f* capitulation
kapitulieren [kapitu'li:rən] *vi* to capitulate
Kappe ['kapə] *f* cap; (*Kapuze*) hood
kappen *vt* to cut
Kapsel ['kapsəl] (-, -n) *f* capsule
kaputt [ka'pʊt] (*umg*) *adj* kaput, broken; (*Person*) exhausted, finished; **am Auto ist etwas** ~ there's something wrong with the car; **~gehen** (*unreg*) *vi* to break; (*Schuhe*) to fall apart; (*Firma*) to go bust; (*Stoff*) to wear out; (*sterben*) to cop it (*umg*); **~machen** *vt* to break; (*Mensch*) to exhaust, to wear out
Kapuze [ka'pu:tsə] *f* hood
Karamell ▲ [kara'mɛl] (-s) *m* caramel; **~bonbon** *nt od m* toffee
Karate [ka'ra:tə] (-s) *nt* karate
Karawane [kara'va:nə] *f* caravan

Kardinal [kardi'na:l] (-s, **Kardinäle**) *m* cardinal; **~zahl** *f* cardinal number
Karfreitag [ka:r'fraita:k] *m* Good Friday
karg [kark] *adj* (*Landschaft, Boden*) barren, (*Lohn*) meagre
kärglich ['kɛrklɪç] *adj* poor, scanty
Karibik [ka'ri:bɪk] (-) *f*: **die** ~ the Caribbean
karibisch [ka'ri:bɪʃ] *adj*: **K~e Inseln** Caribbean Islands
kariert [ka'ri:rt] *adj* (*Stoff*) checked; (*Papier*) squared
Karies ['ka:ries] (-) *f* caries
Karikatur [karika'tu:r] *f* caricature; **~ist** [-'rɪst] *m* cartoonist
Karneval ['karnəval] (-s, -e *od* -s) *m* carnival

Karneval

> *i* **Karneval** *is the time immediately before Lent when people gather to eat, drink and generally have fun before the fasting begins.* **Rosenmontag**, *the day before Shrove Tuesday, is the most important day of* **Karneval** *on the Rhine. Most firms take a day's holiday on that day to enjoy the celebrations. In South Germany and Austria* **Karneval** *is called* **Fasching**.

Karo ['ka:ro] (-s, -s) *nt* square; (*KARTEN*) diamonds
Karosserie [karɔsə'ri:] *f* (*AUT*) body(work)
Karotte [ka'rɔtə] *f* carrot
Karpfen ['karpfən] (-s, -) *m* carp
Karre ['karə] *f* cart, barrow
Karren (-s, -) *m* cart, barrow
Karriere [kari'ɛ:rə] *f* career; ~ **machen** to get on, to get to the top; **~macher** (-s, -) *m* careerist
Karte ['kartə] *f* card; (*Landkarte*) map; (*Speisekarte*) menu; (*Eintrittskarte, Fahrkarte*) ticket; **alles auf eine** ~ **setzen** to put all one's eggs in one basket
Kartei [kar'tai] *f* card index; **~karte** *f* index card
Kartell [kar'tɛl] (-s, -e) *nt* cartel
Karten- *zW*: **~spiel** *nt* card game; pack of cards; **~telefon** *nt* cardphone;

~vorverkauf *m* advance booking office
Kartoffel [kar'tɔfəl] (-, -n) *f* potato; **~brei** *m* mashed potatoes *pl*; **~mus** *nt* mashed potatoes *pl*; **~püree** *nt* mashed potatoes *pl*; **~salat** *m* potato salad
Karton [kar'tõː] (-s, -s) *m* cardboard; (*Schachtel*) cardboard box; **k~iert** [karto'niːrt] *adj* hardback
Karussell [karʊ'sɛl] (-s, -s) *nt* roundabout (*BRIT*), merry-go-round
Karwoche ['kaːrvɔxə] *f* Holy Week
Käse ['kɛːzə] (-s, -) *m* cheese; **~glocke** *f* cheese (plate) cover; **~kuchen** *m* cheesecake
Kaserne [ka'zɛrnə] *f* barracks *pl*; **~nhof** *m* parade ground
Kasino [ka'ziːno] (-s, -s) *nt* club; (*MIL*) officers' mess; (*Spielkasino*) casino
Kaskoversicherung ['kasko-] *f* (*Teilkasko*) ≈ third party, fire and theft insurance; (*Vollkasko*) ≈ fully comprehensive insurance
Kasse ['kasə] *f* (*Geldkasten*) cashbox; (*in Geschäft*) till, cash register; cash desk, checkout; (*Kinokasse, Theaterkasse etc*) box office; ticket office; (*Krankenkasse*) health insurance; (*Sparkasse*) savings bank; **~ machen** to count the money; **getrennte ~ führen** to pay separately; **an der ~** (*in Geschäft*) at the desk; **gut bei ~ sein** to be in the money
Kassen- *zW*: **~arzt** *m* panel doctor (*BRIT*); **~bestand** *m* cash balance; **~patient** *m* panel patient (*BRIT*); **~prüfung** *f* audit; **~sturz** *m*: **~sturz machen** to check one's money; **~zettel** *m* receipt
Kassette [ka'sɛtə] *f* small box; (*Tonband, PHOT*) cassette; (*Bücherkassette*) case
Kassettenrekorder (-s, -) *m* cassette recorder
kassieren [ka'siːrən] *vt* to take ♦ *vi*: **darf ich ~?** would you like to pay now?
Kassierer [ka'siːrər] (-s, -) *m* cashier; (*von Klub*) treasurer
Kastanie [kas'taːniə] *f* chestnut; (*Baum*) chestnut tree
Kasten ['kastən] (-s, ⁸) *m* (*auch SPORT*) box; case; (*Truhe*) chest

kastrieren [kas'triːrən] *vt* to castrate
Katalog [kata'loːk] (-(e)s, -e) *m* catalogue
Katalysator [kataly'zaːtɔr] *m* catalyst; (*AUT*) catalytic converter
katastrophal [katastro'faːl] *adj* catastrophic
Katastrophe [kata'stroːfə] *f* catastrophe, disaster
Kat-Auto ['kat|aʊto] *nt* car fitted with a catalytic converter
Kategorie [katego'riː] *f* category
kategorisch [kate'goːrɪʃ] *adj* categorical
Kater ['kaːtər] (-s, -) *m* tomcat; (*umg*) hangover
kath. *abk* (= *katholisch*) Cath.
Kathedrale [kate'draːlə] *f* cathedral
Katholik [kato'liːk] (-en, -en) *m* Catholic
katholisch [ka'toːlɪʃ] *adj* Catholic
Kätzchen ['kɛtsçən] *nt* kitten
Katze ['katsə] *f* cat; **für die Katz** (*umg*) in vain, for nothing
Katzen- *zW*: **~auge** *nt* cat's eye; (*Fahrrad*) rear light; **~sprung** (*umg*) *m* stone's throw; short journey
Kauderwelsch ['kaʊdərvɛlʃ] (-(s)) *nt* jargon; (*umg*) double Dutch
kauen ['kaʊən] *vt*, *vi* to chew
kauern ['kaʊərn] *vi* to crouch down; (*furchtsam*) to cower
Kauf [kaʊf] (-(e)s, **Käufe**) *m* purchase, buy; (*~en*) buying; **ein guter ~** a bargain; **etw in ~ nehmen** to put up with sth; **k~en** *vt* to buy
Käufer(in) ['kɔʏfər(ɪn)] (-s, -) *m(f)* buyer
Kauf- *zW*: **~frau** *f* businesswoman; **~haus** *nt* department store; **~kraft** *f* purchasing power
käuflich ['kɔʏflɪç] *adj* purchasable, for sale; (*pej*) venal ♦ *adv*: **~ erwerben** to purchase
Kauf- *zW*: **k~lustig** *adj* interested in buying; **~mann** (*pl* **-leute**) *m* businessman; shopkeeper; **k~männisch** *adj* commercial; **k~männischer Angestellter** office worker; **~preis** *m* purchase price; **~vertrag** *m* bill of sale
Kaugummi ['kaʊgʊmi] *m* chewing gum
Kaulquappe ['kaʊlkvapə] *f* tadpole
kaum [kaʊm] *adv* hardly, scarcely

Kaution [kauˈtsiˈoːn] f deposit; (JUR) bail

Kauz [kauts] (**-es, Käuze**) m owl; (fig) queer fellow

Kavalier [kavaˈliːr] (**-s, -e**) m gentleman, cavalier; **~sdelikt** nt peccadillo

Kaviar [ˈkaːviar] m caviar

keck [kɛk] adj daring, bold

Kegel [ˈkeːgəl] (**-s, -**) m skittle; (MATH) cone; **~bahn** f skittle alley; bowling alley; **k~n** vi to play skittles

Kehle [ˈkeːlə] f throat

Kehlkopf m larynx

Kehre [ˈkeːrə] f turn(ing), bend; **k~n** vt, vi (wenden) to turn; (mit Besen) to sweep; **sich an etw** dat **nicht k~n** not to heed sth

Kehricht [ˈkeːriçt] (**-s**) m sweepings pl

Kehrseite f reverse, other side; wrong side; bad side

kehrtmachen vi to turn about, to about-turn

keifen [ˈkaifən] vi to scold, to nag

Keil [kail] (**-(e)s, -e**) m wedge; (MIL) arrowhead; **~riemen** m (AUT) fan belt

Keim [kaim] (**-(e)s, -e**) m bud; (MED, fig) germ; **k~en** vi to germinate; **k~frei** adj sterile; **~zelle** f (fig) nucleus

kein [kain] adj no, not ... any; **~e(r, s)** pron no one, nobody; none; **~erlei** adj attrib no ... whatsoever

keinesfalls adv on no account

keineswegs adv by no means

keinmal adv not once

Keks [keːks] (**-es, -e**) m od nt biscuit

Kelch [kɛlç] (**-(e)s, -e**) m cup, goblet, chalice

Kelle [ˈkɛlə] f (Suppenkelle) ladle; (Maurerkelle) trowel

Keller [ˈkɛlər] (**-s, -**) m cellar

Kellner(in) [ˈkɛlnər(in)] (**-s, -**) m(f) waiter (-tress)

keltern [ˈkɛltərn] vt to press

kennen [ˈkɛnən] (unreg) vt to know; **~ lernen** ▲ to get to know; **sich ~ lernen** to get to know each other; (zum ersten Mal) to meet

Kenner (**-s, -**) m connoisseur

kenntlich adj distinguishable, discernible;

etw ~ machen to mark sth

Kenntnis (**-, -se**) f knowledge no pl; **etw zur ~ nehmen** to note sth; **von etw ~ nehmen** to take notice of sth; **jdn in ~ setzen** to inform sb

Kenn- zW: **~zeichen** nt mark, characteristic; **k~zeichnen** vt insep to characterize; **~ziffer** f reference number

kentern [ˈkɛntərn] vi to capsize

Keramik [keˈraːmik] (**-, -en**) f ceramics pl, pottery

Kerbe [ˈkɛrbə] f notch, groove

Kerker [ˈkɛrkər] (**-s, -**) m prison

Kerl [kɛrl] (**-s, -e**) m chap, bloke (BRIT), guy

Kern [kɛrn] (**-(e)s, -e**) m (Obstkern) pip, stone; (Nusskern) kernel; (Atomkern) nucleus; (fig) heart, core; **~energie** f nuclear energy; **~forschung** f nuclear research; **~frage** f central issue; **k~gesund** adj thoroughly healthy, fit as a fiddle; **k~ig** adj (kraftvoll) robust; (Ausspruch) pithy; **~kraftwerk** nt nuclear power station; **k~los** adj seedless, without pips; **~physik** f nuclear physics sg; **~spaltung** f nuclear fission; **~waffen** pl nuclear weapons

Kerze [ˈkɛrtsə] f candle; (Zündkerze) plug; **k~ngerade** adj straight as a die; **~nständer** m candle holder

kess ▲ [kɛs] adj saucy

Kessel [ˈkɛsəl] (**-s, -**) m kettle; (von Lokomotive etc) boiler; (GEOG) depression; (MIL) encirclement

Kette [ˈkɛtə] f chain; **k~n** vt to chain; **~nrauchen** (**-s**) nt chain smoking; **~nreaktion** f chain reaction

Ketzer [ˈkɛtsər] (**-s, -**) m heretic

keuchen [ˈkɔyçən] vi to pant, to gasp

Keuchhusten m whooping cough

Keule [ˈkɔylə] f club; (KOCH) leg

keusch [kɔyʃ] adj chaste; **K~heit** f chastity

kfm. abk = **kaufmännisch**

Kfz [kaːˈɛfˈtsɛt] nt abk = **Kraftfahrzeug**

KG [kaːˈgeː] (**-, -s**) f abk (= Kommanditgesellschaft) limited partnership

kg abk = **Kilogramm**

kichern [ˈkiçərn] vi to giggle

kidnappen ['kɪtnɛpən] *vt* to kidnap
Kiefer¹ ['kiːfər] **(-s, -)** *m* jaw
Kiefer² ['kiːfər] **(-, -n)** *f* pine; **~nzapfen** *m* pine cone
Kiel [kiːl] **(-(e)s, -e)** *m* (*Federkiel*) quill; (*NAUT*) keel
Kieme ['kiːmə] *f* gill
Kies [kiːs] **(-es, -e)** *m* gravel
Kilo ['kiːlo] *nt* kilo; **~gramm** [kilo'gram] *nt* kilogram; **~meter** [kilo'meːtər] *m* kilometre; **~meterzähler** *m* milometer
Kind [kɪnt] **(-(e)s, -er)** *nt* child; **von ~ auf** from childhood
Kinder- ['kɪndər] *zW*: **~betreuung** *f* crèche; **~ei** [-'raɪ] *f* childishness; **~garten** *m* nursery school, playgroup; **~gärtnerin** *f* nursery school teacher; **~geld** *nt* child benefit (*BRIT*); **~heim** *nt* children's home; **~krippe** *f* crèche; **~lähmung** *f* poliomyelitis; **k~leicht** *adj* childishly easy; **k~los** *adj* childless; **~mädchen** *nt* nursemaid; **k~reich** *adj* with a lot of children; **~sendung** *f* (*RADIO, TV*) children's programme; **~sicherung** *f* (*AUT*) childproof safety catch; **~spiel** *nt* (*fig*) child's play; **~tagesstätte** *f* day nursery; **~wagen** *m* pram, baby carriage (*US*); **~zimmer** *nt* (*für ~*) children's room; (*für Säugling*) nursery

---
Kindergarten

i A **Kindergarten** *is a nursery school for children aged between 3 and 6 years. The children sing and play but do not receive any formal instruction. Most Kindergärten are financed by the town or the church with parents paying a monthly contribution towards the cost.*

Kind- *zW*: **~heit** *f* childhood; **k~isch** *adj* childish; **k~lich** *adj* childlike
Kinn [kɪn] **(-(e)s, -e)** *nt* chin; **~haken** *m* (*BOXEN*) uppercut
Kino ['kiːno] **(-s, -s)** *nt* cinema; **~besucher** *m* cinema-goer; **~programm** *nt* film programme
Kiosk [ki'ɔsk] **(-(e)s, -e)** *m* kiosk

Kippe ['kɪpə] *f* cigarette end; (*umg*) fag; **auf der ~ stehen** (*fig*) to be touch and go
kippen *vi* to topple over, to overturn ♦ *vt* to tilt
Kirch- ['kɪrç] *zW*: **~e** *f* church; **~enlied** *nt* hymn; **~ensteuer** *f* church tax; **~gänger** (**-s, -**) *m* churchgoer; **~hof** *m* churchyard; **k~lich** *adj* ecclesiastical
Kirmes ['kɪrmɛs] **(-, -sen)** *f* fair
Kirsche ['kɪrʃə] *f* cherry
Kissen ['kɪsən] **(-s, -)** *nt* cushion; (*Kopfkissen*) pillow; **~bezug** *m* pillowslip
Kiste ['kɪstə] *f* box; chest
Kitsch [kɪtʃ] **(-(e)s)** *m* kitsch; **k~ig** *adj* kitschy
Kitt [kɪt] **(-(e)s, -e)** *m* putty
Kittel **(-s, -)** *m* overall, smock
kitten *vt* to putty; (*fig: Ehe etc*) to cement
kitzelig ['kɪtsəlɪç] *adj* (*auch fig*) ticklish
kitzeln *vi* to tickle
Kiwi ['kiːvi] **(-, -s)** *f* (*BOT, KOCH*) kiwi fruit
KKW [kaːkaː'veː] *nt abk* = **Kernkraftwerk**
Klage ['klaːgə] *f* complaint; (*JUR*) action; **k~n** *vi* (*wehklagen*) to lament, to wail; (*sich beschweren*) to complain; (*JUR*) to take legal action
Kläger(in) ['klɛːgər(ɪn)] **(-s, -)** *m(f)* plaintiff
kläglich ['klɛːklɪç] *adj* wretched
klamm [klam] *adj* (*Finger*) numb; (*feucht*) damp
Klammer ['klamər] **(-, -n)** *f* clamp; (*in Text*) bracket; (*Büro~*) clip; (*Wäsche~*) peg; (*Zahn~*) brace; **k~n** *vr*: **sich k~n an** +*akk* to cling to
Klang [klaŋ] **(-(e)s, ⁺e)** *m* sound; **k~voll** *adj* sonorous
Klappe ['klapə] *f* valve; (*Ofen~*) damper; (*umg: Mund*) trap; **k~n** *vi* (*Geräusch*) to click; (*Sitz etc*) to tip ♦ *vt* to tip ♦ *vb unpers* to work
Klapper ['klapər] **(-, -n)** *f* rattle; **k~ig** *adj* run-down, worn-out; **k~n** *vi* to clatter, to rattle; **~schlange** *f* rattlesnake; **~storch** *m* stork
Klapp- *zW*: **~messer** *nt* jackknife; **~rad** *nt* collapsible bicycle; **~stuhl** *m* folding chair; **~tisch** *m* folding table
Klaps [klaps] **(-es, -e)** *m* slap

klar[klaːr] *adj* clear; (*NAUT*) ready for sea; (*MIL*) ready for action; **sich** *dat* **(über etw** *akk*) **~ werden** to get (sth) clear in one's mind; **sich** *dat* **im K~en sein über** +*akk* to be clear about; **ins K~e kommen** to get clear; **(na) ~!** of course!; **~ sehen** to see clearly

Kläranlage *f* purification plant

klären['klɛːrən] *vt* (*Flüssigkeit*) to purify; (*Probleme*) to clarify ♦ *vr* to clear (itself) up

Klarheit *f* clarity

Klarinette[klari'nɛtə] *f* clarinet

klar- *zW*: **~legen** *vt* to clear up, to explain; **~machen** *vt* (*Schiff*) to get ready for sea; **jdm etw ~machen** to make sth clear to sb; **~sehen**△ (*unreg*) *vi siehe* **klar**; **K~sichtfolie** *f* transparent film; **~stellen** *vt* to clarify

Klärung['klɛːrʊŋ] *f* (*von Flüssigkeit*) purification; (*von Probleme*) clarification

klarwerden△ (*unreg*) *vi siehe* **klar**

Klasse['klasə] *f* class; (*SCH*) class, form

klasse(*umg*) *adj* smashing

Klassen- *zW*: **~arbeit** *f* test; **~gesellschaft** *f* class society; **~lehrer** *m* form master; **k~los** *adj* classless; **~sprecher(in)** *m(f)* form prefect; **~zimmer** *nt* classroom

klassifizieren[klasifi'tsiːrən] *vt* to classify

Klassik['klasɪk] *f* (*Zeit*) classical period; (*Stil*) classicism; **~er(-s, -)** *m* classic

klassisch *adj* (*auch fig*) classical

Klatsch[klatʃ] (-(e)s, -e) *m* smack, crack; (*Gerede*) gossip; **~base** *f* gossip, scandalmonger; **~e**(*umg*) *f* crib; **k~en** *vi* (*Geräusch*) to clash; (*reden*) to gossip; (*applaudieren*) to applaud, to clap ♦ *vt*: **jdm Beifall k~en** to applaud sb; **~mohn** *m* (corn) poppy; **k~nass**▲ *adj* soaking wet

Klaue['klaʊə] *f* claw; (*umg*: *Schrift*) scrawl; **k~n**(*umg*) *vt* to pinch

Klausel['klaʊzəl] (-, -n) *f* clause

Klausur[klaʊ'zuːr] *f* seclusion; **~arbeit** *f* examination paper

Klavier[kla'viːr] (-s, -e) *nt* piano

Kleb-['kleːb] *zW*: **k~en**['kleːbən] *vt*, *vi*: **k~en (an** +*akk***)** to stick (to); **k~rig** *adj*

sticky; **~stoff** *m* glue; **~streifen** *m* adhesive tape

kleckern['klɛkərn] *vi* to make a mess ♦ *vt* to spill

Klecks[klɛks] (-es, -e) *m* blot, stain

Klee[kleː] (-s) *m* clover; **~blatt** *nt* cloverleaf; (*fig*) trio

Kleid[klaɪt] (-(e)s, -er) *nt* garment; (*Frauenkleid*) dress; **~er** *pl* (~*ung*) clothes; **k~en**['klaɪdən] *vt* to clothe, to dress; to suit ♦ *vr* to dress

Kleider-['klaɪdər] *zW*: **~bügel** *m* coat hanger; **~bürste** *f* clothes brush; **~schrank** *m* wardrobe

Kleid- *zW*: **k~sam** *adj* flattering; **~ung** *f* clothing; **~ungsstück** *nt* garment

klein[klaɪn] *adj* little, small; **~ hacken** to chop, to mince; **~ schneiden** to chop up; **K~e(r, s)** *mf* little one; **K~format** *nt* small size; **im K~format** small-scale; **K~geld** *nt* small change; **K~igkeit** *f* trifle; **K~kind** *nt* infant; **K~kram** *m* details *pl*; **~laut** *adj* dejected, quiet; **~lich** *adj* petty, paltry; **K~od**['klaɪnoːt] (-s, -odien) *nt* gem, jewel; treasure; **K~stadt** *f* small town; **~städtisch** *adj* provincial; **~stmöglich** *adj* smallest possible

Kleister['klaɪstər] (-s, -) *m* paste

Klemme['klɛmə] *f* clip; (*MED*) clamp; (*fig*) jam; **k~n** *vt* (*festhalten*) to jam; (*quetschen*) to pinch, to nip ♦ *vr* to catch o.s.; (*sich hineinzwängen*) to squeeze o.s. ♦ *vi* (*Tür*) to stick, to jam; **sich hinter jdn/etw k~n** to get on to sb/down to sth

Klempner['klɛmpnər] (-s, -) *m* plumber

Klerus['kleːrʊs] (-) *m* clergy

Klette['klɛtə] *f* burr

Kletter-['klɛtər] *zW*: **~er(-s, -)** *m* climber; **k~n** *vi* to climb; **~pflanze** *f* creeper

klicken['klɪkən] *vi* (*COMPUT*) to click

Klient(in)[kli'ɛnt(ɪn)] *m(f)* client

Klima['kliːma] (-s, -s *od* -te) *nt* climate; **~anlage** *f* air conditioning; **~wechsel** *m* change of air

klimpern['klɪmpərn] (*umg*) *vi* (*mit Münzen, Schlüsseln*) to jingle; (*auf Klavier*) to plonk (away)

Spelling Reform: ▲ *new spelling* △ *old spelling (to be phased out)*

Klinge ['klıŋə] f blade; sword

Klingel ['klıŋəl] (-, -n) f bell; **~beutel** m collection bag; **k~n** vi to ring

klingen ['klıŋən] (*unreg*) vi to sound; (*Gläser*) to clink

Klinik ['kli:nık] f hospital, clinic

Klinke ['klıŋkə] f handle

Klippe ['klıpə] f cliff; (*im Meer*) reef; (*fig*) hurdle

klipp und klar ['klıp|ʊntkla:r] adj clear and concise

klirren ['klırən] vi to clank, to jangle; (*Gläser*) to clink; **~de Kälte** biting cold

Klischee [klı'ʃe:] (-s, -s) nt (*Druckplatte*) plate, block; (*fig*) cliché; **~vorstellung** f stereotyped idea

Klo [klo:] (-s, -s) (*umg*) nt loo (*BRIT*), john (*US*)

Kloake [klo'a:kə] f sewer

klobig ['klo:bıç] adj clumsy

Klon [klo:n] (-s, -e) m clone

klonen ['klo:nən] vti to clone

Klopapier (*umg*) nt loo paper (*BRIT*)

klopfen ['klɔpfən] vi to knock; (*Herz*) to thump ♦ vt to beat; **es klopft** somebody's knocking; **jdm auf die Schulter ~** to tap sb on the shoulder

Klopfer (-s, -) m (*Teppichklopfer*) beater; (*Türklopfer*) knocker

Klops [klɔps] (-es, -e) m meatball

Klosett [klo'zet] (-s, -e *od* -s) nt lavatory, toilet; **~papier** nt toilet paper

Kloß [klo:s] (-es, ⁻e) m (*im Hals*) lump; (*KOCH*) dumpling

Kloster ['klo:stər] (-s, ⁻) nt (*Männerkloster*) monastery; (*Frauenkloster*) convent; **klösterlich** ['klø:stərlıç] adj monastic; convent cpd

Klotz [klɔts] (-es, ⁻e) m log; (*Hackklotz*) block; **ein ~ am Bein** (*fig*) a drag, a millstone round (sb's) neck

Klub [klʊp] (-s, -s) m club; **~sessel** m easy chair

Kluft [klʊft] (-, ⁻e) f cleft, gap; (*GEOG*) gorge, chasm

klug [klu:k] adj clever, intelligent; **K~heit** f cleverness, intelligence

Klumpen ['klʊmpən] (-s, -) m (*Erd~*) clod;

(*Blut~*) clot; (*Gold~*) nugget; (*KOCH*) lump

km abk = **Kilometer**

knabbern ['knabərn] vt, vi to nibble

Knabe ['kna:bə] (-n, -n) m boy

Knäckebrot ['knɛkəbro:t] nt crispbread

knacken ['knakən] vt, vi (*auch fig*) to crack

Knacks [knaks] (-es, -e) m crack; (*fig*) defect

Knall [knal] (-(e)s, -e) m bang; (*Peitschenknall*) crack; **~ und Fall** (*umg*) unexpectedly; **~bonbon** nt cracker; **k~en** vi to bang; to crack; **k~rot** adj bright red

knapp [knap] adj tight; (*Geld*) scarce; (*Sprache*) concise; **eine ~e Stunde** just under an hour; **~ unter/neben** just under/ by; **K~heit** f tightness; scarcity; conciseness

knarren ['knarən] vi to creak

Knast [knast] (-(e)s) (*umg*) m (*Haftstrafe*) porridge (*inf*), time (*inf*); (*Gefängnis*) slammer (*inf*), clink (*inf*)

knattern ['knatərn] vi to rattle; (*Maschinengewehr*) to chatter

Knäuel ['knɔyəl] (-s, -) m od nt (*Wollknäuel*) ball; (*Menschenknäuel*) knot

Knauf [knaʊf] (-(e)s, **Knäufe**) m knob; (*Schwertknauf*) pommel

Knebel ['kne:bəl] (-s, -) m gag

kneifen ['knaıfən] (*unreg*) vt to pinch ♦ vi to pinch; (*sich drücken*) to back out; **vor etw ~** to dodge sth

Kneipe ['knaıpə] (*umg*) f pub

kneten ['kne:tən] vt to knead; (*Wachs*) to mould

Knick [knık] (-(e)s, -e) m (*Sprung*) crack; (*Kurve*) bend; (*Falte*) fold; **k~en** vt, vi (*springen*) to crack; (*brechen*) to break; (*Papier*) to fold; **geknickt sein** to be downcast

Knicks [knıks] (-es, -e) m curtsey

Knie [kni:] (-s, -) nt knee; **~beuge** f knee bend; **~bundhose** m knee breeches; **~gelenk** nt knee joint; **~kehle** f back of the knee; **k~n** vi to kneel; **~scheibe** f kneecap; **~strumpf** m knee-length sock

Kniff [knıf] (-(e)s, -e) m (*fig*) trick, knack; **k~elig** adj tricky

knipsen ['knɪpsən] vt (Fahrkarte) to punch; (PHOT) to take a snap of, to snap ♦ vi to take a snap od snaps

Knirps [knɪrps] (-es, -e) m little chap; (®: Schirm) telescopic umbrella

knirschen ['knɪrʃən] vi to crunch; **mit den Zähnen ~** to grind one's teeth

knistern ['knɪstərn] vi to crackle

Knitter- ['knɪtər] zW: **~falte** f crease; **k~frei** adj non-crease; **k~n** vi to crease

Knoblauch ['kno:blaux] (-(e)s) m garlic; **~zehe** f (KOCH) clove of garlic

Knöchel ['knœçəl] (-s, -) m knuckle; (Fußknöchel) ankle

Knochen ['knɔxən] (-s, -) m bone; **~bruch** m fracture; **~gerüst** nt skeleton; **~mark** nt bone marrow

knöchern ['knœçərn] adj bone

knochig ['knɔxɪç] adj bony

Knödel ['knø:dəl] (-s, -) m dumpling

Knolle ['knɔlə] f tuber

Knopf [knɔpf] (-(e)s, ⁻e) m button; (Kragenknopf) stud

knöpfen ['knœpfən] vt to button

Knopfloch nt buttonhole

Knorpel ['knɔrpəl] (-s, -) m cartilage, gristle; **k~ig** adj gristly

Knospe ['knɔspə] f bud

Knoten ['kno:tən] (-s, -) m knot; (BOT) node; (MED) lump; **k~** vt to knot; **~punkt** m junction

Knüller ['knylər] (-s, -) (umg) m hit; (Reportage) scoop

knüpfen ['knypfən] vt to tie; (Teppich) to knot; (Freundschaft) to form

Knüppel ['knypəl] (-s, -) m cudgel; (Polizeiknüppel) baton, truncheon; (AVIAT) (joy)stick

knurren ['knurən] vi (Hund) to snarl, to growl; (Magen) to rumble; (Mensch) to mutter

knusperig ['knuspərɪç] adj crisp; (Keks) crunchy

k. o. [ka:'o:] adj knocked out; (fig) done in

Koalition [koalitsi'o:n] f coalition

Kobold ['ko:bɔlt] (-(e)s, -e) m goblin, imp

Koch [kɔx] (-(e)s, ⁻e) m cook; **~buch** nt

cook(ery) book; **k~en** vt, vi to cook; (Wasser) to boil; **~er** (-s, -) m stove, cooker; **~gelegenheit** f cooking facilities pl

Köchin ['kœçɪn] f cook

Koch- zW: **~löffel** m kitchen spoon; **~nische** f kitchenette; **~platte** f hotplate; **~salz** nt cooking salt; **~topf** m saucepan, pot

Köder ['kø:dər] (-s, -) m bait, lure

ködern vt (Tier) to trap with bait; (Person) to entice, to tempt

Koexistenz [koeksɪs'tɛnts] f coexistence

Koffein [kɔfe'i:n] (-s) nt caffeine; **k~frei** adj decaffeinated

Koffer ['kɔfər] (-s, -) m suitcase; (Schrankkoffer) trunk; **~kuli** m (luggage) trolley; **~radio** nt portable radio; **~raum** m (AUT) boot (BRIT), trunk (US)

Kognak ['kɔnjak] (-s, -s) m brandy, cognac

Kohl [ko:l] (-(e)s, -e) m cabbage

Kohle ['ko:lə] f coal; (Holzkohle) charcoal; (CHEM) carbon; **~hydrat** (-(e)s, -e) nt carbohydrate

Kohlen- zW: **~dioxid** (-(e)s, -e) nt carbon dioxide; **~händler** m coal merchant, coalman; **~säure** f carbon dioxide; **~stoff** m carbon

Kohlepapier nt carbon paper

Koje ['ko:jə] f cabin; (Bett) bunk

Kokain [koka'i:n] (-s) nt cocaine

kokett [ko'kɛt] adj coquettish, flirtatious

Kokosnuss ▲ ['ko:kɔsnus] f coconut

Koks [ko:ks] (-es, -e) m coke

Kolben ['kɔlbən] (-s, -) m (Gewehrkolben) rifle butt; (Keule) club; (CHEM) flask; (TECH) piston; (Maiskolben) cob

Kolik ['ko:lɪk] f colic, the gripes pl

Kollaps [kɔ'laps] (-es, -e) m collapse

Kolleg [kɔ'le:k] (-s, -s od -ien) nt lecture course, **~e** [kɔ'le:gə] m (-n, -n) m colleague; **~in** f colleague; **~ium** nt working party; (SCH) staff

Kollekte [kɔ'lɛktə] f (REL) collection

kollektiv [kɔlɛk'ti:f] adj collective

Köln [kœln] (-s) nt Cologne

Kolonie [kolo'ni:] f colony

Spelling Reform: ▲ new spelling △ old spelling (to be phased out)

kolonisieren [koloni'zi:rən] *vt* to colonize
Kolonne [ko'lɔnə] *f* column; (*von Fahrzeugen*) convoy
Koloss ▲ [ko'lɔs] (**-es, -e**) *m* colossus;
kolo'ssal *adj* colossal
Kölsch [kœlʃ] (**-, -**) *nt* (*Bier*) ≈ (strong) lager
Kombi- ['kɔmbi] *zW:* **~nation** [-natsi'o:n] *f* combination; (*Vermutung*) conjecture; (*Hemdhose*) combinations *pl*; **k~nieren** [-'ni:rən] *vt* to combine ♦ *vi* to deduce, to work out; (*vermuten*) to guess; **~wagen** *m* station wagon; **~zange** *f* (pair of) pliers *pl*
Komet [ko'me:t] (**-en, -en**) *m* comet
Komfort [kɔm'fo:r] (**-s**) *m* luxury
Komik ['ko:mɪk] *f* humour, comedy; **~er** (**-s, -**) *m* comedian
komisch ['ko:mɪʃ] *adj* funny
Komitee [komi'te:] (**-s, -s**) *nt* committee
Komma ['kɔma] (**-s, -s** *od* **-ta**) *nt* comma; **2 ~ 3** 2 point 3
Kommand- [kɔ'mand] *zW:* **~ant** [-'dant] *m* commander, commanding officer; **k~ieren** [-'di:rən] *vt, vi* to command; **~o** (**-s, -s**) *nt* command, order; (*Truppe*) detachment, squad; **auf ~o** to order
kommen ['kɔmən] (*unreg*) *vi* to come; (*näher kommen*) to approach; (*passieren*) to happen; (*gelangen, geraten*) to get; (*Blumen, Zähne, Tränen etc*) to appear; (*in die Schule, das Zuchthaus etc*) to go; **~ lassen** to send for; **das kommt in den Schrank** that goes in the cupboard; **zu sich ~** to come round *od* to; **zu etw ~** to acquire sth; **um etw ~** to lose sth; **nichts auf jdn/etw ~ lassen** to have nothing said against sb/sth; **jdm frech ~** to get cheeky with sb; **auf jeden vierten kommt ein Platz** there's one place for every fourth person; **wer kommt zuerst?** who's first?; **unter ein Auto ~** to be run over by a car; **wie hoch kommt das?** what does that cost?; **komm gut nach Hause!** safe journey (home); **~den Sonntag** next Sunday; **K~** (**-s**) *nt* coming
Kommentar [kɔmɛn'ta:r] *m* commentary; **kein ~** no comment; **k~los** *adj* without comment
Kommentator [kɔmɛn'ta:tɔr] *m* (*TV*) commentator
kommentieren [kɔmɛn'ti:rən] *vt* to comment on
kommerziell [kɔmɛrtsi'el] *adj* commercial
Kommilitone [kɔmili'to:nə] (**-n, -n**) *m* fellow student
Kommissar [kɔmɪ'sa:r] *m* police inspector
Kommission [kɔmɪsi'o:n] *f* (*COMM*) commission; (*Ausschuss*) committee
Kommode [kɔ'mo:də] *f* (chest of) drawers
kommunal [kɔmu'na:l] *adj* local; (*von Stadt auch*) municipal
Kommune [kɔ'mu:nə] *f* commune
Kommunikation [kɔmunɪkatsi'o:n] *f* communication
Kommunion [kɔmuni'o:n] *f* communion
Kommuniqué, Kommunikee ▲ [kɔmyni'ke:] (**-s, -s**) *nt* communiqué
Kommunismus [kɔmu'nɪsmʊs] *m* communism
Kommunist(in) [kɔmu'nɪst(ɪn)] *m(f)* communist; **k~isch** *adj* communist
kommunizieren [kɔmuni'tsi:rən] *vi* to communicate
Komödie [ko'mø:diə] *f* comedy
Kompagnon [kɔmpan'jö:] (**-s, -s**) *m* (*COMM*) partner
kompakt [kɔm'pakt] *adj* compact
Kompanie [kɔmpa'ni:] *f* company
Kompass ▲ ['kɔmpas] (**-es, -e**) *m* compass
kompatibel [kɔmpa'ti:bəl] *adj* compatible
kompetent [kɔmpe'tent] *adj* competent
Kompetenz *f* competence, authority
komplett [kɔm'plet] *adj* complete
Komplex [kɔm'pleks] (**-es, -e**) *m* (*Gebäudekomplex*) complex
Komplikation [kɔmplikatsi'o:n] *f* complication
Kompliment [kɔmpli'mɛnt] *nt* compliment
Komplize [kɔm'pli:tsə] (**-n, -n**) *m* accomplice
kompliziert [kɔmpli'tsi:rt] *adj* complicated
komponieren [kɔmpo'ni:rən] *vt* to compose
Komponist [kɔmpo'nɪst(ɪn)] *m* composer
Komposition [kɔmpozitsi'o:n] *f* composition
Kompost [kɔm'pɔst] (**-(e)s, -e**) *m* compost

Kompott[kɔm'pɔt] (-(e)s, -e) *nt* stewed fruit
Kompromiss▲ [kɔmpro'mɪs] (-es, -e) *m*
compromise; **k~bereit***adj* willing to
compromise
Kondens-[kɔn'dɛns] *zW:* **~ation**
[kɔndɛnzatsi'o:n] *f* condensation; **k~ieren**
[kɔndɛn'zi:rən] *vt* to condense; **~milch***f*
condensed milk
Kondition[kɔnditsi'o:n] *f* (COMM, FIN)
condition; (*Durchhaltevermögen*) stamina;
(*körperliche Verfassung*) physical condition,
state of health
Konditionstraining[kɔnditsi'o:nstre:nɪŋ] *nt*
fitness training
Konditor[kɔn'di:tɔr] *m* pastry cook; **~ei**
[-'raɪ] *f* café; cake shop
Kondom[kɔn'do:m] (-s, -e) *nt* condom
Konferenz[kɔnfe'rɛnts] *f* conference,
meeting
Konfession[kɔnfesi'o:n] *f* (religious)
denomination; **k~ell**[-'nɛl] *adj*
denominational; **k~slos***adj* non-
denominational
Konfirmand[kɔnfɪr'mant] *m* candidate for
confirmation
Konfirmation[kɔnfɪrmatsi'o:n] *f* (REL)
confirmation
konfirmieren[kɔnfɪr'mi:rən] *vt* to confirm
konfiszieren[kɔnfɪs'tsi:rən] *vt* to confiscate
Konfitüre[kɔnfi'ty:rə] *f* jam
Konflikt[kɔn'flɪkt] (-(e)s, -e) *m* conflict
konfrontieren[kɔnfrɔn'ti:rən] *vt* to
confront
konfus[kɔn'fu:s] *adj* confused
Kongress▲ [kɔn'grɛs] (-es, -e) *m*
congress; **~zentrum***nt* conference centre
Kongruenz[kɔngru'ents] *f* agreement,
congruence
König['kø:nɪç] (-(e)s, -e) *m* king; **~in**
['kø:nɪgɪn] *f* queen; **k~lich***adj* royal;
~reich*nt* kingdom
Konjugation[kɔnjugatsi'o:n] *f* conjugation
konjugieren[kɔnju'gi:rən] *vt* to conjugate
Konjunktion[kɔnjʊŋktsi'o:n] *f* conjunction
Konjunktiv['kɔnjʊŋkti:f] (-s, -e) *m*
subjunctive
Konjunktur[kɔnjʊŋk'tu:r] *f* economic

situation; (*Hochkonjunktur*) boom
konkret[kɔn'kre:t] *adj* concrete
Konkurrent(in)[kɔnkʊ'rɛnt(ɪn)] *m(f)*
competitor
Konkurrenz[kɔnkʊ'rɛnts] *f* competition;
k~fähig*adj* competitive; **~kampf***m*
competition; rivalry, competitive situation
konkurrieren[kɔnkʊ'ri:rən] *vi* to compete
Konkurs[kɔn'kʊrs] (-es, -e) *m* bankruptcy
Können(-s) *nt* ability

<hr>
SCHLÜSSELWORT
<hr>

können['kœnən] (*pt* **konnte**, *pp* **gekonnt** *od*
(*als Hilfsverb*) **können**) *vt, vi* 1to be able
to; **ich kann es machen** I can do it, I am
able to do it; **ich kann es nicht machen** I
can't do it, I'm not able to do it; **ich kann
nicht ...** I can't ..., I cannot ...; **ich kann
nicht mehr** I can't go on

2(*wissen, beherrschen*) to know; **können
Sie Deutsch?** can you speak German?; **er
kann gut Englisch** he speaks English well;
sie kann keine Mathematik she can't do
mathematics

3(*dürfen*) to be allowed to; **kann ich
gehen?** can I go?; **könnte ich ...?** could I
...?; **kann ich mit?** (*umg*) can I come with
you?

4(*möglich sein*): **Sie könnten Recht haben**
you may be right; **das kann sein** that's
possible; **kann sein** maybe

<hr>

Könner*m* expert
konnte *etc* ['kɔntə] *vb siehe* **können**
konsequent[kɔnze'kvɛnt] *adj* consistent
Konsequenz[kɔnze'kvɛnts] *f* consistency;
(*Folgerung*) conclusion
Konserv-[kɔn'zɛrv] *zW:* **k~ativ**[-a'ti:f] *adj*
conservative; **~ative(r)**[-a'ti:və(r)] *f(m)* (POL)
conservative; **~ef** tinned food;
~enbüchse*f* tin, can; **k~ieren**[-'vi:rən] *vt*
to preserve; **~ierung***f* preservation;
~ierungsstoff*m* preservatives
Konsonant[kɔnzo'nant] *m* consonant
konstant[kɔn'stant] *adj* constant
konstru-*zW:* **~ieren**[kɔnstru'i:rən] *vt* to
construct; **K~kteur**[kɔnstrʊk'tø:r] *m*

designer; **K~ktion** [kɔnstrʊktsi'oːn] *f* construction; **~ktiv** [kɔnstrʊk'tiːf] *adj* constructive

Konsul ['kɔnzʊl] (**-s, -n**) *m* consul; **~at** [-'laːt] *nt* consulate

konsultieren [kɔnzʊl'tiːrən] *vt* to consult

Konsum [kɔn'zuːm] (**-s**) *m* consumption; **~artikel** *m* consumer article; **~ent** [-'mɛnt] *m* consumer; **k~ieren** [-'miːrən] *vt* to consume

Kontakt [kɔn'takt] (**-(e)s, -e**) *m* contact; **k~arm** *adj* unsociable; **k~freudig** *adj* sociable; **~linsen** *pl* contact lenses

kontern ['kɔntərn] *vt, vi* to counter

Kontinent [kɔnti'nɛnt] *m* continent

Kontingent [kɔntɪŋ'gɛnt] (**-(e)s, -e**) *nt* quota; (*Truppenkontingent*) contingent

kontinuierlich [kɔntinu'iːrlɪç] *adj* continuous

Konto ['kɔnto] (**-s, Konten**) *nt* account; **~auszug** *m* statement (of account); **~inhaber(in)** *m(f)* account holder; **~stand** *m* balance

Kontra ['kɔntra] (**-s, -s**) *nt* (*KARTEN*) double; **jdm ~ geben** (*fig*) to contradict sb; **~bass** ▲ *m* double bass; **~hent** *m* (*COMM*) contracting party; **~punkt** *m* counterpoint

Kontrast [kɔn'trast] (**-(e)s, -e**) *m* contrast

Kontroll- [kɔn'trɔl] *zW:* **~e** *f* control, supervision; (*Passkontrolle*) passport control; **~eur** [-'løːr] *m* inspector; **k~ieren** [-'liːrən] *vt* to control, to supervise; (*nachprüfen*) to check

Konvention [kɔnvɛntsi'oːn] *f* convention; **k~ell** [-'nɛl] *adj* conventional

Konversation [kɔnvɛrzatsi'oːn] *f* conversation; **~slexikon** *nt* encyclop(a)edia

Konvoi ['kɔnvɔy] (**-s, -s**) *m* convoy

Konzentration [kɔntsɛntratsi'oːn] *f* concentration

Konzentrationslager *nt* concentration camp

konzentrieren [kɔntsɛn'triːrən] *vt, vr* to concentrate

konzentriert *adj* concentrated ♦ *adv* (*zuhören, arbeiten*) intently

Konzern [kɔn'tsɛrn] (**-s, -e**) *m* combine

Konzert [kɔn'tsɛrt] (**-(e)s, -e**) *nt* concert; (*Stück*) concerto; **~saal** *m* concert hall

Konzession [kɔntsɛsi'oːn] *f* licence; (*Zugeständnis*) concession

Konzil [kɔn'tsiːl] (**-s, -e** *od* **-ien**) *nt* council

kooperativ [koʔopera'tiːf] *adj* cooperative

koordinieren [koʔɔrdi'niːrən] *vt* to coordinate

Kopf [kɔpf] (**-(e)s, ⁻e**) *m* head; **~haut** *f* scalp; **~hörer** *m* headphones *pl*; **~kissen** *nt* pillow; **k~los** *adj* panic-stricken; **k~rechnen** *vi* to do mental arithmetic; **~salat** *m* lettuce; **~schmerzen** *pl* headache *sg*; **~sprung** *m* header, dive; **~stand** *m* headstand; **~stütze** *f* (*im Auto etc*) headrest, head restraint; **~tuch** *nt* headscarf; **~weh** *nt* headache; **~zerbrechen** *nt:* **jdm ~zerbrechen machen** to be a headache for sb

Kopie [ko'piː] *f* copy; **k~ren** *vt* to copy

Kopiergerät *nt* photocopier

Koppel¹ ['kɔpəl] (**-, -n**) *f* (*Weide*) enclosure

Koppel² ['kɔpəl] (**-s, -**) *nt* (*Gürtel*) belt

koppeln *vt* to couple

Koppelung *f* coupling

Koralle [ko'ralə] *f* coral

Korb [kɔrp] (**-(e)s, ⁻e**) *m* basket; **jdm einen ~ geben** (*fig*) to turn sb down; **~ball** *m* basketball; **~stuhl** *m* wicker chair

Kord [kɔrt] (**-(e)s, -e**) *m* cord, corduroy

Kordel ['kɔrdəl] (**-, -n**) *f* cord, string

Kork [kɔrk] (**-(e)s, -e**) *m* cork; **~en** (**-s, -**) *m* stopper, cork; **~enzieher** (**-s, -**) *m* corkscrew

Korn [kɔrn] (**-(e)s, ⁻er**) *nt* corn, grain; (*Gewehr*) sight

Körper ['kœrpər] (**-s, -**) *m* body; **~bau** *m* build; **k~behindert** *adj* disabled; **~geruch** *m* body odour; **~gewicht** *nt* weight; **~größe** *f* height; **k~lich** *adj* physical; **~pflege** *f* personal hygiene; **~schaft** *f* corporation; **~schaftssteuer** *f* corporation tax; **~teil** *m* part of the body; **~verletzung** *f* bodily *od* physical injury

korpulent [kɔrpu'lɛnt] *adj* corpulent

korrekt [kɔ'rɛkt] *adj* correct; **K~ur** [-'tuːr] *f*

(eines Textes) proofreading; *(Text)* proof; *(SCH)* marking, correction

Korrespond- [kɔrɛspɔnd] *zW:* **~ent(in)** [-'dɛnt(ɪn)] *m(f)* correspondent; **~enz** [-'dɛnts] *f* correspondence; **k~ieren** [-'di:rən] *vi* to correspond

Korridor [ˈkɔridoːr] **(-s, -e)** *m* corridor

korrigieren [kɔriˈgiːrən] *vt* to correct

Korruption [kɔruptsiˈoːn] *f* corruption

Kose- [ˈkoːzə] *zW:* **~form** *f* pet form; **~name** *m* pet name; **~wort** *nt* term of endearment

Kosmetik [kɔsˈmeːtɪk] *f* cosmetics *pl;* **~erin** *f* beautician

kosmetisch *adj* cosmetic; *(Chirurgie)* plastic

kosmisch [ˈkɔsmɪʃ] *adj* cosmic

Kosmo- [kɔsmo] *zW:* **~naut** [-ˈnaut] **(-en, -en)** *m* cosmonaut; **k~politisch** *adj* cosmopolitan; **~s (-)** *m* cosmos

Kost [kɔst] **(-)** *f (Nahrung)* food; *(Verpflegung)* board; **k~bar** *adj* precious; *(teuer)* costly, expensive; **~barkeit** *f* preciousness; costliness, expensiveness; *(Wertstück)* valuable

Kosten *pl* cost(s); *(Ausgaben)* expenses; **auf ~ von** at the expense of; **k~** *vt* to cost; *(versuchen)* to taste ♦ *vi* to taste; **was kostet ...?** what does ... cost?, how much is ...?; **~anschlag** *m* estimate; **k~los** *adj* free (of charge)

köstlich [ˈkœstlɪç] *adj* precious; *(Einfall)* delightful; *(Essen)* delicious; **sich ~ amüsieren** to have a marvellous time

Kostprobe *f* taste; *(fig)* sample

kostspielig *adj* expensive

Kostüm [kɔsˈtyːm] **(-s, -e)** *nt* costume; *(Damenkostüm)* suit; **~fest** *nt* fancy-dress party; **k~ieren** [kɔstyˈmiːrən] *vt, vr* to dress up; **~verleih** *m* costume agency

Kot [koːt] **(-(e)s)** *m* excrement

Kotelett [kɔtaˈlɛt] **(-(e)s, -e od -s)** *nt* cutlet, chop; **~en** *pl (Bart)* sideboards

Köter [ˈkøːtər] **(-s, -)** *m* cur

Kotflügel *m (AUT)* wing

kotzen [ˈkɔtsən] *(umg!)* *vi* to puke *(umg),* to throw up *(umg)*

Krabbe [ˈkrabə] *f* shrimp; **k~ln** *vi* to crawl

Krach [krax] **(-(e)s, -s od -e)** *m* crash; *(andauernd)* noise; *(umg: Streit)* quarrel, argument; **k~en** *vi* to crash; *(beim Brechen)* to crack ♦ *vr (umg)* to argue, to quarrel

krächzen [ˈkrɛçtsən] *vi* to croak

Kraft [kraft] **(-, ²e)** *f* strength; power; force; *(Arbeitskraft)* worker; **in ~ treten** to come into force; **k~** *präp +gen* by virtue of; **~fahrer** *m (motor)* driver; **~fahrzeug** *nt* motor vehicle; **~fahrzeugbrief** *m* logbook; **~fahrzeugsteuer** *f ≈* road tax; **~fahrzeugversicherung** *f* car insurance

kräftig [ˈkrɛftɪç] *adj* strong; **~en** *vt* to strengthen

Kraft- *zW:* **k~los** *adj* weak; powerless; *(JUR)* invalid; **~probe** *f* trial of strength; **~stoff** *m* fuel; **k~voll** *adj* vigorous; **~werk** *nt* power station

Kragen [ˈkraːgən] **(-s, -)** *m* collar; **~weite** *f* collar size

Krähe [ˈkrɛːə] *f* crow; **k~n** *vi* to crow

Kralle [ˈkralə] *f* claw; *(Vogelkralle)* talon; **k~n** *vt* to clutch; *(krampfhaft)* to claw

Kram [kraːm] **(-(e)s)** *m* stuff, rubbish; **k~en** *vi* to rummage; **~laden** *(pej)* *m* small shop

Krampf [krampf] **(-(e)s, ²e)** *m* cramp; *(zuckend)* spasm; **~ader** *f* varicose vein; **k~haft** *adj* convulsive; *(fig: Versuche)* desperate

Kran [kraːn] **(-(e)s, ²e)** *m* crane; *(Wasserkran)* tap, faucet *(US)*

krank [kraŋk] *adj* ill, sick; **K~e(r)** *f(m)* sick person, invalid; patient; **~en** *vi:* **an etw** *dat* **~en** *(fig)* to suffer from sth

kränken [ˈkrɛŋkən] *vt* to hurt

Kranken- *zW:* **~geld** *nt* sick pay; **~gymnastik** *f* physiotherapy; **~haus** *nt* hospital; **~kasse** *f* health insurance; **~pfleger** *m* nursing orderly; **~schein** *m* health insurance card; **~schwester** *f* nurse; **~versicherung** *f* health insurance; **~wagen** *m* ambulance

Krank- *zW:* **k~haft** *adj* diseased; *(Angst etc)* morbid; **~heit** *f* illness; disease; **~heitserreger** *m* disease-causing agent

kränklich [ˈkrɛŋklɪç] *adj* sickly

Kränkung *f* insult, offence

Spelling Reform: ▲ *new spelling* △ *old spelling (to be phased out)*

Kranz [krants] (**-es**, **ᵘe**) *m* wreath, garland

krass ▲ [kras] *adj* crass

Krater ['kraːtər] (**-s**, **-**) *m* crater

Kratz- [krats] *zW:* **~bürste** *f* (*fig*) crosspatch; **k~en** *vt, vi* to scratch; **~er** (**-s**, **-**) *m* scratch; (*Werkzeug*) scraper

Kraul [kraʊl] (**-s**) *nt* crawl; **~ schwimmen** to do the crawl; **k~en** *vi* (*schwimmen*) to do the crawl ♦ *vt* (*streicheln*) to fondle

kraus [kraʊs] *adj* crinkly; (*Haar*) frizzy; (*Stirn*) wrinkled

Kraut [kraʊt] (**-(e)s**, **Kräuter**) *nt* plant; (*Gewürz*) herb; (*Gemüse*) cabbage

Krawall [kra'val] (**-s**, **-e**) *m* row, uproar

Krawatte [kra'vatə] *f* tie

kreativ [krea'tiːf] *adj* creative

Krebs [kreːps] (**-es**, **-e**) *m* crab; (*MED, ASTROL*) cancer; **k~krank** *adj* suffering from cancer

Kredit [kre'diːt] (**-(e)s**, **-e**) *m* credit; **~institut** *nt* bank; **~karte** *f* credit card

Kreide ['kraɪdə] *f* chalk; **k~bleich** *adj* as white as a sheet

Kreis [kraɪs] (**-es**, **-e**) *m* circle; (*Stadtkreis etc*) district; **im ~ gehen** (*auch fig*) to go round in circles

kreischen ['kraɪʃən] *vi* to shriek, to screech

Kreis- *zW:* **~el** ['kraɪzəl] (**-s**, **-**) *m* top; (*~verkehr*) roundabout (*BRIT*), traffic circle (*US*); **k~en** ['kraɪzən] *vi* to spin; **~lauf** *m* (*MED*) circulation; (*fig: der Natur etc*) cycle; **~säge** *f* circular saw; **~stadt** *f* county town; **~verkehr** *m* roundabout traffic

Krematorium [krema'toːriʊm] *nt* crematorium

Kreml ['kreːml] (**-s**) *m* Kremlin

krepieren [kre'piːrən] (*umg*) *vi* (*sterben*) to die, to kick the bucket

Krepp [krep] (**-s**, **-s** *od* **-e**) *m* crepe; **~papier** ▲ *nt* crepe paper

Kresse ['kresə] *f* cress

Kreta ['kreːta] (**-s**) *nt* Crete

Kreuz [krɔyts] (**-es**, **-e**) *nt* cross; (*ANAT*) small of the back; (*KARTEN*) clubs; **k~en** *vt, vr* to cross ♦ *vi* (*NAUT*) to cruise; **~er** (**-s**, **-**) *m* (*Schiff*) cruiser; **~fahrt** *f* cruise; **~feuer** *nt* (*fig*): **ins ~feuer geraten** to be under fire from all sides; **~gang** *m* cloisters *pl*;

k~igen *vt* to crucify; **~igung** *f* crucifixion; **~ung** *f* (*Verkehrskreuzung*) crossing, junction; (*Züchten*) cross; **~verhör** *nt* cross-examination; **~weg** *m* crossroads; (*REL*) Way of the Cross; **~worträtsel** *nt* crossword puzzle; **~zug** *m* crusade

Kriech- ['kriːç] *zW:* **k~en** (*unreg*) *vi* to crawl, to creep; (*pej*) to grovel, to crawl; **~er** (**-s**, **-**) *m* crawler; **~spur** *f* crawler lane; **~tier** *nt* reptile

Krieg [kriːk] (**-(e)s**, **-e**) *m* war

kriegen ['kriːgən] (*umg*) *vt* to get

Kriegs- *zW:* **~erklärung** *f* declaration of war; **~fuß** *m:* **mit jdm/etw auf ~fuß stehen** to be at loggerheads with sb/to have difficulties with sth; **~gefangene(r)** *m* prisoner of war; **~gefangenschaft** *f* captivity; **~gericht** *nt* court-martial; **~schiff** *nt* warship; **~verbrecher** *m* war criminal; **~versehrte(r)** *m* person disabled in the war; **~zustand** *m* state of war

Krim [krɪm] (**-**) *f* Crimea

Krimi ['kriːmi] (**-s**, **-s**) (*umg*) *m* thriller

Kriminal- [krimi'naːl] *zW:* **~beamte(r)** *m* detective; **~i'tät** *f* criminality; **~'polizei** *f ≈* Criminal Investigation Department (*BRIT*), Federal Bureau of Investigation (*US*); **~ro'man** *m* detective story

kriminell [krimi'nɛl] *adj* criminal; **K~e(r)** *m* criminal

Krippe ['krɪpə] *f* crib; (*Kinderkrippe*) crèche

Krise ['kriːzə] *f* crisis; **k~ln** *vi:* **es k~lt** there's a crisis

Kristall [krɪs'tal] (**-s**, **-e**) *m* crystal ♦ *nt* (*Glas*) crystal

Kriterium [kri'teːriʊm] *nt* criterion

Kritik [kri'tiːk] *f* criticism; (*Zeitungskritik*) review, write-up; **~er** ['kriːtikər] (**-s**, **-**) *m* critic; **k~los** *adj* uncritical

kritisch ['kriːtɪʃ] *adj* critical

kritisieren [kriti'ziːrən] *vt, vi* to criticize

kritzeln ['krɪtsəln] *vt, vi* to scribble, to scrawl

Kroatien [kro'aːtsiən] *nt* Croatia

Krokodil [kroko'diːl] (**-s**, **-e**) *nt* crocodile

Krokus ['kroːkʊs] (**-**, **- od -se**) *m* crocus

Krone ['kroːnə] *f* crown; (*Baumkrone*) top

krönen ['krøːnən] *vt* to crown

Kron- *zW:* ~**korken** *m* bottle top;
~**leuchter** *m* chandelier; ~**prinz** *m* crown
prince

Krönung ['krøːnʊŋ] *f* coronation

Kropf [krɔpf] (-(e)s, ¨e) *m* (*MED*) goitre; (*von
Vogel*) crop

Kröte ['krøːtə] *f* toad

Krücke ['krʏkə] *f* crutch

Krug [kruːk] (-(e)s, ¨e) *m* jug; (*Bierkrug*) mug

Krümel ['kryːməl] (-s, -) *m* crumb; **k~n** *vt, vi*
to crumble

krumm [krʊm] *adj* (*auch fig*) crooked;
(*kurvig*) curved; **jdm etw ~ nehmen** to take
sth amiss; ~**beinig** *adj* bandy-legged;
~**lachen** (*umg*) *vr* to laugh o.s. silly

Krümmung ['krʏmʊŋ] *f* bend, curve

Krüppel ['krʏpəl] (-s, -) *m* cripple

Kruste ['krʊstə] *f* crust

Kruzifix [krutsiˈfɪks] (-es, -e) *nt* crucifix

Kübel ['kyːbəl] (-s, -) *m* tub; (*Eimer*) pail

Kubikmeter [kuˈbiːkmeːtər] *m* cubic metre

Küche ['kʏçə] *f* kitchen; (*Kochen*) cooking,
cuisine

Kuchen ['kuːxən] (-s, -) *m* cake; ~**form** *f*
baking tin; ~**gabel** *f* pastry fork

Küchen- *zW:* ~**herd** *m* cooker, stove;
~**schabe** *f* cockroach; ~**schrank** *m*
kitchen cabinet

Kuckuck ['kʊkʊk] (-s, -e) *m* cuckoo; ~**suhr**
f cuckoo clock

Kugel ['kuːgəl] (-, -n) *f* ball; (*MATH*) sphere;
(*MIL*) bullet; (*Erdkugel*) globe; (*SPORT*) shot;
k~förmig *adj* spherical; ~**lager** *nt* ball
bearing; **k~rund** *adj* (*Gegenstand*) round;
(*umg: Person*) tubby; ~**schreiber** *m* ballpoint (pen), Biro ®; **k~sicher** *adj*
bulletproof; ~**stoßen** (-s) *nt* shot put

Kuh [kuː] (-, ¨e) *f* cow

kühl [kyːl] *adj* (*auch fig*) cool; **K~anlage** *f*
refrigeration plant; **K~e** (-) *f* coolness; ~**en**
vt to cool; **K~er** (-s, -) *m* (*AUT*) radiator;
K~erhaube *f* (*AUT*) bonnet (*BRIT*), hood
(*US*); **K~raum** *m* cold storage chamber;
K~schrank *m* refrigerator; **K~truhe** *f*
freezer; **K~ung** *f* cooling; **K~wasser** *nt*
radiator water

kühn [kyːn] *adj* bold, daring; **K~heit** *f*
boldness

Kuhstall *m* byre, cattle shed

Küken ['kyːkən] (-s, -) *nt* chicken

kulant [kuˈlant] *adj* obliging

Kuli ['kuːli] (-s, -s) *m* coolie; (*umg:
Kugelschreiber*) Biro ®

Kulisse [kuˈlɪsə] *f* scenery

kullern ['kʊlərn] *vi* to roll

Kult [kʊlt] (-(e)s, -e) *m* worship, cult; **mit
etw einen ~ treiben** to make a cult out of
sth

kultivieren [kʊltiˈviːrən] *vt* to cultivate

kultiviert *adj* cultivated, refined

Kultur [kʊlˈtuːr] *f* culture; civilization; (*des
Bodens*) cultivation; ~**banause** (*umg*) *m*
philistine, low-brow; ~**beutel** *m* toilet bag;
k~ell [-uˈrɛl] *adj* cultural; ~**ministerium** *nt*
ministry of education and the arts

Kümmel ['kʏməl] (-s, -) *m* caraway seed;
(*Branntwein*) kümmel

Kummer ['kʊmər] (-s) *m* grief, sorrow

kümmerlich ['kʏmərlɪç] *adj* miserable,
wretched

kümmern ['kʏmərn] *vt* to concern ♦ *vr:* **sich
um jdn ~** to look after sb; **das kümmert
mich nicht** that doesn't worry me; **sich
um etw ~** to see to sth

Kumpel ['kʊmpəl] (-s, -) (*umg*) *m* mate

kündbar ['kʏntbaːr] *adj* redeemable,
recallable; (*Vertrag*) terminable

Kunde¹ ['kʊndə] (-n, -n) *m* customer

Kunde² ['kʊndə] *f* (*Botschaft*) news

Kunden- *zW:* ~**dienst** *m* after-sales service;
~**konto** *nt* charge account; ~**nummer** *f*
customer number

Kund- *zW:* **k~geben** (*unreg*) *vt* to
announce; ~**gebung** *f* announcement;
(*Versammlung*) rally

Künd- ['kʏnd] *zW:* **k~igen** *vi* to give in
one's notice ♦ *vt* to cancel; **jdm k~igen** to
give sb his notice; **die Stellung/Wohnung
k~igen** to give notice that one is leaving
one's job/house; **jdm die Stellung/
Wohnung k~igen** to give sb notice to
leave his/her job/house; ~**igung** *f* notice;
~**igungsfrist** *f* period of notice;
~**igungsschutz** *m* protection against

wrongful dismissal

Kundin f customer

Kundschaft f customers pl, clientele

künftig ['kynftɪç] adj future ♦ adv in future

Kunst [kʊnst] (-, ⸚e) f art; (Können) skill; **das ist doch keine ~** it's easy; **~dünger** m artificial manure; **~faser** f synthetic fibre; **~fertigkeit** f skilfulness; **~gegenstand** m art object; **~gerecht** adj skilful; **~geschichte** f history of art; **~gewerbe** nt arts and crafts pl; **~griff** m trick, knack; **~händler** m art dealer

Künstler(in) ['kynstlər(ɪn)] (-s, -) m(f) artist; **k~isch** adj artistic; **~name** m pseudonym

künstlich ['kynstlɪç] adj artificial

Kunst- zW: **~sammler** (-s, -) m art collector; **~seide** f artificial silk; **~stoff** m synthetic material; **~stück** nt trick; **~turnen** nt gymnastics sg; **k~voll** adj artistic; **~werk** nt work of art

kunterbunt ['kʊntərbʊnt] adj higgledy-piggledy

Kupee ▲ [ku'pe:] (-s, -s) nt coupé

Kupfer ['kʊpfər] (-s) nt copper; **k~n** adj copper

Kupon [ku'põ:, ku'pɔŋ] (-s, -s) m coupon; (Stoff~) length of cloth

Kuppe ['kʊpə] f (Bergkuppe) top; (Fingerkuppe) tip

Kuppel (-, -n) f dome; **k~n** vi (JUR) to procure; (AUT) to declutch ♦ vt to join

Kupplung f coupling; (AUT) clutch

Kur [ku:r] (-, -en) f cure, treatment

Kür [ky:r] (-, -en) f (SPORT) free exercises pl

Kurbel ['kʊrbəl] (-, -n) f crank, winder; (AUT) starting handle; **~welle** f crankshaft

Kürbis ['kyrbɪs] (-ses, -se) m pumpkin; (exotisch) gourd

Kurgast m visitor (to a health resort)

kurieren [ku'ri:rən] vt to cure

kurios [kuri'o:s] adj curious, odd; **K~i'tät** f curiosity

Kurort m health resort

Kurs [kʊrs] (-es, -e) m course; (FIN) rate; **~buch** nt timetable; **k~ieren** [kʊr'zi:rən] vi to circulate; **k~iv** [kʊr'zi:f] adv in italics; **~us** ['kʊrzʊs] (-, Kurse) m course; **~wagen**

m (EISENB) through carriage

Kurtaxe [-taksə] (-, -n) f visitors' tax (at health resort or spa)

Kurve ['kʊrvə] f curve; (Straßenkurve) curve, bend; **kurvig** adj (Straße) bendy

kurz [kʊrts] adj short; **~ gesagt** in short; **~ halten** to keep short; **zu ~ kommen** to come off badly; **den Kürzeren ziehen** to get the worst of it; **K~arbeit** f short-time work; **~ärm(e)lig** adj short-sleeved

Kürze ['kyrtsə] f shortness, brevity; **k~n** vt to cut short; (in der Länge) to shorten; (Gehalt) to reduce

kurz- zW: **~erhand** adv on the spot; **~fristig** adj short-term; **K~geschichte** f short story; **~halten** △ (unreg) vt siehe **kurz**; **~lebig** adj short-lived

kürzlich ['kyrtslɪç] adv lately, recently

Kurz- zW: **~schluss** ▲ m (ELEK) short circuit; **k~sichtig** adj short-sighted

Kürzung f (eines Textes) abridgement; (eines Theaterstück, des Gehalts) cut

Kurzwelle f short wave

kuscheln ['kʊʃəln] vr to snuggle up

Kusine [ku'zi:nə] f cousin

Kuss ▲ [kʊs] (-es, ⸚e) m kiss

küssen ['kysən] vt, vr to kiss

Küste ['kystə] f coast, shore

Küstenwache f coastguard

Küster ['kystər] (-s, -) m sexton, verger

Kutsche ['kʊtʃə] f coach, carriage; **~r** (-s, -) m coachman

Kutte ['kʊtə] f habit

Kuvert [ku'vert] (-s, -e od -s) nt envelope; cover

KZ nt abk von **Konzentrationslager**

L, l

l abk = **Liter**

labil [la'bi:l] adj (MED: Konstitution) delicate

Labor [la'bo:r] (-s, -e od -s) nt lab; **~ant(in)** m(f) lab(oratory) assistant

Labyrinth [laby'rɪnt] (-s, -e) nt labyrinth

Lache ['laxə] f (Flüssigkeit) puddle; (von Blut, Benzin etc) pool

lächeln ['lɛçəln] *vi* to smile; **L~** **(-s)** *nt* smile
lachen ['laxən] *vi* to laugh
lächerlich ['lɛçərlɪç] *adj* ridiculous
Lachgas *nt* laughing gas
lachhaft *adj* laughable
Lachs [laks] **(-es, -e)** *m* salmon
Lack [lak] **(-(e)s, -e)** *m* lacquer, varnish; (*von Auto*) paint; **l~ieren** [la'ki:rən] *vt* to varnish; (*Auto*) to spray; **~ierer** [la'ki:rər] **(-s, -)** *m* varnisher
Laden ['la:dən] **(-s, ~)** *m* shop; (*Fensterladen*) shutter
laden ['la:dən] (*unreg*) *vt* (*Lasten*) to load; (*JUR*) to summon; (*einluden*) to invite
Laden- *zW:* **~dieb** *m* shoplifter; **~diebstahl** *m* shoplifting; **~schluss** ▲ *m* closing time; **~tisch** *m* counter
Laderaum *m* freight space; (*AVIAT, NAUT*) hold
Ladung ['la:dʊŋ] *f* (*Last*) cargo, load; (*Beladen*) loading; (*JUR*) summons; (*Einladung*) invitation; (*Sprengladung*) charge
Lage ['la:gə] *f* position, situation; (*Schicht*) layer; **in der ~ sein** to be in a position
Lageplan *m* ground plan
Lager ['la:gər] **(-s, -)** *nt* camp; (*COMM*) warehouse; (*Schlaflager*) bed; (*von Tier*) lair; (*TECH*) bearing; **~bestand** *m* stocks *pl*; **~feuer** *nt* campfire; **~haus** *nt* warehouse, store
lagern ['la:gərn] *vi* (*Dinge*) to be stored; (*Menschen*) to camp ♦ *vt* to store; (*betten*) to lay down; (*Maschine*) to bed
Lagune [la'gu:nə] *f* lagoon
lahm [la:m] *adj* lame; **~ legen** to paralyse; **~en** *vi* to be lame
Lähmung *f* paralysis
Laib [laɪp] **(-s, -e)** *m* loaf
Laie ['laɪə] **(-n, -n)** *m* layman; **l~nhaft** *adj* amateurish
Laken ['la:kən] **(-s, -)** *nt* sheet
Lakritze [la'krɪtsə] *f* liquorice
lallen ['lalən] *vt, vi* to slur; (*Baby*) to babble
Lamelle [la'mɛlə] *f* lamella; (*ELEK*) lamina; (*TECH*) plate
Lametta [la'mɛta] **(-s)** *nt* tinsel

Lamm [lam] **(-(e)s, ~er)** *nt* lamb
Lampe ['lampə] *f* lamp
Lampen- *zW:* **~fieber** *nt* stage fright; **~schirm** *m* lampshade
Lampion [lampi'õː] **(-s, -s)** *m* Chinese lantern
Land [lant] **(-(e)s, ~er)** *nt* land; (*Nation, nicht Stadt*) country; (*Bundesland*) state; **auf dem ~(e)** in the country; *siehe* **hierzulande**; **~besitz** *m* landed property; **~ebahn** *f* runway; **l~en** ['landən] *vt, vi* to land

---
Land

i A **Land** (*plural* **Länder**) *is a member state of the BRD and of Austria. There are 16* **Länder** *in Germany, namely Baden-Württemberg, Bayern, Berlin, Brandenburg, Bremen, Hamburg, Hessen, Mecklenburg-Vorpommern, Niedersachsen, Nordrhein-Westfalen, Rheinland-Pfalz, Saarland, Sachsen, Sachsen-Anhalt, Schleswig-Holstein and Thüringen. Each* **Land** *has its own parliament and constitution. The 9* **Länder** *of Austria are Vorarlberg, Tirol, Salzburg, Oberösterreich, Niederösterreich, Kärnten, Steiermark, Burgenland and Wien.*

Landes- ['landəs] *zW:* **~farben** *pl* national colours; **~innere(s)** *nt* inland region; **~sprache** *f* national language; **l~üblich** *adj* customary; **~verrat** *m* high treason; **~währung** *f* national currency; **l~weit** *adj* nationwide
Land- *zW:* **~haus** *nt* country house; **~karte** *f* map; **~kreis** *m* administrative region; **l~läufig** *adj* customary
ländlich ['lɛntlɪç] *adj* rural
Land- *zW:* **~schaft** *f* countryside; (*KUNST*) landscape; **~schaftsschutzgebiet** *nt* nature reserve; **~sitz** *m* country seat; **~straße** *f* country road; **~streicher** **(-s, -)** *m* tramp; **~strich** *m* region
Landung ['landʊŋ] *f* landing; **~sbrücke** *f* jetty, pier
Land- *zW:* **~weg** *m:* **etw auf dem ~weg befördern** to transport sth by land; **~wirt**

m farmer; **~wirtschaft** *f* agriculture;
~zunge *f* spit

lang [laŋ] *adj* long; (*Mensch*) tall; **~atmig** *adj*
long-winded; **~e** *adv* for a long time;
(*dauern, brauchen*) a long time

Länge ['lɛŋə] *f* length; (*GEOG*) longitude

langen ['laŋən] *vi* (*ausreichen*) to do, to
suffice; (*fassen*): **~ (nach)** to reach (for)
♦ *vt*: **jdm etw ~** to hand *od* pass sb sth; **es
langt mir** I've had enough

Längengrad *m* longitude

Längenmaß *nt* linear measure

lang- *zW*: **L~eweile** *f* boredom; **~fristig**
adj long-term; **~jährig** *adj* (*Freundschaft,
Gewohnheit*) long-standing; **L~lauf** *m* (*SKI*)
cross-country skiing

länglich *adj* longish

längs [lɛŋs] *präp* (+*gen od dat*) along ♦ *adv*
lengthwise

lang- *zW*: **~sam** *adj* slow; **L~samkeit** *f*
slowness; **L~schläfer(in)** *m(f)* late riser

längst [lɛŋst] *adv*: **das ist ~ fertig** that was
finished a long time ago, that has been
finished for a long time; **~e(r, s)** *adj*
longest

lang- *zW*: **~weilen** *vt* to bore ♦ *vr* to be
bored; **~weilig** *adj* boring, tedious;
L~welle *f* long wave; **~wierig** *adj* lengthy,
long-drawn-out

Lanze ['lantsə] *f* lance

Lappalie [la'paːliə] *f* trifle

Lappen ['lapən] (**-s, -**) *m* cloth, rag; (*ANAT*)
lobe

läppisch ['lɛpɪʃ] *adj* foolish

Lapsus ['lapsʊs] (**-, -**) *m* slip

Laptop ['lɛptɔp] (**-s, -s**) *m* laptop
(computer)

Lärche ['lɛrçə] *f* larch

Lärm [lɛrm] (**-(e)s**) *m* noise; **l~en** *vi* to be
noisy, to make a noise

Larve ['larfə] *f* (*BIOL*) larva

lasch [laʃ] *adj* slack

Laser ['leːzər] (**-s, -**) *m* laser

SCHLÜSSELWORT

---

lassen ['lasən] (*pt* **ließ**, *pp* **gelassen** *od* (*als
Hilfsverb*) **lassen**) *vt* **1** (*unterlassen*) to stop;

(*momentan*) to leave; **lass das (sein)!** don't
(do it)!; (*hör auf*) stop it!; **lass mich!** leave
me alone; **lassen wir das!** let's leave it; **er
kann das Trinken nicht lassen** he can't
stop drinking

2 (*zurücklassen*) to leave; **etw lassen, wie
es ist** to leave sth (just) as it is

3 (*überlassen*): **jdn ins Haus lassen** to let
sb into the house

♦ *vi*: **lass mal, ich mache das schon** leave
it, I'll do it

♦ *Hilfsverb* **1** (*veranlassen*): **etw machen
lassen** to have *od* get sth done; **sich** *dat*
etw schicken lassen to have sth sent (to
one)

2 (*zulassen*): **jdn etw wissen lassen** to let
sb know sth; **das Licht brennen lassen** to
leave the light on; **jdn warten lassen** to
keep sb waiting; **das lässt sich machen**
that can be done

3: **lass uns gehen** let's go

---

lässig ['lɛsɪç] *adj* casual; **L~keit** *f* casualness

Last [last] (**-, -en**) *f* load, burden; (*NAUT,
AVIAT*) cargo; (*meist pl*: *Gebühr*) charge; **jdm
zur ~ fallen** to be a burden to sb; **~auto**
nt lorry, truck; **l~en** *vi*: **l~en auf** +*dat* to
weigh on; **~enaufzug** *m* goods lift *od*
elevator (*US*)

Laster ['lastər] (**-s, -**) *nt* vice

lästern ['lɛstərn] *vt*, *vi* (*Gott*) to blaspheme;
(*schlecht sprechen*) to mock

Lästerung *f* jibe; (*Gotteslästerung*)
blasphemy

lästig ['lɛstɪç] *adj* troublesome, tiresome

Last- *zW*: **~kahn** *m* barge; **~kraftwagen**
m heavy goods vehicle; **~schrift** *f* debit;
~wagen *m* lorry, truck; **~zug** *m* articulated
lorry

Latein [la'taɪn] (**-s**) *nt* Latin; **~amerika** *nt*
Latin America

latent [la'tɛnt] *adj* latent

Laterne [la'tɛrnə] *f* lantern; (*Straßenlaterne*)
lamp, light; **~npfahl** *m* lamppost

latschen ['laːtʃən] (*umg*) *vi* (*gehen*) to
wander, to go; (*lässig*) to slouch

Latte ['latə] *f* lath; (*SPORT*) goalpost; (*quer*)

Rechtschreibreform: ▲ *neue Schreibung* △ *alte Schreibung (auslaufend)*

crossbar

Latzhose ['latsho:zə] f dungarees pl

lau [lau] adj (Nacht) balmy; (Wasser) lukewarm

Laub [laup] (-(e)s) nt foliage; ~**baum** m deciduous tree; ~**frosch** m tree frog; ~**säge** f fretsaw

Lauch [laux] (-(e)s, -e) m leek

Lauer ['lauər] f: **auf der ~ sein** od **liegen** to lie in wait; **l~n** vi to lie in wait; (Gefahr) to lurk

Lauf [lauf] (-(e)s, Läufe) m run; (Wettlauf) race; (Entwicklung, ASTRON) course; (Gewehrlauf) barrel; **einer Sache** dat **ihren ~ lassen** to let sth take its course; ~**bahn** f career

laufen ['laufən] (unreg) vt, vi to run; (umg: gehen) to walk; ~**d** adj running; (Monat, Ausgaben) current; **auf dem ~den sein/halten** to be/keep up to date; **am ~den Band** (fig) continuously

Läufer ['lɔyfər] (-s, -) m (Teppich, SPORT) runner; (Fußball) half-back; (Schach) bishop

Lauf- zW: ~**masche** f run, ladder (BRIT); ~**pass** ▲ m: **jdm den ~pass geben** (umg) to send sb packing (inf); ~**stall** m playpen; ~**steg** m catwalk; ~**werk** nt (COMPUT) disk drive

Lauge ['laugə] f soapy water; (CHEM) alkaline solution

Laune ['launə] f mood, humour; (Einfall) caprice; (schlechte) temper; **l~nhaft** adj capricious, changeable

launisch adj moody; bad-tempered

Laus [laus] (-, Läuse) f louse

lauschen ['laufən] vi to eavesdrop, to listen in

lauschig ['laufɪç] adj snug

lausig ['lauzɪç] (umg: pej) adj measly; (Kälte) perishing

laut [laut] adj loud ♦ adv loudly; (lesen) aloud ♦ präp (+gen od dat) according to; **L~** (-(e)s, -e) m sound

Laute ['lautə] f lute

lauten ['lautən] vi to say; (Urteil) to be

läuten ['lɔytən] vt, vi to ring, to sound

lauter ['lautər] adj (Wasser) clear, pure; (Wahrheit, Charakter) honest ♦ adj inv (Freude, Dummheit etc) sheer ♦ adv nothing but, only

laut- zW: ~**hals** adv at the top of one's voice; ~**los** adj noiseless, silent; **L~schrift** f phonetics pl; **L~sprecher** m loudspeaker; ~**stark** adj vociferous; **L~stärke** f (RADIO) volume

lauwarm ['lauvarm] adj (auch fig) lukewarm

Lavendel [la'vɛndəl] (-s, -) m lavender

Lawine [la'vi:nə] f avalanche; ~**ngefahr** f danger of avalanches

lax [laks] adj lax

Lazarett [latsa'rɛt] (-(e)s, -e) nt (MIL) hospital, infirmary

leasen ['li:zən] vt to lease

Leben (-s, -) nt life

leben ['le:bən] vt, vi to live; ~**d** adj living; ~**dig** [le'bɛndɪç] adj living, alive; (lebhaft) lively; **L~digkeit** f liveliness

Lebens- zW: ~**art** f way of life; ~**erwartung** f life expectancy; **l~fähig** adj able to live; ~**freude** f zest for life; ~**gefahr** f: ~**gefahr!** danger!; **in ~gefahr** dangerously ill; **l~gefährlich** adj dangerous; (Verletzung) critical; ~**haltungskosten** pl cost of living sg; ~**jahr** nt year of life; **l~länglich** adj (Strafe) for life; ~**lauf** m curriculum vitae; ~**mittel** pl food sg; ~**mittelgeschäft** nt grocer's (shop); ~**mittelvergiftung** f (MED) food poisoning; **l~müde** adj tired of life; ~**retter** m lifesaver; ~**standard** m standard of living; ~**unterhalt** m livelihood; ~**versicherung** f life insurance; ~**wandel** m way of life; ~**weise** f lifestyle, way of life; **l~wichtig** adj vital, essential; ~**zeichen** nt sign of life

Leber ['le:bər] (-, -n) f liver; ~**fleck** m mole; ~**tran** m cod-liver oil; ~**wurst** f liver sausage

Lebewesen nt creature

leb- ['le:p] zW: ~**haft** adj lively, vivacious; **L~kuchen** m gingerbread; ~**los** adj lifeless

Leck [lɛk] (-(e)s, -e) nt leak; **l~** adj leaky, leaking; **l~en** vi (Loch haben) to leak; (schlecken) to lick ♦ vt to lick

lecker ['lɛkər] *adj* delicious, tasty; **L~bissen** *m* dainty morsel

Leder ['le:dər] (**-s, -**) *nt* leather; **~hose** *f* lederhosen; **l~n** *adj* leather; **~waren** *pl* leather goods

ledig ['le:dɪç] *adj* single; **einer Sache** *gen* ~ **sein** to be free of sth; **~lich** *adv* merely, solely

leer [le:r] *adj* empty; vacant; ~ **machen** to empty; ~ **stehend** empty; **L~e** (**-**) *f* emptiness; **~en** *vt, vr* to empty; **L~gewicht** *nt* weight when empty; **L~gut** *nt* empties *pl*; **L~lauf** *m* neutral; **L~ung** *f* emptying; (*Post*) collection

legal [le'ga:l] *adj* legal, lawful; **~i'sieren** *vt* to legalize

legen ['le:gən] *vt* to lay, to put, to place; (*Ei*) to lay ♦ *vr* to lie down; (*fig*) to subside

Legende [le'gɛndə] *f* legend

leger [le'ʒe:r] *adj* casual

Legierung [le'gi:rʊŋ] *f* alloy

Legislative [legɪsla'ti:və] *f* legislature

legitim [legi'ti:m] *adj* legitimate

legitimieren [legiti'mi:rən] *vt* to legitimate ♦ *vr* to prove one's identity

Lehm [le:m] (**-(e)s, -e**) *m* loam; **l~ig** *adj* loamy

Lehne ['le:nə] *f* arm; back; **l~n** *vt, vr* to lean

Lehnstuhl *m* armchair

Lehr- *zW*: **~amt** *nt* teaching profession; **~buch** *nt* textbook

Lehre ['le:rə] *f* teaching, doctrine; (*beruflich*) apprenticeship; (*moralisch*) lesson; (*TECH*) gauge; **l~n** *vt* to teach

Lehrer(in) (**-s, -**) *m(f)* teacher; **~zimmer** *nt* staff room

Lehr- *zW*: **~gang** *m* course; **~jahre** *pl* apprenticeship *sg*; **~kraft** *f* (*förmlich*) teacher; **~ling** *m* apprentice; **~plan** *m* syllabus; **l~reich** *adj* instructive; **~stelle** *f* apprenticeship; **~zeit** *f* apprenticeship

Leib [laip] (**-(e)s, -er**) *m* body; **halt ihn mir vom ~!** keep him away from me!; **l~haftig** *adj* personified; (*Teufel*) incarnate; **l~lich** *adj* bodily; (*Vater etc*) own; **~schmerzen** *pl* stomach pains; **~wache** *f* bodyguard

Leiche ['laiçə] *f* corpse; **~nhalle** *f* mortuary; **~nwagen** *m* hearse

Leichnam ['laiçna:m] (**-(e)s, -e**) *m* corpse

leicht [laiçt] *adj* light; (*einfach*) easy; **jdm** ~ **fallen** to be easy for sb; **es sich** *dat* ~ **machen** to make things easy for o.s.; **L~athletik** *f* athletics *sg*; **~fertig** *adj* frivolous; **~gläubig** *adj* gullible, credulous; **~hin** *adv* lightly; **L~igkeit** *f* easiness; **mit L~igkeit** with ease; **L~sinn** *m* carelessness; **~sinnig** *adj* careless

Leid [lait] (**-(e)s**) *nt* grief, sorrow; **es tut mir/ihm** ~ I am/he is sorry; **er/das tut mir** ~ I am sorry for him/it; **l~** *adj*: **etw l~ haben** *od* **sein** to be tired of sth; **l~en** (*unreg*) *vt* to suffer; (*erlauben*) to permit ♦ *vi* to suffer; **jdn/etw nicht l~en können** not to be able to stand sb/sth; **~en** ['laidən] (**-s, -**) *nt* suffering; (*Krankheit*) complaint; **~enschaft** *f* passion; **l~enschaftlich** *adj* passionate

leider ['laidər] *adv* unfortunately; **ja, ~** yes, I'm afraid so; **~ nicht** I'm afraid not

leidig ['laidɪç] *adj* worrying, troublesome

leidlich ['laitlɪç] *adj* tolerable ♦ *adv* tolerably

Leid- *zW*: **~tragende(r)** *f(m)* bereaved; (*Benachteiligter*) one who suffers; **~wesen** *nt*: **zu jds ~wesen** to sb's disappointment

Leier ['laiər] (**-, -n**) *f* lyre; (*fig*) old story; **~kasten** *m* barrel organ

Leihbibliothek *f* lending library

Leihbücherei *f* lending library

leihen ['laiən] (*unreg*) *vt* to lend; **sich** *dat* **etw ~** to borrow sth

Leih- *zW*: **~gebühr** *f* hire charge; **~haus** *nt* pawnshop; **~wagen** *m* hired car

Leim [laim] (**-(e)s, -e**) *m* glue; **l~en** *vt* to glue

Leine ['lainə] *f* line, cord; (*Hundeleine*) leash, lead

Leinen *nt* linen; **l~** *adj* linen

Leinwand *f* (*KUNST*) canvas; (*CINE*) screen

leise ['laizə] *adj* quiet; (*sanft*) soft, gentle

Leiste ['laistə] *f* ledge; (*Zierleiste*) strip; (*ANAT*) groin

leisten ['laistən] *vt* (*Arbeit*) to do; (*Gesellschaft*) to keep; (*Ersatz*) to supply; (*vollbringen*) to achieve; **sich** *dat* **etw ~**

können to be able to afford sth
Leistung f performance; (gute) achievement; ~sdruck m pressure; **l~sfähig** adj efficient
Leitartikel m leading article
Leitbild nt model
leiten ['laɪtən] vt to lead; (Firma) to manage; (in eine Richtung) to direct; (ELEK) to conduct
Leiter¹ ['laɪtər] (-s, -) m leader, head; (ELEK) conductor
Leiter² ['laɪtər] (-, -n) f ladder
Leitfaden m guide
Leitplanke f crash barrier
Leitung f (Führung) direction; (CINE, THEAT etc) production; (von Firma) management, directors pl; (Wasserleitung) pipe; (Kabel) cable; **eine lange ~ haben** to be slow on the uptake
Leitungs- zW: **~draht** m wire; **~rohr** nt pipe; **~wasser** nt tap water
Lektion [lɛktsˈoːn] f lesson
Lektüre [lɛkˈtyːrə] f (Lesen) reading; (Lesestoff) reading matter
Lende ['lɛndə] f loin; **~nstück** nt fillet
lenk- ['lɛŋk] zW: **~bar** adj (Fahrzeug) steerable; (Kind) manageable, **~en** vt to steer; (Kind) to guide; (Blick, Aufmerksamkeit) **~en (auf** +akk) to direct (at); **L~rad** nt steering wheel; **L~radschloss ▲** nt steering (wheel) lock; **L~stange** f handlebars pl; **L~ung** f steering
Lepra ['leːpra] (-) f leprosy
Lerche ['lɛrçə] f lark
lernbegierig adj eager to learn
lernen ['lɛrnən] vt to learn
lesbar ['leːsbaːr] adj legible
Lesbierin ['lɛsbiərɪn] f lesbian
lesbisch ['lɛsbɪʃ] adj lesbian
Lese ['leːzə] f (Wein) harvest
Lesebrille f reading glasses
Lesebuch nt reading book, reader
lesen (unreg) vt, vi to read; (ernten) to gather, to pick
Leser(in) (-s, -) m(f) reader; **~brief** m reader's letter; **l~lich** adj legible
Lesezeichen nt bookmark

Lesung ['leːzʊŋ] f (PARL) reading
letzte(r, s) ['lɛtstə(r, s)] adj last; (neueste) latest; **zum ~n Mal** for the last time; **~ns** adv lately; **~re(r, s)** adj latter
Leuchte ['lɔʏçtə] f lamp, light; **l~n** vi to shine, to gleam; **~r (-s, -)** m candlestick
Leucht- zW: **~farbe** f fluorescent colour; **~rakete** f flare; **~reklame** f neon sign; **~röhre** f strip light; **~turm** m lighthouse
leugnen ['lɔʏɡnən] vt to deny
Leukämie [lɔʏkɛˈmiː] f leukaemia
Leukoplast [lɔʏkoˈplast] (®; -(e)s, -e) nt Elastoplast ®
Leumund ['lɔʏmʊnt] (-(e)s, -e) m reputation
Leumundszeugnis nt character reference
Leute ['lɔʏtə] pl people pl
Leutnant ['lɔʏtnant] (-s, -s od -e) m lieutenant
leutselig ['lɔʏtzeːlɪç] adj amiable
Lexikon ['lɛksɪkɔn] (-s, Lexiken od Lexika) nt encyclop(a)edia
Libelle [liˈbɛlə] f dragonfly; (TECH) spirit level
liberal [libeˈraːl] adj liberal; **L~e(r)** f(m) liberal
Licht [lɪçt] (-(e)s, -er) nt light, ~bild nt photograph; (Dia) slide; **~blick** m cheering prospect; **l~empfindlich** adj sensitive to light; **l~en** vt to clear; (Anker) to weigh ♦ vr to clear up; (Haar) to thin; **l~erloh** adv: **l~erloh brennen** to be ablaze; **~hupe** f flashing of headlights; **~jahr** nt light year; **~maschine** f dynamo; **~schalter** m light switch; **~schutzfaktor** m protection factor
Lichtung f clearing, glade
Lid [liːt] (-(e)s, -er) nt eyelid; **~schatten** m eyeshadow
lieb [liːp] adj dear; **das ist ~ von dir** that's kind of you; **~ gewinnen** to get fond of; **~ haben** to be fond of; **~äugeln** ['liːbɔʏɡəln] vi insep: **mit etw ~äugeln** to have one's eye on sth; **mit dem Gedanken ~äugeln, etw zu tun** to toy with the idea of doing sth
Liebe ['liːbə] f love; **l~bedürftig** adj: **l~bedürftig sein** to need love; **l~n** vt to love; to like

liebens- *zW*: **~wert** *adj* loveable; **~würdig** *adj* kind; **~würdigerweise** *adv* kindly; **L~würdigkeit** *f* kindness
lieber ['li:bər] *adv* rather, preferably; **ich gehe ~ nicht** I'd rather not go; *siehe auch* **gern**; **lieb**
Liebes- *zW*: **~brief** *m* love letter; **~kummer** *m*: **~kummer haben** to be lovesick; **~paar** *nt* courting couple, lovers *pl*
liebevoll *adj* loving
lieb- [li:p] *zW*: **~gewinnen** △ (*unreg*) *vt siehe* **lieb; ~haben** △ (*unreg*) *vt siehe* **lieb; L~haber (-s, -)** *m* lover; **L~habe'rei** *f* hobby; **~kosen** ['li:pko:zən] *vt insep* to caress; **~lich** *adj* lovely, charming; **L~ling** *m* darling; **L~lings-** *in zW* favourite; **~los** *adj* unloving; **L~schaft** *f* love affair
Lied [li:t] **(-(e)s, -er)** *nt* song; (*REL*) hymn; **~erbuch** ['li:dər-] *nt* songbook; hymn book
liederlich ['li:dərlıç] *adj* slovenly; (*Lebenswandel*) loose, immoral; **L~keit** *f* slovenliness; immorality
lief *etc* [li:f] *vb siehe* **laufen**
Lieferant [li:fə'rant] *m* supplier
Lieferbedingungen *pl* terms of delivery
liefern ['li:fərn] *vt* to deliver; (*versorgen mit*) to supply; (*Beweis*) to produce
Liefer- *zW*: **~schein** *m* delivery note; **~termin** *m* delivery date; **~ung** *f* delivery; supply; **~wagen** *m* van; **~zeit** *f* delivery period
Liege ['li:gə] *f* bed
liegen ['li:gən] (*unreg*) *vi* to lie; (*sich befinden*) to be; **mir liegt nichts/viel daran** it doesn't matter to me/it matters a lot to me; **es liegt bei Ihnen, ob ...** it's up to you whether ...; **Sprachen ~ mir nicht** languages are not my line; **woran liegt es?** what's the cause?; **~ bleiben** (*im Bett*) to stay in bed; (*nicht aufstehen*) to stay lying down; (*vergessen werden*) to be left (behind); **~ lassen** (*vergessen*) to leave behind
Liege- *zW*: **~sitz** *m* (*AUT*) reclining seat; **~stuhl** *m* deck chair; **~wagen** *m* (*EISENB*) couchette
Lift [lıft] **(-(e)s, -e** *od* **-s)** *m* lift
Likör [li'kø:r] **(-s, -e)** *m* liqueur
lila ['li:la] *adj inv* purple, lilac; **L~ (-s, -s)** *nt* (*Farbe*) purple, lilac
Lilie ['li:liə] *f* lily
Limonade [limo'na:də] *f* lemonade
Limone [li'mo:nə] *f* lime
Linde ['lındə] *f* lime tree, linden
lindern ['lındərn] *vt* to alleviate, to soothe; **Linderung** *f* alleviation
Lineal [line'a:l] **(-s, -e)** *nt* ruler
Linie ['li:niə] *f* line
Linien- *zW*: **~blatt** *nt* ruled sheet; **~flug** *m* scheduled flight; **~richter** *m* linesman
linieren [li'ni:rən] *vt* to line
Linke ['lıŋkə] *f* left side; left hand; (*POL*) left
linkisch *adj* awkward, gauche
links [lıŋks] *adv* left; to *od* on the left; **~ von mir** on *od* to my left; **L~händer(in) (-s, -)** *m(f)* left-handed person; **L~kurve** *f* left-hand bend; **L~verkehr** *m* driving on the left
Linoleum [li'no:leʊm] **(-s)** *nt* lino(leum)
Linse ['lınzə] *f* lentil; (*optisch*) lens *sg*
Lippe ['lıpə] *f* lip; **~nstift** *m* lipstick
lispeln ['lıspəln] *vi* to lisp
Lissabon ['lısabɔn] **(-s)** *nt* Lisbon
List [lıst] **(-, -en)** *f* cunning; trick, ruse
Liste ['lıstə] *f* list
listig ['lıstıç] *adj* cunning, sly
Liter ['li:tər] **(-s, -)** *nt od m* litre
literarisch [lıte'ra:rıʃ] *adj* literary
Literatur [lıtera'tu:r] *f* literature
Litfaßsäule ['lıtfaszɔylə] *f* advertising pillar
Liturgie [litʊr'gi:] *f* liturgy
liturgisch [li'tʊrgıʃ] *adj* liturgical
Litze ['lıtsə] *f* braid; (*ELEK*) flex
Lizenz [li'tsɛnts] *f* licence
Lkw [ɛlka:'ve:] **(-(s), -(s))** *m abk* = **Lastkraftwagen**
Lob [lo:p] **(-(e)s)** *nt* praise
Lobby ['lɔbi] *f* lobby
loben ['lo:bən] *vt* to praise; **~swert** *adj* praiseworthy
löblich ['lø:plıç] *adj* praiseworthy, laudable
Loch [lɔx] **(-(e)s, ⸚er)** *nt* hole; **l~en** *vt* to punch holes in; **~er (-s, -)** *m* punch

löcherig ['lœçərɪç] *adj* full of holes

Lochkarte *f* punch card

Lochstreifen *m* punch tape

Locke ['lɔkə] *f* lock, curl; **l~n** *vt* to entice; (*Haare*) to curl; **~nwickler (-s, -)** *m* curler

locker ['lɔkər] *adj* loose; **~lassen** (*unreg*) *vi*: **nicht ~lassen** not to let up; **~n** *vt* to loosen

lockig ['lɔkɪç] *adj* curly

lodern ['lo:dərn] *vi* to blaze

Löffel ['lœfəl] **(-s, -)** *m* spoon

löffeln *vt* to spoon

Loge ['lo:ʒə] *f* (*THEAT*) box; (*Freimaurer*) (masonic) lodge; (*Pförtnerloge*) office

Logik ['lo:gɪk] *f* logic

logisch ['lo:gɪʃ] *adj* logical

Logopäde [logo'pɛ:də] **(-n, -n)** *m* speech therapist

Lohn [lo:n] **(-(e)s, ⁻e)** *m* reward; (*Arbeitslohn*) pay, wages *pl*; **~büro** *nt* wages office; **~empfänger** *m* wage earner

lohnen ['lo:nən] *vr unpers* to be worth it ♦ *vt*: **(jdm etw) ~** to reward (sb for sth); **~d** *adj* worthwhile

Lohn- *zW*: **~erhöhung** *f* pay rise; **~steuer** *f* income tax; **~steuerkarte** *f* (income) tax card; **~streifen** *m* pay slip; **~tüte** *f* pay packet

Lokal [lo'ka:l] **(-(e)s, -e)** *nt* pub(lic house)

lokal *adj* local; **l~isieren** *vt* to localize

Lokomotive [lokomo'ti:və] *f* locomotive

Lokomotivführer *m* engine driver

Lorbeer ['lɔrbe:r] **(-s, -en)** *m* (*auch fig*) laurel; **~blatt** *nt* (*KOCH*) bay leaf

Los [lo:s] **(-es, -e)** *nt* (*Schicksal*) lot, fate; (*Lotterielos*) lottery ticket

los [lo:s] *adj* (*locker*) loose; **~!** *go onl*: **etw ~ sein** to be rid of sth; **was ist ~?** what's the matter?; **dort ist nichts/viel ~** there's nothing/a lot going on there; **~binden** (*unreg*) *vt* to untie

Löschblatt ['lœʃblat] *nt* sheet of blotting paper

löschen ['lœʃən] *vt* (*Feuer, Licht*) to put out, to extinguish; (*Durst*) to quench; (*COMM*) to cancel; (*COMPUT*) to delete; (*Tonband*) to erase; (*Fracht*) to unload ♦ *vi* (*Feuerwehr*) to

put out a fire; (*Tinte*) to blot

Lösch- *zW*: **~fahrzeug** *nt* fire engine; fire boat; **~gerät** *nt* fire extinguisher; **~papier** *nt* blotting paper

lose ['lo:zə] *adj* loose

Lösegeld *nt* ransom

losen ['lo:zən] *vi* to draw lots

lösen ['lø:zən] *vt* to loosen; (*Rätsel etc*) to solve; (*Verlobung*) to call off; (*CHEM*) to dissolve; (*Partnerschaft*) to break up; (*Fahrkarte*) to buy ♦ *vr* (*aufgehen*) to come loose; (*Zucker etc*) to dissolve; (*Problem, Schwierigkeit*) to (re)solve itself

los- *zW*: **~fahren** (*unreg*) *vi* to leave; **~gehen** (*unreg*) *vi* to set out; (*anfangen*) to start; (*Bombe*) to go off; **auf jdn ~gehen** to go for sb; **~kaufen** *vt* (*Gefangene, Geißeln*) to pay ransom for; **~kommen** (*unreg*) *vi*: **von etw ~kommen** to get away from sth; **~lassen** (*unreg*) *vt* (*Seil*) to let go of; (*Schimpfe*) to let loose; **~laufen** (*unreg*) *vi* to run off

löslich ['lø:slɪç] *adj* soluble; **L~keit** *f* solubility

los- *zW*: **~lösen** *vt*: **(sich) ~lösen** to free (o.s.); **~machen** *vt* to loosen; (*Boot*) to unmoor *vr* to get away; **~schrauben** *vt* to unscrew

Losung ['lo:zʊŋ] *f* watchword, slogan

Lösung ['lø:zʊŋ] *f* (*Lockermachen*) loosening; (*eines Rätsels, CHEM*) solution; **~smittel** *nt* solvent

los- *zW*: **~werden** (*unreg*) *vt* to get rid of; **~ziehen** (*unreg*) (*umg*) *vi* (*sich aufmachen*) to set off

Lot [lo:t] **(-(e)s, -e)** *nt* plumbline; **im ~** vertical; (*fig*) on an even keel

löten ['lø:tən] *vt* to solder

Lothringen ['lo:trɪŋən] **(-s)** *nt* Lorraine

Lotse ['lo:tsə] **(-n, -n)** *m* pilot; (*AVIAT*) air traffic controller; **l~n** *vt* to pilot; (*umg*) to lure

Lotterie [lɔtə'ri:] *f* lottery

Lotto ['lɔto] **(-s, -s)** *nt* national lottery; **~zahlen** *pl* winning lottery numbers

Löwe ['lø:və] **(-n, -n)** *m* lion; (*ASTROL*) Leo; **~nanteil** *m* lion's share; **~nzahn** *m*

dandelion

loyal [loa'jaːl] *adj* loyal; **L~ität** *f* loyalty

Luchs [luks] **(-es, -e)** *m* lynx

Lücke ['lʏkə] *f* gap

Lücken- *zW:* **~büßer (-s, -)** *m* stopgap; **l~haft** *adj* full of gaps; *(Versorgung, Vorräte etc)* inadequate; **l~los** *adj* complete

Luft [luft] **(-, ⁻e)** *f* air; *(Atem)* breath; **in der ~ liegen** to be in the air; **jdn wie ~ behandeln** to ignore sb; **~angriff** *m* air raid; **~ballon** *m* balloon; **~blase** *f* air bubble; **l~dicht** *adj* airtight; **~druck** *m* atmospheric pressure

lüften ['lʏftən] *vt* to air; *(Hut)* to lift, to raise ♦ *vi* to let some air in

Luft- *zW:* **~fahrt** *f* aviation; **~fracht** *f* air freight; **l~gekühlt** *adj* air-cooled; **~gewehr** *nt* air rifle, airgun; **l~ig** *adj* (*Ort*) breezy; (*Raum*) airy; (*Kleider*) summery; **~kissenfahrzeug** *nt* hovercraft; **~kurort** *m* health resort; **l~leer** *adj:* **l~leerer Raum** vacuum; **~linie** *f:* **in der ~linie** as the crow flies; **~loch** *nt* air hole; (*AVIAT*) air pocket; **~matratze** *f* Lilo ® (*BRIT*), air mattress; **~pirat** *m* hijacker; **~post** *f* airmail; **~pumpe** *f* air pump; **~röhre** *f* (*ANAT*) windpipe; **~schlange** *f* streamer; **~schutzkeller** *m* air-raid shelter; **~verkehr** *m* air traffic; **~verschmutzung** *f* air pollution; **~waffe** *f* air force; **~zug** *m* draught

Lüge ['lyːgə] *f* lie; **jdn/etw ~n strafen** to give the lie to sb/sth; **l~n** (*unreg*) *vi* to lie

Lügner(in) (-s, -) *m(f)* liar

Luke ['luːkə] *f* dormer window; hatch

Lump [lump] **(-en, -en)** *m* scamp, rascal

Lumpen ['lumpən] **(-s, -)** *m* rag

lumpen ['lumpən] *vi:* **sich nicht ~ lassen** not to be mean

lumpig ['lumpiç] *adj* shabby

Lupe ['luːpə] *f* magnifying glass; **unter die ~ nehmen** (*fig*) to scrutinize

Lust [lust] **(-, ⁻e)** *f* joy, delight; (*Neigung*) desire; **~ haben zu** *od* **auf etw** *akk* **/etw zu tun** to feel like sth/doing sth

lüstern ['lʏstərn] *adj* lustful, lecherous

lustig ['lustiç] *adj* (*komisch*) amusing, funny;

(*fröhlich*) cheerful

Lust- *zW:* **l~los** *adj* unenthusiastic; **~mord** *m* sex(ual) murder; **~spiel** *nt* comedy

lutschen ['lutʃən] *vt, vi* to suck; **am Daumen ~** to suck one's thumb

Lutscher (-s, -) *m* lollipop

luxuriös [luksuri'øːs] *adj* luxurious

Luxus ['luksus] **(-)** *m* luxury; **~artikel** *pl* luxury goods; **~hotel** *nt* luxury hotel

Luzern [lu'tsɛrn] **(-s)** *nt* Lucerne

Lymphe ['lʏmfə] *f* lymph

lynchen ['lʏnçən] *vt* to lynch

Lyrik ['lyːrik] *f* lyric poetry; **~er (-s, -)** *m* lyric poet

lyrisch ['lyːriʃ] *adj* lyrical

M, m

m *abk* = **Meter**

Machart *f* make

machbar *adj* feasible

SCHLÜSSELWORT
---

machen ['maxən] *vt* **1** to do; (*herstellen, zubereiten*) to make; **was machst du da?** what are you doing (there)?; **das ist nicht zu machen** that can't be done; **das Radio leiser machen** to turn the radio down; **aus Holz gemacht** made of wood

2 (*verursachen, bewirken*) to make; **jdm Angst machen** to make sb afraid; **das macht die Kälte** it's the cold that does that

3 (*ausmachen*) to matter; **das macht nichts** that doesn't matter; **die Kälte macht mir nichts** I don't mind the cold

4 (*kosten, ergeben*) to be; **3 und 5 macht 8** 3 and 5 is *od* are 8; **was** *od* **wie viel macht das?** how much does that make?

5: was macht die Arbeit? how's the work going?; **was macht dein Bruder?** how is your brother doing?; **das Auto machen lassen** to have the car done; **machs gut!** take care!; (*viel Glück*) good luck!

♦ *vi:* **mach schnell!** hurry up!; **Schluss machen** to finish (off); **mach schon!** come on!; **das macht müde** it makes you tired; **in etw** dat **machen** to be od deal in sth ♦ vr to come along (nicely); **sich an etw** akk **machen** to set about sth; **sich verständlich machen** to make o.s. understood; **sich** dat **viel aus jdm/etw machen** to like sb/sth

Macht [maxt] (-, ⸚e) f power; ~**haber** (-s, -) m ruler
mächtig ['mɛçtɪç] adj powerful, mighty; (umg: ungeheuer) enormous
Macht- zW: **m~los** adj powerless; ~**probe** f trial of strength; ~**wort** nt: **ein ~wort sprechen** to exercise one's authority
Mädchen ['mɛːtçən] nt girl; **m~haft** adj girlish; ~**name** m maiden name
Made ['maːdə] f maggot
madig ['maːdɪç] adj maggoty; **jdm etw ~ machen** to spoil sth for sb
mag etc [maːk] vb siehe **mögen**
Magazin [maga'tsiːn] (-s, -e) nt magazine
Magen ['maːgən] (-s, - od ⸚) m stomach; ~**geschwür** nt (MED) stomach ulcer; ~**schmerzen** pl stomachache sg
mager ['maːgər] adj lean; (dünn) thin; **M~keit** f leanness, thinness
Magie [ma'giː] f magic
magisch ['maːgɪʃ] adj magical
Magnet [ma'gneːt] (-s od -en, -en) m magnet; **m~isch** adj magnetic; ~**nadel** f magnetic needle
mähen ['mɛːən] vt, vi to mow
Mahl [maːl] (-(e)s, -e) nt meal; **m~en** (unreg) vt to grind; ~**zeit** f meal ♦ excl enjoy your meal
Mahnbrief m reminder
Mähne ['mɛːnə] f mane
mahn- ['maːn] zW: ~**en** vt to remind; (warnend) to warn; (wegen Schuld) to demand payment from; **M~mal** nt memorial; **M~ung** f reminder; admonition, warning
Mai [maɪ] (-(e)s, -e) m May; ~**glöckchen** nt lily of the valley
Mailand ['maɪlant] nt Milan
mailändisch adj Milanese

mailen ['meːlən] vti to e-mail
Mais [maɪs] (-es, -e) m maize, corn (US); ~**kolben** m corncob; ~**mehl** nt (KOCH) corn meal
Majestät [majɛs'tɛːt] f majesty; **m~isch** adj majestic
Majonäse ▲ [majo'nɛːzə] f mayonnaise
Major [ma'joːr] (-s, -e) m (MIL) major; (AVIAT) squadron leader
Majoran [majo'raːn] (-s, -e) m marjoram
makaber [ma'kaːbər] adj macabre
Makel ['maːkəl] (-s, -) m blemish; (moralisch) stain; **m~los** adj immaculate, spotless
mäkeln ['mɛːkəln] vi to find fault
Makler(in) ['maːklər(ɪn)] (-s, -) m(f) broker
Makrele [ma'kreːlə] f mackerel
Mal [maːl] (-(e)s, -e) nt mark, sign; (Zeitpunkt) time; **ein für alle ~** once and for all; **m~** adv times; (umg) siehe **einmal** ♦ suffix: **-m~** -times
malen vt, vi to paint
Maler (-s, -) m painter; **Male'rei** f painting; **m~isch** adj picturesque
Malkasten m paintbox
Mallorca [ma'jɔrka, ma'lɔrka] (-s) nt Majorca
malnehmen (unreg) vt, vi to multiply
Malz [malts] (-es) nt malt; ~**bier** nt (KOCH) malt beer; ~**bonbon** nt cough drop; ~**kaffee** m malt coffee
Mama ['mama:] (-, -s) (umg) f mum(my) (BRIT), mom(my) (US)
Mami ['mami] (-, -s) = **Mama**
Mammut ['mamʊt] (-s, -e od -s) nt mammoth
man [man] pron one, you; ~ **sagt, ...** they od people say ...; **wie schreibt ~ das?** how do you write it?, how is it written?
Manager(in) ['mɛnɪdʒər(ɪn)] (-s, -) m(f) manager
manch [manç] (unver) pron many a
manche(r, s) ['mançə(r, s)] adj many a; (pl: einige) a number of ♦ pron some
mancherlei [mançər'laɪ] adj inv various ♦ pron inv a variety of things
manchmal adv sometimes
Mandant(in) [man'dant(ɪn)] m(f) (JUR) client
Mandarine [manda'riːnə] f mandarin,

tangerine

Mandat [man'da:t] **(-(e)s, -e)** *nt* mandate

Mandel ['mandəl] **(-, -n)** *f* almond; (*ANAT*) tonsil; **~entzündung** *f* (*MED*) tonsillitis

Manege [ma'ne:ʒə] *f* ring, arena

Mangel ['maŋəl] **(-s, ¨)** *m* lack; (*Knappheit*) shortage; (*Fehler*) defect, fault; **~ an** +*dat* shortage of; **~erscheinung** *f* deficiency symptom; **m~haft** *adj* poor; (*fehlerhaft*) defective, faulty; **m~n** *vi unpers*: **es m~t jdm an etw** *dat* sb lacks sth ♦ *vt* (*Wäsche*) to mangle

mangels *präp* +*gen* for lack of

Manie [ma'ni:] *f* mania

Manier [ma'ni:r] **(-)** *f* manner; style; (*pej*) mannerism; **~en** *pl* (*Umgangsformen*) manners; **m~lich** *adj* well-mannered

Manifest [mani'fɛst] **(-es, -e)** *nt* manifesto

Maniküre [mani'ky:rə] *f* manicure

manipulieren [manipu'li:rən] *vt* to manipulate

Manko ['maŋko] **(-s, -s)** *nt* deficiency; (*COMM*) deficit

Mann [man] **(-(e)s, ¨er)** *m* man; (*Ehemann*) husband; (*NAUT*) hand; **seinen ~ stehen** to hold one's own

Männchen ['mɛnçən] *nt* little man; (*Tier*) male

Mannequin [manə'kɛ̃:] **(-s, -s)** *nt* fashion model

männlich ['mɛnlıç] *adj* (*BIOL*) male; (*fig, GRAM*) masculine

Mannschaft *f* (*SPORT, fig*) team; (*AVIAT, NAUT*) crew; (*MIL*) other ranks *pl*

Manöver [ma'nø:vər] **(-s, -)** *nt* manoeuvre

manövrieren [manø'vri:rən] *vt, vi* to manoeuvre

Mansarde [man'zardə] *f* attic

Manschette [man'ʃɛtə] *f* cuff; (*TECH*) collar; sleeve; **~nknopf** *m* cufflink

Mantel ['mantəl] **(-s, ¨)** *m* coat; (*TECH*) casing, jacket

Manuskript [manu'skrıpt] **(-(e)s, -e)** *nt* manuscript

Mappe ['mapə] *f* briefcase; (*Aktenmappe*) folder

Märchen ['mɛːrçən] *nt* fairy tale; **m~haft**

adj fabulous; **~prinz** *m* Prince Charming

Margarine [marga'ri:nə] *f* margarine

Margerite [margə'ri:tə] *f* (*BOT*) marguerite

Marienkäfer [ma'ri:ənkɛːfər] *m* ladybird

Marine [ma'ri:nə] *f* navy; **m~blau** *adj* navy blue

marinieren [mari'ni:rən] *vt* to marinate

Marionette [mario'nɛtə] *f* puppet

Mark¹ [mark] **(-, -)** *f* (*Münze*) mark

Mark² [mark] **(-(e)s)** *nt* (*Knochenmark*) marrow; **jdm durch ~ und Bein gehen** to go right through sb

markant [mar'kant] *adj* striking

Marke ['markə] *f* mark; (*Warensorte*) brand; (*Fabrikat*) make; (*Rabatt~, Brief~*) stamp; (*Essen~*) ticket; (*aus Metall etc*) token, disc

Markenartikel *m* proprietary article

markieren [mar'ki:rən] *vt* to mark; (*umg*) to act ♦ *vi* (*umg*) to act it

Markierung *f* marking

Markise [mar'ki:zə] *f* awning

Markstück *nt* one-mark piece

Markt [markt] **(-(e)s, ¨e)** *m* market; **~forschung** *f* market research; **~lücke** *f* (*COMM*) opening, gap in the market; **~platz** *m* market place; **m~üblich** *adj* (*Preise, Mieten*) standard, usual; **~wert** *m* (*COMM*) market value; **~wirtschaft** *f* market economy

Marmelade [marmə'la:də] *f* jam

Marmor ['marmɔr] **(-s, -e)** *m* marble; **m~ieren** [-'ri:rən] *vt* to marble

Marokko [ma'rɔko] **(-s)** *nt* Morocco

Marone [ma'ro:nə] **(-, -n** *od* **Maroni)** *f* chestnut

Marotte [ma'rɔtə] *f* fad, quirk

Marsch¹ [marʃ] **(-, -en)** *f* marsh

Marsch² [marʃ] **(-(e)s, ¨e)** *m* march ♦ *excl* march!; **~befehl** *m* marching orders *pl*; **m~bereit** *adj* ready to move; **m~ieren** [mar'ʃi:rən] *vi* to march

Märtyrer(in) ['mɛrtyrər(ın)] **(-s, -)** *m(f)* martyr

März [mɛrts] **(-(es), -e)** *m* March

Marzipan [martsi'pa:n] **(-s, -e)** *nt* marzipan

Masche ['maʃə] *f* mesh; (*Strickmasche*) stitch; **das ist die neueste ~** that's the

latest thing; **~ndraht** *m* wire mesh;
m~nfest *adj* run-resistant

Maschine [ma'fi:nə] *f* machine; (*Motor*)
engine; (*Schreibmaschine*) typewriter; **~
schreiben** to type; **m~ll** [maʃi'nɛl] *adj*
machine(-); mechanical

Maschinen- *zW:* **~bauer** *m* mechanical
engineer; **~gewehr** *nt* machine gun;
~pistole *f* submachine gun; **~schaden** *m*
mechanical fault; **~schlosser** *m* fitter;
~schrift *f* typescript

Maschinist [maʃi'nɪst] *m* engineer

Maser ['ma:zər] (-, -n) *f* (*von Holz*) grain; **~n**
pl (*MED*) measles *sg*

Maske ['maskə] *f* mask; **~nball** *m* fancy-
dress ball

maskieren [mas'ki:rən] *vt* to mask;
(*verkleiden*) to dress up ♦ *vr* to disguise o.s.;
to dress up

Maskottchen [mas'kɔtçən] *nt* (lucky)
mascot

Maß¹ [ma:s] (-es, -e) *nt* measure;
(*Mäßigung*) moderation; (*Grad*) degree,
extent; **~ halten** to exercise moderation

Maß² [ma:s] (-, -(e)) *f* litre of beer

Massage [ma'sa:ʒə] *f* massage

Maßanzug *m* made-to-measure suit

Maßarbeit *f* (*fig*) neat piece of work

Masse ['masə] *f* mass

Maßeinheit *f* unit of measurement

Massen- *zW:* **~artikel** *m* mass-produced
article; **~grab** *nt* mass grave; **m~haft** *adj*
loads of; **~medien** *pl* mass media *pl*;
~veranstaltung *f* mass meeting;
m~weise *adv* on a large scale

Masseur [ma'sø:r] *m* masseur; **~in** *f*
masseuse

maßgebend *adj* authoritative

maßhalten △ (*unreg*) *vi siehe* **Maß¹**

massieren [ma'si:rən] *vt* to massage; (*MIL*)
to mass

massig ['masɪç] *adj* massive; (*umg*) massive
amount of

mäßig ['mɛ:sɪç] *adj* moderate; **~en**
['mɛ:sɪgən] *vt* to restrain, to moderate;
M~keit *f* moderation

Massiv (-s, -e) *nt* massif

massiv [ma'si:f] *adj* solid; (*fig*) heavy, rough

Maß- *zW:* **~krug** *m* tankard; **m~los** *adj*
extreme; **~nahme** *f* measure, step; **~stab**
m rule, measure; (*fig*) standard; (*GEOG*)
scale; **m~voll** *adj* moderate

Mast [mast] (-(e)s, -e(n)) *m* mast; (*ELEK*)
pylon

mästen ['mɛstən] *vt* to fatten

Material [materi'a:l] (-s, -ien) *nt* material(s);
~fehler *m* material defect; **~ismus** [-
'lɪsmʊs] *m* materialism; **m~istisch** [-'lɪstɪʃ]
adj materialistic

Materie [ma'te:riə] *f* matter, substance

materiell [materi'ɛl] *adj* material

Mathematik [matema'ti:k] *f* mathematics
sg; **~er(in)** [mate'ma:tikər(ɪn)] (-s, -) *m(f)*
mathematician

mathematisch [mate'ma:tɪʃ] *adj*
mathematical

Matjeshering ['matjəshe:rɪŋ] *m* (*KOCH*)
young herring

Matratze [ma'tratsə] *f* mattress

Matrixdrucker ['ma:trɪks-] *m* dot-matrix
printer

Matrose [ma'tro:zə] (-n, -n) *m* sailor

Matsch [matʃ] (-(e)s) *m* mud;
(*Schneematsch*) slush; **m~ig** *adj* muddy;
slushy

matt [mat] *adj* weak; (*glanzlos*) dull; (*PHOT*)
matt; (*SCHACH*) mate

Matte ['matə] *f* mat

Mattscheibe *f* (*TV*) screen

Mauer ['mauər] (-, -n) *f* wall; **m~n** *vi* to
build; to lay bricks ♦ *vt* to build

Maul [maul] (-(e)s, Mäuler) *nt* mouth;
m~en (*umg*) *vi* to grumble; **~esel** *m* mule;
~korb *m* muzzle; **~sperre** *f* lockjaw;
~tasche *f* (*KOCH*) pasta envelopes stuffed
and used in soup; **~tier** *nt* mule; **~wurf** *m*
mole

Maurer ['maurər] (-s, -) *m* bricklayer

Maus [maus] (-, Mäuse) *f* (*auch COMPUT*)
mouse

Mause- ['mauzə] *zW:* **~falle** *f* mousetrap;
m~n *vi* to catch mice ♦ *vt* (*umg*) to pinch;
m~tot *adj* stone dead

Maut- ['maut] *zW:* **~gebühr** *f* toll (charge);

~straße *f* toll road

maximal [maksi'ma:l] *adj* maximum ♦ *adv* at most

Mayonnaise [majɔ'nɛːzə] *f* mayonnaise

Mechan- [me'ça:n] *zW:* **~ik** *f* mechanics *sg;* (*Getriebe*) mechanics *pl;* **~iker (-s, -)** *m* mechanic, engineer; **m~isch** *adj* mechanical; **~ismus** *m* mechanism

meckern ['mɛkərn] *vi* to bleat; (*umg*) to moan

Medaille [me'daljə] *f* medal

Medaillon [medal'jõː] **(-s, -s)** *nt* (*Schmuck*) locket

Medikament [medika'mɛnt] *nt* medicine

Meditation [meditatsi'oːn] *f* meditation

meditieren [medi'tiːrən] *vi* to meditate

Medizin [medi'tsiːn] **(-, -en)** *f* medicine; **m~isch** *adj* medical

Meer [meːr] **(-(e)s, -e)** *nt* sea; **~enge** *f* straits *pl;* **~esfrüchte** *pl* seafood *sg;* **~esspiegel** *m* sea level; **~rettich** *m* horseradish; **~schweinchen** *nt* guinea-pig

Mehl [meːl] **(-(e)s, -e)** *nt* flour; **m~ig** *adj* floury; **~schwitze** *f* (*KOCH*) roux; **~speise** *f* (*KOCH*) flummery

mehr [meːr] *adj, adv* more; **~deutig** *adj* ambiguous; **~ere** *adj* several; **~eres** *pron* several things; **~fach** *adj* multiple; (*wiederholt*) repeated; **M~fahrtenkarte** *f* multi-journey ticket; **M~heit** *f* majority; **~malig** *adj* repeated; **~mals** *adv* repeatedly; **~stimmig** *adj* for several voices; **~stimmig singen** to harmonize; **M~wertsteuer** *f* value added tax; **M~zahl** *f* majority; (*GRAM*) plural

Mehrzweck- *in zW* multipurpose

meiden ['maɪdən] (*unreg*) *vt* to avoid

Meile ['maɪlə] *f* mile; **~nstein** *m* milestone; **m~nweit** *adj* for miles

mein(e) [maɪn] *adj* my; **~e(r, s)** *pron* mine

Meineid ['maɪnʔaɪt] *m* perjury

meinen ['maɪnən] *vi* to think ♦ *vt* to think; (*sagen*) to say; (*sagen wollen*) to mean; **das will ich ~** I should think so

mein- *zW:* **~erseits** *adv* for my part; **~etwegen** *adv* (*für mich*) for my sake; (*wegen mir*) on my account; (*von mir aus*) as

far as I'm concerned; I don't care *od* mind; **~etwillen** *adv:* **um ~etwillen** for my sake, on my account

Meinung ['maɪnʊŋ] *f* opinion; **ganz meine ~** I quite agree; **jdm die ~ sagen** to give sb a piece of one's mind

Meinungs- *zW:* **~austausch** *m* exchange of views; **~umfrage** *f* opinion poll; **~verschiedenheit** *f* difference of opinion

Meise ['maɪzə] *f* tit(mouse)

Meißel ['maɪsəl] **(-s, -)** *m* chisel

meist [maɪst] *adj* most ♦ *adv* mostly; **am ~en** the most; **~ens** *adv* generally, usually

Meister ['maɪstər] **(-s, -)** *m* master; (*SPORT*) champion; **m~haft** *adj* masterly; **m~n** *vt* (*Schwierigkeiten etc*) to overcome, conquer; **~schaft** *f* mastery; (*SPORT*) championship; **~stück** *nt* masterpiece; **~werk** *nt* masterpiece

Melancholie [melaŋko'liː] *f* melancholy; **melancholisch** [melaŋ'koːlɪʃ] *adj* melancholy

Melde- ['mɛldə] *zW:* **~frist** *f* registration period; **m~n** *vt* to report ♦ *vr* to report; (*SCH*) to put one's hand up; (*freiwillig*) to volunteer; (*auf etw, am Telefon*) to answer; **sich m~n bei** to report to; to register with; **sich zu Wort m~n** to ask to speak; **~pflicht** *f* obligation to register with the police; **~schluss** ▲ *m* closing date; **~stelle** *f* registration office

Meldung ['mɛldʊŋ] *f* announcement; (*Bericht*) report

meliert [me'liːrt] *adj* (*Haar*) greying; (*Wolle*) flecked

melken ['mɛlkən] (*unreg*) *vt* to milk

Melodie [melo'diː] *f* melody, tune

melodisch [me'loːdɪʃ] *adj* melodious, tuneful

Melone [me'loːnə] *f* melon; (*Hut*) bowler (hat)

Membran [mɛm'braːn] **(-, -en)** *f* (*TECH*) diaphragm

Memoiren [memo'aːrən] *pl* memoirs

Menge ['mɛŋə] *f* quantity; (*Menschenmenge*) crowd; (*große Anzahl*) lot (of); **m~n** *vt* to mix ♦ *vr:* **sich m~n in** +*akk* to meddle

with; **~nlehre** f (MATH) set theory;
~nrabatt m bulk discount

Mensch [mɛnʃ] (**-en, -en**) m human being,
man; person ♦ excl hey!; **kein ~** nobody

Menschen- zW: **~affe** m (ZOOL) ape;
m~freundlich adj philanthropical;
~kenner m judge of human nature;
m~leer adj deserted; **m~möglich** adj
humanly possible; **~rechte** pl human
rights; **m~unwürdig** adj beneath human
dignity; **~verstand** m: **gesunder
~verstand** common sense

Mensch- zW: **~heit** f humanity, mankind;
m~lich adj human; (human) humane;
~lichkeit f humanity

Menstruation [mɛnstruatsi'oːn] f
menstruation

Mentalität [mɛntali'tɛːt] f mentality

Menü [me'nyː] (**-s, -s**) nt (auch COMPUT)
menu

Merk- ['mɛrk] zW: **~blatt** nt instruction
sheet od leaflet; **m~en** vt to notice; **sich**
dat **etw m~en** to remember sth; **m~lich**
adj noticeable; **~mal** nt sign, characteristic;
m~würdig adj odd

messbar ▲ ['mɛsbaːr] adj measurable

Messbecher ▲ m measuring jug

Messe ['mɛsə] f fair; (ECCL) mass; **~gelände**
nt exhibition centre; **~halle** f pavilion at a
fair

messen (unreg) vt to measure ♦ vr to
compete

Messer (**-s, -**) nt knife; **~spitze** f knife
point; (in Rezept) pinch

Messestand m stall at a fair

Messgerät ▲ nt measuring device, gauge

Messing ['mɛsɪŋ] (**-s**) nt brass

Metall [me'tal] (**-s, -e**) nt metal; **m~isch** adj
metallic

Meter ['meːtər] (**-s, -**) nt od m metre; **~maß**
nt tape measure

Methode [me'toːdə] f method;
methodisch adj methodical

Metropole [metro'poːlə] f metropolis

Metzger ['mɛtsgər] (**-s, -**) m butcher; **~ei**
[-'raɪ] f butcher's (shop)

Meute ['mɔʏtə] f pack; **~'rei** f mutiny;

m~rn vi to mutiny

miauen [mi'auən] vi to miaow

mich [mɪç] (akk von **ich**) pron me; myself

Miene ['miːnə] f look, expression

mies [miːs] (umg) adj lousy

Miet- ['miːt] zW: **~auto** nt hired car; **~e** f
rent; **zur ~e wohnen** to live in rented
accommodation; **m~en** vt to rent; (Auto)
to hire; **~er(in)** (**-s, -**) m(f) tenant; **~shaus**
nt tenement, block of (rented) flats;
~vertrag m lease

Migräne [mi'grɛːnə] f migraine

Mikro- ['mikro] zW: **~fon, ~phon**
[-'foːn] (**-s, -e**) nt microphone; **~skop**
[-'skoːp] (**-s, -e**) nt microscope;
m~skopisch adj microscopic;
~wellenherd m microwave (oven)

Milch [mɪlç] (**-**) f milk; **~glas** nt frosted
glass; **m~ig** adj milky; **~kaffee** m white
coffee; **~mann** (pl **-männer**) m milkman;
~mixgetränk nt (KOCH) milkshake;
~pulver nt powdered milk; **~straße** f
Milky Way; **~zahn** m milk tooth

mild [mɪlt] adj mild; (Richter) lenient;
(freundlich) kind, charitable; **M~e** f
mildness; leniency; **m~ern** vt to mitigate, to
soften; (Schmerz) to alleviate; **~ernde
Umstände** extenuating circumstances

Milieu [mili'øː] (**-s, -s**) nt background,
environment; **m~geschädigt** adj
maladjusted

Mili- [mili] zW: **m~tant** [-'tant] adj militant;
~tär [-'tɛːr] (**-s**) nt military, army;
~'tärgericht nt military court; **m~'tärisch**
adj military

Milli- ['mili] zW: **~ardär** [-ar'dɛːr] m
multimillionaire; **~arde** [-'ardə] f milliard;
billion (BES US); **~meter** m millimetre;
~meterpapier nt graph paper

Million [mili'oːn] (**-, -en**) f million; **~är**
[-o'nɛːr] m millionaire

Milz [mɪlts] (**-, -en**) f spleen

Mimik ['miːmɪk] f mime

Mimose [mi'moːzə] f mimosa; (fig) sensitive
person

minder ['mɪndər] adj inferior ♦ adv less;
M~heit f minority; **~jährig** adj minor;

M~jährige(r) *f(m)* minor; **~n** *vt, vr* to decrease, to diminish; **M~ung** *f* decrease; **~wertig** *adj* inferior; **M~wertigkeitskomplex** *m* inferiority complex

Mindest- ['mɪndəst] *zW:* **~alter** *nt* minimum age; **~betrag** *m* minimum amount; **m~e(r, s)** *adj* least; **zum ~en** *od* **m~en** at least; **m~ens** *adv* at least; **~haltbarkeitsdatum** *nt* best-before date; **~lohn** *m* minimum wage; **~maß** *nt* minimum

Mine ['mi:nə] *f* mine; (*Bleistiftmine*) lead; (*Kugelschreibermine*) refill

Mineral [mine'ra:l] (**-s, -e** *od* **-ien**) *nt* mineral; **m~isch** *adj* mineral; **~wasser** *nt* mineral water

Miniatur [minia'tu:r] *f* miniature

Mini- *zW:* **~golf** ['mɪnɪgɔlf] *nt* miniature golf, crazy golf; **m~mal** [mini'ma:l] *adj* minimal; **~mum** ['mi:nimʊm] *nt* minimum; **~rock** *nt* miniskirt

Minister [mi'nɪstər] (**-s, -**) *m* minister; **m~iell** *adj* ministerial; **~ium** *nt* ministry; **~präsident** *m* prime minister

Minus ['mi:nʊs] (**-, -**) *nt* deficit

minus *adv* minus; **M~zeichen** *nt* minus sign

Minute [mi'nu:tə] *f* minute

Minze ['mɪntsə] *f* mint

mir [mi:r] (*dat von* **ich**) *pron* (to) me; **~ nichts, dir nichts** just like that

Misch- ['mɪʃ] *zW:* **~brot** *nt* bread made from more than one kind of flour; **~ehe** *f* mixed marriage; **m~en** *vt* to mix; **~ling** *m* half-caste; **~ung** *f* mixture

miserabel [mizə'ra:bəl] (*umg*) *adj* (*Essen, Film*) dreadful

Miss- ▲ ['mɪs] *zW:* **~behagen** *nt* discomfort, uneasiness; **~bildung** *f* deformity; **m~'billigen** *vt insep* to disapprove of; **~brauch** *m* abuse; (*falscher Gebrauch*) misuse; **m~'brauchen** *vt insep* to abuse; **jdn zu** *od* **für etw m~brauchen** to use sb for *od* to do sth; **~erfolg** *m* failure; **~fallen** (**-s**) *nt* displeasure; **m~'fallen** (*unreg*) *vi insep*: **jdm m~fallen**

to displease sb; **~geschick** *nt* misfortune; **m~glücken** [mɪs'glʏkən] *vi insep* to fail; **jdm m~glückt etw** sb does not succeed with sth; **~griff** *m* mistake; **~gunst** *f* envy; **m~günstig** *adj* envious; **m~'handeln** *vt insep* to ill-treat; **~'handlung** *f* ill-treatment

Mission [mɪsi'o:n] *f* mission; **~ar(in)** *m(f)* missionary

Miss- ▲ *zW:* **~klang** *m* discord; **~kredit** *m* discredit; **m~lingen** [mɪs'lɪŋən] (*unreg*) *vi insep* to fail; **~mut** *m* sullenness; **m~mutig** *adj* sullen; **m~'raten** (*unreg*) *vi insep* to turn out badly ♦ *adj* ill-bred; **~stand** *m* bad state of affairs; abuse; **m~'trauen** *vi insep* to mistrust; **~trauen** (**-s**) *nt* distrust, suspicion; **~trauensantrag** *m* (*POL*) motion of no confidence; **m~trauisch** *adj* distrustful, suspicious; **~verhältnis** *nt* disproportion; **~verständnis** *nt* misunderstanding; **m~verstehen** (*unreg*) *vt insep* to misunderstand; **~wirtschaft** *f* mismanagement

Mist [mɪst] (**-(e)s**) *m* dung; dirt; (*umg*) rubbish

Mistel (**-, -n**) *f* mistletoe

Misthaufen *m* dungheap

mit [mɪt] *präp +dat* with; (*~tels*) by ♦ *adv* along, too; **~ der Bahn** by train; **~ 10 Jahren** at the age of 10; **wollen Sie ~?** do you want to come along?

Mitarbeit ['mɪtʔarbaɪt] *f* cooperation; **m~en** *vi* to cooperate, to collaborate; **~er(in)** *m(f)* collaborator; co-worker ♦ *pl* (*Personal*) staff

Mit- *zW:* **~bestimmung** *f* participation in decision-making; **m~bringen** (*unreg*) *vt* to bring along

miteinander [mɪtʔaɪ'nandər] *adv* together, with one another

miterleben *vt* to see, to witness

Mitesser ['mɪtʔɛsər] (**-s, -**) *m* blackhead

mitfahr- *zW:* **~en** *vi* to accompany; (*auf Reise auch*) to travel with; **M~gelegenheit** *f* lift; **M~zentrale** *f* agency for arranging lifts

mitfühlend *adj* sympathetic, compassionate

Mit- *zW:* **m~geben** (*unreg*) *vt* to give; **~gefühl** *nt* sympathy; **m~gehen** (*unreg*) *vi* to go/come along; **m~genommen** *adj* done in, in a bad way; **~gift** *f* dowry

Mitglied ['mɪtgliːt] *nt* member; **~sbeitrag** *m* membership fee; **~schaft** *f* membership

Mit- *zW:* **m~halten** (*unreg*) *vi* to keep up; **m~helfen** (*unreg*) *vi* to help; **~hilfe** *f* help, assistance; **m~hören** *vt* to listen in to; **m~kommen** (*unreg*) *vi* to come along; (*verstehen*) to keep up, to follow; **~läufer** *m* hanger-on; (*POL*) fellow traveller

Mitleid *nt* sympathy; (*Erbarmen*) compassion; **m~ig** *adj* sympathetic; **m~slos** *adj* pitiless, merciless

Mit- *zW:* **m~machen** *vt* to join in, to take part in; **~mensch** *m* fellow man; **m~nehmen** (*unreg*) *vt* to take along/away; (*anstrengen*) to wear out, to exhaust; **zum ~nehmen** to take away; **m~reden** *vi:* **bei etw m~reden** to have a say in sth; **m~reißen** (*unreg*) *vt* to carry away/along; (*fig*) to thrill, captivate

mitsamt [mɪt'zamt] *präp +dat* together with

Mitschuld *f* complicity; **m~ig** *adj:* **m~ig (an** +*dat*) implicated (in); (*an Unfall*) partly responsible (for)

Mit- *zW:* **~schüler(in)** *m(f)* schoolmate, **m~spielen** *vi* to join in, to take part; **~spieler(in)** *m(f)* partner

Mittag ['mɪtaːk] (**-(e)s, -e**) *m* midday, lunchtime; (**zu**) **~ essen** to have lunch; **heute/morgen ~** today/tomorrow at lunchtime *od* noon; **~essen** *nt* lunch, dinner

mittags *adv* at lunchtime *od* noon; **M~pause** *f* lunch break; **M~schlaf** *m* early afternoon nap, siesta

Mittäter(in) ['mɪttɛːtar(ɪn)] *m(f)* accomplice

Mitte ['mɪtə] *f* middle; (*POL*) centre; **aus unserer ~** from our midst

mitteilen ['mɪttaɪlən] *vt:* **jdm etw ~** to inform sb of sth, to communicate sth to sb

Mitteilung *f* communication

Mittel ['mɪtəl] (**-s, -**) *nt* means; method; (*MATH*) average; (*MED*) medicine; **ein ~ zum Zweck** a means to an end; **~alter** *nt*

Middle Ages *pl*; **m~alterlich** *adj* mediaeval; **~ding** *nt* cross; **~europa** *nt* Central Europe; **~gebirge** *nt* low mountain range; **m~mäßig** *adj* mediocre, middling; **~mäßigkeit** *f* mediocrity; **~meer** *nt* Mediterranean; **~ohrentzündung** *f* inflammation of the middle ear; **~punkt** *m* centre; **~stand** *m* middle class; **~streifen** *m* central reservation; **~stürmer** *m* centre-forward; **~weg** *m* middle course; **~welle** *f* (*RADIO*) medium wave

mitten ['mɪtən] *adv* in the middle; **~ auf der Straße/in der Nacht** in the middle of the street/night

Mitternacht ['mɪtɐnaxt] *f* midnight

mittlere(r, s) ['mɪtlərə(r, s)] *adj* middle; (*durchschnittlich*) medium, average; **~ Reife** ≃ O-levels

---
mittlere Reife

i The **mittlere Reife** is the standard certificate gained at a **Realschule** or **Gymnasium** on successful completion of 6 years' education there. If a pupil at a **Realschule** attains good results in several subjects he is allowed to enter the 11th class of a **Gymnasium** to study for the **Abitur**.

---

mittlerweile ['mɪtlɐvaɪlə] *adv* meanwhile

Mittwoch ['mɪtvɔx] (**-(e)s, -e**) *m* Wednesday; **m~s** *adv* on Wednesdays

mitunter [mɪt'|ʊntɐ] *adv* occasionally, sometimes

Mit- *zW:* **m~verantwortlich** *adj* jointly responsible; **m~wirken** *vi:* **m~wirken (bei)** to contribute (to); (*THEAT*) to take part (in); **~wirkung** *f* contribution; participation

Mobbing ['mɔbɪŋ] (**-s**) *nt* workplace bullying

Möbel ['møːbəl] *pl* furniture *sg;* **~wagen** *m* furniture *od* removal van

mobil [mo'biːl] *adj* mobile; (*MIL*) mobilized; **M~iar** [mobili'aːr] (**-s, -e**) *nt* furnishings *pl;* **M~machung** *f* mobilization; **M~telefon** *nt* mobile phone

möblieren [mø'bliːrən] *vt* to furnish;

möbliert wohnen to live in furnished accommodation

möchte *etc* ['mœçtə] *vb siehe* **mögen**

Mode ['mo:də] *f* fashion

Modell [mo'dɛl] (**-s, -e**) *nt* model; **m~ieren** [-'li:rən] *vt* to model

Modenschau *f* fashion show

moderig ['mo:dərɪç] *adj* (*Keller*) musty; (*Luft*) stale

modern [mo'dɛrn] *adj* modern; (*modisch*) fashionable; **~i'sieren** *vt* to modernize

Mode- *zW*: **~schau** *f* fashion show; **~schmuck** *m* fashion jewellery; **~schöpfer(in)** *m(f)* fashion designer; **~wort** *nt* fashionable word, buzz word

modisch ['mo:dɪʃ] *adj* fashionable

Mofa ['mo:fa] (**-s, -s**) *nt* small moped

mogeln ['mo:gəln] (*umg*) *vi* to cheat

SCHLÜSSELWORT

---

mögen ['mø:gən] (*pt* **mochte**, *pp* **gemocht** *od* (*als Hilfsverb*) **mögen**) *vt, vi* to like; **magst du/mögen Sie ihn?** do you like him?; **ich möchte ...** I would like ..., I'd like ...; **er möchte in die Stadt** he'd like to go into town; **ich möchte nicht, dass du ...** I wouldn't like you to ...; **ich mag nicht mehr** I've had enough

♦ *Hilfsverb* to like to; (*wollen*) to want; **möchtest du etwas essen?** would you like something to eat?; **sie mag nicht bleiben** she doesn't want to stay; **das mag wohl sein** that may well be; **was mag das heißen?** what might that mean?; **Sie möchten zu Hause anrufen** could you please call home?

---

möglich ['mø:klɪç] *adj* possible; **~erweise** *adv* possibly; **M~keit** *f* possibility; **nach M~keit** if possible; **~st** *adv* as ... as possible

Mohn [mo:n] (**-(e)s, -e**) *m* (*~blume*) poppy; (*~samen*) poppy seed

Möhre ['mø:rə] *f* carrot

Mohrrübe ['mo:rry:bə] *f* carrot

mokieren [mo'ki:rən] *vr*: **sich ~ über** +*akk* to make fun of

Mole ['mo:lə] *f* (*harbour*) mole

Molekül [mole'ky:l] (**-s, -e**) *nt* molecule

Molkerei [mɔlkə'rai] *f* dairy

Moll [mɔl] (**-, -**) *nt* (*MUS*) minor (key)

mollig *adj* cosy; (*dicklich*) plump

Moment [mo'mɛnt] (**-(e)s, -e**) *m* moment ♦ *nt* factor; **im ~** at the moment; **~ (mal)!** just a moment; **m~an** [-'ta:n] *adj* momentary ♦ *adv* at the moment

Monarch [mo'narç] (**-en, -en**) *m* monarch; **~ie** [monar'çi:] *f* monarchy

Monat ['mo:nat] (**-(e)s, -e**) *m* month; **m~elang** *adv* for months; **m~lich** *adj* monthly

Monats- *zW*: **~gehalt** *nt*: **das dreizehnte ~gehalt** Christmas bonus (*of one month's salary*); **~karte** *f* monthly ticket

Mönch [mœnç] (**-(e)s, -e**) *m* monk

Mond [mo:nt] (**-(e)s, -e**) *m* moon; **~finsternis** *f* eclipse of the moon; **m~hell** *adj* moonlit; **~landung** *f* moon landing; **~schein** *m* moonlight

Mono- [mono] *in zW* mono; **~log** [-'lo:k] (**-s, -e**) *m* monologue; **~pol** [-'po:l] (**-s, -e**) *nt* monopoly; **m~polisieren** [-poli'zi:rən] *vt* to monopolize; **m~ton** [-'to:n] *adj* monotonous; **~tonie** [-to'ni:] *f* monotony

Montag ['mo:nta:k] (**-(e)s, -e**) *m* Monday

Montage [mɔn'ta:ʒə] *f* (*PHOT etc*) montage; (*TECH*) assembly; (*Einbauen*) fitting

Monteur [mɔn'tø:r] *m* fitter

montieren [mɔn'ti:rən] *vt* to assemble

Monument [monu'mɛnt] *nt* monument; **m~al** [-'ta:l] *adj* monumental

Moor [mo:r] (**-(e)s, -e**) *nt* moor

Moos [mo:s] (**-es, -e**) *nt* moss

Moped ['mo:pet] (**-s, -s**) *nt* moped

Moral [mo'ra:l] (**-, -en**) *f* morality; (*einer Geschichte*) moral; **m~isch** *adj* moral

Morast [mo'rast] (**-(e)s, -e**) *m* morass, mire; **m~ig** *adj* boggy

Mord [mɔrt] (**-(e)s, -e**) *m* murder; **~anschlag** *m* murder attempt

Mörder(in) ['mœrdər(ɪn)] (**-s, -**) *m(f)* murderer (murderess)

mörderisch *adj* (*fig: schrecklich*) terrible, dreadful ♦ *adv* (*umg: entsetzlich*) terribly, dreadfully

---

Rechtschreibreform: ▲ *neue Schreibung* △ *alte Schreibung (auslaufend)*

Mord- *zW:* **~kommission** *f* murder squad; **~glück** (*umg*) *nt* amazing luck; **m~smäßig** (*umg*) *adj* terrific, enormous; **~verdacht** *m* suspicion of murder; **~waffe** *f* murder weapon

morgen ['mɔrgən] *adv* tomorrow; **~ früh** tomorrow morning; **M~** (**-s, -**) *m* morning; **M~mantel** *m* dressing gown; **M~rock** *m* dressing gown; **M~röte** *f* dawn; **~s** *adv* in the morning

morgig ['mɔrgɪç] *adj* tomorrow's; **der ~e Tag** tomorrow

Morphium ['mɔrfiʊm] *nt* morphine

morsch [mɔrʃ] *adj* rotten

Morsealphabet ['mɔrzəalfabeːt] *nt* Morse code

morsen *vi* to send a message by Morse code

Mörtel ['mœrtəl] (**-s, -**) *m* mortar

Mosaik [moza'iːk] (**-s, -en** *od* **-e**) *nt* mosaic

Moschee [mɔ'ʃeː] (**-, -n**) *f* mosque

Moskito [mɔs'kiːto] (**-s, -s**) *m* mosquito

Most [mɔst] (**-(e)s, -e**) *m* (unfermented) fruit juice; (*Apfelwein*) cider

Motel [mo'tel] (**-s, -s**) *nt* motel

Motiv [mo'tiːf] (**-s, -e**) *nt* motive; (*MUS*) theme; **~ation** [-vatsi'oːn] *f* motivation; **m~ieren** [moti'viːrən] *vt* to motivate

Motor ['moːtɔr, *pl* mo'toːrən] (**-s, -en**) *m* engine; (*bes ELEK*) motor; **~boot** *nt* motorboat; **~haube** *f* (*von Auto*) bonnet (*BRIT*), hood (*US*); **m~isieren** *vt* to motorize; **~öl** *nt* engine oil; **~rad** *nt* motorcycle; **~roller** *m* (motor) scooter; **~schaden** *m* engine trouble *od* failure

Motte ['mɔtə] *f* moth; **~nkugel** *f* mothball(s)

Motto ['mɔto] (**-s, -s**) *nt* motto

Möwe ['møːvə] *f* seagull

Mücke ['mʏkə] *f* midge, gnat; **~nstich** *m* midge *od* gnat bite

müde ['myːdə] *adj* tired

Müdigkeit ['myːdɪçkaɪt] *f* tiredness

Muffel (**-s, -**) (*umg*) *m* killjoy, sourpuss

muffig *adj* (*Luft*) musty

Mühe ['myːə] *f* trouble, pains *pl*; **mit Müh und Not** with great difficulty; **sich** *dat* **~**

geben to go to a lot of trouble; **m~los** *adj* without trouble, easy; **m~voll** *adj* laborious, arduous

Mühle ['myːlə] *f* mill; (*Kaffeemühle*) grinder

Müh- *zW:* **~sal** (**-, -e**) *f* tribulation; **m~sam** *adj* arduous, troublesome; **m~selig** *adj* arduous, laborious

Mulde ['mʊldə] *f* hollow, depression

Mull [mʊl] (**-(e)s, -e**) *m* thin muslin

Müll [mʏl] (**-(e)s**) *m* refuse; **~abfuhr** *f* rubbish disposal; (*Leute*) dustmen *pl*; **~abladeplatz** *m* rubbish dump; **~binde** *f* gauze bandage; **~eimer** *m* dustbin, garbage can (*US*); **~haufen** *m* rubbish heap; **~schlucker** (**-s, -**) *m* garbage disposal unit; **~tonne** *f* dustbin; **~verbrennungsanlage** *f* incinerator

mulmig ['mʊlmɪç] *adj* rotten; (*umg*) dodgy; **jdm ist ~** sb feels funny

multiplizieren [mʊltipli'tsiːrən] *vt* to multiply

Mumie ['muːmiə] *f* mummy

Mumm [mʊm] (**-s**) (*umg*) *m* gumption, nerve

Mumps [mʊmps] (**-**) *m od f* (*MED*) mumps

München ['mʏnçən] (**-s**) *nt* Munich

Mund [mʊnt] (**-(e)s, ⁻er**) *m* mouth; **~art** *f* dialect

münden ['mʏndən] *vi:* **~ in** +*akk* to flow into

Mund- *zW:* **m~faul** *adj* taciturn; **~geruch** *m* bad breath; **~harmonika** *f* mouth organ

mündig ['mʏndɪç] *adj* of age; **M~keit** *f* majority

mündlich ['mʏntlɪç] *adj* oral

Mundstück *nt* mouthpiece; (*Zigarettenmundstück*) tip

Mündung ['mʏndʊŋ] *f* (*von Fluss*) mouth; (*Gewehr*) muzzle

Mund- *zW:* **~wasser** *nt* mouthwash; **~werk** *nt:* **ein großes ~werk haben** to have a big mouth; **~winkel** *m* corner of the mouth

Munition [munitsi'oːn] *f* ammunition; **~slager** *nt* ammunition dump

munkeln ['mʊŋkəln] *vi* to whisper, to

mutter

Münster ['mʏnstər] (**-s, -**) *nt* minster

munter ['mʊntər] *adj* lively

Münze ['mʏntsə] *f* coin; **m~n** *vt* to coin, to mint; **auf jdn gemünzt sein** to be aimed at sb

Münzfernsprecher ['mʏntsfɛrnʃprɛçər] *m* callbox (*BRIT*), pay phone

mürb(e) ['mʏrb(ə)] *adj* (*Gestein*) crumbly; (*Holz*) rotten; (*Gebäck*) crisp; **jdn ~ machen** to wear sb down; **M~eteig** ['mʏrbətaɪç] *m* shortcrust pastry

murmeln ['mʊrməln] *vt, vi* to murmur, to mutter

murren ['mʊrən] *vi* to grumble, to grouse

mürrisch ['mʏrɪʃ] *adj* sullen

Mus [muːs] (**-es, -e**) *nt* purée

Muschel ['mʊʃəl] (**-, -n**) *f* mussel; (*~schale*) shell; (*Telefonmuschel*) receiver

Muse ['muːzə] *f* muse

Museum [mu'zeːʊm] (**-s, Museen**) *nt* museum

Musik [mu'ziːk] *f* music; (*Kapelle*) band; **m~alisch** [-kaːlɪʃ] *adj* musical; **~ant(in)** [-'kant(ɪn)] (**-en, -en**) *m(f)* musician; **~box** *f* jukebox; **~er (-s, -)** *m* musician; **~hochschule** *f* college of music; **~instrument** *nt* musical instrument

musisch ['muːzɪʃ] *adj* (*Mensch*) artistic

musizieren [muzi'tsiːrən] *vi* to make music

Muskat [mʊs'kaːt] (**-(e)s, -e**) *m* nutmeg

Muskel ['mʊskəl] (**-s, -n**) *m* muscle; **~kater** *m*: **~kater haben** to be stiff

Muskulatur [mʊskula'tuːr] *f* muscular system

muskulös [mʊsku'løːs] *adj* muscular

Müsli ['myːsli] (**-s, -**) *nt* (*KOCH*) muesli

Muss ▲ [mʊs] (**-**) *nt* necessity, must

Muße ['muːsə] (**-**) *f* leisure

⎡ *SCHLÜSSELWORT* ⎤

müssen ['mʏsən] (*pt* **musste**, *pp* **gemusst** *od* (*als Hilfsverb*) **müssen**) *vi* 1 (*Zwang*) must (*nur im Präsens*), to have to; **ich muss es tun** I must do it, I have to do it; **ich musste es tun** I had to do it; **er muss es**

nicht tun he doesn't have to do it; **muss ich?** must I?, do I have to?; **wann müsst ihr zur Schule?** when do you have to go to school?; **er hat gehen müssen** he (has) had to go; **muss das sein?** is that really necessary?; **ich muss mal** (*umg*) I need the toilet

2 (*sollen*): **das musst du nicht tun!** you oughtn't to *od* shouldn't do that; **Sie hätten ihn fragen müssen** you should have asked him

3: **es muss geregnet haben** it must have rained; **es muss nicht wahr sein** it needn't be true

---

müßig ['myːsɪç] *adj* idle

Muster ['mʊstər] (**-s, -**) *nt* model; (*Dessin*) pattern; (*Probe*) sample; **m~gültig** *adj* exemplary; **m~n** *vt* (*Tapete*) to pattern; (*fig, MIL*) to examine; (*Truppen*) to inspect; **~ung** *f* (*von Stoff*) pattern; (*MIL*) inspection

Mut [muːt] *m* courage; **nur ~!** cheer up!; **jdm ~ machen** to encourage sb; **m~ig** *adj* courageous; **m~los** *adj* discouraged, despondent

mutmaßlich ['muːtmaːslɪç] *adj* presumed ♦ *adv* probably

Mutprobe *f* test *od* trial of courage

Mutter[1] ['mʊtər] (**-, ̈-**) *f* mother

Mutter[2] ['mʊtər] (**-, -n**) *f* (*Schraubenmutter*) nut

mütterlich ['mʏtərlɪç] *adj* motherly; **~erseits** *adv* on the mother's side

Mutter- *zW*: **~liebe** *f* motherly love; **~mal** *nt* birthmark; **~milch** *f* mother's milk; **~schaft** *f* motherhood, maternity; **~schutz** *m* maternity regulations; '**~'seelena|llein** *adj* all alone; **~sprache** *f* native language; **~tag** *m* Mother's Day

Mutti ['mʊti] (**-, -s**) *f* mum(my) (*BRIT*), mom(my) (*US*)

mutwillig ['muːtvɪlɪç] *adj* malicious, deliberate

Mütze ['mʏtsə] *f* cap

MwSt *abk* (= *Mehrwertsteuer*) VAT

mysteriös [mʏsteri'øːs] *adj* mysterious

Mythos ['myːtɔs] (**-, Mythen**) *m* myth

Rechtschreibreform: ▲ *neue Schreibung* △ *alte Schreibung (auslaufend)*

N, n

na [na] *excl* well; **~ gut** okay then
Nabel ['naːbəl] **(-s, -)** *m* navel; **~schnur** *f* umbilical cord

---
SCHLÜSSELWORT
---

nach [naːx] *präp +dat* **1** (*örtlich*) to; **nach Berlin** to Berlin; **nach links/rechts** (to the) left/right; **nach oben/hinten** up/back
2 (*zeitlich*) after; **einer nach dem anderen** one after the other; **nach Ihnen!** after you!; **zehn (Minuten) nach drei** ten (minutes) past three
3 (*gemäß*) according to; **nach dem Gesetz** according to the law; **dem Namen nach** judging by his/her name; **nach allem, was ich weiß** as far as I know

♦ *adv*: **ihm nach!** after him!; **nach und nach** gradually, little by little; **nach wie vor** still

---

nachahmen ['naːxʔaːmən] *vt* to imitate
Nachbar(in) ['naxbaːr(ɪn)] **(-s, -n)** *m(f)* neighbour; **~haus** *nt* im **~haus** next door; **n~lich** *adj* neighbourly; **~schaft** *f* neighbourhood; **~staat** *m* neighbouring state
nach- *zW*: **~bestellen** *vt*: **50 Stück ~bestellen** to order another 50; **N~bestellung** *f* (*COMM*) repeat order; **N~bildung** *f* imitation, copy; **~blicken** *vi* to gaze after; **~datieren** *vt* to postdate
nachdem [naːxˈdeːm] *konj* after; (*weil*) since; **je ~ (ob)** it depends (whether)
nachdenken (*unreg*) *vi*: **~ über** +*akk* to think about; **N~ (-s)** *nt* reflection, meditation
nachdenklich *adj* thoughtful, pensive
Nachdruck ['naːxdrʊk] *m* emphasis; (*TYP*) reprint, reproduction
nachdrücklich ['naːxdrʏklɪç] *adj* emphatic
nacheinander [naːxʔaɪˈnandər] *adv* one after the other
nachempfinden ['naːxʔɛmpfɪndən] (*unreg*)

vt: **jdm etw ~** to feel sth with sb
Nacherzählung ['naːxʔɛrtseːlʊŋ] *f* reproduction (of a story)
Nachfahr ['naːxfaːr] **(-s, -en)** *m* descendant
Nachfolge ['naːxfɔlgə] *f* succession; **n~n** *vi* +*dat* to follow; **~r(in) (-s, -)** *m(f)* successor
nachforschen *vt, vi* to investigate
Nachforschung *f* investigation
Nachfrage ['naːxfraːgə] *f* inquiry; (*COMM*) demand; **n~n** *vi* to inquire
nach- *zW*: **~füllen** *vt* to refill; **~geben** (*unreg*) *vi* to give way, to yield; **N~gebühr** *f* (*POST*) excess postage
nachgehen ['naːxgeːən] (*unreg*) *vi* (+*dat*) to follow; (*erforschen*) to inquire (into); (*Uhr*) to be slow
Nachgeschmack ['naːxgəʃmak] *m* aftertaste
nachgiebig ['naːxgiːbɪç] *adj* soft, accommodating; **N~keit** *f* softness
nachhaltig ['naːxhaltɪç] *adj* lasting; (*Widerstand*) persistent
nachhause *adv* (*österreichisch, schweizerisch*) home
nachhelfen ['naːxhɛlfən] (*unreg*) *vi* +*dat* to assist, to help
nachher [naxˈheːr] *adv* afterwards
Nachhilfeunterricht ['naːxhɪlfəʔʊntərrɪçt] *m* extra tuition
nachholen ['naːxhoːlən] *vt* to catch up with; (*Versäumtes*) to make up for
Nachkomme ['naːxkɔmə] **(-, -n)** *m* descendant
nachkommen (*unreg*) *vi* to follow; (*einer Verpflichtung*) to fulfil; **N~schaft** *f* descendants *pl*
Nachkriegszeit *f* postwar period
Nach- *zW*: **~lass** ▲ **(-es, -lässe)** *m* (*COMM*) discount, rebate; (*Erbe*) estate; **n~lassen** (*unreg*) *vt* (*Strafe*) to remit; (*Summe*) to take off; (*Schulden*) to cancel ♦ *vi* to decrease, to ease off; (*Sturm*) to die down, to ease off; (*schlechter werden*) to deteriorate; **er hat n~gelassen** he has got worse; **n~lässig** *adj* negligent, careless
nachlaufen ['naːxlaʊfən] (*unreg*) *vi* +*dat* to run after, to chase

nachlösen ['naːxløːzən] *vi* (*Zuschlag*) to pay on the train, pay at the other end; (*zur Weiterfahrt*) to pay the supplement

nachmachen ['naːxmaxən] *vt* to imitate, to copy; (*fälschen*) to counterfeit

Nachmittag ['naːxmɪtaːk] *m* afternoon; **am ~** in the afternoon; **n~s** *adv* in the afternoon

Nach- *zW:* **~nahme** *f* cash on delivery; **per ~nahme** C.O.D.; **~name** *m* surname; **~porto** *nt* excess postage

nachprüfen ['naːxpryːfən] *vt* to check, to verify

nachrechnen ['naːxrɛçnən] *vt* to check

nachreichen ['naːxraɪçən] *vt* (*Unterlagen*) to hand in later

Nachricht ['naːxrɪçt] (**-, -en**) *f* (piece of) news; (*Mitteilung*) message; **~en** *pl* (*Neuigkeiten*) news

Nachrichten- *zW:* **~agentur** *f* news agency; **~dienst** *m* (MIL) intelligence service; **~sprecher(in)** *m(f)* newsreader; **~technik** *f* telecommunications *sg*

Nachruf ['naːxruːf] *m* obituary

nachsagen ['naːxzaːgən] *vt* to repeat; **jdm etw ~** to say sth of sb

Nachsaison ['naːxzɛzõ] *f* off-season

nachschicken ['naːxʃɪkən] *vt* to forward

nachschlagen ['naːxʃlaːgən] (*unreg*) *vt* to look up

Nachschlagewerk *nt* reference book

Nachschlüssel *m* duplicate key

Nachschub ['naːxʃuːp] *m* supplies *pl*; (*Truppen*) reinforcements *pl*

nachsehen ['naːxzeːən] (*unreg*) *vt* (*prüfen*) to check ♦ *vi* (*erforschen*) to look and see; **jdm etw ~** to forgive sb sth; **das N~ haben** to come off worst

Nachsendeantrag *m* application to have one's mail forwarded

nachsenden ['naːxzɛndən] (*unreg*) *vt* to send on, to forward

nachsichtig *adj* indulgent, lenient

nachsitzen ['naːxzɪtsən] (*unreg*) *vi:* **~ (müssen)** (SCH) to be kept in

Nachspeise ['naːxʃpaɪzə] *f* dessert, sweet, pudding

Nachspiel ['naːxʃpiːl] *nt* epilogue; (*fig*) sequel

nachsprechen ['naːxʃprɛçən] (*unreg*) *vt:* **(jdm) ~** to repeat (after sb)

nächst [nɛːçst] *präp +dat* (*räumlich*) next to; (*außer*) apart from; **~beste(r, s)** *adj* first that comes along; (*zweitbeste*) next best; **N~e(r)** *f(m)* neighbour; **~e(r, s)** *adj* next; (*~gelegen*) nearest

nachstellen ['naːxʃtɛlən] *vt* (TECH: *neu einstellen*) to adjust

nächst *zW:* **N~enliebe** *f* love for one's fellow men; **~ens** *adv* shortly, soon; **~liegend** *adj* nearest; (*fig*) obvious; **~möglich** *adj* next possible

Nacht [naxt] (**-, ⸚e**) *f* night; **~dienst** *m* night shift

Nachteil ['naːxtaɪl] *m* disadvantage; **n~ig** *adj* disadvantageous

Nachthemd *nt* (*Herrennachthemd*) nightshirt; (*Damennachthemd*) nightdress

Nachtigall ['naxtɪgal] (**-, -en**) *f* nightingale

Nachtisch ['naːxtɪʃ] *m* = **Nachspeise**

Nachtklub *m* night club

Nachtleben *nt* nightlife

nächtlich ['nɛçtlɪç] *adj* nightly

Nachtlokal *nt* night club

Nach- *zW:* **~trag** (**-(e)s, -träge**) *m* supplement; **n~tragen** (*unreg*) *vt* to carry; (*zufügen*) to add; **jdm etw n~tragen** to hold sth against sb; **n~träglich** *adj* later, subsequent; additional ♦ *adv* later, subsequently; additionally; **n~trauern** *vi:* **jdm/etw n~trauern** to mourn the loss of sb/sth

Nacht- *zW:* **n~s** *adv* at *od* by night; **~schicht** *f* nightshift; **~schwester** *f* night nurse; **~tarif** *m* off-peak tariff; **~tisch** *m* bedside table; **~wächter** *m* night watchman

Nach- *zW:* **~untersuchung** *f* checkup; **n~wachsen** (*unreg*) *vi* to grow again; **~wahl** *f* (POL) ≈ by-election

Nachweis ['naːxvaɪs] (**-es, -e**) *m* proof; **n~bar** *adj* provable, demonstrable; **n~en** (*unreg*) *vt* to prove; **jdm etw n~en** to point sth out to sb; **n~lich** *adj* evident, demonstrable

nach- *zW:* **~wirken** *vi* to have after-effects; **N~wirkung** *f* aftereffect; **N~wort** *nt* epilogue; **N~wuchs** *m* offspring; (*beruflich etc*) new recruits *pl*; **~zahlen** *vt, vi* to pay extra; **N~zahlung** *f* additional payment; (*zurückdatiert*) back pay; **~ziehen** (*unreg*) *vt* (*hinter sich herziehen: Bein*) to drag; **N~zügler** **(-s, -)** *m* straggler

Nacken ['nakən] **(-s, -)** *m* nape of the neck

nackt [nakt] *adj* naked; (*Tatsachen*) plain, bare; **N~badestrand** *m* nudist beach; **N~heit** *f* nakedness

Nadel ['na:dəl] **(-, -n)** *f* needle; (*Stecknadel*) pin; **~öhr** *nt* eye of a needle; **~wald** *m* coniferous forest

Nagel ['na:gəl] **(-s, ")** *m* nail, **~bürste** *f* nailbrush; **~feile** *f* nailfile; **~lack** *m* nail varnish *od* polish (*BRIT*); **n~n** *vt, vi* to nail; **n~neu** *adj* brand-new; **~schere** *f* nail scissors *pl*

nagen ['na:gən] *vt, vi* to gnaw

Nagetier ['na:gəti:r] *nt* rodent

nah(e) ['na:(ə)] *adj* (*räumlich*) near(by); (*Verwandte*) near; (*Freunde*) close; (*zeitlich*) near, close ♦ *adv* near(by); near, close; (*verwandt*) closely ♦ *präp (+dat)* near (to), close to; **der Nahe Osten** the Near East; **~ gehen** (*+dat*) to grieve; **~ kommen** (*+dat*) to get close (to); **jdm etw ~ legen** to suggest sth to sb; **~ liegen** to be obvious; **~ liegend** obvious; **~ stehen** (*+dat*) to be close (to); **einer Sache ~ stehen** to sympathize with sth; **~ stehend** close; **jdm (zu) ~ treten** to offend sb

Nahaufnahme *f* close-up

Nähe ['nɛ:ə] **(-)** *f* nearness, proximity; (*Umgebung*) vicinity; **in der ~** close by; at hand; **aus der ~** from close to

nah(e)bei *adv* nearby

nahen *vi, vr* to approach, to draw near

nähen ['nɛ:ən] *vt, vi* to sew

näher *adj, adv* nearer; (*Erklärung, Erkundigung*) more detailed; **(sich) ~ kommen** to get closer; **N~e(s)** *nt* details *pl*, particulars *pl*

Naherholungsgebiet *nt* recreational area

nähern *vr* to approach

nahezu *adv* nearly

Nähgarn *nt* thread

Nahkampf *m* hand-to-hand fighting

Nähkasten *m* sewing basket, workbox

nahm *etc* [na:m] *vb siehe* **nehmen**

Nähmaschine *f* sewing machine

Nähnadel *f* needle

nähren ['nɛ:rən] *vt* to feed ♦ *vr* (*Person*) to feed o.s.; (*Tier*) to feed

nahrhaft ['na:rhaft] *adj* nourishing, nutritious

Nahrung ['na:ruŋ] *f* food; (*fig auch*) sustenance

Nahrungs- *zW:* **~mittel** *nt* foodstuffs *pl*; **~mittelindustrie** *f* food industry; **~suche** *f* search for food

Nährwert *m* nutritional value

Naht [na:t] **(-, "e)** *f* seam; (*MED*) suture; (*TECH*) join; **n~los** *adj* seamless; **n~los ineinander übergehen** to follow without a gap

Nah- *zW:* **~verkehr** *m* local traffic; **~verkehrszug** *m* local train; **~ziel** *nt* immediate objective

Name ['na:mə] **(-ns, -n)** *m* name; **im ~n von** on behalf of; **n~ns** *adv* by the name of; **~nstag** *m* name day, saint's day; **n~ntlich** *adj* by name ♦ *adv* particularly, especially

---

Namenstag

i In Catholic areas of Germany the **Namenstag** is often a more important celebration than a birthday. This is the day dedicated to the saint after whom a person is called, and on that day the person receives presents and invites relatives and friends round to celebrate.

---

namhaft ['na:mhaft] *adj* (*berühmt*) famed, renowned; (*beträchtlich*) considerable; **~ machen** to name

nämlich ['nɛ:mlɪç] *adv* that is to say, namely; (*denn*) since

nannte *etc* ['nantə] *vb siehe* **nennen**

Napf [napf] **(-(e)s, "e)** *m* bowl, dish

Narbe ['narbə] *f* scar; **narbig** *adj* scarred

Narkose [nar'ko:zə] *f* anaesthetic

Narr [nar] (**-en, -en**) *m* fool; **n~en** *vt* to fool; **Närrin** ['nɛrɪn] *f* fool; **närrisch** *adj* foolish, crazy

Narzisse [nar'tsɪsə] *f* narcissus; daffodil

naschen ['naʃən] *vt, vi* to nibble; (*heimlich kosten*) to pinch a bit

naschhaft *adj* sweet-toothed

Nase ['na:zə] *f* nose

Nasen- *zW:* **~bluten** (**-s**) *nt* nosebleed; **~loch** *nt* nostril; **~tropfen** *pl* nose drops

naseweis *adj* pert, cheeky; (*neugierig*) nosey

Nashorn ['na:shɔrn] *nt* rhinoceros

nass ▲ [nas] *adj* wet

Nässe ['nɛsə] (**-**) *f* wetness; **n~n** *vt* to wet

nasskalt ▲ *adj* wet and cold

Nassrasur ▲ *f* wet shave

Nation [natsi'o:n] *f* nation

national [natsio'na:l] *adj* national; **N~feiertag** *m* national holiday; **N~hymne** *f* national anthem; **~isieren** [-i'zi:rən] *vt* to nationalize; **N~ismus** [-'lɪsmʊs] *m* nationalism; **~istisch** [-'lɪstɪʃ] *adj* nationalistic; **N~ität** *f* nationality; **N~mannschaft** *f* national team; **N~sozialismus** *m* national socialism

Natron ['na:trɔn] (**-s**) *nt* soda

Natter ['natər] (**-, -n**) *f* adder

Natur [na'tu:r] *f* nature; (*körperlich*) constitution; **~ell** (**-es, -e**) *nt* disposition; **~erscheinung** *f* natural phenomenon *od* event; **n~farben** *adj* natural coloured; **n~gemäß** *adj* natural; **~gesetz** *nt* law of nature; **n~getreu** *adj* true to life; **~katastrophe** *f* natural disaster

natürlich [na'ty:rlɪç] *adj* natural ♦ *adv* naturally; **ja, ~!** yes, of course; **N~keit** *f* naturalness

Natur- *zW:* **~park** *m* ≈ national park; **~produkt** *nt* natural product; **n~rein** *adj* natural, pure; **~schutz** *m* nature conservation; **unter ~schutz stehen** to be legally protected; **~schutzgebiet** *nt* nature reserve; **~wissenschaft** *f* natural science; **~wissenschaftler(in)** *m(f)*

scientist

nautisch ['nautɪʃ] *adj* nautical

Nazi ['na:tsi] (**-s, -s**) *m* Nazi

NB *abk* (= *nota bene*) nb

n. Chr. *abk* (= *nach Christus*) A.D.

Nebel ['ne:bəl] (**-s, -**) *m* fog, mist; **n~ig** *adj* foggy, misty; **~scheinwerfer** *m* fog lamp

neben ['ne:bən] *präp* (*+akk od dat*) next to; (*+dat*: *außer*) apart from, besides; **~an** [ne:bən'an] *adv* next door; **N~anschluss** ▲ *m* (*TEL*) extension; **N~ausgang** *m* side exit; **~bei** [ne:bən'bai] *adv* at the same time; (*außerdem*) additionally; (*beiläufig*) incidentally; **N~beruf** *m* second job; **N~beschäftigung** *f* second job; **N~buhler(in)** (**-s, -**) *m(f)* rival; **~einander** [ne:bən|ai'nandər] *adv* side by side; **~einander legen** to put next to each other; **N~eingang** *m* side entrance; **N~fach** *nt* subsidiary subject; **N~fluss** ▲ *m* tributary; **N~gebäude** *nt* annexe; **N~geräusch** *nt* (*RADIO*) atmospherics *pl*, interference; **~her** [ne:bən'he:r] *adv* (*zusätzlich*) besides; (*gleichzeitig*) at the same time; (*daneben*) alongside; **N~kosten** *pl* extra charges, extras; **N~produkt** *nt* by-product; **N~sache** *f* trifle, side issue; **~sächlich** *adj* minor, peripheral; **N~saison** *f* low season; **N~straße** *f* side street; **N~verdienst** *m* secondary income; **N~wirkung** *f* side effect; **N~zimmer** *nt* adjoining room

neblig ['ne:blɪç] *adj* foggy, misty

Necessaire [nese'sɛ:r] (**-s, -s**) *nt* (*Nähnecessaire*) needlework box; (*Nagelnecessaire*) manicure case

necken ['nɛkən] *vt* to tease

Neckerei [nɛkə'rai] *f* teasing

Neffe ['nɛfə] (**-n, -n**) *m* nephew

negativ ['ne:gati:f] *adj* negative; **N~** (**-s, -e**) *nt* (*PHOT*) negative

Neger ['ne:gər] (**-s, -**) *m* negro; **~in** *f* negress

nehmen ['ne:mən] (*unreg*) *vt* to take; **jdn zu sich ~** to take sb in; **sich ernst ~** to take o.s. seriously; **nimm dir doch bitte** please help yourself

Neid [naɪt] (-(e)s) m envy; **~er** (-s, -) m envier; **n~isch** ['naɪdɪʃ] adj envious, jealous

neigen ['naɪgən] vt to incline, to lean; (Kopf) to bow ♦ vi: **zu etw ~** to tend to sth

Neigung f (des Geländes) slope; (Tendenz) tendency, inclination; (Vorliebe) liking; (Zuneigung) affection

nein [naɪn] adv no

Nektarine [nɛkta'riːnə] f (Frucht) nectarine

Nelke ['nɛlkə] f carnation, pink; (Gewürz) clove

Nenn- ['nɛn] zW: **n~en** (unreg) vt to name; (mit Namen) to call; **wie n~t man ...?** what do you call ...?; **n~enswert** adj worth mentioning; **~er** (-s, -) m denominator; **~wert** m nominal value; (COMM) par

Neon ['neːɔn] (-s) nt neon; **~licht** nt neon light; **~röhre** f neon tube

Nerv [nɛrf] (-s, -en) m nerve; **jdm auf die ~en gehen** to get on sb's nerves; **n~enaufreibend** adj nerve-racking, **~enbündel** nt bundle of nerves; **~enheilanstalt** f mental home; **n~enkrank** adj mentally ill; **~ensäge** (umg) f pain (in the neck) (umg); **~ensystem** nt nervous system; **~enzusammenbruch** m nervous breakdown, **n~lich** adj (Belastung) affecting the nerves; **n~ös** [nɛr'vøːs] adj nervous; **~osität** f nervousness; **n~tötend** adj nerve-racking; (Arbeit) soul-destroying

Nerz [nɛrts] (-es, -e) m mink

Nessel ['nɛsəl] (-, -n) f nettle

Nessessär ▲ [nesɛ'sɛːr] (-s, -s) nt = **Necessaire**

Nest [nɛst] (-(e)s, -er) nt nest; (umg: Ort) dump

nett [nɛt] adj nice; (freundlich) nice, kind; **~erweise** adv kindly

netto ['nɛtoː] adv net

Netz [nɛts] (-es, -e) nt net; (Gepäcknetz) rack; (Einkaufsnetz) string bag; (Spinnennetz) web; (System) network; **jdm ins ~ gehen** (fig) to fall into sb's trap; **~anschluss** ▲ m mains connection

Netzhaut f retina

neu [nɔy] adj new; (Sprache, Geschichte) modern; **seit ~estem** (since) recently; **die ~esten Nachrichten** the latest news; **~ schreiben** to rewrite, to write again; **N~anschaffung** f new purchase od acquisition; **~artig** adj new kind of; **N~bau** m new building; **N~e(r)** f(m) the new man/woman; **~erdings** adv (kürzlich) (since) recently; (von ~em) again; **N~erscheinung** f (Buch) new publication; (Schallplatte) new release; **N~erung** f innovation, new departure; **N~gier** f curiosity; **~gierig** adj curious; **N~heit** f newness; novelty; **N~igkeit** f news sg; **N~jahr** nt New Year; **~lich** adv recently, the other day; **N~ling** m novice, **N~mond** m new moon

neun [nɔyn] num nine; **~zehn** num nineteen; **~zig** num ninety

neureich adj nouveau riche; **N~e(r)** f(m) nouveau riche

neurotisch adj neurotic

Neuseeland [nɔy'zeːlant] nt New Zealand; **Neuseeländer(in)** [nɔy'zeːlɛndər(ɪn)] m(f) New Zealander

neutral [nɔy'traːl] adj neutral; **~i'sieren** vt to neutralize

Neutrum ['nɔytrum] (-s, -a od -en) nt neuter

Neu- zW: **~wert** m purchase price; **n~wertig** adj (as) new, not used; **~zeit** f modern age; **n~zeitlich** adj modern, recent

─────────────────
SCHLÜSSELWORT
─────────────────

nicht [nɪçt] adv **1** (Verneinung) not; **er ist es nicht** it's not him, it isn't him; **er raucht nicht** (gerade) he isn't smoking; (gewöhnlich) he doesn't smoke; **ich kann das nicht - ich auch nicht** I can't do it - neither od nor can I; **es regnet nicht mehr** it's not raining any more; **nicht rostend** stainless

2 (Bitte, Verbot): **nicht!** don't!, no!; **nicht berühren!** do not touch!; **nicht doch!** don't!

3 (rhetorisch): **du bist müde, nicht (wahr)?** you're tired, aren't you?; **das ist schön,**

nicht (wahr)? it's nice, isn't it?
4: was du nicht sagst! the things you say!

Nichtangriffspakt [nɪçt'|angrɪfspakt] *m* non-aggression pact
Nichte ['nɪçtə] *f* niece
nichtig ['nɪçtɪç] *adj* (*ungültig*) null, void; (*wertlos*) futile
Nichtraucher(in) *m(f)* non-smoker
nichts [nɪçts] *pron* nothing; **für ~ und wieder ~** for nothing at all; **~ sagend** meaningless; **N~ (-)** *nt* nothingness; (*pej: Person*) nonentity
Nichtschwimmer *m* non-swimmer
nichts- *zW:* **~desto'weniger** *adv* nevertheless; **N~nutz (-es, -e)** *m* good-for-nothing; **~nutzig** *adj* worthless, useless; **N~tun (-s)** *nt* idleness
Nichtzutreffende(s) *nt:* **~s od nicht Zutreffendes (bitte) streichen!** (please) delete where appropriate
Nickel ['nɪkəl] **(-s)** *nt* nickel
nicken ['nɪkən] *vi* to nod
Nickerchen ['nɪkərçən] *nt* nap
nie [ni:] *adv* never; **~ wieder** *od* **mehr** never again; **~ und nimmer** never ever
nieder ['ni:dər] *adj* low; (*gering*) inferior ♦ *adv* down; **N~gang** *m* decline; **~gedrückt** *adj* (*deprimiert*) dejected, depressed; **~gehen** (*unreg*) *vi* to descend; (*AVIAT*) to come down; (*Regen*) to fall; (*Boxer*) to go down; **~geschlagen** *adj* depressed, dejected; **N~lage** *f* defeat; **N~lande** *pl* Netherlands; **N~länder(in)** *m(f)* Dutchman(-woman); **~ländisch** *adj* Dutch; **~lassen** (*unreg*) *vr* (*sich setzen*) to sit down; (*an Ort*) to settle (down); (*Arzt, Rechtsanwalt*) to set up a practice; **N~lassung** *f* settlement; (*COMM*) branch; **~legen** *vt* to lay down; (*Arbeit*) to stop; (*Amt*) to resign; **N~sachsen** *nt* Lower Saxony; **N~schlag** *m* (*MET*) precipitation; rainfall; **~schlagen** (*unreg*) *vt* (*Gegner*) to beat down; (*Gegenstand*) to knock down; (*Augen*) to lower; (*Aufstand*) to put down ♦ *vr* (*CHEM*) to precipitate; **~trächtig** *adj* base, mean; **N~trächtigkeit** *f* meanness,

baseness; outrage; **N~ung** *f* (*GEOG*) depression; (*Mündungsgebiet*) flats *pl*
niedlich ['ni:tlɪç] *adj* sweet, cute
niedrig ['ni:drɪç] *adj* low; (*Stand*) lowly, humble; (*Gesinnung*) mean
niemals ['ni:ma:ls] *adv* never
niemand ['ni:mant] *pron* nobody, no-one
Niemandsland ['ni:mantslant] *nt* no-man's-land
Niere ['ni:rə] *f* kidney
nieseln ['ni:zəln] *vi* to drizzle
niesen ['ni:zən] *vi* to sneeze
Niete ['ni:tə] *f* (*TECH*) rivet; (*Los*) blank; (*Reinfall*) flop; (*Mensch*) failure; **n~n** *vt* to rivet

---

St. Nikolaus

i On December 6th, **St. Nikolaus** visits German children to reward those who have been good by filling shoes they have left out with sweets and small presents.

Nikotin [niko'ti:n] **(-s)** *nt* nicotine
Nilpferd [ni:l-] *nt* hippopotamus
Nimmersatt ['nɪmərzat] **(-(e)s, -e)** *m* glutton
nimmst *etc* [nɪmst] *vb siehe* **nehmen**
nippen ['nɪpən] *vt, vi* to sip
nirgend- ['nɪrgənt] *zW:* **~s** *adv* nowhere; **~wo** *adv* nowhere; **~wohin** *adv* nowhere
Nische ['ni:ʃə] *f* niche
nisten ['nɪstən] *vi* to nest
Niveau [ni'vo:] **(-s, -s)** *nt* level
Nixe ['nɪksə] *f* water nymph
nobel ['no:bəl] *adj* (*großzügig*) generous; (*elegant*) posh (*inf*)

SCHLÜSSELWORT

noch [nɔx] *adv* **1** (*weiterhin*) still; **noch nicht** not yet; **noch nie** never (yet); **noch immer** *od* **immer noch** still; **bleiben Sie doch noch** stay a bit longer
2 (*in Zukunft*) still, yet; **das kann noch passieren** that might still happen; **er wird noch kommen** he'll come (yet)
3 (*nicht später als*): **noch vor einer Woche** only a week ago; **noch am selben Tag** the

very same day; **noch im 19. Jahrhundert**
as late as the 19th century; **noch heute**
today

4 (*zusätzlich*): **wer war noch da?** who else
was there?; **noch einmal** once more,
again; **noch dreimal** three more times;
noch einer another one

5 (*bei Vergleichen*): **noch größer** even
bigger; **das ist noch besser** that's better
still; **und wenn es noch so schwer ist**
however hard it is

6: Geld noch und noch heaps (and heaps)
of money; **sie hat noch und noch
versucht, ...** she tried again and again
to ...

♦ *konj*: **weder A noch B** neither A nor B

noch- *zW*: **~mal** ['nɔxma:l] *adv* again, once
more; **~malig** ['nɔxma:lɪç] *adj* repeated;
~mals *adv* again, once more
Nominativ ['no:minati:f] (**-s, -e**) *m*
nominative
nominell [nomi'nɛl] *adj* nominal
Nonne ['nɔnə] *f* nun
Nord(en) ['nɔrd(ən)] (**-s**) *m* north
Nord'irland *nt* Northern Ireland
nordisch *adj* northern
nördlich ['nœrtlɪç] *adj* northerly, northern
♦ *präp* (*gen*) (to the) north of; **~ von** (to
the) north of
Nord- *zW*: **~pol** *m* North Pole; **~rhein-
Westfalen** *nt* North Rhine-Westphalia;
~see *f* North Sea; **n~wärts** *adv*
northwards
nörgeln ['nœrgəln] *vi* to grumble; **Nörgler**
(**-s, -**) *m* grumbler
Norm [nɔrm] (**-, -en**) *f* norm;
(*Größenvorschrift*) standard; **n~al** [nɔr'ma:l]
adj normal; **~al(benzin)** *nt* ≈ 2-star petrol
(*BRIT*), regular petrol (*US*); **n~alerweise**
adv normally; **n~ali'sieren** *vt* to normalize
♦ *vr* to return to normal
normen *vt* to standardize
Norwegen ['nɔrve:gən] *nt* Norway;
norwegisch *adj* Norwegian
Nostalgie [nɔstal'gi:] *f* nostalgia
Not [no:t] (**-, ⁿe**) *f* need; (*Mangel*) want;

(*Mühe*) trouble; (*Zwang*) necessity; **~
leidend** *adj* needy; **zur ~** if necessary; (*gerade
noch*) just about
Notar [no'ta:r] (**-s, -e**) *m* notary; **n~i'ell** *adj*
notarial
Not- *zW*: **~arzt** *m* emergency doctor;
~ausgang *m* emergency exit; **~behelf**
(**-s, -e**) *m* makeshift; **~bremse** *f* emergency brake; **~dienst** *m* (*Bereitschaftsdienst*)
emergency service; **n~dürftig** *adj* scanty;
(*behelfsmäßig*) makeshift
Note ['no:tə] *f* note; (*SCH*) mark (*BRIT*), grade
(*US*)
Noten- *zW*: **~blatt** *nt* sheet of music;
~schlüssel *m* clef; **~ständer** *m* music
stand
Not- *zW*: **~fall** *m* (case of) emergency;
n~falls *adv* if need be; **n~gedrungen** *adj*
necessary, unavoidable; **etw n~gedrungen
machen** to be forced to do sth
notieren [no'ti:rən] *vt* to note; (*COMM*) to
quote
Notierung *f* (*COMM*) quotation
nötig ['nø:tɪç] *adj* necessary; **etw ~ haben** to
need sth; **~en** [-gən] *vt* to compel, to force;
~enfalls *adv* if necessary
Notiz [no'ti:ts] (**-, -en**) *f* note; (*Zeitungsnotiz*)
item; **~ nehmen** to take notice; **~block** *m*
notepad; **~buch** *nt* notebook
Not- *zW*: **~lage** *f* crisis, emergency;
n~landen *vi* to make a forced *od*
emergency landing; **n~leidend** △ *adj*
siehe **Not**; **~lösung** *f* temporary solution;
~lüge *f* white lie
notorisch [no'to:rɪʃ] *adj* notorious
Not- *zW*: **~ruf** *m* emergency call;
~rufsäule *f* emergency telephone;
~stand *m* state of emergency;
~unterkunft *f* emergency
accommodation; **~verband** *m* emergency
dressing; **~wehr** (**-**) *f* self-defence;
n~wendig *adj* necessary; **~wendigkeit** *f*
necessity
Novelle [no'vɛlə] *f* short novel; (*JUR*)
amendment
November [no'vɛmbər] (**-s, -**) *m* November
Nu [nu:] *m*: **im ~** in an instant

Nuance [ny'ã:sə] f nuance
nüchtern ['nʏçtərn] adj sober; (*Magen*) empty; (*Urteil*) prudent; **N~heit** f sobriety
Nudel ['nu:dəl] (-, -n) f noodle; **~n** pl (*Teigwaren*) pasta sg; (*in Suppe*) noodles
Null [nʊl] (-, -en) f nought, zero; (*pej: Mensch*) washout; **n~** m zero; (*Fehler*) no; **n~ Uhr** midnight; **n~ und nichtig** null and void; **~punkt** m zero; **auf dem ~punkt** at zero
numerisch [nu'me:rɪʃ] adj numerical
Nummer ['nʊmər] (-, -n) f number; (*Größe*) size; **n~ieren** ▲ vt to number; **~nschild** nt (*AUT*) number od license (*US*) plate
nun [nu:n] adv now ♦ excl well; **das ist ~ mal so** that's the way it is
nur [nu:r] adv just, only; **wo bleibt er ~?** (just) where is he?
Nürnberg ['nʏrnbɛrk] (-s) nt Nuremberg
Nuss ▲ [nʊs] (-, ⁻e) f nut; **~baum** m walnut tree; **~knacker** (-s, -) m nutcracker
nutz [nʊts] adj: **zu nichts ~ sein** to be no use for anything; **~bringend** adj (*Verwendung*) profitable
nütze ['nʏtsə] adj = nutz
Nutzen (-s) m usefulness; (*Gewinn*) profit; **von ~** useful; **n~** vi to be of use ♦ vt: **etw zu etw n~** to use sth for sth; **was nutzt es?** what's the use?, what use is it?
nützen vi, vt = nutzen
nützlich ['nʏtslɪç] adj useful; **N~keit** f usefulness
Nutz- zW: **n~los** adj useless; **~losigkeit** f uselessness; **~nießer** (-s, -) m beneficiary
Nylon ['naɪlɔn] (-(s)) nt nylon

O, o

Oase [o'a:zə] f oasis
ob [ɔp] konj if, whether; **~ das wohl wahr ist?** can that be true?; **und ~!** you bet!
obdachlos adj homeless
Obdachlose(r) f(m) homeless person; **~nasyl** nt shelter for the homeless
Obduktion [ɔpdʊktsi'o:n] f post-mortem
obduzieren [ɔpdu'tsi:rən] vt to do a post-

mortem on
O-Beine ['o:baɪnə] pl bow od bandy legs
oben ['o:bən] adv above; (*in Haus*) upstairs; **~ erwähnt**, **~ genannt** above-mentioned; **nach ~** up; **von ~** down; **~ ohne** topless; **jdn von ~ bis unten ansehen** to look sb up and down; **~an** adv at the top; **~auf** adv up above, on the top ♦ adj (*munter*) in form; **~drein** adv into the bargain
Ober ['o:bər] (-s, -) m waiter; **die ~en** pl (*umg*) the bosses; (*ECCL*) the superiors; **~arm** m upper arm; **~arzt** m senior physician; **~aufsicht** f supervision; **~bayern** nt Upper Bavaria; **~befehl** m supreme command; **~befehlshaber** m commander-in-chief; **~bekleidung** f outer clothing; **~'bürgermeister** m lord mayor; **~deck** nt upper od top deck; **o~e(r, s)** adj upper; **~fläche** f surface; **o~flächlich** adj superficial; **~geschoss** ▲ nt upper storey; **o~halb** adv above ♦ präp +gen above; **~haupt** nt head, chief; **~haus** nt (*POL*) upper house, House of Lords (*BRIT*); **~hemd** nt shirt; **~herrschaft** f supremacy, sovereignty; **~in** f matron; (*ECCL*) Mother Superior; **~kellner** m head waiter; **~kiefer** m upper jaw; **~körper** m upper part of body; **~leitung** f direction; (*ELEK*) overhead cable; **~licht** nt skylight; **~lippe** f upper lip; **~schenkel** m thigh; **~schicht** f upper classes pl; **~schule** f grammar school (*BRIT*), high school (*US*); **~schwester** f (*MED*) matron
Oberst ['o:bərst] (-en od -s, -en od -e) m colonel; **o~e(r, s)** adj very top, topmost
Ober- zW: **~stufe** f upper school; **~teil** nt upper part; **~weite** f bust/chest measurement
obgleich [ɔp'glaɪç] konj although
Obhut ['ɔphu:t] (-) f care, protection; **in jds ~ sein** to be in sb's care
obig ['o:bɪç] adj above
Objekt [ɔp'jɛkt] (-(e)s, -e) nt object; **~iv** [-'ti:f] (-s, -e) nt lens; **o~iv** adj objective; **~ivi'tät** f objectivity
Oblate [o'bla:tə] f (*Gebäck*) wafer; (*ECCL*) host

obligatorisch [obliga'to:rɪʃ] *adj* compulsory, obligatory

Obrigkeit ['o:brɪçkaɪt] *f* (*Behörden*) authorities *pl*, administration; (*Regierung*) government

obschon [ɔp'ʃo:n] *konj* although

Observatorium [ɔpzɛrva'to:riʊm] *nt* observatory

obskur [ɔps'ku:r] *adj* obscure; (*verdächtig*) dubious

Obst [o:pst] (**-(e)s**) *nt* fruit; **~baum** *m* fruit tree; **~garten** *m* orchard; **~händler** *m* fruiterer, fruit merchant; **~kuchen** *m* fruit tart

obszön [ɔps'tsø:n] *adj* obscene; **O~ität** *f* obscenity

obwohl [ɔp'vo:l] *konj* although

Ochse ['ɔksə] (**-n, -n**) *m* ox; **o~n** (*umg*) *vt, vi* to cram, to swot (BRIT)

Ochsenschwanzsuppe *f* oxtail soup

Ochsenzunge *f* oxtongue

öd(e) ['ø:d(ə)] *adj* (*Land*) waste, barren; (*fig*) dull; **Ö~** *f* desert, waste(land); (*fig*) tedium

oder ['o:dər] *konj* or; **das stimmt, ~?** that's right, isn't it?

Ofen ['o:fən] (**-s, ÿ**) *m* oven; (*Heizofen*) fire, heater; (*Kohlenofen*) stove; (*Hochofen*) furnace; (*Herd*) cooker, stove; **~rohr** *nt* stovepipe

offen ['ɔfən] *adj* open; (*aufrichtig*) frank; (*Stelle*) vacant; **~ bleiben** (*Fenster*) to stay open; (*Frage, Entscheidung*) to remain open; **~ halten** to keep open; **~ lassen** to leave open; **~ stehen** to be open; (*Rechnung*) to be unpaid; **es steht Ihnen ~, es zu tun** you are at liberty to do it; **~ gesagt** to be honest; **~bar** *adj* obvious; **~baren** [ɔfən'ba:rən] *vt* to reveal, to manifest; **O~'barung** *f* (REL) revelation; **O~heit** *f* candour, frankness; **~herzig** *adj* candid, frank; (*Kleid*) revealing; **~kundig** *adj* well-known; (*klar*) evident; **~sichtlich** *adj* evident, obvious

offensiv [ɔfɛn'zi:f] *adj* offensive; **O~e** [-'zi:və] *f* offensive

öffentlich ['œfəntlɪç] *adj* public; **Ö~keit** *f* (*Leute*) public; (*einer Versammlung etc*) public nature; **in aller Ö~keit** in public; **an die Ö~keit dringen** to reach the public ear

offiziell [ɔfitsi'ɛl] *adj* official

Offizier [ɔfi'tsi:r] (**-s, -e**) *m* officer; **~skasino** *nt* officers' mess

öffnen ['œfnən] *vt, vr* to open; **jdm die Tür ~** to open the door for sb

Öffner ['œfnər] (**-s, -**) *m* opener

Öffnung ['œfnʊŋ] *f* opening; **~szeiten** *pl* opening times

oft [ɔft] *adv* often

öfter ['œftər] *adv* more often *od* frequently; **~s** *adv* often, frequently

oh [o:] *excl* oh; **~ je!** oh dear

OHG *abk* (= *Offene Handelsgesellschaft*) general partnership

ohne ['o:nə] *präp +akk* without ♦ *konj* without; **das ist nicht ~** (*umg*) it's not bad; **~ weiteres** without a second thought; (*sofort*) immediately; **~ zu fragen** without asking; **~ dass er es wusste** without him knowing it; **~dies** [o:nə'di:s] *adv* anyway; **~gleichen** [o:nə'glaɪçən] *adj* unsurpassed, without equal; **~hin** [o:nə'hɪn] *adv* anyway, in any case

Ohnmacht ['o:nmaxt] *f* faint; (*fig*) impotence; **in ~ fallen** to faint

ohnmächtig ['o:nmɛçtɪç] *adj* in a faint, unconscious; (*fig*) weak, impotent; **sie ist ~** she has fainted

Ohr [o:r] (**-(e)s, -en**) *nt* ear

Öhr [ø:r] (**-(e)s, -e**) *nt* eye

Ohren- *zW*: **~arzt** *m* ear specialist; **o~betäubend** *adj* deafening; **~schmalz** *nt* earwax; **~schmerzen** *pl* earache *sg*

Ohr- *zW*: **~feige** *f* slap on the face; box on the ears; **o~feigen** *vt*: **jdn o~feigen** to slap sb's face; to box sb's ears; **~läppchen** *nt* ear lobe; **~ring** *m* earring; **~wurm** *m* earwig; (MUS) catchy tune

Öko- [øko] *zW*: **~laden** *m* wholefood shop; **ö~logisch** [-'lo:gɪʃ] *adj* ecological; **ö~nomisch** [-'no:mɪʃ] *adj* economical

Oktober [ɔk'to:bər] (**-s, -**) *m* October; **~fest** *nt* Munich beer festival

---

Spelling Reform: ▲ *new spelling* △ *old spelling (to be phased out)*

Oktoberfest

ⓘ *The annual beer festival, the* **Oktoberfest**, *takes place in Munich at the end of September in a huge area where beer tents and various amusements are set up. People sit at long wooden tables, drink beer from enormous beer mugs, eat pretzels and listen to brass bands. It is a great attraction for tourists and locals alike.*

ökumenisch [øku'me:nɪʃ] *adj* ecumenical

Öl [ø:l] **(-(e)s, -e)** *nt* oil; **~baum** *m* olive tree; **ö~en** *vt* to oil; (TECH) to lubricate; **~farbe** *f* oil paint; **~feld** *nt* oilfield; **~film** *m* film of oil; **~heizung** *f* oil-fired central heating; **ö~ig** *adj* oily; **~industrie** *f* oil industry

oliv [o'li:f] *adj* olive-green; **O~e** *f* olive

Öl- *zW:* **~messstab** ▲ *m* dipstick; **~sardine** *f* sardine; **~stand** *m* oil level; **~standanzeiger** *m* (AUT) oil gauge; **~tanker** *m* oil tanker; **~ung** *f* lubrication; oiling; (ECCL) anointment; **die Letzte ~ung** Extreme Unction; **~wechsel** *m* oil change

Olymp- [o'lymp] *zW:* **~iade** [olympi'a:də] *f* Olympic Games *pl*; **~iasieger(in)** [-iazi:gər(ɪn)] *m(f)* Olympic champion; **~iateilnehmer(in)** *m(f)* Olympic competitor; **o~isch** *adj* Olympic

Ölzeug *nt* oilskins *pl*

Oma ['o:ma] **(-, -s)** (umg) *f* granny

Omelett [ɔm(ə)'lɛt] **(-(e)s, -s)** *nt* omelet(te)

ominös [omi'nø:s] *adj* (unheilvoll) ominous

Onanie [ona'ni:] *f* masturbation; **o~ren** *vi* to masturbate

Onkel ['ɔŋkəl] **(-s, -)** *m* uncle

Opa ['o:pa] **(-s, -s)** (umg) *m* grandpa

Oper ['o:pər] **(-, -n)** *f* opera; opera house

Operation [operatsi'o:n] *f* operation; **~ssaal** *m* operating theatre

Operette [ope'rɛtə] *f* operetta

operieren [ope'ri:rən] *vt* to operate on ♦ *vi* to operate

Opern- *zW:* **~glas** *nt* opera glasses *pl*; **~haus** *nt* opera house

Opfer ['ɔpfər] **(-s, -)** *nt* sacrifice; (Mensch) victim; **o~n** *vt* to sacrifice; **~ung** *f* sacrifice

opponieren [ɔpo'ni:rən] *vi:* **gegen jdn/etw ~** to oppose sb/sth

Opportunist [ɔpɔrtu'nɪst] *m* opportunist

Opposition [ɔpozitsi'o:n] *f* opposition; **o~ell** *adj* opposing

Optik ['ɔptɪk] *f* optics *sg*; **~er (-s, -)** *m* optician

optimal [ɔpti'ma:l] *adj* optimal, optimum

Optimismus [ɔpti'mɪsmʊs] *m* optimism

Optimist [ɔpti'mɪst] *m* optimist; **o~isch** *adj* optimistic

optisch ['ɔptɪʃ] *adj* optical

Orakel [o'ra:kəl] **(-s, -)** *nt* oracle

oral [o'ra:l] *adj* (MED) oral

Orange [o'rã:ʒə] *f* orange; **o~** *adj* orange; **~ade** [orã'ʒa:də] *f* orangeade; **~at** [orã'ʒa:t] **(-s, -e)** *nt* candied peel

Orchester [ɔr'kɛstər] **(-s, -)** *nt* orchestra

Orchidee [ɔrçi'de:ə] *f* orchid

Orden ['ɔrdən] **(-s, -)** *m* (ECCL) order; (MIL) decoration; **~sschwester** *f* nun

ordentlich ['ɔrdəntlɪç] *adj* (anständig) decent, respectable; (geordnet) tidy, neat; (umg: annehmbar) not bad; (: tüchtig) real, proper ♦ *adv* properly; **~er Professor** (full) professor; **O~keit** *f* respectability; tidiness, neatness

ordinär [ɔrdi'nɛ:r] *adj* common, vulgar

ordnen ['ɔrdnən] *vt* to order, to put in order

Ordner (-s, -) *m* steward; (COMM) file

Ordnung *f* order; (Ordnen) ordering; (Geordnetsein) tidiness; **~ machen** to tidy up; **in ~!** okay!

Ordnungs- *zW:* **o~gemäß** *adj* proper, according to the rules; **o~liebend** *adj* orderly, methodical; **~strafe** *f* fine; **o~widrig** *adj* contrary to the rules, irregular; **~widrigkeit** [-vɪdrɪçkaɪt] *f* infringement (of law or rule); **~zahl** *f* ordinal number

Organ [ɔr'ga:n] **(-s, -e)** *nt* organ; (Stimme) voice; **~isation** [-izatsi'o:n] *f* organization; **~isator** [i'za:tɔr] *m* organizer; **o~isch** *adj* organic; **o~isieren** [-i'zi:rən] *vt* to organize, to arrange; (umg: beschaffen) to acquire ♦ *vr* to organize; **~ismus** [-'nɪsmʊs] *m*

organism; **~ist** [-'nɪst] m organist;
~spende f organ donation;
~spenderausweis m donor card

Orgasmus [ɔr'gasmʊs] m orgasm

Orgel ['ɔrgəl] (-, -n) f organ

Orgie ['ɔrgiə] f orgy

Orient ['oːriɛnt] (-s) m Orient, east;
o~alisch [-'taːlɪʃ] adj oriental

orientier- zW: **~en** [-'tiːrən] vt (örtlich) to
locate; (fig) to inform ♦ vr to find one's way
od bearings; to inform o.s.; **O~ung** [-'tiːrʊŋ]
f orientation; (fig) information;
O~ungssinn m sense of direction;
O~ungsstufe f period during which pupils
are selected for different schools

| Orientierungsstufe |

i The *Orientierungsstufe is the name
given to the first two years spent in a
Realschule or **Gymnasium**, during which
a child is assessed as to his or her
suitability for that type of school. At the
end of two years it may be decided to
transfer the child to a school more suited to
his or her ability.*

original [ɔrigi'naːl] adj original; **O** (**-s, -e**)
nt original; **O~fassung** f original version;
O~i'tät f originality

originell [ɔrigi'nɛl] adj original

Orkan [ɔr'kaːn] (-(e)s, -e) m hurricane;
o~artig adj (Wind) gale-force; (Beifall)
thunderous

Ornament [ɔrna'mɛnt] nt decoration,
ornament; **o~al** [-'taːl] adj decorative,
ornamental

Ort [ɔrt] (-(e)s, -e od *ᵁe) m place; **an ~ und
Stelle** on the spot; **o~en** vt to locate

ortho- [ɔrto] zW: **~dox** [-'dɔks] adj orthodox;
O~grafie ▲ [-gra'fiː] f spelling,
orthography; **~'grafisch** ▲ adj
orthographic; **O~päde** [-'pɛːdə] (-n, -n) m
orthopaedist; **O~pädie** [-pɛ'diː] f
orthopaedics sg; **~'pädisch** adj
orthopaedic

örtlich ['œrtlɪç] adj local; **Ö~keit** f locality

ortsansässig adj local

Ortschaft f village, small town

Orts- zW: **o~fremd** adj non-local;
~gespräch nt local (phone)call; **~name**
m place name; **~netz** nt (TEL) local
telephone exchange area; **~tarif** m (TEL)
tariff for local calls; **~zeit** f local time

Ortung f locating

Öse ['øːzə] f loop, eye

Ost'asien [ɔst'aːzjən] nt Eastern Asia

Osten ['ɔstən] (-s) m east

Oster- ['oːstər] zW: **~ei** nt Easter egg; **~fest**
nt Easter; **~glocke** f daffodil; **~hase** m
Easter bunny; **~montag** m Easter Monday;
~n (-s, -) nt Easter

Österreich ['øːstəraɪç] (-s) nt Austria;
~er(in) (-s, -) m(f) Austrian; **ö~isch** adj
Austrian

Ostküste f east coast

östlich ['œstlɪç] adj eastern, easterly

Ostsee f: **die ~** the Baltic (Sea)

Ouvertüre [uver'tyːrə] f overture

oval [o'vaːl] adj oval

Ovation [ovatsi'oːn] f ovation

Oxid, Oxyd [ɔ'ksyːt] (-(e)s, -e) nt oxide;
o~ieren vt, vi to oxidize; **~ierung** f
oxidization

Ozean ['oːtseaːn] (-s, -e) m ocean;
~dampfer m (ocean-going) liner

Ozon [o'tsoːn] (-s) nt ozone; **~loch** nt ozone
hole; **~schicht** f ozone layer

P, p

Paar [paːr] (-(e)s, -e) nt pair; (Ehepaar)
couple; **ein p~** a few; **ein p~ Mal** a few
times; **p~en** vt, vr to couple; (Tiere) to
mate; **~lauf** m pair skating; **~ung** f
combination; mating; **p~weise** adv in
pairs; in couples

Pacht [paxt] (-, -en) f lease; **p~en** vt to
lease

Pächter ['pɛçtər] (-s, -) m leaseholder,
tenant

Pack¹ [pak] (-(e)s, -e od *ᵁe) m bundle,
pack

Pack² [pak] (-(e)s) nt (pej) mob, rabble

Spelling Reform: ▲ new spelling △ old spelling (to be phased out)

Päckchen ['pɛkçən] *nt* small package; (*Zigaretten*) packet; (*Postpäckchen*) small parcel

Pack- *zW*: **p~en** *vt* to pack; (*fassen*) to grasp, to seize; (*umg*: *schaffen*) to manage; (*fig*: *fesseln*) to grip; **~en** (**-s**, **-**) *m* bundle; (*fig*: *Menge*) heaps of; **~esel** *m* (*auch fig*) packhorse; **~papier** *nt* brown paper, wrapping paper; **~ung** *f* packet; (*Pralinenpackung*) box; (*MED*) compress; **~ungsbeilage** *f* enclosed instructions *pl* for use

Pädagog- [peda'go:g] *zW*: **~e** (**-n**, **-n**) *m* teacher; **~ik** *f* education; **p~isch** *adj* educational, pedagogical

Paddel ['padəl] (**-s**, **-**) *nt* paddle; **~boot** *nt* canoe; **p~n** *vi* to paddle

Page ['pa:ʒə] (**-n**, **-n**) *m* page

Paket [pa'ke:t] (**-(e)s**, **-e**) *nt* packet; (*Postpaket*) parcel; **~karte** *f* dispatch note; **~post** *f* parcel post; **~schalter** *m* parcels counter

Pakt [pakt] (**-(e)s**, **-e**) *m* pact

Palast [pa'last] (**-es**, **Paläste**) *m* palace

Palästina [palɛ'sti:na] (**-s**) *nt* Palestine

Palme ['palmə] *f* palm (tree)

Pampelmuse ['pampəlmu:zə] *f* grapefruit

panieren [pa'ni:rən] *vt* (*KOCH*) to bread

Paniermehl [pa'ni:rme:l] *nt* breadcrumbs *pl*

Panik ['pa:nɪk] *f* panic

panisch ['pa:nɪʃ] *adj* panic-stricken

Panne ['panə] *f* (*AUT etc*) breakdown; (*Missgeschick*) slip; **~nhilfe** *f* breakdown service

panschen ['panʃən] *vi* to splash about ♦ *vt* to water down

Pantoffel [pan'tɔfəl] (**-s**, **-n**) *m* slipper

Pantomime [panto'mi:mə] *f* mime

Panzer ['pantsər] (**-s**, **-**) *m* armour; (*Platte*) armour plate; (*Fahrzeug*) tank; **~glas** *nt* bulletproof glass; **p~n** *vt* to armour ♦ *vr* (*fig*) to arm o.s.

Papa [pa'pa:] (**-s**, **-s**) (*umg*) *m* dad, daddy

Papagei [papa'gai] (**-s**, **-en**) *m* parrot

Papier [pa'pi:r] (**-s**, **-e**) *nt* paper; (*Wertpapier*) security; **~fabrik** *f* paper mill; **~geld** *nt* paper money; **~korb** *m* wastepaper basket; **~taschentuch** *nt* tissue

Papp- ['pap] *zW*: **~deckel** *m* cardboard; **~e** *f* cardboard; **~el** (**-**, **-n**) *f* poplar; **p~en** (*umg*) *vt*, *vi* to stick; **p~ig** *adj* sticky

Paprika ['paprika] (**-s**, **-s**) *m* (*Gewürz*) paprika; (*~schote*) pepper

Papst [pa:pst] (**-(e)s**, **ᵉe**) *m* pope

päpstlich ['pɛ:pstlɪç] *adj* papal

Parabel [pa'ra:bəl] (**-**, **-n**) *f* parable; (*MATH*) parabola

Parabolantenne [para'bo:lantenə] *f* satellite dish

Parade [pa'ra:də] *f* (*MIL*) parade, review; (*SPORT*) parry

Paradies [para'di:s] (**-es**, **-e**) *nt* paradise; **p~isch** *adj* heavenly

Paradox [para'dɔks] (**-es**, **-e**) *nt* paradox; **p~** *adj* paradoxical

Paragraf ▲ [para'gra:f] (**-en**, **-en**) *m* paragraph; (*JUR*) section

parallel [para'le:l] *adj* parallel; **P~e** *f* parallel

Parasit [para'zi:t] (**-en**, **-en**) *m* (*auch fig*) parasite

parat [pa'ra:t] *adj* ready

Pärchen ['pɛ:rçən] *nt* couple

Parfüm [par'fy:m] (**-s**, **-s** *od* **-e**) *nt* perfume; **~erie** [-ə'ri:] *f* perfumery; **p~frei** *adj* non-perfumed; **p~ieren** *vt* to scent, to perfume

parieren [pa'ri:rən] *vt* to parry ♦ *vi* (*umg*) to obey

Paris [pa'ri:s] (**-**) *nt* Paris; **~er** *adj* Parisian ♦ *m* Parisian; **~erin** *f* Parisian

Park [park] (**-s**, **-s**) *m* park; (*um Gebäude*) grounds *pl*; **p~en** *vt*, *vi* to park; **~ett** (**-(e)s**, **-e**) *nt* parquet (floor); (*THEAT*) stalls *pl*; **~gebühr** *f* parking fee; **~haus** *nt* multi-storey car park; **~lücke** *f* parking space; **~platz** *m* parking place; car park, parking lot (*US*); **~scheibe** *f* parking disc; **~schein** *m* car park ticket; **~uhr** *f* parking meter; **~verbot** *nt* parking ban

Parlament [parla'mɛnt] *nt* parliament; **~arier** [-'ta:riər] (**-s**, **-**) *m* parliamentarian; **p~arisch** [-'ta:rɪʃ] *adj* parliamentary

Parlaments- *zW*: **~beschluss** ▲ *m* vote of parliament; **~mitglied** *nt* member of parliament; **~sitzung** *f* sitting (of parliament)

Parodie [paro'diː] f parody; **p~ren** vt to parody

Parole [pa'roːlə] f password; (Wahlspruch) motto

Partei [par'taɪ] f party; **~ ergreifen für jdn** to take sb's side; **p~isch** adj partial, bias(s)ed; **p~los** adj neutral, impartial; **~mitglied** nt party member; **~programm** nt (party) manifesto; **~tag** m party conference

Parterre [par'tɛr] (-s, -s) nt ground floor; (THEAT) stalls pl

Partie [par'tiː] f part; (Spiel) game; (Ausflug) outing; (Mann, Frau) catch; (COMM) lot, **mit von der ~ sein** to join in

Partizip [parti'tsiːp] (-s, -ien) nt participle

Partner(in) ['partnər(ɪn)] (-s, -) m(f) partner; **~schaft** f partnership; (von Städten) twinning; **p~schaftlich** adj as partners; **~stadt** f twin town

Party ['paːrti] (-, -s) f party

Pass ▲ [pas] (-es, ⁺e) m pass; (Ausweis) passport

passabel [pa'saːbəl] adj passable, reasonable

Passage [pa'saːʒə] f passage

Passagier [pasa'ʒiːr] (-s, -e) m passenger; **~flugzeug** nt airliner

Passamt ▲ nt passport office

Passant [pa'sant] m passer-by

Passbild ▲ nt passport photograph

passen ['pasən] vi to fit; (Farbe) to go; (auf Frage, KARTEN, SPORT) to pass; **das passt mir nicht** that doesn't suit me; **~ zu** (Farbe, Kleider) to go with; **er passt nicht zu dir** he's not right for you; **~d** adj suitable; (zusammenpassend) matching; (angebracht) fitting; (Zeit) convenient

passier- [pa'siːr] zW: **~bar** adj passable; **~en** vt to pass; (durch Sieb) to strain ♦ vi to happen; **P~schein** m pass, permit

Passion [pasi'oːn] f passion; **p~iert** [-'niːrt] adj enthusiastic, passionate; **~sspiel** nt Passion Play

passiv ['pasiːf] adj passive; **P~** (-s, -e) nt passive; **P~a** pl (COMM) liabilities; **P~ität** f passiveness; **P~rauchen** nt passive smoking

Pass- ▲ zW: **~kontrolle** f passport control; **~stelle** f passport office; **~straße** f (mountain) pass

Paste ['pastə] f paste

Pastete [pas'teːtə] f pie

pasteurisieren [pastøri'ziːrən] vt to pasteurize

Pastor ['pastɔr] m vicar; pastor, minister

Pate ['paːtə] (-n, -n) m godfather; **~nkind** nt godchild

Patent [pa'tɛnt] (-(e)s, -e) nt patent; (MIL) commission; **p~** adj clever; **~amt** nt patent office

Patentante f godmother

patentieren [patɛn'tiːrən] vt to patent

PatentInhaber m patentee

pathetisch [pa'teːtɪʃ] adj emotional; bombastic

Pathologe [pato'loːgə] (-n, -n) m pathologist

pathologisch adj pathological

Pathos ['paːtɔs] (-) nt emotiveness, emotionalism

Patient(in) [patsi'ɛnt(ɪn)] m(f) patient

Patin ['paːtɪn] f godmother

Patriot [patri'oːt] (-en, -en) m patriot; **p~isch** adj patriotic; **~ismus** [-'tɪsmʊs] m patriotism

Patrone [pa'troːnə] f cartridge

Patrouille [pa'trʊljə] f patrol

patrouillieren [patrʊl'jiːrən] vi to patrol

patsch [patʃ] excl splash; **P~e** (umg) f (Bedrängnis) mess, jam; **~en** vi to smack, to slap; (im Wasser) to splash; **~nass** ▲ adj soaking wet

patzig ['patsɪç] (umg) adj cheeky, saucy

Pauke ['paʊkə] f kettledrum; **auf die ~ hauen** to live it up

pauken vt (intensiv lernen) to swot up (inf) ♦ vi to swot (inf), cram (inf)

pausbäckig ['paʊsbɛkɪç] adj chubby-cheeked

pauschal [paʊ'ʃaːl] adj (Kosten) inclusive; (Urteil) sweeping; **P~e** f flat rate; **P~gebühr** f flat rate; **P~preis** m all-in price; **P~reise** f package tour; **P~summe** f lump sum

Pause ['pauzə] f break; (THEAT) interval; (Innehalten) pause; (Kopie) tracing

pausen vt to trace; **~los** adj non-stop; **P~zeichen** nt call sign; (MUS) rest

Pauspapier ['pauspapiːr] nt tracing paper

Pavillon ['paviljõ] (-s, -s) m pavilion

Pazif- [pa'tsiːf-] zW: **~ik** (-s) m Pacific; **p~istisch** adj pacifist

Pech [pεç] (-s, -e) nt pitch; (fig) bad luck; **~ haben** to be unlucky; **p~schwarz** adj pitch-black; **~strähne** (umg) m unlucky patch; **~vogel** (umg) m unlucky person

Pedal [pe'daːl] (-s, -e) nt pedal

Pedant [pe'dant] m pedant; **~e'rie** f pedantry; **p~isch** adj pedantic

Pediküre [pedi'kyːrə] f (Fußpflege) pedicure

Pegel ['peːgəl] (-s, -) m water gauge; **~stand** m water level

peilen ['paɪlən] vt to get a fix on

Pein [paɪn] (-) f agony, pain; **p~igen** vt to torture; (plagen) to torment; **p~lich** adj (unangenehm) embarrassing, awkward, painful; (genau) painstaking

Peitsche ['paɪtʃə] f whip; **p~n** vt to whip; (Regen) to lash

Pelle ['pεlə] f skin; **p~n** vt to skin, to peel

Pellkartoffeln pl jacket potatoes

Pelz [pεlts] (-es, -e) m fur

Pendel ['pεndəl] (-s, -) nt pendulum; **p~n** vi (Zug, Fähre etc) to operate a shuttle service; (Mensch) to commute; **~verkehr** m shuttle traffic; (für Pendler) commuter traffic

Pendler ['pεndlər] (-s, -) m commuter

penetrant [pene'trant] adj sharp; (Person) pushing

Penis ['peːnɪs] (-, -se) m penis

pennen ['pεnən] (umg) vi to kip

Penner (umg: pej) m (Landstreicher) tramp

Pension [penzi'oːn] f (Geld) (Ruhestand) retirement; (für Gäste) boarding od guesthouse; **~är(in)** [-'nεːr(ɪn)] (-s, -e) m(f) pensioner; **p~ieren** vt to pension off; **p~iert** adj retired; **~ierung** f retirement; **~sgast** m boarder, paying guest

Pensum ['pεnzʊm] (-s, **Pensen**) nt quota;

(SCH) curriculum

per [pεr] präp +akk by, per; (pro) per; (bis) by

Perfekt ['pεrfεkt] (-(e)s, -e) nt perfect; **p~** adj perfect

perforieren [pεrfo'riːrən] vt to perforate

Pergament [pεrga'mεnt] nt parchment; **~papier** nt greaseproof paper

Periode [peri'oːdə] f period; **periodisch** adj periodic; (dezimal) recurring

Perle ['pεrlə] f (auch fig) pearl; **p~n** vi to sparkle; (Tropfen) to trickle

Perl- ['pεrl-] zW: **~mutt** (-s) nt mother-of-pearl; **~wein** m sparkling wine

perplex [pεr'plεks] adj dumbfounded

Person [pεr'zoːn] (-, -en) f person; **ich für meine ~ ...** personally I ...

Personal [pεrzo'naːl] (-s) nt personnel; (Bedienung) servants pl; **~ausweis** m identity card; **~computer** m personal computer; **~ien** [-iən] pl particulars; **~mangel** m undermanning; **~pronomen** nt personal pronoun

personell [pεrzo'nεl] adj (Veränderungen) personnel

Personen- zW: **~aufzug** m lift, elevator (US); **~kraftwagen** m private motorcar; **~schaden** m injury to persons; **~zug** m stopping train; passenger train

personifizieren [pεrzonifi'tsiːrən] vt to personify

persönlich [pεr'zøːnlɪç] adj personal ♦ adv in person; personally; **P~keit** f personality

Perspektive [pεrspεk'tiːvə] f perspective

Perücke [pe'rʏkə] f wig

pervers [pεr'vεrs] adj perverse

Pessimismus [pεsi'mɪsmʊs] m pessimism

Pessimist [pεsi'mɪst] m pessimist; **p~isch** adj pessimistic

Pest [pεst] (-) f plague

Petersilie [petər'ziːliə] f parsley

Petroleum [pe'troːleʊm] (-s) nt paraffin, kerosene (US)

Pfad [pfaːt] (-(e)s, -e) m path; **~finder** (-s, -) m boy scout; **~finderin** f girl guide

Pfahl [pfaːl] (-(e)s, -e) m post, stake

Pfand [pfant] (-(e)s, ⁻er) nt pledge, security; (Flaschenpfand) deposit; (im Spiel) forfeit;

~brief m bond
pfänden ['pfɛndən] vt to seize, to distrain
Pfänderspiel nt game of forfeits
Pfandflasche f returnable bottle
Pfandschein m pawn ticket
Pfändung ['pfɛndʊŋ] f seizure, distraint
Pfanne ['pfanə] f (frying) pan
Pfannkuchen m pancake; (Berliner) doughnut
Pfarr- ['pfar] zW: **~ei** f parish; **~er** (-s, -) m priest; (evangelisch) vicar; minister; **~haus** nt vicarage; manse
Pfau [pfaʊ] ((o)o), **-en** m peacock; **~enauge** nt peacock butterfly
Pfeffer ['pfɛfər] (-s, -) m pepper; **~kuchen** m gingerbread; **~minz** (-es, -e) nt peppermint; **~mühle** f pepper mill, **p~n** vt to pepper; (umg: werfen) to fling; **gepfefferte Preise/Witze** steep prices/spicy jokes
Pfeife ['pfaɪfə] f whistle; (Tabakpfeife, Orgelpfeife) pipe; **p~n** (unreg) vt, vi to whistle; **~r** (-s, -) m piper
Pfeil [pfaɪl] (-(e)s, -e) m arrow
Pfeiler ['pfaɪlər] (-s, -) m pillar, prop; (Brückenpfeiler) pier
Pfennig ['pfɛnɪç] ((o)o, o) m pfennig (hundredth part of a mark)
Pferd [pfeːrt] (-(e)s, -e) nt horse
Pferde- ['pfeːrdə] zW: **~rennen** nt horse race; horse racing; **~schwanz** m (Frisur) ponytail; **~stall** m stable
Pfiff [pfɪf] (-(e)s, -e) m whistle
Pfifferling ['pfɪfərlɪŋ] m yellow chanterelle (mushroom); **keinen ~ wert** not worth a thing
pfiffig adj sly, sharp
Pfingsten ['pfɪŋstən] (-, -) nt Whitsun (BRIT), Pentecost
Pfirsich ['pfɪrzɪç] (-s, -e) m peach
Pflanz- ['pflants] zW: **~e** f plant; **p~en** vt to plant; **~enfett** nt vegetable fat; **p~lich** adj vegetable; **~ung** f plantation
Pflaster ['pflastər] (-s, -) nt plaster; (Straße) pavement; **p~n** vt to pave; **~stein** m paving stone
Pflaume ['pflaʊmə] f plum

Pflege ['pfleːgə] f care; (von Idee) cultivation; (Krankenpflege) nursing; **in ~ sein** (Kind) to be fostered out; **p~bedürftig** adj needing care; **~eltern** pl foster parents; **~heim** nt nursing home; **~kind** nt foster child; **p~leicht** adj easy-care; **~mutter** f foster mother; **p~n** vt to look after; (Kranke) to nurse; (Beziehungen) to foster; **~r** (-s, -) m orderly; male nurse; **~rin** f nurse, attendant; **~vater** m foster father
Pflicht [pflɪçt] (-, -en) f duty; (SPORT) compulsory section; **p~bewusst** ▲ adj conscientious; **~fach** nt (SCH) compulsory subject; **~gefühl** nt sense of duty; **p~gemäß** adj dutiful ♦ adv as in duty bound; **~versicherung** f compulsory insurance
pflücken ['pflʏkən] vt to pick; (Blumen) to pick, to pluck
Pflug [pfluːk] (-(e)s, ⁀e) m plough
pflügen ['pflyːgən] vt to plough
Pforte ['pfɔrtə] f gate; door
Pförtner ['pfœrtnər] (-s, -) m porter, doorkeeper, doorman
Pfosten ['pfɔstən] (-s, -) m post
Pfote ['pfoːtə] f paw; (umg: Schrift) scrawl
Pfropfen (-s, -) m (Flaschenpfropfen) stopper; (Blutpropfen) clot
pfui [pfʊɪ] excl ugh!
Pfund [pfʊnt] (-(e)s, -e) nt pound
pfuschen ['pfʊʃən] (umg) vi to be sloppy; **jdm ins Handwerk ~** to interfere in sb's business
Pfuscher ['pfʊʃər] (-s, -) (umg) m sloppy worker; (Kurpfuscher) quack; **~ei** (umg) f sloppy work; quackery
Pfütze ['pfʏtsə] f puddle
Phänomen [fɛnoˈmeːn] (-s, -e) nt phenomenon
phänomenal [-ˈnaːl] adj phenomenal
Phantasie etc [fantaˈziː] f = **Fantasie** etc
phantastisch [fanˈtastɪʃ] adj = **fantastisch**
Phase ['faːzə] f phase
Philologie [filoloˈgiː] f philology
Philosoph [filoˈzoːf] (-en, -en) m philosopher; **~ie** [-ˈfiː] f philosophy; **p~isch** adj philosophical

Spelling Reform: ▲ *new spelling* △ *old spelling (to be phased out)*

phlegmatisch [flɛˈgmaːtɪʃ] *adj* lethargic

Phonetik [foˈneːtɪk] *f* phonetics *sg*

phonetisch *adj* phonetic

Phosphor [ˈfɔsfɔr] **(-s)** *m* phosphorus

Photo *etc* [ˈfoːto] **(-s, -s)** *nt* = **Foto** *etc*

Phrase [ˈfraːzə] *f* phrase; *(pej)* hollow phrase

pH-Wert [peːˈhaːveːrt] *m* pH-value

Physik [fyˈziːk] *f* physics *sg*; **p~alisch** [-ˈkaːlɪʃ] *adj* of physics; **~er(in)** [ˈfyːzɪkər(ɪn)] **(-s, -)** *m(f)* physicist

Physiologie [fyzioloˈgiː] *f* physiology

physisch [ˈfyːzɪʃ] *adj* physical

Pianist(in) [piaˈnɪst(ɪn)] *m(f)* pianist

Pickel [ˈpɪkəl] **(-s, -)** *m* pimple; *(Werkzeug)* pickaxe; *(Bergpickel)* ice axe; **p~ig** *adj* pimply, spotty

picken [ˈpɪkən] *vi* to pick, to peck

Picknick [ˈpɪknɪk] **(-s, -e** *od* **-s)** *nt* picnic; **~ machen** to have a picnic

piepen [ˈpiːpən] *vi* to chirp

piepsen [ˈpiːpsən] *vi* to chirp

Piepser *(umg) m* pager, paging device

Pier [piːər] **(-s, -s** *od* **-e)** *m od f* pier

Pietät [pieˈtɛːt] *f* piety, reverence; **p~los** *adj* impious, irreverent

Pigment [pɪgˈmɛnt] *nt* pigment

Pik [piːk] **(-s, -s)** *nt (KARTEN)* spades

pikant [piˈkant] *adj* spicy, piquant; *(anzüglich)* suggestive

Pilger [ˈpɪlgər] **(-s, -)** *m* pilgrim; **~fahrt** *f* pilgrimage

Pille [ˈpɪlə] *f* pill

Pilot [piˈloːt] **(-en, -en)** *m* pilot

Pilz [pɪlts] **(-es, -e)** *m* fungus; *(essbar)* mushroom; *(giftig)* toadstool; **~krankheit** *f* fungal disease

Pinguin [ˈpɪŋɡuiːn] **(-s, -e)** *m* penguin

Pinie [ˈpiːniə] *f* pine

pinkeln [ˈpɪŋkəln] *(umg) vi* to pee

Pinnwand [ˈpɪnvant] *f* noticeboard

Pinsel [ˈpɪnzəl] **(-s, -)** *m* paintbrush

Pinzette [pɪnˈtsɛtə] *f* tweezers *pl*

Pionier [pioˈniːr] **(-s, -e)** *m* pioneer; *(MIL)* sapper, engineer

Pirat [piˈraːt] **(-en, -en)** *m* pirate

Piste [ˈpɪstə] *f (SKI)* run, piste; *(AVIAT)* runway

Pistole [pɪsˈtoːlə] *f* pistol

Pizza [ˈpɪtsa] **(-, -s)** *f* pizza

Pkw [peːkaːˈveː] **(-(s), -(s))** *m abk* = **Personenkraftwagen**

plädieren [plɛˈdiːrən] *vi* to plead

Plädoyer [plɛdoaˈjeː] **(-s, -s)** *nt* speech for the defence; *(fig)* plea

Plage [ˈplaːgə] *f* plague; *(Mühe)* nuisance; **~geist** *m* pest, nuisance; **p~n** *vt* to torment ♦ *vr* to toil, to slave

Plakat [plaˈkaːt] **(-(e)s, -e)** *nt* placard; poster

Plan [plaːn] **(-(e)s, ⁻e)** *m* plan; *(Karte)* map

Plane *f* tarpaulin

planen *vt* to plan; *(Mord etc)* to plot

Planer **(-s, -)** *m* planner

Planet [plaˈneːt] **(-en, -en)** *m* planet

planieren [plaˈniːrən] *vt* to plane, to level

Planke [ˈplaŋkə] *f* plank

plan- [ˈplaːn] *zW:* **~los** *adj (Vorgehen)* unsystematic; *(Umherlaufen)* aimless; **~mäßig** *adj* according to plan; systematic; *(EISENB)* scheduled

Plansoll **(-s)** *nt* output target

Plantage [planˈtaːʒə] *f* plantation

Plan(t)schbecken [ˈplan(t)ʃbɛkən] *nt* paddling pool

plan(t)schen [ˈplan(t)ʃən] *vi* to splash

Planung *f* planning

Planwirtschaft *f* planned economy

plappern [ˈplapərn] *vi* to chatter

plärren [ˈplɛrən] *vi (Mensch)* to cry, to whine; *(Radio)* to blare

Plasma [ˈplasma] **(-s, Plasmen)** *nt* plasma

Plastik¹ [ˈplastɪk] *f* sculpture

Plastik² [ˈplastɪk] **(-s)** *nt (Kunststoff)* plastic; **~beutel** *m* plastic bag, carrier bag; **~folie** *f* plastic film

plastisch [ˈplastɪʃ] *adj* plastic; **stell dir das ~ vor!** just picture it!

Platane [plaˈtaːnə] *f* plane (tree)

Platin [ˈplaːtiːn] **(-s)** *nt* platinum

platonisch [plaˈtoːnɪʃ] *adj* platonic

platsch [platʃ] *excl* splash; **~en** *vi* to splash

plätschern [ˈplɛtʃərn] *vi* to babble

platschnass ▲ *adj* drenched

platt [plat] *adj* flat; *(umg: überrascht)* flabbergasted; *(fig: geistlos)* flat, boring; **~deutsch** *adj* low German; **P~e** *f*

(*Speisenplatte*, PHOT, TECH) plate; (*Steinplatte*) flag; (*Kachel*) tile; (*Schallplatte*) record; **P~enspieler** *m* record player; **P~enteller** *m* turntable

Platz [plats] **(-es, ⁼e)** *m* place; (*Sitzplatz*) seat; (*Raum*) space, room; (*in Stadt*) square; (*Sportplatz*) playing field; **~ nehmen** to take a seat; **jdm ~ machen** to make room for sb; **~angst** *f* claustrophobia; **~anweiser(in)** **(-s, -)** *m(f)* usher(ette)

Plätzchen [ˈplɛtsçən] *nt* spot; (*Gebäck*) biscuit

platzen *vi* to burst; (*Bombe*) to explode; **vor Wut ~** (*umg*) to be bursting with anger

platzieren ▲ [plaˈtsiːrən] *vt* to place ♦ *vr* (*SPORT*) to be placed; (*TENNIS*) to be seeded

Platz- *zW*: **~karte** *f* seat reservation; **~mangel** *m* lack of space; **~patrone** *f* blank cartridge; **~regen** *m* downpour; **~reservierung** [ˌrezɛrviːruŋ] *f* seat reservation; **~wunde** *f* cut

Plauderei [plaudəˈrai] *f* chat, conversation; (*RADIO*) talk

plaudern [ˈplaudərn] *vi* to chat, to talk

plausibel [plauˈziːbəl] *adj* plausible

plazieren △ [plaˈtsiːrən] *vt, vr siehe* **platzieren**

Pleite [ˈplaitə] *f* bankruptcy; (*umg: Reinfall*) flop; **~ machen** to go bust; **p~** (*umg*) *adj* broke

Plenum [ˈpleːnʊm] **(-s)** *nt* plenum

Plombe [ˈplɔmbə] *f* lead seal; (*Zahnplombe*) filling

plombieren [plɔmˈbiːrən] *vt* to seal; (*Zahn*) to fill

plötzlich [ˈplœtslɪç] *adj* sudden ♦ *adv* suddenly

plump [plʊmp] *adj* clumsy; (*Hände*) coarse; (*Körper*) shapeless; **~sen** (*umg*) *vi* to plump down, to fall

Plunder [ˈplʊndər] **(-s)** *m* rubbish

plündern [ˈplʏndərn] *vt* to plunder; (*Stadt*) to sack ♦ *vi* to plunder; **Plünderung** *f* plundering, sack, pillage

Plural [ˈpluːraːl] **(-s, -e)** *m* plural; **p~istisch** *adj* pluralistic

Plus [plʊs] **(-, -)** *nt* plus; (*FIN*) profit; (*Vorteil*) advantage; **p~** *adv* plus

Plüsch [plyːʃ] **(-(e)s, -e)** *m* plush

Plus- [plʊs] *zW*: **~pol** *m* (*ELEK*) positive pole; **~punkt** *m* point; (*fig*) point in sb's favour

Plutonium [pluˈtoːniʊm] **(-s)** *nt* plutonium

PLZ *abk = **Postleitzahl***

Po [poː] **(-s, -s)** (*umg*) *m* bottom, bum

Pöbel [ˈpøːbəl] **(-s)** *m* mob, rabble; **~ei** *f* vulgarity; **p~haft** *adj* low, vulgar

pochen [ˈpɔxən] *vi* to knock; (*Herz*) to pound; **auf etw** *akk* **~** (*fig*) to insist on sth

Pocken [ˈpɔkən] *pl* smallpox *sg*

Podium [ˈpoːdiʊm] *nt* podium; **~sdiskussion** *f* panel discussion

Poesie [poeˈziː] *f* poetry

Poet [poˈeːt] **(-en, -en)** *m* poet; **p~isch** *adj* poetic

Pointe [poˈɛːtə] *f* point

Pokal [poˈkaːl] **(-s, -e)** *m* goblet; (*SPORT*) cup; **~spiel** *nt* cup tie

pökeln [ˈpøːkəln] *vt* to pickle, to salt

Poker [ˈpoːkər] **(-s)** *nt* od *m* poker

Pol [poːl] **(-s, -e)** *m* pole; **p~ar** *adj* polar; **~arkreis** *m* Arctic circle

Pole [ˈpoːlə] **(-n, -n)** *m* Pole

polemisch [poˈleːmɪʃ] *adj* polemical

Polen [ˈpoːlən] **(-s)** *nt* Poland

Police [poˈliːs(ə)] *f* insurance policy

Polier [poˈliːr] **(-s, -e)** *m* foreman

polieren *vt* to polish

Poliklinik [poliˈkliːnɪk] *f* outpatients (department) *sg*

Polin *f* Pole

Politik [poliˈtiːk] *f* politics *sg*; (*eine bestimmte*) policy; **~er(in)** [poliˈtiːkər(ɪn)] **(-s, -)** *m(f)* politician

politisch [poˈliːtɪʃ] *adj* political

Politur [poliˈtuːr] *f* polish

Polizei [poliˈtsai] *f* police; **~beamte(r)** *m* police officer; **p~lich** *adj* police; **sich p~lich melden** to register with the police; **~revier** *nt* police station; **~staat** *m* police state; **~streife** *f* police patrol; **~stunde** *f* closing time; **~wache** *f* police station

Polizist(in) [poliˈtsɪst(ɪn)] **(-en, -en)** *m(f)* policeman(-woman)

Pollen ['pɔlən] (-s, -) *m* pollen; ~**flug** *m* pollen count

polnisch ['pɔlnɪʃ] *adj* Polish

Polohemd ['po:lohɛmt] *nt* polo shirt

Polster ['pɔlstər] (-s, -) *nt* cushion; (~*ung*) upholstery; (*in Kleidung*) padding; (*fig: Geld*) reserves *pl*; ~**er** (-s, -) *m* upholsterer; ~**möbel** *pl* upholstered furniture *sg*; **p~n** *vt* to upholster; to pad

Polterabend ['pɔltəra:bənt] *m* party on eve of wedding

poltern *vi* (*Krach machen*) to crash; (*schimpfen*) to rant

Polyp [po'ly:p] (-en, -en) *m* polyp; (*umg*) cop; ~**en** *pl* (*MED*) adenoids

Pomade [po'ma:də] *f* pomade

Pommes frites [pɔm'frɪt] *pl* chips, French fried potatoes

Pomp [pɔmp] (-(e)s) *m* pomp; **p~ös** [pɔm'pø:s] *adj* (*Auftritt, Fest, Haus*) ostentatious, showy

Pony ['pɔni] (-s, -s) *nt* (*Pferd*) pony ♦ *m* (*Frisur*) fringe

Popmusik ['pɔpmuzi:k] *f* pop music

Popo [po'po:] (-s, -s) (*umg*) *m* bottom, bum

poppig ['pɔpɪç] *adj* (*Farbe etc*) gaudy

populär [popu'lɛ:r] *adj* popular

Popularität [populari'tɛ:t] *f* popularity

Pore ['po:rə] *f* pore

Pornografie ▲ [pɔrnogra'fi:] *f* pornography; **pornografisch** ▲ [pɔrno'gra:fɪʃ] *adj* pornographic

porös [po'rø:s] *adj* porous

Porree ['pɔre] (-s, -s) *m* leek

Portefeuille [pɔrt(ə)'fø:j] *nt* (*POL, FIN*) portfolio

Portemonnaie [pɔrtmɔ'nɛ:] (-s, -s) *nt* purse

Portier [pɔrti'e:] (-s, -s) *m* porter

Portion [pɔrtsi'o:n] *f* portion, helping; (*umg: Anteil*) amount

Portmonee ▲ [pɔrtmo'ne:] (-s, -s) *nt* = **Portemonnaie**

Porto ['pɔrto] (-s, -s) *nt* postage; **p~frei** *adj* post-free, (postage) prepaid

Portrait [pɔr'trɛ:] (-s, -s) *nt* = **Porträt**; **p~ieren** *vt* = **porträtieren**

Porträt [pɔr'trɛ:] (-s, -s) *nt* portrait; **p~ieren** *vt* to paint, to portray

Portugal ['pɔrtugal] (-s) *nt* Portugal; **Portugiese** [pɔrtu'gi:zə] (-n, -n) *m* Portuguese; **Portu'giesin** *f* Portuguese; **portu'giesisch** *adj* Portuguese

Porzellan [pɔrtse'la:n] (-s, -e) *nt* china, porcelain; (*Geschirr*) china

Posaune [po'zaunə] *f* trombone

Pose ['po:zə] *f* pose

Position [pozitsi'o:n] *f* position

positiv ['po:zitі:f] *adj* positive; **P~** (-s, -e) *nt* (*PHOT*) positive

possessiv ['pɔsesi:f] *adj* possessive; **P~pronomen** (-s, -e) *nt* possessive pronoun

possierlich [po'si:rlɪç] *adj* funny

Post [pɔst] (-, -en) *f* post (office); (*Briefe*) mail; ~**amt** *nt* post office; ~**anweisung** *f* postal order, money order; ~**bote** *m* postman; ~**en** (-s, -) *m* post, position; (*COMM*) item; (*auf Liste*) entry; (*MIL*) sentry; (*Streikposten*) picket; ~**er** (-s, -(s)) *nt* poster; ~**fach** *nt* post office box; ~**karte** *f* postcard; **p~lagernd** *adv* poste restante (*BRIT*), general delivery (*US*); ~**leitzahl** *f* postal code; ~**scheckkonto** *nt* postal giro account; ~**sparbuch** *nt* post office savings book; ~**sparkasse** *f* post office savings bank; ~**stempel** *m* postmark; **p~wendend** *adv* by return of post; ~**wertzeichen** *nt* postage stamp

potent [po'tɛnt] *adj* potent

Potential △ [potentsi'a:l] (-s, -e) *nt siehe* **Potenzial**

potentiell △ [potentsi'ɛl] *adj siehe* **potenziell**

Potenz [po'tɛnts] *f* power; (*eines Mannes*) potency

Potenzial ▲ [poten'tsia:l] (-s, -e) *nt* potential

potenziell ▲ [poten'tsiɛl] *adj* potential

Pracht [praxt] (-) *f* splendour, magnificence; **prächtig** ['prɛçtɪç] *adj* splendid

Prachtstück *nt* showpiece

prachtvoll *adj* splendid, magnificent

Prädikat [prɛdi'ka:t] (-(e)s, -e) *nt* title;

Rechtschreibreform: ▲ *neue Schreibung* △ *alte Schreibung (auslaufend)*

(*GRAM*) predicate; (*Zensur*) distinction
prägen ['prɛːgən] *vt* to stamp; (*Münze*) to mint; (*Ausdruck*) to coin; (*Charakter*) to form
prägnant [prɛ'gnant] *adj* precise, terse
Prägung ['prɛːgʊŋ] *f* minting; forming; (*Eigenart*) character, stamp
prahlen ['praːlən] *vi* to boast, to brag; **Prahle'rei** *f* boasting
Praktik ['praktɪk] *f* practice; **p~abel** [-'kaːbəl] *adj* practicable; **~ant(in)** [-'kant(ɪn)] *m(f)* trainee; **~um** (**-s, Praktika** *od* **Praktiken**) *nt* practical training
praktisch ['praktɪʃ] *adj* practical, handy; **~er Arzt** general practitioner
praktizieren [prakti'tsiːrən] *vt, vi* to practise
Praline [pra'liːnə] *f* chocolate
prall [pral] *adj* firmly rounded; (*Segel*) taut; (*Arme*) plump; (*Sonne*) blazing; **~en** *vi* to bounce, to rebound; (*Sonne*) to blaze
Prämie ['prɛːmiə] *f* premium; (*Belohnung*) award, prize; **p~ren** *vt* to give an award to
Präparat [prɛpa'raːt] (**-(e)s, -e**) *nt* (*BIOL*) preparation; (*MED*) medicine
Präposition [prɛpozitsi'oːn] *f* preposition
Prärie [prɛ'riː] *f* prairie
Präsens ['prɛːzɛns] (**-**) *nt* present tense
präsentieren [prɛzɛn'tiːrən] *vt* to present
Präservativ [prɛzɛrva'tiːf] (**- s, -e**) *nt* contraceptive
Präsident(in) [prɛzi'dɛnt(ɪn)] *m(f)* president; **~schaft** *f* presidency
Präsidium [prɛ'ziːdiʊm] *nt* presidency, chair(manship); (*Polizeipräsidium*) police headquarters *pl*
prasseln ['prasəln] *vi* (*Feuer*) to crackle; (*Hagel*) to drum; (*Wörter*) to rain down
Praxis ['praksɪs] (**-, Praxen**) *f* practice; (*Behandlungsraum*) surgery; (*von Anwalt*) office
Präzedenzfall [prɛtse'dɛnts-] *m* precedent
präzis [prɛ'tsiːs] *adj* precise; **P~ion** [prɛtsizi'oːn] *f* precision
predigen ['preːdɪgən] *vt, vi* to preach; **Prediger** (**-s, -**) *m* preacher
Predigt ['preːdɪçt] (**-, -en**) *f* sermon
Preis [praɪs] (**-es, -e**) *m* price; (*Siegespreis*) prize; **um keinen ~** not at any price;

p~bewusst ▲ *adj* price-conscious
Preiselbeere *f* cranberry
preis- ['praɪz] *zW:* **~en** (*unreg*) *vi* to praise; **~geben** (*unreg*) *vt* to abandon; (*opfern*) to sacrifice; (*zeigen*) to expose; **~gekrönt** *adj* prizewinning; **P~gericht** *nt* jury; **~günstig** *adj* inexpensive; **P~lage** *f* price range; **~lich** *adj* (*Lage, Unterschied*) price, in price; **P~liste** *f* price list; **P~richter** *m* judge (*in a competition*); **P~schild** *nt* price tag; **P~träger(in)** *m(f)* prizewinner; **~wert** *adj* inexpensive
Prell- [prɛl] *zW:* **~bock** *m* buffers *pl*; **p~en** *vt* to bump; (*fig*) to cheat, to swindle; **~ung** *f* bruise
Premiere [prəmi'eːrə] *f* premiere
Premierminister [prəmi'eː mɪnɪstər] *m* prime minister, premier
Presse ['prɛsə] *f* press; **~agentur** *f* press agency; **~freiheit** *f* freedom of the press; **p~n** *vt* to press
Pressluft ▲ ['prɛslʊft] *f* compressed air; **~bohrer** *m* pneumatic drill
Prestige [prɛs'tiːʒə] (**-s**) *nt* prestige
prickeln ['prɪkəln] *vt, vi* to tingle; to tickle
Priester ['priːstər] (**-s, -**) *m* priest
prima *adj inv* first-class, excellent
primär [pri'mɛːr] *adj* primary
Primel ['priːməl] (**-, -n**) *f* primrose
primitiv [primi'tiːf] *adj* primitive
Prinz [prɪnts] (**-en, -en**) *m* prince; **~essin** *f* princess
Prinzip [prɪn'tsiːp] (**-s, -ien**) *nt* principle; **p~iell** [-i'ɛl] *adj, adv* on principle; **p~ienlos** *adj* unprincipled
Priorität [priori'tɛːt] *f* priority
Prise ['priːzə] *f* pinch
Prisma ['prɪsma] (**-s, Prismen**) *nt* prism
privat [pri'vaːt] *adj* private; **P~besitz** *m* private property; **P~fernsehen** *nt* commercial television; **P~patient(in)** *m(f)* private patient; **P~schule** *f* public school
Privileg [privi'leːk] (**-(e)s, -ien**) *nt* privilege
Pro [proː] (**-**) *nt* pro
pro *präp +akk* per
Probe ['proːbə] *f* test; (*Teststück*) sample; (*THEAT*) rehearsal; **jdn auf die ~ stellen** to

put sb to the test; **~exemplar** *nt* specimen copy; **~fahrt** *f* test drive; **p~n** *vt* to try; (*THEAT*) to rehearse; **p~weise** *adv* on approval; **~zeit** *f* probation period

probieren [pro'biːrən] *vt* to try; (*Wein, Speise*) to taste, to sample ♦ *vi* to try; to taste

Problem [pro'bleːm] **(-s, -e)** *nt* problem; **~atik** [-'maːtɪk] *f* problem; **p~atisch** [-'maːtɪʃ] *adj* problematic; **p~los** *adj* problem-free

Produkt [pro'dʊkt] **(-(e)s, -e)** *nt* product; (*AGR*) produce *no pl*; **~ion** [prodʊktsi'oːn] *f* production; output; **p~iv** [-'tiːf] *adj* productive; **~ivität** *f* productivity

Produzent [produ'tsɛnt] *m* manufacturer; (*Film*) producer

produzieren [produ'tsiːrən] *vt* to produce

Professor [pro'fɛsɔr] *m* professor

Profi ['proːfi] **(-s, -s)** *m* (*umg, SPORT*) pro

Profil [pro'fiːl] **(-s, -e)** *nt* profile; (*fig*) image

Profit [pro'fiːt] **(-(e)s, -e)** *m* profit; **p~ieren** *vi*: **p~ieren (von)** to profit (from)

Prognose [pro'gnoːzə] *f* prediction, prognosis

Programm [pro'gram] **(-s, -e)** *nt* programme; (*COMPUT*) program; **p~ieren** [-'miːrən] *vt* to programme; (*COMPUT*) to program; **~ierer(in)** **(-s, -)** *m(f)* programmer

progressiv [progrɛ'siːf] *adj* progressive

Projekt [pro'jɛkt] **(-(e)s, -e)** *nt* project; **~or** [pro'jɛktɔr] *m* projector

proklamieren [prokla'miːrən] *vt* to proclaim

Prokurist(in) [proku'rɪst(ɪn)] *m(f)* ≈ company secretary

Prolet [pro'leːt] **(-en, -en)** *m* prole, pleb; **~arier** [-'taːriər] **(-s, -)** *m* proletarian

Prolog [pro'loːk] **(-(e)s, -e)** *m* prologue

Promenade [promə'naːdə] *f* promenade

Promille [pro'mɪlə] **(-(s), -)** *nt* alcohol level

prominent [promi'nɛnt] *adj* prominent

Prominenz [promi'nɛnts] *f* VIPs *pl*

Promotion [promotsi'oːn] *f* doctorate, Ph.D.

promovieren [promo'viːrən] *vi* to do a doctorate *od* Ph.D.

prompt [prɔmpt] *adj* prompt

Pronomen [pro'noːmɛn] **(-s, -)** *nt* pronoun

Propaganda [propa'ganda] **(-)** *f* propaganda

Propeller [pro'pɛlər] **(-s, -)** *m* propeller

Prophet [pro'feːt] **(-en, -en)** *m* prophet

prophezeien [profe'tsaɪən] *vt* to prophesy; **Prophezeiung** *f* prophecy

Proportion [proportsi'oːn] *f* proportion; **p~al** [-'naːl] *adj* proportional

proportioniert [proportsio'niːrt] *adj*: **gut/schlecht ~** well-/badly-proportioned

Prosa ['proːza] **(-)** *f* prose; **p~isch** [pro'zaːɪʃ] *adj* prosaic

prosit ['proːzɪt] *excl* cheers

Prospekt [pro'spɛkt] **(-(e)s, -e)** *m* leaflet, brochure

prost [proːst] *excl* cheers

Prostituierte [prostitu'iːrtə] *f* prostitute

Prostitution [prostitutsi'oːn] *f* prostitution

Protest [pro'tɛst] **(-(e)s, -e)** *m* protest; **~ant(in)** [protɛs'tant(ɪn)] *m(f)* Protestant; **p~antisch** [protɛs'tantɪʃ] *adj* Protestant; **p~ieren** [protɛs'tiːrən] *vi* to protest

Prothese [pro'teːzə] *f* artificial limb; (*Zahnprothese*) dentures *pl*

Protokoll [proto'kɔl] **(-s, -e)** *nt* register; (*von Sitzung*) minutes *pl*; (*diplomatisch*) protocol; (*Polizeiprotokoll*) statement; **p~ieren** [-'liːrən] *vt* to take down in the minutes

protzen ['prɔtsən] *vi* to show off

Proviant [provi'ant] **(-s, -e)** *m* provisions *pl*, supplies *pl*

Provinz [pro'vɪnts] **(-, -en)** *f* province; **p~iell** *adj* provincial

Provision [provizi'oːn] *f* (*COMM*) commission

provisorisch [provi'zoːrɪʃ] *adj* provisional

Provokation [provokatsi'oːn] *f* provocation

provozieren [provo'tsiːrən] *vt* to provoke

Prozedur [protse'duːr] *f* procedure; (*pej*) carry-on

Prozent [pro'tsɛnt] **(-(e)s, -e)** *nt* per cent, percentage; **~satz** *m* percentage; **p~ual** [-u'aːl] *adj* percentage *cpd*; as a percentage

Prozess ▲ [pro'tsɛs] **(-es, -e)** *m* trial, case

Prozession [protsesi'oːn] *f* procession

prüde ['pryːdə] *adj* prudish; **P~rie** [-'riː] *f* prudery

Prüf- ['pry:f] *zW:* **p~en** *vt* to examine, to test; (*nachprüfen*) to check; **~er** (**-s, -**) *m* examiner; **~ling** *m* examinee; **~ung** *f* examination; checking; **~ungsaus-schuss** ▲ *m* examining board

Prügel ['pry:gəl] (**-s, -**) *m* cudgel ♦ *pl* (*Schläge*) beating; **~ei** [-'laɪ] *f* fight; **p~n** *vt* to beat ♦ *vr* to fight; **~strafe** *f* corporal punishment

Prunk [prʊŋk] (**-(e)s**) *m* pomp, show; **p~voll** *adj* splendid, magnificent

PS [pe:'ɛs] *abk* (= *Pferdestärke*) H.P.

Psych- ['psyç] *zW:* **~iater** [-i'a:tər] (**-s, -**) *m* psychiatrist; **p~iatrisch** *adj* (*MED*) psychiatric; **p~isch** *adj* psychological; **~oanalyse** [-o|ana'ly:zə] *f* psychoanalysis; **~ologe** (**-n, -n**) *m* psychologist; **~olo'gie** *f* psychology; **p~ologisch** *adj* psychological; **~otherapeut(in)** (**-en, -en**) *m(f)* psychotherapist

Pubertät [pubɛr'tɛit] *f* puberty

Publikum ['pu:blikʊm] (**-s**) *nt* audience, (*SPORT*) crowd

publizieren [publi'tsi:rən] *vt* to publish, to publicize

Pudding ['pʊdɪŋ] (**-s, -e** *od* **-s**) *m* blancmange

Pudel ['pu:dəl] (**-s**) *m* poodle

Puder ['pu:dər] (**-s, -**) *m* powder; **~dose** *f* powder compact; **p~n** *vt* to powder; **~zucker** *m* icing sugar

Puff¹ [pʊf] (**-s, -e**) *m* (*Wäschepuff*) linen basket; (*Sitzpuff*) pouf

Puff² [pʊf, *pl* **ᵛe**] (*umg*) *m* (*Stoß*) push

Puff³ [pʊf] (**-s, -**) (*umg*) *m od nt* (*Bordell*) brothel

Puffer (**-s, -**) *m* buffer

Pullover [pʊ'lo:vər] (**-s, -**) *m* pullover, jumper

Puls [pʊls] (**-es, -e**) *m* pulse; **~ader** *f* artery; **p~ieren** *vi* to throb, to pulsate

Pult [pʊlt] (**-(e)s, -e**) *nt* desk

Pulver ['pʊlfər] (**-s, -**) *nt* powder; **p~ig** *adj* powdery; **~schnee** *m* powdery snow

pummelig ['pʊmǝlɪç] *adj* chubby

Pumpe ['pʊmpə] *f* pump; **p~n** *vt* to pump; (*umg*) to lend; to borrow

Punkt [pʊŋkt] (**-(e)s, -e**) *m* point; (*bei Muster*) dot; (*Satzzeichen*) full stop; **p~ieren** [-'ti:rən] *vt* to dot; (*MED*) to aspirate

pünktlich ['pʏŋktlɪç] *adj* punctual; **P~keit** *f* punctuality

Punktsieg *m* victory on points

Punktzahl *f* score

Punsch [pʊnʃ] (**-(e)s, -e**) *m* punch

Pupille [pu'pɪlə] *f* pupil

Puppe ['pʊpə] *f* doll; (*Marionette*) puppet; (*Insektenpuppe*) pupa, chrysalis

Puppen- *zW:* **~spieler** *m* puppeteer; **~stube** *f* doll's house; **~theater** *nt* puppet theatre

pur [pu:r] *adj* pure; (*völlig*) sheer; (*Whisky*) neat

Püree [py're:] (**-s, -s**) *nt* mashed potatoes *pl*

Purzelbaum ['pʊrtsǝlbaʊm] *m* somersault

purzeln ['pʊrtsǝln] *vi* to tumble

Puste ['pu:stə] (**-**) (*umg*) *f* puff; (*fig*) steam; **p~n** *vi* to puff, to blow

Pute ['pu:tə] *f* turkey hen; **~r** (**-s, -**) *m* turkey cock

Putsch [pʊtʃ] (**-(e)s, -e**) *m* revolt, putsch

Putz [pʊts] (**-es**) *m* (*Mörtel*) plaster, roughcast

putzen *vt* to clean; (*Nase*) to wipe, to blow ♦ *vr* to clean o.s.; to dress o.s. up

Putz- *zW:* **~frau** *f* charwoman; **p~ig** *adj* quaint, funny; **~lappen** *m* cloth

Puzzle ['pasǝl] (**-s, -s**) *nt* jigsaw

PVC *nt abk* PVC

Pyjama [pi'dʒa:ma] (**-s, -s**) *m* pyjamas *pl*

Pyramide [pyra'mi:də] *f* pyramid

Pyrenäen [pyre'nɛ:ən] *pl* Pyrenees

Q, q

Quacksalber ['kvakzalbər] (**-s, -**) *m* quack (doctor)

Quader ['kva:dər] (**-s, -**) *m* square stone; (*MATH*) cuboid

Quadrat [kva'dra:t] (**-(e)s, -e**) *nt* square; **q~isch** *adj* square; **~meter** *m* square metre

quaken ['kva:kən] *vi* to croak; (*Ente*) to

quack

quäken ['kvɛːkən] *vi* to screech

Qual [kvaːl] (-, -en) *f* pain, agony; *(seelisch)* anguish; **q~en** *vt* to torment ♦ *vr* to struggle; *(geistig)* to torment o.s.; **~erei** *f* torture, torment

Qualifikation [kvalifikatsi'oːn] *f* qualification

qualifizieren [kvalifi'tsiːrən] *vt* to qualify; *(einstufen)* to label ♦ *vr* to qualify

Qualität [kvali'tɛːt] *f* quality; **~sware** *f* article of high quality

Qualle ['kvalə] *f* jellyfish

Qualm [kvalm] (-(e)s) *m* thick smoke; **q~en** *vt, vi* to smoke

qualvoll ['kvaːlfɔl] *adj* excruciating, painful, agonizing

Quant- ['kvant] *zW:* **~ität** [-i'tɛːt] *f* quantity; **q~itativ** [-ita'tiːf] *adj* quantitative; **~um** (-s) *nt* quantity, amount

Quarantäne [karan'tɛːnə] *f* quarantine

Quark [kvark] (-s) *m* curd cheese

Quartal [kvar'taːl] (-s, -e) *nt* quarter (year)

Quartier [kvar'tiːr] (-s, -e) *nt* accommodation; *(MIL)* quarters *pl*; *(Stadtquartier)* district

Quarz [kvaːrts] (-es, -e) *m* quartz

quasseln ['kvasəln] *(umg) vi* to natter

Quatsch [kvatʃ] (-es) *m* rubbish; **q~en** *vi* to chat, to natter

Quecksilber ['kvɛksɪlbər] *nt* mercury

Quelle ['kvɛlə] *f* spring; *(eines Flusses)* source; **q~n** *(unregt) vi (hervorquellen)* to pour *od* gush forth; *(schwellen)* to swell

quer [kveːr] *adv* crossways, diagonally; *(rechtwinklig)* at right angles; **~ auf dem Bett** across the bed; **Q~balken** *m* crossbeam; **Q~flöte** *f* flute; **Q~format** *nt* *(PHOT)* oblong format; **Q~schnitt** *m* cross-section; **~schnittsgelähmt** *adj* paralysed below the waist; **Q~straße** *f* intersecting road

quetschen ['kvɛtʃən] *vt* to squash, to crush; *(MED)* to bruise

Quetschung *f* bruise, contusion

quieken ['kviːkən] *vi* to squeak

quietschen ['kviːtʃən] *vi* to squeak

Quintessenz ['kvɪntɛsɛnts] *f* quintessence

Quirl [kvɪrl] (-(e)s, -e) *m* whisk

quitt [kvɪt] *adj* quits, even

Quitte *f* quince

quittieren [kvɪ'tiːrən] *vt* to give a receipt for; *(Dienst)* to leave

Quittung *f* receipt

Quiz [kvɪs] (-, -) *nt* quiz

quoll *etc* [kvɔl] *vb siehe* **quellen**

Quote ['kvoːtə] *f* number, rate

R, r

Rabatt [ra'bat] (-(e)s, -e) *m* discount

Rabattmarke *f* trading stamp

Rabe ['raːbə] (-n, -n) *m* raven

rabiat [rabi'aːt] *adj* furious

Rache ['raxə] (-) *f* revenge, vengeance

Rachen (-s, -) *m* throat

rächen ['rɛçən] *vt* to avenge, to revenge ♦ *vr* to take (one's) revenge; **das wird sich ~** you'll pay for that

Rad [raːt] (-(e)s, ᵘer) *nt* wheel; *(Fahrrad)* bike; **~ fahren** to cycle

Radar ['raːdaːr] (-s) *m od nt* radar; **~falle** *f* speed trap; **~kontrolle** *f* radar-controlled speed trap

Radau [ra'dau] (-s) *(umg) m* row

radeln ['raːdəln] *(umg) vi* to cycle

Radfahr- *zW:* **r~en** △ *(unregt) vi siehe* **Rad**; **~er(in)** *m(f)* cyclist; **~weg** *m* cycle track *od* path

Radier- [ra'diːr] *zW:* **r~en** *vt* to rub out, to erase; *(KUNST)* to etch; **~gummi** *m* rubber, eraser; **~ung** *f* etching

Radieschen [ra'diːsçən] *nt* radish

radikal [radi'kaːl] *adj* radical

Radio ['raːdio] (-s, -s) *nt* radio, wireless; **r~ak'tiv** *adj* radioactive; **~aktivi'tät** *f* radioactivity; **~apparat** *m* radio, wireless set

Radius ['raːdiʊs] (-, Radien) *m* radius

Rad- *zW:* **~kappe** *f (AUT)* hub cap; **~ler(in)** *(umg) m(f)* cyclist; **~rennen** *nt* cycle race; cycle racing; **~sport** *m* cycling; **~weg** *m* cycleway

raffen ['rafən] *vt* to snatch, to pick up; *(Stoff)*

to gather (up); (*Geld*) to pile up, to rake in
raffi'niert *adj* crafty, cunning
ragen ['ra:gən] *vi* to tower, to rise
Rahm [ra:m] **(-s)** *m* cream
Rahmen (-s, -) *m* frame(work); **im ~ des Möglichen** within the bounds of possibility; **r~** *vt* to frame
räkeln ['rɛːkln] *vr* = **rekeln**
Rakete [ra'keːtə] *f* rocket; **~nstützpunkt** *m* missile base
rammen ['ramən] *vt* to ram
Rampe ['rampə] *f* ramp; **~nlicht** *nt* (*THEAT*) footlights *pl*
ramponieren [rampo'niːrən] (*umg*) *vt* to damage
Ramsch [ramʃ] **(-(e)s, -e)** *m* junk
ran [ran] (*umg*) *adv* = **heran**
Rand [rant] **(-(e)s, "er)** *m* edge; (*von Brille, Tasse etc*) rim; (*Hutrand*) brim; (*auf Papier*) margin; (*Schmutzrand, unter Augen*) ring; (*fig*) verge, brink; **außer ~ und Band** wild; **am ~e bemerkt** mentioned in passing
randalieren [randa'liːrən] *vi* to (go on the) rampage
Rang [raŋ] **(-(e)s, "e)** *m* rank; (*Stand*) standing; (*Wert*) quality; (*THEAT*) circle
Rangier- [rãʒiːr] *zW*: **~bahnhof** *m* marshalling yard; **r~en** *vt* (*EISENB*) to shunt, to switch (*US*) ♦ *vi* to rank, to be classed; **~gleis** *nt* siding
Ranke ['raŋkə] *f* tendril, shoot
ranzig ['rantsiç] *adj* rancid
Rappen ['rapən] *m* (*FIN*) rappen, centime
rar [raːr] *adj* rare; **sich ~ machen** (*umg*) to keep o.s. to o.s.; **R~i'tät** *f* rarity; (*Sammelobjekt*) curio
rasant [ra'zant] *adj* quick, rapid
rasch [raʃ] *adj* quick
rascheln *vi* to rustle
Rasen ['raːzən] **(-s, -)** *m* lawn; grass
rasen *vi* to rave; (*schnell*) to race; **~d** *adj* furious; **~de Kopfschmerzen** a splitting headache
Rasenmäher (-s, -) *m* lawnmower
Rasier- [ra'ziːr] *zW*: **~apparat** *m* shaver; **~creme** *f* shaving cream; **r~en** *vt, vr* to shave; **~klinge** *f* razor blade; **~messer** *nt*

razor; **~pinsel** *m* shaving brush; **~schaum** *m* shaving foam; **~seife** *f* shaving soap *od* stick; **~wasser** *nt* shaving lotion
Rasse ['rasə] *f* race; (*Tierrasse*) breed; **~hund** *m* thoroughbred dog
rasseln ['rasəln] *vi* to clatter
Rassen- *zW*: **~hass** ▲ *m* race *od* racial hatred; **~trennung** *f* racial segregation
Rassismus [ra'sɪsmʊs] *m* racism
Rast [rast] **(-, -en)** *f* rest; **r~en** *vi* to rest; **~hof** *m* (*AUT*) service station; **r~los** *adj* tireless; (*unruhig*) restless; **~platz** *m* (*AUT*) layby; **~stätte** *f* (*AUT*) service station
Rasur [ra'zuːr] *f* shaving
Rat [raːt] **(-(e)s, Schläge)** *m* advice *no pl*, **ein ~** a piece of advice; **keinen ~ wissen** not to know what to do; *siehe* **zurate**
Rate *f* instalment
raten (*unreg*) *vt, vi* to guess; (*empfehlen*): **jdm ~** to advise sb
Ratenzahlung *f* hire purchase
Ratgeber (-s, -) *m* adviser
Rathaus *nt* town hall
ratifizieren [ratifi'tsiːrən] *vt* to ratify
Ration [ratsi'oːn] *f* ration; **r~al** [-'naːl] *adj* rational; **r~ali'sieren** *vt* to rationalize; **r~ell** [-'nɛl] *adj* efficient; **r~ieren** [-'niːrən] *vt* to ration
Rat- *zW*: **r~los** *adj* at a loss, helpless; **r~sam** *adj* advisable; **~schlag** *m* (piece of) advice
Rätsel ['rɛːtsəl] **(-s, -)** *nt* puzzle; (*Worträtsel*) riddle; **r~haft** *adj* mysterious; **es ist mir r~haft** it's a mystery to me
Ratte ['ratə] *f* rat; **~nfänger (-s, -)** *m* ratcatcher
rattern ['ratərn] *vi* to rattle, to clatter
rau ▲ [rau] *adj* rough, coarse; (*Wetter*) harsh
Raub [raup] **(-(e)s)** *m* robbery; (*Beute*) loot, booty; **~bau** *m* ruthless exploitation; **r~en** ['raubən] *vt* to rob; (*Mensch*) to kidnap, to abduct
Räuber ['rɔybər] **(-s, -)** *m* robber
Raub- *zW*: **~mord** *m* robbery with murder; **~tier** *nt* predator; **~überfall** *m* robbery with violence; **~vogel** *m* bird of prey
Rauch [raux] **(-(e)s)** *m* smoke; **r~en** *vt, vi* to

smoke; **~er(in)** **(-s, -)** *m(f)* smoker;
~erabteil *nt* (*EISENB*) smoker; **räuchern** *vt*
to smoke, to cure; **~fleisch** *nt* smoked
meat; **r~ig** *adj* smoky
rauf [rauf] (*umg*) *adv* = **herauf; hinauf**
raufen *vt* (*Haare*) to pull out ♦ *vi, vr* to fight;
Raufe'rei *f* brawl, fight
rauh △ *etc* [rau] *adj siehe* **rau** *etc*
Raum [raum] **(-(e)s, Räume)** *m* space;
(*Zimmer, Platz*) room; (*Gebiet*) area
räumen ['rɔymən] *vt* to clear; (*Wohnung,
Platz*) to vacate; (*wegbringen*) to shift, to
move; (*in Schrank etc*) to put away
Raum- *zW*: **~fähre** *f* space shuttle; **~fahrt** *f*
space travel; **~inhalt** *m* cubic capacity,
volume
räumlich ['rɔymlɪç] *adj* spatial; **R~keiten** *pl*
premises
Raum- *zW*: **~pflegerin** *f* cleaner; **~schiff**
nt spaceship; **~schifffahrt** ▲ *f* space
travel
Räumung ['rɔymʊŋ] *f* vacating, evacuation;
clearing (away)
Räumungs- *zW*: **~arbeiten** *pl* clearance
operations; **~verkauf** *m* clearance sale; (*bei
Geschäftsaufgabe*) closing down sale
raunen ['raunən] *vt, vi* to whisper
Raupe ['raupə] *f* caterpillar; (*~nkette*)
(caterpillar) track
Raureif ▲ ['rauraɪf] *m* hoarfrost
raus [raus] (*umg*) *adv* = **heraus; hinaus**
Rausch [rauʃ] **(-(e)s, Räusche)** *m*
intoxication
rauschen *vi* (*Wasser*) to rush; (*Baum*) to
rustle; (*Radio etc*) to hiss; (*Mensch*) to
sweep, to sail; **~d** *adj* (*Beifall*) thunderous;
(*Fest*) sumptuous
Rauschgift *nt* drug; **~süchtige(r)** *f(m)*
drug addict
räuspern ['rɔyspərn] *vr* to clear one's throat
Razzia ['ratsia] **(-, Razzien)** *f* raid
Reagenzglas [rea'gɛntsglaːs] *nt* test tube
reagieren [rea'giːrən] *vi*: **~ (auf** +*akk*) to
react (to)
Reakt- *zW*: **~ion** [reaktsi'oːn] *f* reaction;
r~io'när *adj* reactionary; **~or** [re'aktɔr] *m*
reactor

real [re'aːl] *adj* real, material
reali'sieren *vt* (*verwirklichen: Pläne*) to carry
out
Realismus [rea'lɪsmʊs] *m* realism
rea'listisch *adj* realistic
Realschule *f* secondary school

     Realschule

ⓘ   The Realschule *is one of the secondary
schools a German schoolchild may
attend after the* Grundschule*. On the
successful completion of six years of
schooling in the* Realschule *pupils gain the*
mittlere Reife *and usually go on to
vocational training or further education.*

Rebe ['reːbə] *f* vine
rebellieren [rebɛ'liːrən] *vi* to rebel;
Rebelli'on *f* rebellion; **re'bellisch** *adj*
rebellious
Rebhuhn ['rɛphuːn] *nt* (*KOCH, ZOOL*)
partridge
Rechen ['rɛçən] **(-s, -)** *m* rake
Rechen- *zW*: **~fehler** *m* miscalculation;
~maschine *f* calculating machine;
~schaft *f* account; **für etw ~schaft
ablegen** to account for sth; **~schieber** *m*
slide rule
Rech- ['rɛç] *zW*: **r~nen** *vt, vi* to calculate;
jdn/etw r~nen zu to count sb/sth among;
r~nen mit to reckon with; **r~nen auf** +*akk*
to count on; **~nen** *nt* arithmetic; **~ner (-s,
-)** *m* calculator (*COMPUT*) computer; **~nung**
f calculation(s); (*COMM*) bill, check (*US*);
jdm/etw ~nung tragen to take sb/sth into
account; **~nungsbetrag** *m* total amount
of a bill/invoice; **~nungsjahr** *nt* financial
year; **~nungsprüfer** *m* auditor
Recht [rɛçt] **(-(e)s, -e)** *nt* right; (*JUR*) law;
mit ~ rightly, justly; **R~ haben** to be right;
jdm R~ geben to agree with sb; **von ~s
wegen** by rights
recht *adj* right ♦ *adv* (*vor Adjektiv*) really,
quite; **das ist mir ~** that suits me; **jetzt
erst ~** now more than ever
Rechte *f* right (hand); (*POL*) Right; **r~(r, s)**
adj right; (*POL*) right-wing; **ein ~r** a right-

winger; **~(s)** *nt* right thing; **etwas/nichts ~s** something/nothing proper

recht- *zW*: **~eckig** *adj* rectangular; **~fertigen** *vt insep* to justify ♦ *vr insep* to justify o.s.; **R~fertigung** *f* justification; **~haberisch** *(pej) adj (Mensch)* opinionated; **~lich** *adj (gesetzlich: Gleichstellung, Anspruch)* legal; **~los** *adj* with no rights; **~mäßig** *adj* legal, lawful

rechts [rɛçts] *adv* on/to the right; **R~anwalt** *m* lawyer, barrister; **R~anwältin** *f* lawyer, barrister

Rechtschreibung *f* spelling

Rechts- *zW*: **~fall** *m* (law) case; **~händer** **(-s, -)** *m* right-handed person; **r~kräftig** *adj* valid, legal; **~kurve** *f* right-hand bend; **r~verbindlich** *adj* legally binding; **~verkehr** *m* driving on the right; **r~widrig** *adj* illegal; **~wissenschaft** *f* jurisprudence

rechtwinklig *adj* right-angled

rechtzeitig *adj* timely ♦ *adv* in time

Reck [rɛk] **(-(e)s, -e)** *nt* horizontal bar; **r~en** *vt, vr* to stretch

recyceln [riːˈsaikəln] *vt* to recycle; **Recycling** [riːˈsaiklɪŋ] **(-s)** *nt* recycling

Redakteur [redakˈtøːr] *m* editor

Redaktion [redaktsiˈoːn] *f* editing; *(Leute)* editorial staff; *(Büro)* editorial office(s)

Rede [ˈreːdə] *f* speech; *(Gespräch)* talk; **jdn zur ~ stellen** to take sb to task; **~freiheit** *f* freedom of speech; **r~gewandt** *adj* eloquent; **r~n** *vi* to talk, to speak ♦ *vt* to say; *(Unsinn etc)* to talk; **~nsart** *f* set phrase

redlich [ˈreːtlɪç] *adj* honest

Redner **(-s, -)** *m* speaker, orator

redselig [ˈreːtzeːlɪç] *adj* talkative, loquacious

reduzieren [reduˈtsiːrən] *vt* to reduce

Reede [ˈreːdə] *f* protected anchorage; **~r** **(-s, -)** *m* shipowner; **~'rei** *f* shipping line *od* firm

reell [reˈɛl] *adj* fair, honest; *(MATH)* real

Refer- *zW*: **~at** [refeˈraːt] **(-(e)s, -e)** *nt* report; *(Vortrag)* paper; *(Gebiet)* section; **~ent** [refeˈrɛnt] *m* speaker; *(Berichterstatter)* reporter; *(Sachbearbeiter)* expert; **r~ieren** [refeˈriːrən] *vi*: **r~ieren über** +*akk* to speak

od talk on

reflektieren [reflɛkˈtiːrən] *vt (Licht)* to reflect

Reflex [reˈflɛks] **(-es, -e)** *m* reflex; **r~iv** [-ˈksiːf] *adj (GRAM)* reflexive

Reform [reˈfɔrm] **(-, -en)** *f* reform; **~ati'on** *f* reformation; **~ationstag** *m* Reformation Day; **~haus** *nt* health food shop; **r~ieren** [-ˈmiːrən] *vt* to reform

Regal [reˈgaːl] **(-s, -e)** *nt* (book)shelves *pl*, bookcase; stand, rack

rege [ˈreːgə] *adj (lebhaft: Treiben)* lively; *(wach, lebendig: Geist)* keen

Regel [ˈreːgəl] **(-, -n)** *f* rule; *(MED)* period; **r~mäßig** *adj* regular; **~mäßigkeit** *f* regularity; **r~n** *vt* to regulate, to control; *(Angelegenheit)* to settle ♦ *vr*: **sich von selbst r~n** to take care of itself; **r~recht** *adj* regular, proper, thorough; **~ung** *f* regulation; settlement; **r~widrig** *adj* irregular, against the rules

Regen [ˈreːgən] **(-s, -)** *m* rain; **~bogen** *m* rainbow; **~bogenpresse** *f* tabloids *pl*

regenerierbar [regeneˈriːrbaːr] *adj* renewable

Regen- *zW*: **~mantel** *m* raincoat, mac(kintosh); **~schauer** *m* shower (of rain); **~schirm** *m* umbrella; **~wald** *m* *(GEOG)* rainforest; **~wurm** *m* earthworm; **~zeit** *f* rainy season

Regie [reˈʒiː] *f (Film etc)* direction, *(THEAT)* production

Regier- *zW*: **r~en** *vt, vi* to govern, to rule; **~ung** *f* government; *(Monarchie)* reign; **~ungssitz** *m* seat of government; **~ungswechsel** *m* change of government; **~ungszeit** *f* period in government; *(von König)* reign

Regiment [regiˈment] **(-s, -er)** *nt* regiment

Region [regiˈoːn] *f* region

Regisseur [reʒɪˈsøːr] *m* director; *(THEAT)* (stage) producer

Register [reˈgɪstər] **(-s, -)** *nt* register; *(in Buch)* table of contents, index

registrieren [regɪsˈtriːrən] *vt* to register

Regler [ˈreːglər] **(-s, -)** *m* regulator, governor

reglos [ˈreːkloːs] *adj* motionless

regnen [ˈreːgnən] *vi unpers* to rain

regnerisch *adj* rainy

regulär [regu'lɛːr] *adj* regular

regulieren [regu'liːrən] *vt* to regulate; (*COMM*) to settle

Regung ['reːgʊŋ] *f* motion; (*Gefühl*) feeling, impulse; **r~slos** *adj* motionless

Reh [reː] (**-(e)s, -e**) *nt* deer, roe; **~bock** *m* roebuck; **~kitz** *nt* fawn

Reib- ['raɪb] *zW:* **~e** *f* grater; **~eisen** *nt* grater; **r~en** (*unreg*) *vt* to rub; (*KOCH*) to grate; **~fläche** *f* rough surface; **~ung** *f* friction; **r~ungslos** *adj* smooth

Reich (**-(e)s, -e**) *nt* empire, kingdom; (*fig*) realm; **das Dritte R~** the Third Reich

reich [raɪç] *adj* rich

reichen *vi* to reach; (*genügen*) to be enough *od* sufficient ♦ *vt* to hold out; (*geben*) to pass, to hand; (*anbieten*) to offer; **jdm ~** to be enough *od* sufficient for sb

reich- *zW:* **~haltig** *adj* ample, rich; **~lich** *adj* ample, plenty of; **R~tum** (**-s**) *m* wealth; **R~weite** *f* range

Reif (**-(e)s, -e**) *m* (*Ring*) ring, hoop

reif [raɪf] *adj* ripe; (*Mensch, Urteil*) mature

Reife (**-**) *f* ripeness; maturity; **r~n** *vi* to mature; to ripen

Reifen (**-s, -**) *m* ring, hoop; (*Fahrzeugreifen*) tyre; **~druck** *m* tyre pressure; **~panne** *f* puncture

Reihe ['raɪə] *f* row; (*von Tagen etc, umg: Anzahl*) series *sg*; **der ~ nach** in turn; **er ist an der ~** it's his turn; **an die ~ kommen** to have one's turn

Reihen- *zW:* **~folge** *f* sequence; **alphabetische ~folge** alphabetical order; **~haus** *nt* terraced house

reihum [raɪ'ʔʊm] *adv:* **es geht/wir machen das ~** we take turns

Reim [raɪm] (**-(e)s, -e**) *m* rhyme; **r~en** *vt* to rhyme

rein[1] [raɪn] (*umg*) *adv* = **herein; hinein**

rein[2] [raɪn] *adj* pure; (*sauber*) clean ♦ *adv* purely; **etw ins R~e schreiben** to make a fair copy of sth; **etw ins R~e bringen** to clear sth up; **R~fall** (*umg*) *m* let-down; **R~gewinn** *m* net profit; **R~heit** *f* purity; cleanness; **~igen** *vt* to clean; (*Wasser*) to

purify; **R~igung** *f* cleaning; purification; (*Geschäft*) cleaner's; **chemische R~igung** dry cleaning; dry cleaner's; **R~igungsmittel** *nt* cleansing agent; **~rassig** *adj* pedigree; **R~schrift** *f* fair copy

Reis [raɪs] (**-es, -e**) *m* rice

Reise ['raɪzə] *f* journey; (*Schiffsreise*) voyage; **~n** *pl* (*Herumreisen*) travels; **gute ~!** have a good journey; **~apotheke** *f* first-aid kit; **~büro** *nt* travel agency; **r~fertig** *adj* ready to start; **~führer** *m* guide(book); (*Mensch*) travel guide; **~gepäck** *nt* luggage; **~gesellschaft** *f* party of travellers; **~kosten** *pl* travelling expenses; **~leiter** *m* courier; **~lektüre** *f* reading matter for the journey; **r~n** *vi* to travel; **r~n nach** to go to; **~nde(r)** *f(m)* traveller; **~pass** ▲ *m* passport; **~proviant** *m* food and drink for the journey; **~route** *f* route, itinerary; **~ruf** *m* personal message; **~scheck** *m* traveller's cheque; **~veranstalter** *m* tour operator; **~versicherung** *f* travel insurance; **~ziel** *nt* destination

Reißbrett *nt* drawing board

reißen ['raɪsən] (*unreg*) *vt* to tear; (*ziehen*) to pull, to drag; (*Witz*) to crack ♦ *vi* to tear; to pull, to drag; **etw an sich ~** to snatch sth up; (*fig*) to take over sth; **sich um etw ~** to scramble for sth; **~d** *adj* (*Fluss*) raging; (*WIRTS: Verkauf*) rapid

Reiß- *zW:* **~verschluss** ▲ *m* zip(per), zip fastener; **~zwecke** *f* drawing pin (*BRIT*), thumbtack (*US*)

Reit- ['raɪt] *zW:* **r~en** (*unreg*) *vt, vi* to ride; **~er** (**-s, -**) *m* rider; (*MIL*) cavalryman, trooper; **~erin** *f* rider; **~hose** *f* riding breeches *pl*; **~pferd** *nt* saddle horse; **~stiefel** *m* riding boot; **~weg** *n* bridle path; **~zeug** *nt* riding outfit

Reiz [raɪts] (**-es, -e**) *m* stimulus; (*angenehm*) charm; (*Verlockung*) attraction; **r~bar** *adj* irritable; **~barkeit** *f* irritability; **r~en** *vt* to stimulate; (*unangenehm*) to irritate; (*verlocken*) to appeal to, to attract; **r~end** *adj* charming; **r~voll** *adj* attractive

rekeln ['reːkəln] *vr* to stretch out; (*lümmeln*)

to lounge *od* loll about

Reklamation [reklamatsi'o:n] *f* complaint

Reklame [re'kla:mə] *f* advertising; advertisement; **~ machen für etw** to advertise sth

rekonstruieren [rekɔnstru'i:rən] *vt* to reconstruct

Rekord [re'kɔrt] **(-(e)s, -e)** *m* record; **~leistung** *f* record performance

Rektor ['rɛktɔr] *m* (*UNIV*) rector, vice-chancellor; (*SCH*) headteacher (*BRIT*), principal (*US*); **~at** [-'ra:t] **(-(e)s, -e)** *nt* rectorate, vice-chancellorship; headship; (*Zimmer*) rector's *etc* office

Relais [rə'le:] **(-, -)** *nt* relay

relativ [rela'ti:f] *adj* relative; **R~ität** [relativi'tɛ:t] *f* relativity

relevant [rele'vant] *adj* relevant

Relief [reli'ef] **(-s, -s)** *nt* relief

Religion [religi'o:n] *f* religion

religiös [religi'øːs] *adj* religious

Reling ['re:lɪŋ] **(-, -s)** *f* (*NAUT*) rail

Remoulade [remu'la:də] *f* remoulade

Rendezvous [rãde'vu:] **(-, -)** *nt* rendezvous

Renn- ['ren] *zW*: **~bahn** *f* racecourse; (*AUT*) circuit, race track; **r~en** (*unreg*) *vt*, *vi* to run, to race; **~en** **(0, -)** *nt* running; (*Wettbewerb*) race; **~fahrer** *m* racing driver; **~pferd** *nt* racehorse; **~wagen** *m* racing car

renommiert [reno'mi:rt] *adj* renowned

renovieren [reno'vi:rən] *vt* to renovate; **Renovierung** *f* renovation

rentabel [ren'ta:bəl] *adj* profitable, lucrative

Rentabilität [rentabili'tɛ:t] *f* profitability

Rente ['rɛntə] *f* pension

Rentenversicherung *f* pension scheme

rentieren [rɛn'ti:rən] *vr* to pay, to be profitable

Rentner(in) ['rɛntnər(ɪn)] **(-s, -)** *m(f)* pensioner

Reparatur [repara'tu:r] *f* repairing; repair; **~werkstatt** *f* repair shop; (*AUT*) garage

reparieren [repa'ri:rən] *vt* to repair

Reportage [repɔr'ta:ʒə] *f* (on-the-spot) report; (*TV, RADIO*) live commentary *od* coverage

Reporter [re'pɔrtər] **(-s, -)** *m* reporter, commentator

repräsentativ [reprezɛnta'ti:f] *adj* (*stellvertretend, typisch: Menge, Gruppe*) representative; (*beeindruckend: Haus, Auto etc*) impressive

repräsentieren [reprezɛn'ti:rən] *vt* (*Staat, Firma*) to represent; (*darstellen: Wert*) to constitute ♦ *vi* (*gesellschaftlich*) to perform official duties

Repressalie [reprɛ'sa:liə] *f* reprisal

Reprivatisierung [reprivati'zi:rʊŋ] *f* denationalization

Reproduktion [reprodʊktsi'o:n] *f* reproduction

reproduzieren [reprodu'tsi:rən] *vt* to reproduce

Reptil [rɛp'ti:l] **(-s, -ien)** *nt* reptile

Republik [repu'bli:k] *f* republic; **r~anisch** *adj* republican

Reservat [rezɛr'va:t] **(-(e)s, -e)** *nt* reservation

Reserve [re'zɛrvə] *f* reserve; **~rad** *nt* (*AUT*) spare wheel; **~spieler** *m* reserve; **~tank** *m* reserve tank

reservieren [rezɛr'vi:rən] *vt* to reserve

Reservoir [rezɛrvo'a:r] **(-s, -e)** *nt* reservoir

Residenz [rezi'dɛns] *f* residence, seat

resignieren [rezi'gni:rən] *vi* to resign

resolut [rezo'lu:t] *adj* resolute

Resonanz [rezo'nants] *f* resonance; (*fig*) response

Resozialisierung [rezotsiali'zi:rʊŋ] *f* rehabilitation

Respekt [re'spɛkt] **(-(e)s)** *m* respect; **r~ieren** [-'ti:rən] *vt* to respect; **r~los** *adj* disrespectful; **r~voll** *adj* respectful

Ressort [re'so:r] **(-s, -s)** *nt* department

Rest [rɛst] **(-(e)s, -e)** *m* remainder, rest; (*Überrest*) remains *pl*

Restaurant [rɛsto'rã:] **(-s, -s)** *nt* restaurant

restaurieren [rɛstau'ri:rən] *vt* to restore

Rest- *zW*: **~betrag** *m* remainder, outstanding sum; **r~lich** *adj* remaining; **r~los** *adj* complete

Resultat [rezʊl'ta:t] **(-(e)s, -e)** *nt* result

Retorte [re'tɔrtə] *f* retort

Retouren [re'tu:rən] *pl* (*COMM*) returns
retten ['rɛtən] *vt* to save, to rescue
Retter(in) *m(f)* rescuer
Rettich ['rɛtɪç] **(-s, -e)** *m* radish
Rettung *f* rescue; (*Hilfe*) help; **seine letzte ~** his last hope
Rettungs- *zW*: **~boot** *nt* lifeboat; **~dienst** *m* rescue service; **r~los** *adj* hopeless; **~ring** *m* lifebelt, life preserver (*US*); **~wagen** *m* ambulance
retuschieren [retu'ʃi:rən] *vt* (*PHOT*) to retouch
Reue ['rɔyə] **(-)** *f* remorse; (*Bedauern*) regret; **r~n** *vt*: **es reut ihn** he regrets (it) *od* is sorry (about it)
Revanche [re'vã:ʃə] *f* revenge; (*SPORT*) return match
revanchieren [revã'ʃi:rən] *vr* (*sich rächen*) to get one's own back, to have one's revenge; (*erwidern*) to reciprocate, to return the compliment
Revier [re'vi:r] **(-s, -e)** *nt* district; (*Jagdrevier*) preserve; (*Polizeirevier*) police station; beat
Revolte [re'vɔltə] *f* revolt
revol'tieren *vi* (*gegen jdn/etw*) to rebel
Revolution [revolutsi'o:n] *f* revolution; **~är** [-'nɛ:r] **(-s, -e)** *m* revolutionary; **r~ieren** [-'ni:rən] *vt* to revolutionize
Rezept [re'tsɛpt] **(-(e)s, -e)** *nt* recipe; (*MED*) prescription; **r~frei** *adj* available without prescription; **~ion** *f* reception; **r~pflichtig** *adj* available only on prescription
R-Gespräch ['ɛrgəʃprɛːç] *nt* reverse charge call (*BRIT*), collect call (*US*)
Rhabarber [ra'barbər] **(-s)** *m* rhubarb
Rhein [raɪn] **(-s)** *m* Rhine; **r~isch** *adj* Rhenish
Rheinland-Pfalz *nt* (*GEOG*) Rheinland-Pfalz, Rhineland-Palatinate
Rhesusfaktor ['re:zusfaktɔr] *m* rhesus factor
rhetorisch [re'to:rɪʃ] *adj* rhetorical
Rheuma ['rɔyma] **(-s)** *nt* rheumatism; **r~tisch** [-'ma:tɪʃ] *adj* rheumatic
rhythmisch ['rytmɪʃ] *adj* rhythmical
Rhythmus ['rytmʊs] *m* rhythm
richt- ['rɪçt] *zW*: **~en** *vt* to direct; (*Waffe*) to aim; (*einstellen*) to adjust; (*instandsetzen*) to

repair; (*zurechtmachen*) to prepare; (*bestrafen*) to pass judgement on ♦ *vr*: **sich ~en nach** to go by; **~en an** +*akk* to direct at; (*fig*) to direct to; **~en auf** +*akk* to aim at; **R~er(in)** **(-s, -)** *m(f)* judge; **~erlich** *adj* judicial; **R~geschwindigkeit** *f* recommended speed
richtig *adj* right, correct; (*echt*) proper ♦ *adv* (*umg*: *sehr*) really; **bin ich hier ~?** am I in the right place?; **der/die R~e** the right one/person; **das R~e** the right thing; **etw ~ stellen** to correct sth; **R~keit** *f* correctness
Richt- *zW*: **~linie** *f* guideline; **~preis** *m* recommended price
Richtung *f* direction; tendency, orientation
rieb *etc* [ri:p] *vb siehe* **reiben**
riechen ['ri:çən] (*unreg*) *vt, vi* to smell; **an etw** *dat* **~** to smell sth; **nach etw ~** to smell of sth; **ich kann das/ihn nicht ~** (*umg*) I can't stand it/him
rief *etc* [ri:f] *vb siehe* **rufen**
Riegel ['ri:gəl] **(-s, -)** *m* bolt; (*Schokolade usw*) bar
Riemen ['ri:mən] **(-s, -)** *m* strap; (*Gürtel, TECH*) belt; (*NAUT*) oar
Riese ['ri:zə] **(-n, -n)** *m* giant
rieseln *vi* to trickle; (*Schnee*) to fall gently
Riesen- *zW*: **~erfolg** *m* enormous success; **r~groß** *adj* colossal, gigantic, huge; **~rad** *nt* big wheel
riesig ['ri:zɪç] *adj* enormous, huge, vast
riet *etc* [ri:t] *vb siehe* **raten**
Riff [rɪf] **(-(e)s, -e)** *nt* reef
Rille ['rɪlə] *f* groove
Rind [rɪnt] **(-(e)s, -er)** *nt* ox; cow; cattle *pl*; (*KOCH*) beef
Rinde ['rɪndə] *f* rind; (*Baumrinde*) bark; (*Brotrinde*) crust
Rind- [rɪnt] *zW*: **~fleisch** *nt* beef; **~vieh** *nt* cattle *pl*; (*umg*) blockhead, stupid oaf
Ring [rɪŋ] **(-(e)s, -e)** *m* ring; **~buch** *nt* ring binder; **r~en** (*unreg*) *vi* to wrestle; **~en** **(-s)** *nt* wrestling; **~finger** *m* ring finger; **~kampf** *m* wrestling bout; **~richter** *m* referee; **r~s** *adv*: **r~s um** round; **r~sherum** *adv* round about; **~straße** *f*

ring road; **r~sum** *adv* (*rundherum*) round about; (*überall*) all round; **r~sumher** = **ringsum**

Rinn- ['rɪn] *zW:* **~e** *f* gutter, drain; **r~en** (*unreg*) *vi* to run, to trickle; **~stein** *m* gutter

Rippchen ['rɪpçən] *nt* small rib; cutlet

Rippe ['rɪpə] *f* rib

Risiko ['riːziko] (**-s, -s** *od* **Risiken**) *nt* risk

riskant [rɪs'kant] *adj* risky, hazardous

riskieren [rɪs'kiːrən] *vt* to risk

Riss ▲ [rɪs] (**-es, -e**) *m* tear; (*in Mauer, Tasse etc*) crack; (*in Haut*) scratch; (*TECH*) design

rissig ['rɪsɪç] *adj* torn; cracked; scratched

Ritt [rɪt] (**-(e)s, -e**) *m* ride

ritt *etc vb siehe* **reiten**

Ritter (**-s, -**) *m* knight; **r~lich** *adj* chivalrous

Ritze ['rɪtsə] *f* crack, chink

Rivale [ri'vaːlə] (**-n, -n**) *m* rival

Rivalität [rivali'tɛːt] *f* rivalry

Robbe ['rɔbə] *f* seal

Roboter ['rɔbɔtər] (**-s, -**) *m* robot

robust [ro'bʊst] *adj* (*kräftig: Mensch, Gesundheit*) robust

roch *etc* [rɔx] *vb siehe* **riechen**

Rock [rɔk] (**-(e)s, ⁼e**) *m* skirt; (*Jackett*) jacket; (*Uniformrock*) tunic

Rodel ['roːdəl] (**-s, -**) *m* toboggan; **~bahn** *f* toboggan run; **r~n** *vi* to toboggan

Rogen ['roːgən] (**-s, -**) *m* roe, spawn

Roggen ['rɔgən] (**-s, -**) *m* rye; **~brot** *nt* (*KOCH*) rye bread

roh [roː] *adj* raw; (*Mensch*) coarse, crude; **R~bau** *m* shell of a building; **R~material** *nt* raw material; **R~öl** *nt* crude oil

Rohr [roːr] (**-(e)s, -e**) *nt* pipe, tube; (*BOT*) cane; (*Schilf*) reed; (*Gewehrrohr*) barrel; **~bruch** *m* burst pipe

Röhre ['røːrə] *f* tube, pipe; (*RADIO etc*) valve; (*Backröhre*) oven

Rohr- *zW:* **~leitung** *f* pipeline; **~zucker** *m* cane sugar

Rohstoff *m* raw material

Rokoko ['rɔkoko] (**-s**) *nt* rococo

Rolladen △ *m siehe* **Rollladen**

Rollbahn ['rɔlbaːn] *f* (*AVIAT*) runway

Rolle ['rɔlə] *f* roll; (*THEAT, soziologisch*) role; (*Garnrolle etc*) reel, spool; (*Walze*) roller; (*Wäscherolle*) mangle; **keine ~ spielen** not to matter; **eine (wichtige) ~ spielen bei** to play a (major) part *od* role in; **r~n** *vt, vi* to roll; (*AVIAT*) to taxi; **~r** (**-s, -**) *m* scooter; (*Welle*) roller

Roll- *zW:* **~kragen** *m* rollneck, polo neck; **~laden** ▲ *m* shutter; **~mops** *m* pickled herring; **~schuh** *m* roller skate; **~stuhl** *m* wheelchair; **~stuhlfahrer(in)** *m(f)* wheelchair user; **~treppe** *f* escalator

Rom [roːm] (**-s**) *nt* Rome

Roman [ro'maːn] (**-s, -e**) *m* novel; **~tik** *f* romanticism; **~tiker** [ro'mantɪkər] (**-s, -**) *m* romanticist; **r~tisch** [ro'mantɪʃ] *adj* romantic; **~ze** [ro'mantsə] *f* romance

Römer ['røːmər] (**-s, -**) *m* wineglass; (*Mensch*) Roman

römisch ['røːmɪʃ] *adj* Roman; **~-katholisch** *adj* (*REL*) Roman Catholic

röntgen ['rœntgən] *vt* to X-ray; **R~bild** *nt* X-ray; **R~strahlen** *pl* X-rays

rosa ['roːza] *adj inv* pink, rose(-coloured)

Rose ['roːzə] *f* rose

Rosen- *zW:* **~kohl** *m* Brussels sprouts *pl*; **~kranz** *m* rosary; **~montag** *m* Monday before Ash Wednesday

rosig ['roːzɪç] *adj* rosy

Rosine [ro'ziːnə] *f* raisin, currant

Ross ▲ [rɔs] (**-es, -e**) *nt* horse, steed; **~kastanie** *f* horse chestnut

Rost [rɔst] (**-(e)s, -e**) *m* rust; (*Gitter*) grill, gridiron; (*Bettrost*) springs *pl*; **~braten** *m* roast(ed) meat, roast; **r~en** *vi* to rust

rösten ['røːstən] *vt* to roast; to toast; to grill

Rost- *zW:* **r~frei** *adj* rust-free; rustproof; stainless; **r~ig** *adj* rusty; **~schutz** *m* rustproofing

rot [roːt] *adj* red; **in den ~en Zahlen** in the red

Röte ['røːtə] (**-**) *f* redness; **~ln** *pl* German measles *sg*; **r~n** *vt, vr* to redden

rothaarig *adj* red-haired

rotieren [ro'tiːrən] *vi* to rotate

Rot- *zW:* **~kehlchen** *nt* robin; **~stift** *m* red pencil; **~wein** *m* red wine

Rouge [ruːʒ] *nt* blusher

Roulade [ru'laːdə] *f* (*KOCH*) beef olive

Spelling Reform: ▲ *new spelling* △ *old spelling (to be phased out)*

Route ['ruːtə] f route
Routine [ru'tiːnə] f experience; routine
Rübe ['ryːbə] f turnip; **Gelbe ~** carrot; **Rote ~** beetroot (*BRIT*), beet (*US*)
rüber ['ryːbər] (*umg*) *adv* = **herüber**; **hinüber**
Rubrik [ru'briːk] f heading; (*Spalte*) column
Ruck [rʊk] (**-(e)s, -e**) *m* jerk, jolt
Rück- ['rʏk] *zW*: **~antwort** f reply, answer; **r~bezüglich** *adj* reflexive
Rücken ['rʏkən] (**-s, -**) *m* back; (*Bergrücken*) ridge
rücken *vt, vi* to move
Rücken- *zW*: **~mark** *nt* spinal cord; **~schwimmen** *nt* backstroke
Rück- *zW*: **~erstattung** f return, restitution; **~fahrkarte** f return (ticket); **~fahrt** f return journey; **~fall** *m* relapse; **r~fällig** *adj* relapsing; **r~fällig werden** to relapse; **~flug** *m* return flight; **~frage** f question; **r~fragen** *vi* to check, to inquire (further); **~gabe** f return; **~gaberecht** *nt* right of return; **~gang** *m* decline, fall; **r~gängig** *adj*: **etw r~gängig machen** to cancel sth; **~grat** (**-(e)s, -e**) *nt* spine, backbone; **~halt** *m* (*Unterstützung*) backing, support; **~kehr** (**-, -en**) f return; **~licht** *nt* back light; **r~lings** *adv* from behind; backwards; **~nahme** f taking back; **~porto** *nt* return postage; **~reise** f return journey; (*NAUT*) home voyage; **~reiseverkehr** *m* homebound traffic; **~ruf** *m* recall
Rucksack ['rʊkzak] *m* rucksack; **~tourist(in)** *m(f)* backpacker
Rück- *zW*: **~schau** f reflection; **~schlag** *m* (*plötzliche Verschlechterung*) setback; **~schluss** ▲ *m* conclusion; **~schritt** *m* retrogression; **r~schrittlich** *adj* reactionary; retrograde; **~seite** f back; (*von Münze etc*) reverse; **~sicht** f consideration; **~sicht nehmen auf** +*akk* to show consideration for; **r~sichtslos** *adj* inconsiderate; (*Fahren*) reckless; (*unbarmherzig*) ruthless; **r~sichtsvoll** *adj* considerate; **~sitz** *m* back seat; **~spiegel** *m* (*AUT*) rear-view mirror; **~spiel** *nt* return match; **~sprache** f further discussion *od* talk; **~stand** *m* arrears *pl*; **r~ständig** *adj* backward, out-of-date; (*Zahlungen*) in arrears; **~strahler** (**-s, -**) *m* rear reflector; **~tritt** *m* resignation; **~trittbremse** f pedal brake; **~vergütung** f repayment; (*COMM*) refund; **~versicherung** f reinsurance; **r~wärtig** *adj* rear; **r~wärts** *adv* backward(s), back; **~wärtsgang** *m* (*AUT*) reverse gear; **~weg** *m* return journey, way back; **r~wirkend** *adj* retroactive; **~wirkung** f reaction; retrospective effect; **~zahlung** f repayment; **~zug** *m* retreat
Rudel ['ruːdəl] (**-s, -**) *nt* pack; herd
Ruder ['ruːdər] (**-s, -**) *nt* oar; (*Steuer*) rudder; **~boot** *nt* rowing boat; **r~n** *vt, vi* to row
Ruf [ruːf] (**-(e)s, -e**) *m* call, cry; (*Ansehen*) reputation; **r~en** (*unreg*) *vt, vi* to call; to cry; **~name** *m* usual (first) name; **~nummer** f (tele)phone number; **~säule** f (*an Autobahn*) emergency telephone; **~zeichen** *nt* (*RADIO*) call sign; (*TEL*) ringing tone
rügen ['ryːgən] *vt* to rebuke
Ruhe ['ruːə] (**-**) f rest; (*Ungestörtheit*) peace, quiet; (*Gelassenheit, Stille*) calm; (*Schweigen*) silence; **jdn in ~ lassen** to leave sb alone; **sich zur ~ setzen** to retire; **~!** be quiet!, silence!; **r~n** *vi* to rest; **~pause** f break; **~stand** *m* retirement; **~stätte** f: **letzte ~stätte** final resting place; **~störung** f breach of the peace; **~tag** *m* (*von Geschäft*) closing day
ruhig ['ruːɪç] *adj* quiet; (*bewegungslos*) still; (*Hand*) steady; (*gelassen, friedlich*) calm; (*Gewissen*) clear; **kommen Sie ~ herein** just come on in; **tu das ~** feel free to do that
Ruhm [ruːm] (**-(e)s**) *m* fame, glory
rühmen ['ryːmən] *vt* to praise ♦ *vr* to boast
Rühr- [ryːr] *zW*: **~ei** *nt* scrambled egg; **r~en** *vt, vr* (*auch fig*) to move, to stir ♦ *vi*: **r~en von** to come *od* stem from; **r~en an** +*akk* to touch; (*fig*) to touch on; **r~end** *adj* touching, moving; **r~selig** *adj* sentimental, emotional; **~ung** f emotion
Ruin [ru'iːn] (**-s, -e**) *m* ruin; **~e** f ruin; **r~ieren** [-'niːrən] *vt* to ruin
rülpsen ['rʏlpsən] *vi* to burp, to belch
Rum [rʊm] (**-s, -s**) *m* rum

Rumän- [ru'mɛːn] zW: **~ien (-s)** nt Ro(u)mania; **r~isch** adj Ro(u)manian

Rummel ['rʊməl] **(-s)** (umg) m hubbub; (Jahrmarkt) fair; **~platz** m fairground, fair

Rumpf [rʊmpf] **(-(e)s, ⁺e)** m trunk, torso; (AVIAT) fuselage; (NAUT) hull

rümpfen ['rʏmpfən] vt (Nase) to turn up

rund [rʊnt] adj round ♦ adv (etwa) around; **~ um etw** round sth; **R~brief** m circular; **R~e** f round; (in Rennen) lap; (Gesellschaft) circle; **R~fahrt** f (round) trip

Rundfunk ['rʊntfʊŋk] **(-(e)s)** m broadcasting; **im ~** on the radio; **~gerät** nt wireless set; **~sendung** f broadcast, radio programme

Rund- zW: **r~heraus** adv straight out, bluntly; **r~herum** adv round about; all round; **r~lich** adj plump, rounded; **~reise** f round trip; **~schreiben** nt (COMM) circular; **~(wander)weg** m circular path od route

runter ['rʊntər] (umg) adv = **herunter**; **hinunter**

Runzel ['rʊntsəl] **(-, -n)** f wrinkle; **r~ig** adj wrinkled; **r~n** vt to wrinkle; **die Stirn r~n** to frown

rupfen ['rʊpfən] vt to pluck

ruppig ['rʊpɪç] adj rough, gruff

Rüsche ['ryːʃə] f frill

Ruß [ruːs] **(-es)** m soot

Russe ['rʊsə] **(-n, -n)** m Russian

Rüssel ['rʏsəl] **(-s, -)** m snout; (Elefantenrüssel) trunk

rußig ['ruːsɪç] adj sooty

Russin ['rʊsɪn] f Russian

russisch adj Russian

Russland ▲ ['rʊslant] **(-s)** nt Russia

rüsten ['rʏstən] vt to prepare ♦ vi to prepare; (MIL) to arm ♦ vr to prepare (o.s.); to arm o.s.

rüstig ['rʏstɪç] adj sprightly, vigorous

Rüstung ['rʏstʊŋ] f preparation; arming; (Ritterrüstung) armour; (Waffen etc) armaments pl; **~skontrolle** f arms control

Rute ['ruːtə] f rod

Rutsch [rʊtʃ] **(-(e)s, -e)** m slide; (Erdrutsch) landslide; **~bahn** f slide; **r~en** vi to slide;

(ausrutschen) to slip; **r~ig** adj slippery

rütteln ['rʏtəln] vt, vi to shake, to jolt

S, s

S. abk (= Seite) p.; = **Schilling**

s. abk (= siehe) see

Saal [zaːl] **(-(e)s, Säle)** m hall; room

Saarland ['zaːrlant] nt: **das ~** the Saar(land)

Saat [zaːt] **(-, -en)** f seed; (Pflanzen) crop; (Säen) sowing

Säbel ['zɛːbəl] **(-s, -)** m sabre, sword

Sabotage [zabo'taːʒə] f sabotage

Sach- ['zax] zW: **~bearbeiter** m specialist; **s~dienlich** adj relevant, helpful; **~e** f thing; (Angelegenheit) affair, business; (Frage) matter; (Pflicht) task; **zur ~e** to the point; **s~kundig** adj expert; **s~lich** adj matter-of-fact; objective; (Irrtum, Angabe) factual

sächlich ['zɛxlɪç] adj neuter

Sachschaden m material damage

Sachsen ['zaksən] **(-s)** nt Saxony

sächsisch ['zɛksɪʃ] adj Saxon

sacht(e) ['zaxt(ə)] adv softly, gently

Sachverständige(r) f(m) expert

Sack [zak] **(-(e)s, ⁺e)** m sack; **~gasse** f cul-de-sac, dead-end street (US)

Sadismus [za'dɪsmʊs] m sadism

Sadist [za'dɪst] m sadist

säen ['zɛːən] vt, vi to sow

Safersex ▲, Safer Sex m safe sex

Saft [zaft] **(-(e)s, ⁺e)** m juice; (BOT) sap; **s~ig** adj juicy; **s~los** adj dry

Sage ['zaːgə] f saga

Säge ['zɛːgə] f saw; **~mehl** nt sawdust

sagen ['zaːgən] vt, vi to say; (mitteilen): **jdm ~** to tell sb; **~ Sie ihm, dass ...** tell him ...

sagen vt, vi to saw

sagenhaft adj legendary; (umg) great, smashing

sah etc [zaː] vb siehe **sehen**

Sahne ['zaːnə] **(-)** f cream

Saison [zɛ'zõː] **(-, -s)** f season

Saite ['zaɪtə] f string

Sakko ['zako] (**-s, -s**) *m od nt* jacket
Sakrament [zakra'mɛnt] *nt* sacrament
Sakristei [zakrıs'taı] *f* sacristy
Salat [za'la:t] (**-(e)s, -e**) *m* salad; (*Kopfsalat*) lettuce; **~soße** *f* salad dressing
Salbe ['zalbə] *f* ointment
Salbei ['zalbaı] (**-s** *od* **-**) *m od f* sage
Saldo ['zaldo] (**-s, Salden**) *m* balance
Salmiak [zalmi'ak] (**-s**) *m* sal ammoniac; **~geist** *m* liquid ammonia
Salmonellenvergiftung [zalmo'nɛlən-] *f* salmonella (poisoning)
salopp [za'lɔp] *adj* casual
Salpeter [zal'pe:tər] (**-s**) *m* saltpetre; **~säure** *f* nitric acid
Salz [zalts] (**-es, -e**) *nt* salt; **s~en** (*unreg*) *vt* to salt; **s~ig** *adj* salty; **~kartoffeln** *pl* boiled potatoes; **~säure** *f* hydrochloric acid; **~streuer** *m* salt cellar; **~wasser** *nt* (*Meerwasser*) salt water
Samen ['za:mən] (**-s, -**) *m* seed; (*ANAT*) sperm
Sammel- ['zaməl] *zW:* **~band** *m* anthology; **~fahrschein** *m* multi-journey ticket; (*für mehrere Personen*) group ticket
sammeln ['zaməln] *vt* to collect ♦ *vr* to assemble, to gather; (*konzentrieren*) to concentrate
Sammlung ['zamlʊŋ] *f* collection; assembly, gathering; concentration
Samstag ['zamsta:k] *m* Saturday; **s~s** *adv* (on) Saturdays
Samt [zamt] (**-(e)s, -e**) *m* velvet; **s~** *präp* +*dat* (along) with, together with; **s~ und sonders** each and every one (of them)
sämtlich ['zɛmtlıç] *adj* all (the), entire
Sand [zant] (**-(e)s, -e**) *m* sand
Sandale [zan'da:lə] *f* sandal
Sand- *zW:* **~bank** *f* sandbank; **s~ig** ['zandıç] *adj* sandy; **~kasten** *m* sandpit; **~kuchen** *m* Madeira cake; **~papier** *nt* sandpaper; **~stein** *m* sandstone; **s~strahlen** *vt, vi insep* to sandblast; **~strand** *m* sandy beach
sandte *etc* ['zantə] *vb siehe* **senden**
sanft [zanft] *adj* soft, gentle; **~mütig** *adj* gentle, meek

sang *etc* [zaŋ] *vb siehe* **singen**
Sänger(in) ['zɛŋər(ın)] (**-s, -**) *m(f)* singer
Sani- *zW:* **s~eren** [za'ni:rən] *vt* to redevelop; (*Betrieb*) to make financially sound ♦ *vr* to line one's pockets; to become financially sound; **s~tär** [zani'tɛ:r] *adj* sanitary; **s~täre Anlagen** sanitation *sg*; **~täter** [zani'tɛ:tər] (**-s, -**) *m* first-aid attendant; (*MIL*) (medical) orderly
sanktionieren [zaŋktsio'ni:rən] *vt* to sanction
Sardelle [zar'dɛlə] *f* anchovy
Sardine [zar'di:nə] *f* sardine
Sarg [zark] (**-(e)s, ⁴e**) *m* coffin
Sarkasmus [zar'kasmʊs] *m* sarcasm
saß *etc* [za:s] *vb siehe* **sitzen**
Satan ['za:tan] (**-s, -e**) *m* Satan; devil
Satellit [zatɛ'li:t] (**-en, -en**) *m* satellite; **~enfernsehen** *nt* satellite television
Satire [za'ti:rə] *f* satire; **satirisch** *adj* satirical
satt [zat] *adj* full; (*Farbe*) rich, deep; **jdn/etw ~ sein** *od* **haben** to be fed up with sb/sth; **sich ~ hören/sehen an** +*dat* to hear/see enough of; **sich ~ essen** to eat one's fill; **~ machen** to be filling
Sattel ['zatəl] (**-s, ⁴**) *m* saddle; (*Berg*) ridge; **s~n** *vt* to saddle; **~schlepper** *m* articulated lorry
sättigen ['zɛtıgən] *vt* to satisfy; (*CHEM*) to saturate
Satz [zats] (**-es, ⁴e**) *m* (*GRAM*) sentence; (*Nebensatz, Adverbialsatz*) clause; (*Theorem*) theorem; (*MUS*) movement; (*TENNIS: Briefmarken etc*) set; (*Kaffee*) grounds *pl*; (*COMM*) rate; (*Sprung*) jump; **~teil** *m* part of a sentence; **~ung** *f* (*Statut*) statute, rule; **~zeichen** *nt* punctuation mark
Sau [zau] (**-, Säue**) *f* sow; (*umg*) dirty pig
sauber ['zaubər] *adj* clean; (*ironisch*) fine; **~ halten** to keep clean; **S~keit** *f* cleanness; (*einer Person*) cleanliness
säuberlich ['zɔybərlıç] *adv* neatly
säubern *vt* to clean; (*POL etc*) to purge; **Säuberung** *f* cleaning; purge
Sauce ['zo:sə] *f* sauce, gravy
sauer ['zauər] *adj* sour; (*CHEM*) acid; (*umg*)

cross; **saurer Regen** acid rain; **S~braten**
m braised beef marinated in vinegar

Sauerei [zauə'rai] (*umg*) *f* rotten state of
affairs, scandal; (*Schmutz etc*) mess;
(*Unanständigkeit*) obscenity

Sauerkraut *nt* sauerkraut, pickled cabbage

säuerlich ['zɔyərlıç] *adj* (*Geschmack*) sour;
(*missvergnügt: Gesicht*) dour

Sauer- *zW*: **~milch** *f* sour milk; **~rahm** *m*
(*KOCH*) sour cream; **~stoff** *m* oxygen;
~teig *m* leaven

saufen ['zaufən] (*unreg*) (*umg*) *vt, vi* to drink,
to booze; **Säufer** ['zɔyfər] (**-s, -**) (*umg*) *m*
boozer

saugen ['zaugən] (*unreg*) *vt, vi* to suck

säugen ['zɔygən] *vt* to suckle

Sauger ['zaugər] (**-s, -**) *m* dummy,
comforter (*US*); (*auf Flasche*) teat

Säugetier ['zɔygə-] *nt* mammal

Säugling *m* infant, baby

Säule ['zɔylə] *f* column, pillar

Saum [zaum] (**-(e)s, Säume**) *m* hem; (*Naht*)
seam

säumen ['zɔymən] *vt* to hem; to seam ♦ *vi*
to delay, to hesitate

Sauna ['zauna] (**-, -s**) *f* sauna

Säure ['zɔyrə] *f* acid

sausen ['zauzən] *vi* to blow; (*umg: eilen*) to
rush; (*Ohren*) to buzz; **etw ~ lassen** (*umg*)
not to bother with sth

Saxofon, Saxophon [zakso'fo:n] (**-s, -e**)
nt saxophone

SB *abk* = **Selbstbedienung**

S-Bahn *f abk* (= *Schnellbahn*) high speed
railway; (= *Stadtbahn*) suburban railway

schaben ['ʃaːbən] *vt* to scrape

schäbig ['ʃeːbıç] *adj* shabby

Schablone [ʃa'blo:nə] *f* stencil; (*Muster*)
pattern; (*fig*) convention

Schach [ʃax] (**-s, -s**) *nt* chess; (*Stellung*)
check; **~brett** *nt* chessboard; **~figur** *f*
chessman; '**~'matt** *adj* checkmate; **~spiel**
nt game of chess

Schacht [ʃaxt] (**-(e)s, e**) *m* shaft

Schachtel (**-, -n**) *f* box

schade ['ʃaːdə] *adj* a pity *od* shame ♦ *excl*:
(**wie**) **~!** (what a) pity *od* shame; **sich** *dat*

zu ~ sein für etw to consider o.s. too good
for sth

Schädel ['ʃeːdəl] (**-s, -**) *m* skull; **~bruch** *m*
fractured skull

Schaden ['ʃaːdən] (**-s, e**) *m* damage;
(*Verletzung*) injury; (*Nachteil*) disadvantage;
s~ *vi* +*dat* to hurt; **einer Sache s~** to
damage sth; **~ersatz** *m* compensation,
damages *pl*; **~freude** *f* malicious glee;
s~froh *adj* (*Mensch, Lachen*) gloating;
~sfall *m*: **im ~sfall** in the event of a claim

schadhaft ['ʃaːthaft] *adj* faulty, damaged

schäd- ['ʃeːt] *zW*: **~igen** ['ʃeːdıgən] *vt* to
damage; (*Person*) to do harm to, to harm;
~lich *adj*· **~lich (für)** harmful (to);
S~lichkeit *f* harmfulness; **S~ling** *m* pest

Schadstoff ['ʃaːtʃtɔf] *m* harmful substance;
s~arm *adj*: **s~arm sein** to contain a low
level of harmful substances

Schaf [ʃaːf] (**-(e)s, -e**) *nt* sheep

Schäfer ['ʃeːfər] (**-s, -e**) *m* shepherd; **~hund**
m Alsatian (dog) (*BRIT*), German shepherd
(dog) (*US*)

Schaffen ['ʃafən] (**-s**) *nt* (creative) activity

schaffen[1] ['ʃafən] (*unreg*) *vt* to create;
(*Platz*) to make

schaffen[2] ['ʃafən] *vt* (*erreichen*) to manage,
to do; (*erledigen*) to finish; (*Prüfung*) to pass;
(*transportieren*) to take ♦ *vi* (*umg: arbeiten*)
to work; **sich** *dat* **etw ~** to get o.s. sth;
sich an etw *dat* **zu ~ machen** to busy o.s.
with sth

Schaffner(in) ['ʃafnər(ın)] (**-s, -**) *m(f)*
(*Busschaffner*) conductor(-tress); (*EISENB*)
guard

Schaft [ʃaft] (**-(e)s, e**) *m* shaft; (*von Gewehr*)
stock; (*von Stiefel*) leg; (*BOT*) stalk; tree trunk

Schal [ʃaːl] (**-s, -e** *od* **-s**) *m* scarf

schal *adj* flat; (*fig*) insipid

Schälchen ['ʃeːlçən] *nt* cup, bowl

Schale ['ʃaːlə] *f* skin; (*abgeschält*) peel;
(*Nussschale, Muschelschale, Eischale*) shell;
(*Geschirr*) dish, bowl

schälen ['ʃeːlən] *vt* to peel; to shell ♦ *vr* to
peel

Schall [ʃal] (**-(e)s, -e**) *m* sound; **~dämpfer**
(**-s, -**) *m* (*AUT*) silencer; **s~dicht** *adj*

soundproof; **s~en** *vi* to (re)sound; **s~end** *adj* resounding, loud; **~mauer** *f* sound barrier; **~platte** *f* (gramophone) record

Schalt- ['ʃalt] *zW:* **~bild** *nt* circuit diagram; **~brett** *nt* switchboard; **s~en** *vt* to switch, to turn ♦ *vi* (AUT) to change (gear); (*umg: begreifen*) to catch on; **~er** (**-s, -**) *m* counter; (*an Gerät*) switch; **~erbeamte(r)** *m* counter clerk; **~erstunden** *pl* hours of business; **~hebel** *m* switch; (AUT) gear lever; **~jahr** *nt* leap year; **~ung** *f* switching; (ELEK) circuit; (AUT) gear change

Scham [ʃaːm] (**-**) *f* shame; (~*gefühl*) modesty; (*Organe*) private parts *pl*

schämen ['ʃɛːmən] *vr* to be ashamed

schamlos *adj* shameless

Schande [ʃandə] (**-**) *f* disgrace

schändlich ['ʃɛntlɪç] *adj* disgraceful, shameful

Schändung ['ʃɛndʊŋ] *f* violation, defilement

Schanze ['ʃantsə] *f* (*Sprungschanze*) ski jump

Schar [ʃaːr] (**-, -en**) *f* band, company; (*Vögel*) flock; (*Menge*) crowd; **in ~en** in droves; **s~en** *vr* to assemble, to rally

scharf [ʃarf] *adj* sharp; (*Essen*) hot, spicy; (*Munition*) live; **~ nachdenken** to think hard; **auf etw** *akk* **~ sein** (*umg*) to be keen on sth

Schärfe ['ʃɛrfə] *f* sharpness; (*Strenge*) rigour; **s~n** *vt* to sharpen

Scharf- *zW:* **s~machen** (*umg*) *vt* to stir up; **~richter** *m* executioner; **~schütze** *m* marksman, sharpshooter; **s~sinnig** *adj* astute, shrewd

Scharlach ['ʃarlax] (**-s, -e**) *m* (~*fieber*) scarlet fever

Scharnier [ʃarˈniːr] (**-s, -e**) *nt* hinge

scharren ['ʃarən] *vt, vi* to scrape, to scratch

Schaschlik ['ʃaʃlɪk] (**-s, -s**) *m* od *nt* (shish) kebab

Schatten ['ʃatən] (**-s, -**) *m* shadow; **~riss** ▲ *m* silhouette; **~seite** *f* shady side, dark side

schattieren [ʃaˈtiːrən] *vt, vi* to shade

schattig ['ʃatɪç] *adj* shady

Schatulle [ʃaˈtʊlə] *f* casket; (*Geldschatulle*) coffer

Schatz [ʃats] (**-es, ⁻e**) *m* treasure; (*Person*) darling

schätz- [ʃɛts] *zW:* **~bar** *adj* assessable; **S~chen** *nt* darling, love; **~en** *vt* (*abschätzen*) to estimate; (*Gegenstand*) to value; (*würdigen*) to value, to esteem; (*vermuten*) to reckon; **S~ung** *f* estimate; estimation; valuation; **nach meiner S~ung ...** I reckon that ...

Schau [ʃau] (**-**) *f* show; (*Ausstellung*) display, exhibition; **etw zur ~ stellen** to make a show of sth, to show sth off; **~bild** *nt* diagram

Schauder ['ʃaudər] (**-s, -s**) *m* shudder; (*wegen Kälte*) shiver; **s~haft** *adj* horrible; **s~n** *vi* to shudder; to shiver

schauen ['ʃauən] *vi* to look

Schauer ['ʃauər] (**-s, -**) *m* (*Regenschauer*) shower; (*Schreck*) shudder; **~geschichte** *f* horror story; **s~lich** *adj* horrific, spine-chilling

Schaufel ['ʃaufəl] (**-, -n**) *f* shovel; (NAUT) paddle; (TECH) scoop; **s~n** *vt* to shovel, to scoop

Schau- *zW:* **~fenster** *nt* shop window; **~fensterbummel** *m* window shopping (expedition); **~kasten** *m* showcase

Schaukel ['ʃaukəl] (**-, -n**) *f* swing; **s~n** *vi* to swing, to rock; **~pferd** *nt* rocking horse; **~stuhl** *m* rocking chair

Schaulustige(r) ['ʃaulʊstɪɡə(r)] *f(m)* onlooker

Schaum [ʃaum] (**-(e)s, Schäume**) *m* foam; (*Seifenschaum*) lather; **~bad** *nt* bubble bath

schäumen ['ʃɔymən] *vi* to foam

Schaum- *zW:* **~festiger** (**-s, -**) *m* mousse; **~gummi** *m* foam (rubber); **s~ig** *adj* frothy, foamy; **~stoff** *m* foam material; **~wein** *m* sparkling wine

Schauplatz *m* scene

schaurig ['ʃaurɪç] *adj* horrific, dreadful

Schauspiel *nt* spectacle; (THEAT) play; **~er(in)** *m(f)* actor (actress); **s~ern** *vi insep* to act; **Schauspielhaus** *nt* theatre

Scheck [ʃek] (**-s, -s**) *m* cheque; **~gebühr** *f* encashment fee; **~heft** *m* cheque book; **~karte** *f* cheque card

scheffeln ['ʃɛfəln] vt to amass

Scheibe ['ʃaɪbə] f disc; (Brot etc) slice; (Glasscheibe) pane; (MIL) target

Scheiben- zW: **~bremse** f (AUT) disc brake; **~wischer** m (AUT) windscreen wiper

Scheide ['ʃaɪdə] f sheath; (Grenze) boundary; (ANAT) vagina; **s~n** (unreg) vt to separate; (Ehe) to dissolve ♦ vi to depart; to part; **sich s~n lassen** to get a divorce

Scheidung f (Ehescheidung) divorce

Schein [ʃaɪn] (-(e)s, -e) m light; (Anschein) appearance; (Geld) (bank)note; (Bescheinigung) certificate; **zum ~** in pretence; **s~bar** adj apparent; **s~en** (unreg) vi to shine; (Anschein haben) to seem; **s~heilig** adj hypocritical; **~werfer** (-s, -) m floodlight; spotlight; (Suchscheinwerfer) searchlight; (AUT) headlamp

Scheiß- ['ʃaɪs] (umg) in zW bloody

Scheiße ['ʃaɪsə] (-) (umg) f shit

Scheitel ['ʃaɪtl] (-s, -) m top; (Haarscheitel) parting; **s~n** vt to part

scheitern ['ʃaɪtərn] vi to fall

Schelle ['ʃɛlə] f small bell; **s~n** vi to ring

Schellfisch ['ʃɛlfɪʃ] m haddock

Schelm [ʃɛlm] (-(e)s, -e) m rogue; **s~isch** adj mischievous, roguish

Schelte ['ʃɛltə] f scolding; **s~n** (unreg) vt to scold

Schema ['ʃeːma] (-s, -s od -ta) nt scheme, plan; (Darstellung) schema; **nach ~** quite mechanically; **s~tisch** [ʃeˈmaːtɪʃ] adj schematic; (pej) mechanical

Schemel ['ʃeːml] (-s, -) m (foot)stool

Schenkel ['ʃɛŋkl] (-s, -) m thigh

schenken ['ʃɛŋkən] vt (auch fig) to give; (Getränk) to pour; **sich** dat **etw ~** (umg) to skip sth; **das ist geschenkt!** (billig) that's a giveaway!; (nichts wert) that's worthless!

Scherbe ['ʃɛrbə] f broken piece, fragment; (archäologisch) potsherd

Schere ['ʃeːrə] f scissors pl; (groß) shears pl; **s~n** (unreg) vt to cut; (Schaf) to shear; (kümmern) vr to bother ♦ vr to care; **scher dich zum Teufel!** get lost!; **~'rei** (umg) f bother, trouble

Scherz [ʃɛrts] (-es, -e) m joke; fun; **~frage** f conundrum; **s~haft** adj joking, jocular

Scheu [ʃɔʏ] (-) f shyness; (Angst) fear; (Ehrfurcht) awe; **s~** adj shy; **s~en** vr: **sich s~en vor** +dat to be afraid of, to shrink from ♦ vt to shun ♦ vi (Pferd) to shy

scheuern ['ʃɔʏərn] vt to scour, to scrub

Scheune ['ʃɔʏnə] f barn

Scheusal ['ʃɔʏzaːl] (-s, -e) nt monster

scheußlich ['ʃɔʏslɪç] adj dreadful, frightful

Schi [ʃiː] m = **Ski**

Schicht [ʃɪçt] (-, -en) f layer; (Klasse) class, level; (in Fabrik etc) shift; **~arbeit** f shift work; **s~en** vt to layer, to stack

schick [ʃɪk] adj stylish, chic

schicken vt to send ♦ vr: **sich ~ (in** +akk) to resign o.s. (to) ♦ vb unpers (anständig sein) to be fitting

schicklich adj proper, fitting

Schicksal (-s, -e) nt fate; **~sschlag** m great misfortune, blow

Schieb- ['ʃiːb] zW: **~edach** nt (AUT) sun roof; **s~en** (unreg) vt (auch Drogen) to push; (Schuld) to put ♦ vi to push; **~etür** f sliding door; **~ung** f fiddle

Schieds- ['ʃiːts] zW: **~gericht** nt court of arbitration; **~richter** m referee; umpire; (Schlichter) arbitrator

schief [ʃiːf] adj crooked; (Ebene) sloping; (Turm) leaning; (Winkel) oblique; (Blick) funny; (Vergleich) distorted ♦ adv crooked(ly); (ansehen) askance; **etw ~ stellen** to slope sth; **~ gehen** (umg) to go wrong

Schiefer ['ʃiːfər] (-s, -) m slate

schielen ['ʃiːlən] vi to squint; **nach etw ~** (fig) to eye sth

schien etc [ʃiːn] vb siehe **scheinen**

Schienbein nt shinbone

Schiene ['ʃiːnə] f rail; (MED) splint; **s~n** vt to put in splints

schier [ʃiːr] adj (fig) sheer ♦ adv nearly, almost

Schieß- [ʃiːs] zW: **~bude** f shooting gallery; **s~en** (unreg) vt to shoot; (Ball) to kick; (Geschoss) to fire ♦ vi to shoot; (Salat etc) to run to seed; **s~en auf** +akk to shoot at; **~e'rei** *f* shooting incident, shoot-out; **~pulver** *nt* gunpowder; **~scharte** *f* embrasure

Schiff [ʃɪf] **(-(e)s, -e)** *nt* ship, vessel; (*Kirchenschiff*) nave; **s~bar** *adj* (*Fluss*) navigable; **~bruch** *m* shipwreck; **s~brüchig** *adj* shipwrecked; **~chen** *nt* small boat; (*Weben*) shuttle; (*Mütze*) forage cap; **~er** **(-s, -)** *m* bargeman, boatman; **~fahrt** ▲ *f* shipping; (*Reise*) voyage

Schikane [ʃi'kaːnə] *f* harassment; dirty trick; **mit allen ~n** with all the trimmings

schikanieren [ʃika'niːrən] *vt* to harass, to torment

Schikoree ▲ ['ʃikoreː] **(-s)** *m od f* = **Chicorée**

Schild¹ [ʃɪlt] **(-(e)s, -e)** *m* shield; **etw im ~e führen** to be up to sth

Schild² [ʃɪlt] **(-(e)s, -er)** *nt* sign; nameplate; (*Etikett*) label

Schilddrüse *f* thyroid gland

schildern ['ʃɪldərn] *vt* to depict, to portray

Schildkröte *f* tortoise; (*Wasserschildkröte*) turtle

Schilf [ʃɪlf] **(-(e)s, -e)** *nt* (*Pflanze*) reed; (*Material*) reeds *pl*, rushes *pl*; **~rohr** *nt* (*Pflanze*) reed

schillern ['ʃɪlərn] *vi* to shimmer; **~d** *adj* iridescent

Schilling ['ʃɪlɪŋ] *m* schilling

Schimmel ['ʃɪməl] **(-s, -)** *m* mould; (*Pferd*) white horse; **s~ig** *adj* mouldy; **s~n** *vi* to get mouldy

Schimmer ['ʃɪmər] **(-s)** *m* (*Lichtsein*) glimmer; (*Glanz*) shimmer; **s~n** *vi* to glimmer, to shimmer

Schimpanse [ʃɪm'panzə] **(-n, -n)** *m* chimpanzee

schimpfen ['ʃɪmpfən] *vt* to scold ♦ *vi* to curse, to complain; to scold

Schimpfwort *nt* term of abuse

schinden ['ʃɪndən] (*unreg*) *vt* to maltreat, to drive too hard ♦ *vr*: **sich ~ (mit)** to sweat and strain (at), to toil away (at); **Eindruck ~** (*umg*) to create an impression

Schinde'rei *f* grind, drudgery

Schinken ['ʃɪŋkən] **(-s, -)** *m* ham

Schirm [ʃɪrm] **(-(e)s, -e)** *m* (*Regenschirm*) umbrella; (*Sonnenschirm*) parasol, sunshade; (*Wandschirm, Bildschirm*) screen; (*Lampenschirm*) (lamp)shade; (*Mützenschirm*) peak; (*Pilzschirm*) cap; **~mütze** *f* peaked cap; **~ständer** *m* umbrella stand

schizophren [ʃitso'freːn] *adj* schizophrenic

Schlacht [ʃlaxt] **(-, -en)** *f* battle; **s~en** *vt* to slaughter, to kill; **~er** **(-s, -)** *m* butcher; **~feld** *nt* battlefield; **~hof** *m* slaughterhouse, abattoir; **~schiff** *nt* battleship; **~vieh** *nt* animals kept for meat; beef cattle

Schlaf [ʃlaːf] **(-(e)s)** *m* sleep; **~anzug** *m* pyjamas *pl*

Schläfe *f* (*ANAT*) temple

schlafen ['ʃlaːfən] (*unreg*) *vi* to sleep; **~ gehen** to go to bed; **S~szeit** *f* bedtime

schlaff [ʃlaf] *adj* slack; (*energielos*) limp; (*erschöpft*) exhausted

Schlaf- *zW*: **~gelegenheit** *f* sleeping accommodation; **~lied** *nt* lullaby; **s~los** *adj* sleepless; **~losigkeit** *f* sleeplessness, insomnia; **~mittel** *nt* sleeping pill

schläfrig ['ʃleːfrɪç] *adj* sleepy

Schlaf- *zW*: **~saal** *m* dormitory; **~sack** *m* sleeping bag; **~tablette** *f* sleeping pill; **~wagen** *m* sleeping car, sleeper; **s~wandeln** *vi insep* to sleepwalk; **~zimmer** *nt* bedroom

Schlag [ʃlaːk] **(-(e)s, ⁺e)** *m* (*auch fig*) blow; (*auch MED*) stroke; (*Pulsschlag, Herzschlag*) beat; (*ELEK*) shock; (*Blitzschlag*) bolt, stroke; (*Autotür*) car door; (*umg: Portion*) helping; (*Art*) kind, type; **Schläge** *pl* (*Tracht Prügel*) beating *sg*; **mit einem ~** all at once; **~ auf ~** in rapid succession; **~anfall** *m* stroke; **s~artig** *adj* sudden, without warning; **~baum** *m* barrier

Schlägel ['ʃleːgəl] **(-s, -)** *m* (drum)stick; (*Hammer*) mallet, hammer

schlagen ['ʃlaːgən] (*unreg*) *vt, vi* to strike, to hit; (*wiederholt ~, besiegen*) to beat; (*Glocke*) to ring; (*Stunde*) to strike; (*Sahne*) to whip; (*Schlacht*) to fight ♦ *vr* to fight; **nach jdm ~** (*fig*) to take after sb; **sich gut ~** (*fig*) to do well; **Schlager** ['ʃlaːgər] **(-s, -)**

m (auch fig) hit

Schläger ['ʃlɛːɡər] *m* brawler; *(SPORT)* bat; *(TENNIS etc)* racket; *(GOLF)* club; hockey stick; *(Waffe)* rapier; **Schläge'rei** *f* fight, punch-up

Schlagersänger(in) *m(f)* pop singer

Schlag- *zW:* **s~fertig** *adj* quick-witted; **~fertigkeit** *f* ready wit, quickness of repartee; **~loch** *nt* pothole; **~obers** *(ÖSTERR) nt* = **Schlagsahne; ~sahne** *f* (whipped) cream; **~seite** *f (NAUT)* list; **~wort** *nt* slogan, catch phrase; **~zeile** *f* headline; **~zeug** *nt* percussion; drums *pl*; **~zeuger (-s, -)** *m* drummer

Schlamassel [ʃlaˈmasəl] **(-s, -)** *(umg) m* mess

Schlamm [ʃlam] **(-(e)s, -e)** *m* mud; **s~ig** *adj* muddy

Schlamp- ['ʃlamp] *zW:* **~e** *(umg) f* slut; **s~en** *(umg) vi* to be sloppy; **~e'rei** *(umg) f* disorder, untidiness; sloppy work; **s~ig** *(umg) adj (Mensch, Arbeit)* sloppy, messy

Schlange ['ʃlaŋə] *f* snake; *(Menschenschlange)* queue *(BRIT)*, line-up *(US)*; **~ stehen** to (form a) queue, to line up

schlängeln ['ʃlɛŋəln] *vr (Schlange)* to wind; *(Weg)* to wind, twist; *(Fluss)* to meander

Schlangen- *zW:* **~biss ▲** *m* snake bite; **~gift** *nt* snake venom; **~linie** *f* wavy line

schlank [ʃlaŋk] *adj* slim, slender; **S~heit** *f* slimness, slenderness; **S~heitskur** *f* diet

schlapp [ʃlap] *adj* limp; *(locker)* slack; **S~e** *(umg) f* setback

Schlaraffenland [ʃlaˈrafənlant] *nt* land of milk and honey

schlau [ʃlau] *adj* crafty, cunning

Schlauch [ʃlaux] **(-(e)s, Schläuche)** *m* hose; *(in Reifen)* inner tube; *(umg: Anstrengung)* grind; **~boot** *nt* rubber dinghy; **s~en** *(umg) vt* to tell on, to exhaust

Schläue ['ʃlɔyə] **(-)** *f* cunning

Schlaufe ['ʃlaufə] *f* loop; *(Aufhänger)* hanger

Schlauheit *f* cunning

schlecht [ʃlɛçt] *adj* bad ♦ *adv* badly; **~ gelaunt** in a bad mood; **~ und recht** after

a fashion; **jdm ist ~** sb feels sick *od* bad; **jdm geht es ~** sb is in a bad way; **~ machen** to run down; **S~igkeit** *f* badness; bad deed

schlecken ['ʃlɛkən] *vt, vi* to lick

Schlegel ['ʃleːɡəl] **(-s, -)** *m (KOCH)* leg; *siehe* **Schlägel**

schleichen ['ʃlaɪçən] *(unreg) vi* to creep, to crawl; **~d** *adj* gradual; creeping

Schleichwerbung *f (COMM)* plug

Schleier ['ʃlaɪər] **(-s, -)** *m* veil; **s~haft** *(umg) adj:* **jdm s~haft sein** to be a mystery to sb

Schleif- ['ʃlaɪf] *zW:* **~e** *f* loop; *(Band)* bow; **s~en¹** *vt, vi* to drag; **s~en²** *(unreg) vt* to grind; *(Edelstein)* to cut; **~stein** *m* grindstone

Schleim [ʃlaɪm] **(-(e)s, -e)** *m* slime; *(MED)* mucus; *(KOCH)* gruel; **~haut** *f (ANAT)* mucous membrane; **s~ig** *adj* slimy

Schlemm- ['ʃlɛm] *zW:* **s~en** *vi* to feast; **~er (-s, -)** *m* gourmet; **~e'rei** *f* gluttony, feasting

schlendern ['ʃlɛndərn] *vi* to stroll

schlenkern ['ʃlɛŋkərn] *vt, vi* to swing, to dangle

Schlepp- ['ʃlɛp] *zW:* **~e** *f* train; **s~en** *vt* to drag; *(Auto, Schiff)* to tow; *(tragen)* to lug; **s~end** *adj* dragging, slow; **~er (-s, -)** *m* tractor; *(Schiff)* tug

Schlesien ['ʃleːziən] **(-s)** *nt* Silesia

Schleuder ['ʃlɔydər] **(-, -n)** *f* catapult; *(Wäscheschleuder)* spin-drier; *(Butterschleuder etc)* centrifuge; **~gefahr** *f* risk of skidding; **"Achtung ~gefahr"** "slippery road ahead"; **s~n** *vt* to hurl; *(Wäsche)* to spin-dry ♦ *vi (AUT)* to skid; **~preis** *m* give-away price; **~sitz** *m (AVIAT)* ejector seat; *(fig)* hot seat; **~ware** *f* cheap *od* cut-price goods *pl*

schleunigst ['ʃlɔynɪçst] *adv* straight away

Schleuse ['ʃlɔyzə] *f* lock; *(~ntor)* sluice

schlicht [ʃlɪçt] *adj* simple, plain; **~en** *vt (glätten)* to smooth, to dress; *(Streit)* to settle; **S~er (-s, -)** *m* mediator, arbitrator; **S~ung** *f* settlement; arbitration

Schlick [ʃlɪk] **(-(e)s, -e)** *m* mud; *(Ölschlick)* slick

schlief *etc* [ʃliːf] *vb siehe* **schlafen**

Schließ- ['ʃliːs] *zW:* **s~en** (*unreg*) *vt* to close, to shut; (*beenden*) to close; (*Freundschaft, Bündnis, Ehe*) to enter into; (*folgern*): **s~en (aus)** to infer (from) ♦ *vi, vr* to close, to shut; **etw in sich s~en** to include sth; **~fach** *nt* locker; **s~lich** *adv* finally; **s~lich doch** after all

Schliff [ʃlɪf] (-(e)s, -e) *m* cut(ting); (*fig*) polish

schlimm [ʃlɪm] *adj* bad; **~er** *adj* worse; **~ste(r, s)** *adj* worst; **~stenfalls** *adv* at (the) worst

Schlinge ['ʃlɪŋə] *f* loop; (*bes Henkersschlinge*) noose; (*Falle*) snare; (*MED*) sling; **s~n** (*unreg*) *vt* to wind; (*essen*) to bolt, to gobble ♦ *vi* (*essen*) to bolt one's food, to gobble

schlingern *vi* to roll

Schlips [ʃlɪps] (-es, -e) *m* tie

Schlitten ['ʃlɪtən] (-s, -) *m* sledge, sleigh; **~fahren** (-s) *nt* tobogganing

schlittern ['ʃlɪtərn] *vi* to slide

Schlittschuh ['ʃlɪtʃuː] *m* skate; **~ laufen** to skate; **~bahn** *f* skating rink; **~läufer(in)** *m(f)* skater

Schlitz [ʃlɪts] (-es, -e) *m* slit; (*für Münze*) slot; (*Hosenschlitz*) flies *pl*; **s~äugig** *adj* slant-eyed

Schloss ▲ [ʃlɔs] (-es, ⁻er) *nt* lock; (*an Schmuck etc*) clasp; (*Bau*) castle; chateau

schloss ▲ *etc vb siehe* **schließen**

Schlosser ['ʃlɔsər] (-s, -) *m* (*Autoschlosser*) fitter; (*für Schlüssel etc*) locksmith

Schlosserei [-'raɪ] *f* metal (working) shop

Schlot [ʃloːt] (-(e)s, -e) *m* chimney; (*NAUT*) funnel

schlottern ['ʃlɔtərn] *vi* to shake, to tremble; (*Kleidung*) to be baggy

Schlucht [ʃlʊxt] (-, -en) *f* gorge, ravine

schluchzen ['ʃlʊxtsən] *vi* to sob

Schluck [ʃlʊk] (-(e)s, -e) *m* swallow; (*Menge*) drop; **~auf** (-s, -s) *m* hiccups *pl*; **s~en** *vt, vi* to swallow

schludern ['ʃluːdərn] *vi* to skimp, to do sloppy work

schlug *etc* [ʃluːk] *vb siehe* **schlagen**

Schlummer ['ʃlʊmər] (-s) *m* slumber; **s~n**

vi to slumber

Schlund [ʃlʊnt] (-(e)s, ⁻e) *m* gullet; (*fig*) jaw

schlüpfen ['ʃlʏpfən] *vi* to slip; (*Vogel etc*) to hatch (out)

Schlüpfer ['ʃlʏpfər] (-s, -) *m* panties *pl*, knickers *pl*

schlüpfrig ['ʃlʏpfrɪç] *adj* slippery; (*fig*) lewd; **S~keit** *f* slipperiness; (*fig*) lewdness

schlurfen ['ʃlʊrfən] *vi* to shuffle

schlürfen ['ʃlʏrfən] *vt, vi* to slurp

Schluss ▲ [ʃlʊs] (-es, ⁻e) *m* end; (*~folgerung*) conclusion; **am ~** at the end; **~ machen mit** to finish with

Schlüssel ['ʃlʏsəl] (-s, -) *m* (*auch fig*) key; (*Schraubenschlüssel*) spanner, wrench; (*MUS*) clef; **~bein** *nt* collarbone; **~blume** *f* cowslip, primrose; **~bund** *m* bunch of keys; **~dienst** *m* key cutting service; **~loch** *nt* keyhole; **~position** *f* key position; **~wort** *nt* keyword

schlüssig ['ʃlʏsɪç] *adj* conclusive

Schluss- ▲ *zW:* **~licht** *nt* taillight; (*fig*) tailender; **~strich** *m* (*fig*) final stroke; **~verkauf** *m* clearance sale

schmächtig ['ʃmɛçtɪç] *adj* slight

schmackhaft ['ʃmakhaft] *adj* tasty

schmal [ʃmaːl] *adj* narrow; (*Person, Buch etc*) slender, slim; (*karg*) meagre

schmälern ['ʃmɛːlərn] *vt* to diminish; (*fig*) to belittle

Schmalfilm *m* cine film

Schmalz [ʃmalts] (-es, -e) *nt* dripping, lard; (*fig*) sentiment, schmaltz; **s~ig** *adj* (*fig*) schmaltzy

schmarotzen [ʃma'rɔtsən] *vi* to sponge; (*BOT*) to be parasitic; **Schmarotzer** (-s, -) *m* parasite; sponger

Schmarren ['ʃmarən] (-s, -) *m* (*ÖSTERR*) small piece of pancake; (*fig*) rubbish, tripe

schmatzen ['ʃmatsən] *vi* to smack one's lips; to eat noisily

schmecken ['ʃmɛkən] *vt, vi* to taste; **es schmeckt ihm** he likes it

Schmeichel- ['ʃmaɪçəl] *zW:* **~ei** [-'laɪ] *f* flattery; **s~haft** *adj* flattering; **s~n** *vi* to flatter

schmeißen ['ʃmaɪsən] (*unreg*) (*umg*) *vt* to

throw, to chuck

Schmelz [ʃmɛlts] **(-es, -e)** *m* enamel; (*Glasur*) glaze; (*von Stimme*) melodiousness; **s~en** (*unreg*) *vt* to melt; (*Erz*) to smelt ♦ *vi* to melt; **~punkt** *m* melting point; **~wasser** *nt* melted snow

Schmerz [ʃmɛrts] **(-es, -en)** *m* pain; (*Trauer*) grief; **s~empfindlich** *adj* sensitive to pain; **s~en** *vt*, *vi* to hurt; **~ensgeld** *nt* compensation; **s~haft** *adj* painful; **s~lich** *adj* painful; **s~los** *adj* painless; **~mittel** *nt* painkiller; **~tablette** *f* painkiller

Schmetterling [ʃmɛtərlɪŋ] *m* butterfly

schmettern [ʃmɛtərn] *vt* (*werfen*) to hurl; (*TENNIS: Ball*) to smash; (*singen*) to belt out (*inf*)

Schmied [ʃmiːt] **(-(e)s, -e)** *m* blacksmith; **~e** [ʃmiːdə] *f* smithy, forge; **~eeisen** *nt* wrought iron; **s~en** *vt* to forge; (*Pläne*) to devise, to concoct

schmiegen [ʃmiːgən] *vt* to press, to nestle ♦ *vr*: **sich ~ (an** +*akk*) to cuddle up (to), to nestle (up to)

Schmier- [ʃmiːr] *zW*: **~e** *f* grease; (*THEAT*) greasepaint, make-up; **s~en** *vt* to smear; (*ölen*) to lubricate, to grease; (*bestechen*) to bribe, (*schreiben*) to scrawl ♦ *vi* (*schreiben*) to scrawl; **~fett** *nt* grease; **~geld** *nt* bribe; **s~ig** *adj* greasy; **~seife** *f* soft soap

Schminke [ʃmɪŋkə] *f* make-up; **s~n** *vt*, *vr* to make up

schmirgeln [ʃmɪrgəln] *vt* to sand (down)

Schmirgelpapier *nt* emery paper

schmollen [ʃmɔlən] *vi* to sulk, to pout

Schmorbraten *m* stewed *od* braised meat

schmoren [ʃmoːrən] *vt* to stew, to braise

Schmuck [ʃmʊk] **(-(e)s, -e)** *m* jewellery; (*Verzierung*) decoration

schmücken [ʃmʏkən] *vt* to decorate

Schmuck- *zW*: **s~los** *adj* unadorned, plain; **~sachen** *pl* jewels, jewellery *sg*

Schmuggel [ʃmʊgəl] **(-s)** *m* smuggling; **s~n** *vt*, *vi* to smuggle

Schmuggler (-s, -) *m* smuggler

schmunzeln [ʃmʊntsəln] *vi* to smile benignly

schmusen [ʃmuːzən] (*umg*) *vi* (*zärtlich sein*) to cuddle, to canoodle (*inf*)

Schmutz [ʃmʊts] **(-es)** *m* dirt, filth; **~fink** *m* filthy creature; **~fleck** *m* stain; **s~ig** *adj* dirty

Schnabel [ʃnaːbəl] **(-s, ")** *m* beak, bill; (*Ausguss*) spout

Schnalle [ʃnalə] *f* buckle, clasp; **s~n** *vt* to buckle

Schnapp- [ʃnap] *zW*: **s~en** *vt* to grab, to catch ♦ *vi* to snap; **~schloss** ▲ *nt* spring lock; **~schuss** ▲ *m* (*PHOT*) snapshot

Schnaps [ʃnaps] **(-es, "e)** *m* spirits *pl*; schnapps

schnarchen [ʃnarçən] *vi* to snore

schnattern [ʃnatərn] *vi* (*Gänse*) to gabble; (*Ente*) to quack

schnauben [ʃnaubən] *vi* to snort ♦ *vr* to blow one's nose

schnaufen [ʃnaufən] *vi* to puff, to pant

Schnauze *f* snout, muzzle; (*Ausguss*) spout; (*umg*) gob

schnäuzen ▲ [ʃnɔytsən] *vr* to blow one's nose

Schnecke [ʃnɛkə] *f* snail; **~nhaus** *nt* snail's shell

Schnee [ʃneː] **(-s)** *m* snow; (*Eischnee*) beaten egg white; **~ball** *m* snowball; **~flocke** *f* snowflake; **s~frei** *adj* free of snow; **~gestöber** *nt* snowstorm; **~glöckchen** *nt* snowdrop; **~grenze** *f* snow line; **~kette** *f* (*AUT*) snow chain; **~mann** *m* snowman; **~pflug** *m* snowplough; **~regen** *m* sleet; **~schmelze** *f* thaw; **~wehe** *f* snowdrift

Schneide [ʃnaidə] *f* edge; (*Klinge*) blade; **s~n** (*unreg*) *vt* to cut; (*kreuzen*) to cross, to intersect with ♦ *vr* to cut o.s.; to intersect; **s~nd** *adj* cutting; **~r (-s, -)** *m* tailor; **~rei** *f* (*Geschäft*) tailor's; **~rin** *f* dressmaker; **s~rn** *vt* to make ♦ *vi* to be a tailor; **~zahn** *m* incisor

schneien [ʃnaiən] *vi unpers* to snow

Schneise [ʃnaizə] *f* clearing

schnell [ʃnɛl] *adj* quick, fast ♦ *adv* quick, quickly, fast; **S~hefter (-s, -)** *m* loose-leaf binder; **S~igkeit** *f* speed; **S~imbiss** ▲ *m* (*Lokal*) snack bar; **S~kochtopf** *m*

(*Dampfkochtopf*) pressure cooker; **S~reinigung** f dry cleaner's; **~stens** adv as quickly as possible; **S~straße** f expressway; **S~zug** m fast od express train

schneuzen △ ['ʃnɔʏtsən] vr siehe **schnäuzen**

schnippeln ['ʃnɪpəln] (*umg*) vt: **~ (an** +dat) to snip (at)

schnippisch ['ʃnɪpɪʃ] adj sharp-tongued

Schnitt (-(e)s, -e) m cut(ting); (*~punkt*) intersection; (*Querschnitt*) (cross) section; (*Durchschnitt*) average; (*~muster*) pattern; (*an Buch*) edge; (*umg: Gewinn*) profit

schnitt etc vb siehe **schneiden**

Schnitt- zW: **~blumen** pl cut flowers; **~e** f slice; (*belegt*) sandwich; **~fläche** f section; **~lauch** m chive; **~punkt** m (point of) intersection; **~stelle** f (COMPUT) interface; **~wunde** f cut

Schnitz- ['ʃnɪts] zW: **~arbeit** f wood carving; **~el** (-s, -) nt chip; (KOCH) escalope; **s~en** vt to carve; **~er** (-s, -) m carver; (*umg*) blunder; **~e'rei** f carving; carved woodwork

schnodderig ['ʃnɔdərɪç] (*umg*) adj snotty

Schnorchel ['ʃnɔrçəl] (-s, -) m snorkel

Schnörkel ['ʃnœrkəl] (-s, -) m flourish; (ARCHIT) scroll

schnorren ['ʃnɔrən] vt, vi to cadge

schnüffeln ['ʃnʏfəln] vi to sniff

Schnüffler (-s, -) m snooper

Schnuller ['ʃnʊlər] (-s, -) m dummy, comforter (US)

Schnupfen ['ʃnʊpfən] (-s, -) m cold

schnuppern ['ʃnʊpərn] vi to sniff

Schnur [ʃnuːr] (-, ⁻e) f string, cord; (ELEK) flex

schnüren ['ʃnyːrən] vt to tie

schnurgerade adj straight (as a die)

Schnurrbart ['ʃnʊrbaːrt] m moustache

schnurren ['ʃnʊrən] vi to purr; (*Kreisel*) to hum

Schnürschuh m lace-up (shoe)

Schnürsenkel m shoelace

schnurstracks adv straight (away)

Schock [ʃɔk] (-(e)s, -e) m shock; **s~ieren** [ʃɔ'kiːrən] vt to shock, to outrage

Schöffe ['ʃœfə] (-n, -n) m lay magistrate; **Schöffin** f lay magistrate

Schokolade [ʃoko'laːdə] f chocolate

Scholle ['ʃɔlə] f clod; (*Eisscholle*) ice floe; (*Fisch*) plaice

---

SCHLÜSSELWORT

schon [ʃoːn] adv **1** (*bereits*) already; **er ist schon da** he's there already, he's already there; **ist er schon da?** is he there yet?; **warst du schon einmal da?** have you ever been there?; **ich war schon einmal da** I've been there before; **das war schon immer so** that has always been the case; **schon oft** often; **hast du schon gehört?** have you heard?

2 (*bestimmt*) all right; **du wirst schon sehen** you'll see (all right); **das wird schon noch gut** that'll be OK

3 (*bloß*) just; **allein schon das Gefühl ...** just the very feeling ...; **schon der Gedanke** the very thought; **wenn ich das schon höre** I only have to hear that

4 (*einschränkend*): **ja schon, aber ...** yes (well), but ...

5: **schon möglich** possible; **schon gut!** OK!; **du weißt schon** you know; **komm schon!** come on!

---

schön [ʃøːn] adj beautiful; (*nett*) nice; **~e Grüße** best wishes; **~e Ferien** have a nice holiday; **~en Dank** (many) thanks; **sich ~ machen** to make o.s. look nice

schonen ['ʃoːnən] vt to look after ♦ vr to take it easy; **~d** adj careful, gentle

Schön- zW: **~heit** f beauty; **~heitsfehler** m blemish, flaw; **~heitsoperation** f cosmetic surgery

Schonkost (-) f light diet; (*Spezialdiät*) special diet

Schon- zW: **~ung** f good care; (*Nachsicht*) consideration; (*Forst*) plantation of young trees; **s~ungslos** adj unsparing, harsh; **~zeit** f close season

Schöpf- ['ʃœpf] zW: **s~en** vt to scoop, to ladle; (*Mut*) to summon up; (*Luft*) to breathe in; **~er** (-s, -) m creator; **s~erisch** adj

adj creative; **~kelle** *f* ladle; **~ung** *f* creation

Schorf [ʃɔrf] (-(e)s, -e) *m* scab

Schornstein ['ʃɔrnʃtaɪn] *m* chimney; (*NAUT*) funnel; **~feger** (-s, -) *m* chimney sweep

Schoß [ʃoːs] (-es, ⁀e) *m* lap

schoss ▲ *etc vb siehe* **schießen**

Schoßhund *m* pet dog, lapdog

Schote ['ʃoːtə] *f* pod

Schotte ['ʃɔtə] *m* Scot, Scotsman

Schotter ['ʃɔtər] (-s) *m* broken stone, road metal; (*EISENB*) ballast

Schott- [ʃɔt] *zW:* **~in** *f* Scot, Scotswoman; **s~isch** *adj* Scottish, Scots; **~land** *nt* Scotland

schraffieren [ʃra'fiːrən] *vt* to hatch

schräg [ʃrɛːk] *adj* slanting, not straight; **etw ~ stellen** to put sth at an angle; **~gegenüber** diagonally opposite; **S~e** ['ʃrɛːgə] *f* slant; **S~strich** *m* oblique stroke

Schramme ['ʃramə] *f* scratch; **s~n** *vt* to scratch

Schrank [ʃraŋk] (-(e)s, ⁀e) *m* cupboard; (*Kleiderschrank*) wardrobe; **~e** *f* barrier; **~koffer** *m* trunk

Schraube ['ʃraubə] *f* screw; **s~n** *vt* to screw; **~nschlüssel** *m* spanner; **~nzieher** (-s, -) *m* screwdriver

Schraubstock ['ʃraupʃtɔk] *m* (*TECH*) vice

Schreck [ʃrɛk] (-(e)s, -e) *m* terror; fright; **~en** (-s, -) *m* terror; fright; **s~en** *vt* frighten, to scare; **~gespenst** *nt* spectre, nightmare; **s~haft** *adj* jumpy, easily frightened; **s~lich** *adj* terrible, dreadful

Schrei [ʃraɪ] (-(e)s, -e) *m* scream; (*Ruf*) shout

Schreib- ['ʃraɪb] *zW:* **~block** *m* writing pad; **s~en** (*unreg*) *vt, vi* to write; (*buchstabieren*) to spell; **~en** (-s, -) *nt* letter, communication; **s~faul** *adj* bad about writing letters; **~kraft** *f* typist; **~maschine** *f* typewriter; **~papier** *nt* notepaper; **~tisch** *m* desk; **~ung** *f* spelling; **~waren** *pl* stationery *sg*; **~weise** *f* spelling; way of writing; **~zentrale** *f* typing pool; **~zeug** *nt* writing materials *pl*

schreien ['ʃraɪən] (*unreg*) *vt, vi* to scream; (*rufen*) to shout; **~d** *adj* (*fig*) glaring; (*Farbe*) loud

Schrein [ʃraɪn] (-(e)s, -e) *m* shrine

Schreiner ['ʃraɪnər] (-s, -) *m* joiner; (*Zimmermann*) carpenter; (*Möbelschreiner*) cabinetmaker; **~ei** [-'raɪ] *f* joiner's workshop

schreiten ['ʃraɪtən] (*unreg*) *vi* to stride

schrieb *etc* [ʃriːp] *vb siehe* **schreiben**

Schrift [ʃrɪft] (-, -en) *f* writing; handwriting; (*~art*) script; (*Gedrucktes*) pamphlet, work; **~deutsch** *nt* written German; **~führer** *m* secretary; **s~lich** *adj* written ♦ *adv* in writing; **~sprache** *f* written language; **~steller(in)** (-s, -) *m(f)* writer; **~stück** *nt* document; **~wechsel** *m* correspondence

schrill [ʃrɪl] *adj* shrill

Schritt [ʃrɪt] (-(e)s, -e) *m* step; (*Gangart*) walk; (*Tempo*) pace; (*von Hose*) crutch; **~fahren** to drive at walking pace; **~macher** (-s, -) *m* pacemaker; **~tempo** ▲ *nt:* **im ~tempo** at a walking pace

schroff [ʃrɔf] *adj* steep; (*zackig*) jagged; (*fig*) brusque

schröpfen ['ʃrœpfən] *vt* (*fig*) to fleece

Schrot [ʃroːt] (-(e)s, -e) *m od nt* (*Blei*) (small) shot; (*Getreide*) coarsely ground grain, groats *pl*; **~flinte** *f* shotgun

Schrott [ʃrɔt] (-(e)s, -e) *m* scrap metal; **~haufen** *m* scrap heap; **s~reif** *adj* ready for the scrap heap

schrubben ['ʃrʊbən] *vt* to scrub

Schrubber (-s, -) *m* scrubbing brush

schrumpfen ['ʃrʊmpfən] *vi* to shrink; (*Apfel*) to shrivel

Schub- ['ʃuːb] *zW:* **~fach** *nt* drawer; **~karren** *m* wheelbarrow; **~lade** *f* drawer

Schubs [ʃuːps] (-es, -e) (*umg*) *m* shove (*inf*), push

schüchtern ['ʃʏçtərn] *adj* shy; **S~heit** *f* shyness

Schuft [ʃʊft] (-(e)s, -e) *m* scoundrel

schuften (*umg*) *vi* to graft, to slave away

Schuh [ʃuː] (-(e)s, -e) *m* shoe; **~band** *nt* shoelace; **~creme** *f* shoe polish; **~größe** *f* shoe size; **~löffel** *m* shoehorn; **~macher** (-s, -) *m* shoemaker

Schul- *zW:* **~arbeit** *f* homework (*no pl*); **~aufgaben** *pl* homework *sg*; **~besuch** *m*

school attendance; **~buch** nt school book

Schuld [ʃʊlt] (-, -en) f guilt; (FIN) debt; (Verschulden) fault; **~ haben (an** +dat) to be to blame (for); **er hat ~** it's his fault; **jdm ~ geben** to blame sb; siehe **zuschulden**; **s~** adj: **s~ sein (an** +dat) to be to blame (for); **er ist s~** it's his fault; **s~en** [ˈʃʊldən] vt to owe; **s~enfrei** adj free from debt; **~gefühl** nt feeling of guilt; **s~ig** adj guilty; (gebührend) due; **s~ig an etw** dat **sein** to be guilty of sth; **jdm etw s~ig sein** to owe sb sth; **jdm etw s~ig bleiben** not to provide sb with sth; **s~los** adj innocent, without guilt; **~ner (-s, -)** m debtor; **~schein** m promissory note, IOU

Schule [ˈʃuːlə] f school; **s~n** vt to train, to school

Schüler(in) [ˈʃyːlər(ɪn)] (-s, -) m(f) pupil; **~austausch** m school od student exchange; **~ausweis** m (school) student card

Schul- zW: **~ferien** pl school holidays; **s~frei** adj: **s~freier Tag** holiday; **s~frei sein** to be a holiday; **~hof** m playground; **~jahr** nt school year; **~kind** nt schoolchild; **s~pflichtig** adj of school age; **~schiff** nt (NAUT) training ship; **~stunde** f period, lesson; **~tasche** f school bag

Schulter [ˈʃʊltər] (-, -n) f shoulder; **~blatt** nt shoulder blade; **s~n** vt to shoulder

Schulung f education, schooling

Schulzeugnis nt school report

Schund [ʃʊnt] (-(e)s) m trash, garbage

Schuppe [ˈʃʊpə] f scale; **~n** pl (Haarschuppen) dandruff sg

Schuppen (-s, -) m shed

schuppig [ˈʃʊpɪç] adj scaly

Schur [ʃuːr] (-, -en) f shearing

schüren [ˈʃyːrən] vt to rake; (fig) to stir up

schürfen [ˈʃʏrfən] vt, vi to scrape, to scratch; (MIN) to prospect

Schurke [ˈʃʊrkə] (-n, -n) m rogue

Schurwolle f: „**reine ~**" "pure new wool"

Schürze [ˈʃʏrtsə] f apron

Schuss ▲ [ʃʊs] (-es, ⁻e) m shot; (WEBEN) woof; **~bereich** m effective range

Schüssel [ˈʃʏsəl] (-, -n) f bowl

Schuss- ▲ zW: **~linie** f line of fire; **~verletzung** f bullet wound; **~waffe** f firearm

Schuster [ˈʃuːstər] (-s, -) m cobbler, shoemaker

Schutt [ʃʊt] (-(e)s) m rubbish; (Bauschutt) rubble

Schüttelfrost m shivering

schütteln [ˈʃʏtəln] vt, vr to shake

schütten [ˈʃʏtən] vt to pour; (Zucker, Kies etc) to tip; (verschütten) to spill ♦ vi unpers to pour (down)

Schutthalde f dump

Schutthaufen m heap of rubble

Schutz [ʃʊts] (-es) m protection; (Unterschlupf) shelter; **jdn in ~ nehmen** to stand up for sb; **~anzug** m overalls pl; **~blech** nt mudguard

Schütze [ˈʃʏtsə] (-n, -n) m gunman; (Gewehrschütze) rifleman; (Scharfschütze, Sportschütze) marksman; (ASTROL) Sagittarius

schützen [ˈʃʏtsən] vt to protect; **~ vor** +dat od **gegen** to protect from

Schützenfest nt fair featuring shooting matches

Schutz- zW: **~engel** m guardian angel; **~gebiet** nt protectorate; (Naturschutzgebiet) reserve; **~hütte** f shelter, refuge; **~impfung** f immunisation

Schützling [ˈʃʏtslɪŋ] m protégé(e); (bes Kind) charge

Schutz- zW: **s~los** adj defenceless; **~mann** m policeman; **~patron** m patron saint

Schwaben [ˈʃvaːbən] nt Swabia; **schwäbisch** adj Swabian

schwach [ʃvax] adj weak, feeble

Schwäche [ˈʃvɛçə] f weakness; **s~n** vt to weaken

Schwachheit f weakness

schwächlich adj weakly, delicate

Schwächling m weakling

Schwach- zW: **~sinn** m imbecility; **s~sinnig** adj mentally deficient; (Idee) idiotic; **~strom** m weak current

Schwächung [ˈʃvɛçʊŋ] f weakening

Schwager [ˈʃvaːgər] (-s, ⁻) m brother-in-law

Schwägerin [ˈʃvɛːgərɪn] f sister-in-law

Schwalbe ['ʃvalbə] *f* swallow

Schwall [ʃval] **(-(e)s, -e)** *m* surge; *(Worte)* flood, torrent

Schwamm [ʃvam] **(-(e)s, -e)** *m* sponge; *(Pilz)* fungus

schwamm *etc vb siehe* **schwimmen**

schwammig *adj* spongy; *(Gesicht)* puffy

Schwan [ʃvaːn] **(-(e)s, -e)** *m* swan

schwanger ['ʃvaŋər] *adj* pregnant; **S~schaft** *f* pregnancy

schwanken *vi* to sway; *(taumeln)* to stagger, to reel; *(Preise, Zahlen)* to fluctuate; *(zögern)* to hesitate, to vacillate

Schwankung *f* fluctuation

Schwanz [ʃvants] **(-es, -e)** *m* tail

schwänzen ['ʃvɛntsən] *(umg) vt* to skip, to cut ♦ *vi* to play truant

Schwarm [ʃvarm] **(-(e)s, -e)** *m* swarm; *(umg)* heart-throb, idol

schwärm- ['ʃvɛrm] *zW:* **~en** *vi* to swarm; **~en für** to be mad od wild about; **S~erei** [-əˈraɪ] *f* enthusiasm; **~erisch** *adj* impassioned, effusive

Schwarte ['ʃvartə] *f* hard skin; *(Speckschwarte)* rind

schwarz [ʃvarts] *adj* black; **~es Brett** notice board; **ins S~e treffen** *(auch fig)* to hit the bull's eye; **in den ~en Zahlen** in the black; **~ sehen** *(umg)* to see the gloomy side of things; **S~arbeit** *f* illicit work, moonlighting; **S~brot** *nt* black bread; **S~e(r)** *f(m)* black (man/woman)

Schwärze ['ʃvɛrtsə] *f* blackness; *(Farbe)* blacking; *(Druckerschwärze)* printer's ink; **s~n** *vt* to blacken

Schwarz- *zW:* **s~fahren** *(unreg) vi* to travel without paying; to drive without a licence; **~handel** *m* black market (trade); **~markt** *m* black market; **~wald** *m* Black Forest; **s~weiß, s~-weiß** *adj* black and white

schwatzen ['ʃvatsən] *vi* to chatter

schwätzen ['ʃvɛtsən] *vi* to chatter

Schwätzer ['ʃvɛtsər] **(-s, -)** *m* gasbag

schwatzhaft *adj* talkative, gossipy

Schwebe ['ʃveːbə] *f:* **in der ~** *(fig)* in abeyance; **~bahn** *f* overhead railway; **s~n** *vi* to drift, to float; *(hoch)* to soar

Schwed- ['ʃveːd] *zW:* **~e** *m* Swede; **~en** *nt* Sweden; **~in** *f* Swede; **s~isch** *adj* Swedish

Schwefel ['ʃveːfəl] **(-s)** *m* sulphur; **s~ig** *adj* sulphurous; **~säure** *f* sulphuric acid

Schweig- ['ʃvaɪɡ] *zW:* **~egeld** *nt* hush money; **~en (-s)** *nt* silence; **s~en** *(unreg) vi* to be silent; to stop talking; **~epflicht** *f* pledge of secrecy; *(von Anwalt)* requirement of confidentiality; **s~sam** ['ʃvaɪkzaːm] *adj* silent, taciturn; **~samkeit** *f* taciturnity, quietness

Schwein [ʃvaɪn] **(-(e)s, -e)** *nt* pig; *(umg)* (good) luck

Schweine- *zW:* **~fleisch** *nt* pork; **~'rei** *f* mess; *(Gemeinheit)* dirty trick; **~stall** *m* pigsty

schweinisch *adj* filthy

Schweinsleder *nt* pigskin

Schweiß [ʃvaɪs] **(-es)** *m* sweat, perspiration; **s~en** *vt, vi* to weld; **~er (-s, -)** *m* welder; **~füße** *pl* sweaty feet; **~naht** *f* weld

Schweiz [ʃvaɪts] *f* Switzerland; **~er(in)** *m(f)* Swiss; **s~erisch** *adj* Swiss

schwelgen ['ʃvɛlɡən] *vi* to indulge

Schwelle ['ʃvɛlə] *f (auch fig)* threshold; doorstep; *(EISENB)* sleeper *(BRIT)*, tie *(US)*

schwellen *(unreg) vi* to swell

Schwellung *f* swelling

Schwemme ['ʃvɛmə] *f (WIRTS; Überangebot)* surplus

Schwenk- ['ʃvɛŋk] *zW:* **s~bar** *adj* swivel-mounted; **s~en** *vt* to swing; *(Fahne)* to wave; *(abspülen)* to rinse ♦ *vi* to turn, to swivel; *(MIL)* to wheel; **~ung** *f* turn; wheel

schwer [ʃveːr] *adj* heavy; *(schwierig)* difficult, hard; *(schlimm)* serious, bad ♦ *adv (sehr)* very (much); *(verletzt etc)* seriously, badly; **~ erziehbar** difficult (to bring up); **jdm ~ fallen** to be difficult for sb; **jdm/sich etw ~ machen** to make sth difficult for sb/o.s.; **~ nehmen** to take to heart; **sich** *dat od akk* **~ tun** to have difficulties; **~ verdaulich** indigestible, heavy; **~ wiegend** weighty, important; **S~arbeiter** *m* manual worker, labourer; **S~behinderte(r)** *f(m)* seriously handicapped person; **S~e** f weight, heaviness; (*PHYS*) gravity; **~elos** adj weightless; (*Kammer*) zero-G; **~fällig** adj ponderous; **S~gewicht** nt heavyweight; (*fig*) emphasis; **~hörig** adj hard of hearing; **S~industrie** f heavy industry; **S~kraft** f gravity; **S~kranke(r)** f(m) person who is seriously ill; **~lich** adv hardly; **~mütig** adj melancholy; **S~punkt** m centre of gravity; (*fig*) emphasis, crucial point

Schwert [ʃveːrt] (**-(e)s, -er**) nt sword; **~lilie** f iris

schwer- zW: **S~verbrecher(in)** m(f) criminal, serious offender; **S~verletzte(r)** f(m) serious casualty; (*bei Unfall usw auch*) seriously injured person

Schwester [ˈʃvɛstər] (**-, -n**) f sister; (*MED*) nurse; **s~lich** adj sisterly

Schwieger- [ˈʃviːgər] zW: **~eltern** pl parents-in-law; **~mutter** f mother-in-law; **~sohn** m son-in-law; **~tochter** f daughter-in-law; **~vater** m father-in-law

schwierig [ˈʃviːrɪç] adj difficult, hard; **S~keit** f difficulty

Schwimm- [ˈʃvɪm] zW: **~bad** nt swimming baths pl; **~becken** nt swimming pool; **s~en** (*unreg*) vi to swim; (*treiben, nicht sinken*) to float; (*fig: unsicher sein*) to be all at sea; **~er** (**-s, -**) m swimmer; (*Angeln*) float; **~erin** f (female) swimmer; **~lehrer** m swimming instructor; **~weste** f life jacket

Schwindel [ˈʃvɪndəl] (**-s**) m giddiness; dizzy spell; (*Betrug*) swindle, fraud; (*Zeug*) stuff; **s~frei** adj: **s~frei sein** to have a good head for heights; **s~n** (*umg*) vi (*lügen*) to fib; **jdm s~t es** sb feels dizzy

schwinden [ˈʃvɪndən] (*unreg*) vi to disappear; (*sich verringern*) to decrease; (*Kräfte*) to decline

Schwindler [ˈʃvɪndlər] m swindler; (*Lügner*) liar

schwindlig adj dizzy; **mir ist ~** I feel dizzy

Schwing- [ˈʃvɪŋ] zW: **s~en** (*unreg*) vt to swing; (*Waffe etc*) to brandish ♦ vi to swing; (*vibrieren*) to vibrate; (*klingen*) to sound; **~tür** f swing door(s); **~ung** f vibration;

(*PHYS*) oscillation

Schwips [ʃvɪps] (**-es, -e**) m: **einen ~ haben** to be tipsy

schwirren [ˈʃvɪrən] vi to buzz

schwitzen [ˈʃvɪtsən] vi to sweat, to perspire

schwören [ˈʃvøːrən] (*unreg*) vt, vi to swear

schwul [ʃvuːl] (*umg*) adj gay, queer

schwül [ʃvyːl] adj sultry, close; **S~e** (**-**) f sultriness

Schwule(r) (*umg*) f(m) gay (man/woman)

Schwung [ʃvʊŋ] (**-(e)s, ˸e**) m swing; (*Triebkraft*) momentum; (*fig: Energie*) verve, energy; (*umg: Menge*) batch; **s~haft** adj brisk, lively; **s~voll** adj vigorous

Schwur [ʃvuːr] (**-(e)s, ˸e**) m oath; **~gericht** nt court with a jury

sechs [zɛks] num six; **~hundert** num six hundred; **~te(r, s)** adj sixth; **S~tel** (**-s, -**) nt sixth

sechzehn [ˈzɛçtseːn] num sixteen

sechzig [ˈzɛçtsɪç] num sixty

See¹ [zeː] (**-, -n**) f sea

See² [zeː] (**-s, -n**) m lake

See- [zeː] zW: **~bad** nt seaside resort; **~hund** m seal; **~igel** [ˈzeːiːɡəl] m sea urchin; **s~krank** adj seasick; **~krankheit** f seasickness; **~lachs** m rock salmon

Seele [ˈzeːlə] f soul; **s~nruhig** adv calmly

Seeleute [ˈzeːlɔʏtə] pl seamen

Seel- zW: **s~isch** adj mental; **~sorge** f pastoral duties pl; **~sorger** (**-s, -**) m clergyman

See- zW: **~macht** f naval power; **~mann** (*pl* **-leute**) m seaman, sailor; **~meile** f nautical mile; **~möwe** f (*ZOOL*) seagull; **~not** f distress; **~räuber** m pirate; **~rose** f water lily; **~stern** m starfish; **s~tüchtig** adj seaworthy; **~weg** m sea route; **auf dem ~weg** by sea; **~zunge** f sole

Segel [ˈzeːɡəl] (**-s, -**) nt sail; **~boot** nt yacht; **~fliegen** nt gliding; **~flieger** m glider pilot; **~flugzeug** nt glider; **s~n** vt, vi to sail; **~schiff** nt sailing vessel; **~sport** m sailing; **~tuch** nt canvas

Segen [ˈzeːɡən] (**-s, -**) m blessing

Segler [ˈzeːɡlər] (**-s, -**) m sailor, yachtsman

segnen [ˈzeːɡnən] vt to bless

Seh- ['zeː] zW: **s~behindert** adj partially sighted; **s~en** (unreg) vt, vi to see; (in bestimmte Richtung) to look; **mal s~en(, ob ...)** let's see (if ...); **siehe Seite 5** see page 5; **s~enswert** adj worth seeing; **~enswürdigkeiten** pl sights (of a town); **~fehler** m sight defect

Sehne ['zeːnə] f sinew; (an Bogen) string

sehnen vr: **sich ~ nach** to long od yearn for

sehnig adj sinewy

Sehn- zW: **s~lich** adj ardent; **~sucht** f longing; **s~süchtig** adj longing

sehr [zeːr] adv very; (mit Verben) a lot, (very) much; **zu ~** too much; **~ geehrte(r) ...** dear ...

seicht [zaɪçt] adj (auch fig) shallow

Seide ['zaɪdə] f silk; **s~n** adj silk; **~npapier** nt tissue paper

seidig ['zaɪdɪç] adj silky

Seife ['zaɪfə] f soap

Seifen- zW: **~lauge** f soapsuds pl; **~schale** f soap dish; **~schaum** m lather

seihen ['zaɪən] vt to strain, to filter

Seil [zaɪl] (-(e)s, -e) nt rope; cable; **~bahn** f cable railway; **~hüpfen** (-s) nt skipping; **~springen** (-s) nt skipping; **~tänzer(in)** m(f) tightrope walker

sein [zaɪn] (pt war, pp gewesen) vi **1** to be; **ich bin** I am; **du bist** you are; **er/sie/es ist** he/she/it is; **wir sind/ihr seid/sie sind** we/you/they are; **wir waren** we were; **wir sind gewesen** we have been

2: seien Sie nicht böse don't be angry; **sei so gut und ...** be so kind as to ...; **das wäre gut** that would od that'd be a good thing; **wenn ich Sie wäre** if I were od was you; **das wärs** that's all, that's it; **morgen bin ich in Rom** tomorrow I'll od I will be in Rome; **waren Sie mal in Rom?** have you ever been to Rome?

3: wie ist das zu verstehen? how is that to be understood?; **er ist nicht zu ersetzen** he cannot be replaced; **mit ihr ist nicht zu reden** you can't talk to her

4: mir ist kalt I'm cold; **was ist?** what's the matter?, what is it?; **ist was?** is something the matter?; **es sei denn, dass ...** unless ...; **wie dem auch sei** be that as it may; **wie wäre es mit ...?** how od what about ...?; **lass das sein!** stop that!

sein(e) ['zaɪn(ə)] adj his; its; **~e(r, s)** pron his; its; **~er** (gen von **er**) pron of him; **~erseits** adv for his part; **~erzeit** adv in those days, formerly; **~esgleichen** pron people like him; **~etwegen** adv (für ihn) for his sake; (wegen ihm) on his account; (von ihm aus) as far as he is concerned; **~etwillen** adv: **um ~etwillen = seinetwegen; ~ige** pron: **der/die/das ~ige** od **S~ige** his

seit [zaɪt] präp +dat since ♦ konj since; **er ist ~ einer Woche hier** he has been here for a week; **~ langem** for a long time; **~dem** [zaɪt'deːm] adv, konj since

Seite ['zaɪtə] f side; (Buch~) page; (MIL) flank

Seiten- zW: **~airbag** m side-impact airbag; **~ansicht** f side view; **~hieb** m (fig) passing shot, dig; **s~s** präp +gen on the part of; **~schiff** nt aisle; **~sprung** m extramarital escapade; **~stechen** nt (a) stitch; **~straße** f side road; **~streifen** m verge; (der Autobahn) hard shoulder

seither [zaɪt'heːr] adv, konj since (then)

seit- zW: **~lich** adj on one od the side; side cpd; **~wärts** adv sidewards

Sekretär [zekre'tɛːr] m secretary; (Möbel) bureau

Sekretariat [zekretari'aːt] (-(e)s, -e) nt secretary's office, secretariat

Sekretärin f secretary

Sekt [zɛkt] (-(e)s, -e) m champagne

Sekte ['zɛktə] f sect

Sekunde [ze'kʊndə] f second

selber ['zɛlbər] = **selbst**

Selbst [zɛlpst] (-) nt self

selbst [zɛlpst] pron **1: ich/er/wir selbst** I myself/he himself/we ourselves; **sie ist die Tugend selbst** she's virtue itself; **er braut**

sein Bier selbst he brews his own beer; **wie gehts? - gut, und selbst?** how are things? - fine, and yourself? **2** (*ohne Hilfe*) alone, on my/his/one's *etc* own; **von selbst** by itself; **er kam von selbst** he came of his own accord; **selbst gemacht** home-made ♦ *adv* even; **selbst wenn** even if; **selbst Gott** even God (himself)

selbständig *etc* ['zɛlpʃtɛndɪç] = **selbstständig** *etc*

Selbst- *zW:* **~auslöser** *m* (*PHOT*) delayed-action shutter release; **~bedienung** *f* self-service; **~befriedigung** *f* masturbation; **~beherrschung** *f* self-control; **~bestimmung** *f* (*POL*) self-determination; **~beteiligung** *f* (*VERSICHERUNG: bei Kosten*) (voluntary) excess; **s~bewusst** ▲ *adj* (self-)confident; **~bewusstsein** ▲ *nt* self-confidence; **~erhaltung** *f* self-preservation; **~erkenntnis** *f* self-knowledge; **s~gefällig** *adj* smug, self-satisfied; **~gespräch** *nt* conversation with o.s.; **~kostenpreis** *m* cost price; **s~los** *adj* unselfish, selfless; **~mord** *m* suicide; **~mörder(in)** *m(f)* suicide; **s~mörderisch** *adj* suicidal; **s~sicher** *adj* self-assured; **s~ständig** ▲ *adj* independent; **~ständigkeit** ▲ *f* independence; **s~süchtig** *adj* (*Mensch*) selfish; **~versorger** (**-s, -**) *m* (*im Urlaub etc*) self-caterer; **s~verständlich** ['zɛlpstfɛrʃtɛntlɪç] *adj* obvious ♦ *adv* naturally; **ich halte das für s~verständlich** I take that for granted; **~verteidigung** *f* self-defence; **~vertrauen** *nt* self-confidence; **~verwaltung** *f* autonomy, self-government

selig ['zeːlɪç] *adj* happy, blissful; (*REL*) blessed; (*tot*) late; **S~keit** *f* bliss

Sellerie ['zɛlɐriː] (**-s, -(s)** *od* **-, -**) *m od f* celery

selten ['zɛltən] *adj* rare ♦ *adv* seldom, rarely; **S~heit** *f* rarity

Selterswasser ['zɛltɐsvasɐ] *nt* soda water

seltsam ['zɛltzaːm] *adj* strange, curious; **S~keit** *f* strangeness

Semester [zeˈmɛstɐ] (**-s, -**) *nt* semester; **~ferien** *pl* vacation *sg*

Semi- [zemi] *in zW* semi-; **~kolon** [-ˈkoːlɔn] (**-s, -s**) *nt* semicolon

Seminar [zemiˈnaːr] (**-s, -e**) *nt* seminary; (*Kurs*) seminar; (*UNIV: Ort*) department building

Semmel ['zɛməl] (**-, -n**) *f* roll

Senat [zeˈnaːt] (**-(e)s, -e**) *m* senate, council

Sende- ['zɛndə] *zW:* **~bereich** *m* transmission range; **~folge** *f* (*Serie*) series; **s~n** (*unreg*) *vt* to send; (*RADIO, TV*) to transmit, to broadcast ♦ *vi* to transmit, to broadcast; **~r** (**-s, -**) *m* station; (*Anlage*) transmitter; **~reihe** *f* series (of broadcasts)

Sendung ['zɛndʊŋ] *f* consignment; (*Aufgabe*) mission; (*RADIO, TV*) transmission; (*Programm*) programme

Senf [zɛnf] (**-(e)s, -e**) *m* mustard

senil [zeˈniːl] (*pej*) *adj* senile

Senior(in) ['zeːniɔr(ɪn)] (**-s, -en**) *m(f)* (*Mensch im Rentenalter*) (old age) pensioner

Seniorenheim [zeniˈoːrənhaɪm] *nt* old people's home

Senk- ['zɛŋk] *zW:* **~blei** *nt* plumb; **~e** *f* depression; **s~en** *vt* to lower ♦ *vr* to sink, to drop gradually; **s~recht** *adj* vertical, perpendicular; **~rechte** *f* perpendicular; **~rechtstarter** *m* (*AVIAT*) vertical take-off plane; (*fig*) high-flyer

Sensation [zɛnzatsiˈoːn] *f* sensation; **s~ell** [-ˈnɛl] *adj* sensational

sensibel [zɛnˈziːbəl] *adj* sensitive

sentimental [zɛntimɛnˈtaːl] *adj* sentimental; **S~i'tät** *f* sentimentality

separat [zepaˈraːt] *adj* separate

September [zɛpˈtɛmbɐ] (**-(s), -**) *m* September

Serie ['zeːriə] *f* series

serien- *zW:* **~mäßig** *adj* standard; **S~mörder(in)** *m(f)* serial killer; **~weise** *adv* in series

seriös [zeriˈøːs] *adj* serious, bona fide

Service¹ [zɛrˈviːs] (**-(s), -**) *nt* (*Geschirr*) set, service

Service² (**-, -s**) *m* service

servieren [zɛrˈviːrən] *vt, vi* to serve

Serviererin [zɛr'viːrərɪn] f waitress

Serviette [zɛrvi'etə] f napkin, serviette

Servo- ['zɛrvo] zW: **~bremse** f (AUT) servo(-assisted) brake; **~lenkung** f (AUT) power steering

Sessel ['zɛsəl] (**-s, -**) m armchair; **~lift** m chairlift

sesshaft ▲ ['zɛshaft] adj settled; (ansässig) resident

setzen ['zɛtsən] vt to put, to set; (Baum etc) to plant; (Segel, TYP) to set ♦ vr to settle; (Person) to sit down ♦ vi (springen) to leap; (wetten) to bet

Setz- ['zɛts] zW: **~er** (**-s, -**) m (TYP) compositor; **~ling** m young plant

Seuche ['zɔyçə] f epidemic; **~ngebiet** nt infected area

seufzen ['zɔyftsən] vt, vi to sigh

Seufzer ['zɔyftsər] (**-s, -**) m sigh

Sex [zɛks] (**-(es)**) m sex; **~ualität** [-uali'tɛt] f sex, sexuality; **~ualkunde** [zɛksu'aːl-] f (SCH) sex education; **s~uell** [-u'ɛl] adj sexual

Shampoo [ʃam'puː] (**-s, -s**) nt shampoo

Sibirien [zi'biːriən] nt Siberia

sich [zɪç] pron 1 (akk): **er/sie/es ... sich** he/she/it ... himself/herself/itself; **sie** pl/ **man ... sich** they/one ... themselves/ oneself; **Sie ... sich** you ... yourself/ yourselves pl; **sich wiederholen** to repeat oneself/itself

2 (dat): **er/sie/es ... sich** he/she/it ... to himself/herself/itself; **sie** pl/**man ... sich** they/one ... to themselves/oneself; **Sie ... sich** you ... to yourself/yourselves pl; **sie hat sich einen Pullover gekauft** she bought herself a jumper; **sich die Haare waschen** to wash one's hair

3 (mit Präposition): **haben Sie Ihren Ausweis bei sich?** do you have your pass on you?; **er hat nichts bei sich** he's got nothing on him; **sie bleiben gern unter sich** they keep themselves to themselves

4 (einander) each other, one another; **sie bekämpfen sich** they fight each other od

one another

5: **dieses Auto fährt sich gut** this car drives well; **hier sitzt es sich gut** it's good to sit here

Sichel ['zɪçəl] (**-, -n**) f sickle; (Mondsichel) crescent

sicher ['zɪçər] adj safe; (gewiss) certain; (zuverlässig) secure, reliable; (selbstsicher) confident; **vor jdm/etw ~ sein** to be safe from sb/sth; **ich bin nicht ~** I'm not sure od certain; **~ nicht** surely not; **aber ~!** of course!; **~gehen** (unreg) vi to make sure

Sicherheit ['zɪçərhaɪt] f safety; (auch FIN) security; (Gewissheit) certainty; (Selbstsicherheit) confidence

Sicherheits- zW: **~abstand** m safe distance; **~glas** nt safety glass; **~gurt** m safety belt; **s~halber** adv for safety; to be on the safe side; **~nadel** f safety pin; **~schloss ▲** nt safety lock; **~vorkehrung** f safety precaution

sicher- zW: **~lich** adv certainly, surely; **~n** vt to secure; (schützen) to protect; (Waffe) to put the safety catch on; **jdm etw ~n** to secure sth for sb; **sich dat etw ~n** to secure sth (for o.s.); **~stellen** vt to impound; (COMPUT) to save; **S~ung** f (S~n) securing; (Vorrichtung) safety device; (an Waffen) safety catch; (ELEK) fuse; **S~ungskopie** f back-up copy

Sicht [zɪçt] (**-**) f sight; (Aussicht) view; **auf** od **nach ~** (FIN) at sight; **auf lange ~** on a long-term basis; **s~bar** adj visible; **s~en** vt to sight; (auswählen) to sort out; **s~lich** adj evident, obvious; **~verhältnisse** pl visibility sg; **~vermerk** m visa; **~weite** f visibility

sickern ['zɪkərn] vi to trickle, to seep

Sie [ziː] (nom, akk) pron you

sie [ziː] pron (sg: nom) she, it; (: akk) her, it; (pl: nom) they; (: akk) them

Sieb [ziːp] (**-(e)s, -e**) nt sieve; (KOCH) strainer; **s~en**[1] ['ziːbən] vt to sift; (Flüssigkeit) to strain

sieben[2] num seven; **~hundert** num seven hundred; **S~sachen** pl belongings

Spelling Reform: ▲ *new spelling* △ *old spelling (to be phased out)*

siebte(r, s) ['zi:ptə(r, s)] *adj* seventh; **S~l**
(**-s, -**) *nt* seventh

siebzehn ['zi:ptse:n] *num* seventeen

siebzig ['zi:ptsɪç] *num* seventy

siedeln ['zi:dəln] *vi* to settle

sieden ['zi:dən] *vt, vi* to boil, to simmer

Siedepunkt *m* boiling point

Siedler (**-s, -**) *m* settler

Siedlung *f* settlement; (*Häusersiedlung*)
housing estate

Sieg [zi:k] (**-(e)s, -e**) *m* victory

Siegel ['zi:gəl] (**-s, -**) *nt* seal; **~ring** *m* signet
ring

Sieg- *zW:* **s~en** *vi* to be victorious; (*SPORT*)
to win; **~er** (**-s, -**) *m* victor; (*SPORT etc*)
winner; **s~reich** *adj* victorious

siehe *etc* ['zi:ə] *vb siehe* **sehen**

siezen ['zi:tsən] *vt* to address as "Sie"

Signal [zɪ'gna:l] (**-s, -e**) *nt* signal

Silbe ['zɪlbə] *f* syllable

Silber ['zɪlbər] (**-s**) *nt* silver; **~hochzeit** *f*
silver wedding (anniversary); **s~n** *adj* silver;
~papier *nt* silver paper

Silhouette [zilu'ɛtə] *f* silhouette

Silvester [zɪl'vɛstər] (**-s, -**) *nt* New Year's
Eve, Hogmanay (*SCOTTISH*); **~abend** *m* =
Silvester

ⓘ **Silvester** *is the German word for New
Year's Eve. Although not an official
holiday most businesses close early and
shops shut at midday. Most Germans
celebrate in the evening, and at midnight
they let off fireworks and rockets; the revelry
usually lasts until the early hours of the
morning.*

---

simpel ['zɪmpəl] *adj* simple

Sims [zɪms] (**-es, -e**) *nt od m* (*Kaminsims*)
mantelpiece; (*Fenstersims*) (window)sill

simulieren [zimu'li:rən] *vt* to simulate;
(*vortäuschen*) to feign ♦ *vi* to feign illness

simultan [zimʊl'ta:n] *adj* simultaneous

Sinfonie [zɪnfo'ni:] *f* symphony

singen ['zɪŋən] (*unreg*) *vt, vi* to sing

Singular ['zɪŋgula:r] *m* singular

Singvogel ['zɪŋfo:gəl] *m* songbird

sinken ['zɪŋkən] (*unreg*) *vi* to sink; (*Preise etc*)
to fall, to go down

Sinn [zɪn] (**-(e)s, -e**) *m* mind;
(*Wahrnehmungssinn*) sense; (*Bedeutung*)
sense, meaning; **~ für etw** sense of sth;
von ~en sein to be out of one's mind; **es
hat keinen ~** there's no point; **~bild** *nt*
symbol; **s~en** (*unreg*) *vi* to ponder; **auf
etw** *akk* **s~en** to contemplate sth;
~estäuschung *f* illusion; **s~gemäß** *adj*
faithful; (*Wiedergabe*) in one's own words;
s~ig *adj* clever; **s~lich** *adj* sensual,
sensuous; (*Wahrnehmung*) sensory;
~lichkeit *f* sensuality; **s~los** *adj* senseless;
meaningless; **~losigkeit** *f* senselessness;
meaninglessness; **s~voll** *adj* meaningful;
(*vernünftig*) sensible

Sintflut ['zɪntflu:t] *f* Flood

Sippe ['zɪpə] *f* clan, kin

Sippschaft ['zɪpʃaft] (*pej*) *f* relations *pl*,
tribe; (*Bande*) gang

Sirene [zi're:nə] *f* siren

Sirup ['zi:rʊp] (**-s, -e**) *m* syrup

Sitt- ['zɪt] *zW:* **~e** *f* custom; **~en** *pl* (**~lichkeit**)
morals; **~enpolizei** *f* vice squad; **s~sam**
adj modest, demure

Situation [zituatsi'o:n] *f* situation

Sitz [zɪts] (**-es, -e**) *m* seat; **der Anzug hat
einen guten ~** the suit is a good fit; **s~en**
(*unreg*) *vi* to sit; (*Bemerkung, Schlag*) to strike
home, to tell; (*Gelerntes*) to have sunk in;
s~en bleiben to remain seated; (*SCH*) to
have to repeat a year; **auf etw** *dat* **s~en
bleiben** to be lumbered with sth; **s~en
lassen** (*SCH*) to make (sb) repeat a year;
(*Mädchen*) to jilt; (*Wartenden*) to stand up;
etw auf sich *dat* **s~en lassen** to take sth
lying down; **s~end** *adj* (*Tätigkeit*)
sedentary; **~gelegenheit** *f* place to sit
down; **~platz** *m* seat; **~streik** *m* sit-down
strike; **~ung** *f* meeting

Sizilien [zi'tsi:liən] *nt* Sicily

Skala ['ska:la] (**-, Skalen**) *f* scale

Skalpell [skal'pɛl] (**-s, -e**) *nt* scalpel

Skandal [skan'da:l] (**-s, -e**) *m* scandal; **s~ös**
[-'lø:s] *adj* scandalous

Skandinav- [skandi'na:v] *zW:* **~ien** *nt*
Scandinavia; **~ier(in)** *m(f)* Scandinavian;
s~isch *adj* Scandinavian

Skelett [ske'lɛt] **(-(e)s, -e)** *nt* skeleton

Skepsis ['skɛpsɪs] **(-)** *f* scepticism

skeptisch ['skɛptɪʃ] *adj* sceptical

Ski [ʃiː] **(-s, -er)** *m* ski; **~ laufen** *od* **fahren** to
ski; **~fahrer** *m* skier; **~gebiet** *nt* ski(ing)
area; **~läufer** *m* skier; **~lehrer** *m* ski
instructor; **~lift** *m* ski-lift; **~springen** *nt*
ski-jumping; **~stock** *m* ski-pole

Skizze ['skɪtsə] *f* sketch

skizzieren [skɪ'tsiːrən] *vt, vi* to sketch

Sklave ['skla:və] **(-n, -n)** *m* slave; **~'rei** *f*
slavery; **Sklavin** *f* slave

Skonto ['skɔnto] **(-s, -s)** *m od nt* discount

Skorpion [skɔrpi'oːn] **(-s, -e)** *m* scorpion;
(*ASTROL*) Scorpio

Skrupel ['skruːpəl] **(-s, -)** *m* scruple; **s~los**
adj unscrupulous

Skulptur [skʊlp'tuːr] *f* (*Gegenstand*) sculpture

S-Kurve ['ɛskʊrvə] *f* S-bend

Slip [slɪp] **(-s, -s)** *m* (under)pants; **~einlage**
f panty liner

Slowakei [slova'kaɪ] *f:* **die ~** Slovakia

Slowenien [slo've:niən] *nt* Slovenia

Smaragd [sma'rakt] **(-(e)s, -e)** *m* emerald

Smoking ['smoːkɪŋ] **(-s, -s)** *m* dinner jacket

SCHLÜSSELWORT

so [zoː] *adv* **1** (*so sehr*) so; **so groß/schön**
etc so big/nice *etc*; **so groß/schön wie ...**
as big/nice as ...; **so viel (wie)** as much as;
rede nicht so viel don't talk so much; **so**
weit sein to be ready; **so weit wie** *od* **als**
möglich as far as possible; **ich bin so weit**
zufrieden by and large I'm quite satisfied;
so wenig (wie) as little (as); **das hat ihn**
so geärgert, dass ... that annoyed him so
much that ...; **so einer wie ich** somebody
like me; **na so was!** well, well!

2 (*auf diese Weise*) like this; **mach es nicht**
so don't do it like that; **so oder so** in one
way or the other; **und so weiter** and so
on; **... oder so was** ... or something like
that; **das ist gut so** that's fine; **so genannt**
so-called

3 (*umg: umsonst*): **ich habe es so**
bekommen I got it for nothing

♦ *konj:* **so, dass, sodass** so that; **so wie es**
jetzt ist as things are at the moment

♦ *excl:* **so?** really?; **so, das wärs** so, that's
it then

---

s. o. *abk* = **siehe oben**

Söckchen ['zœkçən] *nt* ankle socks

Socke ['zɔkə] *f* sock

Sockel ['zɔkəl] **(-s, -)** *m* pedestal, base

sodass ▲ [zo'das] *konj* so that

Sodawasser ['zo:davasər] *nt* soda water

Sodbrennen ['zo:tbrenən] **(-s, -)** *nt*
heartburn

soeben [zo'|e:bən] *adv* just (now)

Sofa ['zo:fa] **(-s, -s)** *nt* sofa

sofern [zo'fɛrn] *konj* if, provided (that)

sofort [zo'fɔrt] *adv* immediately, at once;
~ig *adj* immediate

Sog [zoːk] **(-(e)s, -e)** *m* (*Strömung*) undertow

sogar [zo'gaːr] *adv* even

sogleich [zo'glaɪç] *adv* straight away, at
once

Sohle ['zo:lə] *f* sole; (*Talsohle etc*) bottom;
(*MIN*) seam

Sohn [zoːn] **(-(e)s, ¨e)** *m* son

Solar- [zo'laːr] *in zW* solar; **~zelle** *f* solar
cell

solch [zɔlç] *pron* such; **ein ~e(r, s) ...** such
a ...

Soldat [zɔl'da:t] **(-en, -en)** *m* soldier

Söldner ['zœldnər] **(-s, -)** *m* mercenary

solidarisch [zoli'da:rɪʃ] *adj* in *od* with
solidarity; **sich ~ erklären** to declare one's
solidarity

Solidari'tät *f* solidarity

solid(e) [zo'li:d(ə)] *adj* solid; (*Leben, Person*)
respectable

Solist(in) [zo'lɪst(ɪn)] *m(f)* soloist

Soll [zɔl] **(-(s), -(s))** *nt* (*FIN*) debit (side);
(*Arbeitsmenge*) quota, target

SCHLÜSSELWORT

sollen ['zɔlən] (*pt* **sollte**, *pp* **gesollt** *od* (*als*
Hilfsverb) **sollen**) *Hilfsverb* **1** (*Pflicht, Befehl*)
to be supposed to; **du hättest nicht gehen**

Spelling Reform: ▲ *new spelling* △ *old spelling (to be phased out)*

sollen you shouldn't have gone, you oughtn't to have gone; **soll ich?** shall I?; **soll ich dir helfen?** shall I help you?; **sag ihm, er soll warten** tell him he's to wait; **was soll ich machen?** what should I do? **2** (*Vermutung*): **sie soll verheiratet sein** she's said to be married; **was soll das heißen?** what's that supposed to mean?; **man sollte glauben, dass ...** you would think that ...; **sollte das passieren, ...** if that should happen ...

♦ *vt, vi:* **was soll das?** what's all this?; **das sollst du nicht** you shouldn't do that; **was solls?** what the hell!

Solo ['zo:lo] *(-s, -s od* **Soli***) nt* solo
somit [zo'mɪt] *konj* and so, therefore
Sommer ['zɔmər] *(-s, -) m* summer; **s~lich** *adj* summery; summer; **~reifen** *m* normal tyre; **~schlussverkauf** ▲ *m* summer sale; **~sprossen** *pl* freckles
Sonde ['zɔndə] *f* probe
Sonder- ['zɔndər] *in zW* special; **~angebot** *nt* special offer; **s~bar** *adj* strange, odd; **~fahrt** *f* special trip; **~fall** *m* special case; **s~lich** *adj* particular; (*außergewöhnlich*) remarkable; (*eigenartig*) peculiar; **~marke** *f* special issue stamp; **s~n** *konj* but ♦ *vt* to separate; **nicht nur ..., s~n auch** not only ..., but also; **~preis** *m* special reduced price; **~zug** *m* special train
Sonnabend ['zɔnˌaːbənt] *m* Saturday
Sonne ['zɔnə] *f* sun; **s~n** *vr* to sun o.s.
Sonnen- *in zW*: **~aufgang** *m* sunrise; **s~baden** *vi* to sunbathe; **~brand** *m* sunburn; **~brille** *f* sunglasses *pl*; **~creme** *f* suntan lotion; **~energie** *f* solar energy, solar power; **~finsternis** *f* solar eclipse; **~kollektor** *m* solar panel; **~schein** *m* sunshine; **~schirm** *m* parasol, sunshade; **~schutzfaktor** *m* protection factor; **~stich** *m* sunstroke; **~uhr** *f* sundial; **~untergang** *m* sunset; **~wende** *f* solstice
sonnig ['zɔnɪç] *adj* sunny
Sonntag ['zɔntaːk] *m* Sunday
sonst [zɔnst] *adv* otherwise; (*mit pron, in Fragen*) else; (*zu anderer Zeit*) at other times,

normally ♦ *konj* otherwise; **~ noch etwas?** anything else?; **~ nichts** nothing else; **~ jemand** anybody (at all); **~ wo** somewhere else; **~ woher** from somewhere else; **~ wohin** somewhere else; **~ig** *adj* other
sooft [zo'ɔft] *konj* whenever
Sopran [zo'praːn] *(-s, -e) m* soprano
Sorge ['zɔrgə] *f* care, worry
sorgen *vi:* **für jdn ~** to look after sb ♦ *vr:* **sich ~ (um)** to worry (about); **für etw ~** to take care of *od* see to sth; **~frei** *adj* carefree; **~voll** *adj* troubled, worried
Sorgerecht *nt* custody (of a child)
Sorg- [zɔrk] *zW:* **~falt** *(-) f* care(fulness); **s~fältig** *adj* careful; **s~los** *adj* careless; (*ohne ~en*) carefree; **s~sam** *adj* careful
Sorte ['zɔrtə] *f* sort; (*Warensorte*) brand; **~n** *pl* (*FIN*) foreign currency *sg*
sortieren [zɔr'tiːrən] *vt* to sort (out)
Sortiment [zɔrti'mɛnt] *nt* assortment
sosehr [zo'zeːr] *konj* as much as
Soße ['zoːsə] *f* sauce; (*Bratensoße*) gravy
soufflieren [zu'fliːrən] *vt, vi* to prompt
Souterrain [zutɛ'rɛ̃ː] *(-s, -s) nt* basement
souverän [zuvə'rɛːn] *adj* sovereign; (*überlegen*) superior
so- *zW:* **~viel** [zo'fiːl] *konj:* **~viel ich weiß** as far as I know; *siehe* **so;** **~weit** [zo'vaɪt] *konj* as far as; *siehe* **so;** **~wenig** [zo'veːnɪç] *konj* little so; *siehe* **so;** **~wie** [zo'viː] *konj* (*~bald*) as soon as; (*ebenso*) as well as; **~wieso** [zovi'zo:] *adv* anyway
sowjetisch [zɔ'vjetɪʃ] *adj* Soviet
Sowjetunion *f* Soviet Union
sowohl [zo'voːl] *konj:* **~ ... als** *od* **wie auch** both ... and
sozial [zotsi'aːl] *adj* social; **S~abgaben** *pl* national insurance contributions; **S~arbeiter(in)** *m(f)* social worker; **S~demokrat** *m* social democrat; **~demokratisch** *adj* social democratic; **S~hilfe** *f* income support (*BRIT*), welfare (aid) (*US*); **~i'sieren** *vt* to socialize; **S~ismus** [-'lɪsmʊs] *m* socialism; **S~ist** [-'lɪst] *m* socialist; **~istisch** *adj* socialist; **S~politik** *f* social welfare policy; **S~produkt** *nt* (net) national product;

S~staat *m* welfare state;
S~versicherung *f* national insurance
(*BRIT*), social security (*US*); **S~wohnung** *f*
council flat
soziologisch [zotsio'lo:gɪʃ] *adj* sociological
sozusagen [zotsu'za:gən] *adv* so to speak
Spachtel ['ʃpaxtəl] (**-s, -**) *m* spatula
spähen ['ʃpɛːən] *vi* to peep, to peek
Spalier [ʃpa'liːr] (**-s, -e**) *nt* (*Gerüst*) trellis;
(*Leute*) guard of honour
Spalt [ʃpalt] (**-(e)s, -e**) *m* crack; (*Türspalt*)
chink; (*fig: Kluft*) split; **~e** *f* crack, fissure;
(*Gletscherspalte*) crevasse; (*in Text*) column;
s~en *vt, vr* (*auch fig*) to split; **~ung** *f*
splitting
Span [ʃpaːn] (**-(e)s, ⁓e**) *m* shaving
Spanferkel *nt* sucking pig
Spange ['ʃpaŋə] *f* clasp; (*Haarspange*) hair
slide; (*Schnalle*) buckle
Spanien ['ʃpaːniən] *nt* Spain; **Spanier(in)**
m(f) Spaniard; **spanisch** *adj* Spanish
Spann- ['ʃpan] *zW:* **~beton** *m* prestressed
concrete; **~betttuch** ▲ *nt* fitted sheet; **~e**
f (*Zeitspanne*) space; (*Differenz*) gap; **s~en**
vt (*straffen*) to tighten, to tauten;
(*befestigen*) to brace ♦ *vi* to be tight;
s~end *adj* exciting, gripping; **~ung** *f*
tension; (*ELEK*) voltage; (*fig*) suspense;
(*unangenehm*) tension
Spar- ['ʃpaːr] *zW:* **~buch** *nt* savings book;
~büchse *f* money box; **s~en** *vt, vi* to
save; **sich** *dat* **etw s~en** to save o.s. sth;
(*Bemerkung*) to keep sth to o.s.; **mit etw
s~en** to be sparing with sth; **an etw** *dat*
s~en to economize on sth; **~er** (**-s, -**) *m*
saver
Spargel ['ʃpargəl] (**-s, -**) *m* asparagus
Sparkasse *f* savings bank
Sparkonto *nt* savings account
spärlich ['ʃpɛːrlɪç] *adj* meagre; (*Bekleidung*)
scanty
Spar- *zW:* **~preis** *m* economy price;
s~sam *adj* economical, thrifty; **~samkeit**
f thrift, economizing; **~schwein** *nt* piggy
bank
Sparte ['ʃpartə] *f* field; line of business;
(*PRESSE*) column

Spaß [ʃpaːs] (**-es, ⁓e**) *m* joke; (*Freude*) fun;
jdm ~ machen to be fun (for sb); **viel ~!**
have fun!; **s~en** *vi* to joke; **mit ihm ist
nicht zu ~en** you can't take liberties with
him; **s~haft** *adj* funny, droll; **s~ig** *adj*
funny, droll
spät [ʃpɛːt] *adj, adv* late; **wie ~ ist es?**
what's the time?
Spaten ['ʃpaːtən] (**-s, -**) *m* spade
später *adj, adv* later
spätestens *adv* at the latest
Spätvorstellung *f* late show
Spatz [ʃpats] (**-en, -en**) *m* sparrow
spazier- [ʃpa'tsiːr] *zW:* **~en** *vi* to stroll, to
walk; **~en fahren** to go for a drive; **~en
gehen** to go for a walk; **S~gang** *m* walk;
S~stock *m* walking stick; **S~weg** *m* path,
walk
Specht [ʃpɛçt] (**-(e)s, -e**) *m* woodpecker
Speck [ʃpɛk] (**-(e)s, -e**) *m* bacon
Spediteur [ʃpedi'tøːr] *m* carrier;
(*Möbelspediteur*) furniture remover
Spedition [ʃpeditsi'oːn] *f* carriage; (*~sfirma*)
road haulage contractor; removal firm
Speer [ʃpeːr] (**-(e)s, -e**) *m* spear; (*SPORT*)
javelin
Speiche ['ʃpaiçə] *f* spoke
Speichel ['ʃpaiçəl] (**-s**) *m* saliva, spit(tle)
Speicher ['ʃpaiçər] (**-s, -**) *m* storehouse;
(*Dachspeicher*) attic, loft; (*Kornspeicher*)
granary; (*Wasserspeicher*) tank; (*TECH*) store;
(*COMPUT*) memory; **s~n** *vt* to store;
(*COMPUT*) to save
speien ['ʃpaiən] (*unreg*) *vt, vi* to spit;
(*erbrechen*) to vomit; (*Vulkan*) to spew
Speise ['ʃpaizə] *f* food; **~eis** [-ais] *nt* ice-
cream; **~kammer** *f* larder, pantry; **~karte**
f menu; **s~n** *vt* to feed ♦ *vi* to dine;
~röhre *f* gullet, oesophagus; **~saal** *m*
dining room; **~wagen** *m* dining car
Speku- [ʃpeku] *zW:* **~lant** *m* speculator;
~lation [latsi'oːn] *f* speculation; **s~lieren**
[-'liːrən] *vi* (*fig*) to speculate; **auf etw** *akk*
s~lieren to have hopes of sth
Spelunke [ʃpe'luŋkə] *f* dive
Spende ['ʃpɛndə] *f* donation; **s~n** *vt* to
donate, to give; **~r** (**-s, -**) *m* donor,

donator

spendieren [ʃpɛn'diːrən] *vt* to pay for, to buy; **jdm etw ~** to treat sb to sth, to stand sb sth

Sperling ['ʃpɛrlɪŋ] *m* sparrow

Sperma ['spɛrma] **(-s, Spermen)** *nt* sperm

Sperr- ['ʃpɛr] *zW*: **~e** *f* barrier; (*Verbot*) ban; **s~en** *vt* to block; (*SPORT*) to suspend, to bar; (*vom Ball*) to obstruct; (*einschließen*) to lock; (*verbieten*) to ban ♦ *vr* to baulk, to jib(e); **~gebiet** *nt* prohibited area; **~holz** *nt* plywood; **s~ig** *adj* bulky; **~müll** *m* bulky refuse; **~sitz** *m* (*THEAT*) stalls *pl*; **~stunde** *f* closing time

Spesen ['ʃpeːzən] *pl* expenses

Spezial- [ʃpetsi'aːl] *in zW* special; **~gebiet** *nt* specialist field; **s~i'sieren** *vr* to specialize; **~i'sierung** *f* specialization; **~ist** [-'lɪst] *m* specialist; **~i'tät** *f* speciality

speziell [ʃpetsi'ɛl] *adj* special

spezifisch [ʃpe'tsiːfɪʃ] *adj* specific

Sphäre ['sfɛːrə] *f* sphere

Spiegel ['ʃpiːgəl] **(-s, -)** *m* mirror; (*Wasserspiegel*) level; (*MIL*) tab; **~bild** *nt* reflection; **s~bildlich** *adj* reversed; **~ei** *nt* fried egg; **s~n** *vt* to mirror, to reflect ♦ *vr* to be reflected ♦ *vi* to gleam; (*widerspiegeln*) to be reflective; **~ung** *f* reflection

Spiel [ʃpiːl] **(-(e)s, -e)** *nt* game; (*Schauspiel*) play; (*Tätigkeit*) play(ing); (*KARTEN*) deck; (*TECH*) (free) play; **s~en** *vt, vi* to play; (*um Geld*) to gamble; (*THEAT*) to perform, to act; **s~end** *adv* easily; **~er (-s, -)** *m* player; (*um Geld*) gambler; **~e'rei** *f* trifling pastime; **~feld** *nt* pitch, field; **~film** *m* feature film; **~kasino** *nt* casino; **~plan** *m* (*THEAT*) programme; **~platz** *m* playground; **~raum** *m* room to manoeuvre, scope; **~regel** *f* rule; **~sachen** *pl* toys; **~uhr** *f* musical box; **~verderber (-s, -)** *m* spoilsport; **~waren** *pl* toys; **~zeug** *nt* toy(s)

Spieß [ʃpiːs] **(-es, -e)** *m* spear; (*Bratspieß*) spit; **~bürger** *m* bourgeois; **~er (-s, -)** (*umg*) *m* bourgeois; **s~ig** (*pej*) *adj* (petit) bourgeois

Spinat [ʃpi'naːt] **(-(e)s, -e)** *m* spinach

Spind [ʃpɪnt] **(-(e)s, -e)** *m od nt* locker

Spinn- ['ʃpɪn] *zW*: **~e** *f* spider; **s~en** (*unreg*) *vt, vi* to spin; (*umg*) to talk rubbish; (*verrückt sein*) to be crazy *od* mad; **~e'rei** *f* spinning mill; **~rad** *nt* spinning wheel; **~webe** *f* cobweb

Spion [ʃpi'oːn] **(-s, -e)** *m* spy; (*in Tür*) spyhole; **~age** [ʃpio'naːʒə] *f* espionage; **s~ieren** [ʃpio'niːrən] *vi* to spy; **~in** *f* (female) spy

Spirale [ʃpi'raːlə] *f* spiral

Spirituosen [ʃpiritu'oːzən] *pl* spirits

Spiritus ['ʃpiːritʊs] **(-, -se)** *m* (methylated) spirit

Spital [ʃpi'taːl] **(-s, ⁻er)** *nt* hospital

spitz [ʃpɪts] *adj* pointed; (*Winkel*) acute; (*fig: Zunge*) sharp; (*: Bemerkung*) caustic

Spitze *f* point, tip; (*Bergspitze*) peak; (*Bemerkung*) taunt, dig; (*erster Platz*) lead, top; (*meist pl: Gewebe*) lace

Spitzel (-s, -) *m* police informer

spitzen *vt* to sharpen

Spitzenmarke *f* brand leader

spitzfindig *adj* (over)subtle

Spitzname *m* nickname

Splitter ['ʃplɪtər] **(-s, -)** *m* splinter

sponsern ['ʃpɔnzərn] *vt* to sponsor

spontan [ʃpɔn'taːn] *adj* spontaneous

Sport [ʃpɔrt] **(-(e)s, -e)** *m* sport; (*fig*) hobby; **~lehrer(in)** *m(f)* games *od* P.E. teacher; **~ler(in) (-s, -)** *m(f)* sportsman(-woman); **s~lich** *adj* sporting; (*Mensch*) sporty; **~platz** *m* playing *od* sports field; **~schuh** *m* (*Turnschuh*) training shoe, trainer; **~stadion** *nt* sports stadium; **~verein** *m* sports club; **~wagen** *m* sports car

Spott [ʃpɔt] **(-(e)s)** *m* mockery, ridicule; **s~billig** *adj* dirt-cheap; **s~en** *vi* to mock; **s~en (über +akk)** to mock (at), to ridicule

spöttisch ['ʃpœtɪʃ] *adj* mocking

sprach *etc* [ʃpraːx] *vb siehe* **sprechen**

Sprach- *zW*: **s~begabt** *adj* good at languages; **~e** *f* language; **~enschule** *f* language school; **~fehler** *m* speech defect; **~führer** *m* phrasebook; **~gefühl** *nt* feeling for language; **~kenntnisse** *pl* linguistic proficiency *sg*; **~kurs** *m* language course; **~labor** *nt* language laboratory; **s~lich** *adj* linguistic; **s~los** adj speechless

sprang etc [ʃpraŋ] vb siehe **springen**

Spray [spre:] (**-s, -s**) m od nt spray

Sprech- [ʃprɛç] zW: **~anlage** f intercom; **s~en** (unreg) vi to speak, to talk ♦ vt to say; (Sprache) to speak; (Person) to speak to; **mit jdm s~en** to speak to sb; **das spricht für ihn** that's a point in his favour; **~er(in)** (**-s, -**) m(f) speaker; (für Gruppe) spokesman(-woman); (RADIO, TV) announcer; **~stunde** f consultation (hour); (doctor's) surgery; **~stundenhilfe** f (doctor's) receptionist; **~zimmer** nt consulting room, surgery, office (US)

spreizen [ʃpraitsən] vt (Beine) to open, to spread; (Finger, Flügel) to spread

Spreng- [ʃprɛŋ] zW: **s~en** vt to sprinkle; (mit ~stoff) to blow up; (Gestein) to blast; (Versammlung) to break up; **~stoff** m explosive(s)

sprichst etc [ʃprɪçst] vb siehe **sprechen**

Sprichwort nt proverb; **sprichwörtlich** adj proverbial

Spring- [ʃprɪŋ] zW: **~brunnen** m fountain; **s~en** (unreg) vi to jump; (Glas) to crack; (mit Kopfsprung) to dive; **~er** (**-s, -**) m jumper; (Schach) knight

Sprit [ʃprɪt] (**-(e)s, -e**) m (umg) m juice, gas

Spritz- [ʃprɪts] zW: **~e** f syringe; injection; (an Schlauch) nozzle; **s~en** vt to spray; (MED) to inject ♦ vi to splash; (herausspritzen) to spurt; (MED) to give injections; **~pistole** f spray gun; **~tour** f (umg) spin

spröde [ʃprø:də] adj brittle; (Person) reserved, coy

Sprosse [ʃprɔsə] f rung

Sprössling ▲ [ʃprœslɪŋ] (umg) m (Kind) offspring (pl inv)

Spruch [ʃprʊx] (**-(e)s, -e**) m saying, maxim; (JUR) judgement

Sprudel [ʃpruːdəl] (**-s, -**) m mineral water; lemonade; **s~n** vi to bubble; **~wasser** nt (KOCH) sparkling od fizzy mineral water

Sprüh- [ʃpry:] zW: **~dose** f aerosol (can); **s~en** vi to spray; (fig) to sparkle ♦ vt to spray; **~regen** m drizzle

Sprung [ʃprʊŋ] (**-(e)s, -e**) m jump; (Riss) crack; **~brett** nt springboard; **s~haft** adj erratic; (Aufstieg) rapid; **~schanze** f ski jump

Spucke [ʃpʊkə] (**-**) f spit; **s~n** vt, vi to spit

Spuk [ʃpuːk] (**-(e)s, -e**) m haunting; (fig) nightmare; **s~en** vi (Geist) to walk; **hier s~t es** this place is haunted

Spülbecken [ʃpy:lbɛkən] nt (in Küche) sink

Spule [ʃpu:lə] f spool; (ELEK) coil

Spül- [ʃpy:l] zW: **~e** f (kitchen) sink; **s~en** vt, vi to rinse; (Geschirr) to wash up; (Toilette) to flush; **~maschine** f dishwasher; **~mittel** nt washing-up liquid; **~stein** m sink; **~ung** f rinsing; flush; (MED) irrigation

Spur [ʃpu:r] (**-, -en**) f trace; (Fußspur, Radspur, Tonbandspur) track; (Fährte) trail; (Fahrspur) lane

spürbar adj noticeable, perceptible

spüren [ʃpy:rən] vt to feel

spurlos adv without (a) trace

Spurt [ʃpʊrt] (**-(e)s, -s od -e**) m spurt; **s~en** vi to spurt

sputen [ʃpu:tən] vr to make haste

St. abk = **Stück** St.; (= Sankt) St.

Staat [ʃta:t] (**-(e)s, -en**) m state; (Prunk) show; (Kleidung) finery; **s~enlos** adj stateless; **s~lich** adj state(-); state-run

Staats- zW: **~angehörige(r)** f(m) national; **~angehörigkeit** f nationality; **~anwalt** m public prosecutor; **~bürger** m citizen; **~dienst** m civil service; **~examen** nt (UNIV) state exam(ination); **s~feindlich** adj subversive; **~mann** (pl **-männer**) m statesman; **~oberhaupt** nt head of state

Stab [ʃta:p] (**-(e)s, -e**) m rod; (Gitterstab) bar; (Menschen) staff; **~hochsprung** m pole vault

stabil [ʃta'bi:l] adj stable; (Möbel) sturdy; **~i'sieren** vt to stabilize

Stachel [ʃtaxəl] (**-s, -n**) m spike; (von Tier) spine; (von Insekten) sting; **~beere** f gooseberry; **~draht** m barbed wire; **s~ig** adj prickly; **~schwein** nt porcupine

Stadion [ʃta:diɔn] (**-s, Stadien**) nt stadium

Stadium [ʃta:diʊm] nt stage, phase

Stadt [ʃtat] (-, ⁻e) *f* town; **~autobahn** *f* urban motorway; **~bahn** *f* suburban railway; **~bücherei** *f* municipal library

Städt- ['ʃtɛːt] *zW:* **~ebau** *m* town planning; **~epartnerschaft** *f* town twinning; **~er(in)** (-s, -) *m(f)* town dweller; **s~isch** *adj* municipal; *(nicht ländlich)* urban

Stadt- *zW:* **~kern** *m* town centre, city centre; **~mauer** *f* city wall(s); **~mitte** *f* town centre; **~plan** *m* street map; **~rand** *m* outskirts *pl*; **~rat** *m (Behörde)* town council, city council; **~rundfahrt** *f* tour of a/the city; **~teil** *m* district, part of town; **~zentrum** *nt* town centre

Staffel ['ʃtafəl] (-, -n) *f* rung; *(SPORT)* relay (team); *(AVIAT)* squadron; **~lauf** *m (SPORT)* relay (race); **s~n** *vt* to graduate

Stahl [ʃtaːl] (-(e)s, ⁻e) *m* steel

stahl *etc vb siehe* **stehlen**

stak *etc* [ʃtaːk] *vb siehe* **stecken**

Stall [ʃtal] (-(e)s, ⁻e) *m* stable; *(Kaninchenstall)* hutch; *(Schweinestall)* sty; *(Hühnerstall)* henhouse

Stamm [ʃtam] (-(e)s, ⁻e) *m (Baumstamm)* trunk; *(Menschenstamm)* tribe; *(GRAM)* stem; **~baum** *m* family tree; *(von Tier)* pedigree; **s~eln** *vt, vi* to stammer; **s~en** *vi:* **s~en von** *od* **aus** to come from; **~gast** *m* regular *(customer)*

stämmig ['ʃtɛmɪç] *adj* sturdy; *(Mensch)* stocky

Stammtisch ['ʃtamtɪʃ] *m* table for the regulars

stampfen ['ʃtampfən] *vt, vi* to stamp; *(stapfen)* to tramp; *(mit Werkzeug)* to pound

Stand [ʃtant] (-(e)s, ⁻e) *m* position; *(Wasserstand, Benzinstand etc)* level; *(Stehen)* standing position; *(Zustand)* state; *(Spielstand)* score; *(Messestand etc)* stand; *(Klasse)* class; *(Beruf)* profession; *siehe* **imstande, zustande**

stand *etc vb siehe* **stehen**

Standard ['ʃtandart] (-s, -s) *m* standard

Ständer ['ʃtɛndər] (-s, -) *m* stand

Standes- ['ʃtandəs] *zW:* **~amt** *nt* registry office; **~beamte(r)** *m* registrar; **s~gemäß** *adj, adv* according to one's social position;

~unterschied *m* social difference

Stand- *zW:* **s~haft** *adj* steadfast; **s~halten** *(unreg) vi:* **(jdm/etw) s~halten** to stand firm (against sb/sth), to resist (sb/sth)

ständig ['ʃtɛndɪç] *adj* permanent; *(ununterbrochen)* constant, continual

Stand- *zW:* **~licht** *nt* sidelights *pl*, parking lights *pl (US)*; **~ort** *m* location; *(MIL)* garrison; **~punkt** *m* standpoint; **~spur** *f* hard shoulder

Stange ['ʃtaŋə] *f* stick; *(Stab)* pole, bar; rod; *(Zigaretten)* carton; **von der ~** *(COMM)* off the peg; **eine ~ Geld** *(umg)* quite a packet

Stängel ▲ ['ʃtɛŋəl] (-s, -) *m* stalk

Stapel ['ʃtaːpəl] (-s, -) *m* pile; *(NAUT)* stocks *pl*; **~lauf** *m* launch; **s~n** *vt* to pile (up)

Star[1] [ʃtaːr] (-(e)s, -e) *m* starling; *(MED)* cataract

Star[2] [ʃtaːr] (-s, -s) *m (Filmstar etc)* star

starb *etc* [ʃtarp] *vb siehe* **sterben**

stark [ʃtark] *adj* strong; *(heftig, groß)* heavy; *(Maßangabe)* thick

Stärke ['ʃtɛrkə] *f* strength; heaviness; thickness; *(KOCH: Wäschestärke)* starch; **s~n** *vt* to strengthen; *(Wäsche)* to starch

Starkstrom *m* heavy current

Stärkung ['ʃtɛrkʊŋ] *f* strengthening; *(Essen)* refreshment

starr [ʃtar] *adj* stiff; *(unnachgiebig)* rigid; *(Blick)* staring; **~en** *vi* to stare; **~en vor** *od* **von** to be covered in; *(Waffen)* to be bristling with; **S~heit** *f* rigidity; **~köpfig** *adj* stubborn; **S~sinn** *m* obstinacy

Start [ʃtart] (-(e)s, -e) *m* start; *(AVIAT)* takeoff; **~automatik** *f (AUT)* automatic choke; **~bahn** *f* runway; **s~en** *vt* to start ♦ *vi* to start; to take off; **~er** (-s, -) *m* starter; **~erlaubnis** *f* takeoff clearance; **~hilfekabel** *nt* jump leads *pl*

Station [ʃtatsi'oːn] *f* station; hospital ward; **s~är** [ʃtatsio'nɛːr] *adj (MED)* in-patient *attr*; **s~ieren** [-'niːrən] *vt* to station

Statist [ʃta'tɪst] *m* extra, supernumerary

Statistik *f* statistics *sg*; **~er** (-s, -) *m* statistician

statistisch *adj* statistical

Stativ [ʃta'tiːf] (-s, -e) *nt* tripod

statt [ʃtat] *konj* instead of ♦ *präp* (+gen od dat) instead of

Stätte [ʃtɛtə] *f* place

statt- *zW:* **~finden** (*unreg*) *vi* to take place; **~haft** *adj* admissible; **~lich** *adj* imposing, handsome

Statue [ʃtaːtuə] *f* statue

Status [ʃtaːtʊs] (**-**, **-**) *m* status

Stau [ʃtaʊ] (**-(e)s**, **-e**) *m* blockage; (*Verkehrsstau*) (traffic) jam

Staub [ʃtaʊp] (**-(e)s**) *m* dust; **~ saugen** to vacuum, to hoover®; **s~en** [ʃtaʊbən] *vi* to be dusty; **s~ig** *adj* dusty; **s~saugen** *vi* to vacuum, to hoover ®; **~sauger** *m* vacuum cleaner; **~tuch** *nt* duster

Staudamm *m* dam

Staude [ʃtaʊdə] *f* shrub

stauen [ʃtaʊən] *vt* (*Wasser*) to dam up; (*Blut*) to stop the flow of ♦ *vr* (*Wasser*) to become dammed up; (*MED: Verkehr*) to become congested; (*Menschen*) to collect; (*Gefühle*) to build up

staunen [ʃtaʊnən] *vi* to be astonished; **S~** (**-s**) *nt* amazement

Stausee [ʃtaʊzeː] (**-s**, **-n**) *m* reservoir, man-made lake

Stauung [ʃtaʊʊŋ] *f* (*von Wasser*) damming-up; (*von Blut, Verkehr*) congestion

Std. *abk* (= *Stunde*) hr.

Steak [ʃteːk] *nt* steak

Stech- [ʃtɛç] *zW:* **s~en** (*unreg*) *vt* (*mit Nadel etc*) to prick; (*mit Messer*) to stab; (*mit Finger*) to poke; (*Biene etc*) to sting; (*Mücke*) to bite; (*Sonne*) to burn; (*KARTEN*) to take; (*ART*) to engrave; (*Torf, Spargel*) to cut; **in See s~en** to put to sea; **~en** (**-s**, **-**) *nt* (*SPORT*) play-off; jump-off; **s~end** *adj* piercing, stabbing; (*Geruch*) pungent; **~palme** *f* holly; **~uhr** *f* time clock

Steck- [ʃtɛk] *zW:* **~brief** *m* "wanted" poster; **~dose** *f* (wall) socket; **s~en** *vt* to put, to insert; (*Nadel*) to stick; (*Pflanzen*) to plant; (*beim Nähen*) to pin ♦ *vi* (*auch unreg*) to be; (*festsitzen*) to be stuck; (*Nadeln*) to stick; **s~en bleiben** to get stuck; **s~en lassen** to leave in; **~enpferd** *nt* hobby-horse; **~er** (**-s**, **-**) *m* plug; **~nadel** *f* pin

Steg [ʃteːk] (**-(e)s**, **-e**) *m* small bridge; (*Anlegesteg*) landing stage; **~reif** *m:* **aus dem ~reif** just like that

stehen [ʃteːən] *vi* (*unreg*) *vi* to stand, (*sich befinden*) to be; (*in Zeitung*) to say; (*stillstehen*) to have stopped ♦ *vi unpers:* **es steht schlecht um jdn/etw** things are bad for sb/sth; **zu jdm/etw ~** to stand by sb/sth; **jdm ~** to suit sb; **wie stehts?** how are things?; (*SPORT*) what's the score?; **~ bleiben** to remain standing; (*Uhr*) to stop; (*Fehler*) to stay as it is; **~ lassen** to leave; (*Bart*) to grow

Stehlampe [ʃteːlampə] *f* standard lamp

stehlen [ʃteːlən] *vt* (*unreg*) *vt* to steal

Stehplatz [ʃteːplats] *m* standing place

steif [ʃtaɪf] *adj* stiff; **S~heit** *f* stiffness

Steig- [ʃtaɪk] *zW:* **~bügel** *m* stirrup; **s~en** [ʃtaɪɡən] (*unreg*) *vi* to rise; (*klettern*) to climb; **s~en in** +*akk* /**auf** +*akk* to get in/on; **s~ern** *vt* to raise; (*GRAM*) to compare ♦ *vi* (*Auktion*) to bid ♦ *vr* to increase; **~erung** *f* raising; (*GRAM*) comparison; **~ung** *f* incline, gradient, rise

steil [ʃtaɪl] *adj* steep; **S~küste** *f* steep coast; (*Klippen*) cliffs *pl*

Stein [ʃtaɪn] (**-(e)s**, **-e**) *m* stone; (*in Uhr*) jewel; **~bock** *m* (*ASTROL*) Capricorn; **~bruch** *m* quarry; **s~ern** *adj* (made of) stone; (*fig*) stony; **~gut** *nt* stoneware; **s~ig** [ʃtaɪnɪç] *adj* stony; **s~igen** *vt* to stone; **~kohle** *f* mineral coal; **~zeit** *f* Stone Age

Stelle [ʃtɛlə] *f* place; (*Arbeit*) post, job; (*Amt*) office; **an Ihrer/meiner ~** in your/my place; *siehe* **anstelle**

stellen *vt* to put; (*Uhr etc*) to set; (*zur Verfügung ~*) to supply; (*fassen: Dieb*) to apprehend ♦ *vr* (*sich aufstellen*) to stand; (*sich einfinden*) to present o.s.; (*bei Polizei*) to give o.s. up; (*vorgeben*) to pretend (to be); **sich zu etw ~** to have an opinion of sth

Stellen- *zW:* **~angebot** *nt* offer of a post; (*in Zeitung*) "vacancies"; **~anzeige** *f* job advertisement; **~gesuch** *nt* application for a post; **~vermittlung** *f* employment agency

---

Spelling Reform: ▲ new spelling △ old spelling (to be phased out)

Stell- *zW:* **~ung** *f* position; (*MIL*) line; **~ung nehmen zu** to comment on; **~ungnahme** *f* comment; **s~vertretend** *adj* deputy, acting; **~vertreter** *m* deputy

Stelze ['ʃtɛltsə] *f* stilt

stemmen ['ʃtɛmən] *vt* to lift (up); (*drücken*) to press; **sich ~ gegen** (*fig*) to resist, to oppose

Stempel ['ʃtɛmpəl] (**-s, -**) *m* stamp; (*BOT*) pistil; **~kissen** *nt* ink pad; **s~n** *vt* to stamp; (*Briefmarke*) to cancel; **s~n gehen** (*umg*) to be *od* go on the dole

Stengel △ ['ʃtɛŋəl] (**-s, -**) *m* = **Stängel**

Steno- [ʃteno] *zW:* **~gramm** [-'gram] *nt* shorthand report; **~grafie** ▲ [-gra'fi:] *f* shorthand; **s~grafieren** ▲ [-gra'fi:rən] *vt, vi* to write (in) shorthand; **~typist(in)** [-ty'pɪst(ɪn)] *m(f)* shorthand typist

Stepp- ['ʃtɛp] *zW:* **~decke** *f* quilt; **~e** *f* prairie; steppe; **s~en** *vt* to stitch ♦ *vi* to tap-dance

Sterb- ['ʃtɛrb] *zW:* **~efall** *m* death; **~ehilfe** *f* euthanasia; **s~en** (*unreg*) *vi* to die; **s~lich** ['ʃtɛrplɪç] *adj* mortal; **~lichkeit** *f* mortality; **~lichkeitsziffer** *f* death rate

stereo- ['ʃtɛːreo] *in zW* stereo(-); **S~anlage** *f* stereo (system); **~typ** [ʃtɛreo'ty:p] *adj* stereotype

steril [ʃte'ri:l] *adj* sterile; **~isieren** *vt* to sterilize; **S~isierung** *f* sterilization

Stern [ʃtɛrn] (**-(e)s, -e**) *m* star; **~bild** *nt* constellation; **~schnuppe** *f* meteor, falling star; **~stunde** *f* historic moment; **~zeichen** *nt* sign of the zodiac

stet [ʃteːt] *adj* steady; **~ig** *adj* constant, continual; **~s** *adv* continually, always

Steuer¹ ['ʃtɔyər] (**-s, -**) *nt* (*NAUT*) helm; (*~ruder*) rudder; (*AUT*) steering wheel

Steuer² ['ʃtɔyər] (**-, -n**) *f* tax; **~berater(in)** *m(f)* tax consultant

Steuerbord *nt* (*NAUT, AVIAT*) starboard

Steuer- ['ʃtɔyər] *zW:* **~erklärung** *f* tax return; **s~frei** *adj* tax-free; **~freibetrag** *m* tax allowance; **~klasse** *f* tax group; **~knüppel** *m* control column; (*AVIAT, COMPUT*) joystick; **~mann** (*pl* **-männer** *od* **-leute**) *m* helmsman; **s~n** *vt, vi* to steer;

(*Flugzeug*) to pilot; (*Entwicklung, Tonstärke*) to control; **s~pflichtig** [-pflɪçtɪç] *adj* taxable; **~rad** *nt* steering wheel; **~ung** *f* (*auch AUT*) steering; piloting; control; (*Vorrichtung*) controls *pl*; **~zahler** (**-s, -**) *m* taxpayer

Steward ['stju:ərt] (**-s, -s**) *m* steward; **~ess** ▲ ['stju:ərdɛs] (**-, -en**) *f* stewardess; air hostess

Stich [ʃtɪç] (**-(e)s, -e**) *m* (*Insektenstich*) sting; (*Messerstich*) stab; (*beim Nähen*) stitch; (*Färbung*) tinge; (*KARTEN*) trick; (*ART*) engraving; **jdn im ~ lassen** to leave sb in the lurch; **s~eln** *vi* (*fig*) to jibe; **s~haltig** *adj* sound, tenable; **~probe** *f* spot check; **~straße** *f* cul-de-sac; **~wahl** *f* final ballot; **~wort** *nt* cue; (*in Wörterbuch*) headword; (*für Vortrag*) note

sticken ['ʃtɪkən] *vt, vi* to embroider

Sticke'rei *f* embroidery

stickig *adj* stuffy, close

Stickstoff *m* nitrogen

Stief- ['ʃti:f] *in zW* step

Stiefel ['ʃti:fəl] (**-s, -**) *m* boot

Stief- *zW:* **~kind** *nt* stepchild; (*fig*) Cinderella; **~mutter** *f* stepmother; **~mütterchen** *nt* pansy; **s~mütterlich** *adj* (*fig*): **jdn/etw s~mütterlich behandeln** to pay little attention to sb/sth; **~vater** *m* stepfather

stiehlst *etc* [ʃti:lst] *vb siehe* **stehlen**

Stiel [ʃti:l] (**-(e)s, -e**) *m* handle; (*BOT*) stalk

Stier (**-(e)s, -e**) *m* bull; (*ASTROL*) Taurus

stieren *vi* to stare

Stierkampf *m* bullfight

Stierkämpfer *m* bullfighter

Stift [ʃtɪft] (**-(e)s, -e**) *m* peg; (*Nagel*) tack; (*Farbstift*) crayon; (*Bleistift*) pencil ♦ *nt* (*charitable*) foundation; (*ECCL*) religious institution; **s~en** *vt* to found; (*Unruhe*) to cause; (*spenden*) to contribute; **~er(in)** (**-s, -**) *m(f)* founder; **~ung** *f* donation; (*Organisation*) foundation; **~zahn** *m* post crown

Stil [ʃti:l] (**-(e)s, -e**) *m* style

still [ʃtɪl] *adj* quiet; (*unbewegt*) still; (*heimlich*) secret; **S~er Ozean** Pacific; **~ halten** to keep still; **~ stehen** to stand still; **S~e** *f*

stillness, quietness; **in aller S~e** quietly;
~en vt to stop; (befriedigen) to satisfy;
(Säugling) to breast-feed; **~legen ▲** vt to
close down; **~schweigen** (unreg) vi to be
silent; **S~schweigen** nt silence;
~schweigend adj silent; (Einverständnis)
tacit ♦ adv silently; tacitly; **S~stand** m
standstill

Stimm- ['ʃtɪm] zW: **~bänder** pl vocal cords;
s~berechtigt adj entitled to vote; **~e** f
voice; (Wahlstimme) vote; **s~en** vt (MUS) to
tune ♦ vi to be right; **das s~te ihn traurig**
that made him feel sad; **s~en für/gegen**
to vote for/against; **s~t so!** that's right;
~enmehrheit f majority (of votes);
~enthaltung f abstention; **~gabel** f
tuning fork; **~recht** nt right to vote; **~ung**
f mood; atmosphere; **s~ungsvoll** adj
enjoyable; full of atmosphere; **~zettel** m
ballot paper

stinken ['ʃtɪŋkən] (unreg) vi to stink

Stipendium ['ʃtiˈpɛndiʊm] nt grant

stirbst etc ['ʃtɪrpst] vb siehe **sterben**

Stirn [ʃtɪrn] (-, -en) f forehead, brow;
(Frechheit) impudence; **~band** nt
headband; **~höhle** f sinus

stöbern ['ʃtøːbərn] vi to rummage

stochern ['ʃtɔxərn] vi to poke (about)

Stock¹ [ʃtɔk] (-(e)s, ᵉᵉ) m stick; (BOT) stock

Stock² [ʃtɔk] (-(e)s, - od **Stockwerke**) m
storey

stocken vi to stop, to pause; **~d** adj halting

Stockung f stoppage

Stockwerk nt storey, floor

Stoff [ʃtɔf] (-(e)s, -e) m (Gewebe) material,
cloth; (Materie) matter; (von Buch etc)
subject (matter); **s~lich** adj material; **~tier**
nt soft toy; **~wechsel** m metabolism

stöhnen ['ʃtøːnən] vi to groan

Stollen ['ʃtɔlən] (-s, -) m (MIN) gallery;
(KOCH) cake eaten at Christmas; (von
Schuhen) stud

stolpern ['ʃtɔlpərn] vi to stumble, to trip

Stolz [ʃtɔlts] (-es) m pride; **s~** adj proud;
s~ieren [ʃtɔlˈtsiːrən] vi to strut

stopfen ['ʃtɔpfən] vt (hineinstopfen) to stuff;
(voll stopfen) to fill (up); (nähen) to darn ♦ vi

(MED) to cause constipation

Stopfgarn nt darning thread

Stoppel ['ʃtɔpəl] (-, -n) f stubble

Stopp- ['ʃtɔp] zW: **s~en** vt to stop; (mit Uhr)
to time ♦ vi to stop; **~schild** nt stop sign;
~uhr f stopwatch

Stöpsel ['ʃtœpsəl] (-s, -) m plug; (für
Flaschen) stopper

Storch [ʃtɔrç] (-(e)s, ᵉᵉ) m stork

Stör- ['ʃtøːr] zW: **s~en** vt to disturb;
(behindern, RADIO) to interfere with ♦ vr:
sich an etw dat **s~en** to let sth bother
one; **s~end** adj disturbing, annoying;
~enfried (-(e)s, -e) m troublemaker

stornieren [ʃtɔrˈniːrən] vt (Auftrag) to
cancel; (Buchung) to reverse

Stornogebühr ['ʃtɔrno-] f cancellation fee

störrisch ['ʃtœrɪʃ] adj stubborn, perverse

Störung f disturbance; interference

Stoß [ʃtoːs] (-es, ᵉᵉ) m (Schub) push; (Schlag)
blow; knock; (mit Schwert) thrust; (mit Fuß)
kick; (Frdstoß) shock; (Haufen) pile;
~dämpfer (-s, -) m shock absorber; **s~en**
(unreg) vt (mit Druck) to shove, to push; (mit
Schlag) to knock, to bump; (mit Fuß) to
kick; (Schwert etc) to thrust; (anstoßen: Kopf
etc) to bump ♦ vr to get a knock ♦ vi: **s~en
an** od **auf** +akk to bump into; (finden) to
come across; (angrenzen) to be next to;
sich s~en an +dat (fig) to take exception
to; **~stange** f (AUT) bumper

stottern ['ʃtɔtərn] vt, vi to stutter

Str. abk (= Straße) St.

Straf- ['ʃtraːf] zW: **~anstalt** f penal
institution; **~arbeit** f (SCH) punishment;
lines pl; **s~bar** adj punishable; **~e** f
punishment; (JUR) penalty; (Gefängnisstrafe)
sentence; (Geldstrafe) fine; **s~en** vt to
punish

straff [ʃtraf] adj tight; (streng) strict; (Stil etc)
concise; (Haltung) erect; **~en** vt to tighten,
to tauten

Strafgefangene(r) f(m) prisoner, convict

Strafgesetzbuch nt penal code

sträflich ['ʃtrɛːflɪç] adj criminal

Sträfling m convict

Straf- zW: **~porto** nt excess postage

Spelling Reform: ▲ *new spelling* △ *old spelling (to be phased out)*

(charge); **~predigt** f telling-off; **~raum** m
(*SPORT*) penalty area; **~recht** nt criminal
law; **~stoß** m (*SPORT*) penalty (kick); **~tat** f
punishable act; **~zettel** m ticket

Strahl [ʃtraːl] **(-s, -en)** m ray, beam;
(*Wasserstrahl*) jet; **s~en** vi to radiate; (*fig*)
to beam; **~ung** f radiation

Strähne [ˈʃtrɛːnə] f strand

stramm [ʃtram] adj tight; (*Haltung*) erect;
(*Mensch*) robust

strampeln [ˈʃtrampəln] vi to kick (about), to
fidget

Strand [ʃtrant] **(-(e)s, ~e)** m shore; (*mit
Sand*) beach; **~bad** nt open-air swimming
pool, lido; **s~en** [ˈʃtrandən] vi to run
aground; (*fig: Mensch*) to fail; **~gut** nt
flotsam; **~korb** m beach chair

Strang [ʃtraŋ] **(-(e)s, ~e)** m cord, rope;
(*Bündel*) skein

Strapaz- zW: **~e** [ʃtraˈpaːtsə] f strain,
exertion; **s~ieren** [ʃtrapaˈtsiːrən] vt
(*Material*) to treat roughly, to punish;
(*Mensch, Kräfte*) to wear out, to exhaust;
s~ierfähig adj hard-wearing; **s~iös**
[ʃtrapatsiˈøːs] adj exhausting, tough

Straße [ˈʃtraːsə] f street, road

Straßen- zW: **~bahn** f tram, streetcar (*US*);
~glätte f slippery road surface; **~karte** f
road map; **~kehrer (-s, -)** m roadsweeper;
~sperre f roadblock; **~verkehr** m (road)
traffic; **~verkehrsordnung** f highway
code

Strateg- [ʃtraˈteːg] zW: **~e (-n, -n)** m
strategist; **~ie** [ʃtrateˈgiː] f strategy; **s~isch**
adj strategic

sträuben [ˈʃtrɔybən] vt to ruffle ♦ vr to
bristle; (*Mensch*): **sich (gegen etw) ~** to
resist (sth)

Strauch [ʃtraux] **(-(e)s, Sträucher)** m bush,
shrub

Strauß¹ [ʃtraus] **(-es, Sträuße)** m bunch;
bouquet

Strauß² [ʃtraus] **(-es, -e)** m ostrich

Streb- [ˈʃtreːb] zW: **s~en** vi to strive, to
endeavour; **s~en nach** to strive for; **~er
(-s, -)** (*pej*) m pusher, climber; (*SCH*) swot
(*BRIT*)

Strecke [ˈʃtrɛkə] f stretch; (*Entfernung*)
distance; (*EISENB, MATH*) line; **s~n** vt to
stretch; (*Waffen*) to lay down; (*KOCH*) to eke
out ♦ vr to stretch (o.s.)

Streich [ʃtraiç] **(-(e)s, -e)** m trick, prank;
(*Hieb*) blow; **s~eln** vt to stroke; **s~en**
(*unreg*) vt (*berühren*) to stroke; (*auftragen*) to
spread; (*anmalen*) to paint; (*durchstreichen*)
to delete; (*nicht genehmigen*) to cancel ♦ vi
(*berühren*) to brush; (*schleichen*) to prowl;
~holz nt match; **~instrument** nt string
instrument

Streif- [ˈʃtraif] zW: **~e** f patrol; **s~en** vt
(*leicht berühren*) to brush against, to graze;
(*Blick*) to skim over; (*Thema, Problem*) to
touch on; (*abstreifen*) to take off ♦ vi
(*gehen*) to roam; **~en (-s, -)** m (*Linie*) stripe;
(*Stück*) strip; (*Film*) film; **~enwagen** m
patrol car; **~schuss** ▲ m graze, grazing
shot; **~zug** m scouting trip

Streik [ʃtraik] **(-(e)s, -s)** m strike; **~brecher
(-s, -)** m blackleg, strikebreaker; **s~en** vi to
strike; **~posten** m (strike) picket

Streit [ʃtrait] **(-(e)s, -e)** m argument;
dispute; **s~en** (*unreg*) vi, vr to argue; to
dispute; **~frage** f point at issue; **s~ig** adj:
jdm etw s~ig machen to dispute sb's right
to sth; **~igkeiten** pl quarrel sg, dispute sg;
~kräfte pl (*MIL*) armed forces

streng [ʃtrɛŋ] adj severe; (*Lehrer, Maßnahme*)
strict; (*Geruch etc*) sharp; **~ genommen**
strictly speaking; **S~e (-)** f severity,
strictness, sharpness; **~gläubig** adj
orthodox, strict; **~stens** adv strictly

Stress ▲ [ʃtrɛs] **(-es, -e)** m stress

stressen vt to put under stress

streuen [ˈʃtrɔyən] vt to strew, to scatter, to
spread

Strich [ʃtriç] **(-(e)s, -e)** m (*Linie*) line;
(*Federstrich, Pinselstrich*) stroke; (*von
Geweben*) nap; (*von Fell*) pile; **auf den ~
gehen** (*umg*) to walk the streets; **jdm
gegen den ~ gehen** to rub sb up the
wrong way; **einen ~ machen durch** to
cross out; (*fig*) to foil; **~kode** m (*auf Waren*)
bar code; **~mädchen** nt streetwalker;
s~weise adv here and there

Strick [ʃtrɪk] **(-(e)s, -e)** m rope; **s~en** vt, vi to knit; **~jacke** f cardigan; **~leiter** f rope ladder; **~nadel** f knitting needle; **~waren** pl knitwear sg

strikt [strɪkt] adj strict

strittig [ˈʃtrɪtɪç] adj disputed, in dispute

Stroh [ʃtroː] **(-(e)s)** nt straw; **~blume** f everlasting flower; **~dach** nt thatched roof; **~halm** m (drinking) straw

Strom [ʃtroːm] **(-(e)s, ⁺e)** m river; (fig) stream; (ELEK) current; **s~abwärts** adv downstream; **s~aufwärts** adv upstream; **~ausfall** m power failure

strömen [ˈʃtrøːmən] vi to stream, to pour

Strom- zW: **~kreis** m circuit; **s~linienförmig** adj streamlined; **~sperre** f power cut

Strömung [ˈʃtrøːmʊŋ] f current

Strophe [ˈʃtroːfə] f verse

strotzen [ˈʃtrɔtsən] vi: **~ vor** od **von** to abound in, to be full of

Strudel [ˈʃtruːdəl] **(-s, -)** m whirlpool, vortex; (KOCH) strudel

Struktur [ʃtrʊkˈtuːr] f structure

Strumpf [ʃtrʊmpf] **(-(e)s, ⁺e)** m stocking; **~band** nt garter; **~hose** f (pair of) tights

Stube [ˈʃtuːbə] f room

Stuben- zW: **~arrest** m confinement to one's room; (MIL) confinement to quarters; **~hocker** (umg) m stay-at-home; **s~rein** adj house-trained

Stuck [ʃtʊk] **(-(e)s)** m stucco

Stück [ʃtyk] **(-(e)s, -e)** nt piece; (etwas) bit; (THEAT) play; **~chen** nt little piece; **~lohn** m piecework wages pl; **s~weise** adv bit by bit, piecemeal; (COMM) individually

Student(in) [ʃtuˈdɛnt(ɪn)] m(f) student; **s~isch** adj student, academic

Studie [ˈʃtuːdiə] f study

Studienfahrt f study trip

studieren [ʃtuˈdiːrən] vt, vi to study

Studio [ˈʃtuːdio] **(-s, -s)** nt studio

Studium [ˈʃtuːdiʊm] nt studies pl

Stufe [ˈʃtuːfə] f step; (Entwicklungsstufe) stage; **s~nweise** adv gradually

Stuhl [ʃtuːl] **(-(e)s, ⁺e)** m chair; **~gang** m bowel movement

stülpen [ˈʃtʏlpən] vt (umdrehen) to turn upside down; (bedecken) to put

stumm [ʃtʊm] adj silent; (MED) dumb

Stummel [ˈʃtʊməl] **(-s, -)** m stump; (Zigarettenstummel) stub

Stummfilm m silent film

Stümper [ˈʃtʏmpər] **(-s, -)** m incompetent, duffer; **s~haft** adj bungling, incompetent; **s~n** vi to bungle

Stumpf [ʃtʊmpf] **(-(e)s, ⁺e)** m stump; **s~** adj blunt; (teilnahmslos, glanzlos) dull; (Winkel) obtuse; **~sinn** m tediousness; **s~sinnig** adj dull

Stunde [ˈʃtʊndə] f hour; (SCH) lesson

stunden vt: **jdm etw ~** to give sb time to pay sth; **S~geschwindigkeit** f average speed per hour; **S~kilometer** pl kilometres per hour; **~lang** adj for hours; **S~lohn** m hourly wage; **S~plan** m timetable; **~weise** adv by the hour; every hour

stündlich [ˈʃtʏntlɪç] adj hourly

Stups [ʃtʊps] **(-es, -e)** (umg) m push; **~nase** f snub nose

stur [ʃtuːr] adj obstinate, pigheaded

Sturm [ʃtʊrm] **(-(e)s, ⁺e)** m storm, gale; (MIL etc) attack, assault

sturm- [ˈʃtʊrm] zW: **~en** vi (Wind) to blow hard, to rage; (rennen) to storm ♦ vt (MIL, fig) to storm ♦ vb unpers: **es ~t** there's a gale blowing; **S~er (-s, -)** m (SPORT) forward, striker; **~isch** adj stormy

Sturmwarnung f gale warning

Sturz [ʃtʊrts] **(-es, ⁺e)** m fall; (POL) overthrow

stürzen [ˈʃtʏrtsən] vt (werfen) to hurl; (POL) to overthrow; (umkehren) to overturn ♦ vr to rush; (hineinstürzen) to plunge ♦ vi to fall; (AVIAT) to dive; (rennen) to dash

Sturzflug m nose dive

Sturzhelm m crash helmet

Stute [ˈʃtuːtə] f mare

Stützbalken m brace, joist

Stütze [ˈʃtʏtsə] f support; help

stutzen [ˈʃtʊtsən] vt to trim; (Ohr, Schwanz) to dock; (Flügel) to clip ♦ vi to hesitate; to become suspicious

stützen vt (auch fig) to support; (Ellbogen

etc) to prop up

stutzig *adj* perplexed, puzzled; *(misstrauisch)* suspicious

Stützpunkt *m* point of support; *(von Hebel)* fulcrum; *(MIL, fig)* base

Styropor [ʃtyro'poːr] (®; **-s**) *nt* polystyrene

s. u. *abk* = siehe unten

Subjekt [zʊp'jɛkt] **(-(e)s, -e)** *nt* subject; **s~iv** [-'tiːf] *adj* subjective; **~ivi'tät** *f* subjectivity

Subsidiarität *f* subsidiarity

Substantiv [zʊpstan'tiːf] **(-s, -e)** *nt* noun

Substanz [zʊp'stants] *f* substance

subtil [zʊp'tiːl] *adj* subtle

subtrahieren [zʊptra'hiːrən] *vt* to subtract

subtropisch ['zʊptroːpɪʃ] *adj* subtropical

Subvention [zʊpvɛntsi'oːn] *f* subsidy; **s~ieren** *vt* to subsidize

Such- ['zuːx] *zW:* **~aktion** *f* search; **~e** *f* search; **s~en** *vt* to look (for), to seek; *(versuchen)* to try ♦ *vi* to seek, to search; **~er (-s, -)** *m* seeker, searcher; *(PHOT)* viewfinder; **~maschine** *f (COMPUT)* search engine

Sucht [zʊxt] **(-, ̈e)** *f* mania; *(MED)* addiction, craving

süchtig ['zʏçtɪç] *adj* addicted; **S~e(r)** *f(m)* addict

Süd- ['zyːt] *zW:* **~en** ['zyːdən] **(-s)** *m* south; **~früchte** *pl* Mediterranean fruit *sg;* **s~lich** *adj* southern; **s~lich von** (to the) south of; **~pol** *m* South Pole; **s~wärts** *adv* southwards

süffig ['zʏfɪç] *adj (Wein)* pleasant to the taste

süffisant [zʏfi'zant] *adj* smug

suggerieren [zʊɡe'riːrən] *vt* to suggest

Sühne ['zyːnə] *f* atonement, expiation; **s~n** *vt* to atone for, to expiate

Sultan ['zʊltan] **(-s, -e)** *m* sultan; **~ine** [zʊlta'niːnə] *f* sultana

Sülze ['zʏltsə] *f* brawn

Summe ['zʊmə] *f* sum, total

summen *vt, vi* to buzz; *(Lied)* to hum

Sumpf [zʊmpf] **(-(e)s, ̈e)** *m* swamp, marsh; **s~ig** *adj* marshy

Sünde ['zʏndə] *f* sin; **~nbock** *(umg) m* scapegoat; **~r(in) (-s, -)** *m(f)* sinner; **sündigen** *vi* to sin

Super ['zuːpər] **(-s)** *nt (Benzin)* four star (petrol) *(BRIT)*, premium *(US)*; **~lativ** [-latiːf] **(-s, -e)** *m* superlative; **~macht** *f* superpower; **~markt** *m* supermarket

Suppe ['zʊpə] *f* soup; **~nteller** *m* soup plate

süß [zyːs] *adj* sweet; **S~e (-)** *f* sweetness; **~en** *vt* to sweeten; **S~igkeit** *f* sweetness; *(Bonbon etc)* sweet *(BRIT)*, candy *(US)*; **~lich** *adj* sweetish; *(fig)* sugary; **~sauer** *adj (Gurke)* pickled; *(Sauce etc)* sweet-and-sour; **S~speise** *f* pudding, sweet; **S~stoff** *m* sweetener; **S~waren** *pl* confectionery *(sing)*; **S~wasser** *nt* fresh water

Symbol [zym'boːl] **(-s, -e)** *nt* symbol; **s~isch** *adj* symbolic(al)

Symmetrie [zyme'triː] *f* symmetry

symmetrisch [zy'meːtrɪʃ] *adj* symmetrical

Sympathie [zympa'tiː] *f* liking, sympathy; **sympathisch** [zym'paːtɪʃ] *adj* likeable; **er ist mir sympathisch** I like him; **sympathi'sieren** *vi* to sympathize

Symphonie [zymfo'niː] *f (MUS)* symphony

Symptom [zymp'toːm] **(-s, -e)** *nt* symptom; **s~atisch** [zympto'maːtɪʃ] *adj* symptomatic

Synagoge [zyna'goːɡə] *f* synagogue

synchron [zyn'kroːn] *adj* synchronous; **~i'sieren** *vt* to synchronize; *(Film)* to dub

Synonym [zyno'nyːm] **(-s, -e)** *nt* synonym; **s~** *adj* synonymous

Synthese [zyn'teːzə] *f* synthesis

synthetisch *adj* synthetic

System [zys'teːm] **(-s, -e)** *nt* system; **s~atisch** *adj* systematic; **s~ati'sieren** *vt* to systematize

Szene ['stseːnə] *f* scene; **~rie** [stsenə'riː] *f* scenery

T, t

t *abk* (= *Tonne*) t

Tabak ['taːbak] **(-s, -e)** *m* tobacco

Tabell- [ta'bɛl] *zW:* **t~arisch** [tabɛ'laːrɪʃ] *adj* tabular; **~e** *f* table

Tablett [ta'blɛt] *nt* tray; **~e** *f* tablet, pill

Tabu [ta'buː] *nt* taboo; **t~** *adj* taboo

Tachometer [taxo'meːtər] **(-s, -)** *m (AUT)*

speedometer

Tadel ['taːdəl] (-s, -) m censure; scolding; (*Fehler*) fault, blemish; **t~los** adj faultless, irreproachable; **t~n** vt to scold

Tafel ['taːfəl] (-, -n) f (*auch* MATH) table; (*Anschlag~*) board; (*Wand~*) blackboard; (*Schiefer~*) slate; (*Gedenk~*) plaque; (*Illustration*) plate; (*Schalt~*) panel; (*Schokolade etc*) bar

Tag [taːk] (-(e)s, -e) m day; daylight; **unter/über ~e** (MIN) underground/on the surface; **an den ~ kommen** to come to light; **guten ~!** good morning/afternoon!; *siehe* **zutage**; **t~aus** adv: **t~aus, ~ein** day in, day out; **~dienst** m day duty

Tage- ['taːgə] zW: **~buch** ['taːgəbuːx] nt diary, journal; **~geld** nt daily allowance; **t~lang** adv for days; **t~n** vi to sit, to meet ♦ vb unpers: **es tagt** dawn is breaking

Tages- zW: **~ablauf** m course of the day; **~anbruch** m dawn; **~fahrt** f day trip; **~karte** f menu of the day; (*Fahrkarte*) day ticket; **~licht** nt daylight; **~ordnung** f agenda; **~zeit** f time of day; **~zeitung** f daily (paper)

täglich ['tɛːklɪç] adj, adv daily

tagsüber ['taːksjyːbər] adv during the day

Tagung f conference

Taille ['taljə] f waist

Takt [takt] (-(e)s, -e) m tact; (MUS) time; **~gefühl** nt tact

Taktik f tactics pl; **taktisch** adj tactical

Takt- zW: **t~los** adj tactless; **~losigkeit** f tactlessness; **~stock** m (conductor's) baton; **t~voll** adj tactful

Tal [taːl] (-(e)s, "er) nt valley

Talent [ta'lɛnt] (-(e)s, -e) nt talent; **t~iert** [talɛn'tiːrt] adj talented, gifted

Talisman ['taːlɪsman] (-s, -e) m talisman

Talsohle f bottom of a valley

Talsperre f dam

Tampon ['tampɔn] (-s, -s) m tampon

Tandem ['tandɛm] (-s, -s) nt tandem

Tang [taŋ] (-(e)s, -e) m seaweed

Tank [taŋk] (-s, -s) m tank; **~anzeige** f fuel gauge; **t~en** vi to fill up with petrol (BRIT) od gas (US); (AVIAT) to (re)fuel; **~er** (-s, -) m tanker; **~schiff** nt tanker; **~stelle** f petrol (BRIT) od gas (US) station; **~wart** m petrol pump (BRIT) od gas station (US) attendant

Tanne ['tanə] f fir

Tannen- zW: **~baum** m fir tree; **~zapten** m fir cone

Tante ['tantə] f aunt

Tanz [tants] (-es, "e) m dance; **t~en** vt, vi to dance

Tänzer(in) ['tɛntsər(ɪn)] (-s, -) m(f) dancer

Tanzfläche f (dance) floor

Tanzschule f dancing school

Tapete [ta'peːtə] f wallpaper; **~nwechsel** m (fig) change of scenery

tapezieren [tape'tsiːrən] vt to (wall)paper; **Tapezierer** [tape'tsiːrər] (-s, -) m (interior) decorator

tapfer ['tapfər] adj brave; **T~keit** f courage, bravery

Tarif [ta'riːf] (-s, -e) m tariff, (scale of) fares od charges; **~lohn** m standard wage rate; **~verhandlungen** pl wage negotiations; **~zone** f fare zone

Tarn- ['tarn] zW: **t~en** vt to camouflage; (*Person, Absicht*) to disguise; **~ung** f camouflaging; disguising

Tasche ['taʃə] f pocket; handbag

Taschen- in zW pocket; **~buch** nt paperback; **~dieb** m pickpocket; **~geld** nt pocket money; **~lampe** f (electric) torch, flashlight (US); **~messer** nt penknife; **~tuch** nt handkerchief

Tasse ['tasə] f cup

Tastatur [tasta'tuːr] f keyboard

Taste ['tastə] f push-button control; (*an Schreibmaschine*) key; **t~n** vt to feel, to touch ♦ vi to feel, to grope ♦ vr to feel one's way

Tat [taːt] (-, -en) f act, deed, action; **in der ~** indeed, as a matter of fact; **t~** etc vb siehe **tun**; **~bestand** m facts pl of the case; **t~enlos** adj inactive

Tät- ['tɛːt] zW: **~er(in)** (-s, -) m(f) perpetrator, culprit; **t~ig** adj active; **in einer Firma t~ig sein** to work for a firm; **~igkeit** f activity; (*Beruf*) occupation; **t~lich** adj violent; **~lichkeit** f violence; **~lichkeiten** pl (*Schlage*) blows

tätowieren [tɛto'viːrən] *vt* to tattoo

Tatsache *f* fact

tatsächlich *adj* actual ♦ *adv* really

Tau¹ [taʊ] **(-(e)s, -e)** *nt* rope

Tau² [taʊ] **(-(e)s)** *m* dew

taub [taʊp] *adj* deaf; (*Nuss*) hollow

Taube ['taʊbə] *f* dove; pigeon; **~nschlag** *m* dovecote; **hier geht es zu wie in einem ~nschlag** it's a hive of activity here

taub- *zW*: **T~heit** *f* deafness; **~stumm** *adj* deaf-and-dumb

Tauch- ['taʊx] *zW*: **t~en** *vt* to dip ♦ *vi* to dive; (*NAUT*) to submerge; **~er (-s, -)** *m* diver; **~eranzug** *m* diving suit; **~erbrille** *f* diving goggles *pl*; **~sieder (-s, -)** *m* immersion coil (*for boiling water*)

tauen ['taʊən] *vt, vi* to thaw ♦ *vb unpers*: **es taut** it's thawing

Tauf- ['taʊf] *zW*: **~becken** *nt* font; **~e** *f* baptism; **t~en** *vt* to christen, to baptize; **~pate** *m* godfather; **~patin** *f* godmother; **~schein** *m* certificate of baptism

taug- ['taʊg] *zW*: **~en** *vi* to be of use; **~en für** to do for, to be good for; **nicht ~en to** be no good *od* useless; **T~enichts (-es, -e)** *m* good-for-nothing; **~lich** ['taʊklɪç] *adj* suitable; (*MIL*) fit (*for service*)

Taumel ['taʊməl] **(-s)** *m* dizziness; (*fig*) frenzy; **t~n** *vi* to reel, to stagger

Tausch [taʊʃ] **(-(e)s, -e)** *m* exchange; **t~en** *vt* to exchange, to swap

täuschen ['tɔʏʃən] *vt* to deceive ♦ *vi* to be deceptive ♦ *vr* to be wrong; **~d** *adj* deceptive

Tauschhandel *m* barter

Täuschung *f* deception; (*optisch*) illusion

tausend ['taʊzənt] *num* (a) thousand

Tauwetter *nt* thaw

Taxi ['taksi] **(-(s), -(s))** *nt* taxi; **~fahrer** *m* taxi driver; **~stand** *m* taxi rank

Tech- ['tɛç] *zW*: **~nik** *f* technique; (*Methode, Kunstfertigkeit*) technology; **~niker (-s, -)** *m* technician; **t~nisch** *adj* technical; **~nolo'gie** *f* technology; **t~no'logisch** *adj* technological

Tee [teː] **(-s, -s)** *m* tea; **~beutel** *m* tea bag; **~kanne** *f* teapot; **~löffel** *m* teaspoon

Teer [teːr] **(-(e)s, -e)** *m* tar; **t~en** *vt* to tar

Teesieb *nt* tea strainer

Teich [taɪç] **(-(e)s, -e)** *m* pond

Teig [taɪk] **(-(e)s, -e)** *m* dough; **t~ig** ['taɪgɪç] *adj* doughy; **~waren** *pl* pasta *sg*

Teil [taɪl] **(-(e)s, -e)** *m od nt* part; (*Anteil*) share; (*Bestandteil*) component; **zum ~** partly; **t~bar** *adj* divisible; **~betrag** *m* instalment; **~chen** *nt* (atomic) particle; **t~en** *vt, vr* to divide; (*mit jdm*) to share; **t~haben** (*unreg*) *vi*: **t~haben an** +*dat* to share in; **~haber (-s, -)** *m* partner; **~kaskoversicherung** *f* third party, fire and theft insurance; **t~möbliert** *adj* partially furnished; **~nahme** *f* participation; (*Mitleid*) sympathy; **t~nahmslos** *adj* disinterested, apathetic; **t~nehmen** (*unreg*) *vi*: **t~nehmen an** +*dat* to take part in; **~nehmer (-s, -)** *m* participant; **t~s** *adv* partly; **~ung** *f* division; **t~weise** *adv* partially, in part; **~zahlung** *f* payment by instalments; **~zeitarbeit** *f* part-time work

Teint [tɛ̃ː] **(-s, -s)** *m* complexion

Telearbeit ['teːleˌʔarbaɪt] *f* teleworking

Telefax ['teːlefaks] *nt* fax

Telefon [tele'foːn] **(-s, -e)** *nt* telephone; **~anruf** *m* (tele)phone call; **~at** [telefo'naːt] **(-(e)s, -e)** *nt* (tele)phone call; **~buch** *nt* telephone directory; **~hörer** *m* (telephone) receiver; **t~ieren** *vi* to telephone; **t~isch** [-ɪʃ] *adj* telephone; (*Benachrichtigung*) by telephone; **~ist(in)** [telefo'nɪst(ɪn)] *m(f)* telephonist; **~karte** *f* phonecard; **~nummer** *f* (tele)phone number; **~zelle** *f* telephone kiosk, callbox; **~zentrale** *f* telephone exchange

Telegraf [tele'graːf] **(-en, -en)** *m* telegraph; **~enmast** *m* telegraph pole; **~ie** [-'fiː] *f* telegraphy; **t~ieren** [-'fiːrən] *vt, vi* to telegraph, to wire

Telegramm [tele'gram] **(-s, -e)** *nt* telegram, cable; **~adresse** *f* telegraphic address

Tele- *zW*: **~objektiv** ['teːleˌʔɔpjɛktiːf] *nt* telephoto lens; **t~pathisch** [tele'paːtɪʃ] *adj* telepathic; **~skop** [tele'skoːp] **(-s, -e)** *nt* telescope

Teller ['tɛlər] (**-s, -**) m plate; **~gericht** nt (KOCH) one-course meal

Tempel ['tɛmpəl] (**-s, -**) m temple

Temperament [tempəra'mɛnt] nt temperament; (Schwung) vivacity, liveliness; **t~voll** adj high-spirited, lively

Temperatur [tempəra'tuːr] f temperature

Tempo¹ ['tɛmpo] (**-s, Tempi**) nt (MUS) tempo

Tempo² ['tɛmpo] (**-s, -s**) nt speed, pace; **~!** get a move on!; **~limit** [-lɪmɪt] (**-s, -s**) nt speed limit; **~taschentuch** ® nt tissue

Tendenz [tɛn'dɛnts] f tendency; (Absicht) intention; **t~iös** [-i'øːs] adj biased, tendentious

tendieren [tɛn'diːrən] vi: **~ zu** to show a tendency to, to incline towards

Tennis ['tɛnɪs] (**-**) nt tennis; **~ball** m tennis ball; **~platz** m tennis court; **~schläger** m tennis racket; **~schuh** m tennis shoe; **~spieler(in)** m(f) tennis player

Tenor [te'noːr] (**-s, ⁺e**) m tenor

Teppich ['tɛpɪç] (**-s, -e**) m carpet; **~boden** m wall-to-wall carpeting

Termin [tɛr'miːn] (**-s, -e**) m (Zeitpunkt) date; (Frist) time limit, deadline; (Arzttermin etc) appointment; **~kalender** m diary, appointments book; **~planer** m personal organizer

Terrasse [tɛ'rasə] f terrace

Terrine [tɛ'riːnə] f tureen

territorial [tɛritori'aːl] adj territorial

Territorium [tɛri'toːriʊm] nt territory

Terror ['tɛrɔr] (**-s**) m terror; reign of terror; **t~isieren** [tɛrori'ziːrən] vt to terrorize; **~ismus** [-'rɪsmʊs] m terrorism; **~ist** [-'rɪst] m terrorist

Tesafilm ['teːzafɪlm] ® m Sellotape ® (BRIT), Scotch tape ® (US)

Tessin [tɛ'siːn] (**-s**) nt: **das ~** Ticino

Test [tɛst] (**-s, -s**) m test

Testament [tɛsta'mɛnt] nt will, testament; (REL) Testament; **t~arisch** [-'taːrɪʃ] adj testamentary

Testamentsvollstrecker m executor (of a will)

testen vt to test

Tetanus ['teːtanʊs] (**-**) m tetanus; **~impfung** f (anti-)tetanus injection

teuer ['tɔyər] adj dear, expensive; **T~ung** f increase in prices; **T~ungszulage** f cost of living bonus

Teufel ['tɔyfəl] (**-s, -**) m devil; **teuflisch** ['tɔyflɪʃ] adj fiendish, diabolical

Text [tɛkst] (**-(e)s, -e**) m text; (Liedertext) words pl; **t~en** vi to write the words

textil [tɛks'tiːl] adj textile; **T~ien** pl textiles; **T~industrie** f textile industry; **T~waren** pl textiles

Textverarbeitung f word processing

Theater [te'aːtər] (**-s, -**) nt theatre; (umg) fuss; **~ spielen** (auch fig) to playact; **~besucher** m playgoer; **~kasse** f box office; **~stück** nt (stage) play

Theke ['teːkə] f (Schanktisch) bar; (Ladentisch) counter

Thema ['teːma] (**-s, Themen** od **-ta**) nt theme, topic, subject

Themse ['tɛmzə] f Thames

Theo- [teo] zW: **~loge** [-'loːgə] (**-n, -n**) m theologian; **~logie** [-lo'giː] f theology; **t~logisch** [-'loːgɪʃ] adj theological; **~retiker** [-'reːtikər] (**-s, -**) m theorist; **t~retisch** [-'reːtɪʃ] adj theoretical; **~rie** [-'riː] f theory

Thera- [tera] zW: **~peut** [-'pɔyt] (**-en, -en**) m therapist; **t~peutisch** [-'pɔytɪʃ] adj therapeutic; **~pie** [-'piː] f therapy

Therm- zW: **~albad** [tɛr'maːlbaːt] nt thermal bath; thermal spa; **~odrucker** [tɛrmo-] m thermal printer; **~ometer** [tɛrmo'meːtər] (**-s, -**) nt thermometer; **~osflasche** ['tɛrmɔsflaʃə] ® f Thermos ® flask

These ['teːzə] f thesis

Thrombose [trɔm'boːzə] f thrombosis

Thron [troːn] (**-(e)s, -e**) m throne; **t~en** vi to sit enthroned; (fig) to sit in state; **~folge** f succession (to the throne); **~folger(in)** (**-s, -**) m(f) heir to the throne

Thunfisch ['tuːnfɪʃ] m tuna

Thüringen ['tyːrɪŋən] (**-s**) nt Thuringia

Thymian ['tyːmiaːn] (**-s, -e**) m thyme

Tick [tɪk] (**-(e)s, -s**) m tic; (Eigenart) quirk;

(*Fimmel*) craze

ticken *vi* to tick

tief [tiːf] *adj* deep; (*~sinnig*) profound; (*Ausschnitt, Preis, Ton*) low; **~ greifend** far-reaching; **~ schürfend** profound; **T~** (**-s, -s**) *nt* (MET) depression; **T~druck** *m* low pressure; **T~e** *f* depth; **T~ebene** *f* plain; **T~enschärfe** *f* (PHOT) depth of focus; **T~garage** *f* underground garage; **~gekühlt** *adj* frozen; **T~kühlfach** *nt* deepfreeze compartment; **T~kühlkost** *f* (deep) frozen food; **T~kühltruhe** *f* deepfreeze, freezer; **T~punkt** *m* low point; (*fig*) low ebb; **T~schlag** *m* (BOXEN, fig) blow below the belt; **T~see** *f* deep sea; **~sinnig** *adj* profound; melancholy; **T~stand** *m* low level; **T~stwert** *m* minimum *od* lowest value

Tier [tiːr] *nt* (**-(e)s, -e**) animal; **~arzt** *m* vet(erinary surgeon); **~garten** *m* zoo(logical gardens *pl*); **~heim** *nt* cat/dog home; **t~isch** *adj* animal; (*auch fig*) brutish; (*fig: Ernst etc*) deadly; **~kreis** *m* zodiac; **~kunde** *f* zoology; **t~liebend** *adj* fond of animals; **~park** *m* zoo; **~quälerei** [-kvɛːlə'raɪ] *f* cruelty to animals; **~schutzverein** *m* society for the prevention of cruelty to animals

Tiger(in) ['tiːɡər(ɪn)] (**-s, -**) *m(f)* tiger(-gress)

tilgen ['tɪlɡən] *vt* to erase; (*Sünden*) to expiate; (*Schulden*) to pay off

Tinte ['tɪntə] *f* ink

Tintenfisch *m* cuttlefish

Tipp ▲ [tɪp] *m* tip; **t~en** *vt, vi* to tap, to touch; (*umg: schreiben*) to type; (*im Lotto etc*) to bet (on); **auf jdn t~en** (*umg: raten*) to tip sb, to put one's money on sb (*fig*)

Tipp- ['tɪp] *zW*: **~fehler** (*umg*) *m* typing error; **t~topp** (*umg*) *adj* tip-top; **~zettel** *m* (pools) coupon

Tirol [ti'roːl] *nt* the Tyrol; **~er(in)** *m(f)* Tyrolean; **t~isch** *adj* Tyrolean

Tisch [tɪʃ] (**-(e)s, -e**) *m* table; **bei ~** at table; **vor/nach ~** before/after eating; **unter den ~ fallen** (*umg*) to be dropped; **~decke** *f* tablecloth; **~ler** (**-s, -**) *m* carpenter, joiner; **~lerei** *f* joiner's workshop; (*Arbeit*)

carpentry, joinery; **t~lern** *vi* to do carpentry *etc*; **~rede** *f* after-dinner speech; **~tennis** *nt* table tennis; **~tuch** *nt* tablecloth

Titel ['tiːtəl] (**-s, -**) *m* title; **~bild** *nt* cover (picture); (*von Buch*) frontispiece; **~rolle** *f* title role; **~seite** *f* cover; (*Buchtitelseite*) title page; **~verteidiger** *m* defending champion, title holder

Toast [toːst] (**-(e)s, -s** *od* **-e**) *m* toast; **~brot** *nt* bread for toasting; **~er** (**-s, -**) *m* toaster

tob- ['toːb] *zW*: **~en** *vi* to rage; (*Kinder*) to romp about; **~süchtig** *adj* maniacal

Tochter ['tɔxtər] (**-, "**) *f* daughter; **~gesellschaft** *f* subsidiary (company)

Tod [toːt] (**-(e)s, -e**) *m* death; **t~ernst** *adj* deadly serious ♦ *adv* in dead earnest

Todes- ['toːdəs] *zW*: **~angst** [-aŋst] *f* mortal fear; **~anzeige** *f* obituary (notice); **~fall** *m* death; **~strafe** *f* death penalty; **~ursache** *f* cause of death; **~urteil** *nt* death sentence; **~verachtung** *f* utter disgust

todkrank *adj* dangerously ill

tödlich ['tøːtlɪç] *adj* deadly, fatal

tod- *zW*: **~müde** *adj* dead tired; **~schick** (*umg*) *adj* smart, classy; **~sicher** (*umg*) *adj* absolutely *od* dead certain; **T~sünde** *f* deadly sin

Toilette [toa'lɛtə] *f* toilet, lavatory; (*Frisiertisch*) dressing table

Toiletten- *zW*: **~artikel** *pl* toiletries, toilet articles; **~papier** *nt* toilet paper; **~tisch** *m* dressing table

toi, toi, toi ['tɔy'tɔy'tɔy] *excl* touch wood

tolerant [tole'rant] *adj* tolerant

Toleranz [tole'rants] *f* tolerance

tolerieren [tole'riːrən] *vt* to tolerate

toll [tɔl] *adj* mad; (*Treiben*) wild; (*umg*) terrific; **~en** *vi* to romp; **T~kirsche** *f* deadly nightshade; **~kühn** *adj* daring; **T~wut** *f* rabies

Tomate [to'maːtə] *f* tomato; **~nmark** *nt* tomato purée

Ton¹ [toːn] (**-(e)s, -e**) *m* (*Erde*) clay

Ton² [toːn] (**-(e)s, "e**) *m* (*Laut*) sound; (MUS) note; (*Redeweise*) tone; (*Farbton, Nuance*) shade; (*Betonung*) stress;

t~angebend *adj* leading; **~art** *f* (musical) key; **~band** *nt* tape; **~bandgerät** *nt* tape recorder

tönen ['tøːnən] *vi* to sound ♦ *vt* to shade; (*Haare*) to tint

tönern ['tøːnərn] *adj* clay

Ton- *zW:* **~fall** *m* intonation; **~film** *m* sound film; **~leiter** *f* (MUS) scale; **t~los** *adj* soundless

Tonne ['tɔnə] *f* barrel; (*Maß*) ton

Ton- *zW:* **~taube** *f* clay pigeon; **~waren** *pl* pottery *sg*, earthenware *sg*

Topf [tɔpf] (**-(e)s, ¨e**) *m* pot; **~blume** *f* pot plant

Töpfer ['tœpfər] (**-s, -**) *m* potter; **~ei** [-'rai] *f* piece of pottery; potter's workshop; **~scheibe** *f* potter's wheel

topografisch ▲ [topo'graːfɪʃ] *adj* topographic

Tor¹ [toːr] (**-en, -en**) *m* fool

Tor² [toːr] (**-(e)s, -e**) *nt* gate, (SPORT) goal; **~bogen** *m* archway

Torf [tɔrf] (**-(e)s**) *m* peat

Torheit *f* foolishness; foolish deed

töricht ['tøːrɪçt] *adj* foolish

torkeln ['tɔrkəln] *vi* to stagger, to reel

Torte ['tɔrtə] *f* cake; (*Obsttorte*) flan, tart

Tortur [tɔr'tuːr] *f* ordeal

Torwart (**-(e)s, -e**) *m* goalkeeper

tosen ['toːzən] *vi* to roar

tot [toːt] *adj* dead; **~ geboren** stillborn; **sich ~ stellen** to pretend to be dead

total [to'taːl] *adj* total; **~itär** [totali'tɛːr] *adj* totalitarian; **T~schaden** *m* (AUT) complete write-off

Tote(r) *f(m)* dead person

töten ['tøːtən] *vt, vi* to kill

Toten- *zW:* **~bett** *nt* death bed; **t~blass** ▲ *adj* deathly pale, white as a sheet; **~kopf** *m* skull; **~schein** *m* death certificate; **t~still** *f* deathly silence

tot- *zW:* **~fahren** (*unreg*) *vt* to run over; **~geboren** △ *adj siehe* **tot**; **~lachen** (*umg*) *vr* to laugh one's head off

Toto ['toːto] (**-s, -s**) *m od nt* pools *pl*; **~schein** *m* pools coupon

tot- *zW:* **T~schlag** *m* manslaughter;

~schlagen (*unreg*) *vt* (*auch fig*) to kill; **~schweigen** (*unreg*) *vt* to hush up; **~stellen** △ *vr siehe* **tot**

Tötung ['tøːtʊŋ] *f* killing

Toupet [tu'peː] (**-s, -s**) *nt* toupee

toupieren [tu'piːrən] *vt* to backcomb

Tour [tuːr] (**-, -en**) *f* tour, trip; (*Umdrehung*) revolution; (*Verhaltensart*) way; **in einer ~** incessantly; **~enzähler** *m* rev counter; **~ismus** [tu'rɪsmʊs] *m* tourism; **~ist** [tu'rɪst] *m* tourist; **~istenklasse** *f* tourist class; **~nee** [tʊr'neː] (**-, -n**) *f* (THEAT *etc*) tour; **auf ~nee gehen** to go on tour

Trab [traːp] (**-(e)s**) *m* trot

Trabantenstadt *f* satellite town

traben ['traːbən] *vi* to trot

Tracht [traxt] (**-, -en**) *f* (*Kleidung*) costume, dress; **eine ~ Prügel** a sound thrashing; **t~en** *vi:* **t~en (nach)** to strive (for); **jdm nach dem Leben t~en** to seek to kill sb; **danach t~en, etw zu tun** to strive *od* endeavour to do sth

trächtig ['trɛçtɪç] *adj* (*Tier*) pregnant

Tradition [traditsi'oːn] *f* tradition; **t~ell** [-'nɛl] *adj* traditional

traf *etc* [traːf] *vb siehe* **treffen**

Tragbahre *f* stretcher

tragbar *adj* (*Gerät*) portable; (*Kleidung*) wearable; (*erträglich*) bearable

träge ['trɛːgə] *adj* sluggish, slow; (PHYS) inert

tragen ['traːgən] (*unreg*) *vt* to carry; (*Kleidung, Brille*) to wear; (*Namen, Früchte*) to bear; (*erdulden*) to endure ♦ *vi* (*schwanger sein*) to be pregnant; (*Eis*) to hold; **sich mit einem Gedanken ~** to have an idea in mind; **zum T~ kommen** to have an effect

Träger ['trɛːgər] (**-s, -**) *m* carrier; wearer; bearer; (*Ordensträger*) holder; (*an Kleidung*) (shoulder) strap; (*Körperschaft etc*) sponsor

Tragetasche *f* carrier bag

Tragfläche *f* (AVIAT) wing

Tragflügelboot *nt* hydrofoil

Trägheit ['trɛːkhait] *f* laziness; (PHYS) inertia

Tragik ['traːgɪk] *f* tragedy; **tragisch** *adj* tragic

Tragödie [tra'gøːdiə] *f* tragedy

Tragweite *f* range; (*fig*) scope

Spelling Reform: ▲ *new spelling* △ *old spelling (to be phased out)*

Train- ['trɛːn] zW: **~er (-s, -)** m (SPORT) trainer, coach; (Fußball) manager; **t~ieren** [trɛ'niːrən] vt, vi to train; (Mensch) to coach; (Übung) to practise; **~ing (-s, -s)** nt training; **~ingsanzug** m track suit

Traktor ['traktɔr] m tractor; (von Drucker) tractor feed

trällern ['trɛlərn] vt, vi to trill, to sing

Tram [tram] **(-, -s)** f tram

trampeln ['trampəln] vt, vi to trample, to stamp

trampen ['trɛmpən] vi to hitch-hike

Tramper(in) [trɛmpər(ɪn)] **(-s, -)** m(f) hitch-hiker

Tran [traːn] **(-(e)s, -e)** m train oil, blubber

tranchieren [trã'ʃiːrən] vt to carve

Träne ['trɛːnə] f tear; **t~n** vi to water; **~ngas** nt teargas

trank etc [traŋk] vb siehe **trinken**

tränken ['trɛŋkən] vt (Tiere) to water

transchieren ▲ [tran'ʃiːrən] vt to carve

Trans- zW: **~formator** [transfɔr'maːtɔr] m transformer; **~istor** [tran'zistɔr] m transistor; **~itverkehr** [tran'ziːtfɛrkeːr] m transit traffic; **~itvisum** nt transit visa; **t~parent** adj transparent; **~parent (-(e)s, -e)** nt (Bild) transparency; (Spruchband) banner; **~plantation** [transplantatsi'oːn] f transplantation; (Hauttransplantation) graft(ing)

Transport [trans'pɔrt] **(-(e)s, -e)** m transport; **t~ieren** [transpɔr'tiːrən] vt to transport; **~kosten** pl transport charges, carriage sg; **~mittel** nt means sg of transportation; **~unternehmen** nt carrier

Traube ['traubə] f grape; bunch (of grapes); **~nzucker** m glucose

trauen ['trauən] vi: **jdm/etw ~** to trust sb/ sth ♦ vr to dare ♦ vt to marry

Trauer ['trauər] **(-)** f sorrow; (für Verstorbenen) mourning; **~fall** m death, bereavement; **~feier** f funeral service; **~kleidung** f mourning; **t~n** vi to mourn; **um jdn t~n** to mourn (for) sb; **~rand** m black border; **~spiel** nt tragedy

traulich ['traulɪç] adj cosy, intimate

Traum [traum] **(-(e)s, Träume)** m dream

Trauma (-s, -men) nt trauma

träum- ['trɔym] zW: **~en** vt, vi to dream; **T~er (-s, -)** m dreamer; **T~e'rei** f dreaming; **~erisch** adj dreamy

traumhaft adj dreamlike; (fig) wonderful

traurig ['trauriç] adj sad; **T~keit** f sadness

Trau- ['trau] zW: **~ring** m wedding ring; **~schein** m marriage certificate; **~ung** f wedding ceremony; **~zeuge** m witness (to a marriage); **~zeugin** f witness (to a marriage)

treffen ['trɛfən] (unreg) vt to strike, to hit; (Bemerkung) to hurt; (begegnen) to meet; (Entscheidung etc) to make; (Maßnahmen) to take ♦ vi to hit ♦ vr (Schiff etc) to meet; **er hat es gut getroffen** he did well; **~ auf** +akk to come across, to meet with; **es traf sich, dass ...** it so happened that ...; **es trifft sich gut** it's convenient; **wie es so trifft** as these things happen; **T~ (-s, -)** nt meeting; **~d** adj pertinent, apposite

Treffer (-s, -) m hit; (Tor) goal; (Los) winner

Treffpunkt m meeting place

Treib- ['traib] zW: **~eis** nt drift ice; **t~en** (unreg) vt to drive; (Studien etc) to pursue; (Sport) to do, to go in for ♦ vi (Schiff etc) to drift; (Pflanzen) to sprout; (KOCH: aufgehen) to rise; (Tee, Kaffee) to be diuretic; **~haus** nt greenhouse; **~hauseffekt** m greenhouse effect; **~hausgas** nt greenhouse gas; **~stoff** m fuel

trenn- ['trɛn] zW: **~bar** adj separable; **~en** vt to separate; (teilen) to divide ♦ vr to separate; **sich ~en von** to part with; **T~ung** f separation; **T~wand** f partition (wall)

Trepp- ['trɛp] zW: **t~ab** adv downstairs; **t~auf** adv upstairs; **~e** f stair(case); **~engeländer** nt banister; **~enhaus** nt staircase

Tresor [tre'zoːr] **(-s, -e)** m safe

Tretboot nt pedalo, pedal boat

treten ['treːtən] (unreg) vi to step; (Tränen, Schweiß) to appear ♦ vt (mit Fußtritt) to kick; (niedertreten) to tread, to trample; **~ nach** to kick at; **~ in** +akk to step in(to); **in Verbindung ~** to get in contact; **in**

Erscheinung ~ to appear
treu [trɔy] *adj* faithful, true; **T~e** (-) *f* loyalty, faithfulness; **T~händer** (-s, -) *m* trustee; **T~handanstalt** *f* trustee organization; **T~handgesellschaft** *f* trust company; **~herzig** *adj* innocent; **~los** *adj* faithless

---

Treuhandanstalt

i The **Treuhandanstalt** was the organization set up in 1990 to take over the nationally-owned companies of the former **DDR**, break them down into smaller units and privatize them. It was based in Berlin and had nine branches. Many companies were closed down by the **Treuhandanstalt** because of their outdated equipment and inability to compete with Western firms which resulted in rising unemployment. Having completed its initial task, the **Treuhandanstalt** was closed down in 1995.

Tribüne [tri'by:nə] *f* grandstand; (*Rednertribüne*) platform
Trichter ['trɪçtər] (-s, -) *m* funnel; (*in Boden*) crater
Trick [trɪk] (-s, -e *od* -s) *m* trick; **~film** *m* cartoon
Trieb [tri:p] (-(e)s, -e) *m* urge, drive; (*Neigung*) inclination; (*an Baum etc*) shoot; **t~** *etc vb siehe* **treiben**; **~kraft** *f* (*fig*) drive; **~täter** *m* sex offender; **~werk** *nt* engine
triefen ['tri:fən] *vi* to drip
triffst *etc* ['trɪfst] *vb siehe* **treffen**
triftig ['trɪftɪç] *adj* good, convincing
Trikot [tri'ko:] (-s, -s) *nt* vest; (*SPORT*) shirt
Trimester [tri'mɛstər] (-s, -) *nt* term
trimmen ['trɪmən] *vr* to do keep fit exercises
trink- ['trɪŋk] *zW*: **~bar** *adj* drinkable; **~en** (*unreg*) *vt, vi* to drink; **T~er** (-s, -) *m* drinker; **T~geld** *nt* tip; **T~halle** *f* refreshment kiosk; **T~wasser** *nt* drinking water
Tripper ['trɪpər] (-s, -) *m* gonorrhoea
Tritt [trɪt] (-(e)s, -e) *m* step; (*Fußtritt*) kick; **~brett** *nt* (*EISENB*) step; (*AUT*) running board

Triumph [tri'ʊmf] (-(e)s, -e) *m* triumph; **~bogen** *m* triumphal arch; **t~ieren** [triʊm'fi:rən] *vi* to triumph; (*jubeln*) to exult
trocken ['trɔkən] *adj* dry; **T~element** *nt* dry cell; **T~haube** *f* hair dryer; **T~heit** *f* dryness; **~legen** *vt* (*Sumpf*) to drain; (*Kind*) to put a clean nappy on; **T~milch** *f* dried milk; **T~rasur** *f* dry shave, electric shave
trocknen ['trɔknən] *vt, vi* to dry
Trödel ['trø:dəl] (-s) (*umg*) *m* junk; **~markt** *m* flea market; **t~n** (*umg*) *vi* to dawdle
Trommel ['trɔməl] (-, -n) *f* drum; **~fell** *nt* eardrum; **t~n** *vt, vi* to drum
Trompete [trɔm'pe:tə] *f* trumpet; **~r** (-s, -) *m* trumpeter
Tropen ['tro:pən] *pl* tropics; **~helm** *m* sun helmet
tröpfeln ['trœpfəln] *vi* to drop, to trickle
Tropfen ['trɔpfən] (-s, -) *m* drop; **t~** *vt, vi* to drip ♦ *vb unpers*: **es tropft** a few raindrops are falling; **t~weise** *adv* in drops
Tropfsteinhöhle *f* stalactite cave
tropisch ['tro:pɪʃ] *adj* tropical
Trost [tro:st] (-es) *m* consolation, comfort
trösten ['trø:stən] *vt* to console, to comfort
trost- *zW*: **~los** *adj* bleak; (*Verhältnisse*) wretched; **T~preis** *m* consolation prize; **~reich** *adj* comforting
Trott [trɔt] (-(o)s, -e) *m* trot, (*Routine*) routine; **~el** (-s, -) (*umg*) *m* fool, dope; **t~en** *vi* to trot
Trotz [trɔts] (-es) *m* pigheadedness; **etw aus ~ tun** to do sth just to show them; **jdm zum ~** in defiance of sb; **t~** *präp* (+*gen od dat*) in spite of; **t~dem** *adv* nevertheless, all the same ♦ *konj* although; **t~en** *vi* (+*dat*) to defy; (*der Kälte, Klima etc*) to withstand; (*der Gefahr*) to brave; (*t~ig sein*) to be awkward; **t~ig** *adj* defiant, pig-headed; **~kopf** *m* obstinate child
trüb [try:p] *adj* dull; (*Flüssigkeit, Glas*) cloudy; (*fig*) gloomy
Trubel ['tru:bəl] (-s) *m* hurly-burly
trüb- *zW*: **~en** ['try:bən] *vt* to cloud ♦ *vr* to become clouded; **T~heit** *f* dullness; cloudiness; gloom; **T~sal** (-, -e) *f* distress; **~sellg** *adj* sad, melancholy; **T~sinn** *m*

depression; **~sinnig** *adj* depressed, gloomy

Trüffel ['tryfəl] (-, **-n**) *f* truffle

trug *etc* [tru:k] *vb siehe* **tragen**

trügen ['try:gən] (*unreg*) *vt* to deceive ♦ *vi* to be deceptive

trügerisch *adj* deceptive

Trugschluss ▲ ['tru:gʃlʊs] *m* false conclusion

Truhe ['tru:ə] *f* chest

Trümmer ['trʏmər] *pl* wreckage *sg*; (*Bautrümmer*) ruins; **~haufen** *m* heap of rubble

Trumpf [trʊmpf] (**-(e)s, ⁓e**) *m* (*auch fig*) trump; **t~en** *vt, vi* to trump

Trunk [trʊŋk] (**-(e)s, ⁓e**) *m* drink; **t~en** *adj* intoxicated; **~enheit** *f* intoxication; **~enheit am Steuer** drunken driving; **~sucht** *f* alcoholism

Trupp [trʊp] (**-s, -s**) *m* troop; **~e** *f* troop; (*Waffengattung*) force; (*Schauspieltruppe*) troupe; **~en** *pl* (*MIL*) troops; **~enübungsplatz** *m* training area

Truthahn ['tru:tha:n] *m* turkey

Tschech- ['tʃɛç] *zW:* **~e** *m* Czech; **~ien** (-s) *nt* the Czech Republic; **~in** *f* Czech; **t~isch** *adj* Czech; **~oslowakei** [-oslova'kaɪ] *f:* **die ~oslowakei** Czechoslovakia; **t~oslowakisch** [-oslo'va:kɪʃ] *adj* Czechoslovak(ian)

tschüs(s) [tʃʏs] *excl* cheerio

T-Shirt ['ti:ʃɜ:t] *nt* T-shirt

Tube ['tu:bə] *f* tube

Tuberkulose [tuberku'lo:zə] *f* tuberculosis

Tuch [tu:x] (**-(e)s, ⁓er**) *nt* cloth; (*Halstuch*) scarf; (*Kopftuch*) headscarf; (*Handtuch*) towel

tüchtig ['tʏçtɪç] *adj* efficient, (cap)able; (*umg: kräftig*) good, sound; **T~keit** *f* efficiency, ability

Tücke ['tʏkə] *f* (*Arglist*) malice; (*Trick*) trick; (*Schwierigkeit*) difficulty, problem

tückisch ['tʏkɪʃ] *adj* treacherous; (*böswillig*) malicious

Tugend ['tu:gənt] (-, **-en**) *f* virtue; **t~haft** *adj* virtuous

Tülle *f* spout

Tulpe ['tʊlpə] *f* tulip

Tumor ['tu:mɔr] (**-s, -e**) *m* tumour

Tümpel ['tʏmpəl] (**-s, -**) *m* pool, pond

Tumult [tu'mʊlt] (**-(e)s, -e**) *m* tumult

tun [tu:n] (*unreg*) *vt* (*machen*) to do; (*legen*) to put ♦ *vi* to act ♦ *vr:* **es tut sich etwas/ viel** something/a lot is happening; **jdm etw ~** (*antun*) to do sth to sb; **etw tut es auch** sth will do; **das tut nichts** that doesn't matter; **das tut nichts zur Sache** that's neither here nor there; **so ~ als ob** to act as if

tünchen ['tʏnçən] *vt* to whitewash

Tunfisch ▲ ['tu:nfɪʃ] *m* = **Thunfisch**

Tunke ['tʊŋkə] *f* sauce; **t~n** *vt* to dip, to dunk

tunlichst ['tu:nlɪçst] *adv* if at all possible; **~ bald** as soon as possible

Tunnel ['tʊnəl] (**-s, -s** *od* **-**) *m* tunnel

Tupfen ['tʊpfən] (**-s, -**) *m* dot, spot; **t~** *vt, vi* to dab; (*mit Farbe*) to dot

Tür [ty:r] (-, **-en**) *f* door

Turbine [tʊr'bi:nə] *f* turbine

Türk- [tʏrk] *zW:* **~e** *m* Turk; **~ei** [tʏr'kaɪ] *f:* **die ~ei** Turkey; **~in** *f* Turk

Türkis [tʏr'ki:s] (**-es, -e**) *m* turquoise; **t~** *adj* turquoise

türkisch ['tʏrkɪʃ] *adj* Turkish

Türklinke *f* doorknob, door handle

Turm [tʊrm] (**-(e)s, ⁓e**) *m* tower; (*Kirchturm*) steeple; (*Sprungturm*) diving platform; (*SCHACH*) castle, rook

türmen ['tʏrmən] *vr* to tower up ♦ *vt* to heap up ♦ *vi* (*umg*) to scarper, to bolt

Turn- [tʊrn] *zW:* **t~en** *vi* to do gymnastic exercises ♦ *vt* to perform; **~en** (**-s**) *nt* gymnastics; (*SCH*) physical education, P.E.; **~er(in)** (**-s, -**) *m(f)* gymnast; **~halle** *f* gym(nasium); **~hose** *f* gym shorts *pl*

Turnier [tʊr'ni:r] (**-s, -e**) *nt* tournament

Turn- *zW:* **~schuh** *m* gym shoe; **~verein** *m* gymnastics club; **~zeug** *nt* gym things *pl*

Tusche ['tʊʃə] *f* Indian ink

tuscheln ['tʊʃəln] *vt, vi* to whisper

Tuschkasten *m* paintbox

Tüte ['ty:tə] *f* bag

tuten ['tu:tən] *vi* (*AUT*) to hoot (*BRIT*), to honk (*US*)

TÜV [tyf] **(-s, -s)** *m abk* (= *Technischer Überwachungs-Verein*) ≈ MOT

Typ [ty:p] **(-s, -en)** *m* type; **~e** *f* (*TYP*) type

Typhus ['ty:fʊs] **(-)** *m* typhoid (fever)

typisch ['ty:pɪʃ] *adj*: **~ (für)** typical (of)

Tyrann [ty'ran] **(-en, -en)** *m* tyrant; **~ei** [-'naɪ] *f* tyranny; **t~isch** *adj* tyrannical; **t~i'sieren** *vt* to tyrannize

U, u

u. a. *abk* = **unter anderem**

U-Bahn ['u:ba:n] *f* underground, tube

übel ['y:bəl] *adj* bad; (*moralisch*) bad, wicked; **jdm ist ~** sb feels sick; **~ gelaunt** bad-tempered; **jdm eine Bemerkung** *etc* **~ nehmen** to be offended at sb's remark *etc*; **Ü~ (-s, -)** *nt* evil; (*Krankheit*) disease; **Ü~keit** *f* nausea

üben ['y:bən] *vt, vi* to exercise, to practise

SCHLÜSSELWORT

über ['y:bər] *präp +dat* **1** (*räumlich*) over, above; **zwei Grad über null** two degrees above zero

2 (*zeitlich*) over; **über der Arbeit einschlafen** to fall asleep over one's work ♦ *präp +akk* **1** (*räumlich*) over; (*hoch über auch*) above; (*quer über auch*) across

2 (*zeitlich*) over; **über Weihnachten** over Christmas; **über kurz oder lang** sooner or later

3 (*mit Zahlen*): **Kinder über 12 Jahren** children over *od* above 12 years of age; **ein Scheck über 200 Mark** a cheque for 200 marks

4 (*auf dem Wege*) via; **nach Köln über Aachen** to Cologne via Aachen; **ich habe es über die Auskunft erfahren** I found out from information

5 (*betreffend*) about; **ein Buch über ...** a book about *od* on ...; **über jdn/etw lachen** to laugh about *od* at sb/sth

6: **Macht über jdn haben** to have power over sb; **sie liebt ihn über alles** she loves him more than everything

♦ *adv* over; **über und über** over and over; **den ganzen Tag über** all day long; **jdm in etw** *dat* **über sein** to be superior to sb in sth

---

überall [y:bər'|al] *adv* everywhere; **~'hin** *adv* everywhere

überanstrengen [y:bər'|anʃtrɛŋən] *vt insep* to overexert ♦ *vr insep* to overexert o.s.

überarbeiten [y:bər'|arbaɪtən] *vt insep* to revise, to rework ♦ *vr insep* to overwork (o.s.)

überaus ['y:bər|aʊs] *adv* exceedingly

überbelichten ['y:bərbəlɪçtən] *vt* (*PHOT*) to overexpose

über'bieten (*unreg*) *vt insep* to outbid; (*übertreffen*) to surpass; (*Rekord*) to break

Überbleibsel ['y:bərblaɪpsəl] **(-s, -)** *nt* residue, remainder

Überblick ['y:bərblɪk] *m* view; (*fig: Darstellung*) survey, overview; (*Fähigkeit*): **~ (über +akk)** grasp (of), overall view (of); **ü~en** [-'blɪkən] *vt insep* to survey

überbring- [y:bər'brɪŋ] *zW*: **~en** (*unreg*) *vt insep* to deliver, to hand over; **Ü~er (-s, -)** *m* bearer

überbrücken [y:bər'brʏkən] *vt insep* to bridge (over)

überbuchen ['y:bərbu:xən] *vt insep* to overbook

über'dauern *vt insep* to outlast

über'denken (*unreg*) *vt insep* to think over

überdies [y:bər'di:s] *adv* besides

überdimensional ['y:bərdimenziona:l] *adj* oversize

Überdruss ▲ ['y:bərdrʊs] **(-es)** *m* weariness; **bis zum ~** ad nauseam

überdurchschnittlich ['y:bərdʊrçʃnɪtlɪç] *adj* above-average ♦ *adv* exceptionally

übereifrig ['y:bər|aɪfrɪç] *adj* over-keen

übereilt [y:bər'|aɪlt] *adj* (over)hasty, premature

überein- [y:bər'|aɪn] *zW*: **~ander** [y:bər|aɪ'nandər] *adv* one upon the other; (*sprechen*) about each other; **~kommen** (*unreg*) *vi* to agree; **Ü~kunft (-, -künfte)** *f* agreement; **~stimmen** *vi* to agree;

Ü~stimmung f agreement

überempfindlich ['y:bər|ɛmpfɪntlɪç] *adj* hypersensitive

überfahren [y:bər'fa:rən] (*unreg*) *vt insep* (AUT) to run over; (*fig*) to walk all over

Überfahrt ['y:bərfa:rt] f crossing

Überfall ['y:bərfal] *m* (*Banküberfall*, MIL) raid; (*auf jdn*) assault; **ü~en** [-'falən] (*unreg*) *vt insep* to attack; (*Bank*) to raid; (*besuchen*) to drop in on, to descend on

überfällig ['y:bərfɛlɪç] *adj* overdue

über'fliegen (*unreg*) *vt insep* to fly over, to overfly; (*Buch*) to skim through

Überfluss ▲ ['y:bərflʊs] *m*: ~ **an** (+*dat*) (super)abundance (of), excess (of)

überflüssig ['y:bərflʏsɪç] *adj* superfluous

über'fordern *vt insep* to demand too much of; (*Kräfte etc*) to overtax

über'führen *vt insep* (*Leiche etc*) to transport; (*Täter*) to have convicted

Über'führung f transport; conviction; (*Brücke*) bridge, overpass

über'füllt *adj* (*Schulen, Straßen*) overcrowded; (*Kurs*) oversubscribed

Übergabe ['y:bərga:bə] f handing over; (MIL) surrender

Übergang ['y:bərgaŋ] *m* crossing; (*Wandel, Überleitung*) transition

Übergangs- *zW*: **~lösung** f provisional solution, stopgap; **~zeit** f transitional period

über'geben (*unreg*) *vt insep* to hand over; (MIL) to surrender ♦ *vr insep* to be sick

übergehen ['y:bərge:ən] (*unreg*) *vi* (*Besitz*) to pass; (*zum Feind etc*) to go over, to defect; ~ **in** +*akk* to turn into; **über'gehen** (*unreg*) *vt insep* to pass over, to omit

Übergewicht ['y:bərgəvɪçt] *nt* excess weight; (*fig*) preponderance

überglücklich ['y:bərglʏklɪç] *adj* overjoyed

Übergröße ['y:bərgrø:sə] f oversize

überhaupt [y:bər'haupt] *adv* at all; (*im Allgemeinen*) in general; (*besonders*) especially; ~ **nicht/keine** not/none at all

überheblich [y:bər'he:plɪç] *adj* arrogant; **Ü~keit** f arrogance

über'holen *vt insep* to overtake; (TECH) to overhaul

über'holt *adj* out-of-date, obsolete

Überholverbot [y:bər'ho:lfɛrbo:t] *nt* restriction on overtaking

über'hören *vt insep* not to hear; (*absichtlich*) to ignore

überirdisch ['y:bər|ɪrdɪʃ] *adj* supernatural, unearthly

über'laden (*unreg*) *vt insep* to overload ♦ *adj* (*fig*) cluttered

über'lassen (*unreg*) *vt insep*: **jdm etw** ~ to leave sth to sb ♦ *vr insep*: **sich einer Sache** *dat* ~ to give o.s. over to sth

über'lasten *vt insep* to overload; (*Mensch*) to overtax

überlaufen ['y:bərlaufən] (*unreg*) *vi* (*Flüssigkeit*) to flow over; (*zum Feind etc*) to go over, to defect; ~ **sein** to be inundated *od* besieged; **über'laufen** (*unreg*) *vt insep* (*Schauer etc*) to come over

über'leben *vt insep* to survive; **Über'lebende(r)** *f(m)* survivor

über'legen *vt insep* to consider ♦ *adj* superior; **ich muss es mir** ~ I'll have to think about it; **Über'legenheit** f superiority

Über'legung f consideration, deliberation

über'liefern *vt insep* to hand down, to transmit

Überlieferung f tradition

überlisten [y:bər'lɪstən] *vt insep* to outwit

überm ['y:bərm] = **über dem**

Übermacht ['y:bərmaxt] f superior force, superiority; **übermächtig** ['y:bərmɛçtɪç] *adj* superior (in strength); (*Gefühl etc*) overwhelming

übermäßig ['y:bərmɛ:sɪç] *adj* excessive

Übermensch ['y:bərmɛnʃ] *m* superman; **ü~lich** *adj* superhuman

übermitteln [y:bər'mɪtəln] *vt insep* to convey

übermorgen ['y:bərmɔrgən] *adv* the day after tomorrow

Übermüdung [y:bər'my:dʊŋ] f fatigue, overtiredness

Übermut ['y:bərmu:t] *m* exuberance

übermütig ['y:bərmy:tɪç] *adj* exuberant,

high-spirited; **~ werden** to get overconfident

übernächste(r, s) ['y:bərnɛːçstə(r, s)] *adj* (*Jahr*) next but one

übernacht- [y:bər'naxt] *zW*: **~en** *vi insep*: **(bei jdm) ~en** to spend the night (at sb's place); **Ü~ung** *f* overnight stay; **Ü~ung mit Frühstück** bed and breakfast; **Ü~ungsmöglichkeit** *f* overnight accommodation *no pl*

Übernahme ['y:bərnaːmə] *f* taking over *od* on, acceptance

über'nehmen (*unreg*) *vt insep* to take on, to accept; (*Amt, Geschäft*) to take over ♦ *vr insep* to take on too much

über'prüfen *vt insep* to examine, to check

überqueren [y:bər'kveːrən] *vt insep* to cross

überragen [y:bər'raːgən] *vt insep* to tower above; (*fig*) to surpass

überraschen [y:bər'raʃən] *vt insep* to surprise

Überraschung *f* surprise

überreden [y:bər'reːdən] *vt insep* to persuade

überreichen [y:bər'raiçən] *vt insep* to present, to hand over

'Überrest *m* remains, remnants

überrumpeln [y:bər'rompəln] *vt insep* to take by surprise

überrunden [y:bər'rondən] *vt insep* to lap

übers ['y:bərs] = **über das**

Überschall- ['y:bərʃal] *zW*: **~flugzeug** *nt* supersonic jet; **~geschwindigkeit** *f* supersonic speed

über'schätzen *vt insep* to overestimate

'überschäumen *vi* (*Bier*) to foam over, bubble over; (*Temperament*) to boil over

Überschlag ['y:bərʃlaːk] *m* (*FIN*) estimate; (*SPORT*) somersault; **ü~en** [-'ʃlaːgən] (*unreg*) *vt insep* (*berechnen*) to estimate; (*auslassen: Seite*) to omit ♦ *vr insep* to somersault; (*Stimme*) to crack; (*AVIAT*) to loop the loop; **'überschlagen** (*unreg*) *vt* (*Beine*) to cross ♦ *vi* (*Wellen*) to break; (*Funken*) to flash

überschnappen ['y:bərʃnapən] *vi* (*Stimme*) to crack; (*umg: Mensch*) to flip one's lid

über'schneiden (*unreg*) *vr insep* (*auch fig*) to overlap; (*Linien*) to intersect

über'schreiben (*unreg*) *vt insep* to provide with a heading; **jdm etw ~** to transfer *od* make over sth to sb

über'schreiten (*unreg*) *vt insep* to cross over; (*fig*) to exceed; (*verletzen*) to transgress

Überschrift ['y:bərʃrift] *f* heading, title

Überschuss ▲ ['y:bərʃʊs] *m*: **~ (an** +*dat*) surplus (of); **überschüssig** ['y:bərʃysiç] *adj* surplus, excess

über'schütten *vt insep*: **jdn/etw mit etw ~** to pour sth over sb/sth; **jdn mit etw ~** (*fig*) to shower sb with sth

überschwänglich ▲ ['y:bərʃvɛŋliç] *adj* effusive

überschwemmen [y:bər'ʃvɛmən] *vt insep* to flood

Überschwemmung *f* flood

Übersee ['y:bərzeː] *f*: **nach/in ~** overseas; **ü~isch** *adj* overseas

über'sehen (*unreg*) *vt insep* to look (out) over; (*fig: Folgen*) to see, to get an overall view of; (: *nicht beachten*) to overlook

über'senden (*unreg*) *vt insep* to send, to forward

übersetz- *zW*: **~en** [y:bər'zɛtsən] *vt insep* to translate; **'übersetzen** *vi* to cross; **Ü~er(in)** [-'zɛtsər(in)] (**-s, -**) *m(f)* translator; **Ü~ung** [-'zɛtsʊŋ] *f* translation; (*TECH*) gear ratio

Übersicht ['y:bərzɪçt] *f* overall view; (*Darstellung*) survey; **ü~lich** *adj* clear; (*Gelände*) open; **~lichkeit** *f* clarity, lucidity

übersiedeln ['y:bərziːdəln] *vi sep* to move; **über'siedeln** *vi* to move

über'spannt *adj* eccentric; (*Idee*) wild, crazy

überspitzt [y:bər'ʃpitst] *adj* exaggerated

über'springen (*unreg*) *vt insep* to jump over; (*fig*) to skip

überstehen [y:bər'ʃteːən] (*unreg*) *vt insep* to overcome, to get over; (*Winter etc*) to survive, to get through; **'überstehen** (*unreg*) *vi* to project

über'steigen (*unreg*) *vt insep* to climb over; (*fig*) to exceed

Spelling Reform: ▲ *new spelling* △ *old spelling (to be phased out)*

über'stimmen *vt insep* to outvote
Überstunden ['y:bərʃtʊndən] *pl* overtime *sg*
über'stürzen *vt insep* to rush ♦ *vr insep* to follow (one another) in rapid succession
überstürzt *adj* (over)hasty
Übertrag ['y:bərtra:k] (-(e)s, -träge) *m* (*COMM*) amount brought forward; **ü~bar** [-'tra:kba:r] *adj* transferable; (*MED*) infectious; **ü~en** [-'tra:gən] (*unreg*) *vt insep* to transfer; (*RADIO*) to broadcast; (*übersetzen*) to render; (*Krankheit*) to transmit ♦ *vr insep* to spread ♦ *adj* figurative; **ü~en auf** +*akk* to transfer to; **jdm etw ü~en** to assign sth to sb; **sich ü~en auf** +*akk* to spread to; **~ung** [-'tra:gʊŋ] *f* transfer(ence); (*RADIO*) broadcast; rendering; transmission
über'treffen (*unreg*) *vt insep* to surpass
über'treiben (*unreg*) *vt insep* to exaggerate; **Übertreibung** *f* exaggeration
übertreten [y:bər'tre:tən] (*unreg*) *vt insep* to cross; (*Gebot etc*) to break; **'übertreten** (*unreg*) *vi* (*über Linie, Gebiet*) to step (over); (*SPORT*) to overstep; (*zu anderem Glauben*) to be converted; **'übertreten (in** +*akk*) (*POL*) to go over (to)
Über'tretung *f* violation, transgression
übertrieben [y:bər'tri:bən] *adj* exaggerated, excessive
übervölkert [y:bər'fœlkərt] *adj* overpopulated
übervoll ['y:bərfɔl] *adj* overfull
übervorteilen [y:bər'fɔrtaɪlən] *vt insep* to dupe, to cheat
über'wachen *vt insep* to supervise; (*Verdächtigen*) to keep under surveillance; **Überwachung** *f* supervision; surveillance
überwältigen [y:bər'vɛltɪgən] *vt insep* to overpower; **~d** *adj* overwhelming
überweisen [y:bər'vaɪzən] (*unreg*) *vt insep* to transfer
Überweisung *f* transfer; **~sauftrag** *m* (credit) transfer order
über'wiegen (*unreg*) *vi insep* to predominate; **~d** *adj* predominant
über'winden (*unreg*) *vt insep* to overcome ♦ *vr insep* to make an effort, to bring o.s. (to do sth)

Überwindung *f* effort, strength of mind
Überzahl ['y:bərtsa:l] *f* superiority, superior numbers *pl*; **in der ~ sein** to be numerically superior
überzählig ['y:bərtsɛ:lɪç] *adj* surplus
über'zeugen *vt insep* to convince; **~d** *adj* convincing
Überzeugung *f* conviction
überziehen ['y:bərtsi:ən] (*unreg*) *vt* to put on; **über'ziehen** (*unreg*) *vt insep* to cover; (*Konto*) to overdraw
Überziehungskredit *m* overdraft provision
Überzug ['y:bərtsu:k] *m* cover; (*Belag*) coating
üblich ['y:plɪç] *adj* usual
U-Boot ['u:bo:t] *nt* submarine
übrig ['y:brɪç] *adj* remaining; **für jdn etwas ~ haben** (*umg*) to be fond of sb; **die Ü~en** the others; **das Ü~e** the rest; **im Ü~en** besides; **~ bleiben** to remain, to be left (over); **~ lassen** to leave (over); **~ens** ['y:brɪgəns] *adv* besides; (*nebenbei bemerkt*) by the way
Übung ['y:bʊŋ] *f* practice; (*Turnübung, Aufgabe etc*) exercise; **~ macht den Meister** practice makes perfect
Ufer ['u:fər] (-s, -) *nt* bank; (*Meeresufer*) shore
Uhr [u:r] (-, -en) *f* clock; (*Armbanduhr*) watch; **wie viel ~ ist es?** what time is it?; **1 ~** 1 o'clock; **20 ~** 8 o'clock, 20.00 (twenty hundred) hours; **~(arm)band** *nt* watch strap; **~band** *nt* watch strap; **~macher** (-s, -) *m* watchmaker; **~werk** *nt* clockwork; works of a watch; **~zeiger** *m* hand; **~zeigersinn** *m*: **im ~zeigersinn** clockwise; **entgegen dem ~zeigersinn** anticlockwise; **~zeit** *f* time (of day)
Uhu ['u:hu] (-s, -s) *m* eagle owl
UKW [u:ka:'ve:] *abk* (= *Ultrakurzwelle*) VHF
ulkig ['ʊlkɪç] *adj* funny
Ulme ['ʊlmə] *f* elm
Ultimatum [ʊlti'ma:tʊm] (-s, **Ultimaten**) *nt* ultimatum
Ultra- ['ʊltra] *zW*: **~schall** *m* (*PHYS*) ultrasound; **u~violett** *adj* ultraviolet

---

um [ʊm] *präp +akk* **1** (*um herum*) (a)round;
um Weihnachten around Christmas; **er
schlug um sich** he hit about him
2 (*mit Zeitangabe*) at; **um acht (Uhr)** at
eight (o'clock)
3 (*mit Größenangabe*) by; **etw um 4 cm
kürzen** to shorten sth by 4 cm; **um 10%
teurer** 10% more expensive; **um vieles
besser** better by far; **um nichts besser**
not in the least bit better
4: der Kampf um den Titel the battle for
the title; **um Geld spielen** to play for
money; **Stunde um Stunde** hour after
hour; **Auge um Auge** an eye for an eye
♦ *präp +gen*: **um ... willen** for the sake of
...; **um Gottes willen** for goodness' *od*
(*stärker*) God's sake
♦ *konj*: **um ... zu** (in order) to ...; **zu klug,
um zu ...** too clever to ...; *siehe* **umso**
♦ *adv* **1** (*ungefähr*) about; **um (die) 30
Leute** about *od* around 30 people
2 (*vorbei*): **die 2 Stunden sind um** the two
hours are up

---

umändern ['ʊmlɛndərn] *vt* to alter
Umänderung *f* alteration
umarbeiten ['ʊmlarbaɪtən] *vt* to remodel;
(*Buch etc*) to revise, to rework
umarmen [ʊmlarmən] *vt insep* to embrace
Umbau ['ʊmbaʊ] **(-(e)s, -e** *od* **-ten)** *m*
reconstruction, alteration(s); **u~en** *vt* to
rebuild, to reconstruct
umbilden ['ʊmbɪldən] *vt* to reorganize; (*POL:
Kabinett*) to reshuffle
umbinden ['ʊmbɪndən] (*unreg*) *vt* (*Krawatte
etc*) to put on
umblättern ['ʊmblɛtərn] *vt* to turn over
umblicken ['ʊmblɪkən] *vr* to look around
umbringen ['ʊmbrɪŋən] (*unreg*) *vt* to kill
umbuchen ['ʊmbuːxən] *vi* to change one's
reservation/flight *etc* ♦ *vt* to change
umdenken ['ʊmdɛŋkən] (*unreg*) *vi* to adjust
one's views
umdrehen ['ʊmdreːən] *vt* to turn (round);
(*Hals*) to wring ♦ *vr* to turn (round)

Um'drehung *f* revolution; rotation
umeinander [ʊmlaɪˈnandər] *adv* round one
another; (*füreinander*) for one another
umfahren ['ʊmfaːrən] (*unreg*) *vt* to run over;
um'fahren (*unreg*) *vt insep* to drive round;
to sail round
umfallen ['ʊmfalən] (*unreg*) *vi* to fall down
od over
Umfang ['ʊmfaŋ] *m* extent; (*von Buch*) size;
(*Reichweite*) range; (*Fläche*) area; (*MATH*)
circumference; **u~reich** *adj* extensive;
(*Buch etc*) voluminous
um'fassen *vt insep* to embrace; (*umgeben*)
to surround; (*enthalten*) to include;
um'fassend *adj* comprehensive, extensive
umformen ['ʊmfɔrmən] *vt* to transform
Umfrage ['ʊmfraːgə] *f* poll
umfüllen ['ʊmfylən] *vt* to transfer; (*Wein*) to
decant
umfunktionieren ['ʊmfʊŋktsioniːrən] *vt* to
convert, to transform
Umgang ['ʊmgaŋ] *m* company; (*mit jdm*)
dealings *pl*; (*Behandlung*) way of behaving
umgänglich ['ʊmgɛŋlɪç] *adj* sociable
Umgangs- *zW*: **~formen** *pl* manners;
~sprache *f* colloquial language
umgeben [ʊmˈgeːbən] (*unreg*) *vt insep* to
surround
Umgebung *f* surroundings *pl*; (*Milieu*)
environment; (*Personen*) people in one's
circle
umgehen ['ʊmgeːən] (*unreg*) *vi* to go
(a)round; **im Schlosse ~** to haunt the
castle; **mit jdm grob etc ~** to treat sb
roughly *etc*; **mit Geld sparsam ~** to be
careful with one's money; **um'gehen** *vt
insep* to bypass; (*MIL*) to outflank; (*Gesetz
etc*) to circumvent; (*vermeiden*) to avoid;
'umgehend *adj* immediate
Um'gehung *f* bypassing; outflanking;
circumvention; avoidance; **~sstraße** *f*
bypass
umgekehrt ['ʊmgəkeːrt] *adj* reverse(d);
(*gegenteilig*) opposite ♦ *adv* the other way
around; **und ~** and vice versa
umgraben ['ʊmgraːbən] (*unreg*) *vt* to dig up
Umhang ['ʊmhaŋ] *m* wrap, cape

Spelling Reform: ▲ *new spelling* △ *old spelling (to be phased out)*

umhauen ['ʊmhaʊən] *vt* to fell; (*fig*) to bowl over

umher [ʊm'he:r] *adv* about, around; **~gehen** (*unreg*) *vi* to walk about; **~ziehen** (*unreg*) *vi* to wander from place to place

umhinkönnen [ʊm'hɪnkœnən] (*unreg*) *vi*: **ich kann nicht umhin, das zu tun** I can't help doing it

umhören ['ʊmhø:rən] *vr* to ask around

Umkehr ['ʊmke:r] (-) *f* turning back; (*Änderung*) change; **u~en** *vi* to turn back ♦ *vt* to turn round, to reverse; (*Tasche etc*) to turn inside out; (*Gefäß etc*) to turn upside down

umkippen ['ʊmkɪpən] *vt* to tip over ♦ *vi* to overturn; (*umg: Mensch*) to keel over; (*fig: Meinung ändern*) to change one's mind

Umkleide- ['ʊmklaɪdə] *zW*: **~kabine** *f* (*im Schwimmbad*) (changing) cubicle; **~raum** *m* changing *od* dressing room

umkommen ['ʊmkɔmən] (*unreg*) *vi* to die, to perish; (*Lebensmittel*) to go bad

Umkreis ['ʊmkraɪs] *m* neighbourhood; **im ~ von** within a radius of

Umlage ['ʊmla:gə] *f* share of the costs

Umlauf ['ʊmlaʊf] *m* (*Geldumlauf*) circulation; (*von Gestirn*) revolution; **~bahn** *f* orbit

Umlaut ['ʊmlaʊt] *m* umlaut

umlegen ['ʊmle:gən] *vt* to put on; (*verlegen*) to move, to shift; (*Kosten*) to share out; (*umkippen*) to tip over; (*umg: töten*) to bump off

umleiten ['ʊmlaɪtən] *vt* to divert

Umleitung *f* diversion

umliegend ['ʊmli:gənt] *adj* surrounding

um'randen *vt insep* to border, to edge

umrechnen ['ʊmrɛçnən] *vt* to convert

Umrechnung *f* conversion; **~skurs** *m* rate of exchange

um'reißen (*unreg*) *vt insep* to outline, to sketch

Umriss ▲ ['ʊmrɪs] *m* outline

umrühren ['ʊmry:rən] *vt, vi* to stir

ums [ʊms] = **um das**

Umsatz ['ʊmzats] *m* turnover; **~steuer** *f* sales tax

umschalten ['ʊmʃaltən] *vt* to switch

umschauen *vr* to look round

Umschlag ['ʊmʃla:k] *m* cover; (*Buchumschlag auch*) jacket; (*MED*) compress; (*Briefumschlag*) envelope; (*Wechsel*) change; (*von Hose*) turn-up; **u~en** [-gən] (*unreg*) *vi* to change; (*NAUT*) to capsize ♦ *vt* to knock over; (*Ärmel*) to turn up; (*Seite*) to turn over; (*Waren*) to transfer; **~platz** *m* (*COMM*) distribution centre

umschreiben ['ʊmʃraɪbən] (*unreg*) *vt* (*neu schreiben*) to rewrite; (*übertragen*) to transfer; **~ auf** +*akk* to transfer to; **um'schreiben** (*unreg*) *vt insep* to paraphrase; (*abgrenzen*) to define

umschulen ['ʊmʃu:lən] *vt* to retrain; (*Kind*) to send to another school

Umschweife ['ʊmʃvaɪfə] *pl*: **ohne ~** without beating about the bush, straight out

Umschwung ['ʊmʃvʊŋ] *m* change (around), revolution

umsehen ['ʊmze:ən] (*unreg*) *vr* to look around *od* about; (*suchen*): **sich ~ (nach)** to look out (for)

umseitig ['ʊmzaɪtɪç] *adv* overleaf

umsichtig ['ʊmzɪçtɪç] *adj* cautious, prudent

umso ▲ ['ʊmzo] *konj*: **~ besser / schlimmer** so much the better/worse

umsonst [ʊm'zɔnst] *adv* in vain; (*gratis*) for nothing

umspringen ['ʊmʃprɪŋən] (*unreg*) *vi* to change; (*Wind auch*) to veer; **mit jdm ~** to treat sb badly

Umstand ['ʊmʃtant] *m* circumstance; **Umstände** *pl* (*fig: Schwierigkeiten*) fuss; **in anderen Umständen sein** to be pregnant; **Umstände machen** to go to a lot of trouble; **unter Umständen** possibly

umständlich ['ʊmʃtɛntlɪç] *adj* (*Methode*) cumbersome, complicated; (*Ausdrucksweise, Erklärung*) long-winded; (*Mensch*) ponderous

Umstandskleid *nt* maternity dress

Umstehende(n) ['ʊmʃte:əndə(n)] *pl* bystanders

umsteigen ['ʊmʃtaɪgən] (*unreg*) *vi* (*EISENB*) to change

umstellen ['ʊmʃtɛlən] *vt* (*an anderen Ort*) to

change round, to rearrange; (*TECH*) to convert ♦ *vr* to adapt (o.s.); **sich auf etw** *akk* ~ to adapt to sth; **um'stellen** *vt insep* to surround

Umstellung ['ʊmʃtɛlʊŋ] *f* change; (*Umgewöhnung*) adjustment; (*TECH*) conversion

umstimmen ['ʊmʃtɪmən] *vt* (*MUS*) to retune; **jdn** ~ to make sb change his mind

umstoßen ['ʊmʃtoːsən] (*unreg*) *vt* to overturn; (*Plan etc*) to change, to upset

umstritten [ʊm'ʃtrɪtən] *adj* disputed

Umsturz ['ʊmʃtʊrts] *m* overthrow

umstürzen ['ʊmʃtʏrtsən] *vt* (*umwerfen*) to overturn ♦ *vi* to collapse, to fall down; (*Wagen*) to overturn

Umtausch ['ʊmtaʊʃ] *m* exchange; **u~en** *vt* to exchange

Umverpackung ['ʊmfɛrpakʊŋ] *f* packaging

umwandeln ['ʊmvandəln] *vt* to change, to convert; (*ELEK*) to transform

umwechseln ['ʊmvɛksəln] *vt* to change

Umweg ['ʊmveːk] *m* detour, roundabout way

Umwelt ['ʊmvɛlt] *f* environment; **u~freundlich** *adj* not harmful to the environment, environment-friendly; **u~schädlich** *adj* ecologically harmful; **~schutz** *m* environmental protection; **~schützer** *m* environmentalist; **~verschmutzung** *f* environmental pollution

umwenden ['ʊmvɛndən] (*unreg*) *vt, vr* to turn (round)

umwerfen ['ʊmvɛrfən] (*unreg*) *vt* to upset, to overturn; (*fig: erschüttern*) to upset, to throw; **~d** (*umg*) *adj* fantastic

umziehen ['ʊmtsiːən] (*unreg*) *vt, vr* to change ♦ *vi* to move

Umzug ['ʊmtsuːk] *m* procession; (*Wohnungsumzug*) move, removal

unab- ['ʊn|ap] *zW:* **~änderlich** *adj* irreversible, unalterable; **~hängig** *adj* independent; **U~hängigkeit** *f* independence; **~kömmlich** *adj* indispensable; **zur Zeit ~kömmlich** not free at the moment; **~lässig** *adj* incessant,

constant; **~sehbar** *adj* immeasurable; (*Folgen*) unforeseeable; (*Kosten*) incalculable; **~sichtlich** *adj* unintentional; **~'wendbar** *adj* inevitable

unachtsam ['ʊn|axtzaːm] *adj* careless; **U~keit** *f* carelessness

unan- ['ʊn|an] *zW:* **~'fechtbar** *adj* indisputable; **~gebracht** *adj* uncalled-for; **~gemessen** *adj* inadequate; **~genehm** *adj* unpleasant; **U~nehmlichkeit** *f* inconvenience; **U~nehmlichkeiten** *pl* (*Ärger*) trouble *sg*; **~sehnlich** *adj* unsightly; **~ständig** *adj* indecent, improper

unappetitlich ['ʊn|apetiːtlɪç] *adj* unsavoury

Unart ['ʊn|aːrt] *f* bad manners *pl*; (*Angewohnheit*) bad habit; **u~ig** *adj* naughty, badly behaved

unauf- ['ʊn|aʊf] *zW:* **~fällig** *adj* unobtrusive; (*Kleidung*) inconspicuous; **~findbar** *adj* not to be found; **~gefordert** *adj* unasked ♦ *adv* spontaneously; **~haltsam** *adj* irresistible; **~'hörlich** *adj* incessant, continuous; **~merksam** *adj* inattentive; **~richtig** *adj* insincere

unaus- ['ʊn|aʊs] *zW:* **~geglichen** *adj* unbalanced; **~'sprechlich** *adj* inexpressible; **~'stehlich** *adj* intolerable

unbarmherzig ['ʊnbarmhɛrtsɪç] *adj* pitiless, merciless

unbeabsichtigt ['ʊnbə|apzɪçtɪçt] *adj* unintentional

unbeachtet ['ʊnbə|axtət] *adj* unnoticed, ignored

unbedenklich ['ʊnbədɛŋklɪç] *adj* (*Plan*) unobjectionable

unbedeutend ['ʊnbədɔʏtənt] *adj* insignificant, unimportant; (*Fehler*) slight

unbedingt ['ʊnbədɪŋt] *adj* unconditional ♦ *adv* absolutely; **musst du ~ gehen?** do you really have to go?

unbefangen ['ʊnbəfaŋən] *adj* impartial, unprejudiced; (*ohne Hemmungen*) uninhibited; **U~heit** *f* impartiality; uninhibitedness

unbefriedigend ['ʊnbəfriːdɪɡənd] *adj* unsatisfactory

unbefriedigt ['ʊnbəfriːdɪçt] *adj* unsatisfied,

dissatisfied

unbefugt ['ʊnbəfuːkt] *adj* unauthorized

unbegreiflich [ʊnbə'graiflɪç] *adj* inconceivable

unbegrenzt ['ʊnbəgrɛntst] *adj* unlimited

unbegründet ['ʊnbəgrʏndət] *adj* unfounded

Unbehagen ['ʊnbəhaːgən] *nt* discomfort; **unbehaglich** ['ʊnbəhaːklɪç] *adj* uncomfortable; (*Gefühl*) uneasy

unbeholfen ['ʊnbəhɔlfən] *adj* awkward, clumsy

unbekannt ['ʊnbəkant] *adj* unknown

unbekümmert ['ʊnbəkʏmərt] *adj* unconcerned

unbeliebt ['ʊnbəliːpt] *adj* unpopular

unbequem ['ʊnbəkveːm] *adj* (*Stuhl*) uncomfortable; (*Mensch*) bothersome; (*Regelung*) inconvenient

unberechenbar [ʊnbə'rɛçənbaːr] *adj* incalculable; (*Mensch, Verhalten*) unpredictable

unberechtigt ['ʊnbərɛçtɪçt] *adj* unjustified; (*nicht erlaubt*) unauthorized

unberührt ['ʊnbərʏrt] *adj* untouched, intact; **sie ist noch ~** she is still a virgin

unbescheiden ['ʊnbəʃaidən] *adj* presumptuous

unbeschreiblich [ʊnbə'ʃraiplɪç] *adj* indescribable

unbeständig ['ʊnbəʃtɛndɪç] *adj* (*Mensch*) inconstant; (*Wetter*) unsettled; (*Lage*) unstable

unbestechlich [ʊnbə'ʃtɛçlɪç] *adj* incorruptible

unbestimmt ['ʊnbəʃtɪmt] *adj* indefinite; (*Zukunft auch*) uncertain

unbeteiligt [ʊnbə'tailɪçt] *adj* unconcerned, indifferent

unbeweglich ['ʊnbəveːklɪç] *adj* immovable

unbewohnt ['ʊnbəvoːnt] *adj* uninhabited; (*Wohnung*) unoccupied

unbewusst ▲ ['ʊnbəvʊst] *adj* unconscious

unbezahlt ['ʊnbətsaːlt] *adj* (*Rechnung*) outstanding, unsettled; (*Urlaub*) unpaid

unbrauchbar ['ʊnbrauxbaːr] *adj* (*Arbeit*) useless; (*Gerät auch*) unusable

und [ʊnt] *konj* and; **~ so weiter** and so on

Undank ['ʊndaŋk] *m* ingratitude; **u~bar** *adj* ungrateful

undefinierbar [ʊndefi'niːrbaːr] *adj* indefinable

undenkbar [ʊn'dɛŋkbaːr] *adj* inconceivable

undeutlich ['ʊndɔʏtlɪç] *adj* indistinct

undicht ['ʊndɪçt] *adj* leaky

Unding ['ʊndɪŋ] *nt* absurdity

undurch- ['ʊndʊrç] *zW*: **~führbar** [-'fyːrbaːr] *adj* impracticable; **~lässig** [-'lɛsɪç] *adj* waterproof, impermeable; **~sichtig** [-'zɪçtɪç] *adj* opaque; (*fig*) obscure

uneben ['ʊnʔeːbən] *adj* uneven

unecht ['ʊnʔɛçt] *adj* (*Schmuck*) fake; (*vorgetäuscht: Freundlichkeit*) false

unehelich ['ʊnʔeːəlɪç] *adj* illegitimate

uneinig ['ʊnʔainɪç] *adj* divided; **~ sein** to disagree; **U~keit** *f* discord, dissension

uneins ['ʊnʔains] *adj* at variance, at odds

unempfindlich ['ʊnʔɛmpfɪntlɪç] *adj* insensitive; (*Stoff*) practical

unendlich [ʊnʔ'ɛntlɪç] *adj* infinite

unent- ['ʊnʔɛnt] *zW*: **~behrlich** [-'beːrlɪç] *adj* indispensable; **~geltlich** [-gɛltlɪç] *adj* free (of charge); **~schieden** [-'ʃiːdən] *adj* undecided; **~schieden enden** (*SPORT*) to end in a draw; **~schlossen** [-'ʃlɔsən] *adj* undecided; irresolute; **~wegt** [-'veːkt] *adj* unswerving; (*unaufhörlich*) incessant

uner- ['ʊnʔɛr] *zW*: **~bittlich** [-'bɪtlɪç] *adj* unyielding, inexorable; **~fahren** [-faːrən] *adj* inexperienced; **~freulich** [-frɔʏlɪç] *adj* unpleasant; **~gründlich** *adj* unfathomable; **~hört** [-høːrt] *adj* unheard-of; (*Bitte*) outrageous; **~lässlich** ▲ [-'lɛslɪç] *adj* indispensable; **~laubt** *adj* unauthorized; **~messlich** ▲ *adj* immeasurable, immense; **~reichbar** *adj* (*Ziel*) unattainable; (*Ort*) inaccessible; (*telefonisch*) unobtainable; **~schöpflich** [-'ʃœpflɪç] *adj* inexhaustible; **~schwinglich** [-'ʃvɪŋlɪç] *adj* (*Preis*) exorbitant; too expensive; **~träglich** [-'trɛːklɪç] *adj* unbearable; (*Frechheit*) insufferable; **~wartet** *adj* unexpected; **~wünscht** *adj* undesirable, unwelcome

unfähig ['ʊnfɛːɪç] *adj* incapable, incompetent; **zu etw ~ sein** to be incapable of sth; **U~keit** *f* incapacity; incompetence

unfair ['ʊnfɛːr] *adj* unfair

Unfall ['ʊnfal] *m* accident; **~flucht** *f* hit-and-run (driving); **~schaden** *m* damages *pl*; **~station** *f* emergency ward; **~stelle** *f* scene of the accident; **~versicherung** *f* accident insurance

unfassbar ▲ [ʊn'fasbaːr] *adj* inconceivable

unfehlbar [ʊn'feːlbaːr] *adj* infallible ♦ *adv* inevitably; **U~keit** *f* infallibility

unförmig ['ʊnfœrmɪç] *adj* (*formlos*) shapeless

unfrei ['ʊnfraɪ] *adj* not free, unfree, (*Paket*) unfranked; **~willig** *adj* involuntary, against one's will

unfreundlich ['ʊnfrɔʏntlɪç] *adj* unfriendly; **U~keit** *f* unfriendliness

Unfriede(n) ['ʊnfriːdə(n)] *m* dissension, strife

unfruchtbar ['ʊnfrʊxtbaːr] *adj* infertile; (*Gespräche*) unfruitful; **U~keit** *f* infertility; unfruitfulness

Unfug ['ʊnfuːk] (**-s**) *m* (*Benehmen*) mischief; (*Unsinn*) nonsense; **grober ~** (*JUR*) gross misconduct; malicious damage

Ungar(in) ['ʊngar(ɪn)] *m(f)* Hungarian; **u~isch** *adj* Hungarian; **~n** *nt* Hungary

ungeachtet ['ʊngəʔaxtət] *präp +gen* notwithstanding

ungeahnt ['ʊngəʔaːnt] *adj* unsuspected, undreamt-of

ungebeten ['ʊngəbeːtən] *adj* uninvited

ungebildet ['ʊngəbɪldət] *adj* uneducated; uncultured

ungedeckt ['ʊngədɛkt] *adj* (*Scheck*) uncovered

Ungeduld ['ʊngədʊlt] *f* impatience; **u~ig** [-dɪç] *adj* impatient

ungeeignet ['ʊngəʔaɪgnət] *adj* unsuitable

ungefähr ['ʊngəfɛːr] *adj* rough, approximate; **das kommt nicht von ~** that's hardly surprising

ungefährlich ['ʊngəfɛːrlɪç] *adj* not dangerous, harmless

ungehalten ['ʊngəhaltən] *adj* indignant

ungeheuer ['ʊngəhɔʏər] *adj* huge ♦ *adv* (*umg*) enormously; **U~** (**-s, -**) *nt* monster;

~lich [-'hɔʏərlɪç] *adj* monstrous

ungehörig ['ʊngəhøːrɪç] *adj* impertinent, improper

ungehorsam ['ʊngəhoːrzaːm] *adj* disobedient; **U~** *m* disobedience

ungeklärt ['ʊngəklɛːrt] *adj* not cleared up; (*Rätsel*) unsolved

ungeladen ['ʊngəlaːdən] *adj* not loaded; (*Gast*) uninvited

ungelegen ['ʊngəleːgən] *adj* inconvenient

ungelernt ['ʊngəlɛrnt] *adj* unskilled

ungelogen ['ʊngəloːgən] *adv* really, honestly

ungemein ['ʊngəmaɪn] *adj* uncommon

ungemütlich ['ʊngəmyːtlɪç] *adj* uncomfortable; (*Person*) disagreeable

ungenau ['ʊngənaʊ] *adj* inaccurate; **U~igkeit** *f* inaccuracy

ungenießbar ['ʊngəniːsbaːr] *adj* inedible; undrinkable; (*umg*) unbearable

ungenügend ['ʊngənyːgənt] *adj* insufficient, inadequate

ungepflegt ['ʊngəpfleːkt] *adj* (*Garten etc*) untended; (*Person*) unkempt; (*Hände*) neglected

ungerade ['ʊngəraːdə] *adj* uneven, odd

ungerecht ['ʊngərɛçt] *adj* unjust; **~fertigt** *adj* unjustified; **U~igkeit** *f* injustice, unfairness

ungern ['ʊngɛrn] *adv* unwillingly, reluctantly

ungeschehen ['ʊngəʃeːən] *adj*: **~ machen** to undo

Ungeschicklichkeit ['ʊngəʃɪklɪçkaɪt] *f* clumsiness

ungeschickt *adj* awkward, clumsy

ungeschminkt ['ʊngəʃmɪŋkt] *adj* without make-up; (*fig*) unvarnished

ungesetzlich ['ʊngəzɛtslɪç] *adj* illegal

ungestört ['ʊngəʃtøːrt] *adj* undisturbed

ungestraft ['ʊngəʃtraːft] *adv* with impunity

ungestüm ['ʊngəʃtyːm] *adj* impetuous; tempestuous

ungesund ['ʊngəzʊnt] *adj* unhealthy

ungetrübt ['ʊngətryːpt] *adj* clear; (*fig*) untroubled; (*Freude*) unalloyed

Ungetüm ['ʊngətyːm] (**-(e)s, -e**) *nt* monster

ungewiss ▲ ['ʊngəvɪs] *adj* uncertain;

U~heit *f* uncertainty

ungewöhnlich ['ʊngəvøːnlɪç] *adj* unusual

ungewohnt ['ʊngəvoːnt] *adj* unaccustomed

Ungeziefer ['ʊngətsiːfər] **(-s)** *nt* vermin

ungezogen ['ʊngətsoːgən] *adj* rude, impertinent; U~heit *f* rudeness, impertinence

ungezwungen ['ʊngətsvʊŋən] *adj* natural, unconstrained

unglaublich [ʊn'glaʊplɪç] *adj* incredible

ungleich ['ʊnglaɪç] *adj* dissimilar; unequal
♦ *adv* incomparably; ~artig *adj* different; U~heit *f* dissimilarity; inequality; ~mäßig *adj* irregular, uneven

Unglück ['ʊnglʏk] **(-(e)s, -e)** *nt* misfortune; (*Pech*) bad luck; (~*sfall*) calamity, disaster; (*Verkehrsunglück*) accident; u~lich *adj* unhappy; (*erfolglos*) unlucky; (*unerfreulich*) unfortunate; u~licherweise [-'vaɪzə] *adv* unfortunately; ~sfall *m* accident, calamity

ungültig ['ʊngʏltɪç] *adj* invalid; U~keit *f* invalidity

ungünstig ['ʊngʏnstɪç] *adj* unfavourable

ungut ['ʊnguːt] *adj* (*Gefühl*) uneasy; **nichts für ~** no offence

unhaltbar [ʊn'haltbaːr] *adj* untenable

Unheil ['ʊnhaɪl] *nt* evil; (*Unglück*) misfortune; ~ **anrichten** to cause mischief; u~bar *adj* incurable

unheimlich ['ʊnhaɪmlɪç] *adj* weird, uncanny
♦ *adv* (*umg*) tremendously

unhöflich ['ʊnhøːflɪç] *adj* impolite; U~keit *f* impoliteness

unhygienisch ['ʊnhygieːnɪʃ] *adj* unhygienic

Uni ['ʊni] **(-, -s)** (*umg*) *f* university

Uniform [uni'fɔrm] *f* uniform; u~iert [-'miːrt] *adj* uniformed

uninteressant ['ʊnǀɪnteresant] *adj* uninteresting

Uni- *zW:* ~versität [univerzi'tɛːt] *f* university; ~versum [uni'verzʊm] **(-s)** *nt* universe

unkenntlich ['ʊnkɛntlɪç] *adj* unrecognizable

Unkenntnis ['ʊnkɛntnɪs] *f* ignorance

unklar ['ʊnklaːr] *adj* unclear; **im U~en sein über** +*akk* to be in the dark about; U~heit *f* unclarity; (*Unentschiedenheit*) uncertainty

unklug ['ʊnkluːk] *adj* unwise

Unkosten ['ʊnkɔstən] *pl* expense(s); ~beitrag *m* contribution to costs *od* expenses

Unkraut ['ʊnkraʊt] *nt* weed; weeds *pl*

unkündbar ['ʊnkʏntbaːr] *adj* (*Stelle*) permanent; (*Vertrag*) binding

unlauter ['ʊnlaʊtər] *adj* unfair

unleserlich ['ʊnleːzərlɪç] *adj* illegible

unlogisch ['ʊnloːgɪʃ] *adj* illogical

unlösbar [ʊn'løːsbar] *adj* insoluble

Unlust ['ʊnlʊst] *f* lack of enthusiasm

Unmenge ['ʊnmɛŋə] *f* tremendous number, hundreds *pl*

Unmensch ['ʊnmɛnʃ] *m* ogre, brute; u~lich *adj* inhuman, brutal; (*ungeheuer*) awful

unmerklich [ʊn'mɛrklɪç] *adj* imperceptible

unmissverständlich ▲ ['ʊnmɪsferʃtɛntlɪç] *adj* unmistakable

unmittelbar ['ʊnmɪtəlbaːr] *adj* immediate

unmodern ['ʊnmodɛrn] *adj* old-fashioned

unmöglich ['ʊnmøːklɪç] *adj* impossible; U~keit *f* impossibility

unmoralisch ['ʊnmoraːlɪʃ] *adj* immoral

Unmut ['ʊnmuːt] *m* ill humour

unnachgiebig ['ʊnnaːxgiːbɪç] *adj* unyielding

unnahbar [ʊn'naːbaːr] *adj* unapproachable

unnötig ['ʊnnøːtɪç] *adj* unnecessary

unnütz ['ʊnnʏts] *adj* useless

unordentlich ['ʊnǀɔrdəntlɪç] *adj* untidy

Unordnung ['ʊnǀɔrdnʊŋ] *f* disorder

unparteiisch ['ʊnpartaɪʃ] *adj* impartial; U~e(r) *f(m)* umpire; (*FUSSBALL*) referee

unpassend ['ʊnpasənt] *adj* inappropriate; (*Zeit*) inopportune

unpässlich ▲ ['ʊnpɛslɪç] *adj* unwell

unpersönlich ['ʊnperzøːnlɪç] *adj* impersonal

unpolitisch ['ʊnpoliːtɪʃ] *adj* apolitical

unpraktisch ['ʊnpraktɪʃ] *adj* unpractical

unpünktlich ['ʊnpʏŋktlɪç] *adj* unpunctual

unrationell ['ʊnratsionel] *adj* inefficient

unrealistisch ['ʊnrealɪstɪʃ] *adj* unrealistic

unrecht ['ʊnrɛçt] *adj* wrong; U~ *nt* wrong; **zu U~** wrongly; **U~ haben** to be wrong; ~mäßig *adj* unlawful, illegal

unregelmäßig ['ʊnreːgəlmɛːsɪç] *adj* irregular; U~keit *f* irregularity

unreif ['ʊnraɪf] *adj* (*Obst*) unripe; (*fig*) immature

unrentabel ['ʊnrɛnta:bəl] *adj* unprofitable

unrichtig ['ʊnrɪçtɪç] *adj* incorrect, wrong

Unruhe ['ʊnru:ə] *f* unrest; **~stifter** *m* troublemaker

unruhig ['ʊnru:ɪç] *adj* restless

uns [ʊns] *pron* (*akk, dat von* **wir**) us; ourselves

unsachlich ['ʊnzaxlɪç] *adj* not to the point, irrelevant

unsagbar [ʊn'za:kba:r] *adj* indescribable

unsanft ['ʊnzanft] *adj* rough

unsauber ['ʊnzaʊbər] *adj* unclean, dirty; (*fig*) crooked; (*MUS*) fuzzy

unschädlich ['ʊnʃɛ:tlɪç] *adj* harmless; **jdn/ etw ~ machen** to render sb/sth harmless

unscharf ['ʊnʃarf] *adj* indistinct; (*Bild etc*) out of focus, blurred

unscheinbar ['ʊnʃaɪnba:r] *adj* insignificant; (*Aussehen, Haus etc*) unprepossessing

unschlagbar [ʊn'ʃla:kba:r] *adj* invincible

unschön ['ʊnʃøːn] *adj* (*hässlich: Anblick*) ugly, unattractive; (*unfreundlich: Benehmen*) unpleasant, ugly

Unschuld ['ʊnʃʊlt] *f* innocence; **u~ig** [-dɪç] *adj* innocent

unselbst(st)ändig ['ʊnzɛlpʃtɛndɪç] *adj* dependent, over-reliant on others

unser(e) ['ʊnzər(ə)] *adj* our; **~e(r, s)** *pron* ours; **~einer** *pron* people like us; **~eins** *pron* = **unsereiner**; **~erseits** *adv* on our part; **~twegen** *adv* (*für uns*) for our sake; (*wegen uns*) on our account; **~twillen** *adv*: **um ~twillen = unsertwegen**

unsicher ['ʊnzɪçər] *adj* uncertain; (*Mensch*) insecure; **U~heit** *f* uncertainty; insecurity

unsichtbar ['ʊnzɪçtba:r] *adj* invisible

Unsinn ['ʊnzɪn] *m* nonsense; **u~ig** *adj* nonsensical

Unsitte ['ʊnzɪtə] *f* deplorable habit

unsozial ['ʊnzotsia:l] *adj* (*Verhalten*) antisocial

unsportlich ['ʊnʃpɔrtlɪç] *adj* not sporty; unfit; (*Verhalten*) unsporting

unsre ['ʊnzrə] = **unsere**

unsterblich ['ʊnʃtɛrplɪç] *adj* immortal

Unstimmigkeit ['ʊnʃtɪmɪçkaɪt] *f* inconsistency; (*Streit*) disagreement

unsympathisch ['ʊnzʏmpa:tɪʃ] *adj* unpleasant; **er ist mir ~** I don't like him

untätig ['ʊntɛ:tɪç] *adj* idle

untauglich ['ʊntaʊklɪç] *adj* unsuitable; (*MIL*) unfit

unteilbar [ʊn'taɪlba:r] *adj* indivisible

unten ['ʊntən] *adv* below; (*im Haus*) downstairs; (*an der Treppe etc*) at the bottom; **nach ~** down; **~ am Berg** *etc* at the bottom of the mountain *etc*; **ich bin bei ihm ~ durch** (*umg*) he's through with me

---

SCHLÜSSELWORT

unter ['ʊntər] *präp +dat* 1 (*räumlich, mit Zahlen*) under; (*drunter*) underneath, below; **unter 18 Jahren** under 18 years
2 (*zwischen*) among(st); **sie waren unter sich** they were by themselves; **einer unter ihnen** one of them; **unter anderem** among other things
♦ *präp +akk* under, below

Unterarm ['ʊntərarm] *m* forearm

unter- *zW*: **~belichten** *vt* (*PHOT*) to underexpose; **U~bewusstsein** ▲ *nt* subconscious; **~bezahlt** *adj* underpaid

unterbieten [ʊntər'bi:tən] (*unreg*) *vt insep* (*COMM*) to undercut; (*Rekord*) to lower

unterbrechen [ʊntər'brɛçən] (*unreg*) *vt insep* to interrupt

Unterbrechung *f* interruption

unterbringen ['ʊntərbrɪŋən] (*unreg*) *vt* (*in Koffer*) to stow; (*in Zeitung*) to place; (*Person: in Hotel etc*) to accommodate, to put up

unterdessen [ʊntər'dɛsən] *adv* meanwhile

Unterdruck ['ʊntərdrʊk] *m* low pressure

unterdrücken [ʊntər'drʏkən] *vt insep* to suppress; (*Leute*) to oppress

untere(r, s) ['ʊntərə(r, s)] *adj* lower

untereinander [ʊntəraɪ'nandər] *adv* with each other; among themselves *etc*

unterentwickelt ['ʊntərɛntvɪkəlt] *adj* underdeveloped

unterernährt ['ʊntərˌɛrnɛːrt] *adj* undernourished, underfed

Unterernährung *f* malnutrition

Unter'führung *f* subway, underpass

Untergang ['ʊntərgaŋ] *m* (down)fall, decline; (*NAUT*) sinking; (*von Gestirn*) setting

unter'gehen *vi* subordinate

untergehen ['ʊntərgeːən] (*unreg*) *vi* to go down; (*Sonne auch*) to set; (*Staat*) to fall; (*Volk*) to perish; (*Welt*) to come to an end; (*im Lärm*) to be drowned

Untergeschoss ▲ ['ʊntərgəʃɔs] *nt* basement

'Untergewicht *nt* underweight

unter'gliedern *vt insep* to subdivide

Untergrund ['ʊntərgrʊnt] *m* foundation; (*POL*) underground; ~**bahn** *f* underground, tube, subway (*US*)

unterhalb ['ʊntərhalp] *präp +gen* below ♦ *adv* below; ~ **von** below

Unterhalt ['ʊntərhalt] *m* maintenance; **u~en** (*unreg*) *vt insep* to maintain; (*belustigen*) to entertain ♦ *vr insep* to talk; (*sich belustigen*) to enjoy o.s.; **u~sam** *adj* (*Abend, Person*) entertaining, amusing; ~**ung** *f* maintenance; (*Belustigung*) entertainment, amusement; (*Gespräch*) talk

Unterhändler ['ʊntərhɛntlər] *m* negotiator

Unter- *zW*: ~**hemd** *nt* vest, undershirt (*US*); ~**hose** *f* underpants *pl*; ~**kiefer** *m* lower jaw

unterkommen ['ʊntərkɔmən] (*unreg*) *vi* to find shelter; to find work; **das ist mir noch nie untergekommen** I've never met with that

unterkühlt [ʊntər'kyːlt] *adj* (*Körper*) affected by hypothermia

Unterkunft ['ʊntərkʊnft] (-, -**künfte**) *f* accommodation

Unterlage ['ʊntərlaːgə] *f* foundation; (*Beleg*) document; (*Schreibunterlage etc*) pad

unter'lassen (*unreg*) *vt insep* (*versäumen*) to fail to do; (*sich enthalten*) to refrain from

unterlaufen [ʊntər'laʊfən] (*unreg*) *vi insep* to happen ♦ *adj*: **mit Blut ~** suffused with blood; (*Augen*) bloodshot

unterlegen ['ʊntərleːgən] *vt* to lay *od* put

under; **unter'legen** *adj* inferior; (*besiegt*) defeated

Unterleib ['ʊntərlaɪp] *m* abdomen

unter'liegen (*unreg*) *vi insep* (+*dat*) to be defeated *od* overcome (by); (*unterworfen sein*) to be subject (to)

Untermiete ['ʊntərmiːtə] *f*: **zur ~ wohnen** to be a subtenant *od* lodger; ~**r(in)** *m(f)* subtenant, lodger

unter'nehmen (*unreg*) *vt insep* to undertake; **Unter'nehmen** (-**s**, -) *nt* undertaking, enterprise (*auch COMM*)

Unternehmer [ʊntər'neːmər] (-**s**, -) *m* entrepreneur, businessman

'unterordnen ['ʊntərɔrdnən] *vr* +*dat* to submit o.s. (to), to give o.s. second place to

Unterredung [ʊntər'reːdʊŋ] *f* discussion, talk

Unterricht ['ʊntərrɪçt] (-(**e**)**s**, -**e**) *m* instruction, lessons *pl*; **u~en** [ʊntər'rɪçtən] *vt insep* to instruct; (*SCH*) to teach ♦ *vr insep*: **sich u~en** (**über** +*akk*) to inform o.s. (about), to obtain information (about); ~**sfach** *nt* subject (on school *etc* curriculum)

Unterrock ['ʊntərrɔk] *m* petticoat, slip

unter'sagen *vt insep* to forbid; **jdm etw ~** to forbid sb to do sth

Untersatz ['ʊntərzats] *m* coaster, saucer

unter'schätzen *vt insep* to underestimate

unter'scheiden (*unreg*) *vt insep* to distinguish ♦ *vr insep* to differ

Unter'scheidung *f* (*Unterschied*) distinction; (*Unterscheiden*) differentiation

Unterschied ['ʊntərʃiːt] (-(**e**)**s**, -**e**) *m* difference, distinction; **im ~ zu** as distinct from; **u~lich** *adj* varying, differing; (*diskriminierend*) discriminatory

unterschiedslos *adv* indiscriminately

unter'schlagen (*unreg*) *vt insep* to embezzle; (*verheimlichen*) to suppress

Unter'schlagung *f* embezzlement

Unterschlupf ['ʊntərʃlʊpf] (-(**e**)**s**, -**schlüpfe**) *m* refuge

unter'schreiben (*unreg*) *vt insep* to sign

Unterschrift ['ʊntərʃrɪft] *f* signature

Unterseeboot ['ʊntərzeːboːt] *nt* submarine
Untersetzer ['ʊntərzɛtsər] *m* tablemat; *(für Gläser)* coaster
untersetzt [ʊntərˈzɛtst] *adj* stocky
unterste(r, s) ['ʊntərstə(r, s)] *adj* lowest, bottom
unterstehen [ʊntərˈʃteːən] *(unreg) vi insep (+dat)* to be under ♦ *vr insep* to dare; **'unterstehen** *(unreg) vi* to shelter
unterstellen [ʊntərˈʃtɛlən] *vt insep* to subordinate; *(fig)* to impute ♦ *vt (Auto)* to garage, to park ♦ *vr* to take shelter
unter'streichen *(unreg) vt insep (auch fig)* to underline
Unterstufe ['ʊntərʃtuːfə] *f* lower grade
unter'stützen *vt insep* to support
Unter'stützung *f* support, assistance
unter'suchen *vt insep (MED)* to examine; *(Polizei)* to investigate
Unter'suchung *f* examination; investigation, inquiry; **~ausschuss** ▲ *m* committee of inquiry; **~shaft** *f* imprisonment on remand
Untertasse ['ʊntərtasə] *f* saucer
untertauchen ['ʊntərtaʊxən] *vi* to dive; *(fig)* to disappear, to go underground
Unterteil ['ʊntərtaɪl] *nt od m* lower part, bottom, **u~en** [ʊntərˈtaɪlən] *vt insep* to divide up
Untertitel ['ʊntərtiːtəl] *m* subtitle
Unterwäsche ['ʊntərvɛʃə] *f* underwear
unterwegs [ʊntərˈveːks] *adv* on the way
unter'werfen *(unreg) vt insep* to subject; *(Volk)* to subjugate ♦ *vr insep (+dat)* to submit (to)
unter'zeichnen *vt insep* to sign
unter'ziehen *(unreg) vt insep* to subject ♦ *vr insep (+dat)* to undergo; *(einer Prüfung)* to take
untragbar [ʊnˈtraːkbaːr] *adj* unbearable, intolerable
untreu ['ʊntrɔy] *adj* unfaithful; **U~e** *f* unfaithfulness
untröstlich [ʊnˈtrøːstlɪç] *adj* inconsolable
unüberlegt ['ʊnlyːbərleːkt] *adj* ill-considered ♦ *adv* without thinking
unübersichtlich *adj (Gelände)* broken;

(Kurve) blind
unumgänglich [ʊn|ʊmˈgɛŋlɪç] *adj* indispensable, vital; absolutely necessary
ununterbrochen ['ʊn|ʊntərbrɔxən] *adj* uninterrupted
unver- ['ʊnfɛr] *zW:* **~änderlich** [-'ɛndərlɪç] *adj* unchangeable; **~antwortlich** [-'antvɔrtlɪç] *adj* irresponsible; *(unentschuldbar)* inexcusable; **~besserlich** *adj* incorrigible; **~bindlich** *adj* not binding; *(Antwort)* curt ♦ *adv (COMM)* without obligation; **~bleit** *adj (Benzin usw)* unleaded; **ich fahre ~bleit** I use unleaded; **~blümt** [-'blyːmt] *adj* plain, blunt ♦ *adv* plainly, bluntly; **~daulich** *adj* indigestible; **~einbar** *adj* incompatible; **~fänglich** [-'fɛŋlɪç] *adj* harmless; **~froren** *adj* impudent; **~gesslich** ▲ *adj (Tag, Erlebnis)* unforgettable; **~hofft** [-'hɔft] *adj* unexpected; **~meidlich** [-'maɪtlɪç] *adj* unavoidable; **~mutet** *adj* unexpected; **~nünftig** [-'nʏnftɪç] *adj* foolish; **~schämt** *adj* impudent; **U~schämtheit** *f* impudence, insolence; **~sehrt** *adj* uninjured; **~söhnlich** [-'zøːnlɪç] *adj* irreconcilable; **~ständlich** [-'ʃtɛntlɪç] *adj* unintelligible; **~träglich** *adj* quarrelsome; *(Meinungen, MED)* incompatible; **~zeihlich** *adj* unpardonable; **~züglich** [-'tsyːklɪç] *adj* immediate
unvollkommen ['ʊnfɔlkɔmən] *adj* imperfect
unvollständig *adj* incomplete
unvor- ['ʊnfoːr] *zW:* **~bereitet** *adj* unprepared; **~eingenommen** *adj* unbiased; **~hergesehen** [-heːrgezeːən] *adj* unforeseen; **~sichtig** [-zɪçtɪç] *adj* careless, imprudent; **~stellbar** [-'ʃtɛlbaːr] *adj* inconceivable; **~teilhaft** *adj* disadvantageous
unwahr ['ʊnvaːr] *adj* untrue; **~scheinlich** *adj* improbable, unlikely ♦ *adv (umg)* incredibly
unweigerlich [ʊnˈvaɪgərlɪç] *adj* unquestioning ♦ *adv* without fail
Unwesen ['ʊnveːzən] *nt* nuisance; *(Unfug)* mischief; **sein ~ treiben** to wreak havoc
unwesentlich *adj* inessential, unimportant; **~ besser** marginally better

Spelling Reform: ▲ *new spelling* △ *old spelling (to be phased out)*

Unwetter ['ʊnvɛtər] *nt* thunderstorm
unwichtig ['ʊnvɪçtɪç] *adj* unimportant
unwider- ['ʊnvi:dər] *zW:* **~legbar** *adj* irrefutable; **~ruflich** *adj* irrevocable; **~stehlich** *adj* irresistible
unwill- ['ʊnvɪl] *zW:* **U~e(n)** *m* indignation; **~ig** *adj* indignant; (*widerwillig*) reluctant; **~kürlich** [-kyːrlɪç] *adj* involuntary ♦ *adv* instinctively; (*lachen*) involuntarily
unwirklich ['ʊnvɪrklɪç] *adj* unreal
unwirksam ['ʊnvɪrkza:m] *adj* (*Mittel, Methode*) ineffective
unwirtschaftlich ['ʊnvɪrtʃaftlɪç] *adj* uneconomical
unwissen- ['ʊnvɪsən] *zW:* **~d** *adj* ignorant; **U~heit** *f* ignorance; **~tlich** *adv* unknowingly, unwittingly
unwohl ['ʊnvoːl] *adj* unwell, ill; **U~sein (-s)** *nt* indisposition
unwürdig ['ʊnvʏrdɪç] *adj* unworthy
unzählig [ʊn'tsɛːlɪç] *adj* innumerable, countless
unzer- [ʊntsɛr] *zW:* **~brechlich** *adj* unbreakable; **~störbar** *adj* indestructible; **~trennlich** *adj* inseparable
Unzucht ['ʊntsʊxt] *f* sexual offence
unzüchtig ['ʊntsʏçtɪç] *adj* immoral; lewd
unzu- ['ʊntsu] *zW:* **~frieden** *adj* dissatisfied; **U~friedenheit** *f* discontent; **~länglich** *adj* inadequate; **~lässig** *adj* inadmissible; **~rechnungsfähig** *adj* irresponsible; **~treffend** *adj* incorrect; **~verlässig** *adj* unreliable
unzweideutig ['ʊntsvaɪdɔytɪç] *adj* unambiguous
üppig ['ʏpɪç] *adj* (*Frau*) curvaceous; (*Busen*) full, ample; (*Essen*) sumptuous; (*Vegetation*) luxuriant, lush
Ur- ['uːr] *in zW* original
uralt ['uːr|alt] *adj* ancient, very old
Uran [u'raːn] (-s) *nt* uranium
Ur- *zW:* **~aufführung** *f* first performance; **~einwohner** *m* original inhabitant; **~eltern** *pl* ancestors; **~enkel(in)** *m(f)* great-grandchild, great-grandson (-daughter); **~großeltern** *pl* great-grandparents; **~heber (-s, -)** *m* originator;

(*Autor*) author; **~heberrecht** *nt* copyright
Urin [u'riːn] (-s, -e) *m* urine
Urkunde ['uːrkʊndə] *f* document, deed
Urlaub ['uːrlaʊp] **(-(e)s, -e)** *m* holiday(s *pl*) (*BRIT*), vacation (*US*); (*MIL etc*) leave; **~er** [-'laʊbər] **(-s, -)** *m* holiday-maker (*BRIT*), vacationer (*US*); **~sort** *m* holiday resort; **~szeit** *f* holiday season
Urne ['ʊrnə] *f* urn
Ursache ['uːrzaxə] *f* cause; **keine ~** that's all right
Ursprung ['uːrʃprʊŋ] *m* origin, source; (*von Fluss*) source
ursprünglich ['uːrʃprʏŋlɪç] *adj* original ♦ *adv* originally
Ursprungsland *nt* country of origin
Urteil ['ʊrtaɪl] **(-s, -e)** *nt* opinion; (*JUR*) sentence, judgement; **u~en** *vi* to judge; **~sspruch** *m* sentence, verdict
Urwald *m* jungle
Urzeit *f* prehistoric times *pl*
USA [uː'ɛs'|aː] *pl abk* (= *Vereinigte Staaten von Amerika*) USA
usw. *abk* (= *und so weiter*) etc
Utensilien [uten'ziːliən] *pl* utensils
Utopie [uto'piː] *f* pipe dream
utopisch [u'toːpɪʃ] *adj* utopian

V, v

vag(e) [vaːk, 'vaːgə] *adj* vague
Vagina [va'giːna] (-, Vaginen) *f* vagina
Vakuum ['vaːkuʊm] **(-s, Vakua od Vakuen)** *nt* vacuum
Vampir [vam'piːr] **(-s, -e)** *m* vampire
Vanille [va'nɪljə] (-) *f* vanilla
Variation [variatsi'oːn] *f* variation
variieren [vari'iːrən] *vt, vi* to vary
Vase ['vaːzə] *f* vase
Vater ['faːtər] **(-s, ⁿ)** *m* father; **~land** *nt* native country; Fatherland
väterlich ['fɛːtərlɪç] *adj* fatherly
Vaterschaft *f* paternity
Vaterunser (-s, -) *nt* Lord's prayer
Vati ['faːti] *m* daddy
v. Chr. *abk* (= *vor Christus*) B.C.

Vegetarier(in) [vege'taːriər(ɪn)] **(-s, -)** *m(f)*
vegetarian

vegetarisch [vege'taːrɪʃ] *adj* vegetarian

Veilchen ['faɪlçən] *nt* violet

Vene ['veːnə] *f* vein

Ventil [vɛn'tiːl] **(-s, -e)** *nt* valve

Ventilator [vɛntiˈlaːtɔr] *m* ventilator

verab- [fɛr'ʔap] *zW:* **~reden** *vt* to agree, to
arrange ♦ *vr:* **sich mit jdm ~reden** to
arrange to meet sb; **mit jdm ~redet sein**
to have arranged to meet sb; **V~redung** *f*
arrangement; (*Treffen*) appointment;
~scheuen *vt* to detest, to abhor;
~schieden *vt* (*Gäste*) to say goodbye to;
(*entlassen*) discharge; (*Gesetz*) to pass
♦ *vr* to take one's leave; **V~schiedung** *f*
leave-taking; discharge; passing

ver- [fɛr] *zW:* **~achten** *vt* to despise;
~ächtlich [-'ʔɛçtlɪç] *adj* contemptuous;
(*~achtenswert*) contemptible; **jdn ~ächtlich
machen** to run sb down; **V~achtung** *f*
contempt

verallgemeinern [fɛrʔalgəˈmaɪnərn] *vt* to
generalize; **Verallgemeinerung** *f*
generalization

veralten [fɛr'ʔaltən] *vi* to become obsolete
od out-of-date

Veranda [ve'randa] **(-, Veranden)** *f* veranda

veränder- [fɛr'ʔɛndər] *zW:* **~lich** *adj*
changeable; **~n** *vt, vr* to change, to alter;
V~ung *f* change, alteration

veran- [fɛr'ʔan] *zW:* **~lagt** *adj* with a ...
nature; **V~lagung** *f* disposition; **~lassen**
vt to cause; **Maßnahmen ~lassen** to take
measures; **sich ~lasst sehen** to feel
prompted; **~schaulichen** *vt* to illustrate;
~schlagen *vt* to estimate; **~stalten** *vt* to
organize, to arrange; **V~stalter (-s, -)** *m*
organizer; **V~staltung** *f* (*V~stalten*)
organizing; (*Konzert etc*) event, function

verantwort- [fɛr'ʔantvɔrt] *zW:* **~en** *vt* to
answer for ♦ *vr* to justify o.s.; **~lich** *adj*
responsible; **V~ung** *f* responsibility;
~ungsbewusst ▲ *adj* responsible;
~ungslos *adj* irresponsible

verarbeiten [fɛr'ʔarbaɪtən] *vt* to process;
(*geistig*) to assimilate; **etw zu etw ~** to

make sth into sth; **Verarbeitung** *f*
processing; assimilation

verärgern [fɛr'ʔɛrgərn] *vt* to annoy

verausgaben [fɛr'ʔaʊsgaːbən] *vr* to run out
of money; (*fig*) to exhaust o.s.

Verb [vɛrp] **(-s, -en)** *nt* verb

Verband [fɛr'bant] **(-(e)s, ⁻e)** *m* (*MED*)
bandage, dressing; (*Bund*) association,
society; (*MIL*) unit; **~kasten** *m* medicine
chest, first-aid box; **~zeug** *nt* bandage

verbannen [fɛr'banən] *vt* to banish

verbergen [fɛr'bɛrgən] (*unreg*) *vt, vr:* (**sich**)
~ (vor +*dat*) to hide (from)

verbessern [fɛr'bɛsərn] *vt, vr* to improve;
(*berichtigen*) to correct (o.s.)

Verbesserung *f* improvement; correction

verbeugen [fɛr'bɔygən] *vr* to bow

Verbeugung *f* bow

ver'biegen (*unreg*) *vi* to bend

ver'bieten (*unreg*) *vt* to forbid; **jdm etw ~**
to forbid sb to do sth

verbilligen [fɛr'bɪlɪgən] *vt* to reduce the
cost of; (*Preis*) to reduce

ver'binden (*unreg*) *vt* to connect;
(*kombinieren*) to combine; (*MED*) to
bandage ♦ *vr* (*auch CHEM*) to combine, to
join; **jdm die Augen ~** to blindfold sb

verbindlich [fɛr'bɪntlɪç] *adj* binding;
(*freundlich*) friendly

Ver'bindung *f* connection;
(*Zusammensetzung*) combination; (*CHEM*)
compound; (*UNIV*) club

verbissen [fɛr'bɪsən] *adj* (*Kampf*) bitter;
(*Gesichtsausdruck*) grim

ver'bitten (*unreg*) *vt:* **sich** *dat* **etw ~** not to
tolerate sth, not to stand for sth

Verbleib [fɛr'blaɪp] **(-(e)s)** *m* whereabouts;
v~en (*unreg*) *vi* to remain

verbleit [fɛr'blaɪt] *adj* (*Benzin*) leaded

verblüffen [fɛr'blyfən] *vt* to stagger, to
amaze; **Verblüffung** *f* stupefaction

ver'blühen *vi* to wither, to fade

ver'bluten *vi* to bleed to death

verborgen [fɛr'bɔrgən] *adj* hidden

Verbot [fɛr'boːt] **(-(e)s, -e)** *nt* prohibition,
ban; **v~en** *adj* forbidden; **Rauchen v~en!**
no smoking; **~sschild** *nt* prohibitory sign

Spelling Reform: ▲ *new spelling* △ *old spelling (to be phased out)*

Verbrauch [fɛr'braʊx] (-(e)s) *m*
consumption; **v~en** *vt* to use up; **~er (-s,**
-) *m* consumer; **v~t** *adj* used up, finished;
(*Luft*) stale; (*Mensch*) worn-out
Verbrechen [fɛr'brɛçən] (**-s, -**) *nt* crime
Verbrecher [fɛr'brɛçər] (**-s, -**) *m* criminal;
v~isch *adj* criminal
ver'breiten *vt, vr* to spread; **sich über etw**
akk **~** to expound on sth
verbreitern [fɛr'braɪtərn] *vt* to broaden
Verbreitung *f* spread(ing), propagation
verbrenn- [fɛr'brɛn] *zW:* **~bar** *adj*
combustible; **~en** (*unreg*) *vt* to burn;
(*Leiche*) to cremate; **V~ung** *f* burning; (*in
Motor*) combustion; (*von Leiche*) cremation;
V~ungsmotor *m* internal combustion
engine
verbringen [fɛr'brɪŋən] (*unreg*) *vt* to spend
verbrühen [fɛr'bry:ən] *vt* to scald
verbuchen [fɛr'bu:xən] *vt* (*FIN*) to register;
(*Erfolg*) to enjoy; (*Misserfolg*) to suffer
verbunden [fɛr'bʊndən] *adj* connected; **jdm
~ sein** to be obliged *od* indebted to sb;
„falsch ~" (*TEL*) "wrong number"
verbünden [fɛr'byndən] *vr* to ally o.s.;
Verbündete(r) *f(m)* ally
ver'bürgen *vr:* **sich ~ für** to vouch for
ver'büßen *vt:* **eine Strafe ~** to serve a
sentence
Verdacht [fɛr'daxt] (-(e)s) *m* suspicion
verdächtig [fɛr'dɛçtɪç] *adj* suspicious,
suspect; **~en** [fɛr'dɛçtɪgən] *vt* to suspect
verdammen [fɛr'damən] *vt* to damn, to
condemn; **verdammt!** damn!
verdammt (*umg*) *adj, adv* damned; **~ noch
mal!** damn!, dammit!
ver'dampfen *vi* to vaporize, to evaporate
ver'danken *vt:* **jdm etw ~** to owe sb sth
verdau- [fɛr'daʊ] *zW:* **~en** *vt* (*auch fig*) to
digest; **~lich** *adj* digestible; **das ist schwer
~lich** that is hard to digest; **V~ung** *f*
digestion
Verdeck [fɛr'dɛk] (-(e)s, -e) *nt* (*AUT*) hood;
(*NAUT*) deck; **v~en** *vt* to cover (up);
(*verbergen*) to hide
Verderb- [fɛr'dɛrp] *zW:* **~en** [-'dɛrbən] (**-s**)
nt ruin; **v~en** (*unreg*) *vt* to spoil; (*schädigen*)

to ruin; (*moralisch*) to corrupt ♦ *vi* (*Essen*) to
spoil, to rot; (*Mensch*) to go to the bad; **es
mit jdm v~en** to get into sb's bad books;
v~lich *adj* (*Einfluss*) pernicious;
(*Lebensmittel*) perishable
verdeutlichen [fɛr'dɔytlɪçən] *vt* to make
clear
ver'dichten *vt, vr* to condense
ver'dienen *vt* to earn; (*moralisch*) to
deserve
Ver'dienst (-(e)s, -e) *m* earnings *pl* ♦ *nt*
merit; (*Leistung*): **~ (um)** service (to)
verdient [fɛr'di:nt] *adj* well-earned; (*Person*)
deserving of esteem; **sich um etw ~
machen** to do a lot for sth
verdoppeln [fɛr'dɔpəln] *vt* to double
verdorben [fɛr'dɔrbən] *adj* spoilt;
(*geschädigt*) ruined; (*moralisch*) corrupt
verdrängen [fɛr'drɛŋən] *vt* to oust, to
displace (*auch PHYS*); (*PSYCH*) to repress
ver'drehen *vt* (*auch fig*) to twist; (*Augen*) to
roll; **jdm den Kopf ~** (*fig*) to turn sb's
head
verdrießlich [fɛr'dri:slɪç] *adj* peevish,
annoyed
Verdruss ▲ [fɛr'drʊs] (-es, -e) *m*
annoyance, worry
verdummen [fɛr'dʊmən] *vt* to make stupid
♦ *vi* to grow stupid
verdunkeln [fɛr'dʊŋkəln] *vt* to darken; (*fig*)
to obscure ♦ *vr* to darken
Verdunk(e)lung *f* blackout; (*fig*) obscuring
verdünnen [fɛr'dynən] *vt* to dilute
verdunsten [fɛr'dʊnstən] *vi* to evaporate
verdursten [fɛr'dʊrstən] *vi* to die of thirst
verdutzt [fɛr'dʊtst] *adj* nonplussed, taken
aback
verehr- [fɛr'|e:r] *zW:* **~en** *vt* to venerate, to
worship (*auch REL*); **jdm etw ~en** to present
sb with sth; **V~er(in)** (-s, -) *m(f)* admirer,
worshipper (*auch REL*); **v~t** *adj* esteemed;
V~ung *f* respect; (*REL*) worship
Verein [fɛr'|aɪn] (-(e)s, -e) *m* club,
association; **v~bar** *adj* compatible;
v~baren *vt* to agree upon; **~barung** *f*
agreement; **v~en** *vt* (*Menschen, Länder*) to
unite; (*Prinzipien*) to reconcile; **mit v~ten**

Kräften having pooled resources, having joined forces; **~te Nationen** United Nations; **v~fachen** vt to simplify; **v~heitlichen** [-haitliçən] vt to standardize; **v~igen** vt, vr to unite; **~igung** f union; (*Verein*) association; **v~t** adj united; **v~zelt** adj isolated

ver'eitern vi to suppurate, to fester

verengen [fɛr'ɛŋən] vr to narrow

vererb- [fɛr'ɛrb] zW: **~en** vt to bequeath; (*BIOL*) to transmit ♦ vr to be hereditary; **V~ung** f bequeathing; (*BIOL*) transmission; (*Lehre*) heredity

verewigen [fɛr'e:vɪgən] vt to Immortalize ♦ vr (*umg*) to immortalize o.s.

ver'fahren (*unreg*) vi to act ♦ vr to get lost ♦ adj tangled; **~ mit** to deal with; **Ver'fahren (-s, -)** nt procedure; (*TECH*) process; (*JUR*) proceedings pl

Verfall [fɛr'fal] **(-(e)s)** m decline; (*von Haus*) dilapidation; (*FIN*) expiry; **v~en** (*unreg*) vi to decline; (*Haus*) to be falling down; (*FIN*) to lapse, **v~en in** +akk to lapse into; **v~en auf** +akk to hit upon; **einem Laster v~en sein** to be addicted to a vice; **~sdatum** nt expiry date; (*der Haltbarkeit*) sell-by date

ver'färben vr to change colour

verfassen [fɛr'fasən] vt (*Rede*) to prepare, work out

Verfasser(in) [fɛr'fasər(ɪn)] **(-s, -)** m(f) author, writer

Verfassung f (*auch POL*) constitution

Verfassungs- zW: **~gericht** nt constitutional court; **v~widrig** adj unconstitutional

ver'faulen vi to rot

ver'fehlen vt to miss; **etw für verfehlt halten** to regard sth as mistaken

verfeinern [fɛr'faɪnərn] vt to refine

ver'filmen vt to film

verflixt [fɛr'flɪkst] (*umg*) adj damned, damn

ver'fluchen vt to curse

verfolg- [fɛr'fɔlg] zW: **~en** vt to pursue; (*gerichtlich*) to prosecute; (*grausam, bes POL*) to persecute; **V~er (-s, -)** m pursuer; **V~ung** f pursuit; prosecution; persecution

verfrüht [fɛr'fry:t] adj premature

verfüg- [fɛr'fy:g] zW: **~bar** adj available; **~en** vt to direct, to order ♦ vr to proceed ♦ vi: **~en über** +akk to have at one's disposal; **V~ung** f direction, order; **zur V~ung** at one's disposal; **jdm zur V~ung stehen** to be available to sb

verführ- [fɛr'fy:r] zW: **~en** vt to tempt; (*sexuell*) to seduce; **V~er** m tempter; seducer; **~erisch** adj seductive; **V~ung** f seduction; (*Versuchung*) temptation

ver'gammeln (*umg*) vi to go to seed; (*Nahrung*) to go off

vergangen [fɛr'gaŋən] adj past; **V~heit** f past

vergänglich [fɛr'gɛŋlɪç] adj transitory

vergasen [fɛr'ga:zən] vt (*töten*) to gas

Vergaser (-s, -) m (*AUT*) carburettor

vergaß etc [fɛr'ga:s] vb siehe **vergessen**

vergeb- [fɛr'ge:b] zW: **~en** (*unreg*) vt (*verzeihen*) to forgive; (*weggeben*) to give away; **jdm etw ~en** to forgive sb (for) sth; **~ens** adv in vain; **~lich** [fɛr'ge:plɪç] adv in vain ♦ adj vain, futile; **V~ung** f forgiveness

ver'gehen (*unreg*) vi to pass by od away ♦ vr to commit an offence; **jdm vergeht etw** sb loses sth; **sich an jdm ~** to (sexually) assault sb; **Ver'gehen (-s, -)** nt offence

ver'gelten (*unreg*) vt: **jdm etw ~** to pay sb back for sth, to repay sb for sth

Ver'geltung f retaliation, reprisal

vergessen [fɛr'gɛsən] (*unreg*) vt to forget; **V~heit** f oblivion

vergesslich ▲ [fɛr'gɛslɪç] adj forgetful; **V~keit** f forgetfulness

vergeuden [fɛr'gɔydən] vt to squander, to waste

vergewaltigen [fɛrgə'valtɪgən] vt to rape; (*fig*) to violate

Vergewaltigung f rape

vergewissern [fɛrgə'vɪsərn] vr to make sure

vergießen (*unreg*) vt to shed

vergiften [fɛr'gɪftən] vt to poison

Vergiftung f poisoning

Vergissmeinnicht ▲ [fɛr'gɪsmaɪnnɪçt] **(-(e)s, -e)** nt forget-me-not

vergisst ▲ etc [fɛr'gɪst] vb siehe **vergessen**

Vergleich [fɛrˈɡlaɪç] (-(e)s, -e) *m*
comparison; (*JUR*) settlement; **im ~ mit** *od*
zu compared with *od* to; **v~bar** *adj*
comparable; **v~en** (*unreg*) *vt* to compare
♦ *vr* to reach a settlement

vergnügen [fɛrˈɡnyːɡən] *vr* to enjoy *od*
amuse o.s.; **V~** (-s, -) *nt* pleasure; **viel V~!**
enjoy yourself!

vergnügt [fɛrˈɡnyːkt] *adj* cheerful

Vergnügung *f* pleasure, amusement;
~spark *m* amusement park

vergolden [fɛrˈɡɔldən] *vt* to gild

verˈgraben *vt* to bury

verˈgreifen (*unreg*) *vr*: **sich an jdm ~** to lay
hands on sb; **sich an etw ~** to
misappropriate sth; **sich im Ton ~** to say
the wrong thing

vergriffen [fɛrˈɡrɪfən] *adj* (*Buch*) out of print;
(*Ware*) out of stock

vergrößern [fɛrˈɡrøːsərn] *vt* to enlarge;
(*mengenmäßig*) to increase; (*Lupe*) to
magnify

Vergrößerung *f* enlargement; increase;
magnification; **~sglas** *nt* magnifying glass

Vergünstigung [fɛrˈɡʏnstɪɡʊŋ] *f*
concession, privilege

Vergütung *f* compensation

verhaften [fɛrˈhaftən] *vt* to arrest

Verhaftung *f* arrest

verˈhalten (*unreg*) *vr* to be, to stand; (*sich
benehmen*) to behave ♦ *vt* to hold *od* keep
back; (*Schritt*) to check; **sich ~ (zu)** (*MATH*)
to be in proportion (to); **Verˈhalten** (-s) *nt*
behaviour

Verhältnis [fɛrˈhɛltnɪs] (-ses, -se) *nt*
relationship; (*MATH*) proportion, ratio; **~se**
pl (*Umstände*) conditions; **über seine ~se
leben** to live beyond one's means;
v~mäßig *adj* relative, comparative ♦ *adv*
relatively, comparatively

verhandeln [fɛrˈhandəln] *vi* to negotiate;
(*JUR*) to hold proceedings ♦ *vt* to discuss;
(*JUR*) to hear; **über etw** *akk* **~** to negotiate
sth *od* about sth

Verhandlung *f* negotiation; (*JUR*)
proceedings *pl*; **~sbasis** *f* (*FIN*) basis for
negotiations

verˈhängen *vt* (*fig*) to impose, to inflict

Verhängnis [fɛrˈhɛŋnɪs] (-ses, -se) *nt* fate,
doom; **jdm zum ~ werden** to be sb's
undoing; **v~voll** *adj* fatal, disastrous

verharmlosen [fɛrˈharmloːzən] *vt* to make
light of, to play down

verhärten [fɛrˈhɛrtən] *vr* to harden

verhasst ▲ [fɛrˈhast] *adj* odious, hateful

verhauen [fɛrˈhaʊən] (*unreg*; *umg*) *vt*
(*verprügeln*) to beat up

verheerend [fɛrˈheːrənt] *adj* disastrous,
devastating

verheimlichen [fɛrˈhaɪmlɪçən] *vt*: **jdm etw
~** to keep sth secret from sb

verheiratet [fɛrˈhaɪraːtət] *adj* married

verˈhelfen (*unreg*) *vi*: **jdm ~ zu** to help sb
to get

verˈhindern *vt* to prevent; **verhindert sein**
to be unable to make it

verhöhnen [fɛrˈhøːnən] *vt* to mock, to
sneer at

Verhör [fɛrˈhøːr] (-(e)s, -e) *nt* interrogation;
(*gerichtlich*) (cross-)examination; **v~en** *vt* to
interrogate; to (cross-)examine ♦ *vr* to
misunderstand, to mishear

verˈhungern *vi* to starve, to die of hunger

verˈhüten *vt* to prevent, to avert

Verˈhütung *f* prevention; **~smittel** *nt*
contraceptive

verirren [fɛrˈ|ɪrən] *vr* to go astray

verˈjagen *vt* to drive away *od* out

verkalken [fɛrˈkalkən] *vi* to calcify; (*umg*) to
become senile

Verkauf [fɛrˈkaʊf] *m* sale; **v~en** *vt* to sell

Verkäufer(in) [fɛrˈkɔʏfər(ɪn)] (-s, -) *m(f)*
seller; salesman(-woman); (*in Laden*) shop
assistant

verkaufsoffen *adj*: **~er Samstag** *Saturday
when the shops stay open all day*

Verkehr [fɛrˈkeːr] (-s, -e) *m* traffic; (*Umgang,
bes sexuell*) intercourse; (*Umlauf*) circulation;
v~en *vi* (*Fahrzeug*) to ply, to run ♦ *vt*, *vr* to
turn, to transform; **v~en mit** to associate
with; **bei jdm v~en** (*besuchen*) to visit sb
regularly

Verkehrs- *zW*: **~ampel** *f* traffic lights *pl*;
~aufkommen *nt* volume of traffic;

~beruhigung f traffic calming; **~delikt** nt traffic offence; **~funk** m radio traffic service; **v~günstig** adj convenient; **~mittel** nt means of transport; **~schild** nt road sign; **~stau** m traffic jam, stoppage; **~unfall** m traffic accident; **~verein** m tourist information office; **~zeichen** nt traffic sign

verkehrt adj wrong; (umgekehrt) the wrong way round

ver'kennen (unreg) vt to misjudge, not to appreciate

ver'klagen vt to take to court

verkleiden [fer'klaɪdən] vr to disguise (o.s.); (sich kostümieren) to get dressed up ♦ vt (Wand) to cover

Verkleidung f disguise; (ARCHIT) wainscoting

verkleinern [fer'klaɪnərn] vt to make smaller, to reduce in size

ver'kneifen (umg) vt: **sich** dat **etw ~** (Lachen) to stifle sth; (Schmerz) to hide sth; (sich versagen) to do without sth

verknüpfen [fer'knʏpfən] vt to tie (up), to knot; (fig) to connect

ver'kommen (unreg) vi to deteriorate, to decay; (Mensch) to go downhill, to come down in the world ♦ adj (moralisch) dissolute, depraved

verkörpern [fer'kœrpərn] vt to embody, to personify

verkraften [fer'kraftən] vt to cope with

ver'kriechen (unreg) vr to creep away, to creep into a corner

verkrüppelt [fer'krʏpəlt] adj crippled

ver'kühlen vr to get a chill

ver'kümmern vi to waste away

ver'künden vt to proclaim; (Urteil) to pronounce

ver'kürzen [fer'kʏrtsən] vt to shorten; (Wort) to abbreviate; **sich** dat **die Zeit ~** to while away the time

Verkürzung f shortening; abbreviation

verladen [fer'laːdən] (unreg) vt (Waren, Vieh) to load; (Truppen: auf Schiff) to embark, (auf Zug) to entrain, (auf Flugzeug) to enplane

Verlag [fer'laːk] (**-(e)s, -e**) m publishing firm

verlangen [fer'laŋən] vt to demand; to desire ♦ vi: **~ nach** to ask for, to desire; **Sie Herrn X** ask for Mr X; **V~ (-s, -)** nt: **V~ (nach)** desire (for); **auf jds V~ (hin)** at sb's request

verlängern [fer'lɛŋərn] vt to extend; (länger machen) to lengthen

Verlängerung f extension; (SPORT) extra time; **~sschnur** f extension cable

verlangsamen [fer'laŋzaːmən] vt, vr to decelerate, to slow down

Verlass ▲ [fer'las] m: **auf ihn/das ist kein ~** he/it cannot be relied upon

ver'lassen (unreg) vt to leave ♦ vr: **sich ~ auf** +akk to depend on ♦ adj desolate; (Mensch) abandoned

verlässlich ▲ [fer'lɛslɪç] adj reliable

Verlauf [fer'lauf] m course; **v~en** (unreg) vi (zeitlich) to pass; (Farben) to run ♦ vr to get lost; (Menschenmenge) to disperse

ver'lauten vi: **etw ~ lassen** to disclose sth; **wie verlautet** as reported

ver'legen vt to move; (verlieren) to mislay; (Buch) to publish ♦ vr: **sich auf etw** akk **~** to take up od to sth ♦ adj embarrassed; **nicht ~ um** never at a loss for; **Ver'legenheit** f embarrassment; (Situation) difficulty, scrape

Verleger [fer'leːɡər] (**-s, -**) m publisher

Verleih [fer'laɪ] (**-(e)s, -e**) m hire service; **v~en** (unreg) vt to lend; (Kraft, Anschein) to confer, to bestow; (Preis, Medaille) to award; **~ung** f lending; bestowal; award

ver'leiten vt to lead astray; **~ zu** to talk into, to tempt into

ver'lernen vt to forget, to unlearn

ver'lesen (unreg) vt to read out; (aussondern) to sort out ♦ vr to make a mistake in reading

verletz- [fer'lɛts] zW: **~en** vt (auch fig) to injure, to hurt; (Gesetz etc) to violate; **~end** adj (fig: Worte) hurtful; **~lich** adj vulnerable, sensitive; **V~te(r)** f(m) injured person; **V~ung** f injury; (Verstoß) violation, infringement

verleugnen [fer'lɔʏɡnən] vt (Herkunft, Glauben) to belie; (Menschen) to disown

verleumden [fɛrˈlɔymdən] *vt* to slander;
Verleumdung *f* slander, libel
ver'lieben *vr*: **sich ~ (in** +*akk*) to fall in love
(with)
verliebt [fɛrˈliːpt] *adj* in love
verlieren [fɛrˈliːrən] (*unreg*) *vt, vi* to lose ♦ *vr*
to get lost
Verlierer *m* loser
verlob- [fɛrˈloːb] *zW*: **~en** *vr*: **sich ~en (mit)**
to get engaged (to); **V~te(r)** [fɛrˈloːptə(r)]
f(m) fiancé *m*, fiancée *f*; **V~ung** *f*
engagement
ver'locken *vt* to entice, to lure
Ver'lockung *f* temptation, attraction
verlogen [fɛrˈloːgən] *adj* untruthful
verlor *etc vb siehe* **verlieren**
verloren [fɛrˈloːrən] *adj* lost; (*Eier*) poached
♦ *vb siehe* **verlieren**; **etw ~ geben** to give
sth up for lost; **~ gehen** to get lost
verlosen [fɛrˈloːzən] *vt* to raffle, to draw lots
for; **Verlosung** *f* raffle, lottery
Verlust [fɛrˈlʊst] **(-(e)s, -e)** *m* loss; (*MIL*)
casualty
ver'machen *vt* to bequeath, to leave
Vermächtnis [fɛrˈmɛçtnɪs] **(-ses, -se)** *nt*
legacy
Vermählung [fɛrˈmɛːlʊŋ] *f* wedding,
marriage
vermarkten [fɛrˈmarktən] *vt* (*COMM*: *Artikel*)
to market
vermehren [fɛrˈmeːrən] *vt, vr* to multiply;
(*Menge*) to increase
Vermehrung *f* multiplying; increase
ver'meiden (*unreg*) *vt* to avoid
vermeintlich [fɛrˈmaɪntlɪç] *adj* supposed
Vermerk [fɛrˈmɛrk] **(-(e)s, -e)** *m* note; (*in
Ausweis*) endorsement; **v~en** *vt* to note
ver'messen (*unreg*) *vt* to survey ♦ *adj*
presumptuous, bold; **Ver'messenheit** *f*
presumptuousness; recklessness
Ver'messung *f* survey(ing)
vermiet- [fɛrˈmiːt] *zW*: **ver'mieten** *vt* to
let, to rent (out); (*Auto*) to hire out, to rent;
Ver'mieter(in) **(-s, -)** *m(f)* landlord(-lady);
Ver'mietung *f* letting, renting (out); (*von
Autos*) hiring (out)
vermindern [fɛrˈmɪndərn] *vt, vr* to lessen, to

decrease; (*Preise*) to reduce
Verminderung *f* reduction
ver'mischen *vt, vr* to mix, to blend
vermissen [fɛrˈmɪsən] *vt* to miss
vermitt- [fɛrˈmɪt] *zW*: **~eln** *vi* to mediate
♦ *vt* (*Gespräch*) to connect; **jdm etw ~eln** to
help sb to obtain sth; **V~ler (-s, -)** *m*
(*Schlichter*) agent, mediator; **V~lung** *f*
procurement; (*Stellenvermittlung*) agency;
(*TEL*) exchange; (*Schlichtung*) mediation;
V~lungsgebühr *f* commission
ver'mögen (*unreg*) *vt* to be capable of; **~
zu** to be able to; **Ver'mögen (-s, -)** *nt*
wealth; (*Fähigkeit*) ability; **ein V~ kosten** to
cost a fortune; **ver'mögend** *adj* wealthy
vermuten [fɛrˈmuːtən] *vt* to suppose, to
guess; (*argwöhnen*) to suspect
vermutlich *adj* supposed, presumed ♦ *adv*
probably
Vermutung *f* supposition; suspicion
vernachlässigen [fɛrˈnaːxlɛsɪgən] *vt* to
neglect
ver'nehmen (*unreg*) *vt* to perceive, to hear;
(*erfahren*) to learn; (*JUR*) to (cross-)examine;
dem V~ nach from what I/we *etc* hear
Vernehmung *f* (cross-)examination
verneigen [fɛrˈnaɪgən] *vr* to bow
verneinen [fɛrˈnaɪnən] *vt* (*Frage*) to answer
in the negative; (*ablehnen*) to deny; (*GRAM*)
to negate; **~d** *adj* negative
Verneinung *f* negation
vernichten [fɛrˈnɪçtən] *vt* to annihilate, to
destroy; **~d** *adj* (*fig*) crushing; (*Blick*)
withering; (*Kritik*) scathing
Vernunft [fɛrˈnʊnft] **(-)** *f* reason,
understanding
vernünftig [fɛrˈnʏnftɪç] *adj* sensible,
reasonable
veröffentlichen [fɛrˈœfəntlɪçən] *vt* to
publish; **Veröffentlichung** *f* publication
verordnen [fɛrˈɔrdnən] *vt* (*MED*) to
prescribe
Verordnung *f* order, decree; (*MED*)
prescription
ver'pachten *vt* to lease (out)
ver'packen *vt* to pack
Ver'packung *f* packing, wrapping;

~**smaterial** *nt* packing, wrapping

ver'**passen** *vt* to miss; **jdm eine Ohrfeige ~** (*umg*) to give sb a clip round the ear

verpfänden [fer'pfɛndən] *vt* (*Besitz*) to mortgage

ver'**pflanzen** *vt* to transplant

ver'**pflegen** *vt* to feed, to cater for

Ver'**pflegung** *f* feeding, catering; (*Kost*) food; (*in Hotel*) board

verpflichten [fer'pflɪçtən] *vt* to oblige, to bind; (*anstellen*) to engage ♦ *vr* to undertake; (*MIL*) to sign on ♦ *vi* to carry obligations; **jdm zu Dank verpflichtet sein** to be obliged to sb

Verpflichtung *f* obligation, duty

verpönt [fer'pø:nt] *adj* disapproved (of), taboo

ver'**prügeln** (*umg*) *vt* to beat up, to do over

Verputz [fer'pʊts] *m* plaster, roughcast; **v~en** *vt* to plaster; (*umg: Essen*) to put away

Verrat [fer'ra:t] (-(e)s) *m* treachery; (*POL*) treason; **v~en** (*unreg*) *vt* to betray; (*Geheimnis*) to divulge ♦ *vr* to give o.s. away

Verräter [fer'rɛ:tər] (-s, -) *m* traitor(-tress); **v~isch** *adj* treacherous

ver'**rechnen** *vt*: **~ mit** to set off against ♦ *vr* to miscalculate

Verrechnungsscheck [fer'rɛçnʊŋsʃɛk] *m* crossed cheque

verregnet [fer're:gnət] *adj* spoilt by rain, rainy

ver'**reisen** *vi* to go away (on a journey)

verrenken [fer'rɛŋkən] *vt* to contort; (*MED*) to dislocate; **sich** *dat* **den Knöchel ~** to sprain one's ankle

ver'**richten** *vt* to do, to perform

verriegeln [fer'ri:gəln] *vt* to bolt up, to lock

verringern [fer'rɪŋərn] *vt* to reduce ♦ *vr* to diminish

Verringerung *f* reduction; lessening

ver'**rinnen** (*unreg*) *vi* to run out *od* away; (*Zeit*) to elapse

ver'**rosten** *vi* to rust

verrotten [fer'rɔtən] *vi* to rot

ver'**rücken** *vt* to move, to shift

verrückt [fer'rʏkt] *adj* crazy, mad; **V~e(r)** *f(m)* lunatic; **V~heit** *f* madness, lunacy

Verruf [fer'ru:f] *m*: **in ~ geraten/bringen** to fall/bring into disrepute; **v~en** *adj* notorious, disreputable

Vers [fɛrs] (-es, -e) *m* verse

ver'**sagen** *vt*: **jdm/sich etw ~** to deny sb/o.s. sth ♦ *vi* to fail; **Ver'sagen** (-s) *nt* failure

ver'**salzen** (*unreg*) *vt* to put too much salt in; (*fig*) to spoil

ver'**sammeln** *vt*, *vr* to assemble, to gather

Ver'**sammlung** *f* meeting, gathering

Versand [fer'zant] (-(e)s) *m* forwarding; dispatch; (*~abteilung*) dispatch department; **~haus** *nt* mail-order firm

ver'**säumen** *vt* to miss; (*unterlassen*) to neglect, to fail

ver'**schaffen** *vt*: **jdm/sich etw ~** to get *od* procure sth for sb/o.s.

verschämt [fer'ʃɛ:mt] *adj* bashful

verschandeln [fer'ʃandəln] (*umg*) *vt* to spoil

verschärfen [fer'ʃɛrfən] *vt* to intensify; (*Lage*) to aggravate ♦ *vr* to intensify; to become aggravated

ver'**schätzen** *vr* to be out in one's reckoning

ver'**schenken** *vt* to give away

verscheuchen [fer'ʃɔyçən] *vt* (*Tiere*) to chase off *od* away

ver'**schicken** *vt* to send off

ver'**schieben** (*unreg*) *vt* to shift; (*EISENB*) to shunt; (*Termin*) to postpone

verschieden [fer'ʃi:dən] *adj* different; (*pl: mehrere*) various; **sie sind ~ groß** they are of different sizes; **~tlich** *adv* several times

verschimmeln [fer'ʃɪməln] *vi* (*Nahrungsmittel*) to go mouldy

verschlafen [fer'ʃla:fən] (*unreg*) *vt* to sleep through; (*fig: versäumen*) to miss ♦ *vi*, *vr* to oversleep ♦ *adj* sleepy

Verschlag [fer'ʃla:k] *m* shed; **v~en** [-gən] (*unreg*) *vt* to board up ♦ *adj* cunning; **jdm den Atem v~en** to take sb's breath away; **an einen Ort v~en werden** to wind up in a place

verschlechtern [fɛrˈʃlɛçtərn] *vt* to make worse ♦ *vr* to deteriorate, to get worse; **Verschlechterung** *f* deterioration

Verschleiß [fɛrˈʃlaɪs] **(-es, -e)** *m* wear and tear; **v~en** (*unreg*) *vt* to wear out

ver'schleppen *vt* to carry off, to abduct; (*Krankheit*) to protract; (*zeitlich*) to drag out

ver'schleudern *vt* to squander; (*COMM*) to sell dirt-cheap

verschließbar *adj* lockable

verschließen [fɛrˈʃliːsən] (*unreg*) *vt* to close; to lock ♦ *vr*: **sich einer Sache** *dat* ~ to close one's mind to sth

verschlimmern [fɛrˈʃlɪmərn] *vt* to make worse, to aggravate ♦ *vr* to get worse, to deteriorate

verschlingen [fɛrˈʃlɪŋən] (*unreg*) *vt* to devour, to swallow up; (*Fäden*) to twist

verschlossen [fɛrˈʃlɔsən] *adj* locked; (*fig*) reserved; **V~heit** *f* reserve

ver'schlucken *vt* to swallow ♦ *vr* to choke

Verschluss ▲ [fɛrˈʃlʊs] *m* lock; (*von Kleid etc*) fastener; (*PHOT*) shutter; (*Stöpsel*) plug

verschlüsseln [fɛrˈʃlʏsəln] *vt* to encode

verschmieren [fɛrˈʃmiːrən] *vt* (*verstreichen: Gips, Mörtel*) to apply, spread on; (*schmutzig machen: Wand etc*) to smear

verschmutzen [fɛrˈʃmʊtsən] *vt* to soil; (*Umwelt*) to pollute

verschneit [fɛrˈʃnaɪt] *adj* snowed up, covered in snow

verschollen [fɛrˈʃɔlən] *adj* lost, missing

ver'schonen *vt*: **jdn mit etw** ~ to spare sb sth

verschönern [fɛrˈʃøːnərn] *vt* to decorate; (*verbessern*) to improve

ver'schreiben (*unreg*) *vt* (*MED*) to prescribe ♦ *vr* to make a mistake (in writing); **sich einer Sache** *dat* ~ to devote o.s. to sth

verschreibungspflichtig *adj* (*Medikament*) available on prescription only

verschrotten [fɛrˈʃrɔtən] *vt* to scrap

verschuld- [fɛrˈʃʊld] *zW*: **~en** *vt* to be guilty of; **V~en (-s)** *nt* fault, guilt; **~et** *adj* in debt; **V~ung** *f* fault; (*Geld*) debts *pl*

ver'schütten *vt* to spill; (*zuschütten*) to fill; (*unter Trümmer*) to bury

ver'schweigen (*unreg*) *vt* to keep secret; **jdm etw** ~ to keep sth from sb

verschwend- [fɛrˈʃvɛnd] *zW*: **~en** *vt* to squander; **V~er (-s, -)** *m* spendthrift; **~erisch** *adj* wasteful, extravagant; **V~ung** *f* waste; extravagance

verschwiegen [fɛrˈʃviːgən] *adj* discreet; (*Ort*) secluded; **V~heit** *f* discretion; seclusion

ver'schwimmen (*unreg*) *vi* to grow hazy, to become blurred

ver'schwinden (*unreg*) *vi* to disappear, to vanish; **Ver'schwinden (-s)** *nt* disappearance

verschwitzt [fɛrˈʃvɪtst] *adj* (*Mensch*) sweaty

verschwommen [fɛrˈʃvɔmən] *adj* hazy, vague

verschwör- [fɛrˈʃvøːr] *zW*: **~en** (*unreg*) *vr* to plot, to conspire; **V~ung** *f* conspiracy, plot

ver'sehen (*unreg*) *vt* to supply, to provide; (*Pflicht*) to carry out; (*Amt*) to fill; (*Haushalt*) to keep ♦ *vr* (*fig*) to make a mistake; **ehe er (es) sich ~ hatte ...** before he knew it ...; **Ver'sehen (-s, -)** *nt* oversight; **aus V~** by mistake; **~tlich** *adv* by mistake

Versehrte(r) [fɛrˈzeːrtə(r)] *f(m)* disabled person

ver'senden (*unreg*) *vt* to forward, to dispatch

ver'senken *vt* to sink ♦ *vr*: **sich ~ in** +*akk* to become engrossed in

versessen [fɛrˈzɛsən] *adj*: ~ **auf** +*akk* mad about

ver'setzen *vt* to transfer; (*verpfänden*) to pawn; (*umg*) to stand up ♦ *vr*: **sich in jdn** *od* **in jds Lage** ~ to put o.s. in sb's place; **jdm einen Tritt/Schlag** ~ to kick/hit sb; **etw mit etw** ~ to mix sth with sth; **jdn in gute Laune** ~ to put sb in a good mood

Ver'setzung *f* transfer

verseuchen [fɛrˈzɔʏçən] *vt* to contaminate

versichern [fɛrˈzɪçərn] *vt* to assure; (*mit Geld*) to insure

Versicherung *f* assurance; insurance

Versicherungs- *zW*: **~gesellschaft** *f* insurance company; **~karte** *f* insurance card; **die grüne ~karte** the green card;

Rechtschreibreform: ▲ *neue Schreibung* △ *alte Schreibung (auslaufend)*

~**police** f insurance policy

ver'**sinken** (*unreg*) vi to sink

ver**söhnen** [fɛrˈzøːnən] vt to reconcile ♦ vr to become reconciled

Ver**söhnung** f reconciliation

ver'**sorgen** vt to provide, to supply; (*Familie etc*) to look after

Ver'**sorgung** f provision; (*Unterhalt*) maintenance; (*Altersversorgung etc*) benefit, assistance

ver**späten** [fɛrˈʃpɛːtən] vr to be late

ver**spätet** adj (*Zug, Abflug, Ankunft*) late; (*Glückwünsche*) belated

Ver**spätung** f delay; ~ **haben** to be late

ver'**sperren** vt to bar, to obstruct

ver**spielt** [fɛrˈʃpiːlt] adj (*Kind, Tier*) playful

ver'**spotten** vt to ridicule, to scoff at

ver'**sprechen** (*unreg*) vt to promise; **sich** dat **etw von etw ~** to expect sth from sth; Ver'**sprechen** (-s, -) nt promise

ver**staatlichen** [fɛrˈʃtaːtlɪçən] vt to nationalize

Ver**stand** [fɛrˈʃtant] m intelligence; mind; **den ~ verlieren** to go out of one's mind; **über jds ~ gehen** to go beyond sb

ver**ständig** [fɛrˈʃtɛndɪç] adj sensible; ~**en** [fɛrˈʃtɛndɪɡən] vt to inform ♦ vr to communicate; (*sich einigen*) to come to an understanding; Ver~**ung** f communication; (*Benachrichtigung*) informing; (*Einigung*) agreement

ver**ständ-** [fɛrˈʃtɛnt] zW: ~**lich** adj understandable, comprehensible; V~**lichkeit** f clarity, intelligibility; V~**nis** (-ses, -se) nt understanding; ~**nislos** adj uncomprehending; ~**nisvoll** adj understanding, sympathetic

ver**stärk-** [fɛrˈʃtɛrk] zW: ~**en** vt to strengthen; (*Ton*) to amplify; (*erhöhen*) to intensify ♦ vr to intensify; V~**er** (-s, -) m amplifier; V~**ung** f strengthening; (*Hilfe*) reinforcements pl; (*von Ton*) amplification

ver**stauchen** [fɛrˈʃtauxən] vt to sprain

ver**stauen** [fɛrˈʃtauən] vt to stow away

Ver**steck** [fɛrˈʃtɛk] (-(e)s, -e) nt hiding (place); ~**en** vt, vr to hide; v~**t** adj hidden

ver'**stehen** (*unreg*) vt to understand ♦ vr to get on; **das versteht sich (von selbst)** that goes without saying

ver**steigern** [fɛrˈʃtaigərn] vt to auction; Ver**steigerung** f auction

ver**stell-** [fɛrˈʃtɛl] zW: ~**bar** adj adjustable, variable; ~**en** vt to move, to shift; (*Uhr*) to adjust; (*versperren*) to block; (*fig*) to disguise ♦ vr to pretend, to put on an act; V~**ung** f pretence

ver**steuern** [fɛrˈʃtɔyərn] vt to pay tax on

ver**stimmt** [fɛrˈʃtɪmt] adj out of tune; (*fig*) cross, put out; (*Magen*) upset

ver'**stopfen** vt to block, to stop up; (*MED*) to constipate

Ver'**stopfung** f obstruction; (*MED*) constipation

ver**storben** [fɛrˈʃtɔrbən] adj deceased, late

ver**stört** [fɛrˈʃtøːrt] adj (*Mensch*) distraught

Ver**stoß** [fɛrˈʃtoːs] m: ~ **(gegen)** infringement (of), violation (of); v~**en** (*unreg*) vt to disown, to reject ♦ vi: v~**en gegen** to offend against

ver'**streichen** (*unreg*) vt to spread ♦ vi to elapse

ver'**streuen** vt to scatter (about)

ver**stümmeln** [fɛrˈʃtʏməln] vt to maim, to mutilate (*auch fig*)

ver**stummen** [fɛrˈʃtʊmən] vi to go silent; (*Lärm*) to die away

Ver**such** [fɛrˈzuːx] (-(e)s, -e) m attempt; (*SCI*) experiment; v~**en** vt to try; (*verlocken*) to tempt ♦ vr: **sich an etw** dat v~**en** to try one's hand at sth; ~**skaninchen** nt (*fig*) guinea-pig; ~**ung** f temptation

ver**tagen** [fɛrˈtaːɡən] vt, vi to adjourn

ver'**tauschen** vt to exchange; (*versehentlich*) to mix up

ver**teidig-** [fɛrˈtaidɪç] zW: ~**en** vt to defend; V~**er** (-s, -) m defender; (*JUR*) defence counsel; V~**ung** f defence

ver'**teilen** vt to distribute; (*Rollen*) to assign; (*Salbe*) to spread

Ver**teilung** f distribution, allotment

ver**tiefen** [fɛrˈtiːfən] vt to deepen ♦ vr: **sich in etw** akk ~ to become engrossed od absorbed in sth

Ver**tiefung** f depression

vertikal [vɛrti'kaːl] *adj* vertical

vertilgen [fɛr'tɪlɡən] *vt* to exterminate; (*umg*) to eat up, to consume

vertonen [fɛr'toːnən] *vt* to set to music

Vertrag [fɛr'traːk] (-(e)s, ⁀e) *m* contract, agreement; (*POL*) treaty; **v~en** [-ɡən] (*unreg*) *vt* to tolerate, to stand ♦ *vr* to get along; (*sich aussöhnen*) to become reconciled; **v~lich** *adj* contractual

verträglich [fɛr'trɛːklɪç] *adj* good-natured, sociable; (*Speisen*) easily digested; (*MED*) easily tolerated; **V~keit** *f* sociability; good nature; digestibility

Vertrags- *zW*: **~bruch** *m* breach of contract; **~händler** *m* appointed retailer; **~partner** *m* party to a contract; **~werkstatt** *f* appointed repair shop; **v~widrig** *adj* contrary to contract

vertrauen [fɛr'trauən] *vi*: **jdm ~** to trust sb; **~ auf** +*akk* to rely on; **V~** (-s) *nt* confidence; **V~ erweckend** inspiring trust; **~svoll** *adj* trustful; **~swürdig** *adj* trustworthy

vertraulich [fɛr'traulɪç] *adj* familiar; (*geheim*) confidential

vertraut [fɛr'traut] *adj* familiar; **V~heit** *f* familiarity

ver'treiben (*unreg*) *vt* to drive away; (*aus Land*) to expel; (*COMM*) to sell; (*Zeit*) to pass

vertret- [fɛr'treːt] *zW*: **~en** (*unreg*) *vt* to represent; (*Ansicht*) to hold, to advocate; **sich** *dat* **die Beine ~en** to stretch one's legs; **V~er** (-s, -) *m* representative; (*Verfechter*) advocate; **V~ung** *f* representation; advocacy

Vertrieb [fɛr'triːp] (-(e)s, -e) *m* marketing (department)

ver'trocknen *vi* to dry up

ver'trösten *vt* to put off

vertun [fɛr'tuːn] (*unreg*) *vt* to waste ♦ *vr* (*umg*) to make a mistake

vertuschen [fɛr'tʊʃən] *vt* to hush *od* cover up

verübeln [fɛr'yːbəln] *vt*: **jdm etw ~** to be cross *od* offended with sb on account of sth

verüben [fɛr'yːbən] *vt* to commit

verun- [fɛr'ʊn] *zW*: **~glimpfen** *vt* to disparage; **~glücken** *vi* to have an accident; **tödlich ~glücken** to be killed in an accident; **~reinigen** *vt* to soil; (*Umwelt*) to pollute; **~sichern** *vt* to rattle; **~treuen** [-trɔyən] *vt* to embezzle

verur- [fɛr'uːr] *zW*: **~sachen** *vt* to cause; **~teilen** [-tailən] *vt* to condemn; **V~teilung** *f* condemnation; (*JUR*) sentence

verviel- [fɛr'fiːl] *zW*: **~fachen** *vt* to multiply; **~fältigen** [-fɛltɪɡən] *vt* to duplicate, to copy; **V~fältigung** *f* duplication, copying

vervollkommnen [fɛr'fɔlkɔmnən] *vt* to perfect

vervollständigen [fɛr'fɔlʃtɛndɪɡən] *vt* to complete

ver'wackeln *vt* (*Foto*) to blur

ver'wählen *vr* (*TEL*) to dial the wrong number

verwahren [fɛr'vaːrən] *vt* to keep, to lock away ♦ *vr* to protest

verwalt- [fɛr'valt] *zW*: **~en** *vt* to manage; to administer; **V~er** (-s, -) *m* manager; (*Vermögensverwalter*) trustee; **V~ung** *f* administration; management

ver'wandeln *vt* to change, to transform ♦ *vr* to change; to be transformed; **Ver'wandlung** *f* change, transformation

verwandt [fɛr'vant] *adj*: **~ (mit)** related (to); **V~e(r)** *f(m)* relative, relation; **V~schaft** *f* relationship; (*Menschen*) relations *pl*

ver'warnen *vt* to caution

Ver'warnung *f* caution

ver'wechseln *vt*: **~ mit** to confuse with; to mistake for; **zum V~ ähnlich** as like as two peas

Ver'wechslung *f* confusion, mixing up

Verwehung [fɛr'veːʊŋ] *f* snowdrift; sand drift

verweichlicht [fɛr'vaiçlɪçt] *adj* effeminate, soft

ver'weigern *vt*: **jdm etw ~** to refuse sb sth; **den Gehorsam/die Aussage ~** to refuse to obey/testify

Ver'weigerung *f* refusal

Verweis [fɛr'vais] (-es, -e) *m* reprimand,

rebuke; *(Hinweis)* reference; **v~en** *(unreg) vt* to refer; **jdn von der Schule v~en** to expel sb (from school); **jdn des Landes v~en** to deport *od* expel sb

ver'welken *vi* to fade

verwend- [fer'vɛnd] *zW:* **~bar** [-'vɛntbaːr] *adj* usable; **ver'wenden** *(unreg) vt* to use; *(Mühe, Zeit, Arbeit)* to spend ♦ *vr* to intercede; **Ver'wendung** *f* use

ver'werfen *(unreg) vt* to reject

verwerflich [fer'vɛrflɪç] *adj* reprehensible

ver'werten *vt* to utilize

Ver'wertung *f* utilization

verwesen [fer'veːzən] *vi* to decay

ver'wickeln *vt* to tangle (up); *(fig)* to involve ♦ *vr* to get tangled (up); **jdn in etw** *akk* **~** to involve sb in sth; **sich in etw** *akk* **~** to get involved in sth

verwickelt [fer'vɪkəlt] *adj (Situation, Fall)* difficult, complicated

verwildern [fer'vɪldərn] *vi* to run wild

verwirklichen [fer'vɪrklɪçən] *vt* to realize, to put into effect

Verwirklichung *f* realization

verwirren [fer'vɪrən] *vt* to tangle (up); *(fig)* to confuse

Verwirrung *f* confusion

verwittern [fer'vɪtərn] *vi* to weather

verwitwet [fer'vɪtvət] *adj* widowed

verwöhnen [fer'vøːnən] *vt* to spoil

verworren [fer'vorən] *adj* confused

verwundbar [fer'vontbaːr] *adj* vulnerable

verwunden [fer'vondən] *vt* to wound

verwunder- [fer'vondər] *zW:* **~lich** *adj* surprising; **V~ung** *f* astonishment

Verwundete(r) *f(m)* injured person

Verwundung *f* wound, injury

ver'wünschen *vt* to curse

verwüsten [fer'vyːstən] *vt* to devastate

verzagen [fer'tsaːgən] *vi* to despair

ver'zählen *vr* to miscount

verzehren [fer'tseːrən] *vt* to consume

ver'zeichnen *vt* to list; *(Niederlage, Verlust)* to register

Verzeichnis [fer'tsaɪçnɪs] **(-ses, -se)** *nt* list, catalogue; *(in Buch)* index

verzeih- [fer'tsaɪ] *zW:* **~en** *(unreg) vt, vi* to

forgive; **jdm etw ~en** to forgive sb for sth; **~lich** *adj* pardonable; **V~ung** *f* forgiveness, pardon; **V~ung!** sorry!, excuse me!

verzichten [fer'tsɪçtən] *vi:* **~ auf** *+akk* to forgo, to give up

ver'ziehen *(unreg) vt* to move ♦ *vt* to put out of shape; *(Kind)* to spoil; *(Pflanzen)* to thin out ♦ *vr* to go out of shape; *(Gesicht)* to contort; *(verschwinden)* to disappear; **das Gesicht ~** to pull a face

verzieren [fer'tsiːrən] *vt* to decorate, to ornament

Verzierung *f* decoration

verzinsen [fer'tsɪnzən] *vt* to pay interest on

ver'zögern *vt* to delay

Ver'zögerung *f* delay, time lag; **~staktik** *f* delaying tactics *pl*

verzollen [fer'tsolən] *vt* to pay duty on

Verzug [fer'tsuːk] *m* delay

verzweif- [fer'tsvaɪf] *zW:* **~eln** *vi* to despair; **~elt** *adj* desperate; **V~lung** *f* despair

Veto ['veːto] **(-s, -s)** *nt* veto

Vetter ['fɛtər] **(-s, -n)** *m* cousin

vgl. *abk (= vergleiche)* cf.

v. H. *abk (= vom Hundert)* p.c.

vibrieren [vi'briːrən] *vi* to vibrate

Video ['viːdeo] *nt* video; **~gerät** *nt* video recorder; **~rekorder** *m* video recorder

Vieh [fiː] **(-(e)s)** *nt* cattle *pl*; **v~isch** *adj* bestial

viel [fiːl] *adj* a lot of, much ♦ *adv* a lot, much; **~ sagend** significant; **~ versprechend** promising; **~e** *pron pl* a lot of, many; **~ zu wenig** much too little; **~erlei** *adj* a great variety of; **~es** *pron* a lot; **~fach** *adj, adv* many times; **auf ~fachen Wunsch** at the request of many people; **V~falt** **(-)** *f* variety; **~fältig** *adj* varied, many-sided

vielleicht [fi'laɪçt] *adv* perhaps

viel- *zW:* **~mal(s)** *adv* many times; **danke ~mals** many thanks; **~mehr** *adv* rather, on the contrary; **~seitig** *adj* many-sided

vier [fiːr] *num* four; **V~eck** **(-(e)s, -e)** *nt* four-sided figure; *(gleichseitig)* square; **~eckig** *adj* four-sided; square; **V~takt-motor** *m* four-stroke engine; **~te(r, s)**

['fiːɐtə(r, s)] *adj* fourth; **V~tel** ['fɪrtəl] (-s, -) *nt* quarter; **V~teljahr** *nt* quarter; **~teljährlich** *adj* quarterly; **~teln** *vt* to divide into four; (*Kuchen usw*) to divide into quarters; **V~telstunde** *f* quarter of an hour; **~zehn** ['fɪrtseːn] *num* fourteen; **in ~zehn Tagen** in a fortnight; **~zehntägig** *adj* fortnightly; **~zig** ['fɪrtsɪç] *num* forty

Villa ['vɪla] (-, **Villen**) *f* villa

violett [vio'lɛt] *adj* violet

Violin- [vio'liːn] *zW:* **~e** *f* violin; **~schlüssel** *m* treble clef

virtuell [vɪrtu'ɛl] *adj* (*COMPUT*) virtual; **~e Realität** virtual reality

Virus ['viːrʊs] (-, **Viren**) *m od nt* (*auch COMPUT*) virus

Visa ['viːza] *pl von* **Visum**

vis-a-vis ▲, **vis-à-vis** [viza'viː] *adv* opposite

Visen ['viːzən] *pl von* **Visum**

Visier [vi'ziːr] (-s, -e) *nt* gunsight; (*am Helm*) visor

Visite [vi'ziːtə] *f* (*MED*) visit; **~nkarte** *f* visiting card

Visum ['viːzʊm] (-s, **Visa** *od* **Visen**) *nt* visa

vital [vi'taːl] *adj* lively, full of life, vital

Vitamin [vita'miːn] (-s, -e) *nt* vitamin

Vogel ['foːgəl] (-s, ⁼) *m* bird; **einen ~ haben** (*umg*) to have bats in the belfry; **jdm den ~ zeigen** (*umg*) to tap one's forehead (*meaning that one thinks sb stupid*); **~bauer** *nt* birdcage; **~perspektive** *f* bird's-eye view; **~scheuche** *f* scarecrow

Vokabel [vo'kaːbəl] (-, -n) *f* word

Vokabular [vokabu'laːr] (-s, -e) *nt* vocabulary

Vokal [vo'kaːl] (-s, -e) *m* vowel

Volk [fɔlk] (-(e)s, ⁼er) *nt* people; nation

Völker- ['fœlkər] *zW:* **~recht** *nt* international law; **v~rechtlich** *adj* according to international law; **~verständigung** *f* international understanding

i *The* **Volkshochschule** *(VHS) is an institution which offers Adult Education classes. No set qualifications are necessary*

to attend. For a small fee adults can attend both vocational and non-vocational classes in the day-time or evening.

Volks- *zW:* **~entscheid** *m* referendum; **~fest** *nt* fair; **~hochschule** *f* adult education classes *pl*; **~lied** *nt* folksong; **~republik** *f* people's republic; **~schule** *f* elementary school; **~tanz** *m* folk dance; **~vertreter(in)** *m(f)* people's representative; **~wirtschaft** *f* economics *sg*

voll [fɔl] *adj* full; **etw ~ machen** to fill sth up; **~ tanken** to fill up; **~ und ganz** completely; **jdn für ~ nehmen** (*umg*) to take sb seriously; **~auf** *adv* amply; **V~bart** *m* full beard; **V~beschäftigung** *f* full employment; **~'bringen** (*unreg*) *vt insep* to accomplish; **~'enden** *vt insep* to finish, to complete; **~endet** *adj* (*~kommen*) completed; **~ends** ['fɔlɛnts] *adv* completely; **V~'endung** *f* completion

Volleyball ['vɔlibal] *m* volleyball

Vollgas *nt:* **mit ~** at full throttle; **~ geben** to step on it

völlig ['fœlɪç] *adj* complete ♦ *adv* completely

voll- *zW:* **~jährig** *adj* of age; **V~kaskoversicherung** ['fɔlkaskofɛrziçərʊŋ] *f* fully comprehensive insurance; **~'kommen** *adj* perfect; **V~'kommenheit** *f* perfection; **V~kornbrot** *nt* wholemeal bread; **V~macht** (-, -en) *f* authority, full powers *pl*; **V~milch** *f* (*KOCH*) full-cream milk; **V~mond** *m* full moon; **V~pension** *f* full board; **~ständig** ['fɔlʃtɛndɪç] *adj* complete; **~'strecken** *vt insep* to execute; **~tanken** △ *vt, vi siehe* **voll**; **V~waschmittel** *nt* detergent;. **V~wertkost** *f* wholefood; **~zählig** ['fɔlsɛːlɪç] *adj* complete; in full number; **~'ziehen** (*unreg*) *vt insep* to carry out ♦ *vr insep* to happen; **V~'zug** *m* execution

Volumen [vo'luːmən] (-s, - *od* **Volumina**) *nt* volume

vom [fɔm] = **von dem**

von [fɔn] *präp +dat* **1** (*Ausgangspunkt*) from;

von from ... to; **von morgens bis abends** from morning till night; **von ... nach ...** from ... to ...; **von ... an** from ...; **von ... aus** from ...; **von dort aus** from there; **etw von sich aus tun** to do sth of one's own accord; **von mir aus** (*umg*) if you like, I don't mind; **von wo/wann ...?** where/when ... from?

2 (*Ursache, im Passiv*) by; **ein Gedicht von Schiller** a poem by Schiller; **von etw müde** tired from sth

3 (*als Genitiv*) of; **ein Freund von mir** a friend of mine; **nett von dir** nice of you; **jeweils zwei von zehn** two out of every ten

4 (*über*) about; **er erzählte vom Urlaub** he talked about his holiday

5: von wegen! (*umg*) no way!

voneinander *adv* from each other

vor [fo:r] *prap +dat* **1** (*raumlich*) in front of; **vor der Kirche links abbiegen** turn left before the church

2 (*zeitlich*) before; **ich war vor ihm da** I was there before him; **vor 2 Tagen** 2 days ago; **5 (Minuten) vor 4** 5 (minutes) to 4; **vor kurzem** a little while ago

3 (*Ursache*) with; **vor Wut/Liebe** with rage/love; **vor Hunger sterben** to die of hunger; **vor lauter Arbeit** because of work

4: vor allem, vor allen Dingen most of all

♦ *präp +akk* (*raumlich*) in front of

♦ *adv:* **vor und zurück** backwards and forwards

Vorabend ['fo:ra:bənt] *m* evening before, eve

voran [fo'ran] *adv* before, ahead; **mach ~!** get on with it!; **~gehen** (*unreg*) *vi* to go ahead; **einer Sache** *dat* **~gehen** to precede sth; **~kommen** (*unreg*) *vi* to come along, to make progress

Voranschlag ['fo:ranʃla:k] *m* estimate

Vorarbeiter ['fo:rarbaitər] *m* foreman

voraus [fo'raus] *adv* ahead; (*zeitlich*) in advance; **jdm ~ sein** to be ahead of sb; **im V~** in advance; **~gehen** (*unreg*) *vi* to go (on) ahead; (*fig*) to precede; **~haben** (*unreg*) *vt:* **jdm etw ~haben** to have the edge on sb in sth; **V~sage** *f* prediction; **~sagen** *vt* to predict; **~sehen** (*unreg*) *vt* to foresee; **~setzen** *vt* to assume; **~gesetzt, dass ...** provided that ...; **V~setzung** *f* requirement, prerequisite; **V~sicht** *f* foresight; **aller V~sicht nach** in all probability; **~sichtlich** *adv* probably

Vorbehalt ['fo:rbəhalt] (-(e)s, -e) *m* reservation, proviso; **v~en** (*unreg*) *vt:* **sich/jdm etw v~en** to reserve sth (for o.s.)/for sb; **v~los** *adj* unconditional ♦ *adv* unconditionally

vorbei [for'bai] *adv* by, past; **das ist ~** that's over; **~gehen** (*unreg*) *vi* to pass by, to go past; **~kommen** (*unreg*) *vi:* **bei jdm ~kommen** to drop in *od* call in on sb

vor- *zW:* **~belastet** ['fo:rbəlastət] *adj* (*fig*) handicapped; **~bereiten** *vt* to prepare; **V~bereitung** *f* preparation; **V~bestellung** *f* advance order; (*von Platz, Tisch etc*) advance booking; **~bestraft** ['fo:rbəʃtra:ft] *adj* previously convicted, with a record

vorbeugen ['fo:rbɔygən] *vt, vr* to lean forward ♦ *vi +dat* to prevent; **~d** *adj* preventive

Vorbeugung *f* prevention; **zur ~ gegen** for the prevention of

Vorbild ['fo:rbilt] *nt* model; **sich** *dat* **jdn zum ~ nehmen** to model o.s. on sb; **v~lich** *adj* model, ideal

vorbringen ['fo:rbrɪŋən] (*unreg*) *vt* to advance, to state

Vorder- ['fɔrdər] *zW:* **~achse** *f* front axle; **v~e(r, s)** *adj* front; **~grund** *m* foreground; **~mann** (*pl* **-männer**) *m* man in front; **jdn auf ~mann bringen** (*umg*) to get sb to shape up; **~seite** *f* front (side); **v~ste(r, s)** *adj* front

vordrängen ['fo:rdrɛŋən] *vr* to push to the front

voreilig ['fo:railiç] *adj* hasty, rash

voreinander [fo:rai'nandər] *adv* (*räumlich*)

in front of each other

voreingenommen ['fo:r|aɪngənɔmən] *adj* biased; **V~heit** *f* bias

vorenthalten ['fo:r|ɛnthaltən] (*unreg*) *vt*: **jdm etw ~** to withhold sth from sb

vorerst ['fo:r|e:rst] *adv* for the moment *od* present

Vorfahr ['fo:rfa:r] (**-en, -en**) *m* ancestor

vorfahren (*unreg*) *vi* to drive (on) ahead; (*vors Haus etc*) to drive up

Vorfahrt *f* (*AUT*) right of way; **~ achten!** give way!

Vorfahrts- *zW*: **~regel** *f* right of way; **~schild** *nt* give way sign; **~straße** *f* major road

Vorfall ['fo:rfal] *m* incident; **v~en** (*unreg*) *vi* to occur

vorfinden ['fo:rfɪndən] (*unreg*) *vt* to find

Vorfreude ['fo:rfrɔʏdə] *f* (joyful) anticipation

vorführen ['fo:rfy:rən] *vt* to show, to display; **dem Gericht ~** to bring before the court

Vorgabe ['fo:rga:bə] *f* (*SPORT*) start, handicap ♦ *in zW* (*COMPUT*) default

Vorgang ['fo:rgaŋ] *m* course of events; (*bes SCI*) process

Vorgänger(in) ['fo:rgɛŋər(ɪn)] (**-s, -**) *m(f)* predecessor

vorgeben ['fo:rge:bən] (*unreg*) *vt* to pretend, to use as a pretext; (*SPORT*) to give an advantage *od* a start of

vorgefertigt ['fo:rgəfɛrtɪçt] *adj* prefabricated

vorgehen ['fo:rge:ən] (*unreg*) *vi* (*voraus*) to go (on) ahead; (*nach vorn*) to go up front; (*handeln*) to act, to proceed; (*Uhr*) to be fast; (*Vorrang haben*) to take precedence; (*passieren*) to go on

Vorgehen (-s) *nt* action

Vorgeschichte ['fo:rgəʃɪçtə] *f* past history

Vorgeschmack ['fo:rgəʃmak] *m* foretaste

Vorgesetzte(r) ['fo:rgəzɛtstə(r)] *f(m)* superior

vorgestern ['fo:rgɛstərn] *adv* the day before yesterday

vorhaben ['fo:rha:bən] (*unreg*) *vt* to intend; **hast du schon was vor?** have you got anything on?; **V~ (-s, -)** *nt* intention

vorhalten ['fo:rhaltən] (*unreg*) *vt* to hold *od* put up ♦ *vi* to last; **jdm etw ~** (*fig*) to reproach sb for sth

vorhanden [fo:r'handən] *adj* existing; (*erhältlich*) available

Vorhang ['fo:rhaŋ] *m* curtain

Vorhängeschloss ▲ ['fo:rhɛŋəʃlɔs] *nt* padlock

vorher [fo:r'he:r] *adv* before(hand); **~bestimmen** *vt* (*Schicksal*) to preordain; **~gehen** (*unreg*) *vi* to precede; **~ig** *adj* previous

Vorherrschaft ['fo:rhɛrʃaft] *f* predominance, supremacy

vorherrschen ['fo:rhɛrʃən] *vi* to predominate

vorher- [fo:r'he:r] *zW*: **V~sage** *f* forecast; **~sagen** *vt* to forecast, to predict; **~sehbar** *adj* predictable; **~sehen** (*unreg*) *vt* to foresee

vorhin [fo:r'hɪn] *adv* not long ago, just now; **V~ein** ▲ *adv*: **im V~ein** beforehand

vorig ['fo:rɪç] *adj* previous, last

Vorkämpfer(in) ['fo:rkɛmpfər(ɪn)] *m(f)* pioneer

Vorkaufsrecht ['fo:rkaʊfsrɛçt] *nt* option to buy

Vorkehrung ['fo:rke:rʊŋ] *f* precaution

vorkommen ['fo:rkɔmən] (*unreg*) *vi* to come forward; (*geschehen, sich finden*) to occur; (*scheinen*) to seem (to be); **sich** *dat* **dumm** *etc* **~** to feel stupid *etc*; **V~ (-s, -)** *nt* occurrence

Vorkriegs- ['fo:rkri:ks] *in zW* prewar

Vorladung ['fo:rla:dʊŋ] *f* summons *sg*

Vorlage ['fo:rla:gə] *f* model, pattern; (*Gesetzesvorlage*) bill; (*SPORT*) pass

vorlassen ['fo:rlasən] (*unreg*) *vt* to admit; (*vorgehen lassen*) to allow to go in front

vorläufig ['fo:rlɔʏfɪç] *adj* temporary, provisional

vorlaut ['fo:rlaʊt] *adj* impertinent, cheeky

vorlesen ['fo:rle:zən] (*unreg*) *vt* to read (out)

Vorlesung *f* (*UNIV*) lecture

vorletzte(r, s) ['fo:rlɛtstə(r, s)] *adj* last but one

vorlieb [fo:r'li:p] *adv*: **~ nehmen mit** to

make do with

Vorliebe ['foːrliːbə] *f* preference, partiality

vorliegen ['foːrliːgən] (*unreg*) *vi* to be (here); **etw liegt jdm vor** sb has sth; **~d** *adj* present, at issue

vormachen ['foːrmaxən] *vt*: **jdm etw ~** to show sb how to do sth; (*fig*) to fool sb; to have sb on

Vormachtstellung ['foːrmaxtʃtɛluŋ] *f* supremacy, hegemony

Vormarsch ['foːrmarʃ] *m* advance

vormerken ['foːrmɛrkən] *vt* to book

Vormittag ['foːrmɪtaːk] *m* morning; **v~s** *adv* in the morning, before noon

vorn [fɔrn] *adv* in front; **von ~ anfangen** to start at the beginning; **nach ~** to the front

Vorname ['foːrnaːmə] *m* first name, Christian name

vorne ['fɔrnə] *adv* = **vorn**

vornehm ['foːrneːm] *adj* distinguished; refined; elegant

vornehmen (*unreg*) *vt* (*fig*) to carry out; **sich** *dat* **etw ~** to start on sth; (*beschließen*) to decide to do sth; **sich** *dat* **jdn ~** to tell sb off

vornherein ['fɔrnhɛraɪn] *adv*: **von ~** from the start

Vorort ['foːrʔɔrt] *m* suburb

Vorrang ['foːrraŋ] *m* precedence, priority; **v~ig** *adj* of prime importance, primary

Vorrat ['foːrraːt] *m* stock, supply

vorrätig ['foːrreːtɪç] *adj* in stock

Vorratskammer *f* pantry

Vorrecht ['foːrreçt] *nt* privilege

Vorrichtung ['foːrrɪçtuŋ] *f* device, contrivance

vorrücken ['foːrrykən] *vi* to advance ♦ *vt* to move forward

Vorsaison ['foːrzɛzõː] *f* early season

Vorsatz ['foːrzats] *m* intention; (*JUR*) intent; **einen ~ fassen** to make a resolution

vorsätzlich ['foːrzɛtslɪç] *adj* intentional; (*JUR*) premeditated ♦ *adv* intentionally

Vorschau ['foːrʃau] *f* (*RADIO, TV*) (programme) preview; (*Film*) trailer

Vorschlag ['foːrʃlaːk] *m* suggestion, proposal; **v~en** (*unreg*) *vt* to suggest, to

propose

vorschreiben ['foːrʃraɪbən] (*unreg*) *vt* to prescribe, to specify

Vorschrift ['foːrʃrɪft] *f* regulation(s); rule(s); (*Anweisungen*) instruction(s); **Dienst nach ~** work-to-rule; **v~smäßig** *adj* as per regulations/instructions

Vorschuss ▲ ['foːrʃʊs] *m* advance

vorsehen ['foːrzeːən] (*unreg*) *vt* to provide for, to plan ♦ *vr* to take care, to be careful ♦ *vi* to be visible

Vorsehung *f* providence

Vorsicht ['foːrzɪçt] *f* caution, care; **~!** look out!, take care!; (*auf Schildern*) caution!, danger!; **~, Stufe!** mind the step!; **v~ig** *adj* cautious, careful; **v~shalber** *adv* just in case

Vorsilbe ['foːrzɪlbə] *f* prefix

vorsingen ['foːrzɪŋən] *vt* (*vor Zuhörern*) to sing (to); (*in Prüfung, für Theater etc*) to audition (for) ♦ *vi* to sing

Vorsitz ['foːrzɪts] *m* chair(manship); **~ende(r)** *f(m)* chairman(-woman)

Vorsorge ['foːrzɔrgə] *f* precaution(s), provision(s); **v~n** *vi*: **v~n für** to make provision(s) for; **~untersuchung** *f* check-up

vorsorglich ['foːrzɔrklɪç] *adv* as a precaution

Vorspeise ['foːrʃpaɪzə] *f* hors d'oeuvre, appetizer

Vorspiel ['foːrʃpiːl] *nt* prelude

vorspielen *vt*: **jdm etw ~** (*MUS*) to play sth for *od* to sb ♦ *vi* (*zur Prüfung etc*) to play for *od* to sb

vorsprechen ['foːrʃprɛçən] (*unreg*) *vt* to say out loud, to recite ♦ *vi*: **bei jdm ~** to call on sb

Vorsprung ['foːrʃpruŋ] *m* projection, ledge; (*fig*) advantage, start

Vorstadt ['foːrʃtat] *f* suburbs *pl*

Vorstand ['foːrʃtant] *m* executive committee; (*COMM*) board (of directors); (*Person*) director, head

vorstehen ['foːrʃteːən] (*unreg*) *vi* to project; **einer Sache** *dat* **~** (*fig*) to be the head of sth

vorstell- ['foːrʃtɛl] *zW*: **~bar** *adj*

Spelling Reform: ▲ *new spelling* △ *old spelling (to be phased out)*

conceivable; **~en** vt to put forward; (*bekannt machen*) to introduce; (*darstellen*) to represent; **~en vor** +*akk* to put in front of; **sich** *dat* **etw ~en** to imagine sth; **V~ung** f (*Bekanntmachen*) introduction; (*THEAT etc*) performance; (*Gedanke*) idea, thought

vorstoßen ['fo:rʃtoːsən] (*unreg*) vi (*ins Unbekannte*) to venture (forth)

Vorstrafe ['fo:rʃtraːfə] f previous conviction

Vortag ['fo:rtak] m: **am ~ einer Sache** *gen* on the day before sth

vortäuschen ['fo:rtɔyʃən] vt to feign, to pretend

Vorteil ['fo:rtail] (**-s, -e**) m: **~ (gegenüber)** advantage (over); **im ~ sein** to have the advantage; **v~haft** adj advantageous

Vortrag ['fo:rtra:k] (**-(e)s, Vorträge**) m talk, lecture; **v~en** [-gən] (*unreg*) vt to carry forward; (*fig*) to recite; (*Rede*) to deliver; (*Lied*) to perform; (*Meinung etc*) to express

vortreten ['fo:rtre:tən] (*unreg*) vi to step forward; (*Augen etc*) to protrude

vorüber [fo'ry:bər] adv past, over; **~gehen** (*unreg*) vi to pass (by); **~gehen an** +*dat* (*fig*) to pass over; **~gehend** adj temporary, passing

Vorurteil ['fo:rʔurtail] nt prejudice

Vorverkauf ['fo:rferkaʊf] m advance booking

Vorwahl ['fo:rva:l] f preliminary election; (*TEL*) dialling code

Vorwand ['fo:rvant] (**-(e)s, Vorwände**) m pretext

vorwärts ['fo:rverts] adv forward; **~ gehen** to progress; **V~gang** m (*AUT etc*) forward gear; **~ kommen** to get on, to make progress

Vorwäsche f prewash

vorweg [fo:r'vek] adv in advance; **~nehmen** (*unreg*) vt to anticipate

vorweisen ['fo:rvaizən] (*unreg*) vt to show, to produce

vorwerfen ['fo:rverfən] (*unreg*) vt: **jdm etw ~** to reproach sb for sth, to accuse sb of sth; **sich** *dat* **nichts vorzuwerfen haben** to have nothing to reproach o.s. with

vorwiegend ['fo:rvi:gənt] adj predominant ♦ adv predominantly

vorwitzig ['fo:rvɪtsɪç] adj (*Mensch, Bemerkung*) cheeky

Vorwort ['fo:rvɔrt] (**-(e)s, -e**) nt preface

Vorwurf ['fo:rvʊrf] m reproach; **jdm/sich Vorwürfe machen** to reproach sb/o.s.; **v~svoll** adj reproachful

vorzeigen ['fo:rtsaigən] vt to show, to produce

vorzeitig ['fo:rtsaitɪç] adj premature

vorziehen ['fo:rtsi:ən] (*unreg*) vt to pull forward; (*Gardinen*) to draw; (*lieber haben*) to prefer

Vorzimmer ['fo:rtsɪmər] nt (*Büro*) outer office

Vorzug ['fo:rtsu:k] m preference; (*gute Eigenschaft*) merit, good quality; (*Vorteil*) advantage

vorzüglich [fo:r'tsy:klɪç] adj excellent

Vorzugspreis m special discount price

vulgär [vʊl'gɛːr] adj vulgar

Vulkan [vʊl'ka:n] (**-s, -e**) m volcano

W, w

Waage ['va:gə] f scales pl; (*ASTROL*) Libra; **w~recht** adj horizontal

Wabe ['va:bə] f honeycomb

wach [vax] adj awake; (*fig*) alert; **W~e** f guard, watch; **W~e halten** to keep watch; **W~e stehen** to stand guard; **~en** vi to be awake; (*Wache halten*) to guard

Wachs [vaks] (**-es, -e**) nt wax

wachsam ['vaxza:m] adj watchful, vigilant, alert

wachsen (*unreg*) vi to grow

Wachstuch ['vakstu:x] nt oilcloth

Wachstum ['vakstu:m] (**-s**) nt growth

Wächter ['veçtər] (**-s, -**) m guard, warden, keeper; (*Parkplatzwächter*) attendant

wackel- ['vakəl] zW: **~ig** adj shaky, wobbly; **W~kontakt** m loose connection; **~n** vi to shake; (*fig: Position*) to be shaky

wacker ['vakər] adj valiant, stout ♦ adv well, bravely

Wade ['va:də] f (ANAT) calf

Waffe ['vafə] f weapon

Waffel ['vafəl] (-, -n) f waffle; wafer

Waffen- zW: **~schein** m gun licence; **~stillstand** m armistice, truce

Wagemut ['va:gəmu:t] m daring

wagen ['va:gən] vt to venture, to dare

Wagen ['va:gən] (-s, -) m vehicle; (Auto) car; (EISENB) carriage; (Pferdewagen) cart; **~heber** (-s, -) m jack

Waggon [va'gõ:] (-s, -s) m carriage; (Güterwaggon) goods van, freight truck (US)

Wagnis ['va:knɪs] (-ses, -se) nt risk

Wagon ▲ [va'gõ:, va'goːn] (-s, -s) m = Waggon

Wahl [va:l] (-, -en) f choice; (POL) election; **zweite ~** (COMM) seconds pl

wähl- ['vɛːl] zW: **~bar** adj eligible; **~en** vt, vi to choose; (POL) to elect, to vote (for); (TEL) to dial; **W~er(in)** (-s, -) m(f) voter; **~erisch** adj fastidious, particular

Wahl- zW: **~fach** nt optional subject; **~gang** m ballot; **~kabine** f polling booth; **~kampf** m election campaign; **~kreis** m constituency; **~lokal** nt polling station; **w~los** adv at random; **~recht** nt franchise; **~spruch** m motto; **~urne** f ballot box

Wahn [va:n] (-(e)s) m delusion; folly; **~sinn** m madness; **w~sinnig** adj insane, mad ♦ adv (umg) incredibly

wahr [va:r] adj true

wahren vt to maintain, to keep

während ['vɛːrənt] präp +gen during ♦ konj while; **~dessen** adv meanwhile

wahr- zW: **~haben** (unreg) vt: **etw nicht ~haben wollen** to refuse to admit sth; **~haft** adv (tatsächlich) truly; **~haftig** [va:r'haftɪç] adj true, real ♦ adv really; **W~heit** f truth; **~nehmen** (unreg) vt to perceive, to observe; **W~nehmung** f perception; **~sagen** vi to prophesy, to tell fortunes; **W~sager(in)** (-s, -) m(f) fortune teller; **~scheinlich** [va:r'ʃaɪnlɪç] adj probable ♦ adv probably; **W~'scheinlichkeit** f probability; **aller W~scheinlichkeit nach** in all probability

Währung ['vɛːrʊŋ] f currency

Wahrzeichen nt symbol

Waise ['vaɪzə] f orphan; **~nhaus** nt orphanage

Wald [valt] (-(e)s, ⁼er) m wood(s); (groß) forest; **~brand** m forest fire; **~sterben** nt trees dying due to pollution

Wales [weɪlz] (-) nt Wales

Wal(fisch) ['va:l(fɪʃ)] (-(e)s, -e) m whale

Waliser [va'li:zər] (-s, -) m Welshman; **Waliserin** [va'li:zərɪn] f Welshwoman; **walisisch** [va'li:zɪʃ] adj Welsh

Walkman ['wɔːkman] (®; -s, **Walkmen**) m Walkman ®, personal stereo

Wall [val] (-(e)s, ⁼e) m embankment; (Bollwerk) rampart

Wallfahr- zW: **~er(in)** m(f) pilgrim; **~t** f pilgrimage

Walnuss ▲ ['valnʊs] f walnut

Walross ▲ ['valrɔs] nt walrus

Walze ['valtsə] f (Gerät) cylinder; (Fahrzeug) roller; **w~n** vt to roll (out)

wälzen ['vɛltsən] vt to roll (over); (Bücher) to hunt through; (Probleme) to deliberate on ♦ vr to wallow; (vor Schmerzen) to roll about; (im Bett) to toss and turn

Walzer ['valtsər] (-s, -) m waltz

Wand [vant] (-, ⁼e) f wall; (Trennwand) partition; (Bergwand) precipice

Wandel ['vandəl] (-s) m change; **w~bar** adj changeable, variable; **w~n** vt, vr to change ♦ vi (gehen) to walk

Wander- ['vandər] zW: **~er** (-s, -) m hiker, rambler; **~karte** f map of country walks; **w~n** vi to hike; (Blick) to wander; (Gedanken) to stray; **~schaft** f travelling; **~ung** f walk, hike; **~weg** m trail, walk

Wandlung f change, transformation

Wange ['vaŋə] f cheek

wanken ['vankən] vi to stagger; (fig) to waver

wann [van] adv when

Wanne ['vanə] f tub

Wanze ['vantsə] f bug

Wappen ['vapən] (-s, -) nt coat of arms, crest; **~kunde** f heraldry

war etc [va:r] vb siehe **sein**

Ware ['va:rə] f ware

Waren- *zW:* **~haus** *nt* department store;
~lager *nt* stock, store; **~muster** *nt* trade
sample; **~probe** *f* sample; **~sendung** *f*
trade sample (*sent by post*); **~zeichen** *nt*:
(eingetragenes) ~zeichen (registered)
trademark

warf *etc* [varf] *vb siehe* **werfen**

warm [varm] *adj* warm; (*Essen*) hot

Wärm- ['verm] *zW:* **~e** *f* warmth; **w~en** *vt,*
vr to warm (up), to heat (up); **~flasche** *f*
hot-water bottle

Warn- ['varn] *zW:* **~blinkanlage** *f* (*AUT*)
hazard warning lights *pl*; **~dreieck** *nt*
warning triangle; **w~en** *vt* to warn; **~ung** *f*
warning

warten ['vartən] *vi:* **~ (auf** +*akk*) to wait
(for); **auf sich ~ lassen** to take a long time

Wärter(in) ['vertər(in)] (**-s, -**) *m(f)* attendant

Warte- ['vartə] *zW:* **~saal** *m* (*EISENB*) waiting
room; **~zimmer** *nt* waiting room

Wartung *f* servicing; service; **~ und
Instandhaltung** maintenance

warum [va'rom] *adv* why

Warze ['vartsə] *f* wart

was [vas] *pron* what; (*umg: etwas*)
something; **~ für (ein) ...** what sort of ...

waschbar *adj* washable

Waschbecken *nt* washbasin

Wäsche ['veʃə] *f* wash(ing); (*Bettwäsche*)
linen; (*Unterwäsche*) underclothing

waschecht *adj* colourfast; (*fig*) genuine

Wäsche- *zW:* **~klammer** *f* clothes peg
(*BRIT*), clothespin (*US*); **~leine** *f* washing
line (*BRIT*)

waschen ['vaʃən] (*unreg*) *vt, vi* to wash ♦ *vr*
to (have a) wash; **sich** *dat* **die Hände ~** to
wash one's hands

Wäsche'rei *f* laundry

Wasch- *zW:* **~gelegenheit** *f* washing
facilities; **~küche** *f* laundry room;
~lappen *m* face flannel, washcloth (*US*);
(*umg*) sissy; **~maschine** *f* washing
machine; **~mittel** *nt* detergent, washing
powder; **~pulver** *nt* detergent, washing
powder; **~raum** *m* washroom; **~salon** *m*
Launderette ®

Wasser ['vasər] (**-s, -**) *nt* water; **~ball** *m*

water polo; **w~dicht** *adj* waterproof; **~fall**
m waterfall; **~farbe** *f* watercolour; **~hahn**
m tap, faucet (*US*); **~kraftwerk** *nt*
hydroelectric power station; **~leitung** *f*
water pipe; **~mann** *n* (*ASTROL*) Aquarius

wässern ['vesərn] *vt, vi* to water

Wasser- *zW:* **w~scheu** *adj* afraid of (the)
water; **~ski** ['vasərʃiː] *nt* water-skiing;
~stoff *m* hydrogen; **~waage** *f* spirit level;
~zeichen *nt* watermark

wässrig ▲ ['vesrɪç] *adj* watery

Watt [vat] (**-(e)s, -en**) *nt* mud flats *pl*

Watte *f* cotton wool, absorbent cotton (*US*)

WC ['veː'tseː] (**-s, -s**) *nt abk* W.C.

Web [veb] (**-s**) *nt* (*COMPUT*) **das ~** the Web

Web- ['veːb] *zW:* **w~en** (*unreg*) *vt* to weave;
~er (**-s, -**) *m* weaver; **~e'rei** *f* (*Betrieb*)
weaving mill

Website ['vebsaɪt] *f* (*COMPUT*) website

Webstuhl ['veːpʃtuːl] *m* loom

Wechsel ['veksəl] (**-s, -**) *m* change; (*COMM*)
bill of exchange; **~geld** *nt* change; **w~haft**
adj (*Wetter*) variable; **~jahre** *pl* change of
life *sg;* **~kurs** *m* rate of exchange; **w~n** *vt*
to change; (*Blicke*) to exchange ♦ *vi* to
change; to vary; (*Geldwechseln*) to have
change; **~strom** *m* alternating current;
~stube *f* bureau de change; **~wirkung** *f*
interaction

Weck- ['vek] *zW:* **~dienst** *m* alarm call
service; **w~en** *vt* to wake (up); to call; **~er**
(**-s, -**) *m* alarm clock

wedeln ['veːdəln] *vi* (*mit Schwanz*) to wag;
(*mit Fächer etc*) to wave

weder ['veːdər] *konj* neither; **~ ... noch ...**
neither ... nor ...

Weg [veːk] (**-(e)s, -e**) *m* way; (*Pfad*) path;
(*Route*) route; **sich auf den ~ machen** to
be on one's way; **jdm aus dem ~ gehen**
to keep out of sb's way; *siehe* **zuwege**

weg [vek] *adv* away, off; **über etw** *akk* **~
sein** to be over sth; **er war schon ~** he
had already left; **Finger ~!** hands off!

wegbleiben (*unreg*) *vi* to stay away

wegen ['veːgən] *präp* +*gen* (*umg: +dat*)
because of

weg- ['vek] *zW:* **~fallen** (*unreg*) *vi* to be left

out; (*Ferien, Bezahlung*) to be cancelled; (*aufhören*) to cease; **~gehen** (*unreg*) *vi* to go away; to leave; **~lassen** (*unreg*) *vt* to leave out; **~laufen** (*unreg*) *vi* to run away *od* off; **~legen** *vt* to put aside; **~machen** (*umg*) *vt* to get rid of; **~müssen** (*unreg*, *umg*) *vi* to have to go; **~nehmen** (*unreg*) *vt* to take away; **~tun** (*unreg*) *vt* to put away; **W~weiser (-s, -)** *m* road sign, signpost; **~werfen** (*unreg*) *vt* to throw away

weh [veː] *adj* sore; **~(e)** *excl*: **~(e), wenn du ...** woe betide you if ...; **o ~!** oh dear!; **~e!** just you dare!

wehen *vt*, *vi* to blow; (*Fahnen*) to flutter

weh- *zW*: **~leidig** *adj* whiny, whining; **~mütig** *adj* melancholy

Wehr [veːr] **(-, -en)** *f*: **sich zur ~ setzen** to defend o.s.; **~dienst** *m* military service; **~dienstverweigerer** *m* ≈ conscientious objector; **w~en** *vr* to defend o.s.; **w~los** *adj* defenceless; **~pflicht** *f* compulsory military service; **w~pflichtig** *adj* liable for military service

---

Wehrdienst

> *Wehrdienst is military service which is still compulsory in Germany. All young men receive their call-up papers at 18 and all those pronounced physically fit are required to spend 10 months in the Bundeswehr. Conscientious objectors are allowed to do Zivildienst as an alternative, after presenting their case.*

---

wehtun ▲ [ˈveːtuːn] (*unreg*) *vt* to hurt, to be sore; **jdm/sich ~** to hurt sb/o.s.

Weib [vaɪp] **(-(e)s, -er)** *nt* woman, female; wife; **~chen** *nt* female; **w~lich** *adj* feminine

weich [vaɪç] *adj* soft; **W~e** *f* points *pl*; **~en** (*unreg*) *vi* to yield, to give way; **W~heit** *f* softness; **~lich** *adj* soft, namby-pamby

Weide [ˈvaɪdə] *f* (*Baum*) willow; (*Gras*) pasture; **w~n** *vi* to graze ♦ *vr*: **sich an etw** *dat* **w~n** to delight in sth

weigern [ˈvaɪgərn] *vr* to refuse

Weigerung [ˈvaɪgərʊŋ] *f* refusal

Weihe [ˈvaɪə] *f* consecration; (*Priesterweihe*) ordination; **w~n** *vt* to consecrate; to ordain

Weihnacht- *zW*: **~en (-)** *nt* Christmas; **w~lich** *adj* Christmas *cpd*

Weihnachts- *zW*: **~abend** *m* Christmas Eve; **~lied** *nt* Christmas carol; **~mann** *m* Father Christmas, Santa Claus; **~markt** *m* Christmas fair; **~tag** *m* Christmas Day; **zweiter ~tag** Boxing Day

---

Weihnachtsmarkt

> *The Weihnachtsmarkt is a market held in most large towns in Germany in the weeks prior to Christmas. People visit it to buy presents, toys and Christmas decorations, and to enjoy the festive atmosphere. Traditional Christmas food and drink can also be consumed there, for example, Lebkuchen and Glühwein.*

Weihwasser *nt* holy water

weil [vaɪl] *konj* because

Weile [ˈvaɪlə] **(-)** *f* while, short time

Wein [vaɪn] **(-(e)s, -e)** *m* wine; (*Pflanze*) vine; **~bau** *m* cultivation of vines; **~berg** *m* vineyard; **~bergschnecke** *f* snail; **~brand** *m* brandy

weinen *vt*, *vi* to cry; **das ist zum W~** it's enough to make you cry *od* weep

Wein- *zW*: **~glas** *nt* wine glass; **~karte** *f* wine list; **~lese** *f* vintage; **~probe** *f* wine-tasting; **~rebe** *f* vine; **w~rot** *adj* burgundy, claret, wine-red; **~stock** *m* vine; **~stube** *f* wine bar; **~traube** *f* grape

weise [ˈvaɪzə] *adj* wise

Weise *f* manner, way; (*Lied*) tune; **auf diese ~** in this way

weisen (*unreg*) *vt* to show

Weisheit [ˈvaɪshaɪt] *f* wisdom; **~szahn** *m* wisdom tooth

weiß [vaɪs] *adj* white ♦ *vb siehe* **wissen**; **W~bier** *nt* weissbier (*light, fizzy beer made using top-fermentation yeast*); **W~brot** *nt* white bread; **~en** *vt* to whitewash; **W~glut** *f* (*TECH*) incandescence; **jdn bis zur W~glut bringen** (*fig*) to make sb see red; **W~kohl**

---

m (white) cabbage; **W~wein** *m* white wine; **W~wurst** *f* veal sausage

weit [vaɪt] *adj* wide; (*Begriff*) broad; (*Reise, Wurf*) long ♦ *adv* far; **wie ~ ist es ...?** how far is it ...?; **in ~er Ferne** in the far distance; **~ blickend** far-seeing; **~ reichend** long-range; (*fig*) far-reaching; **~ verbreitet** widespread; **das geht zu ~** that's going too far; **~aus** *adv* by far; **~blickend** *adj* far-seeing; **W~e** *f* width; (*Raum*) space; (*von Entfernung*) distance; **~en** *vt, vr* to widen

weiter ['vaɪtər] *adj* wider; broader; farther (away); (*zusätzlich*) further ♦ *adv* further; **ohne ~es** without further ado; just like that; **~ nichts/niemand** nothing/nobody else; **~arbeiten** *vi* to go on working; **~bilden** *vr* to continue one's education; **~empfehlen** (*unreg*) *vt* to recommend (to others); **W~fahrt** *f* continuation of the journey; **~führen** *vi* (*Straße*) to lead on (to) ♦ *vt* (*fortsetzen*) to continue, carry on; **~gehen** (*unreg*) *vi* to go on; **~hin** *adv*: **etw ~hin tun** to go on doing sth; **~kommen** (*unreg*) *vi* (*fig: mit Arbeit*) to make progress; **~leiten** *vt* to pass on; **~machen** *vt, vi* to continue

weit- *zW*: **~gehend** *adj* considerable ♦ *adv* largely; **~läufig** *adj* (*Gebäude*) spacious; (*Erklärung*) lengthy; (*Verwandter*) distant; **~reichend** *adj* long-range; (*fig*) far-reaching; **~schweifig** *adj* long-winded; **~sichtig** *adj* (*MED*) long-sighted; (*fig*) far-sighted; **W~sprung** *m* long jump; **~verbreitet** *adj* widespread

Weizen ['vaɪtsən] (**-s, -**) *m* wheat

welche(r, s) *interrogativ pron* which; **welcher von beiden?** which (one) of the two?; **welchen hast du genommen?** which (one) did you take?; **welche eine ...!** what a ...!; **welche Freude!** what joy! ♦ *indef pron* some; (*in Fragen*) any; **ich habe welche** I have some; **haben Sie welche?** do you have any? ♦ *relativ pron* (*bei Menschen*) who; (*bei*

Sachen) which, that; **welche(r, s) auch immer** whoever/whichever/whatever

welk [vɛlk] *adj* withered; **~en** *vi* to wither

Welle ['vɛlə] *f* wave; (*TECH*) shaft

Wellen- *zW*: **~bereich** *m* waveband; **~länge** *f* (*auch fig*) wavelength; **~linie** *f* wavy line; **~sittich** *m* budgerigar

Welt [vɛlt] (**-, -en**) *f* world; **~all** *nt* universe; **~anschauung** *f* philosophy of life; **w~berühmt** *adj* world-famous; **~krieg** *m* world war; **w~lich** *adj* worldly; (*nicht kirchlich*) secular; **~macht** *f* world power; **~meister** *m* world champion; **~raum** *m* space; **~reise** *f* trip round the world; **~stadt** *f* metropolis; **w~weit** *adj* world-wide

wem [veːm] (*dat von* wer) *pron* to whom

wen [veːn] (*akk von* wer) *pron* whom

Wende ['vɛndə] *f* turn; (*Veränderung*) change; **~kreis** *m* (*GEOG*) tropic; (*AUT*) turning circle; **~ltreppe** *f* spiral staircase; **w~n** (*unreg*) *vt, vi, vr* to turn; **sich an jdn w~n** to go/come to sb

wendig ['vɛndɪç] *adj* (*Auto etc*) manœuvrable; (*fig*) agile

Wendung *f* turn; (*Redewendung*) idiom

wenig ['veːnɪç] *adj, adv* little; **~e** *pron pl* few *pl*; **~er** *adj* less; (*mit pl*) fewer ♦ *adv* less; **~ste(r, s)** *adj* least; **am ~sten** least; **~stens** *adv* at least

wenn [vɛn] *konj* **1** (*falls, bei Wünschen*) if; **wenn auch ..., selbst wenn ...** even if ...; **wenn ich doch ...** if only I ...
2 (*zeitlich*) when; **immer wenn** whenever

wennschon ['vɛnʃoːn] *adv*: **na ~** so what?; **~, dennschon!** in for a penny, in for a pound

wer [veːr] *pron* who

Werbe- ['vɛrbə] *zW*: **~fernsehen** *nt* commercial television; **~geschenk** *nt* gift (*from company*); (*zu Gekauftem*) free gift; **w~n** (*unreg*) *vt* to win; (*Mitglied*) to recruit ♦ *vi* to advertise; **um jdn/etw w~n** to try to win sb/sth; **für jdn/etw w~n** to promote sb/sth

Werbung f advertising; (*von Mitgliedern*) recruitment; **~ um jdn/etw** promotion of sb/sth

Werdegang ['veːrdəgaŋ] m (*Laufbahn*) development; (*beruflich*) career

---
SCHLÜSSELWORT
---

werden ['veːrdən] (*pt* **wurde**, *pp* **geworden** *od* (*bei Passiv*) **worden**) *vi* to become; **was ist aus ihm/aus der Sache geworden?** what became of him/it?; **es ist nichts/gut geworden** it came to nothing/turned out well; **es wird Nacht/Tag** it's getting dark/light; **mir wird kalt** I'm getting cold; **mir wird schlecht** I feel ill; **Erster werden** to come *od* be first; **das muss anders werden** that'll have to change; **rot/zu Eis werden** to turn red/to ice; **was willst du (mal) werden?** what do you want to be?; **die Fotos sind gut geworden** the photos have come out nicely

♦ *als Hilfsverb* **1** (*bei Futur*): **er wird es tun** he will *od* he'll do it; **er wird das nicht tun** he will not *od* he won't do it; **es wird gleich regnen** it's going to rain

2 (*bei Konjunktiv*): **ich würde ...** I would ...; **er würde gern ...** he would *od* he'd like to ...; **ich würde lieber ...** I would *od* I'd rather ...

3 (*bei Vermutung*): **sie wird in der Küche sein** she will be in the kitchen

4 (*bei Passiv*): **gebraucht werden** to be used; **er ist erschossen worden** he has *od* he's been shot; **mir wurde gesagt, dass ...** I was told that ...

---

werfen ['vɛrfən] (*unreg*) *vt* to throw

Werft [vɛrft] (-, **-en**) f shipyard, dockyard

Werk [vɛrk] (-(**e**)**s**, **-e**) *nt* work; (*Tätigkeit*) job; (*Fabrik, Mechanismus*) works *pl*; **ans ~ gehen** to set to work; **~statt** (-, **-stätten**) f workshop; (*AUT*) garage; **~tag** m working day; **w~tags** *adv* on working days; **w~tätig** *adj* working; **~zeug** *nt* tool

Wermut ['veːrmuːt] (-(**e**)**s**) m wormwood;

(*Wein*) vermouth

Wert [veːrt] (-(**e**)**s**, **-e**) m worth; (*FIN*) value; **~ legen auf** +*akk* to attach importance to; **es hat doch keinen ~** it's useless; **w~** *adj* worth; (*geschätzt*) dear; worthy; **das ist nichts/viel w~** it's not worth anything/it's worth a lot; **das ist es/er mir w~** it's/he's worth that to me; **~angabe** f declaration of value; **~brief** m registered letter (*containing sth of value*); **w~en** *vt* to rate; **~gegenstände** *mpl* valuables; **w~los** *adj* worthless; **~papier** *nt* security; **w~voll** *adj* valuable

Wesen ['veːzən] (-**s**, -) *nt* (*Geschöpf*) being; (*Natur, Charakter*) nature; **w~tlich** *adj* significant; (*beträchtlich*) considerable

weshalb [vɛsˈhalp] *adv* why

Wespe ['vɛspə] f wasp

wessen ['vɛsən] (*gen von* **wer**) *pron* whose

Weste ['vɛstə] f waistcoat, vest (*US*); (*Wollweste*) cardigan

West- *zW*: **~en** (-**s**) m west; **~europa** *nt* Western Europe; **w~lich** *adj* western ♦ *adv* to the west

weswegen [vɛsˈveːgən] *adv* why

wett [vɛt] *adj* even; **W~bewerb** m competition; **W~e** f bet, wager; **~en** *vt, vi* to bet

Wetter ['vɛtər] (-**s**, -) *nt* weather; **~bericht** m weather report; **~dienst** m meteorological service; **~lage** f (*weather*) situation; **~vorhersage** f weather forecast; **~warte** f weather station

Wett- *zW*: **~kampf** m contest; **~lauf** m race; **w~machen** *vt* to make good

wichtig ['vɪçtɪç] *adj* important; **W~keit** f importance

wickeln ['vɪkəln] *vt* to wind; (*Haare*) to set; (*Kind*) to change; **jdn/etw in etw** *akk* **~** to wrap sb/sth in sth

Wickelraum m mothers' (and babies') room

Widder ['vɪdər] (-**s**, -) m ram; (*ASTROL*) Aries

wider ['viːdər] *präp* +*akk* against; **~'fahren** (*unreg*) *vi* to happen; **~'legen** *vt* to refute

widerlich ['viːdərlɪç] *adj* disgusting, repulsive

wider- ['vi:dər] *zW:* **~rechtlich** *adj*
unlawful; **W~rede** *f* contradiction; **~'rufen**
(*unreg*) *vt insep* to retract; (*Anordnung*) to
revoke; (*Befehl*) to countermand; **~'setzen**
vr insep: **sich jdm/etw ~setzen** to oppose
sb/sth

widerspenstig ['vi:dərʃpɛnstɪç] *adj* wilful

wider- ['vi:dər] *zW:* **~spiegeln** *vt*
(*Entwicklung, Erscheinung*) to mirror, reflect
♦ *vr* to be reflected; **~'sprechen** (*unreg*) *vi*
insep: **jdm ~sprechen** to contradict sb

Widerspruch ['vi:dərʃprʊx] *m*
contradiction; **w~slos** *adv* without arguing

Widerstand ['vi:dərʃtant] *m* resistance

Widerstands- *zW:* **~bewegung** *f*
resistance (movement); **w~fähig** *adj*
resistant, tough; **w~los** *adj* unresisting

wider'stehen (*unreg*) *vi insep*: **jdm/etw ~**
to withstand sb/sth

wider- ['vi:dər] *zW:* **~wärtig** *adj* nasty,
horrid; **W~wille** *m*: **W~wille (gegen)**
aversion (to); **~willig** *adj* unwilling,
reluctant

widmen ['vɪtmən] *vt* to dedicate; to devote
♦ *vr* to devote o.s.

widrig ['vi:drɪç] *adj* (*Umstände*) adverse

SCHLÜSSELWORT
---

wie [vi:] *adv* how; **wie groß/schnell?** how
big/fast?; **wie wärs?** how about it?; **wie ist
er?** what's he like?; **wie gut du das
kannst!** you're very good at it; **wie bitte?**
pardon?; (*entrüstet*) I beg your pardon!;
und wie! and how!; **wie viel** how much;
wie viel Menschen how many people;
wie weit to what extent

♦ *konj* **1** (*bei Vergleichen*): **so schön wie ...**
as beautiful as ...; **wie ich schon sagte** as I
said; **wie du** like you; **singen wie ein ...** to
sing like a ...; **wie (zum Beispiel)** such as
(for example)

2 (*zeitlich*): **wie er das hörte, ging er**
when he heard that he left; **er hörte, wie
der Regen fiel** he heard the rain falling

---

wieder ['vi:dər] *adv* again; **~ da sein** to be
back (again); **~ aufbereiten** to recycle; **~**

aufnehmen to resume; **~ erkennen** to
recognize; **~ gutmachen** to make up for;
(*Fehler*) to put right; **~ herstellen** (*Ruhe,
Frieden etc*) to restore; **~ vereinigen** to
reunite; (*POL*) to reunify; **~ verwerten** to
recycle; **gehst du schon ~?** are you off
again?; **~ ein(e) ...** another ...; **W~aufbau**
m rebuilding; **~bekommen** (*unreg*) *vt* to
get back; **W~gabe** *f* reproduction;
~geben (*unreg*) *vt* (*zurückgeben*) to return;
(*Erzählung etc*) to repeat; (*Gefühle etc*) to
convey; **W~'gutmachung** *f* reparation;
~'herstellen (*Gesundheit, Gebäude*) to
restore; **~'holen** *vt insep* to repeat;
W~'holung *f* repetition; **W~hören** *nt*: **auf
W~hören** (*TEL*) goodbye; **W~kehr** (**-**) *f*
return; (*von Vorfall*) repetition, recurrence;
~sehen (*unreg*) *vt* to see again; **auf
W~sehen** goodbye; **~um** *adv* again;
(*andererseits*) on the other hand;
W~vereinigung *f* (*POL*) reunification;
W~wahl *f* re-election

Wiege ['vi:gə] *f* cradle; **w~n¹** *vt* (*schaukeln*)
to rock

wiegen² (*unreg*) *vt, vi* (*Gewicht*) to weigh

Wien [vi:n] *nt* Vienna

Wiese ['vi:zə] *f* meadow

Wiesel ['vi:zəl] (**-s, -**) *nt* weasel

wieso [vi:'zo:] *adv* why

wieviel △ [vi:'fi:l] *adj siehe* **wie**

wievielmal [vi:'fi:lma:l] *adv* how often

wievielte(r, s) *adj* (*bei Reihenfolge*) zum **~n Mal?** how
many times?; **den W~n haben wir?** what's
the date?; **an ~r Stelle?** in what place?;
der ~ Besucher war er? how many
visitors were there before him?

wild [vɪlt] *adj* wild; **W~ (-(e)s)** *nt* game;
W~e(r) ['vɪldə(r)] *f(m)* savage; **~ern** *vi* to
poach; **~'fremd** (*umg*) *adj* quite strange *od*
unknown; **W~heit** *f* wildness; **W~leder** *nt*
suede; **W~nis** (**-, -se**) *f* wilderness;
W~schwein *nt* (wild) boar

will *etc* [vɪl] *vb siehe* **wollen**

Wille ['vɪlə] (**-ns, -n**) *m* will; **w~n** *präp +gen*:
um ... w~n for the sake of ...; **w~nsstark**
adj strong-willed

will- *zW:* **~ig** *adj* willing; **W~kommen**

Rechtschreibreform: ▲ *neue Schreibung* △ *alte Schreibung (auslaufend)*

[vɪl'kɔmən] **(-s, -)** nt welcome; **~kommen** adj welcome; **jdn ~kommen heißen** to welcome sb; **~kürlich** adj arbitrary; (Bewegung) voluntary

wimmeln ['vɪməln] vi: **~ (von)** to swarm (with)

wimmern ['vɪmərn] vi to whimper

Wimper ['vɪmpər] **(-, -n)** f eyelash

Wimperntusche f mascara

Wind [vɪnt] **(-(e)s, -e)** m wind; **~beutel** m cream puff; (fig) rake; **~e** f (TECH) winch, windlass; (BOT) bindweed; **~el** ['vɪndəl] **(-, -n)** f nappy, diaper (US); **w~en** vi unpers to be windy ♦ vt (unreg) to wind; (Kranz) to weave; (entwinden) to twist ♦ vr (unreg) to wind; (Person) to writhe; **~energie** f wind energy; **w~ig** ['vɪndɪç] adj windy; (fig) dubious; **~jacke** f windcheater; **~mühle** f windmill; **~pocken** pl chickenpox sg; **~schutzscheibe** f (AUT) windscreen (BRIT), windshield (US); **~stärke** f wind force; **w~still** adj (Tag) still, windless; (Platz) sheltered; **~stille** f calm; **~stoß** m gust of wind

Wink [vɪnk] **(-(e)s, -e)** m (mit Hand) wave; (mit Kopf) nod; (Hinweis) hint

Winkel ['vɪnkəl] **(-s, -)** m (MATH) angle; (Gerät) set square; (in Raum) corner

winken ['vɪnkən] vt, vi to wave

winseln ['vɪnzəln] vi to whine

Winter ['vɪntər] **(-s, -)** m winter; **w~fest** adj (Pflanze) hardy; **~garten** m conservatory; **w~lich** adj wintry; **~reifen** m winter tyre; **~sport** m winter sports pl

Winzer ['vɪntsər] **(-s, -)** m vine grower

winzig ['vɪntsɪç] adj tiny

Wipfel ['vɪpfəl] **(-s, -)** m treetop

wir [viːr] pron we; **~ alle** all of us, we all

Wirbel ['vɪrbəl] **(-s, -)** m whirl, swirl; (Trubel) hurly-burly; (Aufsehen) fuss; (ANAT) vertebra; **w~n** vi to whirl, to swirl; **~säule** f spine

wird [vɪrt] vb siehe **werden**

wirfst etc [vɪrfst] vb siehe **werfen**

wirken ['vɪrkən] vi to have an effect; (erfolgreich sein) to work; (scheinen) to seem ♦ vt (Wunder) to work

wirklich ['vɪrklɪç] adj real ♦ adv really;

W~keit f reality

wirksam ['vɪrkzaːm] adj effective

Wirkstoff m (biologisch, chemisch, pflanzlich) active substance

Wirkung ['vɪrkʊŋ] f effect; **w~slos** adj ineffective; **w~slos bleiben** to have no effect; **w~svoll** adj effective

wirr [vɪr] adj confused, wild; **W~warr (-s)** m disorder, chaos

wirst [vɪrst] vb siehe **werden**

Wirt(in) [vɪrt(ɪn)] **(-(e)s, -e)** m(f) landlord(lady); **~schaft** f (Gaststätte) pub; (Haushalt) housekeeping; (eines Landes) economy; (umg: Durcheinander) mess; **w~schaftlich** adj economical; (POL) economic

Wirtschafts- zW: **~krise** f economic crisis; **~politik** f economic policy; **~prüfer** m chartered accountant; **~wunder** nt economic miracle

Wirtshaus nt inn

wischen ['vɪʃən] vt to wipe

Wischer (-s, -) m (AUT) wiper

Wissbegier(de) ▲ ['vɪsbəɡiːr(də)] f thirst for knowledge; **wissbegierig** ▲ adj inquisitive, eager for knowledge

wissen ['vɪsən] (unreg) vt to know; **was weiß ich!** I don't know!; **W~ (-s)** nt knowledge; **W~schaft** f science; **W~schaftler(in) (-s, -)** m(f) scientist; **~schaftlich** adj scientific; **~swert** adj worth knowing

wittern ['vɪtərn] vt to scent; (fig) to suspect

Witterung f weather; (Geruch) scent

Witwe ['vɪtvə] f widow; **~r (-s, -)** m widower

Witz [vɪts] **(-es, -e)** m joke; **~bold (-(e)s, -e)** m joker, wit; **w~ig** adj funny

wo [voː] adv where; (umg: irgendwo) somewhere; **im Augenblick, ~ ...** the moment (that) ...; **die Zeit, ~ ...** the time when ...; **~anders** [voːˈandərs] adv elsewhere; **~bei** [-ˈbaɪ] adv (relativ) by/with which; (interrogativ) what ... in/by/with

Woche ['vɔxə] f week

Wochen- zW: **~ende** nt weekend; **w~lang** adj, adv for weeks; **~markt** m weekly market; **~schau** f newsreel

Spelling Reform: ▲ *new spelling* △ *old spelling (to be phased out)*

wöchentlich ['vœçəntlɪç] *adj, adv* weekly
wodurch [vo'dʊrç] *adv (relativ)* through
which; *(interrogativ)* what ... through
wofür [vo'fy:r] *adv (relativ)* for which;
(interrogativ) what ... for
wog *etc* [vo:k] *vb siehe* **wiegen**
wo- [vo:] *zW:* ~'**gegen** *adv (relativ)* against
which; *(interrogativ)* what ... against; ~**her**
[-'he:r] *adv* where ... from; ~**hin** [-'hɪn] *adv*
where ... to

SCHLÜSSELWORT

wohl [vo:l] *adv* **1**: **sich wohl fühlen**
(zufrieden) to feel happy; *(gesundheitlich)* to
feel well; **jdm wohl tun** to do sb good;
wohl oder übel whether one likes it or not
2 *(wahrscheinlich)* probably; *(gewiss)*
certainly; *(vielleicht)* perhaps; **sie ist wohl**
zu Hause she's probably at home; **das ist**
doch wohl nicht dein Ernst! surely you're
not serious!; **das mag wohl sein** that may
well be; **ob das wohl stimmt?** I wonder if
that's true; **er weiß das sehr wohl** he
knows that perfectly well

Wohl [vo:l] *(-(e)s)* *nt* welfare; **zum ~!**
cheers!; **w~auf** *adv* well; ~**behagen** *nt*
comfort; ~**fahrt** *f* welfare; ~**fahrtsstaat** *m*
welfare state; **w~habend** *adj* wealthy;
w~ig *adj* contented, comfortable;
w~schmeckend *adj* delicious; ~**stand** *m*
prosperity; ~**standsgesellschaft** *f*
affluent society; ~**tat** *f* relief; act of charity;
~**täter(in)** *m(f)* benefactor; **w~tätig** *adj*
charitable; ~**tätigkeits-** *zW* charity,
charitable; **w~tun** *(unreg)* *vi* △ *siehe* **wohl**;
w~verdient *adj* well-earned, well-
deserved; **w~weislich** *adv* prudently;
~**wollen** *(-s)* *nt* good will; **w~wollend** *adj*
benevolent
wohn- [vo:n] *zW:* ~**en** *vi* to live;
W~gemeinschaft *f* *(Menschen)* people
sharing a flat; ~**haft** *adj* resident; **W~heim**
nt (für Studenten) hall of residence; *(für*
Senioren) home; *(bes für Arbeiter)* hostel;
~**lich** *adj* comfortable; **W~mobil** *(-s, -e)*
nt camper; **W~ort** *m* domicile; **W~sitz** *m*

place of residence; **W~ung** *f* house;
(Etagenwohnung) flat, apartment *(US)*;
W~wagen *m* caravan; **W~zimmer** *nt*
living room
wölben ['vœlbən] *vt, vr* to curve
Wolf [vɔlf] *(-(e)s, ⸚e)* *m* wolf
Wolke ['vɔlkə] *f* cloud; ~**nkratzer** *m*
skyscraper; **wolkig** ['vɔlkɪç] *adj* cloudy
Wolle ['vɔlə] *f* wool; **w~n¹** *adj* woollen

SCHLÜSSELWORT

wollen² ['vɔlən] *(pt* **wollte**, *pp* **gewollt** *od*
(als Hilfsverb) **wollen)** *vt, vi* to want; **ich**
will nach Hause I want to go home; **er**
will nicht he doesn't want to; **er wollte**
das nicht he didn't want it; **wenn du**
willst if you like; **ich will, dass du mir**
zuhörst I want you to listen to me
♦ *Hilfsverb:* **er will ein Haus kaufen** he
wants to buy a house; **ich wollte, ich wäre**
... I wish I were ...; **etw gerade tun wollen**
to be going to do sth

---

wollüstig ['vɔlʏstɪç] *adj* lusty, sensual
wo- *zW:* ~**mit** *adv (relativ)* with which;
(interrogativ) what ... with; ~**möglich** *adv*
probably, I suppose; ~**nach** *adv (relativ)*
after/for which; *(interrogativ)* what ... for/
after; ~**ran** *adv (relativ)* on/at which;
(interrogativ) what ... on/at; ~**rauf** *adv*
(relativ) on which; *(interrogativ)* what ... on;
~**raus** *adv (relativ)* from/out of which;
(interrogativ) what ... from/out of; ~**rin** *adv*
(relativ) in which; *(interrogativ)* what ... in
Wort [vɔrt] *(-(e)s, ⸚er* *od* -e)* *nt* word; **jdn**
beim ~ nehmen to take sb at his word;
mit anderen ~en in other words;
w~brüchig *adj* not true to one's word
Wörterbuch ['vœrtərbu:x] *nt* dictionary
Wort- *zW:* ~**führer** *m* spokesman; **w~karg**
adj taciturn; ~**laut** *m* wording
wörtlich ['vœrtlɪç] *adj* literal
Wort- *zW:* **w~los** *adj* mute; **w~reich** *adj*
wordy, verbose; ~**schatz** *m* vocabulary;
~**spiel** *nt* play on words, pun
wo- *zW:* ~**rüber** *adv (relativ)* over/about
which; *(interrogativ)* what ... over/about;

Rechtschreibreform: ▲ *neue Schreibung* △ *alte Schreibung (auslaufend)*

~rum adv (relativ) about/round which; (interrogativ) what ... about/round; **~runter** adv (relativ) under which; (interrogativ) what ... under; **~von** adv (relativ) from which; (interrogativ) what ... from; **~vor** adv (relativ) in front of/before which; (interrogativ) in front of/before what; of what; **~zu** adv (relativ) to/for which; (interrogativ) what ... for/to; (warum) why

Wrack [vrak] (-(e)s, -s) nt wreck

Wucher ['vu:xər] (-s) m profiteering; **~er** (-s, -) m profiteer; **w~isch** adj profiteering; **w~n** vi (Pflanzen) to grow wild; **~ung** f (MED) growth, tumour

Wuchs [vu:ks] (-es) m (Wachstum) growth; (Statur) build

Wucht [vʊxt] (-) f force

wühlen ['vy:lən] vi to scrabble; (Tier) to root; (Maulwurf) to burrow; (umg: arbeiten) to slave away ♦ vt to dig

Wulst [vʊlst] (-es, ⁻e) m bulge; (an Wunde) swelling

wund [vʊnt] adj sore, raw; **W~e** f wound

Wunder ['vʊndər] (-s, -) nt miracle; **es ist kein ~** it's no wonder; **w~bar** adj wonderful, marvellous; **~kerze** f sparkler; **~kind** nt infant prodigy; **w~lich** adj odd, peculiar; **w~n** vr to be surprised ♦ vt to surprise; **sich w~n über** +akk to be surprised at; **w~schön** adj beautiful; **w~voll** adj wonderful

Wundstarrkrampf ['vʊntʃtarkrampf] m tetanus, lockjaw

Wunsch [vʊnʃ] (-(e)s, ⁻e) m wish

wünschen ['vʏnʃən] vt to wish; **sich** dat **etw ~** to want sth, to wish for sth; **~swert** adj desirable

wurde etc ['vʊrdə] vb siehe **werden**

Würde ['vʏrdə] f dignity; (Stellung) honour; **w~voll** adj dignified

würdig ['vʏrdɪç] adj worthy; (würdevoll) dignified; **~en** vt to appreciate

Wurf [vʊrf] (-s, ⁻e) m throw; (Junge) litter

Würfel ['vʏrfəl] (-s, -) m dice; (MATH) cube; **~becher** m (dice) cup; **w~n** vi to play dice ♦ vt to dice; **~zucker** m lump sugar

würgen ['vʏrgən] vt, vi to choke

Wurm [vʊrm] (-(e)s, ⁻er) m worm; **w~stichig** adj worm-ridden

Wurst [vʊrst] (-, ⁻e) f sausage; **das ist mir ~** (umg) I don't care, I don't give a damn

Würstchen ['vʏrstçən] nt sausage

Würze ['vʏrtsə] f seasoning, spice

Wurzel ['vʊrtsəl] (-, -n) f root

würzen ['vʏrtsən] vt to season, to spice

würzig adj spicy

wusch etc [vʊʃ] vb siehe **waschen**

wusste ▲ etc ['vʊstə] vb siehe **wissen**

wüst [vy:st] adj untidy, messy; (ausschweifend) wild; (öde) waste; (umg: heftig) terrible; **W~e** f desert

Wut [vu:t] (-) f rage, fury; **~anfall** m fit of rage

wüten ['vy:tən] vi to rage; **~d** adj furious, mad

X, x

X-Beine ['ɪksbamə] pl knock-knees

x-beliebig [ɪksbə'li:bɪç] adj any (whatever)

xerokopieren [kseroko'pi:rən] vt to xerox, to photocopy

x-mal ['ɪksma:l] adv any number of times, n times

Xylofon ▲, **Xylophon** [ksylo'fo:n] (-s, -e) nt xylophone

Y, y

Yacht (-, -en) f siehe **Jacht**

Ypsilon ['ʏpsilɔn] (-(s), -s) nt the letter Y

Z, z

Zacke ['tsakə] f point; (Bergzacke) jagged peak; (Gabelzacke) prong; (Kammzacke) tooth

zackig ['tsakɪç] adj jagged; (umg) smart; (Tempo) brisk

zaghaft ['tsa:khaft] adj timid

zäh [tse:] adj tough; (Mensch) tenacious;

(*Flüssigkeit*) thick; (*schleppend*) sluggish; Z~igkeit *f* toughness; tenacity

Zahl [tsaːl] (-, -en) *f* number; z~bar *adj* payable; z~en *vt*, *vi* to pay; z~en bitte! the bill please!

zählen ['tsɛːlən] *vt*, *vi* to count; ~ auf +*akk* to count on; ~ zu to be numbered among

Zahlenschloss ▲ *nt* combination lock

Zähler ['tsɛːlər] (-s, -) *m* (*TECH*) meter; (*MATH*) numerator

Zahl- *zW*: z~los *adj* countless; z~reich *adj* numerous; ~tag *m* payday; ~ung *f* payment; ~ungsanweisung *f* giro transfer order; z~ungsfähig *adj* solvent; ~wort *nt* numeral

zahm [tsaːm] *adj* tame

zähmen ['tsɛːmən] *vt* to tame; (*fig*) to curb

Zahn [tsaːn] (-(e)s, ᵘe) *m* tooth; ~arzt *m* dentist; ~ärztin *f* (female) dentist; ~bürste *f* toothbrush; ~fleisch *nt* gums *pl*; ~pasta *f* toothpaste; ~rad *nt* cog(wheel); ~schmerzen *pl* toothache *sg*; ~stein *m* tartar; ~stocher (-s, -) *m* toothpick

Zange ['tsaŋə] *f* pliers *pl*; (*Zuckerzange etc*) tongs *pl*; (*Beißzange, ZOOL*) pincers *pl*; (*MED*) forceps *pl*

zanken ['tsaŋkən] *vi*, *vr* to quarrel

zänkisch ['tsɛŋkɪʃ] *adj* quarrelsome

Zäpfchen ['tsɛpfçən] *nt* (*ANAT*) uvula; (*MED*) suppository

Zapfen ['tsapfən] (-s, -) *m* plug; (*BOT*) cone; (*Eiszapfen*) icicle

zappeln ['tsapəln] *vi* to wriggle; to fidget

zart [tsart] *adj* (*weich, leise*) soft; (*Fleisch*) tender; (*fein, schwächlich*) delicate; Z~heit *f* softness; tenderness; delicacy

zärtlich ['tsɛːrtlɪç] *adj* tender, affectionate

Zauber ['tsaʊbər] (-s, -) *m* magic; (*~bann*) spell; ~ei [-'raɪ] *f* magic; ~er (-s, -) *m* magician; conjuror; z~haft *adj* magical, enchanting; ~künstler *m* conjuror; ~kunststück *nt* conjuring trick; z~n *vi* to conjure, to practise magic

zaudern ['tsaʊdərn] *vi* to hesitate

Zaum [tsaʊm] (-(e)s, Zäume) *m* bridle; etw im ~ halten to keep sth in check

Zaun [tsaʊn] (-(e)s, Zäune) *m* fence

z. B. *abk* (= *zum Beispiel*) e.g.

Zebra ['tseːbra] *nt* zebra; ~streifen *m* zebra crossing

Zeche ['tsɛçə] *f* (*Rechnung*) bill; (*Bergbau*) mine

Zeh [tseː] (-s, -en) *m* toe

Zehe [tseːə] *f* toe; (*Knoblauchzehe*) clove

zehn [tseːn] *num* ten; ~te(r, s) *adj* tenth; Z~tel (-s, -) *nt* tenth (part)

Zeich- ['tsaɪç] *zW*: ~en (-s, -) *nt* sign; z~nen *vt* to draw; (*kennzeichnen*) to mark; (*unterzeichnen*) to sign ♦ *vi* to draw; to sign; ~ner (-s, -) *m* artist; technischer ~ner draughtsman; ~nung *f* drawing; (*Markierung*) markings *pl*

Zeige- ['tsaɪgə] *zW*: ~finger *m* index finger; z~n *vt* to show ♦ *vi* to point ♦ *vr* to show o.s.; z~n auf +*akk* to point to; to point at; es wird sich z~n time will tell; es zeigte sich, dass ... it turned out that ...; ~r (-s, -) *m* pointer; (*Uhrzeiger*) hand

Zeile ['tsaɪlə] *f* line; (*Häuserzeile*) row

Zeit [tsaɪt] (-, -en) *f* time; (*GRAM*) tense; sich *dat* ~ lassen to take one's time; von ~ zu ~ from time to time; *siehe* zurzeit; ~alter *nt* age; ~ansage *f* (*TEL*) speaking clock; ~arbeit *f* (*COMM*) temporary job; z~gemäß *adj* in keeping with the times; ~genosse *m* contemporary; z~ig *adj* early; z~lich *adj* temporal; ~lupe *f* slow motion; z~raubend *adj* time-consuming; ~raum *m* period; ~rechnung *f* time, era; nach/vor unserer ~rechnung A.D./B.C.; ~schrift *f* periodical; ~ung *f* newspaper; ~vertreib *m* pastime, diversion; z~weilig *adj* temporary; z~weise *adv* for a time; ~wort *nt* verb

Zelle ['tsɛlə] *f* cell; (*Telefonzelle*) callbox

Zellstoff *m* cellulose

Zelt [tsɛlt] (-(e)s, -e) *nt* tent; z~en *vi* to camp; ~platz *m* camp site

Zement [tse'mɛnt] (-(e)s, -e) *m* cement; z~ieren *vt* to cement

zensieren [tsɛn'tsiːrən] *vt* to censor; (*SCH*) to mark

Zensur [tsɛn'tsuːr] *f* censorship; (*SCH*) mark

Zentimeter [tsɛnti'meːtər] *m od nt* centimetre

Zentner ['tsɛntnər] **(-s, -)** *m* hundredweight

zentral [tsɛn'traːl] *adj* central; **Z~e** *f* central office; *(TEL)* exchange; **Z~heizung** *f* central heating

Zentrum ['tsɛntrʊm] **(-s, Zentren)** *nt* centre

zerbrechen [tsɛr'brɛçən] *(unreg) vt, vi* to break

zerbrechlich *adj* fragile

zer'drücken *vt* to squash, to crush; *(Kartoffeln)* to mash

Zeremonie [tseremo'niː] *f* ceremony

Zerfall [tsɛr'fal] *m* decay; **z~en** *(unreg) vi* to disintegrate, to decay; *(sich gliedern):* **z~en (in** +*akk)* to fall (into)

zer'gehen *(unreg) vi* to melt, to dissolve

zerkleinern [tsɛr'klaɪnərn] *vt* to reduce to small pieces

zerlegbar [tsɛr'leːkbaːr] *adj* able to be dismantled

zerlegen [tsɛr'leːgən] *vt* to take to pieces; *(Fleisch)* to carve; *(Satz)* to analyse

zermürben [tsɛr'mʏrbən] *vt* to wear down

zerquetschen [tsɛr'kvɛtʃən] *vt* to squash

zer'reißen *(unreg) vt* to tear to pieces ♦ *vi* to tear, to rip

zerren ['tsɛrən] *vt* to drag ♦ *vi.* **~ (an** +*dat)* to tug (at)

zer'rinnen *(unreg) vi* to melt away

zerrissen [tsɛr'rɪsən] *adj* torn, tattered; **Z~heit** *f* tattered state; *(POL)* disunion, discord; *(innere Z~heit)* disintegration

Zerrung *f (MED):* **eine ~** pulled muscle

zerrütten [tsɛr'rʏtən] *vt* to wreck, to destroy

zer'schlagen *(unreg) vt* to shatter, to smash ♦ *vr* to fall through

zer'schneiden *(unreg) vt* to cut up

zer'setzen *vt, vr* to decompose, to dissolve

zer'springen *(unreg) vi* to shatter, to burst

Zerstäuber [tsɛr'ʃtɔʏbər] **(-s, -)** *m* atomizer

zerstören [tsɛr'ʃtøːrən] *vt* to destroy

Zerstörung *f* destruction

zerstreu- [tsɛr'ʃtrɔʏ] *zW:* **~en** *vt* to disperse, to scatter; *(unterhalten)* to divert; *(Zweifel etc)* to dispel ♦ *vr* to disperse, to scatter; to be dispelled; **~t** *adj* scattered; *(Mensch)*

absent-minded; **Z~theit** *f* absent-mindedness; **Z~ung** *f* dispersion; *(Ablenkung)* diversion

zerstückeln [tsɛr'ʃtʏkəln] *vt* to cut into pieces

zer'teilen *vt* to divide into parts

Zertifikat [tsɛrtifi'kaːt] **(-(e)s, -e)** *nt* certificate

zer'treten *(unreg) vt* to crush underfoot

zertrümmern [tsɛr'trʏmərn] *vt* to shatter; *(Gebäude etc)* to demolish

Zettel ['tsɛtəl] **(-s, -)** *m* piece of paper, slip; *(Notizzettel)* note; *(Formular)* form

Zeug [tsɔʏk] **(-(e)s, -e)** *(umg) nt* stuff; *(Ausrüstung)* gear; **dummes ~** (stupid) nonsense; **das ~ haben zu** to have the makings of; **sich ins ~ legen** to put one's shoulder to the wheel

Zeuge ['tsɔʏgə] **(-n, -n)** *m* witness; **z~n** *vi* to bear witness, to testify ♦ *vt (Kind)* to father; **es zeugt von ...** it testifies to ...; **~naussage** *f* evidence; **Zeugin** ['tsɔʏgɪn] *f* witness

Zeugnis ['tsɔʏgnɪs] **(-ses, -se)** *nt* certificate; *(SCH)* report; *(Referenz)* reference; *(Aussage)* evidence, testimony; **~ geben von** to be evidence of, to testify to

z. H(d). *abk (= zu Händen)* attn.

Zickzack ['tsɪktsak] **(-(e)s, -e)** *m* zigzag

Ziege ['tsiːgə] *f* goat

Ziegel ['tsiːgəl] **(-s, -)** *m* brick; *(Dachziegel)* tile

ziehen ['tsiːən] *(unreg) vt* to draw; *(zerren)* to pull; *(SCHACH etc)* to move; *(züchten)* to rear ♦ *vi* to draw; *(umziehen, wandern)* to move; *(Rauch, Wolke etc)* to drift; *(reißen)* to pull ♦ *vb unpers:* **es zieht** there is a draught, it's draughty ♦ *vr (Gummi)* to stretch; *(Grenze etc)* to run; *(Gespräche)* to be drawn out; **etw nach sich ~** to lead to sth, to entail sth

Ziehung ['tsiːʊŋ] *f (Losziehung)* drawing

Ziel [tsiːl] **(-(e)s, -e)** *nt (einer Reise)* destination; *(SPORT)* finish; *(MIL)* target; *(Absicht)* goal; *(SPORT)* finish; *(MIL)* target; *(Absicht)* goal; **z~bewusst** ▲ *adj* decisive; **z~en** *vi:* **z~en (auf** +*akk)* to aim (at); **z~los** *adj* aimless; **~scheibe** *f* target; **z~strebig**

adj purposeful

ziemlich ['tsi:mlıç] *adj* quite a; fair ♦ *adv* rather; quite a bit

zieren ['tsi:rən] *vr* to act coy

zierlich ['tsi:rlıç] *adj* dainty

Ziffer ['tsıfər] (**-, -n**) *f* figure, digit; **~blatt** *nt* dial, clock-face

zig [tsık] (*umg*) *adj* umpteen

Zigarette [tsıga'retə] *f* cigarette

Zigaretten- *zW*: **~automat** *m* cigarette machine; **~schachtel** *f* cigarette packet; **~spitze** *f* cigarette holder

Zigarre [tsı'garə] *f* cigar

Zigeuner(in) [tsı'gɔʏnər(ın)] (**-s, -**) *m(f)* gipsy

Zimmer ['tsımər] (**-s, -**) *nt* room; **~lautstärke** *f* reasonable volume; **~mädchen** *nt* chambermaid; **~mann** *m* carpenter; **z~n** *vt* to make (from wood); **~nachweis** *m* accommodation office; **~pflanze** *f* indoor plant; **~service** *m* room service

zimperlich ['tsımpərlıç] *adj* squeamish; (*pingelig*) fussy, finicky

Zimt [tsımt] (**-(e)s, -e**) *m* cinnamon

Zink [tsıŋk] (**-(e)s**) *nt* zinc

Zinn [tsın] (**-(e)s**) *nt* (*Element*) tin; (*in ~waren*) pewter; **~soldat** *m* tin soldier

Zins [tsıns] (**-es, -en**) *m* interest; **~eszins** *m* compound interest; **~fuß** *m* rate of interest; **z~los** *adj* interest-free; **~satz** *m* rate of interest

Zipfel ['tsıpfəl] (**-s, -**) *m* corner; (*spitz*) tip; (*Hemdzipfel*) tail; (*Wurstzipfel*) end

zirka ['tsırka] *adv* (round) about

Zirkel ['tsırkəl] (**-s, -**) *m* circle; (*MATH*) pair of compasses

Zirkus ['tsırkʊs] (**-, -se**) *m* circus

zischen ['tsıʃən] *vi* to hiss

Zitat [tsi'ta:t] (**-(e)s, -e**) *nt* quotation, quote

zitieren [tsi'ti:rən] *vt* to quote

Zitrone [tsi'tro:nə] *f* lemon; **~nlimonade** *f* lemonade; **~nsaft** *m* lemon juice

zittern ['tsıtərn] *vi* to tremble

zivil [tsi'vi:l] *adj* civil; (*Preis*) moderate; **Z~** (**-s**) *nt* plain clothes *pl*; (*MIL*) civilian clothing; **Z~courage** *f* courage of one's convictions;

Z~dienst *m* community service; **Z~isation** [tsivilizatsi'o:n] *f* civilization; **Z~isationskrankheit** *f* disease peculiar to civilization; **~i'sieren** *vt* to civilize

---
Zivildienst
---

i *A young German has to complete his 13 months' Zivildienst or service to the community if he has opted out of military service as a conscientious objector. This is usually done in a hospital or old people's home. About 18% of young Germans choose to do this as an alternative to the* **Wehrdienst.**

Zivilist [tsivi'lıst] *m* civilian

zögern ['tsø:gərn] *vi* to hesitate

Zoll [tsɔl] (**-(e)s, ⁼e**) *m* customs *pl*; (*Abgabe*) duty; **~abfertigung** *f* customs clearance; **~amt** *nt* customs office; **~beamte(r)** *m* customs official; **~erklärung** *f* customs declaration; **z~frei** *adj* duty-free; **~kontrolle** *f* customs check; **z~pflichtig** *adj* liable to duty, dutiable

Zone ['tso:nə] *f* zone

Zoo [tso:] (**-s, -s**) *m* zoo; **~loge** [tsoo'lo:gə] (**-n, -n**) *m* zoologist; **~lo'gie** *f* zoology; **z~'logisch** *adj* zoological

Zopf [tsɔpf] (**-(e)s, ⁼e**) *m* plait; pigtail; **alter ~** antiquated custom

Zorn [tsɔrn] (**-(e)s**) *m* anger; **z~ig** *adj* angry

zottig ['tsɔtıç] *adj* shaggy

z. T. *abk = zum Teil*

SCHLÜSSELWORT

zu [tsu:] *präp +dat* **1** (*örtlich*) to; **zum Bahnhof/Arzt gehen** to go to the station/ doctor; **zur Schule/Kirche gehen** to go to school/church; **sollen wir zu euch gehen?** shall we go to your place?; **sie sah zu ihm hin** she looked towards him; **zum Fenster herein** through the window; **zu meiner Linken** to *od* on my left

2 (*zeitlich*) at; **zu Ostern** at Easter; **bis zum 1. Mai** until May 1st; (*nicht später als*) by May 1st; **zu meiner Zeit** in my time

3 (*Zusatz*) with; **Wein zum Essen trinken**

to drink wine with one's meal; **sich zu jdm setzen** to sit down beside sb; **setz dich doch zu uns** (come and) sit with us; **Anmerkungen zu etw** notes on sth 4 (*Zweck*) for; **Wasser zum Waschen** water for washing; **Papier zum Schreiben** paper to write on; **etw zum Geburtstag bekommen** to get sth for one's birthday 5 (*Veränderung*) into; **zu etw werden** to turn into sth; **jdn zu etw machen** to make sb (into) sth; **zu Asche verbrennen** to burn to ashes

6 (*mit Zahlen*): **3 zu 2** (*SPORT*) 3-2; **das Stück zu 2 Mark** at 2 marks each; **zum ersten Mal** for the first time

7: **zu meiner Freude** *etc* to my joy *etc*; **zum Glück** luckily; **zu Fuß** on foot; **es ist zum Weinen** it's enough to make you cry ♦ *konj* to; **etw zu essen** sth to eat; **um besser sehen zu können** in order to see better; **ohne es zu wissen** without knowing it; **noch zu bezahlende Rechnungen** bills that are still to be paid ♦ *adv* 1 (*allzu*) too; **zu sehr** too much; **zu viel** too much; **zu wenig** too little 2 (*örtlich*) toward(s); **er kam auf mich zu** he came up to me 3 (*geschlossen*) shut, closed; **die Geschäfte haben zu** the shops are closed; „**auf/zu**" (*Wasserhahn etc*) "on/off" 4 (*umg: los*): **nur zu!** just keep on!; **mach zu!** hurry up!

zualler- [tsu'alər] *zW:* **~erst** [-'ɛːrst] *adv* first of all; **~letzt** [-'lɛtst] *adv* last of all
Zubehör ['tsuːbəhøːr] (**-(e)s, -e**) *nt* accessories *pl*
zubereiten ['tsuːbərattən] *vt* to prepare
zubilligen ['tsuːbılıgən] *vt* to grant
zubinden ['tsuːbındən] (*unreg*) *vt* to tie up
zubringen ['tsuːbrıŋən] (*unreg*) *vt* (*Zeit*) to spend
Zubringer (**-s, -**) *m* (*Straße*) approach *od* slip road
Zucchini [tsu'kiːniː] *pl* (*BOT, KOCH*) courgette (*BRIT*), zucchini (*US*)
Zucht [tsuxt] (**-, -en**) *f* (*von Tieren*) breeding;

(*von Pflanzen*) cultivation; (*Rasse*) breed; (*Erziehung*) raising; (*Disziplin*) discipline
züchten ['tsʏçtən] *vt* (*Tiere*) to breed; (*Pflanzen*) to cultivate, to grow; **Züchter** (**-s, -**) *m* breeder; grower
Zuchthaus *nt* prison, penitentiary (*US*)
züchtigen ['tsʏçtıgən] *vt* to chastise
Züchtung *f* (*Zuchtart, Sorte: von Tier*) breed; (*: von Pflanze*) variety
zucken ['tsʊkən] *vi* to jerk, to twitch; (*Strahl etc*) to flicker ♦ *vt* (*Schultern*) to shrug
Zucker ['tsʊkər] (**-s, -**) *m* sugar; (*MED*) diabetes; **~guss** ▲ *m* icing; **z~krank** *adj* diabetic; **~krankheit** *f* (*MED*) diabetes; **z~n** *vt* to sugar; **~rohr** *nt* sugar cane; **~rübe** *f* sugar beet
Zuckung ['tsʊkʊŋ] *f* convulsion, spasm; (*leicht*) twitch
zudecken ['tsuːdɛkən] *vt* to cover (up)
zudem [tsuˈdeːm] *adv* in addition (to this)
zudringlich ['tsuːdrıŋlıç] *adj* forward, pushing, obtrusive
zudrücken ['tsuːdrʏkən] *vt* to close; **ein Auge ~** to turn a blind eye
zueinander [tsuʔaɪˈnandər] *adv* to one other; (*in Verbindung*) together
zuerkennen ['tsuːʔɛrkɛnən] (*unreg*) *vt* to award; **jdm etw ~** to award sth to sb, to award sb sth
zuerst [tsuˈʔeːrst] *adv* first; (*zu Anfang*) at first; **~ einmal** first of all
Zufahrt ['tsuːfaːrt] *f* approach; **~sstraße** *f* approach road; (*von Autobahn etc*) slip road
Zufall ['tsuːfal] *m* chance; (*Ereignis*) coincidence; **durch ~** by accident; **so ein ~** what a coincidence; **z~en** (*unreg*) *vi* to close, to shut; (*Anteil, Aufgabe*) to fall
zufällig ['tsuːfɛlıç] *adj* chance ♦ *adv* by chance; (*in Frage*) by any chance
Zuflucht ['tsuːflʊxt] *f* recourse; (*Ort*) refuge
zufolge [tsuˈfɔlgə] *präp* (+*dat od gen*) judging by; (*laut*) according to
zufrieden [tsuˈfriːdən] *adj* content(ed), satisfied; **~ geben** to be content *od* satisfied (with); **~ stellen** to satisfy
zufrieren ['tsuːfriːrən] (*unreg*) *vi* to freeze up *od* over

Spelling Reform: ▲ *new spelling* △ *old spelling (to be phased out)*

zufügen ['tsuːfyːɡən] *vt* to add; (*Leid etc*): (*jdm*) **etw ~** to cause (sb) sth

Zufuhr ['tsuːfuːr] (**-, -en**) *f* (*Herbeibringen*) supplying; (*MET*) influx

Zug [tsuːk] (**-(e)s, ⁻e**) *m* (*EISENB*) train; (*Luftzug*) draught; (*Ziehen*) pull(ing); (*Gesichtszug*) feature; (*SCHACH etc*) move; (*Schriftzug*) stroke; (*Atemzug*) breath; (*Charakterzug*) trait; (*an Zigarette*) puff, pull, drag; (*Schluck*) gulp; (*Menschengruppe*) procession; (*von Vögeln*) flight; (*MIL*) platoon; **etw in vollen Zügen genießen** to enjoy sth to the full

Zu- ['tsuː] *zW*: **~gabe** *f* extra; (*in Konzert etc*) encore; **~gang** *m* access, approach; **z~gänglich** *adj* accessible; (*Mensch*) approachable

zugeben ['tsuːɡeːbən] (*unreg*) *vt* (*beifügen*) to add, to throw in; (*zugestehen*) to admit; (*erlauben*) to permit

zugehen ['tsuːɡeːən] (*unreg*) *vi* (*schließen*) to shut; **es geht dort seltsam zu** there are strange goings-on there; **auf jdn/etw ~** to walk towards sb/sth; **dem Ende ~** to be finishing

Zugehörigkeit ['tsuːɡəhøːrɪçkaɪt] *f*: **~ (zu)** membership (of), belonging (to)

Zügel ['tsyːɡəl] (**-s, -**) *m* rein(s); (*fig*) curb; **z~n** *vt* to curb; (*Pferd*) to rein in

zuge- ['tsuːɡə] *zW*: **Z~ständnis** (**-ses, -se**) *nt* concession; **~stehen** (*unreg*) *vt* to admit; (*Rechte*) to concede

Zugführer *m* (*EISENB*) guard

zugig ['tsuːɡɪç] *adj* draughty

zügig ['tsyːɡɪç] *adj* speedy, swift

zugreifen ['tsuːɡraɪfən] (*unreg*) *vi* to seize *od* grab at; (*helfen*) to help; (*beim Essen*) to help o.s.

Zugrestaurant *nt* dining car

zugrunde, zu Grunde [tsuːˈɡrʊndə] *adv*: **~ gehen** to collapse; (*Mensch*) to perish; **einer Sache** *dat* **etw ~ legen** to base sth on sth; **einer Sache** *dat* **~ liegen** to be based on sth; **~ richten** to ruin, to destroy

zugunsten, zu Gunsten [tsuːˈɡʊnstən] *präp* (+*gen od dat*) in favour of

zugute [tsuːˈɡuːtə] *adv*: **jdm etw ~ halten** to concede sth to sb; **jdm ~ kommen** to be of assistance to sb

Zugvogel *m* migratory bird

zuhalten ['tsuːhaltən] (*unreg*) *vt* to keep closed ♦ *vi*: **auf jdn/etw ~** to make a beeline for sb/sth

Zuhälter ['tsuːhɛltər] (**-s, -**) *m* pimp

Zuhause [tsuːˈhaʊzə] (**-**) *nt* home

zuhause [tsuːˈhaʊzə] *adv* (*österreichisch, schweizerisch*) at home

zuhören ['tsuːhøːrən] *vi* to listen

Zuhörer (**-s, -**) *m* listener

zukleben ['tsuːkleːbən] *vt* to paste up

zukommen ['tsuːkɔmən] (*unreg*) *vi* to come up; **auf jdn ~** to come up to sb; **jdm etw ~ lassen** to give sb sth; **etw auf sich ~ lassen** to wait and see; **jdm ~** (*sich gehören*) to be fitting for sb

Zukunft ['tsuːkʊnft] (**-, Zukünfte**) *f* future; **zukünftig** ['tsuːkynftɪç] *adj* future ♦ *adv* in future; **mein zukünftiger Mann** my husband to be

Zulage ['tsuːlaːɡə] *f* bonus

zulassen ['tsuːlasən] (*unreg*) *vt* (*hereinlassen*) to admit; (*erlauben*) to permit; (*Auto*) to license; (*umg: nicht öffnen*) to (keep) shut

zulässig ['tsuːlɛsɪç] *adj* permissible, permitted

Zulassung *f* (*amtlich*) authorization; (*von Kfz*) licensing

zulaufen ['tsuːlaʊfən] (*unreg*) *vi* (*subj: Mensch*): **~ auf jdn/etw** to run up to sb/ sth; (*: Straße*): **~ auf** to lead towards

zuleide, zu Leide [tsuːˈlaɪdə] *adv*: **jdm etw ~ tun** to hurt *od* harm sb

zuletzt [tsuːˈlɛtst] *adv* finally, at last

zuliebe [tsuːˈliːbə] *adv*: **jdm ~** to please sb

zum [tsʊm] = **zu dem**; **~ dritten Mal** for the third time; **~ Scherz** as a joke; **~ Trinken** for drinking

zumachen ['tsuːmaxən] *vt* to shut; (*Kleidung*) to do up, to fasten ♦ *vi* to shut; (*umg*) to hurry up

zu- *zW*: **~mal** [tsuːˈmaːl] *konj* especially (as); **~meist** [tsuːˈmaɪst] *adv* mostly; **~mindest** [tsuːˈmɪndəst] *adv* at least

---

Rechtschreibreform: ▲ *neue Schreibung* △ *alte Schreibung (auslaufend)*

zumutbar ['tsu:mu:tba:r] *adj* reasonable

zumute, zu Mute [tsu'mu:tə] *adv*: **wie ist ihm ~?** how does he feel?

zumuten ['tsu:mu:tən] *vt*: **(jdm) etw ~** to expect *od* ask sth (of sb)

Zumutung ['tsu:mu:tʊŋ] *f* unreasonable expectation *od* demand, impertinence

zunächst [tsu'nɛːçst] *adv* first of all; **~ einmal** to start with

Zunahme ['tsu:na:mə] *f* increase

Zuname ['tsu:na:mə] *m* surname

Zünd- [tsynd] *zW*: **z~en** *vi* (*Feuer*) to light, to ignite; (*Motor*) to fire; (*begeistern*): **bei jdm z~en** to fire sb (with enthusiasm); **z~end** *adj* fiery; **~er (-s, -)** *m* fuse; (*MIL*) detonator; **~holz** ['tsynt-] *nt* match; **~kerze** *f* (*AUT*) spark(ing) plug; **~schloss** ▲ *nt* ignition lock; **~schlüssel** *m* ignition key; **~schnur** *f* fuse wire; **~stoff** *m* (*fig*) inflammatory stuff; **~ung** *f* ignition

zunehmen ['tsu:ne:mən] (*unreg*) *vi* to increase, to grow; (*Mensch*) to put on weight

Zuneigung ['tsu:naɪgʊŋ] *f* affection

Zunft [tsʊnft] **(-, ⸚e)** *f* guild

zünftig ['tsynftɪç] *adj* proper, real; (*Handwerk*) decent

Zunge ['tsʊŋə] *f* tongue

zunichte [tsu'nɪçtə] *adv*: **~ machen** to ruin, to destroy; **~ werden** to come to nothing

zunutze, zu Nutze [tsu'nʊtsə] *adv*: **sich** *dat* **etw ~ machen** to make use of sth

zuoberst [tsu'o:bərst] *adv* at the top

zupfen ['tsʊpfən] *vt* to pull, to pick, to pluck; (*Gitarre*) to pluck

zur [tsu:r] = **zu der**

zurate, zu Rate [tsu'ra:tə] *adv*: **jdn ~ ziehen** to consult sb

zurechnungsfähig ['tsu:rɛçnʊŋsfɛ:ɪç] *adj* responsible, accountable

zurecht- [tsu'rɛçt] *zW*: **~finden** (*unreg*) *vr* to find one's way (about); **~kommen** (*unreg*) *vi* to (be able to) cope, to manage; **~legen** *vt* to get ready; (*Ausrede etc*) to have ready; **~machen** *vt* to prepare ♦ *vr* to get ready; **~weisen** (*unreg*) *vt* to reprimand

zureden ['tsu:re:dən] *vi*: **jdm ~** to persuade *od* urge sb

zurück [tsu'ryk] *adv* back; **~behalten** (*unreg*) *vt* to keep back; **~bekommen** (*unreg*) *vt* to get back; **~bleiben** (*unreg*) *vi* (*Mensch*) to remain behind; (*nicht nachkommen*) to fall behind; (*Schaden*) to remain; **~bringen** (*unreg*) *vt* to bring back; **~fahren** (*unreg*) *vi* to travel back; (*vor Schreck*) to recoil, to start ♦ *vt* to drive back; **~finden** (*unreg*) *vi* to find one's way back; **~fordern** *vt* to demand back; **~führen** *vt* to lead back; **etw auf etw** *akk* **~führen** to trace sth back to sth; **~geben** (*unreg*) *vt* to give back; (*antworten*) to retort with; **~geblieben** *adj* retarded; **~gehen** (*unreg*) *vi* to go back; (*fallen*) to go down, to fall; (*zeitlich*): **~gehen (auf** +*akk*) to date back (to); **~gezogen** *adj* retired, withdrawn; **~halten** (*unreg*) *vt* to hold back, (*Mensch*) to restrain; (*hindern*) to prevent ♦ *vr* (*reserviert sein*) to be reserved; (*im Essen*) to hold back; **~haltend** *adj* reserved; **Z~haltung** *f* reserve; **~kehren** *vi* to return; **~kommen** (*unreg*) *vi* to come back; **auf etw** *akk* **~kommen** to return to sth; **~lassen** (*unreg*) *vt* to leave behind; **~legen** *vt* to put back; (*Geld*) to put by; (*reservieren*) to keep back; (*Strecke*) to cover; **~nehmen** (*unreg*) *vt* to take back; **~stellen** *vt* to put back, to replace; (*aufschieben*) to put off, to postpone; (*Interessen*) to defer; (*Ware*) to keep; **~treten** (*unreg*) *vi* to step back; (*vom Amt*) to retire; **gegenüber etw** *od* **hinter etw** *dat* **~treten** to diminish in importance in view of sth; **~weisen** (*unreg*) *vt* to turn down; (*Mensch*) to reject; **~zahlen** *vt* to repay, to pay back; **~ziehen** (*unreg*) *vt* to pull back; (*Angebot*) to withdraw ♦ *vr* to retire

Zuruf ['tsu:ru:f] *m* shout, cry

zurzeit [tsʊr'tsaɪt] *adv* at the moment

Zusage ['tsu:za:gə] *f* promise; (*Annahme*) consent; **z~n** *vt* to promise ♦ *vi* to accept; **jdm z~n** (*gefallen*) to agree with *od* please sb

zusammen [tsu'zamən] *adv* together;

Z~arbeit f cooperation; **~arbeiten** vi to cooperate; **~beißen** (unreg) vt (Zähne) to clench; **~brechen** (unreg) vi to collapse; (Mensch auch) to break down; **~bringen** (unreg) vt to bring od get together; (Geld) to get; (Sätze) to put together; **Z~bruch** m collapse; **~fassen** vt to summarize; (vereinigen) to unite; **Z~fassung** f summary, résumé; **~fügen** vt to join (together), to unite; **~halten** (unreg) vi to stick together; **Z~hang** m connection; **im/aus dem Z~hang** in/out of context; **~hängen** (unreg) vi to be connected od linked; **~kommen** (unreg) vi to meet, to assemble; (sich ereignen) to occur at once od together; **~legen** vt to put together; (stapeln) to pile up; (falten) to fold; (verbinden) to combine, to unite; (Termine, Fest) to amalgamate; (Geld) to collect; **~nehmen** (unreg) vt to summon up ♦ vr to pull o.s. together; **alles ~genommen** all in all; **~passen** (unreg) vi to go well together, to match; **~schließen** (unreg) vt, vr to join (together); **Z~schluss** ▲ m amalgamation; **~schreiben** (unreg) vt to write as one word; (Bericht) to put together; **Z~sein** (-s) nt get-together; **~setzen** vt to put together ♦ vr (Stoff) to be composed of; (Menschen) to get together; **Z~setzung** f composition; **~stellen** vt to put together; to compile; **Z~stoß** m collision; **~stoßen** (unreg) vi to collide; **~treffen** (unreg) vi to coincide; (Menschen) to meet; **Z~treffen** nt coincidence; meeting; **~zählen** vt to add up; **~ziehen** (unreg) vt (verengern) to draw together; (vereinigen) to bring together; (addieren) to add up ♦ vr to shrink; (sich bilden) to form, to develop

zusätzlich ['tsu:zɛtslɪç] adj additional ♦ adv in addition

zuschauen ['tsu:ʃaʊən] vi to watch, to look on; **Zuschauer(in) (-s, -)** m(f) spectator ♦ pl (THEAT) audience sg

zuschicken ['tsu:ʃɪkən] vt: **(jdm etw) ~** to send od to forward (sth to sb)

Zuschlag ['tsu:ʃla:k] m extra charge,

surcharge; **z~en** (unreg) vt (Tür) to slam; (Ball) to hit; (bei Auktion) to knock down; (Steine etc) to knock into shape ♦ vi (Fenster, Tür) to shut; (Mensch) to hit, to punch; **~karte** f (EISENB) surcharge ticket; **z~pflichtig** adj subject to surcharge

zuschneiden ['tsu:ʃnaɪdən] (unreg) vt to cut out; to cut to size

zuschrauben ['tsu:ʃraʊbən] vt to screw down od up

zuschreiben ['tsu:ʃraɪbən] (unreg) vt (fig) to ascribe, to attribute; (COMM) to credit

Zuschrift ['tsu:ʃrɪft] f letter, reply

zuschulden, zu Schulden [tsu'ʃʊldən] adv: **sich** dat **etw ~ kommen lassen** to make o.s. guilty of sth

Zuschuss ▲ ['tsu:ʃʊs] m subsidy, allowance

zusehen ['tsu:ze:ən] (unreg) vi to watch; (dafür sorgen) to take care; **jdm/etw ~** to watch sb/sth; **~ds** adv visibly

zusenden ['tsu:zɛndən] (unreg) vt to forward, to send on

zusichern ['tsu:zɪçərn] vt: **jdm etw ~** to assure sb of sth

zuspielen ['tsu:ʃpi:lən] vt, vi to pass

zuspitzen ['tsu:ʃpɪtsən] vt to sharpen ♦ vr (Lage) to become critical

zusprechen ['tsu:ʃprɛçən] (unreg) vt (zuerkennen) to award ♦ vi to speak; **jdm etw ~** to award sb sth od sth to sb; **jdm Trost ~** to comfort sb; **dem Essen/ Alkohol ~** to eat/drink a lot

Zustand ['tsu:ʃtant] m state, condition

zustande, zu Stande [tsu'ʃtandə] adv: **~ bringen** to bring about; **~ kommen** to come about

zuständig ['tsu:ʃtɛndɪç] adj responsible; **Z~keit** f competence, responsibility

zustehen ['tsu:ʃte:ən] (unreg) vi: **jdm ~** to be sb's right

zustellen ['tsu:ʃtɛlən] vt (verstellen) to block; (Post etc) to send

Zustellung f delivery

zustimmen ['tsu:ʃtɪmən] vi to agree

Zustimmung f agreement, consent

zustoßen ['tsu:ʃto:sən] (unreg) vi (fig) to happen

Rechtschreibreform: ▲ *neue Schreibung* △ *alte Schreibung (auslaufend)*

zutage, zu Tage [tsu'ta:gə] adv: **~ bringen** to bring to light; **~ treten** to come to light

Zutaten ['tsu:ta:tən] pl ingredients

zuteilen ['tsu:taɪlən] vt (Arbeit, Rolle) to designate, assign; (Aktien, Wohnung) to allocate

zutiefst [tsu'ti:fst] adv deeply

zutragen ['tsu:tra:gən] (unreg) vt to bring; (Klatsch) to tell ♦ vr to happen

zutrau- ['tsu:trau] zW: **Z~en (-s) nt: Z~en (zu)** trust (in); **~en** vt: **jdm etw ~en** to credit sb with sth; **~lich** adj trusting, friendly

zutreffen ['tsu:trefən] (unreg) vi to be correct; to apply; **~d** adj (richtig) accurate, **Z~des bitte unterstreichen** please underline where applicable

Zutritt ['tsu:trɪt] m access, admittance

Zutun ['tsu:tu:n] (-s) nt assistance

zuverlässig ['tsu:ferlesɪç] adj reliable; **Z~keit** f reliability

zuversichtlich ['tsu:ferzɪçtlɪç] adj confident

zuvor [tsu'fo:r] adv before, previously; **~kommen** (unreg) vi +dat to anticipate; **jdm ~kommen** to beat sb to it; **~kommend** adj obliging, courteous

Zuwachs ['tsu:vaks] (-es) m increase, growth; (umg) addition; **z~en** (unreg) vi to become overgrown; (Wunde) to heal (up)

zuwege, zu Wege [tsu've:gə] adv: **etw ~ bringen** to accomplish sth

zuweilen [tsu'vaɪlən] adv at times, now and then

zuweisen ['tsu:vaɪzən] (unreg) vt to assign, to allocate

zuwenden ['tsu:vendən] (unreg) vt (+dat) to turn (towards) ♦ vr: **sich jdm/etw ~** to devote o.s. to sb/sth; to turn to sb/sth

zuwider [tsu'vi:dər] adv: **etw ist jdm ~** sb loathes sth, sb finds sth repugnant; **~handeln** vi: **einer Sache** dat **~handeln** to act contrary to sth; **einem Gesetz ~handeln** to contravene a law

zuziehen ['tsu:tsi:ən] (unreg) vt (schließen: Vorhang) to draw, to close; (herbeirufen: Experten) to call in ♦ vi to move in, to

come; **sich** dat **etw ~** (Krankheit) to catch sth; (Zorn) to incur sth

zuzüglich ['tsu:tsy:klɪç] präp +gen plus, with the addition of

Zwang [tsvaŋ] **(-(e)s, ¨e)** m compulsion, coercion

zwängen ['tsvɛŋən] vt, vr to squeeze

zwanglos adj informal

Zwangs- zW: **~arbeit** f forced labour; (Strafe) hard labour; **~lage** f predicament, tight corner; **z~läufig** adj necessary, inevitable

zwanzig ['tsvantsɪç] num twenty

zwar [tsva:r] adv to be sure, indeed; **das ist ~ ..., aber ...** that may be ... but ...; **und ~ am Sonntag** on Sunday to be precise; **und ~ so schnell, dass ...** in fact so quickly that ...

Zweck [tsvɛk] **(-(e)s, -e)** m purpose, aim; **es hat keinen ~** there's no point; **z~dienlich** adj practical, expedient

Zwecke f hobnail; (Heftzwecke) drawing pin, thumbtack (US)

Zweck- zW: **z~los** adj pointless; **z~mäßig** adj suitable, appropriate; **z~s** präp +gen for the purpose of

zwei [tsvaɪ] num two; **Z~bettzimmer** nt twin room, **~deutig** adj ambiguous; (unanständig) suggestive; **~erlei** adj: **~erlei Stoff** two different kinds of material; **~erlei Meinung** of differing opinions; **~fach** adj double

Zweifel ['tsvaɪfəl] **(-s, -)** m doubt; **z~haft** adj doubtful, dubious; **z~los** adj doubtless; **z~n** vi: **(an etw** dat**) z~n** to doubt (sth)

Zweig [tsvaɪk] **(-(e)s, -e)** m branch; **~stelle** f branch (office)

zwei- zW: **~hundert** num two hundred; **~mal** adv twice; **~sprachig** adj bilingual; **~spurig** adj (AUT) two-lane; **~stimmig** adj for two voices

zweit [tsvaɪt] adv: **zu ~** together; (bei mehreren Paaren) in twos

zweitbeste(r, s) adj second best

zweite(r, s) adj second

zweiteilig ['tsvaɪtaɪlɪç] adj (Gruppe) two-piece; (Fernsehfilm) two-part; (Kleidung) two-piece

zweit- *zW:* **~ens** *adv* secondly; **~größte(r, s)** *adj* second largest; **~klassig** *adj* second-class; **~letzte(r, s)** *adj* last but one, penultimate; **~rangig** *adj* second-rate

Zwerchfell ['tsverçfel] *nt* diaphragm

Zwerg [tsverk] **(-(e)s, -e)** *m* dwarf

Zwetsch(g)e ['tsvetʃ(g)ə] *f* plum

Zwieback ['tsviːbak] **(-(e)s, -e)** *m* rusk

Zwiebel ['tsviːbəl] **(-, -n)** *f* onion; *(Blumenzwiebel)* bulb

Zwie- ['tsviː] *zW:* **~lichtig** *adj* shady, dubious; **~spältig** *adj* *(Gefühle)* conflicting; *(Charakter)* contradictory; **~tracht** *f* discord, dissension

Zwilling ['tsvilɪŋ] **(-s, -e)** *m* twin; **~e** *pl* (*ASTROL*) Gemini

zwingen ['tsvɪŋən] *(unreg)* *vt* to force; **~d** *adj* *(Grund etc)* compelling

zwinkern ['tsvɪŋkərn] *vi* to blink; *(absichtlich)* to wink

Zwirn [tsvɪrn] **(-(e)s, -e)** *m* thread

zwischen ['tsvɪʃən] *präp (+akk od dat)* between; **Z~bemerkung** *f* (incidental) remark; **Z~ding** *nt* cross; **~durch** *adv* in between; *(räumlich)* here and there; **Z~ergebnis** *nt* intermediate result; **Z~fall** *m* incident; **Z~frage** *f* question; **Z~handel** *m* middlemen *pl*; middleman's trade; **Z~landung** *f* (*AVIAT*) stopover; **~menschlich** *adj* interpersonal; **Z~raum** *m* space; **Z~ruf** *m* interjection; **Z~stecker** *m* adaptor (plug); **Z~zeit** *f* interval; **in der Z~zeit** in the interim, meanwhile

zwitschern ['tsvɪtʃərn] *vt, vi* to twitter, to chirp

zwo [tsvoː] *num* two

zwölf [tsvœlf] *num* twelve

Zyklus ['tsyːklus] **(-, Zyklen)** *m* cycle

Zylinder [tsiˈlɪndər] **(-s, -)** *m* cylinder; *(Hut)* top hat

Zyniker ['tsyːnikər] **(-s, -)** *m* cynic

zynisch ['tsyːnɪʃ] *adj* cynical

Zypern ['tsyːpərn] *nt* Cyprus

Zyste ['tsystə] *f* cyst

zz., zzt. *abk* = **zurzeit**

PUZZLES AND WORDGAMES

PUZZLES AND WORDGAMES

Introduction

We are delighted that you have decided to invest in this Collins Pocket Dictionary! Whether you intend to use it in school, at home, on holiday or at work, we are sure that you will find it very useful.

In the pages which follow you will find explanations and wordgames (not too difficult!) designed to give you practice in exploring the dictionary's contents and in retrieving information for a variety of purposes. Answers are provided at the end. If you spend a little time on these pages you should be able to use your dictionary more efficiently and effectively. Have fun!

Supplement by
Roy Simon
reproduced by kind permission of
Tayside Region Education Department

HOW INFORMATION IS PRESENTED IN YOUR DICTIONARY

A great deal of information is packed into your Collins Pocket Dictionary using colour, various typefaces, sizes of type, symbols, abbreviations and brackets. The purpose of this section is to acquaint you with the conventions used in presenting information.

Headwords

A headword is the word you look up in a dictionary. Headwords are listed in alphabetical order throughout the dictionary. They are printed in colour so that they stand out clearly from all the other words on the dictionary page.

Note that at the top of each page a headword appears. This is a guide to the alphabetical order of words on the page. It is there to help you scan through the dictionary more quickly to find the word you want.

The German alphabet consists of the same 26 letters as the English alphabet, plus the letter ß. Although certain letters in the German alphabet take umlaut (ä, ö, ü), this does not affect the order of words in the German-English section of the dictionary.

A Dictionary Entry

An entry is made up of a headword and all the information about that headword. Entries will be short or long depending on how frequently a word is used in either English or German and how many meanings it has. Inevitably, the fuller the dictionary entry the more care is needed in sifting through it to find the information you require.

Meanings

The translations of a headword are given in ordinary type. Where there is more than one meaning or usage, a semi-colon separates one from the other.

abladen ['apla:dən] (*unreg*) *vt* to unload
Ablage ['apla:gə] *f* (*für Akten*) tray; (*für Kleider*) cloakroom
ablassen ['aplasən] (*unreg*) *vt* (*Wasser, Dampf*) to let off; (*vom Preis*) to knock off
♦ *vi*: **von etw ~** to give sth up, to abandon sth

brünett [bry'nɛt] *adj* brunette, dark-haired
Brunnen ['brʊnən] (**-s, -**) *m* fountain; (*tief*) well

Bude ['bu:də] *f* booth, stall; (*umg*) digs *pl* (*BRIT*)

Ohnmacht ['o:nmaxt] *f* faint; (*fig*) impotence; **in ~ fallen** to faint
ohnmächtig ['o:nmɛçtıç] *adj* in a faint, unconscious; (*fig*) weak, impotent; **sie ist ~** she has fainted
Ohr [o:r] (**-(e)s, -en**) *nt* ear
Öhr [ø:r] (**-(e)s, -e**) *nt* eye

Gurt [gʊrt] (**-(e)s, -e**) *m* belt

klar- *zW*: **~legen** *vt* to clear up, to explain; **~machen** *vt* (*Schiff*) to get ready for sea; **jdm etw ~machen** to make sth clear to sb; **~sehen** △ (*unreg*) *vi siehe* **klar**; **K~sichtfolie** *f* transparent film; **~stellen** *vt* to clarify

Zug [tsu:k] (**-(e)s, ⁻e**) *m* (*EISENB*) train; (*Luftzug*) draught; (*Ziehen*) pull(ing); (*Gesichtszug*) feature; (*SCHACH etc*) move; (*Schriftzug*) stroke; (*Atemzug*) breath; (*Charakterzug*) trait; (*an Zigarette*) puff, pull, drag; (*Schluck*) gulp; (*Menschengruppe*) procession; (*von Vögeln*) flight; (*MIL*) platoon; **etw in vollen Zügen genießen** to enjoy sth to the full

In addition, you will often find other words appearing in *italics* in brackets before the translations. These either give some notion of the contexts in which the headword might appear (as with 'scharf' opposite – 'scharfes Essen', 'scharfe Munition', etc.) or else they provide synonyms (as with 'fremd' opposite – 'unvertraut', 'ausländisch', etc.).

Phonetic Spellings

In square brackets immediately after most headwords you will find the phonetic spelling of the word – i.e. its pronunciation. The phonetic transcription of German and English vowels and consonants is given on page xii near the front of your dictionary.

Additional Information About Headwords

Information about the usage or form of certain headwords is given in brackets between the phonetics and the translation or translations. Have a look at the entries for 'KG', 'Filiale', 'löschen' and 'Bruch' opposite.

This information is usually given in abbreviated form. A helpful list of abbreviations is given on pages viii to x at the front of your dictionary.

You should be particularly careful with colloquial words or phrases. Words labelled '(*umg*)' would not normally be used in formal speech, while those labelled '(*umg!*)' would be considered offensive.

Careful consideration of such style labels will provide indications as to the degree of formality and appropriateness of a word and could help you avoid many an embarrassing situation when using German!

Expressions in which the Headword Appears

An entry will often feature certain common expressions in which the headword appears. These expressions are in **bold** type but in black as opposed to colour. A swung dash (–) is used instead of repeating a headword in an entry. 'Schikane' and 'man' opposite illustrate this point.

Related Words

In the Pocket Dictionary words related to certain headwords are sometimes given at the end of an entry, as with 'Lohn' and 'accept' opposite. These are easily picked out as they are also in colour. To help you find these words, they are placed in alphabetical order after the headword to which they belong – see 'acceptable', 'acceptance' etc. opposite.

scharf [ʃarf] *adj* sharp; (*Essen*) hot, spicy; (*Munition*) live; ~ **nachdenken** to think hard; **auf etw** *akk* ~ **sein** (*umg*) to be keen on sth

fremd [frɛmt] *adj* (*unvertraut*) strange; (*ausländisch*) foreign; (*nicht eigen*) someone else's; **etw ist jdm** ~ sth is foreign to sb; **~artig** *adj* strange; **F~enführer** ['frɛmdən-]

gänzlich ['gɛntslɪç] *adj* complete, entire ♦ *adv* completely, entirely

Teufel ['tɔʏfəl] (-s, -) *m* devil, **teuflisch** ['tɔʏflɪʃ] *adj* fiendish, diabolical

KG [kaː'geː] (-, -s) *f abk* (= *Kommanditgesellschaft*) limited partnership

Filiale [fili'aːlə] *f* (*COMM*) branch

löschen ['lœʃən] *vt* (*Feuer, Licht*) to put out, to extinguish; (*Durst*) to quench; (*COMM*) to cancel; (*COMPUT*) to delete; (*Tonband*) to erase; (*Fracht*) to unload ♦ *vi* (*Feuerwehr*) to put out a fire; (*Tinte*) to blot

Bruch [brʊx] (-(e)s, ⁺e) *m* breakage; (*zerbrochene Stelle*) break; (*fig*) split, breach; (*MED: Eingeweidebruch*) rupture, hernia; (*Beinbruch etc*) fracture; (*MATH*) fraction

schenken ['ʃɛŋkən] *vt* (*auch fig*) to give; (*Getränk*) to pour; **sich** *dat* **etw** ~ (*umg*) to skip sth; **das ist geschenkt!** (*billig*) that's a giveaway!; (*nichts wert*) that's worthless!

Bombenerfolg (*umg*) *m* smash hit

Arsch [arʃ] (-es, ⁺e) (*umg!*) *m* arse (*BRIT!*), ass (*US!*)

Schikane [ʃi'kaːnə] *f* harassment; dirty trick; **mit allen ~n** with all the trimmings

man [man] *pron* one, you; ~ **sagt, ...** they *od* people say ...; **wie schreibt** ~ **das?** how do you write it?, how is it written?

Lohn [loːn] (-(e)s, ⁺e) *m* reward; (*Arbeitslohn*) pay, wages *pl*; **~büro** *nt* wages office; **~empfänger** *m* wage earner

accept [ək'sɛpt] *vt* (*take*) annehmen; (*agree to*) akzeptieren; **~able** *adj* annehmbar; **~ance** *n* Annahme *f*

'Key' Words

Your Collins Pocket Dictionary gives special status to certain German and English words which can be looked on as 'key' words in each language. These are words which have many different usages. 'werden', 'alle(r, s)' and 'sich' opposite are typical examples in German. You are likely to become familiar with them in your day-to-day language studies.

There will be occasions, however, when you want to check on a particular usage. Your dictionary can be very helpful here. Note how different parts of speech and different usages are clearly indicated by a combination of lozenges (♦) and numbers. In addition, further guides to usage are given in italics in brackets in the language of the user who needs them.

werden ['veːrdən] (*pt* **wurde**, *pp* **geworden** *od (bei Passiv)* **worden**) *vi* to become; **was ist aus ihm/aus der Sache geworden?** what became of him/it?; **es ist nichts/gut geworden** it came to nothing/turned out well; **es wird Nacht/Tag** it's getting dark/light; **mir wird kalt** I'm getting cold; **mir wird schlecht** I feel ill; **Erster werden** to come *od* be first; **das muss anders werden** that'll have to change; **rot/zu Eis werden** to turn red/to ice; **was willst du (mal) werden?** what do you want to be?; **die Fotos sind gut geworden** the photos have come out nicely

♦ *als Hilfsverb* **1** (*bei Futur*): **er wird es tun** he will *od* he'll do it; **er wird das nicht tun** he will not *od* he won't do it; **es wird gleich regnen** it's going to rain

2 (*bei Konjunktiv*): **ich würde ...** I would ...; **er würde gern ...** he would *od* he'd like to ...; **ich würde lieber ...** I would *od* I'd rather ...

3 (*bei Vermutung*): **sie wird in der Küche sein** she will be in the kitchen

4 (*bei Passiv*): **gebraucht werden** to be used; **er ist erschossen worden** he has *od* he's been shot; **mir wurde gesagt, dass ...** I was told that ...

alle(r, s) ['alə(r,s)] *adj* **1** (*sämtliche*) all; **wir alle** all of us; **alle Kinder waren da** all the children were there; **alle Kinder mögen ...** all children like ...; **alle beide** both of us/them; **sie kamen alle** they all came; **alles Gute** all the best; **alles in allem** all in all **2** (*mit Zeit- oder Maßangaben*) every; **alle vier Jahre** every four years; **alle fünf Meter** every five metres

♦ *pron* everything; **alles was er sagt** everything he says, all that he says

♦ *adv* (*zu Ende, aufgebraucht*) finished; **die Milch ist alle** the milk's all gone, there's no milk left; **etw alle machen** to finish sth up

sich [zɪç] *pron* **1** (*akk*): **er/sie/es ... sich** he/she/it ... himself/herself/itself; **sie** *pl/* **man ... sich** they/one ... themselves/oneself; **Sie ... sich** you ... yourself/yourselves *pl*; **sich wiederholen** to repeat oneself/itself

2 (*dat*): **er/sie/es ... sich** he/she/it ... to himself/herself/itself; **sie** *pl/***man ... sich** they/one ... to themselves/oneself; **Sie ... sich** you ... to yourself/yourselves *pl*; **sie hat sich einen Pullover gekauft** she bought herself a jumper; **sich die Haare waschen** to wash one's hair

3 (*mit Präposition*): **haben Sie Ihren Ausweis bei sich?** do you have your pass on you?; **er hat nichts bei sich** he's got nothing on him; **sie bleiben gern unter sich** they keep themselves to themselves

4 (*einander*) each other, one another; **sie bekämpfen sich** they fight each other *od* one another

5: **dieses Auto fährt sich gut** this car drives well; **hier sitzt es sich gut** it's good to sit here

WORDGAME 1
HEADWORDS

Study the following sentences. In each sentence a wrong word spelt very similarly to the correct word has deliberately been put in and the sentence doesn't make sense. This word is shaded each time. Write out the correct word, which you will find in your dictionary near the wrong word.

Example   Raufen verboten

[‘Raufen’ (= ‘to pull out’) is the wrong word and should be replaced by ‘rauchen’ (= ‘to smoke’)]

1. Hast du das Buch schon gekonnt?

2. Ich habe ein paar VW-Akten gekauft.

3. Wir waren gestern im Kilo.

4. Sollen wir die Theaterkarten schon kauen?

5. Unser Nachbar hat einen kleinen schwarzen Puder.

6. Ich zähle heute die Rechnung.

7. Der Student muss sich für den Kurs einschreiten.

8. Das neue Restaurant ist gar nicht über.

9. Gans viele Leute standen am Unfallort.

10. Ich habe meiner Tanne einen Brief geschrieben.

WORDGAME 2
DICTIONARY ENTRIES

Complete the crossword below by looking up the English words in the list and finding the correct German translations. There is a slight catch, however! All the English words can be translated several ways into German, but only one translation will fit correctly into each part of the crossword. So look carefully through the entries in the English-German section of your dictionary.

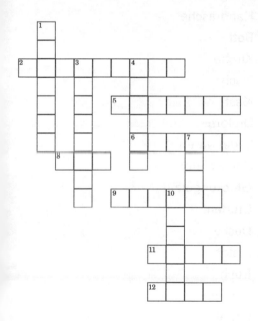

1. FAIR
2. CATCH
3. LEARN
4. FALL
5. HIT
6. HARD
7. CALF
8. PLACE
9. HOLD
10. PLACE
11. TRACK
12. HOME

WORDGAME 3

FINDING MEANINGS

In this list there are eight pairs of words that have some sort of connection with each other. For example, 'Diplom' (= 'diploma') and 'Student' (='student') are linked. Find the other pairs by looking up the words in your dictionary.

1. Morgenrock
2. Handtasche
3. Bett
4. Kirche
5. Fisch
6. Nest
7. Diplom
8. Lederwaren
9. Hausschuhe
10. Glockengeläut
11. Student
12. Decke
13. Elster
14. Buch
15. Schuppe
16. Regal

WORDGAME 4

SYNONYMS

Complete the crossword by supplying synonyms of the words below. You will sometimes find the words you are looking for in italics in brackets in the entries for the words in the list. Sometimes you will have to turn to the English-German section for help.

1. Art
2. probieren
3. Feuer
4. sich ereignen
5. Arroganz
6. namhaft
7. Ladung
8. Plan
9. begegnen
10. Neigung

WORDGAME 5

SPELLING

You will often use your dictionary to check spellings. The person who has compiled this list of ten German words has made <u>three</u> spelling mistakes. Find the three words which have been misspelt and write them out correctly.

1. nachsehen
2. nacht
3. Nagetier
4. Name
5. Nature
6. neuriech
7. Nickerchen
8. Nimmersatt
9. nördlich
10. nötig

WORDGAME 6

ANTONYMS

Complete the crossword by supplying ANTONYMS (i.e. opposites) in German of the words below. Use your dictionary to help.

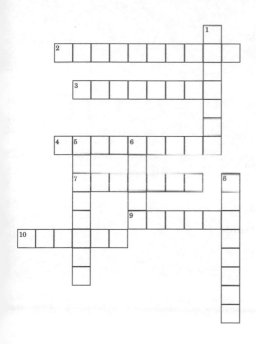

1. gestehen
2. enthüllen
3. unschuldig
4. kaufen
5. verbieten
6. Reichtum
7. ruhig
8. ankommen
9. ängstlich
10. schmutzig

WORDGAME 7
PHONETIC SPELLINGS

The phonetic transcriptions of ten German words are given below. If you study page xii near the front of your dictionary you should be able to work out what the words are.

1. frika'dɛlə
2. ʃpuːr
3. faɪn
4. 'lyːgə
5. 'ʃtaxəl
6. 'naʊtɪʃ
7. gə'vœlbə
8. 'kɔɣçən
9. 'møːgən
10. 'glaʊbvʏrdɪç

WORDGAME 8

EXPRESSIONS IN WHICH THE HEADWORD APPEARS

If you look up the headword 'Satz' in the German-English section of your dictionary you will find that the word can have many meanings. Study the entry carefully and translate the following sentences into English.

1. Der Satz ist viel zu lang.

2. Unterstreicht jeden Satz, der mit einer Konjunktion beginnt.

3. Den Satz von Pythagoras kennt jeder.

4. Das Orchester hat den letzten Satz ganz ausgezeichnet gespielt.

5. Steffi Graf hat in der Meisterschaft keinen Satz verloren.

6. Der ganze Satz war in der Tasse.

7. Bei Lieferungen ins Ausland gilt ein anderer Satz.

8. Sie hat vor lauter Begeisterung einen großen Satz gemacht.

WORDGAME 9
RELATED WORDS

Fill in the blanks in the pairs of sentences below. The missing words are related to the headwords on the left. Choose the correct "relative" each time. You will find it in your dictionary near the headword provided.

HEADWORD	RELATED WORDS
Stellung	1. Ich habe die Uhr auf halb sechs _____. 2. Das Auto steht an der gleichen _____.
Hoffnung	3. _____ bleibt das Wetter so. 4. Sie _____, dass sie bald wieder gesund ist.
Betrug	5. Von ihm lassen wir uns nicht mehr _____. 6. Er ist als _____ bekannt.
sprechen	7. Hat er schon mit seiner Mutter _____? 8. Das Buch wurde in fünf _____ übersetzt.
Student	9. Er hat letztes Semester mit dem _____ begonnen. 10. Sie _____ Medizin.
kurz	11. Ich habe _____ noch mit ihm gesprochen. 12. Der Rock muss _____ werden.

WORDGAME 10

'KEY' WORDS

Study carefully the entry 'machen' in your dictionary and find translations for the following:

1. what are you doing (there)?

2. it's the cold that does that

3. that doesn't matter

4. I don't mind the cold

5. 3 and 5 are 8

6. to have the car done

7. how's the work going?

8. hurry up!

9. to set about sth

10. to turn the radio down

THE DICTIONARY AND GRAMMAR

While it is true that a dictionary can never be a substitute for a detailed grammar book, it nevertheless provides a great deal of grammatical information. If you know how to extract this information you will be able to use German more accurately both in speech and in writing.

The Collins Pocket Dictionary presents grammatical information as follows.

Parts of Speech

Parts of speech are given in italics immediately after the phonetic spellings of headwords. Abbreviated forms are used. Abbreviations can be checked on pages viii to x.

Changes in parts of speech within an entry – for example, from adjective to pronoun to adverb, or from noun to intransitive verb to transitive verb – are indicated by means of lozenges (♦), as with the German 'alle(r, s)' and the English 'fast' opposite.

German Nouns

The gender of each noun in the German-English section of the dictionary is indicated in the following way:

m = Maskulinum
f = Femininum
nt = Neutrum

You will occasionally see '*m od nt*' or '*m od f*' beside an entry. This indicates that the noun can be either masculine or neuter (see 'Knäuel' opposite or masculine or feminine (see 'Sellerie' opposite).

Feminine forms of nouns are shown, as with 'Schaffner(in)' opposite. This is marked *m(f)* to show that the feminine form has the ending '-in'. Nouns which have the ending '-(r)', like 'Angeklagte(r)' opposite, are formed from adjectives and are marked *f(m)* to show that they can be either masculine or feminine. Their spelling changes in the same way as adjectives, depending on their article and position in the sentence.

prosit ['proːzɪt] *excl* cheers

leiten ['laɪtən] *vt* to lead; (*Firma*) to manage; (*in eine Richtung*) to direct; (*ELEK*) to conduct

alle(r, s) ['alə(r,s)] *adj* **1** (*sämtliche*) all; **wir alle** all of us; **alle Kinder waren da** all the children were there; **alle Kinder mögen ...** all children like ...; **alle beide** both of us/ them; **sie kamen alle** they all came; **alles Gute** all the best; **alles in allem** all in all **2** (*mit Zeit- oder Maßangaben*) every; **alle vier Jahre** every four years; **alle fünf Meter** every five metres
♦ *pron* everything; **alles was er sagt** everything he says, all that he says
♦ *adv* (*zu Ende, aufgebraucht*) finished; **die Milch ist alle** the milk's all gone, there's no milk left; **etw alle machen** to finish sth up

fast [faːst] *adj* schnell, (*firm*) fest ♦ *adv* schnell; fest ♦ *n* Fasten *nt* ♦ *vi* fasten; **to be ~** (*clock*) vorgehen

Knäuel ['knɔʏəl] (**-s, -**) *m od nt* (*Wollknäuel*) ball; (*Menschenknäuel*) knot

Sellerie ['zɛləriː] (**-s, -(s)** *od* **-, -**) *m od f* celery

Schaffner(in) ['ʃafnər(ɪn)] (**-s, -**) *m(f)* (*Busschaffner*) conductor(-tress); (*EISENB*) guard

Angeklagte(r) ['angəklaːktə(r)] *f(m)* accused

So many things depend on you knowing the correct gender of a German noun – whether you use 'er', 'sie' or 'es' to translate 'it'; whether you use 'er' or 'es' to translate 'he', 'sie' or 'es' to translate 'she'; the spelling of adjectives etc. If you are in any doubt as to the gender of a noun, it is always best to check it in your dictionary.

Genitive singular and nominative plural forms of many nouns are also given (see 'Bube' and 'Scheitel' opposite). A list of regular noun endings is given on page xi and nouns which have these forms will not show genitive singular and nominative plural at the headword (see 'Rasur' and 'Forelle' opposite). Nouns formed from two or more words do not have genitive singular and nominative plural shown if the last element appears in the dictionary as a headword. For example, if you want to know how to decline 'Backenzahn', you will find the necessary information at 'Zahn'.

Adjectives

Adjectives are given in the form used when they come after a verb. If the adjective comes before a noun, the spelling changes, depending on the gender of the noun and on the article (if any), which comes before the adjective. Compare 'der Hund ist schwarz' with 'der schwarze Hund'. If you find an unfamiliar adjective in a text and want to look it up in the dictionary, you will have to decide what spelling changes have been made before you can know how it will appear in the dictionary.

Some adjectives are never used after a verb. In these cases, the dictionary shows all the possible nominative singular endings.

Adverbs

German adverbs come in three main types.

Some are just adjectives in their after-verb form, used as adverbs. Sometimes the meaning is similar to the meaning of the adjective (see 'laut'), sometimes it is rather different (see 'richtig').

Some adverbs are formed by adding '-weise', '-sweise' or '-erweise' to the adjective.

Other adverbs are not considered to be derived from particular adjectives.

In your dictionary, adjective-adverbs may be shown by a change of part of speech or by the mention 'adj, adv' at the beginning of the entry.

Fuß [fuːs] (-es, ̈e) m foot; (von Glas, Säule etc) base; (von Möbel) leg; **zu ~** on foot;

Stube ['ʃtuːbə] f room

Mädchen ['mɛːtçən] nt girl; **m~haft** adj girlish; **~name** m maiden name

Rasur [ra'zuːr] f shaving

Forelle [fo'rɛlə] f trout

schwarz [ʃvarts] adj black; **~es Brett** notice board; **ins S~e treffen** (auch fig) to hit the bull's eye; **in den ~en Zahlen** in the black; **~ sehen** (umg) to see the gloomy side of things; **S~arbeit** f illicit work, moonlighting; **S~brot** nt black bread; **S~e(r)** f(m) black (man/woman)

laut [laut] adj loud ♦ adv loudly; (lesen) aloud ♦ präp (+gen od dat) according to; **L~** (-(e)s, -e) m sound

richtig adj right, correct; (echt) proper ♦ adv (umg: sehr) really; **bin ich hier ~?** am I in the right place?; **der/die R~e** the right one/person; **das R~e** the right thing; **etw ~ stellen** to correct sth; **R~keit** f correctness

leider ['laɪdər] adv unfortunately; **ja, ~** yes, I'm afraid so; **~ nicht** I'm afraid not

oben ['oːbən] adv above; (in Haus) upstairs; **~ erwähnt, ~ genannt** above-mentioned; **nach ~** up; **von ~** down; **~ ohne** topless;

Bube ['buːbə] (-n, -n) m (Schurke) rogue; (KARTEN) jack

Scheitel ['ʃaɪtəl] (-s, -) m top; (Haarscheitel) parting; **s~n** vt to part

Backenzahn m molar

Zahn [tsaːn] (-(e)s, ̈e) m tooth; **~arzt** m dentist; **~ärztin** f (female) dentist; **~bürste** f toothbrush; **~fleisch** nt gums pl; **~pasta** f toothpaste; **~rad** nt cog(wheel); **~schmerzen** pl toothache sg; **~stein** m tartar; **~stocher** (-s, -) m toothpick

besondere(r, s) [bə'zɔndərə(r, s)] adj special; (eigen) particular; (gesondert) separate; (eigentümlich) peculiar

letzte(r, s) ['lɛtstə(r, s)] adj last; (neueste) latest; **zum ~n Mal** for the last time; **~ns** adv lately; **~re(r, s)** adj latter

nett [nɛt] adj nice; (freundlich) nice, kind; **~erweise** adv kindly

glück- zW: **~lich** adj fortunate; (froh) happy; **~licherweise** adv fortunately; **~'selig** adj blissful

Adjective-plus-ending adverbs will usually appear as subentries.

Adverbs like 'oben' and 'leider' will usually appear as separate headwords.

Where a word in your text seems to be an adverb but does not appear in the dictionary, you should be able to work out a translation from the word it is related to, once you have found that in the dictionary.

Information about Verbs

A major problem facing language learners is that the form of a verb will change according to the subject and/or the tense being used. A typical German verb can take on many different forms – too many to list in a dictionary entry.

Yet, although verbs are listed in your dictionary in their infinitive forms only, this does not mean that the dictionary is of limited value when it comes to handling the verb system of the German language. On the contrary, it contains much valuable information.

First of all, your dictionary will help you with the meanings of unfamiliar verbs. If you came across the word 'füllt' in a text and looked it up in your dictionary you wouldn't find it. What you must do is assume that it is part of a verb and look for the infinitive form. Thus you will deduce that 'füllt' is a form of the verb 'füllen'. You now have the basic meaning of the word you are concerned with – something to do with English verb 'fill' – and this should be enough to help you understand the text you are reading.

It is usually an easy task to make the connection between the form of a verb and the infinitive. For example, 'füllten', 'füllst', 'füllte' and 'gefüllt' are all recognizable as parts of the infinitive 'füllen'. However, sometimes it is less obvious – for example, 'hilft', 'halfen' and 'geholfen' are all parts of 'helfen'. The only real solution to this problem is to learn the various forms of the main German irregular verbs.

And this is the second source of help offered by your dictionary as far as verbs are concerned. The irregular verb lists on pages 609 to 613 at the back of the Collins Pocket Dictionary provide the main forms of the main tenses of the basic irregular verbs. (Verbs which consist of a basic verb with prefix usually follow the rules for the basic verb.) Consider the verb 'sehen' below where the following information is given:

infinitive	present indicative (2nd, 3rd sg)	imperfect	past participle
sehen	siehst, sieht	sah	gesehen

In order to make maximum use of the information contained in these pages, a good working knowledge of the various rules affecting German verbs is required. You will acquire this in the course of your German studies and your Collins dictionary will serve as a useful 'aide-mémoire'. If you happen to forget how to form the second person singular form of the Past Tense of 'sehen' (i.e. how to translate 'You saw'), there will be no need to panic – your dictionary contains the information!

In addition, the main parts of the most common irregular verbs are listed in the body of the dictionary.

WORDGAME 11

PARTS OF SPEECH

In each sentence below a word has been shaded. Put a tick in the appropriate box to indicate the **part of speech** each time.

SENTENCE	Noun	Adj	Adv	Verb
1. Das Essen ist fertig.				
2. Er hat kein Recht dazu.				
3. Warum fahren wir nicht in die Stadt zum Essen?				
4. Ich gehe nicht mit essen.				
5. Rauchen ist strengstens verboten.				
6. Gehen Sie geradeaus und dann die erste Straße links.				
7. Das war aber ein interessanter Vortrag.				
8. Die Schauspielerin trug ein herrliches Kleid.				
9. Hast du schon von deiner Freundin gehört?				
10. Es ist immer noch recht sommerlich.				

WORDGAME 12

MEANING CHANGING WITH GENDER

Some German nouns change meaning according to their gender. Look at the pairs of sentences below and fill in the blanks with either 'ein, einen, eine' or 'der, den, die, das'.

1. Ist das _____ erste Band der Schillerausgabe?

   _____ Band ist nicht lang genug.

2. _____ Mark ist in letzter Zeit wieder gestiegen.

   Der Metzger löst _____ Mark aus den Knochen.

3. Was kostet _____ Bund Petersilie?

   _____ Bund an der Hose ist zu weit.

4. _____ Tau lag noch auf den Wiesen.

   Der Mann konnte _____ Tau nicht heben.

5. Wie steht mir _____ Hut?

   Wir müssen wirklich auf _____ Hut sein.

6. Hinter dem Haus steht _____ Kiefer.

   Er hat sich _____ Kiefer gebrochen.

WORDGAME 13

ADJECTIVES

Try to work out how the adjectives in the following phrases will appear in the dictionary. Write your answer beside the phrase, then check in the dictionary.

1. ein englisches Buch

2. der rote Traktor

3. letzte Nacht

4. mein kleiner Bruder

5. eine lange Reise

6. guter Käse

7. das alte Trikot

8. schwarzes Brot

9. die große Kommode

10. ein heftiger Schlag

11. der siebte Sohn

12. die neuen Nachbarn

WORDGAME 14

VERB TENSES

Use your dictionary to help you fill in the blanks in the table below.
(Remember the important pages at the back of your dictionary.)

INFINITIVE	PRESENT TENSE	IMPERFECT	PERFECT TENSE
sehen		ich	
schlafen	du		
sein			ich
schlagen		ich	
anrufen			ich
abfahren	er		
studieren			ich
haben		ich	
anfangen	du		
waschen	er		
werden		ich	
nehmen			ich

WORDGAME 15

PAST PARTICIPLES

Use your dictionary to find the past participle of these verbs.

INFINITIVE	PAST PARTICIPLE
singen	
beißen	
bringen	
frieren	
reiben	
gewinnen	
helfen	
geschehen	
liegen	
lügen	
schneiden	
kennen	
mögen	
wissen	
können	

WORDGAME 16

IDENTIFYING INFINITIVES

In the sentences below you will see various German verbs shaded. Use your dictionary to help you find the INFINITIVE form of each verb.

1. Leider habe ich Ihren Namen vergessen.

2. Bitte ruf mich doch morgen früh mal an.

3. Er ist um 16 Uhr angekommen.

4. Sie hielt an ihrem Argument fest.

5. Wir waren im Sommer in Italien.

6. Ich würde gerne kommen, wenn ich nur könnte.

7. Die Maschine flog über den Nordpol.

8. Ich würde es ja machen, aber ich habe keine Zeit.

9. Wohin fährst du diesen Winter zum Skilaufen?

10. Wen habt ihr sonst noch eingeladen?

11. Er hat deinen Brief erst gestern bekommen.

12. Liest du das Buch nicht zu Ende?

13. Meine Mutter ist letztes Jahr gestorben.

14. Er hat den Zettel aus Versehen weggeworfen.

15. Ich nahm ihn jeden Tag mit nach Hause.

MORE ABOUT MEANING

In this section we will consider some of the problems associated with using a bilingual dictionary.

Overdependence on your dictionary

That the dictionary is an invaluable tool for the language learner is beyond dispute. Nevertheless, it is possible to become overdependent on your dictionary, turning to it in an almost automatic fashion every time you come up against a new German word or phrase. Tackling an unfamiliar text in this way will turn reading in German into an extremely tedious activity. If you stop to look up every new word you may actually be *hindering* your ability to read in German – you are so concerned with the individual words that you pay no attention to the text as a whole and to the context which gives them meaning. It is therefore important to develop appropriate reading skills – using clues such as titles, headlines, illustrations, etc., understanding relations within a sentence, etc. to predict or infer what a text is about.

A detailed study of the development of reading skills is not within the scope of this supplement; we are concerned with knowing how to use a dictionary, which is only one of several important skills involved in reading. Nevertheless, it may be instructive to look at one example. You see the following text in a German newspaper and are interested in working out what it is about.

Contextual clues here include the word in large type which you would probably recognize as a German name, something that looks like a date below, and the name and address at the bottom. Some 'form' words such as 'wir', 'sind', 'und' and 'Tochter' will be familiar to you from your general studies in German. Given that we are dealing with

> *Wir sind glücklich*
> *über die Geburt*
> *unserer Tochter*
>
> ## Julia
>
> am 5. Juni 1999
>
> *Christine und Artur Landgraf*
> *Vacher Straße 50 B, Köln*

a newspaper, you will probably have worked out by now that this could be an announcement placed in the 'Personal Column'.

So you have used a series of cultural, contextual and word-formation clues to get you to the point where you have understood that Christine and Artur Landgraf have placed this notice in the 'Personal Column' of the newspaper and that something happened to Julia on 5 November 1997. And you have reached this point *without* opening your dictionary once. Common sense and your knowledge of newspaper contents in this country might suggest that this must be an announcement of someone's birth or death. Thus 'glücklich' ('happy') and 'Geburt' ('birth') become the only words that you might have to look up in order to confirm that this is indeed a birth announcement.

When learning German we are helped by the fact that some German and English words look and sound alike and have exactly the same meaning. Such words are called 'COGNATES' i.e. words derived from the same root. Many words come from a common Latin root. Other words are the same or nearly the same in both languages because the German language has borrowed a word from English or vice versa. The dictionary should not be necessary where cognates are concerned – provided you know the English word that the German word resembles!

Words With More Than One Meaning

The need to examine with care *all* the information contained in a dictionary entry must be stressed. This is particularly important with the many German words which have more than one meaning. For example, the German 'Zeit' can mean 'grammatical tense' as well as 'time'. How you translated the word would depend on the context in which you found it.

Similarly, if you were trying to translate a phrase such as 'sich vor etwas drücken', you would have to look through the whole entry for 'drücken' to get the right translation. If you restricted your search to the first couple of lines of the entry and saw that the first meaning given is 'press', you might be tempted to assume that the idiom meant 'to press o.s. in front of sth'. But if you examined the entry closely you would see that 'sich vor etwas drücken' means 'to get out of (doing) sth', as in the sentence 'Sie drückt sich immer vor dem Abwasch'.

The same need for care applies when you are using the English-German section of your dictionary to translate a word from English into German. Watch out in particular for the lozenges indicating changes in parts of speech.

If you want to translate 'You can't fool me', the capital letters at 'Narr' and 'Närrin' will remind you that these words are nouns. But watch what you are doing with the verbs or you could end up with a mistranslation like 'Sie können mich nicht herumalbern'!

Phrasal Verbs

Another potential source of difficulty is English phrasal verbs. These consist of a common verb ('go', 'make', etc.) plus an adverb and/or a preposition to give English expressions such as 'to take after', 'to make out', etc. Entries for such verbs tend to be fairly full; therefore close examination of the contents is required. Note how these verbs appear in colour within the entry.

fool [fuːl] n Narr m, Närrin f ♦ vt (deceive) hereinlegen ♦ vi (also: ~ **around**) (herum)albern; ~**hardy** adj tollkühn; ~**ish** adj albern; ~**proof** adj idiotensicher

make [meɪk] (pt, pp **made**) vt machen; (appoint) ernennen (zu); (cause to do sth) veranlassen; (reach) erreichen; (in time) schaffen; (earn) verdienen ♦ n Marke f; **to ~ sth happen** etw geschehen lassen; **to ~ it** es schaffen; **what time do you ~ it?** wie spät hast du es?; **to ~ do with** auskommen mit; ~ **for** vi gehen/fahren nach; ~ **out** vt (write out) ausstellen; (understand) verstehen; ~ **up** vt machen; (face) schminken; (quarrel) beilegen; (story etc) erfinden ♦ vi sich versöhnen; ~ **up for** vt wieder gutmachen; (COMM) vergüten; ~**believe** n Fantasie f; ~**r** n (COMM) Hersteller m; ~**shift** adj behelfsmäßig, Not-; ~~**up** n Schminke f, Make-up nt; ~**up remover** n Make-up-Entferner m; **making** n: **in the making** im Entstehen; **to have the makings of** das Zeug haben zu

False Friends

Some German and English words have similar forms *and* meanings. There are, however, German words which *look* like English words but have a completely *different* meaning. For example, 'blank' in German means 'bright'; 'Probe' means 'rehearsal'; 'bilden' means 'to educate'. This can easily lead to serious mistranslations.

Sometimes the meaning of the German word is close to the English. For example, 'die Chips' are 'potato crisps' rather than 'chips'; 'der Hund' means a dog of any sort, not just a 'hound'. But some German words have two meanings, one the same as the English, the other completely different! 'Golf' can mean 'gulf' as well as 'golf'; 'senden' can mean 'to send' but can also mean 'to transmit/broadcast'.

Such words are often referred to as 'false friends'. You will have to look at the context in which they appear in order to arrive at the correct meaning. If they seem to fit with the sense of the passage as a whole, it will probably not be necessary to look them up. If they don't make sense, however, you may be dealing with 'false friends'.

WORDGAME 17

WORDS IN CONTEXT

Study the sentences below. Translations of the underlined words are given at the bottom. Match the number of the sentence and the letter of the translation correctly each time.

1. Sprich bitte lauter, ich kann dich nicht hören.

2. Er hört den ganzen Tag Radio.

3. Kannst du das Licht ausmachen, wenn du ins Bett gehst?

4. Können wir heute schon einen Termin ausmachen?

5. Seine Frau saß am Steuer, als der Unfall passierte.

6. Ich muss dieses Jahr viel Steuern nachzahlen.

7. Die Nachfrage nach japanischen Autos ist groß.

8. Aufgrund meiner Nachfrage konnte ich dann doch etwas erfahren.

9. Das Haus wird auf meinen Namen umgeschrieben.

10. Das Referat musst du völlig umschreiben.

11. Sind die Äpfel schon reif?

12. Für ihr Alter wirkt sie schon ziemlich reif.

a.	demand	e.	ripe	i.	steering wheel
b.	transferred	f.	inquiry	j.	listens to
c.	turn off	g.	mature	k.	agree
d.	hear	h.	rewrite	l.	tax

WORDGAME 18
FALSE FRIENDS

Look at the advertisements below. The words which have been shaded
resemble English words but have different meanings here. Find a correct
translation for each word in the context.

1
Reformhaus
Neustr. 23
Sonderangebot:
Vollkornbrot 2, 78 DM

2
Hotel Olympia
Alle Zimmer mit Dusche/WC
Gemütliche Atmosphäre
Bitte Prospekt anfordern

Heinrichstraße 51 –
7000 STUTTGART 25
Tel. 0711/21 56 93

3
KP- Chef Italiens fliegt
morgen nach New York

4
W. Meinzer   Lebensmittel
Heute Chips
im
Sonderangebot

5

Der Mann
im
Smoking

6

Clinton
will wieder
Präsident der
USA werden

7

Nach der
Jahrtausendwende
erst mit 65 in
Rente

8

Europaparlament

Fraktions-Flanke abdecken

9

Reise sorgenfrei
mit diesen Drei

Reisescheck
Devisen
Sparkassenbuch

BEZIRKSSPARKASSE HAUSACH
Hauptstr. 14

WORDGAME 19

WORDS WITH MORE THAN ONE MEANING

Look at the advertisements and headlines below. The words which have been shaded can have more than one meaning. Use your dictionary to help you work out the correct translation in the context.

1

Landespräsident tritt zurück

2

Vermögen:

Vom kleinen zum
großen Geld

3

Ich weiß, wie ich
Schmerzen schnell los werde

Parazetamol
Aus Ihrer Apotheke

4

**Heinrich Wohnmobile
GmbH**

Spezialisten bieten
günstige Preise

5

Hotel Restaurant
Seeberger

Alle Preise inklusive
Bedienung

Marktplatz 12
Loßurg   Telefon (07165) 33 14

6

Müsli – Riegel

von Cadbury

– gibt Kraft und Energie!

7

Hotel – Pension Miramar

Behagliche Atmosphäre
Günstige Nachsaisonpreise

Strandstr. 6,
24340 Eckernförde
Telefon (04269) 29 51

8

Das Blatt
Finanz- und
Wirtschaftszeitung

HAVE FUN WITH YOUR DICTIONARY

Here are some word games for you to try. You will find your dictionary helpful as you attempt the activities.

WORDGAME 20
CODED WORDS

In the boxes below the letters of eight German words have been replaced by numbers. A number represents the same letter each time.

Try to crack the code and find the eight words. If you need help, use your dictionary.

Here is a clue: all the words you are looking for have something to do with TRANSPORT.

1. | W¹ | A² | G³ | 4 | 5 |

2. | 10 | 8 | 11 | 11 | 4 | 10 |

3. | 12 | 2 | 13 | 14 |

4. | 9 | 2 | 7 | 10 | 10 | 2 | 19 |

5. | 9 | 11 | 16 | 3 | 15 | 4 | 16 | 3 |

6. | 6 | 2 | 7 | 5 | 7 | 8 | 9 |

7. | 15 | 16 | 3 |

8. | 11 | 2 | 18 | 12 | 1 | 2 | 3 | 4 | 5 |

314

WORDGAME 21
BEHEADED WORDS

If you 'behead' certain German words, i.e. take away their first letter, you are left with another German word. For example, if you behead 'Kleider' (= 'clothes'), you get 'leider' (= 'unfortunately'), and 'dort' (= 'there') gives 'Ort' (= 'place').

The following words have their heads chopped off, i.e. the first letter has been removed. Use your dictionary to help you form a new German word by adding one letter to the start of each word below. Write down the new German word and its meaning.

1.   ragen (= to tower)

2.   tollen (= to romp)

3.   nie (= never)

4.   Rand (= edge)

5.   oben (= above)

6.   ich (= I)

7.   Rad (= wheel)

8.   innen (= inside)

9.   raten (= to guess)

10.   indisch (= Indian)

11.   eigen (= own)

12.   eben (= level)

13.   Ohr (= ear)

14.   pur (= pure)

WORDGAME 22

CROSSWORD

Complete this crossword by looking up the words listed below in the English-German section of your dictionary. Remember to read through the entry carefully to find the word that will fit.

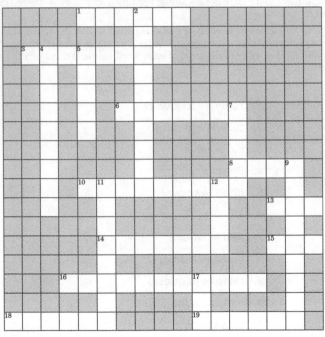

1. Heavily
2. Tearful
3. Meal
4. To record
5. Mood
6. Sad
7. Smooth
8. Deaf
9. To reassure
10. (A piece of) news
11. To start up (a car)
12. Tap
13. Place
14. To withdraw
15. Clock
16. To dirty
17. Day
18. To fold
19. Profit

316

WORDGAME 23

There are twelve German words hidden in the grid below. Each word is made up of five letters but has been split into two parts.

Find the German words. Each group of letters can only be used once.

Use your dictionary to help you.

Re	ten	cke	er	Lad	Na
rbe	Sch	tr	Sip	eh	wei
unt	en	He	am	ank	pe
ren	be	ne	cht	se	ben

WORDGAME 24

Here is a list of German words for things you will find in the kitchen.
Unfortunately, they have all been jumbled up. Try to work out what each
word is and put the word in the boxes on the right. You will see that there
are six shaded boxes below. With the six letters in the shaded boxes make
up <u>another</u> German word for an object you can find in the kitchen.

1. CSIHT   Die Kinder
decken den____

2. DERH   Die Kasserolle
steht auf dem

____

3. RSNAHCK   Ist die
Kaffeekanne in
diesem ____ ?

4. SAETS   Sie gießt den
Tee in die____

5. SRIGHCRE Das____ liegt
im Spülbecken

6. HKRÜHNSKCLA Hol die Milch
aus dem ____
heraus

The word you are looking for is:

WORDGAME 25

Take the four letters given each time and put them in the four empty boxes in the centre of each grid. Arrange them in such a way that you form four six-letter words. Use your dictionary to check the words.

ANSWERS

WORDGAME 1

1	gekannt	6	zahle
2	Aktien	7	einschreiben
3	Kino	8	übel
4	kaufen	9	Ganz
5	Pudel	10	Tante

WORDGAME 2

1	gerecht	7	Wade
2	erreichen	8	Ort
3	erfahren	9	fassen
4	Herbst	10	Stelle
5	treffen	11	Gleis
6	schwer	12	Heim

WORDGAME 3

Morgenrock+Hausschuhe
Handtasche+Lederwaren
Bett+Decke
Kirchturm+Glockengeläut
Fisch+Schuppe
Nest+Elster
Diplom+Student
Buch+Regal

WORDGAME 4

1	Weise *or* Sorte	6	berühmt
2	versuchen	7	Last
3	Brand	8	Karte
4	passieren	9	treffen
5	Überheblichkeit	10	Tendenz

WORDGAME 5

2	Nacht	5	Natur	6	neureich

WORDGAME 6

1	leugnen	6	Armut
2	verstecken	7	lärmend
3	schuldig	8	abreisen
4	verkaufen	9	tapfer
5	erlauben	10	sauber

WORDGAME 7

1	Frikadelle	6	nautisch
2	Spur	7	Gewölbe
3	fein	8	keuchen
4	Lüge	9	mögen
5	Stachel	10	glaubwürdig

WORDGAME 8

1 The sentence is much too long.
2 Underline every clause which starts with a conjunction.
3 Everybody knows Pythagoras' theorem.
4 The orchestra performed the last movement really well.
5 Steffi Graf hasn't lost a set in the championships.
6 All the grounds were in the cup.
7 For deliveries abroad there is a different rate.
8 She jumped for joy.

WORDGAME 9

1	gestellt	7	gesprochen
2	Stelle	8	Sprachen
3	hoffentlich	9	Studium
4	hofft	10	studiert
5	betrügen	11	kürzlich
6	Betrüger	12	gekürzt

WORDGAME 11

1	adj	6	adv
2	noun	7	adj
3	noun	8	verb
4	verb	9	verb
5	adv	10	adj

WORDGAME 12

1 der/das
2 die/das
3 das (or ein)/der
4 der/das
5 der/der
6 eine/den

WORDGAME 13

1	englisch	7	alt
2	rot	8	schwarz
3	letzte(r, s)	9	groß
4	klein	10	heftig
5	lang	11	siebte(r, s)
6	gut	12	neu

WORDGAME 14

ich sah
du schläfst
ich bin gewesen
ich schlug
ich habe angerufen
er fährt ab
ich habe studiert
ich hatte
du fängst an
er wäscht
ich wurde
ich habe genommen

WORDGAME 15

gesungen	gelegen
gebissen	gelogen
gebracht	geschnitten
gefroren	gekannt
gerieben	gemocht
gewonnen	gewusst
geholfen	gekonnt
geschehen	

WORDGAME 16

1	vergessen	9	fahren
2	anrufen	10	einladen
3	ankommen	11	bekommen
4	festhalten	12	lesen
5	sein	13	sterben
6	können	14	wegwerfen
7	fliegen	15	mitnehmen
8	werden		

WORDGAME 17

1	d	5	i	9	b
2	j	6	l	10	h
3	c	7	a	11	e
4	k	8	f	12	g

WORDGAME 18

1 health food shop
2 brochure
3 boss
4 crisps
5 dinner jacket
6 wants
7 pension
8 parliamentary party
9 foreign currency

WORDGAME 19

1 resigns
2 wealth
3 know
4 offer
5 service
6 bar
7 guesthouse
8 newspaper

WORDGAME 20

1 Wagen
2 Roller
3 Taxi
4 Fahrrad
5 Flugzeug
6 Bahnhof
7 Zug
8 Lastwagen

WORDGAME 21

1 tragen (= to carry); fragen (= to ask)
2 Stollen (= gallery)
3 Knie (= knee)
4 Brand (= fire)
5 loben (= to praise)
6 dich (= you); sich (= oneself); mich (= me)
7 Grad (= degree)
8 sinnen (= to ponder); rinnen (= to trickle)
9 braten (= to roast)
10 kindisch (= childish)
11 zeigen (= to show); neigen (= to incline)
12 geben (= to give); leben (= to live); neben (= next to); beben (= to tremble); heben (= to raise); weben (= to weave)
13 Rohr (= pipe, tube)
14 Spur (= race)

WORDGAME 22

1 schwer
2 weinerlich
3 Mahlzeit
4 aufnehmen
5 Laune
6 traurig
7 glatt
8 taub
9 beruhigen
10 Nachricht
11 anlassen
12 Hahn
13 Ort
14 abheben
15 Uhr
16 beschmutzen
17 Tag
18 falten
19 Gewinn

WORDGAME 23

1	Recht	7	neben
2	Laden	8	Sippe
3	Hecke	9	unter
4	ehren	10	Scham
5	beten	11	weise
6	Narbe	12	trank

WORDGAME 24

1	Tisch	4	Tasse
2	Herd	5	Geschirr
3	Schrank	6	Kühlschrank

Hidden word – KESSEL

WORDGAME 25

1
```
  U N
  M I
E I G E L B
K L A S S E
  N E
  G N
```

2
```
    B W
    E Ä
M A C H E N
U N K L A R
    E E
    N R
```

3
```
    F W
    Ü I
S C H E L M
W E R D E N
    E E
    N R
```

ENGLISH – GERMAN
ENGLISCH – DEUTSCH

A, a

A [eɪ] *n* (*MUS*) A *nt*; **~ road** Hauptverkehrsstraße *f*

KEYWORD

a [eɪ, ə] (*before vowel or silent h: an*) *indef art* **1** ein; eine; **a woman** eine Frau; **a book** ein Buch; **an eagle** ein Adler; **she's a doctor** sie ist Ärztin

2 (*instead of the number "one"*) ein; eine; **a year ago** vor einem Jahr; **a hundred/ thousand** *etc* **pounds** (ein) hundert/(ein) tausend *etc* Pfund

3 (*in expressing ratios, prices etc*) pro; **3 a day/week** 3 pro Tag/Woche, 3 am Tag/in der Woche; **10 km an hour** 10 km pro Stunde/in der Stunde

A.A. *n abbr* = **Alcoholics Anonymous**; (*BRIT*) = **Automobile Association**

A.A.A. (*US*) *n abbr* = **American Automobile Association**

aback [ə'bæk] *adv*: **to be taken ~** verblüfft sein

abandon [ə'bændən] *vt* (*give up*) aufgeben; (*desert*) verlassen ♦ *n* Hingabe *f*

abate [ə'beɪt] *vi* nachlassen, sich legen

abattoir ['æbətwɑ:] (*BRIT*) *n* Schlachthaus *nt*

abbey ['æbɪ] *n* Abtei *f*

abbot ['æbət] *n* Abt *m*

abbreviate [ə'bri:vɪeɪt] *vt* abkürzen; **abbreviation** [əbri:vɪ'eɪʃən] *n* Abkürzung *f*

abdicate ['æbdɪkeɪt] *vt* aufgeben ♦ *vi* abdanken

abdomen ['æbdəmɛn] *n* Unterleib *m*

abduct [æb'dʌkt] *vt* entführen

aberration [æbə'reɪʃən] *n* (geistige) Verwirrung *f*

abet [ə'bɛt] *vt see* **aid**

abeyance [ə'beɪəns] *n*: **in ~** in der Schwebe; (*disuse*) außer Kraft

abide [ə'baɪd] *vt* vertragen; leiden; **~ by** *vt* sich halten an *+acc*

ability [ə'bɪlɪtɪ] *n* (*power*) Fähigkeit *f*; (*skill*) Geschicklichkeit *f*

abject ['æbdʒɛkt] *adj* (*liar*) übel; (*poverty*) größte(r, s); (*apology*) zerknirscht

ablaze [ə'bleɪz] *adj* in Flammen

able ['eɪbl] *adj* geschickt, fähig; **to be ~ to do sth** etw tun können; **~-bodied** ['eɪbl'bɒdɪd] *adj* kräftig; (*seaman*) Voll-; **ably** ['eɪblɪ] *adv* geschickt

abnormal [æb'nɔ:məl] *adj* regelwidrig, abnorm

aboard [ə'bɔ:d] *adv*, *prep* an Bord *+gen*

abode [ə'bəud] *n*: **of no fixed ~** ohne festen Wohnsitz

abolish [ə'bɒlɪʃ] *vt* abschaffen; **abolition** [æbə'lɪʃən] *n* Abschaffung *f*

abominable [ə'bɒmɪnəbl] *adj* scheußlich

aborigine [æbə'rɪdʒɪnɪ] *n* Ureinwohner *m*

abort [ə'bɔ:t] *vt* abtreiben; fehlgebären; **~ion** [ə'bɔ:ʃən] *n* Abtreibung *f*; (*miscarriage*) Fehlgeburt *f*; **~ive** *adj* misslungen

abound [ə'baund] *vi* im Überfluss vorhanden sein; **to ~ in** Überfluss haben an *+dat*

KEYWORD

about [ə'baut] *adv* **1** (*approximately*) etwa, ungefähr; **about a hundred/thousand** *etc* etwa hundert/tausend *etc*; **at about 2 o'clock** etwa um 2 Uhr; **I've just about finished** ich bin gerade fertig

2 (*referring to place*) herum, umher; **to leave things lying about** Sachen herumliegen lassen; **to run/walk** *etc* **about** herumrennen/gehen *etc*

3: **to be about to do sth** im Begriff sein, etw zu tun; **he was about to go to bed** er wollte gerade ins Bett gehen

♦ *prep* **1** (*relating to*) über *+acc*; **a book**

about London ein Buch über London; **what is it about?** worum geht es?; (*book etc*) wovon handelt es?; **we talked about it** wir haben darüber geredet; **what** or **how about doing this?** wollen wir das machen? **2** (*referring to place*) um (... herum); **to walk about the town** in der Stadt herumgehen; **her clothes were scattered about the room** ihre Kleider waren über das ganze Zimmer verstreut

about-turn [ə'baut'tə:n] *n* Kehrtwendung *f*
above [ə'bʌv] *adv* oben ♦ *prep* über; **~ all** vor allem; **~ board** *adj* offen, ehrlich
abrasive [ə'breɪzɪv] *adj* Abschleif-; (*personality*) zermürbend, aufreibend
abreast [ə'brɛst] *adv* nebeneinander; **to keep ~ of** Schritt halten mit
abroad [ə'brɔːd] *adv* (*be*) im Ausland; (*go*) ins Ausland
abrupt [ə'brʌpt] *adj* (*sudden*) abrupt, jäh; (*curt*) schroff; **~ly** *adv* abrupt
abscess ['æbsɪs] *n* Geschwür *nt*
abscond [əb'skɔnd] *vi* flüchten, sich davonmachen
abseil ['æbseɪl] *vi* (*also:* **~ down**) sich abseilen
absence ['æbsəns] *n* Abwesenheit *f*
absent ['æbsənt] *adj* abwesend, nicht da; (*lost in thought*) geistesabwesend; **~-minded** *adj* zerstreut
absolute ['æbsəluːt] *adj* absolut; (*power*) unumschränkt; (*rubbish*) vollkommen, rein; **~ly** [æbsə'luːtlɪ] *adv* absolut, vollkommen; **~ly!** ganz bestimmt!
absolve [əb'zɔlv] *vt* entbinden; freisprechen
absorb [əb'zɔːb] *vt* aufsaugen, absorbieren; (*fig*) ganz in Anspruch nehmen, fesseln; **to be ~ed in a book** in ein Buch vertieft sein; **~ent cotton** (*US*) *n* Verbandwatte *f*; **~ing** *adj* aufsaugend; (*fig*) packend; **absorption** [əb'sɔːpʃən] *n* Aufsaugung *f*, Absorption *f*; (*fig*) Versunkenheit *f*
abstain [əb'steɪn] *vi* (*in vote*) sich enthalten; **to ~ from** (*keep from*) sich enthalten +*gen*
abstemious [əb'stiːmɪəs] *adj* enthaltsam
abstinence ['æbstɪnəns] *n* Enthaltsamkeit *f*

abstract ['æbstrækt] *adj* abstrakt
absurd [əb'sɜːd] *adj* absurd
abundance [ə'bʌndəns] *n*: **~ (of)** Überfluss *m* (an +*dat*); **abundant** [ə'bʌndənt] *adj* reichlich
abuse [*n* ə'bjuːs, *vb* ə'bjuːz] *n* (*rude language*) Beschimpfung *f*; (*ill usage*) Missbrauch *m*; (*bad practice*) (Amts)missbrauch *m* ♦ *vt* (*misuse*) missbrauchen; **abusive** [ə'bjuːsɪv] *adj* beleidigend, Schimpf-
abysmal [ə'bɪzməl] *adj* scheußlich; (*ignorance*) bodenlos
abyss [ə'bɪs] *n* Abgrund *m*
AC *abbr* (= *alternating current*) Wechselstrom *m*
academic [ækə'dɛmɪk] *adj* akademisch; (*theoretical*) theoretisch ♦ *n* Akademiker(in) *m(f)*
academy [ə'kædəmɪ] *n* (*school*) Hochschule *f*; (*society*) Akademie *f*
accelerate [æk'sɛləreɪt] *vi* schneller werden; (*AUT*) Gas geben ♦ *vt* beschleunigen; **acceleration** [æksɛlə'reɪʃən] *n* Beschleunigung *f*; **accelerator** [æk'sɛləreɪtə[r]] *n* Gas(pedal) *nt*
accent ['æksənt] *n* Akzent *m*, Tonfall *m*; (*mark*) Akzent *m*; (*stress*) Betonung *f*
accept [ək'sɛpt] *vt* (*take*) annehmen; (*agree to*) akzeptieren; **~able** *adj* annehmbar; **~ance** *n* Annahme *f*
access ['æksɛs] *n* Zugang *m*; **~ible** [æk'sɛsəbl] *adj* (*easy to approach*) zugänglich; (*within reach*) (leicht) erreichbar
accessory [æk'sɛsərɪ] *n* Zubehörteil *nt*; **toilet accessories** Toilettenartikel *pl*
accident ['æksɪdənt] *n* Unfall *m*; (*coincidence*) Zufall *m*; **by ~** zufällig; **~al** [æksɪ'dɛntl] *adj* unbeabsichtigt; **~ally** [æksɪ'dɛntəlɪ] *adv* zufällig; **~ insurance** *n* Unfallversicherung *f*; **~-prone** *adj*: **to be ~-prone** zu Unfällen neigen
acclaim [ə'kleɪm] *vt* zujubeln +*dat* ♦ *n* Beifall *m*
acclimatize [ə'klaɪmətaɪz] *vt*: **to become ~d (to)** sich gewöhnen (an +*acc*), sich akklimatisieren (in +*dat*)
accommodate [ə'kɔmədeɪt] *vt*

unterbringen; (*hold*) Platz haben für; (*oblige*) (aus)helfen für
accommodating [ə'kɔmədeɪtɪŋ] *adj* entgegenkommend
accommodation [əkɔmə'deɪʃən] (*US* **accommodations**) *n* Unterkunft *f*
accompany [ə'kʌmpənɪ] *vt* begleiten
accomplice [ə'kʌmplɪs] *n* Helfershelfer *m*, Komplize *m*
accomplish [ə'kʌmplɪʃ] *vt* (*fulfil*) durchführen; (*finish*) vollenden; (*aim*) erreichen; **~ed** *adj* vollendet, ausgezeichnet; **~ment** *n* (*skill*) Fähigkeit *f*; (*completion*) Vollendung *f*; (*feat*) Leistung *f*
accord [ə'kɔːd] *n* Übereinstimmung *f* ♦ *vt* gewähren; **of one's own ~** freiwillig; **~ing to** nach, laut +*gen*; **~ance** *n*: **in ~ance with** in Übereinstimmung mit; **~ingly** *adv* danach, dementsprechend
accordion [ə'kɔːdɪən] *n* Akkordeon *nt*
accost [ə'kɔst] *vt* ansprechen
account [ə'kaʊnt] *n* (*bill*) Rechnung *f*; (*narrative*) Bericht *m*; (*report*) Rechenschaftsbericht *m*; (*in bank*) Konto *nt*; (*importance*) Geltung *f*; **~s** *npl* (*FIN*) Bücher *pl*; **on ~** auf Rechnung; **of no ~** ohne Bedeutung; **on no ~** keinesfalls; **on ~ of** wegen; **to take into ~** berücksichtigen; **~ for** *vt fus* (*expenditure*) Rechenschaft ablegen für; **how do you ~ for that?** wie erklären Sie (sich) das?; **~able** *adj* verantwortlich; **~ancy** [ə'kaʊntənsɪ] *n* Buchhaltung *f*; **~ant** [ə'kaʊntənt] *n* Wirtschaftsprüfer(in) *m(f)*; **~ number** *n* Kontonummer *f*
accumulate [ə'kjuːmjuleɪt] *vt* ansammeln ♦ *vi* sich ansammeln
accuracy ['ækjʊrəsɪ] *n* Genauigkeit *f*
accurate ['ækjʊrɪt] *adj* genau; **~ly** *adv* genau, richtig
accusation [ækjuːˈzeɪʃən] *n* Anklage *f*, Beschuldigung *f*
accuse [ə'kjuːz] *vt* anklagen, beschuldigen; **~d** *n* Angeklagte(r) *f(m)*
accustom [ə'kʌstəm] *vt*: **to ~ sb (to sth)** jdn (an etw *acc*) gewöhnen; **~ed** *adj* gewohnt
ace [eɪs] *n* Ass *nt*; (*inf*) Ass *nt*, Kanone *f*

ache [eɪk] *n* Schmerz *m* ♦ *vi* (*be sore*) schmerzen, wehtun
achieve [ə'tʃiːv] *vt* zustande *or* zu Stande bringen; (*aim*) erreichen; **~ment** *n* Leistung *f*; (*act*) Erreichen *nt*
acid ['æsɪd] *n* Säure *f* ♦ *adj* sauer, scharf; **~ rain** *n* saure(r) Regen *m*
acknowledge [ək'nɔlɪdʒ] *vt* (*receipt*) bestätigen; (*admit*) zugeben; **~ment** *n* Anerkennung *f*; (*letter*) Empfangsbestätigung *f*
acne ['æknɪ] *n* Akne *f*
acorn ['eɪkɔːn] *n* Eichel *f*
acoustic [ə'kuːstɪk] *adj* akustisch; **~s** *npl* Akustik *f*
acquaint [ə'kweɪnt] *vt* vertraut machen; **to be ~ed with sb** mit jdm bekannt sein; **~ance** *n* (*person*) Bekannte(r) *f(m)*; (*knowledge*) Kenntnis *f*
acquire [ə'kwaɪər] *vt* erwerben; **acquisition** [ækwɪ'zɪʃən] *n* Errungenschaft *f*; (*act*) Erwerb *m*
acquit [ə'kwɪt] *vt* (*free*) freisprechen; **to ~ o.s. well** sich bewähren; **~tal** *n* Freispruch *m*
acre ['eɪkər] *n* Morgen *m*
acrid ['ækrɪd] *adj* (*smell*, *taste*) bitter, (*smoke*) beißend
acrobat ['ækrəbæt] *n* Akrobat *m*
across [ə'krɔs] *prep* über +*acc* ♦ *adv* hinüber, herüber; **he lives ~ the river** er wohnt auf der anderen Seite des Flusses; **ten metres ~** zehn Meter breit; **he lives ~ from us** er wohnt uns gegenüber; **to run/swim ~** hinüberlaufen/schwimmen
acrylic [ə'krɪlɪk] *adj* Acryl-
act [ækt] *n* (*deed*) Tat *f*; (*JUR*) Gesetz *nt*; (*THEAT*) Akt *m*; (: *turn*) Nummer *f* ♦ *vi* (*take ~ion*) handeln; (*behave*) sich verhalten; (*pretend*) vorgeben; (*THEAT*) spielen ♦ *vt* (*in play*) spielen; **to ~ as** fungieren als; **~ing** *adj* stellvertretend ♦ *n* Schauspielkunst *f*; (*performance*) Aufführung *f*
action ['ækʃən] *n* (*deed*) Tat *f*; Handlung *f*; (*motion*) Bewegung *f*; (*way of working*) Funktionieren *nt*; (*battle*) Einsatz *m*, Gefecht *nt*; (*lawsuit*) Klage *f*, Prozess *m*; **out of ~**

(*person*) nicht einsatzfähig; (*thing*) außer Betrieb; **to take ~** etwas unternehmen; **~ replay** n (*TV*) Wiederholung f

activate ['æktɪveɪt] vt (*mechanism*) betätigen; (*CHEM, PHYS*) aktivieren

active ['æktɪv] adj (*brisk*) rege, tatkräftig; (*working*) aktiv; (*GRAM*) aktiv, Tätigkeits-; **~ly** adv aktiv; (*dislike*) offen

activity [æk'tɪvɪtɪ] n Aktivität f; (*doings*) Unternehmungen pl; (*occupation*) Tätigkeit f; **~ holiday** n Aktivurlaub m

actor ['æktə*] n Schauspieler m

actress ['æktrɪs] n Schauspielerin f

actual ['æktjuəl] adj wirklich; **~ly** adv tatsächlich; **~ly no** eigentlich nicht

acumen ['ækjumən] n Scharfsinn m

acute [ə'kju:t] adj (*severe*) heftig, akut; (*keen*) scharfsinnig

ad [æd] n abbr = **advertisement**

A.D. adv abbr (= *Anno Domini*) n. Chr.

adamant ['ædəmənt] adj eisern; hartnäckig

adapt [ə'dæpt] vt anpassen ♦ vi: **to ~ (to)** sich anpassen (an +*acc*); **~able** adj anpassungsfähig; **~ation** [ædæp'teɪʃən] n (*THEAT etc*) Bearbeitung f; (*adjustment*) Anpassung f; **~er, ~or** n (*ELEC*) Zwischenstecker m

add [æd] vt (*join*) hinzufügen; (*numbers: also:* **~ up**) addieren; **~ up** vi (*make sense*) stimmen; **~ up to** vt fus ausmachen

adder ['ædə*] n Kreuzotter f, Natter f

addict ['ædɪkt] n Süchtige(r) f(m); **~ed** [ə'dɪktɪd] adj: **~ed to** -süchtig; **~ion** [ə'dɪkʃən] n Sucht f; **~ive** [ə'dɪktɪv] adj: **to be ~ive** süchtig machen

addition [ə'dɪʃən] n Anhang m, Addition f; (*MATH*) Addition f, Zusammenzählen nt; **in ~** zusätzlich, außerdem; **~al** adj zusätzlich, weiter

additive ['ædɪtɪv] n Zusatz m

address [ə'dres] n Adresse f; (*speech*) Ansprache f ♦ vt (*letter*) adressieren; (*speak to*) ansprechen; (*make speech to*) eine Ansprache halten an +*acc*

adept ['ædept] adj geschickt; **to be ~ at** gut sein in +*dat*

adequate ['ædɪkwɪt] adj angemessen

adhere [əd'hɪə*] vi: **to ~ to** haften an +*dat*; (*fig*) festhalten an +*dat*

adhesive [əd'hi:zɪv] adj klebend; Kleb(e)- ♦ n Klebstoff m; **~ tape** n (*BRIT*) Klebestreifen m; (*US*) Heftpflaster nt

ad hoc [æd'hɔk] adj (*decision, committee*) Ad-hoc- ♦ adv ad hoc

adjacent [ə'dʒeɪsənt] adj benachbart; **~ to** angrenzend an +*acc*

adjective ['ædʒektɪv] n Adjektiv nt, Eigenschaftswort nt

adjoining [ə'dʒɔɪnɪŋ] adj benachbart, Neben-

adjourn [ə'dʒə:n] vt vertagen ♦ vi abbrechen

adjudicate [ə'dʒu:dɪkeɪt] vi entscheiden, ein Urteil fällen

adjust [ə'dʒʌst] vt (*alter*) anpassen; (*put right*) regulieren, richtig stellen ♦ vi sich anpassen; **~able** adj verstellbar

ad-lib [æd'lɪb] vt, vi improvisieren ♦ adv: **ad lib** aus dem Stegreif

administer [əd'mɪnɪstə*] vt (*manage*) verwalten; (*dispense*) ausüben; (*justice*) sprechen; (*medicine*) geben; **administration** [ədmɪnɪs'treɪʃən] n Verwaltung f; (*POL*) Regierung f; **administrative** [əd'mɪnɪstrətɪv] adj Verwaltungs-; **administrator** [əd'mɪnɪstreɪtə*] n Verwaltungsbeamte(r) f(m)

Admiralty ['ædmərəltɪ] (*BRIT*) n Admiralität f

admiration [ædmə'reɪʃən] n Bewunderung f

admire [əd'maɪə*] vt (*respect*) bewundern; (*love*) verehren; **~r** n Bewunderer m

admission [əd'mɪʃən] n (*entrance*) Einlass m; (*fee*) Eintritt(spreis m) m; (*confession*) Geständnis nt; **~ charge** n Eintritt(spreis) m

admit [əd'mɪt] vt (*let in*) einlassen; (*confess*) gestehen; (*accept*) anerkennen; **~tance** n Zulassung f; **~tedly** adv zugegebenermaßen

admonish [əd'mɔnɪʃ] vt ermahnen

ad nauseam [æd'nɔ:sɪæm] adv (*repeat, talk*) endlos

ado [ə'du:] n: **without more ~** ohne weitere Umstände

adolescence [ædəu'lesns] n Jugendalter nt; adolescent [ædəu'lesnt] adj jugendlich ♦ n Jugendliche(r) f(m)

adopt [ə'dɒpt] vt (child) adoptieren; (idea) übernehmen; ~ion [ə'dɒpʃən] n Adoption f; Übernahme f

adore [ə'dɔː] vt anbeten; verehren

adorn [ə'dɔːn] vt schmücken

Adriatic [eɪdrɪ'ætɪk] n: the ~ (Sea) die Adria

adrift [ə'drɪft] adv Wind und Wellen preisgegeben

adult ['ædʌlt] n Erwachsene(r) f(m)

adultery [ə'dʌltərɪ] n Ehebruch m

advance [əd'vɑːns] n (progress) Vorrücken nt; (money) Vorschuss m ♦ vt (move forward) vorrücken; (money) vorschießen; (argument) vorbringen ♦ vi vorwärts gehen; in ~ im Voraus; ~ booking n Vorverkauf m; ~d adj (ahead) vorgerückt; (modern) fortgeschritten; (study) für Fortgeschrittene

advantage [əd'vɑːntɪdʒ] n Vorteil m; to have an ~ over sb jdm gegenüber im Vorteil sein; to take ~ of (misuse) ausnutzen; (profit from) Nutzen ziehen aus; ~ous [ædvən'teɪdʒəs] adj vorteilhaft

advent ['ædvənt] n Ankunft f; A~ Advent m

adventure [əd'ventʃə] n Abenteuer nt; adventurous adj abenteuerlich, waghalsig

adverb ['ædvəːb] n Adverb nt, Umstandswort nt

adversary ['ædvəsərɪ] n Gegner m

adverse ['ædvəːs] adj widrig; adversity [əd'vəːsɪtɪ] n Widrigkeit f, Missgeschick nt

advert ['ædvəːt] n Anzeige f; ~ise ['ædvətaɪz] vt werben für ♦ vi annoncieren; to ~ise for sth etw (per Anzeige) suchen; ~isement [əd'vəːtɪsmənt] n Anzeige f, Inserat nt; ~iser n (in newspaper etc) Inserent m; ~ising n Werbung f

advice [əd'vaɪs] n Rat(schlag) m

advisable [əd'vaɪzəbl] adj ratsam

advise [əd'vaɪz] vt: to ~ (sb) (jdm) raten; ~dly [əd'vaɪzɪdlɪ] adv (deliberately) bewusst; ~r n Berater m; advisory [əd'vaɪzərɪ] adj beratend, Beratungs-

advocate [vb 'ædvəkeɪt, n 'ædvəkət] vt vertreten ♦ n Befürworter(in) m(f)

Aegean [iː'dʒiːən] n: the ~ (Sea) die Ägäis

aerial ['eərɪəl] n Antenne f ♦ adj Luft-

aerobics [ɛə'rəubɪks] n Aerobic nt

aerodynamic ['eərəudaɪ'næmɪk] adj aerodynamisch

aeroplane ['eərəpleɪn] n Flugzeug nt

aerosol ['eərəsɒl] n Aerosol nt; Sprühdose f

aesthetic [iːs'θetɪk] adj ästhetisch

afar [ə'fɑː] adv: from ~ aus der Ferne

affable ['æfəbl] adj umgänglich

affair [ə'feə] n (concern) Angelegenheit f; (event) Ereignis nt; (love ~) Verhältnis nt; ~s npl (business) Geschäfte pl

affect [ə'fekt] vt (influence) (ein)wirken auf +acc; (move deeply) bewegen; this change doesn't ~ us diese Änderung betrifft uns nicht; ~ed adj affektiert, gekünstelt

affection [ə'fekʃən] n Zuneigung f; ~ate adj liebevoll

affiliated [ə'fɪlɪeɪtɪd] adj angeschlossen

affinity [ə'fɪnɪtɪ] n (attraction) gegenseitige Anziehung f; (relationship) Verwandtschaft f

affirmative [ə'fəːmətɪv] adj bestätigend

afflict [ə'flɪkt] vt quälen, heimsuchen

affluence ['æfluəns] n (wealth) Wohlstand m; affluent adj wohlhabend, Wohlstands-

afford [ə'fɔːd] vt sich dat leisten; (yield) bieten, einbringen

afield [ə'fiːld] adv: far ~ weit fort

afloat [ə'fləut] adj: to be ~ schwimmen

afoot [ə'fut] adv im Gang

afraid [ə'freɪd] adj ängstlich; to be ~ of Angst haben vor +dat; to be ~ to do sth sich scheuen, etw zu tun; I am ~ I have ... ich habe leider ...; I'm ~ so/not leider/leider nicht; I am ~ that ... ich fürchte(, dass) ...

afresh [ə'freʃ] adv von neuem

Africa ['æfrɪkə] n Afrika nt; ~n adj afrikanisch ♦ n Afrikaner(in) m(f)

after ['ɑːftə] prep nach; (following, seeking) hinter ... dat ... her; (in imitation) nach, im Stil von ♦ adv: soon ~ bald danach ♦ conj nachdem; what are you ~? was wollen Sie?; ~ he left nachdem er gegangen war; ~ you! nach Ihnen!; ~ all letzten Endes; ~ having shaved als er sich rasiert hatte;

~effects *npl* Nachwirkungen *pl*; **~math** *n* Auswirkungen *pl*; **~noon** *n* Nachmittag *m*; **~s** (*inf*) *n* (*dessert*) Nachtisch *m*; **~sales service** (*BRIT*) *n* Kundendienst *m*; **~shave (lotion)** *n* Rasierwasser *nt*; **~sun** *n* Aftersunlotion *f*; **~thought** *n* nachträgliche(r) Einfall *m*; **~wards** *adv* danach, nachher

again [ə'gɛn] *adv* wieder, noch einmal; (*besides*) außerdem, ferner; **~ and ~** immer wieder

against [ə'gɛnst] *prep* gegen

age [eɪdʒ] *n* (*of person*) Alter *nt*; (*in history*) Zeitalter *nt* ♦ *vi* altern, alt werden ♦ *vt* älter machen; **to come of ~** mündig werden; **20 years of ~** 20 Jahre alt; **it's been ~s since ...** es ist ewig her, seit ...

aged¹ [eɪdʒd] *adj* ... Jahre alt, -jährig

aged² [eɪdʒɪd] *adj* (*elderly*) betagt ♦ *npl*: **the ~** die Alten *pl*

age group *n* Altersgruppe *f*

age limit *n* Altersgrenze *f*

agency ['eɪdʒənsɪ] *n* Agentur *f*; Vermittlung *f*; (*CHEM*) Wirkung *f*; **through** *or* **by the ~ of** ... mithilfe *or* mit Hilfe von ...

agenda [ə'dʒɛndə] *n* Tagesordnung *f*

agent ['eɪdʒənt] *n* (*COMM*) Vertreter *m*; (*spy*) Agent *m*

aggravate ['ægrəveɪt] *vt* (*make worse*) verschlimmern; (*irritate*) reizen

aggregate ['ægrɪɡɪt] *n* Summe *f*

aggression [ə'ɡrɛʃən] *n* Aggression *f*; **aggressive** [ə'ɡrɛsɪv] *adj* aggressiv

aghast [ə'ɡɑːst] *adj* entsetzt

agile ['ædʒaɪl] *adj* flink; agil; (*mind*) rege

agitate ['ædʒɪteɪt] *vt* rütteln; **to ~ for** sich stark machen für

AGM *n abbr* (= *annual general meeting*) JHV *f*

ago [ə'ɡəu] *adv*: **two days ~** vor zwei Tagen; **not long ~** vor kurzem; **it's so long ~** es ist schon so lange her

agog [ə'ɡɒɡ] *adj* gespannt

agonizing ['ægənaɪzɪŋ] *adj* quälend

agony ['ægənɪ] *n* Qual *f*; **to be in ~** Qualen leiden

agree [ə'ɡriː] *vt* (*date*) vereinbaren ♦ *vi* (*have same opinion, correspond*) übereinstimmen; (*consent*) zustimmen; (*be in harmony*) sich vertragen; **to ~ to sth** einer Sache *dat* zustimmen; **to ~ that ...** (*admit*) zugeben, dass ...; **to ~ to do sth** sich bereit erklären, etw zu tun; **garlic doesn't ~ with me** Knoblauch vertrage ich nicht; **I ~** einverstanden, ich stimme zu; **to ~ on sth** sich auf etw *acc* einigen; **~able** *adj* (*pleasing*) liebenswürdig; (*willing to consent*) einverstanden; **~d** *adj* vereinbart; **~ment** *n* (*~ing*) Übereinstimmung *f*; (*contract*) Vereinbarung *f*, Vertrag *m*; **to be in ~ment** übereinstimmen

agricultural [ægrɪ'kʌltʃərəl] *adj* landwirtschaftlich, Landwirtschafts-

agriculture ['ægrɪkʌltʃər] *n* Landwirtschaft *f*

aground [ə'ɡraund] *adv*: **to run ~** auf Grund laufen

ahead [ə'hɛd] *adv* vorwärts; **to be ~** voraus sein; **~ of time** der Zeit voraus; **go right** *or* **straight ~** gehen Sie geradeaus; fahren Sie geradeaus

aid [eɪd] *n* (*assistance*) Hilfe *f*, Unterstützung *f*; (*person*) Hilfe *f*; (*thing*) Hilfsmittel *nt* ♦ *vt* unterstützen, helfen +*dat*; **in ~ of** zugunsten *or* zu Gunsten +*gen*; **to ~ and abet sb** jdm Beihilfe leisten

aide [eɪd] *n* (*person*) Gehilfe *m*; (*MIL*) Adjutant *m*

AIDS [eɪdz] *n abbr* (= *acquired immune deficiency syndrome*) Aids *nt*; **AIDS-related** aidsbedingt

ailing ['eɪlɪŋ] *adj* kränkelnd

ailment ['eɪlmənt] *n* Leiden *nt*

aim [eɪm] *vt* (*gun, camera*) richten ♦ *vi* (*with gun: also*: **take ~**) zielen; (*intend*) beabsichtigen ♦ *n* (*intention*) Absicht *f*, Ziel *nt*; (*pointing*) Zielen *nt*, Richten *nt*; **to ~ at sth** auf etw *dat* richten; (*fig*) etw anstreben; **to ~ to do sth** vorhaben, etw zu tun; **~less** *adj* ziellos; **~lessly** *adv* ziellos

ain't [eɪnt] (*inf*) (= **am not**; **are not**; **is not**; **has not**; **have not**)

air [ɛər] *n* Luft *f*; (*manner*) Miene *f*, Anschein *m*; (*MUS*) Melodie *f* ♦ *vt* lüften; (*fig*) an die Öffentlichkeit bringen ♦ *cpd* Luft-; **by ~** (*travel*) auf dem Luftweg; **to be on the ~**

(*RADIO, TV: programme*) gesendet werden; **~bed** (*BRIT*) *n* Luftmatratze *f;* **~-conditioned** *adj* mit Klimaanlage; **~conditioning** *n* Klimaanlage *f;* **~craft** *n* Flugzeug *nt,* Maschine *f;* **~craft carrier** *n* Flugzeugträger *m;* **~field** *n* Flugplatz *m;* **~force** *n* Luftwaffe *f;* **~freshener** *n* Raumspray *nt;* **~gun** *n* Luftgewehr *nt;* **~hostess** (*BRIT*) *n* Stewardess *f;* **~ letter** (*BRIT*) *n* Luftpostbrief *m;* **~lift** *n* Luftbrücke *f;* **~line** *n* Luftverkehrsgesellschaft *f;* **~liner** *n* Verkehrsflugzeug *nt;* **~lock** *n* Luftblase *f;* **~mail** *n:* **by ~mail** mit Luftpost; **~ miles** *npl* ≈ Flugkilometer *m;* **~plane** (*US*) *n* Flugzeug *nt;* **~port** *n* Flughafen *m,* Flugplatz *m;* **~ raid** *n* Luftangriff *m;* **~sick** *adj* luftkrank; **~space** *n* Luftraum *m;* **~strip** *n* Landestreifen *m;* **~ terminal** *n* Terminal *m;* **~tight** *adj* luftdicht; **~ traffic controller** *n* Fluglotse *m;* **~y** *adj* luftig; (*manner*) leichtfertig

aisle [aɪl] *n* Gang *m;* **~ seat** *n* Sitz *m* am Gang

ajar [ə'dʒɑːr] *adv* angelehnt; einen Spalt offen

alarm [ə'lɑːm] *n* (*warning*) Alarm *m;* (*bell etc*) Alarmanlage *f;* (*anxiety*) Sorge *f* ♦ *vt* erschrecken; **~ call** *n* (*in hotel etc*) Weckruf *m;* **~ clock** *n* Wecker *m*

Albania [æl'beɪnɪə] *n* Albanien *nt*

albeit [ɔːl'biːɪt] *conj* obgleich

album ['ælbəm] *n* Album *nt*

alcohol ['ælkəhɔl] *n* Alkohol *m;* **~-free** *adj* alkoholfrei; **~ic** [ælkə'hɔlɪk] *adj* (*drink*) alkoholisch ♦ *n* Alkoholiker(in) *m(f);* **~ism** *n* Alkoholismus *m*

alert [ə'lɜːt] *adj* wachsam ♦ *n* Alarm *m* ♦ *vt* alarmieren; **to be on the ~** wachsam sein

Algeria [æl'dʒɪərɪə] *n* Algerien *nt*

alias ['eɪlɪəs] *adv* alias ♦ *n* Deckname *m*

alibi ['ælɪbaɪ] *n* Alibi *nt*

alien ['eɪlɪən] *n* Ausländer *m* ♦ *adj* (*foreign*) ausländisch; (*strange*) fremd; **~ to** fremd +*dat;* **~ate** *vt* entfremden

alight [ə'laɪt] *adj* brennend; (*of building*) in Flammen ♦ *vi* (*descend*) aussteigen; (*bird*) sich setzen

align [ə'laɪn] *vt* ausrichten

alike [ə'laɪk] *adj* gleich, ähnlich ♦ *adv* gleich, ebenso; **to look ~** sich *dat* ähnlich sehen

alimony ['ælɪmənɪ] *n* Unterhalt *m,* Alimente *pl*

alive [ə'laɪv] *adj* (*living*) lebend; (*lively*) lebendig, aufgeweckt; **~ (with)** (*full of*) voll (von), wimmelnd (von)

KEYWORD

---

all [ɔːl] *adj* alle(r, s); **all day/night** den ganzen Tag/die ganze Nacht; **all men are equal** alle Menschen sind gleich; **all five came** alle fünf kamen; **all the books/food** die ganzen Bücher/das ganze Essen; **all the time** die ganze Zeit (über); **all his life** sein ganzes Leben (lang)

♦ *pron* **1** alles; **I ate it all, I ate all of it** ich habe alles gegessen; **all of us/the boys went** wir gingen alle/alle Jungen gingen; **we all sat down** wir setzten uns alle

2 (*in phrases*): **above all** vor allem; **after all** schließlich; **at all: not at all** (*in answer to question*) überhaupt nicht; (*in answer to thanks*) gern geschehen; **I'm not at all tired** ich bin überhaupt nicht müde; **anything/all we did** do es ist egal, welche(r, s); **all in all** alles in allem

♦ *adv* ganz; **all alone** ganz allein; **it's not as hard as all that** so schwer ist es nun auch wieder nicht; **all the more/better** umso mehr/besser; **all but** fast; **the score is 2 all** es steht 2 zu 2

---

allay [ə'leɪ] *vt* (*fears*) beschwichtigen

all clear *n* Entwarnung *f*

allegation [ælɪ'geɪʃən] *n* Behauptung *f*

allege [ə'ledʒ] *vt* (*declare*) behaupten; (*falsely*) vorgeben; **~dly** *adv* angeblich

allegiance [ə'liːdʒəns] *n* Treue *f*

allergic [ə'lɜːdʒɪk] *adj:* **~ (to)** allergisch (gegen)

allergy ['ælədʒɪ] *n* Allergie *f*

alleviate [ə'liːvɪeɪt] *vt* lindern

alley ['ælɪ] *n* Gasse *f,* Durchgang *m*

alliance [ə'laɪəns] *n* Bund *m,* Allianz *f*

allied ['ælaɪd] *adj* vereinigt; (*powers*) alliiert; **~ (to)** verwandt (mit)

all: ~**in** (*BRIT*) *adj, adv* (*charge*) alles inbegriffen, Gesamt-; ~**in wrestling** *n* Freistilringen *nt*; ~**night** *adj* (*café, cinema*) die ganze Nacht geöffnet, Nacht-

allocate ['ælәkeɪt] *vt* zuteilen

allot [ә'lɒt] *vt* zuteilen; ~**ment** *n* (*share*) Anteil *m*; (*plot*) Schrebergarten *m*

all-out ['ɔːlaʊt] *adj* total; **all out** *adv* mit voller Kraft

allow [ә'laʊ] *vt* (*permit*) erlauben, gestatten; (*grant*) bewilligen; (*deduct*) abziehen; (*concede*): **to ~ that ...** annehmen, dass ...; **to ~ sb sth** jdm etw erlauben, jdm etw gestatten; **to ~ sb to do sth** jdm erlauben *or* gestatten, etw zu tun; ~ **for** *vt fus* berücksichtigen, einplanen; ~**ance** *n* Beihilfe *f*; **to make ~ances for** berücksichtigen

alloy ['ælɔɪ] *n* Metalllegierung *f*

all: ~ **right** *adv* (*well*) gut; (*correct*) richtig; (*as answer*) okay; ~**round** *adj* (*sportsman*) allseitig, Allround-; (*view*) Rundum-; ~**time** *adj* (*record, high*) ... aller Zeiten, Höchst-

allude [ә'luːd] *vi*: **to ~ to** hinweisen auf +*acc*, anspielen auf +*acc*

alluring [ә'ljʊәrɪŋ] *adj* verlockend

ally [*n* 'ælaɪ, *vb* ә'laɪ] *n* Verbündete(r) *f(m)*; (*POL*) Alliierte(r) *f(m)* ♦ *vr*: **to ~ o.s. with** sich verbünden mit

almighty [ɔːl'maɪtɪ] *adj* allmächtig

almond ['ɑːmәnd] *n* Mandel *f*

almost ['ɔːlmәʊst] *adv* fast, beinahe

alms [ɑːmz] *npl* Almosen *n*

alone [ә'lәʊn] *adj, adv* allein; **to leave sth ~** etw sein lassen; **let ~ ...** geschweige denn ...

along [ә'lɒŋ] *prep* entlang, längs ♦ *adv* (*onward*) vorwärts, weiter; **~ with** zusammen mit; **he was limping ~** er humpelte einher; **all ~** (*all the time*) die ganze Zeit; ~**side** *adv* (*walk*) nebenher; (*come*) nebendran; (*be*) daneben ♦ *prep* (*walk, compared with*) neben +*dat*; (*come*) neben +*acc*; (*be*) entlang, neben +*dat*; (*of ship*) längsseits +*gen*

aloof [ә'luːf] *adj* zurückhaltend ♦ *adv* fern; **to stand ~** abseits stehen

aloud [ә'laʊd] *adv* laut

alphabet ['ælfәbet] *n* Alphabet *nt*; ~**ical** [ælfә'betɪkl] *adj* alphabetisch

alpine ['ælpaɪn] *adj* alpin, Alpen-

Alps [ælps] *npl*: **the ~** die Alpen *pl*

already [ɔːl'redɪ] *adv* schon, bereits

alright ['ɔːl'raɪt] (*BRIT*) *adv* = **all right**

Alsatian [æl'seɪʃәn] *n* (*dog*) Schäferhund *m*

also ['ɔːlsәʊ] *adv* auch, außerdem

altar ['ɔːltә] *n* Altar *m*

alter ['ɔːltә] *vt* ändern; (*dress*) umändern; ~**ation** [ɔːltә'reɪʃәn] *n* Änderung *f*; Umänderung *f*; (*to building*) Umbau *m*

alternate [*adj* ɔ:l'tә:nɪt, *vb* 'ɔːltә:neɪt] *adj* abwechselnd ♦ *vi* abwechseln; **on ~ days** jeden zweiten Tag

alternating ['ɔːltә:neɪtɪŋ] *adj*: ~ **current** Wechselstrom *m*; **alternative** [ɔl'tә:nәtɪv] *adj* andere(r, s) ♦ *n* Alternative *f*; **alternative medicine** Alternativmedizin *f*; **alternatively** *adv* im anderen Falle; **alternatively one could ...** oder man könnte ...; **alternator** ['ɔːltә:neɪtә] *n* (*AUT*) Lichtmaschine *f*

although [ɔːl'ðәʊ] *conj* obwohl

altitude ['æltɪtjuːd] *n* Höhe *f*

alto ['æltәʊ] *n* Alt *m*

altogether [ɔːltә'geðә] *adv* (*on the whole*) im Ganzen genommen; (*entirely*) ganz und gar

aluminium [ælju'mɪnɪәm] (*BRIT*) *n* Aluminium *nt*

aluminum [ә'luːmɪnәm] (*US*) *n* Aluminium *nt*

always ['ɔːlweɪz] *adv* immer

Alzheimer's (disease) ['æltshaɪmәz-] *n* (*MED*) Alzheimerkrankheit *f*

AM *n abbr* (= *Assembly Member*) Mitglied *nt* der walisischen Versammlung

am [æm] *see* **be**

a.m. *adv abbr* (= *ante meridiem*) vormittags

amalgamate [ә'mælgәmeɪt] *vi* (*combine*) sich vereinigen ♦ *vt* (*mix*) amalgamieren

amass [ә'mæs] *vt* anhäufen

amateur ['æmәtә] *n* Amateur *m*; (*pej*) Amateur *m*, Stümper *m*; ~**ish** (*pej*) *adj* dilettantisch, stümperhaft

amaze [ә'meɪz] *vt* erstaunen; **to be ~d (at)** erstaunt sein (über); ~**ment** *n* höchste(s)

Erstaunen *nt*; **amazing** *adj* höchst erstaunlich

Amazon ['æməzən] *n* (GEOG) Amazonas *m*

ambassador [æm'bæsədə'] *n* Botschafter *m*

amber ['æmbə'] *n* Bernstein *m*; **at ~** (BRIT: AUT) auf Gelb, gelb

ambiguous [æm'bɪgjuəs] *adj* zweideutig; (*not clear*) unklar

ambition [æm'bɪʃən] *n* Ehrgeiz *m*; **ambitious** *adj* ehrgeizig

amble ['æmbl] *vi* (*usu*: ~ *along*) schlendern

ambulance ['æmbjuləns] *n* Krankenwagen *m*; **~ man** (*irreg*) *n* Sanitäter *m*

ambush ['æmbuʃ] *n* Hinterhalt *m* ♦ *vt* (aus dem Hinterhalt) überfallen

amenable [ə'mi:nəbl] *adj* gefügig; **~ (to)** (*reason*) zugänglich (+*dat*); (*flattery*) empfänglich (für)

amend [ə'mend] *vt* (*law etc*) abändern, ergänzen; **to make ~s** etw wieder gutmachen; **~ment** *n* Abänderung *f*

amenities [ə'mi:nɪtɪz] *npl* Einrichtungen *pl*

America [ə'merɪkə] *n* Amerika *nt*; **~n** *adj* amerikanisch ♦ *n* Amerikaner(in) *m(f)*

amiable ['eɪmɪəbl] *adj* liebenswürdig

amicable ['æmɪkəbl] *adj* freundschaftlich; (*settlement*) gütlich

amid(st) [ə'mɪd(st)] *prep* mitten in *or* unter +*dat*

amiss [ə'mɪs] *adv*: **to take sth ~** etw übel nehmen; **there's something ~** da stimmt irgendetwas nicht

ammonia [ə'məunɪə] *n* Ammoniak *nt*

ammunition [æmju'nɪʃən] *n* Munition *f*

amnesia [æm'ni:zɪə] *n* Gedächtnisverlust *m*

amnesty ['æmnɪstɪ] *n* Amnestie *f*

amok [ə'mɔk] *adv*: **to run ~** Amok laufen

among(st) [ə'mʌŋ(st)] *prep* unter

amoral [æ'mɔrəl] *adj* unmoralisch

amorous ['æmərəs] *adj* verliebt

amount [ə'maunt] *n* (*of money*) Betrag *m*; (*of water, sand*) Menge *f* ♦ *vi*: **to ~ to** (*total*) sich belaufen auf +*acc*; **a great ~ of time/ energy** ein großer Aufwand an Zeit/ Energie (*dat*); **this ~s to treachery** das kommt Verrat gleich; **he won't ~ to much** aus ihm wird nie was

amp(ere) [æmp(ɛə')] *n* Ampere *nt*

amphibian [æm'fɪbɪən] *n* Amphibie *f*

ample ['æmpl] *adj* (*portion*) reichlich; (*dress*) weit, groß; **~ time** genügend Zeit

amplifier ['æmplɪfaɪə'] *n* Verstärker *m*

amuse [ə'mju:z] *vt* (*entertain*) unterhalten; (*make smile*) belustigen; **~ment** *n* (*feeling*) Unterhaltung *f*; (*recreation*) Zeitvertreib *m*; **~ment arcade** *n* Spielhalle *f*; **~ment park** *n* Vergnügungspark *m*

an [æn, ən] *see* **a**

anaemia [ə'ni:mɪə] *n* Anämie *f*; **anaemic** *adj* blutarm

anaesthetic [ænɪs'θetɪk] *n* Betäubungsmittel *nt*; **under ~** unter Narkose; **anaesthetist** [æ'ni:sθɪtɪst] *n* Anästhesist(in) *m(f)*

analgesic [ænæl'dʒi:sɪk] *n* schmerzlindernde(s) Mittel *nt*

analog(ue) ['ænəlɔg] *adj* Analog-

analogy [ə'nælədʒɪ] *n* Analogie *f*

analyse ['ænəlaɪz] (BRIT) *vt* analysieren

analyses [ə'næləsi:z] (BRIT) *npl of* **analysis**

analysis [ə'næləsɪs] (*pl* **analyses**) *n* Analyse *f*

analyst ['ænəlɪst] *n* Analytiker(in) *m(f)*

analytic(al) [ænə'lɪtɪk(l)] *adj* analytisch

analyze ['ænəlaɪz] (US) *vt* = **analyse**

anarchy ['ænəkɪ] *n* Anarchie *f*

anatomy [ə'nætəmɪ] *n* (*structure*) anatomische(r) Aufbau *m*; (*study*) Anatomie *f*

ancestor ['ænsɪstə'] *n* Vorfahr *m*

anchor ['æŋkə'] *n* Anker *m* ♦ *vi* (*also*: **to drop ~**) ankern, vor Anker gehen ♦ *vt* verankern; **to weigh ~** den Anker lichten

anchovy ['æntʃəvɪ] *n* Sardelle *f*

ancient ['eɪnʃənt] *adj* alt; (*car etc*) uralt

ancillary [æn'sɪlərɪ] *adj* Hilfs-

and [ænd] *conj* und; **~ so on** und so weiter; **try ~ come** versuche zu kommen; **better ~ better** immer besser

Andes ['ændi:z] *npl*: **the ~** die Anden *pl*

anemia *etc* [ə'ni:mɪə] (US) *n* = **anaemia** *etc*

anesthetic *etc* [ænɪs'θetɪk] (US) *n* = **anaesthetic** *etc*

anew [ə'nju:] *adv* von neuem

angel ['eɪndʒəl] *n* Engel *m*

anger ['æŋgə'] *n* Zorn *m* ♦ *vt* ärgern

angina [æn'dʒaɪnə] n Angina f

angle ['æŋgl] n Winkel m; (point of view) Standpunkt m

angler ['æŋglər] n Angler m

Anglican ['æŋglɪkən] adj anglikanisch ♦ n Anglikaner(in) m(f)

angling ['æŋglɪŋ] n Angeln nt

angrily ['æŋgrɪlɪ] adv ärgerlich, böse

angry ['æŋgrɪ] adj ärgerlich, ungehalten, böse; (wound) entzündet; **to be ~ with sb** auf jdn böse sein; **to be ~ at sth** über etw acc verärgert sein

anguish ['æŋgwɪʃ] n Qual f

angular ['æŋgjulər] adj eckig, winkelförmig; (face) kantig

animal ['ænɪməl] n Tier nt; (living creature) Lebewesen nt ♦ adj tierisch

animate [vb 'ænɪmeɪt, adj 'ænɪmɪt] vt beleben ♦ adj lebhaft; **~d** adj lebendig; (film) Zeichentrick-

animosity [ænɪ'mɔsɪtɪ] n Feindseligkeit f, Abneigung f

aniseed ['ænɪsiːd] n Anis m

ankle ['æŋkl] n (Fuß)knöchel m; **~ sock** n Söckchen nt

annex [n 'æneks, vb ə'neks] n (BRIT: also: **~e**) Anbau m ♦ vt anfügen; (POL) annektieren, angliedern

annihilate [ə'naɪəleɪt] vt vernichten

anniversary [ænɪ'vɜːsərɪ] n Jahrestag m

announce [ə'nauns] vt ankündigen, anzeigen; **~ment** n Ankündigung f; (official) Bekanntmachung f; **~r** n Ansager(in) m(f)

annoy [ə'nɔɪ] vt ärgern; **don't get ~ed!** reg dich nicht auf!; **~ance** n Ärgernis nt, Störung f; **~ing** adj ärgerlich; (person) lästig

annual ['ænjuəl] adj jährlich; (salary) Jahres- ♦ n (plant) einjährige Pflanze f; (book) Jahrbuch nt; **~ly** adv jährlich

annul [ə'nʌl] vt aufheben, annullieren

annum ['ænəm] n see **per**

anonymous [ə'nɔnɪməs] adj anonym

anorak ['ænəræk] n Anorak m, Windjacke f

anorexia [ænə'reksɪə] n (MED) Magersucht f

another [ə'nʌðər] adj, pron (different) ein(e) andere(r, s); (additional) noch eine(r, s); see

also **one**

answer ['ɑːnsər] n Antwort f ♦ vi antworten; (on phone) sich melden ♦ vt (person) antworten +dat; (letter, question) beantworten; (telephone) gehen an +acc, abnehmen; (door) öffnen; **in ~ to your letter** in Beantwortung Ihres Schreibens; **to ~ the phone** ans Telefon gehen; **to ~ the bell** or **the door** aufmachen; **~ back** vi frech sein; **~ for** vt fus: **to ~ for sth** für etw verantwortlich sein; **~able** adj: **to be ~able to sb for sth** jdm gegenüber für etw verantwortlich sein; **~ing machine** n Anrufbeantworter m

ant [ænt] n Ameise f

antagonism [æn'tægənɪzəm] n Antagonismus m

antagonize [æn'tægənaɪz] vt reizen

Antarctic [ænt'ɑːktɪk] adj antarktisch ♦ n: **the ~** die Antarktis

antelope ['æntɪləup] n Antilope f

antenatal ['æntɪ'neɪtl] adj vor der Geburt; **~ clinic** n Sprechstunde f für werdende Mütter

antenna [æn'tenə] n (BIOL) Fühler m; (RAD) Antenne f

antennae [æn'teniː] npl of **antenna**

anthem ['ænθəm] n Hymne f; **national ~** Nationalhymne f

anthology [æn'θɔlədʒɪ] n Gedichtsammlung f, Anthologie f

anti- ['æntɪ] prefix Gegen-, Anti-

anti-aircraft ['æntɪ'eəkrɑːft] adj Flugabwehr-

antibiotic ['æntɪbaɪ'ɔtɪk] n Antibiotikum nt

antibody ['æntɪbɔdɪ] n Antikörper m

anticipate [æn'tɪsɪpeɪt] vt (expect: trouble, question) erwarten, rechnen mit; (look forward to) sich freuen auf +acc; (do first) vorwegnehmen; (foresee) ahnen, vorhersehen; **anticipation** [æntɪsɪ'peɪʃən] n Erwartung f; (foreshadowing) Vorwegnahme f

anticlimax ['æntɪ'klaɪmæks] n Ernüchterung f

anticlockwise ['æntɪ'klɔkwaɪz] adv entgegen dem Uhrzeigersinn

antics ['æntɪks] npl Possen pl

anti: **~cyclone** n Hoch nt, Hochdruckgebiet nt; **~depressant** n Antidepressivum nt; **~dote** n Gegenmittel nt; **~freeze** n Frostschutzmittel nt; **~histamine** n Antihistamin nt

antiquated ['æntıkweıtıd] adj antiquiert

antique [æn'ti:k] n Antiquität f ♦ adj antik; (old-fashioned) altmodisch; **~ shop** n Antiquitätenladen m; **antiquity** [æn'tıkwıtı] n Altertum nt

antiseptic [æntı'septık] n Antiseptikum nt ♦ adj antiseptisch

antisocial ['æntı'səʊʃəl] adj (person) ungesellig; (law) unsozial

antlers ['æntləz] npl Geweih nt

anus ['eınəs] n After m

anvil ['ænvıl] n Amboss m

anxiety [æŋ'zaıətı] n Angst f; (worry) Sorge f; **anxious** ['æŋkʃəs] adj ängstlich; (worried) besorgt; **to be anxious to do sth** etw unbedingt tun wollen

---

KEYWORD

---

any ['enı] adj 1 (in questions etc): **have you any butter?** haben Sie (etwas) Butter?; **have you any children?** haben Sie Kinder?; **if there are any tickets left** falls noch Karten da sind

2 (with negative): **I haven't any money/books** ich habe kein Geld/keine Bücher

3 (no matter which) jede(r, s) (beliebige); **any colour (at all)** jede beliebige Farbe; **choose any book you like** nehmen Sie ein beliebiges Buch

4 (in phrases): **in any case** in jedem Fall; **any day now** jeden Tag; **at any moment** jeden Moment; **at any rate** auf jeden Fall

♦ pron 1 (in questions etc): **have you got any?** haben Sie welche?; **can any of you sing?** kann (irgend)einer von euch singen?

2 (with negative): **I haven't any (of them)** ich habe keinen/keines (davon)

3 (no matter which one(s)): **take any of those books (you like)** nehmen Sie irgendeines dieser Bücher

♦ adv 1 (in questions etc): **do you want any more soup/sandwiches?** möchten Sie

noch Suppe/Brote?; **are you feeling any better?** fühlen Sie sich etwas besser?

2 (with negative): **I can't hear him any more** ich kann ihn nicht mehr hören

---

anybody ['enıbɔdı] pron (no matter who) jede(r); (in questions etc) (irgend)jemand, (irgend)eine(r); (with negative): **I can't see ~** ich kann niemanden sehen

anyhow ['enıhaʊ] adv (at any rate): **I shall go ~** ich gehe sowieso; (haphazardly): **do it ~** machen Sie es, wie Sie wollen

anyone ['enıwʌn] pron = **anybody**

KEYWORD

---

anything ['enıθıŋ] pron 1 (in questions etc) (irgend)etwas; **can you see anything?** können Sie etwas sehen?

2 (with negative): **I can't see anything** ich kann nichts sehen

3 (no matter what): **you can say anything you like** Sie können sagen, was Sie wollen; **anything will do** irgendetwas (wird genügen), irgendeine(r, s) (wird genügen); **he'll eat anything** er isst alles

---

anyway ['enıweı] adv (at any rate) auf jeden Fall; (besides): **~, I couldn't come even if I wanted to** jedenfalls könnte ich nicht kommen, selbst wenn ich wollte; **why are you phoning, ~?** warum rufst du überhaupt an?

anywhere ['enıwɛə'] adv (in questions etc) irgendwo; (: with direction) irgendwohin; (no matter where) überall; (: with direction) überallhin; (with negative): **I can't see him ~** ich kann ihn nirgendwo or nirgends sehen; **can you see him ~?** siehst du ihn irgendwo?; **put the books down ~** leg die Bücher irgendwohin

apart [ə'pɑːt] adv (parted) auseinander; (away) beiseite, abseits; **10 miles ~** 10 Meilen auseinander; **to take ~** auseinander nehmen; **~ from** prep außer

apartheid [ə'pɑːteıt] n Apartheid f

apartment [ə'pɑːtmənt] (US) n Wohnung f; **~ building** (US) n Wohnhaus nt

apathy ['æpəθı] n Teilnahmslosigkeit f,

Apathie f

ape [eɪp] n (Menschen)affe m ♦ vt nachahmen

aperitif [əˈpɛntiːf] n Aperitif m

aperture [ˈæpətʃʊəʳ] n Öffnung f; (PHOT) Blende f

APEX [ˈeɪpeks] n abbr (AVIAT: = advance purchase excursion) APEX (im Voraus reservierte(r) Fahrkarte/Flugschein zu reduzierten Preisen)

apex [ˈeɪpeks] n Spitze f

apiece [əˈpiːs] adv pro Stück; (per person) pro Kopf

apologetic [əpɔləˈdʒɛtɪk] adj entschuldigend; **to be ~** sich sehr entschuldigen

apologize [əˈpɔlədʒaɪz] vi: **to ~ (for sth to sb)** sich (für etw bei jdm) entschuldigen; **apology** n Entschuldigung f

apostle [əˈpɔsl] n Apostel m

apostrophe [əˈpɔstrəfi] n Apostroph m

appal [əˈpɔːl] vt erschrecken; **~ling** adj schrecklich

apparatus [æpəˈreɪtəs] n Gerät nt

apparel [əˈpærəl] (US) n Kleidung f

apparent [əˈpærənt] adj offenbar; **~ly** adv anscheinend

apparition [æpəˈrɪʃən] n (ghost) Erscheinung f, Geist m

appeal [əˈpiːl] vi dringend ersuchen; (JUR) Berufung einlegen ♦ n Aufruf m; (JUR) Berufung f; **to ~ for** dringend bitten um; **to ~ to** sich wenden an +acc; (to public) appellieren an +acc; **it doesn't ~ to me** es gefällt mir nicht; **~ing** adj ansprechend

appear [əˈpɪəʳ] vi (come into sight) erscheinen; (be seen) auftauchen; (seem) scheinen; **it would ~ that ...** anscheinend ...; **~ance** n (coming into sight) Erscheinen nt; (outward show) Äußere(s) nt

appease [əˈpiːz] vt beschwichtigen

appendices [əˈpendɪsiːz] npl of **appendix**

appendicitis [əpendɪˈsaɪtɪs] n Blinddarmentzündung f

appendix [əˈpendɪks] (pl **appendices**) n (in book) Anhang m; (MED) Blinddarm m

appetite [ˈæpɪtaɪt] n Appetit m; (fig) Lust f

appetizer [ˈæpɪtaɪzəʳ] n Appetitanreger m; **appetizing** [ˈæpɪtaɪzɪŋ] adj appetitanregend

applaud [əˈplɔːd] vi Beifall klatschen, applaudieren ♦ vt Beifall klatschen +dat; **applause** [əˈplɔːz] n Beifall m, Applaus m

apple [ˈæpl] n Apfel m; **~ tree** n Apfelbaum m

appliance [əˈplaɪəns] n Gerät nt

applicable [əˈplɪkəbl] adj anwendbar; (in forms) zutreffend

applicant [ˈæplɪkənt] n Bewerber(in) m(f)

application [æplɪˈkeɪʃən] n (request) Antrag m; (for job) Bewerbung f; (putting into practice) Anwendung f; (hard work) Fleiß m; **~ form** n Bewerbungsformular nt

applied [əˈplaɪd] adj angewandt

apply [əˈplaɪ] vi (be suitable) zutreffen; (ask): **to ~ (to)** sich wenden (an +acc); (request): **to ~ for** sich melden für +acc ♦ vt (place on) auflegen; (cream) auftragen; (put into practice) anwenden; **to ~ for sth** sich um etw bewerben; **to ~ o.s. to sth** sich bei etw anstrengen

appoint [əˈpɔɪnt] vt (to office) ernennen, berufen; (settle) festsetzen; **~ment** n (meeting) Verabredung f; (at hairdresser etc) Bestellung f; (in business) Termin m; (choice for a position) Ernennung f; (UNIV) Berufung f

appraisal [əˈpreɪzl] n Beurteilung f

appreciable [əˈpriːʃəbl] adj (perceptible) merklich; (able to be estimated) abschätzbar

appreciate [əˈpriːʃɪeɪt] vt (value) zu schätzen wissen; (understand) einsehen ♦ vi (increase in value) im Wert steigen; **appreciation** [əpriːʃɪˈeɪʃən] n Wertschätzung f; (COMM) Wertzuwachs m; **appreciative** [əˈpriːʃɪətɪv] adj (showing thanks) dankbar; (showing liking) anerkennend

apprehend [æprɪˈhend] vt (arrest) festnehmen; (understand) erfassen

apprehension [æprɪˈhenʃən] n Angst f

apprehensive [æprɪˈhensɪv] adj furchtsam

apprentice [əˈprentɪs] n Lehrling m; **~ship** n Lehrzeit f

approach [əˈprəʊtʃ] vi sich nähern ♦ vt herantreten an +acc; (problem) herangehen an +*acc* ♦ *n* Annäherung *f*; (*to problem*) Ansatz *m*; (*path*) Zugang *m*, Zufahrt *f*; **~able** *adj* zugänglich

appropriate [*adj* ə'prəuprıt, *vb* ə'prəuprıeıt] *adj* angemessen; (*remark*) angebracht ♦ *vt* (*take for o.s.*) sich aneignen; (*set apart*) bereitstellen

approval [ə'pru:vəl] *n* (*show of satisfaction*) Beifall *m*; (*permission*) Billigung *f*; **on ~** (*COMM*) bei Gefallen

approve [ə'pru:v] *vt, vi* billigen; **I don't ~ of it/him** ich halte nichts davon/von ihm; **~d school** (*BRIT*) *n* Erziehungsheim *nt*

approximate [*adj* ə'prɔksımıt, *vb* ə'prɔksımeıt] *adj* annähernd, ungefähr ♦ *vt* nahe kommen +*dat*; **~ly** *adv* rund, ungefähr

apricot ['eıprıkɔt] *n* Aprikose *f*

April ['eıprəl] *n* April *m*; **~ Fools' Day** *n* der erste April

apron ['eıprən] *n* Schürze *f*

apt [æpt] *adj* (*suitable*) passend; (*able*) begabt; (*likely*): **to be ~ to do sth** dazu neigen, etw zu tun

aptitude ['æptıtju:d] *n* Begabung *f*

aqualung ['ækwəlʌŋ] *n* Unterwasseratmungsgerät *nt*

aquarium [ə'kweərıəm] *n* Aquarium *nt*

Aquarius [ə'kweərıəs] *n* Wassermann *m*

aquatic [ə'kwætık] *adj* Wasser-

Arab ['ærəb] *n* Araber(in) *m(f)*

Arabia [ə'reıbıə] *n* Arabien *nt*; **~n** *adj* arabisch

Arabic ['ærəbık] *adj* arabisch ♦ *n* Arabisch *nt*

arable ['ærəbl] *adj* bebaubar, Kultur-

arbitrary ['ɑ:bıtrərı] *adj* willkürlich

arbitration [ɑ:bı'treıʃən] *n* Schlichtung *f*

arc [ɑ:k] *n* Bogen *m*

arcade [ɑ:'keıd] *n* Säulengang *m*; (*with video games*) Spielhalle *f*

arch [ɑ:tʃ] *n* Bogen *m* ♦ *vt* überwölben; (*back*) krumm machen

archaeologist [ɑ:kı'ɔlədʒıst] *n* Archäologe *m*

archaeology [ɑ:kı'ɔlədʒı] *n* Archäologie *f*

archaic [ɑ:'keıık] *adj* altertümlich

archbishop [ɑ:tʃ'bıʃəp] *n* Erzbischof *m*

archenemy ['ɑ:tʃ'enəmı] *n* Erzfeind *m*

archeology *etc* [ɑ:kı'ɔlədʒı] (*US*) = **archaeology** *etc*

archery ['ɑ:tʃərı] *n* Bogenschießen *nt*

architect ['ɑ:kıtekt] *n* Architekt(in) *m(f)*; **~ural** [ɑ:kı'tektʃərəl] *adj* architektonisch; **~ure** *n* Architektur *f*

archives ['ɑ:kaıvz] *npl* Archiv *nt*

archway ['ɑ:tʃweı] *n* Bogen *m*

Arctic ['ɑ:ktık] *adj* arktisch ♦ *n*: **the ~** die Arktis

ardent ['ɑıdənt] *adj* glühend

arduous ['ɑ:djuəs] *adj* mühsam

are [ɑ:r] *see* **be**

area ['eərıə] *n* Fläche *f*; (*of land*) Gebiet *nt*; (*part of sth*) Teil *m*, Abschnitt *m*

arena [ə'ri:nə] *n* Arena *f*

aren't [ɑ:nt] = **are not**

Argentina [ɑ:dʒən'ti:nə] *n* Argentinien *nt*; **Argentinian** [ɑ:dʒən'tınıən] *adj* argentinisch ♦ *n* Argentinier(in) *m(f)*

arguably ['ɑ:gjuəblı] *adv* wohl

argue ['ɑ:gju:] *vi* diskutieren; (*angrily*) streiten; **argument** *n* (*theory*) Argument *nt*; (*reasoning*) Argumentation *f*; (*row*) Auseinandersetzung *f*, Streit *m*; **to have an argument** sich streiten; **argumentative** [ɑıgju'mentətıv] *adj* streitlustig

aria ['ɑ:rıə] *n* Arie *f*

Aries ['eərız] *n* Widder *m*

arise [ə'raız] (*pt* **arose**, *pp* **arisen**) *vi* aufsteigen; (*get up*) aufstehen; (*difficulties etc*) entstehen; (*case*) vorkommen; **to ~ from sth** herrühren von etw; **~n** [ə'rızn] *pp* of **arise**

aristocracy [ærıs'tɔkrəsı] *n* Adel *m*, Aristokratie *f*; **aristocrat** ['ærıstəkræt] *n* Adlige(r) *f(m)*, Aristokrat(in) *m(f)*

arithmetic [ə'rıθmətık] *n* Rechnen *nt*, Arithmetik *f*

arm [ɑ:m] *n* Arm *m*; (*branch of military service*) Zweig *m* ♦ *vt* bewaffnen; **~s** *npl* (*weapons*) Waffen *pl*

armaments ['ɑ:məmənts] *npl* Ausrüstung *f*

armchair ['ɑ:mtʃeər] *n* Lehnstuhl *m*

armed [ɑ:md] *adj* (*forces*) Streit-, bewaffnet; **~ robbery** *n* bewaffnete(r) Raubüberfall *m*

armistice ['ɑːmɪstɪs] *n* Waffenstillstand *m*

armour ['ɑːmər] (*US* **armor**) *n* (*knight's*) Rüstung *f*; (*MIL*) Panzerplatte *f*; ~**ed car** *n* Panzerwagen *m*

armpit ['ɑːmpɪt] *n* Achselhöhle *f*

armrest ['ɑːmrɛst] *n* Armlehne *f*

army ['ɑːmɪ] *n* Armee *f*, Heer *nt*; (*host*) Heer *nt*

aroma [ə'rəumə] *n* Duft *m*, Aroma *nt*; ~**therapy** [ərəumə'θerəpɪ] *n* Aromatherapie *f*; ~**tic** [ærə'mætɪk] *adj* aromatisch, würzig

arose [ə'rəuz] *pt of* **arise**

around [ə'raund] *adv* ringsherum; (*almost*) ungefähr ♦ *prep* um ... herum; **is he ~?** ist er hier?

arrange [ə'reɪndʒ] *vt* (*time, meeting*) festsetzen; (*holidays*) festlegen; (*flowers, hair, objects*) anordnen; **I ~d to meet him** ich habe mit ihm ausgemacht, ihn zu treffen; **it's all ~d** es ist alles arrangiert; ~**ment** *n* (*order*) Reihenfolge *f*; (*agreement*) Vereinbarung *f*; ~**ments** *npl* (*plans*) Pläne *pl*

array [ə'reɪ] *n* (*collection*) Ansammlung *f*

arrears [ə'rɪəz] *npl* (*of debts*) Rückstand *m*; (*of work*) Unerledigte(s) *nt*; **in ~** im Rückstand

arrest [ə'rɛst] *vt* (*person*) verhaften; (*stop*) aufhalten ♦ *n* Verhaftung *f*; **under ~** in Haft

arrival [ə'raɪvl] *n* Ankunft *f*

arrive [ə'raɪv] *vi* ankommen; **to ~ at** ankommen in +*dat*, ankommen bei

arrogance ['ærəgəns] *n* Überheblichkeit *f*, Arroganz *f*; **arrogant** ['ærəgənt] *adj* überheblich, arrogant

arrow ['ærəu] *n* Pfeil *m*

arse [ɑːs] (*inf!*) *n* Arsch *m* (*!*)

arsenal ['ɑːsɪnl] *n* Waffenlager *nt*, Zeughaus *nt*

arsenic ['ɑːsnɪk] *n* Arsen *nt*

arson ['ɑːsn] *n* Brandstiftung *f*

art [ɑːt] *n* Kunst *f*; **A~s** *npl* (*UNIV*) Geisteswissenschaften *pl*

artery ['ɑːtərɪ] *n* Schlagader *f*, Arterie *f*

art gallery *n* Kunstgalerie *f*

arthritis [ɑː'θraɪtɪs] *n* Arthritis *f*

artichoke ['ɑːtɪtʃəuk] *n* Artischocke *f*;

Jerusalem ~ Erdartischocke *f*

article ['ɑːtɪkl] *n* (*PRESS, GRAM*) Artikel *m*; (*thing*) Gegenstand *m*, Artikel *m*; (*clause*) Abschnitt *m*, Paragraf *m*; ~ **of clothing** Kleidungsstück *nt*

articulate [*adj* ɑː'tɪkjulɪt, *vb* ɑː'tɪkjuleɪt] *adj* (*able to express o.s.*) redegewandt; (*speaking clearly*) deutlich, verständlich ♦ *vt* (*connect*) zusammenfügen, gliedern; **to be ~** sich gut ausdrücken können; ~**d vehicle** *n* Sattelschlepper *m*

artificial [ɑːtɪ'fɪʃəl] *adj* künstlich, Kunst-; ~ **respiration** *n* künstliche Atmung *f*

artisan ['ɑːtɪzæn] *n* gelernte(r) Handwerker *m*

artist ['ɑːtɪst] *n* Künstler(in) *m(f)*; ~**ic** [ɑː'tɪstɪk] *adj* künstlerisch; ~**ry** *n* künstlerische(s) Können *nt*

art school *n* Kunsthochschule *f*

KEYWORD
---

as [æz] *conj* **1** (*referring to time*) als; **as the years went by** mit den Jahren; **he came in as I was leaving** als er hereinkam, ging ich gerade; **as from tomorrow** ab morgen

2 (*in comparisons*): **as big as** so groß wie; **twice as big as** zweimal so groß wie; **as much/many as** so viel/so viele wie; **as soon as** sobald

3 (*since, because*) da; **he left early as he had to be home by 10** er ging früher, da er um 10 zu Hause sein musste

4 (*referring to manner, way*) wie; **do as you wish** mach was du willst; **as she said** wie sie sagte

5 (*concerning*): **as for** *or* **to that** was das betrifft *or* angeht

6: as if *or* **though** als ob

♦ *prep* als; *see also* **long**; **he works as a driver** er arbeitet als Fahrer; *see also* **such**; **he gave it to me as a present** er hat es mir als Geschenk gegeben; *see also* **well**

---

a.s.a.p. *abbr* = **as soon as possible**

asbestos [æz'bɛstəs] *n* Asbest *m*

ascend [ə'sɛnd] *vi* aufsteigen ♦ *vt* besteigen; **ascent** *n* Aufstieg *m*; Besteigung *f* ascertain [æsə'teɪn] vt feststellen

ascribe [ə'skraɪb] vt: to ~ sth to sth /sth to sb etw einer Sache/jdm etw zuschreiben

ash [æʃ] n Asche f; (tree) Esche f

ashamed [ə'ʃeɪmd] adj beschämt; to be ~ of sth sich für etw schämen

ashen [ˈæʃən] adj (pale) aschfahl

ashore [ə'ʃɔːr] adv an Land

ashtray [ˈæʃtreɪ] n Aschenbecher m

Ash Wednesday n Aschermittwoch m

Asia [ˈeɪʃə] n Asien nt; ~n adj asiatisch ♦ n Asiat(in) m(f)

aside [ə'saɪd] adv beiseite

ask [ɑːsk] vt fragen; (permission) bitten um; ~ him his name frage ihn nach seinem Namen; he ~ed to see you er wollte dich sehen; to ~ sb to do sth jdn bitten, etw zu tun; to ~ sb about sth jdn nach etw fragen; to ~ (sb) a question (jdn) etwas fragen; to ~ sb out to dinner jdn zum Essen einladen; ~ after vt fus fragen nach; ~ for vt fus bitten um

askance [ə'skɑːns] adv: to look ~ at sb jdn schief ansehen

asking price [ˈɑːskɪŋ-] n Verkaufspreis m

asleep [ə'sliːp] adj: to be ~ schlafen; to fall ~ einschlafen

asparagus [əs'pærəgəs] n Spargel m

aspect [ˈæspekt] n Aspekt m

aspersions [əs'pɜːʃənz] npl: to cast ~ on sb/sth sich abfällig über jdn/etw äußern

asphyxiation [æsfɪksɪ'eɪʃən] n Erstickung f

aspirations [æspə'reɪʃənz] npl: to have ~ towards sth etw anstreben

aspire [əs'paɪər] vi: to ~ to streben nach

aspirin [ˈæsprɪn] n Aspirin nt

ass [æs] n (also fig) Esel m; (US: inf!) Arsch m (!)

assailant [ə'seɪlənt] n Angreifer m

assassin [ə'sæsɪn] n Attentäter(in) m(f); ~ate vt ermorden; ~ation [əsæsɪ'neɪʃən] n (geglückte(s)) Attentat nt

assault [ə'sɔːlt] n Angriff m ♦ vt überfallen; (woman) herfallen über +acc

assemble [ə'sembl] vt versammeln; (parts) zusammensetzen ♦ vi sich versammeln; assembly n (meeting) Versammlung f;

(construction) Zusammensetzung f, Montage f; assembly line n Fließband nt

assent [ə'sent] n Zustimmung f

assert [ə'sɜːt] vt erklären; ~ion n Behauptung f

assess [ə'ses] vt schätzen; ~ment n Bewertung f, Einschätzung f; ~or n Steuerberater m

asset [ˈæset] n Vorteil m, Wert m; ~s npl (FIN) Vermögen nt; (estate) Nachlass m

assign [ə'saɪn] vt zuweisen; ~ment n Aufgabe f, Auftrag m

assimilate [ə'sɪmɪleɪt] vt sich aneignen, aufnehmen

assist [ə'sɪst] vt beistehen +dat; ~ance n Unterstützung f, Hilfe f; ~ant n Assistent(in) m(f), Mitarbeiter(in) m(f); (BRIT: also: shop ~ant) Verkäufer(in) m(f)

associate [n ə'səʊʃɪɪt, vb ə'səʊʃɪeɪt] n (partner) Kollege m, Teilhaber m; (member) außerordentliche(s) Mitglied nt ♦ vt verbinden ♦ vi (keep company) verkehren; association [əsəʊsɪ'eɪʃən] n Verband m, Verein m; (PSYCH) Assoziation f; (link) Verbindung f

assorted [ə'sɔːtɪd] adj gemischt

assortment [ə'sɔːtmənt] n Sammlung f; (COMM): ~ (of) Sortiment nt (von), Auswahl f (an +dat)

assume [ə'sjuːm] vt (take for granted) annehmen; (put on) annehmen, sich geben; ~d name n Deckname m

assumption [ə'sʌmpʃən] n Annahme f

assurance [ə'ʃuərəns] n (firm statement) Versicherung f; (confidence) Selbstsicherheit f; (insurance) (Lebens)versicherung f

assure [ə'ʃuər] vt (make sure) sicherstellen; (convince) versichern +dat; (life) versichern

asterisk [ˈæstərɪsk] n Sternchen nt

asthma [ˈæsmə] n Asthma nt

astonish [ə'stɒnɪʃ] vt erstaunen; ~ment n Erstaunen nt

astound [ə'staʊnd] vt verblüffen

astray [ə'streɪ] adv in die Irre; auf Abwege; to go ~ (go wrong) sich vertun; to lead ~ irreführen

astride [ə'straɪd] adv rittlings ♦ prep rittlings

auf
astrologer [əsˈtrɒlədʒəʳ] n Astrologe m, Astrologin f; **astrology** n Astrologie f
astronaut [ˈæstrənɔːt] n Astronaut(in) m(f)
astronomer [əsˈtrɒnəməʳ] n Astronom m
astronomical [æstrəˈnɒmɪkl] adj astronomisch; (success) riesig
astronomy [əsˈtrɒnəmɪ] n Astronomie f
astute [əsˈtjuːt] adj scharfsinnig; schlau, gerissen
asylum [əˈsaɪləm] n (home) Heim nt; (refuge) Asyl nt

KEYWORD

---

at [æt] prep **1** (referring to position, direction) an +dat, bei +dat; (with place) in +dat; **at the top** an der Spitze; **at home/school** zu Hause/in der Schule; **at the baker's** beim Bäcker; **to look at sth** auf etw acc blicken; **to throw sth at sb** etw nach jdm werfen
2 (referring to time): **at 4 o'clock** um 4 Uhr; **at night** bei Nacht; **at Christmas** zu Weihnachten; **at times** manchmal
3 (referring to rates, speed etc): **at £1 a kilo** zu £1 pro Kilo; **two at a time** zwei auf einmal; **at 50 km/h** mit 50 km/h
4 (referring to manner): **at a stroke** mit einem Schlag; **at peace** in Frieden
5 (referring to activity): **to be at work** bei der Arbeit sein; **to play at cowboys** Cowboy spielen; **to be good at sth** gut in etw dat sein
6 (referring to cause): **shocked/surprised/annoyed at sth** schockiert/überrascht/verärgert über etw acc; **I went at his suggestion** ich ging auf seinen Vorschlag hin

---

ate [eɪt] pt of **eat**
atheist [ˈeɪθɪɪst] n Atheist(in) m(f)
Athens [ˈæθɪnz] n Athen nt
athlete [ˈæθliːt] n Athlet m, Sportler m
athletic [æθˈletɪk] adj sportlich, athletisch; **~s** n Leichtathletik f
Atlantic [ətˈlæntɪk] adj atlantisch ♦ n: **the ~ (Ocean)** der Atlantik
atlas [ˈætləs] n Atlas m

ATM abbr (= automated teller machine) Geldautomat m
atmosphere [ˈætməsfɪəʳ] n Atmosphäre f
atom [ˈætəm] n Atom nt; (fig) bisschen nt; **~ic** [əˈtɒmɪk] adj atomar, Atom-; **~(ic) bomb** n Atombombe f
atomizer [ˈætəmaɪzəʳ] n Zerstäuber m
atone [əˈtəun] vi sühnen; **to ~ for sth** etw sühnen
atrocious [əˈtrəuʃəs] adj grässlich
atrocity [əˈtrɒsɪtɪ] n Scheußlichkeit f; (deed) Gräueltat f
attach [əˈtætʃ] vt (fasten) befestigen; **to be ~ed to sb/sth** an jdm/etw hängen; **to ~ importance** etc **to sth** Wichtigkeit etc auf etw acc legen, einer Sache dat Wichtigkeit etc beimessen
attaché case [əˈtæʃeɪ] n Aktenkoffer m
attachment [əˈtætʃmənt] n (tool) Zubehörteil nt; (love): **~ (to sb)** Zuneigung f (zu jdm)
attack [əˈtæk] vt angreifen ♦ n Angriff m; (MED) Anfall m; **~er** n Angreifer(in) m(f)
attain [əˈteɪn] vt erreichen; **~ments** npl Kenntnisse pl
attempt [əˈtempt] n Versuch m ♦ vt versuchen; **~ed murder** Mordversuch m
attend [əˈtend] vt (go to) teilnehmen (an +dat); (lectures) besuchen; **to ~ to** (needs) nachkommen +dat; (person) sich kümmern um; **~ance** n (presence) Anwesenheit f; (people present) Besucherzahl f; **good ~ance** gute Teilnahme; **~ant** n (companion) Begleiter(in) m(f); Gesellschafter(in) m(f); (in car park etc) Wächter(in) m(f); (servant) Bedienstete(r) mf ♦ adj begleitend; (fig) damit verbunden
attention [əˈtenʃən] n Aufmerksamkeit f; (care) Fürsorge f; (for machine etc) Pflege f ♦ excl (MIL) Achtung!; **for the ~ of ...** zu Händen (von) ...
attentive [əˈtentɪv] adj aufmerksam
attic [ˈætɪk] n Dachstube f, Mansarde f
attitude [ˈætɪtjuːd] n (mental) Einstellung f
attorney [əˈtɜːnɪ] n (solicitor) Rechtsanwalt m; **A~ General** n Justizminister m
attract [əˈtrækt] vt anziehen; (attention)

erregen; **~ion** *n* Anziehungskraft *f*; (*thing*)
Attraktion *f*; **~ive** *adj* attraktiv

attribute [*n* ˈætɪbjuːt, *vb* əˈtɪbjuːt] *n*
Eigenschaft *f*, Attribut *nt* ♦ *vt* zuschreiben

attrition [əˈtrɪʃən] *n*: **war of ~**
Zermürbungskrieg *m*

aubergine [ˈəubəʒiːn] *n* Aubergine *f*

auburn [ˈɔːbən] *adj* kastanienbraun

auction [ˈɔːkʃən] *n* (*also*: **sale by ~**)
Versteigerung *f*, Auktion *f* ♦ *vt* versteigern;
~eer [ɔːkʃəˈnɪə] *n* Versteigerer *m*

audacity [ɔːˈdæsɪtɪ] *n* (*boldness*) Wagemut *m*;
(*impudence*) Unverfrorenheit *f*

audible [ˈɔːdɪbl] *adj* hörbar

audience [ˈɔːdɪəns] *n* Zuhörer *pl*, Zuschauer
pl; (*with queen*) Audienz *f*

audiotypist [ˈɔːdɪəuˈtaɪpɪst] *n* Phonotypistin
f, Fonotypistin *f*

audiovisual [ˈɔːdɪəuˈvɪzjuəl] *adj* audiovisuell

audit [ˈɔːdɪt] *vt* prüfen

audition [ɔːˈdɪʃən] *n* Probe *f*

auditor [ˈɔːdɪtə] *n* (*accountant*)
Rechnungsprüfer(in) *m(f)*, Buchprüfer *m*

auditorium [ɔːdɪˈtɔːrɪəm] *n* Zuschauerraum
m

augment [ɔːgˈment] *vt* vermehren

augur [ˈɔːgə] *vi* bedeuten, voraussagen; **this
~s well** das ist ein gutes Omen

August [ˈɔːgəst] *n* August *m*

aunt [ɑːnt] *n* Tante *f*; **~ie** *n* Tantchen *nt*; **~y**
n = **auntie**

au pair [ˈəuˈpeə] *n* (*also*: **~ girl**)
Aupairmädchen *nt*, Au-pair-Mädchen *nt*

aura [ˈɔːrə] *n* Nimbus *m*

auspicious [ɔːsˈpɪʃəs] *adj* günstig;
verheißungsvoll

austere [ɒsˈtɪə] *adj* streng; (*room*) nüchtern;
austerity [ɒsˈtɛrɪtɪ] *n* Strenge *f*; (*POL*)
wirtschaftliche Einschränkung *f*

Australia [ɒsˈtreɪlɪə] *n* Australien *nt*; **~n** *adj*
australisch ♦ *n* Australier(in) *m(f)*

Austria [ˈɒstrɪə] *n* Österreich *nt*; **~n** *adj*
österreichisch ♦ *n* Österreicher(in) *m(f)*

authentic [ɔːˈθentɪk] *adj* echt, authentisch

author [ˈɔːθə] *n* Autor *m*, Schriftsteller *m*;
(*beginner*) Urheber *m*, Schöpfer *m*

authoritarian [ɔːθɒrɪˈtɛərɪən] *adj* autoritär

authoritative [ɔːˈθɒrɪtətɪv] *adj* (*account*)
maßgeblich; (*manner*) herrisch

authority [ɔːˈθɒrɪtɪ] *n* (*power*) Autorität *f*,
(*expert*) Autorität *f*, Fachmann *m*; **the
authorities** *npl* (*ruling body*) die Behörden
pl

authorize [ˈɔːθəraɪz] *vt* bevollmächtigen;
(*permit*) genehmigen

auto [ˈɔːtəu] (*US*) *n* Auto *nt*, Wagen *m*

autobiography [ɔːtəbaɪˈɒgrəfɪ] *n*
Autobiografie *f*

autograph [ˈɔːtəgraːf] *n* (*of celebrity*)
Autogramm *nt* ♦ *vt* mit Autogramm
versehen

automatic [ɔːtəˈmætɪk] *adj* automatisch ♦ *n*
(*gun*) Selbstladepistole *f*; (*car*) Automatik *m*;
~ally *adv* automatisch

automation [ɔːtəˈmeɪʃən] *n* Automatisierung
f

automobile [ˈɔːtəməbiːl] (*US*) *n* Auto(mobil)
nt

autonomous [ɔːˈtɒnəməs] *adj* autonom;
autonomy *n* Autonomie *f*

autumn [ˈɔːtəm] *n* Herbst *m*

auxiliary [ɔːgˈzɪlɪərɪ] *adj* Hilfs-

Av. *abbr* = **avenue**

avail [əˈveɪl] *vt*: **to ~ o.s. of sth** sich einer
Sache *gen* bedienen ♦ *n*: **to no ~** nutzlos

availability [əveɪləˈbɪlɪtɪ] *n* Erhältlichkeit *f*,
Vorhandensein *nt*

available [əˈveɪləbl] *adj* erhältlich; zur
Verfügung stehend; (*person*) erreichbar,
abkömmlich

avalanche [ˈævəlɑːnʃ] *n* Lawine *f*

Ave. *abbr* = **avenue**

avenge [əˈvendʒ] *vt* rächen, sühnen

avenue [ˈævənjuː] *n* Allee *f*

average [ˈævərɪdʒ] *n* Durchschnitt *m* ♦ *adj*
durchschnittlich, Durchschnitts- ♦ *vt*
(*figures*) den Durchschnitt nehmen von;
(*perform*) durchschnittlich leisten; (*in car etc*)
im Schnitt fahren; **on ~** durchschnittlich,
im Durchschnitt; **~ out** *vi*: **to ~ out at** im
Durchschnitt betragen

averse [əˈvɜːs] *adj*: **to be ~ to doing sth**
eine Abneigung dagegen haben, etw zu
tun

avert [ə'vɜːt] *vt* (*turn away*) abkehren; (*prevent*) abwehren

aviary ['eɪvɪərɪ] *n* Vogelhaus *nt*

aviation [eɪvɪ'eɪʃən] *n* Luftfahrt *f*, Flugwesen *nt*

avid ['ævɪd] *adj*: ~ **(for)** gierig (auf +*acc*)

avocado [ævə'kɑːdəʊ] *n* (*BRIT: also:* ~ **pear**) Avocado(birne) *f*

avoid [ə'vɔɪd] *vt* vermeiden

await [ə'weɪt] *vt* erwarten, entgegensehen +*dat*

awake [ə'weɪk] (*pt* **awoke**, *pp* **awoken** *or* **awaked**) *adj* wach ♦ *vt* (auf)wecken ♦ *vi* aufwachen; **to be ~** wach sein; **~ning** *n* Erwachen *nt*

award [ə'wɔːd] *n* (*prize*) Preis *m* ♦ *vt*: **to ~ (sb sth)** (jdm etw) zuerkennen

aware [ə'weəᵊ] *adj* bewusst; **to be ~** sich bewusst sein; **~ness** *n* Bewusstsein *nt*

awash [ə'wɒʃ] *adj* überflutet

away [ə'weɪ] *adv* weg, fort; **two hours ~ by car** zwei Autostunden entfernt; **the holiday was two weeks ~** es war noch zwei Wochen bis zum Urlaub; **two kilometres ~** zwei Kilometer entfernt; ~ **match** *n* (*SPORT*) Auswärtsspiel *nt*

awe [ɔː] *n* Ehrfurcht *f*; **~-inspiring** *adj* Ehrfurcht gebietend; **~some** *adj* Ehrfurcht gebietend

awful ['ɔːfəl] *adj* (*very bad*) furchtbar; **~ly** *adv* furchtbar, sehr

awhile [ə'waɪl] *adv* eine Weile

awkward ['ɔːkwəd] *adj* (*clumsy*) ungeschickt, linkisch; (*embarrassing*) peinlich

awning ['ɔːnɪŋ] *n* Markise *f*

awoke [ə'wəʊk] *pt of* **awake**; **~n** *pp of* **awake**

awry [ə'raɪ] *adv* schief; (*plans*) schief gehen

axe [æks] (*US* **ax**) *n* Axt *f*, Beil *nt* ♦ *vt* (*end suddenly*) streichen

axes¹ ['æksɪz] *npl of* **axe**

axes² ['æksiːz] *npl of* **axis**

axis ['æksɪs] (*pl* **axes**) *n* Achse *f*

axle ['æksl] *n* Achse *f*

ay(e) [aɪ] *excl* (*yes*) ja

azalea [ə'zeɪlɪə] *n* Azalee *f*

B, b

B [biː] *n* (*MUS*) H *nt*; ~ **road** (*BRIT*) Landstraße *f*

B.A. *n abbr* = **Bachelor of Arts**

babble ['bæbl] *vi* schwätzen

baby ['beɪbɪ] *n* Baby *nt*; ~ **carriage** (*US*) *n* Kinderwagen *m*; ~ **food** *n* Babynahrung *f*; **~-sit** *vi* Kinder hüten, babysitten; **~-sitter** *n* Babysitter *m*; **~-sitting** *n* Babysitten *nt*, Babysitting *nt*; ~ **wipe** *n* Ölpflegetuch *nt*

bachelor ['bætʃələᵊ] *n* Junggeselle *m*; **B~ of Arts** Bakkalaureus *m* der philosophischen Fakultät; **B~ of Science** Bakkalaureus *m* der Naturwissenschaften

back [bæk] *n* (*of person, horse*) Rücken *m*; (*of house*) Rückseite *f*; (*of train*) Ende *nt*; (*FOOTBALL*) Verteidiger *m* ♦ *vt* (*support*) unterstützen; (*wager*) wetten auf +*acc*; (*car*) rückwärts fahren ♦ *vi* (*go ~wards*) rückwärts gehen *or* fahren ♦ *adj* hintere(r, s) ♦ *adv* zurück; (*to the rear*) nach hinten; ~ **down** *vi* zurückstecken; ~ **out** *vi* sich zurückziehen; (*inf*) kneifen; ~ **up** *vt* (*support*) unterstützen; (*car*) zurücksetzen; (*COMPUT*) eine Sicherungskopie machen von; **~ache** *n* Rückenschmerzen *pl*; **~bencher** (*BRIT*) *n* Parlamentarier(in) *m(f)*; **~bone** *n* Rückgrat *nt*; (*support*) Rückhalt *m*; **~cloth** *n* Hintergrund *m*; **~date** *vt* rückdatieren; **~drop** *n* (*THEAT*) = **backcloth**; (*~ground*) Hintergrund *m*; **~fire** *vi* (*plan*) fehlschlagen; (*TECH*) fehlzünden; **~ground** *n* Hintergrund *m*; (*person's education*) Vorbildung *f*; **family ~ground** Familienverhältnisse *pl*; **~hand** *n* (*TENNIS: also:* **~hand stroke**) Rückhand *f*; **~hander** (*BRIT*) *n* (*bribe*) Schmiergeld *nt*; **~ing** *n* (*support*) Unterstützung *f*; **~lash** *n* (*fig*) Gegenschlag *m*; **~log** *n* (*of work*) Rückstand *m*; ~ **number** *n* (*PRESS*) alte Nummer *f*; **~pack** *n* Rucksack *m*; **~packer** *n* Rucksacktourist(in) *m(f)*; ~ **pain** *n* Rückenschmerzen *pl*; ~ **pay** *n* (Gehalts- *or* Lohn)nachzahlung *f*; ~ **payments** *npl*

Zahlungsrückstände pl; ~ seat n (AUT) Rücksitz m; ~side (inf) n Hintern m; ~stage adv hinter den Kulissen; ~stroke n Rückenschwimmen nt; ~up adj (COMPUT) Sicherungs- ♦ n (COMPUT) Sicherungskopie f; ~ward adj (less developed) zurückgeblieben; (primitive) rückständig; ~wards adv rückwärts; ~water n (fig) Kaff nt; ~yard n Hinterhof m

bacon ['beɪkən] n Schinkenspeck m

bacteria [bæk'tɪərɪə] npl Bakterien pl

bad [bæd] adj schlecht, schlimm; **to go ~** schlecht werden

bade [bæd] pt of **bid**

badge [bædʒ] n Abzeichen nt

badger ['bædʒər] n Dachs m

badly ['bædlɪ] adv schlecht, schlimm; ~ **wounded** schwer verwundet; **he needs it ~** er braucht es dringend; **to be ~ off (for money)** dringend Geld nötig haben

badminton ['bædmɪntən] n Federball m, Badminton nt

bad-tempered ['bæd'tempəd] adj schlecht gelaunt

baffle ['bæfl] vt (puzzle) verblüffen

bag [bæg] n (sack) Beutel m; (paper) Tüte f; (handbag) Tasche f; (suitcase) Koffer m; (inf: old woman) alte Schachtel f ♦ vt (put in sack) in einen Sack stecken; (hunting) erlegen; ~s **of** (inf: lots of) eine Menge +acc; ~gage ['bægɪdʒ] n Gepäck nt; ~ **allowance** n Freigepäck nt; ~ **reclaim** n Gepäckausgabe f; ~gy ['bægɪ] adj bauschig, sackartig

bagpipes ['bægpaɪps] npl Dudelsack m

bail [beɪl] n (money) Kaution f ♦ vt (prisoner: usu: grant ~ to) gegen Kaution freilassen; (boat: also: ~ **out**) ausschöpfen; **on ~** (prisoner) gegen Kaution freigelassen; **to ~ sb out** die Kaution für jdn stellen; see also **bale**

bailiff ['beɪlɪf] n Gerichtsvollzieher(in) m(f)

bait [beɪt] n Köder m ♦ vt mit einem Köder versehen; (fig) ködern

bake [beɪk] vt, vi backen; ~d **beans** gebackene Bohnen pl; ~d **potatoes** npl in der Schale gebackene Kartoffeln pl; ~r n

Bäcker m; ~ry n Bäckerei f; **baking** n Backen nt; **baking powder** n Backpulver nt

balance ['bæləns] n (scales) Waage f; (equilibrium) Gleichgewicht nt; (FIN: state of account) Saldo m; (difference) Bilanz f; (amount remaining) Restbetrag m ♦ vt (weigh) wägen; (make equal) ausgleichen; ~ **of trade/payments** Handels-/ Zahlungsbilanz f; ~d adj ausgeglichen; ~ **sheet** n Bilanz f, Rechnungsabschluss m

balcony ['bælkənɪ] n Balkon m

bald [bɔːld] adj kahl; (statement) knapp

bale [beɪl] n Ballen m; **bale out** vi (from a plane) abspringen

ball [bɔːl] n Ball m; ~ **bearing** n Kugellager nt

ballet ['bæleɪ] n Ballett nt; ~ **dancer** n Balletttänzer(in) m(f); ~ **shoe** n Ballettschuh m

balloon [bə'luːn] n (Luft)ballon m

ballot ['bælət] n (geheime) Abstimmung f

ballpoint (pen) ['bɔːlpɔɪnt-] n Kugelschreiber m

ballroom ['bɔːlrum] n Tanzsaal m

Baltic ['bɔːltɪk] n: **the ~ (Sea)** die Ostsee

bamboo [bæm'buː] n Bambus m

ban [bæn] n Verbot nt ♦ vt verbieten

banana [bə'nɑːnə] n Banane f

band [bænd] n Band nt; (group) Gruppe f; (of criminals) Bande f; (MUS) Kapelle f, Band f; ~ **together** vi sich zusammentun

bandage ['bændɪdʒ] n Verband m; (elastic) Bandage f ♦ vt (cut) verbinden; (broken limb) bandagieren

Bandaid ['bændeɪd] (® US) n Heftpflaster nt

bandit ['bændɪt] n Bandit m, Räuber m

bandwagon ['bændwægən] n: **to jump on the ~** (fig) auf den fahrenden Zug aufspringen

bandy ['bændɪ] vt wechseln; ~-**legged** adj o-beinig, O-beinig

bang [bæŋ] n (explosion) Knall m; (blow) Hieb m ♦ vt, vi knallen

Bangladesh [bæŋglə'deʃ] n Bangladesch nt

bangle ['bæŋgl] n Armspange f

bangs [bæŋz] (US) npl (fringe) Pony m

banish ['bænɪʃ] *vt* verbannen

banister(s) ['bænɪstə(z)] *n(pl)* (Treppen)geländer *nt*

bank [bæŋk] *n* (*raised ground*) Erdwall *m*; (*of lake etc*) Ufer *nt*; (*FIN*) Bank *f* ♦ *vt* (*tilt: AVIAT*) in die Kurve bringen; (*money*) einzahlen; ~ **on** *vt fus*: **to ~ on sth** mit etw rechnen; ~ **account** *n* Bankkonto *nt*; ~ **card** *n* Scheckkarte *f*; ~**er** *n* Bankier *m*; ~**er's card** (*BRIT*) *n* = **bank card**; **B~ holiday** (*BRIT*) *n* gesetzliche(r) Feiertag *m*; ~**ing** *n* Bankwesen *nt*; ~**note** *n* Banknote *f*; ~ **rate** *n* Banksatz *m*

---

bank holiday

ℹ️ *Als* **bank holiday** *wird in Großbritannien ein gesetzlicher Feiertag bezeichnet, an dem die Banken geschlossen sind. Die meisten dieser Feiertage, abgesehen von Weihnachten und Ostern, fallen auf Montage im Mai und August. An diesen langen Wochenenden (bank holiday weekends) fahren viele Briten in Urlaub, so dass dann auf den Straßen, Flughäfen und bei der Bahn sehr viel Betrieb ist.*

---

bankrupt ['bæŋkrʌpt] *adj*: **to be ~** bankrott sein; **to go ~** Bankrott machen; ~**cy** *n* Bankrott *m*

bank statement *n* Kontoauszug *m*

banned [bænd] *adj*: **he was ~ from driving** (*BRIT*) ihm wurde Fahrverbot erteilt

banner ['bænə*r*] *n* Banner *nt*

banns [bænz] *npl* Aufgebot *nt*

baptism ['bæptɪzəm] *n* Taufe *f*

baptize [bæp'taɪz] *vt* taufen

bar [bɑː*r*] *n* (*rod*) Stange *f*; (*obstacle*) Hindernis *nt*; (*of chocolate*) Tafel *f*; (*of soap*) Stück *nt*; (*for food, drink*) Buffet *nt*, Bar *f*; (*pub*) Wirtschaft *f*; (*MUS*) Takt(strich) *m* ♦ *vt* (*fasten*) verriegeln; (*hinder*) versperren; (*exclude*) ausschließen; **behind ~s** hinter Gittern; **the B~: to be called to the B~** als Anwalt zugelassen werden; ~ **none** ohne Ausnahme

barbaric [bɑː'bærɪk] *adj* primitiv, unkultiviert

barbecue ['bɑːbɪkjuː] *n* Barbecue *nt*

barbed wire ['bɑːbd-] *n* Stacheldraht *m*

barber ['bɑːbə*r*] *n* Herrenfriseur *m*

bar code *n* (*COMM*) Registrierkode *f*

bare [bɛə*r*] *adj* nackt; (*trees, country*) kahl; (*mere*) bloß ♦ *vt* entblößen; ~**back** *adv* ungesattelt; ~**faced** *adj* unverfroren; ~**foot** *adj, adv* barfuß; ~**ly** *adv* kaum, knapp

bargain ['bɑːgɪn] *n* (*sth cheap*) günstiger Kauf; (*agreement: written*) Kaufvertrag *m*; (*: oral*) Geschäft *nt*; **into the ~** obendrein; ~ **for** *vt*: **he got more than he ~ed for** er erlebte sein blaues Wunder

barge [bɑːdʒ] *n* Lastkahn *m*; ~ **in** *vi* hereinplatzen; ~ **into** *vt* rennen gegen

bark [bɑːk] *n* (*of tree*) Rinde *f*; (*of dog*) Bellen *nt* ♦ *vi* (*dog*) bellen

barley ['bɑːlɪ] *n* Gerste *f*; ~ **sugar** *n* Malzbonbon *m*

bar: ~**maid** *n* Bardame *f*; ~**man** (*irreg*) *n* Barkellner *m*; ~ **meal** *n* einfaches Essen in einem Pub

barn [bɑːn] *n* Scheune *f*

barometer [bə'rɒmɪtə*r*] *n* Barometer *nt*

baron ['bærən] *n* Baron *m*; ~**ess** *n* Baronin *f*

barracks ['bærəks] *npl* Kaserne *f*

barrage ['bærɑːʒ] *n* (*gunfire*) Sperrfeuer *nt*; (*dam*) Staudamm *m*; Talsperre *f*

barrel ['bærəl] *n* Fass *nt*; (*of gun*) Lauf *m*

barren ['bærən] *adj* unfruchtbar

barricade [bærɪ'keɪd] *n* Barrikade *f* ♦ *vt* verbarrikadieren

barrier ['bærɪə*r*] *n* (*obstruction*) Hindernis *nt*; (*fence*) Schranke *f*

barring ['bɑːrɪŋ] *prep* außer im Falle +*gen*

barrister ['bærɪstə*r*] (*BRIT*) *n* Rechtsanwalt *m*

barrow ['bærəʊ] *n* (*cart*) Schubkarren *m*

bartender ['bɑːtɛndə*r*] (*US*) *n* Barmann *or* -kellner *m*

barter ['bɑːtə*r*] *vt* handeln

base [beɪs] *n* (*bottom*) Boden *m*, Basis *f*; (*MIL*) Stützpunkt *m* ♦ *vt* gründen; (*opinion, theory*): **to be ~d on** basieren auf +*dat* ♦ *adj* (*low*) gemein; **I'm ~d in London** ich wohne in London; ~**ball** ['beɪsbɔːl] *n* Baseball *m*; ~**ment** ['beɪsmənt] *n* Kellergeschoss *nt*

bases[1] ['beɪsɪz] *npl of* **base**

bases[2] ['beɪsiːz] *npl of* **basis**

bash [bæʃ] (inf) vt (heftig) schlagen
bashful ['bæʃful] adj schüchtern
basic ['beɪsɪk] adj grundlegend; **~s** npl: **the ~s** das Wesentliche sg; **~ally** adv im Grunde
basil ['bæzl] n Basilikum nt
basin ['beɪsn] n (dish) Schüssel f; (for washing, also valley) Becken nt; (dock) (Trocken)becken nt
basis ['beɪsɪs] (pl **bases**) n Basis f, Grundlage f
bask [bɑːsk] vi: **to ~ in the sun** sich sonnen
basket ['bɑːskɪt] n Korb m; **~ball** n Basketball m
bass [beɪs] n (MUS, also instrument) Bass m; (voice) Bassstimme f; **~ drum** n große Trommel
bassoon [bə'suːn] n Fagott nt
bastard ['bɑːstəd] n Bastard m; (inf!) Arschloch nt (!)
bat [bæt] n (SPORT) Schlagholz nt; Schläger m; (ZOOL) Fledermaus f ♦ vt: **he didn't ~ an eyelid** er hat nicht mit der Wimper gezuckt
batch [bætʃ] n (of letters) Stoß m; (of samples) Satz m
bated ['beɪtɪd] adj: **with ~ breath** mit angehaltenem Atem
bath [bɑːθ] n Bad nt; (~ tub) Badewanne f ♦ vt baden; **to have a ~** baden; see also **baths**
bathe [beɪð] vt, vi baden; **~r** n Badende(r) f(m)
bathing ['beɪðɪŋ] n Baden nt; **~ cap** n Badekappe f; **~ costume** n Badeanzug m; **~ suit** (US) n Badeanzug m; **~ trunks** (BRIT) npl Badehose f
bath: **~robe** n Bademantel m; **~room** n Bad(ezimmer nt) nt; **~s** npl (Schwimm)bad nt; **~ towel** n Badetuch nt
baton ['bætən] n (of police) Gummiknüppel m; (MUS) Taktstock m
batter ['bætər] vt verprügeln ♦ n Schlagteig m; (for cake) Biskuitteig m; **~ed** adj (hat, pan) verbeult
battery ['bætərɪ] n (ELEC) Batterie f; (MIL) Geschützbatterie f
battery farming n (Hühner- etc)batterien

pl
battle ['bætl] n Schlacht f; (small) Gefecht nt ♦ vi kämpfen; **~field** n Schlachtfeld nt; **~ship** n Schlachtschiff nt
Bavaria [bə'veərɪə] n Bayern nt; **~n** adj bay(e)risch ♦ n (person) Bayer(in) m(f)
bawdy ['bɔːdɪ] adj unflätig
bawl [bɔːl] vi brüllen
bay [beɪ] n (of sea) Bucht f ♦ vi bellen; **to keep at ~** unter Kontrolle halten; **~ window** n Erkerfenster nt
bazaar [bə'zɑːr] n Basar m
B. & B. abbr = **bed and breakfast**
BBC n abbr (= British Broadcasting Corporation) BBC f or m
B.C. adv abbr (= before Christ) v. Chr.

KEYWORD
---

be [biː] (pt **was, were**, pp **been**) aux vb
1 (with present participle: forming continuous tenses): **what are you doing?** was machst du (gerade)?; **it is raining** es regnet; **I've been waiting for you for hours** ich warte schon seit Stunden auf dich
2 (with pp: forming passives): **to be killed** getötet werden; **the thief was nowhere to be seen** der Dieb war nirgendwo zu sehen
3 (in tag questions): **it was fun, wasn't it?** es hat Spaß gemacht, nicht wahr?
4 (+to +infin): **the house is to be sold** das Haus soll verkauft werden; **he's not to open it** er darf es nicht öffnen
♦ vb +complement **1** (usu) sein; **I'm tired** ich bin müde; **I'm hot/cold** mir ist heiß/kalt; **he's a doctor** er ist Arzt; **2 and 2 are 4** 2 und 2 ist or sind 4; **she's tall/pretty** sie ist groß/hübsch; **be careful/quiet** sei vorsichtig/ruhig
2 (of health): **how are you?** wie geht es dir?; **he's very ill** er ist sehr krank; **I'm fine now** jetzt geht es mir gut
3 (of age): **how old are you?** wie alt bist du?; **I'm sixteen (years old)** ich bin sechzehn (Jahre alt)
4 (cost): **how much was the meal?** was or wie viel hat das Essen gekostet?; **that'll be £5.75, please** das macht £5.75, bitte

♦ *vi* **1** (*exist, occur etc*) sein; **is there a God?** gibt es einen Gott?; **be that as it may** wie dem auch sei; **so be it** also gut **2** (*referring to place*) sein; **I won't be here tomorrow** iche werde morgen nicht hier sein

3 (*referring to movement*): **where have you been?** wo bist du gewesen?; **I've been in the garden** ich war im Garten

♦ *impers vb* **1** (*referring to time, distance, weather*): **it's 5 o'clock** es ist 5 Uhr; **it's 10 km to the village** es sind 10 km bis zum Dorf; **it's too hot/cold** es ist zu heiß/kalt

2 (*emphatic*): **it's me** ich bins; **it's the postman** es ist der Briefträger

beach [biːtʃ] *n* Strand *m* ♦ *vt* (*ship*) auf den Strand setzen

beacon ['biːkən] *n* (*signal*) Leuchtfeuer *nt*; (*traffic ~*) Bake *f*

bead [biːd] *n* Perle *f*; (*drop*) Tropfen *m*

beak [biːk] *n* Schnabel *m*

beaker ['biːkər] *n* Becher *m*

beam [biːm] *n* (*of wood*) Balken *m*; (*of light*) Strahl *m*; (*smile*) strahlende(s) Lächeln *nt* ♦ *vi* strahlen

bean [biːn] *n* Bohne *f*; (*also:* **baked ~s**) gebackene Bohnen *pl*; **~ sprouts** *npl* Sojasprossen *pl*

bear [bɛər] (*pt* **bore**, *pp* **borne**) *n* Bär *m* ♦ *vt* (*weight, crops*) tragen; (*tolerate*) ertragen; (*young*) gebären ♦ *vi*: **to ~ right/left** sich rechts/links halten; **~ out** *vt* (*suspicions etc*) bestätigen; **~ up** *vi* sich halten

beard [bɪəd] *n* Bart *m*; **~ed** *adj* bärtig

bearer ['bɛərər] *n* Träger *m*

bearing ['bɛərɪŋ] *n* (*posture*) Haltung *f*; (*relevance*) Relevanz *f*; (*relation*) Bedeutung *f*; (*TECH*) Kugellager *nt*; **~s** *npl* (*direction*) Orientierung *f*; (*also:* **ball ~s**) (Kugel)lager *nt*

beast [biːst] *n* Tier *nt*, Vieh *nt*; (*person*) Biest *nt*

beat [biːt] (*pt* **beat**, *pp* **beaten**) *n* (*stroke*) Schlag *m*; (*pulsation*) (Herz)schlag *m*; (*police round*) Runde *f*, Revier *nt*; (*MUS*) Takt *m*;

Beat *m* ♦ *vt*, *vi* schlagen; **to ~ it** abhauen; **off the ~en track** abgelegen; **~ off** *vt* abschlagen; **~ up** *vt* zusammenschlagen; **~en** *pp* of **beat**; **~ing** *n* Prügel *pl*

beautiful ['bjuːtɪful] *adj* schön; **~ly** *adv* ausgezeichnet

beauty ['bjuːtɪ] *n* Schönheit *f*; **~ salon** *n* Schönheitssalon *m*; **~ spot** *n* Schönheitsfleck *m*; (*BRIT: TOURISM*) (besonders) schöne(r) Ort *m*

beaver ['biːvər] *n* Biber *m*

became [bɪ'keɪm] *pt* of **become**

because [bɪ'kɔz] *conj* weil ♦ *prep*: **~ of** wegen +*gen*, wegen +*dat* (*inf*)

beck [bɛk] *n*: **to be at the ~ and call of sb** nach jds Pfeife tanzen

beckon ['bɛkən] *vt*, *vi*: **to ~ to sb** jdm ein Zeichen geben

become [bɪ'kʌm] (*irreg: like* **come**) *vi* werden ♦ *vt* werden; (*clothes*) stehen +*dat*

becoming [bɪ'kʌmɪŋ] *adj* (*suitable*) schicklich; (*clothes*) kleidsam

bed [bɛd] *n* Bett *nt*; (*of river*) Flussbett *nt*; (*foundation*) Schicht *f*; (*in garden*) Beet *nt*; **to go to ~** zu Bett gehen; **~ and breakfast** *n* Übernachtung *f* mit Frühstück; **~clothes** *npl* Bettwäsche *f*; **~ding** *n* Bettzeug *nt*

Bed and Breakfast

ⓘ **Bed and Breakfast** *bedeutet „Übernachtung mit Frühstück", wobei sich dies in Großbritannien nicht auf Hotels, sondern auf kleinere Pensionen, Privathäuser und Bauernhöfe bezieht, wo man wesentlich preisgünstiger übernachten kann als in Hotels. Oft wird für Bed and Breakfast, auch B & B genannt, durch ein entsprechendes Schild im Garten oder an der Einfahrt geworben.*

---

bedlam ['bɛdləm] *n* (*uproar*) tolle(s) Durcheinander *nt*

bed linen *n* Bettwäsche *f*

bedraggled [bɪ'dræɡld] *adj* ramponiert

bed: **~ridden** *adj* bettlägerig; **~room** *n* Schlafzimmer *nt*; **~side** *n*: **at the ~side** am Bett; **~sit(ter)** (*BRIT*) *n* Einzimmerwohnung f, möblierte(s) Zimmer nt; ~**spread** n Tagesdecke f; ~**time** n Schlafenszeit f

bee [biː] n Biene f

beech [biːtʃ] n Buche f

beef [biːf] n Rindfleisch nt; **roast ~** Roastbeef nt; ~**burger** n Hamburger m

beehive ['biːhaɪv] n Bienenstock m

beeline ['biːlaɪn] n: **to make a ~ for** schnurstracks zugehen auf +acc

been [biːn] pp of **be**

beer [bɪəʳ] n Bier nt

beet [biːt] n (vegetable) Rübe f; (US: also: **red ~**) Rote Bete f or Rübe f

beetle ['biːtl] n Käfer m

beetroot ['biːtruːt] (BRIT) n Rote Bete f

before [bɪ'fɔːʳ] prep vor ♦ conj bevor ♦ adv (of time) zuvor; früher; **the week ~** die Woche zuvor or vorher; **I've done it ~** das hab ich schon mal getan; ~ **going** bevor er/sie etc geht/ging; ~ **she goes** bevor sie geht; ~**hand** adv im Voraus

beg [beg] vt, vi (implore) dringend bitten; (alms) betteln

began [bɪ'gæn] pt of **begin**

beggar ['begəʳ] n Bettler(in) m(f)

begin [bɪ'gɪn] (pt **began**, pp **begun**) vt, vi anfangen, beginnen; (found) gründen; **to ~ doing** or **to do sth** anfangen or beginnen, etw zu tun; **to ~ with** zunächst (einmal); ~**ner** n Anfänger m; ~**ning** n Anfang m

begun [bɪ'gʌn] pp of **begin**

behalf [bɪ'hɑːf] n: **on ~ of** im Namen +gen; **on my ~** für mich

behave [bɪ'heɪv] vi sich benehmen; **behaviour** [bɪ'heɪvjəʳ] (US **behavior**) n Benehmen nt

beheld [bɪ'held] pt, pp of **behold**

behind [bɪ'haɪnd] prep hinter ♦ adv (late) im Rückstand; (in the rear) hinten ♦ n (inf) Hinterteil nt; ~ **the scenes** (fig) hinter den Kulissen

behold [bɪ'həuld] (irreg: like **hold**) vt erblicken

beige [beɪʒ] adj beige

Beijing [beɪ'dʒɪŋ] n Peking nt

being ['biːɪŋ] n (existence) (Da)sein nt; (person) Wesen nt; **to come into ~**

entstehen

Belarus [belə'rus] n Weißrussland nt

belated [bɪ'leɪtɪd] adj verspätet

belch [beltʃ] vi rülpsen ♦ vt (smoke) ausspeien

belfry ['belfrɪ] n Glockenturm m

Belgian ['beldʒən] adj belgisch ♦ n Belgier(in) m(f)

Belgium ['beldʒəm] n Belgien nt

belie [bɪ'laɪ] vt Lügen strafen +acc

belief [bɪ'liːf] n Glaube m; (conviction) Überzeugung f; ~ **in sb/sth** Glaube an jdn/etw

believe [bɪ'liːv] vt glauben +dat; (think) glauben, meinen, denken ♦ vi (have faith) glauben; **to ~ in sth** an etw acc glauben; ~**r** n Gläubige(r) f(m)

belittle [bɪ'lɪtl] vt herabsetzen

bell [bel] n Glocke f

belligerent [bɪ'lɪdʒərənt] adj (person) streitsüchtig; (country) Krieg führend

bellow ['beləu] vt, vi brüllen

bellows ['beləuz] npl (TECH) Gebläse nt; (for fire) Blasebalg m

belly ['belɪ] n Bauch m

belong [bɪ'lɔŋ] vi gehören; **to ~ to sb** jdm gehören; **to ~ to a club** etc einem Klub etc angehören; ~**ings** npl Habe f

beloved [bɪ'lʌvɪd] adj innig geliebt ♦ n Geliebte(r) f(m)

below [bɪ'ləu] prep unter ♦ adv unten

belt [belt] n (band) Riemen m; (round waist) Gürtel m ♦ vt (fasten) mit Riemen befestigen; (inf: beat) schlagen; ~**way** (US) n (AUT: ring road) Umgehungsstraße f

bemused [bɪ'mjuːzd] adj verwirrt

bench [bentʃ] n (seat) Bank f; (workshop) Werkbank f; (judge's seat) Richterbank f; (judges) Richter pl

bend [bend] (pt, pp **bent**) vt (curve) biegen; (stoop) beugen ♦ vi sich biegen; sich beugen ♦ n Biegung f; (BRIT: in road) Kurve f; ~ **down** or **over** vi sich bücken

beneath [bɪ'niːθ] prep unter ♦ adv darunter

benefactor ['benɪfæktəʳ] n Wohltäter(in) m(f)

beneficial [benɪ'fɪʃəl] adj vorteilhaft; (to

health) heilsam

benefit ['benɪfɪt] n (*advantage*) Nutzen m ♦ vt fördern ♦ vi: **to ~ (from)** Nutzen ziehen (aus)

Benelux ['benɪlʌks] n Beneluxstaaten pl

benevolent [bɪ'nevələnt] adj wohlwollend

benign [bɪ'naɪn] adj (*person*) gütig; (*climate*) mild

bent [bent] pt, pp of **bend** ♦ n (*inclination*) Neigung f ♦ adj (*inf: dishonest*) unehrlich; **to be ~ on** versessen sein auf +acc

bequest [bɪ'kwest] n Vermächtnis nt

bereaved [bɪ'riːvd] npl: **the ~** die Hinterbliebenen pl

beret ['bereɪ] n Baskenmütze f

Berlin [bɜː'lɪn] n Berlin nt

berm [bɜːm] n (*US*) n (*AUT*) Seitenstreifen m

berry ['berɪ] n Beere f

berserk [bə'sɜːk] adj: **to go ~** wild werden

berth [bɜːθ] n (*for ship*) Ankerplatz m; (*in ship*) Koje f; (*in train*) Bett nt ♦ vt am Kai festmachen ♦ vi anlegen

beseech [bɪ'siːtʃ] (*pt, pp* **besought**) vt anflehen

beset [bɪ'set] (*pt, pp* **beset**) vt bedrängen

beside [bɪ'saɪd] prep neben, bei; (*except*) außer; **to be ~ o.s. (with)** außer sich sein (vor +dat); **that's ~ the point** das tut nichts zur Sache

besides [bɪ'saɪdz] prep außer, neben ♦ adv außerdem

besiege [bɪ'siːdʒ] vt (*MIL*) belagern; (*surround*) umlagern, bedrängen

besought [bɪ'sɔːt] pt, pp of **beseech**

best [best] adj beste(r, s) ♦ adv am besten; **the ~ part of** (*quantity*) das meiste +gen; **at ~** höchstens; **to make the ~ of it** das Beste daraus machen; **to do one's ~** sein Bestes tun; **to the ~ of my knowledge** meines Wissens; **to the ~ of my ability** so gut ich kann; **for the ~** zum Besten; **~-before date** n Mindesthaltbarkeitsdatum nt; **~ man** n Trauzeuge m

bestow [bɪ'stəʊ] vt verleihen

bet [bet] (*pt, pp* **bet** or **betted**) n Wette f ♦ vt, vi wetten

betray [bɪ'treɪ] vt verraten

better ['betər] adj, adv besser ♦ vt verbessern ♦ n: **to get the ~ of sb** jdn überwinden; **he thought ~ of it** er hat sich eines Besseren besonnen; **you had ~ leave** Sie gehen jetzt wohl besser; **to get ~** (*MED*) gesund werden; **~ off** adj (*richer*) wohlhabender

betting ['betɪŋ] n Wetten nt; **~ shop** (*BRIT*) n Wettbüro nt

between [bɪ'twiːn] prep zwischen; (*among*) unter ♦ adv dazwischen

beverage ['bevərɪdʒ] n Getränk nt

bevy ['bevɪ] n Schar f

beware [bɪ'weər] vt, vi sich hüten vor +dat; **"~ of the dog"** „Vorsicht, bissiger Hund!"

bewildered [bɪ'wɪldəd] adj verwirrt

beyond [bɪ'jɒnd] prep (*place*) jenseits +gen; (*time*) über ... hinaus; (*out of reach*) außerhalb +gen ♦ adv darüber hinaus; **~ doubt** ohne Zweifel; **~ repair** nicht mehr zu reparieren

bias ['baɪəs] n (*slant*) Neigung f; (*prejudice*) Vorurteil nt; **~(s)ed** adj voreingenommen

bib [bɪb] n Latz m

Bible ['baɪbl] n Bibel f

bicarbonate of soda [baɪ'kɑːbənɪt-] n Natron nt

bicker ['bɪkər] vi zanken

bicycle ['baɪsɪkl] n Fahrrad nt

bid [bɪd] (*pt* **bade** or **bid**, *pp* **bid(den)**) n (*offer*) Gebot nt; (*attempt*) Versuch m ♦ vt, vi (*offer*) bieten; **to ~ farewell** Lebewohl sagen; **~der** n (*person*) Steigerer m; **the highest ~der** der Meistbietende; **~ding** n (*command*) Geheiß nt

bide [baɪd] vt: **to ~ one's time** abwarten

bifocals [baɪ'fəʊklz] npl Bifokalbrille f

big [bɪg] adj groß; **~ dipper** [-'dɪpər] n Achterbahn f; **~-headed** ['bɪg'hedɪd] adj eingebildet

bigot ['bɪgət] n Frömmler m; **~ed** adj bigott; **~ry** n Bigotterie f

big top n Zirkuszelt nt

bike [baɪk] n Rad nt

bikini [bɪ'kiːnɪ] n Bikini m

bile [baɪl] n (*BIOL*) Galle f

bilingual [baɪ'lɪŋgwəl] adj zweisprachig

bill [bɪl] n (*account*) Rechnung f; (*POL*)

Gesetzentwurf *m*; (*US: FIN*) Geldschein *m*; **to fit** *or* **fill the ~** (*fig*) der/die/das Richtige sein; **"post no ~s"** „Plakate ankleben verboten"; **~board** ['bɪlbɔːd] *n* Reklameschild *nt*

billet ['bɪlɪt] *n* Quartier *nt*

billfold ['bɪlfəʊld] (*US*) *n* Geldscheintasche *f*

billiards ['bɪljədz] *n* Billard *nt*

billion ['bɪljən] *n* (*BRIT*) Billion *f*; (*US*) Milliarde *f*

bimbo ['bɪmbəʊ] (*inf: pej*) *n* Puppe *f*, Häschen *nt*

bin [bɪn] *n* Kasten *m*; (*dustbin*) (Abfall)eimer *m*

bind [baɪnd] (*pt, pp* **bound**) *vt* (*tie*) binden; (*tie together*) zusammenbinden; (*oblige*) verpflichten; **~ing** *n* (Buch)einband *m* ♦ *adj* verbindlich

binge [bɪndʒ] (*inf*) *n* Sauferei *f*

bingo ['bɪŋgəʊ] *n* Bingo *nt*

binoculars [bɪ'nɒkjʊləz] *npl* Fernglas *nt*

bio... [baɪəʊ] *prefix*: **~chemistry** *n* Biochemie *f*; **~degradable** *adj* biologisch abbaubar; **~graphy** *n* Biografie *f*; **~logical** [baɪə'lɒdʒɪkl] *adj* biologisch; **~logy** [baɪ'ɒlədʒɪ] *n* Biologie *f*

birch [bɜːtʃ] *n* Birke *f*

bird [bɜːd] *n* Vogel *m*; (*BRIT: inf: girl*) Mädchen *nt*; **~'s-eye view** *n* Vogelschau *f*; **~ watcher** *n* Vogelbeobachter(in) *m(f)*; **~ watching** *n* Vogelbeobachten *nt*

Biro ['baɪərəʊ] ® *n* Kugelschreiber *m*

birth [bɜːθ] *n* Geburt *f*; **to give ~ to** zur Welt bringen; **~ certificate** *n* Geburtsurkunde *f*; **~ control** *n* Geburtenkontrolle *f*; **~day** *n* Geburtstag *m*; **~day card** *n* Geburtstagskarte *f*; **~place** *n* Geburtsort *m*; **~ rate** *n* Geburtenrate *f*

biscuit ['bɪskɪt] *n* Keks *m*

bisect [baɪ'sekt] *vt* halbieren

bishop ['bɪʃəp] *n* Bischof *m*

bit [bɪt] *pt of* **bite** ♦ *n* bisschen, Stückchen *nt*; (*horse's*) Gebiss *nt*; (*COMPUT*) Bit *nt*; **a ~ tired** etwas müde

bitch [bɪtʃ] *n* (*dog*) Hündin *f*; (*unpleasant woman*) Weibsstück *nt*

bite [baɪt] (*pt* **bit**, *pp* **bitten**) *vt, vi* beißen ♦ *n*

Biss *m*; (*mouthful*) Bissen *m*; **to ~ one's nails** Nägel kauen; **let's have a ~ to eat** lass uns etwas essen

bitten ['bɪtn] *pp of* **bite**

bitter ['bɪtər] *adj* bitter; (*memory etc*) schmerzlich; (*person*) verbittert ♦ *n* (*BRIT: beer*) dunkle(s) Bier *nt*; **~ness** *n* Bitterkeit *f*

blab [blæb] *vi* klatschen ♦ *vt* (*also: ~ out*) ausplaudern

black [blæk] *adj* schwarz; (*night*) finster ♦ *vt* schwärzen; (*shoes*) wichsen; (*eye*) blau schlagen; (*BRIT: INDUSTRY*) boykottieren; **to give sb a ~ eye** jdm ein blaues Auge schlagen; **in the ~** (*bank account*) in den schwarzen Zahlen; **~ and blue** grün und blau; **~berry** *n* Brombeere *f*; **~bird** *n* Amsel *f*; **~board** *n* (Wand)tafel *f*; **~ coffee** *n* schwarze(r) Kaffee *m*; **~currant** *n* schwarze Johannisbeere *f*; **~en** *vt* schwärzen; (*fig*) verunglimpfen; **B~ Forest** *n* Schwarzwald *m*; **~ ice** *n* Glatteis *nt*; **~leg** (*BRIT*) *n* Streikbrecher(in) *m(f)*; **~list** *n* schwarze Liste *f*; **~mail** *n* Erpressung *f* ♦ *vt* erpressen; **~ market** *n* Schwarzmarkt *m*; **~out** *n* Verdunklung *f*; (*MED*): **to have a ~out** bewusstlos werden; **~ pudding** *n* ≈ Blutwurst *f*; **B~ Sea** *n*: **the B~ Sea** das Schwarze Meer; **~ sheep** *n* schwarze(s) Schaf *nt*; **~smith** *n* Schmied *m*; **~ spot** *n* (*AUT*) Gefahrenstelle *f*; (*for unemployment etc*) schwer betroffene(s) Gebiet *nt*

bladder ['blædər] *n* Blase *f*

blade [bleɪd] *n* (*of weapon*) Klinge *f*; (*of grass*) Halm *m*; (*of oar*) Ruderblatt *nt*

blame [bleɪm] *n* Tadel *m*, Schuld *f* ♦ *vt* Vorwürfe machen +*dat*; **to ~ sb for sth** jdm die Schuld an etw *dat* geben; **he is to ~** er ist daran schuld

bland [blænd] *adj* mild

blank [blæŋk] *adj* leer, unbeschrieben; (*look*) verdutzt; (*verse*) Blank- ♦ *n* (*space*) Lücke *f*; Zwischenraum *m*; (*cartridge*) Platzpatrone *f*; **~ cheque** *n* Blankoscheck *m*; (*fig*) Freibrief *m*

blanket ['blæŋkɪt] *n* (Woll)decke *f*

blare [bleər] *vi* (*radio*) plärren; (*horn*) tuten; (*MUS*) schmettern

blasé ['blɑːzeɪ] *adj* blasiert

blast [blɑːst] *n* Explosion *f*; (*of wind*) Windstoß *m* ♦ *vt* (*blow up*) sprengen; ~! (*inf*) verflixt!; ~off *n* (*SPACE*) (Raketen)abschuss *m*

blatant ['bleɪtənt] *adj* offenkundig

blaze [bleɪz] *n* (*fire*) lodernde(s) Feuer *nt* ♦ *vi* lodern ♦ *vt*: **to ~ a trail** Bahn brechen

blazer ['bleɪzəʳ] *n* Blazer *m*

bleach [bliːtʃ] *n* (*also:* **household ~**) Bleichmittel *nt* ♦ *vt* bleichen; ~ed *adj* gebleicht

bleachers ['bliːtʃəz] (*US*) *npl* (*SPORT*) unüberdachte Tribüne *f*

bleak [bliːk] *adj* kahl, rau; (*future*) trostlos

bleary-eyed ['blɪərɪˌaɪd] *adj* triefäugig; (*on waking up*) mit verschlafenen Augen

bleat [bliːt] *vi* blöken; (*fig: complain*) meckern

bled [bled] *pt, pp of* **bleed**

bleed [bliːd] (*pt, pp* **bled**) *vi* bluten ♦ *vt* (*draw blood*) zur Ader lassen; **to ~ to death** verbluten

bleeper ['bliːpəʳ] *n* (*of doctor etc*) Funkrufempfänger *m*

blemish ['blemɪʃ] *n* Makel *m* ♦ *vt* verunstalten

blend [blend] *n* Mischung *f* ♦ *vt* mischen ♦ *vi* sich mischen; ~er *n* Mixer *m*, Mixgerät *nt*

bless [bles] (*pt, pp* **blessed**) *vt* segnen; (*give thanks*) preisen; (*make happy*) glücklich machen; ~ **you!** Gesundheit!; ~ing *n* Segen *m*; (*at table*) Tischgebet *nt*; (*happiness*) Wohltat *f*; Segen *m*; (*good wish*) Glück *nt*

blew [bluː] *pt of* **blow**

blimey ['blaɪmɪ] (*BRIT: inf*) *excl* verflucht

blind [blaɪnd] *adj* blind; (*corner*) unübersichtlich ♦ *n* (*for window*) Rouleau *nt* ♦ *vt* blenden; ~ **alley** *n* Sackgasse *f*; ~fold *n* Augenbinde *f* ♦ *adj, adv* mit verbundenen Augen ♦ *vt*: **to ~fold sb** jdm die Augen verbinden; ~ly *adv* blind; (*fig*) blindlings; ~ness *n* Blindheit *f*; ~ **spot** *n* (*AUT*) tote(r) Winkel *m*; (*fig*) schwache(r) Punkt *m*

blink [blɪŋk] *vi* blinzeln; ~ers *npl* Scheuklappen *pl*

bliss [blɪs] *n* (Glück)seligkeit *f*

blister ['blɪstəʳ] *n* Blase *f* ♦ *vi* Blasen werfen

blitz [blɪts] *n* Luftkrieg *m*

blizzard ['blɪzəd] *n* Schneesturm *m*

bloated ['bləutɪd] *adj* aufgedunsen; (*inf: full*) nudelsatt

blob [blɒb] *n* Klümpchen *nt*

bloc [blɒk] *n* (*POL*) Block *m*

block [blɒk] *n* (*of wood*) Block *m*, Klotz *m*; (*of houses*) Häuserblock *m* ♦ *vt* hemmen; ~ade [blɒ'keɪd] *n* Blockade *f* ♦ *vt* blockieren; ~age *n* Verstopfung *f*; ~buster *n* Knüller *m*; ~ **letters** *npl* Blockbuchstaben *pl*; ~ **of flats** (*BRIT*) *n* Häuserblock *m*

bloke [bləuk] (*BRIT: inf*) *n* Kerl *m*, Typ *m*

blond(e) [blɒnd] *adj* blond ♦ *n* Blondine *f*

blood [blʌd] *n* Blut *nt*; ~ **donor** *n* Blutspender *m*; ~ **group** *n* Blutgruppe *f*; ~ **poisoning** *n* Blutvergiftung *f*; ~ **pressure** *n* Blutdruck *m*; ~shed *n* Blutvergießen *nt*; ~shot *adj* blutunterlaufen; ~ **sports** *npl* Jagdsport, Hahnenkampf etc; ~stained *adj* blutbefleckt; ~stream *n* Blut *nt*, Blutkreislauf *m*; ~ **test** *n* Blutprobe *f*; ~thirsty *adj* blutrünstig; ~ **vessel** *n* Blutgefäß *nt*; ~y *adj* blutig; (*BRIT: inf*) verdammt; ~y-minded (*BRIT: inf*) *adj* stur

bloom [bluːm] *n* Blüte *f*; (*freshness*) Glanz *m* ♦ *vi* blühen

blossom ['blɒsəm] *n* Blüte *f* ♦ *vi* blühen

blot [blɒt] *n* Klecks *m* ♦ *vt* beklecksen; (*ink*) (ab)löschen; ~ **out** *vt* auslöschen

blotchy ['blɒtʃɪ] *adj* fleckig

blotting paper ['blɒtɪŋ-] *n* Löschpapier *nt*

blouse [blauz] *n* Bluse *f*

blow [bləu] (*pt* **blew**, *pp* **blown**) *n* Schlag *m* ♦ *vt* blasen ♦ *vi* (*wind*) wehen; **to ~ one's nose** sich *dat* die Nase putzen; ~ **away** *vt* wegblasen; ~ **down** *vt* umwehen; ~ **off** *vt* wegwehen ♦ *vi* wegfliegen; ~ **out** *vi* ausgehen; ~ **over** *vi* vorübergehen; ~ **up** *vi* explodieren ♦ *vt* sprengen; ~-dry *n*: **to have a ~-dry** sich föhnen lassen ♦ *vt* föhnen; ~lamp (*BRIT*) *n* Lötlampe *f*; ~n *pp of* **blow**; ~-out *n* (*AUT*) geplatzte(r) Reifen *m*; ~torch *n* = **blowlamp**

blue [bluː] *adj* blau; (*inf: unhappy*) niedergeschlagen; (*obscene*) pornografisch;

(*joke*) anzüglich ♦ *n*: **out of the ~** (*fig*) aus heiterem Himmel; **to have the ~s** traurig sein; **~bell** *n* Glockenblume *f*; **~bottle** *n* Schmeißfliege *f*; **~ film** *n* Pornofilm *m*; **~print** *n* (*fig*) Entwurf *m*

bluff [blʌf] *vi* bluffen, täuschen ♦ *n* (*deception*) Bluff *m*; **to call sb's ~** es darauf ankommen lassen

blunder ['blʌndə'] *n* grobe(r) Fehler *m*, Schnitzer *m* ♦ *vi* einen groben Fehler machen

blunt [blʌnt] *adj* (*knife*) stumpf; (*talk*) unverblümt ♦ *vt* abstumpfen

blur [blɜ:'] *n* Fleck *m* ♦ *vt* verschwommen machen

blurb [blɜ:b] *n* Waschzettel *m*

blush [blʌʃ] *vi* erröten

blustery ['blʌstərɪ] *adj* stürmisch

boar [bɔ:'] *n* Keiler *m*, Eber *m*

board [bɔ:d] *n* (*of wood*) Brett *nt*; (*of card*) Pappe *f*; (*committee*) Ausschuss *m*; (*of firm*) Aufsichtsrat *m*; (*SCH*) Direktorium *nt* ♦ *vt* (*train*) einsteigen in +*acc*; (*ship*) an Bord gehen +*gen*; **on ~** (*AVIAT, NAUT*) an Bord; **~ and lodging** Unterkunft *f* und Verpflegung; **full/half ~** (*BRIT*) Voll-/Halbpension *f*; **to go by the ~** flachfallen, über Bord gehen; **~ up** *vt* mit Brettern vernageln; **~er** *n* Kostgänger *m*; (*SCH*) Internatsschüler(in) *m(f)*; **~ game** *n* Brettspiel *nt*; **~ing card** *n* (*AVIAT, NAUT*) Bordkarte *f*; **~ing house** *n* Pension *f*; **~ing school** *n* Internat *nt*; **~ room** *n* Sitzungszimmer *nt*

boast [bəust] *vi* prahlen ♦ *vt* sich rühmen +*gen* ♦ *n* Großtuerei *f*; Prahlerei *f*; **to ~ about** *or* **of sth** mit etw prahlen

boat [bəut] *n* Boot *nt*; (*ship*) Schiff *nt*; **~er** *n* (*hat*) Kreissäge *f*; **~swain** *n* = **bosun**; **~train** *n* Zug *m* mit Fährenanschluss

bob [bɔb] *vi* sich auf und nieder bewegen; **~ up** *vi* auftauchen

bobbin ['bɔbɪn] *n* Spule *f*

bobby ['bɔbɪ] (*BRIT*: *inf*) *n* Bobby *m*

bobsleigh ['bɔbsleɪ] *n* Bob *m*

bode [bəud] *vi*: **to ~ well/ill** ein gutes/ schlechtes Zeichen sein

bodily ['bɔdɪlɪ] *adj*, *adv* körperlich

body ['bɔdɪ] *n* Körper *m*; (*dead*) Leiche *f*; (*group*) Mannschaft *f*; (*AUT*) Karosserie *f*; (*trunk*) Rumpf *m*; **~ building** *n* Bodybuilding *nt*; **~guard** *n* Leibwache *f*; **~work** *n* Karosserie *f*

bog [bɔg] *n* Sumpf *m* ♦ *vt*: **to get ~ged down** sich festfahren

boggle ['bɔgl] *vi* stutzen; **the mind ~s** es ist kaum auszumalen

bog-standard *adj* stinknormal (*inf*)

bogus ['bəugəs] *adj* unecht, Schein-

boil [bɔɪl] *vt*, *vi* kochen ♦ *n* (*MED*) Geschwür *nt*; **to come to the** (*BRIT*) **or a** (*US*) **~** zu kochen anfangen; **to ~ down to** (*fig*) hinauslaufen auf +*acc*; **~ over** *vi* überkochen; **~ed egg** *n* (weich) gekochte(s) Ei *nt*; **~ed potatoes** *npl* Salzkartoffeln *pl*; **~er** *n* Boiler *m*; **~er suit** (*BRIT*) *n* Arbeitsanzug *m*; **~ing point** *n* Siedepunkt *m*

boisterous ['bɔɪstərəs] *adj* ungestüm

bold [bəuld] *adj* (*fearless*) unerschrocken; (*handwriting*) fest und klar

bollard ['bɔləd] *n* (*NAUT*) Poller *m*; (*BRIT*: *AUT*) Pfosten *m*

bolt [bəult] *n* Bolzen *m*; (*lock*) Riegel *m* ♦ *adv*: **~ upright** kerzengerade ♦ *vt* verriegeln; (*swallow*) verschlingen ♦ *vi* (*horse*) durchgehen

bomb [bɔm] *n* Bombe *f* ♦ *vt* bombardieren; **~ard** [bɔm'bɑːd] *vt* bombardieren; **~ardment** [bɔm'bɑːdmənt] *n* Beschießung *f*; **~ disposal** *n*: **~ disposal unit** Bombenräumkommando *nt*; **~er** *n* Bomber *m*; (*terrorist*) Bombenattentäter(in) *m(f)*; **~ing** *n* Bomben *nt*; **~shell** *n* (*fig*) Bombe *f*

bona fide ['bəunə'faɪdɪ] *adj* echt

bond [bɔnd] *n* (*link*) Band *nt*; (*FIN*) Schuldverschreibung *f*

bondage ['bɔndɪdʒ] *n* Sklaverei *f*

bone [bəun] *n* Knochen *m*; (*of fish*) Gräte *f*; (*piece of ~*) Knochensplitter *m* ♦ *vt* die Knochen herausnehmen +*dat*; (*fish*) entgräten; **~ dry** *adj* (*inf*) knochentrocken; **~ idle** *adj* stinkfaul; **~ marrow** *n* (*ANAT*) Knochenmark *nt*

bonfire ['bɔnfaɪə'] *n* Feuer *nt* im Freien

bonnet ['bɒnɪt] n Haube f; (for baby) Häubchen nt; (BRIT: AUT) Motorhaube f

bonus ['bəunəs] n Bonus m; (annual ~) Prämie f

bony ['bəunɪ] adj knochig, knochendürr

boo [buː] vt ausspfeifen

booby trap ['buːbɪ-] n Falle f

book [buk] n Buch nt ♦ vt (ticket etc) vorbestellen; (person) verwarnen; ~s npl (COMM) Bücher pl; ~case n Bücherregal nt, Bücherschrank m; ~ing office (BRIT) n (RAIL) Fahrkartenschalter m; (THEAT) Vorverkaufsstelle f; ~-keeping n Buchhaltung f; ~let n Broschüre f; ~maker n Buchmacher m; ~seller n Buchhändler m; ~shelf n Bücherbord nt; ~shop ['bukʃɔp], ~store n Buchhandlung f

boom [buːm] n (noise) Dröhnen nt; (busy period) Hochkonjunktur f ♦ vi dröhnen

boon [buːn] n Wohltat f, Segen m

boost [buːst] n Auftrieb m; (fig) Reklame f ♦ vt Auftrieb geben; ~er n (MED) Wiederholungsimpfung f

boot [buːt] n Stiefel m; (BRIT: AUT) Kofferraum m ♦ vt (kick) einen Fußtritt geben; (COMPUT) laden; **to ~** (in addition) obendrein

booth [buːð] n (at fair) Bude f; (telephone ~) Zelle f; (voting ~) Kabine f

booze [buːz] (inf) n Alkohol m, Schnaps m ♦ vi saufen

border ['bɔːdər] n Grenze f; (edge) Kante f; (in garden) (Blumen)rabatte f ♦ adj Grenz-; **the B~s** Grenzregion zwischen England und Schottland; ~ **on** vt grenzen an +acc; ~line n Grenze f; ~line case n Grenzfall m

bore [bɔːr] pt of **bear** ♦ vt bohren; (weary) langweilen ♦ n (person) Langweiler m; (thing) langweilige Sache f; (of gun) Kaliber nt; **I am ~d** ich langweile mich; ~dom n Langeweile f

boring ['bɔːrɪŋ] adj langweilig

born [bɔːn] adj: **to be ~** geboren werden

borne [bɔːn] pp of **bear**

borough ['bʌrə] n Stadt(gemeinde) f, Stadtbezirk m

borrow ['bɒrəu] vt borgen

Bosnia (and) Herzegovina ['bɒznɪə (ənd) haːtsəgəuˈviːnə] n Bosnien und Herzegowina nt; ~**n** n Bosnier(in) m(f) ♦ adj bosnisch

bosom ['buzəm] n Busen m

boss [bɒs] n Chef m, Boss m ♦ vt: **to ~ around** or **about** herumkommandieren; ~**y** adj herrisch

bosun ['bəusn] n Bootsmann m

botany ['bɒtənɪ] n Botanik f

botch [bɒtʃ] vt (also: ~ **up**) verpfuschen

both [bəuθ] adj beide(s) ♦ pron beide(s) ♦ adv: ~ **X and Y** sowohl X wie or als auch Y; ~ **(of) the books** beide Bücher; ~ **of us went, we ~ went** wir gingen beide

bother ['bɒðər] vt (pester) quälen ♦ vi (fuss) sich aufregen ♦ n Mühe f, Umstand m; **to ~ doing sth** sich dat die Mühe machen, etw zu tun; **what a ~!** wie ärgerlich!

bottle ['bɒtl] n Flasche f ♦ vt (in Flaschen) abfüllen; ~ **up** vt aufstauen; ~ **bank** n Altglascontainer m; ~**d beer** n Flaschenbier nt; ~**d water** n in Flaschen abgefülltes Wasser; ~**neck** n (also fig) Engpass m; ~ **opener** n Flaschenöffner m

bottom ['bɒtəm] n Boden m; (of person) Hintern m; (riverbed) Flussbett nt ♦ adj unterste(r, s)

bough [bau] n Zweig m, Ast m

bought [bɔːt] pt, pp of **buy**

boulder ['bəuldər] n Felsbrocken m

bounce [bauns] vi (person) herumhüpfen; (ball) hochspringen; (cheque) platzen ♦ vt (auf)springen lassen ♦ n (rebound) Aufprall m; ~**r** n Rausschmeißer m

bound [baund] pt, pp of **bind** ♦ n Grenze f; (leap) Sprung m ♦ vi (spring, leap) (auf)springen ♦ adj (obliged) gebunden, verpflichtet; **out of ~s** Zutritt verboten; **to be ~ to do sth** verpflichtet sein, etw zu tun; **it's ~ to happen** es muss so kommen; **to be ~ for ...** nach ... fahren

boundary ['baundrɪ] n Grenze f

bouquet ['bukeɪ] n Strauß m; (of wine) Blume f

bourgeois ['buəʒwaː] adj kleinbürgerlich, bourgeois ♦ n Spießbürger(in) m(f)

bout [baut] n (of illness) Anfall m; (of contest)

Kampf m

bow¹ [bəu] n (ribbon) Schleife f; (weapon, MUS) Bogen m

bow² [bau] n (with head, body) Verbeugung f; (of ship) Bug m ♦ vi sich verbeugen; (submit): **to ~ to** sich beugen +dat

bowels ['bauəlz] npl (ANAT) Darm m

bowl [bəul] n (basin) Schüssel f; (of pipe) (Pfeifen)kopf m; (wooden ball) (Holz)kugel f ♦ vt, vi (die Kugel) rollen

bow-legged ['bəu'legɪd] adj o-beinig, O-beinig

bowler ['bəulə'] n Werfer m; (BRIT: also: ~ hat) Melone f

bowling ['bəulɪŋ] n Kegeln nt; ~ **alley** n Kegelbahn f; ~ **green** n Rasen m zum Bowlingspiel

bowls [bəulz] n (game) Bowlsspiel nt

bow tie [bəu-] n Fliege f

box [bɔks] n (also: **cardboard ~**) Schachtel f; (bigger) Kasten m; (THEAT) Loge f ♦ vt einpacken ♦ vi boxen; ~**er** n Boxer m; ~**er shorts** (BRIT) npl Boxershorts pl; ~**ing** (SPORT) Boxen nt; **B~ing Day** (BRIT) n zweite(r) Weihnachtsfeiertag m; ~**ing gloves** npl Boxhandschuhe pl; ~**ing ring** n Boxring m; ~ **office** n (Theater)kasse f; ~**room** n Rumpelkammer f

Boxing Day

i Boxing Day (26.12.) ist ein Feiertag in Großbritannien. Wenn Weihnachten auf ein Wochenende fällt, wird der Feiertag am nächsten darauf folgenden Wochentag nachgeholt. Der Name geht auf einen alten Brauch zurück; früher erhielten Händler und Lieferanten an diesem Tag ein Geschenk, die so genannte Christmas Box.

boy [bɔɪ] n Junge m

boycott ['bɔɪkɔt] n Boykott m ♦ vt boykottieren

boyfriend ['bɔɪfrɛnd] n Freund m

boyish ['bɔɪʃ] adj jungenhaft

B.R. n abbr = **British Rail**

bra [brɑː] n BH m

brace [breɪs] n (TECH) Stütze f; (MED)

Klammer f ♦ vt stützen; ~**s** npl (BRIT) Hosenträger pl; **to ~ o.s. for sth** (fig) sich auf etw acc gefasst machen

bracelet ['breɪslɪt] n Armband nt

bracing ['breɪsɪŋ] adj kräftigend

bracken ['brækən] n Farnkraut nt

bracket ['brækɪt] n Halter m, Klammer f; (in punctuation) Klammer f; (group) Gruppe f ♦ vt einklammern; (fig) in dieselbe Gruppe einordnen

brag [bræg] vi sich rühmen

braid [breɪd] n (hair) Flechte f; (trim) Borte f

Braille [breɪl] n Blindenschrift f

brain [breɪn] n (ANAT) Gehirn nt; (intellect) Intelligenz f, Verstand m; (person) kluge(r) Kopf m; ~**s** npl (intelligence) Verstand m; ~**child** n Erfindung f; ~**wash** vt eine Gehirnwäsche vornehmen bei; ~**wave** n Geistesblitz m; ~**y** adj gescheit

braise [breɪz] vt schmoren

brake [breɪk] n Bremse f ♦ vt, vi bremsen; ~ **fluid** n Bremsflüssigkeit f; ~ **light** n Bremslicht nt

bramble ['bræmbl] n Brombeere f

bran [bræn] n Klee f; (food) Frühstücksflocken pl

branch [brɑːntʃ] n Ast m; (division) Zweig m ♦ vi (also: ~ **out**: road) sich verzweigen

brand [brænd] n (COMM) Marke f, Sorte f; (on cattle) Brandmal nt ♦ vt brandmarken; (COMM) ein Warenzeichen geben +dat

brandish ['brændɪʃ] vt (drohend) schwingen

brand-new ['brænd'njuː] adj funkelnagelneu

brandy ['brændɪ] n Weinbrand m, Kognak m

brash [bræʃ] adj unverschämt

brass [brɑːs] n Messing nt; **the ~** (MUS) das Blech; ~ **band** n Blaskapelle f

brassière ['bræsɪə'] n Büstenhalter m

brat [bræt] n Gör nt

bravado [brə'vɑːdəu] n Tollkühnheit f

brave [breɪv] adj tapfer ♦ vt die Stirn bieten +dat; ~**ry** n Tapferkeit f

brawl [brɔːl] n Rauferei f

brawn [brɔːn] n (ANAT) Muskeln pl; (strength) Muskelkraft f

bray [breɪ] vi schreien

brazen ['breɪzn] adj (shameless) unverschämt

♦ *vt*: **to ~ it out** sich mit Lügen und Betrügen durchsetzen

brazier ['breɪzɪəʳ] *n* (*of workmen*) offene(r) Kohlenofen *m*

Brazil [brə'zɪl] *n* Brasilien *nt*; **~ian** *adj* brasilianisch ♦ *n* Brasilianer(in) *m(f)*

breach [briːtʃ] *n* (*gap*) Lücke *f*; (*MIL*) Durchbruch *m*; (*of discipline*) Verstoß *m* (gegen die Disziplin); (*of faith*) Vertrauensbruch *m* ♦ *vt* durchbrechen; **~ of contract** Vertragsbruch *m*; **~ of the peace** öffentliche Ruhestörung *f*

bread [bred] *n* Brot *nt*; **~ and butter** Butterbrot *nt*; **~bin** *n* Brotkasten *m*; **~ box** (*US*) *n* Brotkasten *m*; **~crumbs** *npl* Brotkrumen *pl*; (*COOK*) Paniermehl *nt*; **~line** *n*: **to be on the ~line** sich gerade so durchschlagen

breadth [bretθ] *n* Breite *f*

breadwinner ['bredwɪnəʳ] *n* Ernährer *m*

break [breɪk] (*pt* **broke**, *pp* **broken**) *vt* (*destroy*) (ab- or zer)brechen; (*promise*) brechen, nicht einhalten ♦ *vi* (*fall apart*) auseinander brechen; (*collapse*) zusammenbrechen; (*dawn*) anbrechen ♦ *n* (*gap*) Lücke *f*; (*chance*) Chance *f*, Gelegenheit *f*; (*fracture*) Bruch *m*; (*rest*) Pause *f*; **~ down** *vt* (*figures, data*) aufschlüsseln; (*undermine*) überwinden ♦ *vi* (*car*) eine Panne haben; (*person*) zusammenbrechen; **~ even** *vi* die Kosten decken; **~ free** *vi* sich losreißen; **~ in** *vt* (*horse*) zureiten ♦ *vi* (*burglar*) einbrechen; **~ into** *vt* (*house*) einbrechen in +*acc*; (*fig*) überbrücken; **loose** *vi* sich losreißen; **~ off** *vi* abbrechen; **~ open** *vt* (*door etc*) aufbrechen; **~ out** *vi* ausbrechen; **to ~ out in spots** Pikkel bekommen; **~ up** *vi* zerbrechen; (*fig*) sich zerstreuen; (*BRIT*: *SCH*) in die Ferien gehen ♦ *vt* brechen; **~age** *n* Bruch *m*, Beschädigung *f*; **~down** *n* (*TECH*) Panne *f*; (*MED*: *also*: **nervous ~down**) Zusammenbruch *m*; **~down van** (*BRIT*) *n* Abschleppwagen *m*; **~er** *n* Brecher *m*

breakfast ['brekfəst] *n* Frühstück *nt*

break: **~-in** *n* Einbruch *m*; **~ing** *n*: **~ing and entering** (*JUR*) Einbruch *m*; **~through**

n Durchbruch *m*; **~water** *n* Wellenbrecher *m*

breast [brest] *n* Brust *f*; **~-feed** (*irreg*: *like* **feed**) *vt*, *vi* stillen; **~-stroke** *n* Brustschwimmen *nt*

breath [breθ] *n* Atem *m*; **out of ~** außer Atem; **under one's ~** flüsternd

Breathalyzer ['breθəlaɪzəʳ] ® *n* Röhrchen *nt*

breathe [briːð] *vt*, *vi* atmen; **~ in** *vt*, *vi* einatmen; **~ out** *vt*, *vi* ausatmen; **~r** *n* Verschnaufpause *f*; **breathing** *n* Atmung *f*

breathless ['breθlɪs] *adj* atemlos

breathtaking ['breθteɪkɪŋ] *adj* atemberaubend

bred [bred] *pt*, *pp of* **breed**

breed [briːd] (*pt*, *pp* **bred**) *vi* sich vermehren ♦ *vt* züchten ♦ *n* (*race*) Rasse *f*, Zucht *f*; **~ing** *n* Züchtung *f*; (*upbringing*) Erziehung *f*

breeze [briːz] *n* Brise *f*; **breezy** *adj* windig; (*manner*) munter

brevity ['brevɪtɪ] *n* Kürze *f*

brew [bruː] *vt* (*beer*) brauen ♦ *vi* (*storm*) sich zusammenziehen; **~ery** *n* Brauerei *f*

bribe [braɪb] *n* Bestechungsgeld *nt*, Bestechungsgeschenk *nt* ♦ *vt* bestechen; **~ry** ['braɪbərɪ] *n* Bestechung *f*

bric-a-brac ['brɪkəbræk] *n* Nippes *pl*

brick [brɪk] *n* Backstein *m*; **~layer** *n* Maurer *m*; **~works** *n* Ziegelei *f*

bridal ['braɪdl] *adj* Braut-

bride [braɪd] *n* Braut *f*; **~groom** *n* Bräutigam *m*; **~smaid** *n* Brautjungfer *f*

bridge [brɪdʒ] *n* Brücke *f*; (*NAUT*) Kommandobrücke *f*; (*CARDS*) Bridge *nt*; (*ANAT*) Nasenrücken *m* ♦ *vt* eine Brücke schlagen über +*acc*; (*fig*) überbrücken

bridle ['braɪdl] *n* Zaum *m* ♦ *vt* (*fig*) zügeln; (*horse*) aufzäumen; **~ path** *n* Reitweg *m*

brief [briːf] *adj* kurz ♦ *n* (*JUR*) Akten *pl* ♦ *vt* instruieren; **~s** *npl* (*underwear*) Schlüpfer *m*, Slip *m*; **~case** *n* Aktentasche *f*; **~ing** *n* (genaue) Anweisung *f*; **~ly** *adv* kurz

brigadier [brɪgə'dɪəʳ] *n* Brigadegeneral *m*

bright [braɪt] *adj* hell; (*cheerful*) heiter; (*idea*) klug; **~en (up)** ['braɪtn-] *vt* aufhellen; (*person*) aufheitern ♦ *vi* sich aufheitern

brilliance ['brɪljəns] *n* Glanz *m*; (*of person*)

Scharfsinn m

brilliant ['brɪljənt] adj glänzend

brim [brɪm] n Rand m

brine [braɪn] n Salzwasser nt

bring [brɪŋ] (pt, pp **brought**) vt bringen; ~ **about** vt zustande or zu Stande bringen; ~ **back** vt zurückbringen; ~ **down** vt (price) senken; ~ **forward** vt (meeting) vorverlegen; (COMM) übertragen; ~ **in** vt hereinbringen; (harvest) einbringen; ~ **off** vt davontragen; (success) erzielen; ~ **out** vt (object) herausbringen; ~ **round** or **to** vt wieder zu sich bringen; ~ **up** vt aufziehen; (question) zur Sprache bringen

brink [brɪŋk] n Rand m

brisk [brɪsk] adj lebhaft

bristle ['brɪsl] n Borste f ♦ vi sich sträuben; **bristling with** strotzend vor +dat

Britain ['brɪtən] n (also: **Great ~**) Großbritannien nt

British ['brɪtɪʃ] adj britisch ♦ npl: **the ~** die Briten pl; ~ **Isles** npl: **the ~ Isles** die Britischen Inseln pl; ~ **Rail** n die Britischen Eisenbahnen

Briton ['brɪtən] n Brite m, Britin f

Brittany ['brɪtənɪ] n die Bretagne

brittle ['brɪtl] adj spröde

broach [brəʊtʃ] vt (subject) anschneiden

broad [brɔːd] adj breit; (hint) deutlich; (general) allgemein; (accent) stark; **in ~ daylight** am helllichten Tag; ~**cast** (pt, pp **broadcast**) n Rundfunkübertragung f ♦ vt, vi übertragen, senden; ~**en** vt erweitern ♦ vi sich erweitern; ~**ly** adv allgemein gesagt; ~**-minded** adj tolerant

broccoli ['brɒkəlɪ] n Brokkoli pl

brochure ['brəʊʃjʊə] n Broschüre f

broil [brɔɪl] vt (grill) grillen

broke [brəʊk] pt of **break** ♦ adj (inf) pleite

broken ['brəʊkn] pp of **break** ♦ adj: ~ **leg** gebrochenes Bein; **in ~ English** in gebrochenem Englisch; ~**-hearted** adj untröstlich

broker ['brəʊkə] n Makler m

brolly ['brɒlɪ] (BRIT: inf) n Schirm m

bronchitis [brɒŋ'kaɪtɪs] n Bronchitis f

bronze [brɒnz] n Bronze f

brooch [brəʊtʃ] n Brosche f

brood [bruːd] n Brut f ♦ vi brüten

brook [brʊk] n Bach m

broom [brum] n Besen m

Bros. abbr = **Brothers**

broth [brɒθ] n Suppe f, Fleischbrühe f

brothel ['brɒθl] n Bordell nt

brother ['brʌðə] n Bruder m; ~**-in-law** n Schwager m

brought [brɔːt] pt, pp of **bring**

brow [braʊ] n (eyebrow) (Augen)braue f; (forehead) Stirn f; (of hill) Bergkuppe f

brown [braʊn] adj braun ♦ n Braun nt ♦ vt bräunen; ~ **bread** n Mischbrot nt; B~**ie** n Wichtel m; ~ **paper** n Packpapier nt; ~ **sugar** n braune(r) Zucker m

browse [braʊz] vi (in books) blättern; (in shop) schmökern, herumschauen; ~**r** n (COMPUT) Browser m

bruise [bruːz] n Bluterguss m, blaue(r) Fleck m ♦ vt einen blauen Fleck geben ♦ vi einen blauen Fleck bekommen

brunt [brʌnt] n volle Wucht f

brush [brʌʃ] n Bürste f; (for sweeping) Handbesen m; (for painting) Pinsel m; (fight) kurze(r) Kampf m; (MIL) Scharmützel nt; (fig) Auseinandersetzung f ♦ vt (clean) bürsten; (sweep) fegen; (usu: ~ past, ~ against) streifen; ~ **aside** vt abtun; ~ **up** vt (knowledge) auffrischen; ~**wood** n Gestrüpp nt

brusque [bruːsk] adj schroff

Brussels ['brʌslz] n Brüssel nt; ~ **sprout** n Rosenkohl m

brutal ['bruːtl] adj brutal

brute [bruːt] n (person) Scheusal nt ♦ adj: **by ~ force** mit roher Kraft

B.Sc. n abbr = **Bachelor of Science**

BSE n abbr (= bovine spongiform encephalopathy) BSE f

bubble ['bʌbl] n (Luft)blase f ♦ vi sprudeln; (with joy) übersprudeln; ~ **bath** n Schaumbad nt; ~ **gum** n Kaugummi m or nt

buck [bʌk] n Bock m; (US: inf) Dollar m ♦ vi bocken; **to pass the ~ (to sb)** die Verantwortung (auf jdn) abschieben; ~ **up** (inf) vi sich zusammenreißen

bucket ['bʌkɪt] n Eimer m

Buckingham Palace

ⓘ **Buckingham Palace** *ist die offizielle Londoner Residenz der britischen Monarchen und liegt am St James Park. Der Palast wurde 1703 für den Herzog von Buckingham erbaut, 1762 von George III. gekauft, zwischen 1821 und 1836 von John Nash umgebaut, und Anfang des 20. Jahrhunderts teilweise neu gestaltet. Teile des Buckingham Palace sind heute der Öffentlichkeit zugänglich.*

---

buckle ['bʌkl] n Schnalle f ♦ vt (an- or zusammen)schnallen ♦ vi (bend) sich verziehen

bud [bʌd] n Knospe f ♦ vi knospen, keimen

Buddhism ['budɪzəm] n Buddhismus m; **Buddhist** adj buddhistisch ♦ n Buddhist(in) m(f)

budding ['bʌdɪŋ] adj angehend

buddy ['bʌdɪ] (inf) n Kumpel m

budge [bʌdʒ] vt, vi (sich) von der Stelle rühren

budgerigar ['bʌdʒərɪgɑːʳ] n Wellensittich m

budget ['bʌdʒɪt] n Budget nt; (POL) Haushalt m ♦ vi: **to ~ for sth** etw einplanen

budgie ['bʌdʒɪ] n = **budgerigar**

buff [bʌf] adj (colour) lederfarben ♦ n (enthusiast) Fan m

buffalo ['bʌfələu] (pl ~ or ~es) n (BRIT) Büffel m; (US: bison) Bison m

buffer ['bʌfəʳ] n Puffer m; (COMPUT) Pufferspeicher m; **~ zone** n Pufferzone f

buffet[1] ['bʌfɪt] n (blow) Schlag m ♦ vt (herum)stossen

buffet[2] ['bufeɪ] (BRIT) n (bar) Imbissraum m, Erfrischungsraum m; (food) (kaltes) Büfett nt; **~ car** (BRIT) n Speisewagen m

bug [bʌg] n (also fig) Wanze f ♦ vt verwanzen; **the room is bugged** das Zimmer ist verwanzt

bugle ['bjuːgl] n Jagdhorn nt; (MIL: MUS) Bügelhorn m

build [bɪld] (pt, pp **built**) vt bauen ♦ n Körperbau m; **~ up** vt aufbauen; **~er** n

Bauunternehmer m; **~ing** n Gebäude nt; **~ing society** (BRIT) n Bausparkasse f

built [bɪlt] pt, pp of **build**; **~-in** adj (cupboard) eingebaut; **~-up area** n Wohngebiet nt

bulb [bʌlb] n (BOT) (Blumen)zwiebel f; (ELEC) Glühlampe f, Birne f

Bulgaria [bʌlˈgeərɪə] n Bulgarien nt; **~n** adj bulgarisch ♦ n Bulgare m, Bulgarin f; (LING) Bulgarisch nt

bulge [bʌldʒ] n Wölbung f ♦ vi sich wölben

bulk [bʌlk] n Größe f, Masse f; (greater part) Großteil m; **in ~** (COMM) en gros; **the ~ of** der größte Teil +gen; **~head** n Schott nt; **~y** adj (sehr) umfangreich; (goods) sperrig

bull [bul] n Bulle m; (cattle) Stier m; **~dog** n Bulldogge f

bulldozer ['buldəuzəʳ] n Planierraupe f

bullet ['bulɪt] n Kugel f

bulletin ['bulɪtɪn] n Bulletin nt, Bekanntmachung f

bulletproof ['bulɪtpruːf] adj kugelsicher

bullfight ['bulfaɪt] n Stierkampf m; **~er** n Stierkämpfer m; **~ing** n Stierkamp m

bullion ['buljən] n Barren m

bullock ['bulək] n Ochse m

bullring ['bulrɪŋ] n Stierkampfarena f

bull's-eye ['bulzaɪ] n Zentrum nt

bully ['bulɪ] n Raufbold m ♦ vt einschüchtern

bum [bʌm] n (inf: backside) Hintern m; (tramp) Landstreicher m

bumblebee ['bʌmblbiː] n Hummel f

bump [bʌmp] n (blow) Stoß m; (swelling) Beule f ♦ vt, vi stoßen, prallen; **~ into** vt fus stoßen gegen ♦ vt (person) treffen; **~er** n (AUT) Stoßstange f ♦ adj (edition) dick; (harvest) Rekord-

bumpy ['bʌmpɪ] adj holprig

bun [bʌn] n Korinthenbrötchen nt

bunch [bʌntʃ] n (of flowers) Strauß m; (of keys) Bund m; (of people) Haufen m; **~es** npl (in hair) Zöpfe pl

bundle ['bʌndl] n Bündel nt ♦ vt (also: ~ up) bündeln

bungalow ['bʌngələu] n einstöckige(s) Haus nt, Bungalow m

bungle ['bʌngl] vt verpfuschen

bunion ['bʌnjən] n entzündete(r) Fußballen *m*

bunk [bʌŋk] *n* Schlafkoje *f*; ~ **beds** *npl* Etagenbett *nt*

bunker ['bʌŋkər] *n* (*coal store*) Kohlenbunker *m*; (*GOLF*) Sandloch *nt*

bunny ['bʌnɪ] *n* (*also:* ~ **rabbit**) Häschen *nt*

bunting ['bʌntɪŋ] *n* Fahnentuch *nt*

buoy [bɔɪ] *n* Boje *f*; (*lifebuoy*) Rettungsboje *f*; **~ant** *adj* (*floating*) schwimmend; (*fig*) heiter

burden ['bɜːdn] *n* (*weight*) Ladung *f*, Last *f*; (*fig*) Bürde *f* ♦ *vt* belasten

bureau ['bjuərəu] (*pl* **~x**) *n* (*BRIT: writing desk*) Sekretär *m*; (*US: chest of drawers*) Kommode *f*; (*for information etc*) Büro *nt*

bureaucracy [bjuə'rɔkrəsɪ] *n* Bürokratie *f*

bureaucrat ['bjuərəkræt] *n* Bürokrat(in) *m(f)*

bureaux ['bjuərəuz] *npl of* **bureau**

burglar ['bɜːglər] *n* Einbrecher *m*; ~ **alarm** *n* Einbruchssicherung *f*; **~y** *n* Einbruch *m*

burial ['berɪəl] *n* Beerdigung *f*

burly ['bɜːlɪ] *adj* stämmig

Burma ['bɜːmə] *n* Birma *nt*

burn [bɜːn] (*pt, pp* **burned** *or* **burnt**) *vt* verbrennen ♦ *vi* brennen ♦ *n* Brandwunde *f*; ~ **down** *vt, vi* abbrennen; **~er** *n* Brenner *m*; **~ing** *adj* brennend; **~t** [bɜːnt] *pt, pp of* **burn**

burrow ['bʌrəu] *n* (*of fox*) Bau *m*; (*of rabbit*) Höhle *f* ♦ *vt* eingraben

bursar ['bɜːsər] *n* Kassenverwalter *m*, Quästor *m*; **~y** (*BRIT*) *n* Stipendium *nt*

burst [bɜːst] (*pt, pp* **burst**) *vt* zerbrechen ♦ *vi* platzen ♦ *n* Explosion *f*; (*outbreak*) Ausbruch *m*; (*in pipe*) Bruch(stelle *f*) *m*; **to ~ into flames** in Flammen aufgehen; **to ~ into tears** in Tränen ausbrechen; **to ~ out laughing** in Gelächter ausbrechen; ~ **into** *vt fus* (*room etc*) platzen in +*acc*; ~ **open** *vi* aufbrechen

bury ['berɪ] *vt* vergraben; (*in grave*) beerdigen

bus [bʌs] *n* (Auto)bus *m*, Omnibus *m*

bush [buʃ] *n* Busch *m*; **to beat about the ~** wie die Katze um den heißen Brei herumgehen; **~y** ['buʃɪ] *adj* buschig

busily ['bɪzɪlɪ] *adv* geschäftig

business ['bɪznɪs] *n* Geschäft *nt*; (*concern*)

Angelegenheit *f*; **it's none of your ~** es geht dich nichts an; **to mean ~** es ernst meinen; **to be away on ~** geschäftlich verreist sein; **it's my ~ to ...** es ist meine Sache, zu ...; **~like** *adj* geschäftsmäßig; **~man** (*irreg*) *n* Geschäftsmann *m*; ~ **trip** *n* Geschäftsreise *f*; **~woman** (*irreg*) *n* Geschäftsfrau *f*

busker ['bʌskər] (*BRIT*) *n* Straßenmusikant *m*

bus: ~ **shelter** *n* Wartehäuschen *nt*; ~ **station** *n* Busbahnhof *m*; ~ **stop** *n* Bushaltestelle *f*

bust [bʌst] *n* Büste *f* ♦ *adj* (*broken*) kaputt(gegangen); (*business*) pleite; **to go ~** Pleite machen

bustle ['bʌsl] *n* Getriebe *nt* ♦ *vi* hasten

bustling ['bʌslɪŋ] *adj* geschäftig

busy ['bɪzɪ] *adj* beschäftigt; (*road*) belebt ♦ *vt*: **to ~ o.s.** sich beschäftigen; **~body** *n* Übereifrige(r) *mf*; ~ **signal** (*US*) *n* (*TEL*) Besetztzeichen *nt*

KEYWORD

but [bʌt] *conj* **1** (*yet*) aber; **not X but Y** nicht X sondern Y

2 (*however*): **I'd love to come, but I'm busy** ich würde gern kommen, bin aber beschäftigt

3 (*showing disagreement, surprise etc*): **but that's fantastic!** (aber) das ist ja fantastisch!

♦ *prep* (*apart from, except*): **nothing but trouble** nichts als Ärger; **no-one but him can do it** niemand außer ihn kann es machen; **but for you/your help** ohne dich/deine Hilfe; **anything but that** alles, nur das nicht

♦ *adv* (*just, only*): **she's but a child** sie ist noch ein Kind; **had I but known** wenn ich es nur gewusst hätte; **I can but try** ich kann es immerhin versuchen; **all but finished** so gut wie fertig

---

butcher ['butʃər] *n* Metzger *m*; (*murderer*) Schlächter *m* ♦ *vt* (*kill*) abschlachten; **~'s (shop)** *n* Metzgerei *f*

butler ['bʌtlər] *n* Butler *m*

butt [bʌt] n (cask) große(s) Fass nt; (BRIT: fig: target) Zielscheibe f; (of gun) Kolben m; (of cigarette) Stummel m ♦ vt (mit dem Kopf) stoßen; ~ **in** vi sich einmischen

butter ['bʌtə'] n Butter f ♦ vt buttern; ~ **bean** n Wachsbohne f; ~**cup** n Butterblume f

butterfly ['bʌtəflaɪ] n Schmetterling m; (SWIMMING: also: ~ **stroke**) Butterflystil m

buttocks ['bʌtəks] npl Gesäß nt

button ['bʌtn] n Knopf m ♦ vt, vi (also: ~ **up**) zuknöpfen

buttress ['bʌtrɪs] n Strebepfeiler m; Stützbogen m

buxom ['bʌksəm] adj drall

buy [baɪ] (pt, pp **bought**) vt kaufen ♦ n Kauf m; **to ~ sb a drink** jdm einen Drink spendieren; ~**er** n Käufer(in) m(f)

buzz [bʌz] n Summen nt ♦ vi summen; ~**er** ['bʌzə'] n Summer m; ~ **word** n Modewort nt

---
KEYWORD
---

by [baɪ] prep **1** (referring to cause, agent) of, durch; **killed by lightning** vom Blitz getötet; **a painting by Picasso** ein Gemälde von Picasso

2 (referring to method, manner): **by bus/car/train** mit dem Bus/Auto/Zug; **to pay by cheque** per Scheck bezahlen; **by moonlight** bei Mondschein; **by saving hard, he ...** indem er eisern sparte, ... er ...

3 (via, through) über +acc; **he came in by the back door** er kam durch die Hintertür herein

4 (close to, past) bei, an +dat; **a holiday by the sea** ein Urlaub am Meer; **she rushed by me** sie eilte an mir vorbei

5 (not later than): **by 4 o'clock** bis 4 Uhr; **by this time tomorrow** morgen um diese Zeit; **by the time I got here it was too late** als ich hier ankam, war es zu spät

6 (during): **by day** bei Tag

7 (amount): **by the kilo/metre** kiloweise/meterweise; **paid by the hour** stundenweise bezahlt

8 (MATH, measure): **to divide by 3** durch 3

teilen; **to multiply by 3** mit 3 malnehmen; **a room 3 metres by 4** ein Zimmer 3 mal 4 Meter; **it's broader by a metre** es ist (um) einem Meter breiter

9 (according to) nach; **it's all right by me** von mir aus gern

10: **(all) by oneself** etc ganz allein

11: **by the way** übrigens

♦ adv **1** see **go**; **pass** etc

2: **by and by** irgendwann; (with past tenses) nach einiger Zeit; **by and large** (on the whole) im Großen und Ganzen

---

bye(-bye) ['baɪ('baɪ)] excl (auf) Wiedersehen

by(e)-law ['baɪlɔ:] n Verordnung f

by-election ['baɪɪlekʃən] (BRIT) n Nachwahl f

bygone ['baɪgɔn] adj vergangen ♦ n: **let ~s be ~s** lass(t) das Vergangene vergangen sein

bypass ['baɪpɑ:s] n Umgehungsstraße f ♦ vt umgehen

by-product ['baɪprɔdʌkt] n Nebenprodukt nt

bystander ['baɪstændə'] n Zuschauer m

byte [baɪt] n (COMPUT) Byte nt

byword ['baɪwə:d] n Inbegriff m

C, c

C [si:] n (MUS) C nt

C. abbr (= centigrade) C

C.A. abbr = **chartered accountant**

cab [kæb] n Taxi nt; (of train) Führerstand m; (of truck) Führersitz m

cabaret ['kæbəreɪ] n Kabarett nt

cabbage ['kæbɪdʒ] n Kohl(kopf) m

cabin ['kæbɪn] n Hütte f; (NAUT) Kajüte f; (AVIAT) Kabine f; ~ **crew** n (AVIAT) Flugbegleitpersonal nt; ~ **cruiser** n Motorjacht f

cabinet ['kæbɪnɪt] n Schrank m; (for china) Vitrine f; (POL) Kabinett nt; ~-**maker** n Kunsttischler m

cable ['keɪbl] n Drahtseil nt, Tau nt; (TEL) (Leitungs)kabel nt; (telegram) Kabel nt ♦ vt kabeln, telegrafieren; ~ **car** n Seilbahn f; ~ **television** n Kabelfernsehen nt

cache [kæʃ] n geheime(s) (Waffen)lager nt; geheime(s) (Proviant)lager nt

cackle [ˈkækl] vi gackern

cacti [ˈkæktaɪ] npl of **cactus**

cactus [ˈkæktəs] (pl **cacti**) n Kaktus m, Kaktee f

caddie [ˈkædɪ] n (GOLF) Golfjunge m; **caddy** [ˈkædɪ] n = **caddie**

cadet [kəˈdet] n Kadett m

cadge [kædʒ] vt schmarotzen

Caesarean [sɪˈzɛərɪən] adj: ~ **(section)** Kaiserschnitt m

café [ˈkæfeɪ] n Café nt, Restaurant nt

cafeteria [kæfɪˈtɪərɪə] n Selbstbedienungsrestaurant nt

caffein(e) [ˈkæfiːn] n Koffein nt

cage [keɪdʒ] n Käfig m ♦ vt einsperren

cagey [ˈkeɪdʒɪ] adj geheimnistuerisch, zurückhaltend

cagoule [kəˈguːl] n Windhemd nt

Cairo [ˈkaɪərəu] n Kairo nt

cajole [kəˈdʒəul] vt überreden

cake [keɪk] n Kuchen m; (of soap) Stück nt; ~**d** adj verkrustet

calamity [kəˈlæmɪtɪ] n Unglück nt, (Schicksals)schlag m

calcium [ˈkælsɪəm] n Kalzium nt

calculate [ˈkælkjuleɪt] vt berechnen, kalkulieren; **calculating** adj berechnend; **calculation** [kælkjuˈleɪʃən] n Berechnung f; **calculator** n Rechner m

calendar [ˈkæləndəʳ] n Kalender m; ~ **month** n Kalendermonat m

calf [kaːf] (pl **calves**) n Kalb nt; (also: ~**skin**) Kalbsleder nt; (ANAT) Wade f

calibre [ˈkælɪbəʳ] (US **caliber**) n Kaliber nt

call [kɔːl] vt rufen; (name) nennen; (meeting) einberufen; (awaken) wecken; (TEL) anrufen ♦ vi (shout) rufen; (visit: also: ~ **in**, ~ **round**) vorbeikommen ♦ n (shout) Ruf m; (TEL) Anruf m; **to be ~ed** heißen; **on** ~ in Bereitschaft; ~ **back** vi (return) wiederkommen; (TEL) zurückrufen; ~ **for** vt fus (demand) erfordern, verlangen; (fetch) abholen; ~ **off** vt (cancel) absagen; ~ **on** vt fus (visit) besuchen; (turn to) bitten; ~ **out** vi rufen; ~ **up** vt (MIL) einberufen;

~**box** (BRIT) n Telefonzelle f; ~ **centre** n Telefoncenter nt, Callcenter nt; ~**er** n Besucher(in) m(f); (TEL) Anrufer m; ~ **girl** n Callgirl nt; ~-**in** (US) n (phone-in) Phone-in nt; ~**ing** n (vocation) Berufung f; ~**ing card** (US) n Visitenkarte f

callous [ˈkæləs] adj herzlos

calm [kaːm] n Ruhe f; (NAUT) Flaute f ♦ vt beruhigen ♦ adj ruhig; (person) gelassen; ~ **down** vi sich beruhigen ♦ vt beruhigen

Calor gas [ˈkæləʳ-] ® n Propangas nt

calorie [ˈkælərɪ] n Kalorie f

calves [kaːvz] npl of **calf**

Cambodia [kæmˈbəudɪə] n Kambodscha nt

camcorder [ˈkæmkɔːdəʳ] n Camcorder m

came [keɪm] pt of **come**

cameo [ˈkæmɪəu] n Kamee f

camera [ˈkæmərə] n Fotoapparat m; (CINE, TV) Kamera f; **in** ~ unter Ausschluss der Öffentlichkeit; ~**man** (irreg) n Kameramann m

camouflage [ˈkæməflaːʒ] n Tarnung f ♦ vt tarnen

camp [kæmp] n Lager nt ♦ vi zelten, campen ♦ adj affektiert

campaign [kæmˈpeɪn] n Kampagne f; (MIL) Feldzug m ♦ vi (MIL) Krieg führen; (lig) werben, Propaganda machen; (POL) den Wahlkampf führen

camp: ~ **bed** [ˈkæmpˈbed] (BRIT) n Campingbett nt; ~**er** [ˈkæmpəʳ] n Camper(in) m(f); (vehicle) Campingwagen m; ~**ing** [ˈkæmpɪŋ] n: **to go** ~**ing** zelten, Camping machen; ~**ing gas** (US) n Campinggas nt; ~**site** [ˈkæmpsaɪt] n Campingplatz m

campus [ˈkæmpəs] n Universitätsgelände nt, Campus m

can[1] [kæn] n Büchse f, Dose f; (for water) Kanne f ♦ vt konservieren, in Büchsen einmachen

KEYWORD

can[2] [kæn] (negative **cannot**, **can't**, conditional **could**) aux vb 1 (be able to, know how to) können; **I can see you tomorrow, if you like** ich könnte Sie morgen sehen, wenn Sie wollen; **I can swim** ich kann schwimmen; **can you speak German?** sprechen Sie Deutsch? **2** (*may*) können, dürfen; **could I have a word with you?** könnte ich Sie kurz sprechen?

Canada ['kænədə] *n* Kanada *nt*; **Canadian** [kə'neɪdɪən] *adj* kanadisch ♦ *n* Kanadier(in) *m(f)*
canal [kə'næl] *n* Kanal *m*
canapé ['kænəpeɪ] *n* Cocktail- *or* Appetithappen *m*
canary [kə'neəɪ] *n* Kanarienvogel *m*
cancel ['kænsəl] *vt* absagen; (*delete*) durchstreichen; (*train*) streichen; **~lation** [kænsə'leɪʃən] *n* Absage *f*; Streichung *f*
cancer ['kænsəɪ] *n* (ASTROL: C~) Krebs *m*
candid ['kændɪd] *adj* offen, ehrlich
candidate ['kændɪdeɪt] *n* Kandidat(in) *m(f)*
candle ['kændl] *n* Kerze *f*; **~light** *n* Kerzenlicht *nt*; **~stick** *n* (*also:* **~ holder**) Kerzenhalter *m*
candour ['kændəɪ] (*US* **candor**) *n* Offenheit *f*
candy ['kændɪ] *n* Kandis(zucker) *m*; (*US*) Bonbons *pl*; **~floss** (*BRIT*) *n* Zuckerwatte *f*
cane [keɪn] *n* (BOT) Rohr *nt*; (*stick*) Stock *m* ♦ *vt* (*BRIT: beat*) schlagen
canine ['keɪnaɪn] *adj* Hunde-
canister ['kænɪstəɪ] *n* Blechdose *f*
cannabis ['kænəbɪs] *n* Hanf *m*, Haschisch *nt*
canned [kænd] *adj* Büchsen-, eingemacht
cannon ['kænən] (*pl* ~ *or* **~s**) *n* Kanone *f*
cannot ['kænɒt] = **can not**
canny ['kænɪ] *adj* schlau
canoe [kə'nuː] *n* Kanu *nt*; **~ing** *n* Kanusport *m*, Kanufahren *nt*
canon ['kænən] *n* (*clergyman*) Domherr *m*; (*standard*) Grundsatz *m*
can-opener ['kænəupnəɪ] *n* Büchsenöffner *m*
canopy ['kænəpɪ] *n* Baldachin *m*
can't [kænt] = **can not**
cantankerous [kæn'tæŋkərəs] *adj* zänkisch, mürrisch
canteen [kæn'tiːn] *n* Kantine *f*; (*BRIT: of cutlery*) Besteckkasten *m*

canter ['kæntəɪ] *n* Kanter *m* ♦ *vi* in kurzem Galopp reiten
canvas ['kænvəs] *n* Segeltuch *nt*; (*sail*) Segel *nt*; (*for painting*) Leinwand *f*; **under ~** (*camping*) in Zelten
canvass ['kænvəs] *vi* um Stimmen werben; **~ing** *n* Wahlwerbung *f*
canyon ['kænjən] *n* Felsenschlucht *f*
cap [kæp] *n* Mütze *f*; (*of pen*) Kappe *f*; (*of bottle*) Deckel *m* ♦ *vt* (*surpass*) übertreffen; (SPORT) aufstellen; (*put limit on*) einen Höchstsatz festlegen für
capability [keɪpə'bɪlɪtɪ] *n* Fähigkeit *f*
capable ['keɪpəbl] *adj* fähig
capacity [kə'pæsɪtɪ] *n* Fassungsvermögen *nt*; (*ability*) Fähigkeit *f*; (*position*) Eigenschaft *f*
cape [keɪp] *n* (*garment*) Cape *nt*, Umhang *m*; (GEOG) Kap *nt*
caper ['keɪpəɪ] *n* (COOK: *usu:* **~s**) Kaper *f*; (*prank*) Kapriole *f*
capital ['kæpɪtl] *n* (~ *city*) Hauptstadt *f*; (FIN) Kapital *nt*; (~ *letter*) Großbuchstabe *m*; **~ gains tax** *n* Kapitalertragssteuer *f*; **~ism** *n* Kapitalismus *m*; **~ist** *adj* kapitalistisch ♦ *n* Kapitalist(in) *m(f)*; **~ize** *vi*: **to ~ize on** Kapital schlagen aus; **~ punishment** *n* Todesstrafe *f*

Capitol

i **Capitol** *ist das Gebäude in Washington auf dem Capitol Hill, in dem der Kongress der USA zusammentritt. Die Bezeichnung wird in vielen amerikanischen Bundesstaaten auch für das Parlamentsgebäude des jeweiligen Staates verwendet.*

Capricorn ['kæprɪkɔːn] *n* Steinbock *m*
capsize [kæp'saɪz] *vt, vi* kentern
capsule ['kæpsjuːl] *n* Kapsel *f*
captain ['kæptɪn] *n* Kapitän *m*; (MIL) Hauptmann *m* ♦ *vt* anführen
caption ['kæpʃən] *n* (*heading*) Überschrift *f*; (*to picture*) Unterschrift *f*
captivate ['kæptɪveɪt] *vt* fesseln
captive ['kæptɪv] *n* Gefangene(r) *f(m)* ♦ *adj* gefangen (gehalten); **captivity** [kæp'tɪvɪtɪ]

n Gefangenschaft *f*

capture ['kæptʃər] *vt* gefangen nehmen; (*place*) erobern; (*attention*) erregen ♦ *n* Gefangennahme *f*; (*data* ~) Erfassung *f*

car [kɑːʳ] *n* Auto *nt*, Wagen *m*; (*RAIL*) Wagen *m*

caramel ['kærəməl] *n* Karamelle *f*, Karamellbonbon *m or nt*; (*burnt sugar*) Karamell *m*

carat ['kærət] *n* Karat *nt*

caravan ['kærəvæn] *n* (*BRIT*) Wohnwagen *m*; (*in desert*) Karawane *f*; ~**ning** *n* Caravaning *nt*, Urlaub *m* im Wohnwagen; ~ **site** (*BRIT*) *n* Campingplatz *m* für Wohnwagen

carbohydrate [kɑːbəu'haɪdreɪt] *n* Kohlenhydrat *nt*

carbon ['kɑːbən] *n* Kohlenstoff *m*; ~ **copy** *n* Durchschlag *m*; ~ **dioxide** *n* Kohlendioxyd *nt*; ~ **monoxide** *n* Kohlenmonoxyd *nt*; ~ **paper** *n* Kohlepapier *nt*

car boot sale *n* auf einem Parkplatz stattfindender Flohmarkt mit dem Kofferraum als Auslage

carburettor [kɑːbju'rɛtəʳ] (*US* **carburetor**) *n* Vergaser *m*

carcass ['kɑːkəs] *n* Kadaver *m*

card [kɑːd] *n* Karte *f*; ~**board** *n* Pappe *f*; ~ **game** *n* Kartenspiel *nt*

cardiac ['kɑːdiæk] *adj* Herz-

cardigan ['kɑːdɪgən] *n* Strickjacke *f*

cardinal ['kɑːdɪnl] *adj*: ~ **number** Kardinalzahl *f* ♦ *n* (*REL*) Kardinal *m*

card index *n* Kartei *f*; (*in library*) Katalog *m*

cardphone *n* Kartentelefon *nt*

care [kɛəʳ] *n* (*of teeth, car etc*) Pflege *f*; (*of children*) Fürsorge *f*; (~*fulness*) Sorgfalt *f*; (*worry*) Sorge *f* ♦ *vi*: **to ~ about** sich kümmern um; ~ **of** bei; **in sb's** ~ in jds Obhut; **I don't** ~ das ist mir egal; **I couldn't** ~ **less** es ist mir doch völlig egal; **to take** ~ aufpassen; **to take** ~ **of** sorgen für; **to take** ~ **to do sth** sich bemühen, etw zu tun; ~ **for** *vt* sorgen für; (*like*) mögen

career [kə'rɪəʳ] *n* Karriere *f*, Laufbahn *f* ♦ *vi* (*also:* ~ **along**) rasen; ~ **woman** (*irreg*) *n* Karrierefrau *f*

care: ~**free** *adj* sorgenfrei; ~**ful** *adj*

sorgfältig; **(be)** ~**ful!** pass auf!; ~**fully** *adv* vorsichtig; (*methodically*) sorgfältig; ~**less** *adj* nachlässig; ~**lessness** *n* Nachlässigkeit *f*; ~ **r** *n* (*MED*) Betreuer(in) *m(f)*

caress [kə'rɛs] *n* Liebkosung *f* ♦ *vt* liebkosen

caretaker ['kɛəteɪkəʳ] *n* Hausmeister *m*

car ferry *n* Autofähre *f*

cargo ['kɑːgəu] (*pl* ~**es**) *n* Schiffsladung *f*

car hire *n* Autovermietung *f*

Caribbean [kærɪ'biːən] *n*: **the** ~ **(Sea)** die Karibik

caricature ['kærɪkətjuəʳ] *n* Karikatur *f*

caring ['kɛərɪŋ] *adj* (*society, organization*) sozial eingestellt; (*person*) liebevoll

carnage ['kɑːnɪdʒ] *n* Blutbad *nt*

carnation [kɑː'neɪʃən] *n* Nelke *f*

carnival ['kɑːnɪvl] *n* Karneval *m*, Fasching *m*; (*US: fun fair*) Kirmes *f*

carnivorous [kɑː'nɪvərəs] *adj* Fleisch fressend

carol ['kærəl] *n*: **(Christmas)** ~ (Weihnachts)lied *nt*

carp [kɑːp] *n* (*fish*) Karpfen *m*

car park (*BRIT*) *n* Parkplatz *m*; (*covered*) Parkhaus *nt*

carpenter ['kɑːpɪntəʳ] *n* Zimmermann *m*; **carpentry** ['kɑːpɪntrɪ] *n* Zimmerei *f*

carpet ['kɑːpɪt] *n* Teppich *m* ♦ *vt* mit einem Teppich auslegen; ~ **bombing** *n* Flächenbombardierung *f*; ~ **slippers** *npl* Pantoffeln *pl*; ~ **sweeper** ['kɑːpɪtswiːpəʳ] *n* Teppichkehrer *m*

car phone *n* (*TEL*) Autotelefon *nt*

car rental (*US*) *n* Autovermietung *f*

carriage ['kærɪdʒ] *n* Kutsche *f*; (*RAIL, of typewriter*) Wagen *m*; (*of goods*) Beförderung *f*; (*bearing*) Haltung *f*; ~ **return** *n* (*on typewriter*) Rücklauftaste *f*; ~**way** (*BRIT*) *n* (*part of road*) Fahrbahn *f*

carrier ['kærɪəʳ] *n* Träger(in) *m(f)*; (*COMM*) Spediteur *m*; ~ **bag** (*BRIT*) *n* Tragetasche *f*

carrot ['kærət] *n* Möhre *f*, Karotte *f*

carry ['kærɪ] *vt, vi* tragen; **to get carried away** (*fig*) sich nicht mehr bremsen können; ~ **on** *vi* (*continue*) weitermachen; (*inf: complain*) Theater machen; ~ **out** *vt* (*orders*) ausführen; (*investigation*) durchführen; **~cot** (*BRIT*) *n* Babytragetasche *f*; **~-on** (*inf*) *n* (*fuss*) Theater *nt*

cart [kɑːt] *n* Wagen *m*, Karren *m* ♦ *vt* schleppen

cartilage ['kɑːtɪlɪdʒ] *n* Knorpel *m*

carton ['kɑːtən] *n* Karton *m*; (*of milk*) Tüte *f*

cartoon [kɑːˈtuːn] *n* (*PRESS*) Karikatur *f*; (*comic strip*) Comics *pl*; (*CINE*) (Zeichen)trickfilm *m*

cartridge ['kɑːtrɪdʒ] *n* Patrone *f*

carve [kɑːv] *vt* (*wood*) schnitzen; (*stone*) meißeln; (*meat*) (vor)schneiden; **~ up** *vt* aufschneiden; **carving** ['kɑːvɪŋ] *n* Schnitzerei *f*; **carving knife** *n* Tran(s)chiermesser *nt*

car wash *n* Autowäsche *f*

cascade [kæsˈkeɪd] *n* Wasserfall *m* ♦ *vi* kaskadenartig herabfallen

case [keɪs] *n* (*box*) Kasten *m*; (*BRIT: also:* **suitcase**) Koffer *m*; (*JUR, matter*) Fall *m*; **in ~** falls, im Falle; **in any ~** jedenfalls, auf jeden Fall

cash [kæʃ] *n* (Bar)geld *nt* ♦ *vt* einlösen; **~ on delivery** per Nachnahme; **~ book** *n* Kassenbuch *nt*; **~ card** *n* Scheckkarte *f*; **~ desk** (*BRIT*) *n* Kasse *f*; **~ dispenser** *n* Geldautomat *m*

cashew [kæˈʃuː] *n* (*also:* **~ nut**) Cashewnuss *f*

cash flow *n* Cashflow *m*

cashier [kæˈʃɪə*] *n* Kassierer(in) *m(f)*

cashmere ['kæʃmɪə*] *n* Kaschmirwolle *f*

cash register *n* Registrierkasse *f*

casing ['keɪsɪŋ] *n* Gehäuse *nt*

casino [kəˈsiːnəʊ] *n* Kasino *nt*

casket ['kɑːskɪt] *n* Kästchen *nt*; (*US: coffin*) Sarg *m*

casserole ['kæsərəʊl] *n* Kasserolle *f*; (*food*) Auflauf *m*

cassette [kæˈset] *n* Kassette *f*; **~ player** *n* Kassettengerät *nt*

cast [kɑːst] *n* (*pt, pp* **cast**) *vt* werfen; (*horns*) verlieren; (*metal*) gießen; (*THEAT*) besetzen; (*vote*) abgeben ♦ *n* (*THEAT*) Besetzung *f*; (*also:* **plaster ~**) Gipsverband *m*; **~ off** *vi* (*NAUT*) losmachen

castaway ['kɑːstəweɪ] *n* Schiffbrüchige(r) *f(m)*

caste [kɑːst] *n* Kaste *f*

caster sugar ['kɑːstə-] (*BRIT*) *n* Raffinade *f*

casting vote ['kɑːstɪŋ-] (*BRIT*) *n* entscheidende Stimme *f*

cast iron *n* Gusseisen *nt*

castle ['kɑːsl] *n* Burg *f*; Schloss *nt*; (*CHESS*) Turm *m*

castor ['kɑːstə*] *n* (*wheel*) Laufrolle *f*

castor oil *n* Rizinusöl *nt*

castrate [kæsˈtreɪt] *vt* kastrieren

casual ['kæʒjʊl] *adj* (*attitude*) nachlässig; (*dress*) leger; (*meeting*) zufällig; (*work*) Gelegenheits-; **~ly** *adv* (*dress*) zwanglos, leger; (*remark*) beiläufig

casualty ['kæʒjʊltɪ] *n* Verletzte(r) *f(m)*; (*dead*) Tote(r) *f(m)*; (*also:* **~ department**) Unfallstation *f*

cat [kæt] *n* Katze *f*

catalogue ['kætəlɒg] (*US* **catalog**) *n* Katalog *m* ♦ *vt* katalogisieren

catalyst ['kætəlɪst] *n* Katalysator *m*

catalytic converter [kætəˈlɪtɪk kənˈvɜːtə*] *n* Katalysator *m*

catapult ['kætəpʌlt] *n* Schleuder *f*

cataract ['kætərækt] *n* (*MED*) graue(r) Star *m*

catarrh [kəˈtɑː*] *n* Katarr(h) *m*

catastrophe [kəˈtæstrəfɪ] *n* Katastrophe *f*

catch [kætʃ] *n* (*pt, pp* **caught**) *vt* fangen; (*arrest*) fassen; (*train*) erreichen; (*person: by surprise*) ertappen; (*also:* **~ up**) einholen ♦ *vi* (*fire*) in Gang kommen; (*in branches etc*) hängen bleiben ♦ *n* (*fish etc*) Fang *m*; (*trick*) Haken *m*; (*of lock*) Sperrhaken *m*; **to ~ an illness** sich *dat* eine Krankheit holen; **to ~ fire** Feuer fangen; **~ on** *vi* (*understand*) begreifen; (*grow popular*) ankommen; **~ up** *vi* (*fig*) aufholen; **~ing** ['kætʃɪŋ] *adj* ansteckend; **~ment area** ['kætʃmənt-] (*BRIT*) *n* Einzugsgebiet *nt*; **~ phrase** *n* Slogan *m*; **~y** ['kætʃɪ] *adj* (*tune*) eingängig

categoric(al) [kætɪˈgɒrɪk(l)] *adj* kategorisch

category ['kætɪgərɪ] *n* Kategorie *f*

cater ['keɪtə*] *vi* versorgen; **~ for** (*BRIT*) *vt fus* (*party*) ausrichten; (*needs*) eingestellt sein auf +*acc*; **~er** *n* Lieferant(in) *m(f)* von Speisen und Getränken; **~ing** *n*

Gastronomie f

caterpillar ['kætəpılə'] n Raupe f; **~ track**
® n Gleiskette f

cathedral [kə'θiːdrəl] n Kathedrale f, Dom
m

Catholic ['kæθəlık] adj (REL) katholisch ♦ n
Katholik(in) m(f); **c~** adj (tastes etc)
vielseitig

CAT scan [kæt-] n Computertomografie f

Catseye ['kæts'aı] (BRIT: ®) n (AUT)
Katzenauge nt

cattle ['kætl] npl Vieh nt

catty ['kætı] adj gehässig

caucus ['kɔːkəs] n (POL) Gremium nt; (US:
meeting) Sitzung f

caught [kɔːt] pt, pp of **catch**

cauliflower ['kɒlıflauə'] n Blumenkohl m

cause [kɔːz] n Ursache f; (purpose) Sache f
♦ vt verursachen

causeway ['kɔːzweı] n Damm m

caustic ['kɔːstık] adj ätzend; (fig) bissig

caution ['kɔːʃən] n Vorsicht f; (warning)
Verwarnung f ♦ vt verwarnen; **cautious**
['kɔːʃəs] adj vorsichtig

cavalry ['kævəlrı] n Kavallerie f

cave [keıv] n Höhle f; **~ in** vi einstürzen;
~man (irreg) n Höhlenmensch m

cavern ['kævən] n Höhle f

caviar(e) ['kævıɑː'] n Kaviar m

cavity ['kævıtı] n Loch nt

cavort [kə'vɔːt] vi umherspringen

C.B. n abbr (= Citizens' Band (Radio)) CB

C.B.I. n abbr (= Confederation of British
Industry) ≃ BDI m

cc n abbr – **carbon copy**; **cubic
centimetres**

CCTV n abbr (– closed-circuit television)
Videoüberwachung f

CD n abbr (= compact disc) CD f

CDI n abbr (= Compact Disk Interactive) CD-I f

CD player n CD-Spieler m

CD-ROM n abbr (= compact disc read-only
memory) CD-Rom f

cease [siːs] vi aufhören ♦ vt beenden; **~fire**
n Feuereinstellung f; **~less** adj
unaufhörlich

cedar ['siːdə'] n Zeder f

ceiling ['siːlıŋ] n Decke f; (fig) Höchstgrenze
f

celebrate ['selıbreıt] vt, vi feiern; **~d** adj
gefeiert; **celebration** [selı'breıʃən] n Feier f

celebrity [sı'lebrıtı] n gefeierte Persönlichkeit
f

celery ['selərı] n Sellerie m or f

celibacy ['selıbəsı] n Zölibat nt or m

cell [sel] n Zelle f; (ELEC) Element nt

cellar ['selə'] n Keller m

cello ['tʃeləu] n Cello nt

Cellophane ['seləfeın] ® n Cellophan nt ®

cellphone ['selfəun] n Funktelefon nt

cellular ['seljulə'] adj zellular

cellulose ['seljuləus] n Zellulose f

Celt [kelt, selt] n Kelte m, Keltin f; **~ic** ['keltık,
'seltık] adj keltisch

cement [sə'ment] n Zement m ♦ vt
zementieren; **~ mixer** n
Betonmischmaschine f

cemetery ['semıtrı] n Friedhof m

censor ['sensə'] n Zensor m ♦ vt zensieren;
~ship n Zensur f

censure ['senʃə'] vt rügen

census ['sensəs] n Volkszählung f

cent [sent] n (coin) Cent m; see also **per cent**

centenary [sen'tiːnərı] n Jahrhundertfeier f

center ['sentə'] (US) n = **contre**

centigrade ['sentıgreıd] adj Celsius

centimetre ['sentımiːtə'] (US **centimeter**) n
Zentimeter nt

centipede ['sentıpiːd] n Tausendfüßler m

central ['sentrəl] adj zentral; **C~ America** n
Mittelamerika nt; **~ heating** n
Zentralheizung f; **~ize** vt zentralisieren; **~
reservation** (BRIT) n (AUT) Mittelstreifen m

centre ['sentə'] (US **center**) n Zentrum nt
♦ vt zentrieren; **~-forward** n (SPORT) Mittel-
stürmer m; **~-half** n (SPORT) Stopper m

century ['sentjurı] n Jahrhundert nt

ceramic [sı'ræmık] adj keramisch; **~s** npl
Keramiken pl

cereal ['siːrəl] n (grain) Getreide nt; (at
breakfast) Getreideflocken pl

cerebral ['serıbrəl] adj zerebral; (intellectual)
geistig

ceremony ['serımənı] n Zeremonie f; **to**

stand on ~ förmlich sein
certain ['sə:tən] *adj* sicher; (*particular*)
gewiss; **for ~** ganz bestimmt; **~ly** *adv*
sicher, bestimmt; **~ty** *n* Gewissheit *f*
certificate [sə'tɪfɪkɪt] *n* Bescheinigung *f*;
(*SCH etc*) Zeugnis *nt*
certified mail ['sə:tɪfaɪd-] (*US*) *n*
Einschreiben *nt*
certified public accountant ['sə:tɪfaɪd-]
(*US*) *n* geprüfte(r) Buchhalter *m*
certify ['sə:tɪfaɪ] *vt* bescheinigen
cervical ['sə:vɪkl] *adj* (*smear, cancer*)
Gebärmutterhals-
cervix ['sə:vɪks] *n* Gebärmutterhals *m*
cf. *abbr* (= *compare*) vgl.
CFC *n* *abbr* (= *chlorofluorocarbon*) FCKW *m*
ch. *abbr* (= *chapter*) Kap.
chafe [tʃeɪf] *vt* scheuern
chaffinch ['tʃæfɪntʃ] *n* Buchfink *m*
chain [tʃeɪn] *n* Kette *f* ♦ *vt* (*also: ~ up*)
anketten; **~ reaction** *n* Kettenreaktion *f*;
~-smoke *vi* kettenrauchen; **~ store** *n*
Kettenladen *m*
chair [tʃeə'] *n* Stuhl *m*; (*armchair*) Sessel *m*;
(*UNIV*) Lehrstuhl *m* ♦ *vt* (*meeting*) den
Vorsitz führen bei; **~lift** *n* Sessellift *m*;
~man (*irreg*) *n* Vorsitzende(r) *m*
chalet ['ʃæleɪ] *n* Chalet *nt*
chalk [tʃɔ:k] *n* Kreide *f*
challenge ['tʃælɪndʒ] *n* Herausforderung *f*
♦ *vt* herausfordern; (*contest*) bestreiten;
challenging *adj* (*tone*) herausfordernd;
(*work*) anspruchsvoll
chamber ['tʃeɪmbə'] *n* Kammer *f*; **~ of**
commerce Handelskammer *f*; **~maid** *n*
Zimmermädchen *nt*; **~ music** *n*
Kammermusik *f*
chamois ['ʃæmwɑ:] *n* Gämse *f*
champagne [ʃæm'peɪn] *n* Champagner *m*,
Sekt *m*
champion ['tʃæmpɪən] *n* (*SPORT*) Meister(in)
m(f); (*of cause*) Verfechter(in) *m(f)*; **~ship** *n*
Meisterschaft *f*
chance [tʃɑ:ns] *n* (*luck*) Zufall *m*; (*possibility*)
Möglichkeit *f*; (*opportunity*) Gelegenheit *f*,
Chance *f*; (*risk*) Risiko *nt* ♦ *adj* zufällig ♦ *vt*:
to ~ it es darauf ankommen lassen; **by ~**

zufällig; **to take a ~** ein Risiko eingehen
chancellor ['tʃɑ:nsələ'] *n* Kanzler *m*; **C~ of**
the Exchequer (*BRIT*) *n* Schatzkanzler *m*
chandelier [ʃændə'lɪə'] *n* Kronleuchter *m*
change [tʃeɪndʒ] *vt* ändern; (*replace, COMM:*
money) wechseln; (*exchange*) umtauschen;
(*transform*) verwandeln ♦ *vi* sich ändern; (*~*
trains) umsteigen; (*~ clothes*) sich umziehen
♦ *n* Veränderung *f*; (*money returned*)
Wechselgeld *nt*; (*coins*) Kleingeld *nt*; **to ~**
one's mind es sich *dat* anders überlegen;
to ~ into sth (*be transformed*) sich in etw
acc verwandeln; **for a ~** zur Abwechslung;
~able *adj* (*weather*) wechselhaft; **~**
machine *n* Geldwechselautomat *m*;
~over *n* Umstellung *f*
changing ['tʃeɪndʒɪŋ] *adj* veränderlich; **~**
room (*BRIT*) *n* Umkleideraum *m*
channel ['tʃænl] *n* (*stream*) Bachbett *nt*;
(*NAUT*) Straße *f*; (*TV*) Kanal *m*; (*fig*) Weg *m*
♦ *vt* (*efforts*) lenken; **the (English) C~** der
Ärmelkanal; **~-hopping** *n* (*TV*) ständiges
Umschalten; **C~ Islands** *npl*: **the C~**
Islands die Kanalinseln *pl*; **C~ Tunnel** *n*:
the C~ Tunnel der Kanaltunnel
chant [tʃɑ:nt] *n* Gesang *m*; (*of fans*)
Sprechchor *m* ♦ *vt* intonieren
chaos ['keɪɒs] *n* Chaos *nt*
chap [tʃæp] (*inf*) *n* Kerl *m*
chapel ['tʃæpl] *n* Kapelle *f*
chaperon ['ʃæpərəʊn] *n* Anstandsdame *f*
chaplain ['tʃæplɪn] *n* Kaplan *m*
chapped [tʃæpt] *adj* (*skin, lips*) spröde
chapter ['tʃæptə'] *n* Kapitel *nt*
char [tʃɑ:'] *vt* (*burn*) verkohlen
character ['kærɪktə'] *n* Charakter *m*, Wesen
nt; (*in novel, film*) Figur *f*; **~istic**
[kærɪktə'rɪstɪk] *adj*: **~istic (of sb/sth)** (für
jdn/etw) charakteristisch ♦ *n* Kennzeichen
nt; **~ize** *vt* charakterisieren, kennzeichnen
charade [ʃə'rɑ:d] *n* Scharade *f*
charcoal ['tʃɑ:kəʊl] *n* Holzkohle *f*
charge [tʃɑ:dʒ] *n* (*cost*) Preis *m*; (*JUR*)
Anklage *f*; (*explosive*) Ladung *f*; (*attack*)
Angriff *m* ♦ *vt* (*gun, battery*) laden; (*price*)
verlangen; (*JUR*) anklagen; (*MIL*) angreifen
♦ *vi* (*rush*) (an)stürmen; **bank ~s**

Bankgebühren *pl*; **free of ~** kostenlos; **to reverse the ~s** (*TEL*) ein R-Gespräch führen; **to be in ~ of** verantwortlich sein für; **to take ~** (die Verantwortung) übernehmen; **to ~ sth (up) to sb's account** jdm etw in Rechnung stellen; **~ card** *n* Kundenkarte *f*

charitable ['tʃærɪtəbl] *adj* wohltätig; (*lenient*) nachsichtig

charity ['tʃærɪtɪ] *n* (*institution*) Hilfswerk *nt*; (*attitude*) Nächstenliebe *f*

charm [tʃɑːm] *n* Charme *m*; (*spell*) Bann *m*; (*object*) Tallsman *m* ♦ *vt* bezaubern; **~ing** *adj* reizend

chart [tʃɑːt] *n* Tabelle *f*; (*NAUT*) Seekarte *f* ♦ *vt* (*course*) abstecken

charter ['tʃɑːtəʳ] *vt* chartern ♦ *n* Schutzbrief *m*; **~ed accountant** *n* Wirtschafts- prüfer(in) *m(f)*; **~ flight** *n* Charter- flug *m*

chase [tʃeɪs] *vt* jagen, verfolgen ♦ *n* Jagd *f*

chasm ['kæzəm] *n* Kluft *f*

chassis ['ʃæsɪ] *n* Fahrgestell *nt*

chat [tʃæt] *vi* (*also*: **have a ~**) plaudern ♦ *n* Plauderei *f*; **~ show** (*BRIT*) *n* Talkshow *f*

chatter ['tʃætəʳ] *vi* schwatzen, (*teeth*) klappern ♦ *n* Geschwätz *nt*; **~box** *n* Quasselstrippe *f*

chatty ['tʃætɪ] *adj* geschwätzig

chauffeur ['ʃəufəʳ] *n* Chauffeur *m*

chauvinist ['ʃəuvɪnɪst] *n* (*male ~*) Chauvi *m* (*inf*)

cheap [tʃiːp] *adj, adv* billig; **~ day return** *n* Tagesrückfahrkarte *f* (*zu einem günstigeren Tarif*); **~ly** *adv* billig

cheat [tʃiːt] *vt, vi* betrügen; (*SCH*) mogeln ♦ *n* Betrüger(in) *m(f)*

check [tʃɛk] *vt* (*examine*) prüfen; (*make sure*) nachsehen; (*control*) kontrollieren; (*restrain*) zügeln; (*stop*) anhalten ♦ *n* (*examination, restraint*) Kontrolle *f*; (*bill*) Rechnung *f*; (*pattern*) Karo(muster) *nt*; (*US*) = **cheque** ♦ *adj* (*pattern, cloth*) kariert; **~ in** *vi* (*in hotel, airport*) einchecken ♦ *vt* (*luggage*) abfertigen lassen; **~ out** *vi* (*of hotel*) abreisen; **~ up** *vi* nachschauen; **~ up on** *vt* kontrollieren; **~ered** (*US*) *adj* =

chequered; **~ers** (*US*) *n* (*draughts*) Damespiel *nt*; **~-in (desk)** *n* Abfertigung *f*; **~ing account** (*US*) *n* (*current account*) Girokonto *nt*; **~mate** *n* Schachmatt *nt*; **~out** *n* Kasse *f*; **~point** *n* Kontrollpunkt *m*; **~ room** (*US*) *n* (*left-luggage office*) Gepäckaufbewahrung *f*; **~up** *n* (Nach)prüfung *f*; (*MED*) (ärztliche) Untersuchung *f*

cheek [tʃiːk] *n* Backe *f*; (*fig*) Frechheit *f*; **~bone** *n* Backenknochen *m*; **~y** *adj* frech

cheep [tʃiːp] *vi* piepsen

cheer [tʃɪəʳ] *n* (*usu pl*) Hurra- or Beifallsruf *m* ♦ *vt* zujubeln; (*encourage*) aufmuntern ♦ *vi* jauchzen; **~s!** Prost!; **~ up** *vi* bessere Laune bekommen ♦ *vt* aufmuntern; **~ up!** nun lach doch mal!; **~ful** *adj* fröhlich

cheerio [tʃɪərɪ'əu] (*BRIT*) *excl* tschüss!

cheese [tʃiːz] *n* Käse *m*; **~board** *n* (gemischte) Käseplatte *f*

cheetah ['tʃiːtə] *n* Gepard *m*

chef [ʃɛf] *n* Küchenchef *m*

chemical ['kemɪkl] *adj* chemisch ♦ *n* Chemikalie *f*

chemist ['kemɪst] *n* (*BRIT: pharmacist*) Apotheker *m*, Drogist *m*; (*scientist*) Chemiker *m*; **~ry** *n* Chemie *f*; **~'s (shop)** (*BRIT*) *n* Apotheke *f*, Drogerie *f*

cheque [tʃɛk] (*BRIT*) *n* Scheck *m*; **~book** *n* Scheckbuch *nt*; **~ card** *n* Scheckkarte *f*

chequered ['tʃɛkəd] *adj* (*fig*) bewegt

cherish ['tʃerɪʃ] *vt* (*person*) lieben; (*hope*) hegen

cherry ['tʃerɪ] *n* Kirsche *f*

chess [tʃɛs] *n* Schach *nt*; **~board** *n* Schachbrett *nt*; **~man** (*irreg*) *n* Schachfigur *f*

chest [tʃɛst] *n* (*ANAT*) Brust *f*; (*box*) Kiste *f*; **~ of drawers** Kommode *f*

chestnut ['tʃesnʌt] *n* Kastanie *f*

chew [tʃuː] *vt, vi* kauen; **~ing gum** *n* Kaugummi *m*

chic [ʃiːk] *adj* schick, elegant

chick [tʃɪk] *n* Küken *nt*; (*US: inf: girl*) Biene *f*

chicken ['tʃɪkɪn] *n* Huhn *nt*; (*food*) Hähnchen *nt*; **~ out** (*inf*) *vi* knelfen

chickenpox ['tʃɪkɪnpɔks] *n* Windpocken *pl*

chicory ['tʃɪkəri] n (in coffee) Zichorie f; (plant) Chicorée f, Schikoree f

chief [tʃiːf] n (of tribe) Häuptling m; (COMM) Chef m ♦ adj Haupt-; ~ **executive** n Geschäftsführer(in) m(f); **~ly** adv hauptsächlich

chilblain ['tʃɪlbleɪn] n Frostbeule f

child [tʃaɪld] (pl **~ren**) n Kind nt; **~birth** n Entbindung f; **~hood** n Kindheit f; **~ish** adj kindisch; **~like** adj kindlich; **~ minder** (BRIT) n Tagesmutter f; **~ren** ['tʃɪldrən] npl of **child**; ~ **seat** n Kindersitz m

Chile ['tʃɪli] n Chile nt; **~an** adj chilenisch

chill [tʃɪl] n Kühle f; (MED) Erkältung f ♦ vt (CULIN) kühlen

chilli ['tʃɪli] n Peperoni pl; (meal, spice) Chili m

chilly ['tʃɪli] adj kühl, frostig

chime [tʃaɪm] n Geläut nt ♦ vi ertönen

chimney ['tʃɪmni] n Schornstein m; ~ **sweep** n Schornsteinfeger(in) m(f)

chimpanzee [tʃɪmpæn'ziː] n Schimpanse m

chin [tʃɪn] n Kinn nt

China ['tʃaɪnə] n China nt

china ['tʃaɪnə] n Porzellan nt

Chinese [tʃaɪ'niːz] adj chinesisch ♦ n (inv) Chinese m, Chinesin f; (LING) Chinesisch nt

chink [tʃɪŋk] n (opening) Ritze f; (noise) Klirren n

chip [tʃɪp] n (of wood etc) Splitter m; (in poker etc; US: crisp) Chip m ♦ vt absplittern; **~s** npl (BRIT: COOK) Pommes frites pl; ~ **in** vi Zwischenbemerkungen machen

---

Chip shop

ⓘ **Chip shop**, auch *fish-and-chip shop*, ist die traditionelle britische Imbissbude, in der vor allem fritierte Fischfilets und Pommes frites, aber auch andere einfache Mahlzeiten angeboten werden. Früher wurde das Essen zum Mitnehmen in Zeitungspapier verpackt. Manche chip shops haben auch einen Essraum.

---

chiropodist [kɪ'rɔpədɪst] (BRIT) n Fußpfleger(in) m(f)

chirp [tʃəːp] vi zwitschern

chisel ['tʃɪzl] n Meißel m

chit [tʃɪt] n Notiz f

chivalrous ['ʃɪvəlrəs] adj ritterlich; **chivalry** ['ʃɪvəlrɪ] n Ritterlichkeit f

chives [tʃaɪvz] npl Schnittlauch m

chlorine ['klɔːriːn] n Chlor nt

chock-a-block ['tʃɔkə'blɔk] adj voll gepfropft

chock-full [tʃɔk'ful] adj voll gepfropft

chocolate ['tʃɔklɪt] n Schokolade f

choice [tʃɔɪs] n Wahl f; (of goods) Auswahl f ♦ adj Qualitäts-

choir ['kwaɪə'] n Chor m; **~boy** n Chorknabe m

choke [tʃəuk] vi ersticken ♦ vt erdrosseln; (block) (ab)drosseln ♦ n (AUT) Starterklappe f

cholera ['kɔlərə] n Cholera f

cholesterol [kə'lestərɔl] n Cholesterin nt

choose [tʃuːz] (pt **chose**, pp **chosen**) vt wählen; **choosy** ['tʃuːzɪ] adj wählerisch

chop [tʃɔp] vt (wood) spalten; (COOK: also: ~ up) (zer)hacken ♦ n Hieb m; (COOK) Kotelett nt; **~s** npl (jaws) Lefzen pl

chopper ['tʃɔpə'] n (helicopter) Hubschrauber m

choppy ['tʃɔpɪ] adj (sea) bewegt

chopsticks ['tʃɔpstɪks] npl (Ess)stäbchen pl

choral ['kɔːrəl] adj Chor-

chord [kɔːd] n Akkord m

chore [tʃɔːʳ] n Pflicht f; **~s** npl (housework) Hausarbeit f

choreographer [kɔrɪ'ɔgrəfəʳ] n Choreograf(in) m(f)

chorister ['kɔrɪstəʳ] n Chorsänger(in) m(f)

chortle ['tʃɔːtl] vi glucksen

chorus ['kɔːrəs] n Chor m; (in song) Refrain m

chose [tʃəuz] pt of **choose**

chosen ['tʃəuzn] pp of **choose**

chowder ['tʃaudəʳ] (US) n sämige Fischsuppe f

Christ [kraɪst] n Christus m

christen ['krɪsn] vt taufen; **~ing** n Taufe f

Christian ['krɪstɪən] adj christlich ♦ n Christ(in) m(f); **~ity** [krɪstɪ'ænɪtɪ] n Christentum nt; ~ **name** n Vorname m

Christmas ['krɪsməs] n Weihnachten pl;
Happy or Merry ~! frohe or fröhliche
Weihnachten!; ~ card n Weihnachtskarte f;
~ Day n der erste Weihnachtstag; ~ Eve n
Heiligabend m; ~ tree n Weihnachtsbaum
m

chrome [krəʊm] n Verchromung f

chromium ['krəʊmɪəm] n Chrom nt

chronic ['krɒnɪk] adj chronisch

chronicle ['krɒnɪkl] n Chronik f

chronological [krɒnə'lɒdʒɪkl] adj
chronologisch

chubby ['tʃʌbɪ] adj rundlich

chuck [tʃʌk] vt werfen; (BRIT: also: ~ up)
hinwerfen; ~ out vt (person) rauswerfen;
(old clothes etc) wegwerfen

chuckle ['tʃʌkl] vi in sich hineinlachen

chug [tʃʌg] vi tuckern

chunk [tʃʌŋk] n Klumpen m; (of food)
Brocken m

church [tʃɜːtʃ] n Kirche f; ~yard n Kirchhof
m

churn [tʃɜːn] n (for butter) Butterfass nt; (for
milk) Milchkanne f; ~ out (inf) vt
produzieren

chute [ʃuːt] n Rutsche f; (rubbish ~)
Müllschlucker m

chutney ['tʃʌtnɪ] n Chutney nt

CIA (US) n abbr (= Central Intelligence Agency)
CIA m

CID (BRIT) n abbr (= Criminal Investigation
Department) ≈ Kripo f

cider ['saɪdə*] n Apfelwein m

cigar [sɪ'gɑː*] n Zigarre f

cigarette [sɪgə'ret] n Zigarette f; ~ case n
Zigarettenetui nt; ~ end n
Zigarettenstummel m

Cinderella [sɪndə'relə] n Aschenbrödel nt

cinders ['sɪndəz] npl Asche f

cine camera ['sɪnɪ-] (BRIT) n Filmkamera f

cine film (BRIT) n Schmalfilm m

cinema ['sɪnəmə] n Kino nt

cinnamon ['sɪnəmən] n Zimt m

circle ['sɜːkl] n Kreis m; (in cinema etc) Rang
m ♦ vi kreisen ♦ vt (surround) umgeben;
(move round) kreisen um

circuit ['sɜːkɪt] n (track) Rennbahn f; (lap)

Runde f; (ELEC) Stromkreis m

circular ['sɜːkjʊlə*] adj rund ♦ n
Rundschreiben nt

circulate ['sɜːkjʊleɪt] vi zirkulieren ♦ vt in
Umlauf setzen; circulation [sɜːkjʊ'leɪʃən] n
(of blood) Kreislauf m; (of newspaper) Auflage
f; (of money) Umlauf m

circumcise ['sɜːkəmsaɪz] vt beschneiden

circumference [sə'kʌmfərəns] n
(Kreis)umfang m

circumspect ['sɜːkəmspekt] adj umsichtig

circumstances ['sɜːkəmstənsɪz] npl
Umstände pl; (financial) Verhältnisse pl

circumvent [sɜːkəm'vent] vt umgehen

circus ['sɜːkəs] n Zirkus m

CIS n abbr (= Commonwealth of Independent
States) GUS f

cistern ['sɪstən] n Zisterne f; (of W.C.)
Spülkasten m

cite [saɪt] vt zitieren, anführen

citizen ['sɪtɪzn] n Bürger(in) m(f); ~ship n
Staatsbürgerschaft f

citrus fruit ['sɪtrəs-] n Zitrusfrucht f

city ['sɪtɪ] n Großstadt f; the C~ die City, das
Finanzzentrum Londons

city technology college n ≈ Technische
Fachschule f

civic ['sɪvɪk] adj (of town) städtisch; (of citizen)
Bürger-; ~ centre (BRIT) n Stadtverwaltung
f

civil ['sɪvɪl] adj bürgerlich; (not military) zivil;
(polite) höflich; ~ engineer n Bauingenieur
m; ~ian [sɪ'vɪlɪən] n Zivilperson f ♦ adj zivil,
Zivil-

civilization [sɪvɪlaɪ'zeɪʃən] n Zivilisation f

civilized ['sɪvɪlaɪzd] adj zivilisiert

civil: ~ law n Zivilrecht nt; ~ servant n
Staatsbeamte(r) m; C~ Service n
Staatsdienst m; ~ war n Bürgerkrieg m

clad [klæd] adj: ~ in gehüllt in +acc

claim [kleɪm] vt beanspruchen; (have opinion)
behaupten ♦ vi (for insurance) Anspruch
geltend machen ♦ n (demand) Forderung f;
(right) Anspruch m; (pretension) Behauptung
f; ~ant n Antragsteller(in) m(f)

clairvoyant [kleə'vɔɪənt] n Hellseher(in) m(f)

clam [klæm] n Venusmuschel f

clamber ['klæmbər] vi kraxeln

clammy ['klæmɪ] adj klamm

clamour ['klæmər] vi: **to ~ for sth** nach etw verlangen

clamp [klæmp] n Schraubzwinge f ♦ vt einspannen; (AUT: wheel) krallen; **~ down on** vt fus Maßnahmen ergreifen gegen

clan [klæn] n Clan m

clandestine [klæn'destɪn] adj geheim

clang [klæŋ] vi scheppern

clap [klæp] vi klatschen ♦ vt Beifall klatschen +dat ♦ n (of hands) Klatschen nt; (of thunder) Donnerschlag m; **~ping** n Klatschen nt

claret ['klærət] n rote(r) Bordeaux(wein) m

clarify ['klærɪfaɪ] vt klären, erklären

clarinet [klærɪ'net] n Klarinette f

clarity ['klærɪtɪ] n Klarheit f

clash [klæʃ] n (fig) Konflikt m ♦ vi zusammenprallen; (colours) sich beißen; (argue) sich streiten

clasp [klɑːsp] n Griff m; (on jewels, bag) Verschluss m ♦ vt umklammern

class [klɑːs] n Klasse f ♦ vt einordnen; **~-conscious** adj klassenbewusst

classic ['klæsɪk] n Klassiker m ♦ adj klassisch; **~al** adj klassisch

classified ['klæsɪfaɪd] adj (information) Geheim-; **~ advertisement** n Kleinanzeige f

classify ['klæsɪfaɪ] vt klassifizieren

classmate ['klɑːsmeɪt] n Klassenkamerad(in) m(f)

classroom ['klɑːsrum] n Klassenzimmer nt

clatter ['klætər] vi klappern; (feet) trappeln

clause [klɔːz] n (JUR) Klausel f; (GRAM) Satz m

claustrophobia [klɔːstrə'fəubɪə] n Platzangst f

claw [klɔː] n Kralle f ♦ vt (zer)kratzen

clay [kleɪ] n Lehm m; (for pots) Ton m

clean [kliːn] adj sauber ♦ vt putzen; (clothes) reinigen; **~ out** vt gründlich putzen; **~ up** vt aufräumen; **~-cut** adj (person) adrett; (clear) klar; **~er** n (person) Putzfrau f; **~er's** n (also: **dry ~er's**) Reinigung f; **~ing** n Putzen m; (clothes) Reinigung f; **~liness** ['klenlɪnɪs] n Reinlichkeit f

cleanse [klenz] vt reinigen; **~r** n (for face) Reinigungsmilch f

clean-shaven ['kliːn'ʃeɪvn] adj glatt rasiert

cleansing department ['klenzɪŋ-] (BRIT) n Stadtreinigung f

clear [klɪər] adj klar; (road) frei ♦ vt (road etc) freimachen; (obstacle) beseitigen; (JUR: suspect) freisprechen ♦ vi klar werden; (fog) sich lichten ♦ adv: **~ of** von ... entfernt; **to ~ the table** den Tisch abräumen; **~ up** vt aufräumen; (solve) aufklären; **~ance** ['klɪərəns] n (removal) Räumung f; (free space) Lichtung f; (permission) Freigabe f; **~-cut** adj (case) eindeutig; **~ing** n Lichtung f; **~ing bank** (BRIT) n Clearingbank f; **~ly** adv klar; (obviously) eindeutig; **~way** (BRIT) n (Straße f mit) Halteverbot nt

cleaver ['kliːvər] n Hackbeil f

cleft [kleft] n (in rock) Spalte f

clementine ['kleməntaɪn] n (fruit) Klementine f

clench [klentʃ] vt (teeth) zusammenbeißen; (fist) ballen

clergy ['klɜːdʒɪ] n Geistliche(n) pl; **~man** (irreg) n Geistliche(r) m

clerical ['klerɪkl] adj (office) Schreib-, Büro-; (REL) geistlich

clerk [klɑːk, (US) klɜːrk] n (in office) Büroangestellte(r) mf; (US: sales person) Verkäufer(in) m(f)

clever ['klevər] adj klug; (crafty) schlau

cliché ['kliːʃeɪ] n Klischee nt

click [klɪk] vt (tongue) schnalzen mit; (heels) zusammenklappen; **~ on** vt (COMPUT) anklicken

client ['klaɪənt] n Klient(in) m(f); **~ele** [kliːɑ̃ːn'tel] n Kundschaft f

cliff [klɪf] n Klippe f

climate ['klaɪmɪt] n Klima nt

climax ['klaɪmæks] n Höhepunkt m

climb [klaɪm] vt besteigen ♦ vi steigen, klettern ♦ n Aufstieg m; **~-down** n Abstieg m; **~er** n Bergsteiger(in) m(f); **~ing** n Bergsteigen nt

clinch [klɪntʃ] vt (decide) entscheiden; (deal) festmachen

cling [klɪŋ] (pt, pp **clung**) vi (clothes) eng anliegen; **to ~ to** sich festklammern an +dat

clinic ['klɪnɪk] n Klinik f; **~al** adj klinisch

clink [klɪŋk] vi klimpern

clip [klɪp] n Spange f; (also: **paper ~**) Klammer f ♦ vt (papers) heften; (hair, hedge) stutzen; **~pers** npl (for hedge) Heckenschere f; (for hair) Haarschneidemaschine f; **~ping** n Ausschnitt m

cloak [kləuk] n Umhang m ♦ vt hüllen; **~room** n (for coats) Garderobe f; (BRIT: W.C.) Toilette f

clock [klɔk] n Uhr f; **~ in** or **on** vi stempeln; **~ off** or **out** vi stempeln; **~wise** adv im Uhrzeigersinn; **~work** n Uhrwerk nt ♦ adj zum Aufziehen

clog [klɔg] n Holzschuh m ♦ vt verstopfen

cloister ['klɔɪstə*] n Kreuzgang m

clone [kləun] n Klon m ♦ vt klonen

close¹ [kləus] adj (near) in der Nähe; (friend, connection, print) eng; (relative) nahe; (result) knapp; (examination) eingehend; (weather) schwül; (room) stickig ♦ adv nahe, dicht; **~ by** in der Nähe; **~ at hand** in der Nähe; **to have a ~ shave** (fig) mit knapper Not davonkommen

close² [kləuz] vt (shut) schließen; (end) beenden ♦ vi (shop etc) schließen; (door etc) sich schließen ♦ n Ende nt; **~ down** vi schließen; **~d** adj (shop etc) geschlossen; **~d shop** n Gewerkschaftszwang m

close-knit ['kləus'nɪt] adj eng zusammengewachsen

closely ['kləuslɪ] adv eng; (carefully) genau

closet ['klɔzɪt] n Schrank m

close-up ['kləusʌp] n Nahaufnahme f

closure ['kləuʒə*] n Schließung f

clot [klɔt] n (of blood) Blutgerinnsel nt; (fool) Blödmann m ♦ vi gerinnen

cloth [klɔθ] n (material) Tuch nt; (rag) Lappen m

clothe [kləuð] vt kleiden

clothes [kləuðz] npl Kleider pl; **~ brush** n Kleiderbürste f; **~ line** n Wäscheleine f; **~ peg**, **~ pin** (US) n Wäscheklammer f

clothing ['kləuðɪŋ] n Kleidung f

clotted cream ['klɔtɪd-] (BRIT) n Sahne aus erhitzter Milch

cloud [klaud] n Wolke f; **~burst** n Wolkenbruch m; **~y** adj bewölkt; (liquid) trüb

clout [klaut] vt hauen

clove [kləuv] n Gewürznelke f; **~ of garlic** Knoblauchzehe f

clover ['kləuvə*] n Klee m

clown [klaun] n Clown m ♦ vi (also: **~ about**, **~ around**) kaspern

cloying ['klɔɪɪŋ] adj (taste, smell) übersüß

club [klʌb] n (weapon) Knüppel m; (society) Klub m; (also: **golf ~**) Golfschläger m ♦ vt prügeln ♦ vi: **to ~ together** zusammenlegen; **~s** npl (CARDS) Kreuz nt; **~ car** (US) n (RAIL) Speisewagen m; **~ class** n (AVIAT) Club-Klasse f; **~house** n Klubhaus nt

cluck [klʌk] vi glucken

clue [klu:] n Anhaltspunkt m; (in crosswords) Frage f; **I haven't a ~** (ich hab) keine Ahnung

clump [klʌmp] n Gruppe f

clumsy ['klʌmzɪ] adj (person) unbeholfen; (shape) unförmig

clung [klʌŋ] pt, pp of **cling**

cluster ['klʌstə*] n (of trees etc) Gruppe f ♦ vi sich drängen, sich scharen

clutch [klʌtʃ] n Griff m; (AUT) Kupplung f ♦ vt sich festklammern an +dat

clutter ['klʌtə*] vt voll pfropfen; (desk) übersäen

CND n abbr = **Campaign for Nuclear Disarmament**

Co. abbr = **county**; **company**

c/o abbr (= care of) c/o

coach [kəutʃ] n (bus) Reisebus m; (horse-drawn) Kutsche f; (RAIL) (Personen)wagen m; (trainer) Trainer m ♦ vt (SCH) Nachhilfeunterricht geben +dat; (SPORT) trainieren; **~ trip** n Busfahrt f

coal [kəul] n Kohle f; **~ face** n Streb m

coalition [kəuə'lɪʃən] n Koalition f

coalman ['kəulmən] (irreg) n Kohlenhändler m

coal mine n Kohlenbergwerk nt

coarse [kɔ:s] adj grob; (fig) ordinär

coast [kəust] n Küste f ♦ vi dahinrollen; (AUT) im Leerlauf fahren; **~al** adj Küsten-;

~guard n Küstenwache f; **~line** n Küste(nlinie) f

coat [kəut] n Mantel m; (on animals) Fell nt; (of paint) Schicht f ♦ vt überstreichen; **~hanger** n Kleiderbügel m; **~ing** n Überzug m; (of paint) Schicht f; **~ of arms** n Wappen nt

coax [kəuks] vt beschwatzen

cob [kɔb] n see **corn**

cobbler ['kɔblə'] n Schuster m

cobbles ['kɔblz] npl Pflastersteine pl

cobweb ['kɔbweb] n Spinnennetz nt

cocaine [kə'keɪn] n Kokain nt

cock [kɔk] n Hahn m ♦ vt (gun) entsichern; **~erel** ['kɔkərl] n junge(r) Hahn m; **~eyed** adj (fig) verrückt

cockle ['kɔkl] n Herzmuschel f

cockney ['kɔknɪ] n echte(r) Londoner m

cockpit ['kɔkpɪt] n (AVIAT) Pilotenkanzel f

cockroach ['kɔkrəutʃ] n Küchenschabe f

cocktail ['kɔkteɪl] n Cocktail m; **~ cabinet** n Hausbar f; **~ party** n Cocktailparty f

cocoa ['kəukəu] n Kakao m

coconut ['kəukənʌt] n Kokosnuss f

cocoon [kə'ku:n] n Kokon m

cod [kɔd] n Kabeljau m

C.O.D. abbr = **cash on delivery**

code [kəud] n Kode m; (JUR) Kodex m

cod-liver oil ['kɔdlɪvə-] n Lebertran m

coercion [kəu'ə:ʃən] n Zwang m

coffee ['kɔfɪ] n Kaffee m; **~ bar** (BRIT) n Café nt; **~ bean** n Kaffeebohne f; **~ break** n Kaffeepause f; **~pot** n Kaffeekanne f; **~ table** n Couchtisch m

coffin ['kɔfɪn] n Sarg m

cog [kɔg] n (Rad)zahn m

cognac ['kɔnjæk] n Kognak m

coherent [kəu'hɪərənt] adj zusammenhängend; (person) verständlich

coil [kɔɪl] n Rolle f; (ELEC) Spule f; (contraceptive) Spirale f ♦ vt aufwickeln

coin [kɔɪn] n Münze f ♦ vt prägen; **~age** ['kɔɪnɪdʒ] n (word) Prägung f; **~ box** (BRIT) n Münzfernsprecher m

coincide [kəuɪn'saɪd] vi (happen together) zusammenfallen; (agree) übereinstimmen; **~nce** [kəu'ɪnsɪdəns] n Zufall m

coinphone ['kɔɪnfəun] n Münzfernsprecher m

Coke [kəuk] ® n (drink) Coca-Cola ® f

coke [kəuk] n Koks m

colander ['kɔləndə'] n Durchschlag m

cold [kəuld] adj kalt ♦ n Kälte f; (MED) Erkältung f; **I'm ~** mir ist kalt; **to catch ~** sich erkälten; **in ~ blood** kaltblütig; **to give sb the ~ shoulder** jdm die kalte Schulter zeigen; **~ly** adv kalt; **~-shoulder** vt die kalte Schulter zeigen +dat; **~ sore** n Erkältungsbläschen nt

coleslaw ['kəulslɔ:] n Krautsalat m

colic ['kɔlɪk] n Kolik f

collaborate [kə'læbəreɪt] vi zusammenarbeiten

collapse [kə'læps] vi (people) zusammenbrechen; (things) einstürzen ♦ n Zusammenbruch m; Einsturz m; **collapsible** adj zusammenklappbar, Klapp-

collar ['kɔlə'] n Kragen m; **~bone** n Schlüsselbein nt

collateral [kə'lætərl] n (zusätzliche) Sicherheit f

colleague ['kɔli:g] n Kollege m, Kollegin f

collect [kə'lekt] vt sammeln; (BRIT: call and pick up) abholen ♦ vi sich sammeln ♦ adv: **to call ~** (US: TEL) ein R-Gespräch führen; **~ion** [kə'lekʃən] n Sammlung f; (REL) Kollekte f; (of post) Leerung f; **~ive** [kə'lektɪv] adj gemeinsam; (POL) kollektiv; **~or** [kə'lektə'] n Sammler m; (tax ~or) (Steuer)einnehmer m

college ['kɔlɪdʒ] n (UNIV) College nt; (TECH) Fach-, Berufsschule f

collide [kə'laɪd] vi zusammenstoßen

collie ['kɔlɪ] n Collie m

colliery ['kɔlɪərɪ] (BRIT) n Zeche f

collision [kə'lɪʒən] n Zusammenstoß m

colloquial [kə'ləukwɪəl] adj umgangssprachlich

colon ['kəulən] n Doppelpunkt m; (MED) Dickdarm m

colonel ['kə:nl] n Oberst m

colonial [kə'ləunɪəl] adj Kolonial-

colonize ['kɔlənaɪz] vt kolonisieren

colony ['kɒlənɪ] n Kolonie f

colour ['kʌləʳ] (US **color**) n Farbe f ♦ vt (also fig) färben ♦ vi sich verfärben; ~**s** npl (of club) Fahne f; ~ **bar** n Rassenschranke f; ~**blind** adj farbenblind; ~**ed** adj farbig; ~ **film** n Farbfilm m; ~**ful** adj bunt; (personality) schillernd; ~**ing** n (complexion) Gesichtsfarbe f; (substance) Farbstoff m; ~ **scheme** n Farbgebung f; ~ **television** n Farbfernsehen nt

colt [kəʊlt] n Fohlen nt

column ['kɒləm] n Säule f; (MIL) Kolonne f; (of print) Spalte f; ~**ist** ['kɒləmnɪst] n Kolumnist m

coma ['kəʊmə] n Koma nt

comb [kəʊm] n Kamm m ♦ vt kämmen; (search) durchkämmen

combat ['kɒmbæt] n Kampf m ♦ vt bekämpfen

combination [kɒmbɪ'neɪʃən] n Kombination f

combine [vb kəm'baɪn, n 'kɒmbaɪn] vt verbinden ♦ vi sich vereinigen ♦ n (COMM) Konzern m; ~ (**harvester**) n Mähdrescher m

combustion [kəm'bʌstʃən] n Verbrennung f

come [kʌm] (pt **came**, pp **come**) vi kommen; **to ~ undone** aufgehen; ~ **about** vi geschehen; ~ **across** vt fus (find) stoßen auf +acc; ~ **away** vi (person) weggehen; (handle etc) abgehen; ~ **back** vi zurückkommen; ~ **by** vt fus (find): **to ~ by sth** zu etw kommen; ~ **down** vi (price) fallen; ~ **forward** vi (volunteer) sich melden; ~ **from** vt fus (result) kommen von; **where do you ~ from?** wo kommen Sie her?; **I ~ from London** ich komme aus London; ~ **in** vi hereinkommen; (train) einfahren; ~ **in for** vt fus abkriegen; ~ **into** vt fus (inherit) erben; ~ **off** vi (handle) abgehen; (succeed) klappen; ~ **on** vi (progress) vorankommen; ~ **on!** komm!; (hurry) beeil dich!; ~ **out** vi herauskommen; ~ **round** vi (MED) wieder zu sich kommen; ~ **to** vi (MED) wieder zu sich kommen ♦ vt fus (bill) sich belaufen auf +acc; ~ **up** vi hochkommen; (sun)

aufgehen; (problem) auftauchen; ~ **up against** vt fus (resistance, difficulties) stoßen auf +acc; ~ **upon** vt fus stoßen auf +acc; ~ **up with** vt fus sich einfallen lassen

comedian [kə'miːdɪən] n Komiker m; **comedienne** [kəmiːdɪ'ɛn] n Komikerin f

comedown ['kʌmdaʊn] n Abstieg m

comedy ['kɒmɪdɪ] n Komödie f

comet ['kɒmɪt] n Komet m

comeuppance [kʌm'ʌpəns] n: **to get one's ~** seine Quittung bekommen

comfort ['kʌmfət] n Komfort m; (consolation) Trost m ♦ vt trösten; ~**able** adj bequem; ~**ably** adv (sit etc) bequem; (live) angenehm; ~ **station** (US) n öffentliche Toilette f

comic ['kɒmɪk] n Comic(heft) nt; (comedian) Komiker m ♦ adj (also: ~**al**) komisch; ~ **strip** n Comicstrip n

coming ['kʌmɪŋ] n Kommen nt; ~**(s) and going(s)** n(pl) Kommen und Gehen nt

comma ['kɒmə] n Komma nt

command [kə'mɑːnd] n Befehl m; (control) Führung f; (MIL) Kommando nt; (mastery) Beherrschung f ♦ vt befehlen +dat; (MIL) kommandieren; (be able to get) verfügen über +acc; ~**er** [kəmən'dɪəʳ] vt requirieren; ~**er** n Kommandant m; ~**ment** n (REL) Gebot nt

commando [kə'mɑːndəʊ] n Kommandotruppe nt; (person) Mitglied nt einer Kommandotruppe

commemorate [kə'mɛməreɪt] vt gedenken +gen

commence [kə'mɛns] vt, vi beginnen

commend [kə'mɛnd] vt (recommend) empfehlen; (praise) loben

commensurate [kə'mɛnsərɪt] adj: ~ **with sth** einer Sache dat entsprechend

comment ['kɒmɛnt] n Bemerkung f ♦ vi: **to ~ (on)** sich äußern (zu); ~**ary** n Kommentar m; ~**ator** n Kommentator m; (TV) Reporter(in) m(f)

commerce ['kɒmɜːs] n Handel m

commercial [kə'mɜːʃəl] adj kommerziell, geschäftlich; (training) kaufmännisch ♦ n (TV) Fernsehwerbung f; ~ **break** n

Werbespot *m*; **~ize** *vt* kommerzialisieren

commiserate [kə'mɪzəreɪt] *vi*: **to ~ with** Mitleid haben mit

commission [kə'mɪʃən] *n* (*act*) Auftrag *m*; (*fee*) Provision *f*; (*body*) Kommission *f* ♦ *vt* beauftragen; (*MIL*) zum Offizier ernennen; (*work of art*) in Auftrag geben; **out of ~** außer Betrieb; **~er** *n* (*POLICE*) Polizeipräsident *m*

commit [kə'mɪt] *vt* (*crime*) begehen; (*entrust*) anvertrauen; **to ~ o.s.** sich festlegen; **~ment** *n* Verpflichtung *f*

committee [kə'mɪtɪ] *n* Ausschuss *m*

commodity [kə'mɒdɪtɪ] *n* Ware *f*

common ['kɒmən] *adj* (*cause*) gemeinsam; (*pej*) gewöhnlich; (*widespread*) üblich, häufig ♦ *n* Gemeindeland *nt*; **C~s** *npl* (*BRIT*): **the C~s** das Unterhaus; **~er** *n* Bürgerliche(r) *mf*; **~ law** *n* Gewohnheitsrecht *nt*; **~ly** *adv* gewöhnlich; **C~ Market** *n* Gemeinsame(r) Markt *m*; **~place** *adj* alltäglich; **~ room** *n* Gemeinschaftsraum *m*; **~ sense** *n* gesunde(r) Menschenverstand *m*; **C~wealth** *n*: **the C~wealth** das Commonwealth

commotion [kə'məʊʃən] *n* Aufsehen *nt*

communal ['kɒmjuːnl] *adj* Gemeinde-; Gemeinschafts-

commune [*n* 'kɒmjuːn, *vb* kə'mjuːn] *n* Kommune *f* ♦ *vi*: **to ~ with** sich mitteilen +*dat*

communicate [kə'mjuːnɪkeɪt] *vt* (*transmit*) übertragen ♦ *vi* (*be in touch*) in Verbindung stehen; (*make self understood*) sich verständigen; **communication** [kəmjuːnɪ'keɪʃən] *n* (*message*) Mitteilung *f*; (*making understood*) Kommunikation *f*; **communication cord** (*BRIT*) *n* Notbremse *f*

communion [kə'mjuːnɪən] *n* (*also:* **Holy C~**) Abendmahl *nt*, Kommunion *f*

communism ['kɒmjunɪzəm] *n* Kommunismus *m*; **communist** ['kɒmjunɪst] *n* Kommunist(in) *m(f)* ♦ *adj* kommunistisch

community [kə'mjuːnɪtɪ] *n* Gemeinschaft *f*; **~ centre** *n* Gemeinschaftszentrum *nt*; **~**

chest (*US*) *n* Wohltätigkeitsfonds *m*; **~ home** (*BRIT*) *n* Erziehungsheim *nt*

commutation ticket [kɒmju'teɪʃən-] (*US*) *n* Zeitkarte *f*

commute [kə'mjuːt] *vi* pendeln ♦ *vt* umwandeln; **~r** *n* Pendler *m*

compact [*adj* kəm'pækt, *n* 'kɒmpækt] *adj* kompakt ♦ *n* (*for make-up*) Puderdose *f*; **~ disc** *n* Compactdisc *f*, Compact Disc *f*; **~ disc player** *n* CD-Spieler *m*

companion [kəm'pænjən] *n* Begleiter(in) *m(f)*; **~ship** *n* Gesellschaft *f*

company ['kʌmpənɪ] *n* Gesellschaft *f*; (*COMM*) Firma *f*, Gesellschaft *f*; **to keep sb ~** jdm Gesellschaft leisten; **~ secretary** (*BRIT*) *n* ≃ Prokurist(in) *m(f)*

comparable ['kɒmpərəbl] *adj* vergleichbar

comparative [kəm'pærətɪv] *adj* (*relative*) relativ; **~ly** *adv* verhältnismäßig

compare [kəm'peər] *vt* vergleichen ♦ *vi* sich vergleichen lassen; **comparison** [kəm'pærɪsn] *n* Vergleich *m*; **in comparison (with)** im Vergleich (mit *or* zu)

compartment [kəm'pɑːtmənt] *n* (*RAIL*) Abteil *nt*; (*in drawer*) Fach *nt*

compass ['kʌmpəs] *n* Kompass *m*; **~es** *npl* (*MATH etc: also:* **pair of ~es**) Zirkel *m*

compassion [kəm'pæʃən] *n* Mitleid *nt*; **~ate** *adj* mitfühlend

compatible [kəm'pætɪbl] *adj* vereinbar; (*COMPUT*) kompatibel

compel [kəm'pɛl] *vt* zwingen

compensate ['kɒmpənseɪt] *vt* entschädigen ♦ *vi*: **to ~ for** Ersatz leisten für; **compensation** [kɒmpən'seɪʃən] *n* Entschädigung *f*

compère ['kɒmpeər] *n* Conférencier *m*

compete [kəm'piːt] *vi* (*take part*) teilnehmen; (*vie with*) konkurrieren

competent ['kɒmpɪtənt] *adj* kompetent

competition [kɒmpɪ'tɪʃən] *n* (*contest*) Wettbewerb *m*; (*COMM, rivalry*) Konkurrenz *f*; **competitive** [kəm'pɛtɪtɪv] *adj* Konkurrenz-; (*COMM*) konkurrenzfähig; **competitor** [kəm'pɛtɪtər] *n* (*COMM*) Konkurrent(in) *m(f)*; (*participant*) Teilnehmer(in) *m(f)*

compile [kəm'paɪl] vt zusammenstellen
complacency [kəm'pleɪsnsɪ] n
Selbstzufriedenheit f
complacent [kəm'pleɪsnt] adj
selbstzufrieden
complain [kəm'pleɪn] vi sich beklagen;
(formally) sich beschweren; **~t** n Klage f;
(formal ~t) Beschwerde f; (MED) Leiden nt
complement [n 'komplɪmənt, vb
'komplɪment] n Ergänzung f; (ship's crew etc)
Bemannung f ♦ vt ergänzen; **~ary**
[komplɪ'mentərɪ] adj (sich) ergänzend
complete [kəm'pliːt] adj (full) vollkommen,
ganz; (finished) fertig ♦ vt vervollständigen;
(finish) beenden; (fill in: form) ausfüllen; **~ly**
adv ganz; **completion** [kəm'pliːʃən] n
Fertigstellung f; (of contract etc) Abschluss m
complex ['kompleks] adj kompliziert
complexion [kəm'plekʃən] n Gesichtsfarbe
f, (fig) Aspekt m
complexity [kəm'pleksɪtɪ] n Kompliziertheit f
compliance [kəm'plaɪəns] n Fügsamkeit f,
Einwilligung f ♦ vt, **in ~ with sth** einer Sache
dat gemäß
complicate ['komplɪkeɪt] vt komplizieren;
~d adj kompliziert; **complication**
[komplɪ'keɪʃən] n Komplikation f
compliment [n 'komplɪmənt, vb
'komplɪment] n Kompliment nt ♦ vt ein
Kompliment machen +dat; **~s** npl
(greetings) Grüße pl; **to pay sb a ~** jdm ein
Kompliment machen; **~ary** [komplɪ'mentərɪ]
adj schmeichelhaft; (free) Frei-, Gratis-
comply [kəm'plaɪ] vi: **to ~ with** erfüllen +acc;
entsprechen +dat
component [kəm'pəʊnənt] adj Teil- ♦ n
Bestandteil m
compose [kəm'pəʊz] vt (music)
komponieren; (poetry) verfassen; **to ~ o.s.**
sich sammeln; **~d** adj gefasst; **~r** n
Komponist(in) m(f); **composition**
['kompə'zɪʃən] n (MUS) Komposition f; (SCH)
Aufsatz m; (structure) Zusammensetzung f,
Aufbau m
composure [kəm'pəʊʒə'] n Fassung f
compound ['kompaʊnd] n (CHEM)
Verbindung f; (enclosure) Lager nt; (LING)

Kompositum nt ♦ adj zusammengesetzt;
(fracture) kompliziert; **~ interest** n
Zinseszins m
comprehend [komprɪ'hend] vt begreifen;
comprehension n Verständnis nt
comprehensive [komprɪ'hensɪv] adj
umfassend ♦ n = **comprehensive school;**
~ insurance n Vollkasko nt; **~ school**
(BRIT) n Gesamtschule f
compress [vb kəm'pres, n 'kompres] vt
komprimieren ♦ n (MED) Kompresse f
comprise [kəm'praɪz] vt (also: **be ~d of**)
umfassen, bestehen aus
compromise ['komprəmaɪz] n Kompromiss
m ♦ vt kompromittieren ♦ vi einen
Kompromiss schließen
compulsion [kəm'pʌlʃən] n Zwang m;
compulsive [kəm'pʌlsɪv] adj zwanghaft;
compulsory [kəm'pʌlsərɪ] adj obligatorisch
computer [kəm'pjuːtə'] n Computer m,
Rechner m; **~ game** n Computerspiel nt;
~-generated adj computergeneriert; **~ize**
vt (information) computerisieren; (company,
accounts) auf Computer umstellen; **~
programmer** n Programmierer(in) m(f); **~
programming** n Programmieren nt; **~
science** n Informatik f; **computing**
[kəm'pjuːtɪŋ] n (science) Informatik f; (work)
Computerei f
comrade ['komrɪd] n Kamerad m; (POL)
Genosse m
con [kon] vt hereinlegen ♦ n Schwindel nt
concave ['konkeɪv] adj konkav
conceal [kən'siːl] vt (secret) verschweigen;
(hide) verbergen
concede [kən'siːd] vt (grant) gewähren;
(point) zugeben ♦ vi (admit defeat)
nachgeben
conceit [kən'siːt] n Einbildung f; **~ed** adj
eingebildet
conceivable [kən'siːvəbl] adj vorstellbar
conceive [kən'siːv] vt (idea) ausdenken;
(imagine) sich vorstellen; (baby) empfangen
♦ vi empfangen
concentrate ['konsəntreɪt] vi sich
konzentrieren ♦ vt konzentrieren; **to ~ on**
sth sich auf etw acc konzentrieren;

concentration [kɒnsən'treɪʃən] *n* Konzentration *f*; **concentration camp** *n* Konzentrationslager *nt*, KZ *nt*

concept ['kɒnsept] *n* Begriff *m*

conception [kən'sepʃən] *n* (*idea*) Vorstellung *f*; (*BIOL*) Empfängnis *f*

concern [kən'sɜːn] *n* (*affair*) Angelegenheit *f*; (*COMM*) Unternehmen *nt*; (*worry*) Sorge *f* ♦ *vt* (*interest*) angehen; (*be about*) handeln von; (*have connection with*) betreffen; **to be ~ed (about)** sich Sorgen machen (um); **~ing** *prep* hinsichtlich +*gen*

concert ['kɒnsət] *n* Konzert *nt*

concerted [kən'sɜːtɪd] *adj* gemeinsam

concert hall *n* Konzerthalle *f*

concertina [kɒnsə'tiːnə] *n* Handharmonika *f*

concerto [kən'tʃɜːtəʊ] *n* Konzert *nt*

concession [kən'seʃən] *n* (*yielding*) Zugeständnis *nt*; **tax ~** Steuerkonzession *f*

conciliation [kənsɪlɪ'eɪʃən] *n* Versöhnung *f*; (*official*) Schlichtung *f*

concise [kən'saɪs] *adj* präzis

conclude [kən'kluːd] *vt* (*end*) beenden; (*treaty*) (ab)schließen; (*decide*) schließen, folgern; **conclusion** [kən'kluːʒən] *n* (Ab)schluss *m*; (*deduction*) Schluss *m*; **conclusive** [kən'kluːsɪv] *adj* schlüssig

concoct [kən'kɒkt] *vt* zusammenbrauen; **~ion** [kən'kɒkʃən] *n* Gebräu *nt*

concourse ['kɒnkɔːs] *n* (*Bahnhofs*)halle *f*, Vorplatz *m*

concrete ['kɒnkriːt] *n* Beton *m* ♦ *adj* konkret

concur [kən'kɜː] *vi* übereinstimmen

concurrently [kən'kʌrntlɪ] *adv* gleichzeitig

concussion [kən'kʌʃən] *n* (*Gehirn*)erschütterung *f*

condemn [kən'dem] *vt* (*JUR*) verurteilen; (*building*) abbruchreif erklären

condensation [kɒnden'seɪʃən] *n* Kondensation *f*

condense [kən'dens] *vi* (*CHEM*) kondensieren ♦ *vt* (*fig*) zusammendrängen; **~d milk** *n* Kondensmilch *f*

condescending [kɒndɪ'sendɪŋ] *adj* herablassend

condition [kən'dɪʃən] *n* (*state*) Zustand *m*; (*presupposition*) Bedingung *f* ♦ *vt* (*hair etc*)

behandeln; (*accustom*) gewöhnen; **~s** *npl* (*circumstances*) Verhältnisse *pl*; **on ~ that ...** unter der Bedingung, dass ...; **~al** *adj* bedingt; **~er** *n* (*for hair*) Spülung *f*; (*for fabrics*) Weichspüler *m*

condolences [kən'dəʊlənsɪz] *npl* Beileid *nt*

condom ['kɒndəm] *n* Kondom *nt or m*

condominium [kɒndə'mɪnɪəm] (*US*) *n* Eigentumswohnung *f*; (*block*) Eigentumsblock *m*

condone [kən'dəʊn] *vt* gutheißen

conducive [kən'djuːsɪv] *adj*: **~ to** dienlich +*dat*

conduct [*n* 'kɒndʌkt, *vb* kən'dʌkt] *n* (*behaviour*) Verhalten *nt*; (*management*) Führung *f* ♦ *vt* führen; (*MUS*) dirigieren; **~ed tour** *n* Führung *f*; **~or** [kən'dʌktər] *n* (*of orchestra*) Dirigent *m*; (*in bus, US*: *on train*) Schaffner *m*; (*ELEC*) Leiter *m*; **~ress** [kən'dʌktrɪs] *n* (*in bus*) Schaffnerin *f*

cone [kəʊn] *n* (*MATH*) Kegel *m*; (*for ice cream*) (Waffel)tüte *f*; (*BOT*) Tannenzapfen *m*

confectioner's (shop) [kən'fekʃənəz-] *n* Konditorei *f*; **~y** [kən'fekʃənrɪ] *n* Süßigkeiten *pl*

confederation [kənfedə'reɪʃən] *n* Bund *m*

confer [kən'fɜː] *vt* (*degree*) verleihen ♦ *vi* (*discuss*) konferieren, verhandeln; **~ence** ['kɒnfərəns] *n* Konferenz *f*

confess [kən'fes] *vt, vi* gestehen; (*ECCL*) beichten; **~ion** [kən'feʃən] *n* Geständnis *nt*; (*ECCL*) Beichte *f*; **~ional** *n* Beichtstuhl *m*

confide [kən'faɪd] *vi*: **to ~ in** (sich) anvertrauen +*dat*

confidence ['kɒnfɪdns] *n* Vertrauen *nt*; (*assurance*) Selbstvertrauen *nt*; (*secret*) Geheimnis *nt*; **in ~** (*speak, write*) vertraulich; **~ trick** *n* Schwindel *m*

confident ['kɒnfɪdənt] *adj* (*sure*) überzeugt; (*self-assured*) selbstsicher

confidential [kɒnfɪ'denʃəl] *adj* vertraulich

confine [kən'faɪn] *vt* (*limit*) beschränken; (*lock up*) einsperren; **~d** *adj* (*space*) eng; **~ment** *n* (*in prison*) Haft *f*; (*MED*) Wochenbett *nt*; **~s** ['kɒnfaɪnz] *npl* Grenzen *pl*

confirm [kən'fɜːm] *vt* bestätigen; **~ation**

[kɔnfə'meɪʃən] n Bestätigung f; (REL) Konfirmation f; **~ed** adj unverbesserlich; (bachelor) eingefleischt

confiscate ['kɔnfɪskeɪt] vt beschlagnahmen

conflict [n 'kɔnflɪkt, vb kən'flɪkt] n Konflikt m ♦ vi im Widerspruch stehen; **~ing** [kən'flɪktɪŋ] adj widersprüchlich

conform [kən'fɔːm] vi: **to ~ (to)** (things) entsprechen +dat; (people) sich anpassen +dat; (to rules) sich richten (nach)

confound [kən'faund] vt verblüffen; (confuse) durcheinander bringen

confront [kən'frʌnt] vt (enemy) entgegentreten +dat; (problems) sich stellen +dat; **to ~ sb with sth** jdn mit etw konfrontieren; **~ation** [kɔnfrʌn'teɪʃən] n Konfrontation f

confuse [kən'fjuːz] vt verwirren; (sth with sth) verwechseln; **~d** adj verwirrt; **confusing** adj verwirrend; **confusion** [kən'fjuːʒən] n (perplexity) Verwirrung f; (mixing up) Verwechslung f; (tumult) Aufruhr m

congeal [kən'dʒiːl] vi (freeze) gefrieren; (clot) gerinnen

congested [kən'dʒestɪd] adj überfüllt

congestion [kən'dʒestʃən] n Stau m

conglomerate [kən'glɔmərɪt] n (COMM, GEOL) Konglomerat nt

conglomeration [kəglɔmə'reɪʃən] n Anhäufung f

congratulate [kən'grætjuleɪt] vt: **to ~ sb (on sth)** jdn (zu etw) beglückwünschen; **congratulations** [kəngrætju'leɪʃənz] npl Glückwünsche pl; **congratulations!** gratuliere!, herzlichen Glückwunsch!

congregate ['kɔngrɪgeɪt] vi sich versammeln; **congregation** [kɔngrɪ'geɪʃən] n Gemeinde f

congress ['kɔngres] n Kongress m; **C~man** (irreg: US) n Mitglied nt des amerikanischen Repräsentantenhauses

conifer ['kɔnɪfər] n Nadelbaum m

conjunction [kən'dʒʌŋkʃən] n Verbindung f; (GRAM) Konjunktion f

conjunctivitis [kəndʒʌŋktɪ'vaɪtɪs] n Bindehautentzündung f

conjure ['kʌndʒər] vi zaubern; **~ up** vt heraufbeschwören; **~r** n Zauberkünstler(in) m(f)

conk out [kɔŋk-] (inf) vi den Geist aufgeben

con man (irreg) n Schwindler m

connect [kə'nekt] vt verbinden; (ELEC) anschließen; **to be ~ed with** eine Beziehung haben zu; (be related to) verwandt sein mit; **~ion** [kə'nekʃən] n Verbindung f; (relation) Zusammenhang m; (ELEC, TEL, RAIL) Anschluss m

connive [kə'naɪv] vi: **to ~ at** stillschweigend dulden

connoisseur [kɔnɪ'səːr] n Kenner m

conquer ['kɔŋkər] vt (feelings) überwinden; (enemy) besiegen; (country) erobern; **~or** n Eroberer m

conquest ['kɔŋkwest] n Eroberung f

cons [kɔnz] npl see **convenience**; **pro**

conscience ['kɔnʃəns] n Gewissen nt

conscientious [kɔnʃɪ'enʃəs] adj gewissenhaft

conscious ['kɔnʃəs] adj bewusst, (MED) bei Bewusstsein; **~ness** n Bewusstsein nt

conscript ['kɔnskrɪpt] n Wehrpflichtige(r) m; **~ion** [kən'skrɪpʃən] n Wehrpflicht f

consecutive [kən'sekjutɪv] adj aufeinander folgend

consensus [kən'sensəs] n allgemeine Übereinstimmung f

consent [kən'sent] n Zustimmung f ♦ vi zustimmen

consequence ['kɔnsɪkwəns] n (importance) Bedeutung f; (effect) Folge f

consequently ['kɔnsɪkwəntlɪ] adv folglich

conservation [kɔnsə'veɪʃən] n Erhaltung f; (nature ~) Umweltschutz m

conservative [kən'səːvətɪv] adj konservativ; **C~** (BRIT) adj konservativ ♦ n Konservative(r) mf

conservatory [kən'səːvətrɪ] n (room) Wintergarten m

conserve [kən'səːv] vt erhalten

consider [kən'sɪdər] vt überlegen; (take into account) in Betracht ziehen; (regard as) halten für; **to ~ doing sth** daran denken, etw zu tun; **~able** [kən'sɪdərəbl] adj beträchtlich; **~ably** adv beträchtlich; **~ate** adj rücksichtsvoll; **~ation** [kənsɪdə'reɪʃən] n Rücksicht(nahme) f; (thought) Erwägung f; **~ing** prep in Anbetracht +gen

consign [kən'saɪn] vt übergeben; **~ment** n Sendung f

consist [kən'sɪst] vi: **to ~ of** bestehen aus

consistency [kən'sɪstənsɪ] n (of material) Konsistenz f; (of argument, person) Konsequenz f

consistent [kən'sɪstənt] adj (person) konsequent; (argument) folgerichtig

consolation [kɒnsə'leɪʃən] n Trost m

console[1] [kən'səul] vt trösten

console[2] ['kɒnsəul] n Kontroll(pult) nt

consolidate [kən'sɒlɪdeɪt] vt festigen

consommé [kən'sɒmeɪ] n Fleischbrühe f

consonant ['kɒnsənənt] n Konsonant m, Mitlaut m

conspicuous [kən'spɪkjuəs] adj (prominent) auffällig; (visible) deutlich sichtbar

conspiracy [kən'spɪrəsɪ] n Verschwörung f

conspire [kən'spaɪə*] vi sich verschwören

constable ['kʌnstəbl] (BRIT) n Polizist(in) m(f); **chief ~** Polizeipräsident m; **constabulary** [kən'stæbjulərɪ] n Polizei f

constant ['kɒnstənt] adj (continuous) ständig; (unchanging) konstant; **~ly** adv ständig

constellation [kɒnstə'leɪʃən] n Sternbild nt

consternation [kɒnstə'neɪʃən] n Bestürzung f

constipated ['kɒnstɪpeɪtɪd] adj verstopft; **constipation** [kɒnstɪ'peɪʃən] n Verstopfung f

constituency [kən'stɪtjuənsɪ] n Wahlkreis m

constituent [kən'stɪtjuənt] n (person) Wähler m; (part) Bestandteil m

constitute ['kɒnstɪtjuːt] vt (make up) bilden; (amount to) darstellen

constitution [kɒnstɪ'tjuːʃən] n Verfassung f; **~al** adj Verfassungs-

constraint [kən'streɪnt] n Zwang m; (shyness) Befangenheit f

construct [kən'strʌkt] vt bauen; **~ion** [kən'strʌkʃən] n Konstruktion f; (building) Bau m; **~ive** adj konstruktiv

construe [kən'struː] vt deuten

consul ['kɒnsl] n Konsul m; **~ate** n Konsulat nt

consult [kən'sʌlt] vt um Rat fragen; (doctor) konsultieren; (book) nachschlagen in +dat; **~ant** n (MED) Facharzt m; (other specialist) Gutachter m; **~ation** n Beratung f; (MED) Konsultation f; **~ing room** n Sprechzimmer nt

consume [kən'sjuːm] vt verbrauchen; (food) konsumieren; **~r** n Verbraucher m; **~r goods** npl Konsumgüter pl; **~rism** n Konsum m; **~r society** n Konsumgesellschaft f

consummate ['kɒnsʌmeɪt] vt (marriage) vollziehen

consumption [kən'sʌmpʃən] n Verbrauch m; (of food) Konsum m

cont. abbr (= continued) Forts.

contact ['kɒntækt] n (touch) Berührung f; (connection) Verbindung f; (person) Kontakt m ♦ vt sich in Verbindung setzen mit; **~ lenses** npl Kontaktlinsen pl

contagious [kən'teɪdʒəs] adj ansteckend

contain [kən'teɪn] vt enthalten; **to ~ o.s.** sich zügeln; **~er** n Behälter m; (transport) Container m

contaminate [kən'tæmɪneɪt] vt verunreinigen

cont'd abbr (= continued) Forts.

contemplate ['kɒntəmpleɪt] vt (look at) (nachdenklich) betrachten; (think about) überdenken; (plan) vorhaben

contemporary [kən'tempərərɪ] adj zeitgenössisch ♦ n Zeitgenosse m

contempt [kən'tempt] n Verachtung f; **~ of court** (JUR) Missachtung f des Gerichts; **~ible** adj verachtenswert; **~uous** adj verächtlich

contend [kən'tend] vt (argue) behaupten ♦ vi kämpfen; **~er** n (for post) Bewerber(in) m(f); (SPORT) Wettkämpfer(in) m(f)

content [adj, vb kən'tent, n 'kɒntent] adj zufrieden ♦ vt befriedigen ♦ n (also: **~s**) Inhalt m; **~ed** adj zufrieden

contention [kən'tenʃən] n (dispute) Streit m; (argument) Behauptung f

contentment [kən'tentmənt] n Zufriedenheit f

contest [n 'kɔntest, vb kən'test] n
(Wett)kampf m ♦ vt (dispute) bestreiten;
(JUR) anfechten; (POL) kandidieren in +dat;
~**ant** [kən'testənt] n Bewerber(in) m(f)

context ['kɔntekst] n Zusammenhang m

continent ['kɔntɪnənt] n Kontinent m; **the
C~** (BRIT) das europäische Festland; ~**al**
[kɔntɪ'nentl] adj kontinental; ~**al breakfast**
n kleines Frühstück nt; ~**al quilt** (BRIT) n
Federbett nt

contingency [kən'tɪndʒənsɪ] n Möglichkeit f

contingent [kən'tɪndʒənt] n Kontingent nt

continual [kən'tɪnjuəl] adj (endless)
fortwährend; (repeated) immer
wiederkehrend; ~**ly** adv immer wieder

continuation [kəntɪnju'eɪʃən] n Fortsetzung
f

continue [kən'tɪnjuː] vi (person)
weitermachen; (thing) weitergehen ♦ vt
fortsetzen

continuity [kɔntɪ'njuɪtɪ] n Kontinuität f

continuous [kən'tɪnjuəs] adj
ununterbrochen; ~ **stationery** n
Endlospapier nt

contort [kən'tɔːt] vt verdrehen; ~**ion**
[kən'tɔːʃən] n Verzerrung f

contour ['kɔntuə] n Umriss m; (also: ~ **line**)
Höhenlinie f

contraband ['kɔntrəbænd] n
Schmuggelware f

contraception [kɔntrə'sepʃən] n
Empfängnisverhütung f

contraceptive [kɔntrə'septɪv] n
empfängnisverhütende(s) Mittel nt ♦ adj
empfängnisverhütend

contract [n 'kɔntrækt, vb kən'trækt] n Vertrag
m ♦ vi (muscle, metal) sich zusammenziehen
♦ vt zusammenziehen; **to ~ to do sth**
(COMM) sich vertraglich verpflichten, etw zu
tun; ~**ion** [kən'trækʃən] n (shortening)
Verkürzung f; ~**or** [kən'træktə] n
Unternehmer m

contradict [kɔntrə'dɪkt] vt widersprechen
+dat; ~**ion** [kɔntrə'dɪkʃən] n Widerspruch m

contraflow ['kɔntrəfləu] n (AUT)
Gegenverkehr m

contraption [kən'træpʃən] (inf) n Apparat m

contrary[1] ['kɔntrərɪ] adj (opposite)
entgegengesetzt ♦ n Gegenteil nt; **on the ~**
im Gegenteil

contrary[2] [kən'treərɪ] adj (obstinate)
widerspenstig

contrast [n 'kɔntrɑːst, vb kən'trɑːst] n
Kontrast m ♦ vt entgegensetzen; ~**ing**
[kən'trɑːstɪŋ] adj Kontrast-

contravene [kɔntrə'viːn] vt verstoßen
gegen

contribute [kən'trɪbjuːt] vt, vi: **to ~ to**
beitragen zu; **contribution** [kɔntrɪ'bjuːʃən]
n Beitrag m; **contributor** [kən'trɪbjutə] n
Beitragende(r) f(m)

contrive [kən'traɪv] vt ersinnen ♦ vi: **to ~ to
do sth** es schaffen, etw zu tun

control [kən'trəul] vt (direct, test)
kontrollieren ♦ n Kontrolle f; ~**s** npl (of
vehicle) Steuerung f; (of engine) Schalttafel f;
to be in ~ of (business, office) leiten; (group
of children) beaufsichtigen; **out of ~** = außer
Kontrolle; **under ~** unter Kontrolle; ~**led
substance** n verschreibungspflichtiges
Medikament; ~ **panel** n Schalttafel f; ~
room n Kontrollraum m; ~ **tower** n (AVIAT)
Kontrollturm m

controversial [kɔntrə'vəːʃl] adj umstritten;
controversy ['kɔntrəvəːsɪ] n Kontroverse f

conurbation [kɔnə'beɪʃən] n Ballungsgebiet
nt

convalesce [kɔnvə'les] vi genesen;
convalescence [kɔnvə'lesns] n Genesung f

convector [kən'vektə] n Heizlüfter m

convene [kən'viːn] vt zusammenrufen ♦ vi
sich versammeln

convenience [kən'viːnɪəns] n
Annehmlichkeit f; **all modern ~s** or (BRIT)
mod cons mit allem Komfort; **at your ~**
wann es Ihnen passt

convenient [kən'viːnɪənt] adj günstig

convent ['kɔnvənt] n Kloster nt

convention [kən'venʃən] n Versammlung f;
(custom) Konvention f; ~**al** adj
konventionell

convent school n Klosterschule f

converge [kən'vəːdʒ] vi zusammenlaufen

conversant [kən'vɜːsnt] *adj*: **to be ~ with** bewandert sein in +*dat*

conversation [kɒnvə'seɪʃən] *n* Gespräch *nt*; **~al** *adj* Unterhaltungs-

converse [*n* 'kɒnvɜːs, *vb* kən'vɜːs] *n* Gegenteil *nt* ♦ *vi* sich unterhalten

conversion [kən'vɜːʃən] *n* Umwandlung *f*; (*REL*) Bekehrung *f*

convert [*vb* kən'vɜːt, *n* 'kɒnvɜːt] *vt* (*change*) umwandeln; (*REL*) bekehren ♦ *n* Bekehrte(r) *mf*; Konvertit(in) *m(f)*; **~ible** *n* (*AUT*) Kabriolett *nt* ♦ *adj* umwandelbar; (*FIN*) konvertierbar

convex ['kɒnveks] *adj* konvex

convey [kən'veɪ] *vt* (*carry*) befördern; (*feelings*) vermitteln; **~or belt** *n* Fließband *nt*

convict [*vb* kən'vɪkt, *n* 'kɒnvɪkt] *vt* verurteilen ♦ *n* Häftling *m*; **~ion** [kən'vɪkʃən] *n* (*verdict*) Verurteilung *f*; (*belief*) Überzeugung *f*

convince [kən'vɪns] *vt* überzeugen; **~d** *adj*: **~d that** überzeugt davon, dass; **convincing** *adj* überzeugend

convoluted ['kɒnvəluːtɪd] *adj* verwickelt; (*style*) gewunden

convoy ['kɒnvɔɪ] *n* (*of vehicles*) Kolonne *f*; (*protected*) Konvoi *m*

convulse [kən'vʌls] *vt* zusammenzucken lassen; **to be ~d with laughter** sich vor Lachen krümmen; **convulsion** [kən'vʌlʃən] *n* (*esp MED*) Zuckung *f*, Krampf *m*

coo [kuː] *vi* gurren

cook [kuk] *vt*, *vi* kochen ♦ *n* Koch *m*, Köchin *f*; **~ book** *n* Kochbuch *nt*; **~er** *n* Herd *m*; **~ery** *n* Kochkunst *f*; **~ery book** (*BRIT*) *n* = **cook book**; **~ie** (*US*) *n* Plätzchen *nt*; **~ing** *n* Kochen *nt*

cool [kuːl] *adj* kühl ♦ *vt*, *vi* (ab)kühlen; **~ down** *vt*, *vi* (*fig*) (sich) beruhigen; **~ness** *n* Kühle *f*; (*of temperament*) kühle(r) Kopf *m*

coop [kuːp] *n* Hühnerstall *m* ♦ *vt*: **~ up** (*fig*) einpferchen

cooperate [kəu'ɒpəreɪt] *vi* zusammenarbeiten; **cooperation** [kəuɒpə'reɪʃən] *n* Zusammenarbeit *f*

cooperative [kəu'ɒpərətɪv] *adj* hilfsbereit; (*COMM*) genossenschaftlich ♦ *n* (*of farmers*) Genossenschaft *f*; (*~ store*) Konsumladen *m*

coordinate [*vb* kəu'ɔːdɪneɪt, *n* kəu'ɔːdɪnət] *vt* koordinieren ♦ *n* (*MATH*) Koordinate *f*; **~s** *npl* (*clothes*) Kombinationen *pl*;

coordination [kəuɔːdɪ'neɪʃən] *n* Koordination *f*

cop [kɒp] *n* (*inf*) Polyp *m*, Bulle *m*

cope [kəup] *vi*: **to ~ with** fertig werden mit

copious ['kəupɪəs] *adj* reichhaltig

copper ['kɒpə*] *n* (*metal*) Kupfer *nt*; (*inf*: *policeman*) Polyp *m*, Bulle *m*; **~s** *npl* (*money*) Kleingeld *nt*

copse [kɒps] *n* Unterholz *nt*

copy ['kɒpɪ] *n* (*imitation*) Kopie *f*; (*of book etc*) Exemplar *nt*; (*of newspaper*) Nummer *f* ♦ *vt* kopieren, abschreiben; **~right** *n* Copyright *nt*

coral ['kɒrəl] *n* Koralle *f*; **~ reef** *n* Korallenriff *nt*

cord [kɔːd] *n* Schnur *f*; (*ELEC*) Kabel *nt*

cordial ['kɔːdɪəl] *adj* herzlich ♦ *n* Fruchtsaft *m*

cordon ['kɔːdn] *n* Absperrkette *f*; **~ off** *vt* abriegeln

corduroy ['kɔːdərɔɪ] *n* Kord(samt) *m*

core [kɔː*] *n* Kern *m* ♦ *vt* entkernen

cork [kɔːk] *n* (*bark*) Korkrinde *f*; (*stopper*) Korken *m*; **~screw** *n* Korkenzieher *m*

corn [kɔːn] *n* (*BRIT*: *wheat*) Getreide *nt*, Korn *nt*; (*US*: *maize*) Mais *m*; (*on foot*) Hühnerauge *nt*; **~ on the cob** Maiskolben *m*

corned beef ['kɔːnd-] *n* Cornedbeef *nt*, Corned Beef *nt*

corner ['kɔːnə*] *n* Ecke *f*; (*on road*) Kurve *f* ♦ *vt* in die Enge treiben; (*market*) monopolisieren ♦ *vi* (*AUT*) in die Kurve gehen; **~stone** *n* Eckstein *m*

cornet ['kɔːnɪt] *n* (*MUS*) Kornett *nt*; (*BRIT*: *of ice cream*) Eistüte *f*

corn: ~flakes ['kɔːnfleɪks] *npl* Cornflakes *pl* ®; **~flour** ['kɔːnflauə*] (*BRIT*) *n* Maizena *nt* ®; **~starch** ['kɔːnstɑːtʃ] (*US*) *n* Maizena *nt* ®

corny ['kɔːnɪ] *adj* (*joke*) blöd(e)

coronary ['kɒrənərɪ] *n* (*also*: **~ thrombosis**) Herzinfarkt *m*

coronation [kɔrə'neɪʃən] n Krönung f

coroner ['kɔrənər] n Untersuchungsrichter m

corporal ['kɔːpərl] n Obergefreite(r) m ♦ adj: ~ **punishment** Prügelstrafe f

corporate ['kɔːpərɪt] adj gemeinschaftlich, korporativ

corporation [kɔːpə'reɪʃən] n (of town) Gemeinde f; (COMM) Körperschaft f, Aktiengesellschaft f

corps [kɔːr] (pl ~) n (Armee)korps nt

corpse [kɔːps] n Leiche f

corral [kə'rɑːl] n Pferch m, Korral m

correct [kə'rekt] adj (accurate) richtig; (proper) korrekt ♦ vt korrigieren; ~**ion** [kə'rekʃən] n Berichtigung f

correlation [kɔrɪ'leɪʃən] n Wechselbeziehung f

correspond [kɔrɪs'pɔnd] vi (agree) übereinstimmen; (exchange letters) korrespondieren; ~**ence** n (similarity) Entsprechung f; (letters) Briefwechsel m, Korrespondenz f; ~**ence course** n Fernkurs m; ~**ent** n (PRESS) Berichterstatter m

corridor ['kɔrɪdɔːr] n Gang m

corroborate [kə'rɔbəreɪt] vt bestätigen

corrode [kə'rəud] vt zerfressen ♦ vi rosten

corrosion [kə'rəuʒən] n Korrosion f

corrugated ['kɔrəgeɪtɪd] adj gewellt; ~ **iron** n Wellblech n

corrupt [kə'rʌpt] adj korrupt ♦ vt verderben; (bribe) bestechen; ~**ion** [kə'rʌpʃən] n Verdorbenheit f; (bribery) Bestechung f

corset ['kɔːsɪt] n Korsett nt

Corsica ['kɔːsɪkə] n Korsika nt

cosmetics [kɔz'metɪks] npl Kosmetika pl

cosmic ['kɔzmɪk] adj kosmisch

cosmonaut ['kɔzmənɔːt] n Kosmonaut(in) m(f)

cosmopolitan [kɔzmə'pɔlɪtn] adj international; (city) Welt-

cosmos ['kɔzmɔs] n Kosmos m

cost [kɔst] (pt, pp **cost**) n Kosten pl, Preis m ♦ vt, vi kosten; ~**s** npl (JUR) Kosten pl; **how much does it ~?** wie viel kostet das?; **at all ~s** um jeden Preis

co-star ['kəustɑːr] n zweite(r) or weitere(r)

Hauptdarsteller(in) m(f)

cost: ~-**effective** adj rentabel; ~**ly** ['kɔstlɪ] adj kostspielig; ~-**of- living** ['kɔstəv'lɪvɪŋ] adj (index) Lebenshaltungskosten-; ~ **price** (BRIT) n Selbstkostenpreis m

costume ['kɔstjuːm] n Kostüm nt; (fancy dress) Maskenkostüm nt; (BRIT: also: **swimming** ~) Badeanzug m; ~ **jewellery** n Modeschmuck m

cosy ['kəuzɪ] (BRIT) adj behaglich; (atmosphere) gemütlich

cot [kɔt] n (BRIT: child's) Kinderbett(chen) nt; (US: camp bed) Feldbett nt

cottage ['kɔtɪdʒ] n kleine(s) Haus nt; ~ **cheese** n Hüttenkäse m; ~ **industry** n Heimindustrie f; ~ **pie** n Auflauf mit Hackfleisch und Kartoffelbrei

cotton ['kɔtn] n Baumwolle f; (thread) Garn nt; ~ **on to** (inf) vt kapieren; ~ **candy** (US) n Zuckerwatte f; ~ **wool** (BRIT) n Watte f

couch [kautʃ] n Couch f

couchette [kuː'ʃet] n (on train, boat) Liegewagenplatz m

cough [kɔf] vi husten ♦ n Husten m; ~ **drop** n Hustenbonbon nt

could [kud] pt of **can**?

couldn't ['kudnt] = **could not**

council ['kaunsl] n (of town) Stadtrat m; ~ **estate** (BRIT) n Siedlung f des sozialen Wohnungsbaus; ~ **house** (BRIT) n Haus nt des sozialen Wohnungsbaus; ~**lor** ['kaunslər] n Stadtrat m/-rätin f

counsel ['kaunsl] n (barrister) Anwalt m; (advice) Rat(schlag) m ♦ vt beraten; ~**lor** ['kaunslər] n Berater m

count [kaunt] vt, vi zählen ♦ n (reckoning) Abrechnung f; (nobleman) Graf m; ~ **on** vt zählen auf +acc

countenance ['kauntɪnəns] n (old) Antlitz nt ♦ vt (tolerate) gutheißen

counter ['kauntər] n (in shop) Ladentisch m; (in café) Theke f; (in bank, post office) Schalter m ♦ vt entgegnen

counteract ['kauntər'ækt] vt entgegenwirken +dat

counterfeit ['kauntəfɪt] n Fälschung f ♦ vt fälschen ♦ adj gefälscht

counterfoil ['kauntəfɔɪl] *n*
(Kontroll)abschnitt *m*

counterpart ['kauntəpɑːt] *n (object)*
Gegenstück *nt; (person)* Gegenüber *nt*

counterproductive ['kauntəprə'dʌktɪv] *adj*
destruktiv

countersign ['kauntəsaɪn] *vt* gegenzeichnen

countess ['kauntɪs] *n* Gräfin *f*

countless ['kauntlɪs] *adj* zahllos, unzählig

country ['kʌntrɪ] *n* Land *nt; ~ **dancing**
(BRIT) n* Volkstanz *m; ~ **house** n* Landhaus
*nt; ~**man** (irreg) n (national)* Landsmann *m;
(rural)* Bauer *m; ~**side** n* Landschaft *f*

county ['kauntɪ] *n* Landkreis *m; (BRIT)*
Grafschaft *f*

coup [kuː] *(pl ~s) n* Coup *m; (also: ~ **d'état**)*
Staatsstreich *m*, Putsch *m*

couple ['kʌpl] *n* Paar *nt ♦ vt* koppeln; **a ~ of**
ein paar

coupon ['kuːpɒn] *n* Gutschein *m*

coups [kuː] *npl of* **coup**

courage ['kʌrɪdʒ] *n* Mut *m; ~**ous**
[kə'reɪdʒəs] *adj* mutig

courgette [kuə'ʒet] (BRIT) *n* Zucchini *f or pl*

courier ['kurɪər] *n (for holiday)* Reiseleiter *m;
(messenger)* Kurier *m*

course [kɔːs] *n (race)* Bahn *f; (of stream)* Lauf
m; (golf ~) Platz *m; (NAUT, SCH)* Kurs *m; (in
meal)* Gang *m;* **of ~** natürlich

court [kɔːt] *n (royal)* Hof *m; (JUR)* Gericht *nt
♦ vt (woman)* gehen mit; *(danger)*
herausfordern; **to take to ~** vor Gericht
bringen

courteous ['kəːtɪəs] *adj* höflich

courtesy ['kəːtəsɪ] *n* Höflichkeit *f*

courtesy bus, courtesy coach *n*
gebührenfreier Bus *m*

court: ~ house (US) *n* Gerichtsgebäude *nt;
~**ier** ['kɔːtɪər] n* Höfling *m; ~ **martial**
['kɔːt'mɑːʃəl] (pl ~**s martial**) n* Kriegsgericht
nt ♦ vt vor ein Kriegsgericht stellen; **~room**
n Gerichtssaal *m; ~**s martial** npl of* **court
martial; ~yard** ['kɔːtjɑːd] *n* Hof *m*

cousin ['kʌzn] *n* Cousin *m*, Vetter *m;* Kusine
f

cove [kəuv] *n* kleine Bucht *f*

covenant ['kʌvənənt] *n (ECCL)* Bund *m; (JUR)*
Verpflichtung *f*

cover ['kʌvər] *vt (spread over)* bedecken;
(shield) abschirmen; *(include)* sich erstrecken
über +acc; *(protect)* decken; *(distance)*
zurücklegen; *(report on)* berichten über +acc
♦ n (lid) Deckel *m; (for bed)* Decke *f; (MIL)*
Bedeckung *f; (of book)* Einband *m; (of
magazine)* Umschlag *m; (insurance)*
Versicherung *f;* **to take ~** *(from rain)* sich
unterstellen; *(MIL)* in Deckung gehen;
under ~ *(indoors)* drinnen; **~ of** im
Schutze +gen; **under separate ~** *(COMM)*
mit getrennter Post; **to ~ up for sb** jdn
decken; ~**age** *n (PRESS: reports)*
Berichterstattung *f; (distribution)*
Verbreitung *f; ~ **charge** n* Bedienungsgeld
*nt; ~**ing** n* Bedeckung *f; ~**ing letter** (US ~
letter) n* Begleitbrief *m; ~ **note** n*
(INSURANCE) vorläufige(r)
Versicherungsschein *m*

covert ['kʌvət] *adj* geheim

cover-up ['kʌvərʌp] *n* Vertuschung *f*

cow [kau] *n* Kuh *f ♦ vt* einschüchtern

coward ['kauəd] *n* Feigling *m; ~**ice**
['kauədɪs] *n* Feigheit *f; ~**ly** adj* feige

cower ['kauər] *vi* kauern

coy [kɔɪ] *adj* schüchtern

coyote [kɔɪ'əutɪ] *n* Präriewolf *m*

cozy ['kauzɪ] (US) *adj* = **cosy**

CPA (US) *n abbr* = **certified public
accountant**

crab [kræb] *n* Krebs *m*

crab apple *n* Holzapfel *m*

crack [kræk] *n* Riss *m*, Sprung *m; (noise)*
Knall *m; (drug)* Crack *nt ♦ vt (break)*
springen lassen; *(joke)* reißen; *(nut, safe)*
knacken; *(whip)* knallen lassen *♦ vi* springen
♦ adj erstklassig; *(troops)* Elite-; **~ down** *vi:*
to ~ down (on) hart durchgreifen (bei); **~
up** *vi (fig)* zusammenbrechen

cracked [krækt] *adj (glass, plate, ice)*
gesprungen; *(rib, bone)* gebrochen,
angeknackst *(umg); (broken)* gebrochen;
(surface, walls) rissig; *(inf: mad)*
übergeschnappt

cracker ['krækər] *n (firework)* Knallkörper *m*,
Kracher *m; (biscuit)* Keks *m; (Christmas ~)*

Knallbonbon nt

crackle ['krækl] vi knistern; (fire) prasseln

cradle ['kreɪdl] n Wiege f

craft [krɑːft] n (skill) (Hand- or Kunst)fertigkeit f; (trade) Handwerk nt; (NAUT) Schiff nt; **~sman** (irreg) n Handwerker m; **~smanship** n (quality) handwerkliche Ausführung f; (ability) handwerkliche(s) Können nt

crafty ['krɑːftɪ] adj schlau

crag [kræg] n Klippe f

cram [kræm] vt voll stopfen ♦ vi (learn) pauken; **to ~ sth into sth** etw in etw acc stopfen

cramp [kræmp] n Krampf m ♦ vt (limit) einengen; (hinder) hemmen; **~ed** adj (position) verkrampft; (space) eng

crampon ['kræmpən] n Steigeisen nt

cranberry ['krænbərɪ] n Preiselbeere f

crane [kreɪn] n (machine) Kran m, (bird) Kranich m

crank [kræŋk] n (lever) Kurbel f; (person) Spinner m; **~shaft** n Kurbelwelle f

cranny ['krænɪ] n see **nook**

crash [kræʃ] n (noise) Krachen nt; (with cars) Zusammenstoß m; (with plane) Absturz m; (COMM) Zusammenbruch m ♦ vt (plane) abstürzen mit ♦ vi (cars) zusammenstoßen; (plane) abstürzen; (economy) zusammenbrechen; (noise) knallen; **~ course** n Schnellkurs m; **~ helmet** n Sturzhelm m; **~ landing** n Bruchlandung f

crass [kræs] adj krass

crate [kreɪt] n (also fig) Kiste f

crater ['kreɪtə*] n Krater m

cravat(e) [krə'væt] n Halstuch nt

crave [kreɪv] vt verlangen nach

crawl [krɔːl] vi kriechen; (baby) krabbeln ♦ n Kriechen nt; (swim) Kraul nt

crayfish ['kreɪfɪʃ] n inv (freshwater) Krebs m; (saltwater) Languste f

crayon ['kreɪən] n Buntstift m

craze [kreɪz] n Fimmel m

crazy ['kreɪzɪ] adj verrückt

creak [kriːk] vi knarren

cream [kriːm] n (from milk) Rahm m, Sahne f; (polish, cosmetic) Creme f; (fig: people)

Elite f ♦ adj cremefarbig; **~ cake** n Sahnetorte f; **~ cheese** n Rahmquark m; **~y** adj sahnig

crease [kriːs] n Falte f ♦ vt falten; (wrinkle) zerknittern ♦ vi (wrinkle up) knittern; **~d** adj zerknittert, faltig

create [kriː'eɪt] vt erschaffen; (cause) verursachen; **creation** [kriː'eɪʃən] n Schöpfung f; **creative** adj kreativ; **creator** n Schöpfer m

creature ['kriːtʃə*] n Geschöpf nt

crèche [kreʃ] n Krippe f

credence ['kriːdns] n: **to lend** or **give ~ to sth** etw dat Glauben schenken

credentials [krɪ'denʃlz] npl Beglaubigungsschreiben nt

credibility [kredɪ'bɪltɪ] n Glaubwürdigkeit f

credible ['kredɪbl] adj (person) glaubwürdig; (story) glaubhaft

credit ['kredɪt] n (also COMM) Kredit m ♦ vt Glauben schenken +dat; (COMM) gutschreiben; **~s** npl (of film) Mitwirkenden pl; **~able** adj rühmlich; **~ card** n Kreditkarte f; **~or** n Gläubiger m

creed [kriːd] n Glaubensbekenntnis nt

creek [kriːk] n (inlet) kleine Bucht f; (US: river) kleine(r) Wasserlauf m

creep [kriːp] (pt, pp **crept**) vi kriechen; **~er** n Kletterpflanze f; **~y** adj (frightening) gruselig

cremate [krɪ'meɪt] vt einäschern; **cremation** [krɪ'meɪʃən] n Einäscherung f; **crematorium** [kremə'tɔːrɪəm] n Krematorium nt

crêpe [kreɪp] n Krepp m; **~ bandage** (BRIT) n Elastikbinde f

crept [krept] pt, pp of **creep**

crescent ['kresnt] n (of moon) Halbmond m

cress [kres] n Kresse f

crest [krest] n (of cock) Kamm m; (of wave) Wellenkamm m; (coat of arms) Wappen nt

crestfallen ['krestfɔːlən] adj niedergeschlagen

Crete [kriːt] n Kreta nt

crevice ['krevɪs] n Riss m

crew [kruː] n Besatzung f, Mannschaft f; **~-cut** n Bürstenschnitt m; **~ neck** n runde(r)

Ausschnitt *m*

crib [krɪb] *n* (*bed*) Krippe *f* ♦ *vt* (*inf*) spicken

crick [krɪk] *n* Muskelkrampf *m*

cricket ['krɪkɪt] *n* (*insect*) Grille *f*; (*game*) Kricket *nt*

crime [kraɪm] *n* Verbrechen *nt*

criminal ['krɪmɪnl] *n* Verbrecher *m* ♦ *adj* kriminell; (*act*) strafbar

crimson ['krɪmzn] *adj* leuchtend rot

cringe [krɪndʒ] *vi* sich ducken

crinkle ['krɪŋkl] *vt* zerknittern

cripple ['krɪpl] *n* Krüppel *m* ♦ *vt* lahm legen; (*MED*) verkrüppeln

crisis ['kraɪsɪs] (*pl* **crises**) *n* Krise *f*

crisp [krɪsp] *adj* knusprig; ~**s** (*BRIT*) *npl* Chips *pl*

crisscross ['krɪskrɒs] *adj* gekreuzt, Kreuz-

criteria [kraɪ'tɪərɪə] *npl of* **criterion**

criterion [kraɪ'tɪərɪən] (*pl* **criteria**) *n* Kriterium *nt*

critic ['krɪtɪk] *n* Kritiker(in) *m(f)*; ~**al** *adj* kritisch; ~**ally** *adv* kritisch; (*ill*) gefährlich; ~**ism** ['krɪtɪsɪzəm] *n* Kritik *f*; ~**ize** ['krɪtɪsaɪz] *vt* kritisieren

croak [krəʊk] *vi* krächzen; (*frog*) quaken

Croatia [krəʊ'eɪʃə] *n* Kroatien *nt*

crochet ['krəʊʃeɪ] *n* Häkelei *f*

crockery ['krɒkərɪ] *n* Geschirr *nt*

crocodile ['krɒkədaɪl] *n* Krokodil *nt*

crocus ['krəʊkəs] *n* Krokus *m*

croft [krɒft] (*BRIT*) *n* kleine(s) Pachtgut *nt*

crony ['krəʊnɪ] (*inf*) *n* Kumpel *m*

crook [krʊk] *n* (*criminal*) Gauner *m*; (*stick*) Hirtenstab *m*

crooked ['krʊkɪd] *adj* krumm

crop [krɒp] *n* (*harvest*) Ernte *f*; (*riding* ~) Reitpeitsche *f* ♦ *vt* ernten; ~ **up** *vi* passieren

croquet ['krəʊkeɪ] *n* Krocket *nt*

croquette [krə'ket] *n* Krokette *f*

cross [krɒs] *n* Kreuz *nt* ♦ *vt* (*road*) überqueren; (*legs*) übereinander legen; kreuzen ♦ *adj* (*annoyed*) böse; ~ **out** *vt* streichen; ~ **over** *vi* hinübergehen; ~**bar** *n* Querstange *f*; ~**-country** (**race**) *n* Geländelauf *m*; ~**-examine** *vt* ins Kreuzverhör nehmen; ~**-eyed** *adj*: **to be**

~**-eyed** schielen; ~**fire** *n* Kreuzfeuer *nt*; ~**ing** *n* (~*roads*) (Straßen)kreuzung *f*; (*of ship*) Überfahrt *f*; (*for pedestrians*) Fußgängerüberweg *m*; ~**ing guard** (*US*) *n* Schülerlotse *m*; ~ **purposes** *npl*: **to be at** ~ **purposes** aneinander vorbeireden; ~**-reference** *n* Querverweis *m*; ~**roads** *n* Straßenkreuzung *f*; (*fig*) Scheideweg *m*; ~ **section** *n* Querschnitt *m*; ~**walk** (*US*) *n* Fußgängerüberweg *m*; ~**wind** *n* Seitenwind *m*; ~**word** (**puzzle**) *n* Kreuzworträtsel *nt*

crotch [krɒtʃ] *n* Zwickel *m*; (*ANAT*) Unterleib *nt*

crouch [kraʊtʃ] *vi* hocken

crow [krəʊ] *n* (*bird*) Krähe *f*; (*of cock*) Krähen *nt* ♦ *vi* krähen

crowbar ['krəʊbɑːʳ] *n* Stemmeisen *nt*

crowd [kraʊd] *n* Menge *f* ♦ *vt* (*fill*) überfüllen ♦ *vi* drängen; ~**ed** *adj* überfüllt

crown [kraʊn] *n* Krone *f*; (*of head, hat*) Kopf *m* ♦ *vt* krönen; ~ **jewels** *npl* Kronjuwelen *pl*; ~ **prince** *n* Kronprinz *m*

crow's-feet ['krəʊzfiːt] *npl* Krähenfüße *pl*

crucial ['kruːʃl] *adj* entscheidend

crucifix ['kruːsɪfɪks] *n* Kruzifix *nt*; ~**ion** [kruːsɪ'fɪkʃən] *n* Kreuzigung *f*

crude [kruːd] *adj* (*raw*) roh; (*humour, behaviour*) grob; (*basic*) primitiv; ~ (**oil**) *n* Rohöl *nt*

cruel ['kruəl] *adj* grausam; ~**ty** *n* Grausamkeit *f*

cruise [kruːz] *n* Kreuzfahrt *f* ♦ *vi* kreuzen; ~**r** *n* (*MIL*) Kreuzer *m*

crumb [krʌm] *n* Krume *f*

crumble ['krʌmbl] *vt*, *vi* zerbröckeln; **crumbly** *adj* krümelig

crumpet ['krʌmpɪt] *n* Tee(pfann)kuchen *m*

crumple ['krʌmpl] *vt* zerknittern

crunch [krʌntʃ] *n*: **the** ~ (*fig*) der Knackpunkt ♦ *vt* knirschen; ~**y** *adj* knusprig

crusade [kruː'seɪd] *n* Kreuzzug *m*

crush [krʌʃ] *n* Gedränge *nt* ♦ *vt* zerdrücken; (*rebellion*) unterdrücken

crust [krʌst] *n* Kruste *f*

crutch [krʌtʃ] *n* Krücke *f*

crux [krʌks] *n* springende(r) Punkt *m*

cry [kraɪ] vi (shout) schreien; (weep) weinen ♦ n (call) Schrei m; ~ **off** vi (plötzlich) absagen

crypt [krɪpt] n Krypta f

cryptic ['krɪptɪk] adj hintergründig

crystal ['krɪstl] n Kristall m; (glass) Kristallglas nt; (mineral) Bergkristall m; **~-clear** adj kristallklar

crystallize ['krɪstəlaɪz] vt, vi kristallisieren; (fig) klären

CSA n abbr (= Child Support Agency) Amt zur Regelung von Unterhaltszahlungen für Kinder

CTC (BRIT) n abbr = **city technology college**

cub [kʌb] n Junge(s) nt; (also: **C~ scout**) Wölfling m

Cuba ['kjuːbə] n Kuba nt; **~n** adj kubanisch ♦ n Kubaner(in) m(f)

cubbyhole ['kʌbɪhəul] n Eckchen nt

cube [kjuːb] n Würfel m ♦ vt (MATH) hoch drei nehmen

cubic ['kjuːbɪk] adj würfelförmig; (centimetre etc) Kubik-; **~ capacity** n Fassungsvermögen nt

cubicle ['kjuːbɪkl] n Kabine f

cuckoo ['kukuː] n Kuckuck m; ~ **clock** n Kuckucksuhr f

cucumber ['kjuːkʌmbə'] n Gurke f

cuddle ['kʌdl] vt, vi herzen, drücken (inf)

cue [kjuː] n (THEAT) Stichwort nt; (snooker ~) Billardstock m

cuff [kʌf] n (BRIT: of shirt, coat etc) Manschette f; Aufschlag m; (US) = **turn-up**; **off the ~** aus dem Handgelenk; **~link** n Manschettenknopf m

cuisine [kwɪˈziːn] n Kochkunst f, Küche f

cul-de-sac ['kʌldəsæk] n Sackgasse f

culinary ['kʌlɪnərɪ] adj Koch-

cull [kʌl] vt (select) auswählen

culminate ['kʌlmɪneɪt] vi gipfeln; **culmination** [kʌlmɪˈneɪʃən] n Höhepunkt m

culottes [kjuːˈlɒts] npl Hosenrock m

culpable ['kʌlpəbl] adj schuldig

culprit ['kʌlprɪt] n Täter m

cult [kʌlt] n Kult m

cultivate ['kʌltɪveɪt] vt (AGR) bebauen; (mind) bilden; **cultivation** [kʌltɪˈveɪʃən] n

(AGR) Bebauung f; (of person) Bildung f

cultural ['kʌltʃərəl] adj kulturell, Kultur-

culture ['kʌltʃə'] n Kultur f; **~d** adj gebildet

cumbersome ['kʌmbəsəm] adj (object) sperrig

cumulative ['kjuːmjulətɪv] adj gehäuft

cunning ['kʌnɪŋ] n Verschlagenheit f ♦ adj schlau

cup [kʌp] n Tasse f; (prize) Pokal m

cupboard ['kʌbəd] n Schrank m

cup tie (BRIT) n Pokalspiel nt

curate ['kjuərɪt] n (Catholic) Kurat m; (Protestant) Vikar m

curator [kjuəˈreɪtə'] n Kustos m

curb [kəːb] vt zügeln ♦ n (on spending etc) Einschränkung f; (US) Bordstein m

curdle ['kəːdl] vi gerinnen

cure [kjuə'] n Heilmittel nt; (process) Heilverfahren nt ♦ vt heilen

curfew ['kəːfjuː] n Ausgangssperre f; Sperrstunde f

curio ['kjuərɪəu] n Kuriosität f

curiosity [kjuərɪˈɒsɪtɪ] n Neugier f

curious ['kjuərɪəs] adj neugierig; (strange) seltsam

curl [kəːl] n Locke f ♦ vt locken ♦ vi sich locken; ~ **up** vi sich zusammenrollen; (person) sich ankuscheln; **~er** n Lockenwickler m; **~y** ['kəːlɪ] adj lockig

currant ['kʌrnt] n Korinthe f

currency ['kʌrnsɪ] n Währung f; **to gain ~** an Popularität gewinnen

current ['kʌrnt] n Strömung f ♦ adj (expression) gängig, üblich; (issue) neueste; ~ **account** (BRIT) n Girokonto nt; ~ **affairs** npl Zeitgeschehen nt; **~ly** adv zurzeit

curricula [kəˈrɪkjulə] npl of **curriculum**

curriculum [kəˈrɪkjuləm] (pl **~s** or **curricula**) n Lehrplan m; ~ **vitae** [-'viːtaɪ] n Lebenslauf m

curry ['kʌrɪ] n Currygericht nt ♦ vt: **to ~ favour with** sich einschmeicheln bei; ~ **powder** n Curry(pulver) nt

curse [kəːs] vi (swear): **to ~ (at)** fluchen (auf or über +acc) ♦ vt (insult) verwünschen ♦ n Fluch m

cursor ['kəːsə'] n (COMPUT) Cursor m

cursory ['kəːsərɪ] *adj* flüchtig

curt [kəːt] *adj* schroff

curtail [kəː'teɪl] *vt* abkürzen; (*rights*) einschränken

curtain ['kəːtn] *n* Vorhang *m*

curts(e)y ['kəːtsɪ] *n* Knicks *m* ♦ *vi* knicksen

curve [kəːv] *n* Kurve *f*; (*of body, vase etc*) Rundung *f* ♦ *vi* sich biegen; (*hips, breasts*) sich runden; (*road*) einen Bogen machen

cushion ['kuʃən] *n* Kissen *nt* ♦ *vt* dämpfen

custard ['kʌstəd] *n* Vanillesoße *f*

custodian [kʌs'təudɪən] *n* Kustos *m*, Verwalter(in) *m(f)*

custody ['kʌstədɪ] *n* Aufsicht *f*; (*police ~*) Haft *f*; **to take into ~** verhaften

custom ['kʌstəm] *n* (*tradition*) Brauch *m*; (*COMM*) Kundschaft *f*; **~ary** *adj* üblich

customer ['kʌstəmər] *n* Kunde *m*, Kundin *f*

customized ['kʌstəmaɪzd] *adj* (*car etc*) mit Spezialausrüstung

custom-made ['kʌstəm'meɪd] *adj* speziell angefertigt

customs ['kʌstəmz] *npl* Zoll *m*; **~ duty** *n* Zollabgabe *f*; **~ officer** *n* Zollbeamte(r) *m*, Zollbeamtin *f*

cut [kʌt] (*pt, pp* **cut**) *vt* schneiden; (*wages*) kürzen; (*prices*) heruntersetzen ♦ *vi* schneiden; (*intersect*) sich schneiden ♦ *n* Schnitt *m*; (*wound*) Schnittwunde *f*; (*in income etc*) Kürzung *f*; (*share*) Anteil *m*; **to ~ a tooth** zahnen; **~ down** *vt* (*tree*) fällen; (*reduce*) einschränken; **~ off** *vt* (*also fig*) abschneiden; (*allowance*) sperren; **~ out** *vt* (*shape*) ausschneiden; (*delete*) streichen; **~ up** *vt* (*meat*) aufschneiden; **~back** *n* Kürzung *f*

cute [kjuːt] *adj* niedlich

cuticle ['kjuːtɪkl] *n* Nagelhaut *f*

cutlery ['kʌtlərɪ] *n* Besteck *nt*

cutlet ['kʌtlɪt] *n* (*pork*) Kotelett *nt*; (*veal*) Schnitzel *nt*

cut: ~out *n* (*cardboard ~out*) Ausschneidemodell *nt*; **~-price, ~-rate** (*US*) *adj* verbilligt; **~throat** *n* Verbrechertyp *m* ♦ *adj* mörderisch

cutting ['kʌtɪŋ] *adj* schneidend ♦ *n* (*BRIT: PRESS*) Ausschnitt *m*; (: *RAIL*) Durchstich *m*

CV *n abbr* = **curriculum vitae**

cwt *abbr* = **hundredweight(s)**

cyanide ['saɪənaɪd] *n* Zyankali *nt*

cybercafé ['saɪbəkæfeɪ] *n* Internet-Café *nt*

cyberspace ['saɪbəspeɪs] *n* Cyberspace *m*

cycle ['saɪkl] *n* Fahrrad *nt*; (*series*) Reihe *f* ♦ *vi* Rad fahren; **~ hire** *n* Fahrradverleih *m*; **~ lane, ~ path** *n* (Fahr)radweg *m*; **cycling** *n* Radfahren *nt*; **cyclist** *n* Radfahrer(in) *m(f)*

cyclone ['saɪkləun] *n* Zyklon *m*

cygnet ['sɪgnɪt] *n* junge(r) Schwan *m*

cylinder ['sɪlɪndər] *n* Zylinder *m*; (*TECH*) Walze *f*

cymbals ['sɪmblz] *npl* Becken *nt*

cynic ['sɪnɪk] *n* Zyniker(in) *m(f)*; **~al** *adj* zynisch; **~ism** ['sɪnɪsɪzəm] *n* Zynismus *m*

cypress ['saɪprɪs] *n* Zypresse *f*

Cyprus ['saɪprəs] *n* Zypern *nt*

cyst [sɪst] *n* Zyste *f*

cystitis [sɪs'taɪtɪs] *n* Blasenentzündung *f*

czar [zɑːr] *n* Zar *m*

Czech [tʃek] *adj* tschechisch ♦ *n* Tscheche *m*, Tschechin *f*

Czechoslovakia [tʃekəslə'vækɪə] (*HIST*) *n* die Tschechoslowakei; **~n** *adj* tschechoslowakisch ♦ *n* Tschechoslowake *m*, Tchechoslowakin *f*

D, d

D [diː] *n* (*MUS*) D *nt*

dab [dæb] *vt* (*wound, paint*) betupfen ♦ *n* (*little bit*) bisschen *nt*; (*of paint*) Tupfer *m*

dabble ['dæbl] *vi*: **to ~ in sth** in etw *dat* machen

dad [dæd] *n* Papa *m*, Vati *m*; **~dy** ['dædɪ] *n* Papa *m*, Vati *m*; **~dy-long-legs** *n* Weberknecht *m*

daffodil ['dæfədɪl] *n* Osterglocke *f*

daft [dɑːft] (*inf*) *adj* blöd(e), doof

dagger ['dægər] *n* Dolch *m*

daily ['deɪlɪ] *adj* täglich ♦ *n* (*PRESS*) Tageszeitung *f*; (*BRIT: cleaner*) Haushaltshilfe *f* ♦ *adv* täglich

dainty ['deɪntɪ] *adj* zierlich

dairy ['deərɪ] *n* (*shop*) Milchgeschäft *nt*; (*on*

farm) Molkerei *f* ♦ *adj* Milch-; ~ **farm** *n* Hof *m* mit Milchwirtschaft; ~ **produce** *n* Molkereiprodukte *pl*; ~ **products** *npl* Milchprodukte *pl*, Molkereiprodukte *pl*; ~ **store** (*US*) *n* Milchgeschäft *nt*

dais ['deɪs] *n* Podium *nt*

daisy ['deɪzɪ] *n* Gänseblümchen *nt*

dale [deɪl] *n* Tal *nt*

dam [dæm] *n* (Stau)damm *m* ♦ *vt* stauen

damage ['dæmɪdʒ] *n* Schaden *m* ♦ *vt* beschädigen; ~**s** *npl* (*JUR*) Schaden(s)ersatz *m*

damn [dæm] *vt* verdammen ♦ *n* (*inf*): **I don't give a ~** das ist mir total egal ♦ *adj* (*inf*: *also*: ~**ed**) verdammt; ~ **it!** verflucht!; ~**ing** *adj* vernichtend

damp [dæmp] *adj* feucht ♦ *n* Feuchtigkeit *f* ♦ *vt* (*also*: ~**en**) befeuchten; (*discourage*) dämpfen

damson ['dæmzən] *n* Damaszenerpflaume *f*

dance [dɑːns] *n* Tanz *m* ♦ *vi* tanzen; ~ **hall** *n* Tanzlokal *nt*; ~**r** *n* Tänzer(in) *m(f)*; **dancing** *n* Tanzen *nt*

dandelion ['dændɪlaɪən] *n* Löwenzahn *m*

dandruff ['dændrəf] *n* (Kopf)schuppen *pl*

Dane [deɪn] *n* Däne *m*, Dänin *f*

danger ['deɪndʒəʳ] *n* Gefahr *f*; ~**!** (*sign*) Achtung!; **to be in ~ of doing sth** Gefahr laufen, etw zu tun; ~**ous** *adj* gefährlich

dangle ['dæŋgl] *vi* baumeln ♦ *vt* herabhängen lassen

Danish ['deɪnɪʃ] *adj* dänisch ♦ *n* Dänisch *nt*

dare [dɛəʳ] *vt* herausfordern ♦ *vi*: **to ~ (to) do sth** es wagen, etw zu tun; **I ~ say** ich würde sagen; **daring** ['dɛərɪŋ] *adj* (*audacious*) verwegen; (*bold*) wagemutig; (*dress*) gewagt ♦ *n* Mut *m*

dark [dɑːk] *adj* dunkel; (*fig*) düster, trübe; (*deep colour*) dunkel- ♦ *n* Dunkelheit *f*; **to be left in the ~ about** im Dunkeln sein über +*acc*; **after ~** nach Anbruch der Dunkelheit; ~**en** *vt*, *vi* verdunkeln; ~ **glasses** *npl* Sonnenbrille *f*; ~**ness** *n* Finsternis *nt*; ~**room** *n* Dunkelkammer *f*

darling ['dɑːlɪŋ] *n* Liebling *m* ♦ *adj* lieb

darn [dɑːn] *vt* stopfen

dart [dɑːt] *n* (*weapon*) Pfeil *m*; (*in sewing*)

Abnäher *m* ♦ *vi* sausen; ~**s** *n* (*game*) Pfeilwerfen *nt*; ~**board** *n* Zielscheibe *f*

dash [dæʃ] *n* Sprung *m*; (*mark*) (Gedanken)strich *m*; (*small amount*) bisschen *nt* ♦ *vt* (*hopes*) zunichte machen ♦ *vi* stürzen; ~ **away** *vi* davonstürzen; ~ **off** *vi* davonstürzen

dashboard ['dæʃbɔːd] *n* Armaturenbrett *nt*

dashing ['dæʃɪŋ] *adj* schneidig

data ['deɪtə] *npl* Einzelheiten *pl*, Daten *pl*; ~**base** *n* Datenbank *f*; ~ **processing** *n* Datenverarbeitung *f*

date [deɪt] *n* Datum *nt*; (*for meeting etc*) Termin *m*; (*with person*) Verabredung *f*; (*fruit*) Dattel *f* ♦ *vt* (*letter etc*) datieren; (*person*) gehen mit; ~ **of birth** Geburtsdatum *nt*; **to** ~ bis heute; **out of** ~ überholt; **up to** ~ (*clothes*) modisch; (*report*) up-to-date; (*with news*) auf dem Laufenden; ~**d** *adj* altmodisch; ~ **rape** *n* Vergewaltigung *f* nach einem Rendezvous

daub [dɔːb] *vt* beschmieren; (*paint*) schmieren

daughter ['dɔːtəʳ] *n* Tochter *f*; ~**-in-law** *n* Schwiegertochter *f*

daunting ['dɔːntɪŋ] *adj* entmutigend

dawdle ['dɔːdl] *vi* trödeln

dawn [dɔːn] *n* Morgendämmerung *f* ♦ *vi* dämmern; (*fig*): **it ~ed on him that ...** es dämmerte ihm, dass ...

day [deɪ] *n* Tag *m*; **the ~ before/after** am Tag zuvor/danach; **the ~ after tomorrow** übermorgen; **the ~ before yesterday** vorgestern; **by ~** am Tage; ~**break** *n* Tagesanbruch *m*; ~**dream** *vi* mit offenen Augen träumen; ~**light** *n* Tageslicht *nt*; ~ **return** (*BRIT*) *n* Tagesrückfahrkarte *f*; ~**time** *n* Tageszeit *f*; ~**-to-~** *adj* alltäglich

daze [deɪz] *vt* betäuben ♦ *n* Betäubung *f*; **in a ~** benommen

dazzle ['dæzl] *vt* blenden

DC *abbr* (= *direct current*) Gleichstrom *m*

D-day ['diːdeɪ] *n* (*HIST*) Tag der Invasion durch die Alliierten (6.6.44); (*fig*) der Tag X

deacon ['diːkən] *n* Diakon *m*

dead [dɛd] *adj* tot; (*without feeling*) gefühllos ♦ *adv* ganz; (*exactly*) genau ♦ *npl*: **the ~** die

Toten *pl*; **to shoot sb** ~ jdn erschießen; ~
tired todmüde; **to stop** ~ abrupt stehen
bleiben; **~en** *vt* (*pain*) abtöten; (*sound*)
ersticken; ~ **end** *n* Sackgasse *f*; ~ **heat** *n*
tote(s) Rennen *nt*; **~line** *n* Stichtag *m*;
~lock *n* Stillstand *m*; ~ **loss** (*inf*) *n*: **to be**
a ~ loss ein hoffnungsloser Fall sein; **~ly**
adj tödlich; **~pan** *adj* undurchdringlich; **D~**
Sea *n*: **the D~ Sea** das Tote Meer

deaf [def] *adj* taub; **~en** *vt* taub machen;
~ening *adj* (*noise*) ohrenbetäubend; (*noise*)
lautstark; **~-mute** *n* Taubstumme(r) *mf*;
~ness *n* Taubheit *f*

deal [di:l] (*pt, pp* **dealt**) *n* Geschäft *nt* ♦ *vt*
austeilen; (*CARDS*) geben; **a great ~ of** sehr
viel; ~ **in** *vt fus* handeln mit; ~ **with** *vt fus*
(*person*) behandeln; (*subject*) sich befassen
mit; (*problem*) in Angriff nehmen; **~er** *n*
(*COMM*) Händler *m*; (*CARDS*) Kartengeber *m*;
~ings *npl* (*FIN*) Geschäfte *pl*; (*relations*)
Beziehungen *pl*; **~t** [delt] *pt, pp of* **deal**

dean [di:n] *n* (*Protestant*) Superintendent *m*;
(*Catholic*) Dechant *m*; (*UNIV*) Dekan *m*

dear [dɪəʳ] *adj* lieb; (*expensive*) teuer ♦ *n*
Liebling *m* ♦ *excl*: ~ **me!** du liebe Zeit!; **D~**
Sir Sehr geehrter Herr!; **D~ John** Lieber
John!; **~ly** *adv* (*love*) herzlich; (*pay*) teuer

death [dɛθ] *n* Tod *m*; (*statistic*) Todesfall *m*;
~ **certificate** *n* Totenschein *m*; **~ly** *adj*
totenähnlich, Toten-; ~ **penalty** *n*
Todesstrafe *f*; ~ **rate** *n* Sterblichkeitsziffer *f*

debar [dɪˈbɑːʳ] *vt* ausschließen

debase [dɪˈbeɪs] *vt* entwerten

debatable [dɪˈbeɪtəbl] *adj* anfechtbar

debate [dɪˈbeɪt] *n* Debatte *f* ♦ *vt* debattieren,
diskutieren; (*consider*) überlegen

debilitating [dɪˈbɪlɪteɪtɪŋ] *adj* schwächend

debit [ˈdebɪt] *n* Schuldposten *m* ♦ *vt* belasten

debris [ˈdebriː] *n* Trümmer *pl*

debt [dɛt] *n* Schuld *f*; **to be in** ~ verschuldet
sein; **~or** *n* Schuldner *m*

debunk [diːˈbʌŋk] *vt* entlarven

decade [ˈdekeɪd] *n* Jahrzehnt *nt*

decadence [ˈdekədəns] *n* Dekadenz *f*

decaff [ˈdiːkæf] (*inf*) *n* koffeinfreier Kaffee

decaffeinated [dɪˈkæfɪneɪtɪd] *adj* koffeinfrei

decanter [dɪˈkæntəʳ] *n* Karaffe *f*

decay [dɪˈkeɪ] *n* Verfall *m*; (*tooth ~*) Karies *m*
♦ *vi* verfallen; (*teeth, meat etc*) faulen; (*leaves
etc*) verrotten

deceased [dɪˈsiːst] *adj* verstorben

deceit [dɪˈsiːt] *n* Betrug *m*; **~ful** *adj* falsch

deceive [dɪˈsiːv] *vt* täuschen

December [dɪˈsembəʳ] *n* Dezember *m*

decency [ˈdiːsənsɪ] *n* Anstand *m*

decent [ˈdiːsənt] *adj* (*respectable*) anständig;
(*pleasant*) annehmbar

deception [dɪˈsepʃən] *n* Betrug *m*

deceptive [dɪˈseptɪv] *adj* irreführend

decibel [ˈdesɪbel] *n* Dezibel *nt*

decide [dɪˈsaɪd] *vt* entscheiden ♦ *vi* sich
entscheiden; **to ~ on sth** etw beschließen;
~d *adj* entschieden; **~dly** [dɪˈsaɪdɪdlɪ] *adv*
entschieden

deciduous [dɪˈsɪdjuəs] *adj* Laub-

decimal [ˈdesɪməl] *adj* dezimal ♦ *n*
Dezimalzahl *f*; ~ **point** *n* Komma *nt*

decipher [dɪˈsaɪfəʳ] *vt* entziffern

decision [dɪˈsɪʒən] *n* Entscheidung *f*,
Entschluss *m*

decisive [dɪˈsaɪsɪv] *adj* entscheidend;
(*person*) entschlossen

deck [dek] *n* (*NAUT*) Deck *nt*; (*of cards*) Pack
m; **~chair** *n* Liegestuhl *m*

declaration [dekləˈreɪʃən] *n* Erklärung *f*

declare [dɪˈkleəʳ] *vt* erklären; (*CUSTOMS*)
verzollen

decline [dɪˈklaɪn] *n* (*decay*) Verfall *m*;
(*lessening*) Rückgang *m* ♦ *vt* (*invitation*)
ablehnen ♦ *vi* (*say no*) ablehnen; (*of
strength*) nachlassen

decode [ˈdiːˈkəud] *vt* entschlüsseln; **~r** *n* (*TV*)
Decoder *m*

decompose [diːkəmˈpəuz] *vi* (sich)
zersetzen

décor [ˈdeɪkɔːʳ] *n* Ausstattung *f*

decorate [ˈdekəreɪt] *vt* (*room: paper*)
tapezieren; (: *paint*) streichen; (*adorn*)
(aus)schmücken; (*cake*) verzieren; (*honour*)
auszeichnen; **decoration** [dekəˈreɪʃən] *n* (*of
house*) (Wand)dekoration *f*; (*medal*) Orden
m; **decorator** [ˈdekəreɪtəʳ] *n* Maler *m*,
Anstreicher *m*

decorum [dɪˈkɔːrəm] *n* Anstand *m*

decoy ['di:kɔɪ] n Lockvogel m

decrease [n 'di:kri:s, vb di:'kri:s] n Abnahme f ♦ vt vermindern ♦ vi abnehmen

decree [dɪ'kri:] n Erlass m; ~ nisi n vorläufige(s) Scheidungsurteil nt

decrepit [dɪ'krepɪt] adj hinfällig

dedicate ['dedɪkeɪt] vt widmen; ~d adj hingebungsvoll, engagiert; (COMPUT) dediziert; dedication [dedɪ'keɪʃən] n (devotion) Ergebenheit f; (in book) Widmung f

deduce [dɪ'dju:s] vt: to ~ sth (from sth) etw (aus etw) ableiten, etw (aus etw) schließen

deduct [dɪ'dʌkt] vt abziehen; ~ion [dɪ'dʌkʃən] n (of money) Abzug m; (conclusion) (Schluss)folgerung f

deed [di:d] n Tat f; (document) Urkunde f

deem [di:m] vt: to ~ sb/sth (to be) sth jdn/etw für etw halten

deep [di:p] adj tief ♦ adv: the spectators stood 20 ~ die Zuschauer standen in 20 Reihen hintereinander; to be 4m ~ 4 Meter tief sein; ~en vt vertiefen ♦ vi (darkness) tiefer werden; ~ end n: the ~ end (of swimming pool) das Tiefe; ~-freeze n Tiefkühlung f; ~-fry vt frittieren; ~ly adv tief; ~-sea diving n Tiefseetauchen nt; ~-seated adj tief sitzend

deer [dɪə] n Reh nt; ~skin n Hirsch-/Rehleder nt

deface [dɪ'feɪs] vt entstellen

defamation [defə'meɪʃən] n Verleumdung f

default [dɪ'fɔ:lt] n Versäumnis nt; (COMPUT) Standardwert m ♦ vi versäumen; by ~ durch Nichterscheinen

defeat [dɪ'fi:t] n Niederlage f ♦ vt schlagen; ~ist adj defätistisch ♦ n Defätist m

defect [n 'di:fekt, vb dɪ'fekt] n Fehler m ♦ vi überlaufen; ~ive [dɪ'fektɪv] adj fehlerhaft

defence [dɪ'fens] n Verteidigung f; ~less adj wehrlos

defend [dɪ'fend] vt verteidigen; ~ant n Angeklagte(r) m; ~er n Verteidiger m

defense [dɪ'fens] (US) n = defence

defensive [dɪ'fensɪv] adj defensiv ♦ n: on the ~ in der Defensive

defer [dɪ'fɜ:] vt verschieben

deference ['defərəns] n Rücksichtnahme f

defiance [dɪ'faɪəns] n Trotz m, Unnachgiebigkeit f; in ~ of sth einer Sache dat zum Trotz

defiant [dɪ'faɪənt] adj trotzig, unnachgiebig

deficiency [dɪ'fɪʃənsɪ] n (lack) Mangel m; (weakness) Schwäche f

deficient [dɪ'fɪʃənt] adj mangelhaft

deficit ['defɪsɪt] n Defizit nt

defile [vb dɪ'faɪl, n 'di:faɪl] vt beschmutzen ♦ n Hohlweg m

define [dɪ'faɪn] vt bestimmen; (explain) definieren

definite ['defɪnɪt] adj (fixed) definitiv; (clear) eindeutig; ~ly adv bestimmt

definition [defɪ'nɪʃən] n Definition f

deflate [di:'fleɪt] vt die Luft ablassen aus

deflect [dɪ'flekt] vt ablenken

deformity [dɪ'fɔ:mɪtɪ] n Missbildung f

defraud [dɪ'frɔ:d] vt betrügen

defrost [di:'frɒst] vt (fridge) abtauen; (food) auftauen; ~er (US) n (demister) Gebläse nt

deft [deft] adj geschickt

defunct [dɪ'fʌŋkt] adj verstorben

defuse [di:'fju:z] vt entschärfen

defy [dɪ'faɪ] vt (disobey) sich widersetzen +dat; (orders, death) trotzen +dat; (challenge) herausfordern

degenerate [v dɪ'dʒenəreɪt, adj dɪ'dʒenərɪt] vi degenerieren ♦ adj degeneriert

degrading [dɪ'greɪdɪŋ] adj erniedrigend

degree [dɪ'gri:] n Grad m; (UNIV) Universitätsabschluss m; by ~s allmählich; to some ~ zu einem gewissen Grad

dehydrated [di:haɪ'dreɪtɪd] adj (person) ausgetrocknet

de-ice ['di:'aɪs] vt enteisen

deign [deɪn] vi sich herablassen

deity ['di:ɪtɪ] n Gottheit f

dejected [dɪ'dʒektɪd] adj niedergeschlagen

delay [dɪ'leɪ] vt (hold back) aufschieben ♦ vi (linger) sich aufhalten ♦ n Aufschub m, Verzögerung f; (of train etc) Verspätung f; to be ~ed (train) Verspätung haben; without ~ unverzüglich

delectable [dɪ'lektəbl] adj köstlich; (fig) reizend

delegate [n 'dɛlɪgɪt, vb 'dɛlɪgeɪt] n
Delegierte(r) mf ♦ vt delegieren
delete [dɪ'li:t] vt (aus)streichen
deliberate [adj dɪ'lɪbərɪt, vb dɪ'lɪbəreɪt] adj
(intentional) absichtlich; (slow) bedächtig
♦ vi (consider) überlegen; (debate) sich
beraten; ~**ly** adv absichtlich
delicacy ['dɛlɪkəsɪ] n Zartheit f; (weakness)
Anfälligkeit f; (food) Delikatesse f
delicate ['dɛlɪkɪt] adj (fine) fein; (fragile) zart;
(situation) heikel; (MED) empfindlich
delicatessen [dɛlɪkə'tɛsn] n
Feinkostgeschäft nt
delicious [dɪ'lɪʃəs] adj lecker
delight [dɪ'laɪt] n Wonne f ♦ vt entzücken; to
take ~ in sth Freude an etw dat haben;
~**ed** adj: ~**ed (at or with sth)** entzückt
(über +acc etw); ~**ed to do sth** etw sehr
gern tun; ~**ful** adj entzückend, herrlich
delinquency [dɪ'lɪŋkwənsɪ] n Kriminalität f
delinquent [dɪ'lɪŋkwənt] n Straffällige(r) mf
♦ adj straffällig
delirious [dɪ'lɪrɪəs] adj im Fieberwahn
deliver [dɪ'lɪvəʳ] vt (goods) (ab)liefern; (letter)
zustellen; (speech) halten; ~**y** n
(Ab)lieferung f; (of letter) Zustellung f; (of
speech) Vortragsweise f; (MED) Entbindung
f; to take ~**y of** in Empfang nehmen
delude [dɪ'lu:d] vt täuschen
deluge ['dɛlju:dʒ] n Überschwemmung f;
(fig) Flut f ♦ vt (fig) überfluten
delusion [dɪ'lu:ʒən] n (Selbst)täuschung f
de luxe [də'lʌks] adj Luxus-
delve [dɛlv] vi: to ~ **into** sich vertiefen in
+acc
demand [dɪ'mɑ:nd] vt verlangen ♦ n
(request) Verlangen nt; (COMM) Nachfrage f;
in ~ gefragt; **on** ~ auf Verlangen; ~**ing** adj
anspruchsvoll
demean [dɪ'mi:n] vt: to ~ **o.s.** sich
erniedrigen
demeanour [dɪ'mi:nəʳ] (US **demeanor**) n
Benehmen nt
demented [dɪ'mɛntɪd] adj wahnsinnig
demister [di:'mɪstəʳ] n (AUT) Gebläse nt
demo ['dɛməʊ] (inf) n abbr (= demonstration)
Demo f

democracy [dɪ'mɔkrəsɪ] n Demokratie f
democrat ['dɛməkræt] n Demokrat m;
democratic [dɛmə'krætɪk] adj demokratisch
demolish [dɪ'mɔlɪʃ] vt abreißen; (fig)
vernichten
demolition [dɛmə'lɪʃən] n Abbruch m
demon ['di:mən] n Dämon m
demonstrate ['dɛmənstreɪt] vt, vi
demonstrieren; **demonstration**
[dɛmən'streɪʃən] n Demonstration f;
demonstrator ['dɛmənstreɪtəʳ] n (POL)
Demonstrant(in) m(f)
demote [dɪ'məʊt] vt degradieren
demure [dɪ'mjʊəʳ] adj ernst
den [dɛn] n (of animal) Höhle f; (study) Bude
f
denatured alcohol [di:'neɪtʃəd-] (US) n
ungenießbar gemachte(r) Alkohol m
denial [dɪ'naɪəl] n Leugnung f; **official** ~
Dementi nt
denim ['dɛnɪm] adj Denim-; ~**s** npl
Denimjeans pl
Denmark ['dɛnmɑ:k] n Dänemark nt
denomination [dɪnɔmɪ'neɪʃən] n (ECCL)
Bekenntnis nt; (type) Klasse f; (FIN) Wert m
denote [dɪ'nəʊt] vt bedeuten
denounce [dɪ'naʊns] vt brandmarken
dense [dɛns] adj dicht; (stupid) schwer von
Begriff; ~**ly** adv dicht; **density** ['dɛnsɪtɪ] n
Dichte f; **single/double density disk**
Diskette f mit einfacher/doppelter Dichte
dent [dɛnt] n Delle f ♦ vt (also: **make a ~ in**)
einbeulen
dental ['dɛntl] adj Zahn-; ~ **surgeon** n =
dentist
dentist ['dɛntɪst] n Zahnarzt(ärztin) m(f)
dentures ['dɛntʃəz] npl Gebiss nt
deny [dɪ'naɪ] vt leugnen; (officially)
dementieren; (help) abschlagen
deodorant [di:'əʊdərənt] n Deodorant nt
depart [dɪ'pɑ:t] vi abfahren; to ~ **from** (fig:
differ from) abweichen von
department [dɪ'pɑ:tmənt] n (COMM)
Abteilung f; (UNIV) Seminar nt; (POL)
Ministerium nt; ~ **store** n Warenhaus nt
departure [dɪ'pɑ:tʃəʳ] n (of person) Abreise f;
(of train) Abfahrt f; (of plane) Abflug m; **new**

~ Neuerung *f*; ~ **lounge** *n* (*at airport*) Abflughalle *f*

depend [dɪ'pend] *vi*: **to ~ on** abhängen von; (*rely on*) angewiesen sein auf +*acc*; **it ~s** es kommt darauf an; **~ing on the result ...** abhängend vom Resultat ...; **~able** *adj* zuverlässig; **~ant** *n* Angehörige(r) *f(m)*; **~ence** *n* Abhängigkeit *f*; **~ent** *adj* abhängig ♦ *n* = **dependant**; **~ent on** abhängig von

depict [dɪ'pɪkt] *vt* schildern

depleted [dɪ'pliːtɪd] *adj* aufgebraucht

deplorable [dɪ'plɔːrəbl] *adj* bedauerlich

deploy [dɪ'plɔɪ] *vt* einsetzen

depopulation ['diːpɔpju'leɪʃən] *n* Entvölkerung *f*

deport [dɪ'pɔːt] *vt* deportieren; **~ation** [diːpɔː'teɪʃən] *n* Abschiebung *f*

deportment [dɪ'pɔːtmənt] *n* Betragen *nt*

deposit [dɪ'pɔzɪt] *n* (*in bank*) Guthaben *nt*; (*down payment*) Anzahlung *f*; (*security*) Kaution *f*; (CHEM) Niederschlag *m* ♦ *vt* (*in bank*) deponieren; (*put down*) niederlegen; **~ account** *n* Sparkonto *nt*

depot ['depəu] *n* Depot *nt*

depraved [dɪ'preɪvd] *adj* verkommen

depreciate [dɪ'priːʃɪeɪt] *vi* im Wert sinken; **depreciation** [dɪpriːʃɪ'eɪʃən] *n* Wertminderung *f*

depress [dɪ'pres] *vt* (*press down*) niederdrücken; (*in mood*) deprimieren; **~ed** *adj* deprimiert; **~ion** [dɪ'preʃən] *n* (*mood*) Depression *f*; (*in trade*) Wirtschaftskrise *f*; (*hollow*) Vertiefung *f*; (MET) Tief(druckgebiet) *nt*

deprivation [deprɪ'veɪʃən] *n* Not *f*

deprive [dɪ'praɪv] *vt*: **to ~ sb of sth** jdn einer Sache *gen* berauben; **~d** *adj* (*child*) sozial benachteiligt; (*area*) unterentwickelt

depth [depθ] *n* Tiefe *f*; **in the ~s of despair** in tiefster Verzweiflung

deputation [depju'teɪʃən] *n* Abordnung *f*

deputize ['depjutaɪz] *vi*: **to ~ (for sb)** (jdn) vertreten

deputy ['depjutɪ] *adj* stellvertretend ♦ *n* (Stell)vertreter *m*; **~ head** (BRIT: SCOL) *n* Konrektor(in) *m(f)*

derail [dɪ'reɪl] *vt*: **to be ~ed** entgleisen; **~ment** *n* Entgleisung *f*

deranged [dɪ'reɪndʒd] *adj* verrückt

derby ['dɑːrbɪ] (US) *n* Melone *f*

derelict ['derɪlɪkt] *adj* verlassen

deride [dɪ'raɪd] *vt* auslachen

derisory [dɪ'raɪsərɪ] *adj* spöttisch

derivative [dɪ'rɪvətɪv] *n* Derivat *nt* ♦ *adj* abgeleitet

derive [dɪ'raɪv] *vt* (*get*) gewinnen; (*deduce*) ableiten ♦ *vi* (*come from*) abstammen

dermatitis [dəːmə'taɪtɪs] *n* Hautentzündung *f*

derogatory [dɪ'rɔgətərɪ] *adj* geringschätzig

derrick ['derɪk] *n* Drehkran *m*

descend [dɪ'send] *vt*, *vi* hinuntersteigen; **to ~ from** abstammen von; **~ant** *n* Nachkomme *m*; **descent** [dɪ'sent] *n* (*coming down*) Abstieg *m*; (*origin*) Abstammung *f*

describe [dɪs'kraɪb] *vt* beschreiben

description [dɪs'krɪpʃən] *n* Beschreibung *f*; (*sort*) Art *f*

descriptive [dɪs'krɪptɪv] *adj* beschreibend; (*word*) anschaulich

desecrate ['desɪkreɪt] *vt* schänden

desert [*n* 'dezət, *vb* dɪ'zəːt] *n* Wüste *f* ♦ *vt* verlassen; (*temporarily*) im Stich lassen ♦ *vi* (MIL) desertieren; **~s** *npl* (*what one deserves*): **to get one's just ~s** seinen gerechten Lohn bekommen; **~er** *n* Deserteur *m*; **~ion** [dɪ'zəːʃən] *n* (*of wife*) Verlassen *nt*; (MIL) Fahnenflucht *f*; **~ island** *n* einsame Insel *f*

deserve [dɪ'zəːv] *vt* verdienen; **deserving** *adj* verdienstvoll

design [dɪ'zaɪn] *n* (*plan*) Entwurf *m*; (*planning*) Design *nt* ♦ *vt* entwerfen

designate [*vb* 'dezɪgneɪt, *adj* 'dezɪgnɪt] *vt* bestimmen ♦ *adj* designiert

designer [dɪ'zaɪnər] *n* Designer(in) *m(f)*; (TECH) Konstrukteur(in) *m(f)*; (*fashion ~*) Modeschöpfer(in) *m(f)*

desirable [dɪ'zaɪərəbl] *adj* wünschenswert

desire [dɪ'zaɪər] *n* Wunsch *m*, Verlangen *nt* ♦ *vt* (*lust*) begehren; (*ask for*) wollen

desk [desk] *n* Schreibtisch *m*; (BRIT: in shop, restaurant) Kasse *f*; **~top publishing** *n*

Desktop-Publishing *nt*

desolate ['dɛsəlɪt] *adj* öde; (*sad*) trostlos; **desolation** [dɛsə'leɪʃən] *n* Trostlosigkeit *f*

despair [dɪs'pɛəʳ] *n* Verzweiflung *f* ♦ *vi*: **to ~ (of)** verzweifeln (an +*dat*)

despatch [dɪs'pætʃ] *n*, *vt* = **dispatch**

desperate ['dɛspərɪt] *adj* verzweifelt; **~ly** *adv* verzweifelt; **desperation** [dɛspə'reɪʃən] *n* Verzweiflung *f*

despicable [dɪs'pɪkəbl] *adj* abscheulich

despise [dɪs'paɪz] *vt* verachten

despite [dɪs'paɪt] *prep* trotz +*gen*

despondent [dɪs'pɒndənt] *adj* mutlos

dessert [dɪ'zɜːt] *n* Nachtisch *m*; **~spoon** *n* Dessertlöffel *m*

destination [dɛstɪ'neɪʃən] *n* (*of person*) (Reise)ziel *nt*; (*of goods*) Bestimmungsort *m*

destiny ['dɛstɪnɪ] *n* Schicksal *nt*

destitute ['dɛstɪtjuːt] *adj* Not leidend

destroy [dɪs'trɔɪ] *vt* zerstören; **~er** *n* (*NAUT*) Zerstörer *m*

destruction [dɪs'trʌkʃən] *n* Zerstörung *f*

destructive [dɪs'trʌktɪv] *adj* zerstörend

detach [dɪ'tætʃ] *vt* loslösen; **~able** *adj* abtrennbar; **~ed** *adj* (*attitude*) distanziert; (*house*) Einzel-; **~ment** *n* (*fig*) Abstand *m*; (*MIL*) Sonderkommando *nt*

detail ['diːteɪl] *n* Einzelheit *f*, Detail *nt* ♦ *vt* (*relate*) ausführlich berichten; (*appoint*) abkommandieren; **in ~** im Detail; **~ed** *adj* detailliert

detain [dɪ'teɪn] *vt* aufhalten; (*imprison*) in Haft halten

detect [dɪ'tɛkt] *vt* entdecken; **~ion** [dɪ'tɛkʃən] *n* Aufdeckung *f*; **~ive** *n* Detektiv *m*; **~ive story** *n* Kriminalgeschichte *f*, Krimi *m*

détente [deɪ'tɑːnt] *n* Entspannung *f*

detention [dɪ'tɛnʃən] *n* Haft *f*; (*SCH*) Nachsitzen *nt*

deter [dɪ'tɜːʳ] *vt* abschrecken

detergent [dɪ'tɜːdʒənt] *n* Waschmittel *nt*

deteriorate [dɪ'tɪərɪəreɪt] *vi* sich verschlechtern; **deterioration** [dɪtɪərɪə'reɪʃən] *n* Verschlechterung *f*

determination [dɪtɜːmɪ'neɪʃən] *n* Entschlossenheit *f*

determine [dɪ'tɜːmɪn] *vt* bestimmen; **~d** *adj* entschlossen

deterrent [dɪ'tɛrənt] *n* Abschreckungsmittel *nt*

detest [dɪ'tɛst] *vt* verabscheuen

detonate ['dɛtəneɪt] *vt* explodieren lassen ♦ *vi* detonieren

detour ['diːtuəʳ] *n* Umweg *m*; (*US: AUT: diversion*) Umleitung *f* ♦ *vt* (*US: AUT: traffic*) umleiten

detract [dɪ'trækt] *vi*: **to ~ from** schmälern

detriment ['dɛtrɪmənt] *n*: **to the ~ of** zum Schaden +*gen*; **~al** [dɛtrɪ'mɛntl] *adj* schädlich

devaluation [dɪvælju'eɪʃən] *n* Abwertung *f*

devastate ['dɛvəsteɪt] *vt* verwüsten; (*fig: shock*): **to be ~d by** niedergeschmettert sein von; **devastating** *adj* verheerend

develop [dɪ'vɛləp] *vt* entwickeln; (*resources*) erschließen ♦ *vi* sich entwickeln; **~ing country** *n* Entwicklungsland *nt*; **~ment** *n* Entwicklung *f*

deviate ['diːvɪeɪt] *vi* abweichen

device [dɪ'vaɪs] *n* Gerät *nt*

devil ['dɛvl] *n* Teufel *m*

devious ['diːvɪəs] *adj* (*means*) krumm; (*person*) verschlagen

devise [dɪ'vaɪz] *vt* entwickeln

devoid [dɪ'vɔɪd] *adj*: **~ of** ohne

devolution [diːvə'luːʃən] *n* (*POL*) Dezentralisierung *f*

devote [dɪ'vəʊt] *vt*: **to ~ sth (to sth)** etw (einer Sache *dat*) widmen; **~d** *adj* ergeben; **~e** [dɛvəʊ'tiː] *n* Anhänger(in) *m(f)*, Verehrer(in) *m(f)*; **devotion** [dɪ'vəʊʃən] *n* (*piety*) Andacht *f*; (*loyalty*) Ergebenheit *f*, Hingabe *f*

devour [dɪ'vaʊəʳ] *vt* verschlingen

devout [dɪ'vaʊt] *adj* andächtig

dew [djuː] *n* Tau *m*

dexterity [dɛks'tɛrɪtɪ] *n* Geschicklichkeit *f*

DHSS (*BRIT*) *n abbr* = **Department of Health and Social Security**

diabetes [daɪə'biːtiːz] *n* Zuckerkrankheit *f*

diabetic [daɪə'bɛtɪk] *adj* zuckerkrank; (*food*) Diabetiker- ♦ *n* Diabetiker *m*

diabolical [daɪə'bɒlɪkl] (*inf*) *adj* (*weather, behaviour*) saumäßig

diagnose [daɪəg'nəʊz] vt diagnostizieren

diagnoses [daɪəg'nəʊsi:z] npl of **diagnosis**

diagnosis [daɪəg'nəʊsɪs] n Diagnose f

diagonal [daɪ'ægənl] adj diagonal ♦ n Diagonale f

diagram ['daɪəgræm] n Diagramm nt, Schaubild nt

dial ['daɪəl] n (TEL) Wählscheibe f; (of clock) Zifferblatt nt ♦ vt wählen

dialect ['daɪəlɛkt] n Dialekt m

dialling code ['daɪəlɪŋ-] n Vorwahl f

dialling tone n Amtszeichen nt

dialogue ['daɪəlɔg] n Dialog m

dial tone (US) n = **dialling tone**

diameter [daɪ'æmɪtər] n Durchmesser m

diamond ['daɪəmənd] n Diamant m; **~s** npl (CARDS) Karo nt

diaper ['daɪəpər] (US) n Windel f

diaphragm ['daɪəfræm] n Zwerchfell nt

diarrhoea [daɪə'rɪə] (US **diarrhea**) n Durchfall m

diary ['daɪərɪ] n Taschenkalender m; (account) Tagebuch nt

dice [daɪs] n Würfel pl ♦ vt in Würfel schneiden

dictate [dɪk'teɪt] vt diktieren; **~s** ['dɪkteɪts] npl Gebote pl; **dictation** [dɪk'teɪʃən] n Diktat nt

dictator [dɪk'teɪtər] n Diktator m; **~ship** [dɪk'teɪtəʃɪp] n Diktatur f

dictionary ['dɪkʃənrɪ] n Wörterbuch nt

did [dɪd] pt of **do**

didn't ['dɪdnt] = **did not**

die [daɪ] vi sterben; **to be dying for sth** etw unbedingt haben wollen; **to be dying to do sth** darauf brennen, etw zu tun; **~ away** vi schwächer werden; **~ down** vi nachlassen; **~ out** vi aussterben

diesel ['di:zl] n (car) Diesel m; **~ engine** n Dieselmotor m; **~ oil** n Dieselkraftstoff m

diet ['daɪət] n Nahrung f; (special food) Diät f; (slimming) Abmagerungskur f ♦ vi (also: **be on a ~**) eine Abmagerungskur machen

differ ['dɪfər] vi sich unterscheiden; (disagree) anderer Meinung sein; **~ence** n Unterschied m; **~ent** adj anders; (two things) verschieden; **~entiate** [dɪfə'rɛnʃɪeɪt]

vt, vi unterscheiden; **~ently** adv anders; (from one another) unterschiedlich

difficult ['dɪfɪkəlt] adj schwierig; **~y** n Schwierigkeit f

diffident ['dɪfɪdənt] adj schüchtern

diffuse [adj dɪ'fju:s, vb dɪ'fju:z] adj langatmig ♦ vt verbreiten

dig [dɪg] (pt, pp **dug**) vt graben ♦ n (prod) Stoß m; (remark) Spitze f; (archaeological) Ausgrabung f; **~ in** vi (MIL) sich eingraben; **~ into** vt fus (savings) angreifen; **~ up** vt ausgraben; (fig) aufgabeln

digest [vb daɪ'dʒɛst, n 'daɪdʒɛst] vt verdauen ♦ n Auslese f; **~ion** [dɪ'dʒɛstʃən] n Verdauung f

digit ['dɪdʒɪt] n Ziffer f; (ANAT) Finger m; **~al** adj digital, Digital-; **~al camera** n Digitalkamera f; **~al TV** n Digitalfernsehen nt

dignified ['dɪgnɪfaɪd] adj würdevoll

dignity ['dɪgnɪtɪ] n Würde f

digress [daɪ'grɛs] vi abschweifen

digs [dɪgz] (BRIT: inf) npl Bude f

dilapidated [dɪ'læpɪdeɪtɪd] adj baufällig

dilate [daɪ'leɪt] vt weiten ♦ vi sich weiten

dilemma [daɪ'lɛmə] n Dilemma nt

diligent ['dɪlɪdʒənt] adj fleißig

dilute [daɪ'lu:t] vt verdünnen

dim [dɪm] adj trübe, (stupid) schwer von Begriff ♦ vt verdunkeln; **to ~ one's headlights** (esp US) abblenden

dime [daɪm] (US) n Zehncentstück nt

dimension [daɪ'mɛnʃən] n Dimension f

diminish [dɪ'mɪnɪʃ] vt, vi verringern

diminutive [dɪ'mɪnjutɪv] adj winzig ♦ n Verkleinerungsform f

dimmer ['dɪmər] (US) n (AUT) Abblendschalter m; **~s** npl (AUT) Abblendlicht nt; (sidelights) Begrenzungsleuchten pl

dimple ['dɪmpl] n Grübchen nt

din [dɪn] n Getöse nt

dine [daɪn] vi speisen; **~r** n Tischgast m; (RAIL) Speisewagen m

dinghy ['dɪŋgɪ] n Dingi nt; **rubber ~** Schlauchboot nt

dingy ['dɪndʒɪ] adj armselig

dining car (BRIT) n Speisewagen m

dining room ['daɪnɪŋ-] n Esszimmer nt; (in

hotel) Speisezimmer *nt*
dinner ['dɪnəʳ] *n* (*lunch*) Mittagessen *nt*; (*evening*) Abendessen *nt*; (*public*) Festessen *nt*; ~ **jacket** *n* Smoking *m*; ~ **party** *n* Tischgesellschaft *f*; ~ **time** *n* Tischzeit *f*
dinosaur ['daɪnəsɔːʳ] *n* Dinosaurier *m*
dint [dɪnt] *n*: **by** ~ **of** durch
diocese ['daɪəsɪs] *n* Diözese *f*
dip [dɪp] *n* (*hollow*) Senkung *f*; (*bathe*) kurze(s) Baden *nt* ♦ *vt* eintauchen; (*BRIT: AUT*) abblenden ♦ *vi* (*slope*) sich senken, abfallen
diploma [dɪ'pləʊmə] *n* Diplom *nt*
diplomacy [dɪ'pləʊməsɪ] *n* Diplomatie *f*
diplomat ['dɪpləmæt] *n* Diplomat(in) *m(f)*; ~**ic** [dɪplə'mætɪk] *adj* diplomatisch
dip stick *n* Ölmessstab *m*
dipswitch ['dɪpswɪtʃ] (*BRIT*) *n* (*AUT*) Abblendschalter *m*
dire [daɪəʳ] *adj* schrecklich
direct [daɪ'rekt] *adj* direkt ♦ *vt* leiten; (*film*) die Regie führen +*gen*; (*aim*) richten; (*order*) anweisen; **can you** ~ **me to ...?** können Sie mir sagen, wo ich zu ... komme?; ~ **debit** *n* (*BRIT*) Einzugsauftrag *m*; (*transaction*) automatische Abbuchung *f*
direction [dɪ'rekʃən] *n* Richtung *f*; (*CINE*) Regie *f*; Leitung *f*; ~**s** *npl* (*for use*) Gebrauchsanleitung *f*; (*orders*) Anweisungen *pl*; **sense of** ~ Orientierungssinn *m*
directly [dɪ'rektlɪ] *adv* direkt; (*at once*) sofort
director [dɪ'rektəʳ] *n* Direktor *m*; (*of film*) Regisseur *m*
directory [dɪ'rektərɪ] *n* (*TEL*) Telefonbuch *nt*; ~ **enquiries** ~ **assistance** (*US*) *n* (Fernsprech)auskunft *f*
dirt [dɜːt] *n* Schmutz *m*, Dreck *m*; ~-**cheap** *adj* spottbillig; ~**y** *adj* schmutzig ♦ *vt* beschmutzen; ~**y trick** *n* gemeine(r) Trick *m*
disability [dɪsə'bɪlɪtɪ] *n* Körperbehinderung *f*
disabled [dɪs'eɪbld] *adj* körperbehindert
disadvantage [dɪsəd'vɑːntɪdʒ] *n* Nachteil *m*
disagree [dɪsə'griː] *vi* nicht übereinstimmen; (*quarrel*) (sich) streiten; (*food*): **to** ~ **with sb** jdm nicht bekommen; ~**able** *adj*

unangenehm; ~**ment** *n* (*between persons*) Streit *m*; (*between things*) Widerspruch *m*
disallow ['dɪsə'laʊ] *vt* nicht zulassen
disappear [dɪsə'pɪəʳ] *vi* verschwinden; ~**ance** *n* Verschwinden *nt*
disappoint [dɪsə'pɔɪnt] *vt* enttäuschen; ~**ed** *adj* enttäuscht; ~**ment** *n* Enttäuschung *f*
disapproval [dɪsə'pruːvəl] *n* Missbilligung *f*
disapprove [dɪsə'pruːv] *vi*: **to** ~ **of** missbilligen
disarm [dɪs'ɑːm] *vt* entwaffnen; (*POL*) abrüsten; ~**ament** *n* Abrüstung *f*
disarray [dɪsə'reɪ] *n*: **to be in** ~ (*army*) in Auflösung (begriffen) sein; (*clothes*) in unordentlichen Zustand sein
disaster [dɪ'zɑːstəʳ] *n* Katastrophe *f*; **disastrous** [dɪ'zɑːstrəs] *adj* verhängnisvoll
disband [dɪs'bænd] *vt* auflösen ♦ *vi* auseinander gehen
disbelief ['dɪsbə'liːf] *n* Ungläubigkeit *f*
disc [dɪsk] *n* Scheibe *f*; (*record*) (Schall)platte *f*; (*COMPUT*) = **disk**
discard [dɪs'kɑːd] *vt* ablegen
discern [dɪ'sɜːn] *vt* erkennen; ~**ing** *adj* scharfsinnig
discharge [*vb* dɪs'tʃɑːdʒ, *n* 'dɪstʃɑːdʒ] *vt* (*ship*) entladen; (*duties*) nachkommen +*dat*; (*dismiss*) entlassen; (*gun*) abschießen; (*JUR*) freisprechen ♦ *n* (*of ship, ELEC*) Entladung *f*; (*dismissal*) Entlassung *f*; (*MED*) Ausfluss *m*
disciple [dɪ'saɪpl] *n* Jünger *m*
discipline ['dɪsɪplɪn] *n* Disziplin *f* ♦ *vt* (*train*) schulen; (*punish*) bestrafen
disc jockey *n* Diskjockey *m*
disclaim [dɪs'kleɪm] *vt* nicht anerkennen
disclose [dɪs'kləʊz] *vt* enthüllen; **disclosure** [dɪs'kləʊʒəʳ] *n* Enthüllung *f*
disco ['dɪskəʊ] *n abbr* = **discotheque**
discoloured [dɪs'kʌləd] (*US* **discolored**) *adj* verfärbt
discomfort [dɪs'kʌmfət] *n* Unbehagen *nt*
disconcert [dɪskən'sɜːt] *vt* aus der Fassung bringen
disconnect [dɪskə'nekt] *vt* abtrennen
discontent [dɪskən'tent] *n* Unzufriedenheit *f*; ~**ed** *adj* unzufrieden
discontinue [dɪskən'tɪnjuː] *vt* einstellen

discord ['dɪskɔːd] n Zwietracht f; (noise) Dissonanz f

discotheque ['dɪskəʊtek] n Diskothek f

discount [n 'dɪskaʊnt, vb dɪs'kaʊnt] n Rabatt m ♦ vt außer Acht lassen

discourage [dɪs'kʌrɪdʒ] vt entmutigen; (prevent) abraten

discourteous [dɪs'kɜːtɪəs] adj unhöflich

discover [dɪs'kʌvər] vt entdecken; ~y n Entdeckung f

discredit [dɪs'kredɪt] vt in Verruf bringen

discreet [dɪs'kriːt] adj diskret

discrepancy [dɪs'krepənsɪ] n Diskrepanz f

discriminate [dɪs'krɪmɪneɪt] vi unterscheiden; **to ~ against** diskriminieren; **discriminating** adj anspruchsvoll; **discrimination** [dɪskrɪmɪ'neɪʃən] n Urteilsvermögen nt; (pej) Diskriminierung f

discuss [dɪs'kʌs] vt diskutieren, besprechen; ~ion [dɪs'kʌʃən] n Diskussion f, Besprechung f

disdain [dɪs'deɪn] n Verachtung f

disease [dɪ'ziːz] n Krankheit f

disembark [dɪsɪm'bɑːk] vi von Bord gehen

disenchanted ['dɪsɪn'tʃɑːntɪd] adj desillusioniert

disengage [dɪsɪn'geɪdʒ] vt (AUT) auskuppeln

disentangle [dɪsɪn'tæŋgl] vt entwirren

disfigure [dɪs'fɪgər] vt entstellen

disgrace [dɪs'greɪs] n Schande f ♦ vt Schande bringen über +acc; ~ful adj unerhört

disgruntled [dɪs'grʌntld] adj verärgert

disguise [dɪs'gaɪz] vt verkleiden; (feelings) verhehlen ♦ n Verkleidung f; **in ~** verkleidet, maskiert

disgust [dɪs'gʌst] n Abscheu f ♦ vt anwidern; ~ed adj angeekelt; (at sb's behaviour) empört; ~ing adj widerlich

dish [dɪʃ] n Schüssel f; (food) Gericht nt; **to do** or **wash the ~es** abwaschen; ~ **up** vt auftischen; ~ **cloth** n Spüllappen m

dishearten [dɪs'hɑːtn] vt entmutigen

dishevelled [dɪ'ʃevəld] adj (hair) zerzaust; (clothing) ungepflegt

dishonest [dɪs'ɒnɪst] adj unehrlich

dishonour [dɪs'ɒnər] (US **dishonor**) n Unehre f; ~**able** adj unehrenhaft

dishtowel ['dɪʃtaʊəl] n Geschirrtuch nt

dishwasher ['dɪʃwɒʃər] n Geschirrspülmaschine f

disillusion [dɪsɪ'luːʒən] vt enttäuschen, desillusionieren

disincentive [dɪsɪn'sentɪv] n Entmutigung f

disinfect [dɪsɪn'fekt] vt desinfizieren; ~**ant** n Desinfektionsmittel nt

disintegrate [dɪs'ɪntɪgreɪt] vi sich auflösen

disinterested [dɪs'ɪntrəstɪd] adj uneigennützig; (inf) uninteressiert

disjointed [dɪs'dʒɔɪntɪd] adj unzusammenhängend

disk [dɪsk] n (COMPUT) Diskette f; **single/ double sided ~** einseitige/beidseitige Diskette; ~ **drive** n Diskettenlaufwerk nt; ~**ette** [dɪs'ket] (US) n = **disk**

dislike [dɪs'laɪk] n Abneigung f ♦ vt nicht leiden können

dislocate ['dɪsləkeɪt] vt auskugeln

dislodge [dɪs'lɒdʒ] vt verschieben; (MIL) aus der Stellung werfen

disloyal [dɪs'lɔɪəl] adj treulos

dismal ['dɪzml] adj trostlos, trübe

dismantle [dɪs'mæntl] vt demontieren

dismay [dɪs'meɪ] n Bestürzung f ♦ vt bestürzen

dismiss [dɪs'mɪs] vt (employee) entlassen; (idea) von sich weisen; (send away) wegschicken; (JUR) abweisen; ~**al** n Entlassung f

dismount [dɪs'maʊnt] vi absteigen

disobedience [dɪsə'biːdɪəns] n Ungehorsam m; **disobedient** adj ungehorsam

disobey [dɪsə'beɪ] vt nicht gehorchen +dat

disorder [dɪs'ɔːdər] n (confusion) Verwirrung f; (commotion) Aufruhr m; (MED) Erkrankung f

disorderly [dɪs'ɔːdəlɪ] adj (untidy) unordentlich; (unruly) ordnungswidrig

disorganized [dɪs'ɔːgənaɪzd] adj unordentlich

disorientated [dɪs'ɔːrɪenteɪtɪd] adj (person: after journey) verwirrt

disown [dɪs'əʊn] vt (child) verstoßen

disparaging [dɪs'pærɪdʒɪŋ] adj

geringschätzig

dispassionate [dɪs'pæʃənət] *adj* objektiv

dispatch [dɪs'pætʃ] *vt* (*goods*) abschicken, abfertigen ♦ *n* Absendung *f*; (*esp MIL*) Meldung *f*

dispel [dɪs'pel] *vt* zerstreuen

dispensary [dɪs'pensərɪ] *n* Apotheke *f*

dispense [dɪs'pens] *vt* verteilen, austeilen; **~ with** *vt fus* verzichten auf +*acc*; **~r** *n* (*container*) Spender *m*; **dispensing** *adj*: **dispensing chemist** (*BRIT*) Apotheker *m*

dispersal [dɪs'pɜːsl] *n* Zerstreuung *f*

disperse [dɪs'pɜːs] *vt* zerstreuen ♦ *vi* sich verteilen

dispirited [dɪs'pɪrɪtɪd] *adj* niedergeschlagen

displace [dɪs'pleɪs] *vt* verschieben; **~d person** *n* Verschleppte(r) *mf*

display [dɪs'pleɪ] *n* (*of goods*) Auslage *f*; (*of feeling*) Zurschaustellung *f* ♦ *vt* zeigen; (*ostentatiously*) vorführen; (*goods*) ausstellen

displease [dɪs'pliːz] *vt* missfallen +*dat*

displeasure [dɪs'pleʒər] *n* Missfallen *nt*

disposable [dɪs'pəuzəbl] *adj* Wegwerf-; **~ nappy** *n* Papierwindel *f*

disposal [dɪs'pəuzl] *n* (*of property*) Verkauf *m*; (*throwing away*) Beseitigung *f*; **to be at one's ~** einem zur Verfügung stehen

dispose [dɪs'pəuz] *vi*: **to ~ of** loswerden; **~d** *adj* geneigt

disposition [dɪspə'zɪʃən] *n* Wesen *nt*

disproportionate [dɪsprə'pɔːʃənət] *adj* unverhältnismäßig

disprove [dɪs'pruːv] *vt* widerlegen

dispute [dɪs'pjuːt] *n* Streit *m*; (*also:* **industrial ~**) Arbeitskampf *m* ♦ *vt* bestreiten

disqualify [dɪs'kwɒlɪfaɪ] *vt* disqualifizieren

disquiet [dɪs'kwaɪət] *n* Unruhe *f*

disregard [dɪsrɪ'gɑːd] *vt* nicht (be)achten

disrepair ['dɪsrɪ'peər] *n*: **to fall into ~** verfallen

disreputable [dɪs'repjutəbl] *adj* verrufen

disrespectful [dɪsrɪ'spektful] *adj* respektlos

disrupt [dɪs'rʌpt] *vt* stören; (*service*) unterbrechen; **~ion** [dɪs'rʌpʃən] *n* Störung *f*; Unterbrechung *f*

dissatisfaction [dɪssætɪs'fækʃən] *n*

Unzufriedenheit *f*; **dissatisfied** [dɪs'sætɪsfaɪd] *adj* unzufrieden

dissect [dɪ'sekt] *vt* zerlegen, sezieren

dissent [dɪ'sent] *n* abweichende Meinung *f*

dissertation [dɪsə'teɪʃən] *n* wissenschaftliche Arbeit *f*; (*Ph.D.*) Doktorarbeit *f*

disservice [dɪs'sɜːvɪs] *n*: **to do sb a ~** jdm einen schlechten Dienst erweisen

dissident ['dɪsɪdnt] *adj* anders denkend ♦ *n* Dissident *m*

dissimilar [dɪ'sɪmɪlər] *adj*: **~ (to sb/sth)** (jdm/etw) unähnlich

dissipate ['dɪsɪpeɪt] *vt* (*waste*) verschwenden; (*scatter*) zerstreuen

dissociate [dɪ'səuʃɪeɪt] *vt* trennen

dissolve [dɪ'zɒlv] *vt* auflösen ♦ *vi* sich auflösen

dissuade [dɪ'sweɪd] *vt*: **to ~ sb from doing sth** jdn davon abbringen, etw zu tun

distance ['dɪstns] *n* Entfernung *f*; **in the ~** in der Ferne; **distant** *adj* entfernt, fern; (*with time*) fern

distaste [dɪs'teɪst] *n* Abneigung *f*; **~ful** *adj* widerlich

distended [dɪs'tendɪd] *adj* (*stomach*) aufgebläht

distil [dɪs'tɪl] *vt* destillieren; **~lery** *n* Brennerei *f*

distinct [dɪs'tɪŋkt] *adj* (*separate*) getrennt; (*clear*) klar, deutlich; **as ~ from** im Unterschied zu; **~ion** [dɪs'tɪŋkʃən] *n* Unterscheidung *f*; (*eminence*) Auszeichnung *f*; **~ive** *adj* bezeichnend

distinguish [dɪs'tɪŋgwɪʃ] *vt* unterscheiden; **~ed** *adj* (*eminent*) berühmt; **~ing** *adj* bezeichnend

distort [dɪs'tɔːt] *vt* verdrehen; (*misrepresent*) entstellen; **~ion** [dɪs'tɔːʃən] *n* Verzerrung *f*

distract [dɪs'trækt] *vt* ablenken; **~ing** *adj* verwirrend; **~ion** [dɪs'trækʃən] *n* (*distress*) Raserei *f*; (*diversion*) Zerstreuung *f*

distraught [dɪs'trɔːt] *adj* bestürzt

distress [dɪs'tres] *n* Not *f*; (*suffering*) Qual *f* ♦ *vt* quälen; **~ing** *adj* erschütternd; **~ signal** *n* Notsignal *nt*

distribute [dɪs'trɪbjuːt] *vt* verteilen; **distribution** [dɪstrɪ'bjuːʃən] *n* Verteilung *f*;

distributor *n* Verteiler *m*

district ['dɪstrɪkt] *n* (*of country*) Kreis *m*; (*of town*) Bezirk *m*; **~ attorney** (*US*) *n* Oberstaatsanwalt *m*; **~ nurse** *n* Kreiskrankenschwester *f*

distrust [dɪs'trʌst] *n* Misstrauen *nt* ♦ *vt* misstrauen +*dat*

disturb [dɪs'tɜːb] *vt* stören; (*agitate*) erregen; **~ance** *n* Störung *f*; **~ed** *adj* beunruhigt; **emotionally ~ed** emotional gestört; **~ing** *adj* beunruhigend

disuse [dɪs'juːs] *n*: **to fall into ~** außer Gebrauch kommen; **~d** [dɪs'juːzd] *adj* außer Gebrauch; (*mine, railway line*) stillgelegt

ditch [dɪtʃ] *n* Graben *m* ♦ *vt* (*person*) loswerden; (*plan*) fallen lassen

dither ['dɪðəʳ] *vi* verdattert sein

ditto ['dɪtəʊ] *adv* dito, ebenfalls

divan [dɪ'væn] *n* Liegesofa *nt*

dive [daɪv] *n* (*into water*) Kopfsprung *m*; (*AVIAT*) Sturzflug *m* ♦ *vi* tauchen; **~r** *n* Taucher *m*

diverge [daɪ'vɜːdʒ] *vi* auseinander gehen

diverse [daɪ'vɜːs] *adj* verschieden

diversion [daɪ'vɜːʃən] *n* Ablenkung *f*; (*BRIT: AUT*) Umleitung *f*

diversity [daɪ'vɜːsɪtɪ] *n* Vielfalt *f*

divert [daɪ'vɜːt] *vt* ablenken; (*traffic*) umleiten

divide [dɪ'vaɪd] *vt* teilen ♦ *vi* sich teilen; **~d highway** (*US*) *n* Schnellstraße *f*

divine [dɪ'vaɪn] *adj* göttlich

diving ['daɪvɪŋ] *n* (*SPORT*) Turmspringen *nt*; (*underwater ~*) Tauchen *nt*; **~ board** *n* Sprungbrett *nt*

divinity [dɪ'vɪnɪtɪ] *n* Gottheit *f*; (*subject*) Religion *f*

division [dɪ'vɪʒən] *n* Teilung *f*; (*MIL*) Division *f*; (*part*) Abteilung *f*; (*in opinion*) Uneinigkeit *f*; (*BRIT: POL*) Abstimmung *f* durch Hammelsprung *f*

divorce [dɪ'vɔːs] *n* (*Ehe*)scheidung *f* ♦ *vt* scheiden; **~d** *adj* geschieden; **~e** [dɪvɔː'siː] *n* Geschiedene(r) *f(m)*

divulge [daɪ'vʌldʒ] *vt* preisgeben

DIY (*BRIT*) *n abbr* = **do-it-yourself**

dizzy ['dɪzɪ] *adj* schwindlig

DJ *n abbr* = **disc jockey**

DNA fingerprinting *n* genetische Fingerabdrücke *pl*

KEYWORD

---

do [duː] (*pt* **did**, *pp* **done**) *n* (*inf: party etc*) Fete *f*

♦ *aux vb* **1** (*in negative constructions and questions*): **I don't understand** ich verstehe nicht; **didn't you know?** wusstest du das nicht?; **what do you think?** was meinen Sie?

2 (*for emphasis, in polite phrases*): **she does seem rather tired** sie scheint wirklich sehr müde zu sein; **do sit down/help yourself** setzen Sie sich doch hin/greifen Sie doch zu

3 (*used to avoid repeating vb*): **she swims better than I do** sie schwimmt besser als ich; **she lives in Glasgow - so do I** sie wohnt in Glasgow - ich auch

4 (*in tag questions*): **you like him, don't you?** du magst ihn doch, oder?

♦ *vt* **1** (*carry out, perform etc*) tun, machen; **what are you doing tonight?** was machst du heute Abend?; **I've got nothing to do** ich habe nichts zu tun; **to do one's hair/nails** sich die Haare/Nägel machen

2 (*AUT etc*) fahren

♦ *vi* **1** (*act, behave*): **do as I do** mach es wie ich

2 (*get on, fare*): **he's doing well/badly at school** er ist gut/schlecht in der Schule; **how do you do?** guten Tag

3 (*be suitable*) gehen; (*be sufficient*) reichen; **to make do (with)** auskommen mit

do away with *vt* (*kill*) umbringen; (*abolish: law etc*) abschaffen

do up *vt* (*laces, dress, buttons*) zumachen; (*room, house*) renovieren

do with *vt* (*need*) brauchen; (*be connected*) zu tun haben mit

do without *vt, vi* auskommen ohne

---

docile ['dəʊsaɪl] *adj* gefügig

dock [dɒk] *n* Dock *nt*; (*JUR*) Anklagebank *f* ♦ *vi* ins Dock gehen; **~er** *n* Hafenarbeiter *m*; **~yard** *n* Werft *f*

doctor ['dɔktər] n Arzt m, Ärztin f; (UNIV) Doktor m ♦ vt (fig) fälschen; (drink etc) etw beimischen +dat; **D~ of Philosophy** n Doktor m der Philosophie

document ['dɔkjumənt] n Dokument nt; **~ary** [dɔkju'mentəri] n Dokumentarbericht m; (film) Dokumentarfilm m ♦ adj dokumentarisch; **~ation** [dɔkjumən'teɪʃən] n dokumentarische(r) Nachweis m

dodge [dɔdʒ] n Kniff m ♦ vt ausweichen +dat

dodgems ['dɔdʒəmz] (BRIT) npl Autoskooter m

doe [dəʊ] n (roe deer) Ricke f; (red deer) Hirschkuh f; (rabbit) Weibchen nt

does [dʌz] vb see **do**; **~n't** = **does not**

dog [dɔg] n Hund m; **~ collar** n Hundehalsband nt; (ECCL) Kragen m des Geistlichen; **~-eared** adj mit Eselsohren

dogged ['dɔgɪd] adj hartnäckig

dogsbody ['dɔgzbɔdi] n Mädchen nt für alles

doings ['duɪŋz] npl (activities) Treiben nt

do-it-yourself ['duːɪtjɔː'self] n Do-it-yourself nt

doldrums ['dɔldrəmz] npl: **to be in the ~** (business) Flaute haben; (person) deprimiert sein

dole [dəʊl] (BRIT) n Stempelgeld nt; **to be on the ~** stempeln gehen; **~ out** vt ausgeben, austeilen

doleful ['dəʊlful] adj traurig

doll [dɔl] n Puppe f ♦ vt: **to ~ o.s. up** sich aufdonnern

dollar ['dɔlər] n Dollar m

dolphin ['dɔlfɪn] n Delfin m, Delphin m

dome [dəʊm] n Kuppel f

domestic [də'mestɪk] adj häuslich; (within country) Innen-, Binnen-; (animal) Haus-; **~ated** adj (person) häuslich; (animal) zahm

dominant ['dɔmɪnənt] adj vorherrschend

dominate ['dɔmɪneɪt] vt beherrschen

domineering [dɔmɪ'nɪərɪŋ] adj herrisch

dominion [də'mɪnɪən] n (rule) Regierungsgewalt f; (land) Staatsgebiet nt mit Selbstverwaltung

domino ['dɔmɪnəʊ] (pl **~es**) n Dominostein m; **~es** n (game) Domino(spiel) nt

don [dɔn] (BRIT) n akademische(r) Lehrer m

donate [də'neɪt] vt (blood, money) spenden; (lot of money) stiften; **donation** [də'neɪʃən] n Spende f

done [dʌn] pp of **do**

donkey ['dɔŋki] n Esel m

donor ['dəʊnər] n Spender m; **~ card** n Organspenderausweis m

don't [dəʊnt] = **do not**

doodle ['duːdl] vi kritzeln

doom [duːm] n böse(s) Geschick nt; (downfall) Verderben nt ♦ vt: **to be ~ed** zum Untergang verurteilt sein; **~sday** n der Jüngste Tag

door [dɔːr] n Tür f; **~bell** n Türklingel f; **~ handle** n Türklinke f; **~man** (irreg) n Türsteher m; **~mat** n Fußmatte f; **~step** n Türstufe f; **~way** n Türöffnung f

dope [dəʊp] n (drug) Aufputschmittel nt ♦ vt (horse) dopen

dopey ['dəʊpi] (inf) adj bekloppt

dormant ['dɔːmənt] adj latent

dormitory ['dɔːmɪtri] n Schlafsaal m

dormouse ['dɔːmaʊs] (pl **-mice**) n Haselmaus f

DOS [dɔs] n abbr (= disk operating system) DOS nt

dosage ['dəʊsɪdʒ] n Dosierung f

dose [dəʊs] n Dosis f

dosh [dɔʃ] (inf) n (money) Moos nt, Knete f

doss house ['dɔs-] (BRIT) n Bleibe f

dot [dɔt] n Punkt m; **~ted with** übersät mit; **on the ~** pünktlich

dote [dəʊt]: **to ~ on** vt fus vernarrt sein in +acc

dotted line ['dɔtɪd-] n punktierte Linie f

double ['dʌbl] adj, adv doppelt ♦ n Doppelgänger m ♦ vt verdoppeln ♦ vi sich verdoppeln; **~s** npl (TENNIS) Doppel nt; **on or at the ~** im Laufschritt; **~ bass** n Kontrabass m; **~ bed** n Doppelbett nt; **~ bend** (BRIT) n S-Kurve f; **~-breasted** adj zweireihig; **~-cross** vt hintergehen; **~-decker** n Doppeldecker m; **~ glazing** (BRIT) n Doppelverglasung f; **~ room** n Doppelzimmer nt

doubly ['dʌbli] adv doppelt

doubt [daut] *n* Zweifel *m* ♦ *vt* bezweifeln; **~ful** *adj* zweifelhaft; **~less** *adv* ohne Zweifel

dough [dəu] *n* Teig *m*; **~nut** *n* Berliner *m*

douse [dauz] *vt* (*drench*) mit Wasser begießen, durchtränken; (*extinguish*) ausmachen

dove [dʌv] *n* Taube *f*

dovetail ['dʌvteɪl] *vi* (*plans*) übereinstimmen

dowdy ['daudɪ] *adj* unmodern

down [daun] *n* (*fluff*) Flaum *m*; (*hill*) Hügel *m* ♦ *adv* unten; (*motion*) herunter; hinunter ♦ *prep*: **to go ~ the street** die Straße hinuntergehen ♦ *vt* niederschlagen; **~ with X!** nieder mit X!; **~-and-out** *n* Tramp *m*; **~-at-heel** *adj* schäbig; **~cast** *adj* niedergeschlagen; **~fall** *n* Sturz *m*; **~hearted** *adj* niedergeschlagen; **~hill** *adv* bergab; **~ payment** *n* Anzahlung *f*; **~pour** *n* Platzregen *m*; **~right** *adj* ausgesprochen; **~size** *vi* (ECON: *company*) sich verkleinern

Downing Street

i **Downing Street** ist die Straße in London, die von Whitehall zum St James Park führt und in der sich der offizielle Wohnsitz des Premierministers (Nr. 10) und des Finanzministers (Nr. 11) befindet. Im weiteren Sinne bezieht sich der Begriff Downing Street auf die britische Regierung.

Down's syndrome [daunz-] *n* (MED) Down-Syndrom *nt*

down: **~stairs** *adv* unten; (*motion*) nach unten; **~stream** *adv* flussabwärts; **~-to-earth** *adj* praktisch; (*town*) *adv* in der Innenstadt; (*motion*) in die Innenstadt; **~under** (BRIT: *inf*) *adv* in/nach Australien/Neuseeland; **~ward** *adj* Abwärts-, nach unten ♦ *adv* abwärts, nach unten; **~wards** *adv* abwärts, nach unten

dowry ['dauri] *n* Mitgift *f*

doz. *abbr* (= *dozen*) Dtzd.

doze [dəuz] *vi* dösen; **~ off** *vi* einnicken

dozen ['dʌzn] *n* Dutzend *nt*; **a ~ books** ein Dutzend Bücher; **~s of** dutzende *or*

Dutzende von

Dr. *abbr* = **doctor**; **drive**

drab [dræb] *adj* düster, eintönig

draft [drɑːft] *n* Entwurf *m*; (FIN) Wechsel *m*; (US: MIL) Einberufung *f* ♦ *vt* skizzieren; *see also* **draught**

draftsman ['drɑːftsmən] (US: *irreg*) *n* = **draughtsman**

drag [dræg] *vt* schleppen; (*river*) mit einem Schleppnetz absuchen ♦ *vi* sich (dahin)schleppen ♦ *n* (*bore*) etwas Blödes; **in ~** als Tunte; **a man in ~** eine Tunte; **~ on** *vi* sich in die Länge ziehen; **~ and drop** *vt* (COMPUT) Drag & Drop *nt*

dragon ['drægn] *n* Drache *m*; **~fly** ['drægənflaɪ] *n* Libelle *f*

drain [dreɪn] *n* Abfluss *m*; (fig: *burden*) Belastung *f* ♦ *vt* ableiten; (*exhaust*) erschöpfen ♦ *vi* (*of water*) abfließen; **~age** *n* Kanalisation *f*; **~ing board** (US **~board**) *n* Ablaufbrett *nt*; **~pipe** *n* Abflussrohr *nt*

dram [dræm] *n* Schluck *m*

drama ['drɑːmə] *n* Drama *nt*; **~tic** [drə'mætɪk] *adj* dramatisch; **~tist** ['dræmətɪst] *n* Dramatiker *m*; **~tize** ['dræmətaɪz] *vt* (*events*) dramatisieren; (for TV etc) bearbeiten

drank [dræŋk] *pt of* **drink**

drape [dreɪp] *vt* drapieren; **~s** (US) *npl* Vorhänge *pl*

drastic ['dræstɪk] *adj* drastisch

draught [drɑːft] (US **draft**) *n* Zug *m*; (NAUT) Tiefgang *m*; **~s** *n* Damespiel *nt*; **on ~** (*beer*) vom Fass; **~ beer** *n* Bier *nt* vom Fass; **~board** (BRIT) *n* Zeichenbrett *nt*

draughtsman ['drɑːftsmən] (*irreg*) *n* technische(r) Zeichner *m*

draw [drɔː] (*pt* **drew**, *pp* **drawn**) *vt* ziehen; (*crowd*) anlocken; (*picture*) zeichnen; (*money*) abheben; (*water*) schöpfen ♦ *vi* (SPORT) unentschieden spielen ♦ *n* (SPORT) Unentschieden *nt*; (*lottery*) Ziehung *f*; **~ near** *vi* näher rücken; **~ out** *vi* (*train*) ausfahren; (*lengthen*) sich hinziehen; **~ up** *vi* (*stop*) halten ♦ *vt* (*document*) aufsetzen

drawback ['drɔːbæk] *n* Nachteil *m*

drawbridge ['drɔːbrɪdʒ] *n* Zugbrücke *f*

drawer [drɔːʳ] n Schublade f

drawing [ˈdrɔːɪŋ] n Zeichnung f; Zeichnen nt; ~ **board** n Reißbrett nt; ~ **pin** (BRIT) n Reißzwecke f; ~ **room** n Salon m

drawl [drɔːl] n schleppende Sprechweise f

drawn [drɔːn] pp of **draw**

dread [dred] n Furcht f ♦ vt fürchten; **~ful** adj furchtbar

dream [driːm] (pt, pp **dreamed** or **dreamt**) n Traum m ♦ vt träumen ♦ vi: **to ~ (about)** träumen (von); **~er** n Träumer m; **~t** [dremt] pt, pp of **dream**; **~y** adj verträumt

dreary [ˈdrɪərɪ] adj trostlos, öde

dredge [dredʒ] vt ausbaggern

dregs [dregz] npl Bodensatz m; (fig) Abschaum m

drench [drentʃ] vt durchnässen

dress [dres] n Kleidung f; (garment) Kleid nt ♦ vt anziehen; (MED) verbinden; **to get ~ed** sich anziehen; ~ **up** vi sich fein machen; ~ **circle** (BRIT) n erste(r) Rang m; **~er** n (furniture) Anrichte f; **~ing** (MED) Verband m; (COOK) Soße f; **~ing gown** (BRIT) n Morgenrock m; **~ing room** n (THEAT) Garderobe f; (SPORT) Umkleideraum m; **~ing table** n Toilettentisch m; **~maker** n Schneiderin f; **~ rehearsal** n Generalprobe f

drew [druː] pt of **draw**

dribble [ˈdrɪbl] vi sabbern ♦ vt (ball) dribbeln

dried [draɪd] adj getrocknet; (fruit) Dörr-, gedörrte(r, s); ~ **milk** n Milchpulver nt

drier [ˈdraɪəʳ] n = **dryer**

drift [drɪft] n Strömung f; (snowdrift) Schneewehe f; (fig) Richtung f ♦ vi sich treiben lassen; **~wood** n Treibholz nt

drill [drɪl] n Bohrer m; (MIL) Drill m ♦ vt bohren; (MIL) ausbilden ♦ vi: **to ~ (for)** bohren (nach)

drink [drɪŋk] (pt **drank**, pp **drunk**) n Getränk nt; (spirits) Drink m ♦ vt, vi trinken; **to have a ~** etwas trinken; **~er** n Trinker m; **~ing water** n Trinkwasser nt

drip [drɪp] n Tropfen m ♦ vi tropfen; **~-dry** adj bügelfrei; **~ping** n Bratenfett nt

drive [draɪv] (pt **drove**, pp **driven**) n Fahrt f; (road) Einfahrt f; (campaign) Aktion f; (energy) Schwung m; (SPORT) Schlag m;

(also: **disk ~**) Diskettenlaufwerk nt ♦ vt (car) fahren; (animals, people, objects) treiben; (power) antreiben ♦ vi fahren; **left-/right-hand ~** Links-/Rechtssteuerung f; **to ~ sb mad** jdn verrückt machen; **~-by shooting** n Schusswaffenangriff aus einem vorbeifahrenden Wagen

drivel [ˈdrɪvl] n Faselei f

driven [ˈdrɪvn] pp of **drive**

driver [ˈdraɪvəʳ] n Fahrer m; **~'s license** (US) n Führerschein m

driveway [ˈdraɪvweɪ] n Auffahrt f; (longer) Zufahrtsstraße f

driving [ˈdraɪvɪŋ] adj (rain) stürmisch; ~ **instructor** n Fahrlehrer m; ~ **lesson** n Fahrstunde f; ~ **licence** (BRIT) n Führerschein m; ~ **school** n Fahrschule f; ~ **test** n Fahrprüfung f

drizzle [ˈdrɪzl] n Nieselregen m ♦ vi nieseln

droll [drəul] adj drollig

drone [drəun] n (sound) Brummen nt; (bee) Drohne f

drool [druːl] vi sabbern

droop [druːp] vi (schlaff) herabhängen

drop [drɔp] n (of liquid) Tropfen m; (fall) Fall m ♦ vt fallen lassen; (lower) senken; (abandon) fallen lassen ♦ vi (fall) herunterfallen; **~s** npl (MED) Tropfen pl; ~ **off** vi (sleep) einschlafen ♦ vt (passenger) absetzen; ~ **out** vi (withdraw) ausscheiden; **~-out** n Aussteiger m; **~per** n Pipette f; **~pings** npl Kot m

drought [draut] n Dürre f

drove [drəuv] pt of **drive**

drown [draun] vt ertränken; (sound) übertönen ♦ vi ertrinken

drowsy [ˈdrauzɪ] adj schläfrig

drudgery [ˈdrʌdʒərɪ] n Plackerei f

drug [drʌg] n (MED) Arznei f; (narcotic) Rauschgift nt ♦ vt betäuben; ~ **addict** n Rauschgiftsüchtige(r) f(m); **~gist** (US) n Drogist(in) m(f); **~store** (US) n Drogerie f

drum [drʌm] n Trommel f ♦ vi trommeln; **~s** npl (MUS) Schlagzeug nt; **~mer** n Trommler m

drunk [drʌŋk] pp of **drink** ♦ adj betrunken ♦ n (also: **~ard**) Trinker(in) m(f); **~en** adj betrunken

dry [draɪ] *adj* trocken ♦ *vt* (ab)trocknen ♦ *vi* trocknen; **~ up** *vi* austrocknen ♦ *vt* (*dishes*) abtrocknen; **~ cleaner's** *n* chemische Reinigung *f*; **~ cleaning** *n* chemische Reinigung *f*; **~er** *n* Trockner *m*; (*US: spin-dryer*) (Wäsche)schleuder *f*; **~ goods store** (*US*) *n* Kurzwarengeschäft *nt*; **~ness** *n* Trockenheit *f*; **~ rot** *n* Hausschwamm *m*

DSS (*BRIT*) *n abbr* (= *Department of Social Security*) ≈ Sozialministerium *nt*

DTP *n abbr* (= *desktop publishing*) DTP *nt*

dual ['djuːəl] *adj* doppelt; **~ carriageway** (*BRIT*) *n* zweispurige Fahrbahn *f*; **~ nationality** *n* doppelte Staatsangehörigkeit *f*; **~-purpose** *adj* Mehrzweck-

dubbed [dʌbd] *adj* (*film*) synchronisiert

dubious ['djuːbɪəs] *adj* zweifelhaft

duchess ['dʌtʃɪs] *n* Herzogin *f*

duck [dʌk] *n* Ente *f* ♦ *vi* sich ducken; **~ling** *n* Entchen *nt*

duct [dʌkt] *n* Röhre *f*

dud [dʌd] *n* Niete *f* ♦ *adj* (*cheque*) ungedeckt

due [djuː] *adj* fällig; (*fitting*) angemessen ♦ *n* Gebühr *f*; (*right*) Recht *nt* ♦ *adv* (*south etc*) genau; **~s** *npl* (*for club*) Beitrag *m*; (*NAUT*) Gebühren *pl*; **~ to** wegen +*gen*

duel ['djuːəl] *n* Duell *nt*

duet [djuːˈɛt] *n* Duett *nt*

duffel ['dʌfl] *adj*: **~ bag** Matchbeutel *m*, Matchsack *m*

dug [dʌg] *pt, pp of* **dig**

duke [djuːk] *n* Herzog *m*

dull [dʌl] *adj* (*colour, weather*) trübe; (*stupid*) schwer von Begriff; (*boring*) langweilig ♦ *vt* abstumpfen

duly ['djuːlɪ] *adv* ordnungsgemäß

dumb [dʌm] *adj* stumm; (*inf: stupid*) doof, blöde; **~founded** [dʌmˈfaundɪd] *adj* verblüfft

dummy ['dʌmɪ] *n* Schneiderpuppe *f*; (*substitute*) Attrappe *f*; (*BRIT: for baby*) Schnuller *m* ♦ *adj* Schein-

dump [dʌmp] *n* Abfallhaufen *m*; (*MIL*) Stapelplatz *m*; (*inf: place*) Nest *nt* ♦ *vt* abladen, auskippen; **~ing** *n* (*COMM*) Schleuderexport *m*; (*of rubbish*)

Schuttabladen *nt*

dumpling ['dʌmplɪŋ] *n* Kloß *m*, Knödel *m*

dumpy ['dʌmpɪ] *adj* pummelig

dunce [dʌns] *n* Dummkopf *m*

dune [djuːn] *n* Düne *f*

dung [dʌŋ] *n* Dünger *m*

dungarees [dʌŋgəˈriːz] *npl* Latzhose *f*

dungeon ['dʌndʒən] *n* Kerker *m*

dupe [djuːp] *n* Gefoppte(r) *m* ♦ *vt* hintergehen, anführen

duplex ['djuːplɛks] (*US*) *n* zweistöckige Wohnung *f*

duplicate [*n* 'djuːplɪkət, *vb* 'djuːplɪkeɪt] *n* Duplikat *nt* ♦ *vt* verdoppeln; (*make copies*) kopieren; **in ~** in doppelter Ausführung

duplicity [djuːˈplɪsɪtɪ] *n* Doppelspiel *nt*

durable ['djuərəbl] *adj* haltbar

duration [djuəˈreɪʃən] *n* Dauer *f*

duress [djuəˈrɛs] *n*: **under ~** unter Zwang

during ['djuərɪŋ] *prep* während +*gen*

dusk [dʌsk] *n* Abenddämmerung *f*

dust [dʌst] *n* Staub *m* ♦ *vt* abstauben; (*sprinkle*) bestäuben; **~bin** (*BRIT*) *n* Mülleimer *m*; **~er** *n* Staubtuch *nt*; **~ jacket** *n* Schutzumschlag *m*; **~man** (*BRIT: irreg*) *n* Müllmann *m*; **~y** *adj* staubig

Dutch [dʌtʃ] *adj* holländisch, niederländisch ♦ *n* (*LING*) Holländisch *nt*, Niederländisch *nt*, **the ~** *npl* (*people*) die Holländer *pl*, die Niederländer *pl*; **to go ~** getrennte Kasse machen; **~man/woman** (*irreg*) *n* Holländer(in) *m(f)*, Niederländer(in) *m(f)*

dutiful ['djuːtɪful] *adj* pflichtbewusst

duty ['djuːtɪ] *n* Pflicht *f*; (*job*) Aufgabe *f*; (*tax*) Einfuhrzoll *m*; **on ~** im Dienst; **~ chemist's** *n* Apotheke *f* im Bereitschaftsdienst; **~-free** *adj* zollfrei

duvet ['duːveɪ] (*BRIT*) *n* Daunendecke *nt*

DVD *n abbr* (= *digital video disc*) DVD *f*

dwarf [dwɔːf] (*pl* **dwarves**) *n* Zwerg *m* ♦ *vt* überragen

dwell [dwɛl] (*pt, pp* **dwelt**) *vi* wohnen; **~ on** *vt fus* verweilen bei; **~ing** *n* Wohnung *f*

dwelt [dwɛlt] *pt, pp of* **dwell**

dwindle ['dwɪndl] *vi* schwinden

dye [daɪ] *n* Farbstoff *m* ♦ *vt* färben

dying ['daɪɪŋ] *adj* (*person*) sterbend;

(*moments*) letzt
dyke [daɪk] (*BRIT*) n (*channel*) Kanal m;
(*barrier*) Deich m, Damm m
dynamic [daɪˈnæmɪk] adj dynamisch
dynamite [ˈdaɪnəmaɪt] n Dynamit nt
dyslexia [dɪsˈleksɪə] n Legasthenie f

E, e

E [iː] n (*MUS*) E nt
each [iːtʃ] adj jeder/jede/jedes ♦ pron (ein)
jeder/(eine) jede/(ein) jedes; ~ **other**
einander, sich; **they have two books** ~ sie
haben je zwei Bücher
eager [ˈiːgəʳ] adj eifrig
eagle [ˈiːgl] n Adler m
ear [ɪəʳ] n Ohr nt; (*of corn*) Ähre f; ~**ache** n
Ohrenschmerzen pl; ~**drum** n Trommelfell
nt
earl [əːl] n Graf m
earlier [ˈəːlɪəʳ] adj, adv früher; **I can't come
any** ~ ich kann nicht früher or eher
kommen
early [ˈəːlɪ] adj, adv früh; ~ **retirement** n
vorzeitige Pensionierung
earmark [ˈɪəmɑːk] vt vorsehen
earn [əːn] vt verdienen
earnest [ˈəːnɪst] adj ernst; **in** ~ im Ernst
earnings [ˈəːnɪŋz] npl Verdienst m
ear: ~**phones** [ˈɪəfəʊnz] npl Kopfhörer pl;
~**ring** [ˈɪərɪŋ] n Ohrring m; ~**shot** [ˈɪəʃɔt] n
Hörweite f
earth [əːθ] n Erde f; (*BRIT*: *ELEC*) Erdung f ♦ vt
erden; ~**enware** n Steingut nt; ~**quake** n
Erdbeben nt; ~y adj roh
earwig [ˈɪəwɪg] n Ohrwurm m
ease [iːz] n (*simplicity*) Leichtigkeit f; (*social*)
Ungezwungenheit f ♦ vt (*pain*) lindern;
(*burden*) erleichtern; **at** ~ ungezwungen;
(*MIL*) rührt euch!; ~ **off** or **up** vi
nachlassen
easel [ˈiːzl] n Staffelei f
easily [ˈiːzɪlɪ] adv leicht
east [iːst] n Osten m ♦ adj östlich ♦ adv nach
Osten
Easter [ˈiːstəʳ] n Ostern nt; ~ **egg** n Osterei

nt
east: ~**erly** adj östlich, Ost-; ~**ern** adj
östlich; ~**ward(s)** adv ostwärts
easy [ˈiːzɪ] adj (*task*) einfach; (*life*) bequem;
(*manner*) ungezwungen, natürlich ♦ adv
leicht; ~ **chair** n Sessel m; ~**-going** adj
gelassen; (*lax*) lässig
eat [iːt] (*pt* **ate**, *pp* **eaten**) vt essen; (*animals*)
fressen; (*destroy*) (zer)fressen ♦ vi essen;
fressen; ~ **away** vt zerfressen; ~ **into** vt
fus zerfressen; ~**en** pp of **eat**
eau de Cologne [ˈəʊdəkəˈləʊn] n
Kölnischwasser nt
eaves [iːvz] npl Dachrand m
eavesdrop [ˈiːvzdrɔp] vi lauschen; **to** ~ **on
sb** jdn belauschen
ebb [ɛb] n Ebbe f ♦ vi (*fig*: *also*: ~ **away**)
(ab)ebben
ebony [ˈɛbənɪ] n Ebenholz nt
EC n abbr (= *European Community*) EG f
ECB n abbr (= *European Central Bank*) EZB f
eccentric [ɪkˈsɛntrɪk] adj exzentrisch ♦ n
Exzentriker(in) m(f)
ecclesiastical [ɪkliːzɪˈæstɪkl] adj kirchlich
echo [ˈɛkəʊ] (*pl* ~**es**) n Echo nt ♦ vt
zurückwerfen; (*fig*) nachbeten ♦ vi
widerhallen
eclipse [ɪˈklɪps] n Finsternis f ♦ vt verfinstern
ecology [ɪˈkɔlədʒɪ] n Ökologie f
e-commerce [ˈiːkɔməːs] n Onlinehandel m
economic [iːkəˈnɔmɪk] adj wirtschaftlich;
~**al** adj wirtschaftlich; (*person*) sparsam; ~
refugee n Wirtschaftsflüchtling m; ~**s** n
Volkswirtschaft f
economist [ɪˈkɔnəmɪst] n
Volkswirt(schaftler) m
economize [ɪˈkɔnəmaɪz] vi sparen
economy [ɪˈkɔnəmɪ] n (*thrift*) Sparsamkeit f;
(*of country*) Wirtschaft f; ~ **class** n
Touristenklasse f
ecstasy [ˈɛkstəsɪ] n Ekstase f; (*drug*) Ecstasy
nt; **ecstatic** [ɛksˈtætɪk] adj hingerissen
ECU [ˈeɪkjuː] n abbr (= *European Currency
Unit*) ECU m ♦
eczema [ˈɛksɪmə] n Ekzem nt
edge [ɛdʒ] n Rand m; (*of knife*) Schneide f
♦ vt (*SEWING*) einfassen; **on** ~ (*fig*) = **edgy**;

to ~ away from langsam abrücken von; **~ways** *adv*: **he couldn't get a word in ~ways** er kam überhaupt nicht zu Wort

edgy ['edʒɪ] *adj* nervös

edible ['edɪbl] *adj* essbar

edict ['iːdɪkt] *n* Erlass *m*

edit ['edɪt] *vt* redigieren; **~ion** [ɪ'dɪʃən] *n* Ausgabe *f*; **~or** *n* (*of newspaper*) Redakteur *m*; (*of book*) Lektor *m*; **~orial** [edɪ'tɔːrɪəl] *adj* Redaktions- ♦ *n* Leitartikel *m*

educate ['edjukeɪt] *vt* erziehen, (aus)bilden; **~d** *adj* gebildet; **education** [edju'keɪʃən] *n* (*teaching*) Unterricht *m*; (*system*) Schulwesen *nt*; (*schooling*) Erziehung *f*; Bildung *f*; **educational** *adj* pädagogisch

eel [iːl] *n* Aal *m*

eerie ['ɪərɪ] *adj* unheimlich

effect [ɪ'fekt] *n* Wirkung *f* ♦ *vt* bewirken; **~s** *npl* (*sound, visual*) Effekte *pl*; **in ~** in der Tat; **to take ~** (*law*) in Kraft treten; (*drug*) wirken; **~ive** *adj* wirksam, effektiv; **~ively** *adv* wirksam, effektiv

effeminate [ɪ'femɪnɪt] *adj* weibisch

effervescent [efə'vesnt] *adj* (*also fig*) sprudelnd

efficiency [ɪ'fɪʃənsɪ] *n* Leistungsfähigkeit *f*

efficient [ɪ'fɪʃənt] *adj* tüchtig; (*TECH*) leistungsfähig; (*method*) wirksam

effigy ['efɪdʒɪ] *n* Abbild *nt*

effort ['efət] *n* Anstrengung *f*; **~less** *adj* mühelos

effusive [ɪ'fjuːsɪv] *adj* überschwänglich

e.g. *adv abbr* (= *exempli gratia*) z. B.

egalitarian [ɪgælɪ'teərɪən] *adj* Gleichheits-, egalitär

egg [eg] *n* Ei *nt*; **~ on** *vt* anstacheln; **~cup** *n* Eierbecher *m*; **~plant** (*esp US*) *n* Aubergine *f*; **~shell** *n* Eierschale *f*

ego ['iːgəu] *n* Ich *nt*, Selbst *nt*; **~tism** ['egəutɪzəm] *n* Ichbezogenheit *f*; **~tist** ['egəutɪst] *n* Egozentriker *m*

Egypt ['iːdʒɪpt] *n* Ägypten *nt*; **~ian** [ɪ'dʒɪpʃən] *adj* ägyptisch ♦ *n* Ägypter(in) *m(f)*

eiderdown ['aɪdədaun] *n* Daunendecke *f*

eight [eɪt] *num* acht; **~een** *num* achtzehn; **~h** [eɪtθ] *adj* achte(r, s) ♦ *n* Achtel *nt*; **~y** *num* achtzig

Eire ['eərə] *n* Irland *nt*

either ['aɪðər] *conj*: **~ ... or** entweder ... oder ♦ *pron*: **~ of the two** eine(r, s) von beiden ♦ *adj*: **on ~ side** auf beiden Seiten ♦ *adv*: **I don't ~** ich auch nicht; **I don't want ~** ich will keins von beiden

eject [ɪ'dʒekt] *vt* ausstoßen, vertreiben

eke [iːk] *vt*: **to ~ out** strecken

elaborate [*adj* ɪ'læbərɪt, *vb* ɪ'læbəreɪt] *adj* sorgfältig ausgearbeitet, ausführlich ♦ *vt* sorgfältig ausarbeiten ♦ *vi* ausführlich darstellen

elapse [ɪ'læps] *vi* vergehen

elastic [ɪ'læstɪk] *n* Gummiband *nt* ♦ *adj* elastisch; **~ band** (*BRIT*) *n* Gummiband *nt*

elated [ɪ'leɪtɪd] *adj* froh

elation [ɪ'leɪʃən] *n* gehobene Stimmung *f*

elbow ['elbəu] *n* Ellbogen *m*

elder ['eldər] *adj* älter ♦ *n* Ältere(r) *f(m)*; **~ly** *adj* ältere(r, s) ♦ *npl*: **the ~ly** die Älteren *pl*; **eldest** ['eldɪst] *adj* älteste(r, s) ♦ *n* Älteste(r) *f(m)*

elect [ɪ'lekt] *vt* wählen ♦ *adj* zukünftig; **~ion** [ɪ'lekʃən] *n* Wahl *f*; **~ioneering** [ɪlekʃə'nɪərɪŋ] *n* Wahlpropaganda *f*; **~or** *n* Wähler *m*; **~oral** *adj* Wahl-; **~orate** *n* Wähler *pl*, Wählerschaft *f*

electric [ɪ'lektrɪk] *adj* elektrisch, Elektro-; **~al** *adj* elektrisch; **~ blanket** *n* Heizdecke *f*; **~ chair** *n* elektrische(r) Stuhl *m*; **~ fire** *n* elektrische(r) Heizofen *m*

electrician [ɪlek'trɪʃən] *n* Elektriker *m*

electricity [ɪlek'trɪsɪtɪ] *n* Elektrizität *f*

electrify [ɪ'lektrɪfaɪ] *vt* elektrifizieren; (*fig*) elektrisieren

electrocute [ɪ'lektrəkjuːt] *vt* durch elektrischen Strom töten

electronic [ɪlek'trɒnɪk] *adj* elektronisch, Elektronen-; **~ mail** *n* E-Mail *f*; **~s** *n* Elektronik *f*

elegance ['elɪgəns] *n* Eleganz *f*; **elegant** ['elɪgənt] *adj* elegant

element ['elɪmənt] *n* Element *nt*; **~ary** [elɪ'mentərɪ] *adj* einfach; (*primary*) Grund-

elephant ['elɪfənt] *n* Elefant *m*

elevate ['elɪveɪt] *vt* emporheben; **elevation** [elɪ'veɪʃən] *n* (*height*) Erhebung *f*; (*ARCHIT*)

(Quer)schnitt *m*; **elevator** (*US*) *n* Fahrstuhl *m*, Aufzug *m*

eleven [ɪˈlevn] *num* elf; **~ses** (*BRIT*) *npl* ≈ zweite(s) Frühstück *nt*; **~th** *adj* elfte(r, s)

elicit [ɪˈlɪsɪt] *vt* herausbekommen

eligible [ˈelɪdʒəbl] *adj* wählbar; **to be ~ for a pension** pensionsberechtigt sein

eliminate [ɪˈlɪmɪneɪt] *vt* ausschalten

elite [eɪˈliːt] *n* Elite *f*

elm [elm] *n* Ulme *f*

elocution [eləˈkjuːʃən] *n* Sprecherziehung *f*

elongated [ˈiːlɒŋgeɪtɪd] *adj* verlängert

elope [ɪˈləʊp] *vi* entlaufen

eloquence [ˈeləkwəns] *n* Beredsamkeit *f*; **eloquent** *adj* redegewandt

else [els] *adv* sonst; **who ~?** wer sonst?; **somebody ~** jemand anders; **or ~** sonst; **~where** *adv* anderswo, woanders

elude [ɪˈluːd] *vt* entgehen +*dat*

elusive [ɪˈluːsɪv] *adj* schwer fassbar

emaciated [ɪˈmeɪsɪeɪtɪd] *adj* abgezehrt

e-mail [ˈiːmeɪl] *n abbr* (= *electronic mail*) E-Mail *f* ♦ *vti* mailen

emancipation [ɪmænsɪˈpeɪʃən] *n* Emanzipation *f*; Freilassung *f*

embankment [ɪmˈbæŋkmənt] *n* (*of river*) Uferböschung *f*; (*of road*) Straßendamm *m*

embargo [ɪmˈbɑːgəʊ] (*pl* **~es**) *n* Embargo *nt*

embark [ɪmˈbɑːk] *vi* sich einschiffen; **~ on** *vt fus* unternehmen; **~ation** [embɑːˈkeɪʃən] *n* Einschiffung *f*

embarrass [ɪmˈbærəs] *vt* in Verlegenheit bringen; **~ed** *adj* verlegen; **~ing** *adj* peinlich; **~ment** *n* Verlegenheit *f*

embassy [ˈembəsɪ] *n* Botschaft *f*

embed [ɪmˈbed] *vt* einbetten

embellish [ɪmˈbelɪʃ] *vt* verschönern

embers [ˈembəz] *npl* Glut(asche) *f*

embezzle [ɪmˈbezl] *vt* unterschlagen; **~ment** *n* Unterschlagung *f*

embitter [ɪmˈbɪtər] *vt* verbittern

embody [ɪmˈbɒdɪ] *vt* (*ideas*) verkörpern; (*new features*) (in sich) vereinigen

embossed [ɪmˈbɒst] *adj* geprägt

embrace [ɪmˈbreɪs] *vt* umarmen; (*include*) einschließen ♦ *vi* sich umarmen ♦ *n* Umarmung *f*

embroider [ɪmˈbrɔɪdər] *vt* (be)sticken; (*story*) ausschmücken; **~y** *n* Stickerei *f*

emerald [ˈemərəld] *n* Smaragd *m*

emerge [ɪˈmɜːdʒ] *vi* auftauchen; (*truth*) herauskommen; **~nce** *n* Erscheinen *nt*

emergency [ɪˈmɜːdʒənsɪ] *n* Notfall *m*; **~ cord** (*US*) *n* Notbremse *f*; **~ exit** *n* Notausgang *m*; **~ landing** *n* Notlandung *f*; **~ services** *npl* Notdienste *pl*

emery board [ˈemərɪ-] *n* Papiernagelfeile *f*

emigrant [ˈemɪgrənt] *n* Auswanderer *m*

emigrate [ˈemɪgreɪt] *vi* auswandern; **emigration** [emɪˈgreɪʃən] *n* Auswanderung *f*

eminence [ˈemɪnəns] *n* hohe(r) Rang *m*

eminent [ˈemɪnənt] *adj* bedeutend

emission [ɪˈmɪʃən] *n* Ausströmen *nt*; **~s** *npl* Emissionen *fpl*

emit [ɪˈmɪt] *vt* von sich *dat* geben

emotion [ɪˈməʊʃən] *n* Emotion *f*, Gefühl *nt*; **~al** *adj* (*person*) emotional; (*scene*) ergreifend

emotive [ɪˈməʊtɪv] *adj* gefühlsbetont

emperor [ˈempərər] *n* Kaiser *m*

emphases [ˈemfəsiːz] *npl of* **emphasis**

emphasis [ˈemfəsɪs] *n* (*LING*) Betonung *f*; (*fig*) Nachdruck *m*; **emphasize** [ˈemfəsaɪz] *vt* betonen

emphatic [emˈfætɪk] *adj* nachdrücklich; **~ally** *adv* nachdrücklich

empire [ˈempaɪər] *n* Reich *nt*

empirical [emˈpɪrɪkl] *adj* empirisch

employ [ɪmˈplɔɪ] *vt* (*hire*) anstellen; (*use*) verwenden; **~ee** [emplɔɪˈiː] *n* Angestellte(r) *f(m)*; **~er** *n* Arbeitgeber(in) *m(f)*; **~ment** *n* Beschäftigung *f*; **~ment agency** *n* Stellenvermittlung *f*

empower [ɪmˈpaʊər] *vt*: **to ~ sb to do sth** jdn ermächtigen, etw zu tun

empress [ˈempris] *n* Kaiserin *f*

emptiness [ˈemptɪnɪs] *n* Leere *f*

empty [ˈemptɪ] *adj* leer ♦ *n* (*bottle*) Leergut *nt* ♦ *vt* (*contents*) leeren; (*container*) ausleeren ♦ *vi* (*water*) abfließen; (*river*) münden; (*house*) sich leeren; **~-handed** *adj* mit leeren Händen

EMU [ˈiːmjuː] *n abbr* (= *economic and monetary union*) EWU *f*

emulate ['emjuleɪt] vt nacheifern +dat

emulsion [ɪ'mʌlʃən] n Emulsion f

enable [ɪ'neɪbl] vt: **to ~ sb to do sth** es jdm ermöglichen, etw zu tun

enact [ɪ'nækt] vt (law) erlassen; (play) aufführen; (role) spielen

enamel [ɪ'næməl] n Email nt; (of teeth) (Zahn)schmelz m

encased [ɪn'keɪst] adj: **~ in** (enclosed) eingeschlossen in +dat; (covered) verkleidet mit

enchant [ɪn'tʃɑːnt] vt bezaubern; **~ing** adj entzückend

encircle [ɪn'sɜːkl] vt umringen

encl. abbr (= enclosed) Anl.

enclose [ɪn'kləuz] vt einschließen; **to ~ sth (in or with a letter)** etw (einem Brief) beilegen; **~d** (in letter) beiliegend, anbei; **enclosure** [ɪn'kləuʒəʳ] n Einfriedung f; (in letter) Anlage f

encompass [ɪn'kʌmpəs] vt (include) umfassen

encore [ɒŋ'kɔːʳ] n Zugabe f

encounter [ɪn'kauntəʳ] n Begegnung f; (MIL) Zusammenstoß m ♦ vt treffen; (resistance) stoßen auf +acc

encourage [ɪn'kʌrɪdʒ] vt ermutigen; **~ment** n Ermutigung f, Förderung f; **encouraging** adj ermutigend, viel versprechend

encroach [ɪn'krəutʃ] vi: **to ~ (up)on** eindringen in +acc; (time) in Anspruch nehmen

encrusted [ɪn'krʌstɪd] adj: **~ with** besetzt mit

encyclop(a)edia [ensaɪkləu'piːdɪə] n Konversationslexikon nt

end [end] n Ende nt, Schluss m; (purpose) Zweck m ♦ vt (also: **bring to an ~, put an ~ to**) beenden ♦ vi zu Ende gehen; **in the ~** zum Schluss; **on ~** (object) hochkant; **to stand on ~** (hair) zu Berge stehen; **for hours on ~** stundenlang; **~ up** vi landen

endanger [ɪn'deɪndʒəʳ] vt gefährden; **~ed species** n eine vom Aussterben bedrohte Art

endearing [ɪn'dɪərɪŋ] adj gewinnend

endeavour [ɪn'devəʳ] (US **endeavor**) n Bestrebung f ♦ vi sich bemühen

ending ['endɪŋ] n Ende nt

endless ['endlɪs] adj endlos

endorse [ɪn'dɔːs] vt unterzeichnen; (approve) unterstützen; **~ment** n (AUT) Eintrag m

endow [ɪn'dau] vt: **to ~ sb with sth** jdm etw verleihen; (with money) jdm etw stiften

endurance [ɪn'djuərəns] n Ausdauer f

endure [ɪn'djuəʳ] vt ertragen ♦ vi (last) (fort)dauern

enemy ['enəmɪ] n Feind m ♦ adj feindlich

energetic [enə'dʒetɪk] adj tatkräftig

energy ['enədʒɪ] n Energie f

enforce [ɪn'fɔːs] vt durchsetzen

engage [ɪn'geɪdʒ] vt (employ) einstellen; (in conversation) verwickeln; (TECH) einschalten ♦ vi (TECH) ineinander greifen; (clutch) fassen; **to ~ in** sich beteiligen an +dat; **~d** adj verlobt; (BRIT: TEL, toilet) besetzt; (: busy) beschäftigt; **to get ~d** sich verloben; **~d tone** (BRIT) n (TEL) Besetztzeichen nt; **~ment** n (appointment) Verabredung f; (to marry) Verlobung f; (MIL) Gefecht nt; **~ment ring** n Verlobungsring m; **engaging** adj gewinnend

engender [ɪn'dʒendəʳ] vt hervorrufen

engine ['endʒɪn] n (AUT) Motor m; (RAIL) Lokomotive f; **~ driver** n Lok(omotiv)führer(in) m(f)

engineer [endʒɪ'nɪəʳ] n Ingenieur m; (US: RAIL) Lok(omotiv)führer(in) m(f); **~ing** [endʒɪ'nɪərɪŋ] n Technik f

England ['ɪŋglənd] n England nt

English ['ɪŋglɪʃ] adj englisch ♦ n (LING) Englisch nt; **the ~** npl (people) die Engländer pl; **~ Channel** n: **the ~ Channel** der Ärmelkanal m; **~man/woman** (irreg) n Engländer(in) m(f)

engraving [ɪn'greɪvɪŋ] n Stich m

engrossed [ɪn'grəust] adj vertieft

engulf [ɪn'gʌlf] vt verschlingen

enhance [ɪn'hɑːns] vt steigern, heben

enigma [ɪ'nɪgmə] n Rätsel nt; **~tic** [enɪg'mætɪk] adj rätselhaft

enjoy [ɪn'dʒɔɪ] vt genießen; (privilege) besitzen; **to ~ o.s.** sich amüsieren; **~able**

adj erfreulich; **~ment** *n* Genuss *m*, Freude *f*

enlarge [ɪnˈlɑːdʒ] *vt* erweitern; (*PHOT*) vergrößern ♦ *vi*: **to ~ on sth** etw weiter ausführen; **~ment** *n* Vergrößerung *f*

enlighten [ɪnˈlaɪtn] *vt* aufklären; **~ment** *n*: **the E~ment** (*HIST*) die Aufklärung

enlist [ɪnˈlɪst] *vt* gewinnen ♦ *vi* (*MIL*) sich melden

enmity [ˈɛnmɪtɪ] *n* Feindschaft *f*

enormity [ɪˈnɔːmɪtɪ] *n* Ungeheuerlichkeit *f*

enormous [ɪˈnɔːməs] *adj* ungeheuer

enough [ɪˈnʌf] *adj*, *adv* genug; **funnily ~** komischerweise

enquire [ɪnˈkwaɪəʳ] *vt*, *vi* = **inquire**

enrage [ɪnˈreɪdʒ] *vt* wütend machen

enrich [ɪnˈrɪtʃ] *vt* bereichern

enrol [ɪnˈrəul] *vt* einschreiben ♦ *vi* (*register*) sich anmelden; **~ment** *n* (*for course*) Anmeldung *f*

en route [ɔnˈruːt] *adv* unterwegs

ensign [ˈɛnsaɪn, ˈɛnsən] *n* (*NAUT*) Flagge *f*; (*MIL*) Fähnrich *m*

enslave [ɪnˈsleɪv] *vt* versklaven

ensue [ɪnˈsjuː] *vi* folgen, sich ergeben

en suite [ɔnswiːt] *adj*: **room with ~ bathroom** Zimmer *nt* mit eigenem Bad

ensure [ɪnˈʃuəʳ] *vt* garantieren

entail [ɪnˈteɪl] *vt* mit sich bringen

entangle [ɪnˈtæŋgl] *vt* verwirren, verstricken; **~d** *adj*: **to become ~d (in)** (*in net, rope etc*) sich verfangen (in +*dat*)

enter [ˈɛntəʳ] *vt* eintreten in +*dat*, betreten; (*club*) beitreten +*dat*; (*in book*) eintragen ♦ *vi* hereinkommen, hineingehen; **~ for** *vt fus* sich beteiligen an +*dat*; **~ into** *vt fus* (*agreement*) eingehen; (*plans*) eine Rolle spielen bei; **~ (up)on** *vt fus* beginnen

enterprise [ˈɛntəpraɪz] *n* (*in person*) Initiative *f*; (*COMM*) Unternehmen *nt*; **enterprising** [ˈɛntəpraɪzɪŋ] *adj* unternehmungslustig

entertain [ɛntəˈteɪn] *vt* (*guest*) bewirten; (*amuse*) unterhalten; **~er** *n* Unterhaltungskünstler(in) *m(f)*; **~ing** *adj* unterhaltsam; **~ment** *n* Unterhaltung *f*

enthralled [ɪnˈθrɔːld] *adj* gefesselt

enthusiasm [ɪnˈθuːzɪæzəm] *n* Begeisterung *f*

enthusiast [ɪnˈθuːzɪæst] *n* Enthusiast *m*; **~ic** [ɪnθuːzɪˈæstɪk] *adj* begeistert

entice [ɪnˈtaɪs] *vt* verleiten, locken

entire [ɪnˈtaɪəʳ] *adj* ganz; **~ly** *adv* ganz, völlig; **~ty** [ɪnˈtaɪərətɪ] *n*: **in its ~ty** in seiner Gesamtheit

entitle [ɪnˈtaɪtl] *vt* (*allow*) berechtigen; (*name*) betiteln; **~d** *adj* (*book*) mit dem Titel; **to be ~d to sth** das Recht auf etw *acc* haben; **to be ~d to do sth** das Recht haben, etw zu tun

entity [ˈɛntɪtɪ] *n* Ding *nt*, Wesen *nt*

entourage [ɔntuˈrɑːʒ] *n* Gefolge *nt*

entrails [ˈɛntreɪlz] *npl* Eingeweide *pl*

entrance [*n* ˈɛntrns, *vb* ɪnˈtrɑːns] *n* Eingang *m*; (*entering*) Eintritt *m* ♦ *vt* hinreißen; **~ examination** *n* Aufnahmeprüfung *f*; **~ fee** *n* Eintrittsgeld *nt*; **~ ramp** (*US*) *n* (*AUT*) Einfahrt *f*

entrant [ˈɛntrnt] *n* (*for exam*) Kandidat *m*; (*in race*) Teilnehmer *m*

entreat [ɛnˈtriːt] *vt* anflehen

entrenched [ɛnˈtrɛntʃt] *adj* (*fig*) verwurzelt

entrepreneur [ˈɔntrəprəˈnəːʳ] *n* Unternehmer(in) *m(f)*

entrust [ɪnˈtrʌst] *vt*: **to ~ sb with sth** *or* **sth to sb** jdm etw anvertrauen

entry [ˈɛntrɪ] *n* Eingang *m*; (*THEAT*) Auftritt *m*; (*in account*) Eintragung *f*; (*in dictionary*) Eintrag *m*; **"no ~"** „Eintritt verboten"; (*for cars*) „Einfahrt verboten"; **~ form** *n* Anmeldeformular *nt*; **~ phone** *n* Sprechanlage *f*

enumerate [ɪˈnjuːməreɪt] *vt* aufzählen

enunciate [ɪˈnʌnsɪeɪt] *vt* aussprechen

envelop [ɪnˈvɛləp] *vt* einhüllen

envelope [ˈɛnvələup] *n* Umschlag *m*

enviable [ˈɛnvɪəbl] *adj* beneidenswert

envious [ˈɛnvɪəs] *adj* neidisch

environment [ɪnˈvaɪərnmənt] *n* Umgebung *f*; (*ECOLOGY*) Umwelt *f*; **~al** [ɪnvaɪərnˈmɛntl] *adj* Umwelt-; **~-friendly** *adj* umweltfreundlich

envisage [ɪnˈvɪzɪdʒ] *vt* sich *dat* vorstellen

envoy [ˈɛnvɔɪ] *n* Gesandte(r) *mf*

envy [ˈɛnvɪ] *n* Neid *m* ♦ *vt*: **to ~ sb sth** jdn um etw beneiden

enzyme [ˈɛnzaɪm] *n* Enzym *nt*

epic ['ɛpɪk] n Epos nt ♦ adj episch

epidemic [ɛpɪ'dɛmɪk] n Epidemie f

epilepsy ['ɛpɪlɛpsɪ] n Epilepsie f; **epileptic** [ɛpɪ'lɛptɪk] adj epileptisch ♦ n Epileptiker(in) m(f)

episode ['ɛpɪsəʊd] n (incident) Vorfall m; (story) Episode f

epitaph ['ɛpɪtɑːf] n Grabinschrift f

epitomize [ɪ'pɪtəmaɪz] vt verkörpern

equable ['ɛkwəbl] adj ausgeglichen

equal ['iːkwl] adj gleich ♦ n Gleichgestellte(r) mf ♦ vt gleichkommen +dat; ~ **to the task** der Aufgabe gewachsen; **equality** [iː'kwɒlɪti] n Gleichheit f; (equal rights) Gleichberechtigung f; **~ize** vt gleichmachen ♦ vi (SPORT) ausgleichen; **~izer** n (SPORT) Ausgleich(streffer) m; **~ly** adv gleich

equanimity [ɛkwə'nɪmɪtɪ] n Gleichmut m

equate [ɪ'kweɪt] vt gleichsetzen

equation [ɪ'kweɪʃən] n Gleichung f

equator [ɪ'kweɪtər] n Äquator m

equestrian [ɪ'kwɛstrɪən] adj Reit-

equilibrium [iːkwɪ'lɪbrɪəm] n Gleichgewicht nt

equinox ['iːkwɪnɒks] n Tagundnachtgleiche f

equip [ɪ'kwɪp] vt ausrüsten; **to be well ~ped** gut ausgerüstet sein; **~ment** n Ausrüstung f; (TECH) Gerät nt

equitable ['ɛkwɪtəbl] adj gerecht, billig

equities ['ɛkwɪtɪz] (BRIT) npl (FIN) Stammaktien pl

equivalent [ɪ'kwɪvələnt] adj gleichwertig, entsprechend ♦ n Äquivalent nt; (in money) Gegenwert m; ~ **to** gleichwertig +dat, entsprechend +dat

equivocal [ɪ'kwɪvəkl] adj zweideutig

era ['ɪərə] n Epoche f, Ära f

eradicate [ɪ'rædɪkeɪt] vt ausrotten

erase [ɪ'reɪz] vt ausradieren; (tape) löschen; **~r** n Radiergummi m

erect [ɪ'rɛkt] adj aufrecht ♦ vt errichten; **~ion** [ɪ'rɛkʃən] n Errichtung f; (ANAT) Erektion f

ERM n abbr (= Exchange Rate Mechanism) Wechselkursmechanismus m

erode [ɪ'rəʊd] vt zerfressen; (land) auswaschen

erotic [ɪ'rɒtɪk] adj erotisch

err [əːr] vi sich irren

errand ['ɛrənd] n Besorgung f

erratic [ɪ'rætɪk] adj unberechenbar

erroneous [ɪ'rəʊnɪəs] adj irrig

error ['ɛrər] n Fehler m

erupt [ɪ'rʌpt] vi ausbrechen; **~ion** [ɪ'rʌpʃən] n Ausbruch m

escalate ['ɛskəleɪt] vi sich steigern

escalator ['ɛskəleɪtər] n Rolltreppe f

escape [ɪs'keɪp] n Flucht f; (of gas) Entweichen nt ♦ vi entkommen; (prisoners) fliehen; (leak) entweichen ♦ vt entkommen +dat; **escapism** n Flucht f (vor der Wirklichkeit)

escort [n 'ɛskɔːt, vb ɪs'kɔːt] n (person accompanying) Begleiter m; (guard) Eskorte f ♦ vt (lady) begleiten; (MIL) eskortieren

Eskimo ['ɛskɪməʊ] n Eskimo(frau) m(f)

especially [ɪs'pɛʃlɪ] adv besonders

espionage ['ɛspɪənɑːʒ] n Spionage f

esplanade [ɛsplə'neɪd] n Promenade f

Esquire [ɪs'kwaɪər] n: **J. Brown ~** Herrn J. Brown

essay ['ɛseɪ] n Aufsatz m; (LITER) Essay m

essence ['ɛsns] n (quality) Wesen nt; (extract) Essenz f

essential [ɪ'sɛnʃl] adj (necessary) unentbehrlich; (basic) wesentlich ♦ n Allernötigste(s) nt; **~ly** adv eigentlich

establish [ɪs'tæblɪʃ] vt (set up) gründen; (prove) nachweisen; **~ed** adj anerkannt; (belief, laws etc) herrschend; **~ment** n (setting up) Einrichtung f

estate [ɪs'teɪt] n Gut nt; (BRIT: housing ~) Siedlung f; (will) Nachlass m; ~ **agent** (BRIT) n Grundstücksmakler m; ~ **car** (BRIT) n Kombiwagen m

esteem [ɪs'tiːm] n Wertschätzung f

esthetic [ɪs'θɛtɪk] (US) adj = **aesthetic**

estimate [n 'ɛstɪmət, vb 'ɛstɪmeɪt] n Schätzung f; (of price) (Kosten)voranschlag m ♦ vt schätzen; **estimation** [ɛstɪ'meɪʃən] n Einschätzung f; (esteem) Achtung f

estranged [ɪs'treɪndʒd] adj entfremdet

estuary ['ɛstjʊərɪ] n Mündung f

etc *abbr* (= *et cetera*) usw.
etching ['etʃɪŋ] *n* Kupferstich *m*
eternal [ɪ'tɜːnl] *adj* ewig
eternity [ɪ'tɜːnɪtɪ] *n* Ewigkeit *f*
ether ['iːθəʳ] *n* Äther *m*
ethical ['eθɪkl] *adj* ethisch
ethics ['eθɪks] *n* Ethik *f* ♦ *npl* Moral *f*
Ethiopia [iːθɪ'əʊpɪə] *n* Äthiopien *nt*
ethnic ['eθnɪk] *adj* Volks-, ethnisch; ~
minority *n* ethnische Minderheit *f*
ethos ['iːθɒs] *n* Gesinnung *f*
etiquette ['etɪket] *n* Etikette *f*
EU *abbr* (= *European Union*) EU *f*
euphemism ['juːfəmɪzəm] *n* Euphemismus
m
euro ['jʊərəʊ] *n* (*FIN*) Euro *m*
Eurocheque ['jʊərəʊtʃek] *n* Euroscheck *m*
Euroland ['jʊərəʊlænd] *n* Eurozone *f*,
Euroland *nt*
Europe ['jʊərəp] *n* Europa *nt*; ~**an**
[jʊərə'piːən] *adj* europäisch ♦ *n* Europäer(in)
m(f); ~**an Community** *n*: **the ~an**
Community die Europäische Gemeinschaft
Euro-sceptic ['jʊərəʊskeptɪk] *n* Kritiker der
Europäischen Gemeinschaft
evacuate [ɪ'vækjueɪt] *vt* (*place*) räumen;
(*people*) evakuieren; **evacuation**
[ɪvækju'eɪʃən] *n* Räumung *f*; Evakuierung *f*
evade [ɪ'veɪd] *vt* (*escape*) entkommen +*dat*;
(*avoid*) meiden; (*duty*) sich entziehen +*dat*
evaluate [ɪ'væljueɪt] *vt* bewerten;
(*information*) auswerten
evaporate [ɪ'væpəreɪt] *vi* verdampfen ♦ *vt*
verdampfen lassen; ~**d milk** *n*
Kondensmilch *f*
evasion [ɪ'veɪʒən] *n* Umgehung *f*
evasive [ɪ'veɪsɪv] *adj* ausweichend
eve [iːv] *n*: **on the ~ of** am Vorabend +*gen*
even ['iːvn] *adj* eben; gleichmäßig; (*score*
etc) unentschieden; (*number*) gerade ♦ *adv*:
~ **you** sogar du; **to get ~ with sb** jdm
heimzahlen; ~ **if** selbst wenn; ~ **so**
dennoch; ~ **though** obwohl; ~ **more** sogar
noch mehr; ~ **out** *vi* sich ausgleichen
evening ['iːvnɪŋ] *n* Abend *m*; **in the ~**
abends, am Abend; ~ **class** *n* Abendschule
f; ~ **dress** *n* (*man's*) Gesellschaftsanzug *m*;

(*woman's*) Abendkleid *nt*
event [ɪ'vent] *n* (*happening*) Ereignis *nt*;
(*SPORT*) Disziplin *f*; **in the ~ of** im Falle +*gen*;
~**ful** *adj* ereignisreich
eventual [ɪ'ventʃuəl] *adj* (*final*) schließlich;
~**ity** [ɪventʃu'ælɪtɪ] *n* Möglichkeit *f*; ~**ly** *adv*
am Ende; (*given time*) schließlich
ever ['evəʳ] *adv* (*always*) immer; (*at any time*)
je(mals) ♦ *conj* seit; ~ **since** seitdem; **have**
you ~ seen it? haben Sie es je gesehen?;
~**green** *n* Immergrün *nt*; ~**lasting** *adj*
immer während
every ['evrɪ] *adj* jede(r, s); ~ **other/third day**
jeden zweiten/dritten Tag; ~ **one of them**
alle; **I have ~ confidence in him** ich habe
uneingeschränktes Vertrauen in ihn; **we**
wish you ~ success wir wünschen Ihnen
viel Erfolg; **he's ~ bit as clever as his**
brother er ist genauso klug wie sein
Bruder; ~ **now and then** ab und zu;
~**body** *pron* = **everyone**; ~**day** *adj* (*daily*)
täglich; (*commonplace*) alltäglich, Alltags-;
~**one** *pron* jeder, alle *pl*; ~**thing** *pron* alles;
~**where** *adv* überall(hin); (*wherever*) wohin;
~**where you go** wohin du auch gehst
evict [ɪ'vɪkt] *vt* ausweisen; ~**ion** *n* [ɪ'vɪkʃən] *n*
Ausweisung *f*
evidence ['evɪdns] *n* (*sign*) Spur *f*; (*proof*)
Beweis *m*; (*testimony*) Aussage *f*
evident ['evɪdnt] *adj* augenscheinlich; ~**ly**
adv offensichtlich
evil ['iːvl] *adj* böse ♦ *n* Böse *nt*
evocative [ɪ'vɒkətɪv] *adj*: **to be ~ of sth** an
etw *acc* erinnern
evoke [ɪ'vəʊk] *vt* hervorrufen
evolution [iːvə'luːʃən] *n* Entwicklung *f*; (*of*
life) Evolution *f*
evolve [ɪ'vɒlv] *vt* entwickeln ♦ *vi* sich
entwickeln
ewe [juː] *n* Mutterschaf *nt*
ex- [eks] *prefix* Ex-, Alt-, ehemalig
exacerbate [eks'æsəbeɪt] *vt* verschlimmern
exact [ɪg'zækt] *adj* genau ♦ *vt* (*demand*)
verlangen; ~**ing** *adj* anspruchsvoll; ~**ly** *adv*
genau
exaggerate [ɪg'zædʒəreɪt] *vt*, *vi* übertreiben;
exaggeration [ɪgzædʒə'reɪʃən] *n*

Übertreibung *f*

exalted [ɪgˈzɔːltɪd] *adj* (*position, style*) hoch; (*person*) exaltiert

exam [ɪgˈzæm] *n abbr* (*SCH*) = **examination**

examination [ɪgzæmɪˈneɪʃən] *n* Untersuchung *f*; (*SCH*) Prüfung *f*, Examen *nt*; (*customs*) Kontrolle *f*

examine [ɪgˈzæmɪn] *vt* untersuchen; (*SCH*) prüfen; (*consider*) erwägen; ~**r** *n* Prüfer *m*

example [ɪgˈzɑːmpl] *n* Beispiel *nt*; **for** ~ zum Beispiel

exasperate [ɪgˈzɑːspəreɪt] *vt* zur Verzweiflung bringen; **exasperating** *adj* ärgerlich, zum Verzweifeln bringend; **exasperation** [ɪgzɑːspəˈreɪʃən] *n* Verzweiflung *f*

excavate [ˈɛkskəveɪt] *vt* ausgraben; **excavation** [ɛkskəˈveɪʃən] *n* Ausgrabung *f*

exceed [ɪkˈsiːd] *vt* überschreiten; (*hopes*) übertreffen; ~**ingly** *adv* äußerst

excel [ɪkˈsɛl] *vi* sich auszeichnen; ~**lence** [ˈɛksələns] *n* Vortrefflichkeit *f*; **E~lency** [ˈɛksələnsɪ] *n* **His E~lency** Seine Exzellenz *f*; ~**lent** [ˈɛksələnt] *adj* ausgezeichnet

except [ɪkˈsɛpt] *prep* (*also:* ~ **for,** ~**ing**) außer +*dat* ♦ *vt* ausnehmen; ~**ion** [ɪkˈsɛpʃən] *n* Ausnahme *f*, **to take** ~**ion to** Anstoß nehmen an +*dat*; ~**ional** [ɪkˈsɛpʃənl] *adj* außergewöhnlich

excerpt [ˈɛksəːpt] *n* Auszug *m*

excess [ɪkˈsɛs] *n* Übermaß *nt*; **an** ~ **of** ein Übermaß an +*dat*; ~ **baggage** *n* Mehrgepäck *nt*; ~ **fare** *n* Nachlösegebühr *f*; ~**ive** *adj* übermäßig

exchange [ɪksˈtʃeɪndʒ] *n* Austausch *m*; (*also:* **telephone** ~) Zentrale *f* ♦ *vt* (*goods*) tauschen; (*greetings*) austauschen; (*money, blows*) wechseln; ~ **rate** *n* Wechselkurs *m*

Exchequer [ɪksˈtʃɛkər] (*BRIT*) *n*: **the** ~ das Schatzamt

excise [ˈɛksaɪz] *n* Verbrauchssteuer *f*

excite [ɪkˈsaɪt] *vt* erregen; **to get** ~**d** sich aufregen; ~**ment** *n* Aufregung *f*; **exciting** *adj* spannend

exclaim [ɪksˈkleɪm] *vi* ausrufen

exclamation [ɛkskləˈmeɪʃən] *n* Ausruf *m*; ~ **mark** *n* Ausrufezeichen *nt*

exclude [ɪksˈkluːd] *vt* ausschließen

exclusion [ɪksˈkluːʒən] *n* Ausschluss *m*; ~ **zone** *n* Sperrzone *f*

exclusive [ɪksˈkluːsɪv] *adj* (*select*) exklusiv; (*sole*) ausschließlich, Allein-; ~ **of** exklusive +*gen*; ~**ly** *adv* nur, ausschließlich

excrement [ˈɛkskrəmənt] *n* Kot *m*

excruciating [ɪksˈkruːʃɪeɪtɪŋ] *adj* qualvoll

excursion [ɪksˈkəːʃən] *n* Ausflug *m*

excusable [ɪksˈkjuːzəbl] *adj* entschuldbar

excuse [*n* ɪksˈkjuːs, *vb* ɪksˈkjuːz] *n* Entschuldigung *f* ♦ *vt* entschuldigen; ~ **me!** entschuldigen Sie!

ex-directory [ˈɛksdɪˈrɛktərɪ] (*BRIT*) *adj*: **to be** ~ nicht im Telefonbuch stehen

execute [ˈɛksɪkjuːt] *vt* (*carry out*) ausführen; (*kill*) hinrichten; **execution** [ɛksɪˈkjuːʃən] *n* Ausführung *f*; (*killing*) Hinrichtung *f*; **executioner** [ɛksɪˈkjuːʃnər] *n* Scharfrichter *m*

executive [ɪgˈzɛkjutɪv] *n* (*COMM*) Geschäftsführer *m*; (*POL*) Exekutive *f* ♦ *adj* Exekutiv-, ausführend

executor [ɪgˈzɛkjutər] *n* Testamentsvollstrecker *m*

exemplary [ɪgˈzɛmplərɪ] *adj* musterhaft

exemplify [ɪgˈzɛmplɪfaɪ] *vt* veranschaulichen

exempt [ɪgˈzɛmpt] *adj* befreit ♦ *vt* befreien; ~**ion** [ɪgˈzɛmpʃən] *n* Befreiung *f*

exercise [ˈɛksəsaɪz] *n* Übung *f* ♦ *vt* (*power*) ausüben; (*muscle, patience*) üben; (*dog*) ausführen ♦ *vi* Sport treiben; ~ **bike** *n* Heimtrainer *m*; ~ **book** *n* (*Schul*)heft *nt*

exert [ɪgˈzəːt] *vt* (*influence*) ausüben; **to** ~ **o.s.** sich anstrengen; ~**ion** [ɪgˈzəːʃən] *n* Anstrengung *f*

exhale [ɛksˈheɪl] *vt, vi* ausatmen

exhaust [ɪgˈzɔːst] *n* (*fumes*) Abgase *pl*; (*pipe*) Auspuffrohr *nt* ♦ *vt* erschöpfen; ~**ed** *adj* erschöpft; ~**ion** [ɪgˈzɔːstʃən] *n* Erschöpfung *f*; ~**ive** *adj* erschöpfend

exhibit [ɪgˈzɪbɪt] *n* (*JUR*) Beweisstück *nt*; (*ART*) Ausstellungsstück *nt* ♦ *vt* ausstellen; ~**ion** [ɛksɪˈbɪʃən] *n* (*ART*) Ausstellung *f*; (*of temper etc*) Zurschaustellung *f*; ~**ionist** [ɛksɪˈbɪʃənɪst] *n* Exhibitionist *m*

exhilarating [ɪgˈzɪləreɪtɪŋ] *adj* erhebend

ex-husband n Ehemann m
exile ['ɛksaɪl] n Exil nt; (person) Verbannte(r) f(m) ♦ vt verbannen
exist [ɪg'zɪst] vi existieren; **~ence** n Existenz f; **~ing** adj bestehend
exit ['ɛksɪt] n Ausgang m; (THEAT) Abgang m ♦ vi (THEAT) abtreten; (COMPUT) aus einem Programm herausgehen; **~ poll** n bei Wahlen unmittelbar nach Verlassen der Wahllokale durchgeführte Umfrage; **~ ramp** (US) n (AUT) Ausfahrt f
exodus ['ɛksədəs] n Auszug m
exonerate [ɪg'zɔnəreɪt] vt entlasten
exorbitant [ɪg'zɔːbɪtnt] adj übermäßig; (price) Fantasie-
exotic [ɪg'zɔtɪk] adj exotisch
expand [ɪks'pænd] vt ausdehnen ♦ vi sich ausdehnen
expanse [ɪks'pæns] n Fläche f
expansion [ɪks'pænʃən] n Erweiterung f
expatriate [ɛks'pætrɪət] n Ausländer(in) m(f)
expect [ɪks'pɛkt] vt erwarten; (suppose) annehmen ♦ vi: **to be ~ing** ein Kind erwarten; **~ancy** n Erwartung f; **~ant mother** n werdende Mutter f; **~ation** [ɛkspɛk'teɪʃən] n Hoffnung f
expedient [ɪks'piːdɪənt] adj zweckdienlich ♦ n (Hilfs)mittel nt
expedition [ɛkspə'dɪʃən] n Expedition f
expel [ɪks'pɛl] vt ausweisen; (student) (ver)weisen
expend [ɪks'pɛnd] vt (effort) aufwenden; **~iture** n Ausgaben pl
expense [ɪks'pɛns] n Kosten pl; **~s** npl (COMM) Spesen pl; **at the ~ of** auf Kosten von; **~ account** n Spesenkonto nt; **expensive** [ɪks'pɛnsɪv] adj teuer
experience [ɪks'pɪərɪəns] n (incident) Erlebnis nt; (practice) Erfahrung f ♦ vt erleben; **~d** adj erfahren
experiment [ɪks'pɛrɪmənt] n Versuch m, Experiment nt ♦ vi experimentieren; **~al** [ɪkspɛrɪ'mɛntl] adj experimentell
expert ['ɛkspəːt] n Fachmann m; (official) Sachverständige(r) m ♦ adj erfahren; **~ise** [ɛkspəː'tiːz] n Sachkenntnis f
expire [ɪks'paɪəʳ] vi (end) ablaufen; (ticket)

verfallen; (die) sterben; **expiry** n Ablauf m
explain [ɪks'pleɪn] vt erklären
explanation [ɛksplə'neɪʃən] n Erklärung f;
explanatory [ɪks'plænətrɪ] adj erklärend
explicit [ɪks'plɪsɪt] adj ausdrücklich
explode [ɪks'pləʊd] vi explodieren ♦ vt (bomb) sprengen
exploit [n 'ɛksplɔɪt, vb ɪks'plɔɪt] n (Helden)tat f ♦ vt ausbeuten; **~ation** [ɛksplɔɪ'teɪʃən] n Ausbeutung f
exploration [ɛksplə'reɪʃən] n Erforschung f
exploratory [ɪks'plɔrətrɪ] adj Probe-
explore [ɪks'plɔːʳ] vt (travel) erforschen; (search) untersuchen; **~r** n Erforscher(in) m(f)
explosion [ɪks'pləʊʒən] n Explosion f; (fig) Ausbruch m
explosive [ɪks'pləʊsɪv] adj explosiv, Spreng- ♦ n Sprengstoff m
export [vb ɛks'pɔːt, n 'ɛkspɔːt] vt exportieren ♦ n Export m ♦ cpd (trade) Export-; **~er** [ɛks'pɔːtəʳ] n Exporteur m
expose [ɪks'pəʊz] vt (to danger etc) aussetzen; (impostor) entlarven; **to ~ sb to sth** jdn einer Sache dat aussetzen; **~d** adj (position) exponiert; **exposure** [ɪks'pəʊʒəʳ] n (MED) Unterkühlung f; (PHOT) Belichtung f; **exposure meter** n Belichtungsmesser m
express [ɪks'prɛs] adj ausdrücklich; (speedy) Express-, Eil- ♦ n (RAIL) Schnellzug m ♦ adv (send) per Express ♦ vt ausdrücken; **to ~ o.s.** sich ausdrücken; **~ion** [ɪks'prɛʃən] n Ausdruck m; **~ive** adj ausdrucksvoll; **~ly** adv ausdrücklich; **~way** (US) n (urban motorway) Schnellstraße f
expulsion [ɪks'pʌlʃən] n Ausweisung f
exquisite [ɛks'kwɪzɪt] adj erlesen
extend [ɪks'tɛnd] vt (visit etc) verlängern; (building) ausbauen; (hand) ausstrecken; (welcome) bieten ♦ vi (land) sich erstrecken
extension [ɪks'tɛnʃən] n Erweiterung f; (of building) Anbau m; (TEL) Apparat m
extensive [ɪks'tɛnsɪv] adj (knowledge) umfassend; (use) weitgehend, weit gehend
extent [ɪks'tɛnt] n Ausdehnung f; (fig) Ausmaß nt; **to a certain ~** bis zu einem

gewissen Grade; **to such an ~ that ...** dermaßen, dass ...; **to what ~?** inwieweit?

extenuating [ɪks'tenjueɪtɪŋ] *adj* mildernd

exterior [eks'tɪərɪər] *adj* äußere(r, s), Außen- ♦ *n* Äußere(s) *nt*

exterminate [ɪks'tɜːmɪneɪt] *vt* ausrotten

external [eks'tɜːnl] *adj* äußere(r, s), Außen-

extinct [ɪks'tɪŋkt] *adj* ausgestorben; **~ion** [ɪks'tɪŋkʃən] *n* Aussterben *nt*

extinguish [ɪks'tɪŋgwɪʃ] *vt* (aus)löschen

extort [ɪks'tɔːt] *vt* erpressen; **~ion** [ɪks'tɔːʃən] *n* Erpressung *f*; **~ionate** [ɪks'tɔːʃnɪt] *adj* überhöht, erpresserisch

extra ['ekstrə] *adj* zusätzlich ♦ *adv* besonders ♦ *n* (for car etc) Extra *nt*; (charge) Zuschlag *m*; (THEAT) Statist *m* ♦ *prefix* außer...

extract [*v* ɪks'trækt, *n* 'ekstrækt] *vt* (heraus)ziehen ♦ *n* (from book etc) Auszug *m*; (COOK) Extrakt *m*

extracurricular ['ekstrəkə'rɪkjulər] *adj* außerhalb des Stundenplans

extradite ['ekstrədaɪt] *vt* ausliefern

extramarital ['ekstrə'mærɪtl] *adj* außerehelich

extramural ['ekstrə'mjuərl] *adj* (course) Volkshochschul-

extraordinary [ɪks'trɔːdnrɪ] *adj* außerordentlich, (amazing) erstaunlich

extravagance [ɪks'trævəgəns] *n* Verschwendung *f*; (lack of restraint) Zügellosigkeit *f*; (an ~) Extravaganz *f*

extravagant [ɪks'trævəgənt] *adj* extravagant

extreme [ɪks'triːm] *adj* (edge) äußerste(r, s), hinterste(r, s); (cold) äußerste(r, s); (behaviour) außergewöhnlich, übertrieben ♦ *n* Extrem *nt*; **~ly** *adv* äußerst, höchst;

extremist *n* Extremist(in) *m(f)*

extremity [ɪks'tremɪtɪ] *n* (end) Spitze *f*, äußerste(s) Ende *nt*; (hardship) bitterste Not *f*; (ANAT) Hand *f*; Fuß *m*

extricate ['ekstrɪkeɪt] *vt* losmachen, befreien

extrovert ['ekstrəvɜːt] *n* extrovertierte(r) Mensch *m*

exuberant [ɪg'zjuːbərnt] *adj* ausgelassen

exude [ɪg'zjuːd] *vt* absondern

eye [aɪ] *n* Auge *nt*; (of needle) Öhr *nt* ♦ *vt* betrachten; (up and down) mustern; **to**

keep an ~ on aufpassen auf +acc; **~ball** *n* Augapfel *m*; **~bath** *n* Augenbad *nt*; **~brow** *n* Augenbraue *f*; **~brow pencil** *n* Augenbrauenstift *m*; **~drops** *npl* Augentropfen *pl*; **~lash** *n* Augenwimper *f*; **~lid** *n* Augenlid *nt*; **~liner** *n* Eyeliner *nt*; **~opener** *n*: **that was an ~-opener** das hat mir/ihm *etc* die Augen geöffnet; **~shadow** *n* Lidschatten *m*; **~sight** *n* Sehkraft *f*; **~sore** *n* Schandfleck *m*; **~ witness** *n* Augenzeuge *m*

F, f

F [ef] *n* (MUS) F *nt*

F. *abbr* (= Fahrenheit) F

fable ['feɪbl] *n* Fabel *f*

fabric ['fæbrɪk] *n* Stoff *m*; (fig) Gefüge *nt*

fabrication [fæbrɪ'keɪʃən] *n* Erfindung *f*

fabulous ['fæbjuləs] *adj* sagenhaft

face [feɪs] *n* Gesicht *nt*; (surface) Oberfläche *f*; (of clock) Zifferblatt *nt* ♦ *vt* (point towards) liegen nach; (situation, difficulty) sich stellen +dat; **~ down** (person) mit dem Gesicht nach unten; (card) mit der Vorderseite nach unten; **to make** *or* **pull a ~** das Gesicht verziehen; **in the ~ of** angesichts +gen; **on the ~ of it** so, wie es aussieht; **~ to ~** Auge in Auge; **to ~ up to sth** einer Sache *dat* ins Auge sehen; **~ cloth** (BRIT) *n* Waschlappen *m*; **~ cream** *n* Gesichtscreme *f*; **~ lift** *n* Facelifting *nt*; **~ powder** *n* (Gesichts)puder *m*

facet ['fæsɪt] *n* Aspekt *m*; (of gem) Facette *f*, Fassette *f*

facetious [fə'siːʃəs] *adj* witzig

face value *n* Nennwert *m*; **to take sth at (its) ~** (fig) etw für bare Münze nehmen

facial ['feɪʃl] *adj* Gesichts-

facile ['fæsaɪl] *adj* (easy) leicht

facilitate [fə'sɪlɪteɪt] *vt* erleichtern

facilities [fə'sɪlɪtɪz] *npl* Einrichtungen *pl*; **credit ~** Kreditmöglichkeiten *pl*

facing ['feɪsɪŋ] *adj* zugekehrt ♦ *prep* gegenüber

facsimile [fæk'sɪmɪlɪ] *n* Faksimile *nt*;

(*machine*) Telekopierer *m*

fact [fækt] *n* Tatsache *f*; **in ~** in der Tat

faction ['fækʃən] *n* Splittergruppe *f*

factor ['fæktər] *n* Faktor *m*

factory ['fæktərɪ] *n* Fabrik *f*

factual ['fæktjuəl] *adj* sachlich

faculty ['fækəltɪ] *n* Fähigkeit *f*; (*UNIV*) Fakultät *f*; (*US: teaching staff*) Lehrpersonal *nt*

fad [fæd] *n* Tick *m*; (*fashion*) Masche *f*

fade [feɪd] *vi* (*lose colour*) verblassen; (*dim*) nachlassen; (*sound, memory*) schwächer werden; (*wilt*) verwelken

fag [fæg] *n* (*inf*) (*cigarette*) Kippe *f*

fail [feɪl] *vt* (*exam*) nicht bestehen; (*student*) durchfallen lassen; (*courage*) verlassen; (*memory*) im Stich lassen ♦ *vi* (*supplies*) zu Ende gehen; (*student*) durchfallen; (*eyesight*) nachlassen; (*light*) schwächer werden; (*crop*) fehlschlagen; (*remedy*) nicht wirken; **to ~ to do sth** (*neglect*) es unterlassen, etw zu tun; (*be unable*) es nicht schaffen, etw zu tun; **without ~** unbedingt; **~ing** *n* Schwäche *f* ♦ *prep* mangels +*gen*; **~ure** ['feɪljər] *n* (*person*) Versager *m*; (*act*) Versagen *nt*; (*TECH*) Defekt *m*

faint [feɪnt] *adj* schwach ♦ *n* Ohnmacht *f* ♦ *vi* ohnmächtig werden

fair [feər] *adj* (*just*) gerecht, fair; (*hair*) blond; (*skin*) hell; (*weather*) schön; (*not very good*) mittelmäßig; (*sizeable*) ansehnlich ♦ *adv* (*play*) fair ♦ *n* (*COMM*) Messe *f*; (*BRIT: funfair*) Jahrmarkt *m*; **~ly** *adv* (*honestly*) gerecht, fair; (*rather*) ziemlich; **~ness** *n* Fairness *f*

fairy ['feərɪ] *n* Fee *f*; **~ tale** *n* Märchen *nt*

faith [feɪθ] *n* Glaube *m*; (*trust*) Vertrauen *nt*; (*sect*) Bekenntnis *nt*; **~ful** *adj* treu; **~fully** *adv* treu; **yours ~fully** (*BRIT*) hochachtungsvoll

fake [feɪk] *n* (*thing*) Fälschung *f*; (*person*) Schwindler *m* ♦ *adj* vorgetäuscht ♦ *vt* fälschen

falcon ['fɔːlkən] *n* Falke *m*

fall [fɔːl] (*pt* **fell**, *pp* **fallen**) *n* Fall *m*, Sturz *m*; (*decrease*) Fallen *nt*; (*of snow*) (Schnee)fall *m*; (*US: autumn*) Herbst *m* ♦ *vi* (*also fig*) fallen; (*night*) hereinbrechen; **~s** *npl* (*waterfall*) Fälle *pl*; **to ~ flat** platt hinfallen;

(*joke*) nicht ankommen; **~ back** *vi* zurückweichen; **~ back on** *vt fus* zurückgreifen auf +*acc*; **~ behind** *vi* zurückbleiben; **~ down** *vi* (*person*) hinfallen; (*building*) einstürzen; **~ for** *vt fus* (*trick*) hereinfallen auf +*acc*; (*person*) sich verknallen in +*acc*; **~ in** *vi* (*roof*) einstürzen; **~ off** *vi* herunterfallen; (*diminish*) sich vermindern; **~ out** *vi* sich streiten; (*MIL*) wegtreten; **~ through** *vi* (*plan*) ins Wasser fallen

fallacy ['fæləsɪ] *n* Trugschluss *m*

fallen ['fɔːlən] *pp of* **fall**

fallible ['fæləbl] *adj* fehlbar

fallout ['fɔːlaʊt] *n* radioaktive(r) Niederschlag *m*; **~ shelter** *n* Atombunker *m*

fallow ['fæləʊ] *adj* brach(liegend)

false [fɔːls] *adj* falsch; (*artificial*) künstlich; **under ~ pretences** unter Vorspiegelung falscher Tatsachen; **~ alarm** *n* Fehlalarm *m*; **~ teeth** (*BRIT*) *npl* Gebiss *nt*

falter ['fɔːltər] *vi* schwanken; (*in speech*) stocken

fame [feɪm] *n* Ruhm *m*

familiar [fə'mɪlɪər] *adj* bekannt; (*intimate*) familiär; **to be ~ with** vertraut sein mit; **~ize** *vt* vertraut machen

family ['fæmɪlɪ] *n* Familie *f*; (*relations*) Verwandtschaft *f*; **~ business** *n* Familienunternehmen *nt*; **~ doctor** *n* Hausarzt *m*

famine ['fæmɪn] *n* Hungersnot *f*

famished ['fæmɪʃt] *adj* ausgehungert

famous ['feɪməs] *adj* berühmt

fan [fæn] *n* (*folding*) Fächer *m*; (*ELEC*) Ventilator *m*; (*admirer*) Fan *m* ♦ *vt* fächeln; **~ out** *vi* sich (fächerförmig) ausbreiten

fanatic [fə'nætɪk] *n* Fanatiker(in) *m(f)*

fan belt *n* Keilriemen *m*

fanciful ['fænsɪfʊl] *adj* (*odd*) seltsam; (*imaginative*) fantasievoll

fancy ['fænsɪ] *n* (*liking*) Neigung *f*; (*imagination*) Einbildung *f* ♦ *adj* schick ♦ *vt* (*like*) gern haben; wollen; (*imagine*) sich einbilden; **he fancies her** er mag sie; **~ dress** *n* Maskenkostüm *nt*; **~-dress ball** *n* Maskenball *m*

fang [fæŋ] n Fangzahn m; (of snake) Giftzahn m

fantastic [fæn'tæstɪk] adj fantastisch

fantasy ['fæntəsɪ] n Fantasie f

far [fɑːr] adj weit ♦ adv weit entfernt; (very much) weitaus; **by** ~ bei weitem; **so** ~ so weit; bis jetzt; **go as ~ as the station** gehen Sie bis zum Bahnhof; **as ~ as I know** soweit or soviel ich weiß; ~**away** adj weit entfernt

farce [fɑːs] n Farce f; **farcical** ['fɑːsɪkl] adj lächerlich

fare [fɛər] n Fahrpreis m; Fahrgeld nt; (food) Kost f; **half/full** ~ halber/voller Fahrpreis m

Far East n: **the** ~ der Ferne Osten

farewell [fɛə'wɛl] n Abschied(sgruß) m ♦ excl lebe wohl!

farm [fɑːm] n Bauernhof m, Farm f ♦ vt bewirtschaften; ~**er** n Bauer m, Landwirt m; ~**hand** n Landarbeiter m; ~**house** n Bauernhaus nt; ~**ing** n Landwirtschaft f; ~**land** n Ackerland nt; ~**yard** n Hof m

far-reaching ['fɑː'riːtʃɪŋ] adj (reform, effect) weitreichend, weit reichend

fart [fɑːt] (inf!) n Furz m ♦ vi furzen

farther ['fɑːðər] adv weiter; **farthest** ['fɑːðɪst] adj fernste(r, s) ♦ adv am weitesten

fascinate ['fæsɪneɪt] vt faszinieren; **fascinating** adj faszinierend; **fascination** [fæsɪ'neɪʃən] n Faszination f

fascism ['fæʃɪzəm] n Faschismus m

fashion ['fæʃən] n (of clothes) Mode f; (manner) Art f (und Weise f) ♦ vt machen; **in** ~ in Mode; **out of** ~ unmodisch; ~**able** adj (clothes) modisch; (place) elegant; ~ **show** n Mode(n)schau f

fast [fɑːst] adj schnell; (firm) fest ♦ adv schnell; fest ♦ n Fasten nt ♦ vi fasten; **to be** ~ (clock) vorgehen

fasten ['fɑːsn] vt (attach) befestigen; (with rope) zuschnüren; (seat belt) festmachen; (coat) zumachen ♦ vi sich schließen lassen; ~**er** n Verschluss m; ~**ing** n Verschluss m

fast food n Fastfood nt, Fast Food nt

fastidious [fæs'tɪdɪəs] adj wählerisch

fat [fæt] adj dick ♦ n Fett nt

fatal ['feɪtl] adj tödlich; (disastrous)
verhängnisvoll; ~**ity** [fə'tælɪtɪ] n (road death etc) Todesopfer nt; ~**ly** adv tödlich

fate [feɪt] n Schicksal nt; ~**ful** adj (prophetic) schicksalsschwer; (important) schicksalhaft

father ['fɑːðər] n Vater m; (REL) Pater m; ~**-in-law** n Schwiegervater m; ~**ly** adj väterlich

fathom ['fæðəm] n Klafter m ♦ vt ausloten; (fig) ergründen

fatigue [fə'tiːg] n Ermüdung f

fatten ['fætn] vt dick machen; (animals) mästen ♦ vi dick werden

fatty ['fætɪ] adj fettig ♦ n (inf) Dickerchen nt

fatuous ['fætjuəs] adj albern, affig

faucet ['fɔːsɪt] (US) n Wasserhahn m

fault [fɔːlt] n (defect) Defekt m; (ELEC) Störung f; (blame) Schuld f; (GEOG) Verwerfung f; **it's your** ~ du bist daran schuld; **to find** ~ **with (sth/sb)** etwas auszusetzen haben an (etw/jdm); **at** ~ im Unrecht; ~**less** adj tadellos; ~**y** adj fehlerhaft, defekt

fauna ['fɔːnə] n Fauna f

favour ['feɪvə] (US **favor**) n (approval) Wohlwollen nt; (kindness) Gefallen m ♦ vt (prefer) vorziehen; (in ~ of für; zugunsten or zu Gunsten +gen; **to find** ~ **with sb** bei jdm Anklang finden; ~**able** ['feɪvrəbl] adj günstig; ~**ite** ['feɪvrɪt] adj Lieblings- ♦ n (child) Liebling m; (SPORT) Favorit m

fawn [fɔːn] adj rehbraun ♦ n (animal) (Reh)kitz nt ♦ vi: **to** ~ **(up)on** (fig) katzbuckeln vor +dat

fax [fæks] n (document) Fax nt; (machine) Telefax nt ♦ vt: **to** ~ **sth to sb** jdm etw faxen

FBI (US) n abbr (= Federal Bureau of Investigation) FBI m

fear [fɪər] n Furcht f ♦ vt fürchten; ~**ful** adj (timid) furchtsam; (terrible) fürchterlich; ~**less** adj furchtlos

feasible ['fiːzəbl] adj durchführbar

feast [fiːst] n Festmahl nt; (REL: also: ~ **day**) Feiertag m ♦ vi: **to** ~ **(on)** sich gütlich tun (an +dat)

feat [fiːt] n Leistung f

feather ['fɛðər] n Feder f

feature ['fiːtʃər] n (Gesichts)zug m;

(*important part*) Grundzug *m*; (*CINE, PRESS*) Feature *nt* ♦ *vt* darstellen; (*advertising etc*) groß herausbringen ♦ *vi* vorkommen; **featuring X** mit X; ~ **film** *n* Spielfilm *m*

February ['februəri] *n* Februar *m*

fed [fed] *pt, pp* of **feed**

federal ['fedərəl] *adj* Bundes-

federation [fedə'reɪʃən] *n* (*society*) Verband *m*; (*of states*) Staatenbund *m*

fed up *adj*: **to be ~ with sth** etw satt haben; **I'm ~** ich habe die Nase voll

fee [fiː] *n* Gebühr *f*

feeble ['fiːbl] *adj* (*person*) schwach; (*excuse*) lahm

feed [fiːd] (*pt, pp* **fed**) *n* (*for animals*) Futter *nt* ♦ *vt* füttern; (*support*) ernähren; (*data*) eingeben; **to ~ on** fressen; **~back** *n* (*information*) Feed-back *nt*, Feedback *nt*; **~ing bottle** (*BRIT*) *n* Flasche *f*

feel [fiːl] (*pt, pp* **felt**) *n*: **it has a soft ~** es fühlt sich weich an ♦ *vt* (*sense*) fühlen; (*touch*) anfassen; (*think*) meinen ♦ *vi* (*person*) sich fühlen; (*thing*) sich anfühlen; **to get the ~ of sth** sich an etw *acc* gewöhnen; **I ~ cold** mir ist kalt; **I ~ like a cup of tea** ich habe Lust auf eine Tasse Tee; **~ about** *or* **around** *vi* herumsuchen; **~er** *n* Fühler *m*; **~ing** *n* Gefühl *nt*; (*opinion*) Meinung *f*

feet [fiːt] *npl* of **foot**

feign [feɪn] *vt* vortäuschen

feline ['fiːlaɪn] *adj* katzenartig

fell [fel] *pt* of **fall** ♦ *vt* (*tree*) fällen

fellow ['feləu] *n* (*man*) Kerl *m*; **~ citizen** *n* Mitbürger(in) *m(f)*; **~ countryman** (*irreg*) *n* Landsmann *m*; **~ men** *npl* Mitmenschen *pl*; **~ship** *n* (*group*) Körperschaft *f*; (*friendliness*) Kameradschaft *f*; (*scholarship*) Forschungsstipendium *nt*; **~ student** *n* Kommilitone *m*, Kommilitonin *f*

felony ['feləni] *n* schwere(s) Verbrechen *nt*

felt [felt] *pt, pp* of **feel** ♦ *n* Filz *m*; **~-tip pen** *n* Filzstift *m*

female ['fiːmeɪl] *n* (*of animals*) Weibchen *nt* ♦ *adj* weiblich

feminine ['femɪnɪn] *adj* (*LING*) weiblich; (*qualities*) fraulich

feminist ['femɪnɪst] *n* Feminist(in) *m(f)*

fence [fens] *n* Zaun *m* ♦ *vt* (*also*: **~ in**) einzäunen ♦ *vi* fechten; **fencing** ['fensɪŋ] *n* Zaun *m*; (*SPORT*) Fechten *nt*

fend [fend] *vi*: **to ~ for o.s.** sich (allein) durchschlagen; **~ off** *vt* abwehren

fender ['fendər] *n* Kaminvorsetzer *m*; (*US: AUT*) Kotflügel *m*

ferment [*vb* fə'ment, *n* 'fɜːment] *vi* (*CHEM*) gären ♦ *n* (*unrest*) Unruhe *f*

fern [fɜːn] *n* Farn *m*

ferocious [fə'rəuʃəs] *adj* wild, grausam

ferret ['ferɪt] *n* Frettchen *nt* ♦ *vt*: **to ~ out** aufspüren

ferry ['feri] *n* Fähre *f* ♦ *vt* übersetzen

fertile ['fɜːtaɪl] *adj* fruchtbar

fertilize ['fɜːtɪlaɪz] *vt* (*AGR*) düngen; (*BIOL*) befruchten; **~r** *n* (*Kunst*)dünger *m*

fervent ['fɜːvənt] *adj* (*admirer*) glühend; (*hope*) innig

fervour ['fɜːvər] (*US* **fervor**) *n* Leidenschaft *f*

fester ['festər] *vi* eitern

festival ['festɪvəl] *n* (*REL etc*) Fest *nt*; (*ART, MUS*) Festspiele *pl*

festive ['festɪv] *adj* festlich; **the ~ season** (*Christmas*) die Festzeit; **festivities** [fes'tɪvɪtɪz] *npl* Feierlichkeiten *pl*

festoon [fes'tuːn] *vt*: **to ~ with** schmücken mit

fetch [fetʃ] *vt* holen; (*in sale*) einbringen

fetching ['fetʃɪŋ] *adj* reizend

fête [feɪt] *n* Fest *nt*

fetus ['fiːtəs] (*esp US*) *n* = **foetus**

feud [fjuːd] *n* Fehde *f*

feudal ['fjuːdl] *adj* Feudal-

fever ['fiːvər] *n* Fieber *nt*; **~ish** *adj* (*MED*) fiebrig; (*fig*) fieberhaft

few [fjuː] *adj* wenig; **a ~** einige; **~er** *adj* weniger; **~est** *adj* wenigste(r,s)

fiancé [fɪ'ɑ̃ːŋseɪ] *n* Verlobte(r) *m*; **~e** *n* Verlobte *f*

fib [fɪb] *n* Flunkerei *f* ♦ *vi* flunkern

fibre ['faɪbər] (*US* **fiber**) *n* Faser *f*; **~glass** *n* Glaswolle *f*

fickle ['fɪkl] *adj* unbeständig

fiction ['fɪkʃən] *n* (*novels*) Romanliteratur *f*; (*story*) Erdichtung *f*; **~al** *adj* erfunden

fictitious [fɪk'tɪʃəs] *adj* erfunden, fingiert

fiddle ['fɪdl] *n* Geige *f*; (*trick*) Schwindelei *f* ♦ *vt* (*BRIT: accounts*) frisieren; **~ with** *vt fus* herumfummeln an +*dat*

fidelity [fɪ'delɪtɪ] *n* Treue *f*

fidget ['fɪdʒɪt] *vi* zappeln

field [fiːld] *n* Feld *nt*; (*range*) Gebiet *nt*; **~ marshal** *n* Feldmarschall *m*; **~work** *n* Feldforschung *f*

fiend [fiːnd] *n* Teufel *m*

fierce [fɪəs] *adj* wild

fiery ['faɪərɪ] *adj* (*person*) hitzig

fifteen [fɪf'tiːn] *num* fünfzehn

fifth [fɪfθ] *adj* fünfte(r, s) ♦ *n* Fünftel *nt*

fifty ['fɪftɪ] *num* fünfzig; **~-fifty** *adj, adv* halbe-halbe, fifty-fifty (*inf*)

fig [fɪg] *n* Feige *f*

fight [faɪt] (*pt, pp* **fought**) *n* Kampf *m*; (*brawl*) Schlägerei *f*; (*argument*) Streit *m* ♦ *vt* kämpfen gegen; sich schlagen mit; (*fig*) bekämpfen ♦ *vi* kämpfen; sich schlagen; streiten; **~er** *n* Kämpfer(in) *m(f)*; (*plane*) Jagdflugzeug *nt*; **~ing** *n* Kämpfen *nt*; (*war*) Kampfhandlungen *pl*

figment ['fɪgmənt] *n*: **~ of the imagination** reine Einbildung *f*

figurative ['fɪgjurətɪv] *adj* bildlich

figure ['fɪgə*] *n* (*of person*) Figur *f*; (*person*) Gestalt *f*; (*number*) Ziffer *f* ♦ *vt* (*US: imagine*) glauben ♦ *vi* (*appear*) erscheinen; **~ out** *vt* herausbekommen; **~head** *n* (*NAUT, fig*) Galionsfigur *f*; **~ of speech** *n* Redensart *f*

file [faɪl] *n* (*tool*) Feile *f*; (*dossier*) Akte *f*; (*folder*) Aktenordner *m*; (*COMPUT*) Datei *f*; (*row*) Reihe *f* ♦ *vt* (*metal, nails*) feilen; (*papers*) abheften; (*claim*) einreichen ♦ *vi*: **to ~ in/out** hintereinander hereinkommen/ hinausgehen; **to ~ past** vorbeimarschieren; **filing** ['faɪlɪŋ] *n* Ablage *f*; **filing cabinet** *n* Aktenschrank *m*

fill [fɪl] *vt* füllen; (*occupy*) ausfüllen; (*satisfy*) sättigen ♦ *n*: **to eat one's ~** sich richtig satt essen; **~ in** *vt* (*hole*) (auf)füllen; (*form*) ausfüllen; **~ up** *vt* (*container*) auffüllen; (*form*) ausfüllen ♦ *vi* (*AUT*) tanken

fillet ['fɪlɪt] *n* Filet *nt*; **~ steak** *n* Filetsteak *nt*

filling ['fɪlɪŋ] *n* (*COOK*) Füllung *f*; (*for tooth*)

(*Zahn*)plombe *f*; **~ station** *n* Tankstelle *f*

film [fɪlm] *n* Film *m* ♦ *vt* (*scene*) filmen; **~ star** *n* Filmstar *m*

filter ['fɪltə*] *n* Filter *m* ♦ *vt* filtern; **~ lane** (*BRIT*) *n* Abbiegespur *f*; **~-tipped** *adj* Filter-

filth [fɪlθ] *n* Dreck *m*; **~y** *adj* dreckig; (*weather*) scheußlich

fin [fɪn] *n* Flosse *f*

final ['faɪnl] *adj* letzte(r, s); End-; (*conclusive*) endgültig ♦ *n* (*FOOTBALL etc*) Endspiel *nt*; **~s** *npl* (*UNIV*) Abschlussexamen *nt*; (*SPORT*) Schlussrunde *f*

finale [fɪ'nɑːlɪ] *n* (*MUS*) Finale *nt*

final: ~ist *n* (*SPORT*) Schlussrundenteilnehmer *m*; **~ize** *vt* endgültige Form geben +*dat*; abschließen; **~ly** *adv* (*lastly*) zuletzt; (*eventually*) endlich; (*irrevocably*) endgültig

finance [faɪ'næns] *n* Finanzwesen *nt* ♦ *vt* finanzieren; **~s** *npl* (*funds*) Finanzen *pl*; **financial** [faɪ'nænʃəl] *adj* Finanz-; finanziell

find [faɪnd] (*pt, pp* **found**) *vt* finden ♦ *n* Fund *m*; **to ~ sb guilty** jdn für schuldig erklären; **~ out** *vt* herausfinden; **~ings** *npl* (*JUR*) Ermittlungsergebnis *nt*; (*of report*) Befund *m*

fine [faɪn] *adj* fein; (*good*) gut; (*weather*) schön ♦ *adv* (*well*) gut; (*small*) klein ♦ *n* (*JUR*) Geldstrafe *f* ♦ *vt* (*JUR*) mit einer Geldstrafe belegen; **~ arts** *npl* schöne(n) Künste *pl*

finger ['fɪŋgə*] *n* Finger *m* ♦ *vt* befühlen; **~nail** *n* Fingernagel *m*; **~print** *n* Fingerabdruck *m*; **~tip** *n* Fingerspitze *f*

finicky ['fɪnɪkɪ] *adj* pingelig

finish ['fɪnɪʃ] *n* Ende *nt*; (*SPORT*) Ziel *nt*; (*of object*) Verarbeitung *f*; (*of paint*) Oberflächenwirkung *f* ♦ *vt* beenden; (*book*) zu Ende lesen ♦ *vi* aufhören; (*SPORT*) ans Ziel kommen; **to be ~ed with sth** fertig sein mit etw; **to ~ doing sth** mit etw fertig werden; **~ off** *vt* (*complete*) fertig machen; (*kill*) den Gnadenstoß geben +*dat*; (*knock out*) erledigen (*umg*); **~ up** *vt* (*food*) aufessen; (*drink*) austrinken ♦ *vi* (*end up*) enden; **~ing line** *n* Ziellinie *f*; **~ing school** *n* Mädchenpensionat *nt*

finite ['faɪnaɪt] *adj* endlich, begrenzt

Finland ['fɪnlənd] *n* Finnland *nt*

Finn [fɪn] *n* Finne *m*, Finnin *f*; **~ish** *adj*
finnisch ♦ *n* (LING) Finnisch *nt*

fir [fəːʳ] *n* Tanne *f*

fire ['faɪəʳ] *n* Feuer *nt*; (*in house etc*) Brand *m*
♦ *vt* (*gun*) abfeuern; (*imagination*)
entzünden; (*dismiss*) hinauswerfen ♦ *vi*
(AUT) zünden; **to be on ~** brennen; **~
alarm** *n* Feueralarm *m*; **~arm** *n*
Schusswaffe *f*; **~ brigade** (BRIT) *n*
Feuerwehr *f*; **~ department** (US) *n*
Feuerwehr *f*; **~ engine** *n* Feuerwehrauto
nt; **~ escape** *n* Feuerleiter *f*; **~
extinguisher** *n* Löschgerät *nt*; **~man**
(*irreg*) *n* Feuerwehrmann *m*; **~place** *n*
Kamin *m*; **~side** *n* Kamin *m*; **~ station** *n*
Feuerwehrwache *f*; **~wood** *n* Brennholz *nt*;
~works *npl* Feuerwerk *nt*; **~ squad** *n*
Exekutionskommando *nt*

firm [fəːm] *adj* fest ♦ *n* Firma *f*; **~ly** ['fəːmlɪ]
adv (*grasp, speak*) fest; (*push, tug*) energisch;
(*decide*) endgültig

first [fəːst] *adj* erste(r, s) ♦ *adv* zuerst; (*arrive*)
als Erste(r); (*happen*) zum ersten Mal ♦ *n*
(*person: in race*) Erste(r) *mf*; (UNIV) Eins *f*;
(AUT) erste(r) Gang *m*; **at ~** zuerst; **~ of all**
zuallererst; **~ aid** *n* erste Hilfe *f*; **~-aid kit** *n*
Verbandskasten *m*; **~-class** *adj* erstklassig;
(*travel*) erster Klasse; **~-hand** *adj* aus erster
Hand; **~ lady** (US) *n* First Lady *f*; **~ly** *adv*
erstens; **~ name** *n* Vorname *m*; **~-rate** *adj*
erstklassig

fiscal ['fɪskl] *adj* Finanz-

fish [fɪʃ] *n inv* Fisch *m* ♦ *vi* fischen; angeln; **to
go ~ing** angeln gehen; (*in sea*) fischen
gehen; **~erman** (*irreg*) *n* Fischer *m*; **~ farm**
n Fischzucht *f*; **~ fingers** (BRIT) *npl*
Fischstäbchen *pl*; **~ing boat** *n* Fischerboot
nt; **~ing line** *n* Angelschnur *f*; **~ing rod** *n*
Angel(rute) *f*; **~ing tackle** *n* (*for sport*)
Angelgeräte *pl*; **~monger's (shop)** *n*
Fischhändler *m*; **~ slice** *n*
Fischvorlegemesser *nt*; **~ sticks** (US) *npl* =
fish fingers

fishy ['fɪʃɪ] (*inf*) *adj* (*suspicious*) faul

fission ['fɪʃən] *n* Spaltung *f*

fissure ['fɪʃəʳ] *n* Riss *m*

fist [fɪst] *n* Faust *f*

fit [fɪt] *adj* (MED) gesund; (SPORT) in Form, fit;
(*suitable*) geeignet ♦ *vt* passen +*dat*; (*insert,
attach*) einsetzen ♦ *vi* passen; (*in space, gap*)
hineinpassen ♦ *n* (*of clothes*) Sitz *m*; (MED, *of
anger*) Anfall *m*; (*of laughter*) Krampf *m*; **by
~s and starts** (*move*) ruckweise; (*work*)
unregelmäßig; **~ in** *vi* hineinpassen; (*fig:
person*) passen; **~ out** *vt* (*also: ~ up*)
ausstatten; **~ful** *adj* (*sleep*) unruhig; **~ment**
n Einrichtungsgegenstand *m*; **~ness** *n*
(*suitability*) Eignung *f*; (MED) Gesundheit *f*;
(SPORT) Fitness *f*; **~ted carpet** *n*
Teppichboden *m*; **~ted kitchen** *n*
Einbauküche *f*; **~ter** *n* (TECH) Monteur *m*;
~ting *adj* passend ♦ *n* (*of dress*) Anprobe *f*;
(*piece of equipment*) (Ersatz)teil *nt*; **~tings**
npl (*equipment*) Zubehör *nt*; **~ting room** *n*
Anproberaum *m*

five [faɪv] *num* fünf; **~r** (*inf*) *n* (BRIT)
Fünfpfundnote *f*; (US) Fünfdollarnote *f*

fix [fɪks] *vt* befestigen; (*settle*) festsetzen;
(*repair*) reparieren ♦ *n*: **in a ~** in der
Klemme; **~ up** *vt* (*meeting*) arrangieren; **to
~ sb up with sth** jdm etw *acc* verschaffen;
~ation [fɪk'seɪʃən] *n* Fixierung *f*; **~ed** [fɪkst]
adj fest; **~ture** ['fɪkstʃəʳ] *n* Installationsteil *m*;
(SPORT) Spiel *nt*

fizzy ['fɪzɪ] *adj* Sprudel-, sprudelnd

flabbergasted ['flæbəgɑːstɪd] (*inf*) *adj* platt

flabby ['flæbɪ] *adj* wabbelig

flag [flæg] *n* Fahne *f* ♦ *vi* (*strength*)
nachlassen; (*spirit*) erlahmen; **~ down** *vt*
anhalten; **~pole** ['flægpəʊl] *n* Fahnenstange
f

flair [flɛəʳ] *n* Talent *nt*

flak [flæk] *n* Flakfeuer *nt*

flake [fleɪk] *n* (*of snow*) Flocke *f*; (*of rust*)
Schuppe *f* ♦ *vi* (*also: ~ off*) abblättern

flamboyant [flæm'bɔɪənt] *adj* extravagant

flame [fleɪm] *n* Flamme *f*

flamingo [flə'mɪŋɡəʊ] *n* Flamingo *m*

flammable ['flæməbl] *adj* brennbar

flan [flæn] (BRIT) *n* Obsttorte *f*

flank [flæŋk] *n* Flanke *f* ♦ *vt* flankieren

flannel ['flænl] *n* Flanell *m*; (BRIT: *also:* **face
~**) Waschlappen *m*; (: *inf*) Geschwafel *nt*;
~s *npl* (*trousers*) Flanellhose *f*

flap [flæp] *n* Klappe *f*; (*inf: crisis*) (helle) Aufregung *f* ♦ *vt* (*wings*) schlagen mit ♦ *vi* flattern

flare [fleəʳ] *n* (*signal*) Leuchtsignal *nt*; (*in skirt etc*) Weite *f*; ~ **up** *vi* aufflammen; (*fig*) aufbrausen; (*revolt*) (plötzlich) ausbrechen

flash [flæʃ] *n* Blitz *m*; (*also:* **news ~**) Kurzmeldung *f*; (*PHOT*) Blitzlicht *nt* ♦ *vt* aufleuchten lassen ♦ *vi* aufleuchten; **in a ~** im Nu; ~ **by** *or* **past** *vi* vorbeirasen; **~back** *n* Rückblende *f*; **~bulb** *n* Blitzlichtbirne *f*; ~ **cube** *n* Blitzwürfel *m*; **~light** *n* Blitzlicht *nt*

flashy ['flæʃɪ] (*pej*) *adj* knallig

flask [flɑːsk] *n* (*CHEM*) Kolben *m*; (*also:* **vacuum ~**) Thermosflasche *f* ®

flat [flæt] *adj* flach; (*dull*) matt; (*MUS*) erniedrigt; (*beer*) schal; (*tyre*) platt ♦ *n* (*BRIT: rooms*) Wohnung *f*; (*MUS*) b *nt*; (*AUT*) Platte(r) *m*; **to work ~ out** auf Hochtouren arbeiten; **~ly** *adv* glatt; **~screen** *adj* (*TV, COMPUT*) mit flachem Bildschirm; **~ten** *vt* (*also:* **~ten out**) ebnen

flatter ['flætəʳ] *vt* schmeicheln +*dat*; **~ing** *adj* schmeichelhaft; **~y** *n* Schmeichelei *f*

flatulence ['flætjuləns] *n* Blähungen *pl*

flaunt [flɔːnt] *vt* prunken mit

flavour ['fleɪvəʳ] (*US* **flavor**) *n* Geschmack *m* ♦ *vt* würzen; **~ed** *adj*: **strawberry~ed** mit Erdbeergeschmack; **~ing** *n* Würze *f*

flaw [flɔː] *n* Fehler *m*; **~less** *adj* einwandfrei

flax [flæks] *n* Flachs *m*; **~en** *adj* flachsfarben

flea [fliː] *n* Floh *m*

fleck [flek] *n* (*mark*) Fleck *m*; (*pattern*) Tupfen *m*

fled [fled] *pt, pp of* **flee**

flee [fliː] (*pt, pp* **fled**) *vi* fliehen ♦ *vt* fliehen vor +*dat*; (*country*) fliehen aus

fleece [fliːs] *n* Vlies *nt* ♦ *vt* (*inf*) schröpfen

fleet [fliːt] *n* Flotte *f*

fleeting ['fliːtɪŋ] *adj* flüchtig

Flemish ['flemɪʃ] *adj* flämisch

flesh [fleʃ] *n* Fleisch *nt*; ~ **wound** *n* Fleischwunde *f*

flew [fluː] *pt of* **fly**

flex [fleks] *n* Kabel *nt* ♦ *vt* beugen; **~ibility** [fleksɪ'bɪlɪtɪ] *n* Biegsamkeit *f*; (*fig*) Flexibilität

f; **~ible** *adj* biegsam; (*plans*) flexibel

flick [flɪk] *n* leichte(r) Schlag *m* ♦ *vt* leicht schlagen; ~ **through** *vt fus* durchblättern

flicker ['flɪkəʳ] *n* Flackern *nt* ♦ *vi* flackern

flier ['flaɪəʳ] *n* Flieger *m*

flight [flaɪt] *n* Flug *m*; (*fleeing*) Flucht *f*; (*also:* ~ **of steps**) Treppe *f*; **to take ~** die Flucht ergreifen; ~ **attendant** (*US*) *n* Steward(ess) *m(f)*; ~ **deck** *n* Flugdeck *nt*

flimsy ['flɪmzɪ] *adj* (*thin*) hauchdünn; (*excuse*) fadenscheinig

flinch [flɪntʃ] *vi*: **to ~ (away from)** zurückschrecken (vor +*dat*)

fling [flɪŋ] (*pt, pp* **flung**) *vt* schleudern

flint [flɪnt] *n* Feuerstein *m*

flip [flɪp] *vt* werfen

flippant ['flɪpənt] *adj* schnippisch

flipper ['flɪpəʳ] *n* Flosse *f*

flirt [flɜːt] *vi* flirten ♦ *n*: **he/she is a ~** er/sie flirtet gern

flit [flɪt] *vi* flitzen

float [fləʊt] *n* (*FISHING*) Schwimmer *m*; (*esp in procession*) Plattformwagen *m* ♦ *vi* schwimmen; (*in air*) schweben ♦ *vt* (*COMM*) gründen; (*currency*) floaten

flock [flɒk] *n* (*of sheep, REL*) Herde *f*; (*of birds*) Schwarm *m*

flog [flɒg] *vt* prügeln; (*inf: sell*) verkaufen

flood [flʌd] *n* Überschwemmung *f*; (*fig*) Flut *f* ♦ *vt* überschwemmen; **~ing** *n* Überschwemmung *f*; **~light** *n* Flutlicht *nt*

floor [flɔːʳ] *n* (*Fuß*)boden *m*; (*storey*) Stock *m* ♦ *vt* (*person*) zu Boden schlagen; **ground ~** (*BRIT*) Erdgeschoss *nt*; **first ~** (*BRIT*) erste(r) Stock *m*; (*US*) Erdgeschoss *nt*; **~board** *n* Diele *f*; ~ **show** *n* Kabarettvorstellung *f*

flop [flɒp] *n* Plumps *m*; (*failure*) Reinfall *m* ♦ *vi* (*fail*) durchfallen

floppy ['flɒpɪ] *adj* hängend; ~ (**disk**) *n* (*COMPUT*) Diskette *f*

flora ['flɔːrə] *n* Flora *f*; **~l** *adj* Blumen-

florist ['flɒrɪst] *n* Blumenhändler(in) *m(f)*; **~'s (shop)** *n* Blumengeschäft *nt*

flotation [fləʊ'teɪʃən] *n* (*FIN*) Auflegung *f*

flounce [flaʊns] *n* Volant *m*

flounder ['flaʊndəʳ] *vi* (*fig*) ins Schleudern kommen ♦ *n* (*ZOOL*) Flunder *f*

flour ['flauə'] n Mehl nt
flourish ['flʌrɪʃ] vi blühen; gedeihen ♦ n (*waving*) Schwingen nt; (*of trumpets*) Tusch m, Fanfare f
flout [flaut] vt missachten
flow [fləu] n Fließen nt; (*of sea*) Flut f ♦ vi fließen; ~ **chart** n Flussdiagramm nt
flower ['flauə'] n Blume f ♦ vi blühen; ~ **bed** n Blumenbeet nt; ~**pot** n Blumentopf m; ~**y** adj (*style*) blumenreich
flown [fləun] pp of **fly**
flu [flu:] n Grippe f
fluctuate ['flʌktjueɪt] vi schwanken; **fluctuation** [flʌktju'eɪʃən] n Schwankung f
fluency ['flu:ənsɪ] n Flüssigkeit f
fluent ['flu:ənt] adj fließend; ~**ly** adv fließend
fluff [flʌf] n Fussel f; ~**y** adj flaumig
fluid ['flu:ɪd] n Flüssigkeit f ♦ adj flüssig; (*fig: plans*) veränderbar
fluke [flu:k] (*inf*) n Dusel m
flung [flʌŋ] pt, pp of **fling**
fluoride ['fluəraɪd] n Fluorid nt; ~ **toothpaste** n Fluorzahnpasta f
flurry ['flʌrɪ] n (*of snow*) Gestöber nt; (*of activity*) Aufregung f
flush [flʌʃ] n Erröten nt; (*excited*) Glühen nt ♦ vt (aus)spülen ♦ vi erröten ♦ adj glatt; ~ **out** vt aufstöbern; ~**ed** adj rot
flustered ['flʌstəd] adj verwirrt
flute [flu:t] n Querflöte f
flutter ['flʌtə'] n Flattern nt ♦ vi flattern
flux [flʌks] n: **in a state of** ~ im Fluss
fly [flaɪ] (*pt* **flew**, *pp* **flown**) n (*insect*) Fliege f; (*on trousers: also:* **flies**) (Hosen)schlitz m ♦ vt fliegen ♦ vi fliegen; (*flee*) fliehen; (*flag*) wehen; ~ **away** or **off** vi (*bird, insect*) wegfliegen; ~-**drive** n: ~-**drive holiday** Fly & Drive-Urlaub m; ~**ing** n Fliegen nt ♦ adj: **with ~ing colours** mit fliegenden Fahnen; ~**ing start** gute(r) Start m; ~**ing visit** Stippvisite f; ~**ing saucer** n fliegende Untertasse f; ~**over** (*BRIT*) n Überführung f; ~**sheet** n (*for tent*) Regendach nt
foal [fəul] n Fohlen nt
foam [fəum] n Schaum m ♦ vi schäumen; ~ **rubber** n Schaumgummi m
fob [fɔb] vt: **to ~ sb off with sth** jdm etw

andrehen; (*with promise*) jdn mit etw abspeisen
focal ['fəukl] adj Brenn-; ~ **point** n (*of room, activity*) Mittelpunkt m
focus ['fəukəs] (*pl* ~**es**) n Brennpunkt m ♦ vt (*attention*) konzentrieren; (*camera*) scharf einstellen ♦ vi: **to ~ (on)** sich konzentrieren (auf +acc); **in ~** scharf eingestellt; **out of ~** unscharf
fodder ['fɔdə'] n Futter nt
foe [fəu] n Feind m
foetus ['fi:təs] (*US* **fetus**) n Fötus m
fog [fɔg] n Nebel m; ~**gy** adj neblig; ~ **lamp** (*BRIT*), ~ **light** (*US*) n (*AUT*) Nebelscheinwerfer m
foil [fɔɪl] vt vereiteln ♦ n (*metal, also fig*) Folie f; (*FENCING*) Florett nt
fold [fəuld] n (*bend, crease*) Falte f; (*AGR*) Pferch m ♦ vt falten; ~ **up** vt (*map etc*) zusammenfalten ♦ vi (*business*) eingehen; ~**er** n Schnellhefter m; ~**ing** adj (*chair etc*) Klapp-
foliage ['fəulɪɪdʒ] n Laubwerk nt
folk [fəuk] npl Leute pl ♦ adj Volks-; ~**s** npl (*family*) Leute pl; ~**lore** ['fəuklɔ:'] n (*study*) Volkskunde f; (*tradition*) Folklore f; ~ **song** n Volkslied nt; (*modern*) Folksong m
follow ['fɔləu] vt folgen +dat; (*fashion*) mitmachen ♦ vi folgen; ~ **up** vt verfolgen; ~**er** n Anhänger(in) m(f); ~**ing** adj folgend ♦ n (*people*) Gefolgschaft f; ~-**on call** n weiteres Gespräch in einer Telefonzelle um Guthaben zu verbrauchen
folly ['fɔlɪ] n Torheit f
fond [fɔnd] adj: **to be ~ of** gern haben
fondle ['fɔndl] vt streicheln
font [fɔnt] n Taufbecken nt
food [fu:d] n Essen nt; (*fodder*) Futter nt; ~ **mixer** n Küchenmixer m; ~ **poisoning** n Lebensmittelvergiftung f; ~ **processor** n Küchenmaschine f; ~**stuffs** npl Lebensmittel pl
fool [fu:l] n Narr m, Närrin f ♦ vt (*deceive*) hereinlegen ♦ vi (*also:* ~ **around**) (herum)albern; ~**hardy** adj tollkühn; ~**ish** adj albern; ~**proof** adj idiotensicher
foot [fut] (*pl* **feet**) n Fuß m ♦ vt (*bill*)

bezahlen; **on** ~ zu Fuß

footage ['futɪdʒ] n (CINE) Filmmaterial nt

football ['futbɔːl] n Fußball m; (game: BRIT) Fußball m; (: US) Football m; ~ **player** n (BRIT: also: ~**er**) Fußballspieler m, Fußballer m; (US) Footballer m

---

Football Pools

i Football Pools, umgangssprachlich auch the pools genannt, ist das in Großbritannien sehr beliebte Fußballtoto, bei dem auf die Ergebnisse der samstäglichen Fußballspiele gewettet wird. Teilnehmer schicken ihre ausgefüllten Totoschein vor den Spielen an die Totogesellschaft und vergleichen nach den Spielen die Ergebnisse mit ihrem Schein. Die Gewinne können sehr hoch sein und gelegentlich Millionen von Pfund betragen.

---

foot: ~**brake** n Fußbremse f; ~**bridge** n Fußgängerbrücke f; ~**hills** npl Ausläufer pl; ~**hold** n Halt m; ~**ing** n Halt m; (fig) Verhältnis nt; ~**lights** npl Rampenlicht nt; ~**man** (irreg) n Bedienstete(r) m; ~**note** n Fußnote f; ~**path** n Fußweg m; ~**print** n Fußabdruck m; ~**sore** adj fußkrank; ~**step** n Schritt m; ~**wear** n Schuhzeug nt

---

KEYWORD

for [fɔː] prep **1** für; **is this for me?** ist das für mich?; **the train for London** der Zug nach London; **he went for the paper** er ging die Zeitung holen; **give it to me – what for?** gib es mir – warum?

2 (because of) wegen; **for this reason** aus diesem Grunde

3 (referring to distance): **there are roadworks for 5 km** die Baustelle ist 5 km lang; **we walked for miles** wir sind meilenweit gegangen

4 (referring to time) seit; (: with future sense) für; **he was away for 2 years** er war zwei Jahre lang weg

5 (+infin clauses): **it is not for me to decide** das kann ich nicht entscheiden; **for this to be possible ...** damit dies möglich wird/

wurde ...

6 (in spite of) trotz +gen or (inf) dat ; **for all his complaints** obwohl er sich ständig beschwert

♦ conj denn

---

forage ['fɒrɪdʒ] n (Vieh)futter nt

foray ['fɒreɪ] n Raubzug m

forbad(e) [fə'bæd] pt of forbid

forbid [fə'bɪd] (pt forbad(e), pp forbidden) vt verbieten; ~**ding** adj einschüchternd

force [fɔːs] n Kraft f; (compulsion) Zwang m ♦ vt zwingen; (lock) aufbrechen; **the F~s** npl (BRIT) die Streitkräfte; **in ~** (rule) gültig; (group) in großer Stärke; ~**d** adj (smile) gezwungen; (landing) Not-; ~**feed** vt zwangsernähren; ~**ful** adj (speech) kraftvoll; (personality) resolut

forceps ['fɔːseps] npl Zange f

forcibly ['fɔːsəblɪ] adv zwangsweise

ford [fɔːd] n Furt f ♦ vt durchwaten

fore [fɔː] n: **to the ~** in den Vordergrund; ~**arm** ['fɔːrɑːm] n Unterarm m; ~**boding** [fɔː'bəudɪŋ] n Vorahnung f; ~**cast** ['fɔːkɑːst] (irreg: like cast) n Vorhersage f ♦ vt voraussagen; ~**court** ['fɔːkɔːt] n (of garage) Vorplatz m; ~**fathers** ['fɔːfɑːðəz] npl Vorfahren pl; ~**finger** ['fɔːfɪŋɡə] n Zeigefinger m; ~**front** ['fɔːfrʌnt] n Spitze f

forego [fɔː'ɡəu] (irreg: like go) vt verzichten auf +acc

fore: ~**gone** ['fɔːɡɒn] adj: **it's a ~gone conclusion** es steht von vornherein fest; ~**ground** ['fɔːɡraund] n Vordergrund m; ~**head** ['fɒrɪd] n Stirn f

foreign ['fɒrɪn] adj Auslands-; (accent) ausländisch; (trade) Außen-; (body) Fremd-; ~**er** n Ausländer(in) m(f); ~ **exchange** n Devisen pl; F~ **Office** (BRIT) n Außenministerium nt; F~ **Secretary** (BRIT) n Außenminister m

fore ['fɔː-]: ~**leg** n Vorderbein nt; ~**man** (irreg) n Vorarbeiter m; ~**most** adj erste(r, s) ♦ adv: **first and ~most** vor allem

forensic [fə'rensɪk] adj gerichtsmedizinisch

fore ['fɔː-]: ~**runner** n Vorläufer m; ~**see** [fɔː'siː] (irreg: like see) vt vorhersehen;

~**seeable** *adj* absehbar; ~**shadow**
['fɔ:'ʃædəu] *vt* andeuten; ~**sight** ['fɔ:saɪt] *n*
Voraussicht *f*

forest ['fɔrɪst] *n* Wald *m*

forestall [fɔː'stɔːl] *vt* zuvorkommen +*dat*

forestry ['fɔrɪstrɪ] *n* Forstwirtschaft *f*

foretaste ['fɔːteɪst] *n* Vorgeschmack *m*

foretell [fɔː'tel] (*irreg: like* **tell**) *vt*
vorhersagen

forever [fə'revə*] *adv* für immer

foreword ['fɔːwɜːd] *n* Vorwort *nt*

forfeit ['fɔːfɪt] *n* Einbuße *f* ♦ *vt* verwirken

forgave [fə'geɪv] *pt of* **forgive**

forge [fɔːdʒ] *n* Schmiede *f* ♦ *vt* fälschen;
(*iron*) schmieden; ~ **ahead** *vi* Fortschritte
machen; ~**d** *adj* gefälscht; ~**d banknotes**
Blüten (*inf*) *pl*; ~**r** *n* Fälscher *m*; ~**ry** *n*
Fälschung *f*

forget [fə'get] (*pt* **forgot**, *pp* **forgotten**) *vt, vi*
vergessen; ~**ful** *adj* vergesslich; ~**-me-not**
n Vergissmeinnicht *nt*

forgive [fə'gɪv] (*pt* **forgave**, *pp* **forgiven**) *vt*
verzeihen; **to ~ sb (for sth)** jdm (etw)
verzeihen; ~**ness** *n* Verzeihung *f*

forgot [fə'gɒt] *pt of* **forget**; ~**ten** *pp of* **forget**

fork [fɔːk] *n* Gabel *f*; (*in road*) Gabelung *f* ♦ *vi*
(*road*) sich gabeln; ~ **out** (*inf*) *vt* (*pay*)
blechen; ~**-lift truck** *n* Gabelstapler *m*

forlorn [fə'lɔːn] *adj* (*person*) verlassen; (*hope*)
vergeblich

form [fɔːm] *n* Form *f*; (*type*) Art *f*; (*figure*)
Gestalt *f*; (*SCH*) Klasse *f*; (*bench*) (Schul)bank
f; (*document*) Formular *nt* ♦ *vt* formen; (*be
part of*) bilden

formal ['fɔːməl] *adj* formell; (*occasion*)
offiziell; ~**ly** *adv* (*ceremoniously*) formell;
(*officially*) offiziell

format ['fɔːmæt] *n* Format *nt* ♦ *vt* (*COMPUT*)
formatieren

formation [fɔː'meɪʃən] *n* Bildung *f*; (*AVIAT*)
Formation *f*

formative ['fɔːmətɪv] *adj* (*years*) formend

former ['fɔːmə*] *adj* früher; (*opposite of latter*)
erstere(r, s); ~**ly** *adv* früher

formidable ['fɔːmɪdəbl] *adj* furchtbar

formula ['fɔːmjulə] (*pl* ~**e** *or* ~**s**) *n* Formel *f*;
~**e** ['fɔːmjuliː] *npl of* **formula**; ~**te**

['fɔːmjuleɪt] *vt* formulieren

fort [fɔːt] *n* Feste *f*, Fort *nt*

forte ['fɔːtɪ] *n* Stärke *f*, starke Seite *f*

forth [fɔːθ] *adv*: **and so ~** und so weiter;
~**coming** *adj* kommend; (*character*)
entgegenkommend; ~**right** *adj* offen; ~**with** *adv* umgehend

fortify ['fɔːtɪfaɪ] *vt* (ver)stärken; (*protect*)
befestigen

fortitude ['fɔːtɪtjuːd] *n* Seelenstärke *f*

fortnight ['fɔːtnaɪt] (*BRIT*) *n* vierzehn Tage *pl*;
~**ly** (*BRIT*) *adj* zweiwöchentlich ♦ *adv* alle
vierzehn Tage

fortress ['fɔːtrɪs] *n* Festung *f*

fortunate ['fɔːtʃənɪt] *adj* glücklich; ~**ly** *adv*
glücklicherweise, zum Glück

fortune ['fɔːtʃən] *n* Glück *nt*; (*money*)
Vermögen *nt*; ~**-teller** *n* Wahrsager(in)
m(f)

forty ['fɔːtɪ] *num* vierzig

forum ['fɔːrəm] *n* Forum *nt*

forward ['fɔːwəd] *adj* vordere(r, s);
(*movement*) Vorwärts-; (*person*) vorlaut;
(*planning*) Voraus- ♦ *adv* vorwärts ♦ *n*
(*SPORT*) Stürmer *m* ♦ *vt* (*send*) schicken;
(*help*) fördern; ~**s** *adv* vorwärts

fossil ['fɒsl] *n* Fossil *nt*, Versteinerung *f*

foster ['fɒstə*] *vt* (*talent*) fördern; ~ **child** *n*
Pflegekind *nt*; ~ **mother** *n* Pflegemutter *f*

fought [fɔːt] *pt, pp of* **fight**

foul [faul] *adj* schmutzig; (*language*) gemein;
(*weather*) schlecht ♦ *n* (*SPORT*) Foul *nt* ♦ *vt*
(*mechanism*) blockieren; (*SPORT*) foulen; ~
play *n* (*SPORT*) Foulspiel *nt*; (*LAW*)
Verbrechen *nt*

found [faund] *pt, pp of* **find** ♦ *vt* gründen;
~**ation** [faun'deɪʃən] *n* (*act*) Gründung *f*;
(*fig*) Fundament *nt*; (*also:* ~**ation cream**)
Grundierungscreme *f*; ~**ations** *npl* (*of
house*) Fundament *nt*; ~**er** *n* Gründer(in)
m(f) ♦ *vi* sinken

foundry ['faundrɪ] *n* Gießerei *f*

fountain ['fauntɪn] *n* (Spring)brunnen *m*; ~
pen *n* Füllfederhalter *m*

four [fɔː*] *num* vier; **on all ~s** auf allen
vieren; ~**-poster** *n* Himmelbett *nt*; ~**some**
n Quartett *nt*; ~**teen** *num* vierzehn;

~teenth *adj* vierzehnte(r, s); **~th** *adj* vierte(r, s)

fowl [faul] *n* Huhn *nt*; *(food)* Geflügel *nt*

fox [fɔks] *n* Fuchs *m* ♦ *vt* täuschen

foyer ['fɔɪeɪ] *n* Foyer *nt*, Vorhalle *f*

fraction ['frækʃən] *n* (MATH) Bruch *m*; *(part)* Bruchteil *m*

fracture ['fræktʃər] *n* (MED) Bruch *m* ♦ *vt* brechen

fragile ['frædʒaɪl] *adj* zerbrechlich

fragment ['frægmənt] *n* Bruchstück *nt*; *(small part)* Splitter *m*

fragrance ['freɪgrəns] *n* Duft *m*; **fragrant** ['freɪgrənt] *adj* duftend

frail [freɪl] *adj* schwach, gebrechlich

frame [freɪm] *n* Rahmen *m*; *(of spectacles: also:* **~s**) Gestell *nt*; *(body)* Gestalt *f* ♦ *vt* einrahmen; **to ~ sb** *(inf: incriminate)* jdm etwas anhängen; **~ of mind** Verfassung *f*; **~work** *n* Rahmen *m*; *(of society)* Gefüge *nt*

France [frɑːns] *n* Frankreich *nt*

franchise ['fræntʃaɪz] *n* (POL) (aktives) Wahlrecht *nt*; *(COMM)* Lizenz *f*

frank [fræŋk] *adj* offen ♦ *vt* (letter) frankieren; **~ly** *adv* offen gesagt

frantic ['fræntɪk] *adj* verzweifelt

fraternal [frə'tɜːnl] *adj* brüderlich

fraternity [frə'tɜːnɪtɪ] *n* (club) Vereinigung *f*; *(spirit)* Brüderlichkeit *f*; *(US: SCH)* Studentenverbindung *f*

fraternize ['frætənaɪz] *vi* fraternisieren

fraud [frɔːd] *n* (trickery) Betrug *m*; *(person)* Schwindler(in) *m(f)*; **~ulent** ['frɔːdjulənt] *adj* betrügerisch

fraught [frɔːt] *adj*: **~ with** voller +gen

fray [freɪ] *vt, vi* ausfransen; **tempers were ~ed** die Gemüter waren erhitzt

freak [friːk] *n* Monstrosität *f* ♦ *cpd* (storm etc) anormal

freckle ['frekl] *n* Sommersprosse *f*

free [friː] *adj* frei; *(loose)* lose; *(liberal)* freigebig ♦ *vt* (set ~) befreien; *(unblock)* freimachen; **~ (of charge)** gratis, umsonst; **for ~** gratis, umsonst; **~dom** ['friːdəm] *n* Freiheit *f*; **F~fone** ® *n*: **call F~fone 0800 ...** rufen Sie gebührenfrei 0800 ... an; **~-for-all** *n* (fight) allgemeine(s)

Handgemenge *nt*; **~ gift** *n* Geschenk *nt*; **~ kick** *n* Freistoß *m*; **~lance** *adj* frei; *(artist)* freischaffend; **~ly** *adv* frei; *(admit)* offen; **F~post** ® *n* ≃ Gebühr zahlt Empfänger; **~-range** *adj* (hen) Farmhof-; *(eggs)* Land-; **~ trade** *n* Freihandel *m*; **~way** *n* (US) *n* Autobahn *f*; **~wheel** *vi* im Freilauf fahren; **~ will** *n*: **of one's own ~ will** aus freien Stücken

freeze [friːz] (*pt* froze, *pp* frozen) *vi* gefrieren; *(feel cold)* frieren ♦ *vt* (also fig) einfrieren ♦ *n* (fig, FIN) Stopp *m*; **~r** *n* Tiefkühltruhe *f*; *(in fridge)* Gefrierfach *nt*; **freezing** *adj* eisig; *(freezing cold)* eiskalt; **freezing point** *n* Gefrierpunkt *m*

freight [freɪt] *n* Fracht *f*; **~ train** *n* Güterzug *m*

French [frentʃ] *adj* französisch ♦ *n* (LING) Französisch *nt*; **the ~** *npl* (people) die Franzosen *pl*; **~ bean** *n* grüne Bohne *f*; **~ fried potatoes** (BRIT) *npl* Pommes frites *pl*; **~ fries** (US) *npl* Pommes frites *pl*; **~ horn** *n* (MUS) (Wald)horn *nt*; **~ kiss** *n* Zungenkuss *m*; **~ loaf** *n* Baguette *f*; **~man/woman** (irreg) *n* Franzose *m*/Französin *f*; **~ window** *n* Verandatür *f*

frenzy ['frenzɪ] *n* Raserei *f*

frequency ['friːkwənsɪ] *n* Häufigkeit *f*; *(PHYS)* Frequenz *f*

frequent [*adj* 'friːkwənt, *vb* frɪ'kwent] *adj* häufig ♦ *vt* (regelmäßig) besuchen; **~ly** *adv* (often) häufig, oft

fresh [freʃ] *adj* frisch; **~en** *vi* (also: **~en up**) (sich) auffrischen; *(person)* sich frisch machen; **~er** *(inf: BRIT) n* (UNIV) Erstsemester *nt*; **~ly** *adv* gerade; **~man** (irreg) (US) *n* = **fresher**; **~ness** *n* Frische *f*; **~water** *adj* (fish) Süßwasser-

fret [fret] *vi* sich *dat* Sorgen machen

friar ['fraɪər] *n* Klosterbruder *m*

friction ['frɪkʃən] *n* (also fig) Reibung *f*

Friday ['fraɪdɪ] *n* Freitag *m*

fridge [frɪdʒ] (BRIT) *n* Kühlschrank *m*

fried [fraɪd] *adj* gebraten

friend [frend] *n* Freund(in) *m(f)*; **~ly** *adj* freundlich; *(relations)* freundschaftlich; **~ly fire** *n* Beschuss *m* durch die eigene Seite;

~**ship** n Freundschaft f

frieze [friːz] n Fries m

frigate ['frɪgɪt] n Fregatte f

fright [fraɪt] n Schrecken m; **to take ~** es mit der Angst zu tun bekommen; ~**en** vt erschrecken; **to be ~ened** Angst haben; ~**ening** adj schrecklich; ~**ful** (inf) adj furchtbar

frigid ['frɪdʒɪd] adj frigide

frill [frɪl] n Rüsche f

fringe [frɪndʒ] n Besatz m; (BRIT: of hair) Pony m; (fig) Peripherie f; ~ **benefits** npl zusätzliche Leistungen pl

Frisbee ['frɪzbɪ] ® n Frisbee ® nt

frisk [frɪsk] vt durchsuchen

frisky ['frɪskɪ] adj lebendig, ausgelassen

fritter ['frɪtər] vt: **to ~ away** vergeuden

frivolous ['frɪvələs] adj frivol

frizzy ['frɪzɪ] adj kraus

fro [frəu] adv see **to**

frock [frɒk] n Kleid nt

frog [frɒg] n Frosch m; ~**man** (irreg) n Froschmann m

frolic ['frɒlɪk] vi ausgelassen sein

KEYWORD

from [frɒm] prep 1 (indicating starting place) of; (indicating origin etc) aus +dat; **a letter / telephone call from my sister** ein Brief/ Anruf von meiner Schwester; **where do you come from?** woher kommen Sie?; **to drink from the bottle** aus der Flasche trinken

2 (indicating time) von ... an; (: past) seit; **from one o'clock to** or **until** or **till two** von ein Uhr bis zwei; **from January (on)** ab Januar

3 (indicating distance) von ... (entfernt)

4 (indicating price, number etc) ab +dat; **from £10 to £10; there were from 20 to 30 people there** es waren zwischen 20 und 30 Leute da

5 (indicating difference): **he can't tell red from green** er kann nicht zwischen Rot und Grün unterscheiden; **to be different from sb/sth** anders sein als jd/etw

6 (because of, based on): **from what he says** aus dem, was er sagt; **weak from hunger** schwach vor Hunger

front [frʌnt] n Vorderseite f; (of house) Fassade f; (promenade: also: **sea ~**) Strandpromenade f; (MIL, POL, MET) Front f; (fig: appearances) Fassade f ♦ adj (forward) vordere(r, s), Vorder-; (first) vorderste(r, s); **in ~** vorne; **in ~ of** vor; ~**age** n ['frʌntɪdʒ] n Vorderfront f; ~ **door** n (MIL, POL, MET) Haustür f; ~**ier** ['frʌntɪər] n Grenze f; ~ **page** n Titelseite f; ~ **room** n (BRIT) Wohnzimmer nt; ~-**wheel drive** n Vorderradantrieb m

frost [frɒst] n Frost m; ~**bite** n Erfrierung f; ~**ed** adj (glass) Milch-; ~**y** adj frostig

froth [frɒθ] n Schaum m

frown [fraun] n Stirnrunzeln nt ♦ vi die Stirn runzeln

froze [frəuz] pt of **freeze**

frozen ['frəuzn] pp of **freeze**

frugal ['fruːgl] adj sparsam, bescheiden

fruit [fruːt] n inv (as collective) Obst nt; (particular) Frucht f; ~**ful** adj fruchtbar; ~**ion** [fruːˈɪʃən] n: **to come to ~ion** in Erfüllung gehen; ~ **juice** n Fruchtsaft m; ~ **machine** n (BRIT) Spielautomat m; ~ **salad** n Obstsalat m

frustrate [frʌsˈtreɪt] vt vereiteln; ~**d** adj gehemmt; (PSYCH) frustriert

fry [fraɪ] (pt, pp **fried**) vt braten ♦ npl: **small ~** kleine Fische pl; ~**ing pan** n Bratpfanne f

ft. abbr = **foot**; **feet**

fuddy-duddy ['fʌdɪdʌdɪ] n altmodische(r) Kauz m

fudge [fʌdʒ] n Fondant m

fuel ['fjuəl] n Treibstoff m; (for heating) Brennstoff m; (for lighter) Benzin nt; ~ **oil** n (diesel fuel) Heizöl nt; ~ **tank** n Tank m

fugitive ['fjuːdʒɪtɪv] n Flüchtling m

fulfil [ful'fɪl] vt (duty) erfüllen; (promise) einhalten; ~**ment** n Erfüllung f

full [ful] adj (box, bottle, price) voll; (person: satisfied) satt; (member, power, employment) Voll-; (complete) vollständig, Voll-; (speed) höchste(r, s); (skirt) weit ♦ adv: ~ **well** sehr wohl; **in ~** vollständig; **a ~ two hours** volle

zwei Stunden; **~-length** adj (lifesize)
lebensgroß; **a ~-length photograph** eine
Ganzaufnahme; **~ moon** n Vollmond m;
~-scale adj (attack) General-; (drawing) in
Originalgröße; **~ stop** n Punkt m; **~-time**
adj (job) Ganztags- ♦ adv (work) ganztags
♦ n (SPORT) Spielschluss nt; **~y** adv völlig;
~y fledged adj (also fig) flügge; **~y
licensed** adj (hotel, restaurant) mit voller
Schankkonzession or -erlaubnis

fumble ['fʌmbl] vi: **to ~ (with)**
herumfummeln (an +dat)

fume [fjuːm] vi qualmen; (fig) kochen (inf);
~s npl (of fuel, car) Abgase pl

fumigate ['fjuːmɪgeɪt] vt ausräuchern

fun [fʌn] n Spaß m; **to make ~ of** sich lustig
machen über +acc

function ['fʌŋkʃən] n Funktion f; (occasion)
Veranstaltung f ♦ vi funktionieren; **~al** adj
funktionell

fund [fʌnd] n (money) Geldmittel pl, Fonds
m; (store) Vorrat m; **~s** npl (resources) Mittel
pl

fundamental [fʌndə'mentl] adj
fundamental, grundlegend

funeral ['fjuːnərəl] n Beerdigung f; **~
parlour** n Leichenhalle f; **~ service** n
Trauergottesdienst m

funfair ['fʌnfeəʳ] (BRIT) n Jahrmarkt m

fungi ['fʌŋgaɪ] npl of **fungus**

fungus ['fʌŋgəs] n Pilz m

funnel ['fʌnl] n Trichter m; (NAUT)
Schornstein m

funny ['fʌnɪ] adj komisch

fur [fɜːʳ] n Pelz m; **~ coat** n Pelzmantel m

furious ['fjuərɪəs] adj wütend; (attempt)
heftig

furlong ['fɜːlɒŋ] n = 201.17 m

furnace ['fɜːnɪs] n (Brenn)ofen m

furnish ['fɜːnɪʃ] vt einrichten; (supply)
versehen; **~ings** npl Einrichtung f

furniture ['fɜːnɪtʃəʳ] n Möbel pl; **piece of ~**
Möbelstück nt

furrow ['fʌrəʊ] n Furche f

furry ['fɜːrɪ] adj (tongue) pelzig; (animal) Pelz-

further ['fɜːðəʳ] adj weitere(r, s) ♦ adv weiter
♦ vt fördern; **~ education** n Weiterbildung

f; Erwachsenenbildung f; **~more** adv ferner

furthest ['fɜːðɪst] superl of **far**

furtive ['fɜːtɪv] adj verstohlen

fury ['fjuərɪ] n Wut f, Zorn m

fuse [fjuːz] (US **fuze**) n (ELEC) Sicherung f; (of
bomb) Zünder m ♦ vt verschmelzen ♦ vi
(BRIT: ELEC) durchbrennen; **~ box** n
Sicherungskasten m

fuselage ['fjuːzəlɑːʒ] n Flugzeugrumpf m

fusion ['fjuːʒən] n Verschmelzung f

fuss [fʌs] n Theater nt; **~y** adj kleinlich

futile ['fjuːtaɪl] adj zwecklos, sinnlos; **futility**
[fjuː'tɪlɪtɪ] n Zwecklosigkeit f

future ['fjuːtʃəʳ] adj zukünftig ♦ n Zukunft f;
in (the) ~ in Zukunft

fuze [fjuːz] (US) = **fuse**

fuzzy ['fʌzɪ] adj (indistinct) verschwommen;
(hair) kraus

G, g

G [dʒiː] n (MUS) G nt

G7 n abbr (= Group of Seven) G7 f

gabble ['gæbl] vi plappern

gable ['geɪbl] n Giebel m

gadget ['gædʒɪt] n Vorrichtung f

Gaelic ['geɪlɪk] adj gälisch ♦ n (LING) Gälisch
nt

gaffe [gæf] n Fauxpas m

gag [gæg] n Knebel m; (THEAT) Gag m ♦ vt
knebeln

gaiety ['geɪtɪ] n Fröhlichkeit f

gain [geɪn] vt (obtain) erhalten; (win)
gewinnen ♦ vi (clock) vorgehen ♦ n Gewinn
m; **to ~ in sth** an etw dat gewinnen; **~ on**
vt fus einholen

gait [geɪt] n Gang m

gal. abbr = **gallon**

gala ['gɑːlə] n Fest nt

galaxy ['gæləksɪ] n Sternsystem nt

gale [geɪl] n Sturm m

gallant ['gælənt] adj tapfer; (polite) galant

gallbladder [gɔːl-] n Gallenblase f

gallery ['gælərɪ] n Galerie f (also: **art ~**)

galley ['gælɪ] n (ship's kitchen) Kombüse f;
(ship) Galeere f

gallon ['gæln] *n* Gallone *f*

gallop ['gæləp] *n* Galopp *m* ♦ *vi* galoppieren

gallows ['gæləuz] *n* Galgen *m*

gallstone ['gɔːlstəun] *n* Gallenstein *m*

galore [gə'lɔː] *adv* in Hülle und Fülle

galvanize ['gælvənaız] *vt* (*metal*) galvanisieren; (*fig*) elektrisieren

gambit ['gæmbıt] *n* (*fig*): **opening ~** (einleitende(r)) Schachzug *m*

gamble ['gæmbl] *vi* (um Geld) spielen ♦ *vt* (*risk*) aufs Spiel setzen ♦ *n* Risiko *nt*; **~r** *n* Spieler(in) *m(f)*; **gambling** *n* Glücksspiel *nt*

game [geım] *n* Spiel *nt*; (*hunting*) Wild *nt* ♦ *adj*: **~ (for)** bereit (zu); **~keeper** *n* Wildhüter *m*; **~s console** *n* (*COMPUT*) Gameboy *m* ®, Konsole *f*

gammon ['gæmən] *n* geräucherte(r) Schinken *m*

gamut ['gæmət] *n* Tonskala *f*

gang [gæŋ] *n* (*of criminals, youths*) Bande *f*; (*of workmen*) Kolonne *f* ♦ *vi*: **to ~ up on sb** sich gegen jdn verschwören

gangrene ['gæŋgriːn] *n* Brand *m*

gangster ['gæŋstə] *n* Gangster *m*

gangway ['gæŋweı] *n* (*NAUT*) Laufplanke *f*; (*aisle*) Gang *m*

gaol [dʒeıl] (*BRIT*) *n*, *vt* = **jail**

gap [gæp] *n* Lücke *f*

gape [geıp] *vi* glotzen; **gaping** ['geıpıŋ] *adj* (*wound*) klaffend; (*hole*) gähnend

garage ['gærɑːʒ] *n* Garage *f*; (*for repair*) (Auto)reparaturwerkstatt *f*; (*for petrol*) Tankstelle *f*

garbage ['gɑːbıdʒ] *n* Abfall *m*; **~ can** (*US*) *n* Mülltonne *f*

garbled ['gɑːbld] *adj* (*story*) verdreht

garden ['gɑːdn] *n* Garten *m*; **~s** *npl* (*public park*) Park *m*; (*private*) Gartenanlagen *pl*; **~er** *n* Gärtner(in) *m(f)*; **~ing** *n* Gärtnern *nt*

gargle ['gɑːgl] *vi* gurgeln

gargoyle ['gɑːgɔıl] *n* Wasserspeier *m*

garish ['gɛərıʃ] *adj* grell

garland ['gɑːlənd] *n* Girlande *f*

garlic ['gɑːlık] *n* Knoblauch *m*

garment ['gɑːmənt] *n* Kleidungsstück *nt*

garnish ['gɑːnıʃ] *vt* (*food*) garnieren

garrison ['gærısn] *n* Garnison *f*

garter ['gɑːtə] *n* Strumpfband *nt*; (*US*) Strumpfhalter *m*

gas [gæs] *n* Gas *nt*; (*esp US: petrol*) Benzin *nt* ♦ *vt* vergasen; **~ cooker** (*BRIT*) *n* Gasherd *m*; **~ cylinder** *n* Gasflasche *f*; **~ fire** *n* Gasofen *m*

gash [gæʃ] *n* klaffende Wunde *f* ♦ *vt* tief verwunden

gasket ['gæskıt] *n* Dichtungsring *m*

gas mask *n* Gasmaske *f*

gas meter *n* Gaszähler *m*

gasoline ['gæsəliːn] (*US*) *n* Benzin *nt*

gasp [gɑːsp] *vi* keuchen; (*in surprise*) tief Luft holen ♦ *n* Keuchen *nt*

gas: ~ ring *n* Gasring *m*; **~ station** (*US*) *n* Tankstelle *f*; **~ tap** *n* Gashahn *m*

gastric ['gæstrık] *adj* Magen-

gate [geıt] *n* Tor *nt*; (*barrier*) Schranke *f*

gateau ['gætəu] (*pl* **~x**) *n* Torte *f*

gatecrash ['geıtkræʃ] (*BRIT*) *vt* (*party*) platzen in +*acc*

gateway ['geıtweı] *n* Toreingang *m*

gather ['gæðə] *vt* (*people*) versammeln; (*things*) sammeln; (*understand*) annehmen ♦ *vi* (*assemble*) sich versammeln; **to ~ speed** schneller werden; **to ~ (from)** schließen (aus); **~ing** *n* Versammlung *f*

gauche [gəuʃ] *adj* linkisch

gaudy ['gɔːdı] *adj* schreiend

gauge [geıdʒ] *n* (*instrument*) Messgerät *nt*; (*RAIL*) Spurweite *f*; (*dial*) Anzeiger *m*; (*measure*) Maß *nt* ♦ *vt* (ab)messen; (*fig*) abschätzen

gaunt [gɔːnt] *adj* hager

gauze [gɔːz] *n* Gaze *f*

gave [geıv] *pt of* **give**

gay [geı] *adj* (*homosexual*) schwul; (*lively*) lustig

gaze [geız] *n* Blick *m* ♦ *vi* starren; **to ~ at sth** etw *dat* anstarren

gazelle [gə'zɛl] *n* Gazelle *f*

gazumping [gə'zʌmpıŋ] (*BRIT*) *n* Hausverkauf an Höherbietenden trotz Zusage an anderen

GB *n abbr* = **Great Britain**

GCE (*BRIT*) *n abbr* = **General Certificate of Education**

GCSE *(BRIT)* *n abbr* = **General Certificate of Secondary Education**

gear [gɪər] *n* Getriebe *nt*; *(equipment)* Ausrüstung *f*; *(AUT)* Gang *m* ♦ *vt (fig: adapt)*: **to be ~ed to** ausgerichtet sein auf +*acc*; **top** ~ höchste(r) Gang *m*; **high** ~ *(US)* höchste(r) Gang *m*; **low** ~ niedrige(r) Gang *m*; **in** ~ eingekuppelt; ~ **box** *n* Getriebe(gehäuse) *nt*; ~ **lever** *n* Schalthebel *m*; ~ **shift** *(US)* *n* Schalthebel *m*

geese [giːs] *npl of* **goose**

gel [dʒɛl] *n* Gel *nt*

gelatin(e) ['dʒɛlətiːn] *n* Gelatine *f*

gem [dʒɛm] *n* Edelstein *m*; *(fig)* Juwel *nt*

Gemini ['dʒɛmɪnaɪ] *n* Zwillinge *pl*

gender ['dʒɛndər] *n* (GRAM) Geschlecht *nt*

gene [dʒiːn] *n* Gen *nt*

general ['dʒɛnərl] *n* General *m* ♦ *adj* allgemein; ~ **delivery** *(US)* *n* Ausgabe(schalter *m*) *f* postlagernder Sendungen; ~ **election** *n* allgemeine Wahlen *pl*; ~**ize** *vi* verallgemeinern; ~ **knowledge** *n* Allgemeinwissen *nt*; ~**ly** *adv* allgemein, im Allgemeinen; ~ **practitioner** *n* praktische(r) Arzt *m*, praktische Ärztin *f*

generate ['dʒɛnəreɪt] *vt* erzeugen

generation [dʒɛnə'reɪʃən] *n* Generation *f*; *(act)* Erzeugung *f*

generator ['dʒɛnəreɪtər] *n* Generator *m*

generosity [dʒɛnə'rɔsɪtɪ] *n* Großzügigkeit *f*

generous ['dʒɛnərəs] *adj* großzügig

genetic [dʒɪ'nɛtɪk] *adj* genetisch; ~**ally** *adv* genetisch; ~**ally modified** *adj* genmanipuliert; ~ **engineering** *n* Gentechnik *f*; ~ **fingerprinting** [-'fɪŋɡəprɪntɪŋ] *n* genetische Fingerabdrücke *pl*

genetics [dʒɪ'nɛtɪks] *n* Genetik *f*

Geneva [dʒɪ'niːvə] *n* Genf *nt*

genial ['dʒiːnɪəl] *adj* freundlich, jovial

genitals ['dʒɛnɪtlz] *npl* Genitalien *pl*

genius ['dʒiːnɪəs] *n* Genie *nt*

genocide ['dʒɛnəʊsaɪd] *n* Völkermord *m*

gent [dʒɛnt] *n abbr* = **gentleman**

genteel [dʒɛn'tiːl] *adj (polite)* wohlanständig; *(affected)* affektiert

gentle ['dʒɛntl] *adj* sanft, zart

gentleman ['dʒɛntlmən] *(irreg)* *n* Herr *m*; *(polite)* Gentleman *m*

gentleness ['dʒɛntlnɪs] *n* Zartheit *f*, Milde *f*

gently ['dʒɛntlɪ] *adv* zart, sanft

gentry ['dʒɛntrɪ] *n* Landadel *m*

gents [dʒɛnts] *n*: **G~** *(lavatory)* Herren *pl*

genuine ['dʒɛnjuɪn] *adj* echt

geographic(al) [dʒɪə'græfɪk(l)] *adj* geografisch

geography [dʒɪ'ɔɡrəfɪ] *n* Geografie *f*

geological [dʒɪə'lɔdʒɪkl] *adj* geologisch

geology [dʒɪ'ɔlədʒɪ] *n* Geologie *f*

geometric(al) [dʒɪə'mɛtrɪk(l)] *adj* geometrisch

geometry [dʒɪ'ɔmətrɪ] *n* Geometrie *f*

geranium [dʒɪ'reɪnɪəm] *n* Geranie *f*

geriatric [dʒɛrɪ'ætrɪk] *adj* Alten- ♦ *n* Greis(in) *m(f)*

germ [dʒəːm] *n* Keim *m*; *(MED)* Bazillus *m*

German ['dʒəːmən] *adj* deutsch ♦ *n* Deutsche(r) *f(m)*; *(LING)* Deutsch *nt*; ~ **measles** *n* Röteln *pl*; ~**y** *n* Deutschland *nt*

germination [dʒəːmɪ'neɪʃən] *n* Keimen *nt*

gesticulate [dʒɛs'tɪkjuleɪt] *vi* gestikulieren

gesture ['dʒɛstʃər] *n* Geste *f*

KEYWORD

get [ɡɛt] *(pt, pp* **got**, *pp* **gotten** *(US))* *vi* **1** *(become, be)* werden; **to get old/tired** alt/ müde werden; **to get married** heiraten
2 *(go)* (an)kommen, gehen
3 *(begin)*: **to get to know sb** jdn kennen lernen; **let's get going** *or* **started!** fangen wir an!
4 *(modal aux vb)*: **you've got to do it** du musst es tun

♦ *vt* **1**: **to get sth done** *(do)* etw machen; *(have done)* etw machen lassen; **to get sth going** *or* **to go** etw in Gang bringen *or* bekommen; **to get sb to do sth** jdn dazu bringen, etw zu tun
2 *(obtain: money, permission, results)* erhalten; *(find: job, flat)* finden; *(fetch: person, object)* holen; **to get sth for sb** jdm etw besorgen; **get me Mr Jones, please** *(TEL)* verbinden Sie mich bitte mit Mr Jones
3 *(receive: present, letter)* bekommen, kriegen; *(acquire: reputation etc)* erwerben

4 (*catch*) bekommen, kriegen; (*hit: target etc*) treffen, erwischen; **get him!** (*to dog*) fass!

5 (*take, move*) bringen; **to get sth to sb** jdm etw bringen

6 (*understand*) verstehen; (*hear*) mitbekommen; **I've got it!** ich habs!

7 (*have, possess*): **to have got sth** etw haben

get about *vi* herumkommen; (*news*) sich verbreiten

get along *vi* (*people*) (gut) zurechtkommen; (*depart*) sich *acc* auf den Weg machen

get at *vt* (*facts*) herausbekommen; **to get at sb** (*nag*) an jdm herumnörgeln

get away *vi* (*leave*) sich *acc* davonmachen; (*escape*): **to get away from sth** von etw *dat* entkommen; **to get away with sth** mit etw davonkommen

get back *vi* (*return*) zurückkommen ♦ *vt* zurückbekommen

get by *vi* (*pass*) vorbeikommen; (*manage*) zurechtkommen

get down *vi* (her)untergehen ♦ *vt* (*depress*) fertig machen; **to get down to** in Angriff nehmen; (*find time to do*) kommen zu

get in *vi* (*train*) ankommen; (*arrive home*) heimkommen

get into *vt* (*enter*) hinein-/hereinkommen in +*acc*; (: *car, train etc*) einsteigen in +*acc*; (*clothes*) anziehen

get off *vi* (*from train etc*) aussteigen; (*from horse*) absteigen ♦ *vt* aussteigen aus; absteigen von

get on *vi* (*progress*) vorankommen; (*be friends*) auskommen; (*age*) alt werden; (*onto train etc*) einsteigen; (*onto horse*) aufsteigen ♦ *vt* einsteigen in +*acc*; auf etw *acc* aufsteigen

get out *vi* (*of house*) herauskommen; (*of vehicle*) aussteigen ♦ *vt* (*take out*) herausholen

get out of *vt* (*duty etc*) herumkommen um

get over *vt* (*illness*) sich *acc* erholen von;

(*surprise*) verkraften; (*news*) fassen; (*loss*) sich abfinden mit

get round *vt* herumkommen; (*fig: person*) herumkriegen

get through to *vt* (*TEL*) durchkommen zu

get together *vi* zusammenkommen

get up *vi* aufstehen ♦ *vt* hinaufbringen; (*go up*) hinaufgehen; (*organize*) auf die Beine stellen

get up to *vt* (*reach*) erreichen; (*prank etc*) anstellen

getaway ['getəweı] *n* Flucht *f*

get-up ['getʌp] (*inf*) *n* Aufzug *m*

geyser ['giːzəʳ] *n* Geiser *m*; (*heater*) Durchlauferhitzer *m*

ghastly ['gɑːstlɪ] *adj* grässlich

gherkin ['gɜːkɪn] *n* Gewürzgurke *f*

ghetto ['getəʊ] *n* G(h)etto *nt*; ~ **blaster** *n* (große(r)) Radiorekorder *m*

ghost [gəʊst] *n* Gespenst *nt*

giant ['dʒaɪənt] *n* Riese *m* ♦ *adj* riesig, Riesen-

gibberish ['dʒɪbərɪʃ] *n* dumme(s) Geschwätz *nt*

gibe [dʒaɪb] *n* spöttische Bemerkung *f*

giblets ['dʒɪblɪts] *npl* Geflügelinnereien *pl*

giddiness ['gɪdɪnɪs] *n* Schwindelgefühl *nt*

giddy ['gɪdɪ] *adj* schwindlig

gift [gɪft] *n* Geschenk *nt*; (*ability*) Begabung *f*; ~**ed** *adj* begabt; ~ **shop** *n* Geschenkladen *m*; ~ **token**, ~ **voucher** *n* Geschenkgutschein *m*

gigantic [dʒaɪ'gæntɪk] *adj* riesenhaft

giggle ['gɪgl] *vi* kichern ♦ *n* Gekicher *nt*

gild [gɪld] *vt* vergolden

gill [dʒɪl] *n* (1/4 pint) Viertelpinte *f*

gills [gɪlz] *npl* (*of fish*) Kiemen *pl*

gilt [gɪlt] *n* Vergoldung *f* ♦ *adj* vergoldet; ~**-edged** *adj* mündelsicher

gimmick ['gɪmɪk] *n* Gag *m*

gin [dʒɪn] *n* Gin *m*

ginger ['dʒɪndʒəʳ] *n* Ingwer *m*; ~ **ale** *n* Ingwerbier *nt*; ~ **beer** *n* Ingwerbier *nt*; ~**bread** *n* Pfefferkuchen *m*; ~**-haired** *adj* rothaarig

gingerly ['dʒɪndʒəlɪ] *adv* behutsam

gipsy ['dʒɪpsɪ] n Zigeuner(in) m(f)

giraffe [dʒɪ'rɑːf] n Giraffe f

girder ['gɜːdə⁺] n Eisenträger m

girdle ['gɜːdl] n Hüftgürtel m

girl [gɜːl] n Mädchen nt; **an English ~** eine (junge) Engländerin; **~friend** n Freundin f; **~ish** adj mädchenhaft

giro ['dʒaɪrəʊ] n (bank ~) Giro nt; (post office ~) Postscheckverkehr m

girth [gɜːθ] n (measure) Umfang m; (strap) Sattelgurt m

gist [dʒɪst] n Wesentliche(s) nt

give [gɪv] (pt **gave**, pp **given**) vt geben ♦ vi (break) nachgeben; **~ away** vt verschenken; (betray) verraten; **~ back** vt zurückgeben; **~ in** vi nachgeben ♦ vt (hand in) abgeben; **~ off** vt abgeben; **~ out** vt verteilen; (announce) bekannt geben; **~ up** vt, vi aufgeben; **to ~ o.s. up** sich stellen; (after siege) sich ergeben; **~ way** vi (BRIT: traffic) Vorfahrt lassen; (to feelings): **to ~ way to** nachgeben +dat

glacier ['glæsɪə⁺] n Gletscher m

glad [glæd] adj froh; **~ly** ['glædlɪ] adv gern(e)

glamorous ['glæmərəs] adj reizvoll

glamour ['glæmə⁺] n Glanz m

glance [glɑːns] n Blick m ♦ vi: **to ~ (at)** (hin)blicken (auf +acc); **~ off** vt fus (fly off) abprallen von; **glancing** ['glɑːnsɪŋ] adj (blow) Streif-

gland [glænd] n Drüse f

glare [glɛə⁺] n (light) grelle(s) Licht nt; (stare) wilde(r) Blick m ♦ vi grell scheinen; (angrily): **to ~ at** böse ansehen; **glaring** ['glɛərɪŋ] adj (injustice) schreiend; (mistake) krass

glass [glɑːs] n Glas nt; (mirror: also: **looking ~**) Spiegel m; **~es** npl (spectacles) Brille f; **~house** n Gewächshaus nt; **~ware** n Glaswaren pl; **~y** adj glasig

glaze [gleɪz] vt verglasen; (finish with a ~) glasieren ♦ n Glasur f; **~d** adj (eye) glasig; (pot) glasiert; **glazier** ['gleɪzɪə⁺] n Glaser m

gleam [gliːm] n Schimmer m ♦ vi schimmern

glean [gliːn] vt (fig) ausfindig machen

glen [glɛn] n Bergtal nt

glib [glɪb] adj oberflächlich

glide [glaɪd] vi gleiten; **~r** n (AVIAT) Segelflugzeug nt; **gliding** ['glaɪdɪŋ] n Segelfliegen nt

glimmer ['glɪmə⁺] n Schimmer m

glimpse [glɪmps] n flüchtige(r) Blick m ♦ vt flüchtig erblicken

glint [glɪnt] n Glitzern nt ♦ vi glitzern

glisten ['glɪsn] vi glänzen

glitter ['glɪtə⁺] vi funkeln ♦ n Funkeln nt

gloat [gləʊt] vi: **to ~ over** sich weiden an +dat

global ['gləʊbl] adj: **~ warming** globale(r) Temperaturanstieg m

globe [gləʊb] n Erdball m; (sphere) Globus m

gloom [gluːm] n (darkness) Dunkel nt; (depression) düstere Stimmung f; **~y** adj düster

glorify ['glɔːrɪfaɪ] vt verherrlichen

glorious ['glɔːrɪəs] adj glorreich

glory ['glɔːrɪ] n Ruhm m

gloss [glɔs] n (shine) Glanz m; **~ over** vt fus übertünchen

glossary ['glɔsərɪ] n Glossar nt

glossy ['glɔsɪ] adj (surface) glänzend

glove [glʌv] n Handschuh m; **~ compartment** n (AUT) Handschuhfach nt

glow [gləʊ] vi glühen ♦ n Glühen nt

glower ['glaʊə⁺] vi: **to ~ at** finster anblicken

glucose ['gluːkəʊs] n Traubenzucker m

glue [gluː] n Klebstoff m ♦ vt kleben

glum [glʌm] adj bedrückt

glut [glʌt] n Überfluss m

glutton ['glʌtn] n Vielfraß m; **a ~ for work** ein Arbeitstier nt

glycerin(e) ['glɪsəriːn] n Glyzerin nt

GM abbr = **genetically modified**

gnarled [nɑːld] adj knorrig

gnat [næt] n Stechmücke f

gnaw [nɔː] vt nagen an +dat

gnome [nəʊm] n Gnom m

go [gəʊ] (pt **went**, pp **gone**, pl **~es**) vi gehen; (travel) reisen, fahren; (depart: train) (ab)fahren; (be sold) verkauft werden; (work) gehen, funktionieren; (fit, suit) passen; (become) werden; (break etc) nachgeben ♦ n (energy) Schwung m;

(*attempt*) Versuch *m*; **he's ~ing to do it** er wird es tun; **to ~ for a walk** spazieren gehen; **to ~ dancing** tanzen gehen; **how did it ~?** wie wars?; **to ~ with** (*be suitable*) passen zu; **to have a ~ at sth** etw versuchen; **to be on the ~** auf Trab sein; **whose ~ is it?** wer ist dran?; **~ about** *vi* (*rumour*) umgehen ♦ *vt fus*: **how do I ~ about this?** wie packe ich das an?; **~ after** *vt fus* (*pursue: person*) nachgehen +*dat*; **~ ahead** *vi* (*proceed*) weitergehen; **~ along** *vi* dahingehen, dahinfahren ♦ *vt* entlanggehen, entlangfahren ♦ **to ~ along with** (*support*) zustimmen +*dat*; **~ away** *vi* (*depart*) weggehen; **~ back** *vi* (*return*) zurückgehen; **~ back on** *vt fus* (*promise*) nicht halten; **~ by** *vi* (*years, time*) vergehen ♦ *vt fus* (*fetch*) holen (gehen); (*like*) mögen; (*attack*) sich stürzen auf +*acc*; **~ in** *vi* hineingehen; **~ in for** *vt fus* (*competition*) teilnehmen an; (*study*) sich befassen mit; **~ off** *vi* (*depart*) weggehen; (*lights*) ausgehen; (*milk etc*) sauer werden; (*explode*) losgehen ♦ *vt fus* (*dislike*) nicht mehr mögen; **~ on** *vi* (*continue*) weitergehen; (*inf: complain*) meckern; (*lights*) angehen; **to ~ on with sth** mit etw weitermachen; **~ out** *vi* (*fire, light*) ausgehen; (*of house*) hinausgehen; **~ over** *vi* (*ship*) kentern ♦ *vt fus* (*examine, check*) durchgehen; **~ past** *vi*: **to ~ past sth** an etw *dat* vorbeigehen; **~ round** *vi* (*visit*): **to ~ round (to sb's)** (bei jdm) vorbeigehen; **~ through** *vt fus* (*town etc*) durchgehen, durchfahren; **~ up** *vi* (*price*) steigen; **~ with** *vt fus* (*suit*) zu etw passen; **~ without** *vt fus* sich behelfen ohne; (*food*) entbehren

goad [gəud] *vt* anstacheln

go-ahead ['gəuəhɛd] *adj* zielstrebig; (*progressive*) fortschrittlich ♦ *n* grüne(s) Licht *nt*

goal [gəul] *n* Ziel *nt*; (SPORT) Tor *nt*; **~keeper** *n* Torwart *m*; **~ post** *n* Torpfosten *m*

goat [gəut] *n* Ziege *f*

gobble ['gɔbl] *vt* (*also: ~ down, ~ up*) hinunterschlingen

go-between ['gəubɪtwiːn] *n* Mittelsmann *m*

god [gɔd] *n* Gott *m*; **G~** *n* Gott *m*; **~child** *n* Patenkind *nt*; **~daughter** *n* Patentochter *f*; **~dess** *n* Göttin *f*; **~father** *n* Pate *m*; **~forsaken** *adj* gottverlassen; **~mother** *n* Patin *f*; **~send** *n* Geschenk *nt* des Himmels; **~son** *n* Patensohn *m*

goggles ['gɔglz] *npl* Schutzbrille *f*

going ['gəuɪŋ] *n* (HORSE-RACING) Bahn *f* ♦ *adj* (*rate*) gängig; (*concern*) gut gehend; **it's hard ~** es ist schwierig

gold [gəuld] *n* Gold *nt* ♦ *adj* golden; **~en** *adj* golden, Gold-; **~fish** *n* Goldfisch *m*; **~ mine** *n* Goldgrube *f*; **~-plated** *adj* vergoldet; **~smith** *n* Goldschmied(in) *m(f)*

golf [gɔlf] *n* Golf *nt*; **~ ball** *n* Golfball *m*; (*on typewriter*) Kugelkopf *m*; **~ club** *n* (*society*) Golfklub *m*; (*stick*) Golfschläger *m*; **~ course** *n* Golfplatz *m*; **~er** *n* Golfspieler(in) *m(f)*

gondola ['gɔndələ] *n* Gondel *f*

gone [gɔn] *pp of* **go**

gong [gɔŋ] *n* Gong *m*

good [gud] *n* (*benefit*) Wohl *nt*; (*moral excellence*) Güte *f* ♦ *adj* gut; **~s** *npl* (*merchandise etc*) Waren *pl*, Güter *pl*; **a ~ deal (of)** ziemlich viel; **a ~ many** ziemlich viele; **~ morning!** guten Morgen!; **~ afternoon!** guten Tag!; **~ evening!** guten Abend!; **~ night!** gute Nacht!; **would you be ~ enough to ...?** könnten Sie bitte ...?

goodbye [gud'baɪ] *excl* auf Wiedersehen!

good: G~ Friday *n* Karfreitag *m*; **~-looking** *adj* gut aussehend; **~-natured** *adj* gutmütig; (*joke*) harmlos; **~ness** *n* Güte *f*; (*virtue*) Tugend *f*; **~s train** (BRIT) *n* Güterzug *m*; **~will** *n* (*favour*) Wohlwollen *nt*; (COMM) Firmenansehen *nt*

goose [guːs] (*pl* **geese**) *n* Gans *f*

gooseberry ['guzbərɪ] *n* Stachelbeere *f*

gooseflesh ['guːsflɛʃ] *n* Gänsehaut *f*

goose pimples *npl* Gänsehaut *f*

gore [gɔːʳ] *vt* aufspießen ♦ *n* Blut *nt*

gorge [gɔːdʒ] *n* Schlucht *f* ♦ *vt*: **to ~ o.s.** (sich voll) fressen

gorgeous ['gɔːdʒəs] *adj* prächtig

gorilla [gə'rɪlə] *n* Gorilla *m*

gorse [gɔːs] *n* Stechginster *m*

gory ['gɔːrɪ] *adj* blutig

go-slow ['gəu'sləu] (*BRIT*) *n* Bummelstreik *m*

gospel ['gɔspl] *n* Evangelium *nt*

gossip ['gɔsɪp] *n* Klatsch *m*; (*person*) Klatschbase *f* ♦ *vi* klatschen

got [gɔt] *pt, pp of* **get**

gotten ['gɔtn] (*US*) *pp of* **get**

gout [gaut] *n* Gicht *f*

govern ['gʌvən] *vt* regieren; verwalten

governess ['gʌvənɪs] *n* Gouvernante *f*

government ['gʌvnmənt] *n* Regierung *f*

governor ['gʌvənəʳ] *n* Gouverneur *m*

gown [gaun] *n* Gewand *nt*; (*UNIV*) Robe *f*

G.P. *n abbr* = **general practitioner**

grab [græb] *vt* packen

grace [greɪs] *n* Anmut *f*; (*blessing*) Gnade *f*; (*prayer*) Tischgebet *nt* ♦ *vt* (*adorn*) zieren; (*honour*) auszeichnen; **5 days' ~** 5 Tage Aufschub; **~ful** *adj* anmutig

gracious ['greɪʃəs] *adj* gnädig; (*kind*) freundlich

grade [greɪd] *n* Grad *m*; (*slope*) Gefälle *nt* ♦ *vt* (*classify*) einstufen; **~ crossing** (*US*) *n* Bahnübergang *m*; **~ school** (*US*) *n* Grundschule *f*

gradient ['greɪdɪənt] *n* Steigung *f*; Gefälle *nt*

gradual ['grædjuəl] *adj* allmählich; **~ly** *adv* allmählich

graduate [*n* 'grædjuɪt, *vb* 'grædjueɪt] *n*: **to be a ~** das Staatsexamen haben ♦ *vi* das Staatsexamen machen; **graduation** [grædju'eɪʃən] *n* Abschlussfeier *f*

graffiti [grə'fiːtɪ] *npl* Graffiti *pl*

graft [grɑːft] *n* (*hard work*) Schufterei *f*; (*MED*) Verpflanzung *f* ♦ *vt* pfropfen; (*fig*) aufpfropfen; (*MED*) verpflanzen

grain [greɪn] *n* Korn *nt*; (*in wood*) Maserung *f*

gram [græm] *n* Gramm *nt*

grammar ['græməʳ] *n* Grammatik *f*; **~ school** (*BRIT*) *n* Gymnasium *nt*; **grammatical** [grə'mætɪkl] *adj* grammat(ikal)isch

gramme [græm] *n* = **gram**

granary ['grænərɪ] *n* Kornspeicher *m*

grand [grænd] *adj* großartig; **~child** (*pl* **~children**) *n* Enkelkind *nt*, Enkel(in) *m(f)*; **~dad** *n* Opa *m*; **~daughter** *n* Enkelin *f*; **~eur** ['grændjəʳ] *n* Erhabenheit *f*; **~father** *n* Großvater *m*; **~iose** ['grændɪəus] *adj* (*imposing*) großartig; (*pompous*) schwülstig; **~ma** *n* Oma *f*; **~mother** *n* Großmutter *f*; **~pa** *n* = **granddad**; **~parents** *npl* Großeltern *pl*; **~ piano** *n* Flügel *m*; **~son** *n* Enkel *m*; **~stand** *n* Haupttribüne *f*

granite ['grænɪt] *n* Granit *m*

granny ['grænɪ] *n* Oma *f*

grant [grɑːnt] *vt* gewähren ♦ *n* Unterstützung *f*; (*UNIV*) Stipendium *nt*; **to take sth for ~ed** etw als selbstverständlich (an)nehmen

granulated sugar ['grænjuleɪtɪd-] *n* Zuckerraffinade *f*

granule ['grænjuːl] *n* Körnchen *nt*

grape [greɪp] *n* (Wein)traube *f*

grapefruit ['greɪpfruːt] *n* Pampelmuse *f*, Grapefruit *f*

graph [grɑːf] *n* Schaubild *nt*; **~ic** ['græfɪk] *adj* (*descriptive*) anschaulich; (*drawing*) grafisch; **~ics** *npl* Grafik *f*

grapple ['græpl] *vi*: **to ~ with** kämpfen mit

grasp [grɑːsp] *vt* ergreifen; (*understand*) begreifen ♦ *n* Griff *m*; (*of subject*) Beherrschung *f*; **~ing** *adj* habgierig

grass [grɑːs] *n* Gras *nt*; **~hopper** *n* Heuschrecke *f*; **~land** *n* Weideland *nt*; **~roots** *adj* an der Basis; **~ snake** *n* Ringelnatter *f*

grate [greɪt] *n* Kamin *m* ♦ *vi* (*sound*) knirschen ♦ *vt* (*cheese etc*) reiben; **to ~ on the nerves** auf die Nerven gehen

grateful ['greɪtful] *adj* dankbar

grater ['greɪtəʳ] *n* Reibe *f*

gratify ['grætɪfaɪ] *vt* befriedigen; **~ing** *adj* erfreulich

grating ['greɪtɪŋ] *n* (*iron bars*) Gitter *nt* ♦ *adj* (*noise*) knirschend

gratitude ['grætɪtjuːd] *n* Dankbarkeit *f*

gratuity [grə'tjuːɪtɪ] *n* Gratifikation *f*

grave [greɪv] *n* Grab *nt* ♦ *adj* (*serious*) ernst

gravel ['grævl] *n* Kies *m*

gravestone ['greɪvstəun] *n* Grabstein *m*

graveyard ['greɪvjɑːd] *n* Friedhof *m*

gravity ['grævɪtɪ] *n* Schwerkraft *f*; (*seriousness*) Schwere *f*

gravy ['greɪvɪ] *n* (Braten)soße *f*

gray [greɪ] *adj* = **grey**

graze [greɪz] *vi* grasen ♦ *vt* (*touch*) streifen; (*MED*) abschürfen ♦ *n* Abschürfung *f*

grease [griːs] *n* (*fat*) Fett *nt*; (*lubricant*) Schmiere *f* ♦ *vt* (ab)schmieren; **~proof** (*BRIT*) *adj* (*paper*) Butterbrot-; **greasy** ['griːsɪ] *adj* fettig

great [greɪt] *adj* groß; (*inf: good*) prima; **G~ Britain** *n* Großbritannien *nt*; **~~grandfather** *n* Urgroßvater *m*; **~~grandmother** *n* Urgroßmutter *f*; **~ly** *adv* sehr

Greece [griːs] *n* Griechenland *nt*

greed [griːd] *n* (*also:* **~iness**) Gier *f*; (*meanness*) Geiz *m*; **~(iness) for** Gier nach; **~y** *adj* gierig

Greek [griːk] *adj* griechisch ♦ *n* Grieche *m*, Griechin *f*; (*LING*) Griechisch *nt*

green [griːn] *adj* grün ♦ *n* (*village* ~) Dorfwiese *f*; **~ belt** *n* Grüngürtel *m*; **~ card** *n* (*AUT*) grüne Versicherungskarte *f*; **~ery** *n* Grün *nt*; grüne(s) Laub *nt*; **~gage** *n* Reneklode *f*, Reineclaude *f*; **~grocer** (*BRIT*) *n* Obst- und Gemüsehändler *m*; **~house** *n* Gewächshaus *nt*; **~house effect** *n* Treibhauseffekt *m*; **~house gas** *n* Treibhausgas *nt*

Greenland ['griːnlənd] *n* Grönland *nt*

greet [griːt] *vt* grüßen; **~ing** *n* Gruß *m*; **~ing(s) card** *n* Glückwunschkarte *f*

gregarious [grə'gɛərɪəs] *adj* gesellig

grenade [grə'neɪd] *n* Granate *f*

grew [gruː] *pt of* **grow**

grey [greɪ] *adj* grau; **~~haired** *adj* grauhaarig; **~hound** *n* Windhund *m*

grid [grɪd] *n* Gitter *nt*; (*ELEC*) Leitungsnetz *nt*; (*on map*) Gitternetz *nt*

gridlock ['grɪdlɒk] *n* (*AUT: traffic jam*) totale(r) Stau *m*; **~ed** *adj*: **to be ~ed** (*roads*) total verstopft sein; (*talks etc*) festgefahren sein

grief [griːf] *n* Gram *m*, Kummer *m*

grievance ['griːvəns] *n* Beschwerde *f*

grieve [griːv] *vi* sich grämen ♦ *vt* betrüben

grievous ['griːvəs] *adj*: **~ bodily harm** (*JUR*) schwere Körperverletzung *f*

grill [grɪl] *n* Grill *m* ♦ *vt* (*BRIT*) grillen; (*question*) in die Mangel nehmen

grille [grɪl] *n* (*AUT*) (Kühler)gitter *nt*

grim [grɪm] *adj* grimmig; (*situation*) düster

grimace [grɪ'meɪs] *n* Grimasse *f* ♦ *vi* Grimassen schneiden

grime [graɪm] *n* Schmutz *m*; **grimy** ['graɪmɪ] *adj* schmutzig

grin [grɪn] *n* Grinsen *nt* ♦ *vi* grinsen

grind [graɪnd] (*pt, pp* **ground**) *vt* mahlen; (*US: meat*) durch den Fleischwolf drehen; (*sharpen*) schleifen; (*teeth*) knirschen mit ♦ *n* (*bore*) Plackerei *f*

grip [grɪp] *n* Griff *m*; (*suitcase*) Handkoffer *m* ♦ *vt* packen; **~ping** *adj* (*exciting*) spannend

grisly ['grɪzlɪ] *adj* grässlich

gristle ['grɪsl] *n* Knorpel *m*

grit [grɪt] *n* Splitt *m*; (*courage*) Mut *m* ♦ *vt* (*teeth*) zusammenbeißen; (*road*) (mit Splitt be)streuen

groan [grəun] *n* Stöhnen *nt* ♦ *vi* stöhnen

grocer ['grəusə] *n* Lebensmittelhändler *m*; **~ies** *npl* Lebensmittel *pl*; **~'s (shop)** *n* Lebensmittelgeschäft *nt*

groggy ['grɒgɪ] *adj* benommen

groin [grɔɪn] *n* Leistengegend *f*

groom [gruːm] *n* (*also:* **bridegroom**) Bräutigam *m*; (*for horses*) Pferdeknecht *m* ♦ *vt* (*horse*) striegeln; (**well-**)**ed** gepflegt

groove [gruːv] *n* Rille *f*, Furche *f*

grope [grəup] *vi* tasten; **~ for** *vt fus* suchen nach

gross [grəus] *adj* (*coarse*) dick, plump; (*bad*) grob, schwer; (*COMM*) brutto; **~ly** *adv* höchst

grotesque [grə'tɛsk] *adj* grotesk

grotto ['grɒtəu] *n* Grotte *f*

ground [graund] *pt, pp of* **grind** ♦ *n* Boden *m*; (*land*) Grundbesitz *m*; (*reason*) Grund *m*; (*US: also:* ~ **wire**) Erdleitung *f* ♦ *vi* (*run ashore*) stranden, auflaufen; **~s** *npl* (*dregs*) Bodensatz *m*; (*around house*)

(Garten)anlagen *pl*; **on the ~** am Boden; **to the ~** zu Boden; **to gain/lose ~** Boden gewinnen/verlieren; **~ cloth** (*US*) *n* = **groundsheet**; **~ing** *n* (*instruction*) Anfangsunterricht *m*; **~less** *adj* grundlos; **~sheet** (*BRIT*) *n* Zeltboden *m*; **~ staff** *n* Bodenpersonal *nt*; **~work** *n* Grundlage *f*

group [gru:p] *n* Gruppe *f* ♦ *vt* (*also: ~ together*) gruppieren ♦ *vi* sich gruppieren

grouse [graus] *n inv* (*bird*) schottische(s) Moorhuhn *nt*

grove [grəuv] *n* Gehölz *nt*, Hain *m*

grovel ['grɔvl] *vi* (*fig*) kriechen

grow [grəu] (*pt* **grew**, *pp* **grown**) *vi* wachsen; (*become*) werden ♦ *vt* (*raise*) anbauen; **~ up** *vi* aufwachsen; **~er** *n* Züchter *m*; **~ing** *adj* zunehmend

growl [graul] *vi* knurren

grown [grəun] *pp of* **grow**; **~-up** *n* Erwachsene(r) *mf*

growth [grəuθ] *n* Wachstum *nt*; (*increase*) Zunahme *f*; (*of beard etc*) Wuchs *m*

grub [grʌb] *n* Made *f*, Larve *f*; (*inf: food*) Futter *nt*; **~by** ['grʌbɪ] *adj* schmutzig

grudge [grʌdʒ] *n* Groll *m* ♦ *vt*: **to ~ sb sth** jdm etw missgönnen; **to bear sb a ~** einen Groll gegen jdn hegen

gruelling ['gruəlɪŋ] *adj* (*climb, race*) mörderisch

gruesome ['gru:səm] *adj* grauenhaft

gruff [grʌf] *adj* barsch

grumble ['grʌmbl] *vi* murren

grumpy ['grʌmpɪ] *adj* verdrießlich

grunt [grʌnt] *vi* grunzen ♦ *nt* Grunzen *nt*

G-string ['dʒi:strɪŋ] *n* Minislip *m*

guarantee [gærən'ti:] *n* Garantie *f* ♦ *vt* garantieren

guard [gɑ:d] *n* (*sentry*) Wache *f*; (*BRIT: RAIL*) Zugbegleiter *m* ♦ *vt* bewachen

guarded ['gɑ:dɪd] *adj* vorsichtig

guardian ['gɑ:dɪən] *n* Vormund *m*; (*keeper*) Hüter *m*

guard's van ['gɑ:dz-] (*BRIT*) *n* (*RAIL*) Dienstwagen *m*

guerrilla [gə'rɪlə] *n* Guerilla(kämpfer) *m*; **~ warfare** *n* Guerillakrieg *m*

guess [gɛs] *vt, vi* (er)raten, schätzen ♦ *n* Vermutung *f*; **~work** *n* Raterei *f*

guest [gɛst] *n* Gast *m*; **~ house** *n* Pension *f*; **~ room** *n* Gastzimmer *nt*

guffaw [gʌ'fɔ:] *vi* schallend lachen

guidance ['gaɪdəns] *n* (*control*) Leitung *f*; (*advice*) Beratung *f*

guide [gaɪd] *n* Führer *m*; (*also: girl ~*) Pfadfinderin *f* ♦ *vt* führen; **~book** *n* Reiseführer *m*; **~ dog** *n* Blindenhund *m*; **~lines** *npl* Richtlinien *pl*

guild [gɪld] *n* (*HIST*) Gilde *f*

guillotine ['gɪləti:n] *n* Guillotine *f*

guilt [gɪlt] *n* Schuld *f*; **~y** *adj* schuldig

guinea pig ['gɪnɪ-] *n* Meerschweinchen *nt*; (*fig*) Versuchskaninchen *nt*

guise [gaɪz] *n*: **in the ~ of** in der Form +*gen*

guitar [gɪ'tɑ:] *n* Gitarre *f*

gulf [gʌlf] *n* Golf *m*; (*fig*) Abgrund *m*

gull [gʌl] *n* Möwe *f*

gullet ['gʌlɪt] *n* Schlund *m*

gullible ['gʌlɪbl] *adj* leichtgläubig

gully ['gʌlɪ] *n* (Wasser)rinne *f*

gulp [gʌlp] *vt* (*also: ~ down*) hinunterschlucken ♦ *vi* (*gasp*) schlucken

gum [gʌm] *n* (*around teeth*) Zahnfleisch *nt*; (*glue*) Klebstoff *m*; (*also: chewing ~*) Kaugummi *m* ♦ *vt* gummieren; **~boots** (*BRIT*) *npl* Gummistiefel *pl*

gun [gʌn] *n* Schusswaffe *f*; **~boat** *n* Kanonenboot *nt*; **~fire** *n* Geschützfeuer *nt*; **~man** (*irreg*) *n* bewaffnete(r) Verbrecher *m*; **~point** *n*: **at ~point** mit Waffengewalt; **~powder** *n* Schießpulver *nt*; **~shot** *n* Schuss *m*

gurgle ['gə:gl] *vi* gluckern

gush [gʌʃ] *vi* (*rush out*) hervorströmen; (*fig*) schwärmen

gust [gʌst] *n* Windstoß *m*, Bö *f*

gusto ['gʌstəu] *n* Genuss *m*, Lust *f*

gut [gʌt] *n* (*ANAT*) Gedärme *pl*; (*string*) Darm *m*; **~s** *npl* (*fig*) Schneid *m*

gutter ['gʌtər] *n* Dachrinne *f*; (*in street*) Gosse *f*

guttural ['gʌtərl] *adj* guttural, Kehl-

guy [gaɪ] *n* (*also: ~rope*) Halteseil *nt*; (*man*) Typ *m*, Kerl *m*

Guy Fawkes' Night

i **Guy Fawkes' Night**, *auch bonfire night genannt, erinnert an den Gunpowder Plot, einen Attentatsversuch auf James I. und sein Parlament am 5. November 1605. Einer der Verschwörer, Guy Fawkes, wurde auf frischer Tat ertappt, als er das Parlamentsgebäude in die Luft sprengen wollte. Vor der Guy Fawkes' Night basteln Kinder in Großbritannien eine Puppe des Guy Fawkes, mit der sie Geld für Feuerwerkskörper von Passanten erbetteln, und die dann am 5. November auf einem Lagerfeuer mit Feuerwerk verbrannt wird.*

---

guzzle ['gʌzl] *vt, vi* (*drink*) saufen; (*eat*) fressen

gym [dʒɪm] *n* (*also:* ~**nasium**) Turnhalle *f*; (*also:* ~**nastics**) Turnen *nt*

gymnast ['dʒɪmnæst] *n* Turner(in) *m(f)*

gymnastics [dʒɪm'næstɪks] *n* Turnen *nt*, Gymnastik *f*

gym shoes *npl* Turnschuhe *pl*

gynaecologist [gaɪnɪ'kɒlədʒɪst] (*US* **gynecologist**) *n* Frauenarzt(-ärztin) *m(f)*

gypsy ['dʒɪpsɪ] *n* = **gipsy**

gyrate [dʒaɪ'reɪt] *vi* kreisen

H, h

haberdashery [hæbə'dæʃərɪ] (*BRIT*) *n* Kurzwaren *pl*

habit ['hæbɪt] *n* (An)gewohnheit *f*; (*monk's*) Habit *nt or m*

habitable ['hæbɪtəbl] *adj* bewohnbar

habitat ['hæbɪtæt] *n* Lebensraum *m*

habitual [hə'bɪtjuəl] *adj* gewohnheitsmäßig; ~**ly** *adv* gewöhnlich

hack [hæk] *vt* hacken ♦ *n* Hieb *m*; (*writer*) Schreiberling *m*

hacker ['hækər] *n* (*COMPUT*) Hacker *m*

hackneyed ['hæknɪd] *adj* abgedroschen

had [hæd] *pt, pp of* **have**

haddock ['hædək] (*pl* ~ *or* ~**s**) *n* Schellfisch *m*

hadn't ['hædnt] = **had not**

haemorrhage ['hemərɪdʒ] (*US* **hemorrhage**) *n* Blutung *f*

haemorrhoids ['hemərɔɪdz] (*US* **hemorrhoids**) *npl* Hämor(rho)iden *pl*

haggard ['hægəd] *adj* abgekämpft

haggle ['hægl] *vi* feilschen

Hague [heɪg] *n* (*GEOG*) **The** ~ Den Haag *nt*

hail [heɪl] *n* Hagel *m* ♦ *vt* umjubeln ♦ *vi* hageln; ~**stone** *n* Hagelkorn *nt*

hair [hɛər] *n* Haar *nt*, Haare *pl*; (*one* ~) Haar *nt*; ~**brush** *n* Haarbürste *f*; ~**cut** *n* Haarschnitt *m*; **to get a** ~**cut** sich *dat* die Haare schneiden lassen; ~**do** *n* Frisur *f*; ~**dresser** *n* Friseur *m*, Friseuse *f*; ~**dresser's** *n* Friseursalon *m*; ~ **dryer** *n* Trockenhaube *f*; (*hand-held*) Föhn *m*, Fön *m* ®; ~ **gel** *n* Haargel *nt*; ~**grip** *n* Klemme *f*; ~**net** *n* Haarnetz *nt*; ~**pin** *n* Haarnadel *f*; ~**pin bend** (*US* ~**pin curve**) *n* Haarnadelkurve *f*; ~**raising** *adj* haarsträubend; ~ **removing cream** *n* Enthaarungscreme *nt*; ~ **spray** *n* Haarspray *nt*; ~**style** *n* Frisur *f*

hairy ['hɛərɪ] *adj* haarig

hake [heɪk] *n* Seehecht *m*

half [hɑːf] (*pl* **halves**) *n* Hälfte *f* ♦ *adj* halb ♦ *adv* halb, zur Hälfte; ~ **an hour** eine halbe Stunde; **two and a** ~ zweieinhalb; **to cut sth in** ~ etw halbieren; ~ **a dozen** ein halbes Dutzend, sechs; ~ **board** *n* Halbpension *f*; ~**caste** *n* Mischling *m*; ~ **fare** *n* halbe(r) Fahrpreis *m*; ~**hearted** *adj* lustlos; ~**hour** *n* halbe Stunde *f*; ~**price** *n*: (**at**) ~**price** zum halben Preis; ~ **term** (*BRIT*) *n* (*SCH*) Ferien *pl* in der Mitte des Trimesters; ~**time** *n* Halbzeit *f*; ~**way** *adv* halbwegs, auf halbem Wege

halibut ['hælɪbət] *n inv* Heilbutt *m*

hall [hɔːl] *n* Saal *m*; (*entrance* ~) Hausflur *m*; (*building*) Halle *f*; ~ **of residence** (*BRIT*) *n* Studentenwohnheim *nt*

hallmark ['hɔːlmɑːk] *n* Stempel *m*

hallo [hə'ləu] *excl* = **hello**

Hallowe'en ['hæləu'iːn] *n* Tag *m* vor Allerheiligen

Hallowe'en

i Hallowe'en *ist der 31. Oktober, der Vorabend von Allerheiligen und nach altem Glauben der Abend, an dem man Geister und Hexen sehen kann. In Großbritannien und vor allem in den USA feiern die Kinder Hallowe'en, indem sie sich verkleiden und mit selbst gemachten Laternen aus Kürbissen von Tür zu Tür ziehen.*

---

hallucination [həluːsɪ'neɪʃən] *n* Halluzination *f*

hallway ['hɔːlweɪ] *n* Korridor *m*

halo ['heɪləʊ] *n* Heiligenschein *m*

halt [hɔːlt] *n* Halt *m* ♦ *vt, vi* anhalten

halve [hɑːv] *vt* halbieren

halves [hɑːvz] *pl of* **half**

ham [hæm] *n* Schinken *m*

hamburger ['hæmbɜːgəʳ] *n* Hamburger *m*

hamlet ['hæmlɪt] *n* Weiler *m*

hammer ['hæməʳ] *n* Hammer *m* ♦ *vt, vi* hämmern

hammock ['hæmək] *n* Hängematte *f*

hamper ['hæmpəʳ] *vt* (be)hindern ♦ *n* Picknickkorb *m*

hamster ['hæmstəʳ] *n* Hamster *m*

hand [hænd] *n* Hand *f*; (*of clock*) (Uhr)zeiger *m*; (*worker*) Arbeiter *m* ♦ *vt* (*pass*) geben; **to give sb a ~** jdm helfen; **at ~** nahe; **to ~** zur Hand; **in ~** (*under control*) unter Kontrolle; (*being done*) im Gange; (*extra*) übrig; **on ~** zur Verfügung; **on the one ~ ..., on the other ~ ...** einerseits ..., andererseits ...; **~ in** *vt* abgeben; (*forms*) einreichen; **~ out** *vt* austeilen; **~ over** *vt* (*deliver*) übergeben; (*surrender*) abgeben; (: *prisoner*) ausliefern; **~bag** *n* Handtasche *f*; **~book** *n* Handbuch *nt*; **~brake** *n* Handbremse *f*; **~cuffs** *npl* Handschellen *pl*; **~ful** *n* Hand *f* voll; (*inf*: *person*) Plage *f*

handicap ['hændɪkæp] *n* Handikap *nt* ♦ *vt* benachteiligen; **mentally/physically ~ped** geistig/körperlich behindert

handicraft ['hændɪkrɑːft] *n* Kunsthandwerk *nt*

handiwork ['hændɪwɜːk] *n* Arbeit *f*; (*fig*) Werk *nt*

handkerchief ['hæŋkətʃɪf] *n* Taschentuch *nt*

handle ['hændl] *n* (*of door etc*) Klinke *f*; (*of cup etc*) Henkel *m*; (*for winding*) Kurbel *f* ♦ *vt* (*touch*) anfassen; (*deal with: things*) sich befassen mit; (: *people*) umgehen mit; **~bar(s)** *n(pl)* Lenkstange *f*

hand: ~ luggage *n* Handgepäck *nt*; **~made** *adj* handgefertigt; **~out** *n* (*distribution*) Verteilung *f*; (*charity*) Geldzuwendung *f*; (*leaflet*) Flugblatt *nt*; **~rail** *n* Geländer *nt*; (*on ship*) Reling *f*; **~set** *n* (*TEL*) Hörer *m*; **please replace tho ~set** bitte legen Sie auf; **~shake** *n* Händedruck *f*

handsome ['hænsəm] *adj* gut aussehend

handwriting ['hændraɪtɪŋ] *n* Handschrift *f*

handy ['hændɪ] *adj* praktisch; (*shops*) leicht erreichbar; **~man** ['hændɪmæn] (*irreg*) *n* Bastler *m*

hang [hæŋ] (*pt, pp* **hung**) *vt* aufhängen; (*pt, pp* **hanged**: *criminal*) hängen ♦ *vi* hängen ♦ *n*: **to get the ~ of sth** (*inf*) den richtigen Dreh bei etw herauskriegen; **~ about** *vi* sich herumtreiben; **~ around** *vi* sich herumtreiben; **~ on** *vi* (*wait*) warten; **~ up** *vt* (*TEL*) auflegen

hangar ['hæŋəʳ] *n* Hangar *m*

hanger ['hæŋəʳ] *n* Kleiderbügel *m*

hanger-on [hæŋər'ɔn] *n* Anhänger(in) *m(f)*

hang ['hæŋ-]: **~-gliding** *n* Drachenfliegen *nt*; **~over** *n* Kater *m*; **~-up** *n* Komplex *m*

hanker ['hæŋkəʳ] *vi*: **to ~ for** *or* **after** sich sehnen nach

hankie ['hæŋkɪ] *n abbr* = **handkerchief**

hanky ['hæŋkɪ] *n abbr* = **handkerchief**

haphazard [hæp'hæzəd] *adj* zufällig

happen ['hæpən] *vi* sich ereignen, passieren; **as it ~s I'm going there today** zufällig(erweise) gehe ich heute (dort)hin; **~ing** *n* Freignis *nt*

happily ['hæpɪlɪ] *adv* glücklich; (*fortunately*) glücklicherweise

happiness ['hæpɪnɪs] *n* Glück *nt*

happy ['hæpɪ] *adj* glücklich; **~ birthday!** alles Gute zum Geburtstag!; **~-go-lucky** *adj* sorglos; **~ hour** *n* Happy Hour *f*

harass ['hærəs] *vt* plagen; **~ment** *n* Belästigung *f*

harbour ['hɑːbəʳ] (*US* **harbor**) *n* Hafen *m* ♦ *vt* (*hope etc*) hegen; (*criminal etc*) Unterschlupf gewähren

hard [hɑːd] *adj* (*firm*) hart; (*difficult*) schwer; (*harsh*) hart(herzig) ♦ *adv* (*work*) hart; (*try*) sehr; (*push, hit*) fest; **no ~ feelings!** ich nehme es dir nicht übel; **~ of hearing** schwerhörig; **to be ~ done by** übel dran sein; **~back** *n* kartonierte Ausgabe *f*; **~ cash** *n* Bargeld *nt*; **~ disk** *n* (*COMPUT*) Festplatte *f*; **~en** *vt* erhärten; (*fig*) verhärten ♦ *vi* hart werden; (*fig*) sich verhärten; **~-headed** *adj* nüchtern; **~ labour** *n* Zwangsarbeit *f*

hardly ['hɑːdlɪ] *adv* kaum

hard: ~ship *n* Not *f*; **~ shoulder** (*BRIT*) *n* (*AUT*) Seitenstreifen *m*; **~ up** *adj* knapp bei Kasse; **~ware** *n* Eisenwaren *pl*; (*COMPUT*) Hardware *f*; **~ware shop** *n* Eisenwarenhandlung *f*; **~-wearing** *adj* strapazierfähig; **~-working** *adj* fleißig

hardy ['hɑːdɪ] *adj* widerstandsfähig

hare [hεəʳ] *n* Hase *m*; **~-brained** *adj* schwachsinnig

harm [hɑːm] *n* Schaden *m* ♦ *vt* schaden +*dat*; **out of ~'s way** in Sicherheit; **~ful** *adj* schädlich; **~less** *adj* harmlos

harmonica [hɑːˈmɔnɪkə] *n* Mundharmonika *f*

harmonious [hɑːˈməʊnɪəs] *adj* harmonisch

harmonize ['hɑːmənaɪz] *vt* abstimmen ♦ *vi* harmonieren

harmony ['hɑːmənɪ] *n* Harmonie *f*

harness ['hɑːnɪs] *n* Geschirr *nt* ♦ *vt* (*horse*) anschirren; (*fig*) nutzbar machen

harp [hɑːp] *n* Harfe *f* ♦ *vi*: **to ~ on about sth** auf etw *dat* herumreiten

harpoon [hɑːˈpuːn] *n* Harpune *f*

harrowing ['hærəʊɪŋ] *adj* nervenaufreibend

harsh [hɑːʃ] *adj* (*rough*) rau; (*severe*) streng; **~ness** *n* Härte *f*

harvest ['hɑːvɪst] *n* Ernte *f* ♦ *vt, vi* ernten

has [hæz] *vb see* **have**

hash [hæʃ] *vt* klein hacken ♦ *n* (*mess*) Kuddelmuddel *m*

hashish ['hæʃɪʃ] *n* Haschisch *nt*

hasn't ['hæznt] = **has not**

hassle ['hæsl] (*inf*) *n* Theater *nt*

haste [heɪst] *n* Eile *f*; **~n** ['heɪsn] *vt* beschleunigen ♦ *vi* eilen; **hasty** *adj* hastig; (*rash*) vorschnell

hat [hæt] *n* Hut *m*

hatch [hætʃ] *n* (*NAUT: also:* **~way**) Luke *f*; (*in house*) Durchreiche *f* ♦ *vi* (*young*) ausschlüpfen ♦ *vt* (*brood*) ausbrüten; (*plot*) aushecken; **~back** ['hætʃbæk] *n* (*AUT*) (Auto *nt* mit) Heckklappe *f*

hatchet ['hætʃɪt] *n* Beil *nt*

hate [heɪt] *vt* hassen ♦ *n* Hass *m*; **~ful** *adj* verhasst

hatred ['heɪtrɪd] *n* Hass *m*

haughty ['hɔːtɪ] *adj* hochnäsig, überheblich

haul [hɔːl] *vt* ziehen ♦ *n* (*catch*) Fang *m*; **~age** *n* Spedition *f*; **~ier** (*US* **hauler**) *n* Spediteur *m*

haunch [hɔːntʃ] *n* Lende *f*

haunt [hɔːnt] *vt* (*ghost*) spuken in +*dat*; (*memory*) verfolgen; (*pub*) häufig besuchen ♦ *n* Lieblingsplatz *m*; **the castle is ~ed** in dem Schloss spukt es

--- KEYWORD ---

have [hæv] (*pt, pp* **had**) *aux vb* **1** haben; (*esp with vbs of motion*) sein; **to have arrived/ slept** angekommen sein/geschlafen haben; **to have been** gewesen sein; **having eaten** *or* **when he had eaten, he left** nachdem er gegessen hatte, ging er

2 (*in tag questions*): **you've done it, haven't you?** du hast es doch gemacht, oder nicht?

3 (*in short answers and questions*): **you've made a mistake – so I have/no I haven't** du hast einen Fehler gemacht – ja, stimmt/nein; **we haven't paid – yes we have!** wir haben nicht bezahlt – doch; **I've been there before, have you?** ich war schon einmal da, du auch?

♦ *modal aux vb* (*be obliged*): **to have (got) to do sth** etw tun müssen; **you haven't to tell her** du darfst es ihr nicht erzählen

♦ *vt* **1** (*possess*) haben; **he has (got) blue**

eyes er hat blaue Augen; **I have (got) an idea** ich habe eine Idee
2 (*referring to meals etc*): **to have breakfast/a cigarette** frühstücken/eine Zigarette rauchen
3 (*receive, obtain etc*) haben; **may I have your address?** kann ich Ihre Adresse haben?; **to have a baby** ein Kind bekommen
4 (*maintain, allow*): **he will have it that he is right** er besteht darauf, dass er Recht hat; **I won't have it** das lasse ich mir nicht bieten
5: **to have sth done** etw machen lassen; **to have sb do sth** jdn etw machen lassen; **he soon had them all laughing** er brachte sie alle zum Lachen
6 (*experience, suffer*): **she had her bag stolen** man hat ihr die Tasche gestohlen; **he had his arm broken** er hat sich den Arm gebrochen
7 (*+noun: take, hold etc*): **to have a walk/ rest** spazieren gehen/sich ausruhen; **to have a meeting/party** eine Besprechung/ Party haben
have out *vt*: **to have it out with sb** (*settle problem*) etw mit jdm bereden

haven ['heɪvn] *n* Zufluchtsort *m*
haven't ['hævnt] = **have not**
havoc ['hævək] *n* Verwüstung *f*
hawk [hɔːk] *n* Habicht *m*
hay [heɪ] *n* Heu *nt*; **~ fever** *n* Heuschnupfen *m*; **~stack** *n* Heuschober *m*
haywire ['heɪwaɪəʳ] (*inf*) *adj* durcheinander
hazard ['hæzəd] *n* Risiko *nt* ♦ *vt* aufs Spiel setzen; **~ous** *adj* gefährlich; **~ (warning) lights** *npl* (*AUT*) Warnblinklicht *nt*
haze [heɪz] *n* Dunst *m*
hazelnut ['heɪzlnʌt] *n* Haselnuss *f*
hazy ['heɪzɪ] *adj* (*misty*) dunstig; (*vague*) verschwommen
he [hiː] *pron* er
head [hed] *n* Kopf *m*; (*leader*) Leiter *m* ♦ *vt* (an)führen, leiten; (*ball*) köpfen; **~s (or tails)** Kopf (oder Zahl); **~ first** mit dem Kopf nach unten; **~ over heels** kopfüber;

~ for *vt fus* zugehen auf +*acc*; **~ache** *n* Kopfschmerzen *pl*; **~dress** *n* Kopfschmuck *m*; **~ing** *n* Überschrift *f*; **~lamp** (*BRIT*) *n* Scheinwerfer *m*; **~land** *n* Landspitze *f*; **~light** *n* Scheinwerfer *m*; **~line** *n* Schlagzeile *f*; **~long** *adv* kopfüber; **~master** *n* (*of primary school*) Rektor *m*; (*of secondary school*) Direktor *m*; **~mistress** *n* Rektorin *f*; Direktorin *f*; **~ office** *n* Zentrale *f*; **~-on** *adj* Frontal-; **~phones** *npl* Kopfhörer *pl*; **~quarters** *npl* Zentrale *f*; (*MIL*) Hauptquartier *nt*; **~rest** *n* Kopfstütze *f*; **~room** *n* (*of bridges etc*) lichte Höhe *f*; **~scarf** *n* Kopftuch *nt*; **~strong** *adj* eigenwillig; **~teacher** (*BRIT*) *n* Schulleiter(in) *m(f)*; (*of secondary school also*) Direktor(in) *m*; **~ waiter** *n* Oberkellner *m*; **~way** *n* Fortschritte *pl*; **~wind** *n* Gegenwind *m*; **~y** *adj* berauschend
heal [hiːl] *vt* heilen ♦ *vi* verheilen
health [helθ] *n* Gesundheit *f*; **~ food** *n* Reformkost *f*; **H~ Service** (*BRIT*) *n*: **the H~ Service** das Gesundheitswesen; **~y** *adj* gesund
heap [hiːp] *n* Haufen *m* ♦ *vt* häufen
hear [hɪəʳ] (*pt, pp* **heard**) *vt* hören; (*listen to*) anhören ♦ *vi* hören; **~d** [həːd] *pt, pp of* **hear**; **~ing** *n* Gehör *nt*; (*JUR*) Verhandlung *f*; **~ing aid** *n* Hörapparat *m*; **~say** *n* Hörensagen *nt*
hearse [həːs] *n* Leichenwagen *m*
heart [haːt] *n* Herz *nt*; **~s** *npl* (*CARDS*) Herz *nt*; **by ~** auswendig; **~ attack** *n* Herzanfall *m*; **~beat** *n* Herzschlag *m*; **~breaking** *adj* herzzerbrechend; **~broken** *adj* untröstlich; **~burn** *n* Sodbrennen *nt*; **~ failure** *n* Herzschlag *m*; **~felt** *adj* aufrichtig
hearth [haːθ] *n* Herd *m*
heartily ['haːtɪlɪ] *adv* herzlich; (*eat*) herzhaft
heartless ['haːtlɪs] *adj* herzlos
hearty ['haːtɪ] *adj* kräftig; (*friendly*) freundlich
heat [hiːt] *n* Hitze *f*; (*of food, water etc*) Wärme *f*; (*SPORT: also*: **qualifying ~**) Ausscheidungsrunde *f* ♦ *vt* (*house*) heizen; (*substance*) heiß machen, erhitzen; **~ up** *vi* warm werden ♦ *vt* aufwärmen; **~ed** *adj* erhitzt; (*fig*) hitzig; **~er** *n* (Heiz)ofen *m*

heath [hi:θ] (*BRIT*) n Heide f

heathen ['hi:ðn] n Heide m/Heidin f ♦ adj heidnisch, Heiden-

heather ['hɛðəʳ] n Heidekraut nt

heat: ~**ing** n Heizung f; ~~-**seeking** adj Wärme suchend; ~**stroke** n Hitzschlag m; ~ **wave** n Hitzewelle f

heave [hi:v] vt hochheben; (*sigh*) ausstoßen ♦ vi wogen; (*breast*) sich heben ♦ n Heben nt

heaven ['hɛvn] n Himmel m; ~**ly** adj himmlisch

heavily ['hɛvɪlɪ] adv schwer

heavy ['hɛvɪ] adj schwer; ~ **goods vehicle** n Lastkraftwagen m; ~**weight** n (*SPORT*) Schwergewicht nt

Hebrew ['hi:bru:] adj hebräisch ♦ n (*LING*) Hebräisch nt

Hebrides ['hɛbrɪdi:z] npl Hebriden pl

heckle ['hɛkl] vt unterbrechen

hectic ['hɛktɪk] adj hektisch

he'd [hi:d] = he had; he would

hedge [hɛdʒ] n Hecke f ♦ vt einzäunen ♦ vi (*fig*) ausweichen; **to ~ one's bets** sich absichern

hedgehog ['hɛdʒhɔg] n Igel m

heed [hi:d] vt (*also*: **take ~ of**) beachten ♦ n Beachtung f; ~**less** adj achtlos

heel [hi:l] n Ferse f; (*of shoe*) Absatz m ♦ vt mit Absätzen versehen

hefty ['hɛftɪ] adj (*person*) stämmig; (*portion*) reichlich

heifer ['hɛfəʳ] n Färse f

height [haɪt] n (*of person*) Größe f; (*of object*) Höhe f; ~**en** vt erhöhen

heir [ɛəʳ] n Erbe m; ~**ess** ['ɛarɛs] n Erbin f; ~**loom** n Erbstück nt

held [hɛld] pt, pp of **hold**

helicopter ['hɛlɪkɔptəʳ] n Hubschrauber m

heliport ['hɛlɪpɔːt] n Hubschrauber-landeplatz m

hell [hɛl] n Hölle f ♦ excl verdammt!

he'll [hi:l] = he will; he shall

hellish ['hɛlɪʃ] adj höllisch, verteufelt

hello [hə'ləu] excl hallo

helm [hɛlm] n Ruder nt, Steuer nt

helmet ['hɛlmɪt] n Helm m

help [hɛlp] n Hilfe f ♦ vt helfen +dat; **I can't ~ it** ich kann nichts dafür; ~ **yourself** bedienen Sie sich; ~**er** n Helfer m; ~**ful** adj hilfreich; ~**ing** n Portion f; ~**less** adj hilflos

hem [hɛm] n Saum m ♦ vt säumen; ~ **in** vt einengen

hemorrhage ['hɛmərɪdʒ] (*US*) n = **haemorrhage**

hemorrhoids ['hɛmərɔɪdz] (*US*) npl = **haemorrhoids**

hen [hɛn] n Henne f

hence [hɛns] adv von jetzt an; (*therefore*) daher; ~**forth** adv von nun an; (*from then on*) von da an

henchman ['hɛntʃmən] (*irreg*) n Gefolgsmann m

her [hə:ʳ] pron (*acc*) sie; (*dat*) ihr ♦ adj ihr; see also **me; my**

herald ['hɛrəld] n (Vor)bote m ♦ vt verkünden

heraldry ['hɛrəldrɪ] n Wappenkunde f

herb [hə:b] n Kraut nt

herd [hə:d] n Herde f

here [hɪəʳ] adv hier; (*to this place*) hierher; ~**after** [hɪər'ɑːftəʳ] adv hernach, künftig ♦ n Jenseits nt; ~**by** [hɪə'baɪ] adv hiermit

hereditary [hɪ'rɛdɪtrɪ] adj erblich

heredity [hɪ'rɛdɪtɪ] n Vererbung f

heritage ['hɛrɪtɪdʒ] n Erbe nt

hermit ['hə:mɪt] n Einsiedler m

hernia ['hə:nɪə] n Bruch m

hero ['hɪərəu] (pl ~**es**) n Held m; ~**ic** [hɪ'rəuɪk] adj heroisch

heroin ['hɛrəuɪn] n Heroin nt

heroine ['hɛrəuɪn] n Heldin f

heroism ['hɛrəuɪzəm] n Heldentum nt

heron ['hɛrən] n Reiher m

herring ['hɛrɪŋ] n Hering m

hers [hə:z] pron ihre(r, s); see also **mine**[2]

herself [hə:'sɛlf] pron sich (selbst); (*emphatic*) selbst; see also **oneself**

he's [hi:z] = he is; he has

hesitant ['hɛzɪtənt] adj zögernd

hesitate ['hɛzɪteɪt] vi zögern; **hesitation** [hɛzɪ'teɪʃən] n Zögern nt

heterosexual ['hɛtərəu'sɛksjuəl] adj heterosexuell ♦ n Heterosexuelle(r) mf

hew [hju:] (*pt* **hewed**, *pp* **hewn**) *vt* hauen, hacken

hexagonal [hɛkˈsægənl] *adj* sechseckig

heyday [ˈheɪdeɪ] *n* Blüte *f*, Höhepunkt *m*

HGV *n abbr* = **heavy goods vehicle**

hi [haɪ] *excl* he, hallo

hibernate [ˈhaɪbəneɪt] *vi* Winterschlaf *m* halten; **hibernation** [haɪbəˈneɪʃən] *n* Winterschlaf *m*

hiccough [ˈhɪkʌp] *vi* den Schluckauf haben; **~s** *npl* Schluckauf *m*

hiccup [ˈhɪkʌp] – **hiccough**

hid [hɪd] *pt of* **hide**; **~den** [ˈhɪdn] *pp of* **hide**

hide [haɪd] (*pt* **hid**, *pp* **hidden**) *n* (*skin*) Haut *f*, Fell *nt* ♦ *vt* verstecken ♦ *vi* sich verstecken; **~-and-seek** *n* Versteckspiel *nt*; **~away** *n* Versteck *nt*

hideous [ˈhɪdɪəs] *adj* abscheulich

hiding [ˈhaɪdɪŋ] *n* (*beating*) Tracht *f* Prügel; **to be in ~** (*concealed*) sich versteckt halten; **~ place** *n* Versteck *nt*

hi-fi [ˈhaɪfaɪ] *n* Hi-Fi *nt* ♦ *adj* Hi-Fi-

high [haɪ] *adj* hoch; (*wind*) stark ♦ *adv* hoch, **it is 20m ~** es ist 20 Meter hoch; **~brow** *adj* (*betont*) intellektuell; **~chair** *n* Hochstuhl *m*; **~er education** *n* Hochschulbildung *f*; **~-handed** *adj* eigenmächtig; **~-heeled** *adj* hochhackig; **~ jump** *n* (*SPORT*) Hochsprung *m*; **H~lands** *npl*: **the H~lands** das schottische Hochland; **~light** *n* (*fig*) Höhepunkt *m* ♦ *vt* hervorheben; **~ly** *adv* höchst; **~ly strung** *adj* überempfindlich; **~ness** *n* Höhe *f*; **Her H~ness** Ihre Hoheit *f*; **~-pitched** *adj* hoch; **~-rise block** *n* Hochhaus *nt*; **~ school** (*US*) *n* Oberschule *f*; **~ season** (*BRIT*) *n* Hochsaison *f*; **~ street** (*BRIT*) *n* Hauptstraße *f*

highway [ˈhaɪweɪ] *n* Landstraße *f*; **H~ Code** (*BRIT*) *n* Straßenverkehrsordnung *f*

hijack [ˈhaɪdʒæk] *vt* entführen; **~er** *n* Entführer(in) *m(f)*

hike [haɪk] *vi* wandern ♦ *n* Wanderung *f*; **~r** *n* Wanderer *m*; **hiking** *n* Wandern *nt*

hilarious [hɪˈlɛərɪəs] *adj* lustig

hill [hɪl] *n* Berg *m*; **~side** *n* (Berg)hang *m*; **~ walking** *n* Bergwandern *nt*; **~y** *adj* hügelig

hilt [hɪlt] *n* Heft *nt*; **(up) to the ~** ganz und gar

him [hɪm] *pron* (*acc*) ihn; (*dat*) ihm; *see also* **me**; **~self** *pron* sich (selbst); (*emphatic*) selbst; *see also* **oneself**

hind [haɪnd] *adj* hinter, Hinter-

hinder [ˈhɪndə*] *vt* (*stop*) hindern; (*delay*) behindern; **hindrance** *n* (*delay*) Behinderung *f*; (*obstacle*) Hindernis *nt*

hindsight [ˈhaɪndsaɪt] *n*: **with ~** im nachhinein

Hindu [ˈhɪndu:] *n* Hindu *m*

hinge [hɪndʒ] *n* Scharnier *nt*; (*on door*) Türangel *f* ♦ *vi* (*fig*): **to ~ on** abhängen von

hint [hɪnt] *n* Tipp *m*; (*trace*) Anflug *m* ♦ *vt*: **to ~ that** andeuten, dass ♦ *vi*: **to ~ at** andeuten

hip [hɪp] *n* Hüfte *f*

hippie [ˈhɪpɪ] *n* Hippie *m*

hippo [ˈhɪpəu] (*inf*) *n* Nilpferd *nt*

hippopotami [hɪpəˈpɒtəmaɪ] *npl of* **hippopotamus**

hippopotamus [hɪpəˈpɒtəməs] (*pl* **~es** *or* **hippopotami**) *n* Nilpferd *nt*

hire [ˈhaɪə*] *vt* (*worker*) anstellen; (*BRIT*: *car*) mieten ♦ *n* Miete *f*; **for ~** (*taxi*) frei; **~(d) car** (*BRIT*) *n* Mietwagen *m*, Leihwagen *m*; **~ purchase** (*BRIT*) *n* Teilzahlungskauf *m*

his [hɪz] *adj* sein ♦ *pron* seine(r, s); *see also* **my**; **mine[2]**

hiss [hɪs] *vi* zischen ♦ *n* Zischen *nt*

historian [hɪˈstɔːrɪən] *n* Historiker *m*

historic [hɪˈstɒrɪk] *adj* historisch; **~al** *adj* historisch, geschichtlich

history [ˈhɪstərɪ] *n* Geschichte *f*

hit [hɪt] (*pt*, *pp* **hit**) *vt* schlagen; (*injure*) treffen ♦ *n* (*blow*) Schlag *m*; (*success*) Erfolg *m*; (*MUS*) Hit *m*; **to ~ it off with sb** prima mit jdm auskommen; **~-and-run driver** *n* jemand, der Fahrerflucht begeht

hitch [hɪtʃ] *vt* festbinden; (*also*: **~ up**) hochziehen ♦ *n* (*difficulty*) Haken *m*; **to ~ a lift** trampen; **~hike** *vi* trampen; **~hiker** *n* Tramper *m*; **~hiking** *n* Trampen *nt*

hi-tech [ˈhaɪtɛk] *adj* Hightech- ♦ *n* Spitzentechnologie *f*

hitherto [hɪðəˈtu:] *adv* bislang

hit man (*inf*) (*irreg*) *n* Killer *m*

HIV *n abbr:* **HIV-negative / -positive** HIV-negativ/-positiv

hive [haɪv] *n* Bienenkorb *m*

HMS *abbr* = **His / Her Majesty's Ship**

hoard [hɔːd] *n* Schatz *m ♦ vt* horten, hamstern

hoarding ['hɔːdɪŋ] *n* Bretterzaun *m*; (*BRIT: for posters*) Reklamewand *f*

hoarse [hɔːs] *adj* heiser, rau

hoax [həʊks] *n* Streich *m*

hob [hɔb] *n* Kochmulde *f*

hobble ['hɔbl] *vi* humpeln

hobby ['hɔbɪ] *n* Hobby *nt*

hobby-horse ['hɔbɪhɔːs] *n* (*fig*) Steckenpferd *nt*

hobo ['həʊbəʊ] (*US*) *n* Tippelbruder *m*

hockey ['hɔkɪ] *n* Hockey *nt*

hoe [həʊ] *n* Hacke *f ♦ vt* hacken

hog [hɔg] *n* Schlachtschwein *nt ♦ vt* mit Beschlag belegen; **to go the whole ~** aufs Ganze gehen

hoist [hɔɪst] *n* Winde *f ♦ vt* hochziehen

hold [həʊld] (*pt, pp* **held**) *vt* halten; (*contain*) enthalten; (*be able to contain*) fassen; (*breath*) anhalten; (*meeting*) abhalten *♦ vi* (*withstand pressure*) aushalten *♦ n* (*grasp*) Halt *m*; (*NAUT*) Schiffsraum *m*; **~ the line!** (*TEL*) bleiben Sie am Apparat!; **to ~ one's own** sich behaupten; **~ back** *vt* zurückhalten; **~ down** *vt* niederhalten; (*job*) behalten; **~ off** *vt* (*enemy*) abwehren; **~ on** *vi* sich festhalten; (*resist*) durchhalten; (*wait*) warten; **~ on to** *vt fus* festhalten an +*dat*; (*keep*) behalten; **~ out** *vt* hinhalten *♦ vi* aushalten; **~ up** *vt* (*delay*) aufhalten; (*rob*) überfallen; **~-all** (*BRIT*) *n* Reisetasche *f*; **~er** *n* Behälter *m*; **~ing** *n* (*share*) (Aktien)anteil *m*; **~up** *n* (*BRIT: in traffic*) Stockung *f*; (*robbery*) Überfall *m*; (*delay*) Verzögerung *f*

hole [həʊl] *n* Loch *nt*; **~ in the wall** (*inf*) *n* (*cash dispenser*) Geldautomat *m*

holiday ['hɔlɪdeɪ] *n* (*day*) Feiertag *m*; freie(r) Tag *m*; (*vacation*) Urlaub *m*; (*SCH*) Ferien *pl*; **~-maker** (*BRIT*) *n* Urlauber(in) *m(f)*; **~ resort** *n* Ferienort *m*

Holland ['hɔlənd] *n* Holland *nt*

hollow ['hɔləʊ] *adj* hohl; (*fig*) leer *♦ n* Vertiefung *f*; **~ out** *vt* aushöhlen

holly ['hɔlɪ] *n* Stechpalme *f*

holocaust ['hɔləkɔːst] *n* Inferno *nt*

holster ['həʊlstə*] *n* Pistolenhalfter *m*

holy ['həʊlɪ] *adj* heilig; **H~ Ghost** or **Spirit** *n:* **the H~ Ghost** or **Spirit** der Heilige Geist

homage ['hɔmɪdʒ] *n* Huldigung *f*; **to pay ~ to** huldigen +*dat*

home [həʊm] *n* Zuhause *nt*; (*institution*) Heim *nt*, Anstalt *f ♦ adj* einheimisch; (*POL*) inner *♦ adv* heim, nach Hause; **at ~** zu Hause; **~ address** *n* Heimatadresse *f*; **~coming** *n* Heimkehr *f*; **~land** *n* Heimat(land *nt*) *f*; **~less** *adj* obdachlos; **~ly** *adj* häuslich; (*US: ugly*) unscheinbar; **~made** *adj* selbst gemacht; **~ match** *adj* Heimspiel *nt*; **H~ Office** (*BRIT*) *n* Innenministerium *nt*; **~ page** *n* (*COMPUT*) Homepage *f*; **~ rule** *n* Selbstverwaltung *f*; **H~ Secretary** (*BRIT*) *n* Innenminister(in) *m(f)*; **~sick** *adj:* **to be ~sick** Heimweh haben; **~ town** *n* Heimatstadt *f*; **~ward** *adj* (*journey*) Heim-; **~work** *n* Hausaufgaben *pl*

homicide ['hɔmɪsaɪd] (*US*) *n* Totschlag *m*

homeopathic [həʊmɪə'pɔθɪk] (*US* **homeopathic**) *adj* homöopathisch; **homeopathy** [həʊmɪ'ɔpəθɪ] (*US* **homeopathy**) *n* Homöopathie *f*

homogeneous [hɔməʊ'dʒiːnɪəs] *adj* homogen

homosexual [hɔməʊ'sɛksjʊəl] *adj* homosexuell *♦ n* Homosexuelle(r) *mf*

honest ['ɔnɪst] *adj* ehrlich; **~ly** *adv* ehrlich; **~y** *n* Ehrlichkeit *f*

honey ['hʌnɪ] *n* Honig *m*; **~comb** *n* Honigwabe *f*; **~moon** *n* Flitterwochen *pl*, Hochzeitsreise *f*; **~suckle** ['hʌnɪsʌkl] *n* Geißblatt *nt*

honk [hɔŋk] *vi* hupen

honor *etc* ['ɔnə*] (*US*) *vt, n* = **honour** *etc*

honorary ['ɔnərərɪ] *adj* Ehren-

honour ['ɔnə*] (*US* **honor**) *vt* ehren; (*cheque*) einlösen *♦ n* Ehre *f*; **~able** *adj* ehrenwert; (*intention*) ehrenhaft; **~s degree** *n* (*UNIV*) *akademischer Grad mit Prüfung im*

Spezialfach

hood [hud] n Kapuze f; (BRIT: AUT) Verdeck nt; (US: AUT) Kühlerhaube f

hoof [hu:f] (pl hooves) n Huf m

hook [huk] n Haken m ♦ vt einhaken

hooligan ['hu:ligən] n Rowdy m

hoop [hu:p] n Reifen m

hooray [hu:'rei] excl = **hurrah**

hoot [hu:t] vi (AUT) hupen; **~er** n (NAUT) Dampfpfeife f; (BRIT: AUT) (Auto)hupe f

Hoover ['hu:vər] (®; BRIT) n Staubsauger m ♦ vt: **to h~** staubsaugen, Staub saugen

hooves [hu:vz] pl of **hoof**

hop [hɔp] vi hüpfen, hopsen ♦ n (jump) Hopser m

hope [həup] vt, vi hoffen ♦ n Hoffnung f; **I ~ so/not** hoffentlich/hoffentlich nicht; **~ful** adj hoffnungsvoll; (promising) viel versprechend; **~fully** adv hoffentlich; **~less** adj hoffnungslos

hops [hɔps] npl Hopfen m

horizon [hə'raizn] n Horizont m; **~tal** [hɔri'zɔntl] adj horizontal

hormone ['hɔːməun] n Hormon nt

horn [hɔːn] n Horn nt; (AUT) Hupe f

hornet ['hɔːnit] n Hornisse f

horny ['hɔːni] adj schwielig; (US: inf) scharf

horoscope ['hɔrəskəup] n Horoskop nt

horrendous [hə'rendəs] adj (crime) abscheulich; (error) schrecklich

horrible ['hɔribl] adj fürchterlich

horrid ['hɔrid] adj scheußlich

horrify ['hɔrifai] vt entsetzen

horror ['hɔrər] n Schrecken m; **~ film** n Horrorfilm m

hors d'oeuvre [ɔː'dəːvrə] n Vorspeise f

horse [hɔːs] n Pferd nt; **~back** n: **on ~back** beritten; **~ chestnut** n Rosskastanie f; **~man/woman** (irreg) n Reiter(in) m(f); **~power** n Pferdestärke f; **~racing** n Pferderennen nt; **~radish** n Meerrettich m; **~shoe** n Hufeisen nt

horticulture ['hɔːtikʌltʃər] n Gartenbau m

hose [həuz] n (also: **~pipe**) Schlauch m

hosiery ['həuziəri] n Strumpfwaren pl

hospitable ['hɔspitəbl] adj gastfreundlich

hospital ['hɔspitl] n Krankenhaus nt

hospitality [hɔspi'tæliti] n Gastfreundschaft f

host [həust] n Gastgeber m; (innkeeper) (Gast)wirt m; (large number) Heerschar f; (ECCL) Hostie f

hostage ['hɔstidʒ] n Geisel f

hostel ['hɔstl] n Herberge f; (also: **youth ~**) Jugendherberge f

hostess ['həustis] n Gastgeberin f

hostile ['hɔstail] adj feindlich; **hostility** [hɔ'stiliti] n Feindschaft f; **hostilities** npl (fighting) Feindseligkeiten pl

hot [hɔt] adj heiß; (food, water) warm; (spiced) scharf; **I'm ~** mir ist heiß; **~bed** n (fig) Nährboden m; **~ dog** n heiße(s) Würstchen nt

hotel [həu'tel] n Hotel nt; **~ier** [həu'teliər] n Hotelier m

hot: ~house n Treibhaus nt; **~ line** n (POL) heiße(r) Draht m; **~ly** adv (argue) hitzig; **~plate** n Kochplatte f; **~pot** ['hɔtpɔt] (BRIT) n Fleischeintopf m; **~-water bottle** n Wärmflasche f

hound [haund] n Jagdhund m ♦ vt hetzen

hour ['auər] n Stunde f; (time of day) (Tages)zeit f; **~ly** adj, adv stündlich

house [n haus, vb hauz] n Haus nt ♦ vt unterbringen; **on the ~** auf Kosten des Hauses; **~ arrest** n (POL, MIL) Hausarrest m; **~boat** n Hausboot nt; **~breaking** n Einbruch m; **~coat** n Morgenmantel m; **~hold** n Haushalt m; **~keeper** n Haushälterin f; **~keeping** n Haushaltung f; **~-warming party** n Einweihungsparty f; **~wife** (irreg) n Hausfrau f; **~work** n Hausarbeit f

housing ['hauziŋ] n (act) Unterbringung f; (houses) Wohnungen pl; (POL) Wohnungsbau m; (covering) Gehäuse nt; **~ estate** (US **~ development**) n (Wohn)siedlung f

hovel ['hɔvl] n elende Hütte f

hover ['hɔvər] vi (bird) schweben; (person) herumstehen; **~craft** n Luftkissenfahrzeug nt

how [hau] adv wie; **~ are you?** wie geht es Ihnen?; **~ much milk?** wie viel Milch?; **~**

many people? wie viele Leute?

however [hau'ɛvə^r] *adv* (*but*) (je)doch, aber; **~ you phrase it** wie Sie es auch ausdrücken

howl [haul] *n* Heulen *nt* ♦ *vi* heulen

H.P. *abbr* = **hire purchase**

h.p. *abbr* = **horsepower**

H.Q. *abbr* = **headquarters**

HTML *abbr* (= *hypertext markup language*) HTML

hub [hʌb] *n* Radnabe *f*

hubbub [ˈhʌbʌb] *n* Tumult *m*

hubcap [ˈhʌbkæp] *n* Radkappe *f*

huddle [ˈhʌdl] *vi*: **to ~ together** sich zusammendrängen

hue [hjuː] *n* Färbung *f*; **~ and cry** *n* Zetergeschrei *nt*

huff [hʌf] *n*: **to go into a ~** einschnappen

hug [hʌg] *vt* umarmen ♦ *n* Umarmung *f*

huge [hjuːdʒ] *adj* groß, riesig

hulk [hʌlk] *n* (*ship*) abgetakelte(s) Schiff *nt*; (*person*) Koloss *m*

hull [hʌl] *n* Schiffsrumpf *m*

hullo [həˈləu] *excl* = **hello**

hum [hʌm] *vt, vi* summen

human [ˈhjuːmən] *adj* menschlich ♦ *n* (*also*: **~ being**) Mensch *m*

humane [hjuːˈmeɪn] *adj* human

humanitarian [hjuːmænɪˈtɛərɪən] *adj* humanitär

humanity [hjuːˈmænɪtɪ] *n* Menschheit *f*; (*kindliness*) Menschlichkeit *f*

humble [ˈhʌmbl] *adj* demütig; (*modest*) bescheiden ♦ *vt* demütigen

humbug [ˈhʌmbʌg] *n* Humbug *m*; (*BRIT: sweet*) Pfefferminzbonbon *nt*

humdrum [ˈhʌmdrʌm] *adj* stumpfsinnig

humid [ˈhjuːmɪd] *adj* feucht; **~ity** [hjuːˈmɪdɪtɪ] *n* Feuchtigkeit *f*

humiliate [hjuːˈmɪlɪeɪt] *vt* demütigen; **humiliation** [hjuːmɪlɪˈeɪʃən] *n* Demütigung *f*

humility [hjuːˈmɪlɪtɪ] *n* Demut *f*

humor [ˈhjuːmə^r] (*US*) *n, vt* = **humour**

humorous [ˈhjuːmərəs] *adj* humorvoll

humour [ˈhjuːmə^r] (*US* **humor**) *n* (*fun*) Humor *m*; (*mood*) Stimmung *f* ♦ *vt* bei Stimmung halten

hump [hʌmp] *n* Buckel *m*

hunch [hʌntʃ] *n* Buckel *m*; (*premonition*) (Vor)ahnung *f*; **~back** *n* Bucklige(r) *mf*; **~ed** *adj* gekrümmt

hundred [ˈhʌndrəd] *num* hundert; **~weight** *n* Zentner *m* (*BRIT = 50.8 kg; US = 45.3 kg*)

hung [hʌŋ] *pt, pp of* **hang**

Hungarian [hʌŋˈgɛərɪən] *adj* ungarisch ♦ *n* Ungar(in) *m(f)*; (*LING*) Ungarisch *nt*

Hungary [ˈhʌŋgərɪ] *n* Ungarn *nt*

hunger [ˈhʌŋgə^r] *n* Hunger *m* ♦ *vi* hungern

hungry [ˈhʌŋgrɪ] *adj* hungrig; **to be ~** Hunger haben

hunk [hʌŋk] *n* (*of bread*) Stück *nt*

hunt [hʌnt] *vt, vi* jagen ♦ *n* Jagd *f*; **to ~ for** suchen; **~er** *n* Jäger *m*; **~ing** *n* Jagd *f*

hurdle [ˈhɜːdl] *n* (*also fig*) Hürde *f*

hurl [hɜːl] *vt* schleudern

hurrah [huˈrɑː] *n* Hurra *nt*

hurray [huˈreɪ] *n* Hurra *nt*

hurricane [ˈhʌrɪkən] *n* Orkan *m*

hurried [ˈhʌrɪd] *adj* eilig; (*hasty*) übereilt; **~ly** *adv* übereilt, hastig

hurry [ˈhʌrɪ] *n* Eile *f* ♦ *vi* sich beeilen ♦ *vt* (an)treiben; (*job*) übereilen; **to be in a ~** es eilig haben; **~ up** *vi* sich beeilen ♦ *vt* (*person*) zur Eile antreiben; (*work*) vorantreiben

hurt [hɜːt] (*pt, pp* **hurt**) *vt* wehtun +*dat*; (*injure, fig*) verletzen ♦ *vi* wehtun; **~ful** *adj* schädlich; (*remark*) verletzend

hurtle [ˈhɜːtl] *vi* sausen

husband [ˈhʌzbənd] *n* (Ehe)mann *m*

hush [hʌʃ] *n* Stille *f* ♦ *vt* zur Ruhe bringen ♦ *excl* pst, still

husky [ˈhʌskɪ] *adj* (*voice*) rau ♦ *n* Eskimohund *m*

hustle [ˈhʌsl] *vt* (*push*) stoßen; (*hurry*) antreiben ♦ *n*: **~ and bustle** Geschäftigkeit *f*

hut [hʌt] *n* Hütte *f*

hutch [hʌtʃ] *n* (Kaninchen)stall *m*

hyacinth [ˈhaɪəsɪnθ] *n* Hyazinthe *f*

hydrant [ˈhaɪdrənt] *n* (*also*: **fire ~**) Hydrant *m*

hydraulic [haɪˈdrɔːlɪk] *adj* hydraulisch

hydroelectric [ˈhaɪdrəuɪˈlektrɪk] *adj* (*energy*) durch Wasserkraft erzeugt; **~ power station** *n* Wasserkraftwerk *nt*

hydrofoil [ˈhaɪdrəfɔɪl] *n* Tragflügelboot *nt*

hydrogen ['haɪdrədʒən] n Wasserstoff m

hyena [haɪ'iːnə] n Hyäne f

hygiene ['haɪdʒiːn] n Hygiene f; **hygienic** [haɪ'dʒiːnɪk] adj hygienisch

hymn [hɪm] n Kirchenlied nt

hype [haɪp] (inf) n Publicity f

hypermarket ['haɪpəmɑːkɪt] (BRIT) n Hypermarket m

hypertext ['haɪpətekst] n (COMPUT) Hypertext m

hyphen ['haɪfn] n Bindestrich m

hypnosis [hɪp'nəusɪs] n Hypnose f

hypnotize ['hɪpnətaɪz] vt hypnotisieren

hypocrisy [hɪ'pɒkrɪsɪ] n Heuchelei f

hypocrite ['hɪpəkrɪt] n Heuchler m; **hypocritical** [hɪpə'krɪtɪkl] adj scheinheilig, heuchlerisch

hypothermia [haɪpə'θɜːmɪə] n Unterkühlung f

hypotheses [haɪ'pɒθɪsiːz] npl of **hypothesis**

hypothesis [haɪ'pɒθɪsɪs] (pl **hypotheses**) n Hypothese f

hypothetic(al) [haɪpəu'θetɪk(l)] adj hypothetisch

hysterical [hɪ'sterɪkl] adj hysterisch

hysterics [hɪ'sterɪks] npl hysterische(r) Anfall m

I, i

I [aɪ] pron ich

ice [aɪs] n Eis nt ♦ vt (COOK) mit Zuckerguss überziehen ♦ vi (also: ~ up) vereisen; ~ **axe** n Eispickel m; **~berg** n Eisberg m; **~box** (US) n Kühlschrank m; ~ **cream** n Eis nt; ~ **cube** n Eiswürfel m; **~d** [aɪst] adj (cake) mit Zuckerguss überzogen, glasiert; (tea, coffee) Eis-; ~ **hockey** n Eishockey nt

Iceland ['aɪslənd] n Island nt

ice: ~ **lolly** (BRIT) n Eis nt am Stiel; ~ **rink** n (Kunst)eisbahn f; ~ **skating** n Schlittschuhlaufen nt

icicle ['aɪsɪkl] n Eiszapfen m

icing ['aɪsɪŋ] n (on cake) Zuckerguss m; (on window) Vereisung f; ~ **sugar** (BRIT) n Puderzucker m

icon ['aɪkɒn] n Ikone f; (COMPUT) Icon nt

icy ['aɪsɪ] adj (slippery) vereist; (cold) eisig

I'd [aɪd] = **I would; I had**

idea [aɪ'dɪə] n Idee f

ideal [aɪ'dɪəl] n Ideal nt ♦ adj ideal

identical [aɪ'dentɪkl] adj identisch; (twins) eineiig

identification [aɪdentɪfɪ'keɪʃən] n Identifizierung f; **means of ~** Ausweispapiere pl

identify [aɪ'dentɪfaɪ] vt identifizieren; (regard as the same) gleichsetzen

Identikit [aɪ'dentɪkɪt] ® n: ~ **picture** Phantombild nt

identity [aɪ'dentɪtɪ] n Identität f; ~ **card** n Personalausweis m

ideology [aɪdɪ'ɒlədʒɪ] n Ideologie f

idiom ['ɪdɪəm] n (expression) Redewendung f; (dialect) Idiom nt; **~atic** [ɪdɪə'mætɪk] adj idiomatisch

idiosyncrasy [ɪdɪəu'sɪŋkrəsɪ] n Eigenart f

idiot ['ɪdɪət] n Idiot(in) m(f); **~ic** [ɪdɪ'ɒtɪk] adj idiotisch

idle ['aɪdl] adj (doing nothing) untätig; (lazy) faul; (useless) nutzlos, (machine) still(stehend); (threat, talk) leer ♦ vi (machine) leer laufen ♦ vt: **to ~ away the time** die Zeit vertrödeln; **~ness** n Müßiggang m; Faulheit f

idol ['aɪdl] n Idol nt; **~ize** vt vergöttern

i.e. abbr (= id est) d. h.

KEYWORD

if [ɪf] conj **1** wenn; (in case also) falls; **if I were you** wenn ich Sie wäre

2 (although): **(even) if** (selbst or auch) wenn

3 (whether) ob

4: **if so/not** wenn ja/nicht; **if only ...** wenn ... doch nur ...; **if only I could** wenn ich doch nur könnte; see also **as**

ignite [ɪg'naɪt] vt (an)zünden ♦ vi sich entzünden; **ignition** [ɪg'nɪʃən] n Zündung f; **to switch on/off the ignition** den Motor anlassen/abstellen; **ignition key** n (AUT) Zündschlüssel m

ignorance [ˈɪgnərəns] *n* Unwissenheit *f*

ignorant [ˈɪgnərənt] *adj* unwissend; **to be ~ of** nicht wissen

ignore [ɪgˈnɔːʳ] *vt* ignorieren

I'll [aɪl] = **I will**; **I shall**

ill [ɪl] *adj* krank ♦ *n* Übel *nt* ♦ *adv* schlecht; **~-advised** *adj* unklug; **~-at-ease** *adj* unbehaglich

illegal [ɪˈliːgl] *adj* illegal

illegible [ɪˈledʒɪbl] *adj* unleserlich

illegitimate [ɪlɪˈdʒɪtɪmət] *adj* unehelich

ill-fated [ɪlˈfeɪtɪd] *adj* unselig

ill feeling *n* Verstimmung *f*

illicit [ɪˈlɪsɪt] *adj* verboten

illiterate [ɪˈlɪtərət] *adj* ungebildet

ill-mannered [ɪlˈmænəd] *adj* ungehobelt

illness [ˈɪlnɪs] *n* Krankheit *f*

illogical [ɪˈlɒdʒɪkl] *adj* unlogisch

ill-treat [ɪlˈtriːt] *vt* misshandeln

illuminate [ɪˈluːmɪneɪt] *vt* beleuchten; **illumination** [ɪluːmɪˈneɪʃən] *n* Beleuchtung *f*; **illuminations** *pl* (*decorative lights*) festliche Beleuchtung *f*

illusion [ɪˈluːʒən] *n* Illusion *f*; **to be under the ~ that ...** sich *dat* einbilden, dass ...

illustrate [ˈɪləstreɪt] *vt* (*book*) illustrieren; (*explain*) veranschaulichen; **illustration** [ɪləˈstreɪʃən] *n* Illustration *f*; (*explanation*) Veranschaulichung *f*

illustrious [ɪˈlʌstrɪəs] *adj* berühmt

I'm [aɪm] = **I am**

image [ˈɪmɪdʒ] *n* Bild *nt*; (*public ~*) Image *nt*; **~ry** *n* Symbolik *f*

imaginary [ɪˈmædʒɪnəri] *adj* eingebildet; (*world*) Fantasie-

imagination [ɪmædʒɪˈneɪʃən] *n* Einbildung *f*; (*creative*) Fantasie *f*

imaginative [ɪˈmædʒɪnətɪv] *adj* fantasiereich, einfallsreich

imagine [ɪˈmædʒɪn] *vt* sich vorstellen; (*wrongly*) sich einbilden

imbalance [ɪmˈbæləns] *n* Unausgeglichenheit *f*

imbecile [ˈɪmbəsiːl] *n* Schwachsinnige(r) *mf*

imitate [ˈɪmɪteɪt] *vt* imitieren; **imitation** [ɪmɪˈteɪʃən] *n* Imitation *f*

immaculate [ɪˈmækjulət] *adj* makellos;

(*dress*) tadellos; (*ECCL*) unbefleckt

immaterial [ɪməˈtɪərɪəl] *adj* unwesentlich; **it is ~ whether ...** es ist unwichtig, ob ...

immature [ɪməˈtjuəʳ] *adj* unreif

immediate [ɪˈmiːdɪət] *adj* (*instant*) sofortig; (*near*) unmittelbar; (*relatives*) nächste(r, s); (*needs*) dringlich; **~ly** *adv* sofort; **~ly next to** direkt neben

immense [ɪˈmens] *adj* unermesslich

immerse [ɪˈmɜːs] *vt* eintauchen; **to be ~d in** (*fig*) vertieft sein in +*acc*

immersion heater [ɪˈmɜːʃən-] (*BRIT*) *n* Boiler *m*

immigrant [ˈɪmɪgrənt] *n* Einwanderer *m*

immigrate [ˈɪmɪgreɪt] *vi* einwandern; **immigration** [ɪmɪˈgreɪʃən] *n* Einwanderung *f*

imminent [ˈɪmɪnənt] *adj* bevorstehend

immobile [ɪˈməubaɪl] *adj* unbeweglich; **immobilize** [ɪˈməubɪlaɪz] *vt* lähmen

immoral [ɪˈmɒrl] *adj* unmoralisch; **~ity** [ɪmɔˈrælɪtɪ] *n* Unsittlichkeit *f*

immortal [ɪˈmɔːtl] *adj* unsterblich

immune [ɪˈmjuːn] *adj* (*secure*) sicher; (*MED*) immun; **~ from** sicher vor +*dat*; **immunity** *n* (*MED, JUR*) Immunität *f*; (*fig*) Freiheit *f*; **immunize** [ˈɪmjunaɪz] *vt* immunisieren

impact [ˈɪmpækt] *n* Aufprall *m*; (*fig*) Wirkung *f*

impair [ɪmˈpeəʳ] *vt* beeinträchtigen

impart [ɪmˈpɑːt] *vt* mitteilen; (*knowledge*) vermitteln; (*exude*) abgeben

impartial [ɪmˈpɑːʃl] *adj* unparteiisch

impassable [ɪmˈpɑːsəbl] *adj* unpassierbar

impassive [ɪmˈpæsɪv] *adj* gelassen

impatience [ɪmˈpeɪʃəns] *n* Ungeduld *f*; **impatient** *adj* ungeduldig; **impatiently** *adv* ungeduldig

impeccable [ɪmˈpekəbl] *adj* tadellos

impede [ɪmˈpiːd] *vt* (be)hindern; **impediment** [ɪmˈpedɪmənt] *n* Hindernis *nt*; **speech impediment** Sprachfehler *m*

impending [ɪmˈpendɪŋ] *adj* bevorstehend

impenetrable [ɪmˈpenɪtrəbl] *adj* (*also fig*) undurchdringlich

imperative [ɪmˈperətɪv] *adj* (*necessary*) unbedingt erforderlich

imperceptible [ɪmpə'septɪbl] *adj* nicht wahrnehmbar

imperfect [ɪm'pɔːfɪkt] *adj* (*faulty*) fehlerhaft; **~ion** [ɪmpə'fekʃən] *n* Unvollkommenheit *f*; (*fault*) Fehler *m*

imperial [ɪm'pɪərɪəl] *adj* kaiserlich

impersonal [ɪm'pɜːsənl] *adj* unpersönlich

impersonate [ɪm'pɜːsəneɪt] *vt* sich ausgeben als; (*for fun*) imitieren

impertinent [ɪm'pɜːtɪnənt] *adj* unverschämt, frech

impervious [ɪm'pɜːvɪəs] *adj* (*fig*): ~ **(to)** unempfänglich (für)

impetuous [ɪm'petjʊəs] *adj* ungestüm

impetus ['ɪmpətəs] *n* Triebkraft *f*; (*fig*) Auftrieb *m*

impinge [ɪm'pɪndʒ]: **~ on** *vt* beeinträchtigen

implacable [ɪm'plækəbl] *adj* unerbittlich

implement [*n* 'ɪmplɪmənt, *vb* 'ɪmplɪment] *n* Werkzeug *nt* ♦ *vt* ausführen

implicate ['ɪmplɪkeɪt] *vt* verwickeln; **implication** [ɪmplɪ'keɪʃən] *n* (*effect*) Auswirkung *f*; (*in crime*) Verwicklung *f*

implicit [ɪm'plɪsɪt] *adj* (*suggested*) unausgesprochen; (*utter*) vorbehaltlos

implore [ɪm'plɔː*r*] *vt* anflehen

imply [ɪm'plaɪ] *vt* (*hint*) andeuten; (*be evidence for*) schließen lassen auf +*acc*

impolite [ɪmpə'laɪt] *adj* unhöflich

import [*vb* ɪm'pɔːt, *n* 'ɪmpɔːt] *vt* einführen ♦ *n* Einfuhr *f*; (*meaning*) Bedeutung *f*

importance [ɪm'pɔːtns] *n* Bedeutung *f*

important [ɪm'pɔːtənt] *adj* wichtig; **it's not ~** es ist unwichtig

importer [ɪm'pɔːtə*r*] *n* Importeur *m*

impose [ɪm'pəʊz] *vt, vi*: **to ~ (on)** auferlegen (+*dat*); (*penalty, sanctions*) verhängen (gegen); **to ~ (o.s.) on sb** sich jdm aufdrängen

imposing [ɪm'pəʊzɪŋ] *adj* eindrucksvoll

imposition [ɪmpə'zɪʃən] *n* (*of burden, fine*) Auferlegung *f*; **to be an ~** (*on person*) eine Zumutung sein

impossible [ɪm'pɒsɪbl] *adj* unmöglich

impostor [ɪm'pɒstə*r*] *n* Hochstapler *m*

impotent ['ɪmpətnt] *adj* machtlos; (*sexually*) impotent

impound [ɪm'paʊnd] *vt* beschlagnahmen

impoverished [ɪm'pɒvərɪʃt] *adj* verarmt

impracticable [ɪm'præktɪkəbl] *adj* undurchführbar

impractical [ɪm'præktɪkl] *adj* unpraktisch

imprecise [ɪmprɪ'saɪs] *adj* ungenau

impregnable [ɪm'pregnəbl] *adj* (*castle*) uneinnehmbar

impregnate ['ɪmpregneɪt] *vt* (*saturate*) sättigen; (*fertilize*) befruchten

impress [ɪm'pres] *vt* (*influence*) beeindrucken; (*imprint*) (auf)drücken; **to ~ sth on sb** jdm etw einschärfen; **~ed** *adj* beeindruckt; **~ion** [ɪm'preʃən] *n* Eindruck *m*; (*on wax, footprint*) Abdruck *m*; (*of book*) Auflage *f*; (*take-off*) Nachahmung *f*; **I was under the ~ion** ich hatte den Eindruck; **~ionable** *adj* leicht zu beeindrucken; **~ive** *adj* eindrucksvoll

imprint ['ɪmprɪnt] *n* Abdruck *m*

imprison [ɪm'prɪzn] *vt* ins Gefängnis schicken; **~ment** *n* Inhaftierung *f*

improbable [ɪm'prɒbəbl] *adj* unwahrscheinlich

impromptu [ɪm'prɒmptjuː] *adj, adv* aus dem Stegreif, improvisiert

improper [ɪm'prɒpə*r*] *adj* (*indecent*) unanständig; (*unsuitable*) unpassend

improve [ɪm'pruːv] *vt* verbessern ♦ *vi* besser werden; **~ment** *n* (Ver)besserung *f*

improvise ['ɪmprəvaɪz] *vt, vi* improvisieren

imprudent [ɪm'pruːdnt] *adj* unklug

impudent ['ɪmpjudnt] *adj* unverschämt

impulse ['ɪmpʌls] *n* Impuls *m*; **to act on ~** spontan handeln; **impulsive** [ɪm'pʌlsɪv] *adj* impulsiv

impure [ɪm'pjʊə*r*] *adj* (*dirty*) verunreinigt; (*bad*) unsauber; **impurity** [ɪm'pjʊərɪti] *n* Unreinheit *f*; (*TECH*) Verunreinigung *f*

KEYWORD
---

in [ɪn] *prep* **1** (*indicating place, position*) in +*dat*; (*with motion*) in +*acc*; **in here/there** hier/dort; **in London** in London; **in the United States** in den Vereinigten Staaten **2** (*indicating time: during*) in +*dat*; **in summer** im Sommer; **in 1988** (im Jahre)

1988; **in the afternoon** nachmittags, am Nachmittag

3 (*indicating time: in the space of*) innerhalb von; **I'll see you in 2 weeks** *or* **in 2 weeks' time** ich sehe Sie in zwei Wochen

4 (*indicating manner, circumstances, state etc*) in +*dat*; **in the sun/rain** in der Sonne/im Regen; **in English/French** auf Englisch/Französisch; **in a loud/soft voice** mit lauter/leiser Stimme

5 (*with ratios, numbers*): **1 in 10** jeder Zehnte; **20 pence in the pound** 20 Pence pro Pfund; **they lined up in twos** sie stellten sich in Zweierreihe auf

6 (*referring to people, works*): **the disease is common in children** die Krankheit ist bei Kindern häufig; **in Dickens** bei Dickens; **we have a loyal friend in him** er ist uns ein treuer Freund

7 (*indicating profession etc*): **to be in teaching/the army** Lehrer(in)/beim Militär sein; **to be in publishing** im Verlagswesen arbeiten

8 (*with present participle*): **in saying this, I ...** wenn ich das sage, ... ich; **in accepting this view, he ...** weil er diese Meinung akzeptierte, ... er

♦ *adv*: **to be in** (*person: at home, work*) da sein; (*train, ship, plane*) angekommen sein; (*in fashion*) in sein; **to ask sb in** jdn hereinbitten; **to run/limp** *etc* **in** hereingerannt/gehumpelt *etc* kommen

♦ *n*: **the ins and outs** (*of proposal, situation etc*) die Feinheiten

in. *abbr* = **inch**

inability [ɪnəˈbɪlɪtɪ] *n* Unfähigkeit *f*

inaccessible [ɪnəkˈsesɪbl] *adj* unzugänglich

inaccurate [ɪnˈækjurət] *adj* ungenau; (*wrong*) unrichtig

inactivity [ɪnækˈtɪvɪtɪ] *n* Untätigkeit *f*

inadequate [ɪnˈædɪkwət] *adj* unzulänglich

inadvertently [ɪnədˈvɜːtntlɪ] *adv* unabsichtlich

inadvisable [ɪnədˈvaɪzəbl] *adj* nicht ratsam

inane [ɪˈneɪn] *adj* dumm, albern

inanimate [ɪnˈænɪmət] *adj* leblos

inappropriate [ɪnəˈprəuprɪət] *adj* (*clothing*) ungeeignet; (*remark*) unangebracht

inarticulate [ɪnɑːˈtɪkjulət] *adj* unklar

inasmuch as [ɪnəzˈmʌtʃ-] *adv* da; (*in so far as*) so weit

inaudible [ɪnˈɔːdɪbl] *adj* unhörbar

inauguration [ɪnɔːgjuˈreɪʃən] *n* Eröffnung *f*; (*feierliche*) Amtseinführung *f*

inborn [ɪnˈbɔːn] *adj* angeboren

inbred [ɪnˈbred] *adj* angeboren

Inc. *abbr* = **incorporated**

incalculable [ɪnˈkælkjuləbl] *adj* (*consequences*) unabsehbar

incapable [ɪnˈkeɪpəbl] *adj*: ~ **(of doing sth)** unfähig(, etw zu tun)

incapacitate [ɪnkəˈpæsɪteɪt] *vt* untauglich machen

incapacity [ɪnkəˈpæsɪtɪ] *n* Unfähigkeit *f*

incarcerate [ɪnˈkɑːsəreɪt] *vt* einkerkern

incarnation [ɪnkɑːˈneɪʃən] *n* (*ECCL*) Menschwerdung *f*; (*fig*) Inbegriff *m*

incendiary [ɪnˈsendɪərɪ] *adj* Brand-

incense [*n* ˈɪnsens, *vb* ɪnˈsens] *n* Weihrauch *m* ♦ *vt* erzürnen

incentive [ɪnˈsentɪv] *n* Anreiz *m*

incessant [ɪnˈsesnt] *adj* unaufhörlich

incest [ˈɪnsest] *n* Inzest *m*

inch [ɪntʃ] *n* Zoll *m* ♦ *vi*: **to ~ forward** sich Stückchen für Stückchen vorwärts bewegen; **to be within an ~ of** kurz davor sein; **he didn't give an ~** er gab keinen Zentimeter nach

incidence [ˈɪnsɪdns] *n* Auftreten *nt*; (*of crime*) Quote *f*

incident [ˈɪnsɪdnt] *n* Vorfall *m*; (*disturbance*) Zwischenfall *m*

incidental [ɪnsɪˈdentl] *adj* (*music*) Begleit-; (*unimportant*) nebensächlich; (*remark*) beiläufig; **~ly** *adv* übrigens

incinerator [ɪnˈsɪnəreɪtə*] *n* Verbrennungsofen *m*

incision [ɪnˈsɪʒən] *n* Einschnitt *m*

incisive [ɪnˈsaɪsɪv] *adj* (*style*) treffend; (*person*) scharfsinnig

incite [ɪnˈsaɪt] *vt* anstacheln

inclination [ɪnklɪˈneɪʃən] *n* Neigung *f*

incline [*n* ˈɪnklaɪn, *vb* ɪnˈklaɪn] *n* Abhang *m*

♦ *vt* neigen; *(fig)* veranlassen ♦ *vi* sich neigen; **to be ~d to do sth** dazu neigen, etw zu tun

include [ɪnˈkluːd] *vt* einschließen; *(on list, in group)* aufnehmen; **including** *prep*: **including X X** inbegriffen; **inclusion** [ɪnˈkluːʒən] *n* Aufnahme *f*; **inclusive** [ɪnˈkluːsɪv] *adj* einschließlich; *(COMM)* inklusive; **inclusive of** einschließlich +*gen*

incoherent [ɪnkəʊˈhɪərənt] *adj* zusammenhanglos

income [ˈɪnkʌm] *n* Einkommen *nt*; *(from business)* Einkünfte *pl*; **~ tax** *n* Lohnsteuer *f*; *(of self-employed)* Einkommenssteuer *f*

incoming [ˈɪnkʌmɪŋ] *adj*: **~ flight** eintreffende Maschine *f*

incomparable [ɪnˈkɒmpərəbl] *adj* unvergleichlich

incompatible [ɪnkəmˈpætɪbl] *adj* unvereinbar; *(people)* unverträglich

incompetence [ɪnˈkɒmpɪtəns] *n* Unfähigkeit *f*; **incompetent** *adj* unfähig

incomplete [ɪnkəmˈpliːt] *adj* unvollständig

incomprehensible [ɪnkɒmprɪˈhensɪbl] *adj* unverständlich

inconceivable [ɪnkənˈsiːvəbl] *adj* unvorstellbar

incongruous [ɪnˈkɒŋgruəs] *adj* seltsam; *(remark)* unangebracht

inconsiderate [ɪnkənˈsɪdərət] *adj* rücksichtslos

inconsistency [ɪnkənˈsɪstənsɪ] *n* Widersprüchlichkeit *f*; *(state)* Unbeständigkeit *f*

inconsistent [ɪnkənˈsɪstnt] *adj* *(action, speech)* widersprüchlich; *(person, work)* unbeständig; **~ with** nicht übereinstimmend mit

inconspicuous [ɪnkənˈspɪkjuəs] *adj* unauffällig

incontinent [ɪnˈkɒntɪnənt] *adj* *(MED)* nicht fähig, Stuhl und Harn zurückzuhalten

inconvenience [ɪnkənˈviːnjəns] *n* Unbequemlichkeit *f*; *(trouble to others)* Unannehmlichkeiten *pl*

inconvenient [ɪnkənˈviːnjənt] *adj* ungelegen; *(journey)* unbequem

incorporate [ɪnˈkɔːpəreɪt] *vt* *(include)* aufnehmen; *(contain)* enthalten; **~d** *adj*: **~d company** *(US)* eingetragene Aktiengesellschaft *f*

incorrect [ɪnkəˈrekt] *adj* unrichtig

incorrigible [ɪnˈkɒrɪdʒɪbl] *adj* unverbesserlich

incorruptible [ɪnkəˈrʌptɪbl] *adj* unzerstörbar; *(person)* unbestechlich

increase [*n* ˈɪnkriːs, *vb* ɪnˈkriːs] *n* Zunahme *f*; *(pay ~)* Gehaltserhöhung *f*; *(in size)* Vergrößerung *f* ♦ *vt* erhöhen; *(wealth, rage)* vermehren; *(business)* erweitern ♦ *vi* zunehmen; *(prices)* steigen; *(in size)* größer werden; *(in number)* sich vermehren; **increasing** *adj* *(number)* steigend; **increasingly** [ɪnˈkriːsɪŋlɪ] *adv* zunehmend

incredible [ɪnˈkredɪbl] *adj* unglaublich

incredulous [ɪnˈkredjuləs] *adj* ungläubig

increment [ˈɪnkrɪmənt] *n* Zulage *f*

incriminate [ɪnˈkrɪmɪneɪt] *vt* belasten

incubation [ɪnkjuˈbeɪʃən] *n* Ausbrüten *nt*

incubator [ˈɪnkjubeɪtə*r*] *n* Brutkasten *m*

incumbent [ɪnˈkʌmbənt] *n* ♦ *adj*: **it is ~ on him to ...** es obliegt ihm, ...

incur [ɪnˈkɜː*r*] *vt* sich zuziehen; *(debts)* machen

incurable [ɪnˈkjuərəbl] *adj* unheilbar

indebted [ɪnˈdetɪd] *adj* *(obliged)*: **~ (to sb)** (jdm) verpflichtet

indecent [ɪnˈdiːsnt] *adj* unanständig; **~ assault** *(BRIT)* *n* Notzucht *f*; **~ exposure** *n* Exhibitionismus *m*

indecisive [ɪndɪˈsaɪsɪv] *adj* *(battle)* nicht entscheidend; *(person)* unentschlossen

indeed [ɪnˈdiːd] *adv* tatsächlich, in der Tat; **yes ~!** allerdings!

indefinite [ɪnˈdefɪnɪt] *adj* unbestimmt; **~ly** *adv* auf unbestimmte Zeit; *(wait)* unbegrenzt lange

indelible [ɪnˈdelɪbl] *adj* unauslöschlich

indemnity [ɪnˈdemnɪtɪ] *n* *(insurance)* Versicherung *f*; *(compensation)* Entschädigung *f*

independence [ɪndɪˈpendns] *n* Unabhängigkeit *f*; **independent** *adj* unabhängig

---

i **Independence Day** (*der 4. Juli*) *ist in den USA ein gesetzlicher Feiertag zum Gedenken an die Unabhängigkeitserklärung am 4. Juli 1776, mit der die 13 amerikanischen Kolonien ihre Freiheit und Unabhängigkeit von Großbritannien erklärten.*

indestructible [ɪndɪsˈtrʌktəbl] *adj* unzerstörbar

indeterminate [ɪndɪˈtɜːmɪnɪt] *adj* unbestimmt

index [ˈɪndeks] (*pl* **~es** *or* **indices**) *n* Index *m*; **~ card** *n* Karteikarte *f*; **~ finger** *n* Zeigefinger *m*; **~-linked** (*US* **~ed**) *adj* (*salaries*) der Inflationsrate *dat* angeglichen; (*pensions*) dynamisch

India [ˈɪndɪə] *n* Indien *nt*; **~n** *adj* indisch ♦ *n* Inder(in) *m(f)*; **American ~n** Indianer(in) *m(f)*; **~n Ocean** *n*: **the ~n Ocean** der Indische Ozean

indicate [ˈɪndɪkeɪt] *vt* anzeigen; (*hint*) andeuten; **indication** [ɪndɪˈkeɪʃən] *n* Anzeichen *nt*; (*information*) Angabe *f*; **indicative** [ɪnˈdɪkətɪv] *adj*: **indicative of** bezeichnend für; **indicator** *n* (An)zeichen *nt*; (*AUT*) Richtungsanzeiger *m*

indict [ɪnˈdaɪt] *vt* anklagen; **~ment** *n* Anklage *f*

indifference [ɪnˈdɪfrəns] *n* Gleichgültigkeit *f*; Unwichtigkeit *f*; **indifferent** *adj* gleichgültig; (*mediocre*) mäßig

indigenous [ɪnˈdɪdʒɪnəs] *adj* einheimisch

indigestion [ɪndɪˈdʒestʃən] *n* Verdauungsstörung *f*

indignant [ɪnˈdɪgnənt] *adj*: **to be ~ about sth** über etw *acc* empört sein

indignation [ɪndɪgˈneɪʃən] *n* Entrüstung *f*

indignity [ɪnˈdɪgnɪtɪ] *n* Demütigung *f*

indirect [ɪndɪˈrekt] *adj* indirekt

indiscreet [ɪndɪsˈkriːt] *adj* (*insensitive*) taktlos; (*telling secrets*) indiskret; **indiscretion** [ɪndɪsˈkreʃən] *n* Taktlosigkeit *f*; Indiskretion *f*

indiscriminate [ɪndɪsˈkrɪmɪnət] *adj* wahllos;

kritiklos

indispensable [ɪndɪsˈpensəbl] *adj* unentbehrlich

indisposed [ɪndɪsˈpəuzd] *adj* unpässlich

indisputable [ɪndɪsˈpjuːtəbl] *adj* unbestreitbar; (*evidence*) unanfechtbar

indistinct [ɪndɪsˈtɪŋkt] *adj* undeutlich

individual [ɪndɪˈvɪdjuəl] *n* Individuum *nt* ♦ *adj* individuell; (*case*) Einzel-; (*of, for one person*) eigen, individuell; (*characteristic*) eigentümlich; **~ly** *adv* einzeln, individuell

indivisible [ɪndɪˈvɪzɪbl] *adj* unteilbar

indoctrinate [ɪnˈdɒktrɪneɪt] *vt* indoktrinieren

Indonesia [ɪndəˈniːzɪə] *n* Indonesien *nt*

indoor [ˈɪndɔː] *adj* Haus-; Zimmer-; Innen-; (*SPORT*) Hallen-; **~s** [ɪnˈdɔːz] *adv* drinnen, im Haus

induce [ɪnˈdjuːs] *vt* dazu bewegen; (*reaction*) herbeiführen

induction course [ɪnˈdʌkʃən-] (*BRIT*) *n* Einführungskurs *m*

indulge [ɪnˈdʌldʒ] *vt* (*give way*) nachgeben +*dat*; (*gratify*) frönen +*dat* ♦ *vi*: **to ~ (in)** frönen (+*dat*); **~nce** *n* Nachsicht *f*; (*enjoyment*) Genuss *m*; **~nt** *adj* nachsichtig; (*pej*) nachgiebig

industrial [ɪnˈdʌstrɪəl] *adj* Industrie-, industriell; (*dispute, injury*) Arbeits-; **~ action** *n* Arbeitskampfmaßnahmen *pl*; **~ estate** (*BRIT*) *n* Industriegebiet *nt*; **~ist** *n* Industrielle(r) *mf*; **~ize** *vt* industrialisieren; **~ park** (*US*) *n* Industriegebiet *nt*

industrious [ɪnˈdʌstrɪəs] *adj* fleißig

industry [ˈɪndəstrɪ] *n* Industrie *f*; (*diligence*) Fleiß *m*

inebriated [ɪˈniːbrɪeɪtɪd] *adj* betrunken

inedible [ɪnˈedɪbl] *adj* ungenießbar

ineffective [ɪnɪˈfektɪv] *adj* unwirksam; (*person*) untauglich

ineffectual [ɪnɪˈfektʃuəl] *adj* = **ineffective**

inefficiency [ɪnɪˈfɪʃənsɪ] *n* Ineffizienz *f*

inefficient [ɪnɪˈfɪʃənt] *adj* ineffizient; (*ineffective*) unwirksam

inept [ɪˈnept] *adj* (*remark*) unpassend; (*person*) ungeeignet

inequality [ɪnɪˈkwɒlɪtɪ] *n* Ungleichheit *f*

inert [ɪˈnɜːt] *adj* träge; (*CHEM*) inaktiv;

(*motionless*) unbeweglich

inescapable [ɪnɪ'skeɪpəbl] *adj* unvermeidbar

inevitable [ɪn'evɪtəbl] *adj* unvermeidlich;
inevitably *adv* zwangsläufig

inexcusable [ɪnɪks'kjuːzəbl] *adj*
unverzeihlich

inexhaustible [ɪnɪg'zɔːstɪbl] *adj*
unerschöpflich

inexpensive [ɪnɪk'spensɪv] *adj* preiswert

inexperience [ɪnɪk'spɪərɪəns] *n*
Unerfahrenheit *f*; **~d** *adj* unerfahren

inexplicable [ɪnɪk'splɪkəbl] *adj* unerklärlich

inextricably [ɪnɪk'strɪkəblɪ] *adv* untrennbar

infallible [ɪn'fælɪbl] *adj* unfehlbar

infamous ['ɪnfəməs] *adj* (*deed*) schändlich;
(*person*) niederträchtig

infancy ['ɪnfənsɪ] *n* frühe Kindheit *f*; (*fig*)
Anfangsstadium *nt*

infant ['ɪnfənt] *n* kleine(s) Kind *nt*, Säugling
m; **~ile** [-aɪl] *adj* kindisch, infantil; **~
school** (*BRIT*) *n* Vorschule *f*

infatuated [ɪn'fætjueɪtɪd] *adj* vernarrt; **to
become ~ with** sich vernarren in +*acc*,
infatuation [ɪnfætju'eɪʃən] *n*: **infatuation
(with)** Vernarrtheit *f* (in +*acc*)

infect [ɪn'fekt] *vt* anstecken (*also fig*); **~ed
with** (*illness*) infiziert mit; **~ion** [ɪn'fekʃən] *n*
Infektion *f*; **~ious** [ɪn'fekʃəs] *adj* ansteckend

infer [ɪn'fəː] *vt* schließen

inferior [ɪn'fɪərɪə'] *adj* (*rank*) untergeordnet;
(*quality*) minderwertig ♦ *n* Untergebene(r)
m; **~ity** [ɪnfɪərɪ'ɔrɪtɪ] *n* Minderwertigkeit *f*;
(*in rank*) untergeordnete Stellung *f*; **~ity
complex** *n* Minderwertigkeitskomplex *m*

infernal [ɪn'fɜːnl] *adj* höllisch

infertile [ɪn'fɜːtaɪl] *adj* unfruchtbar;
infertility [ɪnfəː'tɪlɪtɪ] *n* Unfruchtbarkeit *f*

infested [ɪn'festɪd] *adj*: **to be ~ with**
wimmeln von

infidelity [ɪnfɪ'delɪtɪ] *n* Untreue *f*

infighting ['ɪnfaɪtɪŋ] *n* Nahkampf *m*

infiltrate ['ɪnfɪltreɪt] *vt* infiltrieren, (*spies*)
einschleusen ♦ *vi* (*MIL, liquid*) einsickern;
(*POL*): **to ~ (into)** unterwandern (+*acc*)

infinite ['ɪnfɪnɪt] *adj* unendlich

infinitive [ɪn'fɪnɪtɪv] *n* Infinitiv *m*

infinity [ɪn'fɪnɪtɪ] *n* Unendlichkeit *f*

infirm [ɪn'fɜːm] *adj* gebrechlich; **~ary** *n*
Krankenhaus *nt*

inflamed [ɪn'fleɪmd] *adj* entzündet

inflammable [ɪn'flæməbl] (*BRIT*) *adj*
feuergefährlich

inflammation [ɪnflə'meɪʃən] *n* Entzündung *f*

inflatable [ɪn'fleɪtəbl] *adj* aufblasbar

inflate [ɪn'fleɪt] *vt* aufblasen; (*tyre*)
aufpumpen; (*prices*) hoch treiben; **inflation**
[ɪn'fleɪʃən] *n* Inflation *f*; **inflationary**
[ɪn'fleɪʃənərɪ] *adj* (*increase*) inflationistisch;
(*situation*) inflationär

inflexible [ɪn'fleksɪbl] *adj* (*person*) nicht
flexibel; (*opinion*) starr; (*thing*) unbiegsam

inflict [ɪn'flɪkt] *vt*: **to ~ sth on sb** jdm etw
zufügen; (*wound*) jdm etw beibringen

influence ['ɪnfluəns] *n* Einfluss *m* ♦ *vt*
beeinflussen

influential [ɪnflu'enʃl] *adj* einflussreich

influenza [ɪnflu'enzə] *n* Grippe *f*

influx ['ɪnflʌks] *n* (*of people*) Zustrom *m*; (*of
ideas*) Eindringen *nt*

infomercial ['ɪnfəumɜːʃl] *n*
Werbeinformationssendung *f*

inform [ɪn'fɔːm] *vt* informieren ♦ *vi*: **to ~ on
sb** jdn denunzieren; **to keep sb ~ed** jdn
auf dem Laufenden halten

informal [ɪn'fɔːml] *adj* zwanglos; **~ity**
[ɪnfɔː'mælɪtɪ] *n* Ungezwungenheit *f*

informant [ɪn'fɔːmənt] *n* Informant(in) *m(f)*

information [ɪnfə'meɪʃən] *n* Auskunft *f*,
Information *f*; **a piece of ~** eine Auskunft,
eine Information; **~ desk** *n*
Auskunftsschalter *m*; **~ office** *n*
Informationsbüro *nt*

informative [ɪn'fɔːmətɪv] *adj* informativ;
(*person*) mitteilsam

informer [ɪn'fɔːmə'] *n* Denunziant(in) *m(f)*

infra-red [ɪnfrə'red] *adj* infrarot

infrequent [ɪn'friːkwənt] *adj* selten

infringe [ɪn'frɪndʒ] *vt* (*law*) verstoßen gegen;
~ upon *vt* verletzen; **~ment** *n* Verstoß *m*,
Verletzung *f*

infuriating [ɪn'fjuərɪeɪtɪŋ] *adj* ärgerlich

ingenuity [ɪndʒɪ'njuːɪtɪ] *n* Genialität *f*

ingenuous [ɪn'dʒenjuəs] *adj* aufrichtig;
(*naive*) naiv

ingot ['ɪŋgət] *n* Barren *m*

ingrained [ɪn'greɪnd] *adj* tief sitzend

ingratiate [ɪn'greɪʃɪeɪt] *vt*: **to ~ o.s. with sb** sich bei jdm einschmeicheln

ingratitude [ɪn'grætɪtjuːd] *n* Undankbarkeit *f*

ingredient [ɪn'griːdɪənt] *n* Bestandteil *m*; (*COOK*) Zutat *f*

inhabit [ɪn'hæbɪt] *vt* bewohnen; **~ant** *n* Bewohner(in) *m(f)*; (*of island, town*) Einwohner(in) *m(f)*

inhale [ɪn'heɪl] *vt* einatmen; (*MED, cigarettes*) inhalieren

inherent [ɪn'hɪərənt] *adj*: **~ (in)** innewohnend (+*dat*)

inherit [ɪn'herɪt] *vt* erben; **~ance** *n* Erbe *nt*, Erbschaft *f*

inhibit [ɪn'hɪbɪt] *vt* hemmen; **to ~ sb from doing sth** jdn daran hindern, etw zu tun; **~ion** [ɪnhɪ'bɪʃən] *n* Hemmung *f*

inhospitable [ɪnhɔs'pɪtəbl] *adj* (*person*) ungastlich; (*country*) unwirtlich

inhuman [ɪn'hjuːmən] *adj* unmenschlich

initial [ɪ'nɪʃl] *adj* anfänglich, Anfangs- ♦ *n* Initiale *f* ♦ *vt* abzeichnen; (*POL*) paraphieren; **~ly** *adv* anfangs

initiate [ɪ'nɪʃɪeɪt] *vt* einführen; (*negotiations*) einleiten; **to ~ proceedings against sb** (*JUR*) gerichtliche Schritte gegen jdn einleiten; **initiation** [ɪnɪʃɪ'eɪʃən] *n* Einführung *f*; Einleitung *f*

initiative [ɪ'nɪʃətɪv] *n* Initiative *f*

inject [ɪn'dʒɛkt] *vt* einspritzen; (*fig*) einflößen; **~ion** [ɪn'dʒɛkʃən] *n* Spritze *f*

injunction [ɪn'dʒʌŋkʃən] *n* Verfügung *f*

injure [ɪn'dʒə*r*] *vt* verletzen; **~d** *adj* (*person, arm*) verletzt; **injury** ['ɪndʒərɪ] *n* Verletzung *f*; **to play injury time** (*SPORT*) nachspielen

injustice [ɪn'dʒʌstɪs] *n* Ungerechtigkeit *f*

ink [ɪŋk] *n* Tinte *f*

inkling ['ɪŋklɪŋ] *n* (dunkle) Ahnung *f*

inlaid [ɪn'leɪd] *adj* eingelegt, Einlege-

inland [*adj* 'ɪnlənd, *adv* ɪn'lænd] *adj* Binnen-; (*domestic*) Inlands- ♦ *adv* landeinwärts; **~ revenue** (*BRIT*) *n* Fiskus *m*

in-laws ['ɪnlɔːz] *npl* (*parents-in-law*) Schwiegereltern *pl*; (*others*) angeheiratete Verwandte *pl*

inlet ['ɪnlɛt] *n* Einlass *m*; (*bay*) kleine Bucht *f*

inmate ['ɪnmeɪt] *n* Insasse *m*

inn [ɪn] *n* Gasthaus *nt*, Wirtshaus *nt*

innate [ɪ'neɪt] *adj* angeboren

inner ['ɪnə*r*] *adj* inner, Innen-; (*fig*) verborgen; **~ city** *n* Innenstadt *f*; **~ tube** *n* (*of tyre*) Schlauch *m*

innings ['ɪnɪŋz] *n* (*CRICKET*) Innenrunde *f*

innocence ['ɪnəsns] *n* Unschuld *f*; (*ignorance*) Unkenntnis *f*

innocent ['ɪnəsnt] *adj* unschuldig

innocuous [ɪ'nɔkjuəs] *adj* harmlos

innovation [ɪnəu'veɪʃən] *n* Neuerung *f*

innuendo [ɪnju'ɛndəu] *n* (versteckte) Anspielung *f*

innumerable [ɪ'njuːmrəbl] *adj* unzählig

inoculation [ɪnɔkju'leɪʃən] *n* Impfung *f*

inopportune [ɪn'ɔpətjuːn] *adj* (*remark*) unangebracht; (*visit*) ungelegen

inordinately [ɪ'nɔːdɪnətlɪ] *adv* unmäßig

inpatient ['ɪnpeɪʃənt] *n* stationäre(r) Patient *m*/stationäre Patientin *f*

input ['ɪnput] *n* (*COMPUT*) Eingabe *f*; (*power ~*) Energiezufuhr *f*; (*of energy, work*) Aufwand *m*

inquest ['ɪnkwɛst] *n* gerichtliche Untersuchung *f*

inquire [ɪn'kwaɪə*r*] *vi* sich erkundigen ♦ *vt* (*price*) sich erkundigen nach; **~ into** *vt* untersuchen; **inquiry** [ɪn'kwaɪərɪ] *n* (*question*) Erkundigung *f*; (*investigation*) Untersuchung *f*; **inquiries** [ɪn'kwaɪərɪz] *n* Auskunft *f*; **inquiry office** (*BRIT*) *n* Auskunft(sbüro *nt*) *f*

inquisitive [ɪn'kwɪzɪtɪv] *adj* neugierig

ins. *abbr* = **inches**

insane [ɪn'seɪn] *adj* wahnsinnig; (*MED*) geisteskrank; **insanity** [ɪn'sænɪtɪ] *n* Wahnsinn *m*

insatiable [ɪn'seɪʃəbl] *adj* unersättlich

inscribe [ɪn'skraɪb] *vt* eingravieren; **inscription** [ɪn'skrɪpʃən] *n* (*on stone*) Inschrift *f*; (*in book*) Widmung *f*

insect ['ɪnsɛkt] *n* Insekt *nt*; **~icide** [ɪn'sɛktɪsaɪd] *n* Insektenvertilgungsmittel *nt*; **~ repellent** *n* Insektenbekämpfungsmittel *nt*

insecure [ɪnsɪ'kjuə*r*] *adj* (*person*) unsicher;

(thing) nicht fest *or* sicher; **insecurity** [ɪnsɪ'kjʊərɪtɪ] *n* Unsicherheit *f*

insemination [ɪnsemɪ'neɪʃən] *n*: **artificial ~** künstliche Befruchtung *f*

insensible [ɪn'sensɪbl] *adj (unconscious)* bewusstlos

insensitive [ɪn'sensɪtɪv] *adj (to pain)* unempfindlich; *(unfeeling)* gefühllos

inseparable [ɪn'sep(ə)rəbl] *adj (people)* unzertrennlich; *(word)* untrennbar

insert [*vb* ɪn'sɜːt, *n* 'ɪnsɜːt] *vt* einfügen; *(coin)* einwerfen; *(stick into)* hineinstecken; *(advertisement)* aufgeben ♦ *n (in book)* Einlage *f*; *(in magazine)* Beilage *f*; **~ion** [ɪn'sɜːʃən] *n* Einfügung *f*; *(PRESS)* Inserat *nt*

in-service ['ɪnsɜːvɪs] *adj (training)* berufsbegleitend

inshore ['ɪn'ʃɔːr] *adj* Küsten- ♦ *adv* an der Küste

inside ['ɪn'saɪd] *n* Innenseite *f*, Innere(s) *nt* ♦ *adj* innere(r, s), Innen- ♦ *adv (place)* innen; *(direction)* nach innen, hinein ♦ *prep (place)* in +*dat*; *(direction)* in +*acc* ... hinein; *(time)* innerhalb +*gen*; **~s** *npl (inf)* Eingeweide *pl*; **~ 10 minutes** unter 10 Minuten; **~ information** *n* interne Informationen *pl*; **~ lane** *n (AUT: in Britain)* linke Spur; **~ out** *adv* linksherum; *(know)* in- und auswendig

insider dealing, insider trading [ɪn'saɪdər-] *n (STOCK EXCHANGE)* Insiderhandel *m*

insidious [ɪn'sɪdɪəs] *adj* heimtückisch

insight ['ɪnsaɪt] *n* Einsicht *f*; **~ into** Einblick *m* in +*acc*

insignificant [ɪnsɪg'nɪfɪknt] *adj* unbedeutend

insincere [ɪnsɪn'sɪər] *adj* unaufrichtig

insinuate [ɪn'sɪnjʊeɪt] *vt (hint)* andeuten

insipid [ɪn'sɪpɪd] *adj* fad(e)

insist [ɪn'sɪst] *vi*: **to ~ (on)** bestehen (auf +*acc*); **~ence** *n* Bestehen *nt*; **~ent** *adj* hartnäckig; *(urgent)* dringend

insole ['ɪnsəʊl] *n* Einlegesohle *f*

insolence ['ɪnsələns] *n* Frechheit *f*

insolent ['ɪnsələnt] *adj* frech

insoluble [ɪn'sɒljʊbl] *adj* unlösbar; *(CHEM)* unlöslich

insolvent [ɪn'sɒlvənt] *adj* zahlungsunfähig

insomnia [ɪn'sɒmnɪə] *n* Schlaflosigkeit *f*

inspect [ɪn'spekt] *vt* prüfen; *(officially)* inspizieren; **~ion** [ɪn'spekʃən] *n* Inspektion *f*; **~or** *n (official)* Inspektor *m*; *(police)* Polizeikommissar *m*; *(BRIT: on buses, trains)* Kontrolleur *m*

inspiration [ɪnspə'reɪʃən] *n* Inspiration *f*

inspire [ɪn'spaɪər] *vt (person)* inspirieren; **to ~ sth in sb** *(respect)* jdm etw einflößen; *(hope)* etw in jdm wecken

instability [ɪnstə'bɪlɪtɪ] *n* Unbeständigkeit *f*, Labilität *f*

install [ɪn'stɔːl] *vt (put in)* installieren; *(telephone)* anschließen; *(establish)* einsetzen; **~ation** [ɪnstə'leɪʃən] *n (of person)* (Amts)einsetzung *f*; *(of machinery)* Installierung *f*; *(machines etc)* Anlage *f*

instalment [ɪn'stɔːlmənt] *(US* **installment)** *n* Rate *f*; *(of story)* Fortsetzung *f*; **to pay in ~s** in Raten zahlen

instance ['ɪnstəns] *n* Fall *m*; *(example)* Beispiel *nt*; **for ~** zum Beispiel; **in the first ~** zunächst

instant ['ɪnstənt] *n* Augenblick *m* ♦ *adj* augenblicklich, sofortig; **~aneous** [ɪnstən'teɪnɪəs] *adj* unmittelbar; **~ coffee** *n* Pulverkaffee *m*; **~ly** *adv* sofort

instead [ɪn'sted] *adv* stattdessen; **~ of** *prep* anstatt +*gen*

instep ['ɪnstep] *n* Spann *m*; *(of shoe)* Blatt *nt*

instil [ɪn'stɪl] *vt (fig)*: **to ~ sth in sb** jdm etw beibringen

instinct ['ɪnstɪŋkt] *n* Instinkt *m*; **~ive** [ɪn'stɪŋktɪv] *adj* instinktiv

institute ['ɪnstɪtjuːt] *n* Institut *nt* ♦ *vt* einführen; *(search)* einleiten

institution [ɪnstɪ'tjuːʃən] *n* Institution *f*; *(home)* Anstalt *f*

instruct [ɪn'strʌkt] *vt* anweisen; *(officially)* instruieren; **~ion** [ɪn'strʌkʃən] *n* Unterricht *m*; **~ions** *npl (orders)* Anweisungen *pl*; *(for use)* Gebrauchsanweisung *f*; **~or** *n* Lehrer *m*

instrument ['ɪnstrumənt] *n* Instrument *nt*; **~al** [ɪnstru'mentl] *adj (MUS)* Instrumental-;

(*helpful*): **~al (in)** behilflich (bei); **~ panel** n
Armaturenbrett
insubordinate [ɪnsəˈbɔːdənɪt] adj aufsässig,
widersetzlich
insufferable [ɪnˈsʌfrəbl] adj unerträglich
insufficient [ɪnsəˈfɪʃənt] adj ungenügend
insular [ˈɪnsjulə] adj (*fig*) engstirnig
insulate [ˈɪnsjuleɪt] vt (*ELEC*) isolieren; (*fig*):
to ~ (from) abschirmen (vor +*dat*);
insulating tape n Isolierband nt;
insulation [ɪnsjuˈleɪʃən] n Isolierung f
insulin [ˈɪnsjulɪn] n Insulin nt
insult [n ˈɪnsʌlt, vb ɪnˈsʌlt] n Beleidigung f
♦ vt beleidigen
insurance [ɪnˈʃuərəns] n Versicherung f;
fire/life ~ Feuer-/Lebensversicherung; **~
agent** n Versicherungsvertreter m; **~
policy** n Versicherungspolice f
insure [ɪnˈʃuə] vt versichern
intact [ɪnˈtækt] adj unversehrt
intake [ˈɪnteɪk] n (*place*) Einlassöffnung f;
(*act*) Aufnahme f; (*BRIT: SCH*): **an ~ of 200 a
year** ein Neuzugang von 200 im Jahr
intangible [ɪnˈtændʒɪbl] adj nicht greifbar
integral [ˈɪntɪɡrəl] adj (*essential*) wesentlich;
(*complete*) vollständig; (*MATH*) Integral-
integrate [ˈɪntɪɡreɪt] vt integrieren ♦ vi sich
integrieren
integrity [ɪnˈtɛɡrɪtɪ] n (*honesty*) Redlichkeit f,
Integrität f
intellect [ˈɪntəlɛkt] n Intellekt m; **~ual**
[ɪntəˈlɛktjuəl] adj geistig, intellektuell ♦ n
Intellektuelle(r) mf
intelligence [ɪnˈtɛlɪdʒəns] n (*understanding*)
Intelligenz f; (*news*) Information f; (*MIL*)
Geheimdienst m; **~ service** n
Nachrichtendienst m, Geheimdienst m
intelligent [ɪnˈtɛlɪdʒənt] adj intelligent; **~ly**
adv klug; (*write, speak*) verständlich
intelligentsia [ɪntɛlɪˈdʒɛntsɪə] n Intelligenz f
intelligible [ɪnˈtɛlɪdʒɪbl] adj verständlich
intend [ɪnˈtɛnd] vt beabsichtigen; **that was
~ed for you** das war für dich gedacht
intense [ɪnˈtɛns] adj stark, intensiv; (*person*)
ernsthaft; **~ly** adv äußerst; (*study*) intensiv
intensify [ɪnˈtɛnsɪfaɪ] vt verstärken,
intensivieren

intensity [ɪnˈtɛnsɪtɪ] n Intensität f
intensive [ɪnˈtɛnsɪv] adj intensiv; **~ care
unit** n Intensivstation f
intent [ɪnˈtɛnt] n Absicht f ♦ adj: **to be ~ on
doing sth** fest entschlossen sein, etw zu
tun; **to all ~s and purposes** praktisch
intention [ɪnˈtɛnʃən] n Absicht f; **~al** adj
absichtlich
intently [ɪnˈtɛntlɪ] adv konzentriert
interact [ɪntərˈækt] vi aufeinander einwirken;
~ion [ɪntərˈækʃən] n Wechselwirkung f;
~ive adj (*COMPUT*) interaktiv
intercept [ɪntəˈsɛpt] vt abfangen
interchange [n ˈɪntətʃeɪndʒ, vb ɪntəˈtʃeɪndʒ]
n (*exchange*) Austausch m; (*on roads*)
Verkehrskreuz n ♦ vt austauschen; **~able**
[ɪntəˈtʃeɪndʒəbl] adj austauschbar
intercom [ˈɪntəkɔm] n (Gegen)sprechanlage
f
intercourse [ˈɪntəkɔːs] n (*exchange*)
Beziehungen pl; (*sexual*) Geschlechtsverkehr
m
interest [ˈɪntrɪst] n Interesse nt; (*FIN*) Zinsen
pl; (*COMM: share*) Anteil m; (*group*)
Interessengruppe f ♦ vt interessieren; **~ed**
adj (*having claims*) beteiligt; (*attentive*)
interessiert; **to be ~ed in** sich interessieren
für; **~ing** adj interessant; **~ rate** n Zinssatz
m
interface [ˈɪntəfeɪs] n (*COMPUT*) Schnittstelle
f, Interface nt
interfere [ɪntəˈfɪə] vi: **to ~ (with)** (*meddle*)
sich einmischen (in +*acc*); (*disrupt*) stören
+*acc*; **~nce** [ɪntəˈfɪərəns] n Einmischung f;
(*TV*) Störung f
interim [ˈɪntərɪm] n: **in the ~** inzwischen
interior [ɪnˈtɪərɪə] n Innere(s) nt ♦ adj
innere(r, s), Innen-; **~ designer** n
Innenarchitekt(in) m(f)
interjection [ɪntəˈdʒɛkʃən] n Ausruf m
interlock [ɪntəˈlɔk] vi ineinander greifen
interlude [ˈɪntəluːd] n Pause f
intermediary [ɪntəˈmiːdɪərɪ] n Vermittler m
intermediate [ɪntəˈmiːdɪət] adj Zwischen-,
Mittel-
interminable [ɪnˈtəːmɪnəbl] adj endlos
intermission [ɪntəˈmɪʃən] n Pause f

intermittent[ɪntə'mɪtnt] *adj* periodisch, stoßweise

intern[*vb* ɪn'tɜːn, *n* 'ɪntɜːn] *vt* internieren ♦ *n* (*US*) Assistenzarzt *m*/-ärztin *f*

internal[ɪn'tɜːnl] *adj* (*inside*) innere(r, s); (*domestic*) Inlands-; **~ly**adv innen; (*MED*) innerlich; **"not to be taken ~ly"** „nur zur äußerlichen Anwendung"; **Internal Revenue Service**(*US*) *n* Finanzamt *nt*

international[ɪntə'næʃənl] *adj* international ♦ *n* (*SPORT*) Nationalspieler(in) *m(f)*; (: *match*) internationale(s) Spiel *nt*

Internet[ɪntənet] *n*: **the ~** das Internet; **~ café**n Internet-Café *nt*

interplay['ɪntəpleɪ] *n* Wechselspiel *nt*

interpret[ɪn'tɜːprɪt] *vt* (*explain*) auslegen, interpretieren; (*translate*) dolmetschen; **~er** *n* Dolmetscher(in) *m(f)*

interrelated[ɪntərɪ'leɪtɪd] *adj* untereinander zusammenhängend

interrogate[ɪn'terəgeɪt] *vt* verhören; **interrogation**[ɪnterə'geɪʃən] *n* Verhör *nt*

interrupt[ɪntə'rʌpt] *vt* unterbrechen; **~ion** [ɪntə'rʌpʃən] *n* Unterbrechung *f*

intersect[ɪntə'sekt] *vt* (*durch*)schneiden ♦ *vi* sich schneiden; **~ion**[ɪntə'sekʃən] *n* (*of roads*) Kreuzung *f*; (*of lines*) Schnittpunkt *m*

intersperse[ɪntə'spɜːs] *vt*: **to ~ sth with sth** etw mit etw durchsetzen

intertwine[ɪntə'twaɪn] *vt* verflechten ♦ *vi* sich verflechten

interval['ɪntəvl] *n* Abstand *m*; (*BRIT*: *THEAT*, *SPORT*) Pause *f*; **at ~s** in Abständen

intervene[ɪntə'viːn] *vi* dazwischenliegen; (*act*): **to ~ (in)** einschreiten (gegen); **intervention**[ɪntə'venʃən] *n* Eingreifen *nt*, Intervention *f*

interview['ɪntəvjuː] *n* (*PRESS etc*) Interview *nt*; (*for job*) Vorstellungsgespräch *nt* ♦ *vt* interviewen; **~er** *n* Interviewer *m*

intestine[ɪn'testɪn] *n*: **large/small ~** Dick-/ Dünndarm *m*

intimacy['ɪntɪməsɪ] *n* Intimität *f*

intimate[*adj* 'ɪntɪmət, *vb* 'ɪntɪmeɪt] *adj* (*inmost*) innerste(r, s); (*knowledge*) eingehend; (*familiar*) vertraut; (*friends*) eng ♦ *vt* andeuten

intimidate[ɪn'tɪmɪdeɪt] *vt* einschüchtern

into['ɪntu] *prep* (*motion*) in +*acc* ... hinein; **5 ~ 25** 25 durch 5

intolerable[ɪn'tɔlərəbl] *adj* unerträglich

intolerant[ɪn'tɔlərnt] *adj*: **~ of** unduldsam gegen(über)

intoxicate[ɪn'tɔksɪkeɪt] *vt* berauschen; **~d** *adj* betrunken; **intoxication**[ɪntɔksɪ'keɪʃən] *n* Rausch *m*

intractable[ɪn'træktəbl] *adj* schwer zu handhaben; (*problem*) schwer lösbar

intranet['ɪntrənet] *n* Intranet *nt*

intransitive[ɪn'trænsɪtɪv] *adj* intransitiv

intravenous[ɪntrə'viːnəs] *adj* intravenös

in-tray['ɪntreɪ] *n* Eingangskorb *m*

intrepid[ɪn'trepɪd] *adj* unerschrocken

intricate[ɪntrɪkət] *adj* kompliziert

intrigue[ɪn'triːg] *n* Intrige *f* ♦ *vt* faszinieren ♦ *vi* intrigieren

intrinsic[ɪn'trɪnsɪk] *adj* innere(r, s); (*difference*) wesentlich

introduce[ɪntrə'djuːs] *vt* (*person*) vorstellen; (*sth new*) einführen; (*subject*) anschneiden; **to ~ sb to sb** jdm jdn vorstellen; **to ~ sb to sth** jdn in etw *acc* einführen; **Introduction** [ɪntrə'dʌkʃən] *n* Einführung *f*; (*to book*) Einleitung *f*; **Introductory**[ɪntrə'dʌktərɪ] *adj* Einführungs-, Vor-

introspective[ɪntrəu'spektɪv] *adj* nach innen gekehrt

introvert['ɪntrəuvɜːt] *n* Introvertierte(r) *mf* ♦ *adj* introvertiert

intrude[ɪn'truːd] *vi*: **to ~ (on sb/sth)** (jdn/ etw) stören; **~r**n Eindringling *m*

intrusion[ɪn'truːʒən] *n* Störung *f*

intrusive[ɪn'truːsɪv] *adj* aufdringlich

intuition[ɪntjuː'ɪʃən] *n* Intuition *f*

inundate['ɪnʌndeɪt] *vt* überschwemmen

invade[ɪn'veɪd] *vt* einfallen in +*acc*; **~r**n Eindringling *m*

invalid[*¹*]['ɪnvəlɪd] *n* (*disabled*) Invalide *mf* ♦ *adj* (*ill*) krank; (*disabled*) invalide

invalid[*²*][ɪn'vælɪd] *adj* (*not valid*) ungültig

invaluable[ɪn'væljuəbl] *adj* unschätzbar

invariable[ɪn'veərɪəbl] *adj* unveränderlich; **invariably**adv ausnahmslos

invent[ɪn'vent] *vt* erfinden; **~ion**[ɪn'venʃən]

n Erfindung *f*; **~ive** *adj* erfinderisch; **~or** *n* Erfinder *m*

inventory ['ɪnvəntrɪ] *n* Inventar *nt*

inverse [ɪn'vɜːs] *n* Umkehrung *f* ♦ *adj* umgekehrt

invert [ɪn'vɜːt] *vt* umdrehen; **~ed commas** (*BRIT*) *npl* Anführungsstriche *pl*

invest [ɪn'vest] *vt* investieren

investigate [ɪn'vestɪgeɪt] *vt* untersuchen; **investigation** [ɪnvestɪ'geɪʃən] *n* Untersuchung *f*; **investigator** [ɪn'vestɪgeɪtə*] *n* Untersuchungsbeamte(r) *m*

investiture [ɪn'vestɪtʃə*] *n* Amtseinsetzung *f*

investment [ɪn'vestmənt] *n* Investition *f*

investor [ɪn'vestə*] *n* (Geld)anleger *m*

invigilate [ɪn'vɪdʒɪleɪt] *vi* (*in exam*) Aufsicht führen ♦ *vt* Aufsicht führen bei

invigorating [ɪn'vɪgəreɪtɪŋ] *adj* stärkend

invincible [ɪn'vɪnsɪbl] *adj* unbesiegbar

invisible [ɪn'vɪzɪbl] *adj* unsichtbar

invitation [ɪnvɪ'teɪʃən] *n* Einladung *f*

invite [ɪn'vaɪt] *vt* einladen

invoice ['ɪnvɔɪs] *n* Rechnung *f* ♦ *vt* (*goods*): **to ~ sb for sth** jdm etw *acc* in Rechnung stellen

invoke [ɪn'vəuk] *vt* anrufen

involuntary [ɪn'vɒləntrɪ] *adj* unabsichtlich

involve [ɪn'vɒlv] *vt* (*entangle*) verwickeln; (*entail*) mit sich bringen; **~d** *adj* verwickelt; **~ment** *n* Verwicklung *f*

inward ['ɪnwəd] *adj* innere(r, s); (*curve*) Innen- ♦ *adv* nach innen; **~ly** *adv* im Innern; **~s** *adv* nach innen

I/O *abbr* (*COMPUT*) (= *input/output*) I/O

iodine ['aɪəudiːn] *n* Jod *nt*

ioniser ['aɪənaɪzə*] *n* Ionisator *m*

iota [aɪ'əutə] *n* (*fig*) bisschen *nt*

IOU *n abbr* (= *I owe you*) Schuldschein *m*

IQ *n abbr* (= *intelligence quotient*) IQ *m*

IRA *n abbr* (= *Irish Republican Army*) IRA *f*

Iran [ɪ'rɑːn] *n* Iran *m*; **~ian** [ɪ'reɪnɪən] *adj* iranisch ♦ *n* Iraner(in) *m(f)*; (*LING*) Iranisch *nt*

Iraq [ɪ'rɑːk] *n* Irak *m*; **~i** *adj* irakisch ♦ *n* Iraker(in) *m(f)*

irate [aɪ'reɪt] *adj* zornig

Ireland ['aɪələnd] *n* Irland *nt*

iris ['aɪrɪs] (*pl* **~es**) *n* Iris *f*

Irish ['aɪrɪʃ] *adj* irisch ♦ *npl*: **the ~** die Iren *pl*, die Irländer *pl*; **~man** (*irreg*) *n* Ire *m*, Irländer *m*; **~ Sea** *n*: **the ~ Sea** die Irische See *f*; **~woman** (*irreg*) *n* Irin *f*, Irländerin *f*

irksome ['ɜːksəm] *adj* lästig

iron ['aɪən] *n* Eisen *nt*; (*for ~ing*) Bügeleisen *nt* ♦ *adj* eisern ♦ *vt* bügeln; **~ out** *vt* (*also fig*) ausbügeln; **Iron Curtain** *n* (*HIST*) Eiserne(r) Vorhang *m*

ironic(al) [aɪ'rɒnɪk(l)] *adj* ironisch; (*coincidence etc*) witzig

iron: ~ing *n* Bügeln *nt*; (*laundry*) Bügelwäsche *f*; **~ing board** *n* Bügelbrett *nt*; **~monger's (shop)** *n* Eisen- und Haushaltswarenhandlung *f*

irony ['aɪrənɪ] *n* Ironie *f*

irrational [ɪ'ræʃənl] *adj* irrational

irrefutable [ɪrɪ'fjuːtəbl] *adj* unwiderlegbar

irregular [ɪ'regjulə*] *adj* unregelmäßig; (*shape*) ungleich(mäßig); (*fig*) unüblich; (*: behaviour*) ungehörig

irrelevant [ɪ'reləvənt] *adj* belanglos, irrelevant

irreparable [ɪ'repərəbl] *adj* nicht wieder gutzumachen

irreplaceable [ɪrɪ'pleɪsəbl] *adj* unersetzlich

irresistible [ɪrɪ'zɪstɪbl] *adj* unwiderstehlich

irrespective [ɪrɪ'spektɪv]: **~ of** *prep* ungeachtet +*gen*

irresponsible [ɪrɪ'spɒnsɪbl] *adj* verantwortungslos

irreverent [ɪ'revərnt] *adj* respektlos

irrevocable [ɪ'revəkəbl] *adj* unwiderrufbar

irrigate ['ɪrɪgeɪt] *vt* bewässern

irritable ['ɪrɪtəbl] *adj* reizbar

irritate ['ɪrɪteɪt] *vt* irritieren, reizen (*also MED*); **irritating** *adj* ärgerlich, irritierend; **he is irritating** er kann einem auf die Nerven gehen; **irritation** [ɪrɪ'teɪʃən] *n* (*anger*) Ärger *m*; (*MED*) Reizung *f*

IRS *n abbr* = **Internal Revenue Service**

is [ɪz] *vb see* **be**

Islam ['ɪzlɑːm] *n* Islam *m*; **~ic** [ɪz'læmɪk] *adj* islamisch

island ['aɪlənd] n Insel f; **~er** n Inselbewohner(in) m(f)

isle [aɪl] n (kleine) Insel f

isn't ['ɪznt] = **is not**

isolate ['aɪsəleɪt] vt isolieren; **~d** adj isoliert; (case) Einzel-; **isolation** [aɪsə'leɪʃən] n Isolierung f

ISP n abbr (= Internet Service Provider) Internet-Anbieter m

Israel ['ɪzreɪl] n Israel nt; **~i** [ɪz'reɪlɪ] adj israelisch ♦ n Israeli mf

issue ['ɪʃjuː] n (matter) Frage f; (outcome) Ausgang m; (of newspaper, shares) Ausgabe f; (offspring) Nachkommenschaft f ♦ vt ausgeben; (warrant) erlassen; (documents) ausstellen; (orders) erteilen; (books) herausgeben; (verdict) aussprechen; **to be at ~** zur Debatte stehen; **to take ~ with sb over sth** jdm in etw dat widersprechen

---

KEYWORD

it [ɪt] pron **1** (specific: subject) er/sie/es; (: direct object) ihn/sie/es; (: indirect object) ihm/ihr/ihm; **about/from/in/of it** darüber/davon/darin/davon
2 (impers) es; **it's raining** es regnet; **it's Friday tomorrow** morgen ist Freitag; **who is it? – it's me** wer ist da? – ich (bin's)

Italian [ɪ'tæljən] adj italienisch ♦ n Italiener(in) m(f); (LING) Italienisch nt

italic [ɪ'tælɪk] adj kursiv; **~s** npl Kursivschrift f

Italy ['ɪtəlɪ] n Italien nt

itch [ɪtʃ] n Juckreiz m; (fig) Lust f ♦ vi jucken; **to be ~ing to do sth** darauf brennen, etw zu tun; **~y** adj juckend

it'd ['ɪtd] = **it would**; **it had**

item ['aɪtəm] n Gegenstand m; (on list) Posten m; (in programme) Nummer f; (in agenda) (Programm)punkt m; (in newspaper) (Zeitungs)notiz f; **~ize** vt verzeichnen

itinerant [ɪ'tɪnərənt] adj umherreisend

itinerary [aɪ'tɪnərərɪ] n Reiseroute f

it'll ['ɪtl] = **it will**; **it shall**

its [ɪts] adj (masculine, neuter) sein; (feminine) ihr

it's [ɪts] = **it is**; **it has**

itself [ɪt'sɛlf] pron sich (selbst); (emphatic) selbst

ITV (BRIT) n abbr = **Independent Television**

I.U.D. n abbr (= intra-uterine device) Pessar nt

I've [aɪv] = **I have**

ivory ['aɪvərɪ] n Elfenbein nt

ivy ['aɪvɪ] n Efeu nt

J, j

jab [dʒæb] vt (hinein)stechen ♦ n Stich m, Stoß m; (inf) Spritze f

jack [dʒæk] n (AUT) (Wagen)heber m; (CARDS) Bube m; **~ up** vt aufbocken

jackal ['dʒækl] n (ZOOL) Schakal m

jackdaw ['dʒækdɔː] n Dohle f

jacket ['dʒækɪt] n Jacke f; (of book) Schutzumschlag m; (TECH) Ummantelung f; **~ potatoes** npl in der Schale gebackene Kartoffeln pl

jackknife ['dʒæknaɪf] vi (truck) sich zusammenschieben

jack plug n (ELEC) Buchsenstecker m

jackpot ['dʒækpɔt] n Haupttreffer m

jaded ['dʒeɪdɪd] adj ermattet

jagged ['dʒægɪd] adj zackig

jail [dʒeɪl] n Gefängnis nt ♦ vt einsperren; **~er** n Gefängniswärter m

jam [dʒæm] n Marmelade f; (also: traffic ~) (Verkehrs)stau m; (inf: trouble) Klemme f ♦ vt (wedge) einklemmen; (cram) hineinzwängen; (obstruct) blockieren ♦ vi sich verklemmen; **to ~ sth into sth** etw in etw acc hineinstopfen

Jamaica [dʒə'meɪkə] n Jamaika nt

jam jar n Marmeladenglas nt

jammed [dʒæmd] adj: **it's ~** es klemmt

jam-packed [dʒæm'pækt] adj überfüllt, proppenvoll

jangle ['dʒæŋgl] vt, vi klimpern

janitor ['dʒænɪtər] n Hausmeister m

January ['dʒænjuərɪ] n Januar m

Japan [dʒə'pæn] n Japan nt; **~ese** [dʒæpə'niːz] adj japanisch ♦ n inv Japaner(in) m(f); (LING) Japanisch nt

jar [dʒɑːr] n Glas nt ♦ vi kreischen; (colours

etc) nicht harmonieren

jargon ['dʒɑːgən] *n* Fachsprache *f*, Jargon *m*

jaundice ['dʒɔːndɪs] *n* Gelbsucht *f*; **~d** *adj* (*fig*) missgünstig

jaunt [dʒɔːnt] *n* Spritztour *f*

javelin ['dʒævlɪn] *n* Speer *m*

jaw [dʒɔː] *n* Kiefer *m*

jay [dʒeɪ] *n* (*ZOOL*) Eichelhäher *m*

jaywalker ['dʒeɪwɔːkə*] *n* unvorsichtige(r) Fußgänger *m*

jazz [dʒæz] *n* Jazz *m*; **~ up** *vt* (*MUS*) verjazzen; (*enliven*) aufpolieren

jealous ['dʒeləs] *adj* (*envious*) missgünstig; (*husband*) eifersüchtig; **~y** *n* Missgunst *f*; Eifersucht *f*

jeans [dʒiːnz] *npl* Jeans *pl*

Jeep [dʒiːp] ® *n* Jeep *m* ®

jeer [dʒɪə*] *vi*: **to ~ (at sb)** (über jdn) höhnisch lachen, (jdn) verspotten

Jehovah's Witness [dʒɪˈheʊvəz-] *n* Zeuge *m*/Zeugin *f* Jehovas

jelly ['dʒelɪ] *n* Gelee *nt*; (*dessert*) Grütze *f*; **~fish** *n* Qualle *f*

jeopardize ['dʒepədaɪz] *vt* gefährden

jeopardy ['dʒepədɪ] *n*: **to be in jeopardy** in Gefahr sein

jerk [dʒɜːk] *n* Ruck *m*; (*inf: idiot*) Trottel *m* ♦ *vt* ruckartig bewegen ♦ *vi* sich ruckartig bewegen

jerky ['dʒɜːkɪ] *adj* (*movement*) ruckartig; (*ride*) rüttelnd

jersey ['dʒɜːzɪ] *n* Pullover *m*

jest [dʒest] *n* Scherz *m* ♦ *vi* spaßen; **in ~** im Spaß

Jesus ['dʒiːzəs] *n* Jesus *m*

jet [dʒet] *n* (*stream: of water etc*) Strahl *m*; (*spout*) Düse *f*; (*AVIAT*) Düsenflugzeug *nt*; **~-black** *adj* rabenschwarz; **~ engine** *n* Düsenmotor *m*; **~ lag** *n* Jetlag *m*

jettison ['dʒetɪsn] *vt* über Bord werfen

jetty ['dʒetɪ] *n* Landesteg *m*, Mole *f*

Jew [dʒuː] *n* Jude *m*

jewel ['dʒuːəl] *n* (*also fig*) Juwel *nt*; **~ler** (*US* **jeweler**) *n* Juwelier *m*; **~ler's (shop)** *n* Juwelier *m*; **~lery** (*US* **jewelry**) *n* Schmuck *m*

Jewess ['dʒuːɪs] *n* Jüdin *f*

Jewish ['dʒuːɪʃ] *adj* jüdisch

jibe [dʒaɪb] *n* spöttische Bemerkung *f*

jiffy ['dʒɪfɪ] (*inf*) *n*: **in a ~** sofort

jigsaw ['dʒɪgsɔː] *n* (*also:* **~ puzzle**) Puzzle(spiel) *nt*

jilt [dʒɪlt] *vt* den Laufpass geben +*dat*

jingle ['dʒɪŋgl] *n* (*advertisement*) Werbesong *m* ♦ *vi* klimpern; (*bells*) bimmeln ♦ *vt* klimpern mit; bimmeln lassen

jinx [dʒɪŋks] *n*: **there's a ~ on it** es ist verhext

jitters ['dʒɪtəz] (*inf*) *npl*: **to get the ~** einen Bammel kriegen

job [dʒɔb] *n* (*piece of work*) Arbeit *f*; (*position*) Stellung *f*; (*duty*) Aufgabe *f*; (*difficulty*) Mühe *f*; **it's a good ~ he ...** es ist ein Glück, dass er ...; **just the ~** genau das Richtige; **J~centre** (*BRIT*) *n* Arbeitsamt *nt*; **~less** *adj* arbeitslos

jockey ['dʒɔkɪ] *n* Jockei *m*, Jockey *m* ♦ *vi*: **to ~ for position** sich in eine gute Position drängeln

jocular ['dʒɔkjulə*] *adj* scherzhaft

jog [dʒɔg] *vt* (an)stoßen ♦ *vi* (*run*) joggen; **to ~ along** vor sich *acc* hinwursteln; (*work*) seinen Gang gehen; **~ging** *nt* Jogging *nt*

join [dʒɔɪn] *vt* (*club*) beitreten +*dat*; (*person*) sich anschließen +*dat*; (*fasten*) **to ~ (sth to sth)** (etw mit etw) verbinden ♦ *vi* (*unite*) sich vereinigen ♦ *n* Verbindungsstelle *f*, Naht *f*; **~ in** *vt, vi*: **to ~ in (sth)** (bei etw) mitmachen; **~ up** *vi* (*MIL*) zur Armee gehen

joiner ['dʒɔɪnə*] *n* Schreiner *m*; **~y** *n* Schreinerei *f*

joint [dʒɔɪnt] *n* (*TECH*) Fuge *f*; (*of bones*) Gelenk *nt*; (*of meat*) Braten *m*; (*inf: place*) Lokal *nt* ♦ *adj* gemeinsam; **~ account** *n* (*with bank etc*) gemeinsame(s) Konto *nt*; **~ly** *adv* gemeinsam

joke [dʒəʊk] *n* Witz *m* ♦ *vi* Witze machen; **to play a ~ on sb** jdm einen Streich spielen

joker [dʒəʊkə*] *n* Witzbold *m*; (*CARDS*) Joker *m*

jolly ['dʒɔlɪ] *adj* lustig ♦ *adv* (*inf*) ganz schön

jolt [dʒəʊlt] *n* (*shock*) Schock *m*; (*jerk*) Stoß *m*

♦ vt (*push*) stoßen; (*shake*) durchschütteln; (*fig*) aufrütteln ♦ vi holpern

Jordan ['dʒɔːdən] n Jordanien nt

jostle ['dʒɔsl] vt anrempeln

jot [dʒɔt] n: **not one ~** kein Jota nt; **~ down** vt notieren; **~ter** n (*BRIT*) Notizblock m

journal ['dʒɜːnl] n (*diary*) Tagebuch nt; (*magazine*) Zeitschrift f; **~ism** n Journalismus m; **~ist** n Journalist(in) m(f)

journey ['dʒɜːnɪ] n Reise f

jovial ['dʒəʊvɪəl] adj jovial

joy [dʒɔɪ] n Freude f; **~ful** adj freudig; **~ous** adj freudig; **~ ride** n Schwarzfahrt f; **~rider** n Autodieb, der den Wagen nur für eine Spritztour stiehlt; **~stick** n Steuerknüppel m; (*COMPUT*) Joystick m

J.P. n abbr = **Justice of the Peace**

Jr abbr = **junior**

jubilant ['dʒuːbɪlnt] adj triumphierend

jubilee ['dʒuːbɪliː] n Jubiläum nt

judge [dʒʌdʒ] n Richter m; (*fig*) Kenner m ♦ vt (*JUR: person*) die Verhandlung führen über +acc; (*case*) verhandeln; (*assess*) beurteilen; (*estimate*) einschätzen; **~ment** n (*JUR*) Urteil nt; (*ECCL*) Gericht nt; (*ability*) Urteilsvermögen nt

judicial [dʒuːˈdɪʃl] adj gerichtlich, Justiz-

judiciary [dʒuːˈdɪʃɪərɪ] n Gerichtsbehörden pl; (*judges*) Richterstand m

judicious [dʒuːˈdɪʃəs] adj weise

judo ['dʒuːdəʊ] n Judo nt

jug [dʒʌɡ] n Krug m

juggernaut ['dʒʌɡənɔːt] (*BRIT*) n (*huge truck*) Schwertransporter m

juggle ['dʒʌɡl] vt, vi jonglieren; **~r** n Jongleur m

Jugoslav etc ['juːɡəʊˈslɑːv] = **Yugoslav** etc

juice [dʒuːs] n Saft m; **juicy** ['dʒuːsɪ] adj (*also fig*) saftig

jukebox ['dʒuːkbɔks] n Musikautomat m

July [dʒuːˈlaɪ] n Juli m

jumble ['dʒʌmbl] n Durcheinander nt ♦ vt (*also: ~ up*) durcheinander werfen; (*facts*) durcheinander bringen

jumble sale (*BRIT*) n Basar m, Flohmarkt m

Jumble sale

ⓘ **Jumble sale** ist ein Wohltätigkeitsbasar, meist in einer Aula oder einem Gemeindehaus abgehalten, bei dem alle möglichen Gebrauchtwaren (vor allem Kleidung, Spielzeug, Bücher, Geschirr und Möbel) verkauft werden. Der Erlös fließt entweder einer Wohltätigkeitsorganisation zu oder wird für örtliche Zwecke verwendet, z.B. die Pfadfinder, die Grundschule, Reparatur der Kirche usw.

---

jumbo (jet) ['dʒʌmbəʊ-] n Jumbo(jet) m

jump [dʒʌmp] vi springen; (*nervously*) zusammenzucken ♦ vt überspringen ♦ n Sprung m; **to ~ the queue** (*BRIT*) sich vordrängeln

jumper ['dʒʌmpə] n (*BRIT: pullover*) Pullover m; (*US: dress*) Trägerkleid nt

jump leads *BRIT*, **jumper cables** US npl Überbrückungskabel nt

jumpy ['dʒʌmpɪ] adj nervös

Jun. abbr = **junior**

junction ['dʒʌŋkʃən] n (*BRIT: of roads*) (Straßen)kreuzung f; (*RAIL*) Knotenpunkt m

juncture ['dʒʌŋktʃə] n: **at this ~** in diesem Augenblick

June [dʒuːn] n Juni m

jungle ['dʒʌŋɡl] n Dschungel m

junior ['dʒuːnɪə] adj (*younger*) jünger; (*after name*) junior; (*SPORT*) Junioren-; (*lower position*) untergeordnet; (*for young people*) Junioren- ♦ n Jüngere(r) mf; **~ school** (*BRIT*) n Grundschule f

junk [dʒʌŋk] n (*rubbish*) Plunder m; (*ship*) Dschunke f; **~ bond** n (*COMM*) niedrig eingestuftes Wertpapier mit hohen Ertragschancen bei erhöhtem Risiko; **~ food** n Junk food nt; **~ mail** n Reklame, die unangefordert in den Briefkasten gesteckt wird; **~ shop** n Ramschladen m

Junr abbr = **junior**

jurisdiction [dʒuərɪsˈdɪkʃən] n Gerichtsbarkeit f; (*range of authority*) Zuständigkeit(sbereich m) f

juror ['dʒuərər] n Geschworene(r) mf; (in competition) Preisrichter m

jury ['dʒuərɪ] n (court) Geschworene pl; (panel) Jury f

just [dʒʌst] adj gerecht ♦ adv (recently, now) gerade, eben; (barely) gerade noch; (exactly) genau, gerade; (only) nur, bloß; (a small distance) gleich; (absolutely) einfach; ~ as I arrived gerade als ich ankam; ~ as nice genauso nett; ~ as well umso besser; ~ now soeben, gerade; ~ try versuch es mal; she's ~ left sie ist gerade or (so)eben gegangen; he's ~ done it er hat es gerade or (so)eben getan; ~ before gerade or kurz bevor; ~ enough gerade genug; he ~ missed er hat fast or beinahe getroffen

justice ['dʒʌstɪs] n (fairness) Gerechtigkeit f; J~ of the Peace n Friedensrichter m

justifiable [dʒʌstɪ'faɪəbl] adj berechtigt

justification [dʒʌstɪfɪ'keɪʃən] n Rechtfertigung f

justify ['dʒʌstɪfaɪ] vt rechtfertigen; (text) justieren

justly ['dʒʌstlɪ] adv (say) mit Recht; (condemn) gerecht

jut [dʒʌt] vi (also: ~ out) herausragen, vorstehen

juvenile ['dʒuːvənaɪl] adj (young) jugendlich; (for the young) Jugend- ♦ n Jugendliche(r) mf

juxtapose ['dʒʌkstəpəuz] vt nebeneinander stellen

K, k

K [keɪ] abbr (= one thousand) Tsd.; (= kilobyte) K

kangaroo [kæŋgə'ruː] n Känguru nt

karate [kə'rɑːtɪ] n Karate nt

kebab [kə'bæb] n Kebab m

keel [kiːl] n Kiel m; on an even ~ (fig) im Lot

keen [kiːn] adj begeistert; (wind, blade, intelligence) scharf; (sight, hearing) gut; to be ~ to do or on doing sth etw unbedingt tun wollen; to be ~ on sth/sb scharf auf etw/jdn sein

keep [kiːp] (pt, pp kept) vt (retain) behalten; (have) haben; (animals, one's word) halten; (support) versorgen; (maintain in state) halten; (preserve) aufbewahren; (restrain) abhalten ♦ vi (continue in direction) sich halten; (food) sich halten; (remain: quiet etc) bleiben ♦ n Unterhalt m; (tower) Burgfried m; (inf): for ~s für immer; to ~ sth to o.s. etw für sich behalten; it ~s happening es passiert immer wieder; ~ back vt fern halten; (information) verschweigen; ~ on vi: ~ on doing sth etw immer weiter tun; ~ out vt nicht hereinlassen; "~ out" „Eintritt verboten!"; ~ up vi Schritt halten ♦ vt aufrechterhalten; (continue) weitermachen; to ~ up with Schritt halten mit; ~er n Wärter(in) m(f); (goalkeeper) Torhüter(in) m(f); ~-fit n Keep-fit nt; ~ing n (care) Obhut f; in ~ing with in Übereinstimmung mit; ~sake n Andenken nt

keg [keg] n Fass nt

kennel ['kenl] n Hundehütte f; ~s npl: to put a dog in ~s (for boarding) einen Hund in Pflege geben

Kenya ['kenjə] n Kenia nt; ~n adj kenianisch ♦ n Kenianer(in) m(f)

kept [kept] pt, pp of keep

kerb [kəːb] (BRIT) n Bordstein m

kernel ['kəːnl] n Kern m

kerosene ['kerəsiːn] n Kerosin nt

kettle ['ketl] n Kessel m; ~drum n Pauke f

key [kiː] n Schlüssel m; (of piano, typewriter) Taste f; (MUS) Tonart f ♦ vt (also: ~ in) eingeben; ~board n Tastatur f; ~ed up adj (person) überdreht; ~hole n Schlüsselloch nt; ~hole surgery n minimal invasive Chirurgie f, Schlüssellochchirurgie f; ~note n Grundton m; ~ ring n Schlüsselring m

khaki ['kɑːkɪ] n K(h)aki nt ♦ adj k(h)aki(farben)

kick [kɪk] vt einen Fußtritt geben +dat, treten ♦ vi treten; (baby) strampeln; (horse) ausschlagen ♦ n (Fuß)tritt m; (thrill) Spaß m; he does it for ~s er macht das aus Jux;

~ off vi (SPORT) anstoßen; **~-off** n (SPORT) Anstoß m

kid [kɪd] n (inf: child) Kind nt; (goat) Zicklein nt; (leather) Glacéleder nt, Glaceeleder nt ♦ vi (inf) Witze machen

kidnap ['kɪdnæp] vt entführen; **~per** n Entführer m; **~ping** n Entführung f

kidney ['kɪdnɪ] n Niere f

kill [kɪl] vt töten, umbringen ♦ vi töten ♦ n (hunting) (Jagd)beute f; **~er** n Mörder(in) m(f); **~ing** n Mord m; **~joy** n Spaßverderber(in) m(f)

kiln [kɪln] n Brennofen m

kilo ['kiːləʊ] n Kilo nt; **~byte** n (COMPUT) Kilobyte nt; **~gram(me)** n Kilogramm nt; **~metre** ['kɪləmiːtəʳ] (US **kilometer**) n Kilometer m; **~watt** n Kilowatt nt

kilt [kɪlt] n Schottenrock m

kind [kaɪnd] adj freundlich ♦ n Art f; **a ~ of** eine Art von; **(two) of a ~** (zwei) von der gleichen Art; **in ~** auf dieselbe Art; (in goods) in Naturalien

kindergarten ['kɪndəgɑːtn] n Kindergarten m

kind-hearted [kaɪnd'hɑːtɪd] adj gutherzig

kindle ['kɪndl] vt (set on fire) anzünden; (rouse) reizen, (er)wecken

kindly ['kaɪndlɪ] adj freundlich ♦ adv liebenswürdig(erweise); **would you ~ ...?** wären Sie so freundlich und ...?

kindness ['kaɪndnɪs] n Freundlichkeit f

kindred ['kɪndrɪd] adj: **~ spirit** Gleichgesinnte(r) mf

king [kɪŋ] n König m; **~dom** n Königreich nt

kingfisher ['kɪŋfɪʃəʳ] n Eisvogel m

king-size(d) ['kɪŋsaɪz(d)] adj (cigarette) Kingsize

kinky ['kɪŋkɪ] (inf) adj (person, ideas) verrückt; (sexual) abartig

kiosk ['kiːɒsk] (BRIT) n (TEL) Telefonhäuschen nt

kipper ['kɪpəʳ] n Räucherhering m

kiss [kɪs] n Kuss m ♦ vt küssen ♦ vi: **they ~ed** sie küssten sich; **~ of life** (BRIT) n: **the ~ of life** Mund-zu-Mund-Beatmung f

kit [kɪt] n Ausrüstung f; (tools) Werkzeug nt

kitchen ['kɪtʃɪn] n Küche f; **~ sink** n

Spülbecken nt

kite [kaɪt] n Drachen m

kitten ['kɪtn] n Kätzchen nt

kitty ['kɪtɪ] n (money) Kasse f

km abbr (= kilometre) km

knack [næk] n Dreh m, Trick m

knapsack ['næpsæk] n Rucksack m; (MIL) Tornister m

knead [niːd] vt kneten

knee [niː] n Knie nt; **~cap** n Kniescheibe f

kneel [niːl] (pt, pp **knelt**) vi (also: **~ down**) knien

knelt [nɛlt] pt, pp of **kneel**

knew [njuː] pt of **know**

knickers ['nɪkəz] (BRIT) npl Schlüpfer m

knife [naɪf] (pl **knives**) n Messer nt ♦ vt erstechen

knight [naɪt] n Ritter m; (chess) Springer m; **~hood** n (title): **to get a ~hood** zum Ritter geschlagen werden

knit [nɪt] vt stricken ♦ vi stricken; (bones) zusammenwachsen; **~ting** n (occupation) Stricken nt; (work) Strickzeug nt; **~ting needle** n Stricknadel f; **~wear** n Strickwaren pl

knives [naɪvz] pl of **knife**

knob [nɒb] n Knauf m; (on instrument) Knopf m; (BRIT: of butter etc) kleine(s) Stück nt

knock [nɒk] vt schlagen; (criticize) heruntermachen ♦ vi: **to ~ at** or **on the door** an die Tür klopfen ♦ n Schlag m; (on door) Klopfen nt; **~ down** vt umwerfen; (with car) anfahren; **~ off** vt (do quickly) hinhauen; (inf: steal) klauen ♦ vi (finish) Feierabend machen; **~ out** vt ausschlagen; (BOXING) k. o. schlagen; **~ over** vt (person, object) umwerfen; (with car) anfahren; **~er** n (on door) Türklopfer m; **~out** n K.-o.-Schlag m; (fig) Sensation f

knot [nɒt] n Knoten m ♦ vt (ver)knoten

knotty ['nɒtɪ] adj (fig) kompliziert

know [nəʊ] (pt **knew**, pp **known**) vt, vi wissen; (be able to) können; (be acquainted with) kennen; (recognize) erkennen; **to ~ how to do sth** wissen, wie man etw macht, etw tun können; **to ~ about** or **of sth/sb** etw/jdn kennen; **~-all** n Alleswisser

m; **~how** *n* Kenntnis *f,* Know-how *nt;*
~ing *adj (look, smile)* wissend; **~ingly** *adv*
wissend; *(intentionally)* wissentlich
knowledge ['nɔlɪdʒ] *n* Wissen *nt,* Kenntnis
f; **~able** *adj* informiert
known [nəun] *pp of* **know**
knuckle ['nʌkl] *n* Fingerknöchel *m*
K.O. *n abbr* = **knockout**
Koran [kɔ'rɑːn] *n* Koran *m*
Korea [kə'rɪə] *n* Korea *nt*
kosher ['kəuʃəʳ] *adj* koscher

L, l

L [el] *abbr (BRIT: AUT) (= learner)* am Auto
angebrachtes Kennzeichen für Fahrschüler; =
lake; (= *large*) gr.; (= *left*) l.
l. *abbr* = **litre**
lab [læb] *(inf) n* Labor *nt*
label ['leɪbl] *n* Etikett *nt ♦ vt* etikettieren
labor *etc* ['leɪbəʳ] *(US)* = **labour** *etc*
laboratory [lə'bɔrətərɪ] *n* Laboratorium *nt*
laborious [lə'bɔːrɪəs] *adj* mühsam
labour ['leɪbəʳ] *(US* **labor**) *n* Arbeit *f;*
(workmen) Arbeitskräfte *pl; (MED)* Wehen *pl*
♦ vi: **to ~ (at)** sich abmühen (mit) *♦ vt*
breittreten *(inf);* **in ~** *(MED)* in den Wehen;
L~ *(BRIT: also:* **the L~ party**) die Labour
Party; **~ed** *adj (movement)* gequält; *(style)*
schwerfällig; **~er** *n* Arbeiter *m;* **farm ~er**
(Land)arbeiter *m*
lace [leɪs] *n (fabric)* Spitze *f; (of shoe)*
Schnürsenkel *m; (braid)* Litze *f ♦ vt (also: ~*
up) (zu)schnüren
lack [læk] *n* Mangel *m ♦ vt* nicht haben; **sb**
~s sth jdm fehlt etw *nom;* **to be ~ing**
fehlen; **sb is ~ing in sth** es fehlt jdm an
etw *dat;* **for** *or* **through ~ of** aus Mangel an
+dat
lacquer ['lækəʳ] *n* Lack *m*
lad [læd] *n* Junge *m*
ladder ['lædəʳ] *n* Leiter *f; (BRIT: in tights)*
Laufmasche *f ♦ vt (BRIT: tights)* Laufmaschen
bekommen in *+dat*
laden ['leɪdn] *adj* beladen, voll
ladle ['leɪdl] *n* Schöpfkelle *f*

lady ['leɪdɪ] *n* Dame *f; (title)* Lady *f;* **young ~**
junge Dame; **the ladies' (room)** die
Damentoilette; **~bird** *(US* **~bug**) *n*
Marienkäfer *m;* **~like** *adj* damenhaft,
vornehm; **~ship** *n:* **your L~ship** Ihre
Ladyschaft
lag [læg] *vi (also: ~* **behind**) zurückbleiben
♦ vt (pipes) verkleiden
lager ['lɑːgəʳ] *n* helle(s) Bier *nt*
lagging ['lægɪŋ] *n* Isolierung *f*
lagoon [lə'guːn] *n* Lagune *f*
laid [leɪd] *pt, pp of* **lay**; **~ back** *(inf) adj* cool
lain [leɪn] *pp of* **lie**
lair [leəʳ] *n* Lager *nt*
lake [leɪk] *n* See *m*
lamb [læm] *n* Lamm *nt; (meat)* Lammfleisch
nt; **~ chop** *n* Lammkotelett *nt;* **~swool** *n*
Lammwolle *f*
lame [leɪm] *adj* lahm; *(excuse)* faul
lament [lə'ment] *n* Klage *f ♦ vt* beklagen
laminated ['læmɪneɪtɪd] *adj* beschichtet
lamp [læmp] *n* Lampe *f; (in street)*
Straßenlaterne *f;* **~post** *n* Laternenpfahl *m;*
~shade *n* Lampenschirm *m*
lance [lɑːns] *n* Lanze *f;* **~ corporal** *(BRIT) n*
Obergefreite(r) *m*
land [lænd] *n* Land *nt ♦ vi (from ship)* an
Land gehen; *(AVIAT, end up)* landen *♦ vt*
(obtain) kriegen; *(passengers)* absetzen;
(goods) abladen; *(troops, space probe)*
landen; **~fill site** ['lændfɪl-] *n* Mülldeponie
f; **~ing** *n* Landung *f; (on stairs)*
(Treppen)absatz *m;* **~ing gear** *n*
Fahrgestell *nt;* **~ing stage** *(BRIT) n*
Landesteg *m;* **~ing strip** *n* Landebahn *f;*
~lady *n* (Haus)wirtin *f;* **~locked** *adj*
landumschlossen, Binnen-; **~lord** *n (of*
house) Hauswirt *m,* Besitzer *m; (of pub)*
Gastwirt *m; (of area)* Grundbesitzer *m;*
~mark *n* Wahrzeichen *nt; (fig)* Meilenstein
m; **~owner** *n* Grundbesitzer *m;* **~scape** *n*
Landschaft *f;* **~ gardener** *n*
Landschaftsgärtner(in) *m(f);* **~slide** *n*
(GEOG) Erdrutsch *m; (POL)*
überwältigende(r) Sieg *m*
lane [leɪn] *n (in town)* Gasse *f; (in country)*
Weg *m; (of motorway)* Fahrbahn *f,* Spur *f;*

(*SPORT*) Bahn *f*; **"get in ~"** „bitte einordnen"

language [ˈlæŋgwɪdʒ] *n* Sprache *f*; **bad ~** unanständige Ausdrücke *pl*; **~ laboratory** *n* Sprachlabor *nt*

languish [ˈlæŋgwɪʃ] *vi* schmachten

lank [læŋk] *adj* dürr

lanky [ˈlæŋkɪ] *adj* schlaksig

lantern [ˈlæntən] *n* Laterne *f*

lap [læp] *n* Schoß *m*; (*SPORT*) Runde *f* ♦ *vt* (*also:* **~ up**) auflecken ♦ *vi* (*water*) plätschern

lapel [ləˈpel] *n* Revers *nt or m*

Lapland [ˈlæplænd] *n* Lappland *nt*

lapse [læps] *n* (*moral*) Fehltritt *m* ♦ *vi* (*decline*) nachlassen; (*expire*) ablaufen; (*claims*) erlöschen; **to ~ into bad habits** sich schlechte Gewohnheiten angewöhnen

laptop (computer) [ˈlæptɒp-] *n* Laptop(-Computer) *m*

lard [lɑːd] *n* Schweineschmalz *nt*

larder [ˈlɑːdə*] *n* Speisekammer *f*

large [lɑːdʒ] *adj* groß; **at ~** auf freiem Fuß; **~ly** *adv* zum größten Teil; **~-scale** *adj* groß angelegt, Groß-

lark [lɑːk] *n* (*bird*) Lerche *f*; (*joke*) Jux *m*; **~ about** (*inf*) *vi* herumalbern

laryngitis [lærɪnˈdʒaɪtɪs] *n* Kehlkopfentzündung *f*

laser [ˈleɪzə*] *n* Laser *m*; **~ printer** *n* Laserdrucker *m*

lash [læʃ] *n* Peitschenhieb *m*; (*eyelash*) Wimper *f* ♦ *vt* (*rain*) schlagen gegen; (*whip*) peitschen; (*bind*) festbinden; **~ out** *vi* (*with fists*) um sich schlagen

lass [læs] *n* Mädchen *nt*

lasso [læˈsuː] *n* Lasso *nt*

last [lɑːst] *adj* letzte(r, s) ♦ *adv* zuletzt; (**~ time**) das letzte Mal ♦ *vi* (*continue*) dauern; (*remain good*) sich halten; (*money*) ausreichen; **at ~** endlich; **~ night** gestern Abend; **~ week** letzte Woche; **~ but one** vorletzte(r, s); **~-ditch** *adj* (*attempt*) in letzter Minute; **~ing** *adj* dauerhaft; (*shame etc*) andauernd; **~ly** *adv* schließlich; **~-minute** *adj* in letzter Minute

latch [lætʃ] *n* Riegel *m*

late [leɪt] *adj* spät; (*dead*) verstorben ♦ *adv* spät; (*after proper time*) zu spät; **to be ~** zu spät kommen; **of ~** in letzter Zeit; **in ~ May** Ende Mai; **~comer** *n* Nachzügler(in) *m(f)*; **~ly** *adv* in letzter Zeit; **later** [ˈleɪtə*] *adj* (*date*) später; (*version*) neuer ♦ *adv* später

lateral [ˈlætərəl] *adj* seitlich

latest [ˈleɪtɪst] *adj* (*fashion*) neueste(r, s) ♦ *n* (*news*) Neu(e)ste(s) *nt*; **at the ~** spätestens

lathe [leɪð] *n* Drehbank *f*

lather [ˈlɑːðə*] *n* (*Seifen*)schaum *m* ♦ *vt* einschäumen ♦ *vi* schäumen

Latin [ˈlætɪn] *n* Latein *nt* ♦ *adj* lateinisch; (*Roman*) römisch; **~ America** *n* Lateinamerika *nt*; **~ American** *adj* lateinamerikanisch

latitude [ˈlætɪtjuːd] *n* (*GEOG*) Breite *f*; (*freedom*) Spielraum *m*

latter [ˈlætə*] *adj* (*second of two*) letztere; (*coming at end*) letzte(r, s), später ♦ *n*: **the ~** der/die/das letztere, die letzteren; **~ly** *adv* in letzter Zeit

lattice [ˈlætɪs] *n* Gitter *nt*

laudable [ˈlɔːdəbl] *adj* löblich

laugh [lɑːf] *n* Lachen *nt* ♦ *vi* lachen; **~ at** *vt* lachen über +*acc*; **~ off** *vt* lachend abtun; **~able** *adj* lachhaft; **~ing stock** *n* Zielscheibe *f* des Spottes; **~ter** *n* Gelächter *nt*

launch [lɔːntʃ] *n* (*of ship*) Stapellauf *m*; (*of rocket*) Abschuss *m*; (*boat*) Barkasse *f*; (*of product*) Einführung *f* ♦ *vt* (*set afloat*) vom Stapel lassen; (*rocket*) (ab)schießen; (*product*) auf den Markt bringen; **~(ing) pad** *n* Abschussrampe *f*

launder [ˈlɔːndə*] *vt* waschen

Launderette [lɔːnˈdret] (® *BRIT*) *n* Waschsalon *m*

Laundromat [ˈlɔːndrəmæt] (® *US*) *n* Waschsalon *m*

laundry [ˈlɔːndrɪ] *n* (*place*) Wäscherei *f*; (*clothes*) Wäsche *f*; **to do the ~** waschen

laureate [ˈlɔːrɪət] *adj see* **poet**

laurel [ˈlɒrl] *n* Lorbeer *m*

lava [ˈlɑːvə] *n* Lava *f*

lavatory [ˈlævətərɪ] *n* Toilette *f*

lavender ['lævəndə[r]] *n* Lavendel *m*

lavish ['lævɪʃ] *adj* (*extravagant*) verschwenderisch; (*generous*) großzügig ♦ *vt* (*money*): **to ~ sth on sth** etw auf etw *acc* verschwenden; (*attention, gifts*): **to ~ sth on sb** jdn mit etw überschütten

law [lɔ:] *n* Gesetz *nt*; (*system*) Recht *nt*; (*as studies*) Jura *no art*; **~-abiding** *adj* gesetzestreu; **~ and order** *n* Recht *nt* und Ordnung *f*; **~ court** *n* Gerichtshof *m*; **~ful** *adj* gesetzlich; **~less** *adj* gesetzlos

lawn [lɔ:n] *n* Rasen *m*; **~mower** *n* Rasenmäher *m*; **~ tennis** *n* Rasentennis *m*

law: **~ school** *n* Rechtsakademie *f*; **~suit** *n* Prozess *m*; **~yer** *n* Rechtsanwalt *m*, Rechtsanwältin *f*

lax [læks] *adj* (*behaviour*) nachlässig; (*standards*) lax

laxative ['læksətɪv] *n* Abführmittel *nt*

lay [leɪ] (*pt, pp* **laid**) *pt* of **lie** ♦ *adj* Laien- ♦ *vt* (*place*) legen; (*table*) decken; (*egg*) legen; (*trap*) stellen; (*money*) wetten; **~ aside** *vt* zurücklegen; **~ by** *vt* (*set aside*) beiseite legen; **~ down** *vt* hinlegen; (*rules*) vorschreiben; (*arms*) strecken; **to ~ down the law** Vorschriften machen; **~ off** *vt* (*workers*) (vorübergehend) entlassen; **~ on** *vt* (*water, gas*) anschließen; (*concert etc*) veranstalten; **~ out** *vt* (her)auslegen; (*money*) ausgeben; (*corpse*) aufbahren; **~ up** *vt* (*subj: illness*) ans Bett fesseln; **~about** *n* Faulenzer *m*; **~-by** *n* (*BRIT*) Parkbucht *f*; (*bigger*) Rastplatz *m*

layer ['leɪə[r]] *n* Schicht *f*

layman ['leɪmən] (*irreg*) *n* Laie *m*

layout ['leɪaʊt] *n* Anlage *f*; (*ART*) Lay-out *nt*, Layout *nt*

laze [leɪz] *vi* faulenzen

laziness ['leɪzɪnɪs] *n* Faulheit *f*

lazy ['leɪzɪ] *adj* faul; (*slow-moving*) träge

lb. *abbr* = **pound** (*weight*)

lead¹ [led] *n* (*chemical*) Blei *nt*; (*of pencil*) (Bleistift)mine *f* ♦ *adj* bleiern, Blei-

lead² [li:d] (*pt, pp* **led**) *n* (*front position*) Führung *f*; (*distance, time ahead*) Vorsprung *f*; (*example*) Vorbild *nt*; (*clue*) Tipp *m*; (*of police*) Spur *f*; (*THEAT*) Hauptrolle *f*; (*dog's*) Leine *f* ♦ *vt* (*guide*) führen; (*group etc*) leiten ♦ *vi* (*be first*) führen; (*SPORT, fig*) in Führung; **in the ~** (*SPORT, fig*) in Führung; **~ astray** *vt* irreführen; **~ away** *vt* wegführen; (*prisoner*) abführen; **~ back** *vi* zurückführen; **~ on** *vt* anführen; **~ on to** *vt* (*induce*) dazu bringen; **~ to** *vt* (*street*) (hin)führen nach; (*result in*) führen zu; **~ up to** *vt* (*drive*) führen zu; (*speaker etc*) hinführen auf +*acc*

leaded petrol ['ledɪd-] *n* verbleites Benzin *nt*

leaden ['ledn] *adj* (*sky, sea*) bleiern; (*heavy: footsteps*) bleischwer

leader ['li:də[r]] *n* Führer *m*, Leiter *m*; (*of party*) Vorsitzende(r) *m*; (*PRESS*) Leitartikel *m*; **~ship** *n* (*office*) Leitung *f*; (*quality*) Führerschaft *f*

lead-free ['ledfri:] *adj* (*petrol*) bleifrei

leading ['li:dɪŋ] *adj* führend; **~ lady** *n* (*THEAT*) Hauptdarstellerin *f*; **~ light** *n* (*person*) führende(r) Geist *m*

lead singer [li:d-] *n* Leadsänger(in) *m(f)*

leaf [li:f] (*pl* **leaves**) *n* Blatt *nt* ♦ *vi*: **to ~ through** durchblättern; **to turn over a new ~** einen neuen Anfang machen

leaflet ['li:flɪt] *n* (*advertisement*) Prospekt *m*; (*pamphlet*) Flugblatt *nt*; (*for information*) Merkblatt *nt*

league [li:g] *n* (*union*) Bund *m*; (*SPORT*) Liga *f*; **to be in ~ with** unter einer Decke stecken mit

leak [li:k] *n* undichte Stelle *f*; (*in ship*) Leck *nt* ♦ *vt* (*liquid etc*) durchlassen ♦ *vi* (*pipe etc*) undicht sein; (*liquid etc*) auslaufen; **the information was ~ed to the enemy** die Information wurde dem Feind zugespielt; **~ out** *vi* (*liquid etc*) auslaufen; (*information*) durchsickern; **~y** ['li:kɪ] *adj* undicht

lean [li:n] (*pt, pp* **leaned** *or* **leant**) *adj* mager ♦ *vi* sich neigen ♦ *vt* (an)lehnen; **to ~ against** sth an etw *dat* angelehnt sein; sich an etw *acc* anlehnen; **~ back** *vi* sich zurücklehnen; **~ forward** *vi* sich vorbeugen; **~ on** *vt fus* sich stützen auf +*acc*; **~ out** *vi* sich hinauslehnen; **~ over** *vi* sich hinüberbeugen; **~ing** *n* Neigung *f* ♦ *adj* schief; **~t** [lent] *pt, pp* of **lean**; **~-to** *n*

Anbau *m*

leap [li:p] (*pt, pp* **leaped** *or* **leapt**) *n* Sprung *m* ♦ *vi* springen; **~frog** *n* Bockspringen *nt*; **~t** [lɛpt] *pt, pp of* **leap**; **~ year** *n* Schaltjahr *nt*

learn [lə:n] (*pt, pp* **learned** *or* **learnt**) *vt, vi* lernen; (*find out*) erfahren; **to ~ how to do sth** etw (er)lernen; **~ed** ['lə:nɪd] *adj* gelehrt; **~er** *n* Anfänger(in) *m(f)*; (*AUT: BRIT: also:* **~er driver**) Fahrschüler(in) *m(f)*; **~ing** *n* Gelehrsamkeit *f*; **~t** [lə:nt] *pt, pp of* **learn**

lease [li:s] *n* (*of property*) Mietvertrag *m* ♦ *vt* pachten

leash [li:ʃ] *n* Leine *f*

least [li:st] *adj* geringste(r, s) ♦ *adv* am wenigsten ♦ *n* Mindeste(s) *nt*; **the ~ possible effort** möglichst geringer Aufwand; **at ~** zumindest; **not in the ~!** durchaus nicht!

leather ['lɛðə'] *n* Leder *nt*

leave [li:v] (*pt, pp* **left**) *vt* verlassen; (*~ behind*) zurücklassen; (*forget*) vergessen; (*allow to remain*) lassen; (*after death*) hinterlassen; (*entrust*): **to ~ sth to sb** jdm etw überlassen ♦ *vi* weggehen, wegfahren; (*for journey*) abreisen; (*bus, train*) abfahren ♦ *n* Erlaubnis *f*; (*MIL*) Urlaub *m*; **to be left** (*remain*) übrig bleiben; **there's some milk left over** es ist noch etwas Milch übrig; **on ~** auf Urlaub; **~ behind** *vt* (*person, object*) dalassen; (*forget*) liegen lassen, stehen lassen; **~ out** *vt* auslassen; **~ of absence** *n* Urlaub *m*

leaves [li:vz] *pl of* **leaf**

Lebanon ['lɛbənən] *n* Libanon *m*

lecherous ['lɛtʃərəs] *adj* lüstern

lecture ['lɛktʃə'] *n* Vortrag *m*; (*UNIV*) Vorlesung *f* ♦ *vi* einen Vortrag halten; (*UNIV*) lesen ♦ *vt* (*scold*) abkanzeln; **to give a ~ on sth** einen Vortrag über etw halten; **~r** ['lɛktʃərə'] *n* Vortragende(r) *mf*; (*BRIT: UNIV*) Dozent(in) *m(f)*

led [lɛd] *pt, pp of* **lead**[2]

ledge [lɛdʒ] *n* Leiste *f*; (*window ~*) Sims *m or nt*; (*of mountain*) (Fels)vorsprung *m*

ledger ['lɛdʒə'] *n* Hauptbuch *nt*

leech [li:tʃ] *n* Blutegel *m*

leek [li:k] *n* Lauch *m*

leer [lɪə'] *vi*: **to ~ (at sb)** (nach jdm) schielen

leeway ['li:weɪ] *n* (*fig*): **to have some ~** etwas Spielraum haben

left [lɛft] *pt, pp of* **leave** ♦ *adj* linke(r, s) ♦ *n* (*side*) linke Seite *f* ♦ *adv* links; **on the ~** links; **to the ~** nach links; **the L~** (*POL*) die Linke *f*; **~-hand** *adj*: **~-hand drive** mit Linkssteuerung; **~-handed** *adj* linkshändig; **~-hand side** *n* linke Seite *f*; **~-luggage locker** *n* Gepäckschließfach *nt*; **~-luggage (office)** (*BRIT*) *n* Gepäckaufbewahrung *f*; **~-overs** *npl* Reste *pl*; **~-wing** *adj* linke(r, s)

leg [lɛg] *n* Bein *nt*; (*of meat*) Keule *f*; (*stage*) Etappe *f*; **1st/2nd ~** (*SPORT*) 1./2. Etappe

legacy ['lɛgəsɪ] *n* Erbe *nt*, Erbschaft *f*

legal ['li:gl] *adj* gesetzlich; (*allowed*) legal; **~ holiday** (*US*) *n* gesetzliche(r) Feiertag *m*; **~ize** *vt* legalisieren; **~ly** *adv* gesetzlich; legal; **~ tender** *n* gesetzliche(s) Zahlungsmittel *nt*

legend ['lɛdʒənd] *n* Legende *f*; **~ary** *adj* legendär

leggings ['lɛgɪŋz] *npl* Leggings *pl*

legible ['lɛdʒəbl] *adj* leserlich

legislation [lɛdʒɪs'leɪʃən] *n* Gesetzgebung *f*; **legislative** ['lɛdʒɪslətɪv] *adj* gesetzgebend; **legislature** ['lɛdʒɪslətʃə'] *n* Legislative *f*

legitimate [lɪ'dʒɪtɪmət] *adj* rechtmäßig, legitim; (*child*) ehelich

legroom ['lɛgru:m] *n* Platz *m* für die Beine

leisure ['lɛʒə'] *n* Freizeit *f*; **to be at ~** Zeit haben; **~ centre** *n* Freizeitzentrum *nt*; **~ly** *adj* gemächlich

lemon ['lɛmən] *n* Zitrone *f*; (*colour*) Zitronengelb *nt*; **~ade** [lɛmə'neɪd] *n* Limonade *f*; **~ tea** *n* Zitronentee *m*

lend [lɛnd] (*pt, pp* **lent**) *vt* leihen; **to ~ sb sth** jdm etw leihen; **~ing library** *n* Leihbibliothek *f*

length [lɛŋθ] *n* Länge *f*; (*of road, pipe etc*) Strecke *f*; (*of material*) Stück *nt*; **at ~** (*lengthily*) ausführlich; (*at last*) schließlich; **~en** *vt* verlängern ♦ *vi* länger werden; **~ways** *adv* längs; **~y** *adj* sehr lang, langatmig

lenient ['li:nɪənt] *adj* nachsichtig

lens [lɛnz] n Linse f; (PHOT) Objektiv nt

Lent [lɛnt] n Fastenzeit f

lent [lɛnt] pt, pp of **lend**

lentil ['lɛntɪl] n Linse f

Leo ['liːəu] n Löwe m

leotard ['liːətɑːd] n Trikot nt, Gymnastikanzug m

leper ['lɛpər] n Leprakranke(r) f(m)

leprosy ['lɛprəsɪ] n Lepra f

lesbian ['lɛzbɪən] adj lesbisch ♦ n Lesbierin f

less [lɛs] adj, adv weniger ♦ n weniger ♦ pron weniger; ~ **than half** weniger als die Hälfte; ~ **than ever** weniger denn je; ~ **and** ~ immer weniger; **the** ~ **he works** je weniger er arbeitet; ~**en** ['lɛsn] vi abnehmen ♦ vt verringern, verkleinern; ~**er** ['lɛsər] adj kleiner, geringer; **to a** ~**er extent** in geringerem Maße

lesson ['lɛsn] n (SCH) Stunde f; (unit of study) Lektion f; (fig) Lehre f; (ECCL) Lesung f; **a maths** ~ eine Mathestunde

lest [lɛst] conj: ~ **it happen** damit es nicht passiert

let [lɛt] (pt, pp **let**) vt lassen; (BRIT: lease) vermieten; **to** ~ **sb do sth** jdn etw tun lassen; **to** ~ **sb know sth** jdn etw wissen lassen; ~**'s go!** gehen wir!; ~ **him come** soll er doch kommen; ~ **down** vt hinunterlassen; (disappoint) enttäuschen; ~ **go** vi loslassen ♦ vt (things) loslassen; (person) gehen lassen; ~ **in** vt hereinlassen; (water) durchlassen; ~ **off** vt (gun) abfeuern; (steam) ablassen; (forgive) laufen lassen; ~ **on** vi durchblicken lassen; (pretend) vorgeben; ~ **out** vt herauslassen; (scream) fahren lassen; ~ **up** vi nachlassen; (stop) aufhören

lethal ['liːθl] adj tödlich

lethargic [lɛ'θɑːdʒɪk] adj lethargisch

letter ['lɛtər] n Brief m; (of alphabet) Buchstabe m; ~ **bomb** n Briefbombe f; ~**box** (BRIT) n Briefkasten m; ~**ing** n Beschriftung f; ~ **of credit** n Akkreditiv m

lettuce ['lɛtɪs] n (Kopf)salat m

let-up ['lɛtʌp] (inf) n Nachlassen nt

leukaemia [luː'kiːmɪə] (US **leukemia**) n Leukämie f

level ['lɛvl] adj (ground) eben; (at same height) auf gleicher Höhe; (equal) gleich gut; (head) kühl ♦ adv auf gleicher Höhe ♦ n (instrument) Wasserwaage f; (altitude) Höhe f; (flat place) ebene Fläche f; (position on scale) Niveau nt; (amount, degree) Grad m ♦ vt (ground) einebnen; **to draw** ~ **with** gleichziehen mit; **to be** ~ **with** auf einer Höhe sein mit; **A** ~**s** (BRIT) ≈ Abitur nt; **O** ~**s** (BRIT) ≈ mittlere Reife f; **on the** ~ (fig: honest) ehrlich; **to** ~ **sth at sb** (blow) jdm etw versetzen; (remark) etw gegen jdn richten; ~ **off** or **out** vi flach or eben werden; (fig) sich ausgleichen; (plane) horizontal fliegen ♦ vt (ground) planieren; (differences) ausgleichen; ~ **crossing** (BRIT) n Bahnübergang m; ~**-headed** adj vernünftig

lever ['liːvər] n Hebel m; (fig) Druckmittel nt ♦ vt (hoch)stemmen; ~**age** n Hebelkraft f; (fig) Einfluss m

levy ['lɛvɪ] n (of taxes) Erhebung f; (tax) Abgaben pl; (MIL) Aushebung f ♦ vt erheben; (MIL) ausheben

lewd [luːd] adj unzüchtig, unanständig

liability [laɪə'bɪlɪtɪ] n (burden) Belastung f; (duty) Pflicht f; (debt) Verpflichtung f; (responsibility) Haftung f; (proneness) Anfälligkeit f

liable ['laɪəbl] adj (responsible) haftbar; (prone) anfällig; **to be** ~ **for sth** etw dat unterliegen; **it's** ~ **to happen** es kann leicht vorkommen

liaise [liː'eɪz] vi: **to** ~ **(with sb)** (mit jdm) zusammenarbeiten; **liaison** n Verbindung f

liar ['laɪər] n Lügner m

libel ['laɪbl] n Verleumdung f ♦ vt verleumden

liberal ['lɪbərl] adj (generous) großzügig; (open-minded) aufgeschlossen; (POL) liberal

liberate ['lɪbəreɪt] vt befreien; **liberation** [lɪbə'reɪʃən] n Befreiung f

liberty ['lɪbətɪ] n Freiheit f; (permission) Erlaubnis f; **to be at** ~ **to do sth** etw tun dürfen; **to take the** ~ **of doing sth** sich dat erlauben, etw zu tun

Libra ['liːbrə] n Waage f

librarian [laɪˈbrɛərɪən] n Bibliothekar(in) m(f)

library [ˈlaɪbrərɪ] n Bibliothek f; (lending ~) Bücherei f

Libya [ˈlɪbɪə] n Libyen nt; ~n adj libysch ♦ n Libyer(in) m(f)

lice [laɪs] npl of **louse**

licence [ˈlaɪsns] (US **license**) n (permit) Erlaubnis f; (also: **driving ~**, (US) **driver's ~**) Führerschein m

license [ˈlaɪsns] (US) = **licence** ♦ vt genehmigen, konzessionieren; ~**d** adj (for alcohol) konzessioniert (für den Alkoholausschank); ~ **plate** (US) n (AUT) Nummernschild nt

lichen [ˈlaɪkən] n Flechte f

lick [lɪk] vt lecken ♦ n Lecken nt; **a ~ of paint** ein bisschen Farbe

licorice [ˈlɪkərɪs] (US) n = **liquorice**

lid [lɪd] n Deckel m; (eyelid) Lid nt

lie [laɪ] (pt **lay**, pp **lain**) vi (rest, be situated) liegen; (put o.s. in position) sich legen; (pt, pp **lied**, tell lies) lügen ♦ n Lüge f; **to ~ low** (fig) untertauchen; ~ **about** vi (things) herumliegen; (people) faulenzen; ~~**down** (BRIT) n: **to have a ~~down** ein Nickerchen machen; ~~**in** (BRIT) n: **to have a ~~in** sich ausschlafen

lieu [luː] n: **in ~ of** anstatt +gen

lieutenant [lefˈtenənt, (US) luːˈtenənt] n Leutnant m

life [laɪf] (pl **lives**) n Leben nt; ~ **assurance** (BRIT) n = **life insurance**; ~**belt** (BRIT) n Rettungsring m; ~**boat** n Rettungsboot nt; ~**guard** n Rettungsschwimmer m; ~ **insurance** n Lebensversicherung f; ~ **jacket** n Schwimmweste f; ~**less** adj (dead) leblos; (dull) langweilig; ~**like** adj lebenswahr, naturgetreu; ~**line** n Rettungsleine f; (fig) Rettungsanker m; ~**long** adj lebenslang; ~ **preserver** (US) n = **lifebelt**; ~~**saver** n Lebensretter(in) m(f); ~~**saving** adj lebensrettend, Rettungs-; ~ **sentence** n lebenslängliche Freiheitsstrafe f; ~ **span** n Lebensspanne f; ~**style** n Lebensstil m; ~ **support system** n (MED) Lebenserhaltungssystem nt; ~**time** n: **in his ~time** während er lebte; **once in a**

~**time** einmal im Leben

lift [lɪft] vt hochheben ♦ vi sich heben ♦ n (BRIT: elevator) Aufzug m, Lift m; **to give sb a ~** jdn mitnehmen; ~~**off** n Abheben nt (vom Boden)

ligament [ˈlɪgəmənt] n Band nt

light [laɪt] (pt, pp **lighted** or **lit**) n Licht nt; (for cigarette etc): **have you got a ~?** haben Sie Feuer? ♦ vt beleuchten; (lamp) anmachen; (fire, cigarette) anzünden ♦ adj (bright) hell; (pale) hell-; (not heavy, easy) leicht; (punishment) milde; (touch) leicht; ~**s** npl (AUT) Beleuchtung f; ~ **up** vi (lamp) angehen; (face) aufleuchten ♦ vt (illuminate) beleuchten; (~s) anmachen; ~ **bulb** n Glühbirne f; ~**en** vi (brighten) hell werden; (~ning) blitzen ♦ vt (give ~ to) erhellen; (hair) aufhellen; (gloom) aufheitern; (make less heavy) leichter machen; (fig) erleichtern; ~**er** n Feuerzeug nt; ~~**headed** adj (thoughtless) leichtsinnig; (giddy) schwindlig; ~~**hearted** adj leichtherzig, fröhlich; ~**house** n Leuchtturm m; ~**ing** n Beleuchtung f; ~**ly** adv leicht; (irresponsibly) leichtfertig; **to get off ~ly** mit einem blauen Auge davonkommen; ~**ness** n (of weight) Leichtigkeit f; (of colour) Helle f

lightning [ˈlaɪtnɪŋ] n Blitz m; ~ **conductor** (US ~ **rod**) n Blitzableiter m

light: ~ **pen** n Lichtstift m; ~**weight** adj (suit) leicht; ~**weight** n (BOXING) Leichtgewichtler m; ~ **year** n Lichtjahr nt

like [laɪk] vt mögen, gern haben ♦ prep wie ♦ adj (similar) ähnlich; (equal) gleich ♦ n: **the ~** dergleichen; **I would** or **I'd ~** ich möchte gern; **would you ~ a coffee?** möchten Sie einen Kaffee?; **to be** or **look ~ sb/sth** jdm/etw ähneln; **that's just ~ him** das ist typisch für ihn; **do it ~ this** mach es so; **it is nothing ~ ...** es ist nicht zu vergleichen mit ...; **what does it look ~?** wie sieht es aus?; **what does it sound ~?** wie hört es sich an?; **what does it taste ~?** wie schmeckt es?; **his ~s and dislikes** was er mag und was er nicht mag; ~**able** adj sympathisch

likelihood [ˈlaɪklɪhud] n Wahrscheinlichkeit f

likely ['laɪklɪ] *adj* wahrscheinlich; **he's ~ to leave** er geht möglicherweise; **not ~!** wohl kaum!

likeness ['laɪknɪs] *n* Ähnlichkeit *f*; (*portrait*) Bild *nt*

likewise ['laɪkwaɪz] *adv* ebenso

liking ['laɪkɪŋ] *n* Zuneigung *f*; (*taste*) Vorliebe *f*

lilac ['laɪlək] *n* Flieder *m* ♦ *adj* (*colour*) fliederfarben

lily ['lɪlɪ] *n* Lilie *f*; **~ of the valley** *n* Maiglöckchen *nt*

limb [lɪm] *n* Glied *nt*

limber up ['lɪmbər-] *vi* sich auflockern; (*fig*) sich vorbereiten

limbo ['lɪmbəʊ] *n*: **to be in ~** (*fig*) in der Schwebe sein

lime [laɪm] *n* (*tree*) Linde *f*; (*fruit*) Limone *f*; (*substance*) Kalk *m*

limelight ['laɪmlaɪt] *n*: **to be in the ~** (*fig*) im Rampenlicht stehen

limestone ['laɪmstəʊn] *n* Kalkstein *m*

limit ['lɪmɪt] *n* Grenze *f*; (*inf*) Höhe *f* ♦ *vt* begrenzen, einschränken; **~ation** [lɪmɪ'teɪʃən] *n* Einschränkung *f*; **~ed** *adj* beschränkt; **to be ~ed to** sich beschränken auf +*acc*; **~ed (liability) company** (*BRIT*) *n* Gesellschaft *f* mit beschränkter Haftung

limousine ['lɪməzi:n] *n* Limousine *f*

limp [lɪmp] *n* Hinken *nt* ♦ *vi* hinken ♦ *adj* schlaff

limpet ['lɪmpɪt] *n* (*fig*) Klette *f*

line [laɪn] *n* Linie *f*; (*rope*) Leine *f*; (*on face*) Falte *f*; (*row*) Reihe *f*; (*of hills*) Kette *f*; (*US: queue*) Schlange *f*; (*company*) Linie *f*, Gesellschaft *f*; (*RAIL*) Strecke *f*; (*TEL*) Leitung *f*; (*written*) Zeile *f*; (*direction*) Richtung *f*; (*fig: business*) Branche *f*; (*range of items*) Kollektion *f* ♦ *vt* (*coat*) füttern; (*border*) säumen; **~s** *npl* (*RAIL*) Gleise *pl*; **in ~ with** in Übereinstimmung mit; **~ up** *vi* sich aufstellen ♦ *vt* aufstellen; (*prepare*) sorgen für; (*support*) mobilisieren; (*surprise*) planen; **~ar** ['lɪnɪər] *adj* gerade; (*measure*) Längen-; **~d** *adj* (*face*) faltig; (*paper*) liniert

linen ['lɪnɪn] *n* Leinen *nt*; (*sheets etc*) Wäsche *f*

liner ['laɪnər] *n* Überseedampfer *m*

linesman ['laɪnzmən] (*irreg*) *n* (*SPORT*) Linienrichter *m*

line-up ['laɪnʌp] *n* Aufstellung *f*

linger ['lɪŋgər] *vi* (*remain long*) verweilen; (*taste*) (zurück)bleiben; (*delay*) zögern, verharren

lingerie ['lænʒəri:] *n* Damenunterwäsche *f*

lingering ['lɪŋgərɪŋ] *adj* (*doubt*) zurückbleibend; (*disease*) langwierig; (*taste*) nachhaltend; (*look*) lang

lingo ['lɪŋgəʊ] (*pl* **~es**) (*inf*) *n* Sprache *f*

linguist ['lɪŋgwɪst] *n* Sprachkundige(r) *mf*; (*UNIV*) Sprachwissenschaftler(in) *m(f)*; **~ic** [lɪŋ'gwɪstɪk] *adj* sprachlich; sprachwissenschaftlich; **~ics** *n* Sprachwissenschaft *f*, Linguistik *f*

lining ['laɪnɪŋ] *n* Futter *nt*

link [lɪŋk] *n* Glied *nt*; (*connection*) Verbindung *f* ♦ *vt* verbinden; **~s** *npl* (*GOLF*) Golfplatz *m*; **~ up** *vt* verbinden ♦ *vi* zusammenkommen; (*companies*) sich zusammenschließen; **~-up** *n* (*TEL*) Verbindung *f*; (*of spaceships*) Kopplung *f*

lino ['laɪnəʊ] *n* = **linoleum**

linoleum [lɪ'nəʊlɪəm] *n* Linoleum *nt*

linseed oil ['lɪnsi:d-] *n* Leinöl *nt*

lion ['laɪən] *n* Löwe *m*; **~ess** *n* Löwin *f*

lip [lɪp] *n* Lippe *f*; (*of jug*) Schnabel *m*; **to pay ~ service (to)** ein Lippenbekenntnis ablegen (zu)

liposuction ['lɪpəʊsʌkʃən] *n* Fettabsaugen *nt*

lip: ~read (*irreg*) *vi* von den Lippen ablesen; **~ salve** *n* Lippenbalsam *m*; **~stick** *n* Lippenstift *m*

liqueur [lɪ'kjʊər] *n* Likör *m*

liquid ['lɪkwɪd] *n* Flüssigkeit *f* ♦ *adj* flüssig

liquidate ['lɪkwɪdeɪt] *vt* liquidieren

liquidize ['lɪkwɪdaɪz] *vt* (*COOK*) (im Mixer) pürieren; **~r** ['lɪkwɪdaɪzər] *n* Mixgerät *nt*

liquor ['lɪkər] *n* Alkohol *m*

liquorice ['lɪkərɪs] (*BRIT*) *n* Lakritze *f*

liquor store (*US*) *n* Spirituosengeschäft *nt*

Lisbon ['lɪzbən] *n* Lissabon *nt*

lisp [lɪsp] *n* Lispeln *nt* ♦ *vt, vi* lispeln

list [lɪst] *n* Liste *f*, Verzeichnis *nt*; (*of ship*) Schlagseite *f* ♦ *vt* (*write down*) eine Liste machen von; (*verbally*) aufzählen ♦ *vi* (*ship*) Schlagseite haben

listen ['lɪsn] *vi* hören; **~ to** *vt* zuhören +*dat*; **~er** *n* (Zu)hörer(in) *m(f)*

listless ['lɪstlɪs] *adj* lustlos

lit [lɪt] *pt, pp of* **light**

liter ['liːtəʳ] (*US*) *n* = **litre**

literacy ['lɪtərəsɪ] *n* Fähigkeit *f* zu lesen und zu schreiben

literal ['lɪtərəl] *adj* buchstäblich; (*translation*) wortwörtlich; **~ly** *adv* wörtlich; buchstäblich

literary ['lɪtərərɪ] *adj* literarisch

literate ['lɪtərət] *adj* des Lesens und Schreibens kundig

literature ['lɪtrɪtʃəʳ] *n* Literatur *f*

litigation [lɪtɪˈɡeɪʃən] *n* Prozess *m*

litre ['liːtəʳ] (*US* **liter**) *n* Liter *m*

litter ['lɪtəʳ] *n* (*rubbish*) Abfall *m*; (*of animals*) Wurf *m* ♦ *vt* in Unordnung bringen; **to be ~ed with** übersät sein mit; **~ bin** (*BRIT*) *n* Abfalleimer *m*

little ['lɪtl] *adj* klein ♦ *adv, n* wenig; **a ~** ein bisschen; **~ by ~** nach und nach

live[1] [laɪv] *adj* lebendig; (*MIL*) scharf; (*ELEC*) geladen; (*broadcast*) live

live[2] [lɪv] *vi* leben; (*dwell*) wohnen ♦ *vt* (*life*) führen; **~ down** *vt*: **I'll never ~ it down** das wird man mir nie vergessen; **~ on** *vt* weiterleben ♦ *vt fus*: **to ~ on sth** von etw leben; **~ together** *vi* zusammenleben; (*share a flat*) zusammenwohnen; **~ up to** *vt* (*standards*) gerecht werden +*dat*; (*principles*) anstreben; (*hopes*) entsprechen +*dat*

livelihood ['laɪvlɪhʊd] *n* Lebensunterhalt *m*

lively ['laɪvlɪ] *adj* lebhaft, lebendig

liven up ['laɪvn-] *vt* beleben

liver ['lɪvəʳ] *n* (*ANAT*) Leber *f*

lives [laɪvz] *pl of* **life**

livestock ['laɪvstɒk] *n* Vieh *nt*

livid ['lɪvɪd] *adj* bläulich; (*furious*) fuchsteufelswild

living ['lɪvɪŋ] *n* (Lebens)unterhalt *m* ♦ *adj* lebendig; (*language etc*) lebend; **to earn or make a ~** sich *dat* seinen Lebensunterhalt verdienen; **~ conditions** *npl*

Wohnverhältnisse *pl*; **~ room** *n* Wohnzimmer *nt*; **~ standards** *npl* Lebensstandard *m*; **~ wage** *n* ausreichender Lohn *m*

lizard ['lɪzəd] *n* Eidechse *f*

load [ləʊd] *n* (*burden*) Last *f*; (*amount*) Ladung *f* ♦ *vt* (*also*: **~ up**) (be)laden; (*COMPUT*) laden; (*camera*) Film einlegen in +*acc*; (*gun*) laden; **a ~ of, ~s of** (*fig*) jede Menge; **~ed** *adj* beladen; (*dice*) präpariert; (*question*) Fang-; (*inf: rich*) steinreich; **~ing bay** *n* Ladeplatz *m*

loaf [ləʊf] (*pl* **loaves**) *n* Brot *nt* ♦ *vi* (*also*: **~ about, ~ around**) herumlungern, faulenzen

loan [ləʊn] *n* Leihgabe *f*; (*FIN*) Darlehen *nt* ♦ *vt* leihen; **on ~** geliehen

loath [ləʊθ] *adj*: **to be ~ to do sth** etw ungern tun

loathe [ləʊð] *vt* verabscheuen

loaves [ləʊvz] *pl of* **loaf**

lobby ['lɒbɪ] *n* Vorhalle *f*; (*POL*) Lobby *f* ♦ *vt* politisch beeinflussen (wollen)

lobster ['lɒbstəʳ] *n* Hummer *m*

local ['ləʊkl] *adj* ortsansässig, Orts- ♦ *n* (*pub*) Stammwirtschaft *f*; **the ~s** *npl* (*people*) die Ortsansässigen *pl*; **~ anaesthetic** *n* (*MED*) örtliche Betäubung *f*; **~ authority** *n* städtische Behörden *pl*; **~ call** *n* (*TEL*) Ortsgespräch *nt*; **~ government** *n* Gemeinde-/Kreisverwaltung *f*; **~ity** [ləʊˈkælɪtɪ] *n* Ort *m*; **~ly** *adv* örtlich, am Ort

locate [ləʊˈkeɪt] *vt* ausfindig machen; (*establish*) errichten; **location** [ləʊˈkeɪʃən] *n* Platz *m*, Lage *f*; **on location** (*CINE*) auf Außenaufnahme

loch [lɒx] (*SCOTTISH*) *n* See *m*

lock [lɒk] *n* Schloss *nt*; (*NAUT*) Schleuse *f*; (*of hair*) Locke *f* ♦ *vt* (*fasten*) (ver)schließen ♦ *vi* (*door etc*) sich schließen (lassen); (*wheels*) blockieren; **~ up** *vt* (*criminal, mental patient*) einsperren; (*house*) abschließen

locker ['lɒkəʳ] *n* Spind *m*

locket ['lɒkɪt] *n* Medaillon *nt*

lock ['lɒk-]: **~out** *n* Aussperrung *f*; **~smith** *n* Schlosser(in) *m(f)*; **~up** *n* (*jail*) Gefängnis *nt*; (*garage*) Garage *f*

locum ['ləʊkəm] *n* (*MED*) Vertreter(in) *m(f)*

lodge [lɔdʒ] n (*gatehouse*) Pförtnerhaus nt; (*freemasons'*) Loge f ♦ vi (*get stuck*) stecken (bleiben); (*in Untermiete*): **to ~ (with)** wohnen (bei) ♦ vt (*protest*) einreichen; **~r** n (Unter)mieter m; **lodgings** n (Miet)wohnung f

loft [lɔft] n (Dach)boden m

lofty [ˈlɔftɪ] adj hoch(ragend); (*proud*) hochmütig

log [lɔg] n Klotz m; (*book*) = **logbook**

logbook [ˈlɔgbuk] n Bordbuch nt; (*for lorry*) Fahrtenschreiber m; (*AUT*) Kraftfahrzeugbrief m

loggerheads [ˈlɔgəhedz] npl: **to be at ~** sich in den Haaren liegen

logic [ˈlɔdʒɪk] n Logik f; **~al** adj logisch

log in or **on** vi (*COMPUT*) einloggen

log off or **out** vi (*COMPUT*) ausloggen

logistics [lɔˈdʒɪstɪks] npl Logistik f

logo [ˈləugəu] n Firmenzeichen nt

loin [lɔɪn] n Lende f

loiter [ˈlɔɪtə*] vi herumstehen

loll [lɔl] vi (*also:* **~ about**) sich rekeln or räkeln

lollipop [ˈlɔlɪpɔp] n (Dauer)lutscher m; **~ man/lady** (*irreg; BRIT*) n ≈ Schülerlotse m

---

Lollipop man/lady

i **Lollipop man/lady** *heißen in Großbritannien die Männer bzw. Frauen, die mit Hilfe eines runden Stoppschildes den Verkehr anhalten, damit Schulkinder die Straße überqueren können. Der Name bezieht sich auf die Form des Schildes, die an einen Lutscher erinnert.*

---

lolly [ˈlɔlɪ] (*inf*) n (*sweet*) Lutscher m

London [ˈlʌndən] n London nt; **~er** n Londoner(in) m(f)

lone [ləun] adj einsam

loneliness [ˈləunlɪnɪs] n Einsamkeit f

lonely [ˈləunlɪ] adj einsam

loner [ˈləunə*] n Einzelgänger(in) m(f)

long [lɔŋ] adj lang; (*distance*) weit ♦ adv lange ♦ vi: **to ~ for** sich sehnen nach; **before ~** bald; **as ~ as** solange; **in the ~ run** auf die Dauer; **don't be ~!** beeil dich!;

how ~ is the street? wie lang ist die Straße?; **how ~ is the lesson?** wie lange dauert die Stunde?; **6 metres ~** 6 Meter lang; **6 months ~** 6 Monate lang; **all night ~** die ganze Nacht; **he no ~er comes** er kommt nicht mehr; **~ ago** vor langer Zeit; **~ before** lange vorher; **at ~ last** endlich; **~-distance** adj Fern-

longevity [lɔnˈdʒɛvɪtɪ] n Langlebigkeit f

long: **~-haired** adj langhaarig; **~hand** n Langschrift f; **~ing** n Sehnsucht f ♦ adj sehnsüchtig

longitude [ˈlɔŋgɪtjuːd] n Längengrad m

long: **~ jump** n Weitsprung m; **~-life** adj (*batteries etc*) mit langer Lebensdauer; **~-lost** adj längst verloren geglaubt; **~-playing record** n Langspielplatte f; **~-range** adj Langstrecken-, Fern-; **~-sighted** adj weitsichtig; **~-standing** adj alt, seit langer Zeit bestehend; **~-suffering** adj schwer geprüft; **~-term** adj langfristig; **~ wave** n Langwelle f; **~-winded** adj langatmig

loo [luː] (*BRIT: inf*) n Klo nt

look [luk] vi schauen; (*seem*) aussehen; (*building etc*): **to ~ on to the sea** aufs Meer gehen ♦ n Blick m; **~s** npl (*appearance*) Aussehen nt; **~ after** vt (*care for*) sorgen für; (*watch*) aufpassen auf +acc; **~ at** vt ansehen; (*consider*) sich überlegen; **~ back** vi sich umsehen; (*fig*) zurückblicken; **~ down on** vt (*fig*) herabsehen auf +acc; **~ for** vt (*seek*) suchen; **~ forward to** vt sich freuen auf +acc; (*in letters*): **we ~ forward to hearing from you** wir hoffen, bald von Ihnen zu hören; **~ into** vt untersuchen; **~ on** vi zusehen; **~ out** vi hinaussehen; (*take care*) aufpassen; **~ out for** vt Ausschau halten nach; (*be careful*) Acht geben auf +acc; **~ round** vi sich umsehen; **~ to** vt (*take care of*) Acht geben auf +acc; (*rely on*) sich verlassen auf +acc; **~ up** vi aufblicken; (*improve*) sich bessern ♦ vt (*word*) nachschlagen; (*person*) besuchen; **~ up to** vt aufsehen zu; **~out** n (*watch*) Ausschau f; (*person*) Wachposten m; (*place*) Ausguck m; (*prospect*) Aussichten pl; **to be on the ~ out**

for sth nach etw Ausschau halten

loom[luːm] *n* Webstuhl *m* ♦ *vi* sich abzeichnen

loony[ˈluːnɪ] (*inf*) *n* Verrückte(r) *mf*

loop[luːp] *n* Schlaufe *f*; **~hole***n* (*fig*) Hintertürchen *nt*

loose[luːs] *adj* lose, locker; (*free*) frei; (*inexact*) unpräzise ♦ *vt* lösen, losbinden; **~ change***n* Kleingeld *nt*; **~ chippings***npl* (*on road*) Rollsplit *m*; **~ end***n*: **to be at a ~ end** (*BRIT*) *or* **at ~ ends** (*US*) nicht wissen, was man tun soll; **~ly***adv* locker, lose; **~n** *vt* lockern, losmachen

loot[luːt] *n* Beute *f* ♦ *vt* plündern

lop off[lɔp-] *vt* abhacken

lopsided[ˈlɔpˈsaɪdɪd] *adj* schief

lord[lɔːd] *n* (*ruler*) Herr *m*; (*BRIT: title*) Lord *m*; **the L~** (*God*) der Herr; **the (House of) L~s** das Oberhaus; **~ship***n*: **Your L~ship** Eure Lordschaft

lorry[ˈlɔrɪ] (*BRIT*) *n* Lastwagen *m*; **~ driver** (*BRIT*) *n* Lastwagenfahrer(in) *m(f)*

lose[luːz] (*pt, pp* **lost**) *vt* verlieren; (*chance*) verpassen ♦ *vi* verlieren; **to ~ (time)** (*clock*) nachgehen; **~r** *n* Verlierer *m*

loss[lɔs] *n* Verlust *m*; **at a ~** (*COMM*) mit Verlust; (*unable*) außerstande, außer Stande

lost[lɔst] *pt, pp of* **lose** ♦ *adj* verloren; **~ property**(*US* **~ and found**) *n* Fundsachen *pl*

lot[lɔt] *n* (*quantity*) Menge *f*; (*fate, at auction*) Los *nt*; (*inf: people, things*) Haufen *m*; **the ~** alles; (*people*) alle; **a ~ of** (*with sg*) viel; (*with pl*) viele; **~s of** massenhaft, viel(e); **I read a ~** ich lese viel; **to draw ~s for sth** etw verlosen

lotion[ˈləʊʃən] *n* Lotion *f*

lottery[ˈlɔtərɪ] *n* Lotterie *f*

loud[laud] *adj* laut; (*showy*) schreiend ♦ *adv* laut; **~ly***adv* laut; **~speaker***n* Lautsprecher *m*

lounge[laundʒ] *n* (*in hotel*) Gesellschaftsraum *m*; (*in house*) Wohnzimmer *nt* ♦ *vi* sich herumlümmeln

louse[laus] (*pl* **lice**) *n* Laus *f*

lousy[ˈlauzɪ] *adj* (*fig*) miserabel

lout[laut] *n* Lümmel *m*

louvre[ˈluːvər] (*US* **louver**) *adj* (*door, window*) Jalousie-

lovable[ˈlʌvəbl] *adj* liebenswert

love[lʌv] *n* Liebe *f*; (*person*) Liebling *m*; (*SPORT*) null ♦ *vt* (*person*) lieben; (*activity*) gerne mögen; **to be in ~ with sb** in jdn verliebt sein; **to make ~** sich lieben; **for the ~ of** aus Liebe zu; **"15 ~"** (*TENNIS*) „15 null"; **to ~ to do sth** etw (sehr) gerne tun; **~ affair***n* (Liebes)verhältnis *nt*; **~ letter***n* Liebesbrief *m*; **~ life***n* Liebesleben *nt*

lovely[ˈlʌvlɪ] *adj* schön

lover[ˈlʌvər] *n* Liebhaber(in) *m(f)*

loving[ˈlʌvɪŋ] *adj* liebend, liebevoll

low[ləʊ] *adj* niedrig; (*rank*) niedere(r, s); (*level, note, neckline*) tief; (*intelligence, density*) gering; (*vulgar*) ordinär; (*not loud*) leise; (*depressed*) gedrückt ♦ *adv* (*not high*) niedrig; (*not loudly*) leise ♦ *n* (*~ point*) Tiefstand *m*; (*MET*) Tief *nt*; **to feel ~** sich mies fühlen; **to turn (down) ~** leiser stellen; **~ alcohol***adj* alkoholarm; **~calorie***adj* kalorienarm; **~cut**(a] (*dress*) tief ausgeschnitten; **~er***vt* herunterlassen; (*eyes, gun*) senken; (*reduce*) herabsetzen, senken ♦ *vr*: **to ~er o.s. to** (*fig*) sich herablassen zu; **~er sixth**(*BRIT*) *n* (*SCOL*) ≈ zwölfte Klasse; **~fat***adj* fettarm, Mager-; **~lands***npl* (*GEOG*) Flachland *nt*; **~ly***adj* bescheiden; **~lying***adj* tief gelegen

loyal[ˈlɔɪəl] *adj* treu; **~ty***n* Treue *f*; **~ty card***n* Kundenkarte *f*

lozenge[ˈlɔzɪndʒ] *n* Pastille *f*

L-plates[ˈelpleɪts] (*BRIT*) *npl* L-Schild *nt*

L-Plates

*Als **L-Plates** werden in Großbritannien die weißen Schilder mit einem roten „L" bezeichnet, die an jedem von einem Fahrschüler geführten Fahrzeug befestigt werden müssen. Fahrschüler bekommen einen vorläufigen Führerschein und dürfen damit unter Aufsicht eines erfahrenen Autofahrers auf allen Straßen außer Autobahnen fahren.*

Ltd*abbr* (= *limited company*) GmbH

lubricant[ˈluːbrɪkənt] *n* Schmiermittel *nt*

lubricate ['lu:brikeit] *vt* schmieren

lucid ['lu:sid] *adj* klar; (*sane*) bei klarem Verstand; (*moment*) licht

luck [lʌk] *n* Glück *nt*; **bad** *or* **hard** *or* **tough ~!** (so ein) Pech!; **good ~!** viel Glück!; **~ily** *adv* glücklicherweise, zum Glück; **~y** *adj* Glücks-; **to be ~y** Glück haben

lucrative ['lu:krətɪv] *adj* einträglich

ludicrous ['lu:dɪkrəs] *adj* grotesk

lug [lʌg] *vt* schleppen

luggage ['lʌgɪdʒ] *n* Gepäck *nt*; **~ rack** *n* Gepäcknetz *nt*

lukewarm ['lu:kwɔ:m] *adj* lauwarm; (*indifferent*) lau

lull [lʌl] *n* Flaute *f* ♦ *vt* einlullen; (*calm*) beruhigen

lullaby ['lʌləbai] *n* Schlaflied *nt*

lumbago [lʌm'beigəu] *n* Hexenschuss *m*

lumber ['lʌmbər] *n* Plunder *m*; (*wood*) Holz *nt*; **~jack** *n* Holzfäller *m*

luminous ['lu:mɪnəs] *adj* Leucht-

lump [lʌmp] *n* Klumpen *m*; (*MED*) Schwellung *f*; (*in breast*) Knoten *m*; (*of sugar*) Stück *nt* ♦ *vt* (*also:* **~ together**) zusammentun; (*judge together*) in einen Topf werfen; **~ sum** *n* Pauschalsumme *f*; **~y** *adj* klumpig

lunacy ['lu:nəsi] *n* Irrsinn *m*

lunar ['lu:nər] *adj* Mond-

lunatic ['lu:nətik] *n* Wahnsinnige(r) *mf* ♦ *adj* wahnsinnig, irr

lunch [lʌntʃ] *n* Mittagessen *nt*; **~eon** ['lʌntʃən] *n* Mittagessen *nt*; **~eon meat** *n* Frühstücksfleisch *nt*; **~eon voucher** (*BRIT*) *n* Essenmarke *f*; **~time** *n* Mittagszeit *f*

lung [lʌŋ] *n* Lunge *f*

lunge [lʌndʒ] *vi* (*also:* **~ forward**) (los)stürzen; **to ~ at** sich stürzen auf +*acc*

lurch [lɔ:tʃ] *vi* taumeln; (*NAUT*) schlingern ♦ *n* Ruck *m*; (*NAUT*) Schlingern *nt*; **to leave sb in the ~** jdn im Stich lassen

lure [luər] *n* Köder *m*; (*fig*) Lockung *f* ♦ *vt* (ver)locken

lurid ['luərid] *adj* (*shocking*) grausig, widerlich; (*colour*) grell

lurk [lɔ:k] *vi* lauern

luscious ['lʌʃəs] *adj* köstlich

lush [lʌʃ] *adj* satt; (*vegetation*) üppig

lust [lʌst] *n* Wollust *f*; (*greed*) Gier *f* ♦ *vi*: **to ~ after** gieren nach

lustre ['lʌstər] (*US* **luster**) *n* Glanz *m*

Luxembourg ['lʌksəmbə:g] *n* Luxemburg *nt*

luxuriant [lʌg'zjuəriənt] *adj* üppig

luxurious [lʌg'zjuəriəs] *adj* luxuriös, Luxus-

luxury ['lʌkʃəri] *n* Luxus *m* ♦ *cpd* Luxus-

lying ['laiɪŋ] *n* Lügen *nt* ♦ *adj* verlogen

lynx [lɪŋks] *n* Luchs *m*

lyric ['lɪrɪk] *n* Lyrik *f* ♦ *adj* lyrisch; **~s** *pl* (*words for song*) (Lied)text *m*; **~al** *adj* lyrisch, gefühlvoll

M, m

m *abbr* = **metre**; **mile**; **million**

M.A. *n abbr* = **Master of Arts**

mac [mæk] (*BRIT: inf*) *n* Regenmantel *m*

macaroni [mækə'rəuni] *n* Makkaroni *pl*

machine [mə'ʃi:n] *n* Maschine *f* ♦ *vt* (*dress etc*) mit der Maschine nähen; **~ gun** *n* Maschinengewehr *nt*; **~ language** *n* (*COMPUT*) Maschinensprache *f*; **~ry** *n* Maschinerie *f*

macho ['mætʃəu] *adj* macho

mackerel ['mækrl] *n* Makrele *f*

mackintosh ['mækɪntɔʃ] (*BRIT*) *n* Regenmantel *m*

mad [mæd] *adj* verrückt; (*dog*) tollwütig; (*angry*) wütend; **~ about** (*fond of*) verrückt nach, versessen auf +*acc*

madam ['mædəm] *n* gnädige Frau *f*

madden ['mædn] *vt* verrückt machen; (*make angry*) ärgern

made [meid] *pt, pp of* **make**

made-to-measure ['meidtə'mɛʒər] (*BRIT*) *adj* Maß-

mad ['mæd-]: **~ly** *adv* wahnsinnig; **~man** (*irreg*) *n* Verrückte(r) *m*, Irre(r) *m*; **~ness** *n* Wahnsinn *m*

magazine [mægə'zi:n] *n* Zeitschrift *f*; (*in gun*) Magazin *nt*

maggot ['mægət] *n* Made *f*

magic ['mædʒɪk] *n* Zauberei *f*, Magie *f*; (*fig*) Zauber *m* ♦ *adj* magisch, Zauber-; **~al** *adj* magisch; **~ian** [mə'dʒɪʃən] n Zauberer m

magistrate ['mædʒɪstreɪt] n (Friedens)richter m

magnanimous [mæg'nænɪməs] adj großmütig

magnet ['mægnɪt] n Magnet m; **~ic** [mæg'netɪk] adj magnetisch; **~ic tape** n Magnetband nt; **~ism** n Magnetismus m; (fig) Ausstrahlungskraft f

magnificent [mæg'nɪfɪsnt] adj großartig

magnify ['mægnɪfaɪ] vt vergrößern; **~ing glass** n Lupe f

magnitude ['mægnɪtjuːd] n (size) Größe f; (importance) Ausmaß nt

magpie ['mægpaɪ] n Elster f

mahogany [mə'hɒgənɪ] n Mahagoni nt ♦ cpd Mahagoni-

maid [meɪd] n Dienstmädchen nt; **old ~** alte Jungfer f

maiden ['meɪdn] n Maid f ♦ adj (flight, speech) Jungfern-; **~ name** n Mädchenname m

mail [meɪl] n Post f ♦ vt aufgeben; **~ box** (US) n Briefkasten m; **~ing list** n Anschreibeliste f; **~ order** n Bestellung f durch die Post; **~ order firm** n Versandhaus nt

maim [meɪm] vt verstümmeln

main [meɪn] adj hauptsächlich, Haupt- ♦ n (pipe) Hauptleitung f; **the ~s** npl (ELEC) das Stromnetz; **in the ~** im Großen und Ganzen; **~frame** n (COMPUT) Großrechner m; **~land** n Festland nt; **~ly** adv hauptsächlich; **~ road** n Hauptstraße f; **~stay** n (fig) Hauptstütze f; **~stream** n Hauptrichtung f

maintain [meɪn'teɪn] vt (machine, roads) instand or in Stand halten; (support) unterhalten; (keep up) aufrechterhalten; (claim) behaupten; (innocence) beteuern

maintenance ['meɪntənəns] n (TECH) Wartung f; (of family) Unterhalt m

maize [meɪz] n Mais m

majestic [mə'dʒestɪk] adj majestätisch

majesty ['mædʒɪstɪ] n Majestät f

major ['meɪdʒə*] n Major m ♦ adj (MUS) Dur; (more important) Haupt-; (bigger) größer

Majorca [mə'jɔːkə] n Mallorca nt

majority [mə'dʒɒrɪtɪ] n Mehrheit f; (JUR) Volljährigkeit f

make [meɪk] (pt, pp **made**) vt machen; (appoint) ernennen (zu); (cause to do sth) veranlassen; (reach) erreichen; (in time) schaffen; (earn) verdienen ♦ n Marke f; **to ~ sth happen** etw geschehen lassen; **to ~ it** es schaffen; **what time do you ~ it?** wie spät hast du es?; **to ~ do with** auskommen mit; **~ for** vi gehen/fahren nach; **~ out** vt (write out) ausstellen; (understand) verstehen; **~ up** vt machen; (face) schminken; (quarrel) beilegen; (story etc) erfinden ♦ vi sich versöhnen; **~ up for** vt wieder gutmachen; (COMM) vergüten; **~believe** n Fantasie f; **~r** n (COMM) Hersteller m; **~shift** adj behelfsmäßig, Not-; **~up** n Schminke f, Make-up nt; **~up remover** n Make-up-Entferner m; **making** n: **in the making** im Entstehen; **to have the makings of** das Zeug haben zu

malaria [mə'leərɪə] n Malaria f

Malaysia [mə'leɪzɪə] n Malaysia nt

male [meɪl] n Mann m; (animal) Männchen nt ♦ adj männlich

malevolent [mə'levələnt] adj übel wollend

malfunction [mæl'fʌŋkʃən] n (MED) Funktionsstörung f; (of machine) Defekt m

malice ['mælɪs] n Bosheit f; **malicious** [mə'lɪʃəs] adj böswillig, gehässig

malign [mə'laɪn] vt verleumden ♦ adj böse

malignant [mə'lɪgnənt] adj bösartig

mall [mɔːl] n (also: **shopping ~**) Einkaufszentrum nt

malleable ['mælɪəbl] adj formbar

mallet ['mælɪt] n Holzhammer m

malnutrition [mælnjuː'trɪʃən] n Unterernährung f

malpractice [mæl'præktɪs] n Amtsvergehen nt

malt [mɔːlt] n Malz nt

Malta ['mɔːltə] n Malta nt; **Maltese** [mɔːl'tiːz] adj inv maltesisch ♦ n inv Malteser(in) m(f)

maltreat [mæl'triːt] vt misshandeln

mammal ['mæml] n Säugetier nt

mammoth ['mæməθ] *n* Mammut *nt* ♦ *adj* Mammut-

man [mæn] (*pl* **men**) *n* Mann *m*; (*human race*) der Mensch, die Menschen *pl* ♦ *vt* bemannen; **an old ~** ein alter Mann, ein Greis *m*; **~ and wife** Mann und Frau

manage ['mænɪdʒ] *vi* zurechtkommen ♦ *vt* (*control*) führen, leiten; (*cope with*) fertig werden mit; **~able** *adj* (*person, animal*) fügsam; (*object*) handlich; **~ment** *n* (*control*) Führung *f*, Leitung *f*; (*directors*) Management *nt*; **~r** *n* Geschäftsführer *m*; **~ress** [mænɪdʒə'rɛs] *n* Geschäftsführerin *f*; **~rial** [mænɪ'dʒɪərɪəl] *adj* (*post*) leitend; (*problem etc*) Management-; **managing** [mænɪdʒɪŋ] *adj*: **managing director** Betriebsleiter *m*

mandarin ['mændərɪn] *n* (*fruit*) Mandarine *f*

mandatory ['mændətərɪ] *adj* obligatorisch

mane [meɪn] *n* Mähne *f*

maneuver [mə'nuːvər] (*US*) = **manoeuvre**

manfully ['mænfəlɪ] *adv* mannhaft

mangle ['mæŋgl] *vt* verstümmeln ♦ *n* Mangel *f*

mango ['mæŋgəʊ] (*pl* **~es**) *n* Mango(pflaume) *f*

mangy ['meɪndʒɪ] *adj* (*dog*) räudig

man ['mæn-]: **~handle** *vt* grob behandeln; **~hole** *n* (Straßen)schacht *m*; **~hood** *n* Mannesalter *nt*; (*~liness*) Männlichkeit *f*; **~hour** *n* Arbeitsstunde *f*; **~hunt** *n* Fahndung *f*

mania ['meɪnɪə] *n* Manie *f*; **~c** ['meɪnɪæk] *n* Wahnsinnige(r) *mf*

manic ['mænɪk] *adj* (*behaviour, activity*) hektisch

manicure ['mænɪkjʊər] *n* Maniküre *f*; **~ set** *n* Necessaire *nt*, Nessessär *nt*

manifest ['mænɪfɛst] *vt* offenbaren ♦ *adj* offenkundig; **~ation** [mænɪfɛs'teɪʃən] *n* (*sign*) Anzeichen *nt*

manifesto [mænɪ'fɛstəʊ] *n* Manifest *nt*

manipulate [mə'nɪpjʊleɪt] *vt* handhaben; (*fig*) manipulieren

man [mæn'-]: **~kind** *n* Menschheit *f*; **~ly** ['mænlɪ] *adj* männlich; mannhaft; **~-made** *adj* (*fibre*) künstlich

manner ['mænər] *n* Art *f*, Weise *f*; **~s** *npl* (*behaviour*) Manieren *pl*; **in a ~ of speaking** sozusagen; **~ism** *n* (*of person*) Angewohnheit *f*; (*of style*) Manieriertheit *f*

manoeuvre [mə'nuːvər] (*US* **maneuver**) *vt, vi* manövrieren ♦ *n* (*MIL*) Feldzug *m*; (*general*) Manöver *nt*, Schachzug *m*

manor ['mænər] *n* Landgut *nt*

manpower ['mænpaʊər] *n* Arbeitskräfte *pl*

mansion ['mænʃən] *n* Villa *f*

manslaughter ['mænslɔːtər] *n* Totschlag *m*

mantelpiece ['mæntlpiːs] *n* Kaminsims *m*

manual ['mænjʊəl] *adj* manuell, Hand- ♦ *n* Handbuch *nt*

manufacture [mænjʊ'fæktʃər] *vt* herstellen ♦ *n* Herstellung *f*; **~r** *n* Hersteller *m*

manure [mə'njʊər] *n* Dünger *m*

manuscript ['mænjʊskrɪpt] *n* Manuskript *nt*

Manx [mæŋks] *adj* der Insel Man

many ['mɛnɪ] *adj, pron* viele; **a great ~** sehr viele; **~ a time** oft

map [mæp] *n* (Land)karte *f*; (*of town*) Stadtplan *m* ♦ *vt* eine Karte machen von; **~ out** *vt* (*fig*) ausarbeiten

maple ['meɪpl] *n* Ahorn *m*

mar [mɑːr] *vt* verderben

marathon ['mærəθən] *n* (*SPORT*) Marathonlauf *m*; (*fig*) Marathon *m*

marble ['mɑːbl] *n* Marmor *m*; (*for game*) Murmel *f*

March [mɑːtʃ] *n* März *m*

march [mɑːtʃ] *vi* marschieren ♦ *n* Marsch *m*

mare [mɛər] *n* Stute *f*

margarine [mɑːdʒə'riːn] *n* Margarine *f*

margin ['mɑːdʒɪn] *n* Rand *m*; (*extra amount*) Spielraum *m*; (*COMM*) Spanne *f*; **~al** *adj* (*note*) Rand-; (*difference etc*) geringfügig; **~al (seat)** *n* (*POL*) Wahlkreis, der nur mit knapper Mehrheit gehalten wird

marigold ['mærɪgəʊld] *n* Ringelblume *f*

marijuana [mærɪ'wɑːnə] *n* Marihuana *nt*

marina [mə'riːnə] *n* Jachthafen *m*

marinate ['mærɪneɪt] *vt* marinieren

marine [mə'riːn] *adj* Meeres-, See- ♦ *n* (*MIL*) Marineinfanterist *m*

marital ['mærɪtl] *adj* ehelich, Ehe-; **~ status** *n* Familienstand *m*

maritime ['mærɪtaɪm] *adj* See-

mark [mɑːk] *n (coin)* Mark *f; (spot)* Fleck *m; (scar)* Kratzer *m; (sign)* Zeichen *nt; (target)* Ziel *nt; (SCH)* Note *f* ♦ *vt (make ~ on)* Flecken/Kratzer machen auf +*acc; (indicate)* markieren; *(exam)* korrigieren; **to ~ time** *(also fig)* auf der Stelle treten; **~ out** *vt* bestimmen; *(area)* abstecken; **~ed** *adj* deutlich; **~er** *n (in book)* (Lese)zeichen *nt; (on road)* Schild *nt*

market ['mɑːkɪt] *n* Markt *m; (stock ~)* Börse *f* ♦ *vt (COMM: new product)* auf den Markt bringen; *(sell)* vertreiben; **~ garden** *(BRIT) n* Handelsgärtnerei *f;* **~ing** *n* Marketing *nt;* **~ research** *n* Marktforschung *f;* **~ value** *n* Marktwert *m*

marksman ['mɑːksmən] *(irreg) n* Scharfschütze *m*

marmalade ['mɑːməleɪd] *n* Orangenmarmelade *f*

maroon [mə'ruːn] *vt* aussetzen ♦ *adj (colour)* kastanienbraun

marquee [mɑː'kiː] *n* große(s) Zelt *nt*

marriage ['mærɪdʒ] *n* Ehe *f; (wedding)* Heirat *f;* **~ bureau** *n* Heiratsinstitut *nt;* **~ certificate** *n* Heiratsurkunde *f*

married ['mærɪd] *adj (person)* verheiratet; *(couple, life)* Ehe-

marrow ['mærəu] *n (Knochen)mark nt; (BOT)* Kürbis *m*

marry ['mærɪ] *vt (join)* trauen; *(take as husband, wife)* heiraten ♦ *vi (also:* **get married)** heiraten

marsh [mɑːʃ] *n* Sumpf *m*

marshal ['mɑːʃl] *n (US)* Bezirkspolizeichef *m* ♦ *vt* (an)ordnen, arrangieren

marshy ['mɑːʃɪ] *adj* sumpfig

martial law ['mɑːʃl] *n* Kriegsrecht *nt*

martyr ['mɑːtər] *n (also fig)* Märtyrer(in) *m(f)* ♦ *vt* zum Märtyrer machen; **~dom** *n* Martyrium *nt*

marvel ['mɑːvl] *n* Wunder *nt* ♦ *vi:* **to ~ (at)** sich wundern (über +*acc*); **~lous** *(US* **marvelous)** *adj* wunderbar

Marxist ['mɑːksɪst] *n* Marxist(in) *m(f)*

marzipan ['mɑːzɪpæn] *n* Marzipan *nt*

mascara [mæs'kɑːrə] *n* Wimperntusche *f*

mascot ['mæskət] *n* Maskottchen *nt*

masculine ['mæskjulɪn] *adj* männlich

mash [mæʃ] *n* Brei *m;* **~ed potatoes** *npl* Kartoffelbrei *m or* -püree *nt*

mask [mɑːsk] *n (also fig)* Maske *f* ♦ *vt* maskieren, verdecken

mason ['meɪsn] *n (stonemason)* Steinmetz *m; (freemason)* Freimaurer *m;* **~ry** *n* Mauerwerk *nt*

masquerade [mæskə'reɪd] *n* Maskerade *f* ♦ *vi:* **to ~ as** sich ausgeben als

mass [mæs] *n* Masse *f; (greater part)* Mehrheit *f; (REL)* Messe *f* ♦ *vi* sich sammeln; **the ~es** *npl (people)* die Masse(n) *f(pl)*

massacre ['mæsəkər] *n* Blutbad *nt* ♦ *vt* niedermetzeln, massakrieren

massage ['mæsɑːʒ] *n* Massage *f* ♦ *vt* massieren

massive ['mæsɪv] *adj* gewaltig, massiv

mass media *npl* Massenmedien *pl*

mass production *n* Massenproduktion *f*

mast [mɑːst] *n* Mast *m*

master ['mɑːstər] *n* Herr *m; (NAUT)* Kapitän *m; (teacher)* Lehrer *m; (artist)* Meister *m* ♦ *vt* meistern; *(language etc)* beherrschen; **~ly** *adj* meisterhaft; **~mind** *n* Kapazität *f* ♦ *vt* geschickt lenken; **M~ of Arts** *n* Magister *m* der philosophischen Fakultät; **M~ of Science** *n* Magister *m* der naturwissenschaftlichen Fakultät; **~piece** *n* Meisterwerk *nt;* **~ plan** *n* kluge(r) Plan *m;* **~y** *n* Können *nt*

masturbate ['mæstəbeɪt] *vi* masturbieren, onanieren

mat [mæt] *n* Matte *f; (for table)* Untersetzer *m* ♦ *adj* = **matt**

match [mætʃ] *n* Streichholz *nt; (sth corresponding)* Pendant *nt; (SPORT)* Wettkampf *m; (ball games)* Spiel *nt* ♦ *vt (be like, suit)* passen zu; *(equal)* gleichkommen +*dat* ♦ *vi* zusammenpassen; **it's a good ~ (for)** es passt gut (zu); **~box** *n* Streichholzschachtel *f;* **~ing** *adj* passend

mate [meɪt] *n (companion)* Kamerad *m; (spouse)* Lebensgefährte *m; (of animal)* Weibchen *nt*/Männchen *nt; (NAUT)* Schiffsoffizier *m* ♦ *vi (animals)* sich paaren

♦ vt (*animals*) paaren

material [məˈtɪərɪəl] n Material nt; (*for book, cloth*) Stoff m ♦ adj (*important*) wesentlich; (*damage*) Sach-; (*comforts etc*) materiell; **~s** npl (*for building etc*) Materialien pl; **~istic** [mətɪərɪəˈlɪstɪk] adj materialistisch; **~ize** vi sich verwirklichen, zustande or zu Stande kommen

maternal [məˈtɜːnl] adj mütterlich, Mutter-

maternity [məˈtɜːnɪtɪ] adj (*dress*) Umstands-; (*benefit*) Wochen-; ~ **hospital** n Entbindungsheim nt

math [mæθ] (*US*) n = **maths**

mathematical [mæθəˈmætɪkl] adj mathematisch; **mathematics** n Mathematik f; **maths** (*US* **math**) n Mathe f

matinée [ˈmætɪneɪ] n Matinee f

matrices [ˈmeɪtrɪsiːz] npl of **matrix**

matriculation [mətrɪkjuˈleɪʃən] n Immatrikulation f

matrimonial [mætrɪˈməʊnɪəl] adj ehelich, Ehe-

matrimony [ˈmætrɪmənɪ] n Ehestand m

matrix [ˈmeɪtrɪks] (*pl* **matrices**) n Matrize f; (*GEOL etc*) Matrix f

matron [ˈmeɪtrən] n (*MED*) Oberin f; (*SCH*) Hausmutter f

matt [mæt] adj (*paint*) matt

matted [ˈmætɪd] adj verfilzt

matter [ˈmætəʳ] n (*substance*) Materie f; (*affair*) Angelegenheit f ♦ vi darauf ankommen; **no ~ how/what** egal wie/was; **what is the ~?** was ist los?; **as a ~ of course** selbstverständlich; **as a ~ of fact** eigentlich; **it doesn't ~** es macht nichts; **~-of-fact** adj sachlich, nüchtern

mattress [ˈmætrɪs] n Matratze f

mature [məˈtjʊəʳ] adj reif ♦ vi reif werden; **maturity** [məˈtjʊərɪtɪ] n Reife f

maul [mɔːl] vt übel zurichten

maxima [ˈmæksɪmə] npl of **maximum**

maximum [ˈmæksɪməm] (*pl* **maxima**) adj Höchst-, Maximal- ♦ n Maximum nt

May [meɪ] n Mai m

may [meɪ] (*conditional* **might**) vi (*be possible*) können; (*have permission*) dürfen; **he ~ come** er kommt vielleicht; **~be** [ˈmeɪbiː]

adv vielleicht

May Day n der 1. Mai

mayhem [ˈmeɪhem] n Chaos nt; (*US*) Körperverletzung f

mayonnaise [meɪəˈneɪz] n Majonäse f, Mayonnaise f

mayor [meəʳ] n Bürgermeister m; **~ess** n Bürgermeisterin f; (*wife*) (die) Frau f Bürgermeister

maypole [ˈmeɪpəʊl] n Maibaum m

maze [meɪz] n Irrgarten m; (*fig*) Wirrwarr nt

M.D. abbr = **Doctor of Medicine**

| KEYWORD |

---

me [miː] pron **1** (*direct*) mich; **it's me** ich bins

2 (*indirect*) mir; **give them to me** gib sie mir

3 (*after prep: +acc*) mich; (: *+dat*) mir; **with/without me** mit mir/ohne mich

---

meadow [ˈmedəʊ] n Wiese f

meagre [ˈmiːgəʳ] (*US* **meager**) adj dürftig, spärlich

meal [miːl] n Essen nt, Mahlzeit f; (*grain*) Schrotmehl nt; **to have a ~** essen (gehen); **~time** n Essenszeit f

mean [miːn] (*pt, pp* **meant**) adj (*stingy*) geizig; (*spiteful*) gemein; (*average*) durchschnittlich, Durchschnitts- ♦ vt (*signify*) bedeuten; (*intend*) vorhaben, beabsichtigen ♦ n (*average*) Durchschnitt m; **~s** npl (*wherewithal*) Mittel pl; (*wealth*) Vermögen nt; **do you ~ me?** meinst du mich?; **do you ~ it?** meinst du das ernst?; **what do you ~?** was willst du damit sagen?; **to be ~t for sb/sth** für jdn/etw bestimmt sein; **by ~s of** durch; **by all ~s** selbstverständlich; **by no ~s** keineswegs

meander [mɪˈændəʳ] vi sich schlängeln

meaning [ˈmiːnɪŋ] n Bedeutung f; (*of life*) Sinn m; **~ful** adj bedeutungsvoll; (*life*) sinnvoll; **~less** adj sinnlos

meanness [ˈmiːnnɪs] n (*stinginess*) Geiz m; (*spitefulness*) Gemeinheit f

meant [ment] pt, pp of **mean**

meantime [ˈmiːntaɪm] adv inzwischen

meanwhile ['mi:nwaɪl] *adv* inzwischen

measles ['mi:zlz] *n* Masern *pl*

measly ['mi:zlɪ] *(inf) adj* poplig

measure ['mɛʒəʳ] *vt, vi* messen ♦ *n* Maß *nt*; *(step)* Maßnahme *f*; **~ments** *npl* Maße *pl*

meat [mi:t] *n* Fleisch *nt*; **cold ~** Aufschnitt *m*; **~ ball** *n* Fleischkloß *m*; **~ pie** *n* Fleischpastete *f*; **~y** *adj* fleischig; *(fig)* gehaltvoll

Mecca ['mɛkə] *n* Mekka *nt (also fig)*

mechanic [mɪ'kænɪk] *n* Mechaniker *m*; **~al** *adj* mechanisch; **~s** *n* Mechanik *f* ♦ *npl* Technik *f*

mechanism ['mɛkənɪzəm] *n* Mechanismus *m*

mechanize ['mɛkənaɪz] *vt* mechanisieren

medal ['mɛdl] *n* Medaille *f*; *(decoration)* Orden *m*; **~list** *(US* **medalist)** *n* Medaillengewinner(in) *m(f)*

meddle ['mɛdl] *vi*: **to ~ (in)** sich einmischen (in +*acc*); **to ~ with sth** sich an etw *dat* zu schaffen machen

media ['mi:dɪə] *npl* Medien *pl*

mediaeval [mɛdɪ'i:vl] *adj* = **medieval**

median ['mi:dɪən] *(US) n (also:* **~ strip)** Mittelstreifen *m*

mediate ['mi:dɪeɪt] *vi* vermitteln; **mediator** *n* Vermittler *m*

Medicaid ['mɛdɪkeɪd] *(®) (US) n* *medizinisches Versorgungsprogramm für sozial Schwache*

medical ['mɛdɪkl] *adj* medizinisch; Medizin-; ärztlich ♦ *n* (ärztliche) Untersuchung *f*

Medicare ['mɛdɪkɛəʳ] *(US) n* staatliche *Krankenversicherung besonders für Ältere*

medicated ['mɛdɪkeɪtɪd] *adj* medizinisch

medication [mɛdɪ'keɪʃən] *n (drugs etc)* Medikamente *pl*

medicinal [mɛ'dɪsɪnl] *adj* medizinisch, Heil-

medicine ['mɛdsɪn] *n* Medizin *f*; *(drugs)* Arznei *f*

medieval [mɛdɪ'i:vl] *adj* mittelalterlich

mediocre [mi:dɪ'əʊkəʳ] *adj* mittelmäßig

meditate ['mɛdɪteɪt] *vi* meditieren; **to ~ (on sth)** (über etw *acc*) nachdenken; **meditation** [mɛdɪ'teɪʃən] *n* Nachsinnen *nt*; Meditation *f*

Mediterranean [mɛdɪtə'reɪnɪən] *adj*

Mittelmeer-; *(person)* südländisch; **the ~ (Sea)** das Mittelmeer

medium ['mi:dɪəm] *adj* mittlere(r, s), Mittel-, mittel- ♦ *n* Mitte *f*; *(means)* Mittel *nt*; *(person)* Medium *nt*; **happy ~** goldener Mittelweg; **~-sized** *adj* mittelgroß; **~ wave** *n* Mittelwelle *f*

medley ['mɛdlɪ] *n* Gemisch *nt*

meek [mi:k] *adj* sanft(mütig)

meet [mi:t] *(pt, pp* **met)** *vt (encounter)* treffen, begegnen +*dat*; *(by arrangement)* sich treffen mit; *(difficulties)* stoßen auf +*acc* *(get to know)* kennen lernen; *(fetch)* abholen; *(join)* zusammentreffen mit; *(satisfy)* entsprechen +*dat* ♦ *vi* sich treffen; *(become acquainted)* sich kennen lernen; **~ with** *vt (problems)* stoßen auf +*acc*; *(US: people)* zusammentreffen mit; **~ing** *n* Treffen *nt*; *(business ~ing)* Besprechung *f*; *(of committee)* Sitzung *f*; *(assembly)* Versammlung *f*

mega- ['mɛgə-] *(inf) prefix* Mega-; **~byte** *n* *(COMPUT)* Megabyte *nt*; **~phone** *n* Megafon *nt*, Megaphon *nt*

melancholy ['mɛlənkəlɪ] *adj (person)* melancholisch; *(sight, event)* traurig

mellow ['mɛləʊ] *adj* mild, weich; *(fruit)* reif; *(fig)* gesetzt ♦ *vi* reif werden

melodious [mɪ'ləʊdɪəs] *adj* wohlklingend

melody ['mɛlədɪ] *n* Melodie *f*

melon ['mɛlən] *n* Melone *f*

melt [mɛlt] *vi* schmelzen; *(anger)* verfliegen ♦ *vt* schmelzen; **~ away** *vi* dahinschmelzen; **~ down** *vt* einschmelzen; **~down** *n (in nuclear reactor)* Kernschmelze *f*; **~ing point** *n* Schmelzpunkt *m*; **~ing pot** *n (fig)* Schmelztiegel *m*

member ['mɛmbəʳ] *n* Mitglied *nt*; *(of tribe, species)* Angehörige(r) *f(m)*; *(ANAT)* Glied *nt*; **M~ of Parliament** *(BRIT) n* Parlamentsmitglied *nt*; **M~ of the European Parliament** *(BRIT) n* Mitglied *nt* des Europäischen Parlaments; **M~ of the Scottish Parliament** *n* Mitglied *nt* des schottischen Parlaments; **~ship** *n* Mitgliedschaft *f*; **to seek ~ship of** einen Antrag auf Mitgliedschaft stellen; **~ship**

card *n* Mitgliedskarte *f*
memento [mə'mentəu] *n* Andenken *nt*
memo ['meməu] *n* Mitteilung *f*
memoirs ['memwɑ:z] *npl* Memoiren *pl*
memorable ['memərəbl] *adj* denkwürdig
memoranda [memə'rændə] *npl of*
memorandum
memorandum [memə'rændəm] (*pl*
memoranda) *n* Mitteilung *f*
memorial [mɪ'mɔ:rɪəl] *n* Denkmal *nt* ♦ *adj*
Gedenk-
memorize ['meməraɪz] *vt* sich einprägen
memory ['meməri] *n* Gedächtnis *nt*; (*of*
computer) Speicher *m*; (*sth recalled*)
Erinnerung *f*
men [men] *pl of* **man** ♦ *n* (*human race*) die
Menschen *pl*
menace ['menɪs] *n* Drohung *f*; Gefahr *f* ♦ *vt*
bedrohen; **menacing** *adj* drohend
menagerie [mɪ'nædʒəri] *n* Tierschau *f*
mend [mend] *vt* reparieren, flicken ♦ *n*
(ver)heilen ♦ *n* ausgebesserte Stelle *f*; **on**
the ~ auf dem Wege der Besserung; **~ing**
n (*articles*) Flickarbeit *f*
menial ['mi:nɪəl] *adj* niedrig
meningitis [menɪn'dʒaɪtɪs] *n*
Hirnhautentzündung *f*, Meningitis *f*
menopause ['menəupɔ:z] *n* Wechseljahre
pl, Menopause *f*
menstruation [menstru'eɪʃən] *n*
Menstruation *f*
mental ['mentl] *adj* geistig, Geistes-;
(*arithmetic*) Kopf-; (*hospital*) Nerven-;
(*cruelty*) seelisch; (*inf: abnormal*) verrückt;
~ity [men'tælɪtɪ] *n* Mentalität *f*
menthol ['menθɒl] *n* Menthol *nt*
mention ['menʃən] *n* Erwähnung *f* ♦ *vt*
erwähnen; **don't ~ it!** bitte (sehr), gern
geschehen
mentor ['mentɔ:'] *n* Mentor *m*
menu ['menju:] *n* Speisekarte *f*
MEP *n abbr* = **Member of the European**
Parliament
mercenary ['mə:sɪnəri] *adj* (*person*)
geldgierig ♦ *n* Söldner *m*
merchandise ['mə:tʃəndaɪz] *n*
(Handels)ware *f*

merchant ['mə:tʃənt] *n* Kaufmann *m*; ~
bank (*BRIT*) *n* Handelsbank *f*; ~ **navy** (*US* ~
marine) *n* Handelsmarine *f*
merciful ['mə:sɪful] *adj* gnädig
merciless ['mə:sɪlɪs] *adj* erbarmungslos
mercury ['mə:kjuri] *n* Quecksilber *nt*
mercy ['mə:sɪ] *n* Erbarmen *nt*; Gnade *f*; **at**
the ~ of ausgeliefert +*dat*
mere [mɪə'] *adj* bloß; **~ly** *adv* bloß
merge [mə:dʒ] *vt* verbinden; (*COMM*)
fusionieren ♦ *vi* verschmelzen; (*roads*)
zusammenlaufen; (*COMM*) fusionieren; **~r** *n*
(*COMM*) Fusion *f*
meringue [mə'ræŋ] *n* Baiser *nt*
merit ['merɪt] *n* Verdienst *nt*; (*advantage*)
Vorzug *m* ♦ *vt* verdienen
mermaid ['mə:meɪd] *n* Wassernixe *f*
merry ['merɪ] *adj* fröhlich; **~-go-round** *n*
Karussell *nt*
mesh [meʃ] *n* Masche *f*
mesmerize ['mezməraɪz] *vt* hypnotisieren;
(*fig*) faszinieren
mess [mes] *n* Unordnung *f*; (*dirt*) Schmutz
m; (*trouble*) Schwierigkeiten *pl*; (*MIL*) Messe
f; ~ **about** *or* **around** *vi* (*play the fool*)
herumalbern; (*do nothing in particular*)
herumgammeln; ~ **about** *or* **around**
with *vt fus* (*tinker with*) herummurksen an
+*dat*; ~ **up** *vt* verpfuschen; (*make untidy*) in
Unordnung bringen
message ['mesɪdʒ] *n* Mitteilung *f*; **to get**
the ~ kapieren
messenger ['mesɪndʒə'] *n* Bote *m*
Messrs ['mesəz] *abbr* (*on letters*) die Herren
messy ['mesɪ] *adj* schmutzig; (*untidy*)
unordentlich
met [met] *pt, pp of* **meet**
metabolism [me'tæbəlɪzəm] *n* Stoffwechsel
m
metal ['metl] *n* Metall *nt*; **~lic** *adj* metallisch;
(*made of ~*) aus Metall
metaphor ['metəfə'] *n* Metapher *f*
meteorology [mi:tɪə'rɔlədʒɪ] *n* Meteorologie
f
meter ['mi:tə'] *n* Zähler *m*; (*US*) = **metre**
method ['meθəd] *n* Methode *f*; **~ical**
[mɪ'θɒdɪkl] *adj* methodisch; **M~ist**

['mεθədıst] *adj* methodistisch ♦ *n* Methodist(in) *m(f)*; ~**ology** [mεθə'dɔlədʒı] *n* Methodik *f*

meths [mεθs] (*BRIT*) *n(pl)* = **methylated spirit(s)**

methylated spirit(s) ['mεθɪleıtıd-] (*BRIT*) *n* (Brenn)spiritus *m*

meticulous [mı'tıkjuləs] *adj* (über)genau

metre ['mi:tər] (*US* **meter**) *n* Meter *m* or *nt*

metric ['mεtrık] *adj* (*also:* ~**al**) metrisch

metropolitan [mεtrə'pɔlıtn] *adj* der Großstadt; **M~ Police** (*BRIT*) *n*: **the M~ Police** die Londoner Polizei

mettle ['mεtl] *n* Mut *m*

mew [mju:] *vi* (*cat*) miauen

mews [mju:z] *n*: ~ **cottage** ehemaliges Kutscherhäuschen

Mexican ['mεksıkən] *adj* mexikanisch ♦ *n* Mexikaner(in) *m(f)*

Mexico ['mεksıkəu] *n* Mexiko *nt*

miaow [mi:'au] *vi* miauen

mice [maıs] *pl of* **mouse**

micro ['maıkrəu] *n* (*also:* ~**computer**) Mikrocomputer *m*; ~**chip** *n* Mikrochip *m*; ~**cosm** ['maıkrəukɔzəm] *n* Mikrokosmos *m*; ~**phone** *n* Mikrofon *nt*, Mikrophon *nt*; ~**scope** *n* Mikroskop *nt*; ~**wave** *n* (*also:* ~**wave oven**) Mikrowelle(nherd *nt*) *f*

mid [mıd] *adj*: **in** ~ **afternoon** am Nachmittag; **in** ~ **air** in der Luft; **in** ~ **May** Mitte Mai

midday [mıd'deı] *n* Mittag *m*

middle ['mıdl] *n* Mitte *f*; (*waist*) Taille *f* ♦ *adj* mittlere(r, s), Mittel-; **in the** ~ **of** mitten in +*dat*; ~-**aged** *adj* mittleren Alters; **M~ Ages** *npl*: **the M~ Ages** das Mittelalter; ~-**class** *adj* Mittelstands-; **M~ East** *n*: **the M~ East** der Nahe Osten; ~**man** (*irreg*) *n* (*COMM*) Zwischenhändler *m*; ~ **name** *n* zweiter Vorname *m*; ~ **weight** *n* (*BOXING*) Mittelgewicht *nt*

middling ['mıdlıŋ] *adj* mittelmäßig

midge [mıdʒ] *n* Mücke *f*

midget ['mıdʒıt] *n* Liliputaner(in) *m(f)*

midnight ['mıdnaıt] *n* Mitternacht *f*

midriff ['mıdrıf] *n* Taille *f*

midst [mıdst] *n*: **in the** ~ **of** (*persons*) mitten

unter +*dat*; (*things*) mitten in +*dat*

mid [mıd'-]: ~**summer** *n* Hochsommer *m*; ~**way** *adv* auf halbem Wege ♦ *adj* Mittel-, ~**week** *adv* in der Mitte der Woche

midwife ['mıdwaıf] (*irreg*) *n* Hebamme *f*; ~**ry** ['mıdwıfərı] *n* Geburtshilfe *f*

midwinter [mıd'wıntər] *n* tiefste(r) Winter *m*

might [maıt] *vi see* **may** ♦ *n* Macht *f*, Kraft *f*; **I** ~ **come** ich komme vielleicht; ~**y** *adj, adv* mächtig

migraine ['mi:greın] *n* Migräne *f*

migrant ['maıgrənt] *adj* Wander-; (*bird*) Zug-

migrate [maı'greıt] *vi* (ab)wandern; (*birds*) (fort)ziehen; **migration** [maı'greıʃən] *n* Wanderung *f*, Zug *m*

mike [maık] *n* = **microphone**

Milan [mı'læn] *n* Mailand *nt*

mild [maıld] *adj* mild; (*medicine, interest*) leicht; (*person*) sanft ♦ *n* (*beer*) leichtes dunkles Bier

mildew ['mıldju:] *n* (*on plants*) Mehltau *m*; (*on food*) Schimmel *m*

mildly ['maıldlı] *adv* leicht; **to put it** ~ gelinde gesagt

mile [maıl] *n* Meile *f*; ~**age** *n* Meilenzahl *f*; ~**ometer** *n* = **milometer**; ~**stone** *n* (*also fig*) Meilenstein *m*

militant ['mılıtnt] *adj* militant ♦ *n* Militante(r) *mf*

military ['mılıtərı] *adj* militärisch, Militär-, Wehr-

militate ['mılıteıt] *vi*: **to** ~ **against** entgegenwirken +*dat*

militia [mı'lıʃə] *n* Miliz *f*

milk [mılk] *n* Milch *f* ♦ *vt* (*also fig*) melken; ~ **chocolate** *n* Milchschokolade *f*; ~**man** (*irreg*) *n* Milchmann *m*; ~ **shake** *n* Milchmixgetränk *nt*; ~**y** *adj* milchig; **M~y Way** *n* Milchstraße *f*

mill [mıl] *n* Mühle *f*; (*factory*) Fabrik *f* ♦ *vt* mahlen ♦ *vi* umherlaufen

millennia [mı'lεnıə] *npl of* **millennium**

millennium [mı'lεnıəm] (*pl* ~**s** *or* **millennia**) *n* Jahrtausend *nt*; ~ **bug** *n* (*COMPUT*) Jahrtausendfehler *m*

miller ['mılər] *n* Müller *m*

milligram(me) ['mılıgræm] *n* Milligramm *nt*

millimetre ['mɪlɪmiːtəʳ] (*US* **millimeter**) *n* Millimeter *m*

million ['mɪljən] *n* Million *f*; **a ~ times** tausendmal; **~aire** [mɪljə'nɛəʳ] *n* Millionär(in) *m(f)*

millstone ['mɪlstəun] *n* Mühlstein *m*

milometer [maɪ'lɒmɪtəʳ] *n* ≈ Kilometerzähler *m*

mime [maɪm] *n* Pantomime *f* ♦ *vt, vi* mimen

mimic ['mɪmɪk] *n* Mimiker *m* ♦ *vt, vi* nachahmen; **~ry** *n* Nachahmung *f*; (*BIOL*) Mimikry *f*

min. *abbr* = **minutes; minimum**

mince [mɪns] *vt* (zer)hacken ♦ *n* (*meat*) Hackfleisch *nt*; **~meat** *n* süße Pastetenfüllung *f*; **~ pie** *n* gefüllte (süße) Pastete *f*; **~r** *n* Fleischwolf *m*

mind [maɪnd] *n* Verstand *m*, Geist *m*; (*opinion*) Meinung *f* ♦ *vt* aufpassen auf +*acc*; (*object to*) etwas haben gegen; **on my ~** auf dem Herzen; **to my ~** meiner Meinung nach; **to be out of one's ~** wahnsinnig sein; **to bear** *or* **keep in ~** bedenken; **to change one's ~** es sich *dat* anders überlegen; **to make up one's ~** sich entschließen; **I don't ~** das macht mir nichts aus; **~ you, ...** allerdings ...; **never ~!** macht nichts!; **"~ the step"** „Vorsicht Stufe"; **~ your own business** kümmern Sie sich um Ihre eigenen Angelegenheiten; **~er** *n* Aufpasser(in) *m(f)*; **~ful** *adj*: **~ful of** achtsam auf +*acc*; **~less** *adj* sinnlos

mine[1] [maɪn] *n* (*coalmine*) Bergwerk *nt*; (*MIL*) Mine *f* ♦ *vt* abbauen; (*MIL*) verminen

mine[2] [maɪn] *pron* meine(r, s); **that book is ~** das Buch gehört mir; **a friend of ~** ein Freund von mir

minefield ['maɪnfiːld] *n* Minenfeld *nt*

miner ['maɪnəʳ] *n* Bergarbeiter *m*

mineral ['mɪnərəl] *adj* mineralisch, Mineral- ♦ *n* Mineral *nt*; **~s** *npl* (*BRIT*: *soft drinks*) alkoholfreie Getränke *pl*; **~ water** *n* Mineralwasser *nt*

minesweeper ['maɪnswiːpəʳ] *n* Minensuchboot *nt*

mingle ['mɪŋgl] *vi*: **to ~ (with)** sich mischen (unter +*acc*)

miniature ['mɪnətʃəʳ] *adj* Miniatur- ♦ *n* Miniatur *f*

minibus ['mɪnɪbʌs] *n* Kleinbus *m*

Minidisc ['mɪnɪdɪsk] *n* Minidisc ® *f*

minimal ['mɪnɪml] *adj* minimal

minimize ['mɪnɪmaɪz] *vt* auf das Mindestmaß beschränken

minimum ['mɪnɪməm] (*pl* **minima**) *n* Minimum *nt* ♦ *adj* Mindest-

mining ['maɪnɪŋ] *n* Bergbau *m* ♦ *adj* Bergbau-, Berg-

miniskirt ['mɪnɪskəːt] *n* Minirock *m*

minister ['mɪnɪstəʳ] *n* (*BRIT*: *POL*) Minister *m*; (*ECCL*) Pfarrer *m* ♦ *vi*: **to ~ to sb/sb's needs** sich um jdn kümmern; **~ial** [mɪnɪs'tɪərɪəl] *adj* ministeriell, Minister-

ministry ['mɪnɪstrɪ] *n* (*BRIT*: *POL*) Ministerium *nt*; (*ECCL*: *office*) geistliche(s) Amt *nt*

mink [mɪŋk] *n* Nerz *m*

minnow ['mɪnəu] *n* Elritze *f*

minor ['maɪnəʳ] *adj* kleiner; (*operation*) leicht; (*problem, poet*) unbedeutend; (*MUS*) Moll ♦ *n* (*BRIT*: *under 18*) Minderjährige(r) *mf*

minority [maɪ'nɒrɪtɪ] *n* Minderheit *f*

mint [mɪnt] *n* Minze *f*; (*sweet*) Pfefferminzbonbon *nt* ♦ *vt* (*coins*) prägen; **the (Royal** (*BRIT*) *or* **US** (*US*)) **M~** die Münzanstalt; **in ~ condition** in tadellosem Zustand

minus ['maɪnəs] *n* Minuszeichen *nt*; (*amount*) Minusbetrag *m* ♦ *prep* minus, weniger

minuscule ['mɪnəskjuːl] *adj* winzig

minute[1] [maɪ'njuːt] *adj* winzig; (*detailed*) minutiös, minuziös

minute[2] ['mɪnɪt] *n* Minute *f*; (*moment*) Augenblick *m*; **~s** *npl* (*of meeting etc*) Protokoll *nt*

miracle ['mɪrəkl] *n* Wunder *nt*

miraculous [mɪ'rækjuləs] *adj* wunderbar

mirage ['mɪrɑːʒ] *n* Fata Morgana *f*

mire ['maɪəʳ] *n* Morast *m*

mirror ['mɪrəʳ] *n* Spiegel *m* ♦ *vt* (wider)spiegeln

mirth [mɜːθ] *n* Heiterkeit *f*

misadventure [mɪsəd'ventʃəʳ] *n* Missgeschick *nt*, Unfall *m*

misanthropist [mɪ'zænθrəpɪst] *n*

Menschenfeind *m*

misapprehension ['mɪsæprɪ'henʃən] *n*
Missverständnis *nt*

misbehave [mɪsbɪ'heɪv] *vi* sich schlecht
benehmen

miscalculate [mɪs'kælkjuleɪt] *vt* falsch
berechnen

miscarriage ['mɪskærɪdʒ] *n* (*MED*)
Fehlgeburt *f*; **~ of justice** Fehlurteil *nt*

miscellaneous [mɪsɪ'leɪnɪəs] *adj*
verschieden

mischief ['mɪstʃɪf] *n* Unfug *m*;
mischievous ['mɪstʃɪvəs] *adj* (*person*)
durchtrieben; (*glance*) verschmitzt; (*rumour*)
bösartig

misconception ['mɪskən'sepʃən] *n*
fälschliche Annahme *f*

misconduct [mɪs'kɒndʌkt] *n* Vergehen *nt*;
professional ~ Berufsvergehen *nt*

misconstrue [mɪskən'struː] *vt*
missverstehen

misdemeanour [mɪsdɪ'miːnəʳ] (*US*
misdemeanor) *n* Vergehen *nt*

miser ['maɪzəʳ] *n* Geizhals *m*

miserable ['mɪzərəbl] *adj* (*unhappy*)
unglücklich; (*headache, weather*)
fürchterlich; (*poor*) elend, (*contemptible*)
erbärmlich

miserly ['maɪzəlɪ] *adj* geizig

misery ['mɪzərɪ] *n* Elend *nt*, Qual *f*

misfire [mɪs'faɪəʳ] *vi* (*gun*) versagen; (*engine*)
fehlzünden; (*plan*) fehlgehen

misfit ['mɪsfɪt] *n* Außenseiter *m*

misfortune [mɪs'fɔːtʃən] *n* Unglück *nt*

misgiving(s) [mɪs'gɪvɪŋ(z)] *n(pl)* Bedenken
pl

misguided [mɪs'gaɪdɪd] *adj* fehlgeleitet;
(*opinions*) irrig

mishandle [mɪs'hændl] *vt* falsch handhaben

mishap ['mɪshæp] *n* Missgeschick *nt*

misinform [mɪsɪn'fɔːm] *vt* falsch
unterrichten

misinterpret [mɪsɪn'təːprɪt] *vt* falsch
auffassen

misjudge [mɪs'dʒʌdʒ] *vt* falsch beurteilen

mislay [mɪs'leɪ] (*irreg: like* **lay**) *vt* verlegen

mislead [mɪs'liːd] (*irreg: like* **lead**[2]) *vt*

(*deceive*) irreführen; **~ing** *adj* irreführend

mismanage [mɪs'mænɪdʒ] *vt* schlecht
verwalten

misnomer [mɪs'nəʊməʳ] *n* falsche
Bezeichnung *f*

misplace [mɪs'pleɪs] *vt* verlegen

misprint ['mɪsprɪnt] *n* Druckfehler *m*

Miss [mɪs] *n* Fräulein *nt*

miss [mɪs] *vt* (*fail to hit, catch*) verfehlen; (*not
notice*) verpassen; (*be too late*) versäumen,
verpassen; (*omit*) auslassen; (*regret the
absence of*) vermissen ♦ *vi* fehlen ♦ *n* (*shot*)
Fehlschuss *m*; (*failure*) Fehlschlag *m*; **I ~ you**
du fehlst mir; **~ out** *vt* auslassen

misshapen [mɪs'ʃeɪpən] *adj* missgestaltet

missile ['mɪsaɪl] *n* Rakete *f*

missing ['mɪsɪŋ] *adj* (*person*) vermisst;
(*thing*) fehlend; **to be ~** fehlen

mission ['mɪʃən] *n* (*work*) Auftrag *m*;
(*people*) Delegation *f*; (*REL*) Mission *f*; **~ary**
n Missionar(in) *m(f)*; **~ statement** *n*
Kurzdarstellung *f* der Firmenphilosophie

misspell ['mɪs'spel] (*irreg: like* **spell**) *vt*
falsch schreiben

misspent ['mɪs'spent] *adj* (*youth*) vergeudet

mist [mɪst] *n* Dunst *m*, Nebel *m* ♦ *vi* (*also: ~
over, ~ up*) sich trüben; (*BRIT: windows*) sich
beschlagen

mistake [mɪs'teɪk] (*irreg: like* **take**) *n* Fehler
m ♦ *vt* (*misunderstand*) missverstehen; (*mix
up*): **to ~ (sth for sth)** (etw mit etw)
verwechseln; **to make a ~** einen Fehler
machen; **by ~** aus Versehen; **to ~ A for B** A
mit B verwechseln; **~n** *pp of* **mistake** ♦ *adj*
(*idea*) falsch; **to be ~n** sich irren

mister ['mɪstəʳ] *n* (*inf*) Herr *m*; *see* **Mr**

mistletoe ['mɪsltəʊ] *n* Mistel *f*

mistook [mɪs'tʊk] *pt of* **mistake**

mistress ['mɪstrɪs] *n* (*teacher*) Lehrerin *f*; (*in
house*) Herrin *f*; (*lover*) Geliebte *f*; *see* **Mrs**

mistrust [mɪs'trʌst] *vt* misstrauen +*dat*

misty ['mɪstɪ] *adj* neblig

misunderstand [mɪsʌndə'stænd] (*irreg: like*
understand) *vt, vi* missverstehen, falsch
verstehen; **~ing** *n* Missverständnis *nt*;
(*disagreement*) Meinungsverschiedenheit *f*

misuse [*n* mɪs'juːs, *vb* mɪs'juːz] *n* falsche(r)

Gebrauch *m* ♦ *vt* falsch gebrauchen

mitigate ['mɪtɪgeɪt] *vt* mildern

mitt(en) ['mɪt(n)] *n* Fausthandschuh *m*

mix [mɪks] *vt (blend)* (ver)mischen ♦ *vi (liquids)* sich (ver)mischen lassen; *(people: get on)* sich vertragen; *(: associate)* Kontakt haben ♦ *n (~ture)* Mischung *f*; ~ **up** *vt* zusammenmischen; *(confuse)* verwechseln; ~**ed** *adj* gemischt; ~**ed-up** *adj* durcheinander; ~**er** *n (for food)* Mixer *m*; ~**ture** *n* Mischung *f*; ~~**up** *n* Durcheinander *nt*

mm *abbr (= millimetre(s))* mm

moan [məun] *n* Stöhnen *nt*; *(complaint)* Klage *f* ♦ *vi* stöhnen; *(complain)* maulen

moat [məut] *n* (Burg)graben *m*

mob [mɔb] *n* Mob *m*; *(the masses)* Pöbel *m* ♦ *vt* herfallen über +acc

mobile ['məubaɪl] *adj* beweglich; *(library etc)* fahrbar ♦ *n (decoration)* Mobile *nt*; ~ **home** *n* Wohnwagen *m*; ~ **phone** *n (TEL)* Mobiltelefon *nt*; **mobility** [məu'bɪlɪtɪ] *n* Beweglichkeit *f*; **mobilize** ['məubɪlaɪz] *vt* mobilisieren

mock [mɔk] *vt* verspotten; *(defy)* trotzen +dat ♦ *adj* Schein-; ~**ery** *n* Spott *m*; *(person)* Gespött *nt*

mod [mɔd] *adj see* **convenience**

mode [məud] *n* (Art *f* und) Weise *f*

model ['mɔdl] *n* Modell *nt*; *(example)* Vorbild *nt*; *(in fashion)* Mannequin *nt* ♦ *adj (railway)* Modell-; *(perfect)* Muster-; vorbildlich ♦ *vt (make)* bilden; *(clothes)* vorführen ♦ *vi* als Mannequin arbeiten

modem ['məudem] *n (COMPUT)* Modem *nt*

moderate [*adj, n* 'mɔdərət, *vb* 'mɔdəreɪt] *adj* gemäßigt ♦ *n (POL)* Gemäßigte(r) *mf* ♦ *vi* sich mäßigen ♦ *vt* mäßigen; **moderation** [mɔdə'reɪʃən] *n* Mäßigung *f*; **in moderation** mit Maßen

modern ['mɔdən] *adj* modern; *(history, languages)* neuere(r, s); ~**ize** *vt* modernisieren

modest ['mɔdɪst] *adj* bescheiden; ~**y** *n* Bescheidenheit *f*

modicum ['mɔdɪkəm] *n* bisschen *nt*

modification [mɔdɪfɪ'keɪʃən] *n*

(Ab)änderung *f*

modify ['mɔdɪfaɪ] *vt* abändern

module ['mɔdjuːl] *n (component)* (Bau)element *nt*; *(SPACE)* (Raum)kapsel *f*

mogul ['məugl] *n (fig)* Mogul *m*

mohair ['məuheəʳ] *n* Mohär *m*, Mohair *m*

moist [mɔɪst] *adj* feucht; ~**en** ['mɔɪsn] *vt* befeuchten; ~**ure** ['mɔɪstʃəʳ] *n* Feuchtigkeit *f*; ~**urizer** ['mɔɪstʃəraɪzəʳ] *n* Feuchtigkeitscreme *f*

molar ['məuləʳ] *n* Backenzahn *m*

molasses [mə'læsɪz] *n* Melasse *f*

mold [məuld] *(US)* = **mould**

mole [məul] *n (spot)* Leberfleck *m*; *(animal)* Maulwurf *m*; *(pier)* Mole *f*

molest [mə'lest] *vt* belästigen

mollycoddle ['mɔlɪkɔdl] *vt* verhätscheln

molt [məult] *(US) vi* = **moult**

molten ['məultən] *adj* geschmolzen

mom [mɔm] *(US) n* = **mum**

moment ['məumənt] *n* Moment *m*, Augenblick *m*; *(importance)* Tragweite *f*; **at the ~** im Augenblick; ~**ary** *adj* kurz; ~**ous** [məu'mentəs] *adj* folgenschwer

momentum [məu'mentəm] *n* Schwung *m*; **to gather ~** in Fahrt kommen

mommy ['mɔmɪ] *(US) n* = **mummy**

Monaco ['mɔnəkəu] *n* Monaco *nt*

monarch ['mɔnək] *n* Herrscher(in) *m(f)*; ~**y** *n* Monarchie *f*

monastery ['mɔnəstərɪ] *n* Kloster *nt*

monastic [mə'næstɪk] *adj* klösterlich, Kloster-

Monday ['mʌndɪ] *n* Montag *m*

monetary ['mʌnɪtərɪ] *adj* Geld-; *(of currency)* Währungs-

money ['mʌnɪ] *n* Geld *nt*; **to make ~** Geld verdienen; ~ **belt** *n* Geldgürtel *nt*; ~**lender** *n* Geldverleiher *m*; ~ **order** *n* Postanweisung *f*; ~~**spinner** *(inf) n* Verkaufsschlager *m*

mongol ['mɔŋgəl] *n (MED)* mongoloide(s) Kind *nt* ♦ *adj* mongolisch; *(MED)* mongoloid

mongrel ['mʌŋgrəl] *n* Promenadenmischung *f*

monitor ['mɔnɪtəʳ] *n (SCH)* Klassenordner *m*; *(television ~)* Monitor *m* ♦ *vt (broadcasts)* abhören; (*control*) überwachen

monk [mʌŋk] *n* Mönch *m*

monkey ['mʌŋkɪ] *n* Affe *m*; ~ **nut** (*BRIT*) Erdnuss *f*; ~ **wrench** *n* (*TECH*) Engländer *m*, Franzose *m*

monochrome ['mɒnəkrəʊm] *adj* schwarz-weiß, schwarzweiß

monopolize [mə'nɒpəlaɪz] *vt* beherrschen

monopoly [mə'nɒpəlɪ] *n* Monopol *nt*

monosyllable ['mɒnəsɪləbl] *n* einsilbige(s) Wort *nt*

monotone ['mɒnətəʊn] *n* gleich bleibende(r) Ton(fall) *m*; **to speak in a ~** monoton sprechen; **monotonous** [mə'nɒtənəs] *adj* eintönig; **monotony** [mə'nɒtənɪ] *n* Eintönigkeit *f*, Monotonie *f*

monsoon [mɒn'suːn] *n* Monsun *m*

monster ['mɒnstəʳ] *n* Ungeheuer *nt*; (*person*) Scheusal *nt*

monstrosity [mɒn'strɒsɪtɪ] *n* Ungeheuerlichkeit *f*; (*thing*) Monstrosität *f*

monstrous ['mɒnstrəs] *adj* (*shocking*) grässlich, ungeheuerlich; (*huge*) riesig

month [mʌnθ] *n* Monat *m*; **~ly** *adj* monatlich, Monats- ♦ *adv* einmal im Monat ♦ *n* (*magazine*) Monatsschrift *f*

monument ['mɒnjumənt] *n* Denkmal *nt*; **~al** [mɒnju'mentl] *adj* (*huge*) gewaltig; (*ignorance*) ungeheuer

moo [muː] *vi* muhen

mood [muːd] *n* Stimmung *f*, Laune *f*; **to be in a good/bad ~** gute/schlechte Laune haben; **~y** *adj* launisch

moon [muːn] *n* Mond *m*; **~light** *n* Mondlicht *nt*; **~lighting** *n* Schwarzarbeit *f*; **~lit** *adj* mondhell

moor [muəʳ] *n* Heide *f*, Hochmoor *nt* ♦ *vt* (*ship*) festmachen, verankern ♦ *vi* anlegen; **~ings** *npl* Liegeplatz *m*; **~land** ['muələnd] *n* Heidemoor *nt*

moose [muːs] *n* Elch *m*

mop [mɒp] *n* Mopp *m* ♦ *vt* (auf)wischen; **~ up** *vt* aufwischen

mope [məʊp] *vi* Trübsal blasen

moped ['məʊped] *n* Moped *nt*

moral ['mɒrl] *adj* moralisch; (*values*) sittlich; (*virtuous*) tugendhaft ♦ *n* Moral *f*; **~s** *npl*

(*ethics*) Moral *f*

morale [mɒ'rɑːl] *n* Moral *f*

morality [mə'rælɪtɪ] *n* Sittlichkeit *f*

morass [mə'ræs] *n* Sumpf *m*

morbid ['mɔːbɪd] *adj* krankhaft; (*jokes*) makaber

KEYWORD

more [mɔːʳ] *adj* (*greater in number etc*) mehr; (*additional*) noch mehr; **do you want (some) more tea?** möchten Sie noch etwas Tee?; **I have no** *or* **I don't have any more money** ich habe kein Geld mehr
♦ *pron* (*greater amount*) mehr; (*further or additional amount*) noch mehr; **is there any more?** gibt es noch mehr?; (*left over*) ist noch etwas da?; **there's no more** es ist nichts mehr da
♦ *adv* mehr; **more dangerous/easily** *etc* **(than)** gefährlicher/einfacher *etc* (als); **more and more** immer mehr; **more and more excited** immer aufgeregter; **more or less** mehr oder weniger; **more than ever** mehr denn je; **more beautiful than ever** schöner denn je

---

moreover [mɔː'rəʊvəʳ] *adv* überdies

morgue [mɔːg] *n* Leichenschauhaus *nt*

Mormon ['mɔːmən] *n* Mormone *m*, Mormonin *f*

morning ['mɔːnɪŋ] *n* Morgen *m*; **in the ~** am Morgen; **7 o'clock in the ~** 7 Uhr morgens; **~ sickness** *n* (Schwangerschafts)übelkeit *f*

Morocco [mə'rɒkəʊ] *n* Marokko *nt*

moron ['mɔːrɒn] *n* Schwachsinnige(r) *mf*

morose [mə'rəʊs] *adj* mürrisch

morphine ['mɔːfiːn] *n* Morphium *nt*

Morse [mɔːs] *n* (*also:* ~ **code**) Morsealphabet *nt*

morsel ['mɔːsl] *n* Bissen *m*

mortal ['mɔːtl] *adj* sterblich; (*deadly*) tödlich; (*very great*) Todes- ♦ *n* (*human being*) Sterbliche(r) *mf*; **~ity** [mɔː'tælɪtɪ] *n* Sterblichkeit *f*; (*death rate*) Sterblichkeitsziffer *f*

mortar ['mɔːtəʳ] *n* (*for building*) Mörtel *m*;

(*MIL*) Granatwerfer *m*

mortgage ['mɔːgɪdʒ] *n* Hypothek *f* ♦ *vt* hypothekarisch belasten; ~ **company** (*US*) *n* ≈ Bausparkasse *f*

mortify ['mɔːtɪfaɪ] *vt* beschämen

mortuary ['mɔːtjuərɪ] *n* Leichenhalle *f*

mosaic [məʊ'zeɪɪk] *n* Mosaik *nt*

Moscow ['mɔskəʊ] *n* Moskau *nt*

Moslem ['mɔzləm] = **Muslim**

mosque [mɔsk] *n* Moschee *f*

mosquito [mɔs'kiːtəʊ] (*pl* ~**es**) *n* Moskito *m*

moss [mɔs] *n* Moos *nt*

most [məʊst] *adj* meiste(r, s) ♦ *adv* am meisten; (*very*) höchst ♦ *n* das meiste, der größte Teil; (*people*) die meisten; ~ **men** die meisten Männer; **at the (very)** ~ allerhöchstens; **to make the** ~ **of** das Beste machen aus; **a** ~ **interesting book** ein höchstinteressantes Buch; ~**ly** *adv* größtenteils

MOT (*BRIT*) *n abbr* (= *Ministry of Transport*): **the MOT (test)** ≈ der TÜV

motel [məʊ'tɛl] *n* Motel *nt*

moth [mɔθ] *n* Nachtfalter *m*; (*wool-eating*) Motte *f*; ~**ball** *n* Mottenkugel *f*

mother ['mʌðəʳ] *n* Mutter *f* ♦ *vt* bemuttern; ~**hood** *n* Mutterschaft *f*; ~**-in-law** *n* Schwiegermutter *f*; ~**ly** *adj* mütterlich; ~**-of-pearl** *n* Perlmut *nt*; **M**~'**s Day** (*BRIT*) *n* Muttertag *m*; ~**-to-be** *n* werdende Mutter *f*; ~ **tongue** *n* Muttersprache *f*

motion ['məʊʃən] *n* Bewegung *f*; (*in meeting*) Antrag *m* ♦ *vt*, *vi*: **to** ~ **(to) sb** jdm winken, jdm zu verstehen geben; ~**less** *adj* regungslos; ~ **picture** *n* Film *m*

motivated ['məʊtɪveɪtɪd] *adj* motiviert

motivation [məʊtɪ'veɪʃən] *n* Motivierung *f*

motive ['məʊtɪv] *n* Motiv *nt*, Beweggrund *m* ♦ *adj* treibend

motley ['mɔtlɪ] *adj* bunt

motor ['məʊtəʳ] *n* Motor *m*; (*BRIT*: *inf*: *vehicle*) Auto *nt* ♦ *adj* Motor-; ~**bike** *n* Motorrad *nt*; ~**boat** *n* Motorboot *nt*; ~**car** (*BRIT*) *n* Auto *nt*; ~**cycle** *n* Motorrad *nt*; ~**cyclist** *n* Motorradfahrer(in) *m(f)*; ~**ing** (*BRIT*) *n* Autofahren *nt* ♦ *adj* Auto-; ~**ist** *n* Autofahrer(in) *m(f)*; ~ **mechanic** *n*

Kraftfahrzeugmechaniker(in) *m(f)*, Kfz-Mechaniker(in) *m(f)*; ~ **racing** (*BRIT*) *n* Autorennen *nt*; ~ **vehicle** *n* Kraftfahrzeug *nt*; ~**way** (*BRIT*) *n* Autobahn *f*

mottled ['mɔtld] *adj* gesprenkelt

mould [məʊld] (*US* **mold**) *n* Form *f*; (*mildew*) Schimmel *m* ♦ *vt* (*also fig*) formen; ~**y** *adj* schimmelig

moult [məʊlt] (*US* **molt**) *vi* sich mausern

mound [maʊnd] *n* (*Erd*)hügel *m*

mount [maʊnt] *n* (*liter*: *hill*) Berg *m*; (*horse*) Pferd *nt*; (*for jewel etc*) Fassung *f* ♦ *vt* (*horse*) steigen auf +*acc*; (*put in setting*) fassen; (*exhibition*) veranstalten; (*attack*) unternehmen ♦ *vi* (*also*: ~ **up**) sich häufen; (*on horse*) aufsteigen

mountain ['maʊntɪn] *n* Berg *m* ♦ *cpd* Berg-; ~ **bike** *n* Mountainbike *nt*; ~**eer** *n* Bergsteiger(in) *m(f)*; ~**eering** [maʊntɪ'nɪərɪŋ] *n* Bergsteigen *nt*; ~**ous** *adj* bergig; ~ **rescue team** *n* Bergwacht *f*; ~**side** *n* Berg(ab)hang *m*

mourn [mɔːn] *vt* betrauen, beklagen ♦ *vi*: **to** ~ **(for sb)** (um jdn) trauern; ~**er** *n* Trauernde(r) *mf*; ~**ful** *adj* traurig; ~**ing** *n* (*grief*) Trauer *f* ♦ *cpd* (*dress*) Trauer-; **in** ~**ing** (*period etc*) in Trauer; (*dress*) in Trauerkleidung *f*

mouse [maʊs] (*pl* **mice**) *n* Maus *f*; ~**trap** *n* Mausefalle *f*; ~ **mat**, ~ **pad** *n* (*COMPUT*) Mousepad *nt*

mousse [muːs] *n* (*COOK*) Creme *f*; (*cosmetic*) Schaumfestiger *m*

moustache [məs'tɑːʃ] *n* Schnurrbart *m*

mousy ['maʊsɪ] *adj* (*colour*) mausgrau; (*person*) schüchtern

mouth [maʊθ] *n* Mund *m*; (*opening*) Öffnung *f*; (*of river*) Mündung *f*; ~**ful** *n* Mund *m* voll; ~ **organ** *n* Mundharmonika *f*; ~**piece** *n* Mundstück *nt*; (*fig*) Sprachrohr *nt*; ~**wash** *n* Mundwasser *nt*; ~**watering** *adj* lecker, appetitlich

movable ['muːvəbl] *adj* beweglich

move [muːv] *n* (~*ment*) Bewegung *f*; (*in game*) Zug *m*; (*step*) Schritt *m*; (*of house*) Umzug *m* ♦ *vt* bewegen; (*people*) transportieren; (*in job*) versetzen;

(*emotionally*) bewegen ♦ *vi* sich bewegen; (*vehicle, ship*) fahren; (*~ house*) umziehen; **to get a ~ on** sich beeilen; **to ~ sb to do sth** jdn veranlassen, etw zu tun; **~ about** *or* **around** *vi* sich hin und her bewegen; (*travel*) unterwegs sein; **~ along** *vi* weitergehen; (*cars*) weiterfahren; **~ away** *vi* weggehen; **~ back** *vi* zurückgehen; (*to the rear*) zurückweichen; **~ forward** *vi* vorwärts gehen, sich vorwärts bewegen ♦ *vt* vorschieben; (*time*) vorverlegen; **~ in** *vi* (*to house*) einziehen; (*troops*) einrücken; **~ on** *vi* weitergehen ♦ *vt* weitergehen lassen; **~ out** *vi* (*of house*) ausziehen; (*troops*) abziehen; **~ over** *vi* zur Seite rücken; **~ up** *vi* aufsteigen; (*in job*) befördert werden ♦ *vt* nach oben bewegen; (*in job*) befördern; **~ment** ['muːvmənt] *n* Bewegung *f*

movie ['muːvɪ] *n* Film *m*; **to go to the ~s** ins Kino gehen; **~ camera** *n* Filmkamera *f*

moving ['muːvɪŋ] *adj* beweglich; (*touching*) ergreifend

mow [məu] (*pt* **mowed**, *pp* **mowed** *or* **mown**) *vt* mähen; **~ down** *vt* (*fig*) niedermähen; **~er** *n* (*lawnmower*) Rasenmäher *m*; **~n** *pp* of **mow**

MP *n abbr* = **Member of Parliament**

m.p.h. *abbr* = **miles per hour**

Mr ['mɪstə] (*US* **Mr.**) *n* Herr *m*

Mrs ['mɪsɪz] (*US* **Mrs.**) *n* Frau *f*

Ms [mɪz] (*US* **Ms.**) *n* (= *Miss or Mrs*) Frau *f*

M.Sc. *n abbr* = **Master of Science**

MSP *n abbr* (= *Member of the Scottish Parliament*) Mitglied *nt* des schottischen Parlaments

much [mʌtʃ] *adj* viel ♦ *adv* sehr; viel ♦ *n* viel, eine Menge; **how ~ is it?** wie viel kostet das?; **too ~** zu viel; **it's not ~** es ist nicht viel; **as ~ as** so sehr, so viel; **however ~ he tries** sosehr er es auch versucht

muck [mʌk] *n* Mist *m*; (*fig*) Schmutz *m*; **~ about** *or* **around** (*inf*) *vi*: **to ~ about** *or* **around (with sth)** (an etw *dat*) herumalbern; **~ up** *vt* (*inf*: *ruin*) vermasseln; (*dirty*) dreckig machen; **~y** *adj* (*dirty*) dreckig

mud [mʌd] *n* Schlamm *m*

muddle ['mʌdl] *n* Durcheinander *nt* ♦ *vt* (*also*: **~ up**) durcheinander bringen; **~ through** *vi* sich durchwursteln

mud [mʌd]: **~dy** *adj* schlammig; **~guard** *n* Schutzblech *nt*; **~-slinging** (*inf*) *n* Verleumdung *f*

muesli ['mjuːzlɪ] *n* Müsli *nt*

muffin ['mʌfɪn] *n* süße(s) Teilchen *nt*

muffle ['mʌfl] *vt* (*sound*) dämpfen; (*wrap up*) einhüllen; **~d** *adj* gedämpft; **~r** *n* (*US*) (*AUT*) Schalldämpfer *m*

mug [mʌg] *n* (*cup*) Becher *m*; (*inf*: *face*) Visage *f*; (: *fool*) Trottel *m* ♦ *vt* überfallen und ausrauben; **~ger** *n* Straßenräuber *m*; **~ging** *n* Überfall *m*

muggy ['mʌgɪ] *adj* (*weather*) schwül

mule [mjuːl] *n* Maulesel *m*

mull [mʌl]: **~ over** *vt* nachdenken über +*acc*

multicoloured ['mʌltɪkʌləd] (*US* **multicolored**) *adj* mehrfarbig

multi-level ['mʌltɪlevl] (*US*) *adj* = **multistorey**

multiple ['mʌltɪpl] *n* Vielfache(s) *nt* ♦ *adj* mehrfach; (*many*) mehrere; **~ sclerosis** *n* multiple Sklerose *f*

multiplex cinema ['mʌltɪpleks-] *n* Kinocenter *nt*

multiplication [mʌltɪplɪ'keɪʃən] *n* Multiplikation *f*; (*increase*) Vervielfachung *f*

multiply ['mʌltɪplaɪ] *vt*: **to ~ (by)** multiplizieren (mit) ♦ *vi* (*BIOL*) sich vermehren

multistorey ['mʌltɪ'stɔːrɪ] (*BRIT*) *adj* (*building, car park*) mehrstöckig

multitude ['mʌltɪtjuːd] *n* Menge *f*

mum [mʌm] *n* (*BRIT*: *inf*) Mutti *f* ♦ *adj*: **to keep ~ (about)** den Mund halten (über +*acc*)

mumble ['mʌmbl] *vt*, *vi* murmeln ♦ *n* Gemurmel *nt*

mummy ['mʌmɪ] *n* (*dead body*) Mumie *f*; (*BRIT*: *inf*) Mami *f*

mumps [mʌmps] *n* Mumps *m*

munch [mʌntʃ] *vt*, *vi* mampfen

mundane [mʌn'deɪn] *adj* banal

municipal [mjuː'nɪsɪpl] *adj* städtisch, Stadt-

mural ['mjuərl] *n* Wandgemälde *nt*

murder ['mɜːdə] *n* Mord *m* ♦ *vt* ermorden; **~er** *n* Mörder *m*; **~ous** *adj* Mord-; (*fig*) mörderisch

murky ['mɜːkɪ] *adj* finster

murmur ['mɜːmər] *n* Murmeln *nt*; (*of water, wind*) Rauschen *nt* ♦ *vt, vi* murmeln

muscle ['mʌsl] *n* Muskel *m*; ~ **in** *vi* mitmischen; **muscular** ['mʌskjulər] *adj* Muskel-; (*strong*) muskulös

museum [mjuː'zɪəm] *n* Museum *nt*

mushroom ['mʌʃrum] *n* Champignon *m*; Pilz *m* ♦ *vi* (*fig*) emporschießen

music ['mjuːzɪk] *n* Musik *f*; (*printed*) Noten *pl*; ~**al** *adj* (*sound*) melodisch; (*person*) musikalisch ♦ *n* (*show*) Musical *nt*; ~**al instrument** *n* Musikinstrument *nt*; ~ **centre** *n* Stereoanlage *f*; ~ **hall** (*BRIT*) *n* Varietee *nt*, Varieté *f*; ~**ian** [mjuː'zɪʃən] *n* Musiker(in) *m(f)*

Muslim ['mʌzlɪm] *adj* moslemisch ♦ *n* Moslem *m*

muslin ['mʌzlɪn] *n* Musselin *m*

mussel ['mʌsl] *n* Miesmuschel *f*

must [mʌst] *vb aux* müssen; (*in negation*) dürfen ♦ *n* Muss *nt*; **the film is a ~** den Film muss man einfach gesehen haben

mustard ['mʌstəd] *n* Senf *m*

muster ['mʌstər] *vt* (*MIL*) antreten lassen; (*courage*) zusammennehmen

mustn't ['mʌsnt] = **must not**

musty ['mʌstɪ] *adj* muffig

mute [mjuːt] *adj* stumm ♦ *n* (*person*) Stumme(r) *mf*; (*MUS*) Dämpfer *m*; ~**d** *adj* gedämpft

mutilate ['mjuːtɪleɪt] *vt* verstümmeln

mutiny ['mjuːtɪnɪ] *n* Meuterei *f* ♦ *vi* meutern

mutter ['mʌtər] *vt, vi* murmeln

mutton ['mʌtn] *n* Hammelfleisch *nt*

mutual ['mjuːtʃuəl] *adj* gegenseitig; beiderseitig; ~**ly** *adv* gegenseitig; für beide Seiten

muzzle ['mʌzl] *n* (*of animal*) Schnauze *f*; (*for animal*) Maulkorb *m*; (*of gun*) Mündung *f* ♦ *vt* einen Maulkorb anlegen +*dat*

my [maɪ] *adj* mein; **this is ~ car** das ist mein Auto; **I've washed ~ hair** ich habe mir die Haare gewaschen

myself [maɪ'self] *pron* mich *acc*; mir *dat*; (*emphatic*) selbst; *see also* **oneself**

mysterious [mɪs'tɪərɪəs] *adj* geheimnisvoll

mystery ['mɪstərɪ] *n* (*secret*) Geheimnis *nt*; (*sth difficult*) Rätsel *nt*

mystify ['mɪstɪfaɪ] *vt* ein Rätsel *nt* sein +*dat*; verblüffen

mystique [mɪs'tiːk] *n* geheimnisvolle Natur *f*

myth [mɪθ] *n* Mythos *m*; (*fig*) Erfindung *f*; ~**ology** [mɪ'θɔlədʒɪ] *n* Mythologie *f*

N, n

n / a *abbr* (= *not applicable*) nicht zutreffend

nab [næb] (*inf*) *vt* schnappen

naff [næf] (*BRIT: inf*) *adj* blöd

nag [næg] *n* (*horse*) Gaul *m*; (*person*) Nörgler(in) *m(f)* ♦ *vt, vi*: **to ~ (at) sb** an jdm herumnörgeln; ~**ging** *adj* (*doubt*) nagend ♦ *n* Nörgelei *f*

nail [neɪl] *n* Nagel *m* ♦ *vt* nageln; **to ~ sb down to doing sth** jdn darauf festnageln, etw zu tun; ~**brush** *n* Nagelbürste *f*; ~**file** *n* Nagelfeile *f*; ~ **polish** *n* Nagellack *m*; ~ **polish remover** *n* Nagellackentferner *m*; ~ **scissors** *npl* Nagelschere *f*; ~ **varnish** (*BRIT*) *n* = **nail polish**

naïve [naɪ'iːv] *adj* naiv

naked ['neɪkɪd] *adj* nackt

name [neɪm] *n* Name *m*; (*reputation*) Ruf *m* ♦ *vt* nennen; (*sth new*) benennen; (*appoint*) ernennen; **by ~** mit Namen; **I know him only by ~** ich kenne ihn nur dem Namen nach; **what's your ~?** wie heißen Sie?; **in the ~ of** im Namen +*gen*; (*for the sake of*) um +*gen* ... willen; ~**less** *adj* namenlos; ~**ly** *adv* nämlich; ~**sake** *n* Namensvetter *m*

nanny ['nænɪ] *n* Kindermädchen *nt*

nap [næp] *n* (*sleep*) Nickerchen *nt*; (*on cloth*) Strich *m* ♦ *vi*: **to be caught ~ping** (*fig*) überrumpelt werden

nape [neɪp] *n* Nacken *m*

napkin ['næpkɪn] *n* (*at table*) Serviette *f*; (*BRIT: for baby*) Windel *f*

nappy ['næpɪ] (*BRIT*) *n* (*for baby*) Windel *f*; ~ **rash** *n* wunde Stellen *pl*

narcotic [naː'kɔtɪk] *adj* betäubend ♦ *n* Betäubungsmittel *nt*

narrative ['nærətɪv] n Erzählung f ♦ adj erzählend

narrator [nə'reɪtə'] n Erzähler(in) m(f)

narrow ['nærəu] adj eng, schmal; (limited) beschränkt ♦ vi sich verengen; **to have a ~ escape** mit knapper Not davonkommen; **to ~ sth down to sth** etw auf etw acc einschränken; **~ly** adv (miss) knapp; (escape) mit knapper Not; **~-minded** adj engstirnig

nasty ['nɑːstɪ] adj ekelhaft, fies; (business, wound) schlimm

nation ['neɪʃən] n Nation f, Volk nt; **~al** ['næʃənl] adj national, National-, Landes- ♦ n Staatsangehörige(r) mf; **~al anthem** (BRIT) n Nationalhymne f; **~al dress** n Tracht f; **N~al Health Service** (BRIT) n staatliche(r) Gesundheitsdienst m; **N~al Insurance** (BRIT) n Sozialversicherung f; **~alism** ['næʃnəlɪzəm] n Nationalismus m; **~alist** ['næʃnəlɪst] n Nationalist(in) m(f) ♦ adj nationalistisch; **~ality** [næʃə'nælɪtɪ] n Staatsangehörigkeit f; **~alize** ['næʃnəlaɪz] vt verstaatlichen; **~ally** ['næʃnəlɪ] adv national, auf Staatsebene; **~al park** (BRIT) n Nationalpark m; **~-wide** ['neɪʃənwaɪd] adj, adv allgemein, landesweit

National Trust

i Der **National Trust** ist ein 1895 gegründeter Natur- und Denkmalschutzverband in Großbritannien, der Gebäude und Gelände von besonderem historischen oder ästhetischen Interesse erhält und der Öffentlichkeit zugänglich macht. Viele Gebäude im Besitz des National Trust sind (z.T. gegen ein Eintrittsgeld) zu besichtigen.

native ['neɪtɪv] n (born in) Einheimische(r) mf; (original inhabitant) Eingeborene(r) mf ♦ adj einheimisch; Eingeborenen-; (belonging by birth) heimatlich, Heimat-; (inborn) angeboren, natürlich; **a ~ of Germany** ein gebürtiger Deutscher; **a ~ speaker of French** ein französischer Muttersprachler; **N~ American** n

Indianer(in) m(f), Ureinwohner(in) m(f) Amerikas; **~ language** n Muttersprache f

Nativity [nə'tɪvɪtɪ] n: **the ~** Christi Geburt no art

NATO ['neɪtəu] n abbr (= North Atlantic Treaty Organization) NATO f

natural ['nætʃrəl] adj natürlich; Natur-; (inborn) (an)geboren; **~ gas** n Erdgas nt; **~ist** n Naturkundler(in) m(f); **~ly** adv natürlich

nature ['neɪtʃə'] n Natur f; **by ~** von Natur (aus)

naught [nɔːt] n = **nought**

naughty ['nɔːtɪ] adj (child) unartig, ungezogen; (action) ungehörig

nausea ['nɔːsɪə] n (sickness) Übelkeit f; (disgust) Ekel m; **~te** ['nɔːsɪeɪt] vt anekeln

nautical ['nɔːtɪkl] adj nautisch; See-; (expression) seemännisch

naval ['neɪvl] adj Marine-, Flotten-; **~ officer** n Marineoffizier m

nave [neɪv] n Kirchen(haupt)schiff nt

navel ['neɪvl] n Nabel m

navigate ['nævɪgeɪt] vi navigieren; **navigation** [nævɪ'geɪʃən] n Navigation f; **navigator** ['nævɪgeɪtə'] n Steuermann m; (AVIAT) Navigator m; (AUT) Beifahrer(in) m(f)

navvy ['nævɪ] (BRIT) n Straßenarbeiter m

navy ['neɪvɪ] n (Kriegs)marine f ♦ adj (also: **~ blue**) marineblau

Nazi ['nɑːtsɪ] n Nazi m

NB abbr (= nota bene) NB

near [nɪə'] adj nah ♦ adv in der Nähe ♦ prep (also: **~ to:** space) in der Nähe +gen; (: time) um +acc ... herum ♦ vt sich nähern +dat; **a ~ miss** knapp daneben; **~by** adj nahe (gelegen) ♦ adv in der Nähe; **~ly** adv fast; **I ~ly fell** ich wäre fast gefallen; **~side** n (AUT) Beifahrerseite f ♦ adj auf der Beifahrerseite; **~-sighted** adj kurzsichtig

neat [niːt] adj (tidy) ordentlich; (solution) sauber; (pure) pur; **~ly** adv (tidily) ordentlich

necessarily ['nesɪsrɪlɪ] adv unbedingt

necessary ['nesɪsrɪ] adj notwendig, nötig; **he did all that was ~** er erledigte alles, was nötig war; **it is ~ to/that ...** man muss ...

necessitate [nɪ'sesɪteɪt] *vt* erforderlich machen

necessity [nɪ'sesɪtɪ] *n* (*need*) Not *f*; (*compulsion*) Notwendigkeit *f*; **necessities** *npl* (*things needed*) das Notwendigste

neck [nɛk] *n* Hals *m* ♦ *vi* (*inf*) knutschen; **~ and ~** Kopf an Kopf; **~lace** ['nɛklɪs] *n* Halskette *f*; **~line** ['nɛklaɪn] *n* Ausschnitt *m*; **~tie** ['nɛktaɪ] (*US*) *n* Krawatte *f*

née [neɪ] *adj* geborene

need [niːd] *n* Bedürfnis *nt*; (*lack*) Mangel *m*; (*necessity*) Notwendigkeit *f*; (*poverty*) Not *f* ♦ *vt* brauchen; **I ~ to do it** ich muss es tun; **you don't ~ to go** du brauchst nicht zu gehen

needle ['niːdl] *n* Nadel *f* ♦ *vt* (*fig: inf*) ärgern

needless ['niːdlɪs] *adj* unnötig; **~ to say** natürlich

needlework ['niːdlwɜːk] *n* Handarbeit *f*

needn't ['niːdnt] = **need not**

needy ['niːdɪ] *adj* bedürftig

negative ['negətɪv] *n* (*PHOT*) Negativ *nt* ♦ *adj* negativ; (*answer*) abschlägig; **~ equity** *n* Differenz zwischen gefallenem Wert und hypothekarischer Belastung eines Wohneigentums

neglect [nɪ'glɛkt] *vt* vernachlässigen ♦ *n* Vernachlässigung *f*; **~ed** *adj* vernachlässigt

negligee ['neglɪʒeɪ] *n* Negligee *nt*, Negligé *nt*

negligence ['neglɪdʒəns] *n* Nachlässigkeit *f*

negligible ['neglɪdʒɪbl] *adj* unbedeutend, geringfügig

negotiable [nɪ'gəʊʃɪəbl] *adj* (*cheque*) übertragbar, einlösbar

negotiate [nɪ'gəʊʃɪeɪt] *vi* verhandeln ♦ *vt* (*treaty*) abschließen; (*difficulty*) überwinden; (*corner*) nehmen; **negotiation** [nɪgəʊʃɪ'eɪʃən] *n* Verhandlung *f*; **negotiator** *n* Unterhändler *m*

neigh [neɪ] *vi* wiehern

neighbour ['neɪbə'] (*US* **neighbor**) *n* Nachbar(in) *m(f)*; **~hood** *n* Nachbarschaft *f*; Umgebung *f*; **~ing** *adj* benachbart, angrenzend; **~ly** *adj* (*person, attitude*) nachbarlich

neither ['naɪðə'] *adj, pron* keine(r, s) (von beiden) ♦ *conj*: **he can't do it, and ~ can I** er kann es nicht und ich auch nicht ♦ *adv*: **~ good nor bad** weder gut noch schlecht; **~ story is true** keine der beiden Geschichten stimmt

neon ['niːɒn] *n* Neon *nt*; **~ light** *n* Neonlampe *f*

nephew ['nevjuː] *n* Neffe *m*

nerve [nɜːv] *n* Nerv *m*; (*courage*) Mut *m*; (*impudence*) Frechheit *f*; **to have a fit of ~s** in Panik geraten; **~-racking** *adj* nervenaufreibend

nervous ['nɜːvəs] *adj* (*of the nerves*) Nerven-; (*timid*) nervös, ängstlich; **~ breakdown** *n* Nervenzusammenbruch *m*; **~ness** *n* Nervosität *f*

nest [nɛst] *n* Nest *nt* ♦ *vi* nisten; **~ egg** *n* (*fig*) Notgroschen *m*

nestle ['nɛsl] *vi* sich kuscheln

Net [nɛt] *n*: **the ~** das Internet

net [nɛt] *n* Netz *nt* ♦ *adj* netto, Netto- ♦ *vt* netto einnehmen; **~ball** *n* Netzball *m*

Netherlands ['neðələndz] *npl*: **the ~** die Niederlande *pl*

nett [nɛt] *adj* = **net**

netting ['netɪŋ] *n* Netz(werk) *nt*

nettle ['netl] *n* Nessel *f*

network ['netwɜːk] *n* Netz *nt*

neurotic [njʊə'rɒtɪk] *adj* neurotisch

neuter ['njuːtə'] *adj* (*BIOL*) geschlechtslos; (*GRAM*) sächlich ♦ *vt* kastrieren

neutral ['njuːtrəl] *adj* neutral ♦ *n* (*AUT*) Leerlauf *m*; **~ity** [njuː'trælɪtɪ] *n* Neutralität *f*; **~ize** *vt* (*fig*) ausgleichen

never ['nevə'] *adv* nie(mals); **I ~ went** ich bin gar nicht gegangen; **~ in my life** nie im Leben; **~-ending** *adj* endlos; **~theless** [nevəðə'les] *adv* trotzdem, dennoch

new [njuː] *adj* neu; **N~ Age** *adj* Newage-, New-Age-; **~born** *adj* neugeboren; **~comer** ['njuːkʌmə'] *n* Neuankömmling *m*; **~fangled** (*pej*) *adj* neumodisch; **~found** *adj* neu entdeckt; **~ly** *adv* frisch, neu; **~lyweds** *npl* Frischvermählte *pl*; **~ moon** *n* Neumond *m*

news [njuːz] *n* Nachricht *f*; (*RAD, TV*) Nachrichten *pl*; **a piece of ~** eine

Nachricht; ~ **agency** n
Nachrichtenagentur f; ~**agent** (BRIT) n
Zeitungshändler m; ~**caster** n
Nachrichtensprecher(in) m(f); ~ **flash** n
Kurzmeldung f; ~**letter** n Rundschreiben
nt; ~**paper** n Zeitung f; ~**print** n
Zeitungspapier nt; ~**reader** n =
newscaster; ~**reel** n Wochenschau f; ~
stand n Zeitungsstand m

newt [njuːt] n Wassermolch m

New Year n Neujahr nt; ~**'s Day** n
Neujahrstag m; ~**'s Eve** n Silvester(abend
m) nt

New Zealand [-'ziːlənd] n Neuseeland nt;
~**er** n Neuseeländer(in) m(f)

next [nɛkst] adj nächste(r, s) ♦ adv (after)
dann, darauf; (~ time) das nächste Mal; **the
~ day** am nächsten or folgenden Tag; ~
time das nächste Mal; ~ **year** nächstes
Jahr; ~ **door** adv nebenan ♦ adj (neighbour,
flat) von nebenan; ~ **of kin** n nächste(r)
Verwandte(r) mf; ~ **to** prep neben; ~ **to
nothing** so gut wie nichts

NHS n abbr = **National Health Service**

nib [nɪb] n Spitze f

nibble ['nɪbl] vt knabbern an +dat

nice [naɪs] adj (person) nett; (thing) schön;
(subtle) fein; ~**-looking** adj gut aussehend;
~**ly** adv gut, nett; ~**ties** ['naɪsɪtɪz] npl
Feinheiten pl

nick [nɪk] n Einkerbung f ♦ vt (inf: steal)
klauen; **in the ~ of time** gerade rechtzeitig

nickel ['nɪkl] n Nickel nt; (US) Nickel m (5
cents)

nickname ['nɪkneɪm] n Spitzname m ♦ vt
taufen

nicotine patch ['nɪkətiːn-] n Nikotinpflaster
nt

niece [niːs] n Nichte f

Nigeria [naɪ'dʒɪərɪə] n Nigeria nt

niggling ['nɪglɪŋ] adj pedantisch; (doubt,
worry) qualend

night [naɪt] n Nacht f; (evening) Abend m;
the ~ before last vorletzte Nacht; **at** or **by
~** (before midnight) abends; (after midnight)
nachts; ~**cap** n (drink) Schlummertrunk m;
~**club** n Nachtlokal nt; ~**dress** n

Nachthemd nt; ~**fall** n Einbruch m der
Nacht; ~ **gown** n = **nightdress**; ~**ie** (inf) n
Nachthemd nt

nightingale ['naɪtɪŋgeɪl] n Nachtigall f

night: ~**life** ['naɪtlaɪf] n Nachtleben nt; ~**ly**
['naɪtlɪ] adj, adv jeden Abend; jede Nacht;
~**mare** ['naɪtmɛəʳ] n Albtraum m; ~ **porter**
n Nachtportier m; ~ **school** n Abendschule
f; ~ **shift** n Nachtschicht f; ~**time** n Nacht
f

nil [nɪl] n Null f

Nile [naɪl] n: **the ~** der Nil

nimble ['nɪmbl] adj beweglich

nine [naɪn] num neun; ~**teen** num
neunzehn; ~**ty** num neunzig

ninth [naɪnθ] adj neunte(r, s)

nip [nɪp] vt kneifen ♦ n Kneifen nt

nipple ['nɪpl] n Brustwarze f

nippy ['nɪpɪ] (inf) adj (person) flink; (BRIT: car)
flott; (: cold) frisch

nitrogen ['naɪtrədʒən] n Stickstoff m

KEYWORD

no [nəu] (pl **noes**) adv (opposite of yes) nein;
to answer no (to question) mit Nein
antworten; (to request) Nein or nein sagen;
no thank you nein, danke
♦ adj (not any) kein(e); **I have no money/
time** ich habe kein Geld/keine Zeit; **"no
smoking"** „Rauchen verboten"
♦ n Nein nt; (no vote) Neinstimme f

---

nobility [nəu'bɪlɪtɪ] n Adel m

noble ['nəubl] adj (rank) adlig; (splendid)
nobel, edel

nobody ['nəubədɪ] pron niemand, keiner

nocturnal [nɔk'təːnl] adj (tour, visit)
nächtlich; (animal) Nacht-

nod [nɔd] vi nicken ♦ vt nicken mit ♦ n
Nicken nt; ~ **off** vi einnicken

noise [nɔɪz] n (sound) Geräusch nt;
(unpleasant, loud) Lärm m; **noisy** ['nɔɪzɪ] adj
laut; (crowd) lärmend

nominal ['nɔmɪnl] adj nominell

nominate ['nɔmɪneɪt] vt (suggest)
vorschlagen; (in election) aufstellen;
(appoint) ernennen; **nomination**

[nɔmɪ'neɪʃən] *n* (*election*) Nominierung *f*; (*appointment*) Ernennung *f*; **nominee** [nɔmɪ'niː] *n* Kandidat(in) *m(f)*

non... [nɔn] *prefix* Nicht-, un-; **~-alcoholic** *adj* alkoholfrei

nonchalant ['nɔnʃələnt] *adj* lässig

non-committal [nɔnkə'mɪtl] *adj* (*reserved*) zurückhaltend; (*uncommitted*) unverbindlich

nondescript ['nɔndɪskrɪpt] *adj* mittelmäßig

none [nʌn] *adj, pron* kein(e, er, es) ♦ *adv*: **he's ~ the worse for it** es hat ihm nicht geschadet; **~ of you** keiner von euch; **I've ~ left** ich habe keinen mehr

nonentity [nɔ'nɛntɪtɪ] *n* Null *f* (*inf*)

nonetheless ['nʌnðə'lɛs] *adv* nichtsdestoweniger

non-existent [nɔnɪg'zɪstənt] *adj* nicht vorhanden

non-fiction [nɔn'fɪkʃən] *n* Sachbücher *pl*

nonplussed [nɔn'plʌst] *adj* verdutzt

nonsense ['nɔnsəns] *n* Unsinn *m*

non: **~-smoker** *n* Nichtraucher(in) *m(f)*; **~-smoking** *adj* Nichtraucher-; **~-stick** *adj* (*pan, surface*) Teflon- ®; **~-stop** *adj* Nonstop-, Non-Stop-

noodles ['nuːdlz] *npl* Nudeln *pl*

nook [nuk] *n* Winkel *m*; **~s and crannies** Ecken und Winkel

noon [nuːn] *n* (12 Uhr) Mittag *m*

no one ['nəuwʌn] *pron* = **nobody**

noose [nuːs] *n* Schlinge *f*

nor [nɔːʳ] *conj* = **neither** ♦ *adv see* **neither**

norm [nɔːm] *n* (*convention*) Norm *f*; (*rule, requirement*) Vorschrift *f*

normal ['nɔːməl] *adj* normal; **~ly** *adv* normal; (*usually*) normalerweise

Normandy ['nɔːməndɪ] *n* Normandie *f*

north [nɔːθ] *n* Norden *m* ♦ *adj* nördlich, Nord- ♦ *adv* nördlich, nach *or* im Norden; **N~ Africa** *n* Nordafrika *nt*; **N~ America** *n* Nordamerika *nt*; **~-east** *n* Nordosten *m*; **~erly** ['nɔːðəlɪ] *adj* nördlich; **~ern** ['nɔːðən] *adj* nördlich, Nord-; **N~ern Ireland** *n* Nordirland *nt*; **N~ Pole** *n* Nordpol *m*; **N~ Sea** *n* Nordsee *f*; **~ward(s)** ['nɔːθwəd(z)] *adv* nach Norden; **~-west** *n* Nordwesten *m*

Norway ['nɔːweɪ] *n* Norwegen *nt*

Norwegian [nɔː'wiːdʒən] *adj* norwegisch ♦ *n* Norweger(in) *m(f)*; (*LING*) Norwegisch *nt*

nose [nəuz] *n* Nase *f* ♦ *vi*: **to ~ about** herumschnüffeln; **~bleed** *n* Nasenbluten *nt*; **~ dive** *n* Sturzflug *m*; **~y** *adj* = **nosy**

nostalgia [nɔs'tældʒɪə] *n* Nostalgie *f*; **nostalgic** *adj* nostalgisch

nostril ['nɔstrɪl] *n* Nasenloch *nt*

nosy ['nəuzɪ] (*inf*) *adj* neugierig

not [nɔt] *adv* nicht; **he is ~** *or* **isn't here** er ist nicht hier; **it's too late, isn't it?** es ist zu spät, oder *or* nicht wahr?; **~ yet/now** noch nicht/nicht jetzt; *see also* **all**; **only**

notably ['nəutəblɪ] *adv* (*especially*) besonders; (*noticeably*) bemerkenswert

notary ['nəutərɪ] *n* Notar(in) *m(f)*

notch [nɔtʃ] *n* Kerbe *f*, Einschnitt *m*

note [nəut] *n* (*MUS*) Note *f*, Ton *m*; (*short letter*) Nachricht *f*; (*POL*) Note *f*; (*comment, attention*) Notiz *f*; (*of lecture etc*) Aufzeichnung *f*; (*banknote*) Schein *m*; (*fame*) Ruf *m* ♦ *vt* (*observe*) bemerken; (*also: ~ down*) notieren; **~book** *n* Notizbuch *nt*; **~d** *adj* bekannt; **~pad** *n* Notizblock *m*; **~paper** *n* Briefpapier *nt*

nothing ['nʌθɪŋ] *n* nichts; **~ new/much** nichts Neues/nicht viel; **for ~** umsonst

notice ['nəutɪs] *n* (*announcement*) Bekanntmachung *f*; (*warning*) Ankündigung *f*; (*dismissal*) Kündigung *f* ♦ *vt* bemerken; **to take ~ of** beachten; **at short ~** kurzfristig; **until further ~** bis auf weiteres; **to hand in one's ~** kündigen; **~able** *adj* merklich; **~ board** *n* Anschlagtafel *f*

notify ['nəutɪfaɪ] *vt* benachrichtigen

notion ['nəuʃən] *n* Idee *f*

notorious [nəu'tɔːrɪəs] *adj* berüchtigt

notwithstanding [nɔtwɪθ'stændɪŋ] *adv* trotzdem; **~ this** ungeachtet dessen

nought [nɔːt] *n* Null *f*

noun [naun] *n* Substantiv *nt*

nourish ['nʌrɪʃ] *vt* nähren; **~ing** *adj* nahrhaft; **~ment** *n* Nahrung *f*

novel ['nɔvl] *n* Roman *m* ♦ *adj* neu(artig); **~ist** *n* Schriftsteller(in) *m(f)*; **~ty** *n* Neuheit *f*

November [nəʊ'vɛmbəʳ] n November m
novice ['nɔvɪs] n Neuling m
now [naʊ] adv jetzt; **right ~** jetzt, gerade; **by ~** inzwischen; **just ~** gerade; **~ and then, ~ and again** ab und zu, manchmal; **from ~ on** von jetzt an; **~adays** adv heutzutage
nowhere ['nəʊwɛəʳ] adv nirgends
nozzle ['nɔzl] n Düse f
nuclear ['nju:klɪəʳ] adj (energy etc) Atom-, Kern-
nuclei ['nju:klɪaɪ] npl of **nucleus**
nucleus ['nju:klɪəs] n Kern m
nude [nju:d] adj nackt ♦ n (ART) Akt m; **in the ~** nackt
nudge [nʌdʒ] vt leicht anstoßen
nudist ['nju:dɪst] n Nudist(in) m(f)
nudity ['nju:dɪtɪ] n Nacktheit f
nuisance ['nju:sns] n Ärgernis nt; **what a ~!** wie ärgerlich!
nuke [nju:k] (inf) n Kernkraftwerk nt ♦ vt atomar vernichten
null [nʌl] adj: **~ and void** null und nichtig
numb [nʌm] adj taub, gefühllos ♦ vt betäuben
number ['nʌmbəʳ] n Nummer f; (numeral also) Zahl f; (quantity) (An)zahl f ♦ vt nummerieren; (amount to) sein; **to be ~ed among** gezahlt werden zu; **a ~ of** (several) einige; **they were ten in ~** sie waren zehn an der Zahl; **~ plate** (BRIT) n (AUT) Nummernschild nt
numeral ['nju:mərəl] n Ziffer f
numerate ['nju:mərɪt] adj rechenkundig
numerical [nju:'mɛrɪkl] adj (order) zahlenmäßig
numerous ['nju:mərəs] adj zahlreich
nun [nʌn] n Nonne f
nurse [nə:s] n Krankenschwester f; (for children) Kindermädchen nt ♦ vt (patient) pflegen; (doubt etc) hegen
nursery ['nə:sərɪ] n (for children) Kinderzimmer nt; (for plants) Gärtnerei f; (for trees) Baumschule f; **~ rhyme** n Kinderreim m; **~ school** n Kindergarten m; **~ slope** (BRIT) n (SKI) Idiotenhügel m (inf), Anfängerhügel m

nursing ['nə:sɪŋ] n (profession) Krankenpflege f; **~ home** n Privatklinik f
nurture ['nə:tʃəʳ] vt aufziehen
nut [nʌt] n Nuss f; (TECH) Schraubenmutter f; (inf) Verrückte(r) mf; **he's ~s** er ist verrückt; **~crackers** ['nʌtkrækəz] npl Nussknacker m
nutmeg ['nʌtmɛg] n Muskat(nuss f) m
nutrient ['nju:trɪənt] n Nährstoff m
nutrition [nju:'trɪʃən] n Nahrung f; **nutritious** [nju:'trɪʃəs] adj nahrhaft
nutshell ['nʌtʃɛl] n Nussschale f; **in a ~** (fig) kurz gesagt
nutter ['nʌtəʳ] (BRIT: inf) n Spinner(in) m(f)
nylon ['naɪlɔn] n Nylon nt ♦ adj Nylon-

O, o

oak [əʊk] n Eiche f ♦ adj Eichen(holz)-
O.A.P. abbr = **old-age pensioner**
oar [ɔ:ʳ] n Ruder nt
oases [əʊ'eɪsi:z] npl of **oasis**
oasis [əʊ'eɪsɪs] n Oase f
oath [əʊθ] n (statement) Eid m, Schwur m; (swearword) Fluch m
oatmeal ['əʊtmi:l] n Haferschrot m
oats [əʊts] npl Hafer m
obedience [ə'bi:dɪəns] n Gehorsam m
obedient [ə'bi:dɪənt] adj gehorsam
obesity [əʊ'bi:sɪtɪ] n Fettleibigkeit f
obey [ə'beɪ] vt, vi: **to ~ (sb)** (jdm) gehorchen
obituary [ə'bɪtjʊərɪ] n Nachruf m
object [n 'ɔbdʒɪkt, vb əb'dʒɛkt] n (thing) Gegenstand m, Objekt nt; (purpose) Ziel nt ♦ vi dagegen sein; **expense is no ~** Ausgaben spielen keine Rolle; **I ~!** ich protestiere!; **to ~ to sth** Einwände gegen etw haben; (morally) Anstoß an etw acc nehmen; **to ~ that** einwenden, dass; **~ion** [əb'dʒɛkʃən] n (reason against) Einwand m, Einspruch m; (dislike) Abneigung f; **I have no ~ion to ...** ich habe nichts gegen ... einzuwenden; **~ionable** [əb'dʒɛkʃənəbl] adj nicht einwandfrei; (language) anstößig
objective [əb'dʒɛktɪv] n Ziel nt ♦ adj objektiv
obligation [ɔblɪ'geɪʃən] n Verpflichtung f; **without ~** unverbindlich; **obligatory**

[ə'blɪɡətəri] *adj* obligatorisch

oblige [ə'blaɪdʒ] *vt* (*compel*) zwingen; (*do a favour*) einen Gefallen tun +*dat*; **to be ~d to sb for sth** jdm für etw verbunden sein

obliging [ə'blaɪdʒɪŋ] *adj* entgegenkommend

oblique [ə'bliːk] *adj* schräg, schief ♦ *n* Schrägstrich *m*

obliterate [ə'blɪtəreɪt] *vt* auslöschen

oblivion [ə'blɪvɪən] *n* Vergessenheit *f*

oblivious [ə'blɪvɪəs] *adj* nicht bewusst

oblong ['ɒblɒŋ] *n* Rechteck *nt* ♦ *adj* länglich

obnoxious [əb'nɒkʃəs] *adj* widerlich

oboe ['əubəu] *n* Oboe *f*

obscene [əb'siːn] *adj* obszön; **obscenity** [əb'senɪtɪ] *n* Obszönität *f*; **obscenities** *npl* (*oaths*) Zoten *pl*

obscure [əb'skjuə*r*] *adj* unklar; (*indistinct*) undeutlich; (*unknown*) unbekannt, obskur; (*dark*) düster ♦ *vt* verdunkeln; (*view*) verbergen; (*confuse*) verwirren; **obscurity** [əb'skjuərɪtɪ] *n* Unklarheit *f*; (*darkness*) Dunkelheit *f*

observance [əb'zɜːvəns] *n* Befolgung *f*

observant [əb'zɜːvənt] *adj* aufmerksam

observation [ɒbzə'veɪʃən] *n* (*noticing*) Beobachtung *f*; (*surveillance*) Überwachung *f*; (*remark*) Bemerkung *f*

observatory [əb'zɜːvətri] *n* Sternwarte *f*, Observatorium *nt*

observe [əb'zɜːv] *vt* (*notice*) bemerken; (*watch*) beobachten; (*customs*) einhalten; **~r** *n* Beobachter(in) *m(f)*

obsess [əb'ses] *vt* verfolgen, quälen; **~ion** [əb'seʃən] *n* Besessenheit *f*, Wahn *m*; **~ive** *adj* krankhaft

obsolete ['ɒbsəliːt] *adj* überholt, veraltet

obstacle ['ɒbstəkl] *n* Hindernis *nt*; **~ race** *n* Hindernisrennen *nt*

obstetrics [ɒb'stetrɪks] *n* Geburtshilfe *f*

obstinate ['ɒbstɪnɪt] *adj* hartnäckig, stur

obstruct [əb'strʌkt] *vt* versperren; (*pipe*) verstopfen; (*hinder*) hemmen; **~ion** [əb'strʌkʃən] *n* Versperrung *f*; Verstopfung *f*; (*obstacle*) Hindernis *nt*

obtain [əb'teɪn] *vt* erhalten, bekommen; (*result*) erzielen

obtrusive [əb'truːsɪv] *adj* aufdringlich

obvious ['ɒbvɪəs] *adj* offenbar, offensichtlich; **~ly** *adv* offensichtlich

occasion [ə'keɪʒən] *n* Gelegenheit *f*; (*special event*) Ereignis *nt*; (*reason*) Anlass *m* ♦ *vt* veranlassen; **~al** *adj* gelegentlich; **~ally** *adv* gelegentlich

occupant ['ɒkjupənt] *n* Inhaber(in) *m(f)*; (*of house*) Bewohner(in) *m(f)*

occupation [ɒkju'peɪʃən] *n* (*employment*) Tätigkeit *f*, Beruf *m*; (*pastime*) Beschäftigung *f*; (*of country*) Besetzung *f*, Okkupation *f*; **~al hazard** *n* Berufsrisiko *nt*

occupier ['ɒkjupaɪə*r*] *n* Bewohner(in) *m(f)*

occupy ['ɒkjupaɪ] *vt* (*take possession of*) besetzen; (*seat*) belegen; (*live in*) bewohnen; (*position, office*) bekleiden; (*position in sb's life*) einnehmen; (*time*) beanspruchen; **to ~ o.s. with sth** sich mit etw beschäftigen; **to ~ o.s. by doing sth** sich damit beschäftigen, etw zu tun

occur [ə'kɜː*r*] *vi* vorkommen; **to ~ to sb** jdm einfallen; **~rence** *n* (*event*) Ereignis *nt*; (*appearing*) Auftreten *nt*

ocean ['əuʃən] *n* Ozean *m*, Meer *nt*; **~-going** *adj* Hochsee-

o'clock [ə'klɒk] *adv*: **it is 5 ~** es ist 5 Uhr

OCR *n abbr* = **optical character reader**

octagonal [ɒk'tægənl] *adj* achteckig

October [ɒk'təubə*r*] *n* Oktober *m*

octopus ['ɒktəpəs] *n* Krake *f*; (*small*) Tintenfisch *m*

odd [ɒd] *adj* (*strange*) sonderbar; (*not even*) ungerade; (*sock etc*) einzeln; (*surplus*) übrig; **60-~** so um die 60; **at ~ times** ab und zu; **to be the ~ one out** (*person*) das fünfte Rad am Wagen sein; (*thing*) nicht dazugehören; **~ity** *n* (*strangeness*) Merkwürdigkeit *f*; (*queer person*) seltsame(r) Kauz *m*; (*thing*) Kuriosität *f*; **~-job man** (*irreg*) *n* Mädchen *nt* für alles; **~ jobs** *npl* gelegentlich anfallende Arbeiten; **~ly** *adv* seltsam; **~ments** *npl* Reste *pl*; **~s** *npl* Chancen *pl*; (*betting*) Gewinnchancen *pl*; **it makes no ~s** es spielt keine Rolle; **~s** uneinig; **~s and ends** *npl* Krimskrams *m*

odometer [ɒ'dɒmɪtə*r*] (*esp US*) *n* Tacho(meter) *m*

odour ['əudə'] (*US* odor) *n* Geruch *m*

KEYWORD

of [ɒv, əv] *prep* **1** von +*dat*; *use of gen*; **the history of Germany** die Geschichte Deutschlands; **a friend of ours** ein Freund von uns; **a boy of 10** ein 10-jähriger Junge; **that was kind of you** das war sehr freundlich von Ihnen
2 (*expressing quantity, amount, dates etc*): **a kilo of flour** ein Kilo Mehl; **how much of this do you need?** wie viel brauchen Sie (davon)?; **there were 3 of them** (*people*) sie waren zu dritt; (*objects*) es gab 3 (davon); **a cup of tea/vase of flowers** eine Tasse Tee/Vase mit Blumen; **the 5th of July** der 5. Juli
3 (*from, out of*) aus; **a bridge made of wood** eine Holzbrücke, eine Brücke aus Holz

off [ɒf] *adj, adv* (*absent*) weg, fort; (*switch*) aus(geschaltet), ab(geschaltet), (*BRIT: food, bad*) schlecht; (*cancelled*) abgesagt ♦ *prep* von +*dat*; **to be ~** (*to leave*) gehen; **to be ~ sick** krank sein; **a day ~** ein freier Tag; **to have an ~ day** einen schlechten Tag haben; **he had his coat ~** er hatte seinen Mantel aus; **10% ~** (*COMM*) 10% Rabatt; **5 km ~ (the road)** 5 km (von der Straße) entfernt; **~ the coast** vor der Küste; **I'm ~ meat** (*no longer eat it*) ich esse kein Fleisch mehr; (*no longer like it*) ich mag kein Fleisch mehr; **on the ~ chance** auf gut Glück

offal ['ɒfl] *n* Innereien *pl*

off-colour ['ɒf'kʌlə'] *adj* nicht wohl

offence [ə'fens] (*US* offense) *n* (*crime*) Vergehen *nt*, Straftat *f*; (*insult*) Beleidigung *f*; **to take ~ at** gekränkt sein wegen

offend [ə'fend] *vt* beleidigen; **~er** *n* Gesetzesübertreter *m*

offense [ə'fens] (*US*) *n* = offence

offensive [ə'fensɪv] *adj* (*unpleasant*) übel, abstoßend; (*weapon*) Kampf-; (*remark*) verletzend ♦ *n* Angriff *m*

offer ['ɒfə'] *n* Angebot *f* ♦ *vt* anbieten; (*opinion*) äußern; (*resistance*) leisten; **on ~**

zum Verkauf angeboten; **~ing** *n* Gabe *f*

offhand [ɒf'hænd] *adj* lässig ♦ *adv* ohne weiteres

office ['ɒfɪs] *n* Büro *nt*; (*position*) Amt *nt*; **doctor's ~** (*US*) Praxis *f*; **to take ~** sein Amt antreten; (*POL*) die Regierung übernehmen; **~ automation** *n* Büroautomatisierung *f*; **~ block** (*US* ~ building) *n* Büro(hoch)haus *nt*; **~ hours** *npl* Dienstzeit *f*; (*US: MED*) Sprechstunde *f*

officer ['ɒfɪsə'] *n* (*MIL*) Offizier *m*; (*public ~*) Beamte(r) *m*

official [ə'fɪʃl] *adj* offiziell, amtlich ♦ *n* Beamte(r) *m*; **~dom** *n* Beamtentum *nt*

officiate [ə'fɪʃɪeɪt] *vi* amtieren

officious [ə'fɪʃəs] *adj* aufdringlich

offing ['ɒfɪŋ] *n*: **in the ~** in (Aus)sicht

Off-licence

i **Off-licence** *ist ein Geschäft (oder eine Theke in einer Gaststätte), wo man alkoholische Getränke kaufen kann, die aber underswo konsumiert werden müssen. In solchen Geschäften, die oft von landesweiten Ketten betrieben werden, kann man auch andere Getränke, Süßigkeiten, Zigaretten und Knabbereien kaufen.*

off: **~-licence** (*BRIT*) *n* (*shop*) Wein- und Spirituosenhandlung *f*; **~-line** *adj* (*COMPUT*) Offline- ♦ *adv* (*COMPUT*) offline; **~-peak** *adj* (*charges*) verbilligt; **~-putting** (*BRIT*) *adj* (*person, remark etc*) abstoßend; **~-road vehicle** *n* Geländefahrzeug *nt*; **~-season** *adj* außer Saison; **~set** (*irreg: like* set) *vt* ausgleichen ♦ *n* (*also:* ~set printing) Offset(druck) *m*; (*fig: of organization*) Zweig *m*; (*: of discussion etc*) Randergebnis *nt*; **~shore** *adv* in einiger Entfernung von der Küste ♦ *adj* küstennah, Küsten-; **~side** *adj* (*SPORT*) im Abseits ♦ *n* (*AUT*) Fahrerseite *f*; **~spring** *n* Nachkommenschaft *f*; (*one*) Sprössling *m*; **~stage** *adv* hinter den Kulissen; **~-the-cuff** *adj* unvorbereitet, aus dem Stegreif; **~-the-peg** (*US* ~-the-rack) *adv* von der Stange; **~-white** *adj* naturweiß

Oftel [ˈɔftɛl] *n* Überwachungsgremium zum Verbraucherschutz nach Privatisierung der Telekommunikationsindustrie

often [ˈɔfn] *adv* oft

Ofwat [ˈɔfwɔt] *n* Überwachungsgremium zum Verbraucherschutz nach Privatisierung der Wasserindustrie

ogle [ˈəʊgl] *vt* liebäugeln mit

oil [ɔɪl] *n* Öl *nt* ♦ *vt* ölen; ~**can** *n* Ölkännchen *nt*; ~**field** *n* Ölfeld *nt*; ~ **filter** *n* (AUT) Ölfilter *m*; ~-**fired** *adj* Öl-; ~ **painting** *n* Ölgemälde *nt*; ~ **rig** *n* Ölplattform *f*; ~**skins** *npl* Ölzeug *nt*; ~ **slick** *n* Ölteppich *m*; ~ **tanker** *n* (Öl)tanker *m*; ~ **well** *n* Ölquelle *f*; ~**y** *adj* ölig; (dirty) ölbeschmiert

ointment [ˈɔɪntmənt] *n* Salbe *f*

O.K. [ˈəʊˈkeɪ] *excl* in Ordnung, O. K., o. k. ♦ *adj* in Ordnung ♦ *vt* genehmigen

okay [ˈəʊˈkeɪ] = **O.K.**

old [əʊld] *adj* alt; **how ~ are you?** wie alt bist du?; **he's 10 years ~** er ist 10 Jahre alt; ~**er brother** ältere(r) Bruder *m*; ~ **age** *n* Alter *nt*; ~-**age pensioner** (BRIT) *n* Rentner(in) *m(f)*; ~-**fashioned** *adj* altmodisch

olive [ˈɔlɪv] *n* (fruit) Olive *f*; (colour) Olive *nt* ♦ *adj* Oliven-; (coloured) olivenfarbig; ~ **oil** *n* Olivenöl *nt*

Olympic [əʊˈlɪmpɪk] *adj* olympisch; **the ~ Games, the ~s** die Olympischen Spiele

omelet(te) [ˈɔmlɪt] *n* Omelett *nt*

omen [ˈəʊmən] *n* Omen *nt*

ominous [ˈɔmɪnəs] *adj* bedrohlich

omission [əʊˈmɪʃən] *n* Auslassung *f*; (neglect) Versäumnis *nt*

omit [əʊˈmɪt] *vt* auslassen; (fail to do) versäumen

─────────────
KEYWORD
─────────────

on [ɔn] *prep* **1** (indicating position) auf +dat; (with vb of motion) auf +acc; (on vertical surface, part of body) an +dat/acc; **it's on the table** es ist auf dem Tisch; **she put the book on the table** sie legte das Buch auf den Tisch; **on the left** links

2 (indicating means, method, condition etc): **on foot** (go, be) zu Fuß; **on the train/plane** (go) mit dem Zug/Flugzeug; (be) im Zug/Flugzeug; **on the telephone/television** am Telefon/im Fernsehen; **to be on drugs** Drogen nehmen; **to be on holiday/business** im Urlaub/auf Geschäftsreise sein

3 (referring to time): **on Friday** (am) Freitag; **on Fridays** freitags; **on June 20th** am 20. Juni; **a week on Friday** Freitag in einer Woche; **on arrival he ...** als er ankam, ... er ...

4 (about, concerning) über +acc ♦ *adv* **1** (referring to dress) an; **she put her boots/hat on** sie zog ihre Stiefel an/setzte ihren Hut auf

2 (further, continuously) weiter; **to walk on** weitergehen ♦ *adj* **1** (functioning, in operation: machine, TV, light) an; (: tap) aufgedreht; (: brakes) angezogen; **is the meeting still on?** findet die Versammlung noch statt?; **there's a good film on** es läuft ein guter Film

2: **that's not on!** (inf: of behaviour) das liegt nicht drin!

─────────────

once [wʌns] *adv* einmal ♦ *conj* wenn ... einmal; ~ **he had left/it was done** nachdem er gegangen war/es fertig war; **at ~** sofort; (at the same time) gleichzeitig; ~ **a week** einmal in der Woche; ~ **more** noch einmal; ~ **and for all** ein für alle Mal; ~ **upon a time** es war einmal

oncoming [ˈɔnkʌmɪŋ] *adj* (traffic) Gegen-, entgegenkommend

─────────────
KEYWORD
─────────────

one [wʌn] *num* eins; (with noun, referring back to noun) ein/eine/ein; **it is one** (o'clock) es ist eins, es ist ein Uhr; **one hundred and fifty** einhundertfünfzig ♦ *adj* **1** (sole) einzige(r, s); **the one book which** das einzige Buch, welches

2 (same) derselbe/dieselbe/dasselbe; **they came in the one car** sie kamen alle in dem einen Auto

3 (indef): **one day I discovered ...** eines Tages bemerkte ich ...

♦ *pron* **1** eine(r, s); **do you have a red one?** haben Sie einen roten/eine rote/ein rotes?; **this one** diese(r, s); **that one** der/die/das; **which one?** welche(r, s)?; **one by one** einzeln

2: one another einander; **do you two ever see one another?** seht ihr beide euch manchmal?

3 (*impers*) man; **one never knows** man kann nie wissen; **to cut one's finger** sich in den Finger schneiden

one: ~-**armed bandit** *n* einarmiger Bandit *m*; ~-**day excursion** (*US*) *n* (*day return*) Tagesrückfahrkarte *f*; ~-**man** *adj* Einmann-; ~-**man band** *n* Einmannkapelle *f*; (*fig*) Einmannbetrieb *m*; ~-**off** (*BRIT: inf*) *n* Einzelfall *m*

oneself [wʌn'sɛlf] *pron* (*reflexive: after prep*) sich, (~ *personally*) sich selbst *or* selber; (*emphatic*) (sich) selbst; **to hurt** ~ sich verletzen

one: ~-**sided** *adj* (*argument*) einseitig; ~-**to-**~ *adj* (*relationship*) eins-zu-eins; ~-**upmanship** *n* die Kunst, anderen um eine Nasenlänge voraus zu sein; ~-**way** *adj* (*street*) Einbahn-

ongoing ['ɔngəʊɪŋ] *adj* momentan; (*progressing*) sich entwickelnd

onion ['ʌnjən] *n* Zwiebel *f*

on-line ['ɔnlaɪn] *adj* (*COMPUT*) Online-

onlooker ['ɔnlʊkəʳ] *n* Zuschauer(in) *m(f)*

only ['əʊnlɪ] *adv* nur, bloß ♦ *adj* einzige(r, s) ♦ *conj* nur, bloß; **an** ~ **child** ein Einzelkind; **not** ~ ... **but also** ... nicht nur ..., sondern auch ...

onset ['ɔnsɛt] *n* (*start*) Beginn *m*

onshore ['ɔnʃɔːʳ] *adj* (*wind*) See-

onslaught ['ɔnslɔːt] *n* Angriff *m*

onto ['ɔntu] *prep* = **on to**

onus ['əʊnəs] *n* Last *f*, Pflicht *f*

onward(s) ['ɔnwəd(z)] *adv* (*place*) voran, vorwärts; **from that day** ~ von dem Tag an; **from today** ~ ab heute

ooze [uːz] *vi* sickern

opaque [əʊ'peɪk] *adj* undurchsichtig

OPEC ['əʊpɛk] *n abbr* (= *Organization of Petroleum-Exporting Countries*) OPEC *f*

open ['əʊpn] *adj* offen; (*public*) öffentlich; (*mind*) aufgeschlossen ♦ *vt* öffnen, aufmachen; (*trial, motorway, account*) eröffnen ♦ *vi* (*begin*) anfangen; (*shop*) aufmachen; (*door, flower*) aufgehen; (*play*) Premiere haben; **in the** ~ **(air)** im Freien; ~ **on to** *vt fus* sich öffnen auf +*acc*; ~ **up** *vt* (*route*) erschließen; (*shop, prospects*) eröffnen ♦ *vi* öffnen; ~**ing** *n* (*hole*) Öffnung *f*; (*beginning*) Anfang *m*; (*good chance*) Gelegenheit *f*; ~**ing hours** *npl* Öffnungszeiten *pl*; ~ **learning centre** *n* Weiterbildungseinrichtung auf Teilzeitbasis; ~**ly** *adv* offen; (*publicly*) öffentlich; ~-**minded** *adj* aufgeschlossen; ~-**necked** *adj* offen; ~-**plan** *adj* (*office*) Großraum-; (*flat etc*) offen angelegt

Open University

i **Open University** *ist eine 1969 in Großbritannien gegründete Fernuniversität für Spätstudierende. Der Unterricht findet durch Fernseh- und Radiosendungen statt, schriftliche Arbeiten werden mit der Post verschickt, und der Besuch von Sommerkursen ist Pflicht. Die Studenten müssen eine bestimmte Anzahl von Unterrichtseinheiten in einem bestimmten Zeitraum absolvieren und für die Verleihung eines akademischen Grades eine Mindestzahl von Scheinen machen.*

opera ['ɔpərə] *n* Oper *f*; ~ **house** *n* Opernhaus *nt*

operate ['ɔpəreɪt] *vt* (*machine*) bedienen; (*brakes, light*) betätigen ♦ *vi* (*machine*) laufen, in Betrieb sein; (*person*) arbeiten; (*MED*): **to** ~ **on** operieren

operatic [ɔpə'rætɪk] *adj* Opern-

operating ['ɔpəreɪtɪŋ] *adj*: ~ **table/theatre** Operationstisch *m*/-saal *m*

operation [ɔpə'reɪʃən] *n* (*working*) Betrieb *m*; (*MED*) Operation *f*; (*undertaking*) Unternehmen *nt*; (*MIL*) Einsatz *m*; **to be in** ~ (*JUR*) in Kraft sein; (*machine*) in Betrieb sein; **to have an** ~ (*MED*) operiert werden;

~al *adj* einsatzbereit

operative ['ɒpərətɪv] *adj* wirksam

operator ['ɒpəreɪtə'] *n* (*of machine*) Arbeiter *m*; (*TEL*) Telefonist(in) *m(f)*

opinion [ə'pɪnjən] *n* Meinung *f*; **in my ~** meiner Meinung nach; **~ated** *adj* starrsinnig; **~ poll** *n* Meinungsumfrage *f*

opponent [ə'pəunənt] *n* Gegner *m*

opportunity [ɒpə'tjuːnɪtɪ] *n* Gelegenheit *f*, Möglichkeit *f*; **to take the ~ of doing sth** die Gelegenheit ergreifen, etw zu tun

oppose [ə'pəuz] *vt* entgegentreten +*dat*; (*argument, idea*) ablehnen; (*plan*) bekämpfen; **to be ~d to sth** gegen etw sein; **as ~d to** im Gegensatz zu; **opposing** *adj* gegnerisch; (*points of view*) entgegengesetzt

opposite ['ɒpəzɪt] *adj* (*house*) gegenüberliegend; (*direction*) entgegengesetzt ♦ *adv* gegenüber ♦ *prep* gegenüber ♦ *n* Gegenteil *nt*

opposition [ɒpə'zɪʃən] *n* (*resistance*) Widerstand *m*; (*POL*) Opposition *f*; (*contrast*) Gegensatz *m*

oppress [ə'pres] *vt* unterdrücken; (*heat etc*) bedrücken; **~ion** [ə'preʃən] *n* Unterdrückung *f*; **~ive** *adj* (*authority, law*) repressiv; (*burden, thought*) bedrückend; (*heat*) drückend

opt [ɒpt] *vi*: **to ~ for** sich entscheiden für; **to ~ to do sth** sich entscheiden, etw zu tun; **to ~ out of** sich drücken vor +*dat*

optical ['ɒptɪkl] *adj* optisch; **~ character reader** *n* optische(s) Lesegerät *nt*

optician [ɒp'tɪʃən] *n* Optiker *m*

optimist ['ɒptɪmɪst] *n* Optimist *m*; **~ic** [ɒptɪ'mɪstɪk] *adj* optimistisch

optimum ['ɒptɪməm] *adj* optimal

option ['ɒpʃən] *n* Wahl *f*; (*COMM*) Option *f*; **to keep one's ~s open** sich alle Möglichkeiten offen halten; **~al** *adj* freiwillig; (*subject*) wahlfrei; **~al extras** *npl* Extras auf Wunsch

or [ɔː'] *conj* oder; **he could not read ~ write** er konnte weder lesen noch schreiben; **~ else** sonst

oral ['ɔːrəl] *adj* mündlich ♦ *n* (*exam*) mündliche Prüfung *f*

orange ['ɒrɪndʒ] *n* (*fruit*) Apfelsine *f*, Orange *f*; (*colour*) Orange *nt* ♦ *adj* orange

orator ['ɒrətə'] *n* Redner(in) *m(f)*

orbit ['ɔːbɪt] *n* Umlaufbahn *f*

orbital (motorway) ['ɔːbɪtəl-] *n* Ringautobahn *f*

orchard ['ɔːtʃəd] *n* Obstgarten *m*

orchestra ['ɔːkɪstrə] *n* Orchester *nt*; (*US: seating*) Parkett *nt*; **~l** [ɔː'kestrəl] *adj* Orchester-, orchestral

orchid ['ɔːkɪd] *n* Orchidee *f*

ordain [ɔː'deɪn] *vt* (*ECCL*) weihen

ordeal [ɔː'diːl] *n* Qual *f*

order ['ɔːdə'] *n* (*sequence*) Reihenfolge *f*; (*good arrangement*) Ordnung *f*; (*command*) Befehl *m*; (*JUR*) Anordnung *f*; (*peace*) Ordnung *f*; (*condition*) Zustand *m*; (*rank*) Klasse *f*; (*COMM*) Bestellung *f*; (*ECCL, honour*) Orden *m* ♦ *vt* (*also:* **put in ~**) ordnen; (*command*) befehlen; (*COMM*) bestellen; **in ~** in der Reihenfolge; **in (working) ~** in gutem Zustand; **in ~ to do sth** um etw zu tun; **on ~** (*COMM*) auf Bestellung; **to ~ sb to do sth** jdm befehlen, etw zu tun; **to ~ sth** (*command*) etw *acc* befehlen; **~ form** *n* Bestellschein *m*; **~ly** *n* (*MIL*) Sanitäter *m*; (*MED*) Pfleger *m* ♦ *adj* (*tidy*) ordentlich; (*well-behaved*) ruhig

ordinary ['ɔːdnrɪ] *adj* gewöhnlich ♦ *n*: **out of the ~** außergewöhnlich

Ordnance Survey ['ɔːdnəns-] (*BRIT*) *n* amtliche(r) Kartografiedienst *m*

ore [ɔː'] *n* Erz *nt*

organ ['ɔːgən] *n* (*MUS*) Orgel *f*; (*BIOL, fig*) Organ *nt*

organic [ɔː'gænɪk] *adj* (*food, farming etc*) biodynamisch

organization [ɔːgənaɪ'zeɪʃən] *n* Organisation *f*; (*make-up*) Struktur *f*

organize ['ɔːgənaɪz] *vt* organisieren; **~r** *n* Organisator *m*, Veranstalter *m*

orgasm ['ɔːgæzəm] *n* Orgasmus *m*

orgy ['ɔːdʒɪ] *n* Orgie *f*

Orient ['ɔːrɪənt] *n* Orient *m*; **o~al** [ɔːrɪ'entl] *adj* orientalisch

origin ['ɒrɪdʒɪn] *n* Ursprung *m*; (*of the world*)

Anfang *m*, Entstehung *f*; **~al** [ə'rɪdʒɪnl] *adj* (*first*) ursprünglich; (*painting*) original; (*idea*) originell ♦ *n* Original *nt*; **~ally** *adv* ursprünglich; originell; **~ate** [ə'rɪdʒɪneɪt] *vi* entstehen ♦ *vt* ins Leben rufen; **to ~ate from** stammen aus

Orkney ['ɔːknɪ] *npl* (*also:* **the ~ Islands**) die Orkneyinseln *pl*

ornament ['ɔːnəmənt] *n* Schmuck *m*; (*on mantelpiece*) Nippesfigur *f*; **~al** [ɔːnə'mentl] *adj* Zier-

ornate [ɔː'neɪt] *adj* reich verziert

orphan ['ɔːfn] *n* Waise *f*, Waisenkind *nt* ♦ *vt*: **to be ~ed** Waise werden; **~age** *n* Waisenhaus *nt*

orthodox ['ɔːθədɒks] *adj* orthodox; **~y** *n* Orthodoxie *f*; (*fig*) Konventionalität *f*

orthopaedic [ɔːθə'piːdɪk] (*US* **orthopedic**) *adj* orthopädisch

ostentatious [ɒsten'teɪʃəs] *adj* großtuerisch, protzig

ostracize ['ɒstrəsaɪz] *vt* ausstoßen

ostrich ['ɒstrɪtʃ] *n* Strauß *m*

other ['ʌðə'] *adj* andere(r, s) ♦ *pron* andere(r, s) ♦ *adv* ~ **than** anders als; **the ~ (one)** der/die/das andere; **the ~ day** neulich; **~s** (*~ people*) andere; **~wise** *adv* (*in a different way*) anders; (*or else*) sonst

otter ['ɒtə'] *n* Otter *m*

ouch [aʊtʃ] *excl* aua

ought [ɔːt] *vb aux* sollen; **I ~ to do it** ich sollte es tun; **this ~ to have been corrected** das hätte korrigiert werden sollen

ounce [aʊns] *n* Unze *f*

our ['aʊə'] *adj* unser; *see also* **my**; **~s** *pron* unsere(r, s); *see also* **mine²**; **~selves** *pron* uns (selbst); (*emphatic*) (wir) selbst; *see also* **oneself**

oust [aʊst] *vt* verdrängen

out [aʊt] *adv* hinaus/heraus; (*not indoors*) draußen; (*not alight*) aus; (*unconscious*) bewusstlos; (*results*) bekannt gegeben; **to eat/go ~** auswärts essen/ausgehen; **~ there** da draußen; **he is ~** (*absent*) er ist nicht da; **he was ~ in his calculations** seine Berechnungen waren nicht richtig; **~**

loud laut; **~ of** aus; (*away from*) außerhalb +*gen*; **to be ~ of milk** *etc* keine Milch *etc* mehr haben; **~ of order** außer Betrieb; **~-and-~** *adj* (*liar, thief etc*) ausgemacht; **~back** *n* Hinterland *nt*; **~board (motor)** *n* Außenbordmotor *m*; **~break** *n* Ausbruch *m*; **~burst** *n* Ausbruch *m*; **~cast** *n* Ausgestoßene(r) *mf*; **~come** *n* Ergebnis *nt*; **~crop** *n* (*of rock*) Felsnase *f*; **~cry** *n* Protest *m*; **~dated** *adj* überholt; **~do** (*irreg: like do*) *vt* übertrumpfen; **~door** *adj* Außen-; (*SPORT*) im Freien; **~doors** *adv* im Freien

outer ['aʊtə'] *adj* äußere(r, s); **~ space** *n* Weltraum *m*

outfit ['aʊtfɪt] *n* Kleidung *f*

out: **~going** *adj* (*character*) aufgeschlossen; **~goings** (*BRIT*) *npl* Ausgaben *pl*; **~grow** (*irreg: like grow*) *vt* (*clothes*) herauswachsen aus; (*habit*) ablegen; **~house** *n* Nebengebäude *nt*

outing ['aʊtɪŋ] *n* Ausflug *m*

outlandish [aʊt'lændɪʃ] *adj* eigenartig

out: **~law** *n* Geächtete(r) *f(m)* ♦ *vt* ächten; (*thing*) verbieten; **~lay** *n* Auslage *f*; **~let** *n* Auslass *m*, Abfluss *m*; (*also:* **retail ~let**) Absatzmarkt *m*; (*US: ELEC*) Steckdose *f*; (*for emotions*) Ventil *nt*

outline ['aʊtlaɪn] *n* Umriss *m*

out: **~live** *vt* überleben; **~look** *n* (*also fig*) Aussicht *f*; (*attitude*) Einstellung *f*; **~lying** *adj* entlegen; (*district*) Außen-; **~moded** *adj* veraltet; **~number** *vt* zahlenmäßig überlegen sein +*dat*; **~of-date** *adj* (*passport*) abgelaufen; (*clothes etc*) altmodisch; (*ideas etc*) überholt; **~of-the-way** *adj* abgelegen; **~patient** *n* ambulante(r) Patient *m*/ambulante Patientin *f*; **~post** *n* (*MIL, fig*) Vorposten *m*; **~put** *n* Leistung *f*, Produktion *f*; (*COMPUT*) Ausgabe *f*

outrage ['aʊtreɪdʒ] *n* (*cruel deed*) Ausschreitung *f*; (*indecency*) Skandal *m* ♦ *vt* (*morals*) verstoßen gegen; (*person*) empören; **~ous** [aʊt'reɪdʒəs] *adj* unerhört

outreach worker [aʊt'riːtʃ-] *n* Streetworker(in) *m(f)*

outright [*adv* aʊt'raɪt, *adj* 'aʊtraɪt] *adv* (*at*

once) sofort; (*openly*) ohne Umschweife
♦ *adj* (*denial*) völlig; (*sale*) Total-; (*winner*)
unbestritten

outset ['autset] *n* Beginn *m*

outside [aut'saɪd] *n* Außenseite *f* ♦ *adj*
äußere(r, s), Außen-; (*chance*) gering ♦ *adv*
außen ♦ *prep* außerhalb +*gen*; **at the ~** (*fig*)
maximal; (*time*) spätestens; **to go ~** nach
draußen gehen; **~ lane** *n* (*AUT*) äußere
Spur *f*; **~ line** *n* (*TEL*) Amtsanschluss *m*; **~r**
n Außenseiter(in) *m(f)*

out: **~size** *adj* übergroß; **~skirts** *npl*
Stadtrand *m*; **~spoken** *adj* freimütig;
~standing *adj* hervorragend; (*debts etc*)
ausstehend; **~stay** *vt*: **to ~stay one's
welcome** länger bleiben als erwünscht;
~stretched *adj* ausgestreckt; **~strip** *vt*
übertreffen; **~ tray** *n* Ausgangskorb *m*

outward ['autwəd] *adj* äußere(r, s); (*journey*)
Hin-; (*freight*) ausgehend ♦ *adv* nach außen;
~ly *adv* äußerlich

outweigh [aut'weɪ] *vt* (*fig*) überwiegen

outwit [aut'wɪt] *vt* überlisten

oval ['əʊvl] *adj* oval ♦ *n* Oval *nt*

Oval Office

ⓘ **Oval Office**, *ein großer ovaler Raum im
Weißen Haus, ist das private Büro des
amerikanischen Präsidenten. Im weiteren
Sinne bezieht sich dieser Begriff oft auf die
Präsidentschaft selbst.*

---

ovary ['əʊvərɪ] *n* Eierstock *m*

ovation [əʊ'veɪʃən] *n* Beifallssturm *m*

oven ['ʌvn] *n* Backofen *m*; **~proof** *adj*
feuerfest

over ['əʊvə] *adv* (*across*) hinüber/herüber;
(*finished*) vorbei; (*left*) übrig; (*again*) wieder,
noch einmal ♦ *prep* über ♦ *prefix* (*excessively*)
übermäßig; **~ here** hier(hin); **~ there**
dort(hin); **all ~** (*everywhere*) überall;
(*finished*) vorbei; **~ and ~** immer wieder; **~
and above** darüber hinaus; **to ask sb ~**
jdn einladen; **to bend ~** sich bücken

overall [*adj*, *n* 'əʊvərɔ:l, *adv* əʊvər'ɔ:l] *adj*
(*situation*) allgemein; (*length*) Gesamt- ♦ *n*
(*BRIT*) Kittel *m* ♦ *adv* insgesamt; **~s** *npl* (*for*

man) Overall *m*

over: **~awe** *vt* (*frighten*) einschüchtern;
(*make impression*) überwältigen; **~balance**
vi Übergewicht bekommen; **~bearing** *adj*
aufdringlich; **~board** *adv* über Bord;
~book *vi* überbuchen

overcast ['əʊvəkɑ:st] *adj* bedeckt

overcharge [əʊvə'tʃɑ:dʒ] *vt*: **to ~ sb** von
jdm zu viel verlangen

overcoat ['əʊvəkəʊt] *n* Mantel *m*

overcome [əʊvə'kʌm] (*irreg: like* come) *vt*
überwinden

over: **~crowded** *adj* überfüllt; **~crowding**
n Überfüllung *f*; **~do** (*irreg: like* do) *vt* (*cook
too much*) verkochen; (*exaggerate*)
übertreiben; **~done** *adj* übertrieben;
(*COOK*) verbraten, verkocht; **~dose** *n*
Überdosis *f*; **~draft** *n* (Konto)überziehung
f; **~drawn** *adj* (*account*) überzogen; **~due**
adj überfällig; **~estimate** *vt* überschätzen;
~excited *adj* überreizt; (*children*) aufgeregt

overflow [əʊvə'fləʊ] *vi* überfließen ♦ *n*
(*excess*) Überschuss *m*; (*also:* **~ pipe**)
Überlaufrohr *nt*

overgrown [əʊvə'grəʊn] *adj* (*garden*)
verwildert

overhaul [*vb* əʊvə'hɔ:l, *n* 'əʊvəhɔ:l] *vt* (*car*)
überholen; (*plans*) überprüfen ♦ *n*
Überholung *f*

overhead [*adv* əʊvə'hed, *adj*, *n* 'əʊvəhed] *adv*
oben ♦ *adj* Hoch-; (*wire*) oberirdisch;
(*lighting*) Decken- ♦ *n* (*US*) = **overheads**; **~s**
npl (*costs*) allgemeine Unkosten *pl*; **~
projector** *n* Overheadprojektor *m*

over: **~hear** (*irreg: like* hear) *vt* (mit
an)hören; **~heat** *vi* (*engine*) heiß laufen;
~joyed *adj* überglücklich; **~kill** *n* (*fig*)
Rundumschlag *m*

overland ['əʊvəlænd] *adj* Überland- ♦ *adv*
(*travel*) über Land

overlap [*vb* əʊvə'læp, *n* 'əʊvəlæp] *vi* sich
überschneiden; (*objects*) sich teilweise
decken ♦ *n* Überschneidung *f*

over: **~leaf** *adv* umseitig; **~load** *vt*
überladen; **~look** *vt* (*view from above*)
überblicken; (*not notice*) übersehen;
(*pardon*) hinwegsehen über +*acc*

overnight [adv əuvə'naɪt, adj 'əuvənaɪt] adv über Nacht ♦ adj (journey) Nacht-; **~ stay** Übernachtung f; **to stay ~** übernachten

overpass ['əuvəpɑːs] n Überführung f

overpower [əuvə'pauə'] vt überwältigen

over: ~rate vt überschätzen; **~ride** (irreg: like **ride**) vt (order, decision) aufheben; (objection) übergehen; **~riding** adj vorherrschend; **~rule** vt verwerfen; **~run** (irreg: like **run**) vt (country) einfallen in; (time limit) überziehen

overseas [əuvə'siːz] adv nach/in Übersee ♦ adj überseeisch, Übersee-

overseer ['əuvəsɪə'] n Aufseher m

overshadow [əuvə'ʃædəu] vt überschatten

overshoot [əuvə'ʃuːt] (irreg: like **shoot**) vt (runway) hinausschießen über +acc

oversight ['əuvəsaɪt] n (mistake) Versehen nt

over: ~sleep (irreg: like **sleep**) vi verschlafen; **~spill** n (Bevölkerungs)überschuss m; **~state** vt übertreiben; **~step** vt: **to ~step the mark** zu weit gehen

overt [əu'vəːt] adj offen(kundig)

overtake [əuvə'teɪk] (irreg: like **take**) vt, vi überholen

over: ~throw (irreg: like **throw**) vt (POL) stürzen; **~time** n Überstunden pl; **~tone** n (fig) Note f

overture ['əuvətʃuə'] n Ouvertüre f

over: ~turn vt, vi umkippen; **~weight** adj zu dick; **~whelm** vt überwältigen; **~work** n Überarbeitung f ♦ vt überlasten ♦ vi sich überarbeiten; **~wrought** adj überreizt

owe [əu] vt schulden; **to ~ sth to sb** (money) jdm etw schulden; (favour etc) jdm etw verdanken; **owing to** prep wegen +gen

owl [aul] n Eule f

own [əun] vt besitzen ♦ adj eigen; **a room of my ~** mein eigenes Zimmer; **to get one's ~ back** sich rächen; **on one's ~** allein; **to ~ up** vi: **to ~ up (to sth)** (etw) zugeben; **~er** n Besitzer(in) m(f); **~ership** n Besitz m

ox [ɔks] (pl **~en**) n Ochse m

oxtail ['ɔksteɪl] n: **~ soup** Ochsenschwanzsuppe f

oxygen ['ɔksɪdʒən] n Sauerstoff m; **~ mask** n Sauerstoffmaske f; **~ tent** n Sauerstoffzelt nt

oyster ['ɔɪstə'] n Auster f

oz. abbr = **ounce(s)**

ozone ['əuzəun] n Ozon nt; **~-friendly** adj (aerosol) ohne Treibgas; (fridge) FCKW-frei; **~ hole** n Ozonloch nt; **~ layer** n Ozonschicht f

P, p

p abbr = **penny; pence**

pa [pɑː] (inf) n Papa m

P.A. n abbr = **personal assistant; public address system**

p.a. abbr = **per annum**

pace [peɪs] n Schritt m; (speed) Tempo nt ♦ vi schreiten; **to keep ~ with** Schritt halten mit; **~maker** n Schrittmacher m

pacific [pə'sɪfɪk] adj pazifisch ♦ n: **the P~ (Ocean)** der Pazifik

pacifist ['pæsɪfɪst] n Pazifist m

pacify ['pæsɪfaɪ] vt befrieden; (calm) beruhigen

pack [pæk] n (of goods) Packung f; (of hounds) Meute f; (of cards) Spiel nt; (gang) Bande f ♦ vt (case) packen; (clothes) einpacken ♦ vi packen; **to ~ sb off to ...** jdn nach ... schicken; **~ it in!** lass es gut sein!

package ['pækɪdʒ] n Paket nt; **~ tour** n Pauschalreise f

packed [pækt] adj abgepackt; **~ lunch** n Lunchpaket nt

packet ['pækɪt] n Päckchen nt

packing ['pækɪŋ] n (action) Packen nt; (material) Verpackung f; **~ case** n (Pack)kiste f

pact [pækt] n Pakt m, Vertrag m

pad [pæd] n (of paper) (Schreib)block m; (stuffing) Polster nt ♦ vt polstern; **~ding** n Polsterung f

paddle ['pædl] n Paddel nt; (US: SPORT) Schläger m ♦ vt (boat) paddeln ♦ vi (in sea) plan(t)schen; **~ steamer** n Raddampfer m

paddling pool ['pædlɪŋ-] (BRIT) n

Plan(t)schbecken *nt*

paddock ['pædək] *n* Koppel *f*

paddy field ['pædɪ-] *n* Reisfeld *nt*

padlock ['pædlɒk] *n* Vorhängeschloss *nt* ♦ *vt* verschließen

paediatrics [piːdɪ'ætrɪks] (*US* **pediatrics**) *n* Kinderheilkunde *f*

pagan ['peɪgən] *adj* heidnisch ♦ *n* Heide *m*, Heidin *f*

page [peɪdʒ] *n* Seite *f*; (*person*) Page *m* ♦ *vt* (*in hotel*) ausrufen lassen

pageant ['pædʒənt] *n* Festzug *m*; **~ry** *n* Gepränge *nt*

pager ['peɪdʒəʳ] *n* (*TEL*) Funkrufempfänger *m*, Piepser *m* (*inf*)

paging device ['peɪdʒɪŋ-] *n* (*TEL*) = **pager**

paid [peɪd] *pt, pp of* **pay** ♦ *adj* bezahlt; **to put ~ to** (*BRIT*) zunichte machen

pail [peɪl] *n* Eimer *m*

pain [peɪn] *n* Schmerz *m*; **to be in ~** Schmerzen haben; **on ~ of death** bei Todesstrafe; **to take ~s to do sth** sich *dat* Mühe geben, etw zu tun; **~ed** *adj* (*expression*) gequält; **~ful** *adj* (*physically*) schmerzhaft; (*embarrassing*) peinlich; (*difficult*) mühsam; **~fully** *adv* (*fig: very*) schrecklich; **~killer** *n* Schmerzmittel *nt*; **~less** *adj* schmerzlos; **~staking** ['zteɪkɪŋ] *adj* gewissenhaft

paint [peɪnt] *n* Farbe *f* ♦ *vt* anstreichen; (*picture*) malen; **to ~ the door blue** die Tür blau streichen; **~brush** *n* Pinsel *m*; **~er** *n* Maler *m*; **~ing** *n* Malerei *f*; (*picture*) Gemälde *nt*; **~work** *n* Anstrich *m*; (*of car*) Lack *m*

pair [peəʳ] *n* Paar *nt*; **~ of scissors** Schere *f*; **~ of trousers** Hose *f*

pajamas [pə'dʒɑːməz] (*US*) *npl* Schlafanzug *m*

Pakistan [pɑːkɪ'stɑːn] *n* Pakistan *nt*; **~i** *adj* pakistanisch ♦ *n* Pakistani *mf*

pal [pæl] (*inf*) *n* Kumpel *m*

palace ['pæləs] *n* Palast *m*, Schloss *nt*

palatable ['pælɪtəbl] *adj* schmackhaft

palate ['pælɪt] *n* Gaumen *m*

palatial [pə'leɪʃəl] *adj* palastartig

pale [peɪl] *adj* blass, bleich ♦ *n*: **to be**

beyond the ~ die Grenzen überschreiten

Palestine ['pælɪstaɪn] *n* Palästina *nt*; **Palestinian** [pælɪs'tɪnɪən] *adj* palästinensisch ♦ *n* Palästinenser(in) *m(f)*

palette ['pælɪt] *n* Palette *f*

paling ['peɪlɪŋ] *n* (*stake*) Zaunpfahl *m*; (*fence*) Lattenzaun *m*

pall [pɔːl] *vi* jeden Reiz verlieren, verblassen

pallet ['pælɪt] *n* (*for goods*) Palette *f*

pallid ['pælɪd] *adj* blass, bleich

pallor ['pæləʳ] *n* Blässe *f*

palm [pɑːm] *n* (*of hand*) Handfläche *f*; (*also:* **~ tree**) Palme *f* ♦ *vt*: **to ~ sth off on sb** jdm etw andrehen; **P~ Sunday** *n* Palmsonntag *m*

palpable ['pælpəbl] *adj* (*also fig*) greifbar

palpitation [pælpɪ'teɪʃən] *n* Herzklopfen *nt*

paltry ['pɔːltrɪ] *adj* armselig

pamper ['pæmpəʳ] *vt* verhätscheln

pamphlet ['pæmflət] *n* Broschüre *f*

pan [pæn] *n* Pfanne *f* ♦ *vi* (*CINE*) schwenken

panache [pə'næʃ] *n* Schwung *m*

pancake ['pænkeɪk] *n* Pfannkuchen *m*

pancreas ['pæŋkrɪəs] *n* Bauchspeicheldrüse *f*

panda ['pændə] *n* Panda *m*; **~ car** (*BRIT*) *n* (Funk)streifenwagen *m*

pandemonium [pændɪ'məʊnɪəm] *n* Hölle *f*; (*noise*) Höllenlärm *m*

pander ['pændəʳ] *vi*: **to ~ to** sich richten nach

pane [peɪn] *n* (*Fenster*)scheibe *f*

panel ['pænl] *n* (*of wood*) Tafel *f*; (*TV*) Diskussionsrunde *f*; **~ling** (*US* **paneling**) *n* Täfelung *f*

pang [pæŋ] *n*: **~s of hunger** quälende(r) Hunger *m*; **~s of conscience** Gewissensbisse *pl*

panic ['pænɪk] *n* Panik *f* ♦ *vi* in Panik geraten; **don't ~** (nur) keine Panik; **~ky** *adj* (*person*) überängstlich; **~-stricken** *adj* von panischem Schrecken erfasst; (*look*) panisch

pansy ['pænzɪ] *n* Stiefmütterchen *nt*; (*inf*) Schwule(r) *m*

pant [pænt] *vi* keuchen; (*dog*) hecheln

panther ['pænθəʳ] *n* Pant(h)er *m*

panties ['pæntɪz] *npl* (Damen)slip *m*
pantihose ['pæntɪhəʊz] *(US)* n Strumpfhose *f*
pantomime ['pæntəmaɪm] *(BRIT)* n Märchenkomödie *f* um Weihnachten

> [!NOTE] Pantomime
>
> **Pantomime** *oder umgangssprachlich* **panto** *ist in Großbritannien ein zur Weihnachtszeit aufgeführtes Märchenspiel mit possenhaften Elementen, Musik, Standardrollen (ein als Frau verkleideter Mann, ein Junge, ein Bösewicht) und aktuellen Witzen. Publikumsbeteiligung wird gern gesehen (z.B. warnen die Kinder den Helden mit dem Ruf „He's behind you" vor einer drohenden Gefahr), und viele der Witze sprechen vor allem Erwachsene an, so dass pantomimes Unterhaltung für die ganze Familie bieten.*

pantry ['pæntrɪ] *n* Vorratskammer *f*
pants [pænts] *npl* (*BRIT: woman's*) Schlüpfer *m*; (: *man's*) Unterhose *f*; (*US: trousers*) Hose *f*
papal ['peɪpəl] *adj* päpstlich
paper ['peɪpə'] *n* Papier *nt*; (*newspaper*) Zeitung *f*; (*essay*) Referat *nt* ♦ *adj* Papier-, aus Papier ♦ *vt* (*wall*) tapezieren; **~s** *npl* (*identity* ~s) Ausweis(papiere *pl*) *m*; **~back** *n* Taschenbuch *nt*; ~ **bag** *n* Tüte *f*; ~ **clip** *n* Büroklammer *f*; ~ **hankie** *n* Tempotaschentuch *nt* ®; **~weight** *n* Briefbeschwerer *m*; **~work** *n* Schreibarbeit *f*
par [pɑː'] *n* (*COMM*) Nennwert *m*; (*GOLF*) Par *nt*; **on a** ~ **with** ebenbürtig +*dat*
parable ['pærəbl] *n* (*REL*) Gleichnis *nt*
parachute ['pærəʃuːt] *n* Fallschirm *m* ♦ *vi* (mit dem Fallschirm) abspringen
parade [pə'reɪd] *n* Parade *f* ♦ *vt* aufmarschieren lassen; (*fig*) zur Schau stellen ♦ *vi* paradieren, vorbeimarschieren
paradise ['pærədaɪs] *n* Paradies *nt*
paradox ['pærədɔks] *n* Paradox *nt*; **~ically** [pærə'dɔksɪklɪ] *adv* paradoxerweise
paraffin ['pærəfɪn] *(BRIT)* n Paraffin *nt*

paragraph ['pærəgrɑːf] *n* Absatz *m*
parallel ['pærəlel] *adj* parallel ♦ *n* Parallele *f*
paralyse ['pærəlaɪz] *(US* **paralyze**) *vt* (*MED*) lähmen, paralysieren; (*fig: organization, production etc*) lahm legen; **~d** *adj* gelähmt; **paralysis** [pə'rælɪsɪs] *n* Lähmung *f*
paralyze ['pærəlaɪz] *(US)* = **paralyse** *vt*
parameter [pə'ræmɪtə'] *n* Parameter *m*; **~s** *npl* (*framework, limits*) Rahmen *m*
paramount ['pærəmaʊnt] *adj* höchste(r, s), oberste(r, s)
paranoid ['pærənɔɪd] *adj* (*person*) an Verfolgungswahn leidend, paranoid; (*feeling*) krankhaft
parapet ['pærəpɪt] *n* Brüstung *f*
paraphernalia [pærəfə'neɪlɪə] *n* Zubehör *nt*, Utensilien *pl*
paraphrase ['pærəfreɪz] *vt* umschreiben
paraplegic [pærə'pliːdʒɪk] *n* Querschnittsgelähmte(r) *f(m)*
parasite ['pærəsaɪt] *n* (*also fig*) Schmarotzer *m*, Parasit *m*
parasol ['pærəsɔl] *n* Sonnenschirm *m*
paratrooper ['pærətruːpə'] *n* Fallschirmjäger *m*
parcel ['pɑːsl] *n* Paket *nt* ♦ *vt* (*also:* ~ **up**) einpacken
parch [pɑːtʃ] *vt* (aus)dörren; **~ed** *adj* ausgetrocknet; (*person*) am Verdursten
parchment ['pɑːtʃmənt] *n* Pergament *nt*
pardon ['pɑːdn] *n* Verzeihung *f* ♦ *vt* (*JUR*) begnadigen; ~ **me!**, **I beg your** ~! verzeihen Sie bitte!; ~ **me?** *(US)* wie bitte?; **(I beg your)** ~? wie bitte?
parent ['peərənt] *n* Elternteil *m*; **~s** *npl* (*mother and father*) Eltern *pl*; **~al** [pə'rentl] *adj* elterlich, Eltern-
parentheses [pə'renθɪsiːz] *npl* of **parenthesis**
parenthesis [pə'renθɪsɪs] *n* Klammer *f*; (*sentence*) Parenthese *f*
Paris ['pærɪs] *n* Paris *nt*
parish ['pærɪʃ] *n* Gemeinde *f*
park [pɑːk] *n* Park *m* ♦ *vt, vi* parken
parking ['pɑːkɪŋ] *n* Parken *nt*; **"no ~"** „Parken verboten"; ~ **lot** *(US)* n Parkplatz *m*; ~ **meter** *n* Parkuhr *f*; ~ **ticket** *n*

Strafzettel *m*

parlance ['pɑːləns] *n* Sprachgebrauch *m*

parliament ['pɑːləmənt] *n* Parlament *nt*;
~ary [pɑːlə'mentəri] *adj* parlamentarisch,
Parlaments-

parlour ['pɑːlər] (*US* **parlor**) *n* Salon *m*

parochial [pə'rəukɪəl] *adj* (*narrow-minded*)
eng(stirnig)

parole [pə'rəul] *n*: **on ~** (*prisoner*) auf
Bewährung

parrot ['pærət] *n* Papagei *m*

parry ['pærɪ] *vt* parieren, abwehren

parsley ['pɑːslɪ] *n* Petersilie *m*

parsnip ['pɑːsnɪp] *n* Pastinake *f*

parson ['pɑːsn] *n* Pfarrer *m*

part [pɑːt] *n* (*piece*) Teil *m*; (*THEAT*) Rolle *f*; (*of
machine*) Teil *nt* ♦ *adv* = **partly**; ♦ *vt*
trennen; (*hair*) scheiteln ♦ *vi* (*people*) sich
trennen; **to take ~ in** teilnehmen an +*dat*;
to take sth in good ~ etw nicht übel
nehmen; **to take sb's ~** sich auf jds Seite
acc stellen; **for my ~** ich für meinen Teil;
for the most ~ meistens, größtenteils; **in ~
exchange** (*BRIT*) in Zahlung; **~ with** *vt fus*
hergeben; (*renounce*) aufgeben; **~ial** ['pɑːʃl]
adj (*incomplete*) teilweise; (*biased*) parteiisch;
to be ~ial to eine (besondere) Vorliebe
haben für

participant [pɑː'tɪsɪpənt] *n* Teilnehmer(in)
m(f)

participate [pɑː'tɪsɪpeɪt] *vi*: **to ~ (in)**
teilnehmen (an +*dat*); **participation**
[pɑːtɪsɪ'peɪʃən] *n* Teilnahme *f*; (*sharing*)
Beteiligung *f*

participle ['pɑːtɪsɪpl] *n* Partizip *nt*

particle ['pɑːtɪkl] *n* (*wall*) Teilchen *nt*

particular [pə'tɪkjulər] *adj* bestimmt; (*exact*)
genau; (*fussy*) eigen; **in ~** besonders; **~ly**
adv besonders

particulars *npl* (*details*) Einzelheiten *pl*; (*of
person*) Personalien *pl*

parting ['pɑːtɪŋ] *n* (*separation*) Abschied *m*;
(*BRIT: of hair*) Scheitel *m* ♦ *adj* Abschieds-

partition [pɑː'tɪʃən] *n* (*wall*) Trennwand *f*;
(*division*) Teilung *f* ♦ *vt* aufteilen

partly ['pɑːtlɪ] *adv* zum Teil, teilweise

partner ['pɑːtnər] *n* Partner *m* ♦ *vt* der

Partner sein von; **~ship** *n* Partnerschaft *f*;
(*COMM*) Teilhaberschaft *f*

partridge ['pɑːtrɪdʒ] *n* Rebhuhn *nt*

part-time ['pɑːt'taɪm] *adj* Teilzeit- ♦ *adv*
stundenweise

party ['pɑːtɪ] *n* (*POL, JUR*) Partei *f*; (*group*)
Gesellschaft *f*; (*celebration*) Party *f* ♦ *adj*
(*dress*) Party-; (*politics*) Partei-; **~ line** *n* (*TEL*)
Gemeinschaftsanschluss *m*

pass [pɑːs] *vt* (*on foot*) vorbeigehen an +*dat*;
(*driving*) vorbeifahren an +*dat*; (*surpass*)
übersteigen; (*hand on*) weitergeben;
(*approve*) genehmigen; (*time*) verbringen;
(*exam*) bestehen ♦ *vi* (*go by*) vorbeigehen;
vorbeifahren; (*years*) vergehen; (*be
successful*) bestehen ♦ *n* (*in mountains,
SPORT*) Pass *m*; (*permission*) Passierschein *m*;
(*in exam*): **to get a ~** bestehen; **to ~ sth
through sth** etw durch etw führen; **to
make a ~ at sb** (*inf*) bei jdm
Annäherungsversuche machen; **~ away** *vi*
(*euph*) verscheiden; **~ by** *vi* vorbeigehen;
vorbeifahren; (*years*) vergehen; **~ on** *vt*
weitergeben; **~ out** *vi* (*faint*) ohnmächtig
werden; **~ up** *vt* vorbeigehen lassen;
~able *adj* (*road*) passierbar; (*fairly good*)
passabel

passage ['pæsɪdʒ] *n* (*corridor*) Gang *m*; (*in
book*) (Text)stelle *f*; (*voyage*) Überfahrt *f*;
~way *n* Durchgang *m*

passbook ['pɑːsbuk] *n* Sparbuch *nt*

passenger ['pæsɪndʒər] *n* Passagier *m*; (*on
bus*) Fahrgast *m*

passer-by [pɑːsə'baɪ] *n* Passant(in) *m(f)*

passing ['pɑːsɪŋ] *adj* (*car*) vorbeifahrend;
(*thought, affair*) momentan ♦ *n*: **in ~**
beiläufig; **~ place** *n* (*AUT*) Ausweichstelle *f*

passion ['pæʃən] *n* Leidenschaft *f*; **~ate** *adj*
leidenschaftlich

passive ['pæsɪv] *adj* passiv; (*LING*) passivisch;
~ smoking *n* Passivrauchen *nt*

Passover ['pɑːsəuvər] *n* Passahfest *nt*

passport ['pɑːspɔːt] *n* (Reise)pass *m*; **~
control** *n* Passkontrolle *f*; **~ office** *n*
Passamt *nt*

password ['pɑːswəːd] *n* Parole *f*, Kennwort
nt, Losung *f*

past [pɑːst] prep (motion) an +dat ... vorbei; (position) hinter +dat; (later than) nach ♦ adj (years) vergangen; (president etc) chemalig ♦ n Vergangenheit f; **he's ~ forty** er ist über vierzig; **for the ~ few/3 days** in den letzten paar/3 Tagen; **to run ~** vorbeilaufen; **ten/quarter ~ eight** zehn/Viertel nach acht

pasta [ˈpæstə] n Teigwaren pl

paste [peɪst] n (fish ~ etc) Paste f; (glue) Kleister m ♦ vt kleben

pasteurized [ˈpæstʃəraɪzd] adj pasteurisiert

pastime [ˈpɑːstaɪm] n Zeitvertreib m

pastor [ˈpɑːstər] n Pfarrer m

pastry [ˈpeɪstrɪ] n Blätterteig m; **pastries** npl (tarts etc) Stückchen pl

pasture [ˈpɑːstʃər] n Weide f

pasty [n ˈpæstɪ, adj ˈpeɪstɪ] n (Fleisch)pastete f ♦ adj blässlich, käsig

pat [pæt] n leichte(r) Schlag m, Klaps m ♦ vt tätscheln

patch [pætʃ] n Fleck m ♦ vt flicken; **(to go through) a bad ~** eine Pechsträhne (haben); **~ up** vt flicken; (quarrel) beilegen; **~ed** adj geflickt; **~y** adj (irregular) ungleichmäßig

pâté [ˈpæteɪ] n Pastete f

patent [ˈpeɪtnt] n Patent n ♦ vt patentieren lassen; (by authorities) patentieren ♦ adj offenkundig; **~ leather** n Lackleder nt

paternal [pəˈtɜːnl] adj väterlich

paternity [pəˈtɜːnɪtɪ] n Vaterschaft f

path [pɑːθ] n Pfad m; Weg m

pathetic [pəˈθetɪk] adj (very bad) kläglich

pathological [pæθəˈlɒdʒɪkl] adj pathologisch

pathology [pəˈθɒlədʒɪ] n Pathologie f

pathos [ˈpeɪθɒs] n Rührseligkeit f

pathway [ˈpɑːθweɪ] n Weg m

patience [ˈpeɪʃns] n Geduld f; (BRIT: CARDS) Patience f

patient [ˈpeɪʃnt] n Patient(in) m(f), Kranke(r) mf ♦ adj geduldig

patio [ˈpætɪəʊ] n Terrasse f

patriotic [pætrɪˈɒtɪk] adj patriotisch

patrol [pəˈtrəʊl] n Patrouille f; (police) Streife f ♦ vt patrouillieren in +dat ♦ vi (police) die Runde machen; (MIL) patrouillieren; **~ car** n Streifenwagen m; **~man** (US) (irreg) n (Streifen)polizist m

patron [ˈpeɪtrən] n (in shop) (Stamm)kunde m; (in hotel) (Stamm)gast m; (supporter) Förderer m; **~ of the arts** Mäzen m; **~age** [ˈpætrɪnɪdʒ] n Schirmherrschaft f; **~ize** [ˈpætrənaɪz] vt (support) unterstützen; (shop) besuchen; (treat condescendingly) von oben herab behandeln; **~ saint** n Schutzpatron(in) m(f)

patter [ˈpætər] n (sound: of feet) Trappeln nt; (: of rain) Prasseln nt; (sales talk) Gerede nt ♦ vi (feet) trappeln; (rain) prasseln

pattern [ˈpætən] n Muster nt; (SEWING) Schnittmuster nt; (KNITTING) Strickanleitung f

pauper [ˈpɔːpər] n Arme(r) mf

pause [pɔːz] n Pause f ♦ vi innehalten

pave [peɪv] vt pflastern; **to ~ the way for** den Weg bahnen für

pavement [ˈpeɪvmənt] (BRIT) n Bürgersteig m

pavilion [pəˈvɪlɪən] n Pavillon m; (SPORT) Klubhaus nt

paving [ˈpeɪvɪŋ] n Straßenpflaster nt; **~ stone** n Pflasterstein m

paw [pɔː] n Pfote f; (of big cats) Tatze f, Pranke f ♦ vt (scrape) scharren; (handle) betatschen

pawn [pɔːn] n Pfand nt; (chess) Bauer m ♦ vt verpfänden; **~broker** n Pfandleiher m; **~shop** n Pfandhaus nt

pay [peɪ] (pt, pp paid) n Bezahlung f, Lohn m ♦ vt bezahlen ♦ vi zahlen; (be profitable) sich bezahlt machen; **to ~ attention (to)** Acht geben (auf +acc); **to ~ sb a visit** jdn besuchen; **~ back** vt zurückzahlen; **~ for** vt fus bezahlen; **~ in** vt einzahlen; **~ off** vt abzahlen ♦ vi (scheme, decision) sich bezahlt machen; **~ up** vi bezahlen; **~able** adj zahlbar, fällig; **~ee** n Zahlungsempfänger m; **~ envelope** (US) n Lohntüte f; **~ment** n Bezahlung f; **advance ~ment** Vorauszahlung f; **monthly ~ment** monatliche Rate f; **~ packet** (BRIT) n Lohntüte f; **~phone** n Münzfernsprecher

m; **~roll** *n* Lohnliste *f*; **~ slip** *n* Lohn-/
Gehaltsstreifen *m*; **~ television** *n*
Abonnenten-Fernsehen *nt*
PC *n abbr* = **personal computer**
p.c. *abbr* = **per cent**
pea [piː] *n* Erbse *f*
peace [piːs] *n* Friede(n) *m*; **~able** *adj*
friedlich; **~ful** *adj* friedlich, ruhig;
~keeping *adj* Friedens-
peach [piːtʃ] *n* Pfirsich *m*
peacock ['piːkɔk] *n* Pfau *m*
peak [piːk] *n* Spitze *f*; (*of mountain*) Gipfel *m*;
(*fig*) Höhepunkt *m*; **~ hours** *npl* (*traffic*)
Hauptverkehrszeit *f*; (*telephone, electricity*)
Hauptbelastungszeit *f*; **~ period** *n* Stoßzeit
f, Hauptzeit *f*
peal [piːl] *n* (Glocken)läuten *nt*; **~s of**
laughter schallende(s) Gelächter *nt*
peanut ['piːnʌt] *n* Erdnuss *f*; **~ butter** *n*
Erdnussbutter *f*
pear [pɛəʳ] *n* Birne *f*
pearl [pɜːl] *n* Perle *f*
peasant ['pɛznt] *n* Bauer *m*
peat [piːt] *n* Torf *m*
pebble ['pɛbl] *n* Kiesel *m*
peck [pɛk] *vt, vi* picken ♦ *n* (*with beak*)
Schnabelhieb *m*; (*kiss*) flüchtige(r) Kuss *m*;
~ing order *n* Hackordnung *f*; **~ish** (*BRIT*:
inf) *adj* ein bisschen hungrig
peculiar [pɪ'kjuːlɪəʳ] *adj* (*odd*) seltsam; **~ to**
charakteristisch für; **~ity** [pɪkjuːlɪ'ærɪtɪ] *n*
(*singular quality*) Besonderheit *f*;
(*strangeness*) Eigenartigkeit *f*
pedal ['pɛdl] *n* Pedal *nt* ♦ *vt, vi* (*cycle*) fahren,
Rad fahren
pedantic [pɪ'dæntɪk] *adj* pedantisch
peddler ['pɛdləʳ] *n* Hausierer(in) *m(f)*; (*of*
drugs) Drogenhändler(in) *m(f)*
pedestal ['pɛdəstl] *n* Sockel *m*
pedestrian [pɪ'dɛstrɪən] *n* Fußgänger *m*
♦ *adj* Fußgänger-; (*humdrum*) langweilig; **~**
crossing (*BRIT*) *n* Fußgängerüberweg *m*;
~ized *n* in eine Fußgängerzone
umgewandelt; **~ precinct** (*BRIT*), **~ zone**
(*US*) *n* Fußgängerzone *f*
pediatrics [piːdɪ'ætrɪks] (*US*) *n* = **paediatrics**
pedigree ['pɛdɪgriː] *n* Stammbaum *m* ♦ *cpd*

(*animal*) reinrassig, Zucht-
pee [piː] (*inf*) *vi* pissen, pinkeln
peek [piːk] *vi* gucken
peel [piːl] *n* Schale *f* ♦ *vt* schälen ♦ *vi* (*paint*
etc) abblättern; (*skin*) sich schälen
peep [piːp] *n* (*BRIT*: *look*) kurze(r) Blick *m*;
(*sound*) Piepsen *nt* ♦ *vi* (*BRIT*: *look*) gucken;
~ out *vi* herausgucken; **~hole** *n* Guckloch
nt
peer [pɪəʳ] *vi* starren; (*peep*) gucken ♦ *n*
(*nobleman*) Peer *m*; (*equal*) Ebenbürtige(r)
m; **~age** *n* Peerswürde *f*
peeved [piːvd] *adj* (*person*) sauer
peg [pɛg] *n* (*stake*) Pflock *m*; (*BRIT*: *also*:
clothes ~) Wäscheklammer *f*
Pekinese [piːkɪ'niːz] *n* (*dog*) Pekinese *m*
pelican ['pɛlɪkən] *n* Pelikan *m*; **~ crossing**
(*BRIT*) *n* (*AUT*) Ampelüberweg *m*
pellet ['pɛlɪt] *n* Kügelchen *nt*
pelmet ['pɛlmɪt] *n* Blende *f*
pelt [pɛlt] *vt* bewerfen ♦ *vi* (*rain*) schütten
♦ *n* Pelz *m*, Fell *nt*
pelvis ['pɛlvɪs] *n* Becken *nt*
pen [pɛn] *n* (*fountain ~*) Federhalter *m*; (*ball-*
point ~) Kuli *m*; (*for sheep*) Pferch *m*
penal ['piːnl] *adj* Straf-; **~ize** *vt* (*punish*)
bestrafen; (*disadvantage*) benachteiligen
penalty ['pɛnltɪ] *n* Strafe *f*; (*FOOTBALL*)
Elfmeter *m*; **~ (kick)** *n* Elfmeter *m*
penance ['pɛnəns] *n* Buße *f*
pence [pɛns] (*BRIT*) *npl of* **penny**
pencil ['pɛnsl] *n* Bleistift *m*; **~ case** *n*
Federmäppchen *nt*; **~ sharpener** *n*
Bleistiftspitzer *m*
pendant ['pɛndnt] *n* Anhänger *m*
pending ['pɛndɪŋ] *prep* bis (zu) ♦ *adj*
unentschieden, noch offen
pendulum ['pɛndjuləm] *n* Pendel *nt*
penetrate ['pɛnɪtreɪt] *vt* durchdringen;
(*enter into*) eindringen in +*acc*;
penetration [pɛnɪ'treɪʃən] *n* Durchdringen
nt; Eindringen *nt*
penfriend ['pɛnfrɛnd] (*BRIT*) *n* Brieffreund(in)
m(f)
penguin ['pɛŋgwɪn] *n* Pinguin *m*
penicillin [pɛnɪ'sɪlɪn] *n* Penizillin *nt*
peninsula [pə'nɪnsjulə] *n* Halbinsel *f*

penis[ˈpiːnɪs] *n* Penis *m*

penitentiary[penɪˈtenʃərɪ] (*US*) *n* Zuchthaus *nt*

penknife[ˈpennaɪf] *n* Federmesser *nt*

pen name*n* Pseudonym *nt*

penniless[ˈpenɪlɪs] *adj* mittellos

penny[ˈpenɪ] (*pl* **pennies** or (*BRIT*) **pence**) *n* Penny *m*; (*US*) Centstück *nt*

penpal[ˈpenpæl] *n* Brieffreund(in) *m(f)*

pension[ˈpenʃən] *n* Rente *f*; ~**er**(*BRIT*) *n* Rentner(in) *m(f)*; ~ **fund***n* Rentenfonds *m*; ~ **plan***n* Rentenversicherung *f*

pensive[ˈpensɪv] *adj* nachdenklich

Pentagon

i **Pentagon** *heißt das fünfeckige Gebäude in Arlington, Virginia, in dem das amerikanische Verteidigungsministerium untergebracht ist. Im weiteren Sinne bezieht sich dieses Wort auf die amerikanische Militärführung.*

---

pentathlon[penˈtæθlən] *n* Fünfkampf *m*

Pentecost[ˈpentɪkɒst] *n* Pfingsten *pl or nt*

penthouse[ˈpenthaus] *n* Dachterrassenwohnung *f*

pent up[ˈpentʌp] *adj* (*feelings*) angestaut

penultimate[peˈnʌltɪmət] *adj* vorletzte(r, s)

people[ˈpiːpl] *n* (*nation*) Volk *nt* ♦ *npl* (*persons*) Leute *pl*; (*inhabitants*) Bevölkerung *f* ♦ *vt* besiedeln; **several ~ came** mehrere Leute kamen; ~ **say that ...** man sagt, dass ...

pepper[ˈpepər] *n* Pfeffer *m*; (*vegetable*) Paprika *m* ♦ *vt* (*pelt*) bombardieren; ~ **mill** *n* Pfeffermühle *f*; ~**mint***n* (*plant*) Pfefferminze *f*; (*sweet*) Pfefferminz *nt*

pep talk[pep-] (*inf*) *n* Anstachelung *f*

per[pɜːr] *prep* pro; ~ **day/person** pro Tag/Person; ~ **annum***adv* pro Jahr; ~ **capita** *adj* (*income*) Pro-Kopf- ♦ *adv* pro Kopf

perceive[pəˈsiːv] *vt* (*realize*) wahrnehmen; (*understand*) verstehen

per cent*n* Prozent *nt*; **percentage** [pəˈsentɪdʒ] *n* Prozentsatz *m*

perception[pəˈsepʃən] *n* Wahrnehmung *f*; (*insight*) Einsicht *f*

perceptive[pəˈseptɪv] *adj* (*person*) aufmerksam; (*analysis*) tief gehend

perch[pɜːtʃ] *n* Stange *f*; (*fish*) Flussbarsch *m* ♦ *vi* sitzen, hocken

percolator[ˈpɜːkəleɪtər] *n* Kaffeemaschine *f*

percussion[pəˈkʌʃən] *n* (*MUS*) Schlagzeug *nt*

perennial[pəˈrenɪəl] *adj* wiederkehrend; (*everlasting*) unvergänglich

perfect[*adj*, *n* ˈpɜːfɪkt, *vb* pəˈfekt] *adj* vollkommen; (*crime, solution*) perfekt ♦ *n* (*GRAM*) Perfekt *nt* ♦ *vt* vervollkommnen; ~**ion***n* Vollkommenheit *f*; ~**ly***adv* vollkommen, perfekt; (*quite*) ganz, einfach

perforate[ˈpɜːfəreɪt] *vt* durchlöchern; **perforation**[pɜːfəˈreɪʃən] *n* Perforieren *nt*; (*line of holes*) Perforation *f*

perform[pəˈfɔːm] *vt* (*carry out*) durch- or ausführen; (*task*) verrichten; (*THEAT*) spielen, geben ♦ *vi* (*THEAT*) auftreten; ~**ance***n* Durchführung *f*; (*efficiency*) Leistung *f*; (*show*) Vorstellung *f*; ~**er** *n* Künstler(in) *m(f)*

perfume[ˈpɜːfjuːm] *n* Duft *m*; (*lady's*) Parfüm *nt*

perhaps[pəˈhæps] *adv* vielleicht

peril[ˈperɪl] *n* Gefahr *f*

perimeter[pəˈrɪmɪtər] *n* Peripherie *f*; (*of circle etc*) Umfang *m*

period[ˈpɪərɪəd] *n* Periode *f*; (*GRAM*) Punkt *m*; (*MED*) Periode *f* ♦ *adj* (*costume*) historisch; ~**ic**[pɪərɪˈɒdɪk] *adj* periodisch; ~**ical**[pɪərɪˈɒdɪkl] *n* Zeitschrift *f*; ~**ically** [pɪərɪˈɒdɪklɪ] *adv* periodisch

peripheral[pəˈrɪfərəl] *adj* Rand-, peripher ♦ *n* (*COMPUT*) Peripheriegerät *nt*

perish[ˈperɪʃ] *vi* umkommen; (*fruit*) verderben; ~**able***adj* leicht verderblich

perjury[ˈpɜːdʒərɪ] *n* Meineid *m*

perk[pɜːk] (*inf*) *n* (*fringe benefit*) Vergünstigung *f*; ~ **up***vi* munter werden; ~**y***adj* keck

perm[pɜːm] *n* Dauerwelle *f*

permanent[ˈpɜːmənənt] *adj* dauernd, ständig

permeate[ˈpɜːmɪeɪt] *vt, vi* durchdringen

permissible[pəˈmɪsɪbl] *adj* zulässig

permission[pəˈmɪʃən] *n* Erlaubnis *f*

permissive [pə'mɪsɪv] *adj* nachgiebig; **the ~ society** die permissive Gesellschaft

permit [*n* 'pə:mɪt, *vb* pə'mɪt] *n* Zulassung *f* ♦ *vt* erlauben, zulassen

perpendicular [pə:pən'dɪkjulər] *adj* senkrecht

perpetrate ['pə:pɪtreɪt] *vt* begehen

perpetual [pə'petjuəl] *adj* dauernd, ständig

perpetuate [pə'petjueɪt] *vt* verewigen, bewahren

perplex [pə'pleks] *vt* verblüffen

persecute ['pə:sɪkjuːt] *vt* verfolgen; **persecution** [pə:sɪ'kjuːʃən] *n* Verfolgung *f*

perseverance [pə:sɪ'vɪərns] *n* Ausdauer *f*

persevere [pə:sɪ'vɪər] *vi* durchhalten

Persian ['pə:ʃən] *adj* persisch ♦ *n* Perser(in) *m(f)*; **the (Persian) Gulf** der Persische Golf

persist [pə'sɪst] *vi* (*in belief etc*) bleiben; (*rain, smell*) andauern; (*continue*) nicht aufhören; **to ~ in** bleiben bei; **~ence** *n* Beharrlichkeit *f*; **~ent** *adj* beharrlich; (*unending*) ständig

person ['pə:sn] *n* Person *f*; **in ~** persönlich; **~able** *adj* gut aussehend; **~al** *adj* persönlich; (*private*) privat; (*of body*) körperlich, Körper-; **~al assistant** *n* Assistent(in) *m(f)*; **~al column** *n* private Kleinanzeigen *pl*; **~al computer** *n* Personalcomputer *m*; **~ality** [pə:sə'nælɪtɪ] *n* Persönlichkeit *f*; **~ally** *adv* persönlich; **~al organizer** *n* Terminplaner *m*, Zeitplaner *m*; (*electronic*) elektronisches Notizbuch *nt*; **~al stereo** *n* Walkman *m* ℝ; **~ify** [pə'sɔnɪfaɪ] *vt* verkörpern

personnel [pə:sə'nel] *n* Personal *nt*

perspective [pə'spektɪv] *n* Perspektive *f*

Perspex ['pə:speks] ℝ *n* Acrylglas *nt*, Akrylglas *nt*

perspiration [pə:spɪ'reɪʃən] *n* Transpiration *f*

perspire [pə'spaɪər] *vi* transpirieren

persuade [pə'sweɪd] *vt* überreden; (*convince*) überzeugen

persuasion [pə'sweɪʒən] *n* Überredung *f*; Überzeugung *f*

persuasive [pə'sweɪsɪv] *adj* überzeugend

pert [pə:t] *adj* keck

pertaining [pə:'teɪnɪŋ]: **~ to** *prep* betreffend +*acc*

pertinent ['pə:tɪnənt] *adj* relevant

perturb [pə'tə:b] *vt* beunruhigen

pervade [pə'veɪd] *vt* erfüllen

perverse [pə'və:s] *adj* pervers; (*obstinate*) eigensinnig

pervert [*n* 'pə:və:t, *vb* pə'və:t] *n* perverse(r) Mensch *m* ♦ *vt* verdrehen; (*morally*) verderben

pessimist ['pesɪmɪst] *n* Pessimist *m*; **~ic** *adj* pessimistisch

pest [pest] *n* (*insect*) Schädling *m*; (*fig: person*) Nervensäge *f*; (*: thing*) Plage *f*; **~er** ['pestər] *vt* plagen; **~icide** ['pestɪsaɪd] *n* Insektenvertilgungsmittel *nt*

pet [pet] *n* (*animal*) Haustier *n* ♦ *vt* liebkosen, streicheln

petal ['petl] *n* Blütenblatt *nt*

peter out ['piːtə-] *vi* allmählich zu Ende gehen

petite [pə'tiːt] *adj* zierlich

petition [pə'tɪʃən] *n* Bittschrift *f*

petrified ['petrɪfaɪd] *adj* versteinert; (*person*) starr (vor Schreck)

petrify ['petrɪfaɪ] *vt* versteinern; (*person*) erstarren lassen

petrol ['petrəl] (*BRIT*) *n* Benzin *nt*, Kraftstoff *m*; **two-/four-star ~** ≃ Normal-/Superbenzin *nt*; **~ can** *n* Benzinkanister *m*

petroleum [pə'trəuliəm] *n* Petroleum *nt*

petrol: ~ pump (*BRIT*) *n* (*in car*) Benzinpumpe *f*; (*at garage*) Zapfsäule *f*; **~ station** (*BRIT*) *n* Tankstelle *f*; **~ tank** (*BRIT*) *n* Benzintank *m*

petticoat ['petɪkəut] *n* Unterrock *m*

petty ['petɪ] *adj* (*unimportant*) unbedeutend; (*mean*) kleinlich; **~ cash** *n* Portokasse *f*; **~ officer** *n* Maat *m*

pew [pjuː] *n* Kirchenbank *f*

pewter ['pjuːtər] *n* Zinn *nt*

phantom ['fæntəm] *n* Phantom *nt*

pharmacist ['fɑːməsɪst] *n* Pharmazeut *m*; (*druggist*) Apotheker *m*

pharmacy ['fɑːməsɪ] *n* Pharmazie *f*; (*shop*) Apotheke *f*

phase [feɪz] *n* Phase *f* ♦ *vt*: **to ~ sth in** etw allmählich einführen; **to ~ sth out** etw auslaufen lassen

Ph.D. n abbr = **Doctor of Philosophy**

pheasant ['feznt] n Fasan m

phenomena [fə'nɔmɪnə] npl of
 phenomenon

phenomenon [fə'nɔmɪnən] n Phänomen nt

philanthropist [fɪ'lænθrəpɪst] n Philanthrop
 m, Menschenfreund m

Philippines ['fɪlɪpiːnz] npl: **the ~** die
 Philippinen pl

philosopher [fɪ'lɔsəfə'] n Philosoph m;
 philosophical [fɪlə'sɔfɪkl] adj
 philosophisch; **philosophy** [fɪ'lɔsəfɪ] n
 Philosophie f

phlegm [flɛm] n (MED) Schleim m

phobia ['fəubjə] n (irrational fear: of insects,
 flying, water etc) Phobie f

phone [fəun] n Telefon nt ♦ vt, vi
 telefonieren, anrufen; **to be on the ~**
 telefonieren; **~ back** vt, vi zurückrufen; **~
 up** vt, vi anrufen; **~ bill** n Telefonrechnung
 f; **~ book** n Telefonbuch nt; **~ booth** n
 Telefonzelle f; **~ box** n Telefonzelle f; **~
 call** n Telefonanruf m, **~card** n (TEL)
 Telefonkarte f; **~-in** n (RAD, TV) Phone-in nt;
 ~ number n Telefonnummer f

phonetics [fə'nɛtɪks] n Phonetik f

phoney ['fəunɪ] (inf) adj unecht ♦ n (person)
 Schwindler m; (thing) Fälschung f;
 (banknote) Blüte f

phony ['fəunɪ] adj, n = **phoney**

photo ['fəutəu] n Foto nt; **~copier**
 ['fəutəukɔpɪə'] n Kopiergerät nt; **~copy**
 ['fəutəukɔpɪ] n Fotokopie f ♦ vt fotokopieren;
 ~genic [fəutəu'dʒɛnɪk] adj fotogen; **~graph**
 n Fotografie f, Aufnahme f ♦ vt
 fotografieren; **~grapher** ['fəutəgræf] n
 Fotograf m; **~graphic** [fəutə'græfɪk] adj
 fotografisch; **~graphy** [fə'tɔgrəfɪ] n
 Fotografie f

phrase [freɪz] n Satz m; (expression)
 Ausdruck m ♦ vt ausdrücken, formulieren; **~
 book** n Sprachführer m

physical ['fɪzɪkl] adj physikalisch; (bodily)
 körperlich, physisch; **~ education** n
 Turnen nt; **~ly** adv physikalisch

physician [fɪ'zɪʃən] n Arzt m

physicist ['fɪzɪsɪst] n Physiker(in) m(f)

physics ['fɪzɪks] n Physik f

physiotherapist [fɪzɪəu'θerəpɪst] n
 Physiotherapeut(in) m(f)

physiotherapy [fɪzɪəu'θerəpɪ] n
 Heilgymnastik f, Physiotherapie f

physique [fɪ'ziːk] n Körperbau m

pianist ['piːənɪst] n Pianist(in) m(f)

piano [pɪ'ænəu] n Klavier nt

pick [pɪk] n (tool) Pickel m; (choice) Auswahl f
 ♦ vt (fruit) pflücken; (choose) aussuchen;
 take your ~ such dir etwas aus; **to ~ sb's
 pocket** jdn bestehlen; **~ on** vt fus (person)
 herumhacken auf +dat; **~ out** vt
 auswählen; **~ up** vi (improve) sich erholen
 ♦ vt (lift up) aufheben; (learn) (schnell)
 mitbekommen; (collect) abholen; (girl) (sich
 dat) anlachen; (AUT: passenger) mitnehmen;
 (speed) gewinnen an +dat; **to ~ o.s. up**
 aufstehen

picket ['pɪkɪt] n (striker) Streikposten m ♦ vt
 (factory) (Streik)posten aufstellen vor +dat
 ♦ vi (Streik)posten stehen

pickle ['pɪkl] n (salty mixture) Pökel m; (inf)
 Klemme f ♦ vt (in Essig) einlegen; einpökeln

pickpocket ['pɪkpɔkɪt] n Taschendieb m

pick-up ['pɪkʌp] n (BRIT: on record player)
 Tonabnehmer m; (small truck) Lieferwagen
 m

picnic ['pɪknɪk] n Picknick nt ♦ vi picknicken;
 ~ area n Rastplatz m

pictorial [pɪk'tɔːrɪəl] adj in Bildern

picture ['pɪktʃə'] n Bild nt ♦ vt (visualize) sich
 dat vorstellen; **the ~s** npl (BRIT) das Kino; **~
 book** n Bilderbuch nt

picturesque [pɪktʃə'rɛsk] adj malerisch

pie [paɪ] n (meat) Pastete f; (fruit) Torte f

piece [piːs] n Stück nt ♦ vt: **to ~ together**
 zusammenstückeln; (fig) sich dat
 zusammenreimen; **to take to ~s** in
 Einzelteile zerlegen; **~meal** adv stückweise,
 Stück für Stück; **~work** n Akkordarbeit f

pie chart n Kreisdiagramm nt

pier [pɪə'] n Pier m, Mole f

pierce [pɪəs] vt durchstechen, durchbohren
 (also look); **~d** adj durchgestochen;
 piercing ['pɪəsɪŋ] adj (cry) durchdringend

pig [pɪg] n Schwein nt

pigeon ['pɪdʒən] n Taube f; **~hole** n (compartment) Ablegefach nt

piggy bank ['pɪgɪ-] n Sparschwein nt

pig: ~headed ['pɪg'hedɪd] adj dickköpfig; **~let** ['pɪglɪt] n Ferkel nt; **~skin** ['pɪgskɪn] n Schweinsleder n; **~sty** ['pɪgstaɪ] n Schweinestall m; **~tail** ['pɪgteɪl] n Zopf m

pike [paɪk] n Pike f; (fish) Hecht m

pilchard ['pɪltʃəd] n Sardine f

pile [paɪl] n Haufen m; (of books, wood) Stapel m; (in ground) Pfahl m; (on carpet) Flausch m ♦ vt (also: ~ up) anhäufen ♦ vi (also: ~ up) sich anhäufen

piles [paɪlz] npl Hämorr(ho)iden pl

pile-up ['paɪlʌp] n (AUT) Massen-zusammenstoß m

pilfering ['pɪlfərɪŋ] n Diebstahl m

pilgrim ['pɪlgrɪm] n Pilger(in) m(f); **~age** n Wallfahrt f

pill [pɪl] n Tablette f, Pille f; **the ~** die (Antibaby)pille

pillage ['pɪlɪdʒ] vt plündern

pillar ['pɪlə*] n Pfeiler m, Säule f (also fig); **~ box** (BRIT) n Briefkasten m

pillion ['pɪljən] n Soziussitz m

pillow ['pɪləʊ] n Kissen nt; **~case** n Kissenbezug m

pilot ['paɪlət] n Pilot m; (NAUT) Lotse m ♦ adj (scheme etc) Versuchs- ♦ vt führen; (ship) lotsen; **~ light** n Zündflamme f

pimp [pɪmp] n Zuhälter m

pimple ['pɪmpl] n Pickel m

PIN n abbr (= personal identification number) PIN f

pin [pɪn] n Nadel f; (for sewing) Stecknadel f; (TECH) Stift m, Bolzen m ♦ vt stecken; (keep in one position) pressen, drücken; **to ~ sth to sth** etw an etw acc heften; **to ~ sth on sb** (fig) jdm etw anhängen; **~s and needles** npl Kribbeln nt; **~ down** vt (fig: person): **to ~ sb down (to sth)** jdn (auf etw acc) festnageln

pinafore ['pɪnəfɔː*] n Schürze f; **~ dress** n Kleiderrock m

pinball ['pɪnbɔːl] n Flipper m

pincers ['pɪnsəz] npl Kneif- or Beißzange f; (MED) Pinzette f

pinch [pɪntʃ] n Zwicken nt, Kneifen nt; (of salt) Prise f ♦ vt zwicken, kneifen; (inf: steal) klauen ♦ vi (shoe) drücken; **at a ~** notfalls, zur Not

pincushion ['pɪnkʊʃən] n Nadelkissen nt

pine [paɪn] n (also: ~ tree) Kiefer f ♦ vi: **to ~ for** sich sehnen nach; **~ away** vi sich zu Tode sehnen

pineapple ['paɪnæpl] n Ananas f

ping [pɪŋ] n Klingeln nt; **~-pong** ® n Pingpong nt

pink [pɪŋk] adj rosa inv ♦ n Rosa nt; (BOT) Nelke f

pinnacle ['pɪnəkl] n Spitze f

PIN (number) n Geheimnummer f

pinpoint ['pɪnpɔɪnt] vt festlegen

pinstripe ['pɪnstraɪp] n Nadelstreifen m

pint [paɪnt] n Pint nt; (BRIT: inf: of beer) große(s) Bier nt

pioneer [paɪə'nɪə*] n Pionier m; (fig also) Bahnbrecher m

pious ['paɪəs] adj fromm

pip [pɪp] n Kern m; **the ~s** npl (BRIT: RAD) das Zeitzeichen

pipe [paɪp] n (smoking) Pfeife f; (tube) Rohr nt; (in house) (Rohr)leitung f ♦ vt (durch Rohre) leiten; (MUS) blasen; **~s** npl (also: bagpipes) Dudelsack m; **~ down** vi (be quiet) die Luft anhalten; **~ cleaner** n Pfeifenreiniger m; **~ dream** n Luftschloss nt; **~line** n (for oil) Pipeline f; **~r** n Pfeifer m; (bagpipes) Dudelsackbläser m

piping ['paɪpɪŋ] adv: **~ hot** siedend heiß

pique ['piːk] n gekränkte(r) Stolz m

pirate ['paɪərət] n Pirat m, Seeräuber m; **~d** adj: **~d version** Raubkopie f; **~ radio** (BRIT) n Piratensender m

Pisces ['paɪsiːz] n Fische pl

piss [pɪs] (inf) vi pissen; **~ed** (inf) adj (drunk) voll

pistol ['pɪstl] n Pistole f

piston ['pɪstən] n Kolben m

pit [pɪt] n Grube f; (THEAT) Parterre nt; (orchestra ~) Orchestergraben m ♦ vt (mark with scars) zerfressen; (compare): **to ~ sb against sb** jdn an jdm messen; **the ~s** npl (MOTOR RACING) die Boxen pl

pitch [pɪtʃ] n Wurf m; (of trader) Stand m; (SPORT) (Spiel)feld nt; (MUS) Tonlage f; (substance) Pech nt ♦ vt werfen; (set up) aufschlagen ♦ vi (NAUT) rollen; **to ~ a tent** ein Zelt aufbauen; **~-black** adj pechschwarz; **~ed battle** n offene Schlacht f

piteous ['pɪtɪəs] adj kläglich, erbärmlich

pitfall ['pɪtfɔːl] n (fig) Falle f

pith [pɪθ] n Mark nt

pithy ['pɪθɪ] adj prägnant

pitiful ['pɪtɪful] adj (deserving pity) bedauernswert; (contemptible) jämmerlich

pitiless ['pɪtɪlɪs] adj erbarmungslos

pittance ['pɪtns] n Hungerlohn m

pity ['pɪtɪ] n (sympathy) Mitleid nt ♦ vt Mitleid haben mit; **what a ~!** wie schade!

pivot ['pɪvət] n Drehpunkt m ♦ vi: **to ~ (on)** sich drehen (um)

pizza ['piːtsə] n Pizza f

placard ['plækɑːd] n Plakat nt, Anschlag m

placate [plə'keɪt] vt beschwichtigen

place [pleɪs] n Platz m; (spot) Stelle f; (town etc) Ort m ♦ vt setzen, stellen, legen; (order) aufgeben; (SPORT) platzieren; (identify) unterbringen; **to take ~** stattfinden, **out of ~** nicht am rechten Platz; (fig: remark) unangebracht; **in the first ~** erstens; **to change ~s with sb** mit jdm den Platz tauschen; **to be ~d third** (in race, exam) auf dem dritten Platz liegen

placid ['plæsɪd] adj gelassen, ruhig

plagiarism ['pleɪdʒərɪzəm] n Plagiat nt

plague [pleɪg] n Pest f; (fig) Plage f ♦ vt plagen

plaice [pleɪs] n Scholle f

plaid [plæd] n Plaid nt

plain [pleɪn] adj (clear) klar, deutlich; (simple) einfach, schlicht; (not beautiful) alltäglich ♦ n Ebene f; **in ~ clothes** (police) in Zivil(kleidung); **~ chocolate** n Bitterschokolade f

plaintiff ['pleɪntɪf] n Kläger m

plaintive ['pleɪntɪv] adj wehleidig

plait [plæt] n Zopf m ♦ vt flechten

plan [plæn] n Plan m ♦ vt, vi planen; **according to ~** planmäßig; **to ~ to do sth**

vorhaben, etw zu tun

plane [pleɪn] n Ebene f; (AVIAT) Flugzeug nt; (tool) Hobel m; (tree) Platane f

planet ['plænɪt] n Planet m

plank [plæŋk] n Brett nt

planning ['plænɪŋ] n Planung f; **family ~** Familienplanung f; **~ permission** n Baugenehmigung f

plant [plɑːnt] n Pflanze f; (TECH) (Maschinen)anlage f; (factory) Fabrik f, Werk nt ♦ vt pflanzen; (set firmly) stellen; **~ation** [plæn'teɪʃən] n Plantage f

plaque [plæk] n Gedenktafel f; (on teeth) (Zahn)belag m

plaster ['plɑːstə] n Gips m; (in house) Verputz m; (BRIT: also: **sticking ~**) Pflaster nt; (for fracture: ~ of Paris) Gipsverband m ♦ vt gipsen; (hole) zugipsen; (ceiling) verputzen; (fig: with pictures etc) bekleben, verkleben; **~ed** (inf) adj besoffen; **~er** n Gipser m

plastic ['plæstɪk] n Plastik nt or f ♦ adj (made of ~) Plastik-; (ART) plastisch, bildend; **~ bag** n Plastiktüte f

plasticine ['plæstɪsiːn] ® n Plastilin nt

plastic surgery n plastische Chirurgie f

plate [pleɪt] n Teller m; (gold/silver ~) vergoldete(s)/versilberte(s) Tafelgeschirr nt; (in book) (Bild)tafel f

plateau ['plætəu] (pl **~s** or **~x**) n (GEOG) Plateau nt, Hochebene f

plateaux ['plætəuz] npl of **plateau**

plate glass n Tafelglas nt

platform ['plætfɔːm] n (at meeting) Plattform f, Podium nt; (RAIL) Bahnsteig m; (POL) Parteiprogramm nt; **~ ticket** n Bahnsteigkarte f

platinum ['plætɪnəm] n Platin nt

platoon [plə'tuːn] n (MIL) Zug m

platter ['plætə] n Platte f

plausible ['plɔːzɪbl] adj (theory, excuse, statement) plausibel; (person) überzeugend

play [pleɪ] n (also TECH) Spiel nt; (THEAT) (Theater)stück nt ♦ vt spielen; (another team) spielen gegen ♦ vi spielen; **to ~ safe** auf Nummer sicher or Sicher gehen; **~ down** vt herunterspielen; **~ up** vi (cause *trouble*) frech werden; (*bad leg etc*) wehtun ♦ *vt* (*person*) plagen; **to ~ up to sb** jdm flattieren; **~-acting** *n* Schauspielerei *f*; **~er** *n* Spieler(in) *m(f)*; **~ful** *adj* spielerisch; **~ground** *n* Spielplatz *m*; **~group** *n* Kindergarten *m*; **~ing card** *n* Spielkarte *f*; **~ing field** *n* Sportplatz *m*; **~mate** *n* Spielkamerad *m*; **~-off** *n* (*SPORT*) Entscheidungsspiel *nt*; **~pen** *n* Laufstall *m*; **~school** *n* = **playgroup**; **~thing** *n* Spielzeug *nt*; **~time** *n* (kleine) Pause *f*; **~wright** ['pleɪraɪt] *n* Theaterschriftsteller *m*

plc *abbr* (= *public limited company*) AG

plea [pliː] *n* Bitte *f*; (*general appeal*) Appell *m*; (*JUR*) Plädoyer *nt*; **~ bargaining** *n* (*LAW*) *Aushandeln der Strafe zwischen Staatsanwaltschaft und Verteidigung*

plead [pliːd] *vt* (*poverty*) zur Entschuldigung anführen; (*JUR: sb's case*) vertreten ♦ *vi* (*beg*) dringend bitten; (*JUR*) plädieren; **to ~ with sb** jdn dringend bitten

pleasant ['plɛznt] *adj* angenehm; **~ries** *npl* (*polite remarks*) Nettigkeiten *pl*

please [pliːz] *vt, vi* (*be agreeable to*) gefallen +*dat*; **~!** bitte!; **~ yourself!** wie du willst!; **~d** *adj* zufrieden; (*glad*): **~d (about sth)** erfreut (über etw *acc*); **~d to meet you** angenehm; **pleasing** ['pliːzɪŋ] *adj* erfreulich

pleasure ['plɛʒər] *n* Freude *f* ♦ *cpd* Vergnügungs-; **"it's a ~"** „gern geschehen"

pleat [pliːt] *n* Falte *f*

plectrum ['plɛktrəm] *n* Plektron *nt*

pledge [plɛdʒ] *n* Pfand *nt*; (*promise*) Versprechen *nt* ♦ *vt* verpfänden; (*promise*) geloben, versprechen

plentiful ['plɛntɪful] *adj* reichlich

plenty ['plɛntɪ] *n* Fülle *f*, Überfluss *m*; **~ of** eine Menge, viel

pleurisy ['pluərɪsɪ] *n* Rippenfellentzündung *f*

pliable ['plaɪəbl] *adj* biegsam; (*person*) beeinflussbar

pliers ['plaɪəz] *npl* (Kneif)zange *f*

plight [plaɪt] *n* (Not)lage *f*

plimsolls ['plɪmsəlz] (*BRIT*) *npl* Turnschuhe *pl*

plinth [plɪnθ] *n* Sockel *m*

P.L.O. *n abbr* (= *Palestine Liberation*

Organization) PLO *f*

plod [plɒd] *vi* (*work*) sich abplagen; (*walk*) trotten

plonk [plɒŋk] *n* (*BRIT: inf: wine*) billige(r) Wein *m* ♦ *vt*: **to ~ sth down** etw hinknallen

plot [plɒt] *n* Komplott *nt*; (*story*) Handlung *f*; (*of land*) Grundstück *nt* ♦ *vt* markieren; (*curve*) zeichnen; (*movements*) nachzeichnen ♦ *vi* (*plan secretly*) sich verschwören

plough [plau] (*US* **plow**) *n* Pflug *m* ♦ *vt* pflügen; **~ back** *vt* (*COMM*) wieder in das Geschäft stecken; **~ through** *vt fus* (*water*) durchpflügen; (*book*) sich kämpfen durch

plow [plau] (*US*) = **plough**

ploy [plɔɪ] *n* Masche *f*

pluck [plʌk] *vt* (*fruit*) pflücken; (*guitar*) zupfen; (*goose etc*) rupfen ♦ *n* Mut *m*; **to ~ up courage** all seinen Mut zusammennehmen

plug [plʌg] *n* Stöpsel *m*; (*ELEC*) Stecker *m*; (*inf: publicity*) Schleichwerbung *f*; (*AUT*) Zündkerze *f* ♦ *vt* (zu)stopfen; (*inf: advertise*) Reklame machen für; **~ in** *vt* (*ELEC*) anschließen

plum [plʌm] *n* Pflaume *f*, Zwetsch(g)e *f*

plumage ['pluːmɪdʒ] *n* Gefieder *nt*

plumber ['plʌmər] *n* Klempner *m*, Installateur *m*; **plumbing** ['plʌmɪŋ] *n* (*craft*) Installieren *nt*; (*fittings*) Leitungen *pl*

plummet ['plʌmɪt] *vi* (ab)stürzen

plump [plʌmp] *adj* rundlich, füllig ♦ *vt* plumpsen lassen; **to ~ for** (*inf: choose*) sich entscheiden für

plunder ['plʌndər] *n* Plünderung *f*; (*loot*) Beute *f* ♦ *vt* plündern

plunge [plʌndʒ] *n* Sturz *m* ♦ *vt* stoßen ♦ *vi* (sich) stürzen; **to take the ~** den Sprung wagen; **plunging** ['plʌndʒɪŋ] *adj* (*neckline*) offenherzig

plural ['pluərl] *n* Plural *m*, Mehrzahl *f*

plus [plʌs] *n* (*also:* **~ sign**) Plus(zeichen) *nt* ♦ *prep* plus, und; **ten/twenty ~** mehr als zehn/zwanzig

plush [plʌʃ] *adj* (*also:* **~y:** *inf*) feudal

ply [plaɪ] *vt* (*trade*) (be)treiben; (*with questions*) zusetzen +*dat*; (*ship, taxi*) befahren ♦ *vi* (*ship, taxi*) verkehren ♦ *n*:

three-~ (*wool*) Dreifach-; **to ~ sb with drink** jdn zum Trinken animieren; **~wood** *n* Sperrholz *nt*

P.M. *n abbr* = prime minister

p.m. *adv abbr* (= post meridiem) nachmittags

pneumatic drill *n* Presslufthammer *m*

pneumonia [njuːˈməʊnɪə] *n* Lungenentzündung *f*

poach [pəʊtʃ] *vt* (COOK) pochieren; (*game*) stehlen ♦ *vi* (*steal*) wildern; **~ed** *adj* (*egg*) verloren; **~er** *n* Wilddieb *m*

P.O. Box *n abbr* = Post Office Box

pocket [ˈpɒkɪt] *n* Tasche *f*; (*of resistance*) (Widerstands)nest *nt* ♦ *vt* einstecken; **to be out of ~** (BRIT) draufzahlen; **~book** *n* Taschenbuch *nt*; **~ calculator** *n* Taschenrechner *m*; **~ knife** *n* Taschenmesser *nt*; **~ money** *n* Taschengeld *nt*

pod [pɒd] *n* Hülse *f*; (*of peas also*) Schote *f*

podgy [ˈpɒdʒɪ] *adj* pummelig

podiatrist [pɒˈdiːətrɪst] (US) *n* Fußpfleger(in) *m(f)*

poem [ˈpəʊɪm] *n* Gedicht *nt*

poet [ˈpəʊɪt] *n* Dichter *m*, Poet *m*; **~ic** [pəʊˈetɪk] *adj* poetisch, dichterisch; **~ laureate** *n* Hofdichter *m*; **~ry** *n* Poesie *f*; (*poems*) Gedichte *pl*

poignant [ˈpɔɪnjənt] *adj* (*touching*) ergreifend

point [pɔɪnt] *n* (*also in discussion, scoring*) Punkt *m*; (*spot*) Punkt *m*, Stelle *f*; (*sharpened tip*) Spitze *f*; (*moment*) (Zeit)punkt *m*; (*purpose*) Zweck *m*; (*idea*) Argument *nt*; (*decimal*) Dezimalstelle *f*; (*personal characteristic*) Seite *f* ♦ *vt* zeigen mit; (*gun*) richten ♦ *vi* zeigen; **~s** *npl* (RAIL) Weichen *pl*; **to be on the ~ of doing sth** drauf und dran sein, etw zu tun; **to make a ~ of** Wert darauf legen; **to get the ~** verstehen, worum es geht; **to come to the ~** zur Sache kommen; **there's no ~ (in doing sth)** es hat keinen Sinn(, etw zu tun); **~ out** *vt* hinweisen auf +*acc*; **~ to** *vt fus* zeigen auf +*acc*; **~-blank** *adv* (*at close range*) aus nächster Entfernung; (*bluntly*) unverblümt; **~ed** *adj* (*also fig*) spitz, scharf;

~edly *adv* (*fig*) spitz; **~er** *n* Zeigestock *m*; (*on dial*) Zeiger *m*; **~less** *adj* sinnlos; **~ of view** *n* Stand- *or* Gesichtspunkt *m*

poise [pɔɪz] *n* Haltung *f*; (*fig*) Gelassenheit *f*

poison [ˈpɔɪzn] *n* (*also fig*) Gift *nt* ♦ *vt* vergiften; **~ing** *n* Vergiftung *f*; **~ous** *adj* giftig, Gift-

poke [pəʊk] *vt* stoßen; (*put*) stecken; (*fire*) schüren; (*hole*) bohren; **~ about** *vi* herumstochern; (*nose around*) herumwühlen

poker [ˈpəʊkər] *n* Schürhaken *m*; (CARDS) Poker *nt*

poky [ˈpəʊkɪ] *adj* eng

Poland [ˈpəʊlənd] *n* Polen *nt*

polar [ˈpəʊlər] *adj* Polar-, polar; **~ bear** *n* Eisbär *m*

Pole [pəʊl] *n* Pole *m*, Polin *f*

pole [pəʊl] *n* Stange *f*, Pfosten *m*; (*flagpole, telegraph ~*) Stange *f*, Mast *m*; (ELEC, GEOG) Pol *m*; (SPORT: *vaulting ~*) Stab *m*; (*ski ~*) Stock *m*; **~ bean** (US) *n* (*runner bean*) Stangenbohne *f*; **~ vault** *n* Stabhochsprung *m*

police [pəˈliːs] *n* Polizei *f* ♦ *vt* kontrollieren; **~ car** *n* Polizeiwagen *m*; **~man** (*irreg*) *n* Polizist *m*; **~ state** *n* Polizeistaat *m*; **~ station** *n* (Polizei)revier *nt*, Wache *f*; **~woman** (*irreg*) *n* Polizistin *f*

policy [ˈpɒlɪsɪ] *n* Politik *f*; (*insurance*) (Versicherungs)police *f*

polio [ˈpəʊlɪəʊ] *n* (*spinale*) Kinderlähmung *f*, Polio *f*

Polish [ˈpəʊlɪʃ] *adj* polnisch ♦ *n* (LING) Polnisch *nt*

polish [ˈpɒlɪʃ] *n* Politur *f*; (*for floor*) Wachs *nt*; (*for shoes*) Creme *f*; (*for nails*) Lack *m*; (*shine*) Glanz *m*; (*of furniture*) Politur *f*; (*fig*) Schliff *m* ♦ *vt* polieren; (*shoes*) putzen; (*fig*) den letzten Schliff geben +*dat*; **~ off** *vt* (*inf: food*) wegputzen; (: *drink*) hinunterschütten; **~ed** *adj* glänzend; (*manners*) verfeinert

polite [pəˈlaɪt] *adj* höflich; **~ly** *adv* höflich; **~ness** *n* Höflichkeit *f*

politic-: ~al [pəˈlɪtɪkl] *adj* politisch; **~ally** [pəˈlɪtɪklɪ] *adv* politisch; **~ally correct**

politisch korrekt; **~ian** [pɔlɪ'tɪʃən] n Politiker m; **~s** npl Politik f

polka dot ['pɔlkə-] n Tupfen m

poll [pəul] n Abstimmung f; (*in election*) Wahl f; (*votes cast*) Wahlbeteiligung f; (*opinion ~*) Umfrage f ♦ vt (*votes*) erhalten

pollen ['pɔlən] n (BOT) Blütenstaub m, Pollen m

polling ['pəulɪŋ-]: **~ booth** (BRIT) n Wahlkabine f; **~ day** (BRIT) n Wahltag m; **~ station** (BRIT) n Wahllokal nt

pollute [pə'luːt] vt verschmutzen, verunreinigen; **~d** adj verschmutzt; **pollution** [pə'luːʃən] n Verschmutzung f

polo ['pəuləu] n Polo nt; **~ neck** n (*also: ~-necked sweater*) Rollkragen m; Rollkragenpullover m; **~ shirt** n Polohemd nt

polystyrene [pɔlɪ'staɪriːn] n Styropor nt

polytechnic [pɔlɪ'tɛknɪk] n technische Hochschule f

polythene ['pɔlɪθiːn] n Plastik nt; **~ bag** n Plastiktüte f

pomegranate ['pɔmɪgrænɪt] n Granatapfel m

pompom ['pɔmpɔm] n Troddel f, Pompon m

pompous ['pɔmpəs] adj aufgeblasen; (*language*) geschwollen

pond [pɔnd] n Teich m, Weiher m

ponder ['pɔndər] vt nachdenken über +acc; **~ous** adj schwerfällig

pong [pɔŋ] (BRIT: inf) n Mief m

pontiff ['pɔntɪf] n Pontifex m

pontoon [pɔn'tuːn] n Ponton m; (CARDS) 17-und-4 nt

pony ['pəunɪ] n Pony nt; **~tail** n Pferdeschwanz m; **~ trekking** (BRIT) n Ponyreiten nt

poodle ['puːdl] n Pudel m

pool [puːl] n (*swimming ~*) Schwimmbad nt; (: *private*) Swimmingpool m; (*of liquid, blood*) Lache f; (*fund*) (gemeinsame) Kasse f; (*billiards*) Poolspiel nt ♦ vt (*money etc*) zusammenlegen; **(football) ~s** Toto nt

poor [puər] adj arm; (*not good*) schlecht ♦ npl: **the ~** die Armen pl; **~ in** (*resources*)

arm an +dat; **~ly** adv schlecht; (*dressed*) ärmlich ♦ adj schlecht

pop [pɔp] n Knall m; (*music*) Popmusik f; (*drink*) Limo(nade) f; (US: inf) Pa m ♦ vt (*put*) stecken; (*balloon*) platzen lassen ♦ vi knallen; **~ in** vi kurz vorbeigehen or vorbeikommen; **~ out** vi (*person*) kurz rausgehen; (*thing*) herausspringen; **~ up** vi auftauchen; **~corn** n Puffmais m

pope [pəup] n Papst m

poplar ['pɔplər] n Pappel f

poppy ['pɔpɪ] n Mohn m

Popsicle ['pɔpsɪkl] (® US) n (*ice lolly*) Eis nt am Stiel

populace ['pɔpjuləs] n Volk nt

popular ['pɔpjulər] adj beliebt, populär; (*of the people*) volkstümlich; (*widespread*) allgemein; **~ity** [pɔpju'lærɪtɪ] n Beliebtheit f, Popularität f; **~ly** adv allgemein, überall

population [pɔpju'leɪʃən] n Bevölkerung f; (*of town*) Einwohner pl

populous ['pɔpjuləs] adj dicht besiedelt

porcelain ['pɔːslɪn] n Porzellan nt

porch [pɔːtʃ] n Vorbau m, Veranda f

porcupine ['pɔːkjupaɪn] n Stachelschwein nt

pore [pɔːr] n Pore f ♦ vi: **to ~ over** brüten über +dat

pork [pɔːk] n Schweinefleisch nt

porn [pɔːn] n Porno m; **~ographic** [pɔːnə'græfɪk] adj pornografisch; **~ography** [pɔː'nɔgrəfɪ] n Pornografie f

porous ['pɔːrəs] adj porös; (*skin*) porig

porpoise ['pɔːpəs] n Tümmler m

porridge ['pɔrɪdʒ] n Haferbrei m

port [pɔːt] n Hafen m; (*town*) Hafenstadt f; (NAUT: *left side*) Backbord nt; (*wine*) Portwein m; **~ of call** Anlaufhafen m

portable ['pɔːtəbl] adj tragbar

porter ['pɔːtər] n Pförtner(in) m(f); (*for luggage*) (Gepäck)träger m

portfolio [pɔːt'fəuliəu] n (*case*) Mappe f; (POL) Geschäftsbereich m; (FIN) Portefeuille nt; (*of artist*) Kollektion f

porthole ['pɔːthəul] n Bullauge nt

portion ['pɔːʃən] n Teil m, Stück nt; (*of food*) Portion f

portrait ['pɔːtreɪt] n Porträt nt

portray [pɔː'treɪ] *vt* darstellen; **~al** *n* Darstellung *f*

Portugal [pɔː'tjugl] *n* Portugal *nt*

Portuguese [pɔːtjuˈgiːz] *adj* portugiesisch ♦ *n inv* Portugiese *m*, Portugiesin *f*; (*LING*) Portugiesisch *nt*

pose [pəʊz] *n* Stellung *f*, Pose *f*; (*affectation*) Pose *f* ♦ *vi* posieren ♦ *vt* stellen

posh [pɒʃ] (*inf*) *adj* (piek)fein

position [pəˈzɪʃən] *n* Stellung *f*; (*place*) Lage *f*; (*job*) Stelle *f*; (*attitude*) Standpunkt *m* ♦ *vt* aufstellen

positive [ˈpɒzɪtɪv] *adj* positiv; (*convinced*) sicher; (*definite*) eindeutig

posse [ˈpɒsɪ] (*US*) *n* Aufgebot *nt*

possess [pəˈzɛs] *vt* besitzen; **~ion** [pəˈzɛʃən] *n* Besitz *m*; **~ive** *adj* besitzergreifend, eigensüchtig

possibility [pɒsɪˈbɪlɪtɪ] *n* Möglichkeit *f*

possible [ˈpɒsɪbl] *adj* möglich; **as big as ~** so groß wie möglich, möglichst groß; **possibly** *adv* möglicherweise, vielleicht; **I cannot possibly come** ich kann unmöglich kommen

post [pəʊst] *n* (*BRIT: letters, delivery*) Post *f*; (*pole*) Pfosten *m*, Pfahl *m*; (*place of duty*) Posten *m*; (*job*) Stelle *f* ♦ *vt* (*notice*) anschlagen; (*BRIT: letters*) aufgeben; (*: appoint*) versetzen; (*soldiers*) aufstellen; **~age** *n* Postgebühr *f*, Porto *nt*; **~al** *adj* Post-; **~al order** *n* Postanweisung *f*; **~box** (*BRIT*) *n* Briefkasten *m*; **~card** *n* Postkarte *f*; **~code** (*BRIT*) *n* Postleitzahl *f*

postdate [ˈpəʊstˈdeɪt] *vt* (*cheque*) nachdatieren

poster [ˈpəʊstəʳ] *n* Plakat *nt*, Poster *nt*

poste restante [pəʊstˈrɛstɑːnt] *n* Aufbewahrungsstelle *f* für postlagernde Sendungen

posterior [pɒsˈtɪərɪəʳ] (*inf*) *n* Hintern *m*

posterity [pɒsˈtɛrɪtɪ] *n* Nachwelt *f*

postgraduate [ˈpəʊstˈgrædjʊət] *n* Weiterstudierende(r) *mf*

posthumous [ˈpɒstjuməs] *adj* post(h)um

postman [ˈpəʊstmən] (*irreg*) *n* Briefträger *m*

postmark [ˈpəʊstmɑːk] *n* Poststempel *m*

post-mortem [pəʊstˈmɔːtəm] *n* Autopsie *f*

post office *n* Postamt *nt*, Post *f*; (*organization*) Post *f*; **Post Office Box** *n* Postfach *nt*

postpone [pəʊsˈpəʊn] *vt* verschieben

postscript [ˈpəʊstskrɪpt] *n* Postskript *nt*; (*to affair*) Nachspiel *nt*

posture [ˈpɒstʃəʳ] *n* Haltung *f* ♦ *vi* posieren

postwar [pəʊstˈwɔː] *adj* Nachkriegs-

postwoman [ˈpəʊstwʊmən] (*irreg*) *n* Briefträgerin *f*

posy [ˈpəʊzɪ] *n* Blumenstrauß *m*

pot [pɒt] *n* Topf *m*; (*teapot*) Kanne *f*; (*inf: marijuana*) Hasch *m* ♦ *vt* (*plant*) eintopfen; **to go to ~** (*inf: work*) auf den Hund kommen

potato [pəˈteɪtəʊ] (*pl ~es*) *n* Kartoffel *f*; **~ peeler** *n* Kartoffelschäler *m*

potent [ˈpəʊtnt] *adj* stark; (*argument*) zwingend

potential [pəˈtɛnʃl] *adj* potenziell, potentiell ♦ *n* Potenzial *nt*, Potential *nt*; **~ly** *adv* potenziell, potentiell

pothole [ˈpɒthəʊl] *n* (*in road*) Schlagloch *nt*; (*BRIT: underground*) Höhle *f*; **potholing** (*BRIT*) *n*: **to go potholing** Höhlen erforschen

potion [ˈpəʊʃən] *n* Trank *m*

potluck [pɒtˈlʌk] *n*: **to take ~ with sth** etw auf gut Glück nehmen

pot plant *n* Topfpflanze *f*

potter [ˈpɒtəʳ] *n* Töpfer *m* ♦ *vi* herumhantieren; **~y** *n* Töpferwaren *pl*; (*place*) Töpferei *f*

potty [ˈpɒtɪ] *adj* (*inf: mad*) verrückt ♦ *n* Töpfchen *nt*

pouch [paʊtʃ] *n* Beutel *m*

pouf(fe) [puːf] *n* Sitzkissen *nt*

poultry [ˈpəʊltrɪ] *n* Geflügel *nt*

pounce [paʊns] *vi* sich stürzen ♦ *n* Sprung *m*, Satz *m*; **to ~ on** sich stürzen auf *+acc*

pound [paʊnd] *n* (*FIN, weight*) Pfund *nt*; (*for cars, animals*) Auslösestelle *f* ♦ *vt* (zer)stampfen ♦ *vi* klopfen, hämmern; **~ sterling** *n* Pfund Sterling *nt*

pour [pɔː] *vt* gießen, schütten ♦ *vi* gießen; (*crowds etc*) strömen; **~ away** *vt* abgießen; **~ in** *vi* (*people*) hereinströmen; **~ off** *vt* abgießen; **~ out** *vi* (*people*) herausströmen

♦ vt (drink) einschenken; **~ing** adj: **~ing rain** strömende(r) Regen m

pout [paut] vi schmollen

poverty ['pɔvətɪ] n Armut f; **~-stricken** adj verarmt, sehr arm

powder ['paudə^r] n Pulver nt; (cosmetic) Puder m ♦ vt pulverisieren; **to ~ one's nose** sich dat die Nase pudern; **~ compact** n Puderdose f; **~ed milk** n Milchpulver nt; **~ room** n Damentoilette f; **~y** adj pulverig

power ['pauə^r] n (also POL) Macht f; (ability) Fähigkeit f; (strength) Stärke f; (MATH) Potenz f; (ELEC) Strom m ♦ vt betreiben, antreiben; **to be in ~** (POL etc) an der Macht sein; **~ cut** n Stromausfall m; **~ed** adj: **~ed by** betrieben mit; **~ failure** (US) n Stromausfall m; **~ful** adj (person) mächtig; (engine, government) stark; **~less** adj machtlos; **~ point** (BRIT) n elektrische(r) Anschluss m; **~ station** n Elektrizitätswerk nt; **~ struggle** n Machtkampf m

p.p. abbr (= per procurationem): **p.p. J. Smith** i. A. J. Smith

PR n abbr = **public relations**

practicable ['præktɪkəbl] adj durchführbar

practical ['præktɪkl] adj praktisch; **~ity** [præktɪ'kælɪtɪ] n (of person) praktische Veranlagung f; (of situation etc) Durchführbarkeit f; **~ joke** n Streich m; **~ly** adv praktisch

practice ['præktɪs] n Übung f; (reality, also of doctor, lawyer) Praxis f; (custom) Brauch m; (in business) Usus m ♦ vt, vi (US) = **practise**; **in ~** (in reality) in der Praxis; **out of ~** außer Übung; **practicing** (US) adj = **practising**

practise ['præktɪs] (US **practice**) vt üben; (profession) ausüben ♦ vi (sich) üben; (doctor, lawyer) praktizieren; **practising** (US **practicing**) adj praktizierend; (Christian etc) aktiv

practitioner [præk'tɪʃənə^r] n praktische(r) Arzt m, praktische Ärztin f

pragmatic [præg'mætɪk] adj pragmatisch

prairie ['prɛərɪ] n Prärie f, Steppe f

praise [preɪz] n Lob nt ♦ vt loben; **~worthy** adj lobenswert

pram [præm] (BRIT) n Kinderwagen m

prance [prɑːns] vi (horse) tänzeln; (person) stolzieren

prank [præŋk] n Streich m

prawn [prɔːn] n Garnele f, Krabbe f; **~ cocktail** n Krabbencocktail m

pray [preɪ] vi beten; **~er** [prɛə^r] n Gebet nt

preach [priːtʃ] vi predigen; **~er** n Prediger m

preamble [prɪ'æmbl] n Einleitung f

precarious [prɪ'kɛərɪəs] adj prekär, unsicher

precaution [prɪ'kɔːʃən] n (Vorsichts)maßnahme f

precede [prɪ'siːd] vi vorausgehen ♦ vt vorausgehen +dat; **~nce** ['presɪdəns] n Vorrang m; **~nt** ['presɪdənt] n Präzedenzfall m; **preceding** [prɪ'siːdɪŋ] adj vorhergehend

precinct ['priːsɪŋkt] n (US: district) Bezirk m; **~s** npl (round building) Gelände nt; (area, environs) Umgebung f; **pedestrian ~** Fußgängerzone f; **shopping ~** Geschäftsviertel nt

precious ['preʃəs] adj kostbar, wertvoll; (affected) pretiös, preziös, geziert

precipice ['presɪpɪs] n Abgrund m

precipitate [adj prɪ'sɪpɪtɪt, vb prɪ'sɪpɪteɪt] adj überstürzt, übereilt ♦ vt hinunterstürzen; (events) heraufbeschwören

precise [prɪ'saɪs] adj genau, präzis; **~ly** adv genau, präzis

precision [prɪ'sɪʒən] n Präzision f

preclude [prɪ'kluːd] vt ausschließen

precocious [prɪ'kəuʃəs] adj frühreif

preconceived [priːkən'siːvd] adj (idea) vorgefasst

precondition ['priːkən'dɪʃən] n Vorbedingung f, Voraussetzung f

precursor [priː'kɜːsə^r] n Vorläufer m

predator ['predətə^r] n Raubtier nt

predecessor ['priːdɪsesə^r] n Vorgänger m

predicament [prɪ'dɪkəmənt] n missliche Lage f

predict [prɪ'dɪkt] vt voraussagen; **~able** adj vorhersagbar; **~ion** [prɪ'dɪkʃən] n Voraussage f

predominantly [prɪ'dɔmɪnəntlɪ] adv

überwiegend, hauptsächlich

predominate [prɪ'dɔmɪneɪt] *vi* vorherrschen; (*fig*) vorherrschen, überwiegen

pre-eminent [priː'emɪnənt] *adj* hervorragend, herausragend

pre-empt [priː'emt] *vt* (*action, decision*) vorwegnehmen

preen [priːn] *vt* putzen; **to ~ o.s.** (*person*) sich brüsten

prefab ['priːfæb] *n* Fertighaus *nt*

preface ['prefəs] *n* Vorwort *nt*

prefect ['priːfekt] *n* Präfekt *m*; (*SCH*) Aufsichtsschüler(in) *m(f)*

prefer [prɪ'fɜːʳ] *vt* vorziehen, lieber mögen; **to ~ to do sth** etw lieber tun; **~ably** ['prefrəblɪ] *adv* vorzugsweise, am liebsten; **~ence** ['prefrəns] *n* Präferenz *f*, Vorzug *m*; **~ential** [prefə'renʃəl] *adj* bevorzugt, Vorzugs-

prefix ['priːfɪks] *n* Vorsilbe *f*, Präfix *nt*

pregnancy ['pregnənsɪ] *n* Schwangerschaft *f*

pregnant ['pregnənt] *adj* schwanger

prehistoric ['priːhɪs'tɔrɪk] *adj* prähistorisch, vorgeschichtlich

prejudice ['predʒudɪs] *n* (*bias*) Voreingenommenheit *f*; (*opinion*) Vorurteil *nt*; (*harm*) Schaden *m* ♦ *vt* beeinträchtigen; **~d** *adj* (*person*) voreingenommen

preliminary [prɪ'lɪmɪnərɪ] *adj* einleitend, Vor-

prelude ['preljuːd] *n* Vorspiel *nt*; (*fig*) Auftakt *m*

premarital ['priː'mærɪtl] *adj* vorehelich

premature ['premətʃuəʳ] *adj* vorzeitig, verfrüht; (*birth*) Früh-

premeditated [priː'medɪteɪtɪd] *adj* geplant; (*murder*) vorsätzlich

premenstrual syndrome [priː'menstruəl-] *n* prämenstruelles Syndrom *nt*

premier ['premɪəʳ] *adj* erste(r, s) ♦ *n* Premier *m*

première ['premɪeəʳ] *n* Premiere *f*; Uraufführung *f*

Premier League [-liːg] *n* ≃ 1. Bundesliga (*höchste Spielklasse im Fußball*)

premise ['premɪs] *n* Voraussetzung *f*,

Prämisse *f*; **~s** *npl* (*shop*) Räumlichkeiten *pl*; (*grounds*) Gelände *nt*; **on the ~s** im Hause

premium ['priːmɪəm] *n* Prämie *f*; **to be at a ~** über pari stehen; **~ bond** (*BRIT*) *n* Prämienanleihe *f*

premonition [premə'nɪʃən] *n* Vorahnung *f*

preoccupation [priːɔkju'peɪʃən] *n* Sorge *f*

preoccupied [priː'ɔkjupaɪd] *adj* (*look*) geistesabwesend

prep [prep] *n* (*SCH*) Hausaufgabe *f*

prepaid [priː'peɪd] *adj* vorausbezahlt; (*letter*) frankiert

preparation [prepə'reɪʃən] *n* Vorbereitung *f*

preparatory [prɪ'pærətərɪ] *adj* Vor(bereitungs)-; **~ school** *n* (*BRIT*) *private Vorbereitungsschule für die Public School*; (*US*) *private Vorbereitungsschule für die Hochschule*

prepare [prɪ'peəʳ] *vt* vorbereiten ♦ *vi* sich vorbereiten; **to ~ for/prepare sth for** sich/etw vorbereiten auf +*acc*; **to be ~d to** ... bereit sein zu ...

preponderance [prɪ'pɔndərns] *n* Übergewicht *nt*

preposition [prepə'zɪʃən] *n* Präposition *f*, Verhältniswort *nt*

preposterous [prɪ'pɔstərəs] *adj* absurd

prep school *n* = **preparatory school**

prerequisite [priː'rekwɪzɪt] *n* (unerlässliche) Voraussetzung *f*

prerogative [prɪ'rɔgətɪv] *n* Vorrecht *nt*

Presbyterian [prezbɪ'tɪərɪən] *adj* presbyterianisch ♦ *n* Presbyteriar(in) *m(f)*

preschool ['priː'skuːl] *adj* Vorschul-

prescribe [prɪ'skraɪb] *vt* vorschreiben; (*MED*) verschreiben

prescription [prɪ'skrɪpʃən] *n* (*MED*) Rezept *nt*

presence ['prezns] *n* Gegenwart *f*; **~ of mind** Geistesgegenwart *f*

present [*adj, n* 'preznt, *vb* prɪ'zent] *adj* (*here*) anwesend; (*current*) gegenwärtig ♦ *n* Gegenwart *f*; (*gift*) Geschenk *nt* ♦ *vt* vorlegen; (*introduce*) vorstellen; (*show*) zeigen; (*give*): **to ~ sb with sth** jdm etw überreichen; **at ~** im Augenblick; **to give sb a ~** jdm ein Geschenk machen; **~able** [prɪ'zentəbl] *adj* präsentabel; **~ation**

[prezn'teɪʃən] n Überreichung f; **~-day** adj heutig; **~er** [prɪ'zɛntər] n (*RAD*, *TV*) Moderator(in) m(f); **~ly** adv bald; (*at ~*) im Augenblick

preservation [prezə'veɪʃən] n Erhaltung f

preservative [prɪ'zɜːvətɪv] n Konservierungsmittel nt

preserve [prɪ'zɜːv] vt erhalten; (*food*) einmachen ♦ n (*jam*) Eingemachte(s) nt; (*reserve*) Schutzgebiet nt

preside [prɪ'zaɪd] vi den Vorsitz haben

president ['prezɪdənt] n Präsident m; **~ial** [prezɪ'denʃl] adj Präsidenten-; (*election*) Präsidentschafts-; (*system*) Präsidial-

press [pres] n Presse f; (*printing house*) Druckerei f ♦ vt drücken; (*iron*) bügeln; (*urge*) (be)drängen ♦ vi (*push*) drücken; **to be ~ed for time** unter Zeitdruck stehen; **to ~ for sth** drängen auf etw acc; **~ on** vi vorwärts drängen; **~ agency** n Presseagentur f; **~ conference** n Pressekonferenz f; **~ed** adj (*clothes*) gebügelt; **~ing** adj dringend; **~ stud** (*BRIT*) n Druckknopf m; **~-up** (*BRIT*) n Liegestütz m

pressure ['preʃər] n Druck m; **~ cooker** n Schnellkochtopf m; **~ gauge** n Druckmesser m

pressurized ['preʃəraɪzd] adj Druck-

prestige [pres'tiːʒ] n Prestige nt;

prestigious [pres'tɪdʒəs] adj Prestige-

presumably [prɪ'zjuːməblɪ] adv vermutlich

presume [prɪ'zjuːm] vt, vi annehmen; **to ~ to do sth** sich erlauben, etw zu tun;

presumption [prɪ'zʌmpʃən] n Annahme f;

presumptuous [prɪ'zʌmpʃəs] adj anmaßend

pretence [prɪ'tens] (*US* **pretense**) n Vorgabe f, Vortäuschung f; (*false claim*) Vorwand m

pretend [prɪ'tend] vt vorgeben, so tun als ob ... ♦ vi so tun; **to ~ to sth** Anspruch erheben auf etw acc

pretense [prɪ'tens] (*US*) n = **pretence**

pretension [prɪ'tenʃən] n Anspruch m; (*impudent claim*) Anmaßung f

pretentious [prɪ'tenʃəs] adj angeberisch

pretext ['priːtekst] n Vorwand m

pretty ['prɪtɪ] adj hübsch ♦ adv (*inf*) ganz

schön

prevail [prɪ'veɪl] vi siegen; (*custom*) vorherrschen; **to ~ against** or **over** siegen über +acc; **to ~ (up)on sb to do sth** jdn dazu bewegen, etw zu tun; **~ing** adj vorherrschend

prevalent ['prevələnt] adj vorherrschend

prevent [prɪ'vent] vt (*stop*) verhindern, verhüten; **to ~ sb from doing sth** jdn (daran) hindern, etw zu tun; **~ative** n Vorbeugungsmittel nt; **~ion** [prɪ'venʃən] n Verhütung f; **~ive** adj vorbeugend, Schutz-

preview ['priːvjuː] n private Voraufführung f; (*trailer*) Vorschau f

previous ['priːvɪəs] adj früher, vorherig; **~ly** adv früher

prewar [priː'wɔːr] adj Vorkriegs-

prey [preɪ] n Beute f; **~ on** vt fus Jagd machen auf +acc; **it was ~ing on his mind** es quälte sein Gewissen

price [praɪs] n Preis m; (*value*) Wert m ♦ vt (*label*) auszeichnen; **~less** adj (*also fig*) unbezahlbar; **~ list** n Preisliste f

prick [prɪk] n Stich m ♦ vt, vi stechen; **to ~ up one's ears** die Ohren spitzen

prickle ['prɪkl] n Stachel m, Dorn m

prickly ['prɪklɪ] adj stachelig; (*fig: person*) reizbar; **~ heat** n Hitzebläschen pl

pride [praɪd] n Stolz m; (*arrogance*) Hochmut m ♦ vt: **to ~ o.s. on sth** auf etw acc stolz sein

priest [priːst] n Priester m; **~hood** n Priesteramt nt

prim [prɪm] adj prüde

primarily ['praɪmərɪlɪ] adv vorwiegend

primary ['praɪmərɪ] adj (*main*) Haupt-; (*SCH*) Grund-; **~ school** (*BRIT*) n Grundschule f

prime [praɪm] adj erste(r, s); (*excellent*) erstklassig ♦ vt vorbereiten; (*gun*) laden; **in the ~ of life** in der Blüte der Jahre; **~ minister** n Premierminister m, Ministerpräsident m; **~r** ['praɪmər] n Fibel f

primeval [praɪ'miːvl] adj vorzeitlich; (*forests*) Ur-

primitive ['prɪmɪtɪv] adj primitiv

primrose ['prɪmrəuz] n (gelbe) Primel f

primus (stove) ['praɪməs-] (®, *BRIT*) n

Primuskocher *m*

prince [prɪns] *n* Prinz *m*; (*ruler*) Fürst *m*; **princess** [prɪn'ses] *n* Prinzessin *f*; Fürstin *f*

principal ['prɪnsɪpl] *adj* Haupt- ♦ *n* (*SCH*) (Schul)direktor *m*, Rektor *m*; (*money*) (Grund)kapital *nt*

principle ['prɪnsɪpl] *n* Grundsatz *m*, Prinzip *nt*; **in ~** im Prinzip; **on ~** aus Prinzip, prinzipiell

print [prɪnt] *n* Druck *m*; (*made by feet, fingers*) Abdruck *m*; (*PHOT*) Abzug *m* ♦ *vt* drucken; (*name*) in Druckbuchstaben schreiben; (*PHOT*) abziehen; **out of ~** vergriffen; **~ed matter** *n* Drucksache *f*; **~er** *n* Drucker *m*; **~ing** *n* Drucken *nt*; (*of photos*) Abziehen *nt*; **~out** *n* (*COMPUT*) Ausdruck *m*

prior ['praɪə'] *adj* früher ♦ *n* Prior *m*; **~ to sth** vor etw *dat*; **~ to going abroad, she had ... bevor sie ins Ausland ging, hatte sie ...

priority [praɪ'ɒrɪtɪ] *n* Vorrang *m*; Priorität *f*

prise [praɪz] *vt*: **to ~ open** aufbrechen

prison ['prɪzn] *n* Gefängnis *nt* ♦ *adj* Gefängnis-; (*system etc*) Strafvollzugs-; **~er** *n* Gefangene(r) *mf*

pristine ['prɪstiːn] *adj* makellos

privacy ['prɪvəsɪ] *n* Ungestörtheit *f*, Ruhe *f*; Privatleben *nt*

private ['praɪvɪt] *adj* privat, Privat-; (*secret*) vertraulich, geheim ♦ *n* einfache(r) Soldat *m*; **"~"** (*on envelope*) "persönlich"; (*on door*) "Privat"; **in ~** privat, unter vier Augen; **~ enterprise** *n* Privatunternehmen *nt*; **~ eye** *n* Privatdetektiv *m*; **~ property** *n* Privatbesitz *m*; **~ school** *n* Privatschule *f*; **privatize** *vt* privatisieren

privet ['prɪvɪt] *n* Liguster *m*

privilege ['prɪvɪlɪdʒ] *n* Privileg *nt*; **~d** *adj* bevorzugt, privilegiert

privy ['prɪvɪ] *adj* geheim, privat; **P~ Council** *n* Geheime(r) Staatsrat *m*

prize [praɪz] *n* Preis *m* ♦ *adj* (*example*) erstklassig; (*idiot*) Voll- ♦ *vt* (hoch) schätzen; **~-giving** *n* Preisverteilung *f*; **~winner** *n* Preisträger(in) *m(f)*

pro [prəʊ] *n* (*professional*) Profi *m*; **the ~s and cons** das Für und Wider

probability [prɒbə'bɪlɪtɪ] *n*

Wahrscheinlichkeit *f*

probable ['prɒbəbl] *adj* wahrscheinlich **probably** *adv* wahrscheinlich

probation [prə'beɪʃən] *n* Probe(zeit) *f*; (*JUR*) Bewährung *f*; **on ~** auf Probe; auf Bewährung

probe [prəʊb] *n* Sonde *f*; (*enquiry*) Untersuchung *f* ♦ *vt*, *vi* erforschen

problem ['prɒbləm] *n* Problem *nt*; **~atic** [prɒblə'mætɪk] *adj* problematisch

procedure [prə'siːdʒə'] *n* Verfahren *nt*

proceed [prə'siːd] *vi* (*advance*) vorrücken; (*start*) anfangen; (*carry on*) fortfahren; (*set about*) vorgehen; **~ings** *npl* Verfahren *nt*

proceeds ['prəʊsiːdz] *npl* Erlös *m*

process ['prəʊses] *n* Prozess *m*; (*method*) Verfahren *nt* ♦ *vt* bearbeiten; (*food*) verarbeiten; (*film*) entwickeln; **~ing** *n* (*PHOT*) Entwickeln *nt*

procession [prə'seʃən] *n* Prozession *f*, Umzug *m*; **funeral ~** Trauerprozession *f*

pro-choice [prəʊ'tʃɔɪs] *adj* (*movement*) Pro-Abtreibungs-, **~ campaigner** Abtreibungsbefürworter(in) *m(f)*

proclaim [prə'kleɪm] *vt* verkünden

procrastinate [prəʊ'kræstɪneɪt] *vi* zaudern

procure [prə'kjʊə'] *vt* beschaffen

prod [prɒd] *vt* stoßen ♦ *n* Stoß *m*

prodigal ['prɒdɪgl] *adj*: **~ (with** *or* **of)** verschwenderisch (mit)

prodigy ['prɒdɪdʒɪ] *n* Wunder *nt*

produce [*n* 'prɒdjuːs, *vb* prə'djuːs] *n* (*AGR*) (Boden)produkte *pl*, (Natur)erzeugnis *nt* ♦ *vt* herstellen, produzieren; (*cause*) hervorrufen; (*farmer*) erzeugen; (*yield*) liefern, bringen; (*play*) inszenieren; **~r** *n* Hersteller *m*, Produzent *m* (also *CINE*); Erzeuger *m*

product ['prɒdʌkt] *n* Produkt *nt*, Erzeugnis *nt*; **~ion** [prə'dʌkʃən] *n* Produktion *f*, Herstellung *f*; (*thing*) Erzeugnis *nt*, Produkt *nt*; (*THEAT*) Inszenierung *f*; **~ion line** *n* Fließband *nt*; **~ive** [prə'dʌktɪv] *adj* produktiv; (*fertile*) ertragreich, fruchtbar

productivity [prɒdʌk'tɪvɪtɪ] *n* Produktivität *f*

profane [prə'feɪn] *adj* weltlich, profan; (*language etc*) gotteslästerlich

profess [prə'fes] *vt* bekennen; (*show*) zeigen; (*claim to be*) vorgeben

profession [prə'feʃən] *n* Beruf *m*; (*declaration*) Bekenntnis *nt*; **~al** *n* Fachmann *m*; (*SPORT*) Berufsspieler(in) *m(f)* ♦ *adj* Berufs-; (*expert*) fachlich; (*player*) professionell; **~ally** *adv* beruflich, fachmännisch

professor [prə'fesər] *n* Professor *m*

proficiency [prə'fiʃənsɪ] *n* Können *nt*

proficient [prə'fiʃənt] *adj* fähig

profile ['prəʊfaɪl] *n* Profil *nt*; (*fig: report*) Kurzbiografie *f*

profit ['prɒfɪt] *n* Gewinn *m* ♦ *vi*: **to ~ (by** *or* **from)** profitieren (von); **~ability** [prɒfɪtə'bɪlɪtɪ] *n* Rentabilität *f*; **~able** *adj* einträglich, rentabel; **~eering** [prɒfɪ'tɪərɪŋ] *n* Profitmacherei *f*

profound [prə'faʊnd] *adj* tief

profuse [prə'fjuːs] *adj* überreich; **~ly** [prə'fjuːslɪ] *adv* überschwänglich; (*sweat*) reichlich; **profusion** [prə'fjuːʒən] *n*: **profusion (of)** Überfülle *f* (von), Überfluss *m* (an +*dat*)

program ['prəʊgræm] *n* (*COMPUT*) Programm *nt* ♦ *vt* (*machine*) programmieren; **~me** (*US* **program**) *n* Programm *nt* ♦ *vt* planen; (*computer*) programmieren; **~mer** (*US* **programer**) *n* Programmierer(in) *m(f)*

progress [*n* 'prəʊgres, *vb* prə'gres] *n* Fortschritt *m* ♦ *vi* fortschreiten, weitergehen; **in ~** im Gang; **~ion** [prə'greʃən] *n* Folge *f*; **~ive** [prə'gresɪv] *adj* fortschrittlich, progressiv

prohibit [prə'hɪbɪt] *vt* verbieten; **to ~ sb from doing sth** jdm untersagen, etw zu tun; **~ion** [prəʊɪ'bɪʃən] *n* Verbot *nt*; (*US*) Alkoholverbot *nt*, Prohibition *f*; **~ive** *adj* unerschwinglich

project [*n* 'prɒdʒekt, *vb* prə'dʒekt] *n* Projekt *nt* ♦ *vt* vorausplanen; (*film etc*) projizieren; (*personality, voice*) zum Tragen bringen ♦ *vi* (*stick out*) hervorragen, (her)vorstehen

projectile [prə'dʒektaɪl] *n* Geschoss *nt*

projection [prə'dʒekʃən] *n* Projektion *f*; (*sth prominent*) Vorsprung *m*

projector [prə'dʒektər] *n* Projektor *m*

proletariat [prəʊlɪ'tɛərɪət] *n* Proletariat *nt*

pro-life [prəʊ'laɪf] *adj* (*movement*) Anti-Abtreibungs-; **~ campaigner** Abtreibungsgegner(in) *m(f)*

prolific [prə'lɪfɪk] *adj* fruchtbar; (*author etc*) produktiv

prologue ['prəʊlɒg] *n* Prolog *m*; (*event*) Vorspiel *nt*

prolong [prə'lɒŋ] *vt* verlängern

prom [prɒm] *n abbr* = **promenade**; **promenade concert**

Prom

i **Prom** (*promenade concert*) ist in Großbritannien ein Konzert, bei dem ein Teil der Zuhörer steht (ursprünglich spazieren ging). *Die seit 1895 alljährlich stattfindenden Proms (seit 1941 immer in der Londoner Royal Albert Hall) zählen zu den bedeutendsten Musikereignissen in England. Der letzte Abend der Proms steht ganz im Zeichen des Patriotismus und gipfelt im Singen des Lieds „Land of Hope and Glory". In den USA und Kanada steht das Wort für* **promenade**, *ein Ball an einer* High School *oder einem* College.

---

promenade [prɒmə'nɑːd] *n* Promenade *f*; **~ concert** *n* Promenadenkonzert *nt*

prominence ['prɒmɪnəns] *n* (große) Bedeutung *f*

prominent ['prɒmɪnənt] *adj* bedeutend; (*politician*) prominent; (*easily seen*) herausragend, auffallend

promiscuous [prə'mɪskjuəs] *adj* lose

promise ['prɒmɪs] *n* Versprechen *nt*; (*hope: ~ of sth*) Aussicht *f* auf etw *acc* ♦ *vt, vi* versprechen; **promising** *adj* viel versprechend

promontory ['prɒməntrɪ] *n* Vorsprung *m*

promote [prə'məʊt] *vt* befördern; (*help on*) fördern, unterstützen; **~r** *n* (*in entertainment, sport*) Veranstalter *m*; (*for charity etc*) Organisator *m*; **promotion** [prə'məʊʃən] *n* (*in rank*) Beförderung *f*; (*furthering*) Förderung *f*; (*COMM*): **promotion (of)** Werbung *f* (für)

prompt [prɒmpt] *adj* prompt, schnell ♦ *adv* (*punctually*) genau ♦ *n* (*COMPUT*) Meldung *f* ♦ *vt* veranlassen; (*THEAT*) soufflieren +*dat*; **to ~ sb to do sth** jdn dazu veranlassen, etw zu tun; **~ly** *adv* sofort

prone [prəun] *adj* hingestreckt; **to be ~ to sth** zu etw neigen

prong [prɒŋ] *n* Zinke *f*

pronoun ['prəunaun] *n* Fürwort *nt*

pronounce [prə'nauns] *vt* aussprechen; (*JUR*) verkünden ♦ *vi*: **to ~ (on)** sich äußern (zu)

pronunciation [prənʌnsi'eiʃən] *n* Aussprache *f*

proof [pru:f] *n* Beweis *m*; (*PRINT*) Korrekturfahne *f*; (*of alcohol*) Alkoholgehalt *m* ♦ *adj* sicher

prop [prɒp] *n* (*also fig*) Stütze *f*; (*THEAT*) Requisit *nt* ♦ *vt* (*also:* **~ up**)stützen

propaganda [prɒpə'gændə] *n* Propaganda *f*

propel [prə'pel] *vt* (an)treiben; **~ler** *n* Propeller *m*; **~ling pencil** (*BRIT*) *n* Drehbleistift *m*

propensity [prə'pensiti] *n* Tendenz *f*

proper ['prɒpə] *adj* richtig; (*seemly*) schicklich; **~ly** *adv* richtig; **~ noun** *n* Eigenname *m*

property ['prɒpəti] *n* Eigentum *nt*; (*quality*) Eigenschaft *f*; (*land*) Grundbesitz *m*; **~ owner** *n* Grundbesitzer *m*

prophecy ['prɒfisi] *n* Prophezeiung *f*

prophesy ['prɒfisai] *vt* prophezeien

prophet ['prɒfit] *n* Prophet *m*

proportion [prə'pɔ:ʃən] *n* Verhältnis *nt*; (*share*) Teil *m* ♦ *vt*: **to ~ (to)** abstimmen (auf +*acc*); **~al** *adj* proportional; **~ate** *adj* verhältnismäßig

proposal [prə'pəuzl] *n* Vorschlag *m*; (*of marriage*) Heiratsantrag *m*

propose [prə'pəuz] *vt* vorschlagen; (*toast*) ausbringen ♦ *vi* (*offer marriage*) einen Heiratsantrag machen; **to ~ to do sth** beabsichtigen, etw zu tun

proposition [prɒpə'ziʃən] *n* Angebot *nt*; (*statement*) Satz *m*

proprietor [prə'praiətə] *n* Besitzer *m*, Eigentümer *m*

propriety [prə'praiəti] *n* Anstand *m*

pro rata [prəu'rɑ:tə] *adv* anteilmäßig

prose [prəuz] *n* Prosa *f*

prosecute ['prɒsikju:t] *vt* (strafrechtlich) verfolgen; **prosecution** [prɒsi'kju:ʃən] *n* (*JUR*) strafrechtliche Verfolgung *f*; (*party*) Anklage *f*; **prosecutor** *n* Vertreter *m* der Anklage; **Public Prosecutor** Staatsanwalt *m*

prospect [*n* 'prɒspekt, *vb* prə'spekt] *n* Aussicht *f* ♦ *vt* auf Bodenschätze hin untersuchen ♦ *vi*: **to ~ (for)** suchen (nach); **~ing** ['prɒspektiŋ] *n* (*for minerals*) Suche *f*; **~ive** [prə'spektiv] *adj* (*son-in-law etc*) zukünftig; (*customer, candidate*) voraussichtlich

prospectus [prə'spektəs] *n* (Werbe)prospekt *m*

prosper ['prɒspə] *vi* blühen, gedeihen; (*person*) erfolgreich sein; **~ity** [prɒ'speriti] *n* Wohlstand *m*; **~ous** *adj* wohlhabend, reich

prostitute ['prɒstitju:t] *n* Prostituierte *f*

prostrate ['prɒstreit] *adj* ausgestreckt (liegend)

protagonist [prə'tægənist] *n* Hauptperson *f*, Held *m*

protect [prə'tekt] *vt* (be)schützen; **~ed species** *n* geschützte Art; **~ion** [prə'tekʃən] *n* Schutz *m*; **~ive** *adj* Schutz-, (be)schützend

protégé ['prəutɛʒei] *n* Schützling *m*

protein ['prəuti:n] *n* Protein *nt*, Eiweiß *nt*

protest [*n* 'prəutest, *vb* prə'test] *n* Protest *m* ♦ *vi* protestieren ♦ *vt* (*affirm*) beteuern

Protestant ['prɒtistənt] *adj* protestantisch ♦ *n* Protestant(in) *m(f)*

protester [prə'testə] *n* (*demonstrator*) Demonstrant(in) *m(f)*

protracted [prə'træktid] *adj* sich hinziehend

protrude [prə'tru:d] *vi* (her)vorstehen

proud [praud] *adj*: **~ (of)** stolz (auf +*acc*)

prove [pru:v] *vt* beweisen ♦ *vi*: **to ~ (to be) correct** sich als richtig erweisen; **to ~ o.s.** sich bewähren

proverb ['prɒvə:b] *n* Sprichwort *nt*; **~ial** [prə'və:biəl] *adj* sprichwörtlich

provide [prə'vaid] *vt* versehen; (*supply*) besorgen; **to ~ sb with sth** jdn mit etw

versorgen; ~ **for** *vt fus* sorgen für;
(*emergency*) Vorkehrungen treffen für; ~**d**
(that) *conj* vorausgesetzt(, dass)

providing [prə'vaɪdɪŋ] *conj* vorausgesetzt(,
dass)

province ['prɒvɪns] *n* Provinz *f*; (*division of
work*) Bereich *m*; **provincial** [prə'vɪnʃəl] *adj*
provinziell, Provinz-

provision [prə'vɪʒən] *n* Vorkehrung *f*;
(*condition*) Bestimmung *f*; ~**s** *npl* (*food*)
Vorräte *pl*, Proviant *m*; ~**al** *adj* provisorisch

proviso [prə'vaɪzəu] *n* Bedingung *f*

provocative [prə'vɒkətɪv] *adj* provozierend

provoke [prə'vəuk] *vt* provozieren; (*cause*)
hervorrufen

prowess ['prauɪs] *n* überragende(s) Können
nt

prowl [praul] *vi* herumstreichen; (*animal*)
schleichen ♦ *n*: **on the ~** umherstreifend;
~**er** *n* Herumtreiber(in) *m(f)*

proximity [prɒk'sɪmɪtɪ] *n* Nähe *f*

proxy ['prɒksɪ] *n* (Stell)vertreter *m*; (*authority,
document*) Vollmacht *f*; **by ~** durch einen
Stellvertreter

prudent ['pru:dnt] *adj* klug, umsichtig

prudish ['pru:dɪʃ] *adj* prüde

prune [pru:n] *n* Backpflaume *f* ♦ *vt*
ausputzen; (*fig*) zurechtstutzen

pry [praɪ] *vi*: **to ~ (into)** seine Nase stecken
(in +*acc*)

PS *n abbr* (= *postscript*) PS

pseudonym ['sju:dənɪm] *n* Pseudonym *nt*,
Deckname *m*

psychiatric [saɪkɪ'ætrɪk] *adj* psychiatrisch

psychiatrist [saɪ'kaɪətrɪst] *n* Psychiater *m*

psychic ['saɪkɪk] *adj* (*also*: ~**al**) übersinnlich;
(*person*) paranormal begabt

psychoanalyse [saɪkəu'ænəlaɪz] (*US*
psychoanalyze) *vt* psychoanalytisch
behandeln; **psychoanalyst** [saɪkəu'ænəlɪst]
n Psychoanalytiker(in) *m(f)*

psychological [saɪkə'lɒdʒɪkl] *adj*
psychologisch; **psychologist** [saɪ'kɒlədʒɪst]
n Psychologe *m*, Psychologin *f*;
psychology [saɪ'kɒlədʒɪ] *n* Psychologie *f*

PTO *abbr* = **please turn over**

pub [pʌb] *n abbr* (= *public house*) Kneipe *f*

Pub

i **Pub** ist ein *Gasthaus mit einer Lizenz
zum Ausschank von alkoholischen
Getränken. Ein Pub besteht meist aus
verschiedenen gemütlichen (**lounge**, **snug**)
oder einfacheren Räumen (**public bar**), in
der oft auch Spiele wie Darts, Domino und
Poolbillard zur Verfügung stehen. In Pubs
werden vor allem mittags oft auch
Mahlzeiten angeboten. Pubs sind
normalerweise von 11 bis 23 Uhr geöffnet,
aber manchmal nachmittags geschlossen.*

pubic ['pju:bɪk] *adj* Scham-

public ['pʌblɪk] *adj* öffentlich ♦ *n* (*also*:
general ~) Öffentlichkeit *f*; **in ~** in der
Öffentlichkeit; ~ **address system** *n*
Lautsprecheranlage *f*

publican ['pʌblɪkən] *n* Wirt *m*

publication [pʌblɪ'keɪʃən] *n*
Veröffentlichung *f*

public: ~ **company** *n* Aktiengesellschaft *f*;
~ **convenience** (*BRIT*) *n* öffentliche
Toiletten *pl*; ~ **holiday** *n* gesetzliche(r)
Feiertag *m*; ~ **house** (*BRIT*) *n* Lokal *nt*,
Kneipe *f*

publicity [pʌb'lɪsɪtɪ] *n* Publicity *f*, Werbung *f*

publicize ['pʌblɪsaɪz] *vt* bekannt machen;
(*advertise*) Publicity machen für

publicly ['pʌblɪklɪ] *adv* öffentlich

public: ~ **opinion** *n* öffentliche Meinung *f*;
~ **relations** *npl* Publicrelations *pl*, Public
Relations *pl*; ~ **school** *n* (*BRIT*) Privatschule
f; (*US*) staatliche Schule *f*; ~~**spirited** *adj*
mit Gemeinschaftssinn; ~ **transport** *n*
öffentliche Verkehrsmittel *pl*

publish ['pʌblɪʃ] *vt* veröffentlichen; (*event*)
bekannt geben; ~**er** *n* Verleger *m*; ~**ing** *n*
(*business*) Verlagswesen *nt*

pub lunch *n* in Pubs servierter Imbiss

pucker ['pʌkər] *vt* (*face*) verziehen; (*lips*)
kräuseln

pudding ['pudɪŋ] *n* (*BRIT: course*) Nachtisch
m; Pudding *m*; **black ~** ≃ Blutwurst *f*

puddle ['pʌdl] *n* Pfütze *f*

puff [pʌf] *n* (*of wind etc*) Stoß *m*; (*cosmetic*)

Puderquaste f ♦ vt blasen, pusten; (*pipe*)
paffen ♦ vi keuchen, schnaufen; (*smoke*)
paffen; **to ~ out smoke** Rauch ausstoßen;
~ pastry (*US* ~ **paste**) n Blätterteig m; **~y**
adj aufgedunsen

pull [pul] n Ruck m; (*influence*) Beziehung f
♦ vt ziehen; (*trigger*) abdrücken ♦ vi ziehen;
to ~ sb's leg jdn auf den Arm nehmen; **to
~ to pieces** in Stücke reißen; (*fig*)
verreißen; **to ~ one's punches** sich
zurückhalten; **to ~ one's weight** sich in die
Riemen legen; **to ~ o.s. together** sich
zusammenreißen; **~ apart** vt (*break*)
zerreißen; (*dismantle*) auseinander nehmen;
(*separate*) trennen; **~ down** vt (*house*)
abreißen; **~ in** vi hineinfahren; (*stop*)
anhalten; (*RAIL*) einfahren; **~ off** vt (*deal
etc*) abschließen; **~ out** vi (*car*)
herausfahren; (*fig: partner*) aussteigen ♦ vt
herausziehen; **~ over** vi (*AUT*) an die Seite
fahren; **~ through** vi durchkommen; **~
up** vi anhalten ♦ vt (*uproot*) herausreißen;
(*stop*) anhalten

pulley ['puli] n Rolle f, Flaschenzug m
pullover ['puləuvəʳ] n Pullover m
pulp [pʌlp] n Brei m; (*of fruit*) Fruchtfleisch nt
pulpit ['pulpit] n Kanzel f
pulsate [pʌl'seit] vi pulsieren
pulse [pʌls] n Puls m; **~s** npl (*BOT*)
Hülsenfrüchte pl
pummel ['pʌml] vt mit den Fäusten
bearbeiten
pump [pʌmp] n Pumpe f; (*shoe*) leichter
(Tanz)schuh m ♦ vt pumpen; **~ up** vt (*tyre*)
aufpumpen
pumpkin ['pʌmpkin] n Kürbis m
pun [pʌn] n Wortspiel nt
punch [pʌntʃ] n (*tool*) Locher m; (*blow*)
(Faust)schlag m; (*drink*) Punsch m, Bowle f
♦ vt lochen; (*strike*) schlagen, boxen; **~ line**
n Pointe f; **~-up** n (*BRIT: inf*) Keilerei f
punctual ['pʌŋktjuəl] adj pünktlich
punctuate ['pʌŋktjueit] vt mit Satzzeichen
versehen; (*fig*) unterbrechen; **punctuation**
[pʌŋktju'eiʃən] n Zeichensetzung f,
Interpunktion f
puncture ['pʌŋktʃəʳ] n Loch nt; (*AUT*)

Reifenpanne f ♦ vt durchbohren
pundit ['pʌndit] n Gelehrte(r) m
pungent ['pʌndʒənt] adj scharf
punish ['pʌniʃ] vt bestrafen; (*in boxing etc*)
übel zurichten; **~ment** n Strafe f; (*action*)
Bestrafung f
punk [pʌŋk] n (*also:* ~ **rocker**) Punker(in)
m(f); (*also:* ~ **rock**) Punk m; (*US: inf:
hoodlum*) Ganove m
punt [pʌnt] n Stechkahn m
punter ['pʌntəʳ] (*BRIT*) n (*better*) Wetter m
puny ['pju:ni] adj kümmerlich
pup [pʌp] n = **puppy**
pupil ['pju:pl] n Schüler(in) m(f), (*in eye*)
Pupille f
puppet ['pʌpit] n Puppe f; Marionette f
puppy ['pʌpi] n junge(r) Hund m
purchase ['pə:tʃis] n Kauf m; (*grip*) Halt m
♦ vt kaufen, erwerben; **~r** n Käufer(in) m(f)
pure [pjuəʳ] adj (*also fig*) rein; **~ly** ['pjuəli]
adv rein
purgatory ['pə:gətəri] n Fegefeuer nt
purge [pə:dʒ] n (*also POL*) Säuberung f ♦ vt
reinigen; (*body*) entschlacken
purify ['pjuərifai] vt reinigen
purity ['pjuəriti] n Reinheit f
purple ['pə:pl] adj violett; (*face*) dunkelrot
purport [pə:'pɔ:t] vi vorgeben
purpose ['pə:pəs] n Zweck m, Ziel nt; (*of
person*) Absicht f; **on ~** absichtlich; **~ful** adj
zielbewusst, entschlossen
purr [pə:ʳ] n Schnurren nt ♦ vi schnurren
purse [pə:s] n Portemonnaie nt, Portmonee
nt, Geldbeutel m ♦ vt (*lips*)
zusammenpressen, schürzen
purser ['pə:səʳ] n Zahlmeister m
pursue [pə'sju:] vt verfolgen; (*study*)
nachgehen +dat; **~r** n Verfolger m; **pursuit**
[pə'sju:t] n Verfolgung f; (*occupation*)
Beschäftigung f
pus [pʌs] n Eiter m
push [puʃ] n Stoß m, Schub m; (*MIL*) Vorstoß
m ♦ vt stoßen, schieben; (*button*) drücken;
(*idea*) durchsetzen ♦ vi stoßen, schieben; **~
aside** vt beiseite schieben; **~ off** (*inf*) vi
abschieben; **~ on** vi weitermachen; **~
through** vt durchdrücken; (*policy*)

durchsetzen; **~ up** *vt* (*total*) erhöhen; (*prices*) hoch treiben; **~chair** (*BRIT*) *n* (Kinder)sportwagen *m*; **~er** *n* (*drug dealer*) Pusher *m*; **~over** (*inf*) *n* Kinderspiel *nt*; **~up** (*US*) *n* (*press-up*) Liegestütz *m*; **~y** (*inf*) *adj* aufdringlich

puss [pus] *n* Mieze(katze) *f*; **~y(cat)** *n* Mieze(katze) *f*

put [put] (*pt, pp* **put**) *vt* setzen, stellen, legen; (*express*) ausdrücken, sagen; (*write*) schreiben; **~ about** *vi* (*turn back*) wenden ♦ *vt* (*spread*) verbreiten; **~ across** *vt* (*explain*) erklären; **~ away** *vt* weglegen; (*store*) beiseite legen; **~ back** *vt* zurückstellen *or* -legen; **~ by** *vt* zurücklegen, sparen; **~ down** *vt* hinstellen *or* -legen; (*rebellion*) niederschlagen; (*animal*) einschläfern; (*in writing*) niederschreiben; **~ forward** *vt* (*idea*) vorbringen; (*clock*) vorstellen; **~ in** *vt* (*application, complaint*) einreichen; **~ off** *vt* verschieben; (*discourage*): **to ~ sb off sth** jdn von etw abbringen; **~ on** *vt* (*clothes etc*) anziehen; (*light etc*) anschalten, anmachen; (*play etc*) aufführen; (*brake*) anziehen; **~ out** *vt* (*hand etc*) (her)ausstrecken; (*news, rumour*) verbreiten; (*light etc*) ausschalten, ausmachen; **~ through** *vt* (*TEL: person*) verbinden; (*: call*) durchstellen; **~ up** *vt* (*tent*) aufstellen; (*building*) errichten; (*price*) erhöhen; (*person*) unterbringen; **~ up with** *vt fus* sich abfinden mit

putrid ['pju:trɪd] *adj* faul

putt [pʌt] *vt* (*golf*) putten ♦ *n* (*golf*) Putten *nt*; **~ing green** *n* kleine(r) Golfplatz *m* nur zum Putten

putty ['pʌtɪ] *n* Kitt *m*; (*fig*) Wachs *nt*

put-up ['putʌp] *adj*: **~ job** abgekartete(s) Spiel *n*

puzzle ['pʌzl] *n* Rätsel *nt*; (*toy*) Geduldspiel *nt* ♦ *vt* verwirren ♦ *vi* sich den Kopf zerbrechen; **~d** *adj* verdutzt, verblüfft; **puzzling** *adj* rätselhaft, verwirrend

pyjamas [pə'dʒɑ:məz] (*BRIT*) *npl* Schlafanzug *m*, Pyjama *m*

pylon ['paɪlən] *n* Mast *m*

pyramid ['pɪrəmɪd] *n* Pyramide *f*

Q, q

quack [kwæk] *n* Quaken *nt*; (*doctor*) Quacksalber *m* ♦ *vi* quaken

quad [kwɔd] *n abbr* = **quadrangle**; **quadruplet**

quadrangle ['kwɔdræŋgl] *n* (*court*) Hof *m*; (*MATH*) Viereck *nt*

quadruple [kwɔ'dru:pl] *adj* ♦ *vi* sich vervierfachen ♦ *vt* vervierfachen

quadruplets [kwɔ'dru:plɪts] *npl* Vierlinge *pl*

quagmire ['kwægmaɪəʳ] *n* Morast *m*

quail [kweɪl] *n* (*bird*) Wachtel *f* ♦ *vi* (*vor Angst*) zittern

quaint [kweɪnt] *adj* kurios; malerisch

quake [kweɪk] *vi* beben, zittern ♦ *n abbr* = **earthquake**

qualification [kwɔlɪfɪ'keɪʃən] *n* Qualifikation *f*; (*sth which limits*) Einschränkung *f*

qualified ['kwɔlɪfaɪd] *adj* (*competent*) qualifiziert; (*limited*) bedingt

qualify ['kwɔlɪfaɪ] *vt* (*prepare*) befähigen; (*limit*) einschränken ♦ *vi* sich qualifizieren; **to ~ as a doctor/lawyer** sein medizinisches/juristisches Staatsexamen machen

quality ['kwɔlɪtɪ] *n* Qualität *f*; (*characteristic*) Eigenschaft *f*

Quality press

i **Quality press** *bezeichnet die seriösen Tages- und Wochenzeitungen, im Gegensatz zu den Massenblättern. Diese Zeitungen sind fast alle großformatig und wenden sich an den anspruchvolleren Leser, der voll informiert sein möchte und bereit ist, für die Zeitungslektüre viel Zeit aufzuwenden. Siehe auch* **tabloid press.**

quality time *n* intensiv genutzte Zeit

qualm [kwɑ:m] *n* Bedenken *nt*

quandary ['kwɔndrɪ] *n*: **to be in a ~** in Verlegenheit sein

quantity ['kwɔntɪtɪ] *n* Menge *f*; **~ surveyor**

n Baukostenkalkulator *m*

quarantine ['kwɒrntiːn] *n* Quarantäne *f*

quarrel ['kwɒrl] *n* Streit *m* ♦ *vi* sich streiten; **~some** *adj* streitsüchtig

quarry ['kwɒrɪ] *n* Steinbruch *m*; (*animal*) Wild *nt*; (*fig*) Opfer *nt*

quarter ['kwɔːtəʳ] *n* Viertel *nt*; (*of year*) Quartal *nt* ♦ *vt* (*divide*) vierteln; (*MIL*) einquartieren; **~s** *npl* (*esp MIL*) Quartier *nt*; **~ of an hour** Viertelstunde *f*; **~ final** *n* Viertelfinale *nt*; **~ly** *adj* vierteljährlich

quartet(te) [kwɔː'tet] *n* Quartett *nt*

quartz [kwɔːts] *n* Quarz *m*

quash [kwɒʃ] *vt* (*verdict*) aufheben

quaver ['kweɪvəʳ] *vi* (*tremble*) zittern

quay [kiː] *n* Kai *m*

queasy ['kwiːzɪ] *adj* übel

queen [kwiːn] *n* Königin *f*; **~ mother** *n* Königinmutter *f*

queer [kwɪəʳ] *adj* seltsam ♦ *n* (*inf: homosexual*) Schwule(r) *m*

quell [kwel] *vt* unterdrücken

quench [kwentʃ] *vt* (*thirst*) löschen

querulous ['kwerʊləs] *adj* nörglerisch

query ['kwɪərɪ] *n* (*question*) (An)frage *f*, (*question mark*) Fragezeichen *nt* ♦ *vt* in Zweifel ziehen, infrage *or* in Frage stellen

quest [kwest] *n* Suche *f*

question ['kwestʃən] *n* Frage *f* ♦ *vt* (*ask*) (be)fragen; (*suspect*) verhören; (*doubt*) infrage *or* in Frage stellen, bezweifeln; **beyond ~** ohne Frage; **out of the ~** ausgeschlossen; **~able** *adj* zweifelhaft; **~ mark** *n* Fragezeichen *nt*

questionnaire [kwestʃə'nɛəʳ] *n* Fragebogen *m*

queue [kjuː] (*BRIT*) *n* Schlange *f* ♦ *vi* (*also: ~ up*) Schlange stehen

quibble ['kwɪbl] *vi* kleinlich sein

quick [kwɪk] *adj* schnell ♦ *n* (*of nail*) Nagelhaut *f*; **be ~!** mach schnell!; **cut to the ~** (*fig*) tief getroffen; **~en** *vt* (*hasten*) beschleunigen ♦ *vi* sich beschleunigen; **~ly** *adv* schnell; **~sand** *n* Treibsand *m*; **~-witted** *adj* schlagfertig

quid [kwɪd] (*BRIT: inf*) *n* Pfund *nt*

quiet ['kwaɪət] *adj* (*without noise*) leise;

(*peaceful, calm*) still, ruhig ♦ *n* Stille *f*, Ruhe *f* ♦ *vt, vi* (*US*) = **quieten**; **keep ~!** sei still!; **~en** *vi* (*also: ~en down*) ruhig werden ♦ *vt* beruhigen; **~ly** *adv* leise, ruhig; **~ness** *n* Ruhe *f*, Stille *f*

quilt [kwɪlt] *n* (*continental ~*) Steppdecke *f*

quin [kwɪn] *n* abbr = **quintuplet**

quintuplets [kwɪn'tjuːplɪts] *npl* Fünflinge *pl*

quip [kwɪp] *n* witzige Bemerkung *f*

quirk [kwɜːk] *n* (*oddity*) Eigenart *f*

quit [kwɪt] (*pt, pp* **quit** *or* **quitted**) *vt* verlassen ♦ *vi* aufhören

quite [kwaɪt] *adv* (*completely*) ganz, völlig; (*fairly*) ziemlich; **~ a few of them** ziemlich viele von ihnen; **~ (so)!** richtig!

quits [kwɪts] *adj* quitt; **let's call it ~** lassen wirs gut sein

quiver ['kwɪvəʳ] *vi* zittern ♦ *n* (*for arrows*) Köcher *m*

quiz [kwɪz] *n* (*competition*) Quiz *nt* ♦ *vt* prüfen; **~zical** *adj* fragend

quota ['kwəʊtə] *n* Anteil *m*; (*COMM*) Quote *f*

quotation [kwəʊ'teɪʃən] *n* Zitat *nt*; (*price*) Kostenvoranschlag *m*; **~ marks** *npl* Anführungszeichen *pl*

quote [kwəʊt] *n* = **quotation** ♦ *vi* (*from book*) zitieren ♦ *vt* zitieren; (*price*) angeben

R, r

rabbi ['ræbaɪ] *n* Rabbiner *m*; (*title*) Rabbi *m*

rabbit ['ræbɪt] *n* Kaninchen *nt*; **~ hole** *n* Kaninchenbau *m*; **~ hutch** *n* Kaninchenstall *m*

rabble ['ræbl] *n* Pöbel *m*

rabies ['reɪbiːz] *n* Tollwut *f*

RAC (*BRIT*) *n abbr* = **Royal Automobile Club**

raccoon [rə'kuːn] *n* Waschbär *m*

race [reɪs] *n* (*species*) Rasse *f*; (*competition*) Rennen *nt*; (*on foot*) Rennen *nt*, Wettlauf *m*; (*rush*) Hetze *f* ♦ *vt* um die Wette laufen mit; (*horses*) laufen lassen ♦ *vi* (*run*) rennen; (*in contest*) am Rennen teilnehmen; **~ car** (*US*) *n* = **racing car**; **~ car driver** (*US*) *n* = **racing driver**; **~course** *n* (*for horses*) Rennbahn *f*; **~horse** *n* Rennpferd *nt*; **~r** *n*

(*person*) Rennfahrer(in) m(f); (*car*)
Rennwagen m; **~track** n (*for cars etc*)
Rennstrecke f
racial ['reɪʃl] adj Rassen-
racing ['reɪsɪŋ] n Rennen nt; **~ car** (*BRIT*) n
Rennwagen m; **~ driver** (*BRIT*) n
Rennfahrer m
racism ['reɪsɪzəm] n Rassismus m; **racist**
['reɪsɪst] n Rassist m ♦ adj rassistisch
rack [ræk] n Ständer m, Gestell nt ♦ vt
plagen; **to go to ~ and ruin** verfallen; **to ~
one's brains** sich dat den Kopf zerbrechen
racket ['rækɪt] n (*din*) Krach m; (*scheme*)
(Schwindel)geschäft nt; (*TENNIS*)
(Tennis)schläger m
racquet ['rækɪt] n (Tennis)schläger m
racy ['reɪsɪ] adj gewagt; (*style*) spritzig
radar ['reɪdɑːˌ] n Radar nt or m
radial ['reɪdɪəl] adj (*also: US:* **~ply**) radial
radiant ['reɪdɪənt] adj strahlend; (*giving out
rays*) Strahlungs-
radiate ['reɪdɪeɪt] vi ausstrahlen; (*roads, lines*)
strahlenförmig wegführen ♦ vt ausstrahlen;
radiation [reɪdɪ'eɪʃən] n (Aus)strahlung f
radiator ['reɪdɪeɪtəˌ] n (*for heating*)
Heizkörper m; (*AUT*) Kühler m
radical ['rædɪkl] adj radikal
radii ['reɪdɪaɪ] npl of **radius**
radio ['reɪdɪəu] n Rundfunk m, Radio nt; (*set*)
Radio nt, Radioapparat m; **on the ~** im
Radio; **~active** ['reɪdɪəu'æktɪv] adj
radioaktiv; **~ cassette** n Radiorekorder m;
~-controlled adj ferngesteuert; **~logy**
[reɪdɪ'ɔlədʒɪ] n Strahlenkunde f; **~ station** n
Rundfunkstation f; **~therapy**
['reɪdɪəu'θerəpɪ] n Röntgentherapie f
radish ['rædɪʃ] n (*big*) Rettich m; (*small*)
Radieschen nt
radius ['reɪdɪəs] n (pl **radii**) Radius m; (*area*)
Umkreis m
RAF n abbr = **Royal Air Force**
raffle ['ræfl] n Verlosung f, Tombola f ♦ vt
verlosen
raft [rɑːft] n Floß nt
rafter ['rɑːftəˌ] n Dachsparren m
rag [ræg] n (*cloth*) Lumpen m, Lappen m;
(*inf: newspaper*) Käseblatt nt; (*UNIV: for*

charity) studentische Sammelaktion f ♦ vt
(*BRIT*) auf den Arm nehmen; **~s** npl (*cloth*)
Lumpen pl; **~ doll** n Flickenpuppe f
rage [reɪdʒ] n Wut f; (*fashion*) große Mode f
♦ vi wüten, toben
ragged ['rægɪd] adj (*edge*) gezackt; (*clothes*)
zerlumpt
raid [reɪd] n Überfall m; (*MIL*) Angriff m; (*by
police*) Razzia f ♦ vt überfallen
rail [reɪl] n (*also RAIL*) Schiene f; (*on stair*)
Geländer nt; (*of ship*) Reling f; **~s** npl (*RAIL*)
Geleise pl; **by ~** per Bahn; **~ing(s)** n(pl)
Geländer nt; **~road** (*US*) n Eisenbahn f;
~way (*BRIT*) n Eisenbahn f; **~way line**
(*BRIT*) n (Eisen)bahnlinie f; (*track*) Gleis nt;
~wayman (*irreg; BRIT*) n Eisenbahner m;
~way station (*BRIT*) n Bahnhof m
rain [reɪn] n Regen m ♦ vt, vi regnen; **in the
~** im Regen; **it's ~ing** es regnet; **~bow** n
Regenbogen m; **~coat** n Regenmantel m;
~drop n Regentropfen m; **~fall** n
Niederschlag m; **~forest** n Regenwald m;
~y adj (*region, season*) Regen-; (*day*)
regnerisch, verregnet
raise [reɪz] n (*esp US: increase*)
(Gehalts)erhöhung f ♦ vt (*lift*) (hoch)heben; (*increase*) erhöhen; (*question*) aufwerfen;
(*doubts*) äußern; (*funds*) beschaffen; (*family*)
großziehen; (*livestock*) züchten; **to ~ one's
voice** die Stimme erheben
raisin ['reɪzn] n Rosine f
rake [reɪk] n Rechen m, Harke f; (*person*)
Wüstling m ♦ vt rechen, harken; (*search*)
(durch)suchen
rally ['rælɪ] n (*POL etc*) Kundgebung f; (*AUT*)
Rallye f ♦ vt (*MIL*) sammeln ♦ vi Kräfte
sammeln; **~ round** vt fus (sich) scharen
um; (*help*) zu Hilfe kommen +dat ♦ vi zu
Hilfe kommen
RAM [ræm] n abbr (= random access memory)
RAM m
ram [ræm] n Widder m ♦ vt (*hit*) rammen;
(*stuff*) (hinein)stopfen
ramble ['ræmbl] n Wanderung f ♦ vi (*talk*)
schwafeln; **~r** n Wanderer m; **rambling** adj
(*speech*) weitschweifig; (*town*) ausgedehnt
ramp [ræmp] n Rampe f; **on / off ~** (*US: AUT*)

Ein-/Ausfahrt f

rampage [ræm'peɪdʒ] *n*: **to be on the ~** randalieren ♦ *vi* randalieren

rampant ['ræmpənt] *adj* wild wuchernd

rampart ['ræmpɑːt] *n* (Schutz)wall *m*

ram raid *n* Raubüberfall, bei dem eine Geschäftsfront mit einem Fahrzeug gerammt wird

ramshackle ['ræmʃækl] *adj* baufällig

ran [ræn] *pt of* **run**

ranch [rɑːntʃ] *n* Ranch f

rancid ['rænsɪd] *adj* ranzig

rancour ['ræŋkər] (*US* **rancor**) *n* Verbitterung f, Groll *m*

random ['rændəm] *adj* ziellos, wahllos ♦ *n*: **at ~** aufs Geratewohl; **~ access** *n* (*COMPUT*) wahlfreie(r) Zugriff *m*

randy ['rændɪ] (*BRIT: inf*) *adj* geil, scharf

rang [ræŋ] *pt of* **ring**

range [reɪndʒ] *n* Reihe f; (*of mountains*) Kette f; (*COMM*) Sortiment *nt*; (*reach*) (Reich)weite f; (*of gun*) Schussweite f; (*for shooting practice*) Schießplatz *m*; (*stove*) (großer) Herd *m* ♦ *vt* (*set in row*) anordnen, aufstellen; (*roam*) durchstreifen ♦ *vi*: **to ~ over** (*wander*) umherstreifen in +*dat*; (*extend*) sich erstrecken auf +*acc*; **a ~ of** (*selection*) eine (große) Auswahl an +*dat*; **prices ranging from £5 to £10** Preise, die sich zwischen £5 und £10 bewegen; **~r** ['reɪndʒər] *n* Förster *m*

rank [ræŋk] *n* (*row*) Reihe f; (*BRIT: also:* **taxi ~**) (Taxi)stand *m*; (*MIL*) Rang *m*; (*social position*) Stand *m* ♦ *vi* (*have ~*): **to ~ among** gehören zu ♦ *adj* (*strong-smelling*) stinkend; (*extreme*) kraß; **the ~ and file** (*fig*) die breite Masse

rankle ['ræŋkl] *vi* nagen

ransack ['rænsæk] *vt* (*plunder*) plündern; (*search*) durchwühlen

ransom ['rænsəm] *n* Lösegeld *nt*; **to hold sb to ~** jdn gegen Lösegeld festhalten

rant [rænt] *vi* hochtrabend reden

rap [ræp] *n* Schlag *m*; (*music*) Rap *m* ♦ *vt* klopfen

rape [reɪp] *n* Vergewaltigung f; (*BOT*) Raps *m* ♦ *vt* vergewaltigen; **~(seed) oil** *n* Rapsöl *nt*

rapid ['ræpɪd] *adj* rasch, schnell; **~ity** [rə'pɪdɪtɪ] *n* Schnelligkeit f; **~s** *npl* Stromschnellen *pl*

rapist ['reɪpɪst] *n* Vergewaltiger *m*

rapport [ræ'pɔːr] *n* gute(s) Verhältnis *nt*

rapture ['ræptʃər] *n* Entzücken *nt*; **rapturous** ['ræptʃərəs] *adj* (*applause*) stürmisch; (*expression*) verzückt

rare [reər] *adj* selten, rar; (*underdone*) nicht durchgebraten; **~ly** ['reəlɪ] *adv* selten

raring ['reərɪŋ] *adj*: **to be ~ to go** (*inf*) es kaum erwarten können, bis es losgeht

rarity ['reərɪtɪ] *n* Seltenheit f

rascal ['rɑːskl] *n* Schuft *m*

rash [ræʃ] *adj* übereilt; (*reckless*) unbesonnen ♦ *n* (Haut)ausschlag *m*

rasher ['ræʃər] *n* Speckscheibe f

raspberry ['rɑːzbərɪ] *n* Himbeere f

rasping ['rɑːspɪŋ] *adj* (*noise*) kratzend; (*voice*) krächzend

rat [ræt] *n* (*animal*) Ratte f; (*person*) Halunke *m*

rate [reɪt] *n* (*proportion*) Rate f, (*price*) Tarif *m*; (*speed*) Tempo *nt* ♦ *vt* (ein)schätzen; **~s** *npl* (*BRIT: tax*) Grundsteuer f; **to ~ as** für etw halten; **~able value** (*BRIT*) *n* Einheitswert *m* (*als Bemessungsgrundlage*); **~payer** (*BRIT*) *n* Steuerzahler(in) *m(f)*

rather ['rɑːðər] *adv* (*in preference*) lieber, eher; (*to some extent*) ziemlich; **I would** or **I'd ~ go** ich würde lieber gehen; **it's ~ expensive** (*quite*) es ist ziemlich teuer; (*too*) es ist etwas zu teuer; **there's ~ a lot** es ist ziemlich viel

ratify ['rætɪfaɪ] *vt* (*POL*) ratifizieren

rating ['reɪtɪŋ] *n* Klasse f

ratio ['reɪʃɪəu] *n* Verhältnis *nt*; **in the ~ of 100 to 1** im Verhältnis 100 zu 1

ration ['ræʃən] *n* (*usu pl*) Ration f ♦ *vt* rationieren

rational ['ræʃənl] *adj* rational

rationale [ræʃə'nɑːl] *n* Grundprinzip *nt*

rationalize ['ræʃnəlaɪz] *vt* rationalisieren

rat race *n* Konkurrenzkampf *m*

rattle ['rætl] *n* (*sound*) Rasseln *nt*; (*toy*) Rassel f ♦ *vi* ratteln, klappern ♦ *vt* rasseln mit; **~snake** *n* Klapperschlange f

raucous ['rɔːkəs] *adj* heiser, rau

rave [reɪv] *vi* (*talk wildly*) fantasieren; (*rage*) toben ♦ *n* (BRIT: *inf: party*) Rave *m*, Fete *f*

raven ['reɪvən] *n* Rabe *m*

ravenous ['rævənəs] *adj* heißhungrig

ravine [rə'viːn] *n* Schlucht *f*

raving ['reɪvɪŋ] *adj*: ~ **lunatic** völlig Wahnsinnige(r) *mf*

ravishing ['rævɪʃɪŋ] *adj* atemberaubend

raw [rɔː] *adj* roh; (*tender*) wund (gerieben); (*inexperienced*) unerfahren; **to get a ~ deal** (*inf*) schlecht wegkommen; ~ **material** *n* Rohmaterial *nt*

ray [reɪ] *n* (*of light*) Strahl *m*; ~ **of hope** Hoffnungsschimmer *m*

raze [reɪz] *vt* (*also*: ~ **to the ground**) dem Erdboden gleichmachen

razor ['reɪzər] *n* Rasierapparat *m*; ~ **blade** *n* Rasierklinge *f*

Rd *abbr* = **road**

RE (BRIT: SCH) *abbr* (= *religious education*) Religionsunterricht *m*

re [riː] *prep* (COMM) betreffs +*gen*

reach [riːtʃ] *n* Reichweite *f*; (*of river*) Strecke *f* ♦ *vt* (*arrive at*) erreichen; (*give*) reichen ♦ *vi* (*stretch*) sich erstrecken; **within ~** (*shops etc*) in erreichbarer Weite *or* Entfernung; **out of ~** außer Reichweite; **to ~ for** (*try to get*) langen nach; ~ **out** *vi* die Hand ausstrecken; **to ~ out for sth** nach etw greifen

react [riː'ækt] *vi* reagieren; ~**ion** [riː'ækʃən] *n* Reaktion *f*; ~**or** [riː'æktər] *n* Reaktor *m*

read¹ [red] *pt, pp* of **read²**

read² [riːd] (*pt, pp* **read**) *vt, vi* lesen; (*aloud*) vorlesen; ~ **out** *vt* vorlesen; ~**able** *adj* leserlich; (*worth ~ing*) lesenswert; ~**er** *n* (*person*) Leser(in) *m(f)*; ~**ership** *n* Leserschaft *f*

readily ['redɪlɪ] *adv* (*willingly*) bereitwillig; (*easily*) prompt

readiness ['redɪnɪs] *n* (*willingness*) Bereitwilligkeit *f*; (*being ready*) Bereitschaft *f*; **in ~** (*prepared*) bereit

reading ['riːdɪŋ] *n* Lesen *nt*

readjust [riːə'dʒʌst] *vt* neu einstellen ♦ *vi* (*person*): **to ~ to** sich wieder anpassen an

+*acc*

ready ['redɪ] *adj* (*prepared, willing*) bereit ♦ *adv*: ~**-cooked** vorgekocht ♦ *n*: **at the ~** bereit; ~**-made** *adj* gebrauchsfertig, Fertig-; (*clothes*) Konfektions-; ~ **money** *n* Bargeld *nt*; ~ **reckoner** *n* Rechentabelle *f*; ~**-to-wear** *adj* Konfektions-

real [rɪəl] *adj* wirklich; (*actual*) eigentlich; (*not fake*) echt; **in ~ terms** effektiv; ~ **estate** *n* Grundbesitz *m*; ~**istic** [rɪə'lɪstɪk] *adj* realistisch

reality [riː'ælɪtɪ] *n* Wirklichkeit *f*, Realität *f*; **in ~** in Wirklichkeit

realization [rɪəlaɪ'zeɪʃən] *n* (*understanding*) Erkenntnis *f*; (*fulfilment*) Verwirklichung *f*

realize ['rɪəlaɪz] *vt* (*understand*) begreifen; (*make real*) verwirklichen; **I didn't ~ ...** ich wusste nicht, ...

really ['rɪəlɪ] *adv* wirklich; ~**?** (*indicating interest*) tatsächlich?; (*expressing surprise*) wirklich?

realm [relm] *n* Reich *nt*

realtor ['rɪəltɔːr] *n* (US) *n* Grundstücks-makler(in) *m(f)*

reap [riːp] *vt* ernten

reappear [riːə'pɪər] *vi* wieder erscheinen

rear [rɪər] *adj* hintere(r, s), Rück- ♦ *n* Rückseite *f*; (*last part*) Schluss *m* ♦ *vt* (*bring up*) aufziehen ♦ *vi* (*horse*) sich aufbäumen; ~**guard** *n* Nachhut *f*

rearmament [riː'ɑːməmənt] *n* Wiederaufrüstung *f*

rearrange [riːə'reɪndʒ] *vt* umordnen

rear-view mirror ['rɪəvjuː-] *n* Rückspiegel *m*

reason ['riːzn] *n* (*cause*) Grund *m*; (*ability to think*) Verstand *m*; (*sensible thoughts*) Vernunft *f* ♦ *vi* (*think*) denken; (*use arguments*) argumentieren; **it stands to ~ that** es ist logisch, dass; **to ~ with sb** mit jdm diskutieren; ~**able** *adj* vernünftig; ~**ably** *adv* vernünftig; (*fairly*) ziemlich; ~**ed** *adj* (*argument*) durchdacht; ~**ing** *n* Urteilen *nt*; (*argumentation*) Beweisführung *f*

reassurance [riːə'ʃuərəns] *n* Beruhigung *f*; (*confirmation*) Bestätigung *f*; **reassure** [riːə'ʃuər] *vt* beruhigen; **to reassure sb of**

sth jdm etw versichern

rebate ['riːbeɪt] n Rückzahlung f

rebel [n 'rɛbl, vb rɪ'bɛl] n Rebell m ♦ vi rebellieren; **~lion** [rɪ'bɛljən] n Rebellion f, Aufstand m; **~lious** [rɪ'bɛljəs] adj rebellisch

rebirth [riː'bɜːθ] n Wiedergeburt f

rebound [vb rɪ'baʊnd, n 'riːbaʊnd] vi zurückprallen ♦ n Rückprall m

rebuff [rɪ'bʌf] n Abfuhr f ♦ vt abblitzen lassen

rebuild [riː'bɪld] (irreg) vt wieder aufbauen; (fig) wieder herstellen

rebuke [rɪ'bjuːk] n Tadel m ♦ vt tadeln, rügen

rebut [rɪ'bʌt] vt widerlegen

recall [vb rɪ'kɔːl, n 'riːkɔːl] vt (call back) zurückrufen; (remember) sich erinnern an +acc ♦ n Rückruf m

recap ['riːkæp] vt, vi wiederholen

rec'd abbr (= received) Eing.

recede [rɪ'siːd] vi zurückweichen; **receding** adj: **receding hairline** Stirnglatze f

receipt [rɪ'siːt] n (document) Quittung f; (receiving) Empfang m; **~s** npl (ECON) Einnahmen pl

receive [rɪ'siːv] vt erhalten; (visitors etc) empfangen; **~r** n (TEL) Hörer m

recent ['riːsnt] adj vor kurzem (geschehen), neuerlich; (modern) neu; **~ly** adv kürzlich, neulich

receptacle [rɪ'sɛptɪkl] n Behälter m

reception [rɪ'sɛpʃən] n Empfang m; **~ desk** n Empfang m; (in hotel) Rezeption f; **~ist** n (in hotel) Empfangschef m, Empfangsdame f; (MED) Sprechstundenhilfe f

receptive [rɪ'sɛptɪv] adj aufnahmebereit

recess [rɪ'sɛs] n (break) Ferien pl; (hollow) Nische f

recession [rɪ'sɛʃən] n Rezession f

recharge [riː'tʃɑːdʒ] vt (battery) aufladen

recipe ['rɛsɪpɪ] n Rezept nt

recipient [rɪ'sɪpɪənt] n Empfänger m

reciprocal [rɪ'sɪprəkl] adj gegenseitig; (mutual) wechselseitig

recital [rɪ'saɪtl] n Vortrag m

recite [rɪ'saɪt] vt vortragen, aufsagen

reckless ['rɛkləs] adj leichtsinnig; (driving) fahrlässig

reckon ['rɛkən] vt (count) rechnen, berechnen, errechnen; (estimate) schätzen; (think): **I ~ that ...** ich nehme an, dass ...; **~ on** vt fus rechnen mit; **~ing** n (calculation) Rechnen nt

reclaim [rɪ'kleɪm] vt (expenses) zurückverlangen; (land): **to ~ (from sth)** (etw dat) gewinnen; **reclamation** [rɛklə'meɪʃən] n (of land) Gewinnung f

recline [rɪ'klaɪn] vi sich zurücklehnen; **reclining** adj Liege-

recluse [rɪ'kluːs] n Einsiedler m

recognition [rɛkəg'nɪʃən] n (recognizing) Erkennen nt; (acknowledgement) Anerkennung f; **transformed beyond ~** völlig verändert

recognizable ['rɛkəgnaɪzəbl] adj erkennbar

recognize ['rɛkəgnaɪz] vt erkennen; (POL, approve) anerkennen; **to ~ as** anerkennen als; **to ~ by** erkennen an +dat

recoil [rɪ'kɔɪl] vi (in horror) zurückschrecken; (rebound) zurückprallen; (person): **to ~ from doing sth** davor zurückschrecken, etw zu tun

recollect [rɛkə'lɛkt] vt sich erinnern an +acc; **~ion** [rɛkə'lɛkʃən] n Erinnerung f

recommend [rɛkə'mɛnd] vt empfehlen; **~ation** [rɛkəmɛn'deɪʃən] n Empfehlung f

recompense ['rɛkəmpɛns] n (compensation) Entschädigung f; (reward) Belohnung f ♦ vt entschädigen; belohnen

reconcile ['rɛkənsaɪl] vt (facts) vereinbaren; (people) versöhnen; **to ~ o.s. to sth** sich mit etw abfinden; **reconciliation** [rɛkənsɪlɪ'eɪʃən] n Versöhnung f

recondition [riːkən'dɪʃən] vt (machine) generalüberholen

reconnoitre [rɛkə'nɔɪtər] (US **reconnoiter**) vt erkunden ♦ vi aufklären

reconsider [riːkən'sɪdər] vt von neuem erwägen, noch einmal überdenken ♦ vi es noch einmal überdenken

reconstruct [riːkən'strʌkt] vt wieder aufbauen; (crime) rekonstruieren

record [n 'rɛkɔːd, vb rɪ'kɔːd] n Aufzeichnung f; (MUS) Schallplatte f; (best performance)

Rekord m ♦ vt aufzeichnen; (*music etc*) aufnehmen; **off the ~** vertraulich, im Vertrauen; **in ~ time** in Rekordzeit; **~ card** n (*in file*) Karteikarte f; **~ed delivery** (*BRIT*) n (*POST*) Einschreiben nt; **~er** n (*TECH*) Registriergerät nt; (*MUS*) Blockflöte f; **~ holder** n (*SPORT*) Rekordinhaber m; **~ing** n (*MUS*) Aufnahme f; **~ player** n Plattenspieler m

recount [rɪ'kaʊnt] vt (*tell*) berichten

re-count ['riːkaʊnt] n Nachzählung f

recoup [rɪ'kuːp] vt: **to ~ one's losses** seinen Verlust wieder gutmachen

recourse [rɪ'kɔːs] n: **to have ~ to** Zuflucht nehmen zu or bei

recover [rɪ'kʌvər] vt (*get back*) zurückerhalten ♦ vi sich erholen

re-cover [riː'kʌvər] vt (*quilt etc*) neu überziehen

recovery [rɪ'kʌvərɪ] n Wiedererlangung f; (*of health*) Erholung f

recreate [riːkrɪ'eɪt] vt wieder herstellen

recreation [rekrɪ'eɪʃən] n Erholung f; **~al** adj Erholungs-; **~al drug** n Freizeitdroge f

recrimination [rɪkrɪmɪ'neɪʃən] n Gegenbeschuldigung f

recruit [rɪ'kruːt] n Rekrut m ♦ vt rekrutieren; **~ment** n Rekrutierung f

rectangle ['rektæŋgl] n Rechteck nt; **rectangular** [rek'tæŋgjələr] adj rechteckig, rechtwinklig

rectify ['rektɪfaɪ] vt berichtigen

rector ['rektər] n (*REL*) Pfarrer m; (*SCH*) Direktor(in) m(f); **~y** ['rektərɪ] n Pfarrhaus nt

recuperate [rɪ'kjuːpəreɪt] vi sich erholen

recur [rɪ'kəːr] vi sich wiederholen; **~rence** n Wiederholung f; **~rent** adj wiederkehrend

recycle [riː'saɪkl] vt wieder verwerten, wieder aufbereiten; **recycling** n Recycling nt

red [red] n Rot nt; (*POL*) Rote(r) m ♦ adj rot; **in the ~** in den roten Zahlen; **~ carpet treatment** n Sonderbehandlung f, große(r) Bahnhof m; **R~ Cross** n Rote(s) Kreuz nt; **~currant** n rote Johannisbeere f; **~den** vi sich röten; (*blush*) erröten ♦ vt röten; **~dish** adj rötlich

redecorate [riː'dekəreɪt] vt neu tapezieren, neu streichen

redeem [rɪ'diːm] vt (*COMM*) einlösen; (*save*) retten; **~ing** adj: **~ing feature** versöhnende(s) Moment nt

redeploy [riːdɪ'plɔɪ] vt (*resources*) umverteilen

red: **~-haired** [red'heəd] adj rothaarig; **~-handed** [red'hændɪd] adv: **to be caught ~-handed** auf frischer Tat ertappt werden; **~head** ['redhed] n Rothaarige(r) mf; **~ herring** n Ablenkungsmanöver nt; **~-hot** [red'hɒt] adj rot glühend

redirect [riːdaɪ'rekt] vt umleiten

red light n: **to go through a ~** (*AUT*) bei Rot über die Ampel fahren; **red-light district** n Strichviertel nt

redo [riː'duː] (*irreg: like* **do**) vt nochmals machen

redolent ['redələnt] adj: **~ of** (*fig*) erinnernd an +acc

redouble [riː'dʌbl] vt: **to ~ one's efforts** seine Anstrengungen verdoppeln

redress [rɪ'dres] vt wieder gutmachen

red: **R~ Sea** n: **the R~ Sea** das Rote Meer; **~skin** ['redskɪn] n Rothaut f; **~ tape** n Bürokratismus m

reduce [rɪ'djuːs] vt (*speed, temperature*) vermindern; (*photo*) verkleinern; **"~ speed now"** (*AUT*) ≈ "langsam"; **to ~ the price (to)** den Preis herabsetzen (auf +acc); **at a ~d price** zum ermäßigten Preis

reduction [rɪ'dʌkʃən] n Verminderung f; Verkleinerung f; Herabsetzung f; (*amount of money*) Nachlass m

redundancy [rɪ'dʌndənsɪ] n Überflüssigkeit f; (*of workers*) Entlassung f

redundant [rɪ'dʌndnt] adj überflüssig; (*workers*) ohne Arbeitsplatz; **to be made ~** arbeitslos werden

reed [riːd] n Schilf nt; (*MUS*) Rohrblatt nt

reef [riːf] n Riff nt

reek [riːk] vi: **to ~ (of)** stinken (nach)

reel [riːl] n Spule f, Rolle f ♦ vt (*also:* **~ in**) wickeln, spulen ♦ vi (*stagger*) taumeln

ref [ref] (*inf*) n abbr (= *referee*) Schiri m

refectory [rɪ'fektərɪ] n (*UNIV*) Mensa f; (*SCH*)

Speisesaal m; (ECCL) Refektorium nt

refer [rɪ'fɜːʳ] vt: **to ~ sb to sth** jdn an jdn/etw verweisen ♦ vi: **to ~ to** (to book) nachschlagen in +dat; (mention) sich beziehen auf +acc

referee [refə'riː] n Schiedsrichter m; (BRIT: for job) Referenz f ♦ vt schiedsrichtern

reference ['refrəns] n (for job) Referenz f; (in book) Verweis m; (number, code) Aktenzeichen nt; (allusion): **~ (to)** Anspielung (auf +acc); **with ~ to** in Bezug auf +acc; **~ book** n Nachschlagewerk nt; **~ number** n Aktenzeichen nt

referenda [refə'rendə] npl of **referendum**

referendum [refə'rendəm] (pl **-da**) n Volksabstimmung f

refill [vb riː'fɪl, n 'riːfɪl] vt nachfüllen ♦ n (for pen) Ersatzmine f

refine [rɪ'faɪn] vt (purify) raffinieren; **~d** adj kultiviert; **~ment** n Kultiviertheit f; **~ry** n Raffinerie f

reflect [rɪ'flekt] vt (light) reflektieren; (fig) (wider)spiegeln ♦ vi (meditate): **to ~ (on)** nachdenken (über +acc); **it ~s badly/well on him** das stellt ihn in ein schlechtes/ gutes Licht; **~ion** [rɪ'flekʃən] n Reflexion f; (image) Spiegelbild nt; (thought) Überlegung f; **on ~ion** wenn man sich dat das recht überlegt

reflex ['riːfleks] adj Reflex- ♦ n Reflex m; **~ive** [rɪ'fleksɪv] adj reflexiv

reform [rɪ'fɔːm] n Reform f ♦ vt (person) bessern; **~atory** (US) n Besserungsanstalt f

refrain [rɪ'freɪn] vi: **to ~ from** unterlassen ♦ n Refrain m

refresh [rɪ'freʃ] vt erfrischen; **~er course** (BRIT) n Wiederholungskurs m; **~ing** adj erfrischend; **~ments** npl Erfrischungen pl

refrigeration [rɪfrɪdʒə'reɪʃən] n Kühlung f

refrigerator [rɪ'frɪdʒəreɪtəʳ] n Kühlschrank m

refuel [riː'fjuːl] vt, vi auftanken

refuge ['refjuːdʒ] n Zuflucht f; **to take ~ in** sich flüchten in +acc; **~e** [refju'dʒiː] n Flüchtling m

refund [n 'riːfʌnd, vb rɪ'fʌnd] n Rückvergütung f ♦ vt zurückerstatten

refurbish [riː'fɜːbɪʃ] vt aufpolieren

refusal [rɪ'fjuːzəl] n (Ver)weigerung f; **first ~** Vorkaufsrecht nt

refuse¹ [rɪ'fjuːz] vt abschlagen ♦ vi sich weigern

refuse² ['refjuːs] n Abfall m, Müll m; **~ collection** n Müllabfuhr f

refute [rɪ'fjuːt] vt widerlegen

regain [rɪ'geɪn] vt wiedergewinnen; (consciousness) wiedererlangen

regal ['riːgl] adj königlich

regalia [rɪ'geɪlɪə] npl Insignien pl

regard [rɪ'gaːd] n Achtung f ♦ vt ansehen; **to send one's ~s to sb** jdn grüßen lassen; **"with kindest ~s"** "mit freundlichen Grüßen"; **~ing** or **as ~s** or **with ~ to** bezüglich +gen, in Bezug auf +acc; **~less** adj: **~less of** ohne Rücksicht auf +acc ♦ adv trotzdem

regenerate [rɪ'dʒenəreɪt] vt erneuern

régime [reɪ'ʒiːm] n Regime nt

regiment [n 'redʒɪmənt, vb 'redʒɪment] n Regiment nt ♦ vt (fig) reglementieren; **~al** [redʒɪ'mentl] adj Regiments-

region ['riːdʒən] n Region f; **in the ~ of** (fig) so um; **~al** adj örtlich, regional

register ['redʒɪstəʳ] n Register nt ♦ vt (list) registrieren; (emotion) zeigen; (write down) eintragen ♦ vi (at hotel) sich eintragen; (with police) sich melden; (make impression) wirken, ankommen; **~ed** (BRIT) adj (letter) Einschreibe-, eingeschrieben; **~ed trademark** n eingetragene(s) Warenzeichen nt

registrar ['redʒɪstraːʳ] n Standesbeamte(r) m

registration [redʒɪs'treɪʃən] n (act) Registrierung f; (AUT: also: **~ number**) polizeiliche(s) Kennzeichen nt

registry ['redʒɪstrɪ] n Sekretariat nt; **~ office** (BRIT) n Standesamt nt; **to get married in a ~ office** standesamtlich heiraten

regret [rɪ'gret] n Bedauern nt ♦ vt bedauern; **~fully** adv mit Bedauern, ungern; **~table** adj bedauerlich

regroup [riː'gruːp] vt umgruppieren ♦ vi sich umgruppieren

regular ['regjuləʳ] adj regelmäßig; (usual) üblich; (inf) regelrecht ♦ n (client etc)

Stammkunde *m*; **~ity** [regjuˈlærɪtɪ] *n* Regelmäßigkeit *f*; **~ly** *adv* regelmäßig

regulate [ˈregjuleɪt] *vt* regeln, regulieren; **regulation** [regjuˈleɪʃən] *n* (*rule*) Vorschrift *f*; (*control*) Regulierung *f*

rehabilitation [ˈriːəbɪlɪˈteɪʃən] *n* (*of criminal*) Resozialisierung *f*

rehearsal [rɪˈhɜːsəl] *n* Probe *f*

rehearse [rɪˈhɜːs] *vt* proben

reign [reɪn] *n* Herrschaft *f* ♦ *vi* herrschen

reimburse [riːɪmˈbɜːs] *vt*: **to ~ sb for sth** jdn für etw entschädigen; jdm etw zurückzahlen

rein [reɪn] *n* Zügel *m*

reincarnation [riːɪnkɑːˈneɪʃən] *n* Wiedergeburt *f*

reindeer [ˈreɪndɪə] *n* Ren *nt*

reinforce [riːɪnˈfɔːs] *vt* verstärken; **~d concrete** *n* Stahlbeton *m*; **~ment** *n* Verstärkung *f*; **~ments** *npl* (*MIL*) Verstärkungstruppen *pl*

reinstate [riːɪnˈsteɪt] *vt* wieder einsetzen

reissue [riːˈɪʃuː] *vt* neu herausgeben

reiterate [riːˈɪtəreɪt] *vt* wiederholen

reject [*n* ˈriːdʒekt, *vb* rɪˈdʒekt] *n* (*COMM*) Ausschuss(artikel) *m* ♦ *vt* ablehnen; **~ion** [rɪˈdʒekʃən] *n* Zurückweisung *f*

rejoice [rɪˈdʒɔɪs] *vi*: **to ~ at** *or* **over** sich freuen über +*acc*

rejuvenate [rɪˈdʒuːvəneɪt] *vt* verjüngen

rekindle [riːˈkɪndl] *vt* wieder anfachen

relapse [rɪˈlæps] *n* Rückfall *m*

relate [rɪˈleɪt] *vt* (*tell*) erzählen; (*connect*) verbinden ♦ *vi*: **to ~ to** zusammenhängen mit; (*form relationship*) eine Beziehung aufbauen zu; **~d** *adj*: **~d (to)** verwandt (mit); **relating** *prep*: **relating to** bezüglich +*gen*; **relation** [rɪˈleɪʃən] *n* Verwandte(r) *mf*; (*connection*) Beziehung *f*; **relationship** *n* Verhältnis *n*, Beziehung *f*

relative [ˈrelətɪv] *n* Verwandte(r) *mf* ♦ *adj* relativ; **~ly** *adv* verhältnismäßig

relax [rɪˈlæks] *vi* (*slacken*) sich lockern; (*muscles, person*) sich entspannen ♦ *vt* (*ease*) lockern, entspannen; **~ation** [riːlækˈseɪʃən] *n* Entspannung *f*; **~ed** *adj* entspannt, locker; **~ing** *adj* entspannend

relay [*n* ˈriːleɪ, *vb* rɪˈleɪ] *n* (*SPORT*) Staffel *f* ♦ *vt* (*message*) weiterleiten; (*RAD, TV*) übertragen

release [rɪˈliːs] *n* (*freedom*) Entlassung *f*; (*TECH*) Auslöser *m* ♦ *vt* befreien; (*prisoner*) entlassen; (*report, news*) verlautbaren, bekannt geben

relegate [ˈreləgeɪt] *vt* (*SPORT*): **to be ~d** absteigen

relent [rɪˈlent] *vi* nachgeben; **~less** *adj* unnachgiebig

relevant [ˈreləvənt] *adj* wichtig, relevant; **~ to** relevant für

reliability [rɪlaɪəˈbɪlɪtɪ] *n* Zuverlässigkeit *f*

reliable [rɪˈlaɪəbl] *adj* zuverlässig; **reliably** *adv* zuverlässig; **to be reliably informed that ...** aus zuverlässiger Quelle wissen, dass ...

reliance [rɪˈlaɪəns] *n*: **~ (on)** Abhängigkeit *f* (von)

relic [ˈrelɪk] *n* (*from past*) Überbleibsel *nt*; (*REL*) Reliquie *f*

relief [rɪˈliːf] *n* Erleichterung *f*; (*help*) Hilfe *f*; (*person*) Ablösung *f*

relieve [rɪˈliːv] *vt* (*ease*) erleichtern; (*help*) entlasten; (*person*) ablösen; **to ~ sb of sth** jdm etw abnehmen; **to ~ o.s.** (*euph*) sich erleichtern (*euph*); **~d** *adj* erleichtert

religion [rɪˈlɪdʒən] *n* Religion *f*; **religious** [rɪˈlɪdʒəs] *adj* religiös

relinquish [rɪˈlɪŋkwɪʃ] *vt* aufgeben

relish [ˈrelɪʃ] *n* Würze *f* ♦ *vt* genießen; **to ~ doing** gern tun

relocate [riːləuˈkeɪt] *vt* verlegen ♦ *vi* umziehen

reluctance [rɪˈlʌktəns] *n* Widerstreben *nt*, Abneigung *f*

reluctant [rɪˈlʌktənt] *adj* widerwillig; **~ly** *adv* ungern

rely [rɪˈlaɪ] *vt fus*: **to ~ on** sich verlassen auf +*acc*

remain [rɪˈmeɪn] *vi* (*be left*) übrig bleiben; (*stay*) bleiben; **~der** *n* Rest *m*; **~ing** *adj* übrig (geblieben); **~s** *npl* Überreste *pl*

remake [ˈriːmeɪk] *n* (*CINE*) Neuverfilmung *f*

remand [rɪˈmɑːnd] *n*: **on ~** in Untersuchungshaft ♦ *vt*: **to ~ in custody** in Untersuchungshaft schicken; **~ home**

(*BRIT*) n Untersuchungsgefängnis nt für Jugendliche

remark [rɪ'maːk] n Bemerkung f ♦ vt bemerken; **~able** adj bemerkenswert; **remarkably** adv außergewöhnlich

remarry [riː'mærɪ] vi sich wieder verheiraten

remedial [rɪ'miːdɪəl] adj Heil-; (*teaching*) Hilfsschul-

remedy ['remədɪ] n Mittel nt ♦ vt (*pain*) abhelfen +dat; (*trouble*) in Ordnung bringen

remember [rɪ'membər] vt sich erinnern an +acc; **remembrance** [rɪ'membrəns] n Erinnerung f; (*official*) Gedenken nt; **R~ Day** n ≈ Volkstrauertag m

---

Remembrance Day

i Remembrance Day oder Remembrance Sunday ist der britische Gedenktag für die Gefallenen der beiden Weltkriege und anderer Konflikte. Er fällt auf einen Sonntag vor oder nach dem 11. November (am 11. November 1918 endete der erste Weltkrieg) und wird mit einer Schweigeminute, Kranzniederlegungen an Kriegerdenkmälern und dem Tragen von Ansteckmadeln in Form einer Mohnblume begangen.

---

remind [rɪ'maɪnd] vt: **to ~ sb to do sth** jdn daran erinnern, etw zu tun; **to ~ sb of sth** jdn an etw acc erinnern; **she ~s me of her mother** sie erinnert mich an ihre Mutter; **~er** n Mahnung f

reminisce [remɪ'nɪs] vi in Erinnerungen schwelgen; **~nt** [remɪ'nɪsnt] adj: **to be ~nt of sth** an etw acc erinnern

remiss [rɪ'mɪs] adj nachlässig

remission [rɪ'mɪʃən] n Nachlass m; (*of debt, sentence*) Erlass m

remit [rɪ'mɪt] vt (*money*): **to ~ (to)** überweisen (an +acc); **~tance** n Geldanweisung f

remnant ['remnənt] n Rest m; **~s** npl (*COMM*) Einzelstücke pl

remorse [rɪ'mɔːs] n Gewissensbisse pl; **~ful** adj reumütig; **~less** adj unbarmherzig

remote [rɪ'məut] adj abgelegen; (*slight*)

gering; **~ control** n Fernsteuerung f; **~ly** adv entfernt

remould ['riːməuld] (*BRIT*) n runderneuerte(r) Reifen m

removable [rɪ'muːvəbl] adj entfernbar

removal [rɪ'muːvəl] n Beseitigung f; (*of furniture*) Umzug m; (*from office*) Entlassung f; **~ van** (*BRIT*) n Möbelwagen m

remove [rɪ'muːv] vt beseitigen, entfernen; **~rs** npl Möbelspedition f

remuneration [rɪmjuːnə'reɪʃən] n Vergütung f, Honorar nt

render ['rendər] vt machen; (*translate*) übersetzen; **~ing** n (*MUS*) Wiedergabe f

rendezvous ['rɒndɪvuː] n (*meeting*) Rendezvous nt; (*place*) Treffpunkt m ♦ vi sich treffen

renew [rɪ'njuː] vt erneuern; (*contract, licence*) verlängern; (*replace*) ersetzen; **~able** adj regenerierbar; **~al** n Erneuerung f; Verlängerung f

renounce [rɪ'nauns] vt (*give up*) verzichten auf +acc; (*disown*) verstoßen

renovate ['renəveɪt] vt renovieren; (*building*) restaurieren

renown [rɪ'naun] n Ruf m; **~ed** adj namhaft

rent [rent] n Miete f; (*for land*) Pacht f ♦ vt (*hold as tenant*) mieten; pachten; (*let*) vermieten; verpachten; (*car etc*) mieten; (*firm*) vermieten; **~al** n Miete f

renunciation [rɪnʌnsɪ'eɪʃən] n: **~ (of)** Verzicht m (auf +acc)

reorganize [riː'ɔːgənaɪz] vt umgestalten, reorganisieren

rep [rep] n abbr (*COMM*) = **representative**; (*THEAT*) = **repertory**

repair [rɪ'peər] n Reparatur f ♦ vt reparieren; (*damage*) wieder gutmachen; **in good/bad ~** in gutem/schlechtem Zustand; **~ kit** n Werkzeugkasten m

repartee [repɑː'tiː] n Witzeleien pl

repatriate [riː'pætrɪeɪt] vt in die Heimat zurückschicken

repay [riː'peɪ] (*irreg*) vt zurückzahlen; (*reward*) vergelten; **~ment** n Rückzahlung f; (*fig*) Vergeltung f

repeal [rɪ'piːl] vt aufheben

repeat [rɪ'piːt] n (RAD, TV)
Wiederholung(ssendung) f ♦ vt
wiederholen; **~edly** adv wiederholt

repel [rɪ'pel] vt (drive back) zurückschlagen;
(disgust) abstoßen; **~lent** adj abstoßend
♦ n: **insect ~lent** Insektenmittel nt

repent [rɪ'pent] vt, vi: **to ~ (of)** bereuen;
~ance n Reue f

repercussion [riːpə'kʌʃən] n Auswirkung f;
to have ~s ein Nachspiel haben

repertory ['repətərɪ] n Repertoire nt

repetition [repɪ'tɪʃən] n Wiederholung f

repetitive [rɪ'petɪtɪv] adj sich wiederholend

replace [rɪ'pleɪs] vt ersetzen; (put back)
zurückstellen; **~ment** n Ersatz m

replay ['riːpleɪ] n (of match)
Wiederholungsspiel nt; (of tape, film)
Wiederholung f

replenish [rɪ'plenɪʃ] vt ergänzen

replica ['replɪkə] n Kopie f

reply [rɪ'plaɪ] n Antwort f ♦ vi antworten; **~
coupon** n Antwortschein m

report [rɪ'pɔːt] n Bericht m; (BRIT: SCH)
Zeugnis nt ♦ vt (tell) berichten; (give
information against) melden; (to police)
anzeigen ♦ vi (make ~) Bericht erstatten;
(present o.s.): **to ~ (to sb)** sich (bei jdm)
melden; **~ card** n (US, SCOTTISH) Zeugnis
nt; **~edly** adv wie verlautet; **~er** n Reporter
m

reprehensible [reprɪ'hensɪbl] adj
tadelnswert

represent [reprɪ'zent] vt darstellen; (speak
for) vertreten; **~ation** n [reprɪzen'teɪʃən] n
Darstellung f; (being ~ed) Vertretung f;
~ations npl (protest) Vorhaltungen pl;
~ative n (person) Vertreter m; (US: POL)
Abgeordnete(r) mf ♦ adj repräsentativ

repress [rɪ'pres] vt unterdrücken; **~ion**
[rɪ'preʃən] n Unterdrückung f

reprieve [rɪ'priːv] n (JUR) Begnadigung f;
(fig) Gnadenfrist f ♦ vt (JUR) begnadigen

reprimand ['reprɪmɑːnd] n Verweis m ♦ vt
einen Verweis erteilen +dat

reprint [n 'riːprɪnt, vb rɪ'prɪnt] n Neudruck m
♦ vt wieder abdrucken

reprisal [rɪ'praɪzl] n Vergeltung f

reproach [rɪ'prəʊtʃ] n Vorwurf m ♦ vt
Vorwürfe machen +dat; **to ~ sb with sth**
jdm etw vorwerfen; **~ful** adj vorwurfsvoll

reproduce [riːprə'djuːs] vt reproduzieren
♦ vi (have offspring) sich vermehren;
reproduction [riːprə'dʌkʃən] n (ART, PHOT)
Reproduktion f; (breeding) Fortpflanzung f;
reproductive [riːprə'dʌktɪv] adj
reproduktiv; (breeding) Fortpflanzungs-

reprove [rɪ'pruːv] vt tadeln

reptile ['reptaɪl] n Reptil nt

republic [rɪ'pʌblɪk] n Republik f

repudiate [rɪ'pjuːdɪeɪt] vt zurückweisen

repugnant [rɪ'pʌgnənt] adj widerlich

repulse [rɪ'pʌls] vt (drive back)
zurückschlagen; (reject) abweisen;
repulsive [rɪ'pʌlsɪv] adj abstoßend

reputable ['repjutəbl] adj angesehen

reputation [repju'teɪʃən] n Ruf m

reputed [rɪ'pjuːtɪd] adj angeblich; **~ly**
[rɪ'pjuːtɪdlɪ] adv angeblich

request [rɪ'kwest] n Bitte f ♦ vt (thing)
erbitten; **to ~ sth of** or **from sb** jdn um etw
bitten; (formally) jdn um etw ersuchen; **~
stop** (BRIT) n Bedarfshaltestelle f

require [rɪ'kwaɪər] vt (need) brauchen;
(demand) erfordern; **~ment** n (condition)
Anforderung f; (need) Bedarf m

requisite ['rekwɪzɪt] adj erforderlich

requisition [rekwɪ'zɪʃən] n Anforderung f
♦ vt beschlagnahmen

rescue ['reskjuː] n Rettung f ♦ vt retten; **~
party** n Rettungsmannschaft f; **~r** n Retter
m

research [rɪ'səːtʃ] n Forschung f ♦ vi
forschen ♦ vt erforschen; **~er** n Forscher m

resemblance [rɪ'zembləns] n Ähnlichkeit f

resemble [rɪ'zembl] vt ähneln +dat

resent [rɪ'zent] vt übel nehmen; **~ful** adj
nachtragend, empfindlich; **~ment** n
Verstimmung f, Unwille m

reservation [rezə'veɪʃən] n (booking)
Reservierung f; (THEAT) Vorbestellung f;
(doubt) Vorbehalt m; (land) Reservat nt

reserve [rɪ'zəːv] n (store) Vorrat m, Reserve
f; (manner) Zurückhaltung f; (game ~)
Naturschutzgebiet nt; (SPORT)

Ersatzspieler(in) *m(f)* ♦ *vt* reservieren; (*judgement*) sich *dat* vorbehalten; **~s** *npl* (*MIL*) Reserve *f*; **in ~** in Reserve; **~d** *adj* reserviert

reshuffle [riːˈʃʌfl] *n* (*POL*): **cabinet ~** Kabinettsumbildung *f* ♦ *vt* (*POL*) umbilden

reside [rɪˈzaɪd] *vi* wohnen, ansässig sein

residence [ˈrezɪdəns] *n* (*house*) Wohnsitz *m*; (*living*) Aufenthalt *m*; **~ permit** (*BRIT*) *n* Aufenthaltserlaubnis *f*

resident [ˈrezɪdənt] *n* (*in house*) Bewohner *m*; (*in area*) Einwohner *m* ♦ *adj* wohnhaft, ansässig; **~ial** [rezɪˈdenʃəl] *adj* Wohn-

residue [ˈrezɪdjuː] *n* Rest *m*; (*CHEM*) Rückstand *m*; (*fig*) Bodensatz *m*

resign [rɪˈzaɪn] *vt* (*office*) aufgeben, zurücktreten von ♦ *vi* (*from office*) zurücktreten; (*employee*) kündigen; **to be ~ed to sth, to ~ o.s. to sth** sich mit etw abfinden; **~ation** [rezɪgˈneɪʃən] *n* (*from job*) Kündigung *f*; (*POL*) Rücktritt *m*; (*submission*) Resignation *f*; **~ed** *adj* resigniert

resilience [rɪˈzɪlɪəns] *n* Spannkraft *f*; (*of person*) Unverwüstlichkeit *f*; **resilient** [rɪˈzɪlɪənt] *adj* unverwüstlich

resin [ˈrezɪn] *n* Harz *nt*

resist [rɪˈzɪst] *vt* widerstehen +*dat*; **~ance** *n* Widerstand *m*

resit [*vb* riːˈsɪt, *n* ˈriːsɪt] *vt* (*exam*) wiederholen ♦ *n* Wiederholung(sprüfung) *f*

resolute [ˈrezəluːt] *adj* entschlossen, resolut; **resolution** [rezəˈluːʃən] *n* (*firmness*) Entschlossenheit *f*; (*intention*) Vorsatz *m*; (*decision*) Beschluss *m*

resolve [rɪˈzɒlv] *n* Entschlossenheit *f* ♦ *vt* (*decide*) beschließen ♦ *vi* sich lösen; **~d** *adj* (*fest*) entschlossen

resonant [ˈrezənənt] *adj* voll

resort [rɪˈzɔːt] *n* (*holiday place*) Erholungsort *m*; (*help*) Zuflucht *f* ♦ *vi*: **to ~ to** Zuflucht nehmen zu; **as a last ~** als letzter Ausweg

resound [rɪˈzaund] *vi*: **to ~ (with)** widerhallen (von); **~ing** *adj* nachhallend; (*success*) groß

resource [rɪˈsɔːs] *n* Findigkeit *f*; **~s** *npl* (*financial*) Geldmittel *pl*; (*natural*) Bodenschätze *pl*; **~ful** *adj* findig

respect [rɪsˈpekt] *n* Respekt *m* ♦ *vt* achten, respektieren; **~s** *npl* (*regards*) Grüße *pl*; **with ~ to** in Bezug auf +*acc*, hinsichtlich +*gen*; **in this ~** in dieser Hinsicht; **~able** *adj* anständig; (*not bad*) leidlich; **~ful** *adj* höflich

respective [rɪsˈpektɪv] *adj* jeweilig; **~ly** *adv* beziehungsweise

respiration [respɪˈreɪʃən] *n* Atmung *f*

respite [ˈrespaɪt] *n* Ruhepause *f*

resplendent [rɪsˈplendənt] *adj* strahlend

respond [rɪsˈpɒnd] *vi* antworten; (*react*): **to ~ (to)** reagieren (auf +*acc*); **response** [rɪsˈpɒns] *n* Antwort *f*; Reaktion *f*; (*to advert*) Resonanz *f*

responsibility [rɪspɒnsɪˈbɪlɪtɪ] *n* Verantwortung *f*

responsible [rɪsˈpɒnsɪbl] *adj* verantwortlich; (*reliable*) verantwortungsvoll

responsive [rɪsˈpɒnsɪv] *adj* empfänglich

rest [rest] *n* Ruhe *f*; (*break*) Pause *f*; (*remainder*) Rest *m* ♦ *vi* sich ausruhen; (*be supported*) (auf)liegen ♦ *vt* (*lean*): **to ~ sth on/against sth** etw gegen etw *acc* lehnen; **the ~ of them** die Übrigen; **it ~s with him to ...** es liegt bei ihm, zu ...

restaurant [ˈrestərɒŋ] *n* Restaurant *nt*, **~ car** (*BRIT*) *n* Speisewagen *m*

restful [ˈrestful] *adj* erholsam, ruhig

rest home *n* Erholungsheim *nt*

restive [ˈrestɪv] *adj* unruhig

restless [ˈrestlɪs] *adj* unruhig

restoration [restəˈreɪʃən] *n* Rückgabe *f*; (*of building etc*) Rückerstattung *f*

restore [rɪsˈtɔː] *vt* (*order*) wieder herstellen; (*customs*) wieder einführen; (*person to position*) wieder einsetzen; (*give back*) zurückgeben; (*renovate*) restaurieren

restrain [rɪsˈtreɪn] *vt* zurückhalten; (*curiosity etc*) beherrschen; (*person*): **to ~ sb from doing sth** jdn davon abhalten, etw zu tun; **~ed** *adj* (*style etc*) gedämpft, verhalten; **~t** *n* (*self-control*) Zurückhaltung *f*

restrict [rɪsˈtrɪkt] *vt* einschränken; **~ion** [rɪsˈtrɪkʃən] *n* Einschränkung *f*; **~ive** *adj* einschränkend

rest room (*US*) *n* Toilette *f*

restructure [riː'strʌktʃəʳ] *vt* umstrukturieren

result [rɪ'zʌlt] *n* Resultat *nt*, Folge *f*; (*of exam, game*) Ergebnis *nt* ♦ *vi*: **to ~ in sth** etw zur Folge haben; **as a ~ of** als Folge +*gen*

resume [rɪ'zjuːm] *vt* fortsetzen; (*occupy again*) wieder einnehmen ♦ *vi* (*work etc*) wieder beginnen

résumé ['reɪzjuːmeɪ] *n* Zusammenfassung *f*

resumption [rɪ'zʌmpʃən] *n* Wiederaufnahme *f*

resurgence [rɪ'sɜːdʒəns] *n* Wiedererwachen *nt*

resurrection [rezə'rekʃən] *n* Auferstehung *f*

resuscitate [rɪ'sʌsɪteɪt] *vt* wieder beleben; **resuscitation** [rɪsʌsɪ'teɪʃən] *n* Wiederbelebung *f*

retail [*n, adj* 'riːteɪl, *vb* 'riːteɪl] *n* Einzelhandel *m* ♦ *adj* Einzelhandels- ♦ *vt* im Kleinen verkaufen ♦ *vi* im Einzelhandel kosten; **~er** ['riːteɪləʳ] *n* Einzelhändler *m*, Kleinhändler *m*; **~ price** *n* Ladenpreis *m*

retain [rɪ'teɪn] *vt* (*keep*) (zurück)behalten; **~er** *n* (*fee*) (Honorar)vorschuss *m*

retaliate [rɪ'tælɪeɪt] *vi* zum Vergeltungsschlag ausholen; **retaliation** [rɪtælɪ'eɪʃən] *n* Vergeltung *f*

retarded [rɪ'tɑːdɪd] *adj* zurückgeblieben

retch [retʃ] *vi* würgen

retentive [rɪ'tentɪv] *adj* (*memory*) gut

reticent ['retɪsnt] *adj* schweigsam

retina ['retɪnə] *n* Netzhaut *f*

retire [rɪ'taɪəʳ] *vi* (*from work*) in den Ruhestand treten; (*withdraw*) sich zurückziehen; (*go to bed*) schlafen gehen; **~d** *adj* (*person*) pensioniert, im Ruhestand; **~ment** *n* Ruhestand *m*

retiring [rɪ'taɪərɪŋ] *adj* zurückhaltend

retort [rɪ'tɔːt] *n* (*reply*) Erwiderung *f* ♦ *vi* (scharf) erwidern

retrace [riː'treɪs] *vt* zurückverfolgen; **to ~ one's steps** denselben Weg zurückgehen

retract [rɪ'trækt] *vt* (*statement*) zurücknehmen; (*claws*) einziehen ♦ *vi* einen Rückzieher machen; **~able** *adj* (*aerial*) ausziehbar

retrain [riː'treɪn] *vt* umschulen

retread ['riːtred] *n* (*tyre*) Reifen *m* mit erneuerter Lauffläche

retreat [rɪ'triːt] *n* Rückzug *m*; (*place*) Zufluchtsort *m* ♦ *vi* sich zurückziehen

retribution [retrɪ'bjuːʃən] *n* Strafe *f*

retrieval [rɪ'triːvəl] *n* Wiedergewinnung *f*

retrieve [rɪ'triːv] *vt* wiederbekommen; (*rescue*) retten; **~r** *n* Apportierhund *m*

retrograde ['retrəgreɪd] *adj* (*step*) Rück-; (*policy*) rückschrittlich

retrospect ['retrəspekt] *n*: **in ~** im Rückblick, rückblickend; **~ive** [retrə'spektɪv] *adj* (*action*) rückwirkend; (*look*) rückblickend

return [rɪ'tɜːn] *n* Rückkehr *f*; (*profits*) Ertrag *m*; (*BRIT: rail ticket etc*) Rückfahrkarte *f*; (*: plane ticket*) Rückflugkarte *f* ♦ *adj* (*journey, match*) Rück- ♦ *vi* zurückkehren, zurückkommen ♦ *vt* zurückgeben, zurücksenden; (*pay back*) zurückzahlen; (*elect*) wählen; (*verdict*) aussprechen; **~s** *npl* (*COMM*) Gewinn *m*; (*receipts*) Einkünfte *pl*; **in ~** dafür; **by ~ of post** postwendend; **many happy ~s!** herzlichen Glückwunsch zum Geburtstag!

reunion [riː'juːnɪən] *n* Wiedervereinigung *f*; (*SCH etc*) Treffen *nt*

reunite [riːjuː'naɪt] *vt* wieder vereinigen

reuse [riː'juːz] *vt* wieder verwenden, wieder verwerten

rev [rev] *n abbr* (*AUT:* = *revolution*) Drehzahl *f*

revamp [riː'væmp] *vt* aufpolieren

reveal [rɪ'viːl] *vt* enthüllen; **~ing** *adj* aufschlussreich

revel ['revl] *vi*: **to ~ in sth/in doing sth** seine Freude an etw *dat* haben/daran haben, etw zu tun

revelation [revə'leɪʃən] *n* Offenbarung *f*

revelry ['revlrɪ] *n* Rummel *m*

revenge [rɪ'vendʒ] *n* Rache *f*; **to take ~ on** sich rächen an +*dat*

revenue ['revənjuː] *n* Einnahmen *pl*

reverberate [rɪ'vɜːbəreɪt] *vi* widerhallen

revere [rɪ'vɪəʳ] *vt* (ver)ehren; **~nce** ['revərəns] *n* Ehrfurcht *f*

Reverend ['revərənd] *adj*: **the ~ Robert Martin** ≈ Pfarrer Robert Martin

reversal [rɪ'vɜːsl] *n* Umkehrung *f*

reverse [rɪ'vɜːs] *n* Rückseite *f*; (*AUT: gear*)

Rückwärtsgang *m* ♦ *adj* (*order, direction*) entgegengesetzt ♦ *vt* umkehren ♦ *vi* (*BRIT: AUT*) rückwärts fahren; **~-charge call** (*BRIT*) *n* R-Gespräch *nt*; **reversing lights** *npl* (*AUT*) Rückfahrscheinwerfer *pl*

revert [rɪ'vɜːt] *vi:* **to ~ to** zurückkehren zu; (*to bad state*) zurückfallen in *+acc*

review [rɪ'vjuː] *n* (*of book*) Rezension *f*; (*magazine*) Zeitschrift *f* ♦ *vt* Rückschau halten auf *+acc*; (*MIL*) mustern; (*book*) rezensieren; (*reexamine*) von neuem untersuchen; **~er** *n* (*critic*) Rezensent *m*

revise [rɪ'vaɪz] *vt* (*book*) überarbeiten; (*reconsider*) ändern, revidieren; **revision** [rɪ'vɪʒən] *n* Prüfung *f*; (*COMM*) Revision *f*; (*SCH*) Wiederholung *f*

revitalize [riː'vaɪtəlaɪz] *vt* neu beleben

revival [rɪ'vaɪvəl] *n* Wiederbelebung *f*; (*REL*) Erweckung *f*; (*THEAT*) Wiederaufnahme *f*

revive [rɪ'vaɪv] *vt* wieder beleben; (*fig*) wieder auffrischen ♦ *vi* wieder erwachen; (*fig*) wieder aufleben

revoke [rɪ'vəuk] *vt* aufheben

revolt [rɪ'vəult] *n* Aufstand *m*, Revolte *f* ♦ *vi* sich auflehnen ♦ *vt* entsetzen; **~ing** *adj* widerlich

revolution [revə'luːʃən] *n* (*turn*) Umdrehung *f*; (*POL*) Revolution *f*; **~ary** *adj* revolutionär ♦ *n* Revolutionär *m*; **~ize** *vt* revolutionieren

revolve [rɪ'vɒlv] *vi* kreisen; (*on own axis*) sich drehen

revolver [rɪ'vɒlvər] *n* Revolver *m*

revolving door [rɪ'vɒlvɪŋ-] *n* Drehtür *f*

revulsion [rɪ'vʌlʃən] *n* Ekel *m*

reward [rɪ'wɔːd] *n* Belohnung *f* ♦ *vt* belohnen; **~ing** *adj* lohnend

rewind [riː'waɪnd] (*irreg: like* wind) *vt* (*tape etc*) zurückspulen

rewire [riː'waɪər] *vt* (*house*) neu verkabeln

reword [riː'wɜːd] *vt* anders formulieren

rewrite [riː'raɪt] (*irreg: like* write) *vt* umarbeiten, neu schreiben

rheumatism ['ruːmətɪzəm] *n* Rheumatismus *m*, Rheuma *nt*

Rhine [raɪn] *n:* **the ~** der Rhein

rhinoceros [raɪ'nɒsərəs] *n* Nashorn *nt*

Rhone [rəun] *n:* **the ~** die Rhone

rhubarb ['ruːbɑːb] *n* Rhabarber *m*

rhyme [raɪm] *n* Reim *m*

rhythm ['rɪðm] *n* Rhythmus *m*

rib [rɪb] *n* Rippe *f* ♦ *vt* (*mock*) hänseln, aufziehen

ribbon ['rɪbən] *n* Band *nt*; **in ~s** (*torn*) in Fetzen

rice [raɪs] *n* Reis *m*; **~ pudding** *n* Milchreis *m*

rich [rɪtʃ] *adj* reich; (*food*) reichhaltig ♦ *npl:* **the ~** die Reichen *pl*; **~es** *npl* Reichtum *m*; **~ly** *adv* reich; (*deserve*) völlig

rickets ['rɪkɪts] *n* Rachitis *f*

rickety ['rɪkɪtɪ] *adj* wack(e)lig

rickshaw ['rɪkʃɔː] *n* Rikscha *f*

ricochet ['rɪkəʃeɪ] *n* Abprallen *nt*; (*shot*) Querschläger *m* ♦ *vi* abprallen

rid [rɪd] (*pt, pp* rid) *vt* befreien; **to get ~ of** loswerden

riddle ['rɪdl] *n* Rätsel *nt* ♦ *vt:* **to be ~d with** völlig durchlöchert sein von

ride [raɪd] (*pt* rode, *pp* ridden) *n* (*in vehicle*) Fahrt *f*; (*on horse*) Ritt *m* ♦ *vt* (*horse*) reiten, (*bicycle*) fahren ♦ *vi* fahren, reiten; **to take sb for a ~** mit jdm eine Fahrt *etc* machen; (*fig*) jdn aufs Glatteis führen; **~r** *n* Reiter *m*

ridge [rɪdʒ] *n* Kamm *m*; (*of roof*) First *m*

ridicule ['rɪdɪkjuːl] *n* Spott *m* ♦ *vt* lächerlich machen

ridiculous [rɪ'dɪkjuləs] *adj* lächerlich

riding ['raɪdɪŋ] *n* Reiten *nt*; **~ school** *n* Reitschule *f*

rife [raɪf] *adj* weit verbreitet; **to be ~** grassieren; **to be ~ with** voll sein von

riffraff ['rɪfræf] *n* Pöbel *m*

rifle ['raɪfl] *n* Gewehr *nt* ♦ *vt* berauben; **~ range** *n* Schießstand *m*

rift [rɪft] *n* Spalte *f*; (*fig*) Bruch *m*

rig [rɪg] *n* (*oil ~*) Bohrinsel *f* ♦ *vt* (*election etc*) manipulieren; **~ out** (*BRIT*) *vt* ausstatten; **~ up** *vt* zusammenbasteln; **~ging** *n* Takelage *f*

right [raɪt] *adj* (*correct, just*) richtig, recht; (*~ side*) rechte(r, s) ♦ *n* Recht *nt*; (*not left, POL*) Rechte *f* ♦ *adv* (*on the ~*) nach rechts; (*to the ~*) nach rechts; (*look, work*) richtig, recht; (*directly*) gerade; (*exactly*) genau ♦ *vt* in

Ordnung bringen, korrigieren ♦ *excl* gut; **on the ~** rechts; **to be in the ~** im Recht sein; **by ~s** von Rechts wegen; **to be ~** Recht haben; **~ away** sofort; **~ now** in diesem Augenblick, eben; **~ in the middle** genau in der Mitte; **~ angle** *n* rechte(r) Winkel *m*; **~eous** ['raɪtʃəs] *adj* rechtschaffen; **~ful** *adj* rechtmäßig; **~-hand** *adj*: **~-hand drive** mit Rechtssteuerung; **~-handed** *adj* rechtshändig; **~-hand man** (*irreg*) *n* rechte Hand *f*; **~-hand side** *n* rechte Seite *f*; **~ly** *adv* mit Recht; **~ of way** *n* Vorfahrt *f*; **~-wing** *adj* rechtsorientiert

rigid ['rɪdʒɪd] *adj* (*stiff*) starr, steif; (*strict*) streng; **~ity** [rɪ'dʒɪdɪtɪ] *n* Starrheit *f*, Strenge *f*

rigmarole ['rɪgmərəul] *n* Gewäsch *nt*

rigor ['rɪgər] (*US*) *n* = **rigour**

rigorous ['rɪgərəs] *adj* streng

rigour ['rɪgər] (*US* **rigor**) *n* Strenge *f*, Härte *f*

rile [raɪl] *vt* ärgern

rim [rɪm] *n* (*edge*) Rand *m*; (*of wheel*) Felge *f*

rind [raɪnd] *n* Rinde *f*

ring [rɪŋ] (*pt* **rang**, *pp* **rung**) *n* Ring *m*; (*of people*) Kreis *m*; (*arena*) Manege *f*; (*of telephone*) Klingeln *nt* ♦ *vt, vi* (*bell*) läuten; (*BRIT*) anrufen; **~ back** (*BRIT*) *vt, vi* zurückrufen; **~ off** (*BRIT*) *vi* aufhängen; **~ up** (*BRIT*) *vt* anrufen; **~ binder** *n* Ringbuch *nt*; **~ing** *n* Klingeln *nt*; (*of large bell*) Läuten *nt*; (*in ears*) Klingen *nt*; **~ing tone** *n* (*TEL*) Rufzeichen *nt*

ringleader ['rɪŋliːdər] *n* Anführer *m*, Rädelsführer *m*

ringlets ['rɪŋlɪts] *npl* Ringellocken *pl*

ring road (*BRIT*) *n* Umgehungsstraße *f*

rink [rɪŋk] *n* (*ice ~*) Eisbahn *f*

rinse [rɪns] *n* Spülen *nt* ♦ *vt* spülen

riot ['raɪət] *n* Aufruhr *m* ♦ *vi* randalieren; **to run ~** (*people*) randalieren; (*vegetation*) wuchern; **~er** *n* Aufrührer *m*; **~ous** *adj* aufrührerisch; (*noisy*) lärmend

rip [rɪp] *n* Schlitz *m*, Riss *m* ♦ *vt, vi* (zer)reißen; **~cord** *n* Reißleine *f*

ripe [raɪp] *adj* reif; **~n** *vi* reifen ♦ *vt* reifen lassen

rip-off ['rɪpɔf] (*inf*) *n*: **it's a ~~~!** das ist Wucher!

ripple ['rɪpl] *n* kleine Welle *f* ♦ *vt* kräuseln ♦ *vi* sich kräuseln

rise [raɪz] (*pt* **rose**, *pp* **risen**) *n* (*slope*) Steigung *f*; (*esp in wages*) Erhöhung *f*; (*growth*) Aufstieg *m* ♦ *vi* (*sun*) aufgehen; (*smoke*) aufsteigen; (*mountain*) sich erheben; (*ground*) ansteigen; (*prices*) steigen; (*in revolt*) sich erheben; **to give ~ to** Anlass geben zu; **to ~ to the occasion** sich der Lage gewachsen zeigen; **~n** [rɪzn] *pp of* **rise**; **~r** ['raɪzər] *n*: **to be an early ~r** ein(e) Frühaufsteher(in) *m(f)* sein; **rising** ['raɪzɪŋ] *adj* (*tide, prices*) steigend; (*sun, moon*) aufgehend ♦ *n* (*uprising*) Aufstand *m*

risk [rɪsk] *n* Gefahr *f*, Risiko *nt* ♦ *vt* (*venture*) wagen; (*chance loss of*) riskieren, aufs Spiel setzen; **to take** *or* **run the ~ of doing sth** das Risiko eingehen, etw zu tun; **at ~** in Gefahr; **at one's own ~** auf eigene Gefahr; **~y** *adj* riskant

risqué ['riːskeɪ] *adj* gewagt

rissole ['rɪsəul] *n* Fleischklößchen *nt*

rite [raɪt] *n* Ritus *m*; **last ~s** Letzte Ölung *f*

ritual ['rɪtjuəl] *n* Ritual *nt* ♦ *adj* ritual, Ritual-; (*fig*) rituell

rival ['raɪvl] *n* Rivale *m*, Konkurrent *m* ♦ *adj* rivalisierend ♦ *vt* rivalisieren mit; (*COMM*) konkurrieren mit; **~ry** *n* Rivalität *f*, Konkurrenz *f*

river ['rɪvər] *n* Fluss *m*, Strom *m* ♦ *cpd* (*port, traffic*) Fluss-; **up/down ~** flussaufwärts/-abwärts; **~bank** *n* Flussufer *nt*; **~bed** *n* Flussbett *nt*

rivet ['rɪvɪt] *n* Niete *f* ♦ *vt* (*fasten*) (ver)nieten

Riviera [rɪvɪ'eərə] *n*: **the ~** die Riviera

road [rəud] *n* Straße *f* ♦ *cpd* Straßen-; **major/minor ~** Haupt-/Nebenstraße *f*; **~ accident** *n* Verkehrsunfall *m*; **~block** *n* Straßensperre *f*; **~hog** *n* Verkehrsrowdy *m*; **~ map** *n* Straßenkarte *f*; **~ rage** *n* Aggressivität *f* im Straßenverkehr; **~ safety** *n* Verkehrssicherheit *f*; **~side** *n* Straßenrand *m* ♦ *adj* an der Landstraße (gelegen); **~ sign** *n* Straßenschild *nt*; **~ user** *n* Verkehrsteilnehmer *m*; **~way** *n* Fahrbahn *f*;

~ **works** *npl* Straßenbauarbeiten *pl*; ~**worthy** *adj* verkehrssicher

roam [rəʊm] *vi* (umher)streifen ♦ *vt* durchstreifen

roar [rɔː] *n* Brüllen *nt*, Gebrüll *nt* ♦ *vi* brüllen; **to ~ with laughter** vor Lachen brüllen; **to do a ~ing trade** ein Riesengeschäft machen

roast [rəʊst] *n* Braten *m* ♦ *vt* braten, schmoren; ~ **beef** *n* Roastbeef *nt*

rob [rɒb] *vt* bestehlen, berauben; (*bank*) ausrauben; **to ~ sb of sth** jdm etw rauben; ~**ber** *n* Räuber *m*; ~**bery** *n* Raub *m*

robe [rəʊb] *n* (*dress*) Gewand *nt*; (*US*) Hauskleid *nt*; (*judge's*) Robe *f*

robin ['rɒbɪn] *n* Rotkehlchen *nt*

robot ['rəʊbɒt] *n* Roboter *m*

robust [rəʊ'bʌst] *adj* (*person*) robust; (*appetite, economy*) gesund

rock [rɒk] *n* Felsen *m*; (*BRIT: sweet*) Zuckerstange *f* ♦ *vt, vi* wiegen, schaukeln; **on the ~s** (*drink*) mit Eis(würfeln); (*marriage*) gescheitert; (*ship*) aufgelaufen; ~ **and roll** *n* Rock and Roll *m*; ~**bottom** *n* (*fig*) Tiefpunkt *m*; ~ **ery** *n* Steingarten *m*

rocket ['rɒkɪt] *n* Rakete *f*

rocking chair ['rɒkɪŋ-] *n* Schaukelstuhl *m*

rocking horse *n* Schaukelpferd *nt*

rocky ['rɒkɪ] *adj* felsig

rod [rɒd] *n* (*bar*) Stange *f*; (*stick*) Rute *f*

rode [rəʊd] *pt of* **ride**

rodent ['rəʊdnt] *n* Nagetier *nt*

roe [rəʊ] *n* (*also:* ~ **deer**) Reh *nt*; (*of fish: also: hard ~*) Rogen *m*; **soft ~** Milch *f*

rogue [rəʊg] *n* Schurke *m*

role [rəʊl] *n* Rolle *f*; ~ **play** *n* Rollenspiel *nt*

roll [rəʊl] *n* Rolle *f*; (*bread*) Brötchen *nt*; (*list*) (Namens)liste *f*; (*of drum*) Wirbel *m* ♦ *vt* (*turn*) rollen, (herum)wälzen; (*grass etc*) walzen ♦ *vi* (*swing*) schlingern; (*sound*) rollen, grollen; ~ **about** *or* **around** *vi* herumkugeln; (*ship*) schlingern; (*dog etc*) sich wälzen; ~ **by** *vi* (*time*) verfließen; ~ **over** *vi* sich (herum)drehen; ~ **up** *vi* (*arrive*) kommen, auftauchen ♦ *vt* (*carpet*) aufrollen; ~ **call** *n* Namensaufruf *m*; ~**er** *n* Rolle *f*, Walze *f*; (*road ~er*) Straßenwalze *f*;

R~erblade ® *n* Rollerblade *m*; ~**er coaster** *n* Achterbahn *f*; ~**er skates** *npl* Rollschuhe *pl*; ~**skating** *n* Rollschuhlaufen *nt*

rolling ['rəʊlɪŋ] *adj* (*landscape*) wellig; ~ **pin** *n* Nudel- *or* Wellholz *nt*; ~ **stock** *n* Wagenmaterial *nt*

ROM [rɒm] *n abbr* (= *read only memory*) ROM *m*

Roman ['rəʊmən] *adj* römisch ♦ *n* Römer(in) *m(f)*; ~ **Catholic** *adj* römisch-katholisch ♦ *n* Katholik(in) *m(f)*

romance [rə'mæns] *n* Romanze *f*; (*story*) (Liebes)roman *m*

Romania [rəʊ'meɪnɪə] *n* = **Rumania**; ~**n** *n* = **Rumanian**

Roman numeral *n* römische Ziffer

romantic [rə'mæntɪk] *adj* romantisch; ~**ism** [rə'mæntɪsɪzəm] *n* Romantik *f*

Rome [rəʊm] *n* Rom *nt*

romp [rɒmp] *n* Tollen *nt* ♦ *vi* (*also:* ~ **about**) herumtollen

rompers ['rɒmpəz] *npl* Spielanzug *m*

roof [ruːf] (*pl* ~**s**) *n* Dach *nt*; (*of mouth*) Gaumen *m* ♦ *vt* überdachen, überdecken; ~**ing** *n* Deckmaterial *nt*; ~ **rack** *n* (*AUT*) Dachgepäckträger *m*

rook [rʊk] *n* (*bird*) Saatkrähe *f*; (*chess*) Turm *m*

room [ruːm] *n* Zimmer *nt*, Raum *m*; (*space*) Platz *m*; (*fig*) Spielraum *m*; ~**s** *npl* (*accommodation*) Wohnung *f*; **"~s to let** (*BRIT*) *or* **for rent** (*US*)" „Zimmer zu vermieten"; **single/double** ~ Einzel-/Doppelzimmer *nt*; ~**ing house** (*US*) *n* Mietshaus *nt* (*mit möblierten Wohnungen*); ~**mate** *n* Mitbewohner(in) *m(f)*; ~ **service** *n* Zimmerbedienung *f*; ~**y** *adj* geräumig

roost [ruːst] *n* Hühnerstange *f* ♦ *vi* auf der Stange hocken

rooster ['ruːstə] *n* Hahn *m*

root [ruːt] *n* (*also fig*) Wurzel *f* ♦ *vi* wurzeln; ~ **about** *vi* (*fig*) herumwühlen; ~ **for** *vt fus* Stimmung machen für; ~ **out** *vt* ausjäten; (*fig*) ausrotten

rope [rəʊp] *n* Seil *nt* ♦ *vt* (*tie*) festschnüren; **to know the ~s** sich auskennen; **to ~ sb in** jdn gewinnen; ~ **off** *vt* absperren;

~ ladder *n* Strickleiter *f*

rosary ['rəuzəri] *n* Rosenkranz *m*

rose [rəuz] *pt of* **rise** ♦ *n* Rose *f* ♦ *adj* Rosen-, rosenrot

rosé ['rəuzeɪ] *n* Rosé *m*

rosebud ['rəuzbʌd] *n* Rosenknospe *f*

rosebush ['rəuzbʊʃ] *n* Rosenstock *m*

rosemary ['rəuzməri] *n* Rosmarin *m*

rosette [rəu'zet] *n* Rosette *f*

roster ['rɒstə'] *n* Dienstplan *m*

rostrum ['rɒstrəm] *n* Rednerbühne *f*

rosy ['rəuzi] *adj* rosig

rot [rɒt] *n* Fäulnis *f*; *(nonsense)* Quatsch *m* ♦ *vi* verfaulen ♦ *vt* verfaulen lassen

rota ['rəutə] *n* Dienstliste *f*

rotary ['rəutəri] *adj* rotierend

rotate [rəu'teɪt] *vt* rotieren lassen; *(take turns)* turnusmäßig wechseln ♦ *vi* rotieren; **rotating** *adj* rotierend; **rotation** [rəu'teɪʃən] *n* Umdrehung *f*

rote [rəut] *n*: **by ~** auswendig

rotten ['rɒtn] *adj* faul; *(fig)* schlecht, gemein; **to feel ~** *(ill)* sich elend fühlen

rotund [rəu'tʌnd] *adj* rundlich

rouble ['ruːbl] *(US* **ruble)** *n* Rubel *m*

rough [rʌf] *adj* *(not smooth)* rau; *(path)* uneben; *(violent)* roh, grob; *(crossing)* stürmisch; *(without comforts)* hart, unbequem; *(unfinished, makeshift)* grob; *(approximate)* ungefähr ♦ *n (BRIT: person)* Rowdy *m*, Rohling *m*; *(GOLF)*: **in the ~** im Rau ♦ *vt*: **to ~ it** primitiv leben; **to sleep ~** im Freien schlafen; **~age** *n* Ballaststoffe *pl*; **~-and-ready** *adj* provisorisch; *(work)* zusammengehauen; **~ copy** *n* Entwurf *m*; **~ draft** *n* Entwurf *m*; **~ly** *adv* grob; *(about)* ungefähr; **~ness** *n* Rauheit *f*; *(of manner)* Ungeschliffenheit *f*

roulette [ruː'let] *n* Roulett(e) *nt*

Roumania [ruː'meɪnɪə] *n* = **Rumania**

round [raund] *adj* rund; *(figures)* aufgerundet ♦ *adv (in a circle)* rundherum ♦ *prep* um ... herum ♦ *n* Runde *f*; *(of ammunition)* Magazin *nt* ♦ *vt (corner)* biegen um; **all ~** überall; **the long way ~** der Umweg; **all the year ~** das ganze Jahr über; **it's just ~ the corner** *(fig)* es ist gerade um die Ecke;

~ the clock rund um die Uhr; **to go ~ to sb's (house)** jdn besuchen; **to go ~ the back** hintenherum gehen; **enough to go ~** genug für alle; **to go the ~s** *(story)* die Runde machen; **a ~ of applause** ein Beifall *m*; **a ~ of drinks** eine Runde Drinks; **a ~ of sandwiches** ein Sandwich *nt or m*, ein belegtes Brot; **~ off** *vt* abrunden; **~ up** *vt (end)* abschließen; *(figures)* aufrunden; *(criminals)* hochnehmen; **~about** *n (BRIT: traffic)* Kreisverkehr *m*; *(: merry-go-~)* Karussell *nt* ♦ *adj* auf Umwegen; **~ers** *npl (game)* ≈ Schlagball *m*; **~ly** *adv (fig)* gründlich; **~-shouldered** *adj* mit abfallenden Schultern; **~ trip** *n* Rundreise *f*; **~up** *n* Zusammentreiben *nt*, Sammeln *nt*

rouse [rauz] *vt (waken)* (auf)wecken; *(stir up)* erregen; **rousing** *adj (welcome)* stürmisch; *(speech)* zündend

route [ruːt] *n* Weg *m*, Route *f*; **~ map** *(BRIT) n (for journey)* Streckenkarte *f*

routine [ruː'tiːn] *n* Routine *f* ♦ *adj* Routine-

row¹ [rau] *n (noise)* Lärm *m*; *(dispute)* Streit *m* ♦ *vi* sich streiten

row² [rəu] *n (line)* Reihe *f* ♦ *vt, vi (boat)* rudern; **in a ~** *(fig)* hintereinander; **~boat** ['rəubaut] *(US) n* Ruderboot *nt*

rowdy ['raudi] *adj* rüpelhaft ♦ *n (person)* Rowdy *m*

rowing ['rəuɪŋ] *n* Rudern *nt*; *(SPORT)* Rudersport *m*; **~ boat** *(BRIT) n* Ruderboot *nt*

royal ['rɔɪəl] *adj* königlich, Königs-; **R~ Air Force** *n* Königliche Luftwaffe *f*; **~ty** ['rɔɪəltɪ] *n (family)* königliche Familie *f*; *(for novel etc)* Tantieme *f*

rpm *abbr (= revs per minute)* U/min

R.S.V.P. *abbr (= répondez s'il vous plaît)* u. A. w. g.

Rt. Hon. *(BRIT) abbr (= Right Honourable)* Abgeordnete(r) *mf*

rub [rʌb] *n (with cloth)* Polieren *nt*; *(on person)* Reiben *nt* ♦ *vt* reiben; **to ~ sb up** *(BRIT) or* **to ~ sb** *(US)* **the wrong way** jdn aufreizen; **~ off** *vi (also fig)*: **to ~ off (on)** abfärben (auf +*acc*); **~ out** *vt* herausreiben; *(with eraser)* ausradieren

rubber ['rʌbə'] *n* Gummi *m*; *(BRIT)*

Radiergummi m; ~ **band** n Gummiband nt; ~ **plant** n Gummibaum m

rubbish ['rʌbɪʃ] n (waste) Abfall m; (nonsense) Blödsinn m, Quatsch m; ~ **bin** (BRIT) n Mülleimer m; ~ **dump** n Müllabladeplatz m

rubble ['rʌbl] n (Stein)schutt m

ruby ['ru:bɪ] n Rubin m ♦ adj rubinrot

rucksack ['rʌksæk] n Rucksack m

rudder ['rʌdə] n Steuerruder nt

ruddy ['rʌdɪ] adj (colour) rötlich; (inf: bloody) verdammt

rude [ru:d] adj unverschämt; (shock) hart; (awakening) unsanft; (unrefined, rough) grob; ~**ness** n Unverschämtheit f, Grobheit f

rudiment ['ru:dɪmənt] n Grundlage f

rueful ['ru:fʊl] adj reuevoll

ruffian ['rʌfɪən] n Rohling m

ruffle ['rʌfl] vt kräuseln

rug [rʌg] n Brücke f; (in bedroom) Bettvorleger m; (BRIT: for knees) (Reise)decke f

rugby ['rʌgbɪ] n (also: ~ **football**) Rugby nt

rugged ['rʌgɪd] adj (coastline) zerklüftet; (features) markig

rugger ['rʌgə] (BRIT: inf) n = **rugby**

ruin ['ru:ɪn] n Ruine f; (downfall) Ruin m ♦ vt ruinieren; ~**s** npl (fig) Trümmer pl; ~**ous** adj ruinierend

rule [ru:l] n Regel f; (government) Regierung f; (for measuring) Lineal nt ♦ vt (govern) herrschen über +acc, regieren; (decide) anordnen, entscheiden; (make lines on) linieren ♦ vi herrschen, regieren; entscheiden; **as a** ~ in der Regel; ~ **out** vt ausschließen; ~**d** adj (paper) liniert; ~**r** n Lineal nt; Herrscher m; **ruling** ['ru:lɪŋ] adj (party) Regierungs-; (class) herrschend ♦ n (JUR) Entscheid m

rum [rʌm] n Rum m

Rumania [ru:'meɪnɪə] n Rumänien nt; ~**n** adj rumänisch ♦ n Rumäne m, Rumänin f; (LING) Rumänisch nt

rumble ['rʌmbl] n Rumpeln nt; (of thunder) Grollen nt ♦ vi rumpeln; grollen

rummage ['rʌmɪdʒ] vi durchstöbern

rumour ['ru:mə] (US **rumor**) n Gerücht nt

♦ vt: **it is ~ed that** man sagt or man munkelt, dass

rump [rʌmp] n Hinterteil nt; ~ **steak** n Rumpsteak nt

rumpus ['rʌmpəs] n Spektakel m

run [rʌn] (pt **ran**, pp **run**) n Lauf m; (in car) (Spazier)fahrt f; (series) Serie f, Reihe f; (ski ~) (Ski)abfahrt f; (in stocking) Laufmasche f ♦ vt (cause to ~) laufen lassen; (car, train, bus) fahren; (race, distance) laufen, rennen; (manage) leiten; (COMPUT) laufen lassen; (pass: hand, eye) gleiten lassen ♦ vi laufen; (move quickly) laufen, rennen; (bus, train) fahren; (flow) fließen, laufen; (colours) (ab)färben; **there was a ~ on** (meat, tickets) es gab einen Ansturm auf +acc; **on the ~** auf der Flucht; **in the long ~** auf die Dauer; **I'll ~ you to the station** ich fahre dich zum Bahnhof; **to ~ a risk** ein Risiko eingehen; ~ **about** or **around** vi (children) umherspringen; ~ **across** vt fus (find) stoßen auf +acc; ~ **away** vi weglaufen; ~ **down** vi (clock) ablaufen ♦ vt (production, factory) allmählich auflösen; (with car) überfahren; (talk against) heruntermachen; **to be ~ down** erschöpft or abgespannt sein; ~ **in** (BRIT) vt (car) einfahren; ~ **into** vt fus (meet: person) zufällig treffen; (trouble) bekommen; (collide with) rennen gegen; fahren gegen; ~ **off** vi fortlaufen; ~ **out** vi (person) hinausrennen; (liquid) auslaufen; (lease) ablaufen; (money) ausgehen; **he ran out of money/petrol** ihm ging das Geld/ Benzin aus; ~ **over** vt (in accident) überfahren; ~ **through** vt (instructions) durchgehen; ~ **up** vt (debt, bill) machen; ~ **up against** vt fus (difficulties) stoßen auf +acc; ~**away** adj (horse) ausgebrochen; (person) flüchtig

rung [rʌŋ] pp of **ring** ♦ n Sprosse f

runner ['rʌnə] n Läufer(in) m(f); (for sleigh) Kufe f; ~ **bean** (BRIT) n Stangenbohne f; ~~**up** n Zweite(r) mf

running ['rʌnɪŋ] n (of business) Leitung f; (of machine) Betrieb m ♦ adj (water) fließend; (commentary) laufend; **to be in/out of the** ~ **for sth** im/aus dem Rennen für etw sein;

3 days ~ 3 Tage lang *or* hintereinander; **~ costs** npl (*of car, machine*) Unterhaltungskosten pl

runny ['rʌnɪ] adj dünn; (*nose*) laufend

run-of-the-mill ['rʌnəvðə'mɪl] adj gewöhnlich, alltäglich

runt [rʌnt] n (*animal*) Kümmerer m

run-up ['rʌnʌp] n: **the ~~~ to** (*election etc*) die Endphase vor +dat

runway ['rʌnweɪ] n Startbahn f

rupture ['rʌptʃə] n (MED) Bruch m

rural ['ruərl] adj ländlich, Land-

ruse [ruːz] n Kniff m, List f

rush [rʌʃ] n Eile f, Hetze f; (FIN) starke Nachfrage f ♦ vt (*carry along*) auf dem schnellsten Wege schaffen *or* transportieren; (*attack*) losstürmen auf +acc ♦ vi (*hurry*) eilen, stürzen; **don't ~ me** dräng mich nicht; **~ hour** n Hauptverkehrszeit f

rusk [rʌsk] n Zwieback m

Russia ['rʌʃə] n Russland nt; **~n** adj russisch ♦ n Russe m, Russin f; (LING) Russisch nt

rust [rʌst] n Rost m ♦ vi rosten

rustic ['rʌstɪk] adj bäuerlich, ländlich

rustle ['rʌsl] vi rauschen, rascheln ♦ vt rascheln lassen

rustproof ['rʌstpruːf] adj rostfrei

rusty ['rʌstɪ] adj rostig

rut [rʌt] n (*in track*) Radspur f; **to be in a ~** im Trott stecken

ruthless ['ruːθlɪs] adj rücksichtslos

rye [raɪ] n Roggen m; **~ bread** n Roggenbrot nt

S, s

sabbath ['sæbəθ] n Sabbat m

sabotage ['sæbətɑːʒ] n Sabotage f ♦ vt sabotieren

saccharin ['sækərɪn] n Sa(c)charin nt

sachet ['sæʃeɪ] n (*of shampoo etc*) Briefchen nt, Kissen nt

sack [sæk] n Sack m ♦ vt (*inf*) hinauswerfen; (*pillage*) plündern; **to get the ~** rausfliegen; **~ing** n (*material*) Sackleinen nt; (*inf*)

Rausschmiss m

sacrament ['sækrəmənt] n Sakrament nt

sacred ['seɪkrɪd] adj heilig

sacrifice ['sækrɪfaɪs] n Opfer nt ♦ vt (*also fig*) opfern

sacrilege ['sækrɪlɪdʒ] n Schändung f

sad [sæd] adj traurig; **~den** vt traurig machen, betrüben

saddle ['sædl] n Sattel m ♦ vt (*burden*): **to ~ sb with sth** jdm etw aufhalsen; **~bag** n Satteltasche f

sadistic [sə'dɪstɪk] adj sadistisch

sadly ['sædlɪ] adv traurig; (*unfortunately*) leider

sadness ['sædnɪs] n Traurigkeit f

s.a.e. abbr (= *stamped addressed envelope*) adressierte(r) Rückumschlag m

safe [seɪf] adj (*careful*) vorsichtig ♦ n Safe m; **~ and sound** gesund und wohl; **(just) to be on the ~ side** um ganz sicherzugehen; **~ from** (*attack*) sicher vor +dat; **~-conduct** n freie(s) Geleit nt; **~-deposit** n (*vault*) Tresorraum m; (*box*) Banksafe m; **~guard** n Sicherung f ♦ vt sichern, schützen; **~keeping** n sichere Verwahrung f; **~ly** adv sicher; (*arrive*) wohlbehalten; **~ sex** n geschützter Sex m

safety ['seɪftɪ] n Sicherheit f; **~ belt** n Sicherheitsgurt m; **~ pin** n Sicherheitsnadel f; **~ valve** n Sicherheitsventil nt

sag [sæg] vi (durch)sacken

sage [seɪdʒ] n (*herb*) Salbei m; (*person*) Weise(r) mf

Sagittarius [sædʒɪ'tɛərɪəs] n Schütze m

Sahara [sə'hɑːrə] n: **the ~ (Desert)** die (Wüste) Sahara

said [sed] pt, pp of **say**

sail [seɪl] n Segel nt; (*trip*) Fahrt f ♦ vt segeln ♦ vi segeln; (*begin voyage: person*) abfahren; (: *ship*) auslaufen; (*fig: cloud etc*) dahinsegeln; **to go for a ~** segeln gehen; **they ~ed into Copenhagen** sie liefen in Kopenhagen ein; **~ through** vt fus, vi (*fig*) (es) spielend schaffen; **~boat** (US) n Segelboot nt; **~ing** n Segeln nt; **~ing ship** n Segelschiff nt; **~or** n Matrose m, Seemann m

saint [seɪnt] *n* Heilige(r) *mf*; **~ly** *adj* heilig, fromm

sake [seɪk] *n*: **for the ~ of** um +*gen* willen

salad ['sæləd] *n* Salat *m*; **~ bowl** *n* Salatschüssel *f*; **~ cream** (*BRIT*) *n* Salatmayonnaise *f*, Salatmajonäse *f*; **~ dressing** *n* Salatsoße *f*

salary ['sælərɪ] *n* Gehalt *nt*

sale [seɪl] *n* Verkauf *m*; (*reduced prices*) Schlussverkauf *m*; **"for ~"** „zu verkaufen"; **on ~** zu verkaufen; **~room** *n* Verkaufsraum *m*; **~s assistant** *n* Verkäufer(in) *m(f)*; **~s clerk** (*US*) *n* Verkäufer(in) *m(f)*; **~sman** (*irreg*) *n* Verkäufer *m*; (*representative*) Vertreter *m*; **~s rep** *n* (*COMM*) Vertreter(in) *m(f)*; **~swoman** (*irreg*) *n* Verkäuferin *f*

salient ['seɪlɪənt] *adj* bemerkenswert

saliva [sə'laɪvə] *n* Speichel *m*

sallow ['sæləʊ] *adj* fahl; (*face*) bleich

salmon ['sæmən] *n* Lachs *m*

salon ['sælɒn] *n* Salon *m*

saloon [sə'luːn] *n* (*BRIT AUT*) Limousine *f*; (*ship's lounge*) Salon *m*; **~ car** (*BRIT*) *n* Limousine *f*

salt [sɔːlt] *n* Salz *nt* ♦ *vt* (*cure*) einsalzen; (*flavour*) salzen; **~cellar** *n* Salzfass *nt*; **~water** *adj* Salzwasser-; **~y** *adj* salzig

salute [sə'luːt] *n* (*MIL*) Gruß *m*; (*with guns*) Salutschüsse *pl* ♦ *vt* (*MIL*) salutieren

salvage ['sælvɪdʒ] *n* (*from ship*) Bergung *f*; (*property*) Rettung *f* ♦ *vt* bergen; retten

salvation [sæl'veɪʃən] *n* Rettung *f*; **S~ Army** *n* Heilsarmee *f*

same [seɪm] *adj, pron* (*similar*) gleiche(r, s); (*identical*) derselbe/dieselbe/dasselbe; **the ~ book as** das gleiche Buch wie; **at the ~ time** zur gleichen Zeit, gleichzeitig; (*however*) zugleich, andererseits; **all** *or* **just the ~** trotzdem; **the ~ to you!** gleichfalls!; **to do the ~ (as sb)** das Gleiche tun (wie jd)

sample ['sɑːmpl] *n* Probe *f* ♦ *vt* probieren

sanctify ['sæŋktɪfaɪ] *vt* weihen

sanctimonious [sæŋktɪ'məʊnɪəs] *adj* scheinheilig

sanction ['sæŋkʃən] *n* Sanktion *f*

sanctity ['sæŋktɪtɪ] *n* Heiligkeit *f*; (*fig*) Unverletzlichkeit *f*

sanctuary ['sæŋktjʊərɪ] *n* (*for fugitive*) Asyl *nt*; (*refuge*) Zufluchtsort *m*; (*for animals*) Schutzgebiet *nt*

sand [sænd] *n* Sand *m* ♦ *vt* (*furniture*) schmirgeln

sandal ['sændl] *n* Sandale *f*

sand: ~box (*US*) *n* = **sandpit**; **~castle** *n* Sandburg *f*; **~ dune** *n* (Sand)düne *f*; **~paper** *n* Sandpapier *nt*; **~pit** *n* Sandkasten *m*; **~stone** *n* Sandstein *m*

sandwich ['sændwɪtʃ] *n* Sandwich *m or nt* ♦ *vt* (*also*: **~ in**) einklemmen; **cheese / ham ~** Käse-/Schinkenbrot; **~ed between** eingeklemmt zwischen; **~ board** *n* Reklametafel *f*; **~ course** (*BRIT*) *n* Theorie und Praxis abwechselnde(r) Ausbildungsgang *m*

sandy ['sændɪ] *adj* sandig; (*hair*) rotblond

sane [seɪn] *adj* geistig gesund *or* normal; (*sensible*) vernünftig, gescheit

sang [sæŋ] *pt of* **sing**

sanitary ['sænɪtərɪ] *adj* hygienisch; **~ towel** *n* (Monats)binde *f*

sanitation [sænɪ'teɪʃən] *n* sanitäre Einrichtungen *pl*; **~ department** (*US*) *n* Stadtreinigung *f*

sanity ['sænɪtɪ] *n* geistige Gesundheit *f*; (*sense*) Vernunft *f*

sank [sæŋk] *pt of* **sink**

Santa Claus [sæntə'klɔːz] *n* Nikolaus *m*, Weihnachtsmann *m*

sap [sæp] *n* (*of plants*) Saft *m* ♦ *vt* (*strength*) schwächen

sapling ['sæplɪŋ] *n* junge(r) Baum *m*

sapphire ['sæfaɪə] *n* Saphir *m*

sarcasm ['sɑːkæzm] *n* Sarkasmus *m*

sarcastic [sɑː'kæstɪk] *adj* sarkastisch

sardine [sɑː'diːn] *n* Sardine *f*

Sardinia [sɑː'dɪnɪə] *n* Sardinien *nt*

sardonic [sɑː'dɒnɪk] *adj* zynisch

sash [sæʃ] *n* Schärpe *f*

sat [sæt] *pt, pp of* **sit**

Satan ['seɪtn] *n* Satan *m*

satchel ['sætʃl] *n* (*for school*) Schulmappe *f*

satellite ['sætəlaɪt] *n* Satellit *m*; **~ dish** *n* (*TECH*) Parabolantenne *f*, Satellitenantenne f; **~ television** n Satellitenfernsehen nt

satisfaction [sætɪsˈfækʃən] n Befriedigung f, Genugtuung f; **satisfactory** [sætɪsˈfæktərɪ] adj zufrieden stellend, befriedigend; **satisfied** adj befriedigt

satisfy [ˈsætɪsfaɪ] vt befriedigen, zufrieden stellen; (convince) überzeugen; (conditions) erfüllen; **~ing** adj befriedigend; (meal) sättigend

saturate [ˈsætʃəreɪt] vt (durch)tränken

Saturday [ˈsætədɪ] n Samstag m, Sonnabend m

sauce [sɔːs] n Soße f, Sauce f; **~pan** n Kasserolle f

saucer [ˈsɔːsəʳ] n Untertasse f

saucy [ˈsɔːsɪ] adj frech, keck

Saudi [ˈsaudɪ]: **~ Arabia** n Saudi-Arabien nt; **~ (Arabian)** adj saudi-arabisch ♦ n Saudi-Araber(in) m(f)

sauna [ˈsɔːnə] n Sauna f

saunter [ˈsɔːntəʳ] vi schlendern

sausage [ˈsɔːsɪdʒ] n Wurst f; **~ roll** n Wurst f im Schlafrock, Wurstpastete f

sauté [ˈsəuteɪ] adj Röst-

savage [ˈsævɪdʒ] adj wild ♦ n Wilde(r) mf ♦ vt (animals) zerfleischen

save [seɪv] vt retten; (money, electricity etc) sparen; (strength etc) aufsparen; (COMPUT) speichern ♦ vi (also: **~ up**) sparen ♦ n (SPORT) (Ball)abwehr f ♦ prep, conj außer, ausgenommen

saving [ˈseɪvɪŋ] adj: **the ~ grace of** das Versöhnende an +dat ♦ n Sparen nt, Ersparnis f; **~s** npl (money) Ersparnisse pl; **~s account** n Sparkonto nt; **~s bank** n Sparkasse f

saviour [ˈseɪvjəʳ] (US **savior**) n (REL) Erlöser m

savour [ˈseɪvəʳ] (US **savor**) vt (taste) schmecken; (fig) genießen; **~y** adj pikant, würzig

saw [sɔː] (pt **sawed**, pp **sawed** or **sawn**) pt of **see** ♦ n (tool) Säge f ♦ vt, vi sägen; **~dust** n Sägemehl nt; **~mill** n Sägewerk nt; **~n** pp of **saw**; **~n-off shotgun** n Gewehr nt mit abgesägtem Lauf

sax [sæks] (inf) n Saxofon nt, Saxophon nt

saxophone [ˈsæksəfəun] n Saxofon nt, Saxophon nt

say [seɪ] (pt, pp **said**) n: **to have a/no ~ in sth** Mitspracherecht/kein Mitspracherecht bei etw haben ♦ vt, vi sagen; **let him have his ~** lass ihn doch reden; **to ~ yes/no** Ja/Nein or ja/nein sagen; **that goes without ~ing** das versteht sich von selbst; **that is to ~** das heißt; **~ing** n Sprichwort nt

scab [skæb] n Schorf m; (pej) Streikbrecher m

scaffold [ˈskæfəld] n (for execution) Schafott nt; **~ing** n (Bau)gerüst nt

scald [skɔːld] n Verbrühung f ♦ vt (burn) verbrühen

scale [skeɪl] n (of fish) Schuppe f; (MUS) Tonleiter f; (on map, size) Maßstab m; (gradation) Skala f ♦ vt (climb) erklimmen; **~s** npl (balance) Waage f; **on a large ~** (fig) im Großen, in großem Umfang; **~ of charges** Gebührenordnung f; **~ down** vt verkleinern; **~ model** n maßstabgetreue(s) Modell nt

scallop [ˈskɔləp] n Kammmuschel f

scalp [skælp] n Kopfhaut f

scamper [ˈskæmpəʳ] vi: **to ~ away** or **off** sich davonmachen

scampi [ˈskæmpɪ] npl Scampi pl

scan [skæn] vt (examine) genau prüfen; (quickly) überfliegen; (horizon) absuchen

scandal [ˈskændl] n Skandal m; (piece of gossip) Skandalgeschichte f

Scandinavia [skændɪˈneɪvɪə] n Skandinavien nt; **~n** adj skandinavisch ♦ n Skandinavier(in) m(f)

scant [skænt] adj knapp; **~ily** adv knapp, dürftig; **~y** adj knapp, unzureichend

scapegoat [ˈskeɪpgəut] n Sündenbock m

scar [skɑːʳ] n Narbe f ♦ vt durch Narben entstellen

scarce [skɛəs] adj selten, rar; (goods) knapp; **~ly** adv kaum; **scarcity** n Mangel m

scare [skɛəʳ] n Schrecken m ♦ vt erschrecken; **bomb ~** Bombendrohung f; **to ~ sb stiff** jdn zu Tode erschrecken; **to be ~d** Angst haben; **~ away** vt (animal) verscheuchen; **~ off** vt = **scare away**;

Saxophon nt

~crow n Vogelscheuche f
scarf [skɑːf] (pl **scarves**) n Schal m; (headscarf) Kopftuch nt
scarlet ['skɑːlɪt] adj scharlachrot ♦ n Scharlachrot nt; **~ fever** n Scharlach m
scarves [skɑːvz] npl of **scarf**
scary ['skɛərɪ] (inf) adj schaurig
scathing ['skeɪðɪŋ] adj scharf, vernichtend
scatter ['skætər] vt (sprinkle) (ver)streuen; (disperse) zerstreuen ♦ vi sich zerstreuen; **~brained** adj flatterhaft, schusselig
scavenger ['skævəndʒər] n (animal) Aasfresser m
scenario [sɪ'nɑːrɪəu] n (THEAT, CINE) Szenarium nt; (fig) Szenario nt
scene [siːn] n (of happening) Ort m; (of play, incident) Szene f; (view) Anblick m; (argument) Szene f, Auftritt m; **~ry** ['siːnərɪ] n (THEAT) Bühnenbild nt; (landscape) Landschaft f
scenic ['siːnɪk] adj landschaftlich
scent [sent] n Parfüm nt; (smell) Duft m ♦ vt parfumieren
sceptical ['skeptɪkl] (US **skeptical**) adj skeptisch
schedule ['ʃedjuːl, (US) 'skedʒuːl] n (list) Liste f; (plan) Programm nt; (of work) Zeitplan m ♦ vt planen; **on ~** pünktlich; **to be ahead of/behind ~** dem Zeitplan voraus/im Rückstand sein; **~d flight** n (not charter) Linienflug m
scheme [skiːm] n Schema nt; (dishonest) Intrige f; (plan of action) Plan m ♦ vi intrigieren ♦ vt planen; **scheming** ['skiːmɪŋ] adj intrigierend
scholar ['skɒlər] n Gelehrte(r) m; (holding ~ship) Stipendiat m; **~ly** adj gelehrt; **~ship** n Gelehrsamkeit f; (grant) Stipendium nt
school [skuːl] n Schule f; (UNIV) Fakultät f ♦ vt schulen; **~ age** n schulpflichtige(s) Alter nt; **~book** n Schulbuch nt; **~boy** n Schüler m; **~children** npl Schüler pl, Schulkinder pl; **~days** npl (alte) Schulzeit f; **~girl** n Schülerin f; **~ing** n Schulung f, Ausbildung f; **~master** n Lehrer m; **~mistress** n Lehrerin f; **~teacher** n Lehrer(in) m(f)

sciatica [saɪ'ætɪkə] n Ischias m or nt
science ['saɪəns] n Wissenschaft f; (natural ~) Naturwissenschaft f; **~ fiction** n Sciencefiction f; **scientific** [saɪən'tɪfɪk] adj wissenschaftlich; (natural ~s) naturwissenschaftlich; **scientist** ['saɪəntɪst] n Wissenschaftler(in) m(f)
scintillating ['sɪntɪleɪtɪŋ] adj sprühend
scissors ['sɪzəz] npl Schere f; **a pair of ~** eine Schere
scoff [skɒf] vt (BRIT: inf: eat) fressen ♦ vi (mock): **to ~ (at)** spotten (über +acc)
scold [skəuld] vt schimpfen
scone [skɒn] n weiche(s) Teegebäck nt
scoop [skuːp] n Schaufel f; (news) sensationelle Erstmeldung f; **~ out** vt herausschaufeln; **~ up** vt aufschaufeln; (liquid) aufschöpfen
scooter ['skuːtər] n Motorroller m; (child's) Roller m
scope [skəup] n Ausmaß nt; (opportunity) (Spiel)raum m
scorch [skɔːtʃ] n Brandstelle f ♦ vt versengen; **~ing** adj brennend
score [skɔːr] n (in game) Punktzahl f; (final ~) (Spiel)ergebnis nt; (MUS) Partitur f; (line) Kratzer m; (twenty) zwanzig, zwanzig Stück ♦ vt (goal) schießen; (points) machen; (mark) einritzen ♦ vi (keep record) Punkte zählen; **on that ~** in dieser Hinsicht; **what's the ~?** wie stehts?; **to ~ 6 out of 10** 6 von 10 Punkten erzielen; **~ out** vt ausstreichen; **~board** n Anschreibetafel f; **~r** n Torschütze m; (recorder) (Auf)schreiber m
scorn [skɔːn] n Verachtung f ♦ vt verhöhnen; **~ful** adj verächtlich
Scorpio ['skɔːpɪəu] n Skorpion m
Scot [skɒt] n Schotte m, Schottin f
Scotch [skɒtʃ] n Scotch m
scotch [skɒtʃ] vt (end) unterbinden
scot-free ['skɒt'friː] adv: **to get off ~~~** (unpunished) ungeschoren davonkommen
Scotland ['skɒtlənd] n Schottland nt
Scots [skɒts] adj schottisch; **~man/woman** (irreg) n Schotte m/Schottin f
Scottish ['skɒtɪʃ] adj schottisch

scoundrel ['skaundrl] *n* Schuft *m*

scour ['skauəʳ] *vt* (*search*) absuchen; (*clean*) schrubben

scourge [skə:dʒ] *n* (*whip*) Geißel *f*; (*plague*) Qual *f*

scout [skaut] *n* (*MIL*) Späher *m*; (*also:* **boy ~**) Pfadfinder *m*; **~ around** *vi*: **to ~ around (for)** sich umsehen (nach)

scowl [skaul] *n* finstere(r) Blick *m* ♦ *vi* finster blicken

scrabble ['skræbl] *vi* (*also:* **~ around**: *search*) (herum)tasten; (*claw*): **to ~ (at)** kratzen (an +*dat*) ♦ *n*: **S~** ® Scrabble *nt* ®

scraggy ['skrægɪ] *adj* dürr, hager

scram [skræm] (*inf*) *vi* abhauen

scramble ['skræmbl] *n* (*climb*) Kletterei *f*; (*struggle*) Kampf *m* ♦ *vi* klettern; (*fight*) sich schlagen; **to ~ out/through** krabbeln aus/ durch; **to ~ for sth** sich um etw raufen; **~d eggs** *npl* Rührei *nt*

scrap [skræp] *n* (*bit*) Stückchen *nt*; (*fight*) Keilerei *f*; (*also:* **~ iron**) Schrott *m* ♦ *vt* verwerfen ♦ *vi* (*fight*) streiten, sich prügeln; **~s** *npl* (*leftovers*) Reste *pl*; (*waste*) Abfall *m*; **~book** *n* Einklebealbum *nt*; **~ dealer** *n* Schrotthändler(in) *m(f)*

scrape [skreɪp] *n* Kratzen *nt*; (*trouble*) Klemme *f* ♦ *vt* kratzen; (*car*) zerkratzen; (*clean*) abkratzen ♦ *vi* (*make harsh noise*) kratzen; **to ~ through** gerade noch durchkommen; **~r** *n* Kratzer *m*

scrap: **~ heap** *n* Schrotthaufen *m*; **on the ~ heap** (*fig*) beim alten Eisen; **~ iron** *n* Schrott *m*; **~ merchant** (*BRIT*) *n* Altwarenhändler(in) *m(f)*; **~ paper** *n* Schmierpapier *nt*

scrappy ['skræpɪ] *adj* zusammengestoppelt

scratch [skrætʃ] *n* (*wound*) Kratzer *m*, Schramme *f* ♦ *adj*: **~ team** zusammengewürfelte Mannschaft ♦ *vt* kratzen; (*car*) zerkratzen ♦ *vi* (sich) kratzen; **to start from ~** ganz von vorne anfangen; **to be up to ~** den Anforderungen entsprechen

scrawl [skrɔ:l] *n* Gekritzel *nt* ♦ *vt, vi* kritzeln

scrawny ['skrɔ:nɪ] *adj* (*person, neck*) dürr

scream [skri:m] *n* Schrei *m* ♦ *vi* schreien

scree [skri:] *n* Geröll(halde *f*) *nt*

screech [skri:tʃ] *n* Schrei *m* ♦ *vi* kreischen

screen [skri:n] *n* (*protective*) Schutzschirm *m*; (*CINE*) Leinwand *f*; (*TV*) Bildschirm *m* ♦ *vt* (*shelter*) (be)schirmen; (*film*) zeigen, vorführen; **~ing** *n* (*MED*) Untersuchung *f*; **~play** *n* Drehbuch *nt*; **~ saver** *n* (*COMPUT*) Bildschirmschoner *m*

screw [skru:] *n* Schraube *f* ♦ *vt* (*fasten*) schrauben; (*vulgar*) bumsen; **~ up** *vt* (*paper etc*) zerknüllen; (*inf: ruin*) vermasseln (*inf*); **~driver** *n* Schraubenzieher *m*

scribble ['skrɪbl] *n* Gekritzel *nt* ♦ *vt* kritzeln

script [skrɪpt] *n* (*handwriting*) Handschrift *f*; (*for film*) Drehbuch *nt*; (*THEAT*) Manuskript *nt*, Text *m*

Scripture ['skrɪptʃəʳ] *n* Heilige Schrift *f*

scroll [skrəul] *n* Schriftrolle *f*

scrounge [skraundʒ] (*inf*) *vt*: **to ~ sth off** *or* **from sb** etw bei jdm abstauben ♦ *n*: **on the ~** beim Schnorren

scrub [skrʌb] *n* (*clean*) Schrubben *nt*; (*in countryside*) Gestrüpp *nt* ♦ *vt* (*clean*) schrubben

scruff [skrʌf] *n*: **by the ~ of the neck** am Genick

scruffy ['skrʌfɪ] *adj* unordentlich, vergammelt

scrum(mage) ['skrʌm(ɪdʒ)] *n* Getümmel *nt*

scruple ['skru:pl] *n* Skrupel *m*, Bedenken *nt*

scrupulous ['skru:pjuləs] *adj* peinlich genau, gewissenhaft

scrutinize ['skru:tɪnaɪz] *vt* genau prüfen; **scrutiny** ['skru:tɪnɪ] *n* genaue Untersuchung *f*

scuff [skʌf] *vt* (*shoes*) abstoßen

scuffle ['skʌfl] *n* Handgemenge *nt*

sculptor ['skʌlptəʳ] *n* Bildhauer(in) *m(f)*

sculpture ['skʌlptʃəʳ] *n* (*ART*) Bildhauerei *f*; (*statue*) Skulptur *f*

scum [skʌm] *n* (*also fig*) Abschaum *m*

scurry ['skʌrɪ] *vi* huschen

scuttle ['skʌtl] *n* (*also:* **coal ~**) Kohleneimer *m* ♦ *vt* (*ship*) versenken ♦ *vi* (*scamper*): **to ~ away** *or* **off** sich davonmachen

scythe [saɪð] *n* Sense *f*

SDP (*BRIT*) *n abbr* = **Social Democratic**

Party

sea[si:] n Meer nt, See f; (fig) Meer nt ♦ adj
Meeres-, See-; **by ~** (travel) auf dem
Seeweg; **on the ~** (boat) auf dem Meer;
(town) am Meer; **out to ~** aufs Meer
hinaus; **out at ~** aufs Meer; **~board**n
Küste f; **~food**n Meeresfrüchte pl; **~ front**
n Strandpromenade f; **~going**adj
seetüchtig, Hochsee-; **~gull**n Möwe f
seal[si:l] n (animal) Robbe f, Seehund m;
(stamp, impression) Siegel nt ♦ vt versiegeln;
~ offvt (place) abriegeln
sea leveln Meeresspiegel m
sea lionn Seelöwe m
seam[si:m] n Saum m; (edges joining) Naht
f; (of coal) Flöz nt
seaman[si:mən] n (irreg) n Seemann m
seaplane[si:pleɪn] n Wasserflugzeug nt
seaport[si:pɔ:t] n Seehafen m
search[sə:tʃ] n (for person, thing) Suche f; (of
drawer, pockets, house) Durchsuchung f ♦ vi
suchen ♦ vt durchsuchen; **in ~ of** auf der
Suche nach, **to ~ for** suchen nach; **~
through**vt durchsuchen; **~ engine**n
(COMPUT) Suchmaschine f; **~ing**adj (look)
forschend; **~light**n Scheinwerfer m; **~
party**n Suchmannschaft f; **~ warrant**n
Durchsuchungsbefehl m
sea: ~shore[si:ʃɔ:] n Meeresküste f; **~sick**
[si:sɪk] adj seekrank; **~side**[si:saɪd] n Küste
f; **~side resort**n Badeort m
season[si:zn] n Jahreszeit f; (Christmas etc)
Zeit f, Saison f ♦ vt (flavour) würzen; **~al**adj
Saison-; **~ed**adj (fig) erfahren; **~ing**n
Gewürz nt, Würze f; **~ ticket**n (RAIL)
Zeitkarte f; (THEAT) Abonnement nt
seat[si:t] n Sitz m, Platz m; (in Parliament)
Sitz m; (part of body) Gesäß nt; (of trousers)
Hosenboden m ♦ vt (place) setzen; (have
space for) Sitzplätze bieten für; **to be ~ed**
sitzen; **~ belt**n Sicherheitsgurt m
sea: ~ watern Meerwasser nt; **~weed**
[si:wi:d] n (See)tang m; **~worthy**[si:wə:ðɪ]
adj seetüchtig
sec.abbr (= second(s)) Sek.
scluded[sɪklu:dɪd] adj abgelegen
seclusion[sɪklu:ʒən] n Zurückgezogenheit f

second[sekənd] adj zweite(r,s) ♦ adv (in ~
position) an zweiter Stelle ♦ n Sekunde f;
(person) Zweite(r) mf; (COMM: imperfect)
zweite Wahl f; (SPORT) Sekundant m; (AUT:
also: ~ gear) zweite(r) Gang m; (BRIT: UNIV:
degree) mittlere Note bei
Abschlussprüfungen ♦ vt (support)
unterstützen; **~ary**adj zweitrangig; **~ary
school**n höhere Schule f, Mittelschule f;
~classadj zweiter Klasse; **~hand**adj aus
zweiter Hand; (car etc) gebraucht; **~ hand**
n (on clock) Sekundenzeiger m; **~ly**adv
zweitens
secondment[sɪkɒndmənt] (BRIT) n
Abordnung f
second-rate[sekənd reɪt] adj mittelmäßig
second thoughtsnpl: **to have ~** es sich
dat anders überlegen; **on ~** (BRIT) or
thought (US) oder lieber (nicht)
secrecy[si:krəsɪ] n Geheimhaltung f
secret[si:krɪt] n Geheimnis nt ♦ adj geheim,
Geheim-; **In ~** geheim
secretarial[sekriteəriəl] adj Sekretärinnen-
secretary[sekrətəri] n Sekretär(in) m(f); **S~
of State**(BRIT) n (POL): **S~ of State (for)**
Minister(in) m(f) (für)
secretion[sɪkri:ʃən] n Absonderung f
secretive[si:krətɪv] adj geheimtuerisch
secretly[si:krɪtlɪ] adv geheim
sectarian[sekteəriən] adj (riots etc)
Konfessions-, zwischen den Konfessionen
section[sekʃən] n Teil m; (department)
Abteilung f; (of document) Abschnitt m
sector[sektə*] n Sektor m
secular[sekjulə*] adj weltlich, profan
secure[sɪkjuə*] adj (safe) sicher; (firmly fixed)
fest ♦ vt (make firm) befestigen, sichern;
(obtain) sichern; **security**[sɪkjuərɪtɪ] n Sicherheit f; (pledge) Pfand nt; (document) Wertpapier nt; (national security) Staatssicherheit f;
security guardn Sicherheitsbeamte(r)
m, Wächter m, Wache f
sedan[sədæn] (US) n (AUT) Limousine f
sedate[sɪdeɪt] adj gesetzt ♦ vt (MED) ein
Beruhigungsmittel geben +dat; **sedation**
[sɪdeɪʃən] n (MED) Einfluss m von
Beruhigungsmitteln; **sedative**[sedɪtɪv] n

Beruhigungsmittel *nt* ♦ *adj* beruhigend, einschläfernd

sediment ['sɛdɪmənt] *n* (Boden)satz *m*

seduce [sɪ'djuːs] *vt* verführen; **seductive** [sɪ'dʌktɪv] *adj* verführerisch

see [siː] (*pt* **saw**, *pp* **seen**) *vt* sehen; (*understand*) (ein)sehen, erkennen; (*visit*) besuchen ♦ *vi* (*be aware*) sehen; (*find out*) nachsehen ♦ *n* (*ECCL: R.C.*) Bistum *nt*; (: *Protestant*) Kirchenkreis *m*; **to ~ sb to the door** jdn hinausbegleiten; **to ~ that** (*ensure*) dafür sorgen, dass; ~ **you soon!** bis bald!; ~ **about** *vt fus* sich kümmern um; ~ **off** *vt*: **to ~ sb off** jdn zum Zug *etc* begleiten; ~ **through** *vt*: **to ~ sth through** etw durchfechten; **to ~ through sb/sth** jdn/ etw durchschauen; ~ **to** *vt fus*: **to ~ to it** dafür sorgen

seed [siːd] *n* Samen *m* ♦ *vt* (*TENNIS*) platzieren; **to go to ~** (*plant*) schießen; (*fig*) herunterkommen; **~ling** *n* Setzling *m*; **~y** *adj* (*café*) übel; (*person*) zweifelhaft

seeing ['siːɪŋ] *conj*: ~ **(that)** da

seek [siːk] (*pt*, *pp* **sought**) *vt* suchen

seem [siːm] *vi* scheinen; **it ~s that ...** es scheint, dass ...; **~ingly** *adv* anscheinend

seen [siːn] *pp* of **see**

seep [siːp] *vi* sickern

seesaw ['siːsɔː] *n* Wippe *f*

seethe [siːð] *vi*: **to ~ with anger** vor Wut kochen

see-through ['siːθruː] *adj* (*dress etc*) durchsichtig

segment ['sɛgmənt] *n* Teil *m*; (*of circle*) Ausschnitt *m*

segregate ['sɛgrɪgeɪt] *vt* trennen

seize [siːz] *vt* (*grasp*) (er)greifen, packen; (*power*) ergreifen; (*take legally*) beschlagnahmen; ~ **(up)on** *vt fus* sich stürzen auf +*acc*; ~ **up** *vi* (*TECH*) sich festfressen; **seizure** ['siːʒəʳ] *n* (*illness*) Anfall *m*

seldom ['sɛldəm] *adv* selten

select [sɪ'lɛkt] *adj* ausgewählt ♦ *vt* auswählen; **~ion** [sɪ'lɛkʃən] *n* Auswahl *f*; **~ive** *adj* (*person*) wählerisch

self [sɛlf] (*pl* **selves**) *pron* selbst ♦ *n* Selbst

nt, Ich *nt*; **the ~** das Ich; **~-assured** *adj* selbstbewusst; **~-catering** (*BRIT*) *adj* für Selbstversorger; **~-centred** (*US* **self-centered**) *adj* egozentrisch; **~-coloured** (*US* **self-colored**) *adj* (*of one colour*) einfarbig, uni; **~-confidence** *n* Selbstvertrauen *nt*, Selbstbewusstsein *nt*; **~-conscious** *adj* gehemmt, befangen; **~-contained** *adj* (*complete*) (in sich) geschlossen; (*person*) verschlossen; (*BRIT: flat*) separat; **~-control** *n* Selbstbeherrschung *f*; **~-defence** (*US* **self-defense**) *n* Selbstverteidigung *f*; (*JUR*) Notwehr *f*; **~-discipline** *n* Selbstdisziplin *f*; **~-employed** *adj* frei(schaffend); **~-evident** *adj* offensichtlich; **~-governing** *adj* selbst verwaltet; **~-indulgent** *adj* zügellos; **~-interest** *n* Eigennutz *m*

selfish ['sɛlfɪʃ] *adj* egoistisch, selbstsüchtig; **~ness** *n* Egoismus *m*, Selbstsucht *f*

self: **~lessly** *adv* selbstlos; **~-made** *adj*: **~-made man** Selfmademan *m*; **~-pity** *n* Selbstmitleid *nt*; **~-portrait** *n* Selbstbildnis *nt*; **~-possessed** *adj* selbstbeherrscht; **~-preservation** *n* Selbsterhaltung *f*; **~-reliant** *adj* unabhängig; **~-respect** *n* Selbstachtung *f*; **~-righteous** *adj* selbstgerecht; **~-sacrifice** *n* Selbstaufopferung *f*; **~-satisfied** *adj* selbstzufrieden; **~-service** *adj* Selbstbedienungs-; **~-sufficient** *adj* selbstgenügsam; **~-taught** *adj* selbst erlernt; **~-taught person** Autodidakt *m*

sell [sɛl] (*pt*, *pp* **sold**) *vt* verkaufen ♦ *vi* verkaufen; (*goods*) sich verkaufen; **to ~ at** *or* **for £10** für £10 verkaufen; ~ **off** *vt* verkaufen; ~ **out** *vi* alles verkaufen; **~-by date** *n* Verfalldatum *nt*; **~er** *n* Verkäufer *m*; **~ing price** *n* Verkaufspreis *m*

Sellotape ['sɛləʊteɪp] (® *BRIT*) *n* Tesafilm *m* ®

sellout ['sɛlaʊt] *n* (*of tickets*): **it was a ~** es war ausverkauft

selves [sɛlvz] *npl* of **self**

semaphore ['sɛməfɔː] *n* Winkzeichen *pl*

semblance ['sɛmblns] *n* Anschein *m*

semen ['siːmən] *n* Sperma *nt*

semester [sɪ'mestə'] (US) n Semester nt

semi ['semɪ] n = **semidetached house**; **~circle** n Halbkreis m; **~colon** n Semikolon nt; **~conductor** n Halbleiter m; **~detached house** (BRIT) n halbe(s) Doppelhaus nt; **~final** n Halbfinale nt

seminary ['semɪnərɪ] n (REL) Priesterseminar nt

semiskilled [semɪ'skɪld] adj angelernt

semi-skimmed [semɪ'skɪmd] adj (milk) teilentrahmt, Halbfett-

senate ['senɪt] n Senat m; **senator** n Senator m

send [send] (pt, pp sent) vt senden, schicken; (inf: inspire) hinreißen; **~ away** vt wegschicken; **~ away for** vt fus anfordern; **~ back** vt zurückschicken; **~ for** vt fus holen lassen; **~ off** vt (goods) abschicken; (BRIT: SPORT: player) vom Feld schicken; **~ out** vt (invitation) aussenden; **~ up** vt hinaufsenden; (BRIT: parody) verulken; **~er** n Absender m; **~-off** n: **to give sb a good ~-off** jdn (ganz) groß verabschieden

senior ['si:nɪə'] adj (older) älter; (higher rank) Ober- ♦ n (older person) Ältere(r) mf; (higher ranking) Rangälteste(r) mf; **~ citizen** n ältere(r) Mitbürger(in) m(f); **~ity** [si:nɪ'ɔrɪtɪ] n (of age) höhere(s) Alter nt; (in rank) höhere(r) Dienstgrad m

sensation [sen'seɪʃən] n Gefühl nt; (excitement) Sensation f, Aufsehen nt; **~al** adj (wonderful) wunderbar; (result) sensationell; (headlines etc) reißerisch

sense [sens] n Sinn m; (understanding) Verstand m, Vernunft f; (feeling) Gefühl nt ♦ vt fühlen, spüren; **~ of humour** Humor m; **to make ~** Sinn ergeben; **~less** adj sinnlos; (unconscious) besinnungslos

sensibility [sensɪ'bɪlɪtɪ] n Empfindsamkeit f; (feeling hurt) Empfindlichkeit f; **sensibilities** npl (feelings) Zartgefühl nt

sensible ['sensɪbl] adj vernünftig

sensitive ['sensɪtɪv] adj: **~ (to)** empfindlich (gegen); **sensitivity** [sensɪ'tɪvɪtɪ] n Empfindlichkeit f; (artistic) Feingefühl nt; (tact) Feinfühligkeit f

sensual ['sensjuəl] adj sinnlich

sensuous ['sensjuəs] adj sinnlich

sent [sent] pt, pp of **send**

sentence ['sentns] n Satz m; (JUR) Strafe f; Urteil nt ♦ vt: **to ~ sb to death/to 5 years** jdn zum Tode/zu 5 Jahren verurteilen

sentiment ['sentɪmənt] n Gefühl nt; (thought) Gedanke m; **~al** [sentɪ'mentl] adj sentimental; (of feelings rather than reason) gefühlsmäßig

sentry ['sentrɪ] n (Schild)wache f

separate [adj 'seprɪt, vb 'sepəreɪt] adj getrennt, separat ♦ vt trennen ♦ vi sich trennen; **~ly** adv getrennt; **~s** npl (clothes) Röcke, Pullover etc; **separation** [sepə'reɪʃən] n Trennung f

September [sep'tembə'] n September m

septic ['septɪk] adj vereitert, septisch; **~ tank** n Klärbehälter m

sequel ['si:kwl] n Folge f

sequence ['si:kwəns] n (Reihen)folge f

sequin ['si:kwɪn] n Paillette f

Serbia ['sə:bɪə] n Serbien nt

serene [sɪ'ri:n] adj heiter

sergeant ['sɑ:dʒənt] n Feldwebel m; (POLICE) (Polizei)wachtmeister m

serial ['sɪərɪəl] n Fortsetzungsroman m; (TV) Fernsehserie f ♦ adj (number) (fort)laufend; **~ize** vt in Fortsetzungen veröffentlichen; in Fortsetzungen senden

series ['sɪərɪz] n inv Serie f, Reihe f

serious ['sɪərɪəs] adj ernst; (injury) schwer; **~ly** adv ernst(haft); (hurt) schwer; **~ness** n Ernst m, Ernsthaftigkeit f

sermon ['sə:mən] n Predigt f

serrated [sɪ'reɪtɪd] adj gezackt

servant ['sə:vənt] n Diener(in) m(f)

serve [sə:v] vt dienen +dat; (guest, customer) bedienen; (food) servieren ♦ vi dienen, nützen; (at table) servieren; (TENNIS) geben, aufschlagen; **it ~s him right** das geschieht ihm recht; **that'll ~ as a table** das geht als Tisch; **to ~ a summons (on sb)** (jdn) vor Gericht laden; **~ out** or **up** vt (food) auftragen, servieren

service ['sə:vɪs] n (help) Dienst m; (trains etc) Verbindung f; (hotel) Service m, Bedienung f; (set of dishes) Service nt; (REL)

Gottesdienst *m*; (*car*) Inspektion *f*; (*for TVs etc*) Kundendienst *m*; (*TENNIS*) Aufschlag *m* ♦ *vt* (*AUT, TECH*) warten, überholen; **the S~s** *npl* (*armed forces*) die Streitkräfte *pl*; **to be of ~ to sb** jdm einen großen Dienst erweisen; **~ included/not included** Bedienung inbegriffen/nicht inbegriffen; **~able** *adj* brauchbar; **~ area** *n* (*on motorway*) Raststätte *f*; **~ charge** (*BRIT*) *n* Bedienung *f*; **~man** (*irreg*) *n* (*soldier etc*) Soldat *m*; **~ station** *n* (Groß)tankstelle *f*

serviette [sɔːvɪˈet] *n* Serviette *f*

servile [ˈsɔːvaɪl] *adj* unterwürfig

session [ˈseʃən] *n* Sitzung *f*; (*POL*) Sitzungsperiode *f*; **to be in ~** tagen

set [set] (*pt, pp* **set**) *n* (*collection of things*) Satz *m*, Set *nt*; (*RAD, TV*) Apparat *m*; (*TENNIS*) Satz *m*; (*group of people*) Kreis *m*; (*CINE*) Szene *f*; (*THEAT*) Bühnenbild *m* ♦ *adj* festgelegt; (*ready*) bereit ♦ *vt* (*place*) setzen, stellen, legen; (*arrange*) (an)ordnen; (*table*) decken; (*time, price*) festsetzen; (*alarm, watch, task*) stellen; (*jewels*) (ein)fassen; (*exam*) ausarbeiten ♦ *vi* (*sun*) untergehen; (*become hard*) fest werden; (*bone*) zusammenwachsen; **to be ~ on doing sth** etw unbedingt tun wollen; **to ~ to music** vertonen; **to ~ on fire** anstecken; **to ~ free** freilassen; **to ~ sth going** etw in Gang bringen; **to ~ sail** losfahren; **~ about** *vt fus* (*task*) anpacken; **~ aside** *vt* beiseite legen; **~ back** *vt*: **to ~ back (by)** zurückwerfen (um); **~ off** *vi* aufbrechen ♦ *vt* (*explode*) sprengen; (*alarm*) losgehen lassen; (*show up well*) hervorheben; **~ out** *vi*: **to ~ out to do sth** vorhaben, etw zu tun ♦ *vt* (*arrange*) anlegen, arrangieren; (*state*) darlegen; **~ up** *vt* (*organization*) aufziehen; (*record*) aufstellen; (*monument*) erstellen; **~back** *n* Rückschlag *m*; **~ meal** *n* Menü *nt*; **~ menu** *n* Tageskarte *f*

settee [seˈtiː] *n* Sofa *nt*

setting [ˈsetɪŋ] *n* Hintergrund *m*

settle [ˈsetl] *vt* ausgleichen; (*pay*) begleichen, bezahlen; (*agree*) regeln ♦ *vi* sich einleben; (*come to rest*) sich niederlassen; (*sink*) sich setzen; (*calm down*) sich beruhigen; **to ~ for**

sth sich mit etw zufrieden geben; **to ~ on** sth sich für etw entscheiden; **to ~ up with sb** mit jdm abrechnen; **~ down** *vi* (*feel at home*) sich einleben; (*calm down*) sich beruhigen; **~ in** *vi* sich eingewöhnen; **~ment** *n* Regelung *f*; (*payment*) Begleichung *f*; (*colony*) Siedlung *f*; **~r** *n* Siedler *m*

setup [ˈsetʌp] *n* (*situation*) Lage *f*

seven [ˈsevn] *num* sieben; **~teen** *num* siebzehn; **~th** *adj* siebte(r, s) ♦ *n* Siebtel *nt*; **~ty** *num* siebzig

sever [ˈsevəʳ] *vt* abtrennen

several [ˈsevərl] *adj* mehrere, verschiedene ♦ *pron* mehrere; **~ of us** einige von uns

severance [ˈsevərəns] *n*: **~ pay** Abfindung *f*

severe [sɪˈvɪəʳ] *adj* (*strict*) streng; (*serious*) schwer; (*climate*) rau; **severity** [sɪˈverɪtɪ] *n* Strenge *f*; Schwere *f*; Rauheit *f*

sew [səu] (*pt* **sewed**, *pp* **sewn**) *vt, vi* nähen; **~ up** *vt* zunähen

sewage [ˈsuːɪdʒ] *n* Abwässer *pl*

sewer [ˈsuːəʳ] *n* (Abwasser)kanal *m*

sewing [ˈsəuɪŋ] *n* Näharbeit *f*; **~ machine** *n* Nähmaschine *f*

sewn [səun] *pp* of **sew**

sex [seks] *n* Sex *m*; (*gender*) Geschlecht *nt*; **to have ~ with sb** mit jdm Geschlechtsverkehr haben; **~ism** *n* Sexismus *m*; **~ist** *adj* sexistisch ♦ *n* Sexist(in) *m(f)*; **~ual** [ˈseksjuəl] *adj* sexuell, geschlechtlich, Geschlechts-; **~uality** [seksjuˈælɪtɪ] *n* Sexualität *f*; **~y** *adj* sexy

shabby [ˈʃæbɪ] *adj* (*also fig*) schäbig

shack [ʃæk] *n* Hütte *f*

shackles [ˈʃæklz] *npl* (*also fig*) Fesseln *pl*, Ketten *pl*

shade [ʃeɪd] *n* Schatten *m*; (*for lamp*) Lampenschirm *m*; (*colour*) Farbton *m* ♦ *vt* abschirmen; **in the ~** im Schatten; **a ~ smaller** ein bisschen kleiner

shadow [ˈʃædəu] *n* Schatten *m* ♦ *vt* (*follow*) beschatten ♦ *adj*: **~ cabinet** (*BRIT: POL*) Schattenkabinett *nt*; **~y** *adj* schattig

shady [ˈʃeɪdɪ] *adj* schattig; (*fig*) zwielichtig

shaft [ʃɑːft] *n* (*of spear etc*) Schaft *m*; (*in mine*) Schacht *m*; (*TECH*) Welle *f*; (*of light*)

Strahl m

shaggy ['ʃægɪ] adj struppig

shake [ʃeɪk] (pt **shook**, pp **shaken**) vt schütteln, rütteln; (shock) erschüttern ♦ vi (move) schwanken; (tremble) zittern, beben ♦ n (jerk) Schütteln nt, Rütteln nt; **to ~ hands with** die Hand geben +dat; **to ~ one's head** den Kopf schütteln; ~ **off** vt abschütteln; ~ **up** vt aufschütteln; (fig) aufrütteln; **~n** ['ʃeɪkn] pp of **shake**; **shaky** ['ʃeɪkɪ] adj zittrig; (weak) unsicher

shall [ʃæl] vb aux: **I ~ go** ich werde gehen; ~ **I open the door?** soll ich die Tür öffnen?; **I'll buy some cake, ~ I?** soll ich Kuchen kaufen?, ich kaufe Kuchen, oder?

shallow ['ʃæləu] adj seicht

sham [ʃæm] n Schein m ♦ adj unecht, falsch

shambles ['ʃæmblz] n Durcheinander nt

shame [ʃeɪm] n Scham f; (disgrace, pity) Schande f ♦ vt beschamen; **it is a ~ that** es ist schade, dass; **it is a ~ to do ...** es ist eine Schande, ... zu tun; **what a ~!** eine Schande!; **~faced** adj beschämt; **~ful** adj schändlich; **~less** adj schamlos

shampoo [ʃæm'puː] n Shampoo(n) nt ♦ vt (hair) waschen; ~ **and set** n Waschen nt und Legen

shamrock ['ʃæmrɔk] n Kleeblatt nt

shandy ['ʃændɪ] n Bier nt mit Limonade

shan't [ʃɑːnt] = **shall not**

shantytown ['ʃæntɪtaun] n Bidonville f

shape [ʃeɪp] n Form f ♦ vt formen, gestalten ♦ vi (also: ~ **up**) sich entwickeln; **to take ~** Gestalt annehmen; **~d** suffix: **heart-~d** herzförmig; **~less** adj formlos; **~ly** adj wohlproportioniert

share [ʃɛəʳ] n (An)teil m; (FIN) Aktie f ♦ vt teilen; **to ~ out (among/between)** verteilen (unter/zwischen); **~holder** n Aktionär(in) m(f)

shark [ʃɑːk] n Hai(fisch) m; (swindler) Gauner m

sharp [ʃɑːp] adj scharf; (pin) spitz; (person) clever; (MUS) erhöht ♦ n Kreuz nt ♦ adv zu hoch; **nine o'clock ~** Punkt neun; **~en** vt schärfen; (pencil) spitzen; **~ener** n (also: **pencil ~ener**) Anspitzer m; **~-eyed** adj

scharfsichtig; **~ly** adv (turn, stop) plötzlich; (stand out, contrast) deutlich; (criticize, retort) scharf

shatter ['ʃætəʳ] vt zerschmettern; (fig) zerstören ♦ vi zerspringen

shave [ʃeɪv] n Rasur f ♦ vt rasieren ♦ vi sich rasieren; **to have a ~** sich rasieren (lassen); **~r** n (also: **electric ~r**) Rasierapparat m

shaving ['ʃeɪvɪŋ] n (action) Rasieren nt; **~s** npl (of wood etc) Späne pl; ~ **brush** n Rasierpinsel m; ~ **cream** n Rasiercreme f; ~ **foam** n Rasierschaum m

shawl [ʃɔːl] n Schal m, Umhang m

she [ʃiː] pron sie ♦ adj weiblich

sheaf [ʃiːf] (pl **sheaves**) n Garbe f

shear [ʃɪəʳ] (pt **sheared**, pp **sheared** or **shorn**) vt scheren; ~ **off** vi abbrechen; **~s** npl Heckenschere f

sheath [ʃiːθ] n Scheide f; (condom) Kondom m or nt

sheaves [ʃiːvz] npl of **sheaf**

shed [ʃed] (pt, pp **shed**) n Schuppen m; (for animals) Stall m ♦ vt (leaves etc) verlieren; (tears) vergießen

she'd [ʃiːd] = **she had; she would**

sheen [ʃiːn] n Glanz m

sheep [ʃiːp] n inv Schaf nt; **~dog** n Schäferhund m; **~ish** adj verlegen; **~skin** n Schaffell nt

sheer [ʃɪəʳ] adj bloß, rein; (steep) steil; (transparent) (hauch)dünn ♦ adv (directly) direkt

sheet [ʃiːt] n Betttuch nt, Bettlaken nt; (of paper) Blatt nt; (of metal etc) Platte f; (of ice) Fläche f

sheik(h) [ʃeɪk] n Scheich m

shelf [ʃelf] (pl **shelves**) n Brett nt, Regal nt

shell [ʃel] n Schale f; (seashell) Muschel f; (explosive) Granate f ♦ vt (peas) schälen; (fire on) beschießen

she'll [ʃiːl] = **she will; she shall**

shellfish ['ʃelfɪʃ] n Schalentier nt; (as food) Meeresfrüchte pl

shell suit n Ballonseidenanzug m

shelter ['ʃeltəʳ] n Schutz m; (air-raid ~) Bunker m ♦ vt schützen, bedecken; (refugees) aufnehmen ♦ vi sich unterstellen;

~ed adj (life) behütet; (spot) geschützt; **~ housing** n (for old people) Altenwohnungen pl; (for handicapped people) Behindertenwohnungen pl

shelve [ʃɛlv] vt aufschieben ♦ vi abfallen

shelves [ʃɛlvz] npl of **shelf**

shepherd [ʃɛpəd] n Schäfer m ♦ vt treiben, führen; **~'s pie** n Auflauf aus Hackfleisch und Kartoffelbrei

sheriff [ʃɛrɪf] n Sheriff m; (SCOTTISH) Friedensrichter m

she's [ʃiːz] = **she is; she has**

Shetland [ʃɛtlənd] n (also: **the ~s, the ~ Isles**) die Shetlandinseln pl

shield [ʃiːld] n Schild m; (fig) Schirm m ♦ vt (be)schirmen; (TECH) abschirmen

shift [ʃɪft] n Verschiebung f; (work) Schicht f ♦ vt (ver)rücken, verschieben; (arm) wegnehmen ♦ vi sich verschieben; **~less** adj (person) träge; **~ work** n Schichtarbeit f; **~y** adj verschlagen

shilly-shally [ʃɪlɪʃælɪ] vi zögern

shin [ʃɪn] n Schienbein nt

shine [ʃaɪn] n (pt, pp **shone**) n Glanz m, Schein m ♦ vt polieren ♦ vi scheinen; (fig) glänzen; **to ~ a torch on sb** jdn (mit einer Lampe) anleuchten

shingle [ʃɪŋgl] n Strandkies m; **~s** npl (MED) Gürtelrose f

shiny [ʃaɪnɪ] adj glänzend

ship [ʃɪp] n Schiff nt ♦ vt verschiffen; **~building** n Schiffbau m; **~ment** n Schiffsladung f; **~per** n Verschiffer m; **~ping** n (act) Verschiffung f; (~s) Schifffahrt f; **~wreck** n Schiffbruch m; (destroyed ~) Wrack nt ♦ vt: **to be ~wrecked** Schiffbruch erleiden; **~yard** n Werft f

shire [ʃaɪə] n (BRIT) Grafschaft f

shirk [ʃəːk] vt ausweichen +dat

shirt [ʃəːt] n (Ober)hemd nt; **in ~ sleeves** in Hemdsärmeln

shit [ʃɪt] (infl) excl Scheiße (!)

shiver [ʃɪvə] n Schauer m ♦ vi frösteln, zittern

shoal [ʃəul] n (Fisch)schwarm m

shock [ʃɔk] n Erschütterung f; (mental) Schock m; (ELEC) Schlag m ♦ vt erschüttern; (offend) schockieren; **~ absorber** n Stoßdämpfer m; **~ed** adj geschockt, schockiert, erschüttert; **~ing** adj unerhört

shod [ʃɔd] pt, pp of **shoe**

shoddy [ʃɔdɪ] adj schäbig

shoe [ʃuː] n (pt, pp **shod**) n Schuh m; (of horse) Hufeisen nt ♦ vt (horse) beschlagen; **~brush** n Schuhbürste f; **~horn** n Schuhlöffel m; **~lace** n Schnürsenkel m; **~ polish** n Schuhcreme f; **~ shop** n Schuhgeschäft nt; **~string** n (fig): **on a ~string** mit sehr wenig Geld

shone [ʃɔn] pt, pp of **shine**

shoo [ʃuː] excl sch; (to dog etc) pfui

shook [ʃuk] pt of **shake**

shoot [ʃuːt] n (pt, pp **shot**) n (branch) Schössling m ♦ vt (gun) abfeuern; (goal, arrow) schießen; (person) anschießen; (kill) erschießen; (film) drehen ♦ vi (move quickly) schießen; **to ~ (at)** schießen (auf +acc); **~ down** vt abschießen; **~ in** vi hineinschießen; **~ out** vi hinausschießen; **~ up** vi (fig) aus dem Boden schießen; **~ing** n Schießerei f; **~ing star** n Sternschnuppe f

shop [ʃɔp] n (esp BRIT) Geschäft nt, Laden m; (workshop) Werkstatt f ♦ vi (also: **go ~ping**) einkaufen gehen; **~ assistant** (BRIT) n Verkäufer(in) m(f); **~ floor** (BRIT) n Werkstatt f; **~keeper** n Geschäftsinhaber m; **~lifting** n Ladendiebstahl m; **~per** n Käufer(in) m(f); **~ping** n Einkaufen nt, Einkauf m; **~ping bag** n Einkaufstasche f; **~ping centre** (US **shopping center**) n Einkaufszentrum nt; **~-soiled** adj angeschmutzt; **~ steward** (BRIT) n (INDUSTRY) Betriebsrat m; **~ window** n Schaufenster nt

shore [ʃɔː] n Ufer nt; (of sea) Strand m ♦ vt: **to ~ up** abstützen

shorn [ʃɔːn] pp of **shear**

short [ʃɔːt] adj kurz; (person) klein; (curt) kurz angebunden; (measure) zu knapp ♦ n (also: **~ film**) Kurzfilm m ♦ adv (suddenly) plötzlich ♦ vi (ELEC) einen Kurzschluss haben; **~s** npl (clothes) Shorts pl; **to be ~ of sth** nicht genug von etw haben; **in ~** kurz gesagt; **~ of doing sth** ohne so weit zu gehen, etw zu tun; **everything ~ of ...** alles außer ...; **it is ~ for** das ist die Kurzform von; **to cut ~** abkürzen; **to fall ~ of sth** etw nicht erreichen; **to stop ~** plötzlich anhalten; **to stop ~ of** Halt machen vor; **~age** n Knappheit f, Mangel m; **~bread** n Mürbegebäck nt; **~-change** vt: **to ~-change sb** jdm zu wenig herausgeben; **~circuit** n Kurzschluss m ♦ vi einen Kurzschluss haben ♦ vt kurzschließen; **~coming** n Mangel m; **~(crust) pastry** (BRIT) n Mürbeteig m; **~ cut** n Abkürzung f; **~en** vt (ab)kürzen; (clothes) kürzer machen; **~fall** n Defizit nt; **~hand** (BRIT) n Stenografie f; **~hand typist** (BRIT) n Stenotypistin f; **~ list** (BRIT) n (for job) engere Wahl f; **~-lived** adj kurzlebig; **~ly** adv bald; **~ notice** n: **at ~ notice** kurzfristig; **~-sighted** (BRIT) adj (also fig) kurzsichtig; **~-staffed** adj: **to be ~-staffed** zu wenig Personal haben; **~-stay** n (car park) Kurzparken nt; **~ story** n Kurzgeschichte f; **~-tempered** adj leicht aufbrausend; **~-term** adj (effect) kurzfristig; **~ wave** n (RAD) Kurzwelle f

shot [ʃɒt] pt, pp of **shoot** ♦ n (from gun) Schuss m; (person) Schütze m; (try) Versuch m; (injection) Spritze f; (PHOT) Aufnahme f; **like a ~** wie der Blitz; **~gun** n Schrotflinte f

should [ʃʊd] vb aux: **I ~ go now** ich sollte jetzt gehen; **he ~ be there now** er sollte eigentlich schon da sein; **I ~ go if I were you** ich würde gehen, wenn ich du wäre; **I ~ like to** ich möchte gerne

shoulder ['ʃəʊldər] n Schulter f; (BRIT: of road): **hard ~** Seitenstreifen m ♦ vt (rifle) schultern; (fig) auf sich nehmen; **~ bag** n Umhängetasche f; **~ blade** n Schulterblatt nt; **~ strap** n (of dress etc) Träger m

shouldn't ['ʃʊdnt] = **should not**

shout [ʃaʊt] n Schrei m; (call) Ruf m ♦ vt rufen ♦ vi schreien; **~ down** vt niederbrüllen; **~ing** n Geschrei nt

shove [ʃʌv] n Schubs m, Stoß m ♦ vt

schieben, stoßen, schubsen; (inf: put): **to ~ sth in(to) sth** etw in etw acc hineinschieben; **~ off** vi (NAUT) abstoßen; (fig: inf) abhauen

shovel ['ʃʌvl] n Schaufel f ♦ vt schaufeln

show [ʃəʊ] (pt **showed**, pp **shown**) n (display) Schau f; (exhibition) Ausstellung f; (CINE, THEAT) Vorstellung f, Show f ♦ vt zeigen; (kindness) erweisen ♦ vi zu sehen sein; **to be on ~** (exhibits etc) ausgestellt sein; **to ~ sb in** jdn hereinführen; **to ~ sb out** jdn hinausbegleiten; **~ off** vi (pej) angeben ♦ vt (display) ausstellen; **~ up** vi (stand out) sich abheben; (arrive) erscheinen ♦ vt aufzeigen; (unmask) bloßstellen; **~ business** n Showbusiness nt; **~down** n Kraftprobe f

shower ['ʃaʊər] n Schauer m; (of stones) (Stein)hagel m; (~ bath) Dusche f ♦ vi duschen ♦ vt: **to ~ sb with sth** jdn mit etw überschütten; **~proof** adj Wasser abstoßend

showing ['ʃəʊɪŋ] n Vorführung f

show jumping n Turnierreiten nt

shown [ʃəʊn] pp of **show**

show: ~-off ['ʃəʊɒf] n Angeber(in) m(f); **~piece** ['ʃəʊpiːs] n Paradestück nt; **~room** ['ʃəʊrʊm] n Ausstellungsraum m

shrank [ʃræŋk] pt of **shrink**

shred [ʃred] n Fetzen m ♦ vt zerfetzen; (COOK) raspeln; **~der** n (COOK) Gemüseschneider m; (for documents) Reißwolf m

shrewd [ʃruːd] adj clever

shriek [ʃriːk] n Schrei m ♦ vt, vi kreischen, schreien

shrill [ʃrɪl] adj schrill

shrimp [ʃrɪmp] n Krabbe f, Garnele f

shrine [ʃraɪn] n Schrein m; (fig) Gedenkstätte f

shrink [ʃrɪŋk] (pt **shrank**, pp **shrunk**) vi schrumpfen, eingehen ♦ vt einschrumpfen lassen; **to ~ from doing sth** davor zurückschrecken, etw zu tun; **~age** n Schrumpfung f; **~-wrap** vt einschweißen

shrivel ['ʃrɪvl] vt, vi (also: **~ up**) schrumpfen, schrumpeln

shroud [ʃraʊd] *n* Leichentuch *nt* ♦ *vt*: **~ed in mystery** mit einem Geheimnis umgeben

Shrove Tuesday ['ʃrəʊv-] *n* Fastnachtsdienstag *m*

shrub [ʃrʌb] *n* Busch *m*, Strauch *m*; **~bery** *n* Gebüsch *nt*

shrug [ʃrʌg] *n* Achselzucken *nt* ♦ *vt, vi*: **to ~ (one's shoulders)** die Achseln zucken; **~ off** *vt* auf die leichte Schulter nehmen

shrunk [ʃrʌŋk] *pp of* **shrink**

shudder ['ʃʌdər] *n* Schauder *m* ♦ *vi* schaudern

shuffle ['ʃʌfl] *vt* (*cards*) mischen; **to ~ (one's feet)** schlurfen

shun [ʃʌn] *vt* scheuen, (ver)meiden

shunt [ʃʌnt] *vt* rangieren

shut [ʃʌt] (*pt, pp* **shut**) *vt* schließen, zumachen ♦ *vi* sich schließen (lassen); **~ down** *vt, vi* schließen; **~ off** *vt* (*supply*) abdrehen; **~ up** *vi* (*keep quiet*) den Mund halten ♦ *vt* (*close*) zuschließen; **~ter** *n* Fensterladen *m*; (*PHOT*) Verschluss *m*

shuttle ['ʃʌtl] *n* (*plane, train etc*) Pendelflugzeug *nt*/-zug *m etc*; (*space ~*) Raumtransporter *m*; (*also:* **~ service**) Pendelverkehr *m*; **~cock** ['ʃʌtlkɔk] *n* Federball *m*; **~ diplomacy** *n* Pendeldiplomatie *f*

shy [ʃaɪ] *adj* schüchtern; **~ness** *n* Schüchternheit *f*

Siamese [saɪə'miːz] *adj*: **~ cat** Siamkatze *f*

Siberia [saɪ'bɪərɪə] *n* Sibirien *nt*

sibling ['sɪblɪŋ] *n* Geschwister *nt*

Sicily ['sɪsɪlɪ] *n* Sizilien *nt*

sick [sɪk] *adj* krank; (*joke*) makaber; **I feel ~** mir ist schlecht; **I was ~** ich habe gebrochen; **to be ~ of sb/sth** jdn/etw satt haben; **~ bay** *n* (Schiffs)lazarett *nt*; **~en** *vt* (*disgust*) krank machen ♦ *vi* krank werden; **~ening** *adj* (*annoying*) zum Weinen

sickle ['sɪkl] *n* Sichel *f*

sick: ~ leave *n*: **to be on ~ leave** krankgeschrieben sein; **~ly** *adj* kränklich, blass; (*causing nausea*) widerlich; **~ness** *n* Krankheit *f*; (*vomiting*) Übelkeit *f*, Erbrechen *nt*; **~ note** *n* Arbeitsunfähigkeits-bescheinigung *f*; **~ pay** *n* Krankengeld *nt*

side [saɪd] *n* Seite *f* ♦ *adj* (*door, entrance*) Seiten-, Neben- ♦ *vi*: **to ~ with sb** jds Partei ergreifen; **by the ~ of** neben; **~ by ~** nebeneinander; **on all ~s** von allen Seiten; **to take ~s (with)** Partei nehmen (für); **from all ~s** von allen Seiten; **~board** *n* Sideboard *nt*; **~boards** (*BRIT*) *npl* Koteletten *pl*; **~burns** *npl* Koteletten *pl*; **~car** *n* Beiwagen *m*; **~ drum** *n* (*MUS*) kleine Trommel; **~ effect** *n* Nebenwirkung *f*; **~light** *n* (*AUT*) Parkleuchte *f*; **~line** *n* (*SPORT*) Seitenlinie *f*; (*fig: hobby*) Nebenbeschäftigung *f*; **~long** *adj* Seiten-; **~ order** *n* Beilage *f*; **~ saddle** *adv* im Damensattel; **~ show** *n* Nebenausstellung *f*; **~step** *vt* (*fig*) ausweichen; **~ street** *n* Seitenstraße *f*; **~track** *vt* (*fig*) ablenken; **~walk** (*US*) *n* Bürgersteig *m*; **~ways** *adv* seitwärts

siding ['saɪdɪŋ] *n* Nebengleis *nt*

sidle ['saɪdl] *vi*: **to ~ up (to)** sich heranmachen (an +*acc*)

siege [siːdʒ] *n* Belagerung *f*

sieve [sɪv] *n* Sieb *nt* ♦ *vt* sieben

sift [sɪft] *vt* sieben; (*fig*) sichten

sigh [saɪ] *n* Seufzer *m* ♦ *vi* seufzen

sight [saɪt] *n* (*power of seeing*) Sehvermögen *nt*; (*look*) Blick *m*; (*fact of seeing*) Anblick *m*; (*of gun*) Visier *nt* ♦ *vt* sichten; **in ~** in Sicht; **out of ~** außer Sicht; **~seeing** *n* Besuch *m* von Sehenswürdigkeiten; **to go ~seeing** Sehenswürdigkeiten besichtigen

sign [saɪn] *n* Zeichen *nt*; (*notice, road ~ etc*) Schild *nt* ♦ *vt* unterschreiben; **to ~ sth over to sb** jdm etw überschreiben; **~ on** *vi* (*as unemployed*) sich (arbeitslos) melden ♦ *vt* (*employee*) anstellen; **~ up** *vi* (*MIL*) sich verpflichten ♦ *vt* verpflichten

signal ['sɪgnl] *n* Signal *nt* ♦ *vt* ein Zeichen geben +*dat*; **~man** (*irreg*) *n* (*RAIL*) Stellwerkswärter *m*

signature ['sɪgnətʃər] *n* Unterschrift *f*; **~ tune** *n* Erkennungsmelodie *f*

signet ring ['sɪgnət-] *n* Siegelring *m*

significance [sɪg'nɪfɪkəns] *n* Bedeutung *f*

significant [sɪg'nɪfɪkənt] *adj* (*meaning sth*)

bedeutsam; *(important)* bedeutend

signify ['sɪgnɪfaɪ] *vt* bedeuten; *(show)* andeuten, zu verstehen geben

sign language *n* Zeichensprache *f*, Fingersprache *f*

signpost ['saɪnpəʊst] *n* Wegweiser *m*

silence ['saɪləns] *n* Stille *f*; *(of person)* Schweigen *nt* ♦ *vt* zum Schweigen bringen; **~r** *n (on gun)* Schalldämpfer *m*; *(BRIT: AUT)* Auspufftopf *m*

silent ['saɪlənt] *adj* still; *(person)* schweigsam; **to remain ~** schweigen; **~ partner** *n (COMM)* stille(r) Teilhaber *m*

silicon chip ['sɪlɪkən-] *n* Siliciumchip *m*, Siliziumchip *m*

silk [sɪlk] *n* Seide *f* ♦ *adj* seiden, Seiden-; **~y** *adj* seidig

silly ['sɪlɪ] *adj* dumm, albern

silt [sɪlt] *n* Schlamm *m*, Schlick *m*

silver ['sɪlvə*] *n* Silber *nt* ♦ *adj* silbern, Silber-; **~ paper** *(BRIT)* *n* Silberpapier *nt*; **~-plated** *adj* versilbert; **~smith** *n* Silberschmied *m*; **~ware** *n* Silber *nt*, **~y** *adj* silbern

similar ['sɪmɪlə*] *adj*: **~ (to)** ähnlich *(+dat)*; **~ity** [sɪmɪ'lærɪtɪ] *n* Ähnlichkeit *f*; **~ly** *adv* in ähnlicher Weise

simmer ['sɪmə*] *vi* sieden ♦ *vt* sieden lassen

simple ['sɪmpl] *adj* einfach; **~(-minded)** *adj* einfältig

simplicity [sɪm'plɪsɪtɪ] *n* Einfachheit *f*; *(of person)* Einfältigkeit *f*

simplify ['sɪmplɪfaɪ] *vt* vereinfachen

simply ['sɪmplɪ] *adv* einfach

simulate ['sɪmjʊleɪt] *vt* simulieren

simultaneous [sɪməl'teɪnɪəs] *adj* gleichzeitig

sin [sɪn] *n* Sünde *f* ♦ *vi* sündigen

since [sɪns] *adv* seither ♦ *prep* seit, seitdem ♦ *conj (time)* seit; *(because)* da, weil; **~ then** seitdem

sincere [sɪn'sɪə*] *adj* aufrichtig; **~ly** *adv*: **yours ~ly** mit freundlichen Grüßen; **sincerity** [sɪn'serɪtɪ] *n* Aufrichtigkeit *f*

sinew ['sɪnjuː] *n* Sehne *f*

sinful ['sɪnfʊl] *adj* sündig, sündhaft

sing [sɪŋ] *(pt* **sang**, *pp* **sung**) *vt*, *vi* singen

Singapore [sɪŋgə'pɔː*] *n* Singapur *nt*

singe [sɪndʒ] *vt* versengen

singer ['sɪŋə*] *n* Sänger(in) *m(f)*

singing ['sɪŋɪŋ] *n* Singen *nt*, Gesang *m*

single ['sɪŋgl] *adj (one only)* einzig; *(bed, room)* Einzel-, einzeln; *(unmarried)* ledig; *(BRIT: ticket)* einfach; *(having one part only)* einzeln ♦ *n (BRIT: also:* **~ ticket**) einfache Fahrkarte *f*; **in ~ file** hintereinander; **~ out** *vt* aussuchen, auswählen; **~ bed** *n* Einzelbett *nt*; **~-breasted** *adj* einreihig; **~-handed** *adj* allein; **~-minded** *adj* zielstrebig; **~ parent** *n* Alleinerziehende(r) *f(m)*; **~ room** *n* Einzelzimmer *nt*; **~s** *n (TENNIS)* Einzel *nt*; **~-track road** *n* einspurige Straße (mit Ausweichstellen); **singly** *adv* einzeln, allein

singular ['sɪŋgjʊlə*] *adj (odd)* merkwürdig, seltsam ♦ *n (GRAM)* Einzahl *f*, Singular *m*

sinister ['sɪnɪstə*] *adj (evil)* böse; *(ghostly)* unheimlich

sink [sɪŋk] *(pt* **sank**, *pp* **sunk**) *n* Spülbecken *nt* ♦ *vt (ship)* versenken ♦ *vi* sinken; **to ~ sth into** *(teeth, claws)* etw schlagen in *+acc*; **~ in** *vi (news etc)* eingehen

sinner ['sɪnə*] *n* Sünder(in) *m(f)*

sinus ['saɪnəs] *n (ANAT)* Sinus *m*

sip [sɪp] *n* Schlückchen *nt* ♦ *vt* nippen an *+dat*

siphon ['saɪfən] *n* Siphon(flasche *f*) *m*; **~ off** *vt* absaugen; *(fig)* abschöpfen

sir [sɜː*] *n (respect)* Herr *m*; *(knight)* Sir *m*; **S~ John Smith** Sir John Smith; **yes ~** ja(wohl, mein Herr)

siren ['saɪərn] *n* Sirene *f*

sirloin ['sɜːlɔɪn] *n* Lendenstück *nt*

sissy ['sɪsɪ] *(inf)* *n* Waschlappen *m*

sister ['sɪstə*] *n* Schwester *f*; *(BRIT: nurse)* Oberschwester *f*; *(nun)* Ordensschwester *f*; **~-in-law** *n* Schwägerin *f*

sit [sɪt] *(pt, pp* **sat**) *vi* sitzen; *(hold session)* tagen ♦ *vt (exam)* machen; **~ down** *vi* sich hinsetzen; **~ in on** *vt fus* dabei sein bei; **~ up** *vi (after lying)* sich aufsetzen; *(straight)* sich gerade setzen; *(at night)* aufbleiben

sitcom ['sɪtkɒm] *n abbr (= situation comedy)* Situationskomödie *f*

site [saɪt] *n* Platz *m*; *(also:* **building ~**)

Baustelle f ♦ vt legen

sitting ['sɪtɪŋ] n (meeting) Sitzung f; ~ **room** n Wohnzimmer nt

situated ['sɪtjʊeɪtɪd] adj: to be ~ liegen

situation [sɪtjʊ'eɪʃən] n Situation f, Lage f; (place) Lage f; (employment) Stelle f; "~s **vacant**" (BRIT) „Stellenangebote" pl

six [sɪks] num sechs; ~**teen** num sechzehn; ~**th** adj sechste(r, s) ♦ n Sechstel nt; ~**ty** num sechzig

size [saɪz] n Größe f; (of project) Umfang m; ~ **up** vt (assess) abschätzen, einschätzen; ~**able** adj ziemlich groß, ansehnlich

sizzle ['sɪzl] vi zischen; (COOK) brutzeln

skate [skeɪt] n Schlittschuh m; (fish: pl inv) Rochen m ♦ vi Schlittschuh laufen; ~**board** n Skateboard nt; ~**boarding** n Skateboardfahren nt; ~**r** n Schlittschuhläufer(in) m(f); **skating** ['skeɪtɪŋ] n Eislauf m; **to go skating** Eis laufen gehen; **skating rink** n Eisbahn f

skeleton ['skelɪtn] n Skelett nt; (fig) Gerüst nt; ~ **key** n Dietrich m; ~ **staff** n Notbesetzung f

skeptical ['skeptɪkl] (US) adj = **sceptical**

sketch [sketʃ] n Skizze f; (THEAT) Sketch m ♦ vt skizzieren; ~**book** n Skizzenbuch nt; ~**y** adj skizzenhaft

skewer ['skjuːər] n Fleischspieß m

ski [skiː] n Ski m, Schi m ♦ vi Ski or Schi laufen; ~ **boot** n Skistiefel m

skid [skɪd] n (AUT) Schleudern nt ♦ vi rutschen; (AUT) schleudern

ski: ~**er** ['skiːər] n Skiläufer(in) m(f); ~**ing** ['skiːɪŋ] n: **to go ~ing** Ski laufen gehen; ~-**jump** n Sprungschanze f ♦ vi Ski springen

skilful ['skɪlful] adj geschickt

ski-lift n Skilift m

skill [skɪl] n Können nt; ~**ed** adj geschickt; (worker) Fach-, gelernt

skim [skɪm] vt (liquid) abschöpfen; (glide over) gleiten über +acc ♦ vi: ~ **through** (book) überfliegen; ~**med milk** n Magermilch f

skimp [skɪmp] vt (do carelessly) oberflächlich tun; ~**y** adj (dress) knapp

skin [skɪn] n Haut f; (peel) Schale f ♦ vt abhäuten; schälen; ~ **cancer** n Hautkrebs m; ~-**deep** adj oberflächlich; ~ **diving** n Schwimmtauchen nt; ~**head** n Skinhead m; ~**ny** adj dünn; ~**tight** adj (dress etc) hauteng

skip [skɪp] n Sprung m ♦ vi hüpfen; (with rope) Seil springen ♦ vt (pass over) übergehen

ski: ~ **pants** npl Skihosen pl; ~ **pass** n Skipass nt; ~ **pole** n Skistock m

skipper ['skɪpər] n Kapitän m ♦ vt führen

skipping rope ['skɪpɪŋ-] (BRIT) n Hüpfseil nt

skirmish ['skɜːmɪʃ] n Scharmützel nt

skirt [skɜːt] n Rock m ♦ vt herumgehen um; (fig) umgehen; ~**ing board** (BRIT) n Fußleiste f

ski suit n Skianzug m

skit [skɪt] n Parodie f

ski tow n Schlepplift m

skittle ['skɪtl] n Kegel m; ~**s** n (game) Kegeln nt

skive [skaɪv] (BRIT: inf) vi schwänzen

skulk [skʌlk] vi sich herumdrücken

skull [skʌl] n Schädel m

skunk [skʌŋk] n Stinktier nt

sky [skaɪ] n Himmel m; ~**light** n Oberlicht nt; ~**scraper** n Wolkenkratzer m

slab [slæb] n (of stone) Platte f

slack [slæk] adj (loose) locker; (business) flau; (careless) nachlässig, lasch ♦ vi nachlässig sein ♦ n: **to take up the** ~ straff ziehen; ~**s** npl (trousers) Hose(n pl) f; ~**en** vi (also: ~**en off**) locker werden; (: slow down) stocken, nachlassen ♦ vt (: loosen) lockern

slag [slæg] (BRIT) vt: ~ **off** (criticize) (he)runtermachen

slag heap [slæg-] n Halde f

slain [sleɪn] pp of **slay**

slam [slæm] n Knall m ♦ vt (door) zuschlagen; (throw down) knallen ♦ vi zuschlagen

slander ['slɑːndər] n Verleumdung f ♦ vt verleumden

slang [slæŋ] n Slang m; (jargon) Jargon m

slant [slɑːnt] n Schräge f; (fig) Tendenz f ♦ vt schräg legen ♦ vi schräg liegen; ~**ed** adj schräg; ~**ing** adj schräg

slap [slæp] n Klaps m ♦ vt einen Klaps geben +dat ♦ adj (directly) geradewegs; **~dash** adj salopp; **~stick** n (comedy) Klamauk m; **~up** (BRIT) adj (meal) erstklassig, prima

slash [slæʃ] n Schnittwunde f ♦ vt (auf)schlitzen

slat [slæt] n Leiste f

slate [sleɪt] n (stone) Schiefer m; (roofing) Dachziegel m ♦ vt (criticize) verreißen

slaughter ['slɔːtər] n (of animals) Schlachten nt; (of people) Gemetzel nt ♦ vt schlachten; (people) niedermetzeln; **~house** n Schlachthof m

Slav [slɑːv] adj slawisch

slave [sleɪv] n Sklave m, Sklavin f ♦ vi schuften, sich schinden; **~ry** n Sklaverei f

slay [sleɪ] (pt **slew**, pp **slain**) vt ermorden

sleazy ['sliːzɪ] adj (place) schmierig

sledge [sledʒ] n Schlitten m

sledgehammer ['sledʒhæmər] n Schmiedehammer m

sledging n Schlittenfahren nt

sleek [sliːk] adj glatt; (shape) rassig

sleep [sliːp] (pt, pp **slept**) n Schlaf m ♦ vi schlafen; **to go to ~** einschlafen; **~ in** vi ausschlafen; (oversleep) verschlafen; **~er** n (person) Schläfer m; (BRIT: RAIL) Schlafwagen m; (: beam) Schwelle f; **~ing bag** n Schlafsack m; **~ing car** n Schlafwagen m; **~ing partner** n = silent partner; **~ing pill** n Schlaftablette f; **~less** adj (night) schlaflos; **~walker** n Schlafwandler(in) m(f); **~y** adj schläfrig

sleet [sliːt] n Schneeregen m

sleeve [sliːv] n Ärmel m; (of record) Umschlag m; **~less** adj ärmellos

sleigh [sleɪ] n Pferdeschlitten m

sleight [slaɪt] n: **~ of hand** Fingerfertigkeit f

slender ['slendər] adj schlank; (fig) gering

slept [slept] pt, pp of **sleep**

slew [sluː] vi (veer) (herum)schwenken ♦ pt of **slay**

slice [slaɪs] n Scheibe f ♦ vt in Scheiben schneiden

slick [slɪk] adj (clever) raffiniert, aalglatt ♦ n Ölteppich m

slid [slɪd] pt, pp of **slide**

slide [slaɪd] (pt, pp **slid**) n Rutschbahn f; (PHOT) Dia(positiv) nt; (BRIT: for hair) (Haar)spange f ♦ vt schieben ♦ vi (slip) gleiten, rutschen; **sliding** ['slaɪdɪŋ] adj (door) Schiebe-; **sliding scale** n gleitende Skala f

slight [slaɪt] adj zierlich; (trivial) geringfügig; (small) gering ♦ n Kränkung f ♦ vt (offend) kränken; **not in the ~est** nicht im Geringsten; **~ly** adv etwas, ein bisschen

slim [slɪm] adj schlank; (book) dünn; (chance) gering ♦ vi eine Schlankheitskur machen

slime [slaɪm] n Schleim m

slimming ['slɪmɪŋ] n Schlankheitskur f

slimy ['slaɪmɪ] adj glitschig; (dirty) schlammig; (person) schmierig

sling [slɪŋ] (pt, pp **slung**) n Schlinge f; (weapon) Schleuder f ♦ vt schleudern

slip [slɪp] n (mistake) Flüchtigkeitsfehler m; (petticoat) Unterrock m; (of paper) Zettel m ♦ vt (put) stecken, schieben ♦ vi (lose balance) ausrutschen; (move) gleiten, rutschen; (decline) nachlassen; (move smoothly): **to ~ in/out** (person) hinein-/hinausschlüpfen; **to give sb the ~** jdm entwischen; **~ of the tongue** Versprecher m; **it ~ped my mind** das ist mir entfallen; **to ~ sth on/off** etw über-/abstreifen; **~ away** vi sich wegstehlen; **~ in** vt hineingleiten lassen ♦ vi (errors) sich einschleichen; **~ped disc** n Bandscheibenschaden m

slipper ['slɪpər] n Hausschuh m

slippery ['slɪpərɪ] adj glatt

slip: ~ road (BRIT) n Auffahrt f/Ausfahrt f; **~shod** adj schlampig; **~-up** n Panne f; **~way** n Auslaufbahn f

slit [slɪt] (pt, pp **slit**) n Schlitz m ♦ vt aufschlitzen

slither ['slɪðər] vi schlittern; (snake) sich schlängeln

sliver ['slɪvər] n (of glass, wood) Splitter m; (of cheese) Scheibchen nt

slob [slɒb] (inf) n Klotz m

slog [slɒg] vi (work hard) schuften ♦ n: **it was a ~** es war eine Plackerei

slogan ['sləʊgən] n Schlagwort nt; (COMM)

Werbespruch *m*

slop [slɒp] *vi* (*also:* ~ **over**) überschwappen ♦ *vt* verschütten

slope [sləup] *n* Neigung *f*; (*of mountains*) (Ab)hang *m* ♦ *vi*: **to ~ down** sich senken; **to ~ up** ansteigen; **sloping** ['sləupɪŋ] *adj* schräg

sloppy ['slɒpɪ] *adj* schlampig

slot [slɒt] *n* Schlitz *m* ♦ *vt*: **to ~ sth in** etw einlegen

sloth [sləuθ] *n* (*laziness*) Faulheit *f*

slot machine *n* (*BRIT*) Automat *m*; (*for gambling*) Spielautomat *m*

slouch [slautʃ] *vi*: **to ~ about** (*laze*) herumhängen (*inf*)

slovenly ['slʌvənlɪ] *adj* schlampig; (*speech*) salopp

slow [sləu] *adj* langsam ♦ *adv* langsam; **to be ~** (*clock*) nachgehen; (*stupid*) begriffsstutzig sein; **"~"** (*road sign*) „Langsam"; **in ~ motion** in Zeitlupe; **~ down** *vi* langsamer werden ♦ *vt* verlangsamen; **~ up** *vi* sich verlangsamen, sich verzögern ♦ *vt* aufhalten, langsamer machen; **~ly** *adv* langsam

sludge [slʌdʒ] *n* Schlamm *m*

slug [slʌg] *n* Nacktschnecke *f*; (*inf: bullet*) Kugel *f*

sluggish ['slʌgɪʃ] *adj* träge; (*COMM*) schleppend

sluice [slu:s] *n* Schleuse *f*

slum [slʌm] *n* (*house*) Elendsquartier *nt*

slump [slʌmp] *n* Rückgang *m* ♦ *vi* fallen, stürzen

slung [slʌŋ] *pt, pp of* **sling**

slur [slɜːʳ] *n* Undeutlichkeit *f*; (*insult*) Verleumdung *f*; **~red** [slɜːd] *adj* (*pronunciation*) undeutlich

slush [slʌʃ] *n* (*snow*) Schneematsch *m*; **~ fund** *n* Schmiergeldfonds *m*

slut [slʌt] *n* Schlampe *f*

sly [slaɪ] *adj* schlau

smack [smæk] *n* Klaps *m* ♦ *vt* einen Klaps geben +*dat* ♦ *vi*: **to ~ of** riechen nach; **to ~ one's lips** schmatzen, sich *dat* die Lippen lecken

small [smɔːl] *adj* klein; **in the ~ hours** in den

frühen Morgenstunden; **~ ads** (*BRIT*) *npl* Kleinanzeigen *pl*; **~ change** *n* Kleingeld *nt*; **~holder** (*BRIT*) *n* Kleinbauer *m*; **~pox** *n* Pocken *pl*; **~ talk** *n* Geplauder *nt*

smart [smɑːt] *adj* (*fashionable*) elegant, schick; (*neat*) adrett; (*clever*) clever; (*quick*) scharf ♦ *vi* brennen, schmerzen; **~ card** *n* Chipkarte *f*; **~en up** *vi* sich in Schale werfen ♦ *vt* herausputzen

smash [smæʃ] *n* Zusammenstoß *m*; (*TENNIS*) Schmetterball *m* ♦ *vt* (*break*) zerschmettern; (*destroy*) vernichten ♦ *vi* (*break*) zersplittern, zerspringen; **~ing** (*inf*) *adj* toll

smattering ['smætərɪŋ] *n* oberflächliche Kenntnis *f*

smear [smɪəʳ] *n* Fleck *m* ♦ *vt* beschmieren

smell [smɛl] (*pt, pp* **smelt** *or* **smelled**) *n* Geruch *m*; (*sense*) Geruchssinn *m* ♦ *vt* riechen ♦ *vi*: **to ~ (of)** riechen (nach); (*fragrantly*) duften (nach); **~y** *adj* übel riechend

smile [smaɪl] *n* Lächeln *nt* ♦ *vi* lächeln

smiling ['smaɪlɪŋ] *adj* lächelnd

smirk [smɜːk] *n* blöde(s) Grinsen *nt*

smock [smɒk] *n* Kittel *m*

smoke [sməuk] *n* Rauch *m* ♦ *vt* rauchen; (*food*) räuchern ♦ *vi* rauchen; **~d** *adj* (*bacon*) geräuchert; (*glass*) Rauch-; **~r** *n* Raucher(in) *m(f)*; (*RAIL*) Raucherabteil *nt*; **~ screen** *n* Rauchwand *f*

smoking ['sməukɪŋ] *n*: **"no ~"** „Rauchen verboten"; **~ compartment** (*BRIT*), **~ car** (*US*) *n* Raucherabteil *nt*

smoky ['sməukɪ] *adj* rauchig; (*room*) verraucht; (*taste*) geräuchert

smolder ['sməuldəʳ] (*US*) *vi* = **smoulder**

smooth [smuːð] *adj* glatt ♦ *vt* (*also:* ~ **out**) glätten, glatt streichen

smother ['smʌðəʳ] *vt* ersticken

smoulder ['sməuldəʳ] (*US* **smolder**) *vi* schwelen

smudge [smʌdʒ] *n* Schmutzfleck *m* ♦ *vt* beschmieren

smug [smʌg] *adj* selbstgefällig

smuggle ['smʌgl] *vt* schmuggeln; **~r** *n* Schmuggler *m*

smuggling ['smʌglɪŋ] *n* Schmuggel *m*

smutty ['smʌtɪ] *adj* schmutzig

snack [snæk] *n* Imbiss *m*; **~ bar** *n* Imbissstube *f*

snag [snæg] *n* Haken *m*

snail [sneɪl] *n* Schnecke *f*

snake [sneɪk] *n* Schlange *f*

snap [snæp] *n* Schnappen *nt*; (*photograph*) Schnappschuss *m* ♦ *adj* (*decision*) schnell ♦ *vt* (*break*) zerbrechen; (*PHOT*) knipsen ♦ *vi* (*break*) brechen; (*speak*) anfauchen; **to ~ shut** zuschnappen; **~ at** *vt fus* schnappen nach; **~ off** *vt* (*break*) abbrechen **~ up** *vt* aufschnappen; **~shot** *n* Schnappschuss *m*

snare [sneəʳ] *n* Schlinge *f* ♦ *vt* mit einer Schlinge fangen

snarl [snɑːl] *n* Zähnefletschen *nt* ♦ *vi* (*dog*) knurren

snatch [snætʃ] *n* (*small amount*) Bruchteil *m* ♦ *vt* schnappen, packen

sneak [sniːk] *vi* schleichen ♦ *n* (*inf*) Petze(r) *mf*; **~ers** ['sniːkəz] (*US*) *npl* Freizeitschuhe *pl*; **~y** ['sniːkɪ] *adj* raffiniert

sneer [snɪəʳ] *n* Hohnlächeln *nt* ♦ *vi* spötteln

sneeze [sniːz] *n* Niesen *nt* ♦ *vi* niesen

sniff [snɪf] *n* Schnuffeln *nt* ♦ *vi* schnieben; (*smell*) schnüffeln ♦ *vt* schnuppern

snigger ['snɪgəʳ] *n* Kichern *nt* ♦ *vi* hämisch kichern

snip [snɪp] *n* Schnippel *m*, Schnipsel *m* ♦ *vt* schnippeln

sniper ['snaɪpəʳ] *n* Heckenschütze *m*

snippet ['snɪpɪt] *n* Schnipsel *m*; (*of conversation*) Fetzen *m*

snivelling ['snɪvlɪŋ] *adj* weinerlich

snob [snɔb] *n* Snob *m*

snooker ['snuːkəʳ] *n* Snooker *nt*

snoop [snuːp] *vi*: **to ~ about** herumschnüffeln

snooze [snuːz] *n* Nickerchen *nt* ♦ *vi* ein Nickerchen machen, dösen

snore [snɔːʳ] *vi* schnarchen ♦ *n* Schnarchen *nt*

snorkel ['snɔːkl] *n* Schnorchel *m*

snort [snɔːt] *n* Schnauben *nt* ♦ *vi* schnauben

snout [snaut] *n* Schnauze *f*

snow [snəu] *n* Schnee *m* ♦ *vi* schneien; **~ball** *n* Schneeball *m* ♦ *vi* eskalieren;

~bound *adj* eingeschneit; **~drift** *n* Schneewehe *f*; **~drop** *n* Schneeglöckchen *nt*; **~fall** *n* Schneefall *m*; **~flake** *n* Schneeflocke *f*; **~man** (*irreg*) *n* Schneemann *m*; **~plough** (*US* **snowplow**) *n* Schneepflug *m*; **~ shoe** *n* Schneeschuh *m*; **~storm** *n* Schneesturm *m*

snub [snʌb] *vt* schroff abfertigen ♦ *n* Verweis *m*; **~-nosed** *adj* stupsnasig

snuff [snʌf] *n* Schnupftabak *m*

snug [snʌg] *adj* gemütlich, behaglich

snuggle ['snʌgl] *vi*: **to ~ up to sb** sich an jdn kuscheln

---

KEYWORD

so [səu] *adv* **1** (*thus*) so; (*likewise*) auch; **so saying he walked away** indem er das sagte, ging er; **if so** wenn ja; **I didn't do it – you did so!** ich hab das nicht gemacht – hast du wohl!; **so do I, so am I** *etc* ich auch; **so it is!** tatsächlich!; **I hope/think so** hoffentlich/ich glaube schon; **so far** bis jetzt

2 (*in comparisons etc: to such a degree*) so; **so quickly/big (that)** so schnell/groß, dass; **I'm so glad to see you** ich freue mich so, dich zu sehen

3: so many so viele; **so much work** so viel Arbeit; **I love you so much** ich liebe dich so sehr

4 (*phrases*): **10 or so** etwa 10; **so long!** (*inf: goodbye*) tschüss!

♦ *conj* **1** (*expressing purpose*): **so as to** um ... zu; **so (that)** damit

2 (*expressing result*) also; **so I was right after all** ich hatte also doch Recht; **so you see ...** wie du siehst ...

---

soak [səuk] *vt* durchnässen; (*leave in liquid*) einweichen ♦ *vi* (ein)weichen; **~ in** *vi* einsickern; **~ up** *vt* aufsaugen; **~ed** *adj* völlig durchnässt; **~ing** *adj* klitschnass, patschnass

so-and-so ['səuənsəu] *n* (*somebody*) Soundso *m*

soap [səup] *n* Seife *f*; **~flakes** *npl* Seifenflocken *pl*; **~ opera** *n* Familienserie *f*

(im Fernsehen, Radio); ~ **powder** n
Waschpulver nt; ~**y** adj seifig, Seifen-

soar ['sɔ:] vi aufsteigen; *(prices)* in die Höhe
schnellen

sob [sɔb] n Schluchzen nt ♦ vi schluchzen

sober ['səubər] adj *(also fig)* nüchtern; ~ **up**
vi nüchtern werden

so-called ['səu'kɔ:ld] adj so genannt

soccer ['sɔkər] n Fußball m

sociable ['səuʃəbl] adj gesellig

social ['səuʃl] adj sozial; *(friendly, living with
others)* gesellig ♦ n gesellige(r) Abend m; ~
club n Verein m *(für Freizeitgestaltung)*;
~**ism** n Sozialismus m; ~**ist** n Sozialist(in)
m(f) ♦ adj sozialistisch; ~**ize** vi: **to ~ize
(with)** gesellschaftlich verkehren (mit); ~**ly**
adv gesellschaftlich, privat; ~ **security** n
Sozialversicherung f; ~ **work** n Sozialarbeit
f; ~ **worker** n Sozialarbeiter(in) m(f)

society [sə'saiəti] n Gesellschaft f;
(fashionable world) die große Welt

sociology [səusi'ɔlədʒi] n Soziologie f

sock [sɔk] n Socke f

socket ['sɔkit] n *(ELEC)* Steckdose f; *(of eye)*
Augenhöhle f

sod [sɔd] n Rasenstück nt; *(inf!)* Saukerl m *(!)*

soda ['səudə] n Soda f; *(also: ~ water)*
Soda(wasser) nt; *(US: also: ~ pop)*
Limonade f

sodden ['sɔdn] adj durchweicht

sodium ['səudiəm] n Natrium nt

sofa ['səufə] n Sofa nt

soft [sɔft] adj weich; *(not loud)* leise; *(weak)*
nachgiebig; ~ **drink** n alkoholfreie(s)
Getränk nt; ~**en** ['sɔfn] vt weich machen;
(blow) abschwächen, mildern ♦ vi weich
werden; ~**ly** adv sanft; leise; ~**ness** n
Weichheit f, *(fig)* Sanftheit f

software ['sɔftweər] n *(COMPUT)* Software f

soggy ['sɔgi] adj *(ground)* sumpfig; *(bread)*
aufgeweicht

soil [sɔil] n Erde f ♦ vt beschmutzen

solace ['sɔlis] n Trost m

solar ['səulər] adj Sonnen-; ~ **cell** n
Solarzelle f; ~ **energy** n Sonnenenergie f;
~ **panel** n Sonnenkollektor m; ~ **power** n
Sonnenenergie f

sold [səuld] pt, pp of **sell**; ~ **out** *(COMM)*
ausverkauft

solder ['səuldər] vt löten

soldier ['səuldʒər] n Soldat m

sole [səul] n Sohle f; *(fish)* Seezunge f ♦ adj
alleinig, Allein-; ~**ly** adv ausschließlich

solemn ['sɔləm] adj feierlich

sole trader n *(COMM)* Einzelunternehmen
nt

solicit [sə'lisit] vt *(request)* bitten um ♦ vi
(prostitute) Kunden anwerben

solicitor [sə'lisitər] n Rechtsanwalt m/-
anwältin f

solid ['sɔlid] adj *(hard)* fest; *(of same material,
not hollow)* massiv; *(without break)* voll,
ganz; *(reliable, sensible)* solide ♦ n Festkörper
m; ~**arity** [sɔli'dæriti] n Solidarität f; ~**ify**
[sə'lidifai] vi fest werden

solitary ['sɔlitəri] adj einsam, einzeln; ~
confinement n Einzelhaft f

solitude ['sɔlitju:d] n Einsamkeit f

solo ['səuləu] n Solo nt; ~**ist** ['səuləuist] n
Solist(in) m(f)

soluble ['sɔljubl] adj *(substance)* löslich;
(problem) (auf)lösbar

solution [sə'lu:ʃən] n *(also fig)* Lösung f; *(of
mystery)* Erklärung f

solve [sɔlv] vt (auf)lösen

solvent ['sɔlvənt] adj *(FIN)* zahlungsfähig ♦ n
(CHEM) Lösungsmittel nt

sombre ['sɔmbər] *(US* **somber)** adj düster

KEYWORD
---

some [sʌm] adj **1** *(a certain amount or
number of)* einige; *(a few)* ein paar; *(with
singular nouns)* etwas; **some tea/biscuits**
etwas Tee/ein paar Plätzchen; **I've got
some money, but not much** ich habe ein
bisschen Geld, aber nicht viel

2 *(certain: in contrasts)* manche(r, s); **some
people say that ...** manche Leute sagen,
dass ...

3 *(unspecified)* irgendein(e); **some woman
was asking for you** da hat eine Frau nach
Ihnen gefragt; **some day** eines Tages;
some day next week irgendwann nächste
Woche

♦ pron 1 (a certain number) einige; **have you got some?** haben Sie welche? 2 (a certain amount) etwas; **I've read some of the book** ich habe das Buch teilweise gelesen
♦ adv: **some 10 people** etwa 10 Leute

somebody ['sʌmbədɪ] pron = **someone**
somehow ['sʌmhau] adv (in some way, for some reason) irgendwie
someone ['sʌmwʌn] pron jemand; (direct obj) jemand(en); (indirect obj) jemandem
someplace ['sʌmpleɪs] (US) adv = **somewhere**
somersault ['sʌməsɔːlt] n Salto m ♦ vi einen Salto machen
something ['sʌmθɪŋ] pron etwas
sometime ['sʌmtaɪm] adv (irgend)einmal
sometimes ['sʌmtaɪmz] adv manchmal
somewhat ['sʌmwɔt] adv etwas
somewhere ['sʌmweəʳ] adv irgendwo; (to a place) irgendwohin; **~ else** irgendwo anders
son [sʌn] n Sohn m
sonar ['səunɑːʳ] n Echolot nt
song [sɒŋ] n Lied nt
sonic boom ['sɒnɪk-] n Überschallknall m
son-in-law ['sʌnɪnlɔː] n Schwiegersohn m
soon [suːn] adv bald; **~ afterwards** kurz danach; **~er** adv (time) früher; (for preference) lieber; **~er or later** früher oder später
soot [sut] n Ruß m
soothe [suːð] vt (person) beruhigen; (pain) lindern
sophisticated [sə'fɪstɪkeɪtɪd] adj (person) kultiviert; (machinery) hoch entwickelt
sophomore ['sɒfəmɔːʳ] (US) n College-student m im 2. Jahr
soporific [sɒpə'rɪfɪk] adj einschläfernd
sopping ['sɒpɪŋ] adj patschnass
soppy ['sɒpɪ] (inf) adj schmalzig
soprano [sə'prɑːnəu] n Sopran m
sorcerer ['sɔːsərəʳ] n Hexenmeister m
sordid ['sɔːdɪd] adj erbärmlich
sore [sɔːʳ] adj schmerzend; (point) wund ♦ n Wunde f; **~ly** adv (tempted) stark, sehr

sorrow ['sɒrəu] n Kummer m, Leid nt; **~ful** adj sorgenvoll
sorry ['sɒrɪ] adj traurig, erbärmlich; **~!** Entschuldigung!; **to feel ~ for sb** jdn bemitleiden; **I feel ~ for him** er tut mir Leid; **~?** (pardon) wie bitte?
sort [sɔːt] n Art f, Sorte f ♦ vt (also: **~ out**: papers) sortieren; (: problems) sichten, in Ordnung bringen; **~ing office** n Sortierstelle f
SOS n SOS nt
so-so ['səusəu] adv so(so) lala
sought [sɔːt] pt, pp of **seek**
soul [səul] n Seele f; (music) Soul m; **~-destroying** adj trostlos; **~ful** adj seelenvoll
sound [saund] adj (healthy) gesund; (safe) sicher; (sensible) vernünftig; (theory) stichhaltig; (thorough) tüchtig, gehörig ♦ adv: **to be ~ asleep** fest schlafen ♦ n (noise) Geräusch nt, Laut m, (GEOG) Sund m ♦ vt erschallen lassen; (alarm) (Alarm) schlagen ♦ vi (make a ~) schallen, tönen; (seem) klingen; **to ~ like** sich anhören wie; **~ out** vt erforschen; (person) auf den Zahn fühlen +dat; **~ barrier** n Schallmauer f, **~ bite** n (RAD, TV) prägnante(s) Zitat nt; **~ effects** npl Toneffekte pl; **~ly** adv (sleep) fest; (beat) tüchtig; **~proof** adj (room) schalldicht; **~ track** n Tonstreifen m; (music) Filmmusik f
soup [suːp] n Suppe f; **~ plate** n Suppenteller m; **~spoon** n Suppenlöffel m
sour ['sauəʳ] adj (also fig) sauer; **it's ~ grapes** (fig) die Trauben hängen zu hoch
source [sɔːs] n (also fig) Quelle f
south [sauθ] n Süden m ♦ adj Süd-, südlich ♦ adv nach Süden, südwärts; **S~ Africa** n Südafrika nt; **S~ African** adj südafrikanisch ♦ n Südafrikaner(in) m(f); **S~ America** n Südamerika nt; **S~ American** adj südamerikanisch ♦ n Südamerikaner(in) m(f); **~-east** n Südosten m; **~erly** ['sʌðəlɪ] adj südlich; **~ern** ['sʌðən] adj südlich, Süd-; **S~ Pole** n Südpol m; **S~ Wales** n Südwales nt; **~ward(s)** adv südwärts, nach Süden; **~-west** n Südwesten m
souvenir [suːvə'nɪəʳ] n Souvenir nt

sovereign ['sɒvrɪn] n (*ruler*) Herrscher(in) m(f) ♦ adj (*independent*) souverän

soviet ['səʊvɪət] adj sowjetisch; **the S~ Union** die Sowjetunion

sow¹ [saʊ] n (*place*) Sau f

sow² [səʊ] (*pt* **sowed**, *pp* **sown**) vt (*also fig*) säen

soya ['sɔɪə] (*US* **soy**) n: **~ bean** Sojabohne f; **~ sauce** Sojasauce f

spa [spɑː] n (*place*) Kurort m

space [speɪs] n Platz m, Raum m; (*universe*) Weltraum m, All nt; (*length of time*) Abstand m ♦ vt (*also:* **~ out**) verteilen; **~craft** n Raumschiff nt; **~man** (*irreg*) n Raumfahrer m; **~ ship** n Raumschiff nt

spacing ['speɪsɪŋ] n Abstand m; (*also:* **~ out**) Verteilung f

spacious ['speɪʃəs] adj geräumig, weit

spade [speɪd] n Spaten m; **~s** npl (*CARDS*) Pik nt

Spain [speɪn] n Spanien nt

span [spæn] n Spanne f; (*of bridge etc*) Spannweite f ♦ vt überspannen

Spaniard ['spænjəd] n Spanier(in) m(f)

spaniel ['spænjəl] n Spaniel m

Spanish ['spænɪʃ] adj spanisch ♦ n (*LING*) Spanisch nt; **the ~** npl (*people*) die Spanier pl

spank [spæŋk] vt verhauen, versohlen

spanner ['spænər] (*BRIT*) n Schraubenschlüssel m

spar [spɑːr] n (*NAUT*) Sparren m ♦ vi (*BOXING*) einen Sparring machen

spare [speər] adj Ersatz- ♦ n = **spare part** ♦ vt (*lives, feelings*) verschonen; (*trouble*) ersparen; **to ~** (*surplus*) übrig; **~ part** n Ersatzteil nt; **~ time** n Freizeit f; **~ wheel** n (*AUT*) Reservereifen m

sparing ['speərɪŋ] adj: **to be ~ with** geizen mit; **~ly** adv sparsam; (*eat, spend etc*) in Maßen

spark [spɑːk] n Funken m; **~(ing) plug** n Zündkerze f

sparkle ['spɑːkl] n Funkeln nt; (*gaiety*) Schwung m ♦ vi funkeln; **sparkling** adj funkelnd; (*wine*) Schaum-; (*mineral water*) mit Kohlensäure; (*conversation*) spritzig,

geistreich

sparrow ['spærəʊ] n Spatz m

sparse [spɑːs] adj spärlich

spasm ['spæzəm] n (*MED*) Krampf m; (*fig*) Anfall m; **~odic** [spæz'mɔdɪk] adj (*fig*) sprunghaft

spastic ['spæstɪk] (*old*) n Spastiker(in) m(f) ♦ adj spastisch

spat [spæt] pt, pp of **spit**

spate [speɪt] n (*fig*) Flut f, Schwall m; **in ~** (*river*) angeschwollen

spatter ['spætər] vt bespritzen, verspritzen

spatula ['spætjʊlə] n Spatel m

spawn [spɔːn] vi laichen ♦ n Laich m

speak [spiːk] (*pt* **spoke**, *pp* **spoken**) vt sprechen, reden; (*truth*) sagen; (*language*) sprechen ♦ vi: **to ~ (to)** sprechen (mit or zu); **to ~ to sb** of or **about sth** mit jdm über etw acc sprechen; **~ up!** sprich lauter!; **~er** n Sprecher(in) m(f), Redner(in) m(f); (*loudspeaker*) Lautsprecher m; (*POL*): **the S~er** der Vorsitzende des Parlaments (*BRIT*) or des Kongresses (*US*)

spear [spɪər] n Speer m ♦ vt aufspießen; **~head** vt (*attack etc*) anführen

spec [spek] (*inf*) n: **on ~** auf gut Glück

special ['speʃl] adj besondere(r, s); **~ist** n (*TECH*) Fachmann m; (*MED*) Facharzt m/ Fachärztin f; **~ity** [speʃɪ'ælɪtɪ] n Spezialität f; (*study*) Spezialgebiet nt; **~ize** vi: **to ~ize (in)** sich spezialisieren (auf +acc); **~ly** adv besonders; (*explicitly*) extra; **~ needs** adj: **~ needs children** behinderte Kinder pl; **~ty** (*esp US*) n = **speciality**

species ['spiːʃiːz] n Art f

specific [spə'sɪfɪk] adj spezifisch; **~ally** adv spezifisch

specification [spesɪfɪ'keɪʃən] n Angabe f; (*stipulation*) Bedingung f; **~s** npl (*TECH*) technische Daten pl

specify ['spesɪfaɪ] vt genau angeben

specimen ['spesɪmən] n Probe f

speck [spek] n Fleckchen nt

speckled ['spekld] adj gesprenkelt

specs [speks] (*inf*) npl Brille f

spectacle ['spektəkl] n Schauspiel nt; **~s** npl (*glasses*) Brille f

spectacular [spɛk'tækjuləʳ] *adj* sensationell; (*success etc*) spektakulär

spectator [spɛk'teɪtəʳ] *n* Zuschauer(in) *m(f)*

spectre ['spɛktəʳ] (*US* **specter**) *n* Geist *m*, Gespenst *nt*

speculate ['spɛkjuleɪt] *vi* spekulieren

speech [spiːtʃ] *n* Sprache *f*; (*address*) Rede *f*; (*way one speaks*) Sprechweise *f*; **~less** *adj* sprachlos

speed [spiːd] *n* Geschwindigkeit *f*; (*gear*) Gang *m* ♦ *vi* (*JUR*) (zu) schnell fahren; **at full** *or* **top ~** mit Höchstgeschwindigkeit; **~ up** *vt* beschleunigen ♦ *vi* schneller werden; schneller fahren; **~boat** *n* Schnellboot *nt*; **~ily** *adv* schleunigst; **~ing** *n* Geschwindigkeitsüberschreitung *f*; **~ limit** *n* Geschwindigkeitsbegrenzung *f*; **~ometer** [spɪ'dɒmɪtəʳ] *n* Tachometer *m*; **~way** *n* (*bike racing*) Motorradrennstrecke *f*; **~y** *adj* schnell

spell [spɛl] (*pt, pp* **spelt** (*BRIT*) *or* **spelled**) *n* (*magic*) Bann *m*; (*period of time*) (eine) Zeit lang ♦ *vt* buchstabieren; (*imply*) bedeuten; **to cast a ~ on sb** jdn verzaubern; **~bound** *adj* (*wie*) gebannt; **~ing** *n* Rechtschreibung *f*

spelt [spɛlt] (*BRIT*) *pt, pp of* **spell**

spend [spɛnd] (*pt, pp* **spent**) *vt* (*money*) ausgeben; (*time*) verbringen; **~thrift** *n* Verschwender(in) *m(f)*

spent [spɛnt] *pt, pp of* **spend**

sperm [spɜːm] *n* (*BIOL*) Samenflüssigkeit *f*

spew [spjuː] *vt* (er)brechen

sphere [sfɪəʳ] *n* (*globe*) Kugel *f*; (*fig*) Sphäre *f*, Gebiet *nt*; **spherical** ['sfɛrɪkl] *adj* kugelförmig

spice [spaɪs] *n* Gewürz *nt* ♦ *vt* würzen

spick-and-span ['spɪkən'spæn] *adj* blitzblank

spicy ['spaɪsɪ] *adj* (*food*) stark gewürzt; (*fig*) pikant

spider ['spaɪdəʳ] *n* Spinne *f*

spike [spaɪk] *n* Dorn *m*, Spitze *f*

spill [spɪl] (*pt, pp* **spilt** *or* **spilled**) *vt* verschütten ♦ *vi* sich ergießen; **~ over** *vi* überlaufen; (*fig*) sich ausbreiten

spilt [spɪlt] *pt, pp of* **spill**

spin [spɪn] (*pt, pp* **spun**) *n* (*trip in car*) Spazierfahrt *f*; (*AVIAT*) (Ab)trudeln *nt*; (*on ball*) Drall *m* ♦ *vt* (*thread*) spinnen; (*like top*) (herum)wirbeln ♦ *vi* sich drehen; **~ out** *vt* in die Länge ziehen

spinach ['spɪnɪtʃ] *n* Spinat *m*

spinal ['spaɪnl] *adj* Rückgrat-; **~ cord** *n* Rückenmark *nt*

spindly ['spɪndlɪ] *adj* spindeldürr

spin doctor *n* PR-Fachmann *m*, PR-Fachfrau *f*

spin-dryer [spɪn'draɪəʳ] (*BRIT*) *n* Wäscheschleuder *f*

spine [spaɪn] *n* Rückgrat *nt*; (*thorn*) Stachel *m*; **~less** *adj* (*also fig*) rückgratlos

spinning ['spɪnɪŋ] *n* Spinnen *nt*; **~ top** *n* Kreisel *m*; **~ wheel** *n* Spinnrad *nt*

spin-off ['spɪnɒf] *n* Nebenprodukt *nt*

spinster ['spɪnstəʳ] *n* unverheiratete Frau *f*; (*pej*) alte Jungfer *f*

spiral ['spaɪərl] *n* Spirale *f* ♦ *adj* spiralförmig; (*movement etc*) in Spiralen ♦ *vi* sich (hoch)winden; **~ staircase** *n* Wendeltreppe *f*

spire ['spaɪəʳ] *n* Turm *m*

spirit ['spɪrɪt] *n* Geist *m*; (*humour, mood*) Stimmung *f*; (*courage*) Mut *m*; (*verve*) Elan *m*; (*alcohol*) Alkohol *m*; **~s** *npl* (*drink*) Spirituosen *pl*; **in good ~s** gut aufgelegt; **~ed** *adj* beherzt; **~ level** *n* Wasserwaage *f*

spiritual ['spɪrɪtjuəl] *adj* geistig, seelisch; (*REL*) geistlich ♦ *n* Spiritual *nt*

spit [spɪt] (*pt, pp* **spat**) *n* (*for roasting*) (Brat)spieß *m*; (*saliva*) Spucke *f* ♦ *vi* spucken; (*rain*) sprühen; (*make a sound*) zischen; (*cat*) fauchen

spite [spaɪt] *n* Gehässigkeit *f* ♦ *vt* kränken; **in ~ of** trotz; **~ful** *adj* gehässig

spittle ['spɪtl] *n* Speichel *m*, Spucke *f*

splash [splæʃ] *n* Spritzer *m*; (*of colour*) (Farb)fleck *m* ♦ *vt* bespritzen ♦ *vi* spritzen

spleen [spliːn] *n* (*ANAT*) Milz *f*

splendid ['splendɪd] *adj* glänzend

splendour ['splendəʳ] (*US* **splendor**) *n* Pracht *f*

splint [splɪnt] *n* Schiene *f*

splinter ['splɪntəʳ] *n* Splitter *m* ♦ *vi* (zer)splittern

split [splɪt] (*pt, pp* **split**) *n* Spalte *f*; (*fig*) Spaltung *f*; (*division*) Trennung *f* ♦ *vt* spalten *vi* ♦ *vi* (*divide*) reißen; **~ up** *vi* sich trennen

splutter ['splʌtər] *vi* stottern

spoil [spɔɪl] (*pt, pp* **spoilt** *or* **spoiled**) *vt* (*ruin*) verderben; (*child*) verwöhnen; **~s** *npl* Beute *f*; **~sport** *n* Spielverderber *m*; **~t** *pt, pp of* **spoil**

spoke [spəʊk] *pt of* **speak** ♦ *n* Speiche *f*; **~n** *pp of* **speak**

spokesman ['spəʊksmən] (*irreg*) *n* Sprecher *m*; **spokeswoman** ['spəʊkswʊmən] (*irreg*) *n* Sprecherin *f*

sponge [spʌndʒ] *n* Schwamm *m* ♦ *vt* abwaschen ♦ *vi*: **to ~ on** auf Kosten +*gen* leben; **~ bag** (*BRIT*) *n* Kulturbeutel *m*; **~ cake** *n* Rührkuchen *m*

sponsor ['spɒnsər] *n* Sponsor *m* ♦ *vt* fördern; **~ship** *n* Finanzierung *f*; (*public*) Schirmherrschaft *f*

spontaneous [spɒn'teɪnɪəs] *adj* spontan

spooky ['spuːkɪ] (*inf*) *adj* gespenstisch

spool [spuːl] *n* Spule *f*, Rolle *f*

spoon [spuːn] *n* Löffel *m*; **~feed** (*irreg*) *vt* mit dem Löffel füttern; (*fig*) hochpäppeln; **~ful** *n* Löffel *m* (voll)

sport [spɔːt] *n* Sport *m*; (*person*) feine(r) Kerl *m*; **~ing** *adj* (*fair*) sportlich, fair; **to give sb a ~ing chance** jdm eine faire Chance geben; **~ jacket** (*US*) *n* = **sports jacket**; **~s car** *n* Sportwagen *m*; **~s jacket** *n* Sportjackett *nt*; **~sman** (*irreg*) *n* Sportler *m*; **~smanship** *n* Sportlichkeit *f*; **~swear** *n* Sportkleidung *f*; **~swoman** (*irreg*) *n* Sportlerin *f*; **~y** *adj* sportlich

spot [spɒt] *n* Punkt *m*; (*dirty*) Fleck(en) *m*; (*place*) Stelle *f*; (*MED*) Pickel *m* ♦ *vt* erspähen; (*mistake*) bemerken; **on the ~** an Ort und Stelle; (*at once*) auf der Stelle; **~ check** *n* Stichprobe *f*; **~less** *adj* fleckenlos; **~light** *n* Scheinwerferlicht *nt*; (*lamp*) Scheinwerfer *m*; **~ted** *adj* gefleckt; **~ty** *adj* (*face*) pickelig

spouse [spaʊs] *n* Gatte *m*/Gattin *f*

spout [spaʊt] *n* (*of pot*) Tülle *f*; (*jet*) Wasserstrahl *m* ♦ *vi* speien

sprain [spreɪn] *n* Verrenkung *f* ♦ *vt* verrenken

sprang [spræŋ] *pt of* **spring**

sprawl [sprɔːl] *vi* sich strecken

spray [spreɪ] *n* Spray *nt*; (*off sea*) Gischt *f*; (*of flowers*) Zweig *m* ♦ *vt* besprühen, sprayen

spread [spred] (*pt, pp* **spread**) *n* (*extent*) Verbreitung *f*; (*inf: meal*) Schmaus *m*; (*for bread*) Aufstrich *m* ♦ *vt* ausbreiten; (*scatter*) verbreiten; (*butter*) streichen ♦ *vi* sich ausbreiten; **~ out** *vi* (*move apart*) sich verteilen; **~-eagled** ['spredɪːgld] *adj*: **to be ~-eagled** alle viere von sich strecken; **~sheet** *n* Tabellenkalkulation *f*

spree [spriː] *n* (*shopping*) Einkaufsbummel *m*; **to go on a ~** einen draufmachen

sprightly ['spraɪtlɪ] *adj* munter, lebhaft

spring [sprɪŋ] (*pt* **sprang**, *pp* **sprung**) *n* (*leap*) Sprung *m*; (*TECH*) Feder *f*; (*season*) Frühling *m*; (*water*) Quelle *f* ♦ *vi* (*leap*) springen; **~ up** *vi* (*problem*) auftauchen; **~board** *n* Sprungbrett *nt*; **~-clean** *n* (*also:* **~-cleaning**) Frühjahrsputz *m*; **~time** *n* Frühling *m*; **~y** *adj* federnd, elastisch

sprinkle ['sprɪŋkl] *vt* (*salt*) streuen; (*liquid*) sprenkeln; **to ~ water on, to ~ with water** mit Wasser besprengen; **~r** ['sprɪŋklər] *n* (*for lawn*) Sprenger *m*; (*for fire fighting*) Sprinkler *m*

sprint [sprɪnt] *n* (*race*) Sprint *m* ♦ *vi* (*run fast*) rennen; (*SPORT*) sprinten; **~er** *n* Sprinter(in) *m(f)*

sprout [spraʊt] *vi* sprießen

sprouts [spraʊts] *npl* (*also:* **Brussels ~**) Rosenkohl *m*

spruce [spruːs] *n* Fichte *f* ♦ *adj* schmuck, adrett

sprung [sprʌŋ] *pp of* **spring**

spry [spraɪ] *adj* flink, rege

spun [spʌn] *pt, pp of* **spin**

spur [spəːr] *n* Sporn *m*; (*fig*) Ansporn *m* ♦ *vt* (*also:* **~ on**: *fig*) anspornen; **on the ~ of the moment** spontan

spurious ['spjʊərɪəs] *adj* falsch

spurn [spəːn] *vt* verschmähen

spurt [spəːt] *n* (*jet*) Strahl *m*; (*acceleration*) Spurt *m* ♦ *vi* (*liquid*) schießen

spy [spaɪ] *n* Spion(in) *m(f)* ♦ *vi* spionieren ♦ *vt* erspähen; **~ing** *n* Spionage *f*

sq. *abbr* = **square**

squabble [ˈskwɒbl] *n* Zank *m* ♦ *vi* sich zanken

squad [skwɒd] *n* (*MIL*) Abteilung *f*; (*POLICE*) Kommando *nt*

squadron [ˈskwɒdrn] *n* (*cavalry*) Schwadron *f*; (*NAUT*) Geschwader *nt*; (*air force*) Staffel *f*

squalid [ˈskwɒlɪd] *adj* verkommen

squall [skwɔ:l] *n* Bö(e) *f*, Windstoß *m*

squalor [ˈskwɒlə^r] *n* Verwahrlosung *f*

squander [ˈskwɒndə^r] *vt* verschwenden

square [skweə^r] *n* Quadrat *nt*; (*open space*) Platz *m*; (*instrument*) Winkel *m*; (*inf: person*) Spießer *m* ♦ *adj* viereckig; (*inf: ideas, tastes*) spießig ♦ *vt* (*arrange*) ausmachen; (*MATH*) ins Quadrat erheben ♦ *vi* (*agree*) übereinstimmen; **all ~** quitt; **a ~ meal** eine ordentliche Mahlzeit; **2 metres ~** 2 Meter im Quadrat; **1 ~ metre** 1 Quadratmeter; **~ly** *adv* fest, gerade

squash [skwɒʃ] *n* (*BRIT: drink*) Saft *m*; (*game*) Squash *nt* ♦ *vt* zerquetschen

squat [skwɒt] *adj* untersetzt ♦ *vi* hocken; **~ter** *n* Hausbesetzer *m*

squawk [skwɔ:k] *vi* kreischen

squeak [skwi:k] *vi* quiek(s)en; (*spring, door etc*) quietschen

squeal [skwi:l] *vi* schrill schreien

squeamish [ˈskwi:mɪʃ] *adj* empfindlich

squeeze [skwi:z] *vt* pressen, drücken; (*orange*) auspressen; **~ out** *vt* ausquetschen

squelch [skweltʃ] *vi* platschen

squib [skwɪb] *n* Knallfrosch *m*

squid [skwɪd] *n* Tintenfisch *m*

squiggle [ˈskwɪgl] *n* Schnörkel *m*

squint [skwɪnt] *vi* schielen ♦ *n*: **to have a ~** schielen; **to ~ at sb/sth** nach jdm/etw schielen

squirm [skwə:m] *vi* sich winden

squirrel [ˈskwɪrəl] *n* Eichhörnchen *nt*

squirt [skwə:t] *vt, vi* spritzen

Sr *abbr* (= *senior*) sen.

St *abbr* (= *saint*) hl., St.; (= *street*) Str.

stab [stæb] *n* (*blow*) Stich *m*; (*inf: try*) Versuch *m* ♦ *vt* erstechen

stabilize [ˈsteɪbəlaɪz] *vt* stabilisieren ♦ *vi* sich stabilisieren

stable [ˈsteɪbl] *adj* stabil ♦ *n* Stall *m*

stack [stæk] *n* Stapel *m* ♦ *vt* stapeln

stadium [ˈsteɪdɪəm] *n* Stadion *nt*

staff [stɑ:f] *n* (*stick, MIL*) Stab *m*; (*personnel*) Personal *nt*; (*BRIT: SCH*) Lehrkräfte *pl* ♦ *vt* besetzen

stag [stæg] *n* Hirsch *m*

stage [steɪdʒ] *n* Bühne *f*; (*of journey*) Etappe *f*; (*degree*) Stufe *f*; (*point*) Stadium *nt* ♦ *vt* (*put on*) aufführen; (*simulate*) inszenieren; (*demonstration*) veranstalten; **in ~s** etappenweise; **~coach** *n* Postkutsche *f*; **~ door** *n* Bühneneingang *m*; **~ manager** *n* Intendant *m*

stagger [ˈstægə^r] *vi* wanken, taumeln ♦ *vt* (*amaze*) verblüffen; (*hours*) staffeln; **~ing** *adj* unglaublich

stagnant [ˈstægnənt] *adj* stagnierend; (*water*) stehend; **stagnate** [stægˈneɪt] *vi* stagnieren

stag party *n* Männerabend *m* (*vom Bräutigam vor der Hochzeit gegeben*)

staid [steɪd] *adj* gesetzt

stain [steɪn] *n* Fleck *m* ♦ *vt* beflecken; **~ed glass window** buntes Glasfenster *nt*; **~less** *adj* (*steel*) rostfrei; **~ remover** *n* Fleckentferner *m*

stair [steə^r] *n* (*Treppen*)stufe *f*; **~s** *npl* (*flight of steps*) Treppe *f*; **~case** *n* Treppenhaus *nt*, Treppe *f*; **~way** *n* Treppenaufgang *m*

stake [steɪk] *n* (*post*) Pfahl *m*; (*money*) Einsatz *m* ♦ *vt* (*bet: money*) setzen; **to be at ~** auf dem Spiel stehen

stale [steɪl] *adj* alt; (*bread*) altbacken

stalemate [ˈsteɪlmeɪt] *n* (*CHESS*) Patt *nt*; (*fig*) Stillstand *m*

stalk [stɔ:k] *n* Stängel *m*, Stiel *m* ♦ *vt* (*game*) jagen; **~ off** *vi* abstolzieren

stall [stɔ:l] *n* (*in stable*) Stand *m*, Box *f*; (*in market*) (Verkaufs)stand *m* ♦ *vt* (*AUT*) abwürgen ♦ *vi* (*AUT*) stehen bleiben; (*fig*) Ausflüchte machen; **~s** *npl* (*BRIT: THEAT*) Parkett *nt*

stallion [ˈstæljən] *n* Zuchthengst *m*

stalwart ['stɔ:lwət] *n* treue(r) Anhänger *m*

stamina ['stæminə] *n* Durchhaltevermögen *nt*, Zähigkeit *f*

stammer ['stæmə'] *n* Stottern *nt* ♦ *vt, vi* stottern, stammeln

stamp [stæmp] *n* Briefmarke *f*; (*for document*) Stempel *m* ♦ *vi* stampfen ♦ *vt* (*mark*) stempeln; (*mail*) frankieren; (*foot*) stampfen mit; ~ **album** *n* Briefmarkenalbum *nt*; ~ **collecting** *n* Briefmarkensammeln *nt*

stampede [stæm'pi:d] *n* panische Flucht *f*

stance [stæns] *n* Haltung *f*

stand [stænd] (*pt, pp* **stood**) *n* (*for objects*) Gestell *nt*; (*seats*) Tribüne *f* ♦ *vi* stehen; (*rise*) aufstehen; (*decision*) feststehen ♦ *vt* setzen, stellen; (*endure*) aushalten; (*person*) ausstehen; (*nonsense*) dulden; **to make a ~** Widerstand leisten; **to ~ for parliament** (*BRIT*) für das Parlament kandidieren; ~ **by** *vi* (*be ready*) bereitstehen ♦ *vt fus* (*opinion*) treu bleiben +*dat*; ~ **down** *vi* (*withdraw*) zurücktreten; ~ **for** *vt fus* (*signify*) stehen für; (*permit, tolerate*) hinnehmen; ~ **in for** *vt fus* einspringen für; ~ **out** *vi* (*be prominent*) hervorstechen; ~ **up** *vi* (*rise*) aufstehen; ~ **up for** *vt fus* sich einsetzen für; ~ **up to** *vt fus*: **to ~ up to sth** einer Sache *dat* gewachsen sein; **to ~ up to sb** sich jdm gegenüber behaupten

standard ['stændəd] *n* (*measure*) Norm *f*; (*flag*) Fahne *f* ♦ *adj* (*size etc*) Normal-; ~**s** *npl* (*morals*) Maßstäbe *pl*; ~**ize** *vt* vereinheitlichen; ~ **lamp** (*BRIT*) *n* Stehlampe *f*; ~ **of living** *n* Lebensstandard *m*

stand: ~~**by** *n* Reserve *f*; **to be on** ~**by** in Bereitschaft sein; ~~**by ticket** *n* (*AVIAT*) Standbyticket *nt*; ~~**in** ['stændɪn] *n* Ersatz *m*

standing ['stændɪŋ] *adj* (*erect*) stehend; (*permanent*) ständig; (*invitation*) offen ♦ *n* (*duration*) Dauer *f*; (*reputation*) Ansehen *nt*; **of many years'** ~ langjährig; ~ **order** (*BRIT*) *n* (*at bank*) Dauerauftrag *m*; ~ **room** *n* Stehplatz *m*

stand: ~~**offish** [stænd'ɔfif] *adj* zurückhaltend, sehr reserviert; ~~**point** ['stændpɔint] *n* Standpunkt *m*; ~~**still**

['stændstɪl] *n*: **to be at a** ~**still** stillstehen; **to come to a** ~**still** zum Stillstand kommen

stank [stæŋk] *pt of* **stink**

staple ['steɪpl] *n* (*in paper*) Heftklammer *f*; (*article*) Haupterzeugnis *nt* ♦ *adj* Grund-, Haupt- ♦ *vt* (*fest*)klammern; ~**r** *n* Heftmaschine *f*

star [stɑ:'] *n* Stern *m*; (*person*) Star *m* ♦ *vi* die Hauptrolle spielen ♦ *vt*: ~**ring** ... in der Hauptrolle/den Hauptrollen ...

starboard ['stɑ:bɔːd] *n* Steuerbord *nt*

starch [stɑ:tf] *n* Stärke *f*

stardom ['stɑ:dəm] *n* Berühmtheit *f*

stare [stɛə'] *n* starre(r) Blick *m* ♦ *vi*: **to ~ at** starren auf +*acc*, anstarren

starfish ['stɑ:fɪf] *n* Seestern *m*

stark [stɑ:k] *adj* öde ♦ *adv*: ~ **naked** splitternackt

starling ['stɑ:lɪŋ] *n* Star *m*

starry ['stɑ:rɪ] *adj* Sternen-; ~~**eyed** *adj* (*innocent*) blauäugig

start [stɑ:t] *n* Anfang *m*; (*SPORT*) Start *m*; (*lead*) Vorsprung *m* ♦ *vt* in Gang setzen; (*car*) anlassen ♦ *vi* anfangen; (*car*) anspringen; (*on journey*) aufbrechen; (*SPORT*) starten; (*with fright*) zusammenfahren; **to ~ doing** *or* **to do sth** anfangen, etw zu tun; ~ **off** *vi* anfangen; (*begin moving*) losgehen; losfahren; ~ **up** *vi* anfangen ♦ *vt* beginnen; (*car*) anlassen; (*engine*) starten; ~**er** *n* (*AUT*) Anlasser *m*; (*for race*) Starter *m*; (*BRIT: COOK*) Vorspeise *f*; ~**ing point** *n* Ausgangspunkt *m*

startle ['stɑ:tl] *vt* erschrecken; **startling** *adj* erschreckend

starvation [stɑ:'veɪ∫ən] *n* Verhungern *nt*

starve [stɑ:v] *vi* verhungern ♦ *vt* verhungern lassen; **I'm starving** ich sterbe vor Hunger

state [steɪt] *n* (*condition*) Zustand *m*; (*POL*) Staat *m* ♦ *vt* erklären; (*facts*) angeben; **the S~s** (*USA*) die Staaten; **to be in a** ~ durchdrehen; ~**ly** *adj* würdevoll; ~**ly home** *n* herrschaftliches Anwesen *nt*, Schloss *nt*; ~**ment** *n* Aussage *f*; (*POL*) Erklärung *f*; ~**sman** (*irreg*) *n* Staatsmann *m*

static ['stætɪk] *n* (*also*: ~ **electricity**) Reibungselektrizität *f*

station ['steɪʃən] n (*RAIL etc*) Bahnhof m; (*police etc*) Wache f; (*in society*) Stand m ♦ vt stationieren

stationary ['steɪʃnərɪ] adj stillstehend; (*car*) parkend

stationer's n (*shop*) Schreibwarengeschäft nt; ~**y** n Schreibwaren pl

station master n Bahnhofsvorsteher m

station wagon n Kombiwagen m

statistics [stə'tɪstɪks] n Statistik f

statue ['stætjuː] n Statue f

stature ['stætʃər] n Größe f

status ['steɪtəs] n Status m

statute ['stætjuːt] n Gesetz nt; **statutory** ['stætjutrɪ] adj gesetzlich

staunch [stɔːntʃ] adj standhaft

stay [steɪ] n Aufenthalt m ♦ vi bleiben; (*reside*) wohnen; **to ~ put** an Ort und Stelle bleiben; **to ~ the night** übernachten; ~ **behind** vi zurückbleiben; ~ **in** vi (*at home*) zu Hause bleiben; ~ **on** vi (*continue*) länger bleiben; ~ **out** vi (*of house*) wegbleiben; ~ **up** vi (*at night*) aufbleiben; ~**ing power** n Durchhaltevermögen nt

stead [stɛd] n: **in sb's** ~ an jds Stelle dat; **to stand sb in good** ~ jdm zugute kommen

steadfast ['stɛdfɑːst] adj standhaft, treu

steadily ['stɛdɪlɪ] adv stetig, regelmäßig

steady ['stɛdɪ] adj (*firm*) fest, stabil; (*regular*) gleichmäßig; (*reliable*) beständig; (*hand*) ruhig; (*job, boyfriend*) fest ♦ vt festigen; **to ~ o.s. on/against sth** sich stützen auf/gegen sth acc

steak [steɪk] n Steak nt; (*fish*) Filet nt

steal [stiːl] (*pt* **stole**, *pp* **stolen**) vt stehlen ♦ vi stehlen; (*go quietly*) sich stehlen

stealth [stɛlθ] n Heimlichkeit f; ~**y** adj verstohlen, heimlich

steam [stiːm] n Dampf m ♦ vt (*COOK*) im Dampfbad erhitzen ♦ vi dampfen; ~ **engine** n Dampfmaschine f; ~**er** n Dampfer m; ~**roller** n Dampfwalze f; ~**ship** n = **steamer**; ~**y** adj dampfig

steel [stiːl] n Stahl m ♦ adj Stahl-; (*fig*) stählern; ~**works** n Stahlwerke pl

steep [stiːp] adj steil; (*price*) gepfeffert ♦ vt einweichen

steeple ['stiːpl] n Kirchturm m; ~**chase** n Hindernisrennen nt

steer [stɪər] vt, vi steuern; (*car etc*) lenken; ~**ing** n (*AUT*) Steuerung f; ~**ing wheel** n Steuer- or Lenkrad nt

stem [stɛm] n Stiel m ♦ vt aufhalten; ~ **from** vt fus abstammen von

stench [stɛntʃ] n Gestank m

stencil ['stɛnsl] n Schablone f ♦ vt (auf)drucken

stenographer [stɛ'nɔgrəfər] (*US*) n Stenograf(in) m(f)

step [stɛp] n Schritt m; (*stair*) Stufe f ♦ vi treten, schreiten; ~**s** npl (*BRIT*) = **stepladder**; **to take ~s** Schritte unternehmen; **in/out of** ~ (**with**) im/nicht im Gleichklang (mit); ~ **down** vi (*fig*) abtreten; ~ **off** vt fus aussteigen aus; ~ **up** vt steigern

stepbrother ['stɛpbrʌðər] n Stiefbruder m

stepdaughter ['stɛpdɔːtər] n Stieftochter f

stepfather ['stɛpfɑːðər] n Stiefvater m

stepladder ['stɛplædər] n Trittleiter f

stepmother ['stɛpmʌðər] n Stiefmutter f

stepping stone ['stɛpɪŋ-] n Stein m; (*fig*) Sprungbrett n

stepsister ['stɛpsɪstər] n Stiefschwester f

stepson ['stɛpsʌn] n Stiefsohn m

stereo ['stɛrɪəʊ] n Stereoanlage f ♦ adj (*also:* ~**phonic**) stereofonisch, stereophonisch

stereotype ['stɪərətaɪp] n (*fig*) Klischee nt ♦ vt stereotypieren; (*fig*) stereotyp machen

sterile ['stɛraɪl] adj steril; (*person*) unfruchtbar; **sterilize** vt sterilisieren

sterling ['stɜːlɪŋ] adj (*FIN*) Sterling-; (*character*) gediegen ♦ n (*ECON*) das Pfund Sterling; **a pound** ~ ein Pfund Sterling

stern [stɜːn] adj streng ♦ n Heck nt, Achterschiff nt

stew [stjuː] n Eintopf m ♦ vt, vi schmoren

steward ['stjuːəd] n Steward m; ~**ess** n Stewardess f

stick [stɪk] (*pt, pp* **stuck**) n Stock m; (*of chalk etc*) Stück nt ♦ vt (*stab*) stechen; (*fix*) stecken; (*put*) stellen; (*gum*) (an)kleben; (*inf: tolerate*) vertragen ♦ vi (*stop*) stecken bleiben; (*get stuck*) klemmen; (*hold fast*)

kleben, haften; **~ out** vi (project)
hervorstehen; **~ up** vi (project) in die Höhe
stehen; **~ up for** vt fus (defend) eintreten
für; **~er** n Aufkleber m; **~ing plaster** n
Heftpflaster nt

stickler ['stɪklə*] n: **~ (for)** Pedant m (in
+acc)

stick-up ['stɪkʌp] (inf) n (Raub)überfall m

sticky ['stɪkɪ] adj klebrig; (atmosphere) stickig

stiff [stɪf] adj steif; (difficult) hart; (paste) dick;
(drink) stark; **to have a ~ neck** einen steifen
Hals haben; **~en** vt versteifen, (ver)stärken
♦ vi sich versteifen

stifle ['staɪfl] vt unterdrücken; **stifling** adj
drückend

stigma ['stɪgmə] (pl BOT, MED, REL **~ta**; fig **~s**)
n Stigma nt

stigmata [stɪg'mɑːtə] npl of **stigma**

stile [staɪl] n Steige f

stiletto [stɪ'letəu] (BRIT) n (also: **~ heel**)
Pfennigabsatz m

still [stɪl] adj still ♦ adv (immer) noch;
(anyhow) immerhin; **~born** adj tot
geboren; **~ life** n Stillleben nt

stilt [stɪlt] n Stelze f

stilted ['stɪltɪd] adj gestelzt

stimulate ['stɪmjuleɪt] vt anregen,
stimulieren

stimuli ['stɪmjulaɪ] npl of **stimulus**

stimulus ['stɪmjuləs] (pl **-li**) n Anregung f,
Reiz m

sting [stɪŋ] (pt, pp **stung**) n Stich m; (organ)
Stachel m ♦ vi stechen; (on skin) brennen
♦ vt stechen

stingy ['stɪndʒɪ] adj geizig, knauserig

stink [stɪŋk] (pt **stank**, pp **stunk**) n Gestank
m ♦ vi stinken; **~ing** adj (fig) widerlich

stint [stɪnt] n (period) Betätigung f; **to do
one's ~** seine Arbeit tun; (share) seinen Teil
beitragen

stipulate ['stɪpjuleɪt] vt festsetzen

stir [stɜː*] n Bewegung f; (COOK) Rühren nt;
(sensation) Aufsehen nt ♦ vt (um)rühren ♦ vi
sich rühren; **~ up** vt (mob) aufhetzen;
(mixture) umrühren; (dust) aufwirbeln

stirrup ['stɪrəp] n Steigbügel m

stitch [stɪtʃ] n (with needle) Stich m; (MED)

Faden m; (of knitting) Masche f; (pain) Stich
m ♦ vt nähen

stoat [stəut] n Wiesel nt

stock [stɔk] n Vorrat m; (COMM)
(Waren)lager nt; (livestock) Vieh nt; (COOK)
Brühe f; (FIN) Grundkapital nt ♦ adj stets
vorrätig; (standard) Normal- ♦ vt (in shop)
führen; **~s** npl (FIN) Aktien pl; **in/out of ~**
vorrätig/nicht vorrätig; **to take ~ of**
Inventur machen von; (fig) Bilanz ziehen
aus; **~s and shares** Effekten pl; **~ up** vi: **to
~ up (with)** Reserven anlegen (von);
~broker ['stɔkbrəukə*] n Börsenmakler m; **~
cube** n Brühwürfel m; **~ exchange** n
Börse f

stocking ['stɔkɪŋ] n Strumpf m

stock: ~ market n Börse f; **~ phrase** n
Standardsatz m; **~pile** n Vorrat m ♦ vt
aufstapeln; **~taking** (BRIT) n (COMM)
Inventur f, Bestandsaufnahme f

stocky ['stɔkɪ] adj untersetzt

stodgy ['stɔdʒɪ] adj pampig

stoke [stəuk] vt schüren

stole [stəul] pt of **steal** ♦ n Stola f

stolen ['stəuln] pp of **steal**

stomach ['stʌmək] n Bauch m, Magen m
♦ vt vertragen; **~-ache** n Magen- or
Bauchschmerzen pl

stone [stəun] n Stein m; (BRIT: weight)
Gewichtseinheit = 6.35 kg ♦ vt (olive)
entkernen; (kill) steinigen; **~-cold** adj
eiskalt; **~-deaf** adj stocktaub; **~work** n
Mauerwerk nt; **stony** ['stəunɪ] adj steinig

stood [stud] pt, pp of **stand**

stool [stuːl] n Hocker m

stoop [stuːp] vi sich bücken

stop [stɔp] n Halt m; (bus ~) Haltestelle f;
(punctuation) Punkt m ♦ vt anhalten; (bring
to an end) aufhören (mit), sein lassen ♦ vi
aufhören; (clock) stehen bleiben; (remain)
bleiben; **to ~ doing sth** aufhören, etw zu
tun; **to ~ dead** innehalten; **~ off** vi kurz
Halt machen; **~ up** vt (hole) zustopfen,
verstopfen; **~gap** n Notlösung f; **~lights**
npl (AUT) Bremslichter pl; **~over** n (on
journey) Zwischenaufenthalt m; **~page**
['stɔpɪdʒ] n (An)halten nt; (traffic)

Verkehrsstockung f; (strike)
Arbeitseinstellung f; ~per ['stɔpər] n
Propfen m, Stöpsel m; ~ press n letzte
Meldung f; ~watch ['stɔpwɔtʃ] n Stoppuhr f

storage ['stɔ:rɪdʒ] n Lagerung f; ~ heater n
(Nachtstrom)speicherofen m

store [stɔ:r] n Vorrat m; (place) Lager nt,
Warenhaus nt; (BRIT: large shop) Kaufhaus
nt; (US) Laden m ♦ vt lagern; ~s npl
(supplies) Vorräte pl; ~ up vt sich
eindecken mit; ~room n Lagerraum m,
Vorratsraum m

storey ['stɔ:rɪ] (US story) n Stock m

stork [stɔ:k] n Storch m

storm [stɔ:m] n (also fig) Sturm m ♦ vt, vi
stürmen; ~y adj stürmisch

story ['stɔ:rɪ] n Geschichte f; (lie) Märchen
nt; (US) = storey; ~book n
Geschichtenbuch nt; ~teller n
Geschichtenerzähler m

stout [staut] adj (bold) tapfer; (fat) beleibt
♦ n Starkbier nt; (also: **sweet ~**) ≈ Malzbier
nt

stove [stəuv] n (Koch)herd m; (for heating)
Ofen m

stow [stəu] vt verstauen; ~away n blinde(r)
Passagier m

straddle ['strædl] vt (horse, fence) rittlings
sitzen auf (+dat); (fig) überbrücken

straggle ['strægl] vi (people) nachhinken; ~r
n Nachzügler m; **straggly** adj (hair) zottig

straight [streɪt] adj gerade; (honest) offen,
ehrlich; (drink) pur ♦ adv (direct) direkt,
geradewegs; **to put** or **get sth ~** etw in
Ordnung bringen; ~ **away** sofort; ~ **off**
sofort; ~en vt (also: **~en out**) gerade
machen; (fig) klarstellen; ~-faced adv ohne
die Miene zu verziehen ♦ adj: **to be ~-
faced** keine Miene verziehen; ~forward
adj einfach, unkompliziert

strain [streɪn] n Belastung f; (streak, trace)
Zug m; (of music) Fetzen m ♦ vt
überanstrengen; (stretch) anspannen;
(muscle) zerren; (filter) (durch)seihen ♦ vi
sich anstrengen; ~ed adj (laugh)
gezwungen; (relations) gespannt; ~er n
Sieb nt

strait [streɪt] n Straße f, Meerenge f;
~jacket n Zwangsjacke f; ~-laced adj
engherzig, streng

strand [strænd] n (of hair) Strähne f; (also fig)
Faden m

stranded ['strændɪd] adj (also fig) gestrandet

strange [streɪndʒ] adj fremd; (unusual)
seltsam; ~r n Fremde(r) mf

strangle ['stræŋgl] vt erwürgen; ~hold n
(fig) Umklammerung f

strap [stræp] n Riemen m; (on clothes) Träger
m ♦ vt (fasten) festschnallen

strapping ['stræpɪŋ] adj stramm

strata ['strɑ:tə] npl of **stratum**

strategic [strə'ti:dʒɪk] adj strategisch

strategy ['strætɪdʒɪ] n (fig) Strategie f

stratum ['strɑ:təm] (pl -ta) n Schicht f

straw [strɔ:] n Stroh nt; (single stalk, drinking
~) Strohhalm m; **that's the last ~!** das ist
der Gipfel!

strawberry ['strɔ:bərɪ] n Erdbeere f

stray [streɪ] adj (animal) verirrt ♦ vi
herumstreunen

streak [stri:k] n Streifen m; (in character)
Einschlag m; (in hair) Strähne f ♦ vt streifen
♦ vi zucken; (move quickly) flitzen; ~ **of bad
luck** Pechsträhne f; ~y adj gestreift; (bacon)
durchwachsen

stream [stri:m] n (brook) Bach m; (fig) Strom
m ♦ vt (SCH) in (Leistungs)gruppen einteilen
♦ vi strömen; **to ~ in/out** (people) hinein-/
hinausströmen

streamer ['stri:mər] n (flag) Wimpel m; (of
paper) Luftschlange f

streamlined ['stri:mlaɪnd] adj
stromlinienförmig; (effective) rationell

street [stri:t] n Straße f ♦ adj Straßen-; ~car
(US) n Straßenbahn f; ~ lamp n
Straßenlaterne f; ~ plan n Stadtplan m;
~wise (inf) adj: **to be ~wise** wissen, wo es
langgeht

strength [streŋθ] n (also fig) Stärke f; Kraft f;
~en vt (ver)stärken

strenuous ['strenjuəs] adj anstrengend

stress [stres] n Druck m; (mental) Stress m;
(GRAM) Betonung f ♦ vt betonen

stretch [stretʃ] n Strecke f ♦ vt ausdehnen,

strecken ♦ *vi* sich erstrecken; (*person*) sich strecken; ~ **out** *vi* sich ausstrecken ♦ *vt* ausstrecken

stretcher ['stretʃə'] *n* Tragbahre *f*

stretchy ['stretʃɪ] *adj* elastisch, dehnbar

strewn [struːn] *adj*: ~ **with** übersät mit

stricken ['strɪkən] *adj* (*person*) ergriffen; (*city, country*) heimgesucht; ~ **with** (*disease*) leidend unter +*dat*

strict [strɪkt] *adj* (*exact*) genau; (*severe*) streng; ~**ly** *adv* streng, genau

stridden ['strɪdn] *pp of* **stride**

stride [straɪd] (*pt* **strode**, *pp* **stridden**) *n* lange(r) Schritt *m* ♦ *vi* schreiten

strident ['straɪdnt] *adj* schneidend, durchdringend

strife [straɪf] *n* Streit *m*

strike [straɪk] (*pt*, *pp* **struck**) *n* Streik *m*; (*attack*) Schlag *m* ♦ *vt* (*hit*) schlagen; (*collide*) stoßen gegen; (*come to mind*) einfallen +*dat*; (*stand out*) auffallen +*dat*; (*find*) finden ♦ *vi* (*stop work*) streiken; (*attack*) zuschlagen; (*clock*) schlagen; **on** ~ (*workers*) im Streik; **to** ~ **a match** ein Streichholz anzünden; ~ **down** *vt* (*lay low*) niederschlagen; ~ **out** *vt* (*cross out*) ausstreichen; ~ **up** *vt* (*music*) anstimmen; (*friendship*) schließen; ~**r** *n* Streikende(r) *mf*; **striking** ['straɪkɪŋ] *adj* auffallend

string [strɪŋ] (*pt*, *pp* **strung**) *n* Schnur *f*; (*row*) Reihe *f*; (*MUS*) Saite *f* ♦ *vt*: **to** ~ **together** aneinander reihen ♦ *vi*: **to** ~ **out** (sich) verteilen; **the** ~**s** *npl* (*MUS*) die Streichinstrumente *pl*; **to pull** ~**s** (*fig*) Fäden ziehen; ~ **bean** *n* grüne Bohne *f*; ~(**ed**) **instrument** *n* (*MUS*) Saiteninstrument *nt*

stringent ['strɪndʒənt] *adj* streng

strip [strɪp] *n* Streifen *m* ♦ *vt* (*uncover*) abstreifen, abziehen; (*clothes*) ausziehen; (*TECH*) auseinander nehmen ♦ *vi* (*undress*) sich ausziehen; ~ **cartoon** *n* Bildserie *f*

stripe [straɪp] *n* Streifen *m*; ~**d** *adj* gestreift

strip lighting *n* Neonlicht *nt*

stripper ['strɪpə'] *n* Stripteasetänzerin *f*

strip-search ['strɪpsɜːtʃ] *n* Leibesvisitation *f* (*bei der man sich ausziehen muss*) ♦ *vt*: **to be** ~~**ed** sich ausziehen müssen und

durchsucht werden

stripy ['straɪpɪ] *adj* gestreift

strive [straɪv] (*pt* **strove**, *pp* **striven**) *vi*: **to** ~ **(for)** streben (nach)

strode [strəʊd] *pt of* **stride**

stroke [strəʊk] *n* Schlag *m*; (*SWIMMING, ROWING*) Stoß *m*; (*MED*) Schlaganfall *m*; (*caress*) Streicheln *nt* ♦ *vt* streicheln; **at a** ~ mit einem Schlag

stroll [strəʊl] *n* Spaziergang *m* ♦ *vi* schlendern; ~**er** (*US*) *n* (*pushchair*) Sportwagen *m*

strong [strɒŋ] *adj* stark; (*firm*) fest; **they are 50** ~ sie sind 50 Mann stark; ~**box** *n* Kassette *f*; ~**hold** *n* Hochburg *f*; ~**ly** *adv* stark; ~**room** *n* Tresor *m*

strove [strəʊv] *pt of* **strive**

struck [strʌk] *pt*, *pp of* **strike**

structure ['strʌktʃə'] *n* Struktur *f*, Aufbau *m*; (*building*) Bau *m*

struggle ['strʌgl] *n* Kampf *m* ♦ *vi* (*fight*) kämpfen

strum [strʌm] *vt* (*guitar*) klimpern auf +*dat*

strung [strʌŋ] *pt*, *pp of* **string**

strut [strʌt] *n* Strebe *f*, Stütze *f* ♦ *vi* stolzieren

stub [stʌb] *n* Stummel *m*; (*of cigarette*) Kippe *f* ♦ *vt*: **to** ~ **one's toe** sich *dat* den Zeh anstoßen; ~ **out** *vt* ausdrücken

stubble ['stʌbl] *n* Stoppel *f*

stubborn ['stʌbən] *adj* hartnäckig

stuck [stʌk] *pt*, *pp of* **stick** ♦ *adj* (*jammed*) klemmend; ~~**up** *adj* hochnäsig

stud [stʌd] *n* (*button*) Kragenknopf *m*; (*place*) Gestüt *nt* ♦ *vt* (*fig*): ~**ded with** übersät mit

student ['stjuːdənt] *n* Student(in) *m(f)*; (*US*) Student(in) *m(f)*, Schüler(in) *m(f)* ♦ *adj* Studenten-; ~ **driver** (*US*) *n* Fahrschüler(in) *m(f)*

studio ['stjuːdɪəʊ] *n* Studio *nt*; (*for artist*) Atelier *nt*; ~ **apartment** (*US*) *n* Appartement *nt*; ~ **flat** *n* Appartement *nt*

studious ['stjuːdɪəs] *adj* lernbegierig

study ['stʌdɪ] *n* Studium *nt*; (*investigation*) Studium *nt*, Untersuchung *f*; (*room*) Arbeitszimmer *nt*; (*essay etc*) Studie *f* ♦ *vt* studieren; (*face*) erforschen; (*evidence*) prüfen ♦ *vi* studieren

stuff [stʌf] n Stoff m; (inf) Zeug nt ♦ vt stopfen, füllen; (animal) ausstopfen; ~ing n Füllung f; ~y adj (room) schwül; (person) spießig

stumble ['stʌmbl] vi stolpern; **to ~ across** (fig) zufällig stoßen auf +acc

stumbling block ['stʌmblɪŋ-] n Hindernis nt

stump [stʌmp] n Stumpf m

stun [stʌn] vt betäuben; (shock) niederschmettern

stung [stʌŋ] pt, pp of **sting**

stunk [stʌŋk] pp of **stink**

stunned adj benommen, fassungslos

stunning ['stʌnɪŋ] adj betäubend; (news) überwältigend, umwerfend

stunt [stʌnt] n Kunststück nt, Trick m

stunted ['stʌntɪd] adj verkümmert

stuntman ['stʌntmæn] (irreg) n Stuntman m

stupefy ['stju:pɪfaɪ] vt betäuben; (by news) bestürzen

stupendous [stju:'pɛndəs] adj erstaunlich, enorm

stupid ['stju:pɪd] adj dumm; ~ity [stju:'pɪdɪtɪ] n Dummheit f

stupor ['stju:pə'] n Betäubung f

sturdy ['stɜ:dɪ] adj kräftig, robust

stutter ['stʌtə'] n Stottern nt ♦ vi stottern

sty [staɪ] n Schweinestall m

stye [staɪ] n Gerstenkorn nt

style [staɪl] n Stil m; (fashion) Mode f; **stylish** ['staɪlɪʃ] adj modisch; **stylist** ['staɪlɪst] n (hair stylist) Friseur m, Friseuse f

stylus ['staɪləs] n (Grammofon)nadel f

suave [swɑːv] adj zuvorkommend

sub... [sʌb] prefix Unter...; ~**conscious** adj unterbewusst ♦ n: **the ~conscious** das Unterbewusste; ~**contract** vt (vertraglich) untervermieten; ~**divide** vt unterteilen; ~**dued** adj (lighting) gedämpft; (person) still

subject [n, adj 'sʌbdʒɪkt, vb səb'dʒɛkt] n (of kingdom) Untertan m; (citizen) Staatsangehörige(r) mf; (topic) Thema nt; (SCH) Fach nt; (GRAM) Subjekt m ♦ adj: **to be ~ to** unterworfen sein +dat; (exposed) ausgesetzt sein +dat ♦ vt (subdue) unterwerfen; (expose) aussetzen; ~**ive**

[səb'dʒɛktɪv] adj subjektiv; ~ **matter** n Thema nt

sublet [sʌb'lɛt] (irreg: like **let**) vt untervermieten

sublime [sə'blaɪm] adj erhaben

submachine gun ['sʌbmə'ʃiːn-] n Maschinenpistole f

submarine [sʌbmə'riːn] n Unterseeboot nt, U-Boot nt

submerge [səb'mɜːdʒ] vt untertauchen; (flood) überschwemmen ♦ vi untertauchen

submission [səb'mɪʃən] n (obedience) Gehorsam m; (claim) Behauptung f; (of plan) Unterbreitung f; **submissive** [səb'mɪsɪv] adj demütig, unterwürfig (pej)

submit [səb'mɪt] vt behaupten; (plan) unterbreiten ♦ vi sich ergeben

subnormal [sʌb'nɔːml] adj minderbegabt

subordinate [sə'bɔːdɪnət] adj untergeordnet ♦ n Untergebene(r) mf

subpoena [sə'piːnə] n Vorladung f ♦ vt vorladen

subscribe [səb'skraɪb] vi: **to ~ to** (view etc) unterstützen; (newspaper) abonnieren; ~**r** n (to periodical) Abonnent m; (TEL) Telefonteilnehmer m

subscription [səb'skrɪpʃən] n Abonnement nt; (money subscribed) (Mitglieds)beitrag m

subsequent ['sʌbsɪkwənt] adj folgend, später; ~**ly** adv später

subside [səb'saɪd] vi sich senken; ~**nce** [səb'saɪdns] n Senkung f

subsidiarity [sʌbsɪdɪ'ærɪtɪ] n (POL) Subsidiarität f

subsidiary [səb'sɪdɪərɪ] adj Neben- ♦ n Tochtergesellschaft f

subsidize ['sʌbsɪdaɪz] vt subventionieren

subsidy ['sʌbsɪdɪ] n Subvention f

subsistence [səb'sɪstəns] n Unterhalt m

substance ['sʌbstəns] n Substanz f

substantial [səb'stænʃl] adj (strong) fest, kräftig; (important) wesentlich; ~**ly** adv erheblich

substantiate [səb'stænʃɪeɪt] vt begründen, belegen

substitute ['sʌbstɪtjuːt] n Ersatz m ♦ vt ersetzen; **substitution** [sʌbstɪ'tjuːʃən] n

Ersetzung *f*

subterfuge ['sʌbtəfju:dʒ] *n* Vorwand *m*; (*trick*) Trick *m*

subterranean [sʌbtə'reɪnɪən] *adj* unterirdisch

subtitle ['sʌbtaɪtl] *n* Untertitel *m*; ~d *adj* untertitelt, mit Untertiteln versehen

subtle ['sʌtl] *adj* fein; ~ty *n* Feinheit *f*

subtotal [sʌb'təʊtl] *n* Zwischensumme *f*

subtract [səb'trækt] *vt* abziehen; ~ion [səb'trækʃən] *n* Abziehen *nt*, Subtraktion *f*

suburb ['sʌbə:b] *n* Vorort *m*; **the ~s** die Außenbezirke *pl*; ~an [sə'bə:bən] *adj* Vorort(s)-; ~ia [sə'bə:bɪə] *n* Vorstadt *f*

subversive [səb'və:sɪv] *adj* subversiv

subway ['sʌbweɪ] *n* (*US*) U-Bahn *f*; (*BRIT*) Unterführung *f*

succeed [sək'si:d] *vi* (*person*) erfolgreich sein, Erfolg haben; (*plan etc also*) gelingen ♦ *vt* (nach)folgen +*dat*; **he ~ed in doing it** es gelang ihm, es zu tun; ~ing *adj* (nach)folgend

success [sək'ses] *n* Erfolg *m*; ~ful *adj* erfolgreich; **to be ~ful (in doing sth)** Erfolg haben (bei etw); ~fully *adv* erfolgreich

succession [sək'seʃən] *n* (Aufeinander)folge *f*; (*to throne*) Nachfolge *f*

successive [sək'sesɪv] *adj* aufeinander folgend

successor [sək'sesər] *n* Nachfolger(in) *m(f)*

succinct [sək'sɪŋkt] *adj* knapp

succulent ['sʌkjulənt] *adj* saftig

succumb [sə'kʌm] *vi*: **to ~ (to)** erliegen (+*dat*); (*yield*) nachgeben (+*dat*)

such [sʌtʃ] *adj* solche(r, s); **~ a book** so ein Buch; **~ courage** so ein Mut; **~ a long trip** so eine lange Reise; **~ a lot of** so viel(e); **~ as** wie; **a noise ~ as to** ein derartiger Lärm, dass; **as ~** an sich; **~-and-~ a time** die und die Zeit

suck [sʌk] *vt* saugen; (*lollipop etc*) lutschen

sucker ['sʌkər] (*inf*) *n* Idiot *m*

suction ['sʌkʃən] *n* Saugkraft *f*

sudden ['sʌdn] *adj* plötzlich; **all of a ~** auf einmal; ~ly *adv* plötzlich

suds [sʌdz] *npl* Seifenlauge *f*; (*lather*) Seifenschaum *m*

sue [su:] *vt* verklagen

suede [sweɪd] *n* Wildleder *nt*

suet ['suɪt] *n* Nierenfett *nt*

Suez ['su:ɪz] *n*: **the ~ Canal** der Suezkanal

suffer ['sʌfər] *vt* (er)leiden ♦ *vi* leiden; ~er *n* Leidende(r) *mf*; ~ing *n* Leiden *nt*

suffice [sə'faɪs] *vi* genügen

sufficient [sə'fɪʃənt] *adj* ausreichend; ~ly *adv* ausreichend

suffix ['sʌfɪks] *n* Nachsilbe *f*

suffocate ['sʌfəkeɪt] *vt, vi* ersticken

suffrage ['sʌfrɪdʒ] *n* Wahlrecht *nt*

sugar ['ʃugər] *n* Zucker *m* ♦ *vt* zuckern; **~ beet** *n* Zuckerrübe *f*; **~ cane** *n* Zuckerrohr *nt*; ~y *adj* süß

suggest [sə'dʒest] *vt* vorschlagen; (*show*) schließen lassen auf +*acc*; ~ion [sə'dʒestʃən] *n* Vorschlag *m*; ~ive *adj* anregend; (*indecent*) zweideutig

suicide ['suɪsaɪd] *n* Selbstmord *m*; **to commit ~** Selbstmord begehen

suit [su:t] *n* Anzug *m*; (*CARDS*) Farbe *f* ♦ *vt* passen +*dat*; (*clothes*) stehen +*dat*; **well ~ed** (*well matched*) gut zusammenpassend; ~able *adj* geeignet, passend; ~ably *adv* passend, angemessen

suitcase ['su:tkeɪs] *n* (Hand)koffer *m*

suite [swi:t] *n* (*of rooms*) Zimmerflucht *f*; (*of furniture*) Einrichtung *f*; (*MUS*) Suite *f*

suitor ['su:tər] *n* (*JUR*) Kläger(in) *m(f)*

sulfur ['sʌlfər] (*US*) *n* = **sulphur**

sulk [sʌlk] *vi* schmollen; ~y *adj* schmollend

sullen ['sʌlən] *adj* mürrisch

sulphur ['sʌlfər] (*US* **sulfur**) *n* Schwefel *m*

sultana [sʌl'tɑ:nə] *n* (*fruit*) Sultanine *f*

sultry ['sʌltrɪ] *adj* schwül

sum [sʌm] *n* Summe *f*; (*money*) Betrag *m*, Summe *f*; (*arithmetic*) Rechenaufgabe *f*; **~ up** *vt, vi* zusammenfassen

summarize ['sʌməraɪz] *vt* kurz zusammenfassen

summary ['sʌmərɪ] *n* Zusammenfassung *f* ♦ *adj* (*justice*) kurzerhand erteilt

summer ['sʌmər] *n* Sommer *m* ♦ *adj* Sommer-; **~house** *n* (*in garden*) Gartenhaus *nt*; **~time** *n* Sommerzeit *f*

summit ['sʌmɪt] *n* Gipfel *m*; ~

(conference) n Gipfelkonferenz f
summon ['sʌmən] vt herbeirufen; (JUR)
vorladen; (gather up) aufbringen; ~**s** (JUR) n
Vorladung f ♦ vt vorladen
sump [sʌmp] (BRIT) n (AUT) Ölwanne f
sumptuous ['sʌmptjuəs] adj prächtig
sun [sʌn] n Sonne f; ~**bathe** vi sich sonnen;
~**block** n Sonnenschutzcreme f; ~**burn** n
Sonnenbrand m; ~**burnt** adj
sonnenverbrannt, sonnengebräunt; **to be**
~**burnt** (painfully) einen Sonnenbrand
haben
Sunday ['sʌndɪ] n Sonntag m; ~ **school** n
Sonntagsschule f
sundial ['sʌndaɪəl] n Sonnenuhr f
sundown ['sʌndaun] n Sonnenuntergang m
sundries ['sʌndrɪz] npl (miscellaneous items)
Verschiedene(s) nt
sundry ['sʌndrɪ] adj verschieden; **all and** ~
alle
sunflower ['sʌnflauə^r] n Sonnenblume f
sung [sʌŋ] pp of **sing**
sunglasses ['sʌnɡlɑːsɪz] npl Sonnenbrille f
sunk [sʌŋk] pp of **sink**
sun: ~**light** ['sʌnlaɪt] n Sonnenlicht nt; ~**lit**
['sʌnlɪt] adj sonnenbeschienen; ~**ny** ['sʌnɪ]
adj sonnig; ~**rise** n Sonnenaufgang m; ~
roof n (AUT) Schiebedach nt; ~**screen**
['sʌnskriːn] n Sonnenschutzcreme f; ~**set**
['sʌnset] n Sonnenuntergang m; ~**shade**
['sʌnʃeɪd] n Sonnenschirm m; ~**shine**
['sʌnʃaɪn] n Sonnenschein m; ~**stroke**
['sʌnstrəuk] n Hitzschlag m; ~**tan** [sʌntæn] n
(Sonnen)bräune f; ~**tan oil** n Sonnenöl nt
super ['suːpə^r] (inf) adj prima, klasse
superannuation [suːpərænjuːˈeɪʃən] n
Pension f
superb [suːˈpəːb] adj ausgezeichnet,
hervorragend
supercilious [suːpəˈsɪlɪəs] adj herablassend
superficial [suːpəˈfɪʃəl] adj oberflächlich
superfluous [suːˈpəːfluəs] adj überflüssig
superhuman [suːpəˈhjuːmən] adj (effort)
übermenschlich
superimpose ['suːpərɪmˈpəuz] vt
übereinander legen
superintendent [suːpərɪnˈtendənt] n

Polizeichef m
superior [suːˈpɪərɪə^r] adj überlegen; (better)
besser ♦ n Vorgesetzte(r) mf; ~**ity**
[suːpɪərɪˈɒrɪtɪ] n Überlegenheit f
superlative [suːˈpəːlətɪv] adj überragend
super: ~**man** ['suːpəmæn] (irreg) n
Übermensch m; ~**market** ['suːpəmɑːkɪt] n
Supermarkt m; ~**natural** [suːpəˈnætʃərəl] adj
übernatürlich; ~**power** ['suːpəpauə^r] n
Weltmacht f
supersede [suːpəˈsiːd] vt ersetzen
supersonic ['suːpəˈsɒnɪk] adj Überschall-
superstition [suːpəˈstɪʃən] n Aberglaube m;
superstitious [suːpəˈstɪʃəs] adj
abergläubisch
supervise ['suːpəvaɪz] vt beaufsichtigen,
kontrollieren; **supervision** [suːpəˈvɪʒən] n
Aufsicht f; **supervisor** ['suːpəvaɪzə^r] n
Aufsichtsperson f; **supervisory**
['suːpəvaɪzərɪ] adj Aufsichts-
supper ['sʌpə^r] n Abendessen nt
supplant [səˈplɑːnt] vt (person, thing)
ersetzen
supple ['sʌpl] adj geschmeidig
supplement [n 'sʌplɪmənt, vb sʌplɪˈment] n
Ergänzung f; (in book) Nachtrag m ♦ vt
ergänzen; ~**ary** [sʌplɪˈmentərɪ] adj
ergänzend; ~**ary benefit** (BRIT: old) n ≈
Sozialhilfe f
supplier [səˈplaɪə^r] n Lieferant m
supplies [səˈplaɪz] npl (food) Vorräte pl; (MIL)
Nachschub m
supply [səˈplaɪ] vt liefern ♦ n Vorrat m; (~ing)
Lieferung f; see also **supplies**; ~ **teacher**
(BRIT) n Vertretung f
support [səˈpɔːt] n Unterstützung f; (TECH)
Stütze f ♦ vt (hold up) stützen, tragen;
(provide for) ernähren; (be in favour of)
unterstützen; ~**er** n Anhänger(in) m(f)
suppose [səˈpəuz] vt, vi annehmen; **to be**
~**d to do sth** etw tun sollen; ~**dly**
[səˈpəuzɪdlɪ] adv angeblich; **supposing** conj
angenommen; **supposition** [sʌpəˈzɪʃən] n
Voraussetzung f
suppress [səˈpres] vt unterdrücken
supremacy [suːˈpreməsɪ] n Vorherrschaft f,
Oberhoheit f

supreme [su'pri:m] *adj* oberste(r, s), höchste(r, s)

surcharge ['sɜ:tʃɑ:dʒ] *n* Zuschlag *m*

sure [ʃʊəʳ] *adj* sicher, gewiss; ~! (*of course*) klar!; **to make ~ of sth/that** sich einer Sache *gen* vergewissern/vergewissern, dass; ~ **enough** (*with past*) tatsächlich; (*with future*) ganz bestimmt; ~**-footed** *adj* sicher (auf den Füßen); ~**ly** *adv* (*certainly*) sicherlich, gewiss; ~**ly it's wrong** das ist doch wohl falsch

surety ['ʃʊərətɪ] *n* Sicherheit *f*

surf [sɜ:f] *n* Brandung *f*

surface ['sɜ:fɪs] *n* Oberfläche *f* ♦ *vt* (*roadway*) teeren ♦ *vi* auftauchen; ~ **mail** *n* gewöhnliche Post *f*

surfboard ['sɜ:fbɔ:d] *n* Surfbrett *nt*

surfeit ['sɜ:fɪt] *n* Übermaß *nt*

surfing ['sɜ:fɪŋ] *n* Surfen *nt*

surge [sɜ:dʒ] *n* Woge *f* ♦ *vi* wogen

surgeon ['sɜ:dʒən] *n* Chirurg(in) *m(f)*

surgery ['sɜ:dʒərɪ] *n* (*BRIT: place*) Praxis *f*; (: *time*) Sprechstunde *f*; (*treatment*) Operation *f*; **to undergo ~** operiert werden; ~ **hours** (*BRIT*) *npl* Sprechstunden *pl*

surgical ['sɜ:dʒɪkl] *adj* chirurgisch; ~ **spirit** (*BRIT*) *n* Wundbenzin *nt*

surly ['sɜ:lɪ] *adj* verdrießlich, grob

surmount [sɜ:'maunt] *vt* überwinden

surname ['sɜ:neɪm] *n* Zuname *m*

surpass [sɜ:'pɑ:s] *vt* übertreffen

surplus ['sɜ:pləs] *n* Überschuss *m* ♦ *adj* überschüssig, Über(schuss)-

surprise [sə'praɪz] *n* Überraschung *f* ♦ *vt* überraschen; ~**d** *adj* überrascht; **surprising** *adj* überraschend; **surprisingly** *adv* überraschend(erweise)

surrender [sə'rendəʳ] *n* Kapitulation *f* ♦ *vi* sich ergeben

surreptitious [sʌrəp'tɪʃəs] *adj* heimlich; (*look also*) verstohlen

surrogate ['sʌrəgɪt] *n* Ersatz *m*; ~ **mother** *n* Leihmutter *f*

surround [sə'raund] *vt* umgeben; ~**ing** *adj* (*countryside*) umliegend; ~**ings** *npl* Umgebung *f*; (*environment*) Umwelt *f*

surveillance [sə'veɪləns] *n* Überwachung *f*

survey [*n* 'sə:veɪ, *vb* sə:'veɪ] *n* Übersicht *f* ♦ *vt* überblicken; (*land*) vermessen; ~**or** [sə'veɪəʳ] *n* Land(ver)messer(in) *m(f)*

survival [sə'vaɪvl] *n* Überleben *nt*

survive [sə'vaɪv] *vt, vi* überleben; **survivor** [sə'vaɪvəʳ] *n* Überlebende(r) *mf*

susceptible [sə'septəbl] *adj*: ~ (**to**) empfindlich (gegen); (*charms etc*) empfänglich (für)

suspect [*n* 'sʌspekt, *vb* səs'pekt] *n* Verdächtige(r) *mf* ♦ *adj* verdächtig ♦ *vt* verdächtigen; (*think*) vermuten

suspend [səs'pend] *vt* verschieben; (*from work*) suspendieren; (*hang up*) aufhängen; (*SPORT*) sperren; ~**ed sentence** *n* (*JUR*) zur Bewährung ausgesetzte Strafe; ~**er belt** *n* Strumpf(halter)gürtel *m*; ~**ers** *npl* (*BRIT*) Strumpfhalter *m*; (*US*) Hosenträger *m*

suspense [səs'pens] *n* Spannung *f*

suspension [səs'penʃən] *n* (*from work*) Suspendierung *f*; (*SPORT*) Sperrung *f*; (*AUT*) Federung *f*; ~ **bridge** *n* Hängebrücke *f*

suspicion [səs'pɪʃən] *n* Misstrauen *nt*; Verdacht *m*; **suspicious** [səs'pɪʃəs] *adj* misstrauisch; (*causing ~*) verdächtig

sustain [səs'teɪn] *vt* (*maintain*) aufrechterhalten; (*confirm*) bestätigen; (*injury*) davontragen; ~**able** *adj* (*development, growth etc*) aufrechtzuerhalten; ~**ed** *adj* (*effort*) anhaltend

sustenance ['sʌstɪnəns] *n* Nahrung *f*

swab [swɔb] *n* (*MED*) Tupfer *m*

swagger ['swægəʳ] *vi* stolzieren

swallow ['swɔləu] *n* (*bird*) Schwalbe *f*; (*of food etc*) Schluck *m* ♦ *vt* (ver)schlucken; ~ **up** *vt* verschlingen

swam [swæm] *pt of* swim

swamp [swɔmp] *n* Sumpf *m* ♦ *vt* überschwemmen

swan [swɔn] *n* Schwan *m*

swap [swɔp] *n* Tausch *m* ♦ *vt*: **to ~ sth (for sth)** etw (gegen etw) tauschen *or* eintauschen

swarm [swɔ:m] *n* Schwarm *m* ♦ *vi*: **to ~ or be ~ing with** wimmeln von

swarthy ['swɔːðɪ] *adj* dunkel, braun

swastika ['swɒstɪkə] *n* Hakenkreuz *nt*

swat [swɒt] *vt* totschlagen

sway [sweɪ] *vi* schwanken; (*branches*) schaukeln, sich wiegen ♦ *vt* schwenken; (*influence*) beeinflussen

swear [sweəʳ] (*pt* **swore**, *pp* **sworn**) *vi* (*promise*) schwören; (*curse*) fluchen; **to ~ to sth** schwören auf etw *acc*; **~word** *n* Fluch *m*

sweat [swɛt] *n* Schweiß *m* ♦ *vi* schwitzen

sweater ['swɛtəʳ] *n* Pullover *m*

sweatshirt ['swɛtʃəːt] *n* Sweatshirt *nt*

sweaty ['swɛtɪ] *adj* verschwitzt

Swede [swiːd] *n* Schwede *m*, Schwedin *f*

swede [swiːd] (*BRIT*) *n* Steckrübe *f*

Sweden ['swiːdn] *n* Schweden *nt*

Swedish ['swiːdɪʃ] *adj* schwedisch ♦ *n* (*LING*) Schwedisch

sweep [swiːp] (*pt, pp* **swept**) *n* (*chimney ~*) Schornsteinfeger *m* ♦ *vt* fegen, kehren; **~ away** *vt* wegfegen; **~ past** *vi* vorbeisausen; **~ up** *vt* zusammenkehren; **~ing** *adj* (*gesture*) schwungvoll; (*statement*) verallgemeinernd

sweet [swiːt] *n* (*course*) Nachtisch *m*; (*candy*) Bonbon *nt* ♦ *adj* süß; **~corn** *n* Zuckermais *m*; **~en** *vt* süßen; (*fig*) versüßen; **~heart** *n* Liebste(r) *mf*; **~ness** *n* Süße *f*; **~ pea** *n* Gartenwicke *f*

swell [swɛl] (*pt* **swelled**, *pp* **swollen** or **swelled**) *n* Seegang *m* ♦ *adj* (*inf*) todschick ♦ *vt* (*numbers*) vermehren ♦ *vi* (*also: ~ up*) (an)schwellen; **~ing** *n* Schwellung *f*

sweltering ['swɛltərɪŋ] *adj* drückend

swept [swɛpt] *pt, pp of* **sweep**

swerve [swəːv] *vt, vi* ausscheren

swift [swɪft] *n* Mauersegler *m* ♦ *adj* geschwind, schnell, rasch; **~ly** *adv* geschwind, schnell, rasch

swig [swɪg] *n* Zug *m*

swill [swɪl] *n* (*for pigs*) Schweinefutter *nt* ♦ *vt* spülen

swim [swɪm] (*pt* **swam**, *pp* **swum**) *n*: **to go for a ~** schwimmen gehen ♦ *vi* schwimmen ♦ *vt* (*cross*) (durch)schwimmen; **~mer** *n* Schwimmer(in) *m(f)*; **~ming** *n* Schwimmen *nt*; **~ming cap** *n* Badehaube *f*, Badekappe *f*; **~ming costume** (*BRIT*) *n* Badeanzug *m*; **~ming pool** *n* Schwimmbecken *nt*; (*private*) Swimmingpool *m*; **~ming trunks** *npl* Badehose *f*; **~suit** *n* Badeanzug *m*

swindle ['swɪndl] *n* Schwindel *m*, Betrug *m* ♦ *vt* betrügen

swine [swaɪn] *n* (*also fig*) Schwein *nt*

swing [swɪŋ] (*pt, pp* **swung**) *n* (*child's*) Schaukel *f*; (*movement*) Schwung *m* ♦ *vt* schwingen ♦ *vi* schwingen, schaukeln; (*turn quickly*) schwenken; **in full ~** in vollem Gange; **~ bridge** *n* Drehbrücke *f*; **~ door** (*BRIT*) *n* Schwingtür *f*

swingeing ['swɪndʒɪŋ] (*BRIT*) *adj* hart; (*taxation, cuts*) extrem

swinging door ['swɪŋɪŋ-] (*US*) *n* Schwingtür *f*

swipe [swaɪp] *n* Hieb *m* ♦ *vt* (*inf: hit*) hart schlagen; (*: steal*) klauen

swirl [swəːl] *vi* wirbeln

swish [swɪʃ] *adj* (*inf: smart*) schick ♦ *vi* zischen; (*grass, skirts*) rascheln

Swiss [swɪs] *adj* Schweizer, schweizerisch ♦ *n* Schweizer(in) *m(f)*; **the ~** *npl* (*people*) die Schweizer *pl*

switch [swɪtʃ] *n* (*ELEC*) Schalter *m*; (*change*) Wechsel *m* ♦ *vt* (*ELEC*) schalten; (*change*) wechseln ♦ *vi* wechseln; **~ off** *vt* ab- or ausschalten; **~ on** *vt* an- or einschalten; **~board** *n* Zentrale *f*; (*board*) Schaltbrett *nt*

Switzerland ['swɪtsələnd] *n* die Schweiz

swivel ['swɪvl] *vt* (*also: ~ round*) drehen ♦ *vi* (*also: ~ round*) sich drehen

swollen ['swəʊlən] *pp of* **swell**

swoon [swuːn] *vi* (*old*) in Ohnmacht fallen

swoop [swuːp] *n* Sturzflug *m*; (*esp by police*) Razzia *f* ♦ *vi* (*also: ~ down*) stürzen

swop [swɒp] = **swap**

sword [sɔːd] *n* Schwert *nt*; **~fish** *n* Schwertfisch *m*

swore [swɔːʳ] *pt of* **swear**

sworn [swɔːn] *pp of* **swear**

swot [swɒt] *vt, vi* pauken

swum [swʌm] *pp of* **swim**

swung [swʌŋ] *pt, pp of* **swing**

sycamore ['sɪkəmɔːr] n (US) Platane f; (BRIT) Bergahorn m

syllable ['sɪləbl] n Silbe f

syllabus ['sɪləbəs] n Lehrplan m

symbol ['sɪmbl] n Symbol nt; ~ic(al) [sɪm'bɒlɪk(l)] adj symbolisch

symmetry ['sɪmɪtrɪ] n Symmetrie f

sympathetic [sɪmpə'θetɪk] adj mitfühlend

sympathize ['sɪmpəθaɪz] vi mitfühlen; ~r n (POL) Sympathisant(in) m(f)

sympathy ['sɪmpəθɪ] n Mitleid nt, Mitgefühl nt; (condolence) Beileid nt; **with our deepest ~** mit tief empfundenem Beileid

symphony ['sɪmfənɪ] n Sinfonie f

symptom ['sɪmptəm] n Symptom nt; ~atic [sɪmptə'mætɪk] adj (fig): **~atic of** bezeichnend für

synagogue ['sɪnəgɒg] n Synagoge f

synchronize ['sɪŋkrənaɪz] vt synchronisieren

syndicate ['sɪndɪkɪt] n Konsortium nt

synonym ['sɪnənɪm] n Synonym nt; ~ous [sɪ'nɒnɪməs] adj gleichbedeutend

synopsis [sɪ'nɒpsɪs] n Zusammenfassung f

synthetic [sɪn'θetɪk] adj synthetisch; ~s npl (man-made fabrics) Synthetik f

syphon ['saɪfən] = **siphon**

Syria ['sɪrɪə] n Syrien nt

syringe [sɪ'rɪndʒ] n Spritze f

syrup ['sɪrəp] n Sirup m; (of sugar) Melasse f

system ['sɪstəm] n System nt; ~atic [sɪstə'mætɪk] adj systematisch; **~ disk** n (COMPUT) Systemdiskette f; **~s analyst** n Systemanalytiker(in) m(f)

T, t

ta [tɑː] (BRIT: inf) excl danke!

tab [tæb] n Aufhänger m; (name ~) Schild nt; **to keep ~s on** (fig) genau im Auge behalten

tabby ['tæbɪ] n (also: **~ cat**) getigerte Katze f

table ['teɪbl] n Tisch m; (list) Tabelle f ♦ vt (PARL: propose) vorlegen, einbringen; **to lay** or **set the ~** den Tisch decken; ~cloth n Tischtuch nt; **~ d'hôte** [tɑːbl'dəut] n Tagesmenü nt; **~ lamp** n Tischlampe f;

~mat n Untersatz m; **~ of contents** n Inhaltsverzeichnis nt; **~spoon** n Esslöffel m; **~spoonful** n Esslöffel m (voll)

tablet ['tæblɪt] n (MED) Tablette f

table tennis n Tischtennis nt

table wine n Tafelwein m

tabloid ['tæblɔɪd] n Zeitung f in kleinem Format; (pej) Boulevardzeitung f

tabulate ['tæbjuleɪt] vt tabellarisch ordnen

tacit ['tæsɪt] adj stillschweigend

taciturn ['tæsɪtɜːn] adj wortkarg

tack [tæk] n (small nail) Stift m; (US: thumbtack) Reißzwecke f; (stitch) Heftstich m; (NAUT) Lavieren nt; (course) Kurs m ♦ vt (nail) nageln; (stitch) heften ♦ vi aufkreuzen

tackle ['tækl] n (for lifting) Flaschenzug m; (NAUT) Takelage f; (SPORT) Tackling nt ♦ vt (deal with) anpacken, in Angriff nehmen; (person) festhalten; (player) angehen

tacky ['tækɪ] adj klebrig

tact [tækt] n Takt m; ~ful adj taktvoll

tactical ['tæktɪkl] adj taktisch

tactics ['tæktɪks] npl Taktik f

tactless ['tæktlɪs] adj taktlos

tadpole ['tædpəʊl] n Kaulquappe f

taffy ['tæfɪ] (US) n Sahnebonbon nt

tag [tæg] n (label) Schild nt, Anhänger m; (maker's name) Etikett nt; **~ along** vi mitkommen

tail [teɪl] n Schwanz m; (of list) Schluss m ♦ vt folgen +dat; **~ away** or **off** vi abfallen, schwinden; ~back n (BRIT) in (AUT) (Rück)stau m; **~ coat** n Frack m; **~ end** n Schluss m, Ende nt; ~gate n (AUT) Heckklappe f

tailor ['teɪlər] n Schneider m; ~ing n

Schneidern nt; ~-made adj maßgeschneidert; (fig): ~-made for sb jdm wie auf den Leib geschnitten

tailwind ['teɪlwɪnd] n Rückenwind m

tainted ['teɪntɪd] adj verdorben

take [teɪk] (pt **took**, pp **taken**) vt nehmen; (trip, exam, PHOT) machen; (capture: person) fassen; (: town; also COMM, FIN) einnehmen; (carry to a place) bringen; (get for o.s.) sich dat nehmen; (gain, obtain) bekommen; (put up with) hinnehmen; (respond to) aufnehmen; (interpret) auffassen; (assume) annehmen; (contain) Platz haben für; (GRAM) stehen mit; **to ~ sth from sb** jdm etw wegnehmen; **to ~ sth from sth** (MATH: subtract) etw von etw abziehen; (extract, quotation) etw einer Sache dat entnehmen; ~ **after** vt fus ähnlich sein +dat; ~ **apart** vt auseinander nehmen; ~ **away** vt (remove) wegnehmen; (carry off) wegbringen; ~ **back** vt (return) zurückbringen; (retract) zurücknehmen; ~ **down** vt (pull down) abreißen; (write down) aufschreiben; ~ **in** vt (deceive) hereinlegen; (understand) begreifen; (include) einschließen; ~ **off** vi (plane) starten ♦ vt (remove) wegnehmen; (clothing) ausziehen; (imitate) nachmachen; ~ **on** vt (undertake) übernehmen; (engage) einstellen; (opponent) antreten gegen; ~ **out** vt (girl, dog) ausführen; (extract) herausnehmen; (insurance) abschließen; (licence) sich dat geben lassen; (book) ausleihen; (remove) entfernen; **to ~ sth out of sth** (drawer, pocket etc) etw aus etw herausnehmen; ~ **over** vt übernehmen ♦ vi: **to ~ over from sb** jdn ablösen; ~ **to** vt fus (like) mögen; (adopt as practice) sich dat angewöhnen; ~ **up** vt (raise) aufnehmen; (dress etc) kürzer machen; (occupy) in Anspruch nehmen; (engage in) sich befassen mit; ~**away** adj zum Mitnehmen; ~~**home pay** n Nettolohn m; ~**n** pp of **take**; ~**off** n (AVIAT) Start m; (imitation) Nachahmung f; ~**out** (US) adj = **takeaway**; ~**over** n (COMM) Übernahme f; **takings** ['teɪkɪŋz] npl (COMM) Einnahmen pl

talc [tælk] n (also: ~**um powder**) Talkumpuder m

tale [teɪl] n Geschichte f, Erzählung f; **to tell ~s** (fig: lie) Geschichten erfinden

talent ['tælnt] n Talent nt; ~**ed** adj begabt

talk [tɔːk] n (conversation) Gespräch nt; (rumour) Gerede nt; (speech) Vortrag m ♦ vi sprechen, reden; ~**s** npl (POL etc) Gespräche pl; **to ~ about** sprechen von +dat or über +acc; **to ~ sb into doing sth** jdn überreden, etw zu tun; **to ~ sb out of doing sth** jdm ausreden, etw zu tun; **to ~ shop** fachsimpeln; ~ **over** vt besprechen; ~**ative** adj gesprächig

tall [tɔːl] adj groß; (building) hoch; **to be 1 m 80 ~** 1,80 m groß sein; ~**boy** (BRIT) n Kommode f; ~ **story** n übertriebene Geschichte f

tally ['tælɪ] n Abrechnung f ♦ vi übereinstimmen

talon ['tælən] n Kralle f

tame [teɪm] adj zahm; (fig) fade

tamper ['tæmpə*] vi: **to ~ with** herumpfuschen an +dat

tampon ['tæmpɒn] n Tampon m

tan [tæn] n (Sonnen)bräune f; (colour) Gelbbraun nt ♦ adj (colour) (gelb)braun ♦ vt bräunen ♦ vi braun werden

tang [tæŋ] n Schärfe f

tangent ['tændʒənt] n Tangente f; **to go off at a ~** (fig) vom Thema abkommen

tangerine [tændʒə'riːn] n Mandarine f

tangible ['tændʒəbl] adj greifbar

tangle ['tæŋgl] n Durcheinander nt; (trouble) Schwierigkeiten pl; **to get in(to) a ~** sich verheddern

tank [tæŋk] n (container) Tank m, Behälter m; (MIL) Panzer m; ~**er** ['tæŋkə*] n (ship) Tanker m; (vehicle) Tankwagen m

tanned [tænd] adj gebräunt

tantalizing ['tæntəlaɪzɪŋ] adj verlockend; (annoying) quälend

tantamount ['tæntəmaunt] adj: ~ **to** gleichbedeutend mit

tantrum ['tæntrəm] n Wutanfall m

tap [tæp] n Hahn m; (gentle blow) Klopfen nt ♦ vt (strike) klopfen; (supply) anzapfen;

(*telephone*) abhören; **on ~** (*fig: resources*) zur Hand; **~-dancing** n Steppen nt

tape [teɪp] n Band nt; (*magnetic*) (Ton)band nt; (*adhesive*) Klebstreifen m ♦ vt (*record*) aufnehmen; **~ deck** n Tapedeck nt; **~ measure** n Maßband nt

taper ['teɪpər] vi spitz zulaufen

tape recorder n Tonbandgerät nt

tapestry ['tæpɪstrɪ] n Wandteppich m

tar [tɑː] n Teer m

target ['tɑːgɪt] n Ziel nt; (*board*) Zielscheibe f

tariff ['tærɪf] n (*duty paid*) Zoll m; (*list*) Tarif m

tarmac ['tɑːmæk] n (AVIAT) Rollfeld nt

tarnish ['tɑːnɪʃ] vt matt machen; (*fig*) beflecken

tarpaulin [tɑːˈpɔːlɪn] n Plane f

tarragon ['tærəgən] n Estragon m

tart [tɑːt] n (Obst)torte f; (*inf*) Nutte f ♦ adj scharf; **~ up** (*inf*) vt aufmachen; (*person*) auftakeln

tartan ['tɑːtn] n Schottenkaro nt ♦ adj mit Schottenkaro

tartar ['tɑːtər] n Zahnstein m

tartar(e) sauce ['tɑːtə-] n Remoulade f

task [tɑːsk] n Aufgabe f; **to take sb to ~** sich dat jdn vornehmen; **~ force** n Sondertrupp m

tassel ['tæsl] n Quaste f

taste [teɪst] n Geschmack m; (*sense*) Geschmackssinn m; (*small quantity*) Kostprobe f; (*liking*) Vorliebe f ♦ vt schmecken; (*try*) probieren ♦ vi schmecken; **can I have a ~ of this wine?** kann ich diesen Wein probieren?; **to have a ~ for sth** etw mögen; **in good/bad ~** geschmackvoll/geschmacklos; **you can ~ the garlic (in it)** man kann den Knoblauch herausschmecken; **to ~ of sth** nach einer Sache schmecken; **~ful** adj geschmackvoll; **~less** adj (*insipid*) fade; (*in bad ~*) geschmacklos; **tasty** ['teɪstɪ] adj schmackhaft

tattered ['tætəd] adj = **in tatters**

tatters ['tætəz] npl: **in ~** in Fetzen

tattoo [təˈtuː] n (MIL) Zapfenstreich m; (*on skin*) Tätowierung f ♦ vt tätowieren

tatty ['tætɪ] (BRIT: *inf*) adj schäbig

taught [tɔːt] pt, pp of **teach**

taunt [tɔːnt] n höhnische Bemerkung f ♦ vt verhöhnen

Taurus ['tɔːrəs] n Stier m

taut [tɔːt] adj straff

tawdry ['tɔːdrɪ] adj (bunt und) billig

tax [tæks] n Steuer f ♦ vt besteuern; (*strain*) strapazieren; (*strength*) angreifen; **~able** adj (*income*) steuerpflichtig; **~ation** [tækˈseɪʃən] n Besteuerung f; **~ avoidance** n Steuerumgehung f; **~ disc** (BRIT) n (AUT) Kraftfahrzeugsteuerplakette f; **~ evasion** n Steuerhinterziehung f; **~-free** adj steuerfrei

taxi ['tæksɪ] n Taxi nt ♦ vi (*plane*) rollen; **~ driver** n Taxifahrer m; **~ rank** (BRIT) n Taxistand m; **~ stand** n Taxistand m

tax: ~payer n Steuerzahler m; **~ relief** n Steuerermäßigung f; **~ return** n Steuererklärung f

TB n abbr (= *tuberculosis*) Tb f, Tbc f

tea [tiː] n Tee m; (*meal*) (frühes) Abendessen nt; **high ~** (BRIT) Abendessen nt; **~ bag** n Teebeutel m; **~ break** (BRIT) n Teepause f

teach [tiːtʃ] (pt, pp **taught**) vt lehren; (SCH) lehren, unterrichten; (*show*): **to ~ sb sth** jdm etw beibringen ♦ vi lehren, unterrichten; **~er** n Lehrer(in) m(f); **~er's pet** n Lehrers Liebling m; **~ing** n (~er's work) Unterricht m; (*doctrine*) Lehre f

tea: ~ cloth n Geschirrtuch nt; **~ cosy** n Teewärmer m; **~cup** n Teetasse f; **~ leaves** npl Teeblätter pl

team [tiːm] n (*workers*) Team nt; (SPORT) Mannschaft f; (*animals*) Gespann nt; **~work** n Gemeinschaftsarbeit f, Teamarbeit f

teapot ['tiːpɒt] n Teekanne f

tear[1] [teər] (pt **tore**, pp **torn**) n Riss m ♦ vt zerreißen; (*muscle*) zerren ♦ vi (zer)reißen; (*rush*) rasen; **~ along** vi (*rush*) entlangrasen; **~ up** vt (*sheet of paper etc*) zerreißen

tear[2] [tɪər] n Träne f; **~ful** adj ['tɪəful] weinend; (*voice*) weinerlich; **~ gas** ['tɪəgæs] n Tränengas nt

tearoom ['tiːruːm] n Teestube f

tease [tiːz] n Hänsler m ♦ vt necken

tea set n Teeservice nt

teaspoon ['tiːspuːn] n Teelöffel m
teat [tiːt] n Brustwarze f; (of animal) Zitze f; (of bottle) Sauger m
tea time n (in the afternoon) Teestunde f; (mealtime) Abendessen nt
tea towel n Geschirrtuch nt
technical ['tɛknɪkl] adj technisch; (knowledge, terms) Fach-; **~ity** [tɛknɪ'kælɪtɪ] n technische Einzelheit f; (JUR) Formsache f; **~ly** adv technisch; (speak) spezialisiert; (fig) genau genommen
technician [tɛk'nɪʃən] n Techniker m
technique [tɛk'niːk] n Technik f
techno ['tɛknəu] n Techno m
technological [tɛknə'lɔdʒɪkl] adj technologisch
technology [tɛk'nɔlədʒɪ] n Technologie f
teddy (bear) ['tɛdɪ-] n Teddybär m
tedious ['tiːdɪəs] adj langweilig, ermüdend
tee [tiː] n (GOLF: object) Tee nt
teem [tiːm] vi (swarm): **to ~ (with)** wimmeln (von); **it is ~ing (with rain)** es gießt in Strömen
teenage ['tiːneɪdʒ] adj (fashions etc) Teenager-, jugendlich; **~r** n Teenager m, Jugendliche(r) mf
teens [tiːnz] npl Teenageralter nt
tee-shirt ['tiːʃəːt] n T-Shirt nt
teeter ['tiːtər] vi schwanken
teeth [tiːθ] npl of **tooth**
teethe [tiːð] vi zahnen; **teething ring** n Beißring m; **teething troubles** npl (fig) Kinderkrankheiten pl
teetotal ['tiː'təutl] adj abstinent
tele: **~communications** npl Fernmeldewesen nt; **~conferencing** n Telefon- or Videokonferenz f; **~gram** n Telegramm nt; **~graph** n Telegraf m; **~graph pole** n Telegrafenmast m
telephone ['tɛlɪfəun] n Telefon nt, Fernsprecher m ♦ vt anrufen; (message) telefonisch mitteilen; **to be on the ~** (talking) telefonieren; (possessing phone) Telefon haben; **~ booth** n Telefonzelle f; **~ box** (BRIT) n Telefonzelle f; **~ call** n Telefongespräch nt, Anruf m; **~ directory** n Telefonbuch nt; **~ number** n

Telefonnummer f; **telephonist** [tə'lɛfənɪst] (BRIT) n Telefonist(in) m(f)
telephoto lens ['tɛlɪ'fəutəu-] n Teleobjektiv nt
telesales ['tɛlɪseɪlz] n Telefonverkauf m
telescope ['tɛlɪskəup] n Teleskop nt, Fernrohr nt ♦ vt ineinander schieben
televise ['tɛlɪvaɪz] vt durch das Fernsehen übertragen
television ['tɛlɪvɪʒən] n Fernsehen nt; **on ~** im Fernsehen; **~ (set)** n Fernsehapparat m, Fernseher m
teleworking ['tɛlɪwəːkɪŋ] n Telearbeit f
telex ['tɛlɛks] n Telex nt ♦ vt per Telex schicken
tell [tɛl] (pt, pp **told**) vt (story) erzählen; (secret) ausplaudern; (say, make known) sagen; (distinguish) erkennen; (be sure) wissen ♦ vi (talk) sprechen; (be sure) wissen; (divulge) es verraten; (have effect) sich auswirken; **to ~ sb to do sth** jdm sagen, dass er etw tun soll; **to ~ sb sth** or **sth to sb** jdm etw sagen; **to ~ sth by** **sth** jdn an etw dat erkennen; **to ~ sth from** etw unterscheiden von; **to ~ of sth** von etw sprechen; **~ off** vt: **to ~ sb off** jdn ausschimpfen
teller ['tɛlər] n Kassenbeamte(r) mf
telling ['tɛlɪŋ] adj verräterisch; (blow) hart
telltale ['tɛlteɪl] adj verräterisch
telly ['tɛlɪ] (BRIT: inf) n abbr (= television) TV nt
temp [tɛmp] n abbr (= temporary) Aushilfssekretärin f
temper ['tɛmpər] n (disposition) Temperament nt; (anger) Zorn m ♦ vt (tone down) mildern; (metal) härten; **to be in a (bad) ~** wütend sein; **to lose one's ~** die Beherrschung verlieren
temperament ['tɛmprəmənt] n Temperament nt; **~al** [tɛmprə'mɛntl] adj (moody) launisch
temperate ['tɛmprət] adj gemäßigt
temperature ['tɛmprətʃər] n Temperatur f; (MED: high ~) Fieber nt; **to have** or **run a ~** Fieber haben
template ['tɛmplɪt] n Schablone f
temple ['tɛmpl] n Tempel m; (ANAT) Schlä-

fe *f*

temporal ['tempərl] *adj (of time)* zeitlich; *(worldly)* irdisch, weltlich

temporarily ['tempərərılı] *adv* zeitweilig, vorübergehend

temporary ['tempərərı] *adj* vorläufig; *(road, building)* provisorisch

tempt [tempt] *vt (persuade)* verleiten; *(attract)* reizen, (ver)locken; **to ~ sb into doing sth** jdn dazu verleiten, etw zu tun; **~ation** [temp'teıʃən] *n* Versuchung *f*; **~ing** *adj (person)* verführerisch; *(object, situation)* verlockend

ten [ten] *num* zehn

tenable ['tenəbl] *adj* haltbar

tenacious [tə'neıʃəs] *adj* zäh, hartnäckig

tenacity [tə'næsıtı] *n* Zähigkeit *f*, Hartnäckigkeit *f*

tenancy ['tenənsı] *n* Mietverhältnis *nt*

tenant ['tenənt] *n* Mieter *m*; *(of larger property)* Pächter *m*

tend [tend] *vt (look after)* sich kümmern um ♦ *vi*: **to ~ to do sth** etw gewöhnlich tun

tendency ['tendənsı] *n* Tendenz *f*; *(of person)* Tendenz *f*, Neigung *f*

tender ['tendər] *adj* zart; *(loving)* zärtlich ♦ *n (COMM: offer)* Kostenanschlag *m* ♦ *vt* (an)bieten; *(resignation)* einreichen; **~ness** *n* Zartheit *f*; *(being loving)* Zärtlichkeit *f*

tendon ['tendən] *n* Sehne *f*

tenement ['tenəmənt] *n* Mietshaus *nt*

tennis ['tenıs] *n* Tennis *nt*; **~ ball** *n* Tennisball *m*; **~ court** *n* Tennisplatz *m*; **~ player** *n* Tennisspieler(in) *m(f)*; **~ racket** *n* Tennisschläger *m*; **~ shoes** *npl* Tennisschuhe *pl*

tenor ['tenər] *n* Tenor *m*

tenpin bowling ['tenpın-] *n* Bowling *nt*

tense [tens] *adj* angespannt ♦ *n* Zeitform *f*

tension ['tenʃən] *n* Spannung *f*

tent [tent] *n* Zelt *nt*

tentacle ['tentəkl] *n* Fühler *m*; *(of sea animals)* Fangarm *m*

tentative ['tentətıv] *adj (movement)* unsicher; *(offer)* Probe-; *(arrangement)* vorläufig; *(suggestion)* unverbindlich; **~ly** *adv* versuchsweise; *(try, move)* vorsichtig

tenterhooks ['tentəhuks] *npl*: **to be on ~** auf die Folter gespannt sein

tenth [tenθ] *adj* zehnte(r, s)

tent peg *n* Hering *m*

tent pole *n* Zeltstange *f*

tenuous ['tenjuəs] *adj* schwach

tenure ['tenjuər] *n (of land)* Besitz *m*; *(of office)* Amtszeit *f*

tepid ['tepıd] *adj* lauwarm

term [tə:m] *n (period of time)* Zeit(raum *m*) *f*; *(limit)* Frist *f*; *(SCH)* Quartal *nt*; *(UNIV)* Trimester *nt*; *(expression)* Ausdruck *m* ♦ *vt* (be)nennen; **~s** *npl (conditions)* Bedingungen *pl*; **in the short/long ~** auf kurze/lange Sicht; **to be on good ~s with sb** gut mit jdm auskommen; **to come to ~s with** *(person)* sich einigen mit; *(problem)* sich abfinden mit

terminal ['tə:mınl] *n (BRIT: also: **coach** ~)* Endstation *f*; *(AVIAT)* Terminal *m*; *(COMPUT)* Terminal *nt* or *m* ♦ *adj* Schluss-; *(MED)* unheilbar; **~ly** *adj (MED)*: **~ly ill** unheilbar krank

terminate ['tə:mıneıt] *vt* beenden ♦ *vi* enden, aufhören

termini ['tə:mınaı] *npl* of **terminus**

terminus ['tə:mınəs] *(pl* **termini***)* *n* Endstation *f*

terrace ['terəs] *n (BRIT: row of houses)* Häuserreihe *f*; *(in garden etc)* Terrasse *f*; **the ~s** *npl (BRIT: SPORT)* die Ränge; **~d** *adj (garden)* terrassenförmig angelegt; *(house)* Reihen-

terrain [te'reın] *n* Gelände *nt*

terrible ['terıbl] *adj* schrecklich, entsetzlich, fürchterlich; **terribly** *adv* fürchterlich

terrier ['terıər] *n* Terrier *m*

terrific [tə'rıfık] *adj* unwahrscheinlich; **~!** klasse!

terrified *adj*: **to be ~ of sth** vor etw schreckliche Angst haben

terrify ['terıfaı] *vt* erschrecken

territorial [terı'tɔ:rıəl] *adj* Gebiets-, territorial

territory ['terıtərı] *n* Gebiet *nt*

terror ['terər] *n* Schrecken *m*

terrorism ['terərızəm] *n* Terrorismus *m*; **~ist** *n* Terrorist(in) *m(f)*; **~ize** *vt* terrorisieren

terse [tɜːs] adj knapp, kurz, bündig

test [test] n Probe f; (examination) Prüfung f; (PSYCH, TECH) Test m ♦ vt prüfen; (PSYCH) testen

testicle ['tɛstɪkl] n (ANAT) Hoden m

testify ['tɛstɪfaɪ] vi aussagen; **to ~ to sth** etw bezeugen

testimony ['tɛstɪmənɪ] n (JUR) Zeugenaussage f; (fig) Zeugnis nt

test match n (SPORT) Länderkampf m

test tube n Reagenzglas nt

tetanus ['tɛtənəs] n Wundstarrkrampf m, Tetanus m

tether ['tɛðə*] vt anbinden ♦ n: **at the end of one's ~** völlig am Ende

text [tɛkst] n Text m; (of document) Wortlaut m; **~book** n Lehrbuch nt

textiles ['tɛkstaɪlz] npl Textilien pl

texture ['tɛkstʃə*] n Beschaffenheit f

Thai [taɪ] adj thailändisch ♦ n Thailänder(in) m(f); **~land** n Thailand nt

Thames [tɛmz] n: **the ~** die Themse

than [ðæn, ðən] prep (in comparisons) als

thank [θæŋk] vt danken +dat; **you've him to ~ for your success** Sie haben Ihren Erfolg ihm zu verdanken; **~ you (very much)** danke (vielmals), danke schön; **~ful** adj dankbar; **~less** adj undankbar; **~s** npl Dank m ♦ excl danke!; **~s to** dank +gen; **T~sgiving (Day)** n (US) Thanksgiving Day m

---

Thanksgiving (Day)

> Thanksgiving (Day) ist ein Feiertag in den USA, der auf den vierten Donnerstag im November fällt. Er soll daran erinnern, wie die Pilgerväter die gute Ernte im Jahre 1621 feierten. In Kanada gibt es einen ähnlichen Erntedanktag (der aber nichts mit dem Pilgervätern zu tun hat) am zweiten Montag im Oktober.

KEYWORD

that [ðæt, ðət] adj (demonstrative: pl those) der/die/das; jene(r, s); **that one** das da
♦ pron **1** (demonstrative: pl those) das; **who's/what's that?** wer ist da/was ist das?; **is that you?** bist du das?; **that's what he said** genau das hat er gesagt; **what happened after that?** was passierte danach?; **that is** das heißt

2 (relative: subj) der/die/das, die; (: direct obj) den/die/das, die; (: indirect obj) dem/der/dem, denen; **all (that) I have** alles, was ich habe

3 (relative: of time): **the day (that)** an dem Tag, als; **the winter (that) he came** in dem Winter, in dem er kam

♦ conj dass; **he thought that I was ill** er dachte, dass ich krank sei, er dachte, ich sei krank

♦ adv (demonstrative) so; **I can't work that much** ich kann nicht so viel arbeiten

---

thatched [θætʃt] adj strohgedeckt; (cottage) mit Strohdach

thaw [θɔː] n Tauwetter nt ♦ vi tauen; (frozen foods, fig: people) auftauen ♦ vt (auf)tauen lassen

---

KEYWORD

the [ðiː, ðə] def art **1** der/die/das; **to play the piano/violin** Klavier/Geige spielen; **I'm going to the butcher's/the cinema** ich gehe zum Fleischer/ins Kino; **Elizabeth the First** Elisabeth die Erste

2 (+adj to form noun) das, die; **the rich and the poor** die Reichen und die Armen

3 (in comparisons): **the more he works the more he earns** je mehr er arbeitet, desto mehr verdient er

---

theatre ['θɪətə*] (US **theater**) n Theater nt; (for lectures etc) Saal m; (MED) Operationssaal m; **~goer** n Theaterbesucher(in) m(f); **theatrical** [θɪ'ætrɪkl] adj Theater-; (career) Schauspieler-; (showy) theatralisch

theft [θɛft] n Diebstahl m

their [ðɛə*] adj ihr; see also **my**; **~s** pron ihre(r, s); see also **mine²**

them [ðɛm, ðəm] pron (acc) sie; (dat) ihnen; see also **me**

theme [θi:m] *n* Thema *nt*; (*MUS*) Motiv *nt*; ~
park *n* (thematisch gestalteter) Freizeitpark
m; ~ **song** *n* Titelmusik *f*

themselves [ðəm'selvz] *pl pron* (*reflexive*)
sich (selbst); (*emphatic*) selbst; *see also*
oneself

then [ðen] *adv* (*at that time*) damals; (*next*)
dann ♦ *conj* also, folglich; (*furthermore*)
ferner ♦ *adj* damalig; **from ~ on** von da an;
by ~ bis dahin; **the ~ president** der
damalige Präsident

theology [θɪ'ɔlədʒɪ] *n* Theologie *f*

theoretical [θɪə'retɪkl] *adj* theoretisch; ~**ly**
adv theoretisch

theory ['θɪərɪ] *n* Theorie *f*

therapist ['θerəpɪst] *n* Therapeut(in) *m(f)*

therapy ['θerəpɪ] *n* Therapie *f*

KEYWORD
---

there [ðeə] *adv* **1**: **there is, there are** es *or*
da ist/sind; (*there exists/exist also*) es gibt;
there are 3 of them (*people, things*) es gibt
3 davon; **there has been an accident** da
war ein Unfall
2 (*place*) da, dort; (*direction*) dahin, dorthin;
put it in/on there leg es dahinein/
dorthinauf
3: **there, there** (*esp to child*) na, na

there: ~**abouts** ['ðeərə'bauts] *adv* (*place*)
dort in der Nähe, dort irgendwo; (*amount*):
20 or ~abouts ungefähr 20; ~**after**
[ðeər'ɑ:ftə] *adv* danach; ~**by** ['ðeəbaɪ] *adv*
dadurch, damit

therefore ['ðeəfɔ:] *adv* deshalb, daher

there's ['ðeəz] = **there is**; **there has**

thermometer [θə'mɔmɪtə] *n* Thermometer
nt

Thermos ['θɜ:məs] ® *n* Thermosflasche *f*

thesaurus [θɪ'sɔ:rəs] *n* Synonymwörterbuch
nt

these [ði:z] *pron, adj* (*pl*) diese

theses ['θi:si:z] *npl of* **thesis**

thesis ['θi:sɪs] (*pl* **theses**) *n* (*for discussion*)
These *f*; (*UNIV*) Dissertation *f*, Doktorarbeit *f*

they [ðeɪ] *pl pron* sie; (*people in general*) man;
~ **say that ...** (*it is said that*) es wird gesagt,

dass ; ~'**d** = **they had**; **they would**; ~=
they shall; **they will**; ~= **they are**; ~= **they
have**

thick [θɪk] *adj* dick; (*forest*) dicht; (*liquid*)
dickflüssig; (*slow, stupid*) dumm, schwer
von Begriff ♦ *n*: **in the ~ of** mitten in +*dat*;
it's 20 cm ~ es ist 20 cm dick *or* stark; ~**en**
vi (*fog*) dichter werden ♦ *vt* (*sauce etc*)
verdicken; ~**ness** *n* Dicke *f*; Dichte *f*;
Dickflüssigkeit *f*; ~**set** *adj* untersetzt; ~-
skinned *adj* dickhäutig

thief [θi:f] (*pl* **thieves**) *n* Dieb(in) *m(f)*

thieves [θi:vz] *npl of* **thief**

thieving ['θi:vɪŋ] *n* Stehlen *nt* ♦ *adj* die-
bisch

thigh [θaɪ] *n* Oberschenkel *m*

thimble ['θɪmbl] *n* Fingerhut *m*

thin [θɪn] *adj* dünn; (*person*) dünn, mager;
(*excuse*) schwach ♦ *vt*: **to ~ (down)** (*sauce,
paint*) verdünnen

thing [θɪŋ] *n* Ding *nt*; (*affair*) Sache *f*; **my ~s**
meine Sachen *pl*; **the best ~ would be to
...** das Beste wäre, ...; **how are ~s?** wie
gehts?

think [θɪŋk] (*pt, pp* **thought**) *vt, vi* denken;
what did you ~ of them? was halten Sie
von ihnen?; **to ~ about sth/sb**
nachdenken über etw/jdn; **I'll ~ about it**
ich überlege es mir; **to ~ of doing sth**
vorhaben *or* beabsichtigen, etw zu tun; **I ~
so/not** ich glaube (schon)/glaube nicht; **to
~ well of sb** viel von jdm halten; ~ **over**
vt überdenken; ~ **up** *vt* sich *dat*
ausdenken

think tank *n* Expertengruppe *f*

thinly ['θɪnlɪ] *adv* dünn; (*disguised*) kaum

third [θɜ:d] *adj* dritte(r, s) ♦ *n* (*person*)
Dritte(r) *mf*; (*part*) Drittel *nt*; ~**ly** *adv*
drittens; ~ **party insurance** (*BRIT*) *n*
Haftpflichtversicherung *f*; ~-**rate** *adj*
minderwertig; **T~ World** *n*: **the T~ World**
die Dritte Welt *f*

thirst [θɜ:st] *n* (*also fig*) Durst *m*; ~**y** *adj*
(*person*) durstig; (*work*) durstig machend; **to
be ~y** Durst haben

thirteen [θɜ:'ti:n] *num* dreizehn

thirty ['θɜ:tɪ] *num* dreißig

┌─ KEYWORD ─┐

this [ðɪs] adj (demonstrative: pl these) diese(r, s); **this evening** heute Abend; **this one** diese(r, s) (da)
♦ pron (demonstrative: pl these) dies, das; **who/what is this?** wer/was ist das?; **this is where I live** hier wohne ich; **this is what he said** das hat er gesagt; **this is Mr Brown** dies ist Mr Brown; (on telephone) hier ist Mr Brown
♦ adv (demonstrative): **this high/long** etc so groß/lang etc

thistle ['θɪsl] n Distel f
thorn [θɔːn] n Dorn m; **~y** adj dornig; (problem) schwierig
thorough ['θʌrə] adj gründlich; **~bred** n Vollblut nt ♦ adj reinrassig, Vollblut-; **~fare** n Straße f; **"no ~fare"** „Durchfahrt verboten"; **~ly** adv gründlich; (extremely) äußerst
those [ðəuz] pl pron die (da), jene ♦ adj die, jene
though [ðəu] conj obwohl ♦ adv trotzdem
thought [θɔːt] pt, pp of **think** ♦ n (idea) Gedanke m; (thinking) Denken nt, Denkvermögen nt; **~ful** adj (thinking) gedankenvoll, nachdenklich; (kind) rücksichtsvoll, aufmerksam; **~less** adj gedankenlos, unbesonnen; (unkind) rücksichtslos
thousand ['θauzənd] num tausend; **two ~** zweitausend; **~s of** tausende or Tausende (von); **~th** adj tausendste(r, s)
thrash [θræʃ] vt verdreschen; (fig) (vernichtend) schlagen; **~ about** vi um sich schlagen; **~ out** vt ausdiskutieren
thread [θrɛd] n Faden m, Garn nt; (TECH) Gewinde nt; (in story) Faden m ♦ vt (needle) einfädeln; **~bare** adj fadenscheinig
threat [θrɛt] n Drohung f; (danger) Gefahr f; **~en** vt bedrohen ♦ vi drohen; **to ~en sb with sth** jdm etw androhen
three [θriː] num drei; **~-dimensional** adj dreidimensional; **~-piece suite** n dreiteilige Polstergarnitur f; **~-wheeler** n

Dreiradwagen m
thresh [θrɛʃ] vt, vi dreschen
threshold ['θrɛʃhəuld] n Schwelle f
threw [θruː] pt of **throw**
thrift [θrɪft] n Sparsamkeit f; **~y** adj sparsam
thrill [θrɪl] n Reiz m, Erregung f ♦ vt begeistern, packen; **to be ~ed with** (gift etc) sich unheimlich freuen über +acc; **~er** n Krimi m; **~ing** adj spannend; (news) aufregend
thrive [θraɪv] (pt thrived, pp thrived) vi: **to ~ (on)** gedeihen (bei); **thriving** ['θraɪvɪŋ] adj blühend
throat [θrəut] n Hals m, Kehle f; **to have a sore ~** Halsschmerzen haben
throb [θrɔb] vi klopfen, pochen
throes [θrəuz] npl: **in the ~ of** mitten in +dat
throne [θrəun] n Thron m; **on the ~** auf dem Thron
throng ['θrɔŋ] n (Menschen)schar f ♦ vt sich drängen in +dat
throttle ['θrɔtl] n Gashebel m ♦ vt erdrosseln
through [θruː] prep durch; (time) während +gen; (because of) aus, durch ♦ adv durch ♦ adj (ticket, train) durchgehend; (finished) fertig; **to put sb ~ (to)** jdn verbinden (mit); **to be ~** (TEL) eine Verbindung haben; (have finished) fertig sein; **no ~ way** (BRIT) Sackgasse f; **~out** [θruːˈaut] prep (place) überall in +dat; (time) während +gen ♦ adv überall; die ganze Zeit
throw [θrəu] (pt threw, pp thrown) n Wurf m ♦ vt werfen; **to ~ a party** eine Party geben; **~ away** vt wegwerfen; (waste) verschenken; (money) verschwenden; **~ off** vt abwerfen; (pursuer) abschütteln; **~ out** vt hinauswerfen; (rubbish) wegwerfen; (plan) verwerfen; **~ up** vt, vi (vomit) speien; **~away** adj Wegwerf-; **~in** n Einwurf m; **~n** pp of **throw**
thru [θruː] (US) = **through**
thrush [θrʌʃ] n Drossel f
thrust [θrʌst] (pt, pp thrust) vt, vi (push) stoßen
thud [θʌd] n dumpfe(r) (Auf)schlag m
thug [θʌg] n Schlägertyp m

thumb [θʌm] *n* Daumen *m* ♦ *vt* (*book*) durchblättern; **to ~ a lift** per Anhalter fahren (wollen); **~tack** (*US*) *n* Reißzwecke *f*

thump [θʌmp] *n* (*blow*) Schlag *m*; (*noise*) Bums *m* ♦ *vi* hämmern, pochen ♦ *vt* schlagen auf +*acc*

thunder ['θʌndəʳ] *n* Donner *m* ♦ *vi* donnern; (*train etc*): **to ~ past** vorbeidonnern ♦ *vt* brüllen; **~bolt** *n* Blitz *nt*; **~clap** *n* Donnerschlag *m*; **~storm** *n* Gewitter *nt*, Unwetter *nt*; **~y** *adj* gewitterschwül

Thursday ['θɜːzdɪ] *n* Donnerstag *m*

thus [ðʌs] *adv* (*in this way*) so; (*therefore*) somit, also, folglich

thwart [θwɔːt] *vt* vereiteln, durchkreuzen; (*person*) hindern

thyme [taɪm] *n* Thymian *m*

thyroid ['θaɪrɔɪd] *n* Schilddrüse *f*

tiara [tɪ'ɑːrə] *n* Diadem *nt*

tic [tɪk] *n* Tick *m*

tick [tɪk] *n* (*sound*) Ticken *nt*; (*mark*) Häkchen *nt* ♦ *vi* ticken ♦ *vt* abhaken; **in a ~** (*BRIT: inf*) sofort; **~ off** *vt* abhaken; (*person*) ausschimpfen; **~ over** *vi* (*engine*) im Leerlauf laufen; (*fig*) auf Sparflamme laufen

ticket ['tɪkɪt] *n* (*for travel*) Fahrkarte *f*; (*for entrance*) (Eintritts)karte *f*; (*price ~*) Preisschild *nt*; (*luggage ~*) (Gepäck)schein *m*; (*raffle ~*) Los *nt*; (*parking ~*) Strafzettel *m*; (*in car park*) Parkschein *m*; **~ collector** *n* Fahrkartenkontrolleur *m*; **~ inspector** *n* Fahrkartenkontrolleur *m*; **~ office** *n* (*THEAT etc*) Kasse *f*; (*RAIL etc*) Fahrkartenschalter *m*

tickle ['tɪkl] *n* Kitzeln *nt* ♦ *vt* kitzeln; (*amuse*) amüsieren; **ticklish** ['tɪklɪʃ] *adj* (*also fig*) kitzlig

tidal ['taɪdl] *adj* Flut-, Tide-; **~ wave** *n* Flutwelle *f*

tidbit ['tɪdbɪt] (*US*) *n* Leckerbissen *m*

tiddlywinks ['tɪdlɪwɪŋks] *n* Floh(hüpf)spiel *nt*

tide [taɪd] *n* Gezeiten *pl*; **high/low ~** Flut *f*/ Ebbe *f*

tidy ['taɪdɪ] *adj* ordentlich ♦ *vt* aufräumen, in Ordnung bringen

tie [taɪ] *n* (*BRIT: neck*) Krawatte *f*, Schlips *m*; (*sth connecting*) Band *nt*; (*SPORT*) Unentschieden *nt* ♦ *vt* (*fasten, restrict*) binden ♦ *vi* (*SPORT*) unentschieden spielen; (*in competition*) punktgleich sein; **to ~ in a bow** zur Schleife binden; **to ~ a knot in sth** einen Knoten in etw *acc* machen; **~ down** *vt* festbinden; **to ~ sb down to** jdn binden an +*acc*; **~ up** *vt* (*dog*) anbinden; (*parcel*) verschnüren; (*boat*) festmachen; (*person*) fesseln; **to be ~d up** (*busy*) beschäftigt sein

tier [tɪəʳ] *n* Rang *m*; (*of cake*) Etage *f*

tiff [tɪf] *n* Krach *m*

tiger ['taɪgəʳ] *n* Tiger *m*

tight [taɪt] *adj* (*close*) eng, knapp; (*schedule*) gedrängt; (*firm*) fest; (*control*) streng; (*stretched*) stramm, (an)gespannt; (*inf: drunk*) blau, stramm ♦ *adv* (*squeeze*) fest; **~en** *vt* anziehen, anspannen; (*restrictions*) verschärfen ♦ *vi* sich spannen; **~-fisted** *adj* knauserig; **~ly** *adv* eng; fest; (*stretched*) straff; **~rope** *n* Seil *nt*; **~s** *npl* (*esp BRIT*) Strumpfhose *f*

tile [taɪl] *n* (*on roof*) Dachziegel *m*; (*on wall or floor*) Fliese *f*; **~d** *adj* (*roof*) gedeckt, Ziegel-; (*floor, wall*) mit Fliesen belegt

till [tɪl] *n* Kasse *f* ♦ *vt* bestellen ♦ *prep, conj* = **until**

tiller ['tɪləʳ] *n* Ruderpinne *f*

tilt [tɪlt] *vt* kippen, neigen ♦ *vi* sich neigen

timber ['tɪmbəʳ] *n* (*wood*) Holz *nt*

time [taɪm] *n* Zeit *f*; (*occasion*) Mal *nt*; (*rhythm*) Takt *m* ♦ *vt* zur rechten Zeit tun, zeitlich einrichten; (*SPORT*) stoppen; **in 2 weeks' ~** in 2 Wochen; **a long ~** lange; **for the ~ being** vorläufig; **4 at a ~** zu jeweils 4; **from ~ to ~** gelegentlich; **to have a good ~** sich amüsieren; **in ~** (*soon enough*) rechtzeitig; (*after some ~*) mit der Zeit; (*MUS*) im Takt; **in no ~** im Handumdrehen; **any ~** jederzeit; **on ~** pünktlich, rechtzeitig; **five ~s 5** fünfmal 5; **what ~ is it?** wie viel Uhr ist es?, wie spät ist es?; **at ~s** manchmal; **~ bomb** *n* Zeitbombe *f*; **~less** *adj* (*beauty*) zeitlos; **~ limit** *n* Frist *f*; **~ly** *adj* rechtzeitig; günstig; **~ off** *n* freie Zeit *f*; **~r** *n* (*timer switch: in kitchen*) Schaltuhr *f*; **~ scale** *n* Zeitspanne *f*; **~-share** *adj* Timesharing-; **~ switch**

(*BRIT*) *n* Zeitschalter *m*; ~**table** *n* Fahrplan *m*; (*SCH*) Stundenplan *m*; ~ **zone** *n* Zeitzone *f*

timid ['tɪmɪd] *adj* ängstlich, schüchtern

timing ['taɪmɪŋ] *n* Wahl *f* des richtigen Zeitpunkts, Timing *nt*

timpani ['tɪmpənɪ] *npl* Kesselpauken *pl*

tin [tɪn] *n* (*metal*) Blech *nt*; (*BRIT*: *can*) Büchse *f*, Dose *f*; ~**foil** *n* Stanniolpapier *nt*

tinge [tɪndʒ] *n* (*colour*) Färbung *f*; (*fig*) Anflug *m* ♦ *vt* färben; ~**d with** mit einer Spur von

tingle ['tɪŋgl] *n* Prickeln *nt* ♦ *vi* prickeln

tinker ['tɪŋkər] *n* Kesselflicker *m*; ~ **with** *vt fus* herumpfuschen an +*dat*

tinkle ['tɪŋkl] *vi* klingeln

tinned [tɪnd] (*BRIT*) *adj* (*food*) Dosen-, Büchsen-

tin opener [-əupnər] (*BRIT*) *n* Dosen- *or* Büchsenöffner *m*

tinsel ['tɪnsl] *n* Rauschgold *nt*

tint [tɪnt] *n* Farbton *m*; (*slight colour*) Anflug *m*; (*hair*) Tönung *f*; ~**ed** *adj* getönt

tiny ['taɪnɪ] *adj* winzig

tip [tɪp] *n* (*pointed end*) Spitze *f*; (*money*) Trinkgeld *nt*; (*hint*) Wink *m*, Tipp *m* ♦ *vt* (*slant*) kippen; (*hat*) antippen; (~ *over*) umkippen; (*waiter*) ein Trinkgeld geben +*dat*; ~**off** *n* Hinweis *m*, Tipp *m*; ~**ped** (*BRIT*) *adj* (*cigarette*) Filter-

tipsy ['tɪpsɪ] *adj* beschwipst

tiptoe ['tɪptəu] *n*: **on** ~ auf Zehenspitzen

tiptop [tɪp'tɔp] *adj*: **in** ~ **condition** tipptopp, erstklassig

tire ['taɪər] *n* (*US*) = **tyre** ♦ *vt*, *vi* ermüden, müde machen/werden; ~**d** *adj* müde; **to be ~d of sth** etw satt haben; ~**less** *adj* unermüdlich; ~**some** *adj* lästig

tiring ['taɪərɪŋ] *adj* ermüdend

tissue ['tɪʃu:] *n* Gewebe *nt*; (*paper handkerchief*) Papiertaschentuch *nt*; ~ **paper** *n* Seidenpapier *nt*

tit [tɪt] *n* (*bird*) Meise *f*; ~ **for tat** wie du mir, so ich dir

titbit ['tɪtbɪt] (*US* **tidbit**) *n* Leckerbissen *m*

titillate ['tɪtɪleɪt] *vt* kitzeln

title ['taɪtl] *n* Titel *m*; ~ **deed** *n* Eigentumsurkunde *f*; ~ **role** *n* Hauptrolle *f*

titter ['tɪtər] *vi* kichern

titular ['tɪtjulər] *adj* (*in name only*) nominell

TM *abbr* (= *trademark*) Wz

---

to [tu:, tə] *prep* **1** (*direction*) zu, nach; **I go to France/school** ich gehe nach Frankreich/zur Schule; **to the left** nach links

2 (*as far as*) bis

3 (*with expressions of time*) vor; **a quarter to 5** Viertel vor 5

4 (*for, of*) für; **secretary to the director** Sekretärin des Direktors

5 (*expressing indirect object*): **to give sth to sb** jdm etw geben; **to talk to sb** mit jdm sprechen; **I sold it to a friend** ich habe es einem Freund verkauft

6 (*in relation to*) zu; **30 miles to the gallon** 30 Meilen pro Gallone

7 (*purpose, result*) zu; **to my surprise** zu meiner Überraschung

♦ *with vb* **1** (*infin*): **to go/eat** gehen/essen; **to want to do sth** etw tun wollen; **to try/start to do sth** versuchen/anfangen, etw zu tun; **he has a lot to lose** er hat viel zu verlieren

2 (*with vb omitted*): **I don't want to** ich will (es) nicht

3 (*purpose, result*) um; **I did it to help you** ich tat es, um dir zu helfen

4 (*after adj etc*): **ready to use** gebrauchsfertig; **too old/young to ...** zu alt/jung, um ... zu ...

♦ *adv*: **push/pull the door to** die Tür zuschieben/zuziehen

---

toad [təud] *n* Kröte *f*; ~**stool** *n* Giftpilz *m*

toast [təust] *n* (*bread*) Toast *m*; (*drinking*) Trinkspruch *m* ♦ *vt* trinken auf +*acc*; (*bread*) toasten; (*warm*) wärmen; ~**er** *n* Toaster *m*

tobacco [tə'bækəu] *n* Tabak *m*; ~**nist** [tə'bækənɪst] *n* Tabakhändler *m*; ~**nist's (shop)** *n* Tabakladen *m*

toboggan [tə'bɔgən] *n* (*Rodel*)schlitten *m*; ~**ing** *n* Rodeln *nt*

today [tə'deɪ] *adv* heute; (*at the present time*) heutzutage

toddler ['tɒdlər] *n* Kleinkind *nt*

toddy ['tɒdɪ] *n* (Whisky)grog *m*

to-do [tə'du:] *n* Theater *nt*

toe [təu] *n* Zehe *f*; (*of sock, shoe*) Spitze *f*
♦ *vt*: **to ~ the line** (*fig*) sich einfügen; **~nail**
n Zehennagel *m*

toffee ['tɒfɪ] *n* Sahnebonbon *nt*; **~ apple**
(*BRIT*) *n* kandierte(r) Apfel *m*

together [tə'geðər] *adv* zusammen; (*at the
same time*) gleichzeitig; **~ with** zusammen
mit; gleichzeitig mit

toil [tɔɪl] *n* harte Arbeit *f*, Plackerei *f* ♦ *vi* sich
abmühen, sich plagen

toilet ['tɔɪlət] *n* Toilette *f* ♦ *cpd* Toiletten-; **~
bag** *n* Waschbeutel *m*; **~ paper** *n*
Toilettenpapier *nt*; **~ries** ['tɔɪlətrɪz] *npl*
Toilettenartikel *pl*; **~ roll** *n* Rolle *f*
Toilettenpapier; **~ water** *n* Toilettenwasser
nt

token ['təukən] *n* Zeichen *nt*; (*gift ~*)
Gutschein *m*; **book/record ~** (*BRIT*)
Bücher-/Plattengutschein *m*

Tokyo ['təukjəu] *n* Tokio *nt*

told [təuld] *pt, pp of* **tell**

tolerable ['tɒlərəbl] *adj* (*bearable*) erträglich;
(*fairly good*) leidlich

tolerant ['tɒlərnt] *adj*: **be ~ (of)** vertragen
+*acc*

tolerate ['tɒləreɪt] *vt* dulden; (*noise*) ertragen

toll [təul] *n* Gebühr *f* ♦ *vi* (*bell*) läuten

tomato [tə'mɑ:təu] *n* (*pl ~es*) Tomate *f*

tomb [tu:m] *n* Grab(mal) *nt*

tomboy ['tɒmbɔɪ] *n* Wildfang *m*

tombstone ['tu:mstəun] *n* Grabstein *m*

tomcat ['tɒmkæt] *n* Kater *m*

tomorrow [tə'mɒrəu] *n* Morgen *nt* ♦ *adv*
morgen; **the day after ~** übermorgen; **~
morning** morgen früh; **a week ~** morgen
in einer Woche

ton [tʌn] *n* Tonne *f* (*BRIT* = 1016kg; *US
= 907kg*); **~s of** (*inf*) eine Unmenge von

tone [təun] *n* Ton *m*; **~ down** *vt* (*criticism,
demands*) mäßigen; (*colours*) abtonen; **~ up**
vt in Form bringen; **~-deaf** *adj* ohne
musikalisches Gehör

tongs [tɒŋz] *npl* Zange *f*; (*curling ~*)
Lockenstab *m*

tongue [tʌŋ] *n* Zunge *f*; (*language*) Sprache
f; **with ~ in cheek** scherzhaft; **~-tied** *adj*
stumm, sprachlos; **~ twister** *n*
Zungenbrecher *m*

tonic ['tɒnɪk] *n* (*drink*) Tonic *nt*; (*MED*)
Stärkungsmittel *nt*

tonight [tə'naɪt] *adv* heute Abend

tonsil ['tɒnsl] *n* Mandel *f*; **~litis** [tɒnsɪ'laɪtɪs] *n*
Mandelentzündung *f*

too [tu:] *adv* zu; (*also*) auch; **~ bad!** Pech!; **~
many** zu viele

took [tuk] *pt of* **take**

tool [tu:l] *n* (*also fig*) Werkzeug *nt*; **~box** *n*
Werkzeugkasten *m*

toot [tu:t] *n* Hupen *nt* ♦ *vi* tuten; (*AUT*)
hupen

tooth [tu:θ] *n* (*pl* **teeth**) *n* Zahn *m*; **~ache** *n*
Zahnschmerzen *pl*, Zahnweh *nt*; **~brush** *n*
Zahnbürste *f*; **~paste** *n* Zahnpasta *f*;
~pick *n* Zahnstocher *m*

top [tɒp] *n* Spitze *f*; (*of mountain*) Gipfel *m*;
(*of tree*) Wipfel *m*; (*toy*) Kreisel *m*; (*~ gear*)
vierte(r)/fünfte(r) Gang *m* ♦ *adj* oberste(r, s)
♦ *vt* (*list*) an erster Stelle stehen auf +*dat*;
on ~ of oben auf +*dat*; **from ~ to bottom**
von oben bis unten; **~ off** (*US*) *vt* auffüllen;
~ up *vt* auffüllen; **~ floor** *n* oberste(s)
Stockwerk *nt*; **~ hat** *n* Zylinder *m*; **~-
heavy** *adj* kopflastig

topic ['tɒpɪk] *n* Thema *nt*,
Gesprächsgegenstand *m*; **~al** *adj* aktuell

top: ~less ['tɒplɪs] *adj* (*bather etc*) oben
ohne; **~-level** ['tɒplevl] *adj* auf höchster
Ebene; **~most** ['tɒpməust] *adj* oberste(r, s)

topple ['tɒpl] *vt, vi* stürzen, kippen

top-secret ['tɒp'si:krɪt] *adj* streng geheim

topsy-turvy ['tɒpsɪ'tɜ:vɪ] *adv* durcheinander
♦ *adj* auf den Kopf gestellt

torch [tɔ:tʃ] *n* (*BRIT: ELEC*) Taschenlampe *f*;
(*with flame*) Fackel *f*

tore [tɔ:r] *pt of* **tear¹**

torment [*n* 'tɔ:mɛnt, *vb* tɔ:'mɛnt] *n* Qual *f*
♦ *vt* (*distress*) quälen

torn [tɔ:n] *pp of* **tear¹** ♦ *adj* hin- und
hergerissen

torrent ['tɒrnt] *n* Sturzbach *m*; **~ial** [tɔ'rɛnʃl]
adj wolkenbruchartig

torrid ['torɪd] adj heiß

tortoise ['tɔːtəs] n Schildkröte f; ~shell ['tɔːtəʃel] n Schildpatt m

torture ['tɔːtʃəʳ] n Folter f ♦ vt foltern

Tory ['tɔːrɪ] (BRIT) n (POL) Tory m ♦ adj Tory-, konservativ

toss [tɔs] vt schleudern; to ~ a coin or to ~ up for sth etw mit einer Münze entscheiden; to ~ and turn (in bed) sich hin und her werfen

tot [tɔt] n (small quantity) bisschen nt; (small child) Knirps m

total ['təutl] n Gesamtheit f; (money) Endsumme f ♦ adj Gesamt-, total ♦ vt (add up) zusammenzählen; (amount to) sich belaufen auf

totalitarian [təutælɪ'tɛərɪən] adj totalitär

totally ['təutəlɪ] adv total

totter ['tɔtəʳ] vi wanken, schwanken

touch [tʌtʃ] n Berührung f; (sense of feeling) Tastsinn m ♦ vt (feel) berühren; (come against) leicht anstoßen; (emotionally) rühren; a ~ of (fig) eine Spur von; to get in ~ with sb sich mit jdm in Verbindung setzen; to lose ~ (friends) Kontakt verlieren; ~ on vt fus (topic) berühren, erwähnen; ~ up vt (paint) auffrischen; ~-and-go adj riskant, knapp; ~down n Landen nt, Niedergehen nt; ~ed adj (moved) gerührt; ~ing adj rührend; ~line n Seitenlinie f; ~-sensitive screen n (COMPUT) berührungsempfindlicher Bildschirm m; ~y adj empfindlich, reizbar

tough [tʌf] adj zäh; (difficult) schwierig ♦ n Schläger(typ) m; ~en vt zäh machen; (make strong) abhärten

toupee ['tuːpeɪ] n Toupet nt

tour ['tuəʳ] n Tour f ♦ vi umherreisen; (THEAT) auf Tour sein; auf Tour gehen; ~ guide n Reiseleiter(in) m(f)

tourism ['tuərɪzm] n Fremdenverkehr m, Tourismus m

tourist ['tuərɪst] n Tourist(in) m(f) ♦ cpd (class) Touristen-; ~ office n Verkehrsamt nt

tournament ['tuənəmənt] n Turnier nt

tousled ['tauzld] adj zerzaust

tout [taut] vi: to ~ for auf Kundenfang gehen für ♦ n: ticket ~ Kundenschlepper(in) m(f)

tow [təu] vt (ab)schleppen; on (BRIT) or in (US) ~ (AUT) im Schlepp

toward(s) [tə'wɔːd(z)] prep (with time) gegen; (in direction of) nach

towel ['tauəl] n Handtuch nt; ~ling n (fabric) Frottee nt or m; ~ rack (US) n Handtuchstange f; ~ rail n Handtuchstange f

tower ['tauəʳ] n Turm m; ~ block (BRIT) n Hochhaus nt; ~ing adj hochragend

town [taun] n Stadt f; to go to ~ (fig) sich ins Zeug legen; ~ centre n Stadtzentrum nt; ~ clerk n Stadtdirektor m; ~ council n Stadtrat m; ~ hall n Rathaus nt; ~ plan n Stadtplan m; ~ planning n Stadtplanung f

towrope ['təurəup] n Abschlepptau nt

tow truck (US) n Abschleppwagen m

toxic ['tɔksɪk] adj giftig, Gift-

toy [tɔɪ] n Spielzeug nt; ~ with vt fus spielen mit; ~shop n Spielwarengeschäft nt

trace [treɪs] n Spur f ♦ vt (follow a course) nachspüren +dat; (find out) aufspüren; (copy) durchpausen; tracing paper n Pauspapier nt

track [træk] n (mark) Spur f; (path) Weg m; (racetrack) Rennbahn f; (RAIL) Gleis nt ♦ vt verfolgen; to keep ~ of sb jdn im Auge behalten; ~ down vt aufspüren; ~suit n Trainingsanzug m

tract [trækt] n (of land) Gebiet nt

traction ['trækʃən] n (power) Zugkraft f; (AUT: grip) Bodenhaftung f; (MED): in ~ im Streckverband

tractor ['træktəʳ] n Traktor m

trade [treɪd] n (commerce) Handel m; (business) Geschäft nt, Gewerbe nt; (people) Geschäftsleute pl; (skilled manual work) Handwerk nt ♦ vi: to ~ (in) handeln (mit) ♦ vt tauschen; ~ in vt in Zahlung geben; ~ fair n Messe f; ~-in price n Preis, zu dem etw in Zahlung genommen wird; ~mark n Warenzeichen nt; ~ name n Handelsbezeichnung f; ~r n Händler m; ~sman (irreg) n (shopkeeper) Geschäftsmann m; (workman) Handwerker *m*; (*delivery man*) Lieferant *m*; ~ **union** *n* Gewerkschaft *f*; ~ **unionist** *n* Gewerkschaftler(in) *m(f)*

trading ['treɪdɪŋ] *n* Handel *m*; ~ **estate** (*BRIT*) *n* Industriegelände *nt*

tradition [trə'dɪʃən] *n* Tradition *f*; ~**al** *adj* traditionell, herkömmlich

traffic ['træfɪk] *n* Verkehr *m*; (*esp in drugs*): ~ **(in)** Handel *m* (mit) ♦ *vi*: **to ~ in** (*esp drugs*) handeln mit; ~ **calming** *n* Verkehrsberuhigung *f*; ~ **circle** (*US*) *n* Kreisverkehr *m*; ~ **jam** *n* Verkehrsstauung *f*; ~ **lights** *npl* Verkehrsampel *f*; ~ **warden** *n* ≈ Verkehrspolizist *m* (*ohne amtliche Befugnisse*), Politesse *f* (*ohne amtliche Befugnisse*)

tragedy ['trædʒədɪ] *n* Tragödie *f*

tragic ['trædʒɪk] *adj* tragisch

trail [treɪl] *n* (*track*) Spur *f*; (*of smoke*) Rauchfahne *f*; (*of dust*) Staubwolke *f*; (*road*) Pfad *m*, Weg *m* ♦ *vt* (*animal*) verfolgen; (*person*) folgen +*dat*; (*drag*) schleppen ♦ *vi* (*hang loosely*) schleifen; (*plants*) sich ranken; (*be behind*) hinterherhinken; (*SPORT*) weit zurückliegen; (*walk*) zuckeln; ~ **behind** *vi* zurückbleiben; ~**er** *n* Anhänger *m*; (*US: caravan*) Wohnwagen *m*; (*for film*) Vorschau *f*; ~**er truck** (*US*) *n* Sattelschlepper *m*

train [treɪn] *n* Zug *m*; (*of dress*) Schleppe *f*; (*series*) Folge *f* ♦ *vt* (*teach: person*) ausbilden; (: *animal*) abrichten; (: *mind*) schulen; (*SPORT*) trainieren; (*aim*) richten ♦ *vi* (*exercise*) trainieren; (*study*) ausgebildet werden; ~ **of thought** Gedankengang *m*; **to ~ sth on** (*aim*) etw richten auf +*acc*; ~**ed** *adj* (*eye*) geschult; (*person, voice*) ausgebildet; ~**ee** *n* Lehrling *m*; Praktikant(in) *m(f)*; ~**er** *n* (*SPORT*) Trainer *m*; Ausbilder *m*; ~**ers** *npl* Turnschuhe *pl*; ~**ing** *n* (*for occupation*) Ausbildung *f*; (*SPORT*) Training *nt*; **in ~ing** im Training; ~**ing college** *n* pädagogische Hochschule *f*, Lehrerseminar *nt*; ~**ing shoes** *npl* Turnschuhe *pl*

traipse [treɪps] *vi* latschen

trait [treɪt] *n* Zug *m*, Merkmal *nt*

traitor ['treɪtə'] *n* Verräter *m*

trajectory [trə'dʒɛktərɪ] *n* Flugbahn *f*

tram [træm] (*BRIT*) *n* (*also:* ~**car**) Straßenbahn *f*

tramp [træmp] *n* Landstreicher *m* ♦ *vi* (*trudge*) stampfen, stapfen

trample ['træmpl] *vt* (*nieder*)trampeln ♦ *vi* (*herum*)trampeln; **to ~ (underfoot)** herumtrampeln auf +*dat*

trampoline ['træmpəliːn] *n* Trampolin *m*

tranquil ['træŋkwɪl] *adj* ruhig, friedlich; ~**lity** [træŋ'kwɪlɪtɪ] (*US* **tranquility**) *n* Ruhe *f*; ~**lizer** (*US* **tranquilizer**) *n* Beruhigungsmittel *nt*

transact [træn'zækt] *vt* abwickeln; ~**ion** [træn'zækʃən] *n* Abwicklung *f*; (*piece of business*) Geschäft *nt*, Transaktion *f*

transcend [træn'sɛnd] *vt* übersteigen

transcription [træn'skrɪpʃən] *n* Transkription *f*; (*product*) Abschrift *f*

transfer [*n* 'trænsfə', *vb* træns'fɜː'] *n* (~*ring*) Übertragung *f*; (*of business*) Umzug *m*; (*being ~red*) Versetzung *f*; (*design*) Abziehbild *nt*; (*SPORT*) Transfer *m* ♦ *vt* (*business*) verlegen; (*person*) versetzen; (*prisoner*) überführen; (*drawing*) übertragen; (*money*) überweisen; **to ~ the charges** (*BRIT: TEL*) ein R-Gespräch führen; ~ **desk** *n* (*AVIAT*) Transitschalter *m*

transform [træns'fɔːm] *vt* umwandeln; ~**ation** [trænsfə'meɪʃən] *n* Umwandlung *f*, Verwandlung *f*

transfusion [træns'fjuːʒən] *n* Blutübertragung *f*, Transfusion *f*

transient ['trænzɪənt] *adj* kurz(lebig)

transistor [træn'zɪstə'] *n* (*ELEC*) Transistor *m*; (*RAD*) Transistorradio *nt*

transit ['trænzɪt] *n*: **in ~** unterwegs

transition [træn'zɪʃən] *n* Übergang *m*; ~**al** *adj* Übergangs-

transit lounge *n* Warteraum *m*

translate [trænz'leɪt] *vt, vi* übersetzen; **translation** [trænz'leɪʃən] *n* Übersetzung *f*; **translator** [trænz'leɪtə'] *n* Übersetzer(in) *m(f)*

transmission [trænz'mɪʃən] *n* (*of information*) Übermittlung *f*; (*ELEC, MED, TV*) Übertragung *f*; (*AUT*) Getriebe *nt*

transmit [trænz'mɪt] *vt* (*message*) übermitteln; (*ELEC, MED, TV*) übertragen; **~ter** *n* Sender *m*

transparency [træns'pɛərnsɪ] *n* Durchsichtigkeit *f*; (*BRIT: PHOT*) Dia(positiv) *nt*

transparent [træns'pærnt] *adj* durchsichtig; (*fig*) offenkundig

transpire [træns'paɪər] *vi* (*turn out*) sich herausstellen; (*happen*) passieren

transplant [*vb* træns'plɑːnt, *n* 'trænsplɑːnt] *vt* umpflanzen; (*MED, also fig: person*) verpflanzen ♦ *n* (*MED*) Transplantation *f*; (*organ*) Transplantat *nt*

transport [*n* 'trænspɔːt, *vb* træns'pɔːt] *n* Transport *m*, Beförderung *f* ♦ *vt* befördern; transportieren; **means of ~** Transportmittel *nt*; **~ation** ['trænspɔː'teɪʃən] *n* Transport *m*, Beförderung *f*; (*means*) Beförderungsmittel *nt*; (*cost*) Transportkosten *pl*; **~ café** (*BRIT*) *n* Fernfahrerlokal *nt*

trap [træp] *n* Falle *f*; (*carriage*) zweirädrige(r) Einspänner *m*; (*inf: mouth*) Klappe *f* ♦ *vt* fangen; (*person*) in eine Falle locken; **~door** *n* Falltür *f*

trappings ['træpɪŋz] *npl* Aufmachung *f*

trash [træʃ] *n* (*rubbish*) Plunder *m*; (*nonsense*) Mist *m*; **~ can** (*US*) *n* Mülleimer *m*; **~y** (*inf*) *adj* minderwertig, wertlos; (*novel*) Schund-

traumatic [trɔː'mætɪk] *adj* traumatisch

travel ['trævl] *n* Reisen *nt* ♦ *vi* reisen ♦ *vt* (*distance*) zurücklegen; (*country*) bereisen; **~s** *npl* (*journeys*) Reisen *pl*; **~ agency** *n* Reisebüro *nt*; **~ agent** *n* Reisebürokaufmann(-frau) *m(f)*; **~ler** (*US* **traveler**) *n* Reisende(r) *mf*; (*salesman*) Handlungsreisende(r) *m*; **~ler's cheque** (*US* **traveler's check**) *n* Reisescheck *m*; **~ling** (*US* **traveling**) *n* Reisen *nt*; **~sick** *adj* reisekrank; **~ sickness** *n* Reisekrankheit *f*

trawler ['trɔːlər] *n* (*NAUT, FISHING*) Fischdampfer *m*, Trawler *m*

tray [treɪ] *n* (*tea ~*) Tablett *nt*; (*for mail*) Ablage *f*

treacherous ['tretʃərəs] *adj* verräterisch; (*road*) tückisch

treachery ['tretʃərɪ] *n* Verrat *m*

treacle ['triːkl] *n* Sirup *m*, Melasse *f*

tread [tred] (*pt* **trod**, *pp* **trodden**) *n* Schritt *m*, Tritt *m*; (*of stair*) Stufe *f*; (*on tyre*) Profil *nt* ♦ *vi* treten; **~ on** *vt fus* treten auf +*acc*

treason ['triːzn] *n* Verrat *m*

treasure ['treʒər] *n* Schatz *m* ♦ *vt* schätzen

treasurer ['treʒərər] *n* Kassenverwalter *m*, Schatzmeister *m*

treasury ['treʒərɪ] *n* (*POL*) Finanzministerium *nt*

treat [triːt] *n* besondere Freude *f* ♦ *vt* (*deal with*) behandeln; **to ~ sb to sth** jdm etw spendieren

treatise ['triːtɪz] *n* Abhandlung *f*

treatment ['triːtmənt] *n* Behandlung *f*

treaty ['triːtɪ] *n* Vertrag *m*

treble ['trebl] *adj* dreifach ♦ *vt* verdreifachen; **~ clef** *n* Violinschlüssel *m*

tree [triː] *n* Baum *m*; **~ trunk** *n* Baumstamm *m*

trek [trek] *n* Treck *m*, Zug *m*; (*inf*) anstrengende(r) Weg *m* ♦ *vi* trecken

trellis ['trelɪs] *n* Gitter *nt*; (*for gardening*) Spalier *nt*

tremble ['trembl] *vi* zittern; (*ground*) beben

tremendous [trɪ'mendəs] *adj* gewaltig, kolossal; (*inf: good*) prima

tremor ['tremər] *n* Zittern *nt*; (*of earth*) Beben *nt*

trench [trentʃ] *n* Graben *m*; (*MIL*) Schützengraben *m*

trend [trend] *n* Tendenz *f*; **~y** (*inf*) *adj* modisch

trepidation [trepɪ'deɪʃən] *n* Beklommenheit *f*

trespass ['trespəs] *vi*: **to ~ on** widerrechtlich betreten; **"no ~ing"** „Betreten verboten"

trestle ['tresl] *n* Bock *m*; **~ table** *n* Klapptisch *m*

trial ['traɪəl] *n* (*JUR*) Prozess *m*; (*test*) Versuch *m*, Probe *f*; (*hardship*) Prüfung *f*; **by ~ and error** durch Ausprobieren; **~ period** *n* Probezeit *f*

triangle ['traɪæŋgl] *n* Dreieck *nt*; (*MUS*) Triangel *f*; **triangular** [traɪ'æŋgjulər] *adj* dreieckig

tribal ['traɪbl] *adj* Stammes-

tribe [traɪb] *n* Stamm *m*; **~sman** (*irreg*) *n*

Stammesangehörige(r) *m*

tribulation [trɪbjuˈleɪʃən] *n* Not *f*, Mühsal *f*

tribunal [traɪˈbjuːnl] *n* Gericht *nt*; (*inquiry*) Untersuchungsausschuss *m*

tributary [ˈtrɪbjutərɪ] *n* Nebenfluss *m*

tribute [ˈtrɪbjuːt] *n* (*admiration*) Zeichen *nt* der Hochachtung; **to pay ~ to sb/sth** jdm/einer Sache Tribut zollen

trick [trɪk] *n* Trick *m*; (*CARDS*) Stich *m* ♦ *vt* überlisten, beschwindeln; **to play a ~ on sb** jdm einen Streich spielen; **that should do the ~** daß müsste eigentlich klappen; **~ery** *n* Tricks *pl*

trickle [ˈtrɪkl] *n* Tröpfeln *nt*; (*small river*) Rinnsal *nt* ♦ *vi* tröpfeln; (*seep*) sickern

tricky [ˈtrɪkɪ] *adj* (*problem*) schwierig; (*situation*) kitzlig

tricycle [ˈtraɪsɪkl] *n* Dreirad *nt*

trifle [ˈtraɪfl] *n* Kleinigkeit *f*; (*COOK*) Trifle *m* ♦ *adv*: **a ~ ...** ein bisschen ...; **trifling** *adj* geringfügig

trigger [ˈtrɪgəʳ] *n* Drücker *m*; **~ off** *vt* auslösen

trim [trɪm] *adj* gepflegt; (*figure*) schlank ♦ *n* (gute) Verfassung *f*; (*embellishment, on car*) Verzierung *f* ♦ *vt* (*clip*) schneiden; (*trees*) stutzen; (*decorate*) besetzen; (*sails*) trimmen; **~mings** *npl* (*decorations*) Verzierung *f*, Verzierungen *pl*; (*extras*) Zubehör *nt*

Trinity [ˈtrɪnɪtɪ] *n*: **the ~** die Dreieinigkeit *f*

trinket [ˈtrɪŋkɪt] *n* kleine(s) Schmuckstück *nt*

trip [trɪp] *n* (*kurze*) Reise *f*; (*outing*) Ausflug *m*; (*stumble*) Stolpern *nt* ♦ *vi* (*stumble*) stolpern; **on a ~** auf Reisen; **~ up** *vi* stolpern; (*fig*) stolpern, einen Fehler machen ♦ *vt* zu Fall bringen; (*fig*) hereinlegen

tripe [traɪp] *n* (*food*) Kutteln *pl*; (*rubbish*) Mist *m*

triple [ˈtrɪpl] *adj* dreifach

triplets [ˈtrɪplɪts] *npl* Drillinge *pl*

triplicate [ˈtrɪplɪkət] *n*: **in ~** in dreifacher Ausfertigung

tripod [ˈtraɪpɒd] *n* (*PHOT*) Stativ *nt*

trite [traɪt] *adj* banal

triumph [ˈtraɪʌmf] *n* Triumph *m* ♦ *vi*: **to ~**

(over) triumphieren (über +*acc*); **~ant** [traɪˈʌmfənt] *adj* triumphierend

trivia [ˈtrɪvɪə] *npl* Trivialitäten *pl*

trivial [ˈtrɪvɪəl] *adj* gering(fügig), trivial

trod [trɒd] *pt of* **tread**; **~den** *pp of* **tread**

trolley [ˈtrɒlɪ] *n* Handwagen *m*; (*in shop*) Einkaufswagen *m*; (*for luggage*) Kofferkuli *m*; (*table*) Teewagen *m*; **~ bus** *n* Oberleitungsbus *m*, Obus *m*

trombone [trɒmˈbəun] *n* Posaune *f*

troop [truːp] *n* Schar *f*; (*MIL*) Trupp *m*; **~s** *npl* (*MIL*) Truppen *pl*; **~ in/out** *vi* hinein-/hinausströmen; **~ing the colour** *n* (*ceremony*) Fahnenparade *f*

trophy [ˈtrəufɪ] *n* Trophäe *f*

tropic [ˈtrɒpɪk] *n* Wendekreis *m*; **~al** *adj* tropisch

trot [trɒt] *n* Trott *m* ♦ *vi* trotten; **on the ~** (*BRIT: fig: inf*) in einer Tour

trouble [ˈtrʌbl] *n* (*problems*) Ärger *m*; (*worry*) Sorge *f*; (*in country, industry*) Unruhen *pl*; (*effort*) Mühe *f*; (*MED*) **stomach ~** Magenbeschwerden *pl* ♦ *vt* (*disturb*) stören; **~s** *npl* (*POL etc*) Unruhen *pl*; **to ~ to do sth** sich bemühen, etw zu tun; **to be in ~** Probleme *or* Ärger haben; **to go to the ~ of doing sth** sich die Mühe machen, etw zu tun; **what's the ~?** was ist los?; (*to sick person*) wo fehlts?; **~d** *adj* (*person*) beunruhigt; (*country*) geplagt; **~-free** *adj* sorglos; **~maker** *n* Unruhestifter *m*; **~shooter** *n* Vermittler *m*; **~some** *adj* lästig, unangenehm; (*child*) schwierig

trough [trɒf] *n* Trog *m*; (*channel*) Rinne *f*, Kanal *m*; (*MET*) Tief *nt*

trousers [ˈtrauzəz] *npl* Hose *f*

trout [traut] *n* Forelle *f*

trowel [ˈtrauəl] *n* Kelle *f*

truant [ˈtruənt] *n*: **to play ~** (*BRIT*) (die Schule) schwänzen

truce [truːs] *n* Waffenstillstand *m*

truck [trʌk] *n* Lastwagen *m*; (*RAIL*) offene(r) Güterwagen *m*; **~ driver** *n* Lastwagenfahrer *m*; **~ farm** (*US*) *n* Gemüsegärtnerei *f*

trudge [trʌdʒ] *vi* sich (mühselig) dahinschleppen

true [tru:] adj (exact) wahr; (genuine) echt; (friend) treu

truffle ['trʌfl] n Trüffel f or m

truly ['tru:lɪ] adv wirklich; **yours ~** Ihr sehr ergebener

trump [trʌmp] n (CARDS) Trumpf m

trumpet ['trʌmpɪt] n Trompete f

truncheon ['trʌntʃən] n Gummiknüppel m

trundle ['trʌndl] vt schieben ♦ vi: **to ~ along** entlangrollen

trunk [trʌŋk] n (of tree) (Baum)stamm m; (ANAT) Rumpf m; (box) Truhe f, Überseekoffer m; (of elephant) Rüssel m; (US: AUT) Kofferraum m; **~s** npl (also: **swimming ~s**) Badehose f

truss [trʌs] vt (also: **~ up**) fesseln

trust [trʌst] n (confidence) Vertrauen nt; (for land etc) Treuhandvermögen nt ♦ vt (rely on) vertrauen +dat, sich verlassen auf +acc; (hope) hoffen, (entrust): **to ~ sth to sb** jdm etw anvertrauen; **~ed** adj treu; **~ee** [trʌs'ti:] n Vermögensverwalter m; **~ful** adj vertrauensvoll; **~ing** adj vertrauensvoll; **~worthy** adj vertrauenswürdig; (account) glaubwürdig

truth [tru:θ] n Wahrheit f; **~ful** adj ehrlich

try [traɪ] n Versuch m ♦ vt (attempt) versuchen; (test) (aus)probieren; (JUR: person) unter Anklage stellen; (: case) verhandeln; (courage, patience) auf die Probe stellen ♦ vi (make effort) versuchen, sich bemühen; **to have a ~** es versuchen; **to ~ to do sth** versuchen, etw zu tun; **~ on** vt (dress) anprobieren; (hat) aufprobieren; **~ out** vt ausprobieren; **~ing** adj schwierig

T-shirt ['ti:ʃɔ:t] n T-Shirt nt

T-square ['ti:skweər] n Reißschiene f

tub [tʌb] n Wanne f, Kübel m; (for margarine etc) Becher m

tubby ['tʌbɪ] adj rundlich

tube [tju:b] n Röhre f, Rohr nt; (for toothpaste etc) Tube f; (underground) U-Bahn f; (AUT) Schlauch m

tuberculosis [tjubə:kju'ləusɪs] n Tuberkulose f

tube station n (in London) U-Bahnstation f

tubing ['tju:bɪŋ] n Schlauch m; **tubular** ['tju:bjulər] adj röhrenförmig

TUC (BRIT) n abbr = **Trades Union Congress**

tuck [tʌk] n (fold) Falte f, Einschlag m ♦ vt (put) stecken; (gather) fälteln, einschlagen; **~ away** vt wegstecken; **~ in** vt hineinstecken; (blanket etc) feststecken; (person) zudecken ♦ vi (eat) hineinhauen, zulangen; **~ up** vt (child) warm zudecken; **~ shop** n Süßwarenladen m

Tuesday ['tju:zdɪ] n Dienstag m

tuft [tʌft] n Büschel m

tug [tʌg] n (jerk) Zerren nt, Ruck m; (NAUT) Schleppdampfer m ♦ vt, vi zerren, ziehen; (boat) schleppen; **~ of war** n Tauziehen nt

tuition [tju:'ɪʃən] n (BRIT) Unterricht m; (: private ~) Privatunterricht m; (US: school fees) Schulgeld nt

tulip ['tju:lɪp] n Tulpe f

tumble ['tʌmbl] n (fall) Sturz m ♦ vi fallen, stürzen; **~ to** vt fus kapieren; **~down** adj baufällig; **~ dryer** (BRIT) n Trockner m; **~r** ['tʌmblər] n (glass) Trinkglas nt

tummy ['tʌmɪ] n (inf) n Bauch m; **~ upset** n Magenverstimmung f

tumour ['tju:mər] (US **tumor**) n Geschwulst f, Tumor m

tumultuous [tju:'mʌltjuəs] adj (welcome, applause etc) stürmisch

tuna ['tju:nə] n T(h)unfisch m

tune [tju:n] n Melodie f ♦ vt (MUS) stimmen; (AUT) richtig einstellen; **to sing in ~/out of ~** richtig/falsch singen; **to be out of ~ with** nicht harmonieren mit; **~ in** vi einschalten; **~ up** vi (MUS) stimmen; **~ful** adj melodisch; **~r** n (RAD) Tuner m; (person) (Instrumenten)stimmer m; **piano ~r** Klavierstimmer(in) m(f)

tunic ['tju:nɪk] n Waffenrock m; (loose garment) lange Bluse f

tuning ['tju:nɪŋ] n (RAD, AUT) Einstellen nt; (MUS) Stimmen nt; **~ fork** n Stimmgabel f

Tunisia [tju:'nɪzɪə] n Tunesien nt

tunnel ['tʌnl] n Tunnel m, Unterführung f ♦ vi einen Tunnel anlegen

turbulent ['tə:bjulənt] adj stürmisch

tureen [tə'ri:n] *n* Terrine *f*

turf [tə:f] *n* Rasen *m*; (*piece*) Sode *f* ♦ *vt* mit Grassoden belegen; **~ out** (*inf*) *vt* rauswerfen

turgid ['tə:dʒɪd] *adj* geschwollen

Turk [tə:k] *n* Türke *m*, Türkin *f*

Turkey ['tə:kɪ] *n* Türkei *f*

turkey ['tə:kɪ] *n* Puter *m*, Truthahn *m*

Turkish ['tə:kɪʃ] *adj* türkisch ♦ *n* (LING) Türkisch *nt*

turmoil ['tə:mɔɪl] *n* Aufruhr *m*, Tumult *m*

turn [tə:n] *n* (*rotation*) (Um)drehung *f*; (*performance*) (Programm)nummer *f*; (MED) Schock *m* ♦ *vt* (*rotate*) drehen; (*change position of*) umdrehen, wenden; (*page*) umblättern; (*transform*): **to ~ sth into sth** etw in etw *acc* verwandeln; (*direct*) zuwenden ♦ *vi* (*rotate*) sich drehen; (*change direction: in car*) abbiegen; (: *wind*) drehen; (*~ round*) umdrehen, wenden; (*become*) werden; (*leaves*) sich verfärben; (*milk*) sauer werden; (*weather*) umschlagen; **to do sb a good ~** jdm etwas Gutes tun; **it's your ~** du bist dran *or* an der Reihe; **in ~, by ~s** abwechselnd; **to take ~s** sich abwechseln; **it gave me quite a ~** das hat mich schön erschreckt; **"no left ~"** (AUT) „Linksabbiegen verboten"; **~ away** *vi* sich abwenden; **~ back** *vt* umdrehen; (*person*) zurückschicken; (*clock*) zurückstellen ♦ *vi* umkehren; **~ down** *vt* (*refuse*) ablehnen; (*fold down*) umschlagen; **~ in** *vi* (*go to bed*) ins Bett gehen ♦ *vt* (*fold inwards*) einwärts biegen; **~ off** *vi* abbiegen ♦ *vt* ausschalten; (*tap*) zudrehen; (*machine, electricity*) abstellen; **~ on** *vt* (*light*) anschalten, einschalten; (*tap*) aufdrehen; (*machine*) anstellen; **~ out** *vi* (*prove to be*) sich erweisen; (*people*) sich entwickeln ♦ *vt* (*light*) ausschalten; (*gas*) abstellen; (*produce*) produzieren; **how did the cake ~ out?** wie ist der Kuchen geworden?; **~ over** *vi* (*person*) sich umdrehen ♦ *vt* (*object*) umdrehen, wenden; (*page*) umblättern; **~ round** *vi* (*person, vehicle*) sich herumdrehen; (*rotate*) sich drehen; **~ up** *vi* auftauchen ♦ *vt* (*collar*) hochklappen,

hochstellen; (*nose*) rümpfen; (*increase: radio*) lauter stellen; (: *heat*) höher drehen; **~ing** *n* (*in road*) Abzweigung *f*; **~ing point** *n* Wendepunkt *m*

turnip ['tə:nɪp] *n* Steckrübe *f*

turnout ['tə:naut] *n* (*Besucher*)zahl *f*

turnover ['tə:nəuvə'] *n* Umsatz *m*; (*of staff*) Wechsel *m*

turnpike ['tə:npaɪk] (US) *n* gebührenpflichtige Straße *f*

turn: ~stile ['tə:nstaɪl] *n* Drehkreuz *nt*; **~table** ['tə:nteɪbl] *n* (*of record player*) Plattenteller *m*; (RAIL) Drehscheibe *f*; **~-up** ['tə:nʌp] (BRIT) *n* (*on trousers*) Aufschlag *m*

turpentine ['tə:pəntaɪn] *n* Terpentin *nt*

turquoise ['tə:kwɔɪz] *n* (*gem*) Türkis *m*; (*colour*) Türkis *nt* ♦ *adj* türkisfarben

turret ['tʌrɪt] *n* Turm *m*

turtle ['tə:tl] *n* Schildkröte *f*; **~ neck (sweater)** *n* Pullover *m* mit Schildkrötkragen

tusk [tʌsk] *n* Stoßzahn *m*

tussle ['tʌsl] *n* Balgerei *f*

tutor ['tju:tə'] *n* (*teacher*) Privatlehrer *m*; (*college instructor*) Tutor *m*; **~ial** [tju:'tɔ:rɪəl] *n* (UNIV) Kolloquium *nt*, Seminarübung *f*

tuxedo [tʌk'si:dəu] (US) *n* Smoking *m*

TV [ti:'vi:] *n abbr* (= *television*) TV *nt*

twang [twæŋ] *n* scharfe(r) Ton *m*; (*of voice*) Näseln *nt*

tweezers ['twi:zəz] *npl* Pinzette *f*

twelfth [twelfθ] *adj* zwölfte(r, s)

twelve [twelv] *num* zwölf; **at ~ o'clock** (*midday*) um 12 Uhr; (*midnight*) um null Uhr

twentieth ['twentɪθ] *adj* zwanzigste(r, s)

twenty ['twentɪ] *num* zwanzig

twice [twaɪs] *adv* zweimal; **~ as much** doppelt so viel

twiddle ['twɪdl] *vt, vi*: **to ~ (with) sth** an etw *dat* herumdrehen; **to ~ one's thumbs** (*fig*) Däumchen drehen

twig [twɪg] *n* dünne(r) Zweig *m* ♦ *vt* (*inf*) kapieren, merken

twilight ['twaɪlaɪt] *n* Zwielicht *nt*

twin [twɪn] *n* Zwilling *m* ♦ *adj* Zwillings-; (*very similar*) Doppel- ♦ *vt* (*towns*) zu

Partnerstädten machen; **~-bedded room**
n Zimmer nt mit zwei Einzelbetten; **~ beds**
npl zwei (gleiche) Einzelbetten pl
twine [twaɪn] n Bindfaden m ♦ vi (plants)
sich ranken
twinge [twɪndʒ] n stechende(r) Schmerz m,
Stechen nt
twinkle ['twɪŋkl] n Funkeln nt, Blitzen nt ♦ vi
funkeln
twinned adj: **to be ~ with** die Partnerstadt
von ... sein
twirl [twɜːl] n Wirbel m ♦ vt, vi
(herum)wirbeln
twist [twɪst] n (~ing) Drehung f; (bend) Kurve
f ♦ vt (turn) drehen; (make crooked)
verbiegen; (distort) verdrehen ♦ vi (wind)
sich drehen; (curve) sich winden
twit [twɪt] (inf) n Idiot m
twitch [twɪtʃ] n Zucken nt ♦ vi zucken
two [tuː] num zwei; **to put ~ and ~ together**
seine Schlüsse ziehen, **~-door** adj
zweitürig; **~-faced** adj falsch; **~fold** adj,
adv zweifach, doppelt; **to increase ~fold**
verdoppeln; **~-piece** adj zweiteilig; **~-
piece (suit)** n Zweiteiler m; **~-piece
(swimsuit)** n zweiteilige(r) Badeanzug m;
~-seater n (plane, car) Zweisitzer m;
~some n Paar nt; **~-way** adj (traffic)
Gegen-
tycoon [taɪˈkuːn] n: **(business) ~**
(Industrie)magnat m
type [taɪp] n Typ m, Art f; (PRINT) Type f ♦ vt,
vi Maschine schreiben, tippen; **~cast**
(THEAT, TV) auf eine Rolle festgelegt; **~face**
n Schrift f; **~script** n
maschinegeschriebene(r) Text m; **~writer**
n Schreibmaschine f; **~written** adj
maschinegeschrieben
typhoid ['taɪfɔɪd] n Typhus m
typical ['tɪpɪkl] adj: **~ (of)** typisch (für)
typify ['tɪpɪfaɪ] vt typisch sein für
typing ['taɪpɪŋ] n Maschineschreiben nt
typist ['taɪpɪst] n Maschinenschreiber(in)
m(f), Tippse f (inf)
tyrant ['taɪərənt] n Tyrann m
tyre ['taɪə*] (US **tire**) n Reifen m; **~ pressure**
n Reifendruck m

U, u

U-bend ['juːbend] n (in pipe) U-Bogen m
udder ['ʌdə*] n Euter nt
UFO ['juːfəu] n abbr (= unidentified flying
object) UFO nt
ugh [əːh] excl hu
ugliness ['ʌglɪnɪs] n Hässlichkeit f
ugly ['ʌglɪ] adj hässlich; (bad) böse, schlimm
UHT abbr (= ultra heat treated): **UHT milk**
H-Milch f
UK n abbr = **United Kingdom**
ulcer ['ʌlsə*] n Geschwür nt
Ulster ['ʌlstə*] n Ulster nt
ulterior [ʌlˈtɪərɪə*] adj: **~ motive**
Hintergedanke m
ultimate ['ʌltɪmət] adj äußerste(r, s),
allerletzte(r, s); **~ly** adv schließlich, letzten
Endes
ultrasound ['ʌltrəsaund] n (MED) Ultraschall
m
umbilical cord [ʌmˈbɪlɪkl-] n Nabelschnur f
umbrella [ʌmˈbrɛlə] n Schirm m
umpire ['ʌmpaɪə*] n Schiedsrichter m ♦ vt, vi
schiedsrichtern
umpteenth [ʌmpˈtiːnθ] (inf) adj zig; **for the
~ time** zum x-ten Mal
UN n abbr = **United Nations**
unable [ʌnˈeɪbl] adj: **to be ~ to do sth** etw
nicht tun können
unacceptable [ʌnəkˈsɛptəbl] adj
unannehmbar, nicht akzeptabel
unaccompanied [ʌnəˈkʌmpənɪd] adj ohne
Begleitung
unaccountably [ʌnəˈkauntəblɪ] adv
unerklärlich
unaccustomed [ʌnəˈkʌstəmd] adj nicht
gewöhnt; (unusual) ungewohnt; **~ to** nicht
gewöhnt an +acc
unanimous [juːˈnænɪməs] adj einmütig;
(vote) einstimmig; **~ly** adv einmütig;
einstimmig
unarmed [ʌnˈɑːmd] adj unbewaffnet
unashamed [ʌnəˈʃeɪmd] adj schamlos
unassuming [ʌnəˈsjuːmɪŋ] adj bescheiden

unattached [ʌnə'tætʃt] *adj* ungebunden

unattended [ʌnə'tɛndɪd] *adj* (*person*) unbeaufsichtigt; (*thing*) unbewacht

unauthorized [ʌn'ɔ:θəraɪzd] *adj* unbefugt

unavoidable [ʌnə'vɔɪdəbl] *adj* unvermeidlich

unaware [ʌnə'wɛəʳ] *adj*: **to be ~ of sth** sich *dat* einer Sache *gen* nicht bewusst sein; **~s** *adv* unversehens

unbalanced [ʌn'bælənst] *adj* unausgeglichen; (*mentally*) gestört

unbearable [ʌn'bɛərəbl] *adj* unerträglich

unbeatable [ʌn'bi:təbl] *adj* unschlagbar

unbeknown(st) [ʌnbɪ'nəʊn(st)] *adv*: **~ to me** ohne mein Wissen

unbelievable [ʌnbɪ'li:vəbl] *adj* unglaublich

unbend [ʌn'bɛnd] (*irreg: like* **bend**) *vt* gerade biegen ♦ *vi* aus sich herausgehen

unbias(s)ed [ʌn'baɪəst] *adj* unparteiisch

unborn [ʌn'bɔ:n] *adj* ungeboren

unbreakable [ʌn'breɪkəbl] *adj* unzerbrechlich

unbridled [ʌn'braɪdld] *adj* ungezügelt

unbroken [ʌn'brəʊkən] *adj* (*period*) ununterbrochen; (*spirit*) ungebrochen; (*record*) unübertroffen

unburden [ʌn'bɜ:dn] *vt*: **to ~ o.s.** (jdm) sein Herz ausschütten

unbutton [ʌn'bʌtn] *vt* aufknöpfen

uncalled-for [ʌn'kɔ:ldfɔ:ʳ] *adj* unnötig

uncanny [ʌn'kænɪ] *adj* unheimlich

unceasing [ʌn'si:sɪŋ] *adj* unaufhörlich

unceremonious [ʌnsɛrɪ'məʊnɪəs] *adj* (*abrupt, rude*) brüsk; (*exit, departure*) überstürzt

uncertain [ʌn'sɜ:tn] *adj* unsicher; (*doubtful*) ungewiss; (*unreliable*) unbeständig; (*vague*) undeutlich, vag(e); **~ty** *n* Ungewissheit *f*

unchanged [ʌn'tʃeɪndʒd] *adj* unverändert

unchecked [ʌn'tʃɛkt] *adj* ungeprüft; (*not stopped: advance*) ungehindert

uncivilized [ʌn'sɪvɪlaɪzd] *adj* unzivilisiert

uncle [ʌŋkl] *n* Onkel *m*

uncomfortable [ʌn'kʌmfətəbl] *adj* unbequem, ungemütlich

uncommon [ʌn'kɔmən] *adj* ungewöhnlich; (*outstanding*) außergewöhnlich

uncompromising [ʌn'kɔmprəmaɪzɪŋ] *adj* kompromisslos, unnachgiebig

unconcerned [ʌnkən'sɜ:nd] *adj* unbekümmert; (*indifferent*) gleichgültig

unconditional [ʌnkən'dɪʃənl] *adj* bedingungslos

unconscious [ʌn'kɔnʃəs] *adj* (MED) bewusstlos; (*not meant*) unbeabsichtigt ♦ *n*: **the ~** das Unbewusste; **~ly** *adv* unbewusst

uncontrollable [ʌnkən'trəʊləbl] *adj* unkontrollierbar, unbändig

unconventional [ʌnkən'vɛnʃənl] *adj* unkonventionell

uncouth [ʌn'ku:θ] *adj* grob

uncover [ʌn'kʌvəʳ] *vt* aufdecken

undecided [ʌndɪ'saɪdɪd] *adj* unschlüssig

undeniable [ʌndɪ'naɪəbl] *adj* unleugbar

under ['ʌndəʳ] *prep* unter ♦ *adv* darunter; **~ there** da drunter; **~ repair** in Reparatur

underage [ʌndər'eɪdʒ] *adj* minderjährig

undercarriage ['ʌndəkærɪdʒ] (BRIT) *n* (AVIAT) Fahrgestell *nt*

undercharge [ʌndə'tʃɑ:dʒ] *vt*: **to ~ sb** jdm zu wenig berechnen

undercoat ['ʌndəkəʊt] *n* (*paint*) Grundierung *f*

undercover [ʌndə'kʌvəʳ] *adj* Geheim-

undercurrent ['ʌndəkʌrnt] *n* Unterströmung *f*

undercut [ʌndə'kʌt] (*irreg: like* **cut**) *vt* unterbieten

underdeveloped ['ʌndədɪ'vɛləpt] *adj* Entwicklungs-, unterentwickelt

underdog ['ʌndədɔg] *n* Unterlegene(r) *mf*

underdone [ʌndə'dʌn] *adj* (COOK) nicht gar, nicht durchgebraten

underestimate ['ʌndər'ɛstɪmeɪt] *vt* unterschätzen

underexposed ['ʌndərɪks'pəʊzd] *adj* unterbelichtet

underfoot [ʌndə'fut] *adv* am Boden

undergo [ʌndə'gəʊ] (*irreg: like* **go**) *vt* (*experience*) durchmachen; (*test, operation*) sich unterziehen +*dat*

undergraduate [ʌndə'grædjuɪt] *n* Student(in) *m(f)*

underground ['ʌndəgraʊnd] *n* U-Bahn *f*

♦ *adj* Untergrund-

undergrowth ['ʌndəgrəuθ] *n* Gestrüpp *nt*, Unterholz *nt*

underhand(ed) [ʌndə'hænd(ɪd)] *adj* hinterhältig

underlie [ʌndə'laɪ] (*irreg: like* lie) *vt* zugrunde *or* zu Grunde liegen +*dat*

underline [ʌndə'laɪn] *vt* unterstreichen; (*emphasize*) betonen

underling ['ʌndəlɪŋ] *n* Handlanger *m*

undermine [ʌndə'maɪn] *vt* untergraben

underneath [ʌndə'niːθ] *adv* darunter ♦ *prep* unter

underpaid [ʌndə'peɪd] *adj* unterbezahlt

underpants ['ʌndəpænts] *npl* Unterhose *f*

underpass ['ʌndəpɑːs] (*BRIT*) *n* Unterführung *f*

underprivileged [ʌndə'prɪvɪlɪdʒd] *adj* benachteiligt, unterprivilegiert

underrate [ʌndə'reɪt] *vt* unterschätzen

undershirt ['ʌndəʃəːt] (*US*) *n* Unterhemd *nt*

undershorts ['ʌndəʃɔːts] (*US*) *npl* Unterhose *f*

underside ['ʌndəsaɪd] *n* Unterseite *f*

underskirt ['ʌndəskəːt] (*BRIT*) *n* Unterrock *m*

understand [ʌndə'stænd] (*irreg: like* stand) *vt*, *vi* verstehen; **I ~ that ...** ich habe gehört, dass ...; **am I to ~ that ...?** soll das (etwa) heißen, dass ...?; **what do you ~ by that?** was verstehen Sie darunter?; **it is understood that ...** es wurde vereinbart, dass ...; **to make o.s. understood** sich verständlich machen; **is that understood?** ist das klar?; **~able** *adj* verständlich; **~ing** *n* Verständnis *nt* ♦ *adj* verständnisvoll

understatement ['ʌndəsteɪtmənt] *n* (*quality*) Untertreibung *f*; **that's an ~!** das ist untertrieben!

understood [ʌndə'stud] *pt*, *pp of* **understand** ♦ *adj* klar; (*implied*) angenommen

understudy ['ʌndəstʌdɪ] *n* Ersatz(schau)spieler(in) *m(f)*

undertake [ʌndə'teɪk] (*irreg: like* take) *vt* unternehmen ♦ *vi*: **to ~ to do sth** sich verpflichten, etw zu tun

undertaker ['ʌndəteɪkə'] *n* Leichenbestatter *m*

undertaking ['ʌndəteɪkɪŋ] *n* (*enterprise*) Unternehmen *nt*; (*promise*) Verpflichtung *f*

undertone ['ʌndətəun] *n*: **in an ~** mit gedämpfter Stimme

underwater ['ʌndə'wɔːtə'] *adv* unter Wasser ♦ *adj* Unterwasser-

underwear ['ʌndəwɛə'] *n* Unterwäsche *f*

underworld ['ʌndəwəːld] *n* (*of crime*) Unterwelt *f*

underwriter ['ʌndəraɪtə'] *n* Assekurant *m*

undesirable [ʌndɪ'zaɪərəbl] *adj* unerwünscht

undies ['ʌndɪz] (*inf*) *npl* (Damen)unterwäsche *f*

undisputed ['ʌndɪs'pjuːtɪd] *adj* unbestritten

undo [ʌn'duː] (*irreg: like* do) *vt* (*unfasten*) öffnen, aufmachen; (*work*) zunichte machen; **~ing** *n* Verderben *nt*

undoubted [ʌn'dautɪd] *adj* unbezweifelt; **~ly** *adv* zweifellos, ohne Zweifel

undress [ʌn'drɛs] *vt* ausziehen ♦ *vi* sich ausziehen

undue [ʌn'djuː] *adj* übermäßig

undulating ['ʌndjuleɪtɪŋ] *adj* wellenförmig; (*country*) wellig

unduly [ʌn'djuːlɪ] *adv* übermäßig

unearth [ʌn'əːθ] *vt* (*dig up*) ausgraben; (*discover*) ans Licht bringen

unearthly [ʌn'əːθlɪ] *adj* (*hour*) nachtschlafen

uneasy [ʌn'iːzɪ] *adj* (*worried*) unruhig; (*feeling*) ungut

uneconomic(al) ['ʌniːkə'nɔmɪk(l)] *adj* unwirtschaftlich

uneducated [ʌn'ɛdjukeɪtɪd] *adj* ungebildet

unemployed [ʌnɪm'plɔɪd] *adj* arbeitslos ♦ *npl*: **the ~** die Arbeitslosen *pl*

unemployment [ʌnɪm'plɔɪmənt] *n* Arbeitslosigkeit *f*

unending [ʌn'ɛndɪŋ] *adj* endlos

unerring [ʌn'əːrɪŋ] *adj* unfehlbar

uneven [ʌn'iːvn] *adj* (*surface*) uneben; (*quality*) ungleichmäßig

unexpected [ʌnɪks'pɛktɪd] *adj* unerwartet; **~ly** *adv* unerwartet

unfailing [ʌn'feɪlɪŋ] *adj* nie versagend

unfair [ʌn'fɛə'] *adj* ungerecht, unfair

unfaithful [ʌn'feɪθful] *adj* untreu

unfamiliar [ʌnfə'mɪlɪə] *adj* ungewohnt; *(person, subject)* unbekannt; **to be ~ with** nicht kennen +*acc*, nicht vertraut sein mit

unfashionable [ʌn'fæʃnəbl] *adj* unmodern; *(area etc)* nicht in Mode

unfasten [ʌn'fɑ:sn] *vt* öffnen, aufmachen

unfavourable [ʌn'feɪvrəbl] *(US* **unfavorable)** *adj* ungünstig

unfeeling [ʌn'fi:lɪŋ] *adj* gefühllos, kalt

unfinished [ʌn'fɪnɪʃt] *adj* unvollendet

unfit [ʌn'fɪt] *adj* ungeeignet; *(in bad health)* nicht fit; **~ for sth** zu *or* für etw ungeeignet

unfold [ʌn'fəʊld] *vt* entfalten; *(paper)* auseinander falten ♦ *vi (develop)* sich entfalten

unforeseen ['ʌnfɔ:'si:n] *adj* unvorhergesehen

unforgettable [ʌnfə'getəbl] *adj* unvergesslich

unforgivable [ʌnfə'gɪvəbl] *adj* unverzeihlich

unfortunate [ʌn'fɔ:tʃənət] *adj* unglücklich, bedauerlich; **~ly** *adv* leider

unfounded [ʌn'faʊndɪd] *adj* unbegründet

unfriendly [ʌn'frendlɪ] *adj* unfreundlich

ungainly [ʌn'geɪnlɪ] *adj* linkisch

ungodly [ʌn'gɔdlɪ] *adj (hour)* nachtschlafend; *(row)* heillos

ungrateful [ʌn'greɪtful] *adj* undankbar

unhappiness [ʌn'hæpɪnɪs] *n* Unglück *nt*, Unglückseligkeit *f*

unhappy [ʌn'hæpɪ] *adj* unglücklich; **~ with** *(arrangements etc)* unzufrieden mit

unharmed [ʌn'hɑ:md] *adj* wohlbehalten, unversehrt

UNHCR *n abbr (= United Nations High Commission for Refugees)* Flüchtlingshochkommissariat der Vereinten Nationen

unhealthy [ʌn'helθɪ] *adj* ungesund

unheard-of [ʌn'hə:dɔv] *adj* unerhört

unhurt [ʌn'hə:t] *adj* unverletzt

unidentified [ʌnaɪ'dentɪfaɪd] *adj* unbekannt, nicht identifiziert

uniform ['ju:nɪfɔ:m] *n* Uniform *f* ♦ *adj* einheitlich; **~ity** [ju:nɪ'fɔ:mɪtɪ] *n* Einheitlichkeit *f*

unify ['ju:nɪfaɪ] *vt* vereinigen

unilateral [ju:nɪ'lætərəl] *adj* einseitig

uninhabited [ʌnɪn'hæbɪtɪd] *adj* unbewohnt

unintentional [ʌnɪn'tenʃənəl] *adj* unabsichtlich

union ['ju:njən] *n (uniting)* Vereinigung *f*; *(alliance)* Bund *m*, Union *f*; *(trade ~)* Gewerkschaft *f*; **U~ Jack** *n* Union Jack *m*

unique [ju:'ni:k] *adj* einzig(artig)

UNISON ['ju:nɪsn] *n Gewerkschaft der Angestellten im öffentlichen Dienst*

unison ['ju:nɪsn] *n* Einstimmigkeit *f*; **in ~** einstimmig

unit ['ju:nɪt] *n* Einheit *f*; **kitchen ~** Küchenelement *nt*

unite [ju:'naɪt] *vt* vereinigen ♦ *vi* sich vereinigen; **~d** *adj* vereinigt; *(together)* vereint; **U~d Kingdom** *n* Vereinigte(s) Königreich *nt*; **U~d Nations (Organization)** *n* Vereinte Nationen *pl*; **U~d States (of America)** *n* Vereinigte Staaten *pl* (von Amerika)

unit trust *(BRIT) n* Treuhandgesellschaft *f*

unity ['ju:nɪtɪ] *n* Einheit *f*; *(agreement)* Einigkeit *f*

universal [ju:nɪ'və:sl] *adj* allgemein

universe ['ju:nɪvə:s] *n* (Welt)all *nt*

university [ju:nɪ'və:sɪtɪ] *n* Universität *f*

unjust [ʌn'dʒʌst] *adj* ungerecht

unkempt [ʌn'kempt] *adj* ungepflegt

unkind [ʌn'kaɪnd] *adj* unfreundlich

unknown [ʌn'nəʊn] *adj:* **~ (to sb)** (jdm) unbekannt

unlawful [ʌn'lɔ:ful] *adj* illegal

unleaded ['ʌn'ledɪd] *adj* bleifrei, unverbleit; **I use ~** ich fahre bleifrei

unleash [ʌn'li:ʃ] *vt* entfesseln

unless [ʌn'les] *conj* wenn nicht, es sei denn; **~ he comes** es sei denn, er kommt; **~ otherwise stated** sofern nicht anders angegeben

unlike [ʌn'laɪk] *adj* unähnlich ♦ *prep* im Gegensatz zu

unlikely [ʌn'laɪklɪ] *adj (not likely)* unwahrscheinlich; *(unexpected: combination etc)* merkwürdig

unlimited [ʌn'lɪmɪtɪd] *adj* unbegrenzt

unlisted ['ʌn'lɪstɪd] *(US) adj* nicht im

Telefonbuch stehend
unload [ʌn'ləud] vt entladen
unlock [ʌn'lɔk] vt aufschließen
unlucky [ʌn'lʌki] adj unglücklich; (person) unglückselig; **to be ~** Pech haben
unmarried [ʌn'mærɪd] adj unverheiratet, ledig
unmask [ʌn'mɑːsk] vt entlarven
unmistakable [ʌnmɪs'teɪkəbl] adj unverkennbar
unmitigated [ʌn'mɪtɪgeɪtɪd] adj ungemildert, ganz
unnatural [ʌn'nætʃrəl] adj unnatürlich
unnecessary [ʌn'nesəsərɪ] adj unnötig
unnoticed [ʌn'nəutɪst] adj: **to go ~** unbemerkt bleiben
UNO ['juːnəu] n abbr = **United Nations Organization**
unobtainable [ʌnəb'teɪnəbl] adj: **this number is ~** kein Anschluss unter dieser Nummer
unobtrusive [ʌnəb'truːsɪv] adj unauffällig
unofficial [ʌnə'fɪʃl] adj inoffiziell
unpack [ʌn'pæk] vt, vi auspacken
unparalleled [ʌn'pærəleld] adj beispiellos
unpleasant [ʌn'pleznt] adj unangenehm
unplug [ʌn'plʌg] vt den Stecker herausziehen von
unpopular [ʌn'pɔpjulə] adj (person) unbeliebt; (decision etc) unpopulär
unprecedented [ʌn'presɪdentɪd] adj beispiellos
unpredictable [ʌnprɪ'dɪktəbl] adj unvorhersehbar; (weather, person) unberechenbar
unprofessional [ʌnprə'feʃənl] adj unprofessionell
UNPROFOR n abbr (= United Nations Protection Force) UNPROFOR f
unqualified [ʌn'kwɔlɪfaɪd] adj (success) uneingeschränkt, voll; (person) unqualifiziert
unquestionably [ʌn'kwestʃənəblɪ] adv fraglos
unravel [ʌn'rævl] vt (disentangle) ausfasern, entwirren; (solve) lösen
unreal [ʌn'rɪəl] adj unwirklich
unrealistic ['ʌnrɪə'lɪstɪk] adj unrealistisch

unreasonable [ʌn'riːznəbl] adj unvernünftig; (demand) übertrieben
unrelated [ʌnrɪ'leɪtɪd] adj ohne Beziehung; (family) nicht verwandt
unrelenting [ʌnrɪ'lentɪŋ] adj unerbittlich
unreliable [ʌnrɪ'laɪəbl] adj unzuverlässig
unremitting [ʌnrɪ'mɪtɪŋ] adj (efforts, attempts) unermüdlich
unreservedly [ʌnrɪ'zɜːvɪdlɪ] adv offen; (believe, trust) uneingeschränkt; (cry) rückhaltlos
unrest [ʌn'rest] n (discontent) Unruhe f; (fighting) Unruhen pl
unroll [ʌn'rəul] vt aufrollen
unruly [ʌn'ruːlɪ] adj (child) undiszipliniert; schwer lenkbar
unsafe [ʌn'seɪf] adj nicht sicher
unsaid [ʌn'sed] adj: **to leave sth ~** etw ungesagt lassen
unsatisfactory ['ʌnsætɪs'fæktərɪ] adj unbefriedigend; unzulänglich
unsavoury [ʌn'seɪvərɪ] (US **unsavory**) adj (fig) widerwärtig
unscathed [ʌn'skeɪðd] adj unversehrt
unscrew [ʌn'skruː] vt aufschrauben
unscrupulous [ʌn'skruːpjuləs] adj skrupellos
unsettled [ʌn'setld] adj (person) rastlos; (weather) wechselhaft
unshaven [ʌn'ʃeɪvn] adj unrasiert
unsightly [ʌn'saɪtlɪ] adj unansehnlich
unskilled [ʌn'skɪld] adj ungelernt
unspeakable [ʌn'spiːkəbl] adj (joy) unsagbar; (crime) scheußlich
unstable [ʌn'steɪbl] adj instabil; (mentally) labil
unsteady [ʌn'stedɪ] adj unsicher
unstuck [ʌn'stʌk] adj: **to come ~** sich lösen; (fig) ins Wasser fallen
unsuccessful [ʌnsək'sesful] adj erfolglos
unsuitable [ʌn'suːtəbl] adj unpassend
unsure [ʌn'ʃuə] adj unsicher; **to be ~ of o.s.** unsicher sein
unsuspecting [ʌnsəs'pektɪŋ] adj nichts ahnend
unsympathetic ['ʌnsɪmpə'θetɪk] adj gefühllos; (response) abweisend; (unlikeable)

unsympathisch

untapped [ʌnˈtæpt] *adj* (*resources*) ungenützt

unthinkable [ʌnˈθɪŋkəbl] *adj* unvorstellbar

untidy [ʌnˈtaɪdɪ] *adj* unordentlich

untie [ʌnˈtaɪ] *vt* aufschnüren

until [ənˈtɪl] *prep, conj* bis; ~ **he comes** bis er kommt; ~ **then** bis dann; ~ **now** bis jetzt

untimely [ʌnˈtaɪmlɪ] *adj* (*death*) vorzeitig

untold [ʌnˈtəʊld] *adj* unermesslich

untoward [ʌntəˈwɔːd] *adj* widrig

untranslatable [ʌntrænzˈleɪtəbl] *adj* unübersetzbar

unused [ʌnˈjuːzd] *adj* unbenutzt

unusual [ʌnˈjuːʒʊəl] *adj* ungewöhnlich

unveil [ʌnˈveɪl] *vt* enthüllen

unwanted [ʌnˈwɒntɪd] *adj* unerwünscht

unwavering [ʌnˈweɪvərɪŋ] *adj* standhaft, unerschütterlich

unwelcome [ʌnˈwelkəm] *adj* (*at a bad time*) unwillkommen; (*unpleasant*) unerfreulich

unwell [ʌnˈwel] *adj*: **to feel** *or* **be** ~ sich nicht wohl fühlen

unwieldy [ʌnˈwiːldɪ] *adj* sperrig

unwilling [ʌnˈwɪlɪŋ] *adj*: **to be** ~ **to do sth** nicht bereit sein, etw zu tun; ~**ly** *adv* widerwillig

unwind [ʌnˈwaɪnd] (*irreg: like* **wind**[2]) *vt* abwickeln ♦ *vi* (*relax*) sich entspannen

unwise [ʌnˈwaɪz] *adj* unklug

unwitting [ʌnˈwɪtɪŋ] *adj* unwissentlich

unworkable [ʌnˈwɜːkəbl] *adj* (*plan*) undurchführbar

unworthy [ʌnˈwɜːðɪ] *adj* (*person*): ~ **(of sth)** (einer Sache *gen*) nicht wert

unwrap [ʌnˈræp] *vt* auspacken

unwritten [ʌnˈrɪtn] *adj* ungeschrieben

KEYWORD
---

up [ʌp] *prep*: **to be up sth** oben auf etw *dat* sein; **to go up sth** (auf) etw *acc* hinaufgehen; **go up that road** gehen Sie die Straße hinauf
♦ *adv* 1 (*upwards, higher*) oben; **put it up a bit higher** stell es etwas weiter nach oben; **up there** da oben, dort oben; **up above** hoch oben

2: **to be up** (*out of bed*) auf sein; (*prices, level*) gestiegen sein; (*building, tent*) stehen

3: **up to** (*as far as*) bis; **up to now** bis jetzt

4: **up to** (*depending on*): **it's up to you** das hängt von dir ab; (*equal to*): **he's not up to it** (*job, task etc*) er ist dem nicht gewachsen; (*inf: be doing: showing disapproval, suspicion*): **what is he up to?** was führt er im Schilde?; **it's not up to me to decide** die Entscheidung liegt nicht bei mir; **his work is not up to the required standard** seine Arbeit entspricht nicht dem geforderten Niveau

♦ *n*: **ups and downs** (*in life, career*) Höhen und Tiefen *pl*

---

up-and-coming [ʌpəndˈkʌmɪŋ] *adj* aufstrebend

upbringing [ˈʌpbrɪŋɪŋ] *n* Erziehung *f*

update [ʌpˈdeɪt] *vt* auf den neuesten Stand bringen

upgrade [ʌpˈɡreɪd] *vt* höher einstufen

upheaval [ʌpˈhiːvl] *n* Umbruch *m*

uphill [ˈʌpˈhɪl] *adj* ansteigend; (*fig*) mühsam
♦ *adv*: **to go** ~ bergauf gehen/fahren

uphold [ʌpˈhəʊld] (*irreg: like* **hold**) *vt* unterstützen

upholstery [ʌpˈhəʊlstərɪ] *n* Polster *nt*; Polsterung *f*

upkeep [ˈʌpkiːp] *n* Instandhaltung *f*

upon [əˈpɒn] *prep* auf

upper [ˈʌpə] *n* (*on shoe*) Oberleder *nt* ♦ *adj* obere(r, s), höhere(r, s); **to have the** ~ **hand** die Oberhand haben; ~-**class** *adj* vornehm; ~**most** *adj* oberste(r, s), höchste(r, s); **what was** ~**most in my mind** was mich in erster Linie beschäftigte; ~ **sixth** (*BRIT: SCOL*) *n* Abschlussklasse *f*

upright [ˈʌpraɪt] *adj* aufrecht

uprising [ˈʌpraɪzɪŋ] *n* Aufstand *m*

uproar [ˈʌprɔː] *n* Aufruhr *m*

uproot [ʌpˈruːt] *vt* ausreißen

upset [*n* ˈʌpset, *vb, adj* ʌpˈset] (*irreg: like* **set**) *n* Aufregung *f* ♦ *vt* (*overturn*) umwerfen; (*disturb*) aufregen, bestürzen; (*plans*) durcheinander bringen ♦ *adj* (*person*) aufgeregt; (*stomach*) verdorben

upshot ['ʌpʃɔt] n (End)ergebnis nt
upside-down ['ʌpsaɪd-] adv verkehrt herum
upstairs [ʌp'stɛəz] adv oben; (go) nach oben ♦ adj (room) obere(r, s), Ober- ♦ n obere(s) Stockwerk nt
upstart ['ʌpstɑːt] n Emporkömmling m
upstream [ʌp'striːm] adv stromaufwärts
uptake ['ʌpteɪk] n: **to be quick on the ~** schnell begreifen; **to be slow on the ~** schwer von Begriff sein
uptight [ʌp'taɪt] (inf) adj (nervous) nervös; (inhibited) verklemmt
up-to-date ['ʌptə'deɪt] adj (clothes) modisch, modern; (information) neueste(r, s)
upturn ['ʌptəːn] n Aufschwung m
upward ['ʌpwəd] adj nach oben gerichtet; **~(s)** adv aufwärts
uranium [juə'reɪnɪəm] n Uran nt
urban ['əːbən] adj städtisch, Stadt-; **~ clearway** [w] n Stadtautobahn f
urchin ['əːtʃɪn] n (boy) Schlingel m; (sea ~) Seeigel m
urge [əːdʒ] n Drang m ♦ vt: **to ~ sb to do sth** jdn (dazu) drängen, etw zu tun
urgency ['əːdʒənsɪ] n Dringlichkeit f
urgent ['əːdʒənt] adj dringend
urinal ['juərɪnl] n (public) Pissoir nt
urinate ['juərɪneɪt] vi urinieren
urine ['juərɪn] n Urin m, Harn m
urn [əːn] n Urne f; (tea ~) Teemaschine f
US n abbr = **United States**
us [ʌs] pron uns; see also **me**
USA n abbr = **United States of America**
usage ['juːzɪdʒ] n Gebrauch m; (esp LING) Sprachgebrauch m
use [n juːs, vb juːz] n (employment) Gebrauch m; (point) Zweck m ♦ vt gebrauchen; **in ~** in Gebrauch; **out of ~** außer Gebrauch; **to be of ~** nützlich sein; **it's no ~** es hat keinen Zweck; **what's the ~?** was solls?; **~d to** (accustomed to) gewöhnt an +acc; **she ~d to live here** (formerly) sie hat früher mal hier gewohnt; **~ up** vt aufbrauchen, verbrauchen; **~d** adj (car) Gebraucht-; **~ful** adj nützlich; **~fulness** n Nützlichkeit f; **~less** adj nutzlos, unnütz; **~r** n Benutzer m; **~r-friendly** adj (computer) benutzerfreundlich
usher ['ʌʃəʳ] n Platzanweiser m; **~ette** [ʌʃə'ret] n Platzanweiserin f
usual ['juːʒuəl] adj gewöhnlich, üblich; **as ~** wie üblich; **~ly** adv gewöhnlich
usurp [juː'zəːp] vt an sich reißen
utensil [juː'tensl] n Gerät nt; **kitchen ~s** Küchengeräte pl
uterus ['juːtərəs] n Gebärmutter f
utilitarian [juːtɪlɪ'tɛərɪən] adj Nützlichkeits-
utility [juː'tɪlɪtɪ] n (usefulness) Nützlichkeit f; (also: **public ~**) öffentliche(r) Versorgungsbetrieb m; **~ room** n Hauswirtschaftsraum m
utilize ['juːtɪlaɪz] vt benützen
utmost ['ʌtməust] adj äußerste(r, s) ♦ n: **to do one's ~** sein Möglichstes tun
utter ['ʌtəʳ] adj äußerste(r, s), höchste(r, s), völlig ♦ vt äußern, aussprechen; **~ance** n Äußerung f; **~ly** adv äußerst, absolut, völlig
U-turn ['juː'təːn] n (AUT) Kehrtwendung f

V, v

v. abbr = **verse; versus; volt**; (= vide) see
vacancy ['veɪkənsɪ] n (BRIT: job) offene Stelle f; (room) freie(s) Zimmer nt; **"no vacancies"** "belegt"
vacant ['veɪkənt] adj leer; (unoccupied) frei; (house) leer stehend, unbewohnt; (stupid) (gedanken)leer; **~ lot** (US) n unbebaute(s) Grundstück nt
vacate [və'keɪt] vt (seat) frei machen; (room) räumen
vacation [və'keɪʃən] n Ferien pl, Urlaub m; **~ist** (US) n Ferienreisende(r) f(m)
vaccinate ['væksɪneɪt] vt impfen
vaccine ['væksiːn] n Impfstoff m
vacuum ['vækjum] n Vakuum nt; **~ bottle** (US) n Thermosflasche f; **~ cleaner** n Staubsauger m; **~ flask** (BRIT) n Thermosflasche f; **~-packed** adj vakuumversiegelt
vagina [və'dʒaɪnə] n Scheide f
vague [veɪg] adj vag(e); (absent-minded) geistesabwesend; **~ly** adv unbestimmt,

vag(e)

vain [veɪn] *adj* eitel; (*attempt*) vergeblich; **in ~** vergebens, umsonst

valentine ['væləntaɪn] *n* (*also:* **~ card**) Valentinsgruß *m*; **V~'s Day** *n* Valentinstag *m*

valet ['vælɪt] *n* Kammerdiener *m*

valiant ['væliənt] *adj* tapfer

valid ['vælɪd] *adj* gültig; (*argument*) stichhaltig; (*objection*) berechtigt; **~ity** [vəˈlɪdɪtɪ] *n* Gültigkeit *f*

valley ['vælɪ] *n* Tal *nt*

valour ['vælər] (*US* **valor**) *n* Tapferkeit *f*

valuable ['væljuəbl] *adj* wertvoll; (*time*) kostbar; **~s** *npl* Wertsachen *pl*

valuation [væljuˈeɪʃən] *n* (*FIN*) Schätzung *f*; Beurteilung *f*

value ['vælju:] *n* Wert *m*; (*usefulness*) Nutzen *m* ♦ *vt* (*prize*) (hoch) schätzen, werthalten; (*estimate*) schätzen; **~ added tax** (*BRIT*) *n* Mehrwertsteuer *f*; **~d** *adj* (hoch) geschätzt

valve [vælv] *n* Ventil *nt*; (*BIOL*) Klappe *f*; (*RAD*) Röhre *f*

van [væn] *n* Lieferwagen *m*; (*BRIT: RAIL*) Waggon *m*

vandal ['vændl] *n* Rowdy *m*; **~ism** *n* mutwillige Beschädigung *f*; **~ize** *vt* mutwillig beschädigen

vanguard ['vænga:d] *n* (*fig*) Spitze *f*

vanilla [vəˈnɪlə] *n* Vanille *f*; **~ ice cream** *n* Vanilleeis *nt*

vanish ['vænɪʃ] *vi* verschwinden

vanity ['vænɪtɪ] *n* Eitelkeit *f*; **~ case** *n* Schminkkoffer *m*

vantage ['va:ntɪdʒ] *n*: **~ point** gute(r) Aussichtspunkt *m*

vapour ['veɪpər] (*US* **vapor**) *n* (*mist*) Dunst *m*; (*gas*) Dampf *m*

variable ['veəriəbl] *adj* wechselhaft, veränderlich; (*speed, height*) regulierbar

variance ['veəriəns] *n*: **to be at ~ (with)** nicht übereinstimmen (mit)

variation [veərɪˈeɪʃən] *n* Variation *f*; (*in prices etc*) Schwankung *f*

varicose ['værɪkəus] *adj*: **~ veins** Krampfadern *pl*

varied ['veərɪd] *adj* unterschiedlich; (*life*) abwechslungsreich

variety [vəˈraɪətɪ] *n* (*difference*) Abwechslung *f*; (*varied collection*) Vielfalt *f*; (*COMM*) Auswahl *f*; (*sort*) Sorte *f*, Art *f*; **~ show** *n* Varietee *nt*, Varieté *nt*

various ['veəriəs] *adj* verschieden; (*several*) mehrere

varnish ['va:nɪʃ] *n* Lack *m*; (*on pottery*) Glasur *f* ♦ *vt* lackieren

vary ['veəri] *vt* (*alter*) verändern; (*give variety to*) abwechslungsreicher gestalten ♦ *vi* sich (ver)ändern; (*prices*) schwanken; (*weather*) unterschiedlich sein

vase [va:z] *n* Vase *f*

Vaseline ['væsɪli:n] ® *n* Vaseline *f*

vast [va:st] *adj* weit, groß, riesig

VAT [væt] *n abbr* (= value added tax) MwSt *f*

vat [væt] *n* große(s) Fass *nt*

vault [vɔ:lt] *n* (*of roof*) Gewölbe *nt*; (*tomb*) Gruft *f*; (*in bank*) Tresorraum *m*; (*leap*) Sprung *m* ♦ *vt* (*also:* **~ over**) überspringen

vaunted ['vɔ:ntɪd] *adj*: **much-~** viel gerühmt

VCR *n abbr* = **video cassette recorder**

VD *n abbr* = **venereal disease**

VDU *n abbr* = **visual display unit**

veal [vi:l] *n* Kalbfleisch *nt*

veer [vɪər] *vi* sich drehen; (*of car*) ausscheren

vegan ['vi:gən] *n* Vegan *m*, radikale(r) Vegetarier(in) *m(f)*

vegeburger ['vedʒɪbə:gər] *n* vegetarische Frikadelle *f*

vegetable ['vedʒtəbl] *n* Gemüse *nt* ♦ *adj* Gemüse-; **~s** *npl* (*CULIN*) Gemüse *nt*

vegetarian [vedʒɪˈteəriən] *n* Vegetarier(in) *m(f)* ♦ *adj* vegetarisch

vegetate ['vedʒɪteɪt] *vi* (dahin)vegetieren

veggieburger ['vedʒɪbə:gər] *n* = **vegeburger**

vehement ['vi:ɪmənt] *adj* heftig

vehicle ['vi:ɪkl] *n* Fahrzeug *nt*; (*fig*) Mittel *nt*

veil [veɪl] *n* (*also fig*) Schleier *m* ♦ *vt* verschleiern

vein [veɪn] *n* Ader *f*; (*mood*) Stimmung *f*

velocity [vɪˈlɔsɪtɪ] *n* Geschwindigkeit *f*

velvet ['velvɪt] *n* Samt *m* ♦ *adj* Samt-

vendetta [venˈdetə] *n* Fehde *f*; (*in family*)

Blutrache f

vending machine ['vendɪŋ-] n Automat m

vendor ['vendər] n Verkäufer m

veneer [və'nɪər] n Furnier(holz) nt; (fig) äußere(r) Anstrich m

venereal disease [vɪ'nɪərɪəl-] n Geschlechtskrankheit f

Venetian blind [vɪ'niːʃən-] n Jalousie f

vengeance ['vendʒəns] n Rache f; **with a ~** gewaltig

venison ['venɪsn] n Reh(fleisch) nt

venom ['venəm] n Gift nt

vent [vent] n Öffnung f, (in coat) Schlitz m; (fig) Ventil nt ♦ vt (emotion) abreagieren

ventilate ['ventɪleɪt] vt belüften; **ventilator** ['ventɪleɪtə'] n Ventilator m

ventriloquist [ven'trɪləkwɪst] n Bauchredner m

venture ['ventʃə'] n Unternehmung f, Projekt nt ♦ vt wagen; (life) aufs Spiel setzen ♦ vi sich wagen

venue ['venjuː] n Schauplatz m

verb [vɜːb] n Zeitwort nt, Verb nt; **~al** adj (spoken) mündlich; (translation) wörtlich; **~ally** adv mündlich

verbatim [vɜː'beɪtɪm] adv Wort für Wort ♦ adj wörtlich

verbose [vɜː'bəus] adj wortreich

verdict ['vɜːdɪkt] n Urteil nt

verge [vɜːdʒ] n (BRIT) Rand m ♦ vi: **to ~ on** grenzen an +acc; **"soft ~s"** (BRIT: AUT) „Seitenstreifen nicht befahrbar"; **on the ~ of doing sth** im Begriff, etw zu tun

verify ['verɪfaɪ] vt (über)prüfen; (confirm) bestätigen; (theory) beweisen

veritable ['verɪtəbl] adj wirklich, echt

vermin ['vɜːmɪn] npl Ungeziefer nt

vermouth ['vɜːməθ] n Wermut m

versatile ['vɜːsətaɪl] adj vielseitig

verse [vɜːs] n (poetry) Poesie f; (stanza) Strophe f; (of Bible) Vers m; **in ~** in Versform

version ['vɜːʃən] n Version f; (of car) Modell nt

versus ['vɜːsəs] prep gegen

vertebrate ['vɜːtɪbrɪt] adj Wirbel-

vertical ['vɜːtɪkl] adj senkrecht

vertigo ['vɜːtɪgəu] n Schwindel m

very ['verɪ] adv sehr ♦ adj (extreme) äußerste(r, s); **the ~ book which** genau das Buch, welches; **the ~ last ...** der/die/das allerletzte ...; **at the ~ least** allerwenigstens; **~ much** sehr

vessel ['vesl] n (ship) Schiff nt; (container) Gefäß nt

vest [vest] n (BRIT) Unterhemd nt; (US: waistcoat) Weste f

vested interests ['vestɪd-] npl finanzielle Beteiligung f; (people) finanziell Beteiligte pl; (fig) persönliche(s) Interesse nt

vestige ['vestɪdʒ] n Spur f

vestry ['vestrɪ] n Sakristei f

vet [vet] n abbr (= veterinary surgeon) Tierarzt m/-ärztin f

veteran ['vetərn] n Veteran(in) m(f)

veterinarian [vetrɪ'neərɪən] n (US) Tierarzt m/-ärztin f

veterinary ['vetrɪnərɪ] adj Veterinär-, **~ surgeon** (BRIT) n Tierarzt m/-ärztin f

veto ['viːtəu] n (pl ~es) n Veto nt ♦ vt sein Veto einlegen gegen

vex [veks] vt ärgern; **~ed** adj verärgert; **~ed question** umstrittene Frage f

VHF abbr (= very high frequency) UKW f

via ['vaɪə] prep über +acc

viable ['vaɪəbl] adj (plan) durchführbar; (company) rentabel

vibrant ['vaɪbrnt] adj (lively) lebhaft; (bright) leuchtend; (full of emotion: voice) bebend

vibrate [vaɪ'breɪt] vi zittern, beben; (machine, string) vibrieren; **vibration** [vaɪ'breɪʃən] n Schwingung f; (of machine) Vibrieren nt

vicar ['vɪkə'] n Pfarrer m; **~age** n Pfarrhaus nt

vice [vaɪs] n (evil) Laster nt; (TECH) Schraubstock m

vice-chairman [vaɪs'tʃeəmən] n stellvertretende(r) Vorsitzende(r) m

vice-president [vaɪs'prezɪdənt] n Vizepräsident m

vice squad n ≃ Sittenpolizei f

vice versa ['vaɪsɪ'vɜːsə] adv umgekehrt

vicinity [vɪ'sɪnɪtɪ] n Umgebung f; (closeness) Nähe f

vicious ['vɪʃəs] *adj* gemein, böse; ~ **circle** *n* Teufelskreis *m*

victim ['vɪktɪm] *n* Opfer *nt*

victor ['vɪktə'] *n* Sieger *m*

Victorian [vɪk'tɔːrɪən] *adj* viktorianisch; *(fig)* (sitten)streng

victorious [vɪk'tɔːrɪəs] *adj* siegreich

victory ['vɪktərɪ] *n* Sieg *m*

video ['vɪdɪəʊ] *adj* Fernseh-, Bild- ♦ *n* (~ *film*) Video *nt*; *(also:* ~ **cassette**) Videokassette *f*; *(also:* ~ **cassette recorder**) Videorekorder *m*; ~ **tape** *n* Videoband *nt*; ~ **wall** *n* Videowand *m*

vie [vaɪ] *vi* wetteifern

Vienna [vɪ'enə] *n* Wien *nt*

Vietnam ['vjet'næm] *n* Vietnam *nt*; ~**ese** *adj* vietnamesisch ♦ *n inv* (person) Vietnamese *m*, Vietnamesin *f*

view [vjuː] *n* (sight) Sicht *f*, Blick *m*; (scene) Aussicht *f*; (opinion) Ansicht *f*; (intention) Absicht *f* ♦ *vt* (situation) betrachten; (house) besichtigen; **to have sth in** ~ etw beabsichtigen; **on** ~ ausgestellt; **in** ~ **of** wegen +gen, angesichts +gen; ~**er** *n* (PHOT: small projector) Gucki *m*; (TV) Fernsehzuschauer(in) *m(f)*; ~**finder** *n* Sucher *m*; ~**point** *n* Standpunkt *m*

vigil ['vɪdʒɪl] *n* (Nacht)wache *f*; ~**ant** *adj* wachsam

vigorous ['vɪgərəs] *adj* kräftig; (protest) energisch, heftig

vile [vaɪl] *adj* (mean) gemein; (foul) abscheulich

villa ['vɪlə] *n* Villa *f*

village ['vɪlɪdʒ] *n* Dorf *nt*; ~**r** *n* Dorfbewohner(in) *m(f)*

villain ['vɪlən] *n* Schurke *m*

vindicate ['vɪndɪkeɪt] *vt* rechtfertigen

vindictive [vɪn'dɪktɪv] *adj* nachtragend, rachsüchtig

vine [vaɪn] *n* Rebstock *m*, Rebe *f*

vinegar ['vɪnɪgə'] *n* Essig *m*

vineyard ['vɪnjɑːd] *n* Weinberg *m*

vintage ['vɪntɪdʒ] *n* (of wine) Jahrgang *m*; ~ **car** *n* Oldtimer *m* (zwischen 1919 und 1930 gebaut); ~ **wine** *n* edle(r) Wein *m*

viola [vɪ'əʊlə] *n* Bratsche *f*

violate ['vaɪəleɪt] *vt* (law) übertreten; (rights, rule, neutrality) verletzen; (sanctity, woman) schänden; **violation** [vaɪə'leɪʃən] *n* Übertretung *f*; Verletzung *f*

violence ['vaɪələns] *n* (force) Heftigkeit *f*; (brutality) Gewalttätigkeit *f*

violent ['vaɪələnt] *adj* (strong) heftig; (brutal) gewalttätig, brutal; (contrast) krass; (death) gewaltsam

violet ['vaɪələt] *n* Veilchen *nt* ♦ *adj* veilchenblau, violett

violin [vaɪə'lɪn] *n* Geige *f*, Violine *f*; ~**ist** *n* Geiger(in) *m(f)*

VIP *n abbr* (= *very important person*) VIP *m*

virgin ['vɜːdʒɪn] *n* Jungfrau *f* ♦ *adj* jungfräulich, unberührt; ~**ity** [vɜː'dʒɪnɪtɪ] *n* Unschuld *f*

Virgo ['vɜːgəʊ] *n* Jungfrau *f*

virile ['vɪraɪl] *adj* männlich; **virility** [vɪ'rɪlɪtɪ] *n* Männlichkeit *f*

virtually ['vɜːtjʊəlɪ] *adv* praktisch, fast

virtual reality ['vɜːtjʊəl-] *n* (COMPUT) virtuelle Realität *f*

virtue ['vɜːtjuː] *n* (moral goodness) Tugend *f*; (good quality) Vorteil *m*, Vorzug *m*; **by** ~ **of** aufgrund or auf Grund +gen

virtuous ['vɜːtjʊəs] *adj* tugendhaft

virulent ['vɪrʊlənt] *adj* (poisonous) bösartig; (bitter) scharf, geharnischt

virus ['vaɪərəs] *n* (also COMPUT) Virus *m*

visa ['viːzə] *n* Visum *nt*

vis-à-vis [viːzə'viː] *prep* gegenüber

viscous ['vɪskəs] *adj* zähflüssig

visibility [vɪzɪ'bɪlɪtɪ] *n* (MET) Sicht(weite) *f*

visible ['vɪzəbl] *adj* sichtbar; **visibly** *adv* sichtlich

vision ['vɪʒən] *n* (ability) Sehvermögen *nt*; (foresight) Weitblick *m*; (in dream, image) Vision *f*

visit ['vɪzɪt] *n* Besuch *m* ♦ *vt* besuchen; (town, country) fahren nach; ~**ing hours** *npl* (in hospital etc) Besuchszeiten *pl*; ~**or** *n* (in house) Besucher(in) *m(f)*; (in hotel) Gast *m*; ~**or centre** *n* Touristeninformation *f*

visor ['vaɪzə'] *n* Visier *nt*; (on cap) Schirm *m*; (AUT) Blende *f*

vista ['vɪstə] *n* Aussicht *f*

visual ['vɪzjuəl] adj Seh-, visuell; ~ **aid** n Anschauungsmaterial nt; ~ **display unit** n Bildschirm(gerät nt) m; ~**ize** vt sich +dat vorstellen; ~**ly-impaired** adj sehbehindert

vital ['vaɪtl] adj (important) unerlässlich; (necessary for life) Lebens-, lebenswichtig; (lively) vital; ~**ity** [vaɪ'tælɪtɪ] n Vitalität f; ~**ly** adv: **vitally important** adj äußerst wichtig; ~ **statistics** npl (fig) Maße pl

vitamin ['vɪtəmɪn] n Vitamin nt

vivacious [vɪ'veɪʃəs] adj lebhaft

vivid ['vɪvɪd] adj (graphic) lebhaft; (memory) lebhaft; (bright) leuchtend; ~**ly** adv lebendig; lebhaft; leuchtend

V-neck ['viːnɛk] n V-Ausschnitt m

vocabulary [vəu'kæbjulərɪ] n Wortschatz m, Vokabular nt

vocal ['vəukl] adj Vokal-, Gesang-; (fig) lautstark; ~ **cords** npl Stimmbänder pl

vocation [vəu'keɪʃən] n (calling) Berufung f; ~**al** adj Berufs-

vociferous [və'sɪfərəs] adj lautstark

vodka ['vɔdkə] n Wodka m

vogue [vəuɡ] n Mode f

voice [vɔɪs] n Stimme f; (fig) Mitspracherecht nt ♦ vt äußern; ~ **mail** n (TEL) Voicemail f

void [vɔɪd] n Leere f ♦ adj (invalid) nichtig, ungültig; (empty): ~ **of** ohne, bar +gen; see **null**

volatile ['vɔlətaɪl] adj (gas) flüchtig; (person) impulsiv; (situation) brisant

volcano [vɔl'keɪnəu] n Vulkan m

volition [və'lɪʃən] n Wille m; **of one's own ~** aus freiem Willen

volley ['vɔlɪ] n (of guns) Salve f; (of stones) Hagel m; (tennis) Flugball m; ~**ball** n Volleyball m

volt [vəult] n Volt nt; ~**age** n Spannung f

volume ['vɔljuːm] n (book) Band m; (size) Umfang m; (space) Rauminhalt m; (of sound) Lautstärke f

voluntarily ['vɔləntrɪlɪ] adv freiwillig

voluntary ['vɔləntərɪ] adj freiwillig

volunteer [vɔlən'tɪər] n Freiwillige(r) mf ♦ vi sich freiwillig melden; **to ~ to do sth** sich anbieten, etw zu tun

vomit ['vɔmɪt] n Erbrochene(s) nt ♦ vt spucken ♦ vi sich übergeben

vote [vəut] n Stimme f; (ballot) Abstimmung f; (result) Abstimmungsergebnis nt; (franchise) Wahlrecht nt ♦ vt, vi wählen; ~ **of thanks** n Dankesworte pl; ~**r** n Wähler(in) m(f); **voting** ['vəutɪŋ] n Wahl f

voucher ['vautʃər] n Gutschein m

vouch for [vautʃ-] vt bürgen für

vow [vau] n Versprechen nt; (REL) Gelübde nt ♦ vt geloben

vowel ['vauəl] n Vokal m

voyage ['vɔɪdʒ] n Reise f

vulgar ['vʌlɡər] adj (rude) vulgär; ~**ity** [vʌl'ɡærɪtɪ] n Vulgarität f

vulnerable ['vʌlnərəbl] adj (easily injured) verwundbar; (sensitive) verletzlich

vulture ['vʌltʃər] n Geier m

W, w

wad [wɔd] n (bundle) Bündel nt; (of paper) Stoß m; (of money) Packen m

waddle ['wɔdl] vi watscheln

wade [weɪd] vi: **to ~ through** waten durch

wafer ['weɪfər] n Waffel f; (REL) Hostie f; (COMPUT) Wafer f

waffle ['wɔfl] n Waffel f; (inf: empty talk) Geschwafel nt ♦ vi schwafeln

waft [wɔft] vt, vi wehen

wag [wæɡ] vt (tail) wedeln mit ♦ vi wedeln

wage [weɪdʒ] n (also: ~**s**) (Arbeits)lohn m ♦ vt: **to ~ war** Krieg führen; ~ **earner** n Lohnempfänger(in) m(f); ~ **packet** n Lohntüte f

wager ['weɪdʒər] n Wette f ♦ vt, vi wetten

waggle ['wæɡl] vi wackeln

wag(g)on ['wæɡən] n (horse-drawn) Fuhrwerk nt; (US: AUT) Wagen m; (BRIT: RAIL) Wag(g)on m

wail [weɪl] n Wehgeschrei nt ♦ vi wehklagen, jammern

waist [weɪst] n Taille f; ~**coat** (BRIT) n Weste f; ~**line** n Taille f

wait [weɪt] n Wartezeit f ♦ vi warten; **to lie in ~ for sb** jdm auflauern, **I can't ~ to see**

him ich kanns kaum erwarten ihn zu sehen; **"no ~ing"** (*BRIT: AUT*) „Halteverbot"; **~ behind** *vi* zurückbleiben; **~ for** *vt fus* warten auf +*acc*; **~ on** *vt fus* bedienen; **~er** *n* Kellner *m*; **~ing list** *n* Warteliste *f*; **~ing room** *n* (*MED*) Wartezimmer *nt*; (*RAIL*) Wartesaal *m*; **~ress** *n* Kellnerin *f*

waive [weɪv] *vt* verzichten auf +*acc*

wake [weɪk] (*pt* woke, waked, *pp* woken) *vt* wecken ♦ *vi* (*also:* **~ up**) aufwachen ♦ *n* (*NAUT*) Kielwasser *nt*; (*for dead*) Totenwache *f*; **to ~ up to** (*fig*) sich bewusst werden +*gen*

waken [weɪkn] *vt* aufwecken

Wales [weɪlz] *n* Wales *nt*

walk [wɔːk] *n* Spaziergang *m*; (*gait*) Gang *m*; (*route*) Weg *m* ♦ *vi* gehen; (*stroll*) spazieren gehen; (*longer*) wandern; **~s of life** Sphären *pl*; **a 10-minute ~** 10 Minuten zu Fuß; **to ~ out on sb** (*inf*) jdn sitzen lassen; **~er** *n* Spaziergänger *m*; (*hiker*) Wanderer *m*; **~ie-talkie** [wɔːkɪˈtɔːkɪ] *n* tragbare(s) Sprechfunkgerät *nt*; **~ing** *n* Gehen *nt*; (*hiking*) Wandern *nt* ♦ *adj* Wander-; **~ing shoes** *npl* Wanderschuhe *pl*; **~ing stick** *n* Spazierstock *m*; **W~man** [wɔːkmən] ® *n* Walkman *m* ®; **~out** *n* Streik *m*; **~over** (*inf*) *n* leichte(r) Sieg *m*; **~way** *n* Fußweg *m*

wall [wɔːl] *n* (*inside*) Wand *f*; (*outside*) Mauer *f*; **~ed** *adj* von Mauern umgeben

wallet [wɒlɪt] *n* Brieftasche *f*

wallflower [wɔːlflauəʳ] *n* Goldlack *m*; **to be a ~** (*fig*) ein Mauerblümchen sein

wallop [wɒləp] (*inf*) *vt* schlagen, verprügeln

wallow [wɒləu] *vi* sich wälzen

wallpaper [wɔːlpeɪpəʳ] *n* Tapete *f*

walnut [wɔːlnʌt] *n* Walnuss *f*

walrus [wɔːlrəs] *n* Walross *nt*

waltz [wɔːlts] *n* Walzer *m* ♦ *vi* Walzer tanzen

wan [wɒn] *adj* bleich

wand [wɒnd] *n* (*also:* **magic ~**) Zauberstab *m*

wander [wɒndəʳ] *vi* (*roam*) (herum)wandern; (*fig*) abschweifen

wane [weɪn] *vi* abnehmen; (*fig*) schwinden

wangle [wæŋgl] (*BRIT: inf*) *vt*: **to ~ sth** etw richtig hindrehen

want [wɒnt] *n* (*lack*) Mangel *m* ♦ *vt* (*need*) brauchen; (*desire*) wollen; (*lack*) nicht haben; **~s** *npl* (*needs*) Bedürfnisse *pl*; **for ~ of** aus Mangel an +*dat*; mangels +*gen*; **to ~ to do sth** etw tun wollen; **to ~ sb to do sth** wollen, dass jd etw tut; **~ed** *adj* (*criminal etc*) gesucht; **"cook ~ed"** (*in adverts*) „Koch/Köchin gesucht"; **~ing** *adj*: **to be found ~ing** sich als unzulänglich erweisen

wanton [wɒntn] *adj* mutwillig, zügellos

war [wɔːʳ] *n* Krieg *m*; **to make ~** Krieg führen

ward [wɔːd] *n* (*in hospital*) Station *f*; (*of city*) Bezirk *m*; (*child*) Mündel *nt*; **~ off** *vt* abwenden, abwehren

warden [wɔːdn] *n* (*guard*) Wächter *m*, Aufseher *m*; (*BRIT: in youth hostel*) Herbergsvater *m*; (*UNIV*) Heimleiter *m*; (*BRIT: also:* **traffic ~**) ≃ Verkehrspolizist *m*, ≃ Politesse *f*

warder [wɔːdəʳ] (*BRIT*) *n* Gefängniswärter *m*

wardrobe [wɔːdrəub] *n* Kleiderschrank *m*; (*clothes*) Garderobe *f*

warehouse [wɛəhaus] *n* Lagerhaus *nt*

wares [wɛəz] *npl* Ware *f*

warfare [wɔːfɛəʳ] *n* Krieg *m*; Kriegsführung *f*

warhead [wɔːhed] *n* Sprengkopf *m*

warily [wɛərɪlɪ] *adv* vorsichtig

warlike [wɔːlaɪk] *adj* kriegerisch

warm [wɔːm] *adj* warm; (*welcome*) herzlich ♦ *vt, vi* wärmen; **I'm ~** mir ist warm; **it's ~** es ist warm; **~ up** *vt* aufwärmen ♦ *vi* warm werden; **~-hearted** *adj* warmherzig; **~ly** *adv* warm; herzlich; **~th** *n* Wärme *f*; Herzlichkeit *f*

warn [wɔːn] *vt*: **to ~ (of** *or* **against)** warnen (vor +*dat*); **~ing** *n* Warnung *f*; **without ~ing** unerwartet; **~ing light** *n* Warnlicht *nt*; **~ing triangle** *n* (*AUT*) Warndreieck *nt*

warp [wɔːp] *vt* verziehen; **~ed** *adj* wellig; (*fig*) pervers

warrant [wɒrnt] *n* (*for arrest*) Haftbefehl *m*

warranty [wɒrəntɪ] *n* Garantie *f*

warren [wɒrən] *n* Labyrinth *nt*

Warsaw [wɔːsɔː] *n* Warschau *nt*

warship [wɔːʃɪp] *n* Kriegsschiff *nt*

wart [wɔːt] *n* Warze *f*

wartime ['wɔːtaɪm] n Krieg m

wary ['wɛərɪ] adj misstrauisch

was [wɒz] pt of **be**

wash [wɒʃ] n Wäsche f ♦ vt waschen; (dishes) abwaschen ♦ vi sich waschen; (do ~ing) waschen; **to have a ~** sich waschen; **~ away** vt abwaschen, wegspülen; **~ off** vt abwaschen; **~ up** vi (BRIT) spülen; (US) sich waschen; **~able** adj waschbar; **~basin** n Waschbecken nt; **~ bowl** (US) n Waschbecken nt; **~ cloth** (US) n (face cloth) Waschlappen m; **~er** n (TECH) Dichtungsring m; (machine) Waschmaschine f; **~ing** n Wäsche f; **~ing machine** n Waschmaschine f; **~ing powder** (BRIT) n Waschpulver nt; **~ing-up** n Abwasch m; **~ing-up liquid** n Spülmittel nt; **~-out** (inf) n (event) Reinfall m; (person) Niete f; **~room** n Waschraum m

wasn't ['wɒznt] = **was not**

wasp [wɒsp] n Wespe f

wastage ['weɪstɪdʒ] n Verlust m; **natural ~** Verschleiß m

waste [weɪst] n Verschwendung f; (what is ~d) Abfall m ♦ adj (useless) überschüssig, Abfall- ♦ vt (object) verschwenden; (time, life) vergeuden ♦ vi: **to ~ away** verfallen, verkümmern; **~s** npl (land) Einöde f; **~ disposal unit** (BRIT) n Müllschlucker m; **~ful** adj verschwenderisch; (process) aufwändig, aufwendig; **~ ground** (BRIT) n unbebaute(s) Grundstück nt; **~land** n Ödland nt; **~paper basket** n Papierkorb m; **~ pipe** n Abflussrohr nt

watch [wɒtʃ] n Wache f; (for time) Uhr f ♦ vt ansehen; (observe) beobachten; (be careful of) aufpassen auf +acc; (guard) bewachen ♦ vi zusehen; **to be on the ~ (for sth)** (auf etw acc) aufpassen; **to ~ TV** fernsehen; **to ~ sb doing sth** jdm bei etw zuschauen; **~ out** vi Ausschau halten; (be careful) aufpassen; **~ out!** pass auf!; **~dog** n Wachhund m; (fig) Wächter m; **~ful** adj wachsam; **~maker** n Uhrmacher m; **~man** (irreg) n (also: **night ~man**) (Nacht)wächter m; **~ strap** n Uhrarmband nt

water ['wɔːtər] n Wasser nt ♦ vt (be)gießen; (river) bewässern; (horses) tränken ♦ vi (eye) tränen; **~s** npl (of sea, river etc) Gewässer nt; **~ down** vt verwässern; **~ closet** (BRIT) n (Wasser)klosett nt; **~colour** (US **watercolor**) n (painting) Aquarell nt; (paint) Wasserfarbe f; **~cress** n (Brunnen)kresse f; **~fall** n Wasserfall m; **~ heater** n Heißwassergerät nt; **~ing can** n Gießkanne f; **~ level** n Wasserstand m; **~lily** n Seerose f; **~line** n Wasserlinie f; **~logged** adj (ground) voll Wasser; **~ main** n Haupt(wasser)leitung f; **~mark** n Wasserzeichen nt; (on wall) Wasserstandsmarke f; **~melon** n Wassermelone f; **~ polo** n Wasserball(spiel) nt; **~proof** adj wasserdicht; **~shed** n Wasserscheide f; **~-skiing** n Wasserskilaufen nt; **~ tank** n Wassertank m; **~tight** adj wasserdicht; **~way** n Wasserweg m; **~works** npl Wasserwerk nt; **~y** adj wäss(e)rig

watt [wɒt] n Watt nt

wave [weɪv] n Welle f; (with hand) Winken nt ♦ vt (move to and fro) schwenken; (hand, flag) winken mit ♦ vi (person) winken; (flag) wehen; **~length** n (also fig) Wellenlänge f

waver ['weɪvər] vi schwanken

wavy ['weɪvɪ] adj wellig

wax [wæks] n Wachs nt; (sealing ~) Siegellack m; (in ear) Ohrenschmalz nt ♦ vt (floor) (ein)wachsen ♦ vi (moon) zunehmen; **~works** npl Wachsfigurenkabinett nt

way [weɪ] n Weg m; (method) Art und Weise f; (direction) Richtung f; (habit) Gewohnheit f; (distance) Entfernung f; (condition) Zustand m; **which ~? - this ~** welche Richtung? - hier entlang; **on the ~** (en route) unterwegs; **to be in the ~** im Weg sein; **to go out of one's ~ to do sth** sich besonders anstrengen, um etw zu tun; **to lose one's ~** sich verirren; **"give ~"** (BRIT: AUT) „Vorfahrt achten!"; **in a ~** in gewisser Weise; **by the ~** übrigens; **in some ~s** in gewisser Hinsicht; **"~ in"** (BRIT) „Eingang"; **"~ out"** (BRIT) „Ausgang"

waylay [weɪ'leɪ] (irreg: like **lay**) vt auflauern

+*dat*

wayward ['weɪwəd] *adj* eigensinnig

W.C. (*BRIT*) *n* WC *nt*

we [wiː] *pl pron* wir

weak [wiːk] *adj* schwach; **~en** *vt* schwächen ♦ *vi* schwächer werden; **~ling** *n* Schwächling *m*; **~ness** *n* Schwäche *f*

wealth [welθ] *n* Reichtum *m*; (*abundance*) Fülle *f*; **~y** *adj* reich

wean [wiːn] *vt* entwöhnen

weapon ['wepən] *n* Waffe *f*

wear [weəʳ] (*pt* **wore**, *pp* **worn**) *n* (*clothing*): **sports/baby ~** Sport-/Babykleidung *f*; (*use*) Verschleiß *m* ♦ *vt* (*have on*) tragen; (*smile etc*) haben; (*use*) abnutzen ♦ *vi* (*last*) halten; (*become old*) (sich) verschleißen; **evening ~** Abendkleidung *f*; **~ and tear** Verschleiß *m*; **~ away** *vt* verbrauchen ♦ *vi* schwinden; **~ down** *vt* (*people*) zermürben; **~ off** *vi* sich verlieren; **~ out** *vt* verschleißen; (*person*) erschöpfen

weary ['wɪərɪ] *adj* müde ♦ *vt* ermüden ♦ *vi* überdrüssig werden

weasel ['wiːzl] *n* Wiesel *nt*

weather ['weðəʳ] *n* Wetter *nt* ♦ *vt* verwittern lassen; (*resist*) überstehen; **under the ~** (*fig: ill*) angeschlagen (*inf*); **~-beaten** *adj* verwittert; **~cock** *n* Wetterhahn *m*; **~ forecast** *n* Wettervorhersage *f*; **~ vane** *n* Wetterfahne *f*

weave [wiːv] (*pt* **wove**, *pp* **woven**) *vt* weben; **~r** *n* Weber(in) *m(f)*; **weaving** *n* (*craft*) Webkunst *f*

Web [web] *n*: **the ~** das Web

web [web] *n*; (*membrane*) Schwimmhaut *f*; **~ site** *n* (*COMPUT*) Website *f*, Webseite *f*

wed [wed] (*pt*, *pp* **wedded**) *vt* heiraten ♦ *n*: **the newly-~s** *npl* die Frischvermählten *pl*

we'd [wiːd] = **we had**; **we would**

wedding ['wedɪŋ] *n* Hochzeit *f*; **silver/golden ~ anniversary** Silberhochzeit *f*/goldene Hochzeit *f*; **~ day** *n* Hochzeitstag *m*; **~ dress** *n* Hochzeitskleid *nt*; **~ ring** *n* Trauring *m*, Ehering *m*

wedge [wedʒ] *n* Keil *m*; (*of cheese etc*) Stück *nt* ♦ *vt* (*fasten*) festklemmen; (*pack tightly*) einkeilen

Wednesday ['wenzdɪ] *n* Mittwoch *m*

wee [wiː] (*SCOTTISH*) *adj* klein, winzig

weed [wiːd] *n* Unkraut *nt* ♦ *vt* jäten; **~-killer** *n* Unkrautvertilgungsmittel *nt*

weedy ['wiːdɪ] *adj* (*person*) schmächtig

week [wiːk] *n* Woche *f*; **a ~ today/on Friday** heute/Freitag in einer Woche; **~day** *n* Wochentag *m*; **~end** *n* Wochenende *nt*; **~ly** *adj* wöchentlich; (*wages, magazine*) Wochen- ♦ *adv* wöchentlich

weep [wiːp] (*pt*, *pp* **wept**) *vi* weinen; **~ing willow** *n* Trauerweide *f*

weigh [weɪ] *vt*, *vi* wiegen; **to ~ anchor** den Anker lichten; **~ down** *vt* niederdrücken; **~ up** *vt* abschätzen

weight [weɪt] *n* Gewicht *nt*; **to lose/put on ~** abnehmen/zunehmen; **~ing** *n* (*allowance*) Zulage *f*; **~lifter** *n* Gewichtheber *m*; **~lifting** *n* Gewichtheben *nt*; **~y** *adj* (*heavy*) gewichtig; (*important*) schwerwiegend, schwer wiegend

weir [wɪəʳ] *n* (Stau)wehr *nt*

weird [wɪəd] *adj* seltsam

welcome ['welkəm] *n* Willkommen *nt*, Empfang *m* ♦ *vt* begrüßen; **thank you - you're ~!** danke - nichts zu danken

welder ['weldəʳ] *n* (*person*) Schweißer(in) *m(f)*

welding ['weldɪŋ] *n* Schweißen *nt*

welfare ['welfeəʳ] *n* Wohl *nt*; (*social*) Fürsorge *f*; **~ state** *n* Wohlfahrtsstaat *m*; **~ work** *n* Fürsorge *f*

well [wel] *n* Brunnen *m*; (*oil ~*) Quelle *f* ♦ *adj* (*in good health*) gesund ♦ *adv* gut ♦ *excl* nun!, na schön!; **I'm ~** es geht mir gut; **get ~ soon!** gute Besserung!; **as ~** auch; **as ~ as** sowohl als auch; **~ done!** gut gemacht!; **to do ~** (*person*) gut zurechtkommen; (*business*) gut gehen; **~ up** *vi* emporsteigen; (*fig*) aufsteigen

we'll [wiːl] = **we will**; **we shall**

well: **~-behaved** ['welbɪ'heɪvd] *adj* wohlerzogen; **~-being** n ['wel'biːɪŋ] *n* Wohl *nt*; **~-built** ['wel'bɪlt] *adj* kräftig gebaut; **~-deserved** ['weldɪ'zɜːvd] *adj* wohlverdient; **~-dressed** ['wel'drest] *adj* gut gekleidet; **~-heeled** ['wel'hiːld] (*inf*) *adj* (*wealthy*) gut

gepolstert
wellingtons ['wɛlɪŋtənz] npl (also:
wellington boots) Gummistiefel pl
well: ~-**known** ['wɛl'nəun] adj bekannt; ~-
mannered ['wɛl'mænəd] adj wohlerzogen;
~-**meaning** ['wɛl'miːnɪŋ] adj (person)
wohlmeinend; (action) gut gemeint; ~-**off**
['wɛl'ɔf] adj gut situiert; ~-**read** ['wɛl'rɛd] adj
(sehr) belesen; ~-**to-do** ['wɛltə'duː] adj
wohlhabend; ~-**wisher** ['wɛlwɪʃəʳ] n
Gönner m
Welsh [wɛlʃ] adj walisisch ♦ n (LING)
Walisisch nt; **the** ~ npl (people) die Waliser
pl; ~ **Assembly** n walisische Versammlung
f; ~**man/woman** (irreg) n Waliser(in) m(f)
went [wɛnt] pt of **go**
wept [wɛpt] pt, pp of **weep**
were [wəːʳ] pt pl of **be**
we're [wɪəʳ] = **we are**
weren't [wəːnt] = **were not**
west [wɛst] n Westen m ♦ adj West-, westlich
♦ adv westwärts, nach Westen; **the W**~ der
Westen; **W**~ **Country** (BRIT) n: **the W~
Country** der Südwesten Englands; ~**erly**
adj westlich; ~**ern** adj westlich, West- ♦ n
(CINE) Western m; **W~ Indian** adj
westindisch ♦ n Westindier(in) m(f); **W~
Indies** npl Westindische Inseln pl;
~**ward(s)** adv westwärts
wet [wɛt] adj nass; **to get** ~ nass werden; **"~
paint"** „frisch gestrichen"; ~ **blanket** n
(fig) Triefel m; ~ **suit** n Taucheranzug m
we've [wiːv] = **we have**
whack [wæk] n Schlag m ♦ vt schlagen
whale [weɪl] n Wal m
wharf [wɔːf] n Kai m
wharves [wɔːvz] npl of **wharf**

KEYWORD

what [wɔt] adj 1 (in questions) welche(r, s),
was für ein(e); **what size is it?** welche
Größe ist das?
2 (in exclamations) was für ein(e); **what a
mess!** was für ein Durcheinander!
♦ pron (interrogative/relative) was; **what are
you doing?** was machst du gerade?; **what
are you talking about?** wovon reden Sie?;

what is it called? wie heißt das?; **what
about ...?** wie wärs mit ...?; **I saw what
you did** ich habe gesehen, was du
gemacht hast
♦ excl (disbelieving) wie, was; **what, no
coffee!** wie, kein Kaffee?; **I've crashed the
car - what!** Ich hatte einen Autounfall -
was!

whatever [wɔt'ɛvəʳ] adj: ~ **book** welches
Buch auch immer ♦ pron: **do** ~ **is
necessary** tu, was (immer auch) nötig ist;
~ **happens** egal, was passiert; **nothing** ~
überhaupt or absolut gar nichts; **do** ~ **you
want** tu, was (immer) du (auch) möchtest;
no reason ~ or **whatsoever** überhaupt or
absolut kein Grund
whatsoever [wɔtsəu'ɛvəʳ] adj see **whatever**
wheat [wiːt] n Weizen m
wheedle ['wiːdl] vt: **to** ~ **sb into doing sth**
jdn dazu überreden, etw zu tun; **to** ~ **sth
out of sb** jdm etw abluchsen
wheel [wiːl] n Rad nt; (steering ~) Lenkrad
nt; (disc) Scheibe f ♦ vt schieben; ~**barrow**
n Schubkarren m; ~**chair** n Rollstuhl m; ~
clamp n (AUT) Parkkralle f
wheeze [wiːz] vi keuchen

KEYWORD

when [wɛn] adv wann
♦ conj 1 (at, during, after the time that)
wenn; (in past) als; **she was reading when
I came in** sie las, als ich hereinkam; **be
careful when you cross the road** seien Sie
vorsichtig, wenn Sie über die Straße gehen
2 (on, at which) als; **on the day when I met
him** an dem Tag, an dem ich ihn traf
3 (whereas) wo ... doch

whenever [wɛn'ɛvəʳ] adv wann (auch)
immer; (every time that) jedes Mal wenn
♦ conj (any time) wenn
where [wɛəʳ] adv (place) wo; (direction)
wohin; ~ **from** woher; **this is** ~ ... hier ...;
~**abouts** ['wɛərəbauts] adv wo ♦ n
Aufenthaltsort m; **nobody knows his
~abouts** niemand weiß, wo er ist; ~**as**

[wɛər'æz] *conj* während, wo ... doch; **~by** *pron* woran, wodurch, womit, wovon; **~upon** *conj* worauf, wonach; (*at beginning of sentence*) daraufhin; **~ver** [wɛər'ɛvər] *adv* wo (immer)

wherewithal ['wɛəwɪðɔːl] *n* nötige (Geld)mittel *pl*

whet [wɛt] *vt* (*appetite*) anregen

whether ['wɛðər] *conj* ob; **I don't know ~ to accept or not** ich weiß nicht, ob ich es annehmen soll oder nicht; **~ you go or not** ob du gehst oder nicht; **it's doubtful/ unclear ~ ...** es ist zweifelhaft/nicht klar, ob ...

[KEYWORD]

which [wɪtʃ] *adj* **1** (*interrogative: direct, indirect*) welche(r, s); **which one?** welche(r, s)?
2: in which case in diesem Fall; **by which time** zu dieser Zeit
♦ *pron* **1** (*interrogative*) welche(r, s); (*of people also*) wer
2 (*relative*) der/die/das; (*referring to people*) was; **the apple which you ate/which is on the table** der Apfel, den du gegessen hast/der auf dem Tisch liegt; **he said he saw her, which is true** er sagte, er habe sie gesehen, was auch stimmt

whichever [wɪtʃ'ɛvər] *adj* welche(r, s) auch immer; (*no matter which*) ganz gleich welche(r, s); **~ book you take** welches Buch du auch nimmst; **~ car you prefer** egal welches Auto du vorziehst

whiff [wɪf] *n* Hauch *m*

while [waɪl] *n* Weile *f* ♦ *conj* während; **for a ~** eine Zeit lang; **~ away** *vt* (*time*) sich *dat* vertreiben

whim [wɪm] *n* Laune *f*

whimper ['wɪmpər] *n* Wimmern *nt* ♦ *vi* wimmern

whimsical ['wɪmzɪkəl] *adj* launisch

whine [waɪn] *n* Gewinsel *nt*, Gejammer *nt* ♦ *vi* heulen, winseln

whip [wɪp] *n* Peitsche *f*; (*POL*) Fraktionsführer *m* ♦ *vt* (*beat*) peitschen; (*snatch*) reißen;

~ped cream *n* Schlagsahne *f*

whip-round ['wɪpraund] (*BRIT: inf*) *n* Geldsammlung *f*

whirl [wəːl] *n* Wirbel *m* ♦ *vt, vi* (herum)wirbeln; **~pool** *n* Wirbel *m*; **~wind** *n* Wirbelwind *m*

whirr [wəːr] *vi* schwirren, surren

whisk [wɪsk] *n* Schneebesen *m* ♦ *vt* (*cream etc*) schlagen; **to ~ sb away** *or* **off** mit jdm davon sausen

whisker ['wɪskər] *n*: **~s** (*of animal*) Barthaare *pl*; (*of man*) Backenbart *m*

whisky ['wɪskɪ] (*US, IRISH* **whiskey**) *n* Whisky *m*

whisper ['wɪspər] *n* Flüstern *nt* ♦ *vt, vi* flüstern

whistle ['wɪsl] *n* Pfiff *m*; (*instrument*) Pfeife *f* ♦ *vt, vi* pfeifen

white [waɪt] *n* Weiß *nt*; (*of egg*) Eiweiß *nt* ♦ *adj* weiß; **~ coffee** (*BRIT*) *n* Kaffee *m* mit Milch; **~-collar worker** *n* Angestellte(r) *m*; **~ elephant** *n* (*fig*) Fehlinvestition *f*; **~ lie** *n* Notlüge *f*; **~ paper** *n* (*POL*) Weißbuch *nt*; **~wash** *n* (*paint*) Tünche *f*; (*fig*) Ehrenrettung *f* ♦ *vt* weißen, tünchen; (*fig*) rein waschen

whiting ['waɪtɪŋ] *n* Weißfisch *m*

Whitsun ['wɪtsn] *n* Pfingsten *nt*

whittle ['wɪtl] *vt*: **to ~ away** *or* **down** stutzen, verringern

whizz [wɪz] *vi*: **to ~ past** *or* **by** vorbeizischen, vorbeischwirren; **~ kid** (*inf*) *n* Kanone *f*

[KEYWORD]

who [huː] *pron* **1** (*interrogative*) wer; (*acc*) wen; (*dat*) wem; **who is it?, who's there?** wer ist da?
2 (*relative*) der/die/das; **the woman/man who spoke to me** die Frau/der Mann, die/ der mit mir sprach

whodu(n)nit [huː'dʌnɪt] (*inf*) *n* Krimi *m*

whoever [huː'ɛvər] *pron* wer/wen/wem auch immer; (*no matter who*) ganz gleich wer/ wen/wem

whole [həul] *adj* ganz ♦ *n* Ganze(s) *nt*; **the ~ of the town** die ganze Stadt; **on the ~** im

Großen und Ganzen; **as a ~** im Großen und Ganzen; **~food(s)** ['hɔːlfuːd(z)] *n(pl)* Vollwertkost *f*; **~hearted** [həʊl'hɑːtɪd] *adj* rückhaltlos; **~heartedly** *adv* von ganzem Herzen; **~meal** *adj* (*bread, flour*) Vollkorn-; **~sale** *n* Großhandel *m* ♦ *adj* (*trade*) Großhandels-; (*destruction*) Massen-; **~saler** *n* Großhändler *m*; **~some** *adj* bekömmlich, gesund; **~wheat** *adj* = **wholemeal**

wholly ['hɔːlɪ] *adv* ganz, völlig

[KEYWORD]

whom [huːm] *pron* **1** (*interrogative: acc*) wen; (: *dat*) wem; **whom did you see?** wen haben Sie gesehen?; **to whom did you give it?** wem haben Sie es gegeben?
2 (*relative: acc*) den/die/das; (: *dat*) dem/der/dem; **the man whom I saw/to whom I spoke** der Mann, den ich sah/mit dem ich sprach

whooping cough ['huːpɪŋ-] *n* Keuchhusten *m*

whore [hɔːr] *n* Hure *f*

whose [huːz] *adj* (*possessive: interrogative*) wessen; (: *relative*) dessen; (*after f and pl*) deren ♦ *pron* wessen; **~ book is this?**, **~ is this book?** wessen Buch ist dies?; **~ is this?** wem gehört das?

[KEYWORD]

why [waɪ] *adv* warum, weshalb
♦ *conj* warum, weshalb; **that's not why I'm here** ich bin nicht deswegen hier; **that's the reason why** deshalb
♦ *excl* (*expressing surprise, shock*) na so was; (*explaining*) also dann; **why, it's you!** na so was, du bist es!

wick [wɪk] *n* Docht *m*
wicked ['wɪkɪd] *adj* böse
wicker ['wɪkər] *n* (*also:* **~work**) Korbgeflecht *nt*
wicket ['wɪkɪt] *n* Tor *nt*, Dreistab *m*
wide [waɪd] *adj* breit; (*plain*) weit; (*in firing*) daneben ♦ *adv*: **to open ~** weit öffnen; **to shoot ~** danebenschießen; **~-angle lens** *n*

Weitwinkelobjektiv *nt*; **~-awake** *adj* hellwach; **~ly** *adv* weit; (*known*) allgemein; **~n** *vt* erweitern; **~ open** *adj* weit geöffnet; **~spread** *adj* weitverbreitet, weit verbreitet

widow ['wɪdəʊ] *n* Witwe *f*; **~ed** *adj* verwitwet; **~er** *n* Witwer *m*

width [wɪdθ] *n* Breite *f*, Weite *f*

wield [wiːld] *vt* schwingen, handhaben

wife [waɪf] (*pl* **wives**) *n* (Ehe)frau *f*, Gattin *f*

wig [wɪg] *n* Perücke *f*

wiggle ['wɪgl] *n* Wackeln *nt* ♦ *vt* wackeln mit ♦ *vi* wackeln

wild [waɪld] *adj* wild; (*violent*) heftig; (*plan, idea*) verrückt; **~erness** ['wɪldənɪs] *n* Wildnis *f*, Wüste *f*; **~-goose chase** *n* (*fig*) fruchtlose(s) Unternehmen *nt*; **~life** *n* Tierwelt *f*; **~ly** *adv* wild, ungestüm; (*exaggerated*) irrsinnig; **~s** *npl*: **the ~s** die Wildnis *f*

wilful ['wɪlful] (*US* **willful**) *adj* (*intended*) vorsätzlich; (*obstinate*) eigensinnig

[KEYWORD]

will [wɪl] *aux vb* **1** (*forms future tense*) werden; **I will finish it tomorrow** ich mache es morgen zu Ende
2 (*in conjectures, predictions*): **he will** *or* **he'll be there by now** er dürfte jetzt da sein; **that will be the postman** das wird der Postbote sein
3 (*in commands, requests, offers*): **will you be quiet!** sei endlich still!; **will you help me?** hilfst du mir?; **will you have a cup of tea?** trinken Sie eine Tasse Tee?; **I won't put up with it!** das lasse ich mir nicht gefallen!
♦ *vt* wollen
♦ *n* Wille *m*; (*JUR*) Testament *nt*

willing ['wɪlɪŋ] *adj* gewillt, bereit; **~ly** *adv* bereitwillig, gern; **~ness** *n* (Bereit)willigkeit *f*

willow ['wɪləʊ] *n* Weide *f*

willpower ['wɪl'paʊər] *n* Willenskraft *f*

willy-nilly ['wɪlɪ'nɪlɪ] *adv* einfach so

wilt [wɪlt] *vi* (ver)welken

wily ['waɪlɪ] *adj* gerissen

win [wɪn] (*pt, pp* **won**) *n* Sieg *m* ♦ *vt, vi*

gewinnen; **to ~ sb over** or **round** jdn gewinnen, jdn dazu bringen

wince [wɪns] vi zusammenzucken

winch [wɪntʃ] n Winde f

wind¹ [wɪnd] n Wind m; (MED) Blähungen pl

wind² [waɪnd] (pt, pp **wound**) vt (rope) winden; (bandage) wickeln ♦ vi (turn) sich winden; **~ up** vt (clock) aufziehen; (debate) (ab)schließen

windfall ['wɪndfɔ:l] n unverhoffte(r) Glücksfall m

winding ['waɪndɪŋ] adj (road) gewunden

wind instrument ['wɪnd-] n Blasinstrument nt

windmill ['wɪndmɪl] n Windmühle f

window ['wɪndəʊ] n Fenster nt; **~ box** n Blumenkasten m; **~ cleaner** n Fensterputzer m; **~ envelope** n Fensterbriefumschlag m; **~ ledge** n Fenstersims m; **~ pane** n Fensterscheibe f; **~-shopping** n Schaufensterbummel m; **to go ~-shopping** einen Schaufensterbummel machen; **~sill** n Fensterbank f

wind: **~pipe** n Luftröhre f; **~power** n Windenergie f; **~screen** (BRIT) n Windschutzscheibe f; **~screen washer** n Scheibenwaschanlage f; **~screen wiper** n Scheibenwischer m; **~shield** (US) n = **windscreen;** **~swept** adj vom Wind gepeitscht; (person) zerzaust; **~y** adj windig

wine [waɪn] n Wein m; **~ bar** n Weinlokal nt; **~ cellar** n Weinkeller m; **~glass** n Weinglas nt; **~ list** n Weinkarte f; **~ merchant** n Weinhändler m; **~ tasting** n Weinprobe f; **~ waiter** n Weinkellner m

wing [wɪŋ] n Flügel m; (MIL) Gruppe f; **~s** npl (THEAT) Seitenkulisse f; **~er** n (SPORT) Flügelstürmer m

wink [wɪŋk] n Zwinkern nt ♦ vi zwinkern, blinzeln

winner ['wɪnər] n Gewinner m; (SPORT) Sieger m

winning ['wɪnɪŋ] adj (team) siegreich, Sieger-; (goal) entscheidend; **~ post** n Ziel nt; **~s** npl Gewinn m

winter ['wɪntər] n Winter m ♦ adj (clothes) Winter- ♦ vi überwintern; **~ sports** npl

Wintersport m; **wintry** ['wɪntrɪ] adj Winter-, winterlich

wipe [waɪp] n: **to give sth a ~** etw (ab)wischen ♦ vt wischen; **~ off** vt abwischen; **~ out** vt (debt) löschen; (destroy) auslöschen; **~ up** vt aufwischen

wire ['waɪər] n Draht m; (telegram) Telegramm nt ♦ vt telegrafieren; **to ~ sb** jdm telegrafieren; **~less** ['waɪəlɪs] (BRIT) n Radio(apparat m) nt

wiring ['waɪərɪŋ] n elektrische Leitungen pl

wiry ['waɪərɪ] adj drahtig

wisdom ['wɪzdəm] n Weisheit f; (of decision) Klugheit f; **~ tooth** n Weisheitszahn m

wise [waɪz] adj klug, weise ♦ suffix: **timewise** zeitlich gesehen

wisecrack ['waɪzkræk] n Witzelei f

wish [wɪʃ] n Wunsch m ♦ vt wünschen; **best ~es** (on birthday etc) alles Gute; **with best ~es** herzliche Grüße; **to ~ sb goodbye** jdn verabschieden; **he ~ed me well** er wünschte mir Glück; **to ~ to do sth** etw tun wollen; **~ for** vt fus sich dat wünschen; **~ful thinking** n Wunschdenken nt

wishy-washy ['wɪʃɪ'wɒʃɪ] (inf) adj (ideas, argument) verschwommen

wisp [wɪsp] n (Haar)strähne f; (of smoke) Wölkchen nt

wistful ['wɪstfʊl] adj sehnsüchtig

wit [wɪt] n (also: **~s**) Verstand m no pl; (amusing ideas) Witz m; (person) Witzbold m

witch [wɪtʃ] n Hexe f; **~craft** n Hexerei f

KEYWORD
---

with [wɪð, wɪθ] prep **1** (accompanying, in the company of) mit; **we stayed with friends** wir übernachteten bei Freunden; **I'll be with you in a minute** einen Augenblick, ich bin sofort da; **I'm not with you** (I don't understand) das verstehe ich nicht; **to be with it** (inf: up-to-date) auf dem Laufenden sein; (: alert) (voll) da sein (inf)

2 (descriptive, indicating manner etc) mit; **the man with the grey hat** der Mann mit dem grauen Hut; **red with anger** rot vor Wut

---

withdraw [wɪθ'drɔ:] (irreg: like **draw**) vt

zurückziehen; (*money*) abheben; (*remark*) zurücknehmen ♦ *vi* sich zurückziehen; ~al *n* Zurückziehung *f*; Abheben *nt*; Zurücknahme *f*; ~n *adj* (*person*) verschlossen

wither ['wɪðə'] *vi* (ver)welken

withhold [wɪθ'həuld] (*irreg: like* hold) *vt*: to ~ sth (from sb) (jdm) etw vorenthalten

within [wɪð'ɪn] *prep* innerhalb +*gen* ♦ *adv* innen; ~ sight of in Sichtweite von; ~ the week innerhalb dieser Woche; ~ a mile of weniger als eine Meile von

without [wɪð'aut] *prep* ohne; ~ sleeping *etc* ohne zu schlafen *etc*

withstand [wɪθ'stænd] (*irreg: like* stand) *vt* widerstehen +*dat*

witness ['wɪtnɪs] *n* Zeuge *m*, Zeugin *f* ♦ *vt* (*see*) sehen, miterleben; (*document*) beglaubigen; ~ box *n* Zeugenstand *m*; ~ stand (*US*) *n* Zeugenstand *m*

witticism ['wɪtɪsɪzəm] *n* witzige Bemerkung *f*

witty ['wɪtɪ] *adj* witzig, geistreich

wives [waɪvz] *pl of* wife

wk *abbr* = week

wobble ['wɔbl] *vi* wackeln

woe [wəu] *n* Kummer *m*

woke [wəuk] *pt of* wake

woken ['wəukn] *pp of* wake

wolf [wulf] (*pl* wolves) *n* Wolf *m*

woman ['wumən] (*pl* women) *n* Frau *f*; ~ doctor *n* Ärztin *f*; ~ly *adj* weiblich

womb [wu:m] *n* Gebärmutter *f*

women ['wɪmɪn] *npl of* woman; ~'s lib (*inf*) *n* Frauenrechtsbewegung *f*

won [wʌn] *pt, pp of* win

wonder ['wʌndə'] *n* (*marvel*) Wunder *nt*; (*surprise*) Staunen *nt*, Verwunderung *f* ♦ *vi* sich wundern ♦ *vt*: I ~ whether ... ich frage mich, ob ...; **it's no ~ that** es ist kein Wunder, dass; **to ~ at** sich wundern über +*acc*; **to ~ about** sich Gedanken machen über +*acc*; ~ful *adj* wunderbar, herrlich

won't [wəunt] = **will not**

woo [wu:] *vt* (*audience etc*) umwerben

wood [wud] *n* Holz *nt*; (*forest*) Wald *m*; ~ carving *n* Holzschnitzerei *f*; ~ed *adj* bewaldet; ~en *adj* (*also fig*) hölzern;

~pecker *n* Specht *m*; ~wind *n* Blasinstrumente *pl*; ~work *n* Holzwerk *nt*; (*craft*) Holzarbeiten *pl*; ~worm *n* Holzwurm *m*

wool [wul] *n* Wolle *f*; **to pull the ~ over sb's eyes** (*fig*) jdm Sand in die Augen streuen; ~len (*US* woolen) *adj* Woll-; ~lens *npl* Wollsachen *pl*; ~ly (*US* wooly) *adj* wollig; (*fig*) schwammig

word [wə:d] *n* Wort *nt*; (*news*) Bescheid *m* ♦ *vt* formulieren; **in other ~s** anders gesagt; **to break/keep one's ~** sein Wort brechen/halten; ~ing *n* Wortlaut *m*; ~ processing *n* Textverarbeitung *f*; ~ processor *n* Textverarbeitung *f*

wore [wɔ:'] *pt of* wear

work [wə:k] *n* Arbeit *f*; (*ART, LITER*) Werk *nt* ♦ *vi* arbeiten; (*machine*) funktionieren; (*medicine*) wirken; (*succeed*) klappen; ~s *n sg* (*BRIT: factory*) Fabrik *f*, Werk *nt* ♦ *npl* (*of watch*) Werk *nt*; **to be out of ~** arbeitslos sein; **in ~ing order** in betriebsfähigem Zustand; ~ loose *vi* sich lockern; ~ on *vi* weiterarbeiten ♦ *vt fus* arbeiten an +*dat*; (*influence*) bearbeiten; ~ out *vi* (*sum*) aufgehen; (*plan*) klappen ♦ *vt* (*problem*) lösen; (*plan*) ausarbeiten; **it ~s out at £100** das gibt or macht £100; ~ up *vt*: **to get ~ed up** sich aufregen; ~ahle *adj* (*soil*) bearbeitbar; (*plan*) ausführbar; ~aholic [wə:kə'hɔlɪk] *n* Arbeitssüchtige(r) *f(m)*; ~er *n* Arbeiter(in) *m(f)*; ~ experience *n* Praktikum *nt*; ~force *n* Arbeiterschaft *f*; ~ing class *n* Arbeiterklasse *f*; ~ing-class *adj* Arbeiter-; ~man (*irreg*) *n* Arbeiter *m*; ~manship *n* Arbeit *f*, Ausführung *f*; ~sheet *n* Arbeitsblatt *nt*; ~shop *n* Werkstatt *f*; ~ station *n* Arbeitsplatz *m*; ~-to-rule (*BRIT*) *n* Dienst *m* nach Vorschrift

world [wə:ld] *n* Welt *f*; **to think the ~ of sb** große Stücke auf jdn halten; ~ly *adj* weltlich, irdisch; ~-wide *adj* weltweit

World-Wide Web ['wə:ld'waɪd-] *n* World Wide Web *nt*

worm [wə:m] *n* Wurm *m*

worn [wɔ:n] *pp of* wear ♦ *adj* (*clothes*) abgetragen; ~-out *adj* (*object*) abgenutzt;

(*person*) völlig erschöpft

worried ['wʌrɪd] *adj* besorgt, beunruhigt

worry ['wʌrɪ] *n* Sorge *f* ♦ *vt* beunruhigen ♦ *vi* (*feel uneasy*) sich sorgen, sich *dat* Gedanken machen; **~ing** *adj* beunruhigend

worse [wəːs] *adj* schlechter, schlimmer ♦ *adv* schlimmer, ärger ♦ *n* Schlimmere(s) *nt*, Schlechtere(s) *nt*; **a change for the ~** eine Verschlechterung; **~n** *vt* verschlimmern ♦ *vi* sich verschlechtern; **~ off** *adj* (*fig*) schlechter dran

worship ['wəːʃɪp] *n* Verehrung *f* ♦ *vt* anbeten; **Your W~** (*BRIT: to mayor*) Herr/ Frau Bürgermeister; (: *to judge*) Euer Ehren

worst [wəːst] *adj* schlimmste(r, s), schlechteste(r, s) ♦ *adv* am schlimmsten, am ärgsten ♦ *n* Schlimmste(s) *nt*, Ärgste(s) *nt*; **at ~** schlimmstenfalls

worth [wəːθ] *n* Wert *m* ♦ *adj* wert; **it's ~ it** es lohnt sich; **to be ~ one's while (to do sth)** die Mühe wert sein(, etw zu tun); **~less** *adj* wertlos; (*person*) nichtsnutzig; **~while** *adj* lohnend, der Mühe wert; **~y** *adj* wert, würdig

---

KEYWORD

would [wʊd] *aux vb* **1** (*conditional tense*): **if you asked him he would do it** wenn du ihn fragtest, würde er es tun; **if you had asked him he would have done it** wenn du ihn gefragt hättest, hätte er es getan

2 (*in offers, invitations, requests*): **would you like a biscuit?** möchten Sie ein Plätzchen?; **would you ask him to come in?** würden Sie ihn bitte hineinbitten?

3 (*in indirect speech*): **I said I would do it** ich sagte, ich würde es tun

4 (*emphatic*): **it WOULD have to snow today!** es musste ja ausgerechnet heute schneien!

5 (*insistence*): **she wouldn't behave** sie wollte sich partout nicht anständig benehmen

6 (*conjecture*): **it would have been midnight** es mag ungefähr Mitternacht gewesen sein; **it would seem so** es sieht wohl so aus

7 (*indicating habit*): **he would go there on Mondays** er ging jeden Montag dorthin

---

would-be ['wʊdbiː] (*pej*) *adj* Möchtegern-

wouldn't ['wʊdnt] = **would not**

wound[1] [wuːnd] *n* (*also fig*) Wunde *f* ♦ *vt* verwunden, verletzen (*also fig*)

wound[2] [waʊnd] *pt, pp of* **wind**[2]

wove [wəʊv] *pt of* **weave**; **~n** *pp of* **weave**

wrangle ['ræŋgl] *n* Streit *m* ♦ *vi* sich zanken

wrap [ræp] *vt* einwickeln; **~ up** *vt* einwickeln; (*deal*) abschließen; **~per** *n* Umschlag *m*, Schutzhülle *f*; **~ping paper** *n* Einwickelpapier *nt*

wrath [rɔθ] *n* Zorn *m*

wreak [riːk] *vt* (*havoc*) anrichten; (*vengeance*) üben

wreath [riːθ] *n* Kranz *m*

wreck [rɛk] *n* (*ship*) Wrack *nt*; (*sth ruined*) Ruine *f* ♦ *vt* zerstören; **~age** *n* Trümmer *pl*

wren [rɛn] *n* Zaunkönig *m*

wrench [rɛntʃ] *n* (*spanner*) Schraubenschlüssel *m*; (*twist*) Ruck *m* ♦ *vt* reißen, zerren; **to ~ sth from sb** jdm etw entreißen *or* entwinden

wrestle ['rɛsl] *vi*: **to ~ (with sb)** (mit jdm) ringen; **~r** *n* Ringer(in) *m(f)*; **wrestling** *n* Ringen *nt*

wretched ['rɛtʃɪd] *adj* (*inf*) verflixt

wriggle ['rɪgl] *n* Schlängeln *n* ♦ *vi* sich winden

wring [rɪŋ] (*pt, pp* **wrung**) *vt* wringen

wrinkle ['rɪŋkl] *n* Falte *f*, Runzel *f* ♦ *vt* runzeln ♦ *vi* sich runzeln; (*material*) knittern; **~d** *adj* faltig, schrumpelig

wrist [rɪst] *n* Handgelenk *nt*; **~watch** *n* Armbanduhr *f*

writ [rɪt] *n* gerichtliche(r) Befehl *m*

write [raɪt] (*pt* **wrote**, *pp* **written**) *vt, vi* schreiben; **~ down** *vt* aufschreiben; **~ off** *vt* (*dismiss*) abschreiben; **~ out** *vt* (*essay*) abschreiben; (*cheque*) ausstellen; **~ up** *vt* schreiben; **~-off** *n*: **it is a ~-off** das kann man abschreiben; **~r** *n* Schriftsteller *m*

writhe [raɪð] *vi* sich winden

writing ['raɪtɪŋ] *n* (*act*) Schreiben *nt*; (*handwriting*) (Hand)schrift *f*; **in ~** schriftlich;

~ paper n Schreibpapier nt
written ['rɪtn] pp of **write**
wrong [rɒŋ] adj (incorrect) falsch; (morally) unrecht ♦ n Unrecht nt ♦ vt Unrecht tun +dat; **he was ~ in doing that** es war nicht recht von ihm, das zu tun; **you are ~ about that, you've got it ~** da hast du Unrecht; **to be in the ~** im Unrecht sein; **what's ~ with your leg?** was ist mit deinem Bein los?; **to go ~** (plan) schief gehen; (person) einen Fehler machen; **~ful** adj unrechtmäßig; **~ly** adv falsch; (accuse) zu Unrecht
wrong number n (TEL): **you've got the ~** Sie sind falsch verbunden
wrote [rəut] pt of **write**
wrought [rɔːt] adj: **~ iron** Schmiedeeisen nt
wrung [rʌŋ] pt, pp of **wring**
wry [raɪ] adj ironisch
wt. abbr = **weight**
WWW n abbr (= World Wide Web): **the ~** das WWW.

X, x

Xmas ['ɛksməs] n abbr = **Christmas**
X-ray ['ɛksreɪ] n Röntgenaufnahme f ♦ vt röntgen; **~~s** npl Röntgenstrahlen pl
xylophone ['zaɪləfəun] n Xylofon nt, Xylophon nt

Y, y

yacht [jɒt] n Jacht f; **~ing** n (Sport)segeln nt; **~sman** (irreg) n Sportsegler m
Yank [jæŋk] (inf) n Ami m
yap [jæp] vi (dog) kläffen
yard [jɑːd] n Hof m; (measure) (englische) Elle f, Yard nt (0,91 m); **~stick** n (fig) Maßstab m
yarn [jɑːn] n (thread) Garn nt; (story) (Seemanns)garn nt
yawn [jɔːn] n Gähnen nt ♦ vi gähnen; **~ing** adj (gap) gähnend
yd. abbr = **yard(s)**

yeah [jɛə] (inf) adv ja
year [jɪəʳ] n Jahr nt; **to be 8 ~s old** acht Jahre alt sein; **an eight-year-old child** ein achtjähriges Kind; **~ly** adj, adv jährlich
yearn [jɜːn] vi: **to ~ (for)** sich sehnen (nach); **~ing** n Verlangen nt, Sehnsucht f
yeast [jiːst] n Hefe f
yell [jɛl] n gellende(r) Schrei m ♦ vi laut schreien
yellow ['jɛləu] adj gelb ♦ n Gelb nt
yelp [jɛlp] n Gekläff nt ♦ vi kläffen
yes [jɛs] adv ja ♦ n Ja nt, Jawort nt; **to say ~** Ja or ja sagen; **to answer ~** mit Ja antworten
yesterday ['jɛstədɪ] adv gestern ♦ n Gestern nt; **~ morning/evening** gestern Morgen/Abend; **all day ~** gestern den ganzen Tag; **the day before ~** vorgestern
yet [jɛt] adv noch; (in question) schon; (up to now) bis jetzt ♦ conj doch, dennoch; **it is not finished ~** es ist noch nicht fertig; **the best ~** das bisher Beste; **as ~** bis jetzt; (in past) bis dahin
yew [juː] n Eibe f
yield [jiːld] n Ertrag m ♦ vt (result, crop) hervorbringen; (interest, profit) abwerfen; (concede) abtreten ♦ vi nachgeben; (MIL) sich ergeben; **"~"** (US: AUT) „Vorfahrt gewähren"
YMCA n abbr (= Young Men's Christian Association) CVJM m
yob [jɒb] (BRIT: inf) n Halbstarke(r) f(m)
yoga ['jəugə] n Joga m
yog(h)urt ['jəugət] n Jog(h)urt m
yoke [jəuk] n (also fig) Joch nt
yolk [jəuk] n Eidotter m, Eigelb nt

KEYWORD

you [juː] pron 1 (subj, in comparisons: familiar form: sg) du; (: pl) ihr; (in letters also) du, ihr; (: polite form) Sie; **you Germans** ihr Deutschen; **she's younger than you** sie ist jünger als du/Sie
2 (direct object, after prep +acc: familiar form: sg) dich; (: pl) euch; (in letters also) dich, euch; (: polite form) Sie; **I know you** ich kenne dich/euch/Sie

3 (*indirect object, after prep +dat: familiar form: sg*) dir; (: *pl*) euch; (*in letters also*) dir, euch; (: *polite form*) Ihnen; **I gave it to you** ich gab es dir/euch/Ihnen
4 (*impers: one: subj*) man; (: *direct object*) einen; (: *indirect object*) einem; **fresh air does you good** frische Luft tut gut

you'd [ju:d] = **you had**; **you would**
you'll [ju:l] = **you will**; **you shall**
young [jʌŋ] *adj* jung ♦ *npl*: **the ~** die Jungen *pl*; ~**ster** *n* Junge *m*, junge(r) Bursche *m*, junge(s) Mädchen *nt*
your [jɔːʳ] *adj* (*familiar: sg*) dein; (: *pl*) euer, eure *pl*; (*polite*) Ihr; *see also* **my**
you're [juəʳ] = **you are**
yours [jɔːz] *pron* (*familiar: sg*) deine(r, s); (: *pl*) eure(r, s); (*polite*) Ihre(r, s); *see also* **mine²**
yourself [jɔː'sɛlf] *pron* (*emphatic*) selbst; (*familiar: sg: acc*) dich (selbst); (: *dat*) dir (selbst); (: *pl*) euch (selbst); (*polite*) sich (selbst); *see also* **oneself; yourselves** *pl pron* (*reflexive: familiar*) euch; (: *polite*) sich; (*emphatic*) selbst; *see also* **oneself**
youth [ju:θ] *n* Jugend *f*; (*young man*) junge(r) Mann *m*; ~**s** *npl* (*young people*) Jugendliche *pl*; ~ **club** *n* Jugendzentrum *nt*; ~**ful** *adj* jugendlich; ~ **hostel** *n* Jugendherberge *f*
you've [ju:v] = **you have**
YTS (*BRIT*) *n abbr* (= *Youth Training Scheme*) staatliches Förderprogramm für arbeitslose Jugendliche
Yugoslav ['ju:gəuslɑːv] *adj* jugoslawisch ♦ *n* Jugoslawe *m*, Jugoslawin *f*; ~**ia**

[ju:gəu'slɑːvɪə] *n* Jugoslawien *nt*
yuppie ['jʌpɪ] (*inf*) *n* Yuppie *m* ♦ *adj* yuppiehaft, Yuppie-
YWCA *n abbr* (= *Young Women's Christian Association*) CVJF *m*

Z, z

zany ['zeɪnɪ] *adj* (*ideas, sense of humour*) verrückt
zap [zæp] *vt* (*COMPUT*) löschen
zeal [zi:l] *n* Eifer *m*; ~**ous** ['zɛləs] *adj* eifrig
zebra ['zi:brə] *n* Zebra *nt*; ~ **crossing** (*BRIT*) *n* Zebrastreifen *m*
zero ['zɪərəu] *n* Null *f*; (*on scale*) Nullpunkt *m*
zest [zɛst] *n* Begeisterung *f*
zigzag ['zɪgzæg] *n* Zickzack *m*
Zimbabwe [zɪm'bɑːbwɪ] *n* Zimbabwe *nt*
Zimmer frame ['zɪmə-] *n* Laufgestell *nt*
zip [zɪp] *n* Reißverschluss *m* ♦ *vt* (*also:* ~ **up**) den Reißverschluss zumachen +*gen*
zip code (*US*) *n* Postleitzahl *f*
zipper ['zɪpəʳ] (*US*) *n* Reißverschluss *m*
zit [zɪt] (*inf*) *n* Pickel *m*
zodiac ['zəudiæk] *n* Tierkreis *m*
zombie ['zɒmbɪ] *n*: **like a ~** (*fig*) wie im Tran
zone [zəun] *n* (*also MIL*) Zone *f*, Gebiet *nt*; (*in town*) Bezirk *m*
zoo [zu:] *n* Zoo *m*
zoology [zu:'ɒlədʒɪ] *n* Zoologie *f*
zoom [zu:m] *vi*: **to ~ past** vorbeisausen; ~ **lens** *n* Zoomobjektiv *nt*
zucchini [zu:'ki:nɪ] (*US*) *npl* Zucchini *pl*

GERMAN IRREGULAR VERBS

*with 'sein'

infinitive	present indicative (2nd, 3rd sg)	imperfect	past participle
aufschrecken*	schrickst auf, schrickt auf	schrak or schreckte auf	aufgeschreckt
ausbedingen	bedingst aus, bedingt aus	bedang or bedingte aus	ausbedungen
backen	bäckst, bäckt	backte or buk	gebacken
befehlen	befiehlst, befiehlt	befahl	befohlen
beginnen	beginnst, beginnt	begann	begonnen
beißen	beißt, beißt	biss	gebissen
bergen	birgst, birgt	barg	geborgen
bersten*	birst, birst	barst	geborsten
bescheißen*	bescheißt, bescheißt	beschiss	beschissen
bewegen	bewegst, bewegt	bewog	bewogen
biegen	biegst, biegt	bog	gebogen
bieten	bietest, bietet	bot	geboten
binden	bindest, bindet	band	gebunden
bitten	bittest, bittet	bat	gebeten
blasen	bläst, bläst	blies	geblasen
bleiben*	bleibst, bleibt	blieb	geblieben
braten	brätst, brät	briet	gebraten
brechen*	brichst, bricht	brach	gebrochen
brennen	brennst, brennt	brannte	gebrannt
bringen	bringst, bringt	brachte	gebracht
denken	denkst, denkt	dachte	gedacht
dreschen	drisch(e)st, drischt	drosch	gedroschen
dringen*	dringst, dringt	drang	gedrungen
dürfen	darfst, darf	durfte	gedurft
empfehlen	empfiehlst, empfiehlt	empfahl	empfohlen
erbleichen*	erbleichst, erbleicht	erbleichte	erblichen
erlöschen*	erlischst, erlischt	erlosch	erloschen
erschrecken*	erschrickst, erschrickt	erschrak	erschrocken
essen	isst, isst	aß	gegessen
fahren*	fährst, fährt	fuhr	gefahren
fallen*	fällst, fällt	fiel	gefallen

infinitive	present indicative (2nd, 3rd sg)	imperfect	past participle
fangen	fängst, fängt	fing	gefangen
fechten	fichtst, ficht	focht	gefochten
finden	findest, findet	fand	gefunden
flechten	flichtst, flicht	flocht	geflochten
fliegen*	fliegst, fliegt	flog	geflogen
fliehen*	fliehst, flieht	floh	geflohen
fließen*	fließt, fließt	floss	geflossen
fressen	frisst, frisst	fraß	gefressen
frieren	frierst, friert	fror	gefroren
gären*	gärst, gärt	gor	gegoren
gebären	gebierst, gebiert	gebar	geboren
geben	gibst, gibt	gab	gegeben
gedeihen*	gedeihst, gedeiht	gedieh	gediehen
gehen*	gehst, geht	ging	gegangen
gelingen*	——, gelingt	gelang	gelungen
gelten	giltst, gilt	galt	gegolten
genesen*	gene(se)st, genest	genas	genesen
genießen	genießt, genießt	genoss	genossen
geraten*	gerätst, gerät	geriet	geraten
geschehen*	——, geschieht	geschah	geschehen
gewinnen	gewinnst, gewinnt	gewann	gewonnen
gießen	gießt, gießt	goss	gegossen
gleichen	gleichst, gleicht	glich	geglichen
gleiten*	gleitest, gleitet	glitt	geglitten
glimmen	glimmst, glimmt	glomm	geglommen
graben	gräbst, gräbt	grub	gegraben
greifen	greifst, greift	griff	gegriffen
haben	hast, hat	hatte	gehabt
halten	hältst, hält	hielt	gehalten
hängen	hängst, hängt	hing	gehangen
hauen	haust, haut	haute	gehauen
heben	hebst, hebt	hob	gehoben
heißen	heißt, heißt	hieß	geheißen
helfen	hilfst, hilft	half	geholfen
kennen	kennst, kennt	kannte	gekannt
klimmen*	klimmst, klimmt	klomm	geklommen
klingen	klingst, klingt	klang	geklungen
kneifen	kneifst, kneift	kniff	gekniffen
kommen*	kommst, kommt	kam	gekommen
können	kannst, kann	konnte	gekonnt
kriechen*	kriechst, kriecht	kroch	gekrochen
laden	lädst, lädt	lud	geladen
lassen	lässt, lässt	ließ	gelassen
laufen*	läufst, läuft	lief	gelaufen
leiden	leidest, leidet	litt	gelitten

610

infinitive	present indicative (2nd, 3rd sg)	imperfect	past participle
leihen	leihst, leiht	lieh	geliehen
lesen	liest, liest	las	gelesen
liegen*	liegst, liegt	lag	gelegen
lügen	lügst, lügt	log	gelogen
mahlen	mahlst, mahlt	mahlte	gemahlen
meiden	meidest, meidet	mied	gemieden
melken	melkst, melkt	melkte	gemolken
messen	misst, misst	maß	gemessen
misslingen*	——, misslingt	misslang	misslungen
mögen	magst, mag	mochte	gemocht
müssen	musst, muss	musste	gemusst
nehmen	nimmst, nimmt	nahm	genommen
nennen	nennst, nennt	nannte	genannt
pfeifen	pfeifst, pfeift	pfiff	gepfiffen
preisen	preist, preist	pries	gepriesen
quellen*	quillst, quillt	quoll	gequollen
raten	rätst, rät	riet	geraten
reiben	reibst, reibt	rieb	gerieben
reißen*	reißt, reißt	riss	gerissen
reiten*	reitest, reitet	ritt	geritten
rennen*	rennst, rennt	rannte	gerannt
riechen	riechst, riecht	roch	gerochen
ringen	ringst, ringt	rang	gerungen
rinnen*	rinnst, rinnt	rann	geronnen
rufen	rufst, ruft	rief	gerufen
salzen	salzt, salzt	salzte	gesalzen
saufen	säufst, säuft	soff	gesoffen
saugen	saugst, saugt	sog	gesogen
schaffen	schaffst, schafft	schuf	geschaffen
scheiden	scheidest, scheidet	schied	geschieden
scheinen	scheinst, scheint	schien	geschienen
schelten	schiltst, schilt	schalt	gescholten
scheren	scherst, schert	schor	geschoren
schieben	schiebst, schiebt	schob	geschoben
schießen	schießt, schießt	schoss	geschossen
schinden	schindest, schindet	schindete	geschunden
schlafen	schläfst, schläft	schlief	geschlafen
schlagen	schlägst, schlägt	schlug	geschlagen
schleichen*	schleichst, schleicht	schlich	geschlichen
schleifen	schleifst, schleift	schliff	geschliffen
schließen	schließt, schließt	schloss	geschlossen
schlingen	schlingst, schlingt	schlang	geschlungen

infinitive	present indicative (2nd, 3rd sg)	imperfect	past participle
schmeißen	schmeißt, schmeißt	schmiss	geschmissen
schmelzen*	schmilzt, schmilzt	schmolz	geschmolzen
schneiden	schneidest, schneidet	schnitt	geschnitten
schreiben	schreibst, schreibt	schrieb	geschrieben
schreien	schreist, schreit	schrie	geschrie(e)n
schreiten	schreitest, schreitet	schritt	geschritten
schweigen	schweigst, schweigt	schwieg	geschwiegen
schwellen*	schwillst, schwillt	schwoll	geschwollen
schwimmen*	schwimmst, schwimmt	schwamm	geschwommen
schwinden*	schwindest, schwindet	schwand	geschwunden
schwingen	schwingst, schwingt	schwang	geschwungen
schwören	schwörst, schwört	schwor	geschworen
sehen	siehst, sieht	sah	gesehen
sein*	bist, ist	war	gewesen
senden	sendest, sendet	sandte	gesandt
singen	singst, singt	sang	gesungen
sinken*	sinkst, sinkt	sank	gesunken
sinnen	sinnst, sinnt	sann	gesonnen
sitzen*	sitzt, sitzt	saß	gesessen
sollen	sollst, soll	sollte	gesollt
speien	speist, speit	spie	gespie(e)n
spinnen	spinnst, spinnt	spann	gesponnen
sprechen	sprichst, spricht	sprach	gesprochen
sprießen*	sprießt, sprießt	spross	gesprossen
springen*	springst, springt	sprang	gesprungen
stechen	stichst, sticht	stach	gestochen
stecken	steckst, steckt	steckte or stak	gesteckt
stehen	stehst, steht	stand	gestanden
stehlen	stiehlst, stiehlt	stahl	gestohlen
steigen*	steigst, steigt	stieg	gestiegen
sterben*	stirbst, stirbt	starb	gestorben
stinken	stinkst, stinkt	stank	gestunken
stoßen	stößt, stößt	stieß	gestoßen
streichen	streichst, streicht	strich	gestrichen
streiten*	streitest, streitet	stritt	gestritten
tragen	trägst, trägt	trug	getragen
treffen	triffst, trifft	traf	getroffen
treiben*	treibst, treibt	trieb	getrieben

infinitive	present indicative (2nd, 3rd sg)	imperfect	past participle
treten*	trittst, tritt	trat	getreten
trinken	trinkst, trinkt	trank	getrunken
trügen	trügst, trügt	trog	getrogen
tun	tust, tut	tat	getan
verderben	verdirbst, verdirbt	verdarb	verdorben
verdrießen	verdrießt, verdrießt	verdross	verdrossen
vergessen	vergisst, vergisst	vergaß	vergessen
verlieren	verlierst, verliert	verlor	verloren
verschleißen	verschleißt, verschleißt	verschliss	verschlissen
wachsen*	wächst, wächst	wuchs	gewachsen
weben	webst, webt	webte *or* wob	gewoben
wägen	wägst, wägt	wog	gewogen
waschen	wäschst, wäscht	wusch	gewaschen
weichen*	weichst, weicht	wich	gewichen
weisen	weist, weist	wies	gewiesen
wenden	wendest, wendet	wandte	gewandt
werben	wirbst, wirbt	warb	geworben
werden*	wirst, wird	wurde	geworden
werfen	wirfst, wirft	warf	geworfen
wiegen	wiegst, wiegt	wog	gewogen
winden	windest, windet	wand	gewunden
wissen	weißt, weiß	wusste	gewusst
wollen	willst, will	wollte	gewollt
wringen	wringst, wringt	wrang	gewrungen
zeihen	zeihst, zeiht	zieh	geziehen
ziehen*	ziehst, zieht	zog	gezogen
zwingen	zwingst, zwingt	zwang	gezwungen

GERMAN SPELLING CHANGES

In July 1996, all German-speaking countries signed a declaration concerning the reform of German spelling, with the result that the new spelling rules are now taught in all schools. To ensure that you have the most up-to-date information at your fingertips, the following list contains the old and new spellings of all German headwords and translations in this dictionary which are affected by the reform.

ALT/OLD	NEU/NEW	ALT/OLD	NEU/NEW
abend	**Abend**	aufsein	**auf sein**
Abfluß	**Abfluss**	aufwendig	**aufwendig**
Abflußrohr	**Abflussrohr**		or **aufwändig**
Abschluß	**Abschluss**	auseinanderbrechen	**auseinander brechen**
Abschlußexamen	**Abschlussexamen**	auseinanderbringen	**auseinander bringen**
Abschlußfeier	**Abschlussfeier**	auseinanderfallen	**auseinander fallen**
Abschlußklasse	**Abschlussklasse**	auseinanderfalten	**auseinander falten**
Abschlußprüfung	**Abschlussprüfung**	auseinandergehen	**auseinander gehen**
Abschuß	**Abschuss**	auseinanderhalten	**auseinander halten**
Abschußrampe	**Abschussrampe**	auseinandernehmen	**auseinander nehmen**
Abszeß	**Abszess**	auseinandersetzen	**auseinander setzen**
achtgeben	**Acht geben**	Ausfluß	**Ausfluss**
Adreßbuch	**Adressbuch**	Ausguß	**Ausguss**
Alleinerziehende(r)	**Alleinerziehende(r)**	Auslaß	**Auslass**
	or **allein Erziehende(r)**	Ausschluß	**Ausschluss**
alleinstehend	**allein stehend**	Ausschuß	**Ausschuss**
allgemeingültig	**allgemein gültig**	Ausschuß(artikel)	**Ausschuss(artikel)**
allzuoft	**allzu oft**	aussein	**aus sein**
allzuviel	**allzu viel**	außerstande	**außer Stande**
Alptraum	**Alptraum**	Autobiographie	**Autobiographie**
	or **Albtraum**		or **Autobiografie**
Amboß	**Amboss**	Baß	**Bass**
Amtsanschluß	**Amtsanschluss**	Baßstimme	**Bassstimme**
(Amts)mißbrauch	**(Amts)missbrauch**		or **Bass-Stimme**
andersdenkend	**anders denkend**	Ballettänzer(in)	**Balletttänzer(in)**
aneinandergeraten	**aneinander geraten**		or **Ballett-Tänzer(in)**
aneinanderreihen	**aneinander reihen**	beeinflußbar	**beeinflussbar**
Anlaß	**Anlass**	beiseitelegen	**beiseite legen**
anläßlich	**anlässlich**	bekanntgeben	**bekannt geben**
Anschluß	**Anschluss**	bekanntmachen	**bekannt machen**
Anschlußflug	**Anschlussflug**	Beschluß	**Beschluss**
As	**Ass**	Beschuß	**Beschuss**
aufeinanderfolgen	**aufeinander folgen**	bessergehen	**besser gehen**
aufeinanderfolgend	**aufeinander folgend**	Bettuch	**Betttuch**
aufeinanderlegen	**aufeinander legen**		or **Bett-Tuch**
aufeinanderprallen	**aufeinander prallen**	(Bevölkerungs)überschuß	**(Bevölkerungs)überschuss**
Aufschluß	**Aufschluss**		
aufschlußreich	**aufschlussreich**	bewußt	**bewusst**
aufsehenerregend	**Aufsehen erregend**	bewußtlos	**bewusstlos**

ALT/OLD	NEU/NEW	ALT/OLD	NEU/NEW
Bewußtlosigkeit	Bewusstlosigkeit	durchnumerieren	durchnummerieren
Bewußtsein	Bewusstsein	ehrfurchtgebietend	Ehrfurcht gebietend
bezug	Bezug	Einfluß	Einfluss
Bibliographie	Bibliographie	Einflußbereich	Einflussbereich
	or Bibliografie	einflußreich	einflussreich
Biographie	Biographie	einigemal	einige Mal
	or Biografie	einiggehen	einig gehen
Biß	Biss	Einlaß	Einlass
biß	biss	ekelerregend	Ekel erregend
bißchen	bisschen	Elsaß	Elsass
blaß	blass	Engpaß	Engpass
bläßlich	blässlich	Entschluß	Entschluss
bleibenlassen	bleiben lassen	entschlußfreudig	entschlussfreudig
Bluterguß	Bluterguss	Entschlußkraft	Entschlusskraft
Boß	Boss	epochemachend	Epoche machend
braungebrannt	braun gebrannt	Erdgeschoß	Erdgeschoss
breitmachen	breit machen	Erdnuß	Erdnuss
Brennessel	Brennnessel	Erdnußbutter	Erdnussbutter
	or Brenn-Nessel	erfolgversprechend	Erfolg versprechend
Büroschluß	Büroschluss	Erguß	Erguss
Butterfaß	Butterfass	Erlaß	Erlass
Cashewnuß	Cashewnuss	ernstgemeint	ernst gemeint
Chicorée	Chicorée	erstemal	erste Mal
	or Schikoree	Eß-	Ess-
Choreograph(in)	Choreograph(in)	erstenmal	ersten Mal
	or Choreograf(in)	eßbar	essbar
Computertomographie	Computertomographie	Eßbesteck	Essbesteck
	or Computertomografie	Eßecke	Essecke
dabeisein	dabei sein	Eßgeschirr	Essgeschirr
dafürkönnen	dafür können	Eßkastanie	Esskastanie
dahinterkommen	dahinter kommen	Eßlöffel	Esslöffel
darauffolgend	darauf folgend	Eßlöffel(voll)	Esslöffel (voll)
dasein	da sein	(Eß)stäbchen	(Ess)stäbchen
daß	dass		or (Ess-)Stäbchen
Dekolleté	Dekolleté	Eßtisch	Esstisch
	or Dekolletee	Eßwaren	Esswaren
Delphin	Delphin	Eßzimmer	Esszimmer
	or Delfin	Expreß	Express
dessenungeachtet	dessen ungeachtet	Expreß-	Express-
dichtbevölkert	dicht bevölkert	Expreßgut	Expressgut
diensthabend	Dienst habend	Expreßzug	Expresszug
differential	differential	Exzeß	Exzess
	or differenzial	Facette	Facette
Differentialrechnung	Differentialrechnung		or Fassette
	or Differenzialrechnung	Fährenanschluß	Fährenanschluss
Diktaphon	Diktaphon	Fairneß	Fairness
	or Diktafon	fallenlassen	fallen lassen
dreiviertel	drei Viertel	Faß	Fass
durcheinanderbringen	durcheinander bringen	faßbar	fassbar
durcheinanderreden	durcheinander reden	Fehlschuß	Fehlschuss
durcheinanderwerfen	durcheinander werfen	fernhalten	fern halten

ALT/OLD	NEU/NEW	ALT/OLD	NEU/NEW
fertigbringen	fertig bringen	gewiß	gewiss
fertigmachen	fertig machen	Gewißheit	Gewissheit
fertigstellen	fertig stellen	gewußt	gewusst
fertigwerden	fertig werden	glattrasiert	glatt rasiert
festangestellt	fest angestellt	glattstreichen	glatt streichen
Fitneß	Fitness	gleichbleibend	gleich bleibend
fleischfressend	Fleisch fressend	gleichgesinnt	gleich gesinnt
floß	floss	Glimmstengel	Glimmstängel
Fluß	Fluss	Grammophon	Grammophon
Fluß–	Fluss–		or Grammofon
flußabwärts	flussabwärts	(Grammophon)nadel	(Grammophon)nadel
Flußbarsch	Flussbarsch		or (Grammofon)nadel
Flußbett	Flussbett	Graphiker(in)	Graphiker(in)
Flußdiagramm	Flussdiagramm		or Grafiker(in)
flüssigmachen	flüssig machen	graphisch	graphisch
Flußufer	Flussufer		or grafisch
Fön ®	Fön	gräßlich	grässlich
	or Föhn ®	Greuel	Gräuel
fönen	föhnen	Greueltat	Gräueltat
Fönfrisur	Föhnfrisur	greulich	gräulich
Friedensschluß	Friedensschluss	Grundriß	Grundriss
Frischvermählte	frisch Vermählte	Guß	Guss
Frischvermählten	frisch Vermählten	Gußeisen	Gusseisen
frißt	frisst	gutaussehend	gut aussehend
fritieren	frittieren	gutgehen	gut gehen
Gebiß	Gebiss	gutgehend	gut gehend
Gebührenerlaß	Gebührenerlass	gutgemeint	gut gemeint
gefangen(gehalten)	gefangen (gehalten)	guttun	gut tun
gefangenhalten	gefangen halten	haftenbleiben	haften bleiben
gefangennehmen	gefangen nehmen	halboffen	halb offen
gefaßt	gefasst	haltmachen	Halt machen
geheimhalten	geheim halten	Hämorrhoiden	Hämorrhoiden
gehenlassen	gehen lassen		or Hämorriden
Gemeinschaftsanschluß		Handvoll	Hand voll
	Gemeinschaftsanschluss	hängenbleiben	hängen bleiben
Gemse	Gämse	hängenlassen	hängen lassen
gemußt	gemusst	hartgekocht	hart gekocht
genaugenommen	genau genommen	Haselnuß	Haselnuss
Genuß	Genuss	Haß	Hass
genüßlich	genüsslich	häßlich	hässlich
Genußmittel	Genussmittel	Häßlichkeit	Hässlichkeit
Geograph	Geograph	haushalten	haushalten
	or Geograf		or Haus halten
Geographie	Geographie	heiligsprechen	heilig sprechen
	or Geografie	Hexenschuß	Hexenschuss
geographisch	geographisch	hierbehalten	hier behalten
	or geografisch	hierbleiben	hier bleiben
geringachten	gering achten	hierlassen	hier lassen
Geschäftsschluß	Geschäftsschluss	hierzulande	hierzulande
Geschoß	Geschoss		or hier zu Lande
gewinnbringend	Gewinn bringend	hochachten	hoch achten

ALT/OLD	NEU/NEW	ALT/OLD	NEU/NEW
hochbegabt	hoch begabt	kompromißlos	kompromisslos
hochdotiert	hoch dotiert	Kompromißlösung	Kompromisslösung
hochentwickelt	hoch entwickelt	Kongreß	Kongress
(hoch)geschätzt	(hoch) geschätzt	Kongreßzentrum	Kongresszentrum
(hoch)schätzen	(hoch) schätzen	Kontrabaß	Kontrabass
(Honorar)vorschuß	(Honorar)vorschuss	kraß	krass
Imbiß	Imbiss	Kreppapier	Krepppapier
Imbißhalle	Imbisshalle		or Krepp-Papier
Imbißraum	Imbissraum	kriegführend	Krieg führend
Imbißstube	Imbissstube	krummnehmen	krumm nehmen
	or Imbiss-Stube	Kurzbiographie	Kurzbiographie
immerwährend	immer während		or Kurzbiografie
imstande	imstande	kurzhalten	kurz halten
	or im Stande	Kurzschluß	Kurzschluss
ineinandergreifen	ineinander greifen	Kuß	Kuss
ineinanderschieben	ineinander schieben	Ladenschluß	Ladenschluss
Intercity-Expreßzug	Intercity-Expresszug	Laufpaß	Laufpass
ißt	isst	leerlaufen	leer laufen
Jahresabschluß	Jahresabschluss	leerstehend	leer stehend
jedesmal	jedes Mal	leichtfallen	leicht fallen
Joghurt	Joghurt	leichtmachen	leicht machen
	or Jogurt	Lenkradschloß	Lenkradschloss
kahlgeschoren	kahl geschoren	letztemal	letzte Mal
kaltbleiben	kalt bleiben	liebgewinnen	lieb gewinnen
Kammuschel	Kammmuschel	liebhaben	lieb haben
	or Kamm-Muschel	liegenbleiben	liegen bleiben
Känguruh	Känguru	liegenlassen	liegen lassen
Karamel	Karamell	Litfaßsäule	Litfasssäule
Karamelbonbon	Karamellbonbon		or Litfass-Säule
Katarrh	Katarrh	Lithographie	Lithographie
	or Katarr		or Lithografie
Kellergeschoß	Kellergeschoss	Luftschloß	Luftschloss
kennenlernen	kennen lernen	maschineschreiben	Maschine schreiben
keß	kess	maßhalten	Maß halten
klarsehen	klar sehen	Megaphon	Megaphon
klarwerden	klar werden		or Megafon
klassenbewußt	klassenbewusst	Meldeschluß	Meldeschluss
Klassenbewußtsein	Klassenbewusstsein	meßbar	messbar
klatschnaß	klatschnass	Meßbecher	Messbecher
kleinhacken	klein hacken	Meßgerät	Messgerät
kleinschneiden	klein schneiden	Mikrophon	Mikrophon
klitschnaß	klitschnass		or Mikrofon
knapphalten	knapp halten	Miß-	Miss-
Kokosnuß	Kokosnuss	mißachten	missachten
Koloß	Koloss	Mißachtung	Missachtung
Kombinationsschloß	Kombinationsschloss	Mißbehagen	Missbehagen
Communiqué	Kommuniqué	Mißbildung	Missbildung
	or Kommunikee	mißbilligen	missbilligen
Kompaß	Kompass	Mißbilligung	Missbilligung
Kompromiß	Kompromiss	Mißbrauch	Missbrauch
kompromißbereit	kompromissbereit	mißbrauchen	missbrauchen

ALT/OLD	NEU/NEW	ALT/OLD	NEU/NEW
Mißerfolg	Misserfolg	Nebenanschluß	Nebenanschluss
Mißfallen	Missfallen	nebeneinanderlegen	nebeneinander legen
mißfallen	missfallen	nebeneinanderstellen	nebeneinander stellen
Mißgeburt	Missgeburt	Nebenfluß	Nebenfluss
Mißgeschick	Missgeschick	Necessaire	Necessaire
mißgestaltet	missgestaltet		or Nessessär
mißglücken	missglücken		
mißgönnen	missgönnen	Negligé	Negligé
Mißgriff	Missgriff		or Negligee
Mißgunst	Missgunst	Netzanschluß	Netzanschluss
mißgünstig	missgünstig	neuentdeckt	neu entdeckt
mißhandeln	misshandeln	nichtsahnend	nichts ahnend
Mißhandlung	Misshandlung	nichtssagend	nichts sagend
Mißklang	Missklang	Nonstop–	Nonstop–
Mißkredit	Misskredit		or Non-Stop–
mißlich	misslich	notleidend	Not leidend
mißlingen	misslingen	numerieren	nummerieren
mißlungen	misslungen	Nuß	Nuss
Mißmut	Missmut	Nußbaum	Nussbaum
mißmutig	missmutig	Nußknacker	Nussknacker
mißraten	missraten	Nußschale	Nussschale
Mißstand	Missstand		or Nuss–Schale
	or Miss–Stand	obenerwähnt	oben erwähnt
Mißtrauen	Misstrauen	obengenannt	oben genannt
mißtrauen	misstrauen	Obergeschoß	Obergeschoss
Mißtrauensantrag	Misstrauensantrag	offenbleiben	offen bleiben
Mißtrauensvotum	Misstrauensvotum	offenhalten	offen halten
mißtrauisch	misstrauisch	offenlassen	offen lassen
Mißverhältnis	Missverhältnis	offenstehen	offen stehen
Mißverständnis	Missverständnis	Ölmeßstab	Ölmessstab
mißverstehen	missverstehen		or Ölmess–Stab
Mißwirtschaft	Misswirtschaft	Orthographie	Orthographie
mittag	Mittag		or Orthografie
Mop	Mopp	orthographisch	orthographisch
Muß	Muss		or orthografisch
mußte	musste	paarmal	paar Mal
nachhinein	Nachhinein	Panther	Panther
Nachlaß	Nachlass		or Panter
nahegehen	nahe gehen	Paragraph	Paragraph
nahekommen	nahe kommen		or Paragraf
nahelegen	nahe legen	Paranuß	Paranuss
naheliegen	nahe liegen	Parlamentsbeschluß	Parlamentsbeschluss
naheliegend	nahe liegend	Paß	Pass
näherkommen	näher kommen	Paß–	Pass–
näherrücken	näher rücken	Paßamt	Passamt
nahestehen	nahe stehen	Paßbild	Passbild
nahestehend	nahe stehend	Paßkontrolle	Passkontrolle
nahetreten	nahe treten	Paßstelle	Passstelle
naß	nass		or Pass–Stelle
naßkalt	nasskalt	Paßstraße	Passstraße
Naßrasur	Nassrasur		or Pass–Straße
		patschnaß	patschnass

ALT/OLD	NEU/NEW	ALT/OLD	NEU/NEW
pflichtbewußt	pflichtbewusst	rotglühend	rot glühend
Phantasie	Phantasie	Rückschluß	Rückschluss
	or Fantasie	Rußland	Russland
Phantasie–	Phantasie–	Safe(r) Sex	Safe(r) Sex
	or Fantasie–		or Safe(r)-sex
phantasielos	phantasielos	Salzfaß	Salzfass
	or fantasielos	sauberhalten	sauber halten
phantasiereich	phantasiereich	Saxophon	Saxophon
	or fantasiereich		or Saxofon
phantasieren	phantasieren	Schattenriß	Schattenriss
	or fantasieren	schiefgehen	schief gehen
phantasievoll	phantasievoll	Schiffahrt	Schifffahrt
	or fantasievoll		or Schiff–Fahrt
phantastisch	phantastisch	Schiffahrtslinie	Schifffahrtslinie
	or fantastisch	Schlangenbiß	Schlangenbiss
platschnaß	platschnass	schlechtgehen	schlecht gehen
lazieren	platzieren	schlechtmachen	schlecht machen
Pornographie	Pornographie	Schlegel	Schlägel
	or Pornografie	Schloß	Schloss
pornographisch	pornographisch	schloß	schloss
	or pornografisch	Schluß	Schluss
Portemonnaie	Portemonnaie	Schluß–	Schluss–
	or Portmonee	(Schluß)folgerung	(Schluss)folgerung
Potential	Potential	Schlußlicht	Schlusslicht
	or Potenzial	Schlußrunde	Schlussrunde
potentiell	potentiell	Schlußrundenteilnehmer	
	or potenziell		Schlussrundenteilnehmer
preisbewußt	preisbewusst	Schlußstrich	Schlussstrich
Preßluft	Pressluft		or Schluss–Strich
Preßluftbohrer	Pressluftbohrer	Schlußverkauf	Schlussverkauf
Preßlufthammer	Presslufthammer	Schmiß	Schmiss
Prozeß	Prozess	Schnappschloß	Schnappschloss
Prüfungsausschuß	Prüfungsausschuss	Schnappschuß	Schnappschuss
Rad fahren	Rad fahren	Schnellimbiß	Schnellimbiss
(Raketen)abschuß	(Raketen)abschuss	schneuzen	schnäuzen
Rassenhaß	Rassenhass	schoß	schoss
rauh	rau	Schößling	Schössling
Rauhreif	Raureif	Schrittempo	Schritttempo
Raumschiffahrt	Raumschifffahrt		or Schritt–Tempo
	or Raumschiff–Fahrt	Schuß	Schuss
Rausschmiß	Rausschmiss	Schußbereich	Schussbereich
Rechnungsabschluß	Rechnungsabschluss	Schußlinie	Schusslinie
reinwaschen	rein waschen	Schußverletzung	Schussverletzung
Reisepaß	Reisepass	Schußwaffe	Schusswaffe
Reißverschluß	Reißverschluss	Schußweite	Schussweite
richtigstellen	richtig stellen	schwererziehbar	schwer erziehbar
Riß	Riss	schwerfallen	schwer fallen
Rolladen	Rollladen	schwermachen	schwer machen
	or Roll–Laden	schwernehmen	schwer nehmen
Roß	Ross	schwertun	schwer tun
Roßkastanie	Rosskastanie	schwerverdaulich	schwer verdaulich

619

ALT/OLD	NEU/NEW	ALT/OLD	NEU/NEW
schwerverletzt	schwer verletzt		or telegrafieren
Seismograph	Seismograph	Thunfisch	Thunfisch
	or Seismograf		or Tunfisch
selbständig	selbständig	tiefausgeschnitten	tief ausgeschnitten
	or selbstständig	tiefgehend	tief gehend
Selbständigkeit	Selbständigkeit	tiefgekühlt	tief gekühlt
	or Selbstständigkeit	tiefgreifend	tief greifend
selbstbewußt	selbstbewusst	tiefschürfend	tief schürfend
Selbstbewußtsein	Selbstbewusstsein	Tip	Tipp
selbstgemacht	selbst gemacht	topographisch	topographisch
selbstverständlich	selbst verständlich		or topografisch
selbstverwaltet	selbst verwaltet	totenblaß	totenblass
seßhaft	sesshaft	totgeboren	tot geboren
Showbusineß	Showbusiness	Trugschluß	Trugschluss
Sicherheitsschloß	Sicherheitsschloss	tschüs	tschüs
sitzenbleiben	sitzen bleiben		or tschüss
sitzenlassen	sitzen lassen	übelgelaunt	übel gelaunt
Skipaß	Skipass	übelnehmen	übel nehmen
sogenannt	so genannt	übelriechend	übel riechend
Sommerschlußverkauf		übelwollend	übel wollend
	Sommerschlussverkauf	Überdruß	Überdruss
sonstjemand	sonst jemand	übereinanderlegen	übereinander legen
sonstwo	sonst wo	Überfluß	Überfluss
sonstwoher	sonst woher	Überschuß	Überschuss
sonstwohin	sonst wohin	überschwenglich	überschwänglich
Spannbettuch	Spannbetttuch	übrigbleiben	übrig bleiben
	or Spannbett-Tuch	übriggeblieben	übrig geblieben
spazierenfahren	spazieren fahren	übriglassen	übrig lassen
spazierengehen	spazieren gehen	Umriß	Umriss
Sprößling	Sprössling	unbewußt	unbewusst
steckenbleiben	stecken bleiben	Unbewußte	Unbewusste
steckenlassen	stecken lassen	unerläßlich	unerlässlich
stehenbleiben	stehen bleiben	unermeßlich	unermesslich
stehenlassen	stehen lassen	unfaßbar	unfassbar
Stengel	Stängel	ungewiß	ungewiss
Stenographie	Stenographie	Ungewißheit	Ungewissheit
	or Stenografie	unmißverständlich	unmissverständlich
stenographieren	stenographieren	unpäßlich	unpässlich
	or stenografieren	unselbständig	unselbständig
Stenograph(in)	Stenograph(in)		or unselbstständig
	or Stenograf(in)		unterbewusst
stereophonisch	stereophonisch	unterbewußt	unterbewusst
	or stereofonisch	Unterbewußte	Unterbewusste
		Unterbewußtsein	Unterbewusstsein
Stewardeß	Stewardess	Untergeschoß	Untergeschoss
Stilleben	Stillleben	Untersuchungsausschuß	
	or Still-Leben		Untersuchungsausschu
stillegen	stilllegen	unvergeßlich	unvergesslich
Streifschuß	Streifschuss	Varieté	Varieté
strenggenommen	streng genommen		or Varietee
Streß	Stress	verantwortungsbewußt	
telegraphieren	telegraphieren		verantwortungsbewus

ALT/OLD	NEU/NEW	ALT/OLD	NEU/NEW
erdruß	Verdruss	wiedergutzumachen	wieder gutzumachen
ergeßlich	vergesslich	wiederherstellen	wieder herstellen
ergeßlichkeit	Vergesslichkeit	wiedersehen	wieder sehen
ergißmeinnicht	Vergissmeinnicht	wiedervereinigen	wieder vereinigen
ergißt	vergisst	wiederverwenden	wieder verwenden
erhaßt	verhasst	wiederverwerten	wieder verwerten
erlaß	Verlass	wieviel	wie viel
erläßlich	verlässlich	Wißbegier(de)	Wissbegier(de)
erlorengehen	verloren gehen	wißbegierig	wissbegierig
ermißt	vermisst	wohltun	wohl tun
erschluß	Verschluss	wußte	wusste
ertrauenerweckend	Vertrauen erweckend	Xylophon	Xylophon
elsagend	viel sagend		or Xylofon
elversprechend	viel versprechend	Zahlenschloß	Zahlenschloss
oll)fressen	(voll) fressen	zeitlang	Zeit lang
ollgepfropft	voll gepfropft	zielbewußt	zielbewusst
ollpfropfen	voll pfropfen	Zuckerguß	Zuckerguss
ollstopfen	voll stopfen	zufriedengeben	zufrieden geben
olltanken	voll tanken	zufriedenstellen	zufrieden stellen
orgefaßt	vorgefasst	zufriedenstellend	zufrieden stellend
orhängeschluß	Vorhängeschloss	zugrunde	zugrunde
orhinein	Vorhinein		or zu Grunde
orliebnehmen	vorlieb nehmen	zugunsten	zugunsten
orschluß	Vorschuss		or zu Gunsten
orwärtsbewegen	vorwärts bewegen	zuleide	zuleide
orwärtsdrängen	vorwärts drängen		or zu Leide
orwärtsgehen	vorwärts gehen	zumute	zumute
orwärtskommen	vorwärts kommen		or zu Mute
aggon	Waggon	Zündschloß	Zündschloss
	or Wagon	Zungenkuß	Zungenkuss
alnuß	Walnuss	zunutze	zunutze
alroß	Walross		or zu Nutze
asserabstoßend	Wasser abstoßend	Zusammenschluß	Zusammenschluss
äßrig	wässrig	zuschulden	zuschulden
eißrußland	Weißrussland		or zu Schulden
eitblickend	weitblickend	Zuschuß	Zuschuss
	or weit blickend	zustande	zustande
eitreichend	weitreichend		or zu Stande
	or weit reichend	zustande bringen	zustande bringen
eitverbreitet	weitverbreitet		or zu Stande bringen
	or weit verbreitet	zustande kommen	zustande kommen
ederaufbauen	wieder aufbauen		or zu Stande kommen
ederaufbereiten	wieder aufbereiten	zutage	zutage
ederaufnehmen	wieder aufnehmen		or zu Tage
ederbeleben	wieder beleben	zuviel	zu viel
edereinsetzen	wieder einsetzen	zuwege	zuwege
edererkennen	wieder erkennen		or zu Wege
edererwachen	wieder erwachen	zuwenig	zu wenig
edergutmachen	wieder gutmachen		